HISTORICAL DICTIONARY

The historical dictionaries present essential information on a broad range of subjects, including American and world history, art, business, cities, countries, cultures, customs, film, global conflicts, international relations, literature, music, philosophy, religion, sports, and theater. Written by experts, all contain highly informative introductory essays of the topic and detailed chronologies that, in some cases, cover vast historical time periods but still manage to heavily feature more recent events.

Brief A–Z entries describe the main people, events, politics, social issues, institutions, and policies that make the topic unique, and entries are cross-referenced for ease of browsing. Extensive bibliographies are divided into several general subject areas, providing excellent access points for students, researchers, and anyone wanting to know more. Additionally, maps, photographs, and appendixes of supplemental information aid high school and college students doing term papers or introductory research projects. In short, the historical dictionaries are the perfect starting point for anyone looking to research in these fields.

HISTORICAL DICTIONARIES OF LITERATURE AND THE ARTS

Jon Woronoff, Series Editor

Spanish Cinema, by Alberto Mira, 2010.

Film Noir, by Andrew Spicer, 2010.

French Theater, by Edward Forman, 2010.

Choral Music, by Melvin P. Unger, 2010.

Westerns in Literature, by Paul Varner, 2010.

Baroque Art and Architecture, by Lilian H. Zirpolo, 2010.

Surrealism, by Keith Aspley, 2010.

Science Fiction Cinema, by M. Keith Booker, 2010.

Latin American Literature and Theater, by Richard A. Young and Odile Cisneros, 2011.

Children's Literature, by Emer O'Sullivan, 2010.

German Literature to 1945, by William Grange, 2011.

Neoclassical Art and Architecture, by Allison Lee Palmer, 2011.

American Cinema, by M. Keith Booker, 2011.

American Theater: Contemporary, by James Fisher, 2011.

English Music: ca. 1400–1958, by Charles Edward McGuire and Steven E. Plank, 2011.

Rococo Art, by Jennifer D. Milam, 2011.

Romantic Art and Architecture, by Allison Lee Palmer, 2011.

Japanese Cinema, by Jasper Sharp, 2011.

Modern and Contemporary Classical Music, by Nicole V. Gagné, 2012.

Russian Music, by Daniel Jaffé, 2012.

Music of the Classical Period, by Bertil van Boer, 2012.

Holocaust Cinema, by Robert C. Reimer and Carol J. Reimer, 2012.

Asian American Literature and Theater, by Wenjing Xu, 2012.

Beat Movement, by Paul Varner, 2012.

Jazz, by John S. Davis, 2012.

Crime Films, by Geoff Mayer, 2013.

Scandinavian Cinema, by John Sundholm, Isak Thorsen, Lars Gustaf Andersson, Olof Hedling, Gunnar Iversen, and Birgir Thor Møller, 2013.

Chinese Cinema, by Tan Ye and Yun Zhu, 2013.

Taiwan Cinema, by Daw-Ming Lee, 2013.

Russian Literature, by Jonathan Stone, 2013.

Gothic Literature, by William Hughes, 2013.

French Literature, by John Flower, 2013.

Baroque Music, by Joseph P. Swain, 2013.

Opera, by Scott L. Balthazar, 2013.

British Cinema, by Alan Burton and Steve Chibnall, 2013.

Romantic Music, by John Michael Cooper with Randy Kinnett, 2013.

Historical Dictionary of Romantic Music

John Michael Cooper
with Randy Kinnett

The Scarecrow Press, Inc.
Lanham • Toronto • Plymouth, UK
2013

Published by Scarecrow Press, Inc.
A wholly owned subsidiary of Rowman & Littlefield
4501 Forbes Boulevard, Suite 200, Lanham, Maryland 20706
http://www.scarecrowpress.com

10 Thornbury Road, Plymouth PL6 7PP, United Kingdom

British Library Cataloguing in Publication Information Available

Library of Congress Cataloging-in-Publication Data

Cooper, John Michael.
Historical dictionary of romantic music / John Michael Cooper with Randy Kinnett.
pages cm. — (Historical dictionaries of literature and the arts)
Includes bibliographical references.
ISBN 978-0-8108-7230-1 (cloth : alk. paper) — ISBN 978-0-8108-7484-8 (ebook)
1. Music—19th century—Dictionaries. I. Kinnett, Randy, 1979–. II. Title.
ML100.C77 2013
780.9'03403—dc23
2013015481

♾™   The paper used in this publication meets the minimum requirements of American
National Standard for Information Sciences Permanence of Paper for Printed Library
Materials, ANSI/NISO Z39.48-1992.

Printed in the United States of America.

In memoriam William G. Cooper (1931–2012): an able musician and lover of music, and ever a student of history, he was also my teacher, my mentor, my father, my friend.
—JMC

For my father, Mac, whose love of reading and learning he has always shared with me.
—RK

Contents

Editor's Foreword

This *Historical Dictionary of Romantic Music* includes information about not only numerous composers of what became Romantic music but also notable performers, publishers, and critics. More famous works have their own entries and others are included within other entries (on their composers, for example). Romantic music is also embedded in a period that generated a great deal of art and literature, with which it often interacted. Since this period was a transitional one, not only in music but also in technology and politics, the broader historical context is also addressed.

Romantic music is the gift of the "long 19th century," the term that applies to a lengthy and complex period. The chronology highlights not only musical events but others that provided a backdrop as well, and the meaning of the music is described in the introduction. But the most important part of the book is contained in the dictionary section, with hundreds of entries on the topics mentioned above. These entries focus not only on the main, canonical composers we all know but also on so many more who are worthy of mention—some of whom lived outside the core areas of France and what became Germany and made significant contributions. Other entries describe those involved in the business of music, instruments, and perhaps unfamiliar concepts and technical terms. Finally, there is a substantial bibliography, directing readers to many of the best resources on the music, its composers, and the surrounding environment.

This volume was written largely by John Michael Cooper, professor of music and holder of the Margarett Root Brown Chair in Fine Arts at Southwestern University. In this capacity, he has been both teaching and writing about Romantic music for two decades. His previous publications are all on the Mendelssohns, with a fourth in progress on music and secular religion in the long 19th century. His interests are quite broad, and he has written articles on many other Romantic composers as well as aesthetics, performance practice, and other topics for a variety of academic journals. In addition, he has published several editions of musical scores used in live performances and recordings. He was aided in the compilation of this volume by Randy Kinnett, who completed his PhD in musicology. He has also written and lectured on the music of Gustav Mahler and Alban Berg as well as more general topics, such as reception history and interwar Viennese culture.

Thanks to their painstaking work, we now have an abundance of information in one location.

Jon Woronoff
Series Editor

Preface

Readers of this book will naturally wonder how it relates to the plethora of other current English-language music reference books that include Romantic music—books such as the second edition of the *New Grove Dictionary of Music and Musicians*, the *New Harvard Biographical Dictionary of Music*, the *New Harvard Dictionary of Music*, the *New Oxford Companion to Music*, and the *New Oxford Dictionary of Music*, as well as similar resources in other languages. Since Romantic music remains the core of the modern performance canon and consequently has figured prominently in most music reference sources not specifically devoted to other periods, one might guess that the contents of a historical dictionary of that music would largely replicate the corresponding entries in these other authoritative sources.

They do not. The main reason is that this book attempts to complement and supplement those resources, not supersede them. Because those sources are all general in nature, their coverage of 19th-century topics is geared toward general readerships. Here, by contrast, we have the luxury of being able to include items that may be too specific to the 19th century to warrant substantive discussion in some of those other resources, for example, Mexican composer Cenobio Paniagua y Vásques, Lisinsky's Croatian national opera *Ljubav i zloba* (Love and Malice, 1846), Fanny Hensel's piano cycle *Das Jahr* (1841–1842), Robert Schumann's "entirely new genre for the concert hall" *Das Paradies und die Peri* (1844), or the "intentional fallacy." While the discussion of these and other such topics in this book can claim to be neither encyclopedic nor definitive, we hope that they, collectively, will give modern, musically literate readers a sense of the dynamic, kaleidoscopic, and often socially and politically charged Romantic musical landscape as it developed in different ways in different places during the long 19th century.

That task presents its fair share of challenges. Among the more daunting is that of inclusiveness, for while Romantic music is nothing if not all-embracing in its interests and aspirations, no book can be so comprehensive. We eagerly include canonical composers and works as well as concepts central to the Western European canon but avoid handing out medals to those composers, works, and concepts (e.g., Beethoven, Wagner's *Tristan*, and organicism) that latter-day musicians generally revere, and we avoid language that tends to be dismissive of composers, works, and concepts that the long 19th century celebrated as its own (e.g., Meyerbeer's *Les Huguenots*). In that same spirit, we include noncanonical composers, works, and concepts and, in some sense, venture beyond the strict chronological purview of 19th-century music in the interest of presenting the topography of the landscape of 19th-century music as its inhabitants, in various times and places, would have viewed it. Johann Sebastian Bach and Wolfgang Amadeus Mozart are thus included here and discussed as the Romantics understood them rather than through the lens of latter-day historians and musicians. At the same time, limitations of space made it necessary to exclude a great many composers and works of note—and again we must explain that we want this book to serve as a reliable and handy gateway for more detailed and in-depth research.

ACKNOWLEDGMENTS

This book would have been impossible without the generous support of Southwestern University; the Brown Foundation of Houston, Texas; Lisa Anderson and the outstanding workers in the Interlibrary Loan Department of Southwestern University; and the generally excellent staff of Southwestern University's Smith Library Center. The cover photograph of the 1906 Chopin monument by Jacques Froment-Meurice (1864–1947) in the Parc Monceau (Paris) is by photographer/filmmaker/pianist extraordinaire Anthony Tobin (Austin, Texas); thanks to Tony's fine work, we will be pleased if readers, despite the old admonition to the contrary, judge this book at least in part by its cover. At Scarecrow Press we owe a special debt of gratitude to Kellie Hagan and April Snider, for their patience in shepherding a hefty manuscript through the production process. Much help during the volume's initial stages of organization and development was provided by Southwestern University alumna Megan McCarty, now pursuing the PhD in musicology at Duke University: to her we owe the compilation of a master spreadsheet of prospective entries and preparatory work on some of the entries; in particular, this book makes several references to a song cycle by Liszt (on texts by Hugo) whose cyclicity was first recognized by Megan in work that has been formally presented but not yet published. We also offer our gratitude to a number of professional colleagues for input both general and specific in making this book's content as strong as possible: Jonathan Bellman (University of Northern Colorado, Greeley), Lorraine Byrne Bodley (National University of Ireland, Maynooth), Melissa Byrnes (Southwestern University), Bill F. Faucett (Tampa, Florida), Bryan Gilliam (Duke University), Nicole Grimes (University of California, Irvine), Janita Hall-Swadley (Parkin, Arkansas), Angela R. Mace (Colorado State University, Fort Collins), Petronel Malan (Dallas, Texas), Donald Mintz (Montclair State University), Michelle

Perrin Blair (University of Houston), Douglass Seaton (Florida State University), R. Larry Todd (Duke University), and Ralf Wehner (Sächsische Akademie der Wissenschaften, Leipzig).

Finally, thanks are due to our families for their patience and support along the way. In particular, we thank Mrs. Jackie Cooper for her constant encouragement and Cindy Cooper for encouraging and prodding at every step along the way.

Reader's Notes

The entries in this dictionary are written by John Michael Cooper, Randy Kinnett, or (in a few cases) Megan Marie McCarty; for clarity of attribution, the entries are thus initialed either JMC, RK, or MMM. The dictionary portion consists primarily of biographical entries, but we also include entries for musical genres as well as historical, political, and theoretical topics. In all, Old System Russian dates are tacitly converted to New System dates. Russian names and titles are transliterated (Romanized) as they are in *The New Grove Dictionary of Music and Musicians* (2nd ed.) and *Grove Music Online*. We translate the titles of works but generally give titles of organizations only in the original language.

Nation, nationality, and race are always tricky matters. In the biographical entries of this historical dictionary we identify figures by their country or countries of origin and affiliation; we specifically avoid the familiar custom of allowing those from the United States to be identified by their continent (i.e., as "Americans") while segregating other affiliates of that continent out by country (Brazilian, Canadian, Cuban, Mexican, etc.). Race and ethnicity are mentioned when we deem them material to a musician's self-identification and/or reception history, and we sometimes avail ourselves of nuanced phrasing in order to clarify our understanding. Thus, we identify Ernst Bloch as a "Jewish composer" but Leopold Auer as a Hungarian of Jewish descent. The Berwalds are identified as a Swedish family of German descent, while we deem it relevant that Anthony Philip Heinrich was a U.S. composer of German-Bohemian descent and Mexican composer Chiquinha Gonzaga was born of a Brazilian father and mulatto mother.

The plural of *opus* (Latin, "work") is not "opuses" but *opera*—the same word generally used to denote staged musical drama (typically comprised, in the genre's early years, of multiple "works"). This dictionary thus uses "opera" (not italicized) to denote staged musical dramas and *opera* to denote two or more works with opus numbers (e.g., Beethoven's "13 *opera* of songs").

The parenthetical information at the head of biographical entries provides only years of birth and death since readers can easily find information concerning the places and exact dates of years of birth and death in other readily available resources. Our biographical entries also focus primarily on professional information rather than, for example, details of parentage or family life, love life, and so on except when we deem that information material to what has to be said in the space available here. In the initial presentation of our biographical subjects' names, we include in parentheses any authorized names that were not used and place variants and spurious, changed, or rejected names in brackets.

In identifying works, we abide by the composers' own formulations wherever possible, first providing title and subtitle as they are generally given in the English-speaking world, followed by the original titles and subtitles, catalog numbers, and opus or WoO numbers as available. Thus, the work usually known as Hector Berlioz's *Symphonie fantastique* or *Fantastic Symphony* is identified by the composer's own consistent formulation of the title: *Episode in the Life of an Artist: Symphonie fantastique* (Fr., *Episode de la vie d'un artiste: Symphonie fantastique en cinq parties*), H. 48/Op. 14(A). Song titles are provided in italics and text incipits in quotation marks (e.g., *Erlkönig* but "Wer reitet so spät"). In providing dates for compositions, we generally privilege the date of the final authorized or first published version(s) rather than their dates of conception or initial completion; when possible and appropriate according to context, we often also provide dates of earlier composition, revision, and (especially in the case of operas) performance. Thus, Berlioz's *Episode in the Life of an Artist* is thus dated either 1845 (the year of its publication in parts and full score) or, when Franz Liszt's piano arrangement is the subject of discussion, 1834 (the year of that arrangement's publication). This differs from the practice of many other texts, but our reasoning is straightforward and, we think, convincing: the later dates, not the earlier ones, are the dates at which the compositions achieved the form in which they are best known today and discussed here. Assigning the year 1840 to the 1850 version of Robert Schumann's *Eichendorff-Liederkreis*, as most discussions do, is understandable (since much of the music was composed in 1840) but is also false since Schumann's critical replacement of the original opening song, *Der frohe Wandersmann*, with the moving *In der Fremde*, with its overt references to the violence that attended the Revolutions of 1848, occurred well after the date of initial composition and profoundly reframed the cycle as a whole—and the latter version is the one that is generally known today.

In order to facilitate the rapid and efficient location of information and to make this book as useful a reference tool as possible, extensive cross-references have been provided in the dictionary section. Within individual entries, terms that have their own entries are in boldface type the first time they appear. Related terms that do not appear in the text are indicated via a *see also* at the end of the entry. *See* refers to other entries that deal with this topic.

The space limitations of this book make it impossible for us to provide entries on anything more than a very few works that are iconic and occupy a special place in their respective genres. If readers find our decisions as to what to include or omit frustrating or confusing, we can only respond that we share their frustrations. We have endeavored to be as thorough as space permits and to provide information commensurate with the level of detail called for by this historical dictionary focused on the vast world of Romantic music.

Acronyms and Abbreviations

GENERAL

ADMv	Allgemeiner Deutscher Musikverein
GMO	*Grove Music Online*
HD MCCM	Gagné, Nicole V. *Historical Dictionary of Modern and Contemporary Classical Music.* Lanham, MD: Scarecrow Press, 2012.
HD MCP	Boer, Bertil van. *Historical Dictionary of Music of the Classical Period.* Lanham, MD: Scarecrow Press, 2012
LAMZ	[Leipzig] *Allgemeine musikalische Zeitung*
NGS	New German School
NZfM	*Neue Zeitschrift für Musik*

CATALOGING AND REFERENCING

Abbr.	Catalogue/Cataloguer Name	Composer Name
AV	Allroggen, Gerhard. *E. T. A. Hoffmanns Kompositionen: Ein chronologisch-thematisches Verzeichnis seiner musikalischen Werke mit einer Einführung.* Regensburg: Gustav Bosse, 1970.	E. T. A. Hoffmann
BWV	Schmieder, Wolfgang. *Thematisch-systematisches Verzeichnis der musikalischen Werke von Johann Sebastian Bach: Bach-Werke-Verzeichnis (BWV).* 2nd ed. Wiesbaden: Breitkopf & Härtel, 1990.	Johann Sebastian Bach

CT	Chomiński, Józef M., and Teresa Dalila Turło. *Katalog dzieł Fryderyka Chopina*. Kraków: Polskie Wydawn, Muzyczne, 1990	Fryderyk Chopin
D.	Deutsch, Otto Erich, Werner Aderhold, and Walter Dürr. *Franz Schubert: Thematisches Verzeichnis seiner Werke in chronologischer Folge*. 2nd ed. Kassel: Bärenreiter, 1990.	Franz Schubert
EG	Fog, Dan, Kirsti Grinde, and Øyvind Norheim. *Edvard Grieg (1843–1907): Thematisch-bibliographisches Werkverzeichnis*. Frankfurt: C. F. Peters, 2008.	Edvard Grieg
EHWV	*Humperdinck, Eva. Engelbert Humperdinck: Werkverzeichnis zum 140. Geburtstag "Der unbekannte Engelbert Humperdinck—Seine Werke."* Koblenz: Görres-Verlag, 1994.	Engelbert Humperdinck
FS	Fog, Dan, and Torben Schousboe. *Carl Nielsen, kompositioner: En bibliografi*. Copenhagen: Nyt Nordisk Forlag, 1965.	Carl Nielsen
H.	Holoman, D. Kern. *Catalogue of the Works of Hector Berlioz*. Kassel: Bärenreiter, 1987.	Hector Berlioz
Hob.	Hoboken, Anthony von. *Joseph Haydn: Thematisch-bibliographisches Werkverzeichnis*. 3 vols. Mainz: B. Schott's Söhne, 1957–1978.	Franz Joseph Haydn
H-U	Hellwig-Unruh, Renate. *Fanny Hensel geb. Mendelssohn Bartholdy: Thematisches Verzeichnis der Kompositionen*. Adliswil: Kunzelman, 2000.	Fanny Hensel
HWV	Baselt, B. *Händel-Handbuch*. Vols. 1–3. Kassel: Bärenreiter, 1978–1986.	George Frideric Handel

J.	Jähns, Friedrich Wilhelm. *Carl Maria von Weber in seinen Werken: Chronologisch-thematisches Verzeichnis seiner sämmtlichen Compositionen.* Berlin: Schlesinger, 1871.	Carl Maria von Weber
JB	Berkovec, Jirí. *Tematický katalog skladeb Bedřicha Smetany.* Manuscript, 1999; cited from *GMO.*	Bedřich Smetana
JW	Simeone, Nigel, John Tyrrell, and Alena Němcová. *Janáček's Works: A Catalogue of the Music and Writings of Leoš Janáček.* Oxford: Clarendon, 1997.	Leoš Janáček
K./ K⁶	Köchel, Ludwig Ritter von. *Chronologisch-thematisches Verzeichnis sämmtlicher Tonwerke W. A. Mozarts.* Leipzig: Breitkopf & Härtel, 1862. K⁶ = 6th ed., rev. Franz Giegling, Alexander Weinmann, and Gerd Sievers. Wiesbaden: Breitkopf & Härtel, 1964.	Wolfgang Amadeus Mozart
LoWV	Capelle, Irmlind. *Chronologisch-thematisches Verzeichnis der Werke von Gustav Albert Lortzing.* Cologne: Studio, 1994.	Albert Lortzing
LW	Mueller, Rena Charnin, and Maria Eckhardt. *Thematisches Verzeichnis der Werke Franz Liszts.* In preparation; cited from *GMO.*	Franz Liszt
M.	Mohr, Wilhelm. *César Franck.* 2nd ed. Tutzing: Hans Schneider, 1969.	César Franck
McCorkle	McCorkle, Margit L. *Johannes Brahms: Thematisch-bibliographisches Werkverzeichnis.* Munich: G. Henle, 1984.	Johannes Brahms
MWV	Wehner, Ralf. *Felix Mendelssohn Bartholdy: Thematisch-*	Felix Mendelssohn Bartholdy

	systematisches Verzeichnis der musikalischen Werke (MWV). Wiesbaden: Breitkopf & Härtel, 2009.	
S.	Šourek, Otakar. *Dvořák's Werke: Ein vollständiges Verzeichnis in chronologischer, thematischer und systematischer Anordnung.* Berlin: N. Simrock, 1917.	Antonín Dvořák
WWV	Deathridge, John, Martin Geck, and Egon Voss. *Wagner Werk-Verzeichnis (WWV): Verzeichnis der musikalischen Werke Richard Wagners und ihrer Quellen.* Mainz: Schott, 1986.	Richard Wagner

Chronology

Note: The entries in this year-by-year survey begin with general societal and cultural events and then proceed through literature and the other arts to events pertaining directly to music. The latter proceed in the following categorical order:

- institutional events (founding of ensembles, journals, and so on)
- notable biographical milestones
- premieres of select major works
- publications of select major works

The entries note composers' deaths but not their births because their deaths frequently were widely noted and influential, while their births were at that point significant only in familial circles. Due to limitations of space, entries privilege completion dates for works rather than the points at which they were begun, citing first publication rather than publication in full score (since the latter frequently occurred substantially later). Berlioz's *Episode in the Life of an Artist* thus appears in the year 1845 with the parenthetical note "beg. 1830."

When an event other than the composition of a work unfolds over the course of several years, the generally accepted range of years is given parenthetically within the entry for the nearest year, rounded off. Thus, the collaborative process that led to the development of the modern clarinet is given in the year 1840 with a parenthetical "(1839–1843)" at the end.

1789 Outbreak of French Revolution; George Washington is elected first president of the U.S. *Journal des débats* (Journal of Debates) is founded (Paris). William Blake publishes *Songs of Innocence*. Viennese music publisher Artaria sets up own shops. Composition of Haydn's Symphony No. 92 ("Oxford") and Mozart's Clarinet Quintet (K. 581).

1790 Habsburg emperor Joseph II dies; Leopold II proclaimed new emperor. Haydn and Beethoven meet for the first time. Gerber, *Historisch-biographisches Lexikon der Tonkünstler* vol. 1 publ. (vol. 2, 1792). Anton Walter named Royal-Imperial Chamber Organ Builder and Instrument Maker. Rode makes public debut. Premieres: Méhul, *Euphrosine*; Mozart, *Così fan tutte, ossia La scuola degli amanti* (Thus Do They All, or The School for Lovers). Publications: Haydn, String Quartets Op. 64.

1791 The French royal family attempts to flee the country but is discovered in Varennes. In Berlin, Brandenburg Gate is finished. Érard makes its first square piano. Mozart completes part of his Requiem before dying (K. 626; work completed by Süßmaier). Premieres: Cherubini, *Lodoïska*; Mozart, *Die Zauberflöte* (The Magic Flute) and *La clemenza di Tito* (The Clemency of Titus), Piano Concerto No. 27 in B-flat major (K. 595), Clarinet Concerto (K. 622); Haydn, Symphonies No. 95 and 96. Deaths: Mozart.

1792 French Republic declared; the newly invented guillotine is first used; Franz II becomes Holy Roman emperor; the War of the First Coalition begins. British Mary Wollstonecraft publishes *A Vindication of the Rights of Woman*. Beethoven arrives in Vienna; Rouget de Lisle composes *La Marseillaise*. Premieres: Haydn, Symphonies No. 93, 94, 97, and 98; Méhul, *Stratonice*.

1793 Reign of Terror in France begins. Louis XVI and Marie Antoinette are beheaded; the Louvre Palace in Paris becomes a museum. Nikolaus Simrock founds a music-publishing company in Bonn. Premieres: Méhul, *Le jeune sage et le vieux fou* (The Wise Young Man and the Old Fool). Deaths: Goldoni, Hasse.

1794 Robespierre is executed; Reign of Terror comes to an end. The U.S. federal government quells the Whiskey Rebellion; Eli Whitney patents cotton gin. Thomas Paine issues the first part of *The Age of Reason* (the other two follow in 1785 and 1807); Blake publishes *Songs of Experience*. Premieres: Haydn, Symphonies No. 99, 100, and 101. Publications: Billings, *The Continental Harmony*; Méhul, *Hymne à la raison* (later renamed *Hymne patriotique*).

1795 France takes the Netherlands and forms the Batavian Republic; Britain, Russia, and Austria form Alliance of St. Petersburg. Goethe, *Wilhelm Meisters Lehrjahre* (Wilhelm Meister's Apprenticeship), and Schiller, *Briefe über die ästhetische Erziehung des Menschen* (Letters on the Aesthetic Education of Man), published. The *Maison Pleyel* opens in Paris; Haydn returns to Vienna. Premieres: Haydn, Symphonies No. 102, 103, and 104. Publications: Beethoven, Three Piano Trios, Op. 1. Deaths: J. C. F. Bach and G. Benda.

1796 France defeats Austria at Battle of Lodi; Catherine II of Russia dies in Saint Petersburg. Alouis Senefelder invents lithography. Jean Paul Richter's *Blumen-, Frucht- und Dornenstücke*, 1 and Schiller, *Über naïve und sentimentalische Dichtung* (On Naïve and Sentimental Poetry) are published. Gottfried Christoph Härtel buys and takes over the Breitkopf publishing firm. The Conservatoire National Superieur de Musique (the Paris Conservatory) opens. Premieres: Haydn: *Missa in tempore belli*.

1797 Bonaparte conquers Venice, ending over a millennium of independence. Death of feminist author Mary Wollstonecraft. Paer takes over direction of Kärtnertor Theater (Vienna). Premieres: *Gott erhalte Franze den Kaiser* (God preserve Emperor Franz) with lyrics by Haschka and music by Haydn; Cherubini, *Medée*.

1798 French forces invade Papal States, remove pope from power, establish Roman Republic; Bonaparte invades and conquers Egypt. Anonymous publication of Wordsworth and Coleridge, *Lyrical Ballads, with a Few Other Poems* (first work of English literary romanticism) and Thomas Malthus, *An Essay on the Principle of Population*. *Allgemeine musikalische Zeitung* founded, edited by Rochlitz, continues until 1848 then is reinstated between 1866 and 1882. Weber begins private study with Michael Haydn. Premieres: Haydn, *The Creation*; Paer, *Griselda*.

1799 Napoléon Bonaparte overthrows French Directory, becomes first consul of France; Rosetta Stone is discovered in Egypt. Invention of armory system of manufacturing, important influence for industrial revolution. Premieres: Beethoven, Piano Sonatas Op. 13 and 14 (including the "Pathétique"); Field, Piano Concerto No. 1; Paer, *Camilla*. Deaths: Dittersdorf.

1800 Founding of U.S. Library of Congress; Napoléon Bonaparte crosses the Alps and invades Italian states. Kant's *Logik* and Parson Weems's *Life of Washington* published. Zelter becomes director of Berlin Singakademie; public debut of Carl Czerny in Vienna. Premieres: Cherubini, *Les deux journées*; Beethoven: Symphony No. 1; Boieldieu, *Le calife de Bagdad* (The Caliph of Baghdad). Deaths: Billings, Fasch, and Piccini.

1801 Tsar Alexander I ascends to Russian throne; French troops defeated by British at Second Battle of Abukir and Battle of Cairo; Bonaparte signs Concordate of 1801 with Pope Pius VII establishing Catholic Church as majority church of France. In Paris, restoration of Théâtre-Italien, merging of Comédie-Italienne and Opéra-Comique. Forkel publishes *Allgemeine Geschichte der Musik* (General History of Music), vol. 2. Premieres: Haydn: *Die Jahreszeiten* (The Seasons); Paer, *Achille*. Publications: Beethoven, Six String Quartets, Op. 18; Field, Three Piano Sonatas, Op. 1; Spohr, Violin Concerto Op. 1; Tomášek, *Leonore*.

1802 Napoleon Bonaparte becomes president of the Italian Republic and first consul of France. Chateaubriand publishes *Génie du christianisme* (The Genius of Christianity), a defense of Christianity against Enlightenment philosophy. Streicher piano firm is established; Beethoven pens Heiligenstadt Testament; Leipzig *Singakademie* is founded; Philharmonic Society is established in St. Petersburg; Pleyel launches series *Bibliothèque musicale*, making works of Beethoven and Haydn available to French public in score form.

Publications: Forkel, *Ueber Johann Sebastian Bachs Leben, Kunst und Kunstwerke* (On J. S. Bach's Life, Art, and Artworks); Beethoven, Piano Sonatas Op. 22, 26, and 27.

1803 German lands reconstituted as Confederation of the Rhine under French and Russian influence. The United States roughly doubles in size with Louisiana Purchase from France. Jean Paul publishes *Titan*; Schiller premieres *Die Braut von Messina*. Gewandhaus Quartet founded in Leipzig; the Académie des Beaux Arts establishes the Prix de Rome (Rome Prize); Zelter edits and publishes five motets of J. S. Bach. Baillot, R. Kreutzer, and Rode, *Méthode de violon* (Violin Method) published. Premieres: Beethoven: Symphony No. 2 and Violin Sonata Op. 47 ("Kreutzer"); Hummel, Trumpet Concerto; Paisiello, *Proserpine*. Publications: Beethoven, Piano Sonatas Op. 31 Nos. 1–2 and "Eroica" Variations, Op. 35; Reicha, 36 Fugues; Rode, Piano Concerto No. 7 in A minor, Op. 9. Deaths: Süßmaier.

1804 Bonaparte has himself crowned Emperor Napoleon I by the pope. *Code Napoléon* established in France. Jean Paul publishes *Vorschule der Ästhetik* (Preparatory School of Aesthetics). Graf piano firm founded; Schuppanzigh establishes Quartet Evenings in Vienna; Boieldieu is appointed conductor of Imperial Opera in St. Petersburg (–1810). Publications: Beethoven, Piano Sonata Op. 31 No. 3; Reichard, *Liederspiele*. Premieres: Le Sueur, *Ossian*; Paer, *Leonora*; Schiller, *Wilhelm Tell* (William Tell).

1805 Austrian and Russian armies defeated by French at Austerlitz; Austria gives up territories to France, including Italian ones. Renewal of *Concerts spirituels* in Paris. The first volume of Arnim and Brentano's *Des knaben Wunderhorn* (The Boy's Miraculous Posthorn) appears. Premieres: Beethoven, "Eroica" Symphony and *Leonore, ou l'amour conjugal* (later revised and retitled *Fidelio*). Publications: Beethoven, Violin Sonata Op. 47 "Kreutzer," the "Waldstein" Piano Sonata, and *Ah, perfido!*; Tomášek, Symphony in E-flat major. Deaths: Boccherini.

1806 France defeats Prussia in Battle of Jena; French troops occupy Berlin; Holy Roman Empire dissolved. Momigny's *Cours complet d'harmonie et de composition* (Complete Harmony and Composition Course) and A. F. C. Kollman's *A New Theory of Musical Harmony* published. Premieres: Beethoven, "Rasumovsky" String Quartets, Op. 59; Méhul, *Uthal*. Deaths: Michael Haydn.

1807 Prussia cedes possession of lands west of the Elbe and Polish lands to form French Duchy of Warsaw. Charles and Mary Lamb coauthor *Tales from Shakespeare*. Publication of Hegel, *Phänomenologie des Geistes* (Phenomenology of Spirit). Milan Conservatory founded; Dreyssigsche Singakademie founded in Dresden, modeled on Berlin counterpart. Friedrich Hofmeister begins publishing music, and Breitkopf & Härtel begins making pianos. Premieres: Beethoven, Symphony No. 4; Méhul, *Joseph*; Spontini, *La Vestale* (The Virgin). Publications: Beethoven, Piano Sonata Op. 57 (Appasionata).

1808 France occupies Rome; France invades Spain, installing Joseph Bonaparte as king; publication of Goethe, *Faust: Der Tragödie erster Teil* (Faust: Part One of the Tragedy); Kleist, *Penthesilea*; Oehlenschläger, *Hakon Jarl*, and the first of Thomas Moore's *Irish Melodies*. Founding of Ricordi (Milan) and Philharmonic Society (Brno). Premieres: Beethoven, Symphonies No. 5 and 6, Choral Fantasy, Op. 80, and Piano Concerto No. 4. Publications: Beethoven, Piano Concerto No. 4.

1809 France occupies Vienna; Metternich becomes chief minister of Austria. Founding of Phil-Harmonic Society in Boston. Zelter founds Berlin Liedertafel. Griesinger publishes *Biographische Notizen über Joseph Haydn* serially in *LAMZ*. Weber begins *Tonkünstlers Leben* (never completed). Premieres: Bishop, *The Circassian Bride*; Spontini, *Fernand Cortez* (first version). Publications: Beethoven, Symphonies No. 5 and 6, Cello Sonata; A. Romberg, *Das Lied von der Glocke* (Song of the Bell). Deaths: Albrechtsberger, Haydn.

1810 Start of Mexican War of Independence. Founding of University of Berlin (later Friedrich-Wilhelms-Universität, today Humboldt-Universität), the German lands' first university to articulate unity of research and teaching as its goal. Publication of de Staël, *De l'Allemagne*, advocating for German culture to French readers, and Scott, *The Lady of the Lake*; invention of valve trumpet. E. T. A. Hoffmann's "Beethoven's Instrumental Music" published in *LAMZ*; Maria Szymanowska makes her public debut in Warsaw and Vienna. Premieres: Beethoven's incidental music for *Egmont*; Weber, *Silvana*. Publications: Beethoven, "Lebewohl" Piano Sonata Op. 81a; Spohr, *6 deutsche Lieder*, Op. 25.

1811 In Sweden, founding of Gothic League to promote nationalist sentiment. Publication of Jane Austen, *Sense and Sensibility*. Prague Conservatory founded; invention of damper piano by J. A. Stein (Vienna); publication of Choron and Fayolle, *Dictionnaire des musiciens*. Novello begins publishing music in London; Thibaut founds Singverein in Heidelberg. Premieres: Beethoven, Piano Concerto No. 5; Spohr, Symphony No. 1; Tomášek, *Seraphine*; Weber, *Abu Hassan*. Publications: Field, Piano Concertos No. 1–3.

1812 Napoléon Bonaparte invades Russia, occupies Moscow, followed by disastrous retreat. Publication of first two cantos of Byron, *Childe Harold's Pilgrimage*, and L. Tieck, *Phantasus*. Carl Möser's first subscription concert in Berlin. Beethoven and Goethe meet in Teplitz. Premieres: Beethoven, Symphony No. 8; Boieldieu, *Jean de Paris* (John of Paris). Publications: Field, Nocturnes No. 1, 2, and 3. Deaths: Schikaneder.

1813 Sixth Coalition forces drive the French out of Spain, Germany, and Italy; following the Leipzig "Battle of Nations," Napoleon Bonaparte's men fall back to France. Austen publishes *Pride and Prejudice*; Percy Shelley writes *Queen Mab*. Philharmonic Society of London established. Premieres: Beethoven, Symphony No. 7 and *Wellington's Victory*; Rossini, *Tancredi* and *L'italiana in Algeri* (The Italian Girl in Algiers).

1814 Napoléon Bonaparte defeated, exiled to Elba; Louis XVIII becomes king, and France recognizes 1729 borders. Congress of Vienna begins in September and extends through June 1815. The British army burns Washington, D.C. Francis Scott Key writes poem "Defense of Fort McHenry," later set to music of "Anacreon in Heaven" to become U.S. national anthem ("The Star Spangled Banner"). Publication of Scott, *Waverly*; Fichte, *Reden an die deutsche Nation* (Speeches to the German Nation); Austen, *Mansfield Park*. Stalybridge Old Band (first brass band) founded; Academia de Música established in Cuba; Viennese *Gesellschaft der Musikfreunde* chartered. Reicha publishes *Traité de mélodie* (Treatise on Melody); Winkel patents metronome ("chronometer"); Baillot's quartet concert series begins in Paris. Schubert composes *Gretchen am Spinnrade*, milestone in Romantic art song. Premieres: Beethoven, "Archduke" Piano Trio and final version of *Fidelio*; Hummel, Piano Concerto in E major; Schubert, Mass in F major, D. 105. Deaths: Burney.

1815 Congress of Vienna organizes German lands into 38 separate states to form the German Confederation; the Rhineland annexed to Prussia. Grimm brothers' *Kinder- und Hausmärchen* and Hoffmann, *Die Elixiere des Teufels* (The Devil's Elixirs), published. Handel and Haydn Society founded in Boston. Maelzel patents his metronome; Maria Szymanowska begins tour of Russia and Europe; Moscheles wins public acclaim in Vienna; Beethoven's final public performance. Publications: Hummel, *La bella capriciosa*; F. Fesca, String Quartets Opp. 1 and 2.

1816 Estonia emancipates its serfs; Argentina declares independence. New pedagogical works include Garcia, *Esercizj per la voce con accompto. del pianoforte* (Exercises for the Voice with Piano Accompaniment), and Reicha, *Cours de composition musicale* (Course of Musical Composition). Premieres: Hoffmann, *Undine*; Rossini, *Il barbiere di Siviglia* (The Barber of Seville) and *Otello*; Schubert, Symphony No. 5, D. 485; Spohr, *Faust*. Publications: Beethoven, *An die ferne Geliebte;* F. Fesca, String Quartets Opp. 3 and 4; Hummel, Septet in D minor, Op. 74. Deaths: Paisiello.

1817 Publication of Byron, *Manfred*, and Scott, *Rob Roy*. Choron founds Institution Royale de Musique Classique et Religieuse in Paris; establishment of Dresden's Italian Court Opera and German Opera, with Weber as Royal Saxon Kapellmeister; Vienna Conservatory founded. Cipriani Potter travels to Vienna to study with Beethoven; Heinrich conducts first known U.S. performance of a Beethoven symphony (probably First Symphony) in Lexington, Kentucky; Clementi publishes *Gradus ad Parnassum*, vol. 1. Premieres: Rossini, *La Cenerentola* (Cinderella) and *La gazza ladra* (The Thieving Magpie); Schubert, Symphony No. 6, D. 589. Publications: F. Fesca, String Quartets Op. 7 and String Quintets Opp. 8 and 9; Field, Nocturnes No. 4, 5, and 6 and Piano Concerto No. 5; Reicha, Wind Quintets Op. 88. Deaths: Méhul.

1818 Publication of Goethe, *Italienische Reise*; Schopenhauer, *Die Welt als Wille und Vorstellung* (1st ed.; 2nd ed. in 1844); Shelley, *Frankenstein; or, The Modern Prometheus*. Caspar David Friedrich paints *Wanderer above the Sea of Fog*. Founding of Niederrheinisches Musikfest in Düsseldorf (to rotate between Düsseldorf, Cologne, and Aachen annually). Chopin plays at a benefit concert in Warsaw, followed by numerous invitations to visit aristocratic homes; Franz Gruber and Josef Mohr compose *Silent Night*. Premieres: Boieldieu, *Le petit chaperon rouge* (Little Red Riding Hood). Deaths: Forkel.

1819 In Manchester, popular assembly demanding reform of parliamentary representation disrupted in Peterloo Massacre (important early reaction to Congress of Vienna and political structure of Restoration culture). Spain cedes Florida to the U.S. Publication of Scott, *Ivanhoe* and *The Bride of Lammermoor*; Goethe, *West-Östlicher Divan*. Vienna *Singverein* founded under direction of Salieri; Giuditta Pasta debuts in Venice. Premieres: Hummel, Piano Concerto in B minor; Rossini, *Ermione* and *La donna del lago* (The Lady of the Lake); Spontini, *Olympie*. Publications: Beethoven, Piano Sonata Op. 106 "Hammerklavier"; Fesca, String Quartets Opp. 12 and 14; Field, Piano Concerto No. 4; Reicha, Wind Quintets Opp. 91 and 96; Spohr, Nonet Op. 31 and Octet Op. 32. Deaths: Gerber.

1820 The Venus de Milo is discovered. Premieres: Mercadante, *Violenza e costanza* (Violence and Faith); Spohr, Symphony No. 2. Publications: F. Fesca, String Quintet Op. 15; Heinrich, *The Dawning of Music in Kentucky, or The Pleasures of Harmony in the Solitudes of Nature*; Paganini, 24 Caprices (comp. ca. 1805) and 6 Guitar Quartets; Reicha, Wind Quintet Op. 100; Tomášek, *Requiem*. Deaths: Bigot.

1821 Napoléon Bonaparte dies in exile; Mexico wins independence from Spain. Goethe publishes *Wilhelm Meisters Wanderjahre*, 1st ed. Liszt moves to Vienna, where he studies with Czerny and Salieri; Habeneck becomes director of Paris Opéra (–1846); Giuditta Pasta acclaimed in Paris in role of Desdemona in Rossini's *Otello*; Mendelssohns hold their first *Sonntagsmusiken*. Premieres: Mercadante, *Elisa e Claudio*; Schubert, *Erlkönig* and *Der Wanderer*; Weber, *Der Freischütz* and *Konzertstück*. Publications: Beethoven, Piano Sonata No. 30 in E major, Op. 109; F. Fesca, String Quintet Op. 20; Field, Nocturnes No. 7 and 8; Hummel, Piano Concertos in A minor and B minor; Schubert, *Gretchen am Spinnrade, Heidenröslein, Der König von Thule, Der Tod und das Mädchen*, and *Wandrers Nachtlied*. Deaths: A. Romberg.

1822 Royal Academy of Music founded in London. Liszt begins career as virtuoso pianist; Lowell Mason anonymously publishes *The Boston Handel and Haydn Society Collection of Church Music*; Érard patents double-escapement action. Premieres: Spontini, *Nurmahal*. Publications: Beethoven, Piano Sonata No. 31 in A-flat major, Op. 110; Spohr, Mass in C minor. Deaths: Hoffmann.

1823 U.S. Monroe Doctrine introduced. Premieres: Rossini, *Semiramide*; Schubert, incidental music to Chézy, *Rosamunde*; Spohr, *Jessonda*; Voříšek, Symphony; Weber, *Euryanthe*. Publications: Beethoven, Piano Sonata No. 32 in C minor, Op. 111 and Diabelli Variations, Op. 120; Field, Piano Concerto No. 6; Mendelssohn, Piano Quartet in C Minor, Op. 1.

1824 Charles X becomes King of France. Liszt makes his Paris debut. Premieres: Beethoven, "Choral" Symphony No. 9 and *Missa Solemnis*; Meyerbeer, *Il crociato in Egitto* (The Crusader in Egypt). Publications: F. Fesca, String Quartet Op. 34; Schubert, *Die schöne Müllerin*. Deaths: Byron, Viotti.

1825 The Panic of 1825 begins at Bank of England; Erie Canal opens. Alpheus Babcock patents a one-piece cast-iron square piano frame; Schubert presents his "Great" Symphony in C major to the *Gesellschaft der Musikfreunde*; it goes unperformed for 14 years; Thibaut publishes *Über Reinheit der Tonkunst* (On the Purity of the Musical Art); Malibran debuts in London as Rosina in Rossini's *Barber of Seville*. Premieres: Boieldieu, *La dame blanche* (The White Lady); Mendelssohn, Octet; Schubert, Mass in C Major, D. 452. Publications: F. Fesca, String Quartet Op. 36. Deaths: Salieri, Voříšek.

1826 Cooper's *The Last of the Mohicans* and Disraeli's *Vivian Grey* appear. Reicha, *Traité de haute composition musicale* (Treatise on Advanced Musical Composition) published. Premieres: Beethoven, "Choral" Symphony No. 9; Mendelssohn, *Midsummer Night's Dream Overture* (Op. 21); Mercadante, *Caritea, regina di Spagna* (Caritea, Queen of Spain); Spohr, *Die letzten Dinge* (The End of Days); Weber, *Oberon*. Publications: Beethoven, String Quartet in E-flat major, Op. 127; Hummel, Piano Concerto in E major;

Potter, *Studies in All the Major and Minor Keys*; Schubert, Piano Sonatas in A minor and D major (D. 845 and 850), and String Quartet in D minor "Death and the Maiden." Deaths: Arriaga, Danzi, F. Fesca, Weber.

1827 Audubon's *The Birds of America* begins serial publication; Heine publishes *Buch der Lieder* (Book of Songs). Fétis founds *La Revue et gazette musicale de Paris*, which continues until 1880. Premieres: Schubert, Octet in F major. Publications: Beethoven, String Quartets Opp. 130–133; Hensel, three songs in Felix Mendelssohn, *Zwölf Gesänge*, Op. 8; Schubert, *Gesänge aus Wilhelm Meister*, *Valses nobles*, and Piano Sonata in G major. Deaths: Beethoven.

1828 Habaneck founds Orchestre de la Société des Concerts du Conservatoire; Heller and Parish-Alvars begin first major concert tours; Hummel publishes *Ausführliche theoretisch-practische Anweisung zum Pianofortespiel* (Detailed Theoretical and Practical Method for Playing Piano); R. Schumann begins piano study with Friedrich Wieck. Premieres: Auber, *La muette de Portici*; Kuhnau, *Elverhøj* (The Elf Hill); Lortzing, *Die Himmelfahrt Jesu Christi* (The Ascension of Jesus Christ); Marschner, *Der Vampyr* (The Vampire); Mercadante, *Gabriella di Vergy*. Publications: Schubert, *Winterreise*, Piano Trio in E-flat major, D. 929; Spohr, Symphony No. 3. Deaths: Schubert.

1829 Louis Braille introduces braille system. Goethe publishes final versions of *Wilhelm Meisters Wanderjahre, oder Die Entsagenden* (Wilhelm Meister's Journeyman Years, or The Renunciants) and *Faust: Der Tragödie erster Teil* (Faust: Part One of the Tragedy). Mendelssohn and Berlin Singakademie perform Bach, *St. Matthew Passion*; beginning of public Bach revival. Chopin gives Viennese debut. Premieres: Loewe, *Die Zerstörung Jerusalems* (The Destruction of Jerusalem); Marschner, *Der Templer und die Jüdin* (The Templar and the Jewess); Rossini, *Guillaume Tell* (William Tell). Publications: Czerny, *48 Études en forme de préludes et cadences* (48 Etudes in the Form of Preludes and Cadenzas) and vol. 1 of *Fantasie-Schule* (School of Improvisation); Schubert, "Trout" Piano Quintet in A major, D. 667. Deaths: Gossec.

1830 July Revolution in France; William IV becomes king of United Kingdom. Publication of *Book of Mormon* and Stendhal, *The Red and the Black*; Delacroix finishes *Liberty Leading the People*; Hugo's *Hernani* premieres. García publishes *Esercizj per la voce con accompto. del pianoforte* (Exercises for the Voice with Piano Accompaniment); Spohr's *Die letzten Dinge* well received (in English) at Norwich Festival. Hector Berlioz wins Prix de Rome. Premieres: Auber, *Fra Diavolo* (Brother Devil); Berlioz, first version of *Episode in the Life of an Artist*; Donizetti, *Anna Bolena*; Spohr, *Der Alchymist*. Publications: Chopin, Variations on "Là ci darem la mano" from

Mozart's *Don Giovanni*, Op. 2; Hensel, three songs in Felix Mendelssohn, *Zwölf Lieder*, Op. 9; Hummel, Piano Concerto in A-flat major; Mendelssohn, String Quartets No. 1 and 2, Opp. 12 and 13. Deaths: Rode, Schuppanzigh.

1831 France invades Algiers; Nat Turner's slave rebellion occurs in Virginia. HMS *Beagle* heads to sea with Darwin aboard; publication of Hugo, *Notre-Dame de Paris* (The Hunchback of Notre Dame); Pushkin, *Boris Godunov*. Chopin settles in Paris; R. Schumann reviews Chopin's Op. 2 Variations in *LAMZ*. Premieres: Bellini, *La sonnambula* and *Norma*; Chopin, Piano Concerto No. 2; Meyerbeer, *Robert le diable*. Publications: R. Schumann, *Abegg* Variations and *Papillons*. Deaths: Érard, R. Kreutzer, Pleyel, Szymanowska.

1832 Greek War of Independence ends. Publication of Hugo, *Le roi s'amuse* (The King Amuses Himself). Premieres: Donizetti, *L'elisir d'amore* (The Elixir of Love); Mendelssohn, *Hebrides Overture* (beg. 1829). Mercadante, *I normanni a Parigi* (The Normans in Paris). Publications: Chopin, Mazurkas Opp. 6 and 7, Nocturnes Op. 9, and Piano Trio in G minor; Field, Piano Concerto No. 7; Mendelssohn, first volume of *Lieder ohne Worte* (Songs without Words) publ. in London (later publ. Simrock as Op. 19[b], 1833); Potter, Symphony No. 10 in G minor (in piano-duet arrangement); R. Schumann, *Studien nach Capricen von Paganini*. Deaths: Clementi, García, Kuhlau, Zelter.

1833 Computer pioneers Ada Lovelace and Charles Babbage meet. Pushkin's *Eugene Onegin* published. Berlioz marries Harriet Smithson. Premieres: Cherubini, *Ali-Baba*; Donizetti, *Lucrezia Borgia*; Hummel, Piano Concerto in F major; Marschner, *Hans Heiling*. Publications: Bennett, Piano Concerto No. 1; Chopin, Nocturnes Op. 15; Spohr, 3 Psalms, Op. 85.

1834 Pushkin's *The Queen of Spades* printed. Delecroix paints *The Women of Algiers*. *Neue Zeitschrift für Musik* begins in Leipzig, edited by R. Schumann; new pedagogical works include Baillot, *L'art du violon: nouvelle method* (The Art of the Violin: A New Method); Czerny, *Die Schule des Legato und Staccato* (School of Legato and Staccato). Premieres: Conradin Kreutzer, *Das Nachtlager von Granada* (first version). Publications: Cherubini, *Ali-Baba*; Field, Piano Concerto No. 7; R. Schumann, *Toccata* in C major; Spohr, *Die Weihe der Töne: Charakteristisches Tongemälde in Form einer Sinfonie* (The Consecration of Tones: Characteristic Tone-Painting in the Form of a Symphony). Deaths: Boieldieu.

1835 Publication of H.C. Anderson, vol. 1 of *Eventyr, fortalte for Børn* (Fairy Tales Told for Children); Gogol, *Taras Bulba*; Tocqueville, vol. 1 of *De la démocratie en Amérique* (Democracy in America). Publication of Liszt, "De la situation des artistes et de leur condition dans la Société" (On the Situation of Artists and Their Position in Society); vol. 1 of Fétis, *Bio-*

graphie universelle des musiciens et bibliographie générale de musique (1st ed.). Premieres: Bellini, *I Puritani*; Donizetti, *Lucia di Lammermoor* and *Maria Stuarda*; Halévy, *La juive* (The Jewess); C. Schumann, Piano Concerto in A minor; Verstovsky, *Askol'dova mogila* (Askold's Tomb). Publications: Bennett, Piano Concerto No. 2; Chopin, Scherzo in B minor, Op. 20; *Lieder ohne Worte* Op. 30. Deaths: Bellini, W. Müller.

1836 Chopin introduced to Baroness Amandine Dupin, pseud. George Sand; Czerny publishes *Die Schule des Fugenspiels und des Vortrags mehrstimmiger Sätze und deren besonderer Schwierigkeiten auf dem Piano-Forte* (School of Playing Fugue and of Performing Polyphonic Music, and of Its Particular Difficulties on the Piano). Premieres: Cherubini, Requiem No. 2; Glinka, *Zhizn' za tsarya* (A Life for the Tsar); Mendelssohn, *St. Paul*; Mercadante, *I briganti* (The Pirates); Meyerbeer, *Les Huguenots*. Publications: Bennett, Piano Concerto No. 3; Chopin, Ballade in G minor, Op. 23 and Nocturnes, Op. 27; Schubert, Piano Trio in B-flat major, D. 898; Tomášek, *Coronation Mass*. Deaths: Burgmüller, Malibran, Nägeli, Reicha, Rouget de Lisle.

1837 Victoria becomes queen of United Kingdom, moves into Buckingham Palace; Panic of 1837 begins in the United States; Louis Daguerre invents daguerreotype. Carlyle publishes *The French Revolution: A History*. A. B. Marx publishes vol. 1 of *Die Lehre von der musikalischen Komposition, praktisch-theoretisch* (Theory and Practice of Musical Composition; final vol. in 1847); piano duel between Liszt and Thalberg. Premieres: Donizetti, *Roberto Devereux, ossia Il conte di Essex* (Robert Devereux, or The Earl of Essex); Hartmann, Symphony No. 1; Lortzing, *Zar und Zimmermann* (Tsar and Carpenter); Mercadante, *Il giuramento* (The Oath); Onslow, *Guise, ou Les états de Blois* (Guise, or The Estates of Blois); A. Thomas, *La double échelle* (The Step Ladder). Publications: Cherubini, Requiem No. 2; Chopin, Scherzo, Op. 31, 12 Etudes, Op. 25, and Nocturnes, Op. 32; Mendelssohn, *Six Preludes and Fugues for Piano, Op. 35* Op. 38; R. Schumann, *Carnaval*. Deaths: Field, Hummel.

1838 Delacroix paints *Portrait of Frédéric Chopin and George Sand*; publication of Dickens, *Oliver Twist*; Hugo, *Ruy Blas*. Schumann discovers Schubert's "Great" C-major Symphony, D. 944. Premieres: Berlioz, *Benvenuto Cellini*; Mercadante, *I due illustri rivali* (The Distinguished Rivals). Publications: Berlioz, *Grande Messe des Morts*. Deaths: Thomas Attwood, Ferdinand Ries.

1839 Kingdom of Belgium established; First Opium War begins. Faraday publishes "Experimental Researches in Electricity"; Goodyear claims discovery of vulcanization; publication of Balzac, *Béatrix*; Darwin, *The Voyage of the Beagle*; Poe, "The Fall of the House of Usher." Jenny Lind first performs at Stockholm Opera; Czerny publishes *Vollständige theoretisch-praktische Pianoforte-Schule* (Complete Theoretical and Practical School of Piano). Premieres: Mercadante, *Elena da Felta* and *Il bravo* (The Good Man); Schubert, "Great" Symphony in C major, D. 944. Publications: Bennett, Piano Concerto No. 4; Chopin, 24 Preludes, Op. 28; Hummel, Piano Concerto in F major; Mendelssohn, *Psalm 42*, Op. 42, and String Quartets, Op. 44. Deaths: Berger, Paer, Sor.

1840 Queen Victoria marries Prince Albert of Saxe-Coburg and Gotha. J. M. W. Turner paints *Slavers Throwing Overboard the Dead and Dying*; publication of Cooper, *The Pathfinder*; Thackaray, *Catherine*; Schindler, *Biographie von Ludwig van Beethoven*; Edward William Lane completes translation of *1,001 Nights*. Clarinetist Hyacinthe Eléonore Klosé and maker Louis-Auguste Buffet collaborate to produce clarinette à anneaux mobiles, first modern clarinet (1839–1843). Premieres: Donizetti, *La fille du régiment* (The Daughter of the Regiment); Mendelssohn, symphony-cantata "Lobgesang," Op. 52; Mercadante, *La Vestale* (The Virgin). Publications: Bennett, Caprice in E major; Berlioz, *King Lear* concert overture; Chopin, Piano Sonata in B-flat minor, Ballade Op. 38, Nocturnes, Op. 37, and Scherzo in C-sharp minor, Op. 39; Liszt, *Etudes d'exécution transcendante d'après Paganini* (Transcendental Etudes after Paganini) and *Album d'un voyageur*; Mendelssohn, Piano Trio No. 1; R. Schumann, Heine-Liederkreis and *Myrthen*; Spohr, Symphony No. 5. Deaths: Paganini, Thibaut, Johann Michael Vogl.

1841 The United Kingdom takes Hong Kong. First issue of *Punch*. Hensel composes *Das Jahr* (–1842). Publications: Chopin, Ballade in A-flat major, Op. 47, Nocturnes, Op. 48, and Fantasy in F minor, Op. 49; Mendelssohn, *Lieder ohne Worte* Op. 53; Molique, Violin Concerto No. 5 in A minor, Op. 21; C. and R. Schumann, *Liebesfrühling* (Spring of Love); R. Schumann, Symphony No. 1 in B-flat major ("Spring"). Deaths: B. Romberg.

1842 China and United Kingdom sign Treaty of Nanking. Emerson's *The Transcendentalist* published. New York and Vienna Philharmonic Orchestras founded. Premieres: Berwald, *Erinnerung an die norwegischen Alpen* (Memory of the Norwegian Alps), *Humoristisches Capriccio*, and *Elfenspiel* (Elf Play); Glinka, *Ruslan and Ludmila*; Lortzing, *Der Wildschutz* (The Poacher); Mendelssohn, Symphony No. 3, Op. 56 ("Scottish"); Rossini, *Stabat Mater*; Verdi, *Nabucco*; Wagner, *Rienzi*. Publications: Loewe, *Johann Hus*; R. Schumann, Eichendorff-Liederkreis; Spohr, Symphony No. 6, *Historische Symphonie im Styl und Geschmack vier verschiedener Zeitabschnitte* (Historical Symphony in the Style and Taste of Four Different Periods), and Symphony No. 7, *Irdisches und Göttliches im Menschenleben* (The Worldly and Godly in the Life of Man). Deaths: Baillot, Cherubini, Momigny, Costanze Mozart.

1843 Publication of Dickens, *A Christmas Carol*; Kierkegaard, *Either/Or*; Poe, "The Tell-Tale Heart"; *The Economist* newspaper. Chickering patents full cast-iron frame for grand pianos. Mendelssohn founds Leipzig Conservatory. Berlioz prints *Grand traité d'instrumentation et d'orchestration modernes* (Grand Treatise on Instrumentation and Modern Orchestration) in book form. Premieres: Berwald, *Sinfonie sérieuse*; Donizetti, *Don Pasquale*; Gade, Symphony No. 1; R. Schumann, *Das Paradies und die Peri*; Wagner, *Der fliegende Holländer* (The Flying Dutchman). Publications: Chopin, Ballade in F minor, Op. 52 and Scherzo in E major, Op. 54; Franck, Piano Trios, Op. 1; R. Schumann, *Frauenliebe und -leben* (Woman's Love and Life) and Piano Quintet Op. 44. Deaths: Joseph Lanner.

1844 Electrical telegraph line opens between Baltimore and Washington, D.C.; Marx and Engels first meet in Paris; Dumas *père* publishes *The Count of Monte Cristo* and *The Three Musketeers*. Final volume of Fétis, *Biographie universelle des musiciens et bibliographie générale de musique* (Universal Biography of Musicians and General Musical Bibliography, 1st ed.) appears. Premieres: David, *Le désert*; Mercadante, *Leonora*. Publications: Berlioz, *Roman Carnival* Overture; Chopin, Nocturnes, Op. 55; Mendelssohn, *Lieder ohne Worte* Op. 62; C. Schumann, 6 *Lieder*, Op. 13; R. Schumann, *Dichterliebe* (Poet's Love). Deaths: Baini.

1845 Great Famine begins in Ireland. Publication of Douglass, *Narrative of the Life of Frederick Douglass, an American Slave*; Mérimée, *Carmen*; Poe, "The Raven." First Beethoven Festival held in Bonn. Franz Brendel becomes editor in chief of *NZfM*. Premieres: Fry, *Leonora*; Lortzing, *Undine*; Mendelssohn, Violin Concerto in E minor; Wagner, *Tannhäuser*. Publications: Berlioz, *Episode in the Life of an Artist: Fantastic Symphony in Five Parts* (beg. 1830); Chopin, Piano Sonata in B minor; Mendelssohn, *Lieder ohne Worte* Op. 67; R. Schumann, Piano Quartet Op. 47. Deaths: Mayr.

1846 Adolphe Saxe patents first saxophone. Premieres: Lisinski, *Ljubav i zloba (Love and Malice)*; Lortzing, *Der Waffenschmied* (The Armorer); Mendelssohn, *Elijah*; Mercadante, *Gli Orazi ed i Curiazi* (The Horatii and the Curiatii); R. Schumann, Piano Concerto in A minor and Symphony No. 2 in C major; Suppé, *Dichter und Bauer* (Poet and Peasant). Publications: Chopin, Barcarolle, Op. 60 and Nocturnes, Op. 62; Hensel, *6 Lieder*, Op. 1 and *4 Lieder* for piano, Op. 2; Mendelssohn, Piano Trio No. 2, Op. 66. Deaths: Dragonetti.

1847 Publication of Charlotte Brontë, *Jane Eyre*; Emily Brontë, *Wuthering Heights*; Longfellow, *Evangeline*; Thackeray, *Vanity Fair*. Franz Liszt retires from piano-virtuoso career. Premieres: Verdi, *Macbeth* (first version). Publications: Berlioz, *Roméo et Juliette* (comp. 1839); Chopin, Cello Sonata Op.

65; Hensel, 6 *Gesänge* for SATB, Op. 3, piano *Mélodies*, Opp. 4 and 5, and *4 Lieder* for piano, Op. 6; Henselt, Piano Concerto in F minor; C. Schumann, Piano Trio Op. 17. Deaths: Hensel, Mendelssohn.

1848 Revolutions occur across Europe; French Second Republic established with Louis-Napoléon Bonaparte elected president; Franz Joseph I becomes emperor of Austria. Publication of Marx/Engels, *The Communist Manifesto*; Veit paints *Germania*. Liszt settles in Weimar as Kapellmeister; Kastner publishes *Manuel général de musique militaire à l'usage des armées françaises* (General Handbook on Military Music as Used by the Armies of France). Premieres: Mercadante, *La schiava saracena* (The Saracen Slave Girl). Publications: Alkan, Grand Sonata Op. 33; Berlioz, *Harold en Italie* (beg. 1834); Foster, *Susanna* and *Uncle Ned*; Hensel, *6 Lieder*, Op. 7; Molique, Piano Quintet Op. 35; R. Schumann, Piano Trio No. 1 in D minor, String Quartets Op. 41, and *Album für die Jugend* (Album for the Young); Spohr, *An sie am Klavier*; J. Strauss (I), *Radetsky March*. Deaths: Donizetti.

1849 European revolutions and rebellions continue, reaching Dresden in May Uprising, and new republican and national governments are predominantly suppressed. Pre-Raphaelites hold first exhibition in London; publication of Dickens, *David Copperfield*, and Hawthorne, *The Scarlet Letter*. William Sterndale Bennett helps found the English Bach Society; Wagner publishes *Die Kunst und die Revolution* (Art and Revolution) and *Das Kunstwerk der Zukunft* (The Artwork of the Future). Premieres: Liszt, *Tasso: Lamento e Trionfo*; Meyerbeer, *Le prophète*; Nicolai, *Die lustigen Weiber von Windsor* (The Merry Wives of Windsor); A. Thomas, *Le Caïd* (The Ringleader); Verdi, *Luisa Miller*. Publications: Czerny, *Schule der praktischen Tonsetzkunst* (School of Practical Composition); Gottschalk, *Bamboula* and *La savane* (The Savanna); Onslow, Wind Nonet in A major; R. Schumann, *Fantasiestücke, Romanzen und Balladen*, vol. 1, and Piano Trio No. 2 in F major. Deaths: Chopin, Habaneck, Kalkbrenner, C. Kreutzer, Nicolai, J. Strauss (I).

1850 U.S. Congress passes Fugitive Slave Act. Soprano Jenny Lind tours the United States under P. T. Barnum's sponsorship. The German Bach-Gesellschaft is founded; Wagner anonymously publishes "Das Judenthum in der Musik" (Jewry in Music). Premieres: Barbieri, *Gloria y peluca* (Gloria and Wig); Wagner, *Lohengrin*. Publications: Gottschalk, *Le bananier* (The Banana Tree); Foster, *Nelly Bly* and *De Camptown Races*; Hensel, Piano Trio, Op. post. 11; Mendelssohn, String Quartet Op. posth. 80; R. Schumann, *Genoveva* and *Romanzen und Balladen* , vol. 2. Deaths: Tomášek.

1851 The *New York Times* founded. Hawthorne, *The House of the Seven Gables*, and Melville, *Moby-Dick* published. Chickering pianos receive accolades at London Great Exposition; ex-slave Elizabeth Greenfield (later known as "the black swan") begins performing in New York; complete edition of J. S. Bach's works begun; Wagner publishes *Oper und Drama* (Opera and Drama). Premieres: Barbieri, *Jugar con fuego* (To Play with Fire); R. Schumann, Symphony No. 3 in E-flat major "Rhenish"; Verdi, *Rigoletto*. Publications: Gottschalk, *Le mancenillier* (The Manchineel); Liszt, *Hungarian Rhapsodies* Nos. 1 and 2 and *Etudes d'exécution transcendante pour le piano*. Deaths: Lortzing, Spontini.

1852 French President Louis-Napoléon Bonaparte ends Second Republic, becomes Emperor Napoléon III. Stowe publishes *Uncle Tom's Cabin*; Millais completes painting *Ophelia*. First issue of *Dwight's Journal of Music* (cont. until 1881). Liszt publishes first edition of biography *F. Chopin*. Premieres: R. Schumann, *Manfred, Der Rose Pilgerfahrt*, and Symphony No. 4 in D minor (final version; orig. No. 2 [1841]); Söderman, *Urdur*. Publications: Foster, *Massa's In de Cold Ground*; Onslow, Wind Quintet in F major; R. Schumann, Piano Trio No. 3 in G minor. Deaths: Moore.

1853 Crimean War begins. Dickens publishes *Bleak House*. Normal Music Institute, first U.S. school for music-teacher training, opens in New York. Concert in Memphis, Tennesseee, by Ole Bull draws 10,000 listeners; Brahms meets the Schumanns, and Robert publishes "Neue Bahnen" essay on Brahms; publication of Sechter, vol. 1 of *Die Grundsätze der musikalischen Komposition* (Principles of Musical Composition), and Köhler, *Die Melodie der Sprache in ihrer Anwendung besonders auf das Lied und die Oper* (The Melody of Speech as Applied Specifically to Song and Opera). Premieres: Fry, *Santa Claus: A Christmas Symphony*; Verdi, *Il trovatore* (The Troubadour) and *La traviata* (The Fallen Woman). Publications: Foster, *My Old Kentucky Home*; Gounod, *Méditation sur le 1er Prélude de S. Bach*; Liszt, *Hungarian Rhapsodies* Nos. 3–16; McCarty, *Fleurs de salon: 2 Favorite Polkas*; Molique, Cello Concerto Op. 45. Deaths: Onslow.

1854 In Crimean War, allies besiege Russian naval port city of Sevastopol. Tennyson, *The Charge of the Light Brigade*, and Thoreau, *Walden*, published. Robert Schumann attempts suicide and is institutionalized. Publication of Hanslick, *Vom Musikalisch-Schönen* (On the Musically Beautiful, 1st ed.), and A. B. Marx, vol. 1 of *Die Musik des 19. Jahrhunderts und ihre Pflege* (The Music of the Nineteenth Century and Its Culture; 2nd vol. in 1855). Premieres: Fry, *Niagara Symphony*; Liszt, *Les Préludes, Mazeppa*, and *Orpheus*. Publications: Berlioz, *La damnation de Faust* (The Damnation of Faust) and *Te Deum*; Foster, *Jeanie with the Light Brown Hair*; Gottschalk, *The Last Hope*; Liszt, Piano Sonata in B minor.

1855 French and British troops take Sevastopol. Longfellow, *The Song of Hiawatha* and Whitman, *Leaves of Grass*, 1st ed, published. Premieres: Liszt, *Prometheus* and Piano Concerto No. 1; Verdi, *Les vêpres siciliennes*

(The Sicilian Vespers). Publications: Berlioz, *Lélio, ou Le retour à la vie* (Lélio, or The Return to Life); Gottschalk, *Le banjo*; Gounod, *Messe solennelle de Ste. Cécile*; Liszt, *Première Année: Suisse* (First Year: Switzerland) from *Années de pèlerinage* (Years of Pilgrimage); C. Schumann, 3 *Romanzen* Op. 22; Spohr, Septet Op. 147.

1856 David Livingstone completes his journey across Africa. Flaubert finishes *Madame Bovary*, which appears serially. Henry Engelhard Steinway creates his first piano; Chrysander organizes founding of *Händel-Gesellschaft*. Premieres: Dargomïzhsky, *Rusalka*; Söderman, *Hin Ondes första lärospån* (The Devil's First Lesson). Publications: C. Schumann, 6 *Lieder*, Op. 23. Deaths: Adolphe Adam, Lindpaintner, R. Schumann.

1857 The U.S. Supreme Court rules that people there of African descent are not citizens and do not receive constitutional protection in *Dred Scott v. Sanford*. Panic of 1857 begins in the United States and spreads to Europe. Emperor Franz Joseph I orders demolition of Vienna's city walls, making room for *Ringstrasse*. Premieres: Liszt, *A "Faust" Symphony*, *Die Ideale*, and *Hunnenschlacht*; Verdi, *Simon Boccanegra* (first version, Venice). Publications: Foster, *Gentle Annie*; Pierpont, *One Horse Open Sleigh* (today "Jingle Bells"). Deaths: Castil-Blaze, Czerny, Glinka.

1858 France begins conquest of Vietnam. Gray's *Anatomy* appears. Harvard Glee Club founded. Publications: Liszt, *Première année: Suisse* (First Year: Switzerland) from *Années de pèlerinage* (Years of Pilgrimage). Premieres: Cornelius, *Der Barbier von Baghdad* (The Barber of Baghdad); Offenbach, *Orphée aux enfers* (Orpheus in the Underworld); Söderman, *Svenskt festspel* (Swedish Festival). Deaths: Cramer, Diabelli, J. Kinkel.

1859 Completion of Westminster Palace's Elizabeth Tower, featuring bell "Big Ben." Oil rush in Pennsylvania. Publication of Darwin, *On the Origin of Species*; Dickens, *A Tale of Two Cities*; and John Stuart Mill, *On Liberty*. Manet paints *The Absinthe Drinker*. *Versammlung deutscher Tonkünstler* (Conference of German Musicians) convenes for the first time. Anton and Nikolay Rubinstein found Russian Musical Society. Premieres: Brahms, Piano Concerto No. 1; Gounod, *Faust*; Meyerbeer, *Le pardon de Ploërmel*; Paniagua, *Catalina de Guisa*; Verdi, *Un ballo in maschera* (A Masked Ball); Wagner, Prelude to *Tristan und Isolde*. Publications: Alkan, 12 Etudes in Minor Keys, Op. 39; Liszt, *Deuxième année: Italie* (Second Year: Italy) from *Années de pèlerinage*; Raff, 3 *Klavier-Soli*, Op. 72. Deaths: Spohr.

1860 South Carolina secedes from the United States; 10 states follow within five months. Longfellow publishes "Paul Revere's Ride." Brahms, Joachim, Grimm, and Scholz prematurely publish manifesto against New German School in the *NZfM* and Berliner *Musik-Zeitung Echo*. Liszt issues *Des bohé-*

miens et de leur musique en Hongrie (On Gypsies and Their Music in Hungary). Premieres: Suppé, *Das Pensionat* (The Boarding School). Publications: Foster, *Old Black Joe*. Deaths: Jullien, Carl Friedrich Zöllner.

1861 Italy is unified; Civil War begins in the United States (–1865); Wilhelm I becomes Prussian emperor. Charles Dickens's *Great Expectations* and George Eliot's *Silas Marner* appear. *Tannhäuser* meets scandal in Paris; the *Allgemeiner Deutscher Musikverein* is founded by Franz Brendel and Franz Liszt. Publications: Molique, *Abraham*. Deaths: Heinrich, Marschner, Louis Niedermeyer, Vincent Novello.

1862 Victor Hugo's *Les Misérables* appears. Publication of Ambros, *Geschichte der Musik*, vol. 1, and Helmholtz, *Die Lehre von den Tonempfindungen als physiologische Grundlage für die Theorie der Musik* (On the Sensations of Tone as a Physiological Basis for the Theory of Music). Köchel's Mozart catalog first published. Anton Rubinstein founds St. Petersburg Conservatory. Premieres: Berlioz, *Béatrice et Bénédict*; Verdi, *La forza del destino* (The Force of Destiny, first version, St. Petersburg). Deaths: Halévy, Verstovsky.

1863 U.S. President Abraham Lincoln signs Emancipation Proclamation. Gevaert: *Traité général d'instrumentation: Exposé méthodique* (General Treatise on Instrumentation). Premieres: Berlioz, *Les Troyens* (The Trojans); Bizet, *Les pêcheurs de perles* (The Pearl Fishers); Suppé, *Flotte Bursche* (Jolly Students). Publications: Liszt, Piano Concerto No. 2.

1864 Ludwig II becomes king of Bavaria, begins supporting Wagner financially. Publication of Dostoyevsky's *Notes from Underground*, Tennyson's *Enoch Arden*, and Verne's *Journey to the Center of the Earth*. Rheinberger begins directing Munich *Oratorienverein* (Oratorio Club). Premieres: Barbieri, *Pan y toros* (Bread and Bulls); Offenbach, *La belle Hélène*; Suppé, *Franz Schubert*. Publications: Foster, *Beautiful Dreamer*. Deaths: Foster, Lindblad, Meyerbeer.

1865 Civil War ends in the United States with surrender of Confederate forces to General U. S. Grant; President Lincoln assassinated. Wilhelm Busch's *Max und Moritz* and Lewis Carroll's *Alice's Adventures in Wonderland* are published. Nottebohm publishes *Ein Skizzenbuch von Beethoven* (A Beethoven Sketchbook). Premieres: Liszt, *Die Legende von der heiligen Elisabeth* (The Legend of St. Elisabeth); Meyerbeer, *L'Africaine*; Wagner, *Tristan und Isolde*. Publications: Castillon, Piano Quintet in E flat; Liszt, *Totentanz* (second version); Wagner, *Die Walküre*. Deaths: Pasta.

1866 Prussia defeats Austria at Battle of Königgrätz. Dostoyevsky publishes *Crime and Punishment*. Premieres: Bizet, *La jolie fille de Perth* (The Fair Maid of Perth); Offenbach, *Barbe-Bleu* (Bluebeard) and *La vie parisienne*

(Parisian Life); Smetana, *Braniboři v Čechách* (Brandenburgers in Bohemia); Suppé, *Leichte Kavallerie* (Light Cavalry); A. Thomas, *Mignon*. Publications: Paine, Mass in D major. Deaths: A. B. Marx.

1867 The Dominion of Canada and the North German Confederation are formed. The Suez Canal opens. The United States purchases Alaska from Russia. Ibsen publishes *Peer Gynt*. Founding of Copenhagen Conservatory (today the Royal Danish Academy of Music). Music publishers Novello and Ewer merge into Novello, Ewer & Co. Premieres: Gounod, *Roméo et Juliette*; Offenbach, *La Grande Duchesse de Gérolstein*; Verdi, *Don Carlos* (first version, Paris). Publications: J. Strauss (II), *An der schönen blauen Donau* (The Beautiful Blue Danube); Svendsen, String Octet in A major. Deaths: Sechter.

1868 Meiji Restoration begins in Japan. Alcott's *Little Women* and Dostoyevsky's *The Idiot* are published. Bruckner moves to Vienna. Premieres: Bruch, Violin Concerto in G minor; Offenbach, *La Périchole*; A. Thomas, *Hamlet*; Wagner, *Die Meistersinger von Nürnberg*. Publications: Svendsen, String Quartet in A minor, String Quintet in C major, and Symphony No. 1. Deaths: Berwald, Brendel, Rossini.

1869 First U.S. Transcontinental Railroad completed. Tolstoy, *War and Peace*, and Twain, *Innocents Abroad*, published. Publication of Bottesini, *Metodo completo per contrabbasso* (Complete Method for Contrabass), and Wagner, *Über das Dirigiren* (On Conducting). Premieres: Brahms, *Ein deutsches Requiem* (A German Requiem, first performance of all seven movements); Cui, *Vil'yam Ratklif* (William Ratcliff); Verdi, *La forza del destino* (rev. version, Milan); Wagner, *Das Rheingold*. Publications: Cunha, *A Sertaneja*; J. Strauss (II), *Wein, Weib und Gesang* (Wine, Women, and Song). Deaths: Berlioz, Dargomïzhsky, Gottschalk; Molique.

1870 The United States extends suffrage to African American men by constitutional amendment; Napoléon III is captured and imprisoned weeks after declaring war on Prussia; France declares Third Republic. Verne publishes *Twenty-Thousand Leagues under the Sea*. Francis7 Xaver Witt founds *Allgemeiner Deutscher Cäcilienverein*. Wagner publishes monograph *Beethoven*. Premieres: Delibes, *Coppélia*; Gomes, *Il Guarany*; Raff, Symphony No. 3 *Im Walde* (In the Woods); Smetana, *Bartered Bride* (4th definitive ed.) and *Dalibor*; Wagner, *Die Walküre*. Deaths: Mercadante, Moscheles, Josef Strauss.

1871 Prussia defeats France in Franco-Prussian War. The German Empire is formed. Paris Commune suppressed. Publication of Eliot, *Middlemarch*, and Darwin, *The Descent of Man*. Whistler paints *Arrangement in Grey and Black No. 1*, or *Whistler's Mother*. Société Nationale de Musique founded by

Bussine and Saint-Saëns. Brahms moves to Vienna. Premieres: Gounod, *Gallia*; Verdi, *Aida*. Publications: Bizet, *Jeux d'enfants* (Childrens' Games); Castillon, Piano Quartet in G minor. Deaths: Fétis, Potter, Tausig, Thalberg.

1872 *Akademischer Wagnerverein* founded by Guido Adler, Felix Mottl, and Karl Wolf. Publication of Rückert, *Kindertodtenlieder* (posthumous). Coussemaker issues *Oeuvres complètes du trouvère Adam de la Halle* (Complete Works of the Trouvère Adam de la Halle). Premieres: Bizet, incidental music to Daudet, *L'arlésienne* (The Maid of Arles); Dargomïzhsky, *Kamennïy gost'* (The Stone Guest, completed by Cui); Ponchielli, *I promessi sposi* (The Betrothed, rev. version; orig. 1856); Söderman, incidental music for Shakespeare's *Richard III*. Publications: Liszt, *Christus*; Mussorgsky, *Detskaya* (The Nursery); Paine, *St. Peter*; Widor, Organ Symphonies No. 1–4, Op. 13. Deaths: Lowell Mason.

1873 The Panic of 1873 kicks off the Long Depression of 1873–1879. Jules Verne publishes *Around the World in 80 Days*. Publication of Spitta, *Johann Sebastian Bach*, vol. 1, and Wagner, *Eine Kapitulation* (A Capitulation). Premieres: Massenet, *Marie-Magdeleine*; Montero, *Virginia*; Paine, *St. Peter*; Ponchielli, *Le due gemelle* (The Twin Sisters); Raff, *Maria Stuarda*; Tchaikovsky, *The Snow Maiden* and *The Tempest*. Publications: J. Strauss (II), *Wiener Blut* (Viennese Blood). Deaths: Castillon, Ferdinand David, Friedrich Wieck.

1874 Art critic Louis Leroy labels Claude Monet's *Impression: Soleil levant* (Impression: Sunrise) "impressionist." Mallarmé completes *L'après-midi d'un faune* (The Afternoon of a Faun). Premieres: Caballero, *La Marsellesa* (The Girl from Marseilles); Mussorgsky, *Boris Godunov* (first version); Ponchielli, *I Lituani* (The Lithuanians); Smetana, *Vltava* (The Moldau); J. Strauss (II), *Die Fledermaus* (The Bat); Verdi, *Requiem*. Publications: Berwald, Symphony No. 1 (*Symphonie sérieuse*). Deaths: Cornelius, Tellefsen.

1875 Gevaert, *Nouveau traité d'instrumentation* (New Treatise on Instrumentation), and Hanslick, *Die moderne Oper: Kritiken und Studien* (Modern Opera: Criticisms and Studies), published. Premieres: Bizet, *Carmen*; Sullivan, *Trial by Jury*; Tchaikovsky, Piano Concerto No. 1. Publications: Lalo, *Symphonie espagnole*; Reinecke, Symphony No. 2; Saint-Saëns, *Danse macabre*. Deaths: Bennett, Bizet.

1876 The United States defeated at the Battle of Little Bighorn. Queen Victoria becomes empress of India. Premiere of Ibsen, *Peer Gynt*. Mark Twain publishes *The Adventures of Tom Sawyer*. Opening of Bayreuth Festival; Rameau Festival. Premieres: Brahms, Symphony No. 1; Delibes, *Sylvia*; Ponchielli, *La gioconda* (The Happy Woman); Stanford, incidental music to

Tennyson, *Queen Mary*; Suppé, *Fatinitza*; Wagner, *Der Ring des Nibelungen.* Publications: Grieg, incidental music to *Peer Gynt.* Deaths: Ambros, Félicien David, Mary Shaw, Samuel Wesley.

1877 Thomas Edison gives first demonstration of phonograph. Tolstoy publishes *Anna Karenina.* Tchaikovsky and Nadezhda von Meck begin corresponding. Premieres: Brahms, Symphony No. 2; Franck, *Les Eolides* (The Breezes); Massenet, *Le roi de Lahore* (The King of Lahore); Saint-Saëns, *Samson et Dalila*; Sullivan, *The Sorcerer*; Tchaikovsky, *Swan Lake* and *Francesca da Rimini.* Publications: Gonzaga, *Atraente* (Attractive); Lalo, Cello Concerto in D minor; Svendsen, *Karnival i Paris* (Carnival in Paris), three *Norwegian Rhapsodies*, and Symphony No. 2; Tchaikovsky, *The Tempest.*

1878 Paris Exhibition Opens. Publication of Hardy, *The Return of the Native.* First volume of Grove, *Dictionary of Music and Musicians* (1st ed.) issued. Premieres: Marqués, *El anillo de hierro* (The Iron Ring); Sullivan, *H.M.S. Pinafore*; Tchaikovsky, Symphony No. 4; Wagner, Prelude to *Parsifal.* Publications: Dvořák, *Slavonic Dances*, Op. 46.

1879 Ibsen publishes *A Doll's House.* Premieres: Brahms, Violin Concerto in D major; Stanford, Symphony No. 1; Sullivan, *The Pirates of Penzance*; Suppé, *Boccaccio*; Tchaikovsky, *Eugene Onegin.* Publications: Dvořák, *Moravské dvojzpěvy* (Moravian Duets).

1880 Thomas Edison opens first commercial power station. Publication of Dostoyevsky's *The Brothers Karamazov* and Twain's *A Tramp Abroad.* Hans von Bülow begins conducting Meiningen Orchestra; Amy Fay publishes *Music Study in Germany.* Premieres: Brahms, *Tragic Overture*, and Tchaikovsky, *Capriccio italien.* Publications: Franck, *Les béatitudes*; Smetana, String Quartet No. 1 "Z mého života" (From My Life) and *Vltava* (The Moldau); Tchaikovsky, Symphony No. 2 "Little Russian" (final version, beg. 1872) and Symphony No. 4. Deaths: Bull, Offenbach.

1881 U.S. President James Garfield assassinated. Savoy Theatre in London becomes first public building lit by incandescent light; Clara Barton founds American Red Cross. Henry Lee Higginson founds Boston Symphony Orchestra. Premieres: Brahms, *Academic Festival Overture*, *Nänie*, and Piano Concerto No. 2; Bruch, Scottish Fantasy for Violin and Orchestra; Bruckner, Symphony No. 4 (second version); Mackenzie, *The Bride*; Offenbach, *Les contes d'Hoffmann* (The Tales of Hoffmann; completed by Guiraud); R. Strauss, Symphony No. 1; Tchaikovsky, Violin Concerto and Piano Concerto No. 2; Verdi, *Simon Boccanegra* (rev. version, Milan). Publications: Bruch, *Kol Nidrei*; Svendsen, *Romance.* Deaths: Boehm, Mussorgsky, N. Rubinstein, Vieuxtemps.

1882 Publication of Nietzsche, *Die fröhliche Wissenschaft* (The Gay Science), and Twain, *The Prince and the Pauper*. Manet paints *A Bar at the Folies-Bergère*. Fifth volume of Ambros's *Geschichte der Musik* issued posthumously. Premieres: Tchaikovsky, *1812* Overture; Wagner, *Parsifal*. Publications: Balakirev, *Overture on the Themes of Three Russian Songs*; Borodin, Symphony No. 1 and *V sredney Azii* (In Central Asia); Brahms, Piano Trio No. 2; Mussorgsky, *Pesni i plyaski smerti* (Songs and Dances of Death; ed. Rimsky-Korsakov); Reinecke, Flute Sonata *Undine*. Deaths: Raff.

1883 The volcanos of Krakatoa explode, destroying most of the island with worldwide effects. Nietsche's *Also sprach Zarathustra* and Stevenson's *Treasure Island* published. Opening of Metropolitan Opera, New York. Premieres: Brahms, Symphony No. 3 and *Gesang der Parzen*; Chabrier, *España*; Delibes, *Lakmé*; Franck, *Le chasseur maudit* (The Accursed Huntsman). Publications: Chabrier, *España*; Lalo, *Concerto russe* for violin; Liszt, *Troisième année* (Third Year) from *Années de pèlerinage* (Years of Pilgrimage). Deaths: Flotow, Volkmann, Wagner.

1884 Washington Monument completed. Publication of Abbott's *Flatland* and Twain's *The Adventures of Huckleberry Finn*. Debussy wins the Prix de Rome; Dubois issues *L'accompagnement pratique du plainchant* (Practical Rules for Accompanying Plainchant); Grove publishes first edition of *Beethoven's Nine Symphonies*. Premieres: Bruckner, Symphony No. 7; Fibich, *Nevěsta messinská* (The Bride of Messina); Mackenzie, *The Rose of Sharon* (first version); Marqués, *El reloj de Lucerna* (The Lucerne Clock); Massenet, *Manon*; Sousa, *Désirée*; R. Strauss, Suite in B-flat major; Sullivan, *Princess Ida*; Verdi, *Don Carlo* (rev. version, Milan). Publications: Balakirev, *Tamara*; Borodin, String Quartet No. 1; MacDowell, Piano Concerto No. 1; Massenet, *Manon*; Smetana, *Dalibor*. Deaths: Smetana.

1885 *Revue Wagnerienne* in print (1885–1888). Premieres: Brahms, Symphony No. 4; Dvořák, Symphony No. 7 and *Svatební košile* (The Spectre's Bride); Franck, *Prélude, choral et fugue* and *Les Djinns* (The Genies); Stanford, *The Three Holy Children*; J. Strauss (II), *Die Zigeunerbaron* (The Gypsy Baron); Sullivan, *The Mikado*. Publications: Grieg, *Fra Holberg tid* (From Holberg's Time); Liszt, *Hungarian Rhapsodies* Nos. 17–19; Reinecke, Harp Concerto. Deaths: Hiller.

1886 New York City's Statue of Liberty completed. Publication of Hardy's *The Mayor of Casterbridge* and Stevenson's *The Strange Case of Dr. Jeckyll and Mr. Hyde*; Seurat completes painting *A Sunday Afternoon on the Island of La Grande Jatte*. Parry publishes *Studies of Great Composers*. Premieres: Bruckner, *Te Deum*; Dvořák, *Svatá Ludmila* (St. Ludmilla); Saint-Saëns, Symphony No. 3 ("Organ"); Stanford, *The Revenge*. Publications: Chaminade, Six Concert Etudes, Op. 35; Franck, Violin Sonata; Mussorgsky, *Kar-*

tinki s vïstavki (Pictures at an Exhibition, ed. Rimsky-Korsakov) and *Ivanova noch' na Lïsoy gore* (St John's Night on Bald Mountain, ed. Rimsky-Korsakov); Sousa, *The Gladiator*. Deaths: Köhler, Liszt, Ponchielli.

1887 Emil Berliner patents gramophone disc record. Nietzsche publishes *Zur Genealogie der Moral* (On the Genealogy of Morality). Premieres: Berutti, *Obertura Andes*; Brahms, Concerto for Violin and Cello; Parry, *Blest Pair of Sirens*; Sullivan, *Ruddigore*; Verdi, *Otello*. Publications: Borodin, Symphony No. 2 and Piano Trio No. 3; Dvořák, *Svatá Ludmila* (St. Ludmilla); Widor, Organ Symphonies No. 5–8, Op. 42. Deaths: Borodin, Lind, Malpiero, Marxsen.

1888 Wilhelm II becomes German emperor. Several London murders are attributed to Jack the Ripper; Van Gogh paints Arles *Sunflowers* series and cuts off ear. Premieres: Bruckner, Symphony No. 4 (third version); Fauré, *Requiem*; Franck, *Psyché*; Parry, *Judith*; Sullivan, *The Yeomen of the Guard*; Tchaikovsky, Symphony No. 5. Publications: Borodin, String Quartet No. 2 and Symphony No. 3 (completed by Glazunov); Grieg, *Peer Gynt* Suite No. 1; Mackenzie, Overture to *Twelfth Night*; Parry, *Judith*; Sousa, *Semper Fidelis*. Deaths: Alkan, Heller, Witt.

1889 Universal Exhibition in Paris; Eiffel Tower completed (beg. 1887). Van Gogh paints *The Starry Night*. Publication of Tolstoy's *The Kreutzer Sonata* and Twain's *A Connecticut Yankee in King Arthur's Court*. Premieres: Bretón, *Los amantes de Teruel* (The Lovers of Teruel); Dubois, *Fantaisie triomphale*; Franck, Symphony in D minor; R. Strauss, *Don Juan*; Sullivan, *The Gondoliers*. Publications: Franck, String Quartet; Rimsky-Korsakov, *Sheherazade*; Smetana, String Quartet No. 2; Sousa, *Washington Post*; Wolf, *Mörike-* and *Eichendorff-Lieder*. Deaths: Bottesini, Henselt.

1890 Emperor Wilhelm II dismisses Chancellor Bismarck. Wounded Knee Massacre occurs in South Dakota. Publication of Ibsen's *Hedda Gabler*, Frazer's *The Golden Bough*, and Wilde's *The Picture of Dorian Gray*. Monet begins *Haystacks* series. Gevaert, *Cours méthodique d'orchestration* (Methodical Course of Instruction in Orchestration), published. Tchaikovsky's patroness von Meck terminates their relationship. Premieres: Borodin, *Knyaz' Igor'* (Prince Igor); Franck, String Quartet; Mascagni, *Cavalleria rusticana* (Rustic Chivalry); Smyth, *Serenade* and *Anthony and Cleopatra*; R. Strauss, *Tod und Verklärung* (Death and Transfiguration); Tchaikovsky, *The Sleeping Beauty* and *The Queen of Spades*. Publications: Debussy, *Cinq poèmes de Baudelaire*; Dubois, *Fantaisie triomphale*; MacDowell, Piano Concerto No. 2; Rimsky-Korsakov, *Russian Easter Overture*; Wolf, *Goethe-Lieder*. Deaths: Franck, Gade, Lachner.

1891 Frank Wedekind completes *Spring Awakening*; Gaugin paints *Tahitian Women on the Beach*. Carnegie Hall opens in New York City. Premieres: Arensky, *Son na Volga* (A Dream on the Volga); Chausson, Symphony in B-flat major; Fauré, *Cinq mélodies*; Gomes, *Condor*; Marqués, *El montaguillo* (The Altar Boy); Stanford, *Eden*. Publications: Wolf, *Spanisches Liederbuch*. Deaths: Delibes.

1892 Doyle publishes *The Adventures of Sherlock Holmes*. Premieres: Bruckner, Symphony No. 8; Dvořák, *Příroda, Život a Láska* (Nature, Life and Love); Massenet, *Werther*; Parry, *Job*; Sibelius, *Kullervo*; Tchaikovsky, *The Nutcracker*. Publications: Albéniz, *Chant d'Espagne*; Brahms, Trio in A minor for Clarinet, Cello, and Piano (Op. 114) and Clarinet Quintet in B minor, Op. 115; Franck, *Trois chorals*; Gomes, *Colombo*; Wolf, *Italienisches Liederbuch*, vol. 1. Deaths: Dessoff, Franz, Guiraud, Lalo.

1893 World's Fair in Chicago; Panic of 1893. Wilde publishes *Salomé*; premiere of Maeterlinck, *Pelléas et Mélisande*; Munch paints *The Scream*. Parry publishes *The Art of Music* (rev. as *The Evolution of the Art of Music*, 1896). Premieres: Albéniz, *The Magic Opal*; Bretón, *La verbena de la poloma* (The Paloma Fair); Caballero, *El dúo de La africana* (The Duet from *L'Africaine*); Debussy, *Prélude à "L'apres-midi d'un faune"*; Franck, *Les Eolides* (The Breezes) and *Les Djinns* (The Genies); Grieg, *Peer Gynt* Suite No. 2; Humperdinck, *Hänsel und Gretel*; Leoncavallo, *I Pagliacci*; Parker, *Hora novissima*; Puccini, *Manon Lescaut*; Tchaikovsky, Symphony No. 6; Verdi, *Falstaff*. Publications: Sousa, *The Liberty Bell*. Deaths: Gounod, Tchaikovsky.

1894 French army officer Alfred Dreyfus, of Jewish descent, accused of spying for Germans. Publication of Fontane, *Effi Briest*; Kipling, *The Jungle Book*; Twain, *Pudd'nhead Wilson*. Founding of Schola Cantorum. Premieres: Massenet, *Thaïs*; Parry, *King Saul*; Rachmaninoff, *Trio élégiaque* No. 2; R. Strauss, *Guntram* and Symphony No. 2. Publications: Arensky, Piano Trio No. 1 in D minor; Debussy, String Quartet in G minor; Dvořák, Piano Trio ("Dumky") and String Quartet in F major; Fauré, *La bonne chanson*; Magnard, Symphony No. 1. Deaths: Bülow, Chabrier, A. Rubinstein.

1895 Alfred Dreyfus sentenced to life on Devil's Island. Oscar Wilde sentenced to two years' imprisonment on sodomy charges. Caruso debuts in Naples. Publication of Crane, *The Red Badge of Courage*; Hardy, *Jude the Obscure*; Wells, *The Time Machine*. Publication begins of "complete" Rameau edition (–1913). Premieres: Bretón, *La Dolores*; Mahler, Symphony No. 2; Tchaikovsky, Piano Concerto No. 3. Publications: Mackenzie, *Britannia* Overture; Reinecke, Symphony No. 3. Deaths: Suppé.

1896 The Olympic Games are revived in Athens. Publication of Herzl, *The Jewish State*, and Wells, *The Island of Dr. Moreau*. Premieres: Dvořák, *The Water Goblin* and Cello Concerto in B minor; Puccini, *La bohème*; Sousa, *El Capitan* (operetta); Stanford, *Shamus O'Brien*; R. Strauss, *Also sprach Zarathustra*. Publications: Chausson, *Poème de l'amour et de la mer* (Poem of Love and the Sea); Franck, Symphony in D minor; MacDowell, *Woodland Sketches*; Wolf, *Italienisches Liederbuch*, vol. 2. Deaths: Bruckner, Gomes, Pohl, Clara Schumann.

1897 Klimt and others found the Vienna Secession. Publication of Rostand, *Cyrano de Bergerac*; Stoker, *Dracula*; and Wells, *The Invisible Man*. Mahler becomes director of Court Opera (Vienna). George Chadwick publishes *Harmony: A Course of Study*. Premieres: Caballero, *La viejecita* (The Little Old Lady); Dukas, *L'aprenti sorcier* (The Sorcerer's Apprentice); Fibich, *Šarka*; Humperdinck, *Königskinder* (melodrama version); Scriabin, Piano Concerto. Publications: MacDowell, "Indian" Suite No. 2; Sousa, *The Stars and Stripes Forever*. Deaths: Woldemar Bargiel, Brahms.

1898 The USS *Maine* explodes in Cuba; the United States declares war on Spain. Evidence emerges that the French military suppressed evidence of Alfred Dreyfus's innocence, leading to Zola's famously titled open letter, "J'Accuse . . . !" (I Accuse You!). Premieres: Caballero, *Gigantes y cabezudos* (Giants and Big-Heads); Dvořák, *The Wild Dove*; Glazunov, *Raymonda*; Granados, *María del Carmen*; Rimsky-Korsakov, *Sadko*; Smyth, *Fantasio*; Richard Strauss, *Don Quixote*. Publications: Grieg, *Haugtussa* (The Mountain Maid); Reger, Chorale Fantasy on *Ein' feste Burg ist unser Gott*. Deaths: George Frederick Bristow.

1899 Alfred Dreyfus is returned to France, retried for treason, convicted again despite evidence in his defense, and nevertheless pardoned; official exoneration would not come until 1906. Publication of Kate Chopin, *The Awakening*; Conrad, *Heart of Darkness*; Freud, *The Interpretation of Dreams*; and Norris, *McTeague*. Scott Joplin's success begins with *Maple Leaf Rag*. Premieres: Elgar, *Enigma* Variations and *Sea Pictures*; R. Strauss, *Ein Heldenleben* (A Heroic Life). Publications: Balakirev, Symphony No. 1; Mackenzie, "Scottish" Piano Concerto; Magnard, Symphony No. 2; Mahler, *Des Knaben Wunderhorn* (The Boy's Miraculous Posthorn); Reger, Chorale Fantasy on *Freu'dich sehr, o meine Seele*. Deaths: Chausson, J. Strauss (II).

1900 Paris World Exhibition; international forces arrive in China to suppress Boxer Rebellion. Publication of Baum, *The Wonderful Wizard of Oz*; Conrad, *Lord Jim*; Dreiser, *Sister Carrie*; Schnitzler, *Reigen*. Premieres: Elgar, *The Dream of Gerontius*; Fauré, *Prométhée*; Puccini, *Tosca*; Rimsky-Korsakov, *The Tale of Tsar Saltan*; Sibelius, *Finlandia* and Symphony No. 1 (final version); Zemlinsky, *Es war einmal* (Once upon a Time). Publications: Reger, Two Chorale Fantasias, Op. 40 and *Fantasia and Fugue on B-A-C-H.* Deaths: Fibich, Grove, Hartmann, J. Schalk, Sullivan.

1901 Queen Victoria dies and is succeeded by son Edward VII; U.S. President McKinley is assassinated. Oil is discovered near Beaumont, Texas. Publication of Kipling, *Kim*; Mann, *Buddenbrooks*; Potter, *The Tale of Peter Rabbit.* Dubois releases *Traité de contrepoint et de fugue* (Treatise on Counterpoint and Fugue). Premieres: Delius, *Paris: A Nocturne*; Dvořák, *Rusalka*; Elgar, *Pomp and Circumstance* March No. 1; Mackenzie, *The Cricket on the Hearth*; Mahler, Symphony No. 4; Rachmaninoff, Piano Concerto No. 2; Scriabin, Symphony No. 1; R. Strauss, *Feuersnot* (Fire Famine). Publications: Debussy, *Nocturnes*; Paine, *Azara*; Reger, 3 Chorale Fantasias, Op. 52. Deaths: Chrysander, Verdi.

1902 Second Boer War ends. Publication of Doyle, *The Hound of the Baskervilles* and Kipling, *Just So Stories.* Klimt paints Beethoven Frieze in the Vienna Secession Building; Rodin completes *The Thinker.* Caruso does his first recording sessions. Premieres: Castro, *Atzimba*; Debussy, *Pelléas et Mélisande*; Elorduy, *Zulema*; Lehár, *Gold und Silber*; Mahler, Symphony No. 3; Scriabin, Symphony No. 2; Sibelius, Symphony No. 2; Smyth, *Der Wald* (The Forest). Publications: Magnard, Symphony No. 3; Reger, Piano Quintet No. 2.

1903 Orville Wright is first to fly an airplane. Kandinsky paints *Der blaue Reiter* (The Blue Rider). Publication of London, *The Call of the Wild*, and Romain Rolland, *Vie de Beethoven* (Life of Beethoven). Caruso joins the Metropolitan Opera. Premieres: Bruckner, Symphony No. 9, first three movements (ed. Ferdinand Löwe). Publications: Franck, *Psyché*; Magnard, *Hymne à la justice.* Deaths: Wolf.

1904 Russia completes Trans-Siberian Railroad; Japan declares war on Russia. Publication of London, *The Sea-Wolf*; premiere of Barrie, *Peter Pan*, and Wedekind, *Pandora's Box.* Premieres: Janáček, *Její pastorkyňa: Jenůfa* (Her Stepdaughter Jenůfa); Mahler, Symphony No. 5; R. Strauss, *Symphonia Domestica.* Publications: Magnard, *Chant funèbre*; Reger, *Variations and Fugue on a Theme of Bach.* Deaths: Dvořák.

1905 Japan defeats Russia in Russo-Japanese War. Russian Revolution of 1905. Publication of Burnett, *A Little Princess* and Orczy, *The Scarlet Pimpernel.* Einstein publishes on special theory of relativity. Premieres: Debussy, *La mer*; Glazunov, Violin Concerto; Lehár, *Die lustige Witwe* (The Merry Widow); Lyadov, *Baba Yaga*; Mahler, *Kindertotenlieder*; Sibelius, Violin Concerto (final version; orig. 1904); R. Strauss, *Salome.* Publications: Scriabin, Symphony No. 3. Deaths: Cervantes, Theodore Thomas.

1906 Earthquakes on American Pacific coast largely destroy San Francisco and Valparaíso. Publication of London, *White Fang*. Premieres: Mahler, Symphony No. 6; Parry, *The Soul's Ransom*; Rachmaninoff, *Francesca da Rimini*; Smyth, *Standrecht* (orig. titled *Les naufrageurs* or *The Wreckers*). Publications: Albéniz, *Iberia*, book 1; Lyadov, *Eight Russian Folksongs*; Sibelius, *Karelia* Overture and Symphony No. 3. Deaths: Arensky, Paine.

1907 Picasso paints *The Young Ladies of Avignon*. Stieglitz photographs *The Steerage*. Busoni prints *Entwurf einer neuen Ästhetik der Tonkunst* (Sketch of a New Compositional Aesthetics). Premieres: Dukas, *Ariane et Barbe-bleue* (Arianna and Bluebeard); Mahler, Symphony No. 7; Parry, *The Vision of Life*. Publications: Albéniz, *Iberia*, books 2 and 3; Glazunov, Symphony No. 8. Deaths: Grieg, Joachim, Ludwig Thuille.

1908 First Ford Model T automobile produced. Publication of Chesterton, *The Man Who Was Thursday*; Forster, *A Room with a View*; Grahame, *The Wind in the Willows*; and Montgomery, *Anne of Green Gables*. Klimt paints *The Kiss*. Premieres: Delius, *Brigg Fair* and *In a Summer Garden*; Elgar, Symphony No. 1; Rachmaninoff, Symphony No. 2; Scriabin, *The Poem of Ecstasy*. Publications: Albéniz, *Iberia*, book 4; Balakirev, Symphony No. 2; Debussy, *Children's Corner*; Reinecke, Flute Concerto. Deaths: Gevaert, MacDowell, Rimsky-Korsakov, Sarasate.

1909 Publication of Leroux, *The Phantom of the Opera*. Premieres: Lehár, *Der Graf von Luxemburg* (The Count of Luxemburg); Rachmaninoff, Piano Concerto No. 3; Rimsky-Korsakov, *The Golden Cockerel*; R. Strauss, *Elektra*. Publications: Bartók, String Quartet No. 1; Lyadov, *The Enchanted Lake*; Reger, *Symphonischer Prolog zu einer Tragödie*; Sibelius, *Karelia* Suite. Deaths: Albéniz.

1910 King George V succeeds father Edward VII as king of United Kingdom. Publication of Forster, *Howards End*. Matisse paints *Dance*. Premieres: Bloch, *Macbeth*; Elgar, Violin Concerto in B minor; Humperdinck, *Königskinder* (opera version); Lehár, *Zigeunerliebe* (Gypsy Love); Mahler, Symphony No. 8; Puccini, *La fanciulla del West* (The Golden Girl of the West); Rachmaninoff, *Liturgiya svyatovo Ioanna Zlatousta* (Liturgy of St. John Chrysostom); Stravinsky, *The Firebird*; Zemlinsky, *Kleider machen Leute* (The Clothes Make the Man). Publications: Debussy, *Préludes*, book 1; Lyadov, *Kikimora*. Deaths: Balakirev, Reinecke, Viardot.

1911 Triangle Shirtwaist Factory fire in New York City kills 146 workers. Amundsen expedition is first to reach South Pole. Publication of Barrie, *Peter and Wendy*; Bierce, *The Devil's Dictionary*; Burnett, *The Secret Garden*; Wharton, *Ethan Frome*. *Blaue Reiter* exhibition in Munich features works of Kandinsky and others. Premieres: Elgar, Symphony No. 2; Magnard, *Bérénice*; Mahler, *Das Lied von der Erde*; Scriabin, *Prometheus: The Poem of Fire*; Sibelius, Symphony No. 4; Smyth, "The March of the Women"; R. Strauss, *Der Rosenkavalier*; Stravinsky, *Petrushka*. Deaths: Mahler.

1912 Duchamp paints *Nude Descending a Staircase, No. 2*. Publication of Burroughs, *Tarzan of the Apes* and *A Princess of Mars*; Grey, *Riders of the Purple Sage*; and Mann, *Der Tod in Venedig* (Death in Venice). Ethel Smyth briefly imprisoned for militant activity as suffragette. Premieres: Dukas, *La péri*; Elgar, *The Music Makers*; Gonzaga, *Forrobodó*; Mahler, Symphony No. 9; Parker, *Mona*; Schoenberg, *Pierrot lunaire*; R. Strauss, *Ariadne auf Naxos* (first version, rev. 1916). Publications: Granados, *Goyescas, o Los majos enamorados* (Goyescas; or, The Gallants in Love), book 1; Reger, *Romantic Suite*. Deaths: Samuel Coleridge-Taylor, Massenet.

1913 The United States amends the Constitution to allow popular election of senators. R. J. Reynolds produces first packaged cigarettes. Publication of Cather, *O Pioneers!* and premiere of Shaw, *Pygmalion*. Luigi Rossolo publishes *The Art of Noises: A Futurist Manifesto*. Performances of Berg's *Altenberg Lieder* (Vienna) and the Ballets Russes's *The Rite of Spring* (Paris, with music by Stravinsky) are met with riots. Premieres: Fauré, *Pénélope*; Mussorgsky, *Sorochinskaya yamarka* (Sorochintsky Fair, completed by Lyadov et al.); Stravinsky, *The Rite of Spring*. Publications: Debussy, *Trois poèmes de Mallarmé* and *Préludes*, book 2; Granados, *Goyescas*, book 2; Reger, *4 Tone Poems after Arnold Böcklin*. Deaths: Draeseke.

1914 World War I begins. Panama Canal opens. Publications: Reger, *Variations and Fugue on a Theme of Mozart* and *8 Geistliche Gesänge* (Eight Sacred Songs); Scriabin, *Vers la flamme*; Stravinsky, *The Nightingale*. Deaths: Lyadov, Magnard, Giovanni Sgambati.

Introduction

MUSIC'S ROMANTICISMS

"Romantic music" is a term that means so many different things to so many different people that it effectively possesses no stable and reliable meaning for anyone. Even setting aside, for practical reasons, the vast world of vernacular musics, the repertoires to which the adjective "Romantic" is commonly applied range from the late Baroque (especially Johann Sebastian Bach) through Sergei Rachmaninoff, Jean Sibelius, Richard Strauss, and Ralph Vaughan-Williams, to say nothing of the Neo-Romantic movement that emerged in the late 20th century in the works of, for example, George Rochberg, David Del Tredici, and Ellen Taafe Zwillich. It is easy to see how 20th- and 21st-century composers were able to seize upon a corpus of stylistic traits familiar from 19th-century music and somehow merge them with ideas, styles, and compositional techniques developed more recently—but we must also remember that 19th-century composers and performers who offered what today would be considered "romanticized" renditions of the music of Bach did not feel that they were appropriating that music and adapting it to their own needs. Rather, in their own view, they were discovering in Bach's music an adumbration of their own and reviving it. Similarly, when self-evidently Romantic composers and commentators such as E. T. A. Hoffmann, Franz Liszt, Robert Schumann, and Richard Wagner spoke of Wolfgang Amadeus Mozart as a Romantic, their intention was neither to appropriate and assimilate Mozart nor to project their own agendas onto "Classical" music but to acknowledge the commonalities between Mozart's music and their own—diverse though their own styles were.

Nor are these broader applications of the term "Romantic" limited to figures who are uncredentialed in more inherently scholarly disciplines, such as history and historiography. Beginning in 1917, musicologist Alfred Einstein's widely used *Short History of Western Music* famously exploited a dichotomy between Classicism and Romanticism by bestowing semantically attractive but historically specious monikers on composers such as Schubert and Mendelssohn while also portraying Mozart in a light that, in historical retrospect, is heavily *romanticized* (as the term *Romantic* was understood in the early 20th century).[1] A generation later, Paul Henry Lang adopted the opposite strategy, emphasizing "the confluence of Classicism and Romanticism" in chapter 15 of his seminal *Music in Western Civilization*.[2] The terrain has shifted—sometimes subtly, sometimes significantly—as numerous other scholars, such as Marshall Brown, Carl Dahlhaus, John Daverio, Hans Lenneberg, David Montgomery, and Leon Plantinga (to name but a few), have attempted to clarify what music qualifies as Romantic.[3] Indeed, extrapolating from these stylistic exponents and scholarly ventures a chronological framework for "Romantic music," one might reasonably argue that in all of music history since about 1700, Romantic music has been absent from newly composed music for only about one generation of major composers, from the death of Vaughan-Williams (1958) to George Rochberg's turn to tonality in the early 1970s.

How, then, is one to determine which ideas and composers, and what music, does or does not warrant coverage in a historical dictionary of Romantic music? Traditional attempts to define such a scope have been based on criteria that are stylistic, chronological, or both. Although some stylistic approaches refine the inquiry by distinguishing between *romantic* and *romanticist*,[4] foundational to most is a conceptual dichotomy between Romanticism and Classicism, a presupposition that Romanticism in music is an oppositional or (at most) complementary force to Classicism. Romanticism, in this view, celebrates the sublime over the beautiful, the individual over the collective, the nationalist over the cosmopolitan, the secular over the sacred, the daemonic and Dionysian over the quotidian and Apollonian. It values subjectivity over objectivity, prizes extremism and radicalism while shunning moderation and establishmentarianism, celebrates idealism while looking askance at prudence and pragmatism. Composers and works are labeled "Romantic" to the extent that they are perceived to cultivate the antecedents in each of the above pairings, un-Romantic to the extent that they (supposedly) do not.

But such dualities are fundamentally flawed. To begin with, they make little allowance for any nuanced and symbiotic coexistence of "Classical" and "Romantic" impulses within a given work or a given composer's life and/or career. More importantly, there is no single set of criteria that fit both the Romanticism of the early 19th century and that of the early 20th century: the values cultivated late in the century are worlds removed from—indeed, often antipodal to—those cultivated in its early years. Gustav Mahler and Richard Strauss, like Johannes Brahms, Anton Bruckner, Wagner, Liszt, Schumann, and Felix Mendelssohn Bartholdy before them, certainly enjoyed a profound and extraordinarily creative retrospective empathy with Beethoven and Schubert—but Beethoven almost certainly would not have recognized the Romanticism of Ferrucio Busoni's arrangement (1916) of the Benedictus from the *Missa solemnis*, and neither he nor Schubert would likely have recognized the Romantic spirit that spoke in Mahler's Ninth Symphony (1911). Similarly, the inherently cosmopolitan spirit of both Friedrich Schiller's "An die Freude" and the final movement of Beethoven's Ninth Symphony could hardly be further from the fierce German nationalism that just a generation later inspired the interpretations of Adolf Bernhard Marx and Wagner[5] as well as other composers who responded to the Ninth in their own works.

The Classic/Romantic dichotomy is also false because the Enlightenment, as the intellectual and cultural progenitor of Classicism, was itself inherently radical and prefigurative of Romanticism.[6] When the early self-described Romantics rejected the values they perceived as normative of late 18th-century culture, what they opposed was not the Enlightenment but a retrenchment of sorts, an attempt by the philosophes and their followers to moderate the radical revolution of the mind that had been unleashed at the beginning of the 17th century by philosophers such as Pierre Bayle (1647–1706), Thomas Hobbes (1588–1679), and Baruch Spinoza (1632–1677)—ideas that had quickly spread to the reading public and exerted momentous influence in the realms of jurisprudence, theology, and the study of history. As members of the clergy, the political elite, and the reading public quickly realized, the original Enlightenment facilitated—*demanded*—changes in society that would profoundly destabilize the existing order: making the individual rather than the collective the basis of politics and asserting values of atheism, secularism, and religious tolerance; the need for greater equality for women under the law and the renunciation of slavery; and an empirical, naturalist approach to the sciences and history alike. Those currents—all obvious adumbrations of ideas that would figure significantly in Romanticism—met with widespread resistance, and that resistance impelled Voltaire, Jean-Jacques Rousseau, Immanuel Kant, and other late Enlightenment figures to salvage those principles by formulating the comparatively moderate theses against which Romanticism is commonly perceived to have revolted.[7] The revolutionary impulse of Romanticism is thus more accurately viewed as an affirmation of the principles that originally defined the Enlightenment, not a rejection of them. If Classicism is Enlightenment's progeny, then Romanticism is the maturation and fruition of Classicism. This dictionary thus declines to acknowledge any meaningful distinction between Romantic and Classical music—and with that the concept of Romantic music (the subject of this book) threatens to become as all-encompassing as the concept of music itself.

At the other end of the methodological spectrum is a definition of Romantic music that relies on chronology. Although no one would dispute that the 19th century is (in the formulation of Jacques Barzun) "the Romantic century,"[8] few would argue that the era of Romantic music was born on 1 January 1800 and ended on 31 December 1899. Some scholars have dated the Romantic movement as beginning with the death of Beethoven, others with Beethoven's embarking on his "new path" around 1802, and so on. None of these composer-centric approaches is satisfactory, however, because they tacitly sweep aside vast amounts of Romantic music in the interest of defining the concept in terms of an individual who participated in and contributed to music's Romanticisms rather than creating them.

Instead, we adopt a methodological compromise between two opposite methodological extremes in defining our subject—discussing all music conventionally labeled "Romantic" or only all music and composers active between 1800 and 1900—by centering our volume on what is commonly referred to as "the long 19th century"—the period from the outbreak of the French Revolution (1789) to the beginning of World War I (1914).[9] Starting with that framework, we aspire to a primarily synchronic perspective, privileging composers, works, and ideas that were considered Romantic at the time of their creation and initial dissemination and approaching chronologically circumjacent entries (e.g., J. S. Bach, Wolfgang Amadeus Mozart, Claude Debussy, or impressionism) from a perspective centered on values cultivated during the long 19th century. Thus, our entries on Mozart and Haydn will bear little resemblance to their counterparts in Bertil van Boer's *Historical Dictionary of the Music of the Classical Period*[10] because they focus on 19th-century musicians' inevitably subjective knowledge and assessment of those figures. At the same time, we by no means pretend that our readers' needs and perspectives are defined by those that conditioned the way the 19th century saw itself. We thus complement our deliberately synchronic approach with other topics that have emerged subsequently—some of them factual (recently acquired information about individual works or composers' lives or issues such as copyright and performance right), others conceptual, methodological, or theoretical (e.g., editorial method, performance practice, or reception history).

ROMANTICISM'S UPHEAVALS

Within that broad historical framework, this book treats neither the long 19th century nor Romantic music of that century as a more-or-less smooth or even mildly bumpy continuum. Instead, we underscore the many and often profoundly disruptive political and social events that characterized the long 19th century in the eyes of its inhabitants. The century commenced in the 1790s with what historian Jay Winik has called "the great upheaval"[11]—the rise and establishment of democracy, industrialism, liberalism, nationalism, republicanism, and revolution; the emergence of a savage Holy War between Muslims and Christians and a tumultuous societal debate in Europe about whether Jews should or should not be "tolerated" as members of European society; the fledgling United States' survival of three separate rebellions and much internal discord and its initial growth toward stable nationhood; the beginnings of organized dissent against colonial rule in Latin America; and, coterminous with these momentous changes, a vain but also consequential transferral of late Enlightenment ideas concerning order and reason into the constellation of new forces now identified as Romanticism.

At century's end, the existing order wrought by those developments was again thrown into chaos with World War I and, in the worlds of music and the other arts, the firm establishment of technologies that made it possible for sound to be transported across vast distances, transcending (by means of recorded and broadcast sound) even time and space themselves. By the time of Gustav Mahler's *Kindertotenlieder*, Ethel Smyth's "The March of the Women," or Richard Strauss's *Der Rosenkavalier*, it was possible for the experience of music to be an entirely passive act of consumption rather than one that required performers and listeners to share a common space and experience music actively together—thus obliterating those subtle but powerful listener/performer interactions that continue to inform live performances today. That transformation of the sociology of musical creation, performance, and consumption created the structures of musical listening that have predominated ever since—structures that in principle are utterly alien to music's Romanticisms as they had existed up to then.

At the epicenter of that long century bookended by upheaval, we find another widespread surge of paroxysmal change in the Revolutions of 1848 in Europe and the lead-up to and eruption of the Civil War in the United States, the latter being the bloodiest war in human history to that date. The two half-centuries surrounding the mid-century upheavals may also be seen as each subdividing into two parts (demarcating the revolutions of 1830 and the wars of the 1870s), and the first of these four sections must also be further subdivided around 1815, the end of the Napoleonic Wars that had consummated the societal upheavals set in motion with the French Revolution. Comparably important, albeit in more elusive terms, is a further subdivision at around 1890—the point where the forces of modernism acquired critical mass[12] and the major industrial powers embarked on what was to be the final phase of the New Imperialism.

These societal caesurae were not just the current events that formed a context for music's Romanticisms. They also affected the resources available for the arts and learning, the demographics of domestic and public music making, and the institutions of music themselves. In recognition of these circumstances, we proceed from the reasonable assumptions that artworks are conditioned by the cultural, intellectual, and political worlds that bear them and that composers—themselves also a product of those worlds—address themselves to performers and listeners whose responses to and interpretations of music are conditioned by those same worlds. Readers will thus find that this dictionary includes topic entries for "purely" political topics, such as the Congress of Vienna, the Restoration and Bourbon Restoration, or the Franco-Prussian War, as well as frequent reference to them.

THE GENERATIONS OF ROMANTICISM

But while music reflects and refracts its contexts, it is composed, performed, and consumed by humans, not "-isms." We address this human agency by differentiating among four reasonably discrete generations of Romantics, using the above-mentioned major societal events as our guideposts in doing so and framing the individual generations in terms of how those societal guideposts align with composers' formative years (upbringing and education) and professional careers.

The *Early Romantic Generation* is thus viewed here as the group of composers whose upbringing and education coincided with the initiation of the great societal upheaval of the late 18th century and began trying to establish their reputations at the turn of the 19th century, as young professionals addressing themselves to the musical public as it existed during the Napoleonic Wars. The composers of this generation thus matured during the final years of the system of aristocratic and institutional patronage that had dominated musical culture since time immemorial and witnessed the first flourishing of a new culture of public patronage. The potency of church and court as sponsors and consumers of musical production was now rivaled or surpassed by the commercial power of an increasingly urbanized and literate middle class whose interests were often secular as well as sacred and whose sympathies with the political status quo were anything but assured. In pedestrian terms, those socioeconomic developments that coincided with the development of these composers' emergent self-identification as professional musicians informed their worldviews. They also determined whether they would be able to make a living in their chosen vocation or be forced to corral it into the nooks and crannies of a life whose subsistence was provided by other means.

Such were the defining circumstances of composers born during the last three decades of the 18th century—an extraordinary generation that includes not only the oft-cited Ludwig van Beethoven, Nicolò Paganini, Gioacchino Rossini, Franz Schubert, and Carl Maria von Weber but also less celebrated generational compeers, such as Franz Berwald, Johann Nepomuk Hummel, Étienne-Nicolas Méhul, Giacomo Meyerbeer, Georges Onslow, Cipriani Potter, Louis Spohr, Maria Szymanowska, Václav Tomášek, and Aleksey Verstovsky, among many others.

Although many members of that Early Romantic Generation lived well into the new century, their perspective on that new and tumultuous time differed substantively from that of the *Romantic Generation* born in the first two decades of the 19th century—an equally or even more extraordinary group whose exponents included (to name just a few) Vincenzo Bellini, Hector Berlioz, Olé Bull, Fryderyk Chopin, Félicien David, William Henry Fry, Fanny Hensel, Franz Liszt, Maria Malibran, Felix Mendelssohn Bartholdy, Jacques Offenbach, Clara Schumann, Robert Schumann, Thomas Tellefsen, Sigismond Thalberg, Giuseppe Verdi, and Richard Wagner. For those younger composers, the societal tumult of the Napoleonic Wars and the radical assumptions of liberalism that had first flourished in the early or middle careers of the Early Romantic Generation were simply the way of the world during their youth—but Bonaparte's defeat in 1814 and the establishment of a new, more conservative social order that centered on domestic values combined with major developments in industry and communication during the first part of the century to make the general issues and quotidian realities that defined these musicians' careers substantially different than those that accompanied their rise to maturity.

The growth of Romantic nationalism and its attendant cults of Romantic constructions of historical figures who suited its needs (J. S. Bach, Miguel de Cervantes, Albrecht Dürer, Ossian, and William Shakespeare) further informed their perspectives, and for German and Austrian composers especially, the deaths of Weber (1826) and Beethoven (1827), along with the de facto retirement of Rossini (1829), created a sudden and enormous vacuum where the dominant figures of European cultivated music had been just a few years earlier. When the Bach Revival became a public affair after the Berlin Singakademie's three performances of the Baroque master's *St. Matthew Passion* in the spring of 1829, leading to a surge in editions and performances of Bach's music in the mid- and late 19th century, many of the Romantic Generation's composers found in the styles, techniques, and musical rhetoric of the early 18th century an array of sources of inspiration for infusing the musical languages of modernity with "new" (i.e., Baroque) gestures and techniques that, by virtue of Bach's growing reputation as a great German composer whose music had fallen into obscurity because of the increasingly outmoded values of the mid-18th century, imbued those idioms with historical authority.

Then there were the mid-century revolutions. The significance of these events is attested to in part by the fact that virtually every composer who lived past them, whether from the Romantic Generation or the Early Romantic Generation, exhibited a marked difference in style and technique around mid-century. More telling still are the heated, eloquent, and often polemical writings about music's past, present, and future that proliferated in the 1850s and the fact that the nationalist concerns that had taken root and begun to grow during the century's first half became decisive aspects of musical life at mid-century.

A review of the explicit and implicit importance of national style as an aspect of musical style for the *Late Romantic Generation* attests to this new, emphatically social and political character in the musical discourse of the century's third quarter. In the Italian lands, the composers and others who came of age around mid-century achieved the unification of their country under a single ruler for the first time since the fifth century—not least of all by making the name of the successful Romantic Generation composer Giuseppe Verdi into an acronym for the slogan of the unification movement and appropriating his works for their own cause. The German lands were deeply riven by polemics. On the one hand, the second half of the century witnessed the maturation and flourishing of a conception of "pure" music as the superior manifestation of Germanness (as represented in mythologized readings of the symphonies of Haydn, Mozart, and Beethoven; many works of the Late Romantic Generation's own Bruckner and Brahms; and the rise to prominence of the Viennese critic Eduard Hanslick). Set against this cult—and argued with great eloquence—was a self-consciously progressive stance represented by the New German School and personified by Liszt and Wagner, who were championed in writings of Franz Brendel, Adolf Bernhard Marx, Richard Pohl, and others.

The mid-19th century was also the age in which Russia's Mighty Handful began to develop their ideas and coalesce as a group, the age that witnessed Britain's strongest effort yet at emancipation from the hegemony of continental composers, the strongest attempt by the young United States to do the same, and a momentous (and at least partially successful) effort of the former and continuing colonies in Latin America to do the same. Amid it all, developments in transportation and communications had made it possible to travel faster and farther than ever before, facilitating a broader intercourse among competing ideas around the musical world, and the music-publishing industry's own technologies had made possible the production and sale of more music in more formats, at lower cost, than ever before. Church and court remained staunch and important constituents of music and its publics—but for the musicians of the Late Romantic Generation more than ever before, the second half of the 19th century was a world in which the middle classes and the forces of liberalism, more than church, court, and state, were central and essential to professional success in leaving a meaningful legacy for posterity. The Late Romantic Generation's best-known members include Mily Balakirev, Georges Bizet, Aleksandr Borodin, Johannes Brahms, Max Bruch, Anton Bruckner, Feruccio Busoni, Emmanuel Chabrier, César Cui, Antonín Dvořák, Stephen Foster, César Franck, Louis Moreau Gottschalk, Charles Gounod, Edvard Grieg, Jules Massenet, Joseph Rheinberger, Camille Saint-

Saëns, Bedřich Smetana, Modest Mussorgsky, and Pyotor Tchaikovsky, but to these must be added any number of other notable composers—among them Alexis de Castillon, Peter Cornelius, Brasílio da Cunha, Théodore Dubois, Amy Fay, Carlos Gomes, Chiquinha Gonzaga, Alexander Mackenzie, José Angel Montero, John Knowles Paine, Hubert Parry, Franz von Suppé, Severin Svendsen, and Charles-Marie Widor.

The fourth generation of musical Romanticism comprised that extraordinary group of musicians who were born in the 1860s and 1870s—the *Modern Romantic Generation*, whose best-known representatives include Claude Debussy, Edward Elgar, Enrique Granados, Gustav Mahler, Giacomo Puccini, Arnold Schoenberg, Jean Sibelius, Aleksandr Scriabin, Ethel Smyth, John Philip Sousa, Richard Strauss, and Hugo Wolf. In Britain, Central Europe, North and South America, Scandinavia, and Spain, where the work of nation building and/or emancipation from French, German, or Italian musical hegemony was still incomplete, this generation's Romanticism was still preoccupied with the notion that music should express the collective people to whose cultural experience its creators gave voice in composing and performing it; thus attest numerous compositions by Isaac Albéniz, Daniel Alomía Robles, Thomas Bretón, Ricardo Castro, George Whitefield Chadwick, Ernesto Elorduy, Leoš Janáček, Charles Villiers Stanford, José Maria Valle Riestra, and Carl Nielsen. In France and Germany, too, nationalist impulses figured prominently—in Germany as part of the political muscle flexing of the newly unified Prussian state under Bismarck, via celebrations of the splendors of a German musical past that now included the late Wagner (a messianic figure whose force rivaled Beethoven's), and in Third Republic France via a variety of currents set in motion by the homeland's humiliating defeat in the Franco-Prussian War. Yet even at their most nationalistic, the Romanticisms cultivated by the modern Romantics during the 19th century's closing decades were more resolutely modernist than those of the previous generation, more aware that a new century was dawning, and more determined to cultivate music as an expression of the modern condition.

Additionally, in the world of the Modern Romantic Generation, the early Romantics' celebration of music's ability to express the inexpressible and achieve greater potency through its subjective nature became a celebration of consummately subjective individualistic self-expression, an aesthetic realm in which musical worth was often inversely proportional to collective accessibility. Many—in fact, most—of these musicians lived well into the 20th century, witnessing not only the revolutions in the sociology of music effected by the widespread use of recorded and broadcast musical sound but also one or (in a few cases) both world wars and the collapse of functional tonality as the conceptual cornerstone of music's organization. By the time music's Romanticisms reached their twilight, they bore little resemblance to what had been understood as Romantic at the beginning or even middle of the long 19th century.

Finally, this book attempts to correct one misperception that is fueled and perpetuated by many other English-language surveys of Romantic music: the notion that Romanticism was a predominantly European force whose leaders were all or mostly French, German, Italian, and Russian males. It was not. While it is true that the latter-day canon of Romantic music is dominated by French, Germans, and Italians, with a few Russians thrown in for good measure, especially in Western Europe and the United States, that canon is itself a culturally and politically self-affirming construct whose cult of "masters" and "masterworks" either implicitly or explicitly excluded composers, ideas, and repertoires that it deemed alien or (in the verbiage of the long 19th century itself) "inferior" or "primitive." We are no longer bound by the cultural and political needs of that century—and we recognize that the Romanticisms of music were in fact very nearly a global movement. We thus acknowledge and celebrate the music of Beethoven and Brahms, Franck and Fauré, Rossini and Verdi, Mussorgsky and Tchaikovsky—but do not make it our business to privilege those composers' music over that of women composers or over the equally Romantic and musically rich musical Romanticisms of Britain, Scandinavia, Central Europe, or North, Central, and South America. We therefore aim to be inclusive in our coverage and not to perpetuate the gendered, cultural, and political biases that have excluded or marginalized a great many remarkable composers and works from many standard accounts' portrayals of Romanticism in music. No entry in this book is as long or as detailed as it might be or should be, and in that sense all are deficient: this, too, is a reflection of the fact (discussed in the preface) that this book is intended to be a complement to other resources rather than a competitor to or superseding of them.

* * *

Whether by projecting an orderly and ever-expanding future course characterized by increased complexity, sophistication, and depth or by rewriting or reconstructing the past in order to make the needs of the present and a projected future, many—perhaps most—of the various phases of Romanticism have gone hand in hand with aspirations toward historical transcendence. Such comprehensiveness, expansiveness, and aspirations to universality may reflect Romanticism's roots in the Enlightenment—but they are far beyond the scope of this book, even though the final tally of entries included here is just over half those initially projected. The same would be true of any book, the Web, or any other knowledge base: such is the nature of human experience and knowledge. But it does not change the fact that many readers are bound to find that we have omitted items we should have included, given short shrift to some and undue length to others, and generally erred in any number of other ways. Of those readers, we ask forgiveness and patience. We hope that the present attempt to lexiconize the vast and multifaceted worlds of music's Romanticisms will serve as a stepping-stone for more satisfactory future contributions. Beyond that—and more affirmatively—we hope that this book will prove a resource that helps its readers to learn and understand more about the music, the composers, and the ideas that are its starting point and raison d'être and to enjoy the worlds offered them by Romantic music more than might otherwise have been the case.

NOTES

1. Alfred Einstein, *Geschichte der Musik* (Leipzig: B. G. Teubner, 1917; 5th ed., 1948); *A Short History of Music* (New York: Alfred A. Knopf, 1937; numerous eds. through 1996). The verbiage in question is present in all German and English editions. In the 1937 English edition, it occurs on pp. 196–97.

2. Paul Henry Lang, *Music in Western Civilization* (New York: Norton, 1941), 734–800.

3. Marshall Brown, "German Romanticism and Music," in his *The Tooth That Nibbles at the Soul: Essays on Music and Poetry* (Seattle: University of Washington Press, 2010), 63–78; Carl Dahlhaus, "Studien zur romantischen Musikästhetik," *Archiv für Musikwissenschaft* 42 (1985): 157–65; John Daverio, *Nineteenth-Century Music and the German Romantic Ideology* (New York: Macmillan, 1993); Hans Lenneberg, "Classic and Romantic: The First Usage of the Terms," *Musical Quarterly* 78 (1994): 610–25; David Montgomery, "North German Romanticism: Origins and Structural Language in Music, Poetry and Painting" (PhD diss., University of California, Los Angeles, 1987); Leon Plantinga, "'Classic' and 'Romantic,' Beethoven and Schubert," in *Schubert's Vienna*, ed. Raymond Erickson (New Haven, CT: Yale University Press), 79–97.

4. See Jacques Barzun, *Classic, Romantic, and Modern*, 2nd ed. (Boston: Little, Brown, 1961), 4–6.

5. See especially Elisabeth Eleonore Bauer, *Wie Beethoven auf den Sockel kam: Zur Entstehung eines musikalischen Mythos* (Stuttgart: J. B. Metzler, 1992).

6. The standard English-language text in the conventional portrayal of the Enlightenment as a quintessentially conservative movement is Peter Gay's *The Enlightenment: An Interpretation*, 2 vols. (New York: Alfred A. Knopf, 1966–1969). This portrayal has more recently been challenged by Jonathan Israel. See his *Radical Enlightenment: Philosophy and the Making of Modernity, 1650–1750* (Oxford: Oxford University Press, 2001) or the more compact *A Revolution of the Mind: Radical Enlightenment and the Intellectual Origins of Modern Democracy* (Princeton, NJ: Princeton University Press, 2010).

7. See Jonathan Israel, *Enlightenment Contested: Philosophy, Modernity, and the Emancipation of Man, 1670–1752* (Oxford: Oxford University Press, 2006).

8. Jacques Barzun, *Berlioz and the Romantic Century* (New York: Columbia University Press, 1969).

9. See Eric J. Hobsbawm, *The Age of Revolution: Europe, 1789–1848* (London: Weidenfeld and Nicolson, 1962); *The Age of Capital, 1848–1875* (London: Weidenfeld and Nicolson, 1975); and *The Age of Empire, 1875–1914* (London: Weidenfeld and Nicolson, 1987).

10. Bertil van Boer, *Music of the Classical Period* (Lanham, MD: Scarecrow Press, 2012).

11. Jay Winik, *The Great Upheaval: America and the Birth of the Modern World, 1788–1800* (New York: HarperCollins, 2007).

12. For an excellent discussion of the emergence of musical modernism, see the entry on the term (pp. 178–80) and the introduction (pp. 1–7) in Nicole V. Gagné, *Historical Dictionary of Modern and Contemporary Classical Music* (Lanham, MD: Scarecrow Press, 2012).

A

ABSOLUTE MUSIC. (Fr., musique pure; Ger., absolute Musik.) Music that is considered to be free of (Lat. *absolutus*) any coherence, logic, or meaning that is not itself inherently and solely musical. Since it supposedly is neither inspired nor formed by extramusical ideas or experiences and employs no extramusical elements (texts, titles, and so on) in order to convey its meaning, absolute music is by definition instrumental; in the polemics of the **long 19th century**, it was usually considered the antithesis of **program music.**

The notion of absolute music is controversial and polemical since in positing a dichotomy between "absolute" and "program" music it begs the question of whether music, as a physical phenomenon of sound created by vibrations, is in fact capable of expressing anything other than sound itself. Moreover, even if one accepts that ordered sounds can convey a content that they themselves do not possess or contain (as opposed to merely stimulating impressions, perceptions, or thoughts of some extramusical content or simply eliciting an emotional response in performers and listeners), the question remains whether there can in fact be such a thing as music that is truly autonomous rather than born and therefore suggestive of ideas or experiences that are not themselves musical. Even if such a music is conceivable and practicable, one must still inquire whether it is aesthetically desirable (as proponents of the idea of absolute music asserted). Many prominent mid-19th-century intellectuals and musicians asserted that music devoid of some explicitly "poetic" content (i.e., absolute music) was inherently deficient, an artifact of an approach to musical aesthetics that belonged to an earlier stage in music's evolutionary history.

Finally, there has been—and still is—disagreement as to whether the concept of absolute music embraces only music that is truly pure and abstract (if such music exists) or only music that does not *explicitly* employ or invoke some extramusical semantic structure. For example, if a composer publishes an instrumental work with no verbal, **paratextual**, or other extramusical semantic elements, then that work naturally qualifies as potentially absolute music. Yet if the work's genesis and the composer's private materials contain programmatic references or other semantic indicators, then one might reasonably object that the composer's decision to suppress the discursive references in the published edition is a matter of gesture rather than substance. That decision, however, does not alter the fact that the work was conceived and shaped as programmatic or characteristic music. In this case—the first movement of **Gustav Mahler**'s **Symphony** No. 2 ("Resurrection," 1894, rev. 1903), which was conceived as an instrumental **symphonic poem** titled *Totenfeier* (Funeral Rites, 1888)—the work is "absolute" only in a superficial and essentially misleading sense; its nature and content are anything but absolute. Such cases—and they are many—are often said to be "between absolute and program music" (after an important 1963 essay by Walter Wiora; refer to the bibliography).

The idea of music without a content, object, or purpose (in the words of 20th-century musicologist Carl Dahlhaus) originated in the writings of early Romantic aestheticians such as **Johann Wolfgang von Goethe**, Johann Gottfried Herder (1744–1803), **E. T. A. Hoffmann, Jean Paul Richter**, and **Ludwig Tieck** and is a backlash against what they considered the abuses of hermeneutic readings of instrumental music. On the one hand, there were approaches such as **Jérôme-Joseph de Momigny**'s reading of the first movement of **Wolfgang Amadeus Mozart**'s **String Quartet** in D Minor, K. 421/417b, which includes extremely detailed intrinsically musical analyses (focusing on the music's motivic, phrasal, periodic, and harmonic construction) but also attempts to "convey the true expression" of the movement (representing, in Momigny's view, nobility and pathos) by setting words to the melody in the Violin I part—the words themselves taken from a French translation of Dido's farewell to Aeneas in Virgil's *Aeneid*. At the other extreme is Hoffmann's lengthy and influential essay on **Ludwig van Beethoven**'s instrumental music, which eloquently asserts that "music that scorns every aid from and mixing with any other art (poetry)" is more expressive, not less, than programmatic or characteristic music precisely because "the inner structure of the movements . . . everything, leads to a single point," "the spiritual realm of the infinite" (*Allgemeine Musikalische Zeitung* 12, no. 40 [4 July 1810]: col. 631–32). Yet Hoffmann then describes the first movement's second subject in unabashedly poetic terms: "The breast that is oppressed and alarmed by intimations of things monstrous, destructive, and threatening wheezes for air with wrenching gasps, but just then a friendly, luminous figure appears and brings light into the dark night."

Moreover, Hoffmann's "absolute" elucidation of Beethoven's Op. 67 directly contradicts the view of absolute music as music "without a content, object, or purpose," for his reading makes clear that the aim of instrumental music without programmatic or characteristic associations is to become "the most Romantic of all the arts" not by expressing less but by expressing more. Finally, somewhere between these two views lies the notion (espoused by Goethe and Arthur Schopenhauer in the realms of literature and philosophy and by **Fanny Hensel** and **Felix Mendelssohn Bartholdy** in the realms of music) that instrumental music without descriptive verbal indicators possesses superior expressive power not because of its greater abstraction but because verbal language itself is inherently vague and incapable of clear communication: if (as is often the case) the same word can mean radically different things to different readers or listeners, then music that relies on words for its inspiration or expression is inevitably ambiguous, less expressive rather than more so. In this view, the issue is not the expressive capacity of music but the expressive deficiency of words.

A critical new stage in the debate about absolute music arrived in the wake of the **Revolutions of 1848**. In his Zurich writings, **Richard Wagner** developed the notion of the *Gesamtkunstwerk* and the **music drama** as rejections of all "partial arts" (*Teilkünste*), the latter embracing all "absolute music" (*Oper und Drama* [Opera and Drama, 1849] and *Das Kunstwerk der Zukunft* [**The Artwork of the Future**, 1850]). Music, Wagner asserted, was inherently meaningful; any attempt to create music that did not explicitly embrace its poetic dimension was aesthetically anachronistic, a throwback to a stage in the evolution of the art before the last movement of Beethoven's Ninth (**"Choral"**) **Symphony**. This ambitious and socially engaged aesthetic agenda was embraced also by **Franz Brendel**, **Franz Liszt**, and the **New German School** (as well as the New German School's official outgrowth, the **Allgemeiner Deutscher Musikverein**). But in 1854, the Viennese music critic **Eduard Hanslick** published his influential treatise *Vom Musikalisch-Schönen* (On the Musically Beautiful), which was widely translated and went through 11 editions by 1910. Hanslick did not dispute that music could express extramusical ideas, subjects, or actions, nor did he argue that music must or should be abstract and autonomous and hence beautiful solely in musical terms. Rather, he and his followers asserted that music that did not explicitly entail some extramusical content was not (as the New German School maintained) necessarily aesthetically or expressively deficient, while music that relied on words to make its meaning coherent and comprehensible was musically deficient because poetry was unable to meet that challenge. The musically beautiful, then, could embrace both program music and music that was not explicitly programmatic (i.e., "absolute" music) as well as vocal music.

The problems attendant to the concepts and aesthetics of absolute music and program music continued to multiply over the subsequent course of the long 19th century as well as the 20th century. Important factors in the concept's increasingly problematic status were the spread of new compositional techniques (one doubts that even the most radical advocate of "absolute" music from the 1870s would have approved of dodecaphony, even though its techniques correspond closely to those of formalist absolutists), the advent of new theories and aesthetics of objectivity and expression, and the development of new scholarly understanding of how music—even "absolute" music—is inevitably **narrative** in nature and implicitly imbued with extramusical meaning by means of musical **topics** and styles. [JMC]

AGUIRRE, JULIÁN (1868–1924). Argentine composer, critic, and pianist of the Modern Romantic Generation; one of the most important figures in Argentine musical **nationalism** in the **long 19th century**. His output consists mostly of works for solo **piano** and a number of **songs** for voice with piano, many of them employing authentic Argentine **folk song** and others drawing on melodic, harmonic, rhythmic, and cadential characteristics of that repertoire. He composed a **sonata** and a *Soneto del Petrarca* for cello and **piano** and several works for violin and piano, and his symphonic **suite** *De mi país* (From My Country, 1910) is an important contribution to the nationalist orchestral repertoire. He was also active as a music critic, writing numerous reviews and articles for the journal *El Hogar* (The Home) between 1920 and 1924. He is best known today for his four volumes of *Aires Nacionales Argentinos* and his *Aires criollos*, which, though voiced in the genres and styles of Western European piano music, were strongly influenced by Argentine folk music.

Aguirre was born in Buenos Aires but as a boy moved with his family to Madrid, where he studied and excelled in composition, counterpoint, and harmony between 1882 and 1886 and favorably impressed **Isaac Albéniz**. There he was deeply influenced by the ideas of Spanish Romantic nationalism. Upon his return to Argentina in 1886, he established himself as a pianist and composer, following the lead of **Alberto Williams** in drawing on folk music in his works whose instrumentation and intended performance venues belonged to the European tradition. He taught harmony at the Conservatorio Nacional de Música and the Conservatorio de Buenos Aires. His importance as an Argentine cultural luminary was acknowledged by the erection of a bronze bust of him in the Rose Garden of the Parque Tres de Febrero in Buenos Aires in 1934 and the naming of the **Conservatory** in Banfield (in the Buenos Aires Province) after him in 1960. Aaron Copland acknowledged Aguirre's and the Cuban **Ignacio Cervantes**'s importance as voices in Latin American nationalism in his 1952 essay "Musical Imagination in the Americas." [JMC]

ALBÉNIZ, ISAAC (MANUEL FRANCISCO) (1860–1909). Spanish pianist and composer of the Modern Romantic Generation; his generation's most influential exponent of Spanish **nationalism** and **impressionism** in music. He was a child **prodigy** on **piano** (giving his first public performance at the Teatro Romea in Barcelona at age four or five; sources disagree) and by 1867 was studying informally with Antoine-François Marmontel

(1816–1898), renowned piano pedagogue of the Paris **Conservatory**, in Paris. When his father lost his government post after the Glorious Revolution of 1868, he and his sister Clementina toured the provinces to raise money; eventually, the family settled in Madrid. There he enrolled at the Escuela Nacional de Música y Declamación (now the Real Conservatorio Superior de Música) but continued to interrupt his studies for tours—in 1869 stowing away on a ship to the New World, where he toured Argentina, Brazil, Cuba, Puerto Rico, and the United States.

In 1876, Albéniz returned to Europe and began studies at the Leipzig Conservatory before relocating to the Brussels Conservatory; many biographers claim that he went on to study with **Franz Liszt**, but this claim is untrue. He later toured Spain and Latin America, and by 1882 he had become an administrator in a touring **zarzuela** company. He settled in Barcelona in 1883 but by late 1885 had relocated again to Madrid, where he became an important contributor to the city's **salon** culture and further developed his abilities as a composer. His reputation as a pianist-composer led to his works being featured in a series of 20 concerts hosted by the **Érard** firm at the Barcelona Universal Exhibition of 1888. After further successes as a performer in Paris and London, he relocated to the latter city, where his **comic opera** *The Magic Opal* was a great success. He relocated to Paris in 1894 but continued concertizing in Spain, over the next eight years becoming increasingly involved in entrepreneurial ventures designed to promote Spanish music as well as Catalán culture. His success abroad produced skepticism at home about his national authenticity, however, and in 1902 he moved to Paris yet again, convinced that he could better promote the Spanish cause there than in a homeland where he was viewed as tainted by foreign influence. His health failed increasingly over the next few years and consigned several ambitious projects to incompletion, but he was able to complete his magnum opus, the four-volume set of impressionist piano pieces published in 1906–1908 under the collective title of *Iberia*.

Albéniz is best known today for his piano music—including, in addition to the sometimes phenomenally difficult and always colorful music of *Iberia*, five **sonatas**, two *Suites españolas* (1886 and 1889), the *Suite antigua* (1887), *Recuerdos de viaje* (Travel Memories, 1887), *España*, (1890), and *Cantos de España* (Songs of Spain, 1896) as well as two piano **concertos**. He also completed three zarzuelas and several other serious and comic operas, one **symphonic poem** and numerous suites and other works for **orchestra** on Iberian themes, several instrumental **chamber** compositions, and **songs** on English, French, Italian, and Spanish texts. [JMC]

ALBUMBLATT. (pl. Albumblätter; Ger., "album leaf"; Fr., feuille d'album *or* page d'album; It., foglio d'album.) Literally, a page ("leaf") in a guest book or **autograph** book, widely cultivated in domestic social use during the long 19th century; more practically, informal term for a composition written on such pages. Frequently during the long 19th century, households purchased prebound, elegant or ornamental volumes (usually oblong in format) in which their guests could write brief notes, poems, musical compositions, or simply signatures to be kept as mementos. Over time, these volumes became records of the home's history of visitors and sources of recollection. Composers typically inscribed a short piece or a few bars of a familiar longer work in such albums. Because the volumes rarely contained music staves, composers would usually hand rule a staff or staff system, write the musical passage on the page, and then pen a short greeting (e.g., "in fond remembrance") followed by their signature. Sometimes they would write a new work—invariably a short one (given the limited space on the page). When they did so, it usually was titled *Albumblatt* if/when it was later published.

Over the course of the long 19th century, the term became increasingly common as an informal title for pieces that were not actually written in or for albums but retained the slight dimensions and simple style of those that were. **Ludwig van Beethoven**'s *Für Elise* (WoO 59, 1810) is probably the best-known *Albumblatt* of the century as a whole. Other examples were penned by **Hans von Bülow** (1879), **Fryderyk Chopin** (1843), **Antonín Dvořák** (1880 and 1888), **Niels W.** Gade (1882), **Edvard Grieg** (1888), **Stephen Heller** (1864), **Ferdinand Hiller** (1875), **Franz Liszt** (ca. 1841), **Felix Mendelssohn Bartholdy** (ca. 1836), **Modest Mussorgsky** (1880), **Camille Saint-Saëns** (1921), **Franz Schubert** (1825), **Pyotor Il'yich Tchaikovsky** (1874), and **Richard Wagner** (1853, 1861, and 1875).

The term could also be applied to collections of short works bearing these general characteristics; such collections sometimes dropped the prefatory "Album" and were designated simply *Blätter* (leaves; sing. *Blatt*). Such collections were published by **Ferrucco Busoni** (*Drei Albumblätter*, 1917–1921), Grieg (*Fire/Albumblade*, Op. 28, 1878), **Max Reger** (*Lose Blätter* [Loose Leaves, Op. 13, 1894] and *Bunte Blätter* [Colorful Leaves, Op. 36, 1899]), and **Robert Schumann** (*Albumblätter* [Op. 124, 1854], *Album für die Jugend* [Album for the Young, Op. 68, 1848]; nos. 4–8 of *Bunte Blätter* [Colorful Leaves, Op. 99, 1852]). [JMC]

See also CHARACTER (CHARACTERISTIC) PIECE; COMPOSITIONAL PROCESS, CREATIVE PROCESS; HOLOGRAPH.

ALKAN, CHARLES-VALENTIN (1813–1888). French composer and **virtuoso** pianist of the Romantic Generation. He was born Charles-Valentin Morhange, but, like his elder sister and his four younger brothers, he adopted his father's first name as his own surname. He began studies at the Paris **Conservatory** at the age of six, studying there with renowned pedagogue Joseph Zimmermann (1785–1853) and winning high praise from **Luigi Cherubini** among others. He was promoted (justifiably) as a **prodigy**, winning prizes in harmony, organ, **piano**, and solfège at the Conservatory and publishing his op. 1 at the age of 14. He was admired by **Fryderyk Chopin**, with whom he shared the stage in 1838, and **Franz Liszt**, with whom he participated in the Parisian **salon** of the Princesse de la Moskova. His circle of close friends included Eugène Delacroix, Alexandre Dumas *fils*, **Victor Hugo**, Félicité Robert de Lamennais, and George Sand, as well as Chopin.

Alkan's career and music are highly idiosyncratic. Apart from two trips to London (1833 and 1835), he spent his entire career in and around Paris, but despite his close friendships with prominent public artists and intellectuals in the French capital, he was shy and reclusive, dropping from the public stage almost entirely after 1839 despite the considerable—and increasing—acclaim with which his performances and music were met. He gave a total of two public recitals in 1844, another two in 1845, and two more in 1853, then disappeared from public performance until 1873. Between 1873 and 1880, he organized a series of "petits concerts de musique classique" (small concerts of classical [in modern parlance, "Baroque"] music) in which he performed little-known and generally little-understood music of the 18th century (**J. S. Bach**, Louis Couperin, **Franz Joseph Haydn**, **Wolfgang Amadeus Mozart**, André Grétry, and Jean-Philippe Rameau), and the 19th century (**Ludwig van Beethoven**'s late **sonatas** as well as works by Chopin, **Felix Mendelssohn Bartholdy**, and **Camille Saint-Saëns**). After the end of this series, he made no further public appearances, nor did he compose after about 1873. Later in life, he was an ardent promoter of the **pedal piano**. His demise—a piece of furniture fell on him and captured him for more than 24 hours, when he was found dead—ranks as one of the more remarkable deaths in the history of 19th-century music, though the popular myth that a bookshelf fell on and killed him as he was reaching for a copy of the Talmud is untrue.

Most of Alkan's 75 numbered *opera* are for piano solo, and many of his works are overtly programmatic or characteristic in nature—*see* PROGRAM (PROGRAMMATIC) MUSIC. The 1844 *Chemin de fer* (Railroad, Op. 27) is perhaps the most famous of these, and apparently the earliest musical depiction of the newly developed railway, although its musical rewards are slight compared to rich harmonies and adventurous textures of many of the compositions in the *48 Motifs ou esquisses* (48 Motives or Sketches, Op. 63, 1861). Among his other more remarkable works are the Grand **Sonata** ("The Four Ages"), Op. 33 (1848), the cycle of 12 **character pieces** *Les mois* (The Months, Op. 74, 1838 and ca. 1872), and especially the *12 Études in Minor Keys*, Op. 39—the latter a deceptively simple title that belies the expansive scope of most of the works as well as the fact that **cycle** includes a "**symphony** for piano solo" (Études 4–7), a "**concerto** for piano alone" (Études 8–10; Etude 8 alone runs to nearly 30 minutes), and an "**overture**" (Étude 11). Although his music is seldom heard today, his influence is evident in the many and substantive parallels between his music and that of **Claude De-**

bussy and **Gabriel Fauré** and from the fact that his *Allegro barbaro* (No. 12 of the *12 Études in the Major Keys*, Op. 35, 1848) was clearly a conceptual model for Bartók's work of the same title (1911). [JMC]

ALLGEMEINE MUSIKALISCHE ZEITUNG. (Ger., "General Musical Periodical.") Leipzig-based music periodical with sporadically released musical supplements. It was published in two series, the first running from 3 October 1798 to 6 December 1848 and the second from 1 January 1863 to 27 December 1882. Until 1866, the journal was published by **Breitkopf & Härtel** (Leipzig); thereafter, it was published by J. Rieter-Biedermann (also Leipzig). The editorial board was headed first by the journal's two founders, Friedrich Rochlitz (1798–1818) and Gottfried Christoph Härtel (1819–1827), then by a series of other influential composers, critics, and theorists: Gottfried Wilhelm Fink (1827–1842), C. F. Becker (1842), Moritz Hauptmann (1843–1846), and J. C. Lobe (1846–1848). The editors in chief of the *neue Folge* (new series) were Selmar Bagge (1863–1868), Arrey von Dommer (1868) and Robert Eitner (1868), **Friedrich Chrysander** (1868–1871 and 1875–1882), and Joseph Müller (1871–1875). The journal's long history included a remarkable roster of contributors, such as **Hector Berlioz**, G. A. Griesinger (author of the first biography of **Franz Joseph Haydn**, published in serialized form), **Eduard Hanslick, E. T. A. Hoffmann** (including his influential essay on **Ludwig van Beethoven**'s instrumental music and the Fifth **Symphony** in particular), **Franz Liszt**, G. A. MacFarren, A. B. Marx, and **Robert Schumann** (the latter's celebrated review of **Fryderyk Chopin**'s *Variations on "La ci darem la mano,"* Op. 2).

Despite the vast changes in musical life between 1798 and 1882 and significant shifts in editorial direction and outlook, the contents of the *LAmZ* issues were generally organized into seven sections. Issues typically began with one or two lengthy technical articles (often serialized) on issues ranging from aesthetics through historical repertoires, music theory, and specific works or groups of works to issues such as **performance practice** and the construction and design of musical instruments. These were typically followed by short biographical articles on contemporary and earlier composers, performers, theorists, and other musicians, then by a section of reviews (sometimes lengthy) of recently published music and writings about music, and then (as opportunity arose) descriptions of newly invented musical instruments. Typically, the last prose sections of the issues were devoted to reports and reviews of concerts both in the German lands and abroad, sometimes as far away as South America; by a section of miscellaneous notes; and by advertisements for new and forthcoming books and music as well as musical manufacturers, teachers of private lessons, and so on.

As the musical world became increasingly polemical during the years leading up to 1848, the *LAmZ*, as the most established and influential commercial and critical organ in the German lands, was increasingly open to charges of conservatism—all the more so because it was published by a firm (Breitkopf & Härtel) whose promotion of composers of the long 19th century (including Beethoven, **Vincenzo Bellini, Gaetano Donizetti, Felix Mendelssohn Bartholdy, Giacomo Meyerbeer, Wolfgang Amadeus Mozart, Franz Schubert**, and **Clara** and **Robert Schumann**) was well known but had little to do with the progressive currents that would eventually be championed by the **New German School**. These criticisms are less well suited to the journal's pre-1848 existence than they are to its second series, in which it increasingly centered on matters of musical philology and of Renaissance and Baroque music while paying little heed to the eruption of musical **modernism** that characterized the late 1870s and early 1880s. Nevertheless, the weekly issues of the *LAmZ* provide a detailed, vivid, and sustained glimpse into the complex and constantly shifting musical landscape of its day that was unparalleled at the time and has few peers even today.

The reasons for the cessation of publication of the first series in December 1848 remain unclear. In the last issue, the publisher included a note citing the proliferation of local music periodicals and journals relating to various specialized disciplines and the increasingly fractious nature of musical life at that point, noting that "in such a whirlpool there is no more room for a *general* music periodical," and to this the editor in chief appended a note making clear that the publisher, not he or the other editors, had decided to terminate the journal after 50 successful years. These reasons are plausible enough, but they raise the question of why the press then reinitiated the journal in 1863. [JMC]

See also NEUE ZEITSCHRIFT FÜR MUSIK.

ALLGEMEINER DEUTSCHER MUSIKVEREIN. (Ger., "General German Musical Union.") Musical organization founded in 1861, product of the less formal Tonkünstler-Versammlung (Conference of Musicians) that had met for the first time in Leipzig in 1859 (*see* NEW GERMAN SCHOOL). Like the Tonkünstler-Versammlung, the Allgemeiner Deutscher Musikverein was by charter avowedly progressive in its agenda. Its principal organizers were **Franz Brendel** and **Franz Liszt**, although the initial membership of 202 included many musical notables who contributed in a variety of capacities. Brendel remained president of the organization until his death in 1868. He was succeeded in that post by a number of luminaries of late 19th-century and early 20th-century German music, among them Peter Raabe (1920–1937), Carl Riedel (1868–1888), Max von Schillings (1909–1920), and **Richard Strauss** (1901–1909). Over the course of its long history, the society's demographic and philosophical profile evolved in accordance with changing issues and ideas in the musical world. During these later years it promoted music by Germans not usually considered progressive (among them **Johannes Brahms**) as well as music by non-Germans (**Hector Berlioz, Aleksandr Borodin, César Cui, Antonín Dvořák, Aleksandr Glazunov, Nikolay Rimsky-Korsakov, Camille Saint-Säens,** and **Pyotor Il'yich Tchaikovsky**). The most prominent non-German in the later history was Béla Bartók (*HD MCCM*). The ADMv was dissolved in 1937 as part of the Nazi reorganization of German cultural organization.

The Allgemeiner Deutscher Musikverein was chartered in order to support new music and young musicians. The most visible efforts to these ends were its annual festivals, which offered premieres by such leading contemporary composers as Bartók, Berg, **Peter Cornelius, Frederick Delius,** Hindemith, Kodály, Krenek, Liszt, Pfitzner, **Max Reger,** Schoenberg, **Jean Sibelius,** Richard Strauss, Wagner, and Webern as well as (in the 1890s) older music by, for example, **J. S. Bach, George Frideric Handel,** and Alessandro Scarlatti. The organization also sponsored numerous chapters and financially supported important foundations created during its existence (including a **Beethoven**-Stiftung, a Liszt-Stiftung, and a **Richard-Wagner**-Stiftung). Perhaps most important, through these foundations it offered scholarships to rising young composers, among them Reger and Schoenberg. [JMC]

ALOMÍA ROBLES, DANIEL (1871–1942). Peruvian composer and ethnomusicologist of the Modern Romantic Generation, best known today for the song "El condor pasa" (later parodied by Simon and Garfunkel) in the context of his two-act **zarzuela** of the same title. In his teens, he studied **piano** and solfège in Lima and performed as an extra in the capital city's lively culture of **operetta**, moving on to study medicine at the Lima Facultad de San Fernando from 1892 to 1894, but devoted himself to the study of indigenous musics beginning in 1896. He traveled widely in Ecuador and Bolivia as well as his native Peru, transcribing the texts and music of Andean **folk song**. In 1920, Victor and Brunswick released 13 albums of his transcriptions of Andean folk song with orchestral accompaniment. Alomía Robles resided in New York City from 1922 to 1933 and from 1939 to his death was director of the Fine Arts section of the Peruvian Ministry of Education. In addition to transcribing nearly 700 Andean melodies and arranging 319 of these for voice(s) with orchestra, he composed 238 original compositions, including short **piano** compositions and **character** pieces, vocal and instrumental **chamber music,** some **orchestral** works, one four-act **opera,** and several zarzuelas. His commitment to indigenous musics and success in integrating them into the musical idioms of European post-Romanticism made him an important figure in Peruvian musical **nationalism.** [JMC]

AMBROS, AUGUST WILHELM (1816–1876). Austrian music historian, art critic, and composer. Though he received his doctorate in law in 1839 from Prague University and would work in the civil service for much of his adult life, music figured centrally in his life from early childhood on. As an admirer of **Robert Schumann**, Ambros, together with **Eduard Hanslick**, participated in the **Davidsbund** of Prague to counter musical conservatism; Schumann and **Jean Paul Richter** would continue to be an inspiration for Ambros in his later music journalism writing for Schumann's *Neue Zeitschrift für Musik*, *Bohemia* (Prague), and the *Wiener Allgemeine Musik-Zeitung*, among others, across Germany and Austria.

In 1869, Ambros achieved a lifelong goal of becoming a professor of the history of music and professor of art at the Prague Conservatory; after his move to Vienna in 1871, he would continue to lecture at the Vienna Conservatory and the university. In Vienna, he worked with the Central Commission for the Study and Preservation of Artistic and Historical Monuments and the Austrian Museum as well as other artistic institutions.

Although Ambros was a composer, his most significant contributions to musical thought in the 19th century can be found in his works in aesthetics and music history. His first publication, *Die Grenzen der Musik und Poesie* (The Boundaries of Music and Poetry, 1856), sought a balance between the formalist views of Hanslick and those of the **New German School** in the mid-century debate over **program music**. Ambros believed that music could embody ideas or extramusical content as long as the formal aspects of the music were "appropriately" aligned to convey such ideas; formal architecture and poetic content should be combined in the music. Extramusical content should not be relied upon to create organization or unification in an otherwise unorganized, incoherent work. Programs as well, in any work, were unacceptable due to their "inorganic" nature separate from the organic musical workings of a piece. Despite all this, Ambros was cordial with **Hector Berlioz** and **Franz Liszt** and admired some of their music.

Even more important is Ambros's five-volume *Geschichte der Musik* (History of Music, 1862–1882), research for which he conducted throughout the 1860s with archival materials from Germany, Austria, and especially Italy. Though some criticized this tome for a lack of rigorous scientific method and stylistic analysis, it was one of the first surveys of music history to employ any sort of scientific basis. Ambros traces the origins of music back to Greek antiquity, attempting, as **Franz Brendel** did in his *Geschichte der Musik in Italien, Deutschland und Frankreich* (History of Music in Italy, Germany, and France, 1852), to create a narrative of progress and continuity from antiquity to the present day. Perhaps showing how deeply influenced he was by Hegelian ideas, Ambros also insisted that each musical phenomenon be considered as a separate historical event, outside of any overarching narrative. The volume was influenced by Hegelian notions of artworks as individual historical phenomena that embodied a *Zeitgeist* (an underlying spirit that connects each epoch of art) and thus were intimately tied to culture and cultural history. Ambros was also apparently influenced by his uncle Raphael Georg Kiesewetter (1773–1850) in that his view of music and its history included not only Western classical music but also non-Western musics from China, Egypt, and India. In that sense, Ambros was unique to his generation of music historians and a significant influence on later music historians in formulating an understanding of *Musikwissenschaft* that embraced non-Western as well as Western musics.

Ambros would die before he could complete the entire series of the *Geschichte*. The last volume he worked upon was the fourth, which extended only to the mid-17th century. **Gustav Nottebohm** was engaged to edit and complete the series from Ambros's notes. The last two volumes, *Geschichte der Musik des 17., 18. und 19. Jahrhunderts* (History of Music in the 17th–19th Centuries, 1881 and 1886), were entrusted to Wilhelm Langhans and were written for a wider audience. [MMM/JMC]

AN DIE FERNE GELIEBTE, **OP. 98.** (Ger., "To the Distant Beloved.") Iconic **song cycle** by **Ludwig van Beethoven** on texts by Alois Jeitteles [Jeiteles] (1794–1858). Jeitteles is an otherwise obscure figure who studied philosophy in Prague and medicine in Vienna, becoming a physician in Brünn in 1819, working as a publicist for insurgent causes during the **Revolutions of 1848**, and publishing well-read translations of Spanish renaissance drama and poetry (especially **Calderón de la Barca**). He had published individual lyric poems in the years before Beethoven penned *An die ferne Geliebte*, but the poems of the cycle itself are not published, suggesting that Beethoven received them privately and personally or perhaps commissioned them. Beethoven in 1816 described the cycle as a *Liederkreis an die Entfernte* (Song Cycle to the Distant Woman), but the autograph is titled *"An die entfernte Geliebte,"/Sechs Lieder von/Aloys Jeittels* [sic]/*in Musik gesetzt/von L. v. Beethoven* (To the Distant Beloved/Six Songs by/Aloys Jeittels [sic]/Set to Music/by L. v. Beethoven), while the first edition (Vienna: S. A. Stainer & Co.) is titled *"An die ferne Geliebte"/Ein Liederkreis von Al. Jeitteles [. . .]*. The latter two versions highlight that the woman in question is not only distant but also beloved, while the final version of the title underscores that the work is not a group of six **songs** but an indivisible cyclical unity (*see* CYCLIC FORM).

Despite Jeitteles's obscurity, the poems are significant among literary sources of the song cycle because they trope the **topic** of the *Wanderlieder* cycle by making the distance traversed psychological rather than physical (the travel is only within the fantasy of the lyric persona). They also construct the travel as a journey that is imagined and then re-created through song rather than in person, operating within a **narrative** frame rather than as a linear plot progression: the first song establishes the distance between the lyric persona and his beloved; the central four songs, topically related poems centered on love, make up a package of song sent to the beloved; and the final song then asks the recipient/beloved to "take these songs that I sang to you, Beloved, and sing them to yourself with the lute in the evening," for "what separates us evaporates in the face of song." Beethoven's setting of the poems is significant in the history of the song cycle not least of all because of the emphasis it places on indivisibility. Most obviously, none of the songs but the last has a conclusive final cadence, and the music is continuous. The cycle also employs a clear, rounded, and carefully coordinated tonal plan, and the last song thematically recalls the first, creating a musical reprise that underscores the completion of the textual cycle.

Although *An die ferne Geliebte* is by no means the first song cycle or even necessarily the first such work by a major composer, it exerted a significant influence over the mid- and later 19th century, being quoted or substantively alluded to in dozens of other compositions—most notably **Felix Mendelssohn Bartholdy**'s symphony-cantata *Lobgesang* (MW A18/Op. 52, 1841); **Robert Schumann**'s **Fantasy** in C Major for Piano (Op. 17, 1839) and **Symphony** No. 2, Op. 61 (1846); and **Johannes Brahms**'s **Piano Trio** in B Major, Op. 8 (1854, rev. 1891). It is best understood as a turning point or pivot from earlier concepts of the song cycle, which made little effort to generate cyclicity by purely musical means and entrusted those aspects primarily to the poetry, to a model in which musical coherence was the predominant concern. [JMC]

See also LA BONNE CHANSON, OP. 61; DICHTERLIEBE, OP 48; GE-SANG (PL. GESÄNGE); KINDERTOTENLIEDER; DES KNABEN WUN-DERHORN; DAS LIED VON DER ERDE; SONGS AND DANCES OF DEATH; WINTERREISE.

ANNÉES DE PÈLERINAGE. (Fr., "Years of Pilgrimage.") Title of three **cyclical** books of **programmatic** pieces for **piano** solo by **Franz Liszt**. The nine pieces of the first book, titled *Première année: Suisse* (First Year: Switzerland, LW A159, comp. 1848–1855, publ. 1858), were based in part on works published in the earlier *Album d'un voyageur* (Album of a Traveler, LW A40a–c, 1837–1838, publ. 1842) with some thematic material also appropriated from the *Fantaisie romantique sur deux mélodies suisses* (Romantic Fantasy on Two Swiss Melodies, LW A21, 1837). The second book (*Deuxième année: Italie* [Second Year: Italy]) exists in two versions. The first (LW A55), inspired by Liszt's travels in the Italian lands in 1837–1838, originally comprised seven pieces that were published by Schott (Mainz) in 1858; nos. 4–6 of this collection were revisions of the first version of the *Tre*

Sonnetti di Petrarca (Three Sonnets by Petrarch, LW N14, 1842–1846). The second version appends to these six three more pieces collectively titled *Venezia e Napoli* (Venice and Naples, LW A197), comp. 1859, publ. 1861. The third book (titled simply *Troisième année*, LW A283, 1877–1882, publ. 1883) consists of seven pieces that are less conspicuously virtuosic than those of the first two books, focusing instead on contemplative and religious themes consistent with Liszt's having taken the Lower Orders in the Roman Catholic Church in 1865. The titles of three of its pieces (Nos. 2–4) refer to Liszt's residence during his frequent visits to Rome, the Villa d'Este, while No. 5 (*Sunt lacrymae rerum, en mode hongrois*, no. 5) was originally titled *Thrénodie hongroise* (Hungarian Threnody), reflecting its inspiration in the defeat of the Hungarian movement for independence from Austria in 1848. No. 6 (*Marche funèbre*/Funereal March) was written in memory of Emperor Maximilian I of Mexico, executed by insurgent Republicans in 1867. Altogether, the final versions of the three volumes comprise 23 pieces based on geographical, literary, musical, pictorial, and political sources of inspiration, including Lord Byron, Dante Alighieri (1265–1321), Michelangelo Buonarotti (1475–1564), Petrarch (Francesco Petraca, 1304–1374), Raphael Sanzio da Urbino (1483–1520), **Friedrich Schiller**, and Étienne Pivert de Senancour (1770–1845). Books 1 and 2 especially are landmarks in the literature of **program music** and pianistic **virtuosity**, and all three volumes are milestones in the 19th-century fascination with musical cyclicity. [JMC]
    See also FASSUNG LETZTER HAND.

ARENSKY, ANTON (STEPANOVICH) (1861–1906). Russian composer, **conductor**, and **pianist** of the Modern Romantic Generation. With the exception of his **Piano Trio** No. 1 in D Minor and orchestral *Variations on a Theme of Tchaikovsky* (both 1894), Arensky's compositional output is not often heard today; **Nikolay Rimsky-Korsakov** famously predicted this. Nevertheless, Arensky's oeuvre spans many genres—including **chamber music, concerto, opera, song**, and **symphony**—and exhibits the stylistic marks of teacher Rimsky-Korsakov, friend **Pyotor Il'yich Tchaikovsky, Fryderyk Chopin**, and **Felix Mendelssohn Bartholdy**.
    With mother and father amateur musicians, Arensky was immersed in a musical environment early on. By the time he entered the St. Petersburg **Conservatory** in 1879, Arensky was an excellent pianist who had begun to compose short pieces. There, he studied composition under Rimsky-Korsakov, whose mentorship—pivotal to Arensky's career—included recruiting the younger composer to assist in the preparations for *Snegurochka* (The Snow Maiden, 1881). Arensky also began composing what would become his most successful opera, *Son na Volga* (A Dream on the Volga, 1891), under Rimsky-Korsakov's tutelage. In 1882, Arensky joined the Moscow Conservatory faculty and taught harmony and counterpoint; among his stu-

dents there were **Sergei Rachmaninoff** and **Aleksandr Scriabin.** Arensky moved back to St. Petersburg in 1895 to replace **Mily Balakirev** as director of the Russian imperial court chapel, and the pension he drew upon leaving in 1901 supported him for the last five years of his life, during which he made frequent public appearances at the **piano** and podium. [RK]

ART SONG. *See* SONG.

ARTARIA. Influential Austrian firm of publishers in art, cartography, and music, founded as a shop in Mainz in 1765 but based in Vienna by 1768. Headed by Giovanni Casimiro Artaria (1725–1797) and his nephews Carlo and Francesco, the firm was originally listed in Vienna as Cugini Artaria, becoming Artaria & Comp. in 1771. The shop began dealing printed music in 1776 and, responsive to the rapidly growing market for the international trade in Joseph II's Vienna, had published its own first edition of music by 1778. By 1789, it had set up its own printing shop, and by 1791, it had begun experimenting with new printing methods. It quickly became Vienna's pre-eminent publisher of maps as well as music over the course of the 1790s. The years of the Napoleonic Wars proved challenging, and during the **Restoration** the Artaria house had difficulty competing with newer firms, such as **Diabelli** (founded in 1818), Haslinger (founded in 1803), and Mechetti (publishing music from ca. 1807). Nevertheless, it remained one of the leading Austrian publishers of music and maps until 1858, when it ceased publishing music. It was **Wolfgang Amadeus Mozart**'s principal publisher during his lifetime and one of **Ludwig van Beethoven**'s most important publishers. Other prominent composers whose music it published included **Adrien Boieldieu, Carl Czerny, Gaetano Donizetti, Johann Nepomuk Hummel, Franz Liszt, Ignaz Moscheles, Elias Parish-Alvars, Ignaz Pleyel, Gioachino Rossini, Franz Schubert. Simon Sechter,** and **Sigismond Thalberg.** [JMC]
  See also PRINTING AND PUBLISHING OF MUSIC.

ARTWORK OF THE FUTURE. (Ger., *Das Kunstwerk der Zukunft.*) Title of an extended pamphlet by **Richard Wagner**, published in 1850 with a dedication to the philosopher of history and religion Ludwig Feuerbach (1804–1872). Preceded by *Die Kunst und die Revolution* (Art and Revolution, 1849) and followed by *Das Judenthum in der Musik* (Jewry in Music, 1850), *Das Kunstwerk der Zukunft* is one of the most important of the tracts written and published during Wagner's willed hiatus from composition during his exile following the **Revolutions of 1848.** Like many other reformist tracts of Western civilization, it sought to revive and theorize in modern terms the artistic (specifically theatrical) legacy of a mythologized ancient

Greece. Together with Wagner's other postrevolutionary writings, it laid the philosophical and theoretical groundwork for the approach to composition that he would employ in the *Ring of the Nibelung, Tristan und Isolde*, and (to a lesser extent) *Die Meistersinger von Nürmberg* and *Parsifal*.

Das Kunstwerk der Zukunft brilliantly enunciates several themes that not only reflect mid-19th century issues in European politics, society, and art but also would inspire countless tropes and responses that were crucial to developments in subsequent cultural history. First, it asserts that the cultivation of the various arts as intersecting but autonomous spheres of endeavor (e.g., as in contemporary **opera** and **oratorio**) was unnatural and that the natural state of art was that of an indivisible totality. Moreover, it asserts that if art would address this challenge and aspired to totality, it would naturally be embraced by "das Volk" (the folk; i.e., the strong and the non-Jewish from among the people—as opposed to the public at large, which embraced and in Wagner's view was detrimentally influenced by Jews and other weaklings). It names **Johann Wolfgang von Goethe, William Shakespeare**, and **Ludwig van Beethoven** as champions of this renunciation of superficiality and proposes that the history of music up to Beethoven's Late Vienna Period had been a quest driving toward such a goal. The incursion of the voice into the formerly "absolute musical language" ("absolute Tonsprache") of the **symphony** with the entry of the recitative in the Finale of Beethoven's Ninth **("Choral")** **Symphony** had been comparable to Christopher Columbus's laying down anchor on the shores of the New World.

Finally, drawing on ideas developed in *Art and Revolution, The Artwork of the Future* asserted that this *Volk*-led revolution of artistic ideals would bind society and art, making art itself into a new religion that would supersede Christianity (and all other religions) in a modern revival of the artistic and societal oneness of ancient Greece (as Wagner understood it). In conspicuously and deliberately religious verbiage, Wagner asserted that Beethoven's Ninth—a work that at that point still remained only rarely performed and little understood—thus represented the "salvation of music out of its most unique elements to become the most universalizing of the arts." The Ninth, Wagner argued, was "the *human* gospel of the art of the future" and the "key" "forged for us by Beethoven" to "*unified drama*" (emphasis Wagner's).

Were it not for Wagner's success in developing further and implementing these ideas and those of his other postrevolutionary writings in his subsequent operas, *The Artwork of the Future* might well have had no more impact than most of the other enthusiastic and often brilliant (but now forgotten) artistic, social, and theoretical polemics of the years immediately following the Revolutions of 1848. As it turned out—and perhaps inevitably—many who tried to take up Wagner's challenge and make good on these ideas failed miserably. The essay's thesis of an eventual *Zukunftsmusik* that represented the telos for all of humanity's artistic strivings became a derisive tool for detractors who began mocking the notion of a *Zukunftsmusik* (or, among skeptics such as **Hector Berlioz**, "la musique de l'avenir"; both mean *music of the future*). Those criticisms led Wagner to return to the concept of the artwork of the future in another, significantly shorter essay titled *Zukunftsmusik* in September 1860—discouraging use of the term *Zukunftsmusik* but reiterating his main theses and continuing to argue for the syncretic artwork of the future.

Nevertheless, the sweeping reframing of the theoretical and social structures of art in society that Wagner developed in this and his other mid-century essays yielded a significant change in his own style that produced seven further operas that remain indispensable to any appreciation of the history of music and European culture in the late 19th and 20th centuries, works without which subsequent compositions by composers as diverse as **Anton Bruckner, Ernest Chausson, Claude Debussy, Edward Elgar, César Franck, Gustav Mahler,** and **Richard Strauss**, among countless others, would have been virtually unthinkable. [JMC]
See also RECEPTION.

AUBER, (DANIEL-FRANÇOIS-) ESPRIT (1782–1871). French composer of the Early Romantic Generation; his generation's leading composer of **opéras comiques**, best known today for the opéra comique *Fra Diavolo* (Brother Devil, 1830) and the **grand opera** *La muette de Portici* (The Mute Girl of Portici, 1828). His parents intended for him to be an art dealer and sent him to London in 1802–1803 to learn that trade, but on returning to France he decided to pursue his long-standing interest in music instead. He studied with **Luigi Cherubini** beginning in 1805 and grew rapidly as a composer, but the failure of *Le séjour militaire* (The Military Station, 1813) at the Opéra-Comique led him to disavow that genre. He returned to it in 1819, however, after his father declared bankruptcy, Thereafter, he wrote regularly for the French stage until his output began to slow in the mid-1850s. The success of works such as *La bergère châtelaine* (The Lady Shepherdess, 1820), *Emma* (1821), *Le Cheval de bronze* (The Bronze Horse, 1835), *Le Domino noir* (The Black Domino, 1837), *Les Diamants de la couronne* (The Crown Diamonds, 1841), and *Manon Lescaut* (1856), together with the sensation created by *La muette de Portici*, led to his appointment as director of the Paris **Conservatory** in 1842, a post he held until 1871, and director of the Imperial Chapel in 1857. Other important compositions include the extravagant *Gustav III* (1833), which requires some 300 people on the stage at one point; the five-act biblical opera *L'enfant prodigue* (The Prodigal Son, 1850); and the opéra comique *Le premier jour de bonheur* (The First Day of Happiness, 1868).

Over the course of his career, Auber penned a total of 49 **operas**, 36 of them in collaboration with **Eugène Scribe**. He also composed much worthwhile sacred music, including one *Messe solennelle* (Solemn Mass, 1812), one **Stabat mater** (n.d.), numerous settings of movements from the Mass Ordinary, and **motets**. There are also several **concert arias** and secular **cantatas** and a sizable corpus of instrumental **chamber music**. Although the genres with which he is most commonly associated today stereotypically have little cultivation of learned counterpoint, Auber was fascinated by the subject and published several works on it. [JMC]

AUER, LEOPOLD (1845–1930). Hungarian violinist and teacher of the Late Romantic Generation; of Jewish descent. Though he was also a conductor, music editor, and composer, he is most widely recognized as one of the most important violinists and pedagogues, particularly within the Russian School, of the 19th and 20th centuries. He began violin lessons at six years old; two years later, in 1853, he started formal studies at the Budapest **Conservatory**, moving to Vienna in 1855 to study violin and eventually **piano** with Jakob Dont (1815–1888). At the encouragement of Dont, Auer enrolled at the Vienna Conservatory in 1857–1858; after receiving his diploma, he began a freelance touring career to support himself but stayed close enough to Vienna to be able to see traveling **virtuosi** such as Antonio Bazzini (1818–1897), Ferdinand Laub (1832–1875), and Henri Vieuxtemps (1820–1881). In 1862, he moved to Hanover to study with **Joseph Joachim**. Through his connection with Joachim, Auer became acquainted with **Johannes Brahms, Ferdinand David, Niels Gade,** and **Clara Schumann**. He toured around Europe after leaving Joachim's tutelage in 1865, making his debut in Leipzig at the Gewandhaus and giving acclaimed performances in other cities in Germany, Holland, and Scandinavia and in London, where he met and performed with **Anton Rubinstein**.

In 1868, Auer accepted an offer to take the place of Henryk Wieniawski (1835–1880) at the Imperial Conservatory at St. Petersburg, where he would remain until 1917. During his tenure at St. Petersburg, he served as soloist to the Imperial **Ballet**, first violinist for the **string quartet** of the Russian Music Society and occasionally as conductor of the society's orchestral concerts. Auer became acquainted with **Franz Liszt** and **Pyotr Tchaikovsky** in St. Petersburg, the latter of whom wished to dedicate his Violin Concerto to him. Auer refused, declaring the concerto unplayable, although he would later go on to perform the work, with his own edits added. He was also influential as a teacher, both in Russia and in the United States (whence he moved in 1918), working first at the Institute of Musical Art in New York City (1926–1928) and then at the Curtis Institute of Music in Philadelphia (1928). His pupils included Elman, Heifetz, Milstein, Max Rosen, and Zimbalist. Along with an autobiography, *My Long Life in Music* (1923), Auer wrote several manuals on violin technique and method, including *Violin Playing as I Teach It* (1921) and *Violin Master Works and Their Interpretations* (1925). [MMM/JMC]

See also PERFORMANCE PRACTICE.

AUFFÜHRUNGSPRAXIS. *See* PERFORMANCE PRACTICE.

AUTOGRAPH. A manuscript wholly written by an author or composer who can be named on the basis of that manuscript or a portion of any given document in the handwriting of the named author or composer. Common types of autographs during the **long 19th century** are letters, diaries, *Albumblätter* (*see* ALBUMBLATT), scores, and sometimes parts or arrangements of musical compositions. Autograph sources such as sketches, drafts, and fair-copy scores are typically the most important documents of musical compositions' genesis and provide valuable information for editors, performers, and other interpreters. Many other manuscripts and proofs for printed editions survive with autograph corrections and changes; these, too, are important tools for establishing an authoritative musical text. [JMC]

See also COMPOSITIONAL PROCESS, CREATIVE PROCESS; EDITING AND EDITIONS; HOLOGRAPH; URTEXT.

BACH, JOHANN SEBASTIAN (1685–1750). German Baroque composer, organist, and teacher; along with **Albrecht Dürer, Wolfgang Amadeus Mozart, William Shakespeare,** and eventually **Johann Wolfgang von Goethe,** iconic figure for numerous important themes and issues in Romantic music. One of more than 60 musicians spread across seven generations in his family, Bach was also father to four sons who were respected and influential composers in their own right: W. F. Bach (1710–1784), C. P. E. Bach (1714–1788), J. C. F. Bach (1732–1795), and J. C. Bach (1735–1782). He traveled only within a limited geographic range during his lifetime but voraciously absorbed other national and regional styles by copying, arranging, and performing other composers' works, in turn integrating these styles into his own music. He composed in virtually every genre available to the early 18th century composer, except for **opera**—although many of these works exerted little influence until late in the 19th century because they existed only in manuscript and remained unknown to 19th-century composers for much of the century. He was also admired as a harpsichordist and organist and for his technical knowledge of organ construction and repair.

Bach published only a handful of works during his lifetime, and what music was known during the late 18th century and early 19th century was performed only in limited circles. Consequently, the Romantics' understandings of his life, music, and significance changed continually as more of his music was revived and more was learned about his life and career. His name was appropriated by diverse causes, and views of his music and its significance varied widely according to geography, changing substantially over the course of the **long 19th century.** On the one hand, the fact that his reputation during his lifetime rested in part on his skills as an organist and harpsichordist combined with his increasingly sacralized status in the 19th century to make him an important symbolic progenitor of the cult of **virtuosity,** lending historical legitimacy to a phenomenon whose aesthetic validity was sometimes regarded with suspicion.

More commonly, because so little was known of early 18th-century French and Italian styles in the early 19th century, the Romantics generally overlooked Bach's cultivation of contemporary Italian and French musical styles. They thus viewed him as a traditionalist who regarded his contemporaries' music with skepticism, instead pursuing the expressive potentials of intricate counterpoint and **chorale**-based composition to their fullest. In this capacity, Bach became the cause célèbre of **historicism**, German **nationalism**, a revival of organ composition, and the specifically Prussian vision for German national unification that centered on Protestantism (what eventually became known as the *Kleindeutsche Lösung*). More generally, Bach's potency as a symbol for broader cultural causes generated greater interest in and appreciation for the styles and techniques of musical composition represented in his works than would otherwise likely have been the case. Bach's music thus became an agent for change in the 19th century, enriching the overall palette of ideas, styles, and techniques available to Romantic composers by adding appeal to the angular, affective melodic lines, complicated fugal techniques, and *stile antico* polyphony they discovered in his music. [JMC]

See also BACH REVIVAL, BACH AWAKENING, BACH RENAISSANCE; CECILIAN MOVEMENT; FORKEL, JOHANN NICOLAUS (1749–1818); RECEPTION.

BACH REVIVAL, BACH AWAKENING, BACH RENAISSANCE. Term for the resurgence of interest in the study and public performance of the music of **Johann Sebastian Bach** that unfolded over the course of the long 19th century; one of the most important currents of **historicism** and German **nationalism**. In the second half of the 18th century, Bach's music was best known in Prussia, where C. P. E. Bach; the theorists Johann Friedrich Agricola (1720–1774), J. P. Kirnberger (1721–1783), Christoph Nichelmann (1717–1762), and Friedrich Wilhelm Marpurg (1718–1795); and the composers and conductors C. F. Fasch (1736–1800) and Carl Friedrich Zelter (1758–1832) worked assiduously to stimulate interest in his music and cultivate understanding for the increasingly old-fashioned theoretical and contrapuntal premises that underlay his music—namely, the two volumes of *The Well-Tempered Clavier* and the **motets** that were performed by the Berlin Singakademie. During this time in Austria, the same repertoires were promoted by **salonnière** Fanny von Arnstein (1758–1818) and the Prussian diplomat Gottfried van Swieten (1733–1803). A similar situation obtained in England, where Bach figured in John Hawkins's *General History of the Science and Practice of Music* (1776) and other figures began to publish individual keyboard works (e.g., John Casper Heck's inclusion of Bach's Fugue in C Major, BWV 953, without attribution, in his *The Art of Playing the Harpsichord*, 1770). The still-encountered assertion that Bach's music was completely unknown during the decades after his death is a serious exaggeration, but it is true to say that his works were familiar primarily to connoisseurs and operated only on the outer peripheries of public musical life.

That situation began to change during the first decade of the 19th century. On the Continent, the first major milestone was the first serious attempt at a complete edition of Bach's harpsichord works beginning in 1800 (*Oeuvres complettes de Jean Sebastien Bach* [Complete Works of J. S. Bach]) under the editorship of **Johann Nicolaus Forkel** and the first book-length Bach biography, also by Forkel, in 1802 (*Ueber Johann Sebastian Bachs Leben, Kunst und Kunstwerke* [On Johann Sebastian Bach's Life, Art, and Artworks]). Although Forkel's portrayal of Bach contained gaps and significant inaccuracies, it was fundamentally shaped by the need to discover or construct a German and Protestant icon who could serve as an ideological rallying point for German speakers in search of a sense of national unity in the face of the ever-increasing probability of the German lands' becoming a part of the growing First **French Empire** of Napoléon Bonaparte. It succeeded in promoting public interest in the Baroque composer. The year 1802 also saw the publication of new editions of *Die Kunst der Fuge* (The Art of Fugue, BWV 1050). In 1802–1803, the Sonatas and Partitas for Unaccompanied Violin (BWV 1001–06) were published in facsimile, and the first edition of five of Bach's motets (BWV 225–29) was published under the editorship of J. C. Bach and J. G. Schicht (1753–1823).

A few further editions of the motets and some of the cantatas followed over the course of the early 19th century, but during the early years of the **Restoration**, the principal means of disseminating Bach's music appears to have been individual musicians' manuscript copies of Bach's **autographs** and **holograph** copies of those manuscripts. As musicians such as the tenor and vocal pedagogue Franz Hauser (1794–1870) made or procured these copies and shared them with others in the course of their travels and relocations, musicians were exposed to scores whose very appearance was strikingly different from any repertoire easily available in print or regularly encountered in public performance—but private readings by amateur choirs brought Bach's music to light in sound and experience among musicians and music-loving amateurs nevertheless. The nascent Bach Project was thus abetted by freedom to travel in the newly peaceful political stability of the Restoration, fueled by growing nationalist sentiment, and given momentum by essentially private means.

Important new developments began quietly early in 1824, when salonnière Bella Salomon (1749–1824) gave her grandson **Felix Mendelssohn Bartholdy**, then 16, a manuscript copy of Bach's *St. Matthew Passion*. Most of the Mendelssohn family was a part of the circle of Berlin initiates into Bach's music led by Zelter, and young Felix Mendelssohn had both received a thorough instruction in Bachian counterpoint as part of his composition lessons with Zelter and encountered Bach's motets in connection with his teacher's direction of the Berlin Singakademie as well as readings of the Frankfurt am Main Cäcilienverein in 1827. On returning to Berlin in the fall of 1827, he began assembling a small group of musical intimates, among them the baritone Eduard Devrient (1801–1877) and the theorist and composer **Adolf Bernhard Marx**, for readings of "rarely heard works," and by 13 December 1828, Mendelssohn and Devrient together, presumably with the support of Zelter, petitioned the directorial board of the Singakademie for use of its hall and participation of its membership in a performance of the work on 11 March 1829. Rehearsals followed, directed by Mendelssohn at the piano, with more singers and instrumentalists showing up for each session, and copyists had difficulty producing enough manuscript parts to supply them all. Word of the elaborate preparations and the wonder experienced by the ensemble's participants spread, producing a general and increasing sense of anticipation well beyond Berlin itself and generating attention in the German lands' flourishing industry of daily newspapers, abetted not least of all by the tireless efforts of Marx in the *Berliner allgemeine musikalische Zeitung* (Berlin General Music Periodical).

The performance for which Devrient and Mendelssohn had requested permission took place to a packed hall in the Singakademie on 11 March 1829, with eight soloists, about 30 instrumentalists, and a chorus of 158 performing Mendelssohn's edited and cut version of the *St. Matthew Passion* (with Mendelssohn himself **conducting** with a baton from the **piano**) before an audience of about 900, with 1,000 more members of the public being turned away ticketless at the door. The extraordinary success accorded that first performance led to a repeat performance (also with Mendelssohn conducting) on 21 March, the 144th anniversary of Bach's birth, and that performance's likewise brilliant success led to a third performance (this time directed by Zelter since Mendelssohn had in the meantime left for his first trip to England) on 17 April (Good Friday).

With those three sensational performances, the Bach Revival became a public affair and one of the most important driving forces in 19th-century German historicism and nationalism, establishing Bach as a composer whose works were indeed viable for public performance in Romantic Europe. The 1830s witnessed a flood of new editions of Bach's choral music and performances of Bach's vocal music—not only Marx's edition of BWV 244 but also editions of some of the **cantatas**, plus editions of *The Art of Fugue*, a new edition by **Carl Czerny** of both volumes of *The Well-Tempered Clavier* (1837), and some of the organ works. An important new chapter opened on 29 February 1840, when **Ferdinand David** gave the first public performance of the **Chaconne** from the Partita in D Minor for Unaccompanied Violin (BWV 1004) and the Preludio from the Partita in E Major (BWV 1006), with Mendelssohn improvising an accompaniment at the piano for both works.

Although the autograph of both pieces had been published in facsimile in 1802, neither had been committed to print, and there is no record of any prior public performance. Now, however, a new surge of public performances of Bach's concerted instrumental music emerged—not only the **Sonatas** and Partitas but also the **concertos**, the orchestral **suites**, and the accompanied sonatas.

The enthusiasm for Bach also spread to England, France, and (to a lesser extent) the Italian lands. As noted above, by the early 19th century there was an existing English appreciation for Bach as a personification of Protestantism, a situation reflected partly in Samuel Wesley's efforts on behalf of the Lutheran composer but also in other developments, such as the composer and theorist Augustus Kollmann's (1756–1829) emphasis on Bachian counterpoint in his writings on music beginning around 1796 and a robust cult of performance of Bach's keyboard works in England already in the first two decades of the century. These efforts gained momentum when Mendelssohn arrived in London in April 1829—the toast of the city's musical culture and awash in the sensational successes of the performances he had just organized and directed in Berlin. He impressed British musicians by performing Bach's organ works, with pedals, in St. Paul's Cathedral with a degree of understanding and confidence unusual in the Isles at that point. **Ignaz Moscheles** performed Bach's D-Minor Keyboard Concerto (BWV 1063) with the Philharmonic Society of London in 1836, and the 1837 Birmingham Festival included parts of the *St. Matthew Passion*, B-Minor Mass, and *Magnificat* (BWV 243).

In predominantly Catholic France, Bach's Protestantism was, if anything, a peculiar and in some ways **exotic** qualifier to the qualities of his music with which 19th-century French musicians identified more readily—namely, its expansive scope and grandeur. The Bach Revival caught on more slowly in the Italian lands, but it found an energetic and influential advocate in the person of the abbot Fortunato Santini (1778–1861), who translated the texts of the motets and the *St. John Passion* (BWV 243) into Italian, and in the music of **Gioachino Rossini**, who had been introduced to Bach's music during his youthful studies with Stanislao Mattei (1750–1825) and emulated Bach's elaborate imitative counterpoint in works such as the finale of the **Stabat mater** (1832, rev. 1841–1842) and the Gloria, Credo, and especially the "Prélude religieux" of the *Petite messe solennelle* (1863, rev. 1867; *see* SOLEMN MASS).

As a result of these developments, by the end of the 1840s Bach was widely regarded as a worthy compeer of or superior to **George Frideric Handel** in many circles. One of the first Bach Societies was founded in England (after the model of that country's Handel Society) primarily through the agency of **William Sterndale Bennett** in 1849. The English Bach Society's goals included the promotion of Bach's music through performance and education but not print. That latter, more ambitious goal was undertaken by the German lands' Bach-Gesellschaft, plans for which were begun already in the mid-1830s and which was finally formed in 1850 principally through the efforts of Moritz Hauptmann (1792–1868; cantor of the Leipzig Thomaskirche), Mozart biographer Otto Jahn (1813–1869), organist and musicologist C. F. Becker (1804–1877), and **Robert Schumann.** Collaborating with preeminent music publisher **Breitkopf & Härtel,** the Bach-Gesellschaft undertook a musical and cultural project of extraordinary scope—one that encountered many difficulties as its rapidly growing membership struggled to develop an accurate inventory of the Baroque composer's oeuvre, gain access to the vast and complex body of surviving sources, and disseminate Bach's music in print in a fashion that was both faithful to the surviving sources and approachable to mid-19th-century musicians (*see* EDITING AND EDITIONS). The editorial and philological methods of the Gesellschaft reflected the nascent state of musical scholarship regarding the critical editing of music, and its editions are now largely obsolete (although many currently circulating editions of Bach's music, most notably the Dover Reprints series, are knockoffs of them). Nevertheless, the corpus of works it presented in 66 volumes between December 1851 and January 1900 was the largest and most authoritative such endeavor up to that point, and it made Bach's music available for the first time (and in quantity) to scholars and other musicians around the world. Those editions in turn facilitated the production of new, significantly more scholarly life-and-works studies, such as Philipp Spitta's (1841–1894) two-volume biography (vol. 1, 1873; vol. 2, 1880; Engl. trans., 1884).

These developments did much more than simply introduce Bach's life, career, and music into public life in the mid- and later 19th century; they also made it possible for composers to draw on Bach's music and his compositional techniques in enriching the stylistic discourses of Romantic music. The roster of major composers who actively drew on Bach's music in creating new music—whether consciously archaic in style of integrating Bachian elements into contemporary idioms—after the mid-19th century is enormous, including **Charles-Valentin Alkan, Hector Berlioz, Johannes Brahms, Anton Bruckner, Ferruccio Busoni, Paul Dukas, César Franck, Robert Franz, Niels W. Gade, Charles Hallé, Fanny Hensel, Franz Liszt,** Mendelssohn, **John Knowles Paine, Jules Étienne Pasdeloup, Serge Rachmaninoff, Max Reger,** Rossini, **Camille Saint-Saëns,** Clara and Robert Schumann, **Giuseppe Verdi, Richard Wagner,** and **Charles-Marie Widor,** among countless others. [JMC]

See also CECILIAN MOVEMENT; RECEPTION.

BAGATELLE. (Fr., "trifle," from It. bagattella; Ger., Kleinigkeit.) Term for a short, unimposing piece of music, usually for **piano** solo. Bagatelles may be considered a variety of **character piece**, but unlike most character pieces, they have no particular stylistic or topical connotations (e.g., as **marches**, **mazurkas**, and **nocturnes** do). The term also denotes a game in which the players must put nine balls through a series of arches into cups at the end of an oblong table on which pins have been placed as obstacles; perhaps in derivation from (or association with) this lighthearted parlor game, most bagatelles were published in sets. The term was first used in the 17th century by composers including François Couperin (1668–1733) and Marin Marais (1656–1728) and occurred sporadically during the 18th century, including a set of *Musikalische Bagatellen* published by **Breitkopf & Härtel** in 1797. Drawing on these meanings, *Bagatelle* is also the name of a one-act *opéra comique* by **Jacques Offenbach**. The term was also occasionally used for unimposing compositions based on other composers' works (e.g., Théodore Döhler's [1814–1856] *La Renaissance*, subtitled "Bagatelle à la valse sur l'opéra *Lucie de Lammermoor* [by **Gaetano Donizetti**], 1843).

The best-known bagatelles of the **long 19th century** are those of **Ludwig van Beethoven** (opp. 13, 119, and 126), and more famous than these is his *Albumblatt* bagatelle *Für Elise* (WoO 59, 1810). Others were composed by **César Cui, Antonín Dvořák, Leopold Godowsky, Stephen Heller, Henri Herz, Johann Nepomuk Hummel, Franz Liszt, Anatoly Lyadov, Camille Saint-Saëns, Bedřich Smetana**, and **Johann Strauss (II)**, among many others. [JMC]

BAILLOT, PIERRE (1771–1842). French violin **virtuoso**, composer, and pedagogue of the Early Romantic Generation; with **Rudolfe Kreutzer** and **Pierre Rode**, one of the most enduringly influential figures in developing and promulgating the Franco-Belgian school of violin playing. He founded France's first professional instrumental chamber ensemble and gave a total of 154 solo performances over the course of his career between 1814 and 1840. He demonstrated musical talent at a very early age and at age 10 was inspired by the playing of G. B. Viotti (1755–1824) to dedicate himself to the violin, subsequently taking lessons with the composer and theorist Charles-Simon Catel (1773–1830), **Luigi Cherubini**, and **Antoine Reicha**. He was appointed to the newly opened Paris **Conservatory** in 1795, joined Napoléon Bonaparte's private orchestra in 1802, and toured Russia to great acclaim in 1805–1808. During the resurgence of instrumental **chamber music** that attended the **Restoration**, he gained great fame as a chamber musician, also touring the Low Countries and England in 1815–1816. From 1821 to 1831, he served as concertmaster of the Paris Opéra (arguably the single most important public position for an instrumentalist at the time) and in 1825 began serving in the same position in the Chapelle Royale.

Baillot was also an able composer, with nine violin **concertos** to his credit plus several other **orchestral** works with solo violin and several dozen instrumental **chamber** works (including one violin **sonata**, three **string quartets**, and numerous **trios**, among other works). His greatest influence, however, was as a teacher, in particular through his *L'art du violon: Nouvelle méthode* (The Art of the Violin: A New Method, 1834), his *Méthode de violoncelle* (Cello Method, 1834; coauthored with Catel, Nicholas Baudiot [1773–1849], and Jean-Henri Levasseur [1764–1823]), and his first pedagogical publication, *Méthode de violon* (Violin Method, 1803; coauthored with Rode and Kreutzer). [JMC]

BALAKIREV, MILY ALEKSEYEVICH (1837–1910). Russian composer, **conductor**, pianist, and teacher of the Late Romantic Generation; influential member of the **Mighty Handful** and one of his generation's most important exponents of Russian musical **nationalism** as well as **exoticism**. His completed works include **incidental music** to **William Shakespeare**'s *King Lear* (1858–1861, rev. 1902–1905), sacred and secular a cappella choral music, 45 **songs**, two **symphonies**, four **overtures**, one **symphonic poem**, one piano **concerto**, other **orchestral** compositions, and a sizable body of virtuosic **piano** music. Of these works, the two *Overtures on Russian Themes* (1858 and 1864, rev. 1881 and 1884), the two symphonies (1866, rev. 1897, and 1900–1908), the symphonic poem *Tamara* (1867–1882, publ. 1884), and the orientalist piano **fantasy** *Islamey* (1869, publ. 1870; rev. and publ. 1902) are best known today.

Balakirev began his studies in music with his mother and by age 10 was formally studying piano. He entered the University of Kazan as a mathematic student in 1853 but continued to perform on the piano, and a trip to St. Petersburg in 1855 earned him the support of **Aleksandr Dargomïzhsky, Mikhail Glinka,** and influential critic Vladimir Stasov (1824–1906), whose nationalist aspirations would remain a powerful influence on his thinking thereafter. His reputation spread widely in the reformist climate of the early reign of Tsar Alexander II (fl. 1855–1881), and his first published compositions (a collection of 20 songs) appeared in print in 1858. During the early 1860s, his growing reputation earned him the allegiance first of **César Cui,** then of other emergent Russian nationalists, including **Aleksandr Borodin, Modest Mussorgsky, Nikolay Rimsky-Korsakov,** and **Pyotor Il'yich Tchaikovsky.** His increasingly purist (anti-German) Russian nationalist sentiments made him an influential voice in the founding of the Free School of Music founded as a counterbalance to the French and German influences reflected in the newly instituted St. Petersburg and Moscow Conservatories.

Vacations in the Caucasus in 1862, 1863, and 1868 provided occasion for Balakirev to study and absorb the **folk song** of that region. These influences are reflected not least of all in the completion of the first version of *Islamey* in 1869 (premiered by **Nikolay Rubinstein** in December of that year), and in 1867 he succeeded **Anton Rubinstein** to become conductor of the Russian Musical Society. In the latter capacity, he assiduously promoted the music of other Russian composers, giving the premieres of works by Borodin, Mussorgsky, Rimsky-Korsakov, and Tchaikovsky. Many of these compositions had been prompted or encouraged to completion by Balakirev. His mentorship is reflected in the fact that Tchaikovsky dedicated his **concert overtures** *Fatum* and *Romeo and Juliet* as well as his *"Manfred" Symphony* (after **Lord Byron**) to Balakirev. (Stasov had suggested the idea for the latter to Balakirev, who had proposed it to **Hector Berlioz** before prompting Tchaikovsky on the subject.)

By the early 1870s, the composers whom Balakirev had mentored increasingly gathered public attention and began developing away from him; he felt increasingly isolated in the Russian musical life he had helped to reinvigorate. A nervous breakdown in 1871 forced him to retire from public life in music and composition, instead taking a mediocre job with the railroad in order to make ends meet. Increasingly depressed, he resigned from his position at the Free School in 1874. These dark years of Balakirev's life witnessed little musical activity, but in the 1880s he began to reenter musical life, resuming his work at the Free School in 1881, completing the symphonic poem *Tamara* in 1882, and being appointed director of the Imperial Chapel in 1883. He officially retired with a pension in 1895 and once again withdrew into seclusion but this time was able to complete a number of important compositional projects—most importantly a revised version of *Islamey* (1902) (*see* FASSUNG LETZTER HAND), the Second Symphony (1900–1908, publ. 1908), and an orchestral **suite** based on pieces by **Fryderyk Chopin**. [JMC]

BALLAD. In general, a slow, simple, or historical song, often related to folk stories or legend, usually with a narrator and strophic in form. Unlike the **Lied**, it is usually **narrative** in nature. The term derives from the Latin *ballare* ("to dance") and embraces vernacular and folk music as well as works in the cultivated tradition. Applied to vernacular music, the term more specifically denotes a short, often slow, and strophic song that could be treated as a contrafactum for other songs, sometimes with texts on significantly different subjects. The texts of such songs typically are composed in ballad meter, with four lines per strophe, eight syllables in the first and third lines and six in the second and fourth lines, and four stresses in the longer lines and three in the shorter ones. Their music is conspicuously simple, with balanced two- and four-measure phrases, treble-dominated textures, and overwhelmingly diatonic harmony. This mix-and-match process of transmitting text and music, like that of hymnody (*see* CHORALE), was well established before the **long 19th century** and facilitated the musical transmission of widely varying texts to enormous nonexpert audiences.

By the turn of the 19th century, collections of ballad texts had begun to appear, and by the end of the long 19th century, the subject had attracted scholarly attention, resulting in the publication of multivolume collections of texts and/or tunes (most importantly, Svend Grundtvig's [1824–1883] collection of Danish ballads [1843ff], Francis James Child's collection of English and Scottish ballads [1882–1898], and George Doncieux's [1856–1903] collection of French *romancéros* [1904]). The century's increasing interest in **folk song** led to the translation and publication of some of these in other languages. Composers including **Ludwig van Beethoven, Johannes Brahms, Joseph Joachim, Carl Loewe,** and **Franz Schubert** in turn set these translated texts to new music more germane to the cultivated sphere, thus effecting a reappropriation of folk and popular music for the recital and concert hall.

As the examples just named suggest, in cultivated music the simplicity of works designated "ballad" is often feigned or illusory; more often it is scarcely applicable at all. The term occurs most commonly in German narrative song, where its roots trace (paradoxically) back to English balladry. In 1765, Thomas Percy (Bishop of Dromore, Ireland; 1729–1811) published a collection of English ballads, popular songs, and sonnets titled *Reliques of Popular Song* that attracted widespread attention on the Continent as well as in England. The collection attracted the attention of many Germans, including Johann Gottfried Herder (1744–1803), who would publish many of Percy's ballads in German translation as *Stimmen der Völker in Leidern* (Voices of the People in Songs) by 1779. One well-known set of compositions produced by this process is the corpus of settings of the ballad "Edward" by Brahms, Loewe, and Schubert.

Along with the Arnim/Brentano collection *Des Knaben Wunderhorn*, the Grimm brothers' studies of German and Northern European folktales and fairy tales, and the Scottish poet James Macpherson's forged collection of ostensibly Gaelic prehistoric poetry (*see* OSSIAN), Herder's collection represented the European reading publics' deep-seated need to rediscover the supposed truth and understated artfulness of natural beauty as it had been cultivated outside the realms of "art" music and literature up to that point. Some composers began setting many of these original folk ballads, while poets emulated what they considered the poems' salient stylistic traits—most often works with a third-person narrator, one or more nonnarrative **lyric personae**, and a subject based in folklore or legend—in newly created texts whose literary technique and subject matter remained firmly rooted in the cultivated tradition. These new, folk-like texts were in turn set to music by composers and performed in **salons** as well as public recitals and concerts.

Goethe's *Erlkönig* is one such text, and its settings by Schubert and Loewe are but the two best known of a great many (others include settings by Alselm Hüttenbrenner, Bernhard Klein, Luise Reichardt, **Bernhard Romberg**, Friedrich Schneider, Corona Schröter, **Louis Spohr**, and **Václav Tomášek**). The most prolific and influential composer of this sort of ballad was **Zumsteeg**, who produced seven volumes of *Kleine Balladen und Lieder* (Short Ballads and Songs) between 1800 and 1805.

The long 19th century's exploration of new dramatic and narrative strategies resulted in other expansions of the term "ballad." Goethe referred to his 1799 poem *Die erste Walpurgisnacht* (The First Walpurgis Night), later set by Loewe for solo voice and piano and **Felix Mendelssohn Bartholdy** for soloists, chorus, and full orchestra, as a "dramatic ballad," indicating that its plot unfolded through the utterances of different lyric personae without the presence of a third-person narrator. Ludwig Uhland and Emanuel Geibel composed new ballad texts on historical or pseudohistorical subjects that were set as cantatas by **Robert Schumann** (*Der Königssohn*, Op. 116, 1851; *Des Sängers Fluch*, Op. 139, 1852; *Vom Pagen und der Königstochter*, Op. 140, 1852). By the Modern Romantic Generation, the term had become so broad as to be almost amorphous and undesirable as a generic delimiter: for example, **Hugo Wolf** composed a number of works that are clear descendants of the ballads of Loewe and Schubert but are not designated ballads, and **Gustav Mahler**'s early cantata *Das klagende Lied* (1878–1880, rev. 1892–1893, 1898–1899) is a ballad in all but name. [JMC]
See also BALLADE.

BALLADE. A long, often episodic, one-movement instrumental piece, usually for **piano** solo, in a **narrative** or dramatic style and possessing an epic or archaic tone in at least some sections. Some possess clear literary models (most famously those of **Johannes Brahms**, whose op. 10, no. 1 ballade is headed "After the Scottish Ballad 'Edward'" [as Brahms knew it from Johann Gottfried Herder's *Stimmen der Völker*]). Others invite programmatic or characteristic associations with literature because of their generic designation, their narrative tone, and their loose adherence to the structural norms of **absolute music** (as represented in **sonatas, theme and variations**, and so on). The first instrumental works in the genre are the four ballades of **Fryderyk Chopin** (opp. 23 [ca. 1835], 38 [1839], 47 [1841], and 52 [1843]), and these have essentially defined the instrumental ballade ever since. Other important ballades for piano solo were composed by **César Franck** (1844), **Franz Liszt** (LW A117, 1849; A181, 1853), Brahms (Op. 10, 1854; Op. 118, no. 3, 1893), and **Edvard Grieg** (Op. 24, 1876; Op. 65, 1896); the most important instrumental ballades not for piano alone are **Gabriel Fauré**'s Op. 19 (1881, for piano and orchestra) and **Paul Dukas**'s *L'apprenti sorcier* (The Sorcerer's Apprentice, after **Johann Wolfgang von Goethe**, 1897, for orchestra). Other contributions to the genre are by **Hans von Bülow** (1858), **George Chadwick** (1915), **Clause Debussy** (1891), **Felix Draeseke** (1868), **Aleksandr Glazunov** (1902), **Louis Moreau Gottschalk** (Opp. 109 and 135, both 1850), **Joseph Joachim** (1853), **Anatoly Lyadov** (1890), and **William Mason** (1864), among many others.

As a genre, the instrumental ballade represents a milestone in the history of program music. Conceptually, it belongs to the category of the **character piece**, but it is significantly longer and more dramatic than most individual character pieces, and despite the parallel between its generic designation and an established vocal genre, its musical style does not invoke a prototype (e.g., as the *Lieder ohne Worte* do). Rather, the designation "ballade" suggests that these instrumental works somehow narrate, as their vocal counterparts do, treating of topics that are alternately universal and timeless (love, betrayal, heroism, defeat, exploitation) or particular and recounted in bardic fashion in the past tense. This **narrative** tone, of course, implies a subject to be narrated and thus moves the instrumental ballade into the proximity of **program music** simply by means of this potent gesture, even though none explicitly identifies any extramusical idea or subject (another parallel with the *Lieder ohne Worte*). The musical style may imply the presence of a narrator, or it might suggest the style of narration that simply mediates among characters in an unfolding drama of historical import, as in Goethe's *Die erste Walpurgisnacht*. Most often they adopt a lilting compound meter, thus further evoking with the vocal ballade and suggesting the character of a wordless narration. [JMC]

See also BALLAD; NARRATIVE.

BALLET. An art that combines dance, mime, and music in order to evoke a mood, illustrate a scene, or tell a story. It has been used in the context of **opera** since that genre's emergence, attained a new level of prominence beginning in the 1660s (notably in the operas and *ballets de cour* of Lully [1632–1687]), and continues to serve an important purpose in such works today (among the more recent notable compositions employing ballet is Philip Glass's *Akhnaten*, 1984). The 18th century also witnessed a more autonomous form of ballet, however, the *ballet d'action*, whose music is primarily instrumental, producing an inherently dramatic art form that conveys ideas and plot solely through dance and music without recourse to spoken or sung language.

The **long 19th century** witnessed a flourishing of both ballet within opera and *ballet d'action*. Within opera, the musical and textual reforms of Christoph Willibald Ritter von Gluck (1714–1787) and Ranieri de' Calzabighi (1714–1795) in the French versions of their reform operas combined with similar reform movements in the world of dance (represented chiefly by Franz Hilverding, Gasparo Angiolini, and Jean-Georges Noverre) to produce a heightened desire for aesthetic unity within staged musicodramatic compositions and a greater integration of the ballet into the plot of the opera; indeed, Gluck collaborated with Angiolini and Noverre. The same can be said of operas of Niccolò Jommelli (1714–1774) in Rome, Vienna, and Stuttgart and of Tommaso Traetta (1727–1779) in Parma, Vienna, Mannheim, and the Imperial court of Catherine II in Russia. Important milestones in this process were marked by **Carl Maria von Weber**'s *Silvana* (1810) and the Berlin version of his *Euryanthe* (1825); **Gioachino Rossini**'s *Guillaume Tell* (1829); **Giacomo Meyerbeer**'s *Robert le diable* (Robert the Devil, 1831); **Mikhail Glinka**'s *Zhizn' za tsarya* (A Life for the Tsar, 1834–1836) and *Ruslan and Lyudmila* (1842); **Giuseppe Verdi**'s *Les vêspres siciliennes* (1855) and the French versions of his *I Lombardi* (as *Jérusalem*, 1847), *Il trovatore* (as *Le trouvère*, 1857), *Macbeth* (1865), and *Otello* (1894); **Modest Mussorgsky**'s *Boris Godunov* (1868–1874); **Aleksandr Borodin**'s *Prince Igor* (1869–1897), **Nikolay Rimsky-Korsakov**'s *Snegurochka* (The Snow Maiden, 1882–1898); and **Pyotor Il'yich Tchaikovsky**'s *Yevgeny Onegin* (Eugene Onegin, 1878–1879) and *Pikovaya dama* (The Queen of Spades, 1890), among others. **Hector Berlioz**, ever aware of Parisian audiences' expectations (not to say demands) that opera include ballet, orchestrated Weber's *Auffӧrderung zum Tanze* (Invitation to the Dance, J. 260) to serve as an inserted ballet in Act 1 of the French version of **Der Freischütz** (as *Le Freyschütz*, H. 90) when he conducted it in Paris in 1841.

The same time span witnessed a new flourishing and reform of *ballet d'action*. By late 18th-century convention, the usual practice was that the plot and choreography of these pieces were worked out by the director and choreographer, who would then bring in the composer at the last minute with specific instructions as to the tempos, steps, and durations of each musical selection, resulting in a made-to-order score whose claims to musical integrity were at best coincidental. **Ludwig van Beethoven**'s *Die Geschӧpfe des Prometheus* (**The Creatures of Prometheus**, Op. 43; 1800–1801) marked an important departure from this convention: Beethoven was commissioned to write the music on the basis of a plot drafted by the well-known choreographer Salvatore Viganó (1769–1821), and the two collaborated to produce a work that is entirely consistent with Novarre's reforms. Another advance was made with **Fromenthal Halévy**'s score for **Eugène Scribe**'s ballet *Manon Lescaut* (1830), which is considered to have been the first to use melody to identify character—a technique related to the contemporaneous employment of **idée fixe** and *Leitmotiv* in the works of Berlioz and Weber.

Romantic ballet as it is best known today was revolutionized above all by the innovations of a specific dancer—Marie Taglione (1804–1884), who danced on the tips of her toes with a seemingly supernatural grace—and the efforts of composers to accommodate this style. **Adolphe Adam** was among the early leaders in this trend, composing some 14 ballets between 1830 and

1856—among them *Faust* (1833), *La fille du Danube* (The Daughter of the Danube, 1836), and *Giselle* (1841)—and his role was taken over by **Léo Delibes**, whose *Coppélia* (1870) and *Sylvia* (1876) have remained among the most-performed Romantic ballets. The iconic composer in the genre in the late 19th century, however, is Tchaikovsky, whose four-act *Lebedinoe ozero* (*Swan Lake*, 1875–1877), *Spyashchaya krasavitsa* (The Sleeping Beauty, 1889–1890), and *Shchelkunchik* (*Nutcracker*, 1892) set new standards of dramatic imagination, musical variety, and orchestration and (especially in the case of *The Nutcracker*) have remained perennial favorites. Tchaikovsky's ballets provided the starting point not only for **Aleksandr Glazunov**'s *Raymonda* (1896–1897), *Barïshnya-sluzhanka* (*Les ruses d'amour*/The Wiles of Love, 1898), and *Vremena goda* (The Seasons, 1899) but also Stravinsky's *Zhar'-ptitsa* (The Firebird, 1909–1910) and *Petrushka* (1910–1911) and **Richard Strauss**'s *Der Bürger als Edelmann* (The Middle-Class Aristocrat, 1900, after Molière), *Josephslegende* (The Legend of Joseph, 1912–1914), *Schlagobers* (Whipped Cream, 1921–1922), and the little-known late chamber ballet *Verklungene Feste* (Fading Festivals, 1941). [JMC]

BAR FORM. (Ger., Barform.) Umbrella term for the form AAB or aa'B, common in many varieties of music—vocal and instrumental, cultivated and vernacular—but stereotypically associated with **chorales** and other German strophic **songs** (both sacred and secular) of the Middle Ages and Renaissance. Its association with the latter two contexts made it an important agent for evoking archaicness, particularly German archaicness, in **historicist** and **nationalist** music during the **long 19th century**. **Franz Schubert** set Gretchen's strophic song *Der König in Thule* (D. 367/Op. 5, no. 5, 1816) in bar form in response to the poem's depiction of a king in the long-lost land at the northernmost portion of the world, and the form was also employed by **Johannes Brahms, Felix Mendelssohn Bartholdy, Gustav Mahler**, and **Robert Schumann**, among many others, in order to evoke the "epic style" (*see* TOPIC). Its best-known use in the long 19th century is in the Prize Song in Act III of **Richard Wagner**'s *Die Meistersinger* (1867), though Wagner also used it extensively elsewhere.

Nineteenth-century composers and poets sometimes applied the term "bar form" loosely, whether out of misunderstanding (as in the case of Wagner's use in *Die Meistersinger*) or as a deliberate modernization. In the sense cultivated in the poetry and music of the Reformation chorales and the Minne- and Meisterlieder, the term denotes an entire song, not a strophe within it (an individual strophe was known as a *Gesätz, Liet*, or *Ton*). Within each song in bar form, each strophe comprised two main parts: an *Aufgesang* (introductory song) and an *Abgesang* (after-song). The *Aufgesang* comprised two lines with different text but the same rhyme scheme (known as *Stollen* [sing. *Stoll*] or *pes*), while the *Abgesang* comprised another pair of lines, the second of which concluded with a rhyme of the second *Stoll* of the *Aufgesang*. In musical settings, the same melody was typically used for both *Stollen* and recurred near the close of the *Abgesang*. In strict usage, the bar form must also comprise at least three strophes. [JMC]

See also GESANG (PL. GESÄNGE); LIED (PL. LIEDER).

BARBIERI, FRANCISCO (DE ASIS) ASENJO (1823–1894). Spanish composer, musicologist, critic, clarinetist, and music educator of the Late Romantic Generation. Described by **François-Joseph Fétis** in volume 1 of the Supplément et Complément to the *Biographie universelle des musiciens* (1878) as "one of the most imaginative, popular, and distinguished Spanish composers of our time," he was known as a composer for his **comic operas** and **zarzuelas**, while his scholarly investigations into then-obscure archaic musical instruments and musical heritages of Spain (especially the *viheula* and the late Renaissance songbooks known as *cancioneros*) represented important Iberian contributions to the **historicist** movement and rescued his country's distinctive traditions from the threat of oblivion. On the whole, he is one of the most important representatives of Spanish musical **nationalism**.

Barbieri's family wanted him to pursue a career in medicine or engineering, but in 1837 he embraced music as a vocation, enrolling in the newly founded Madrid **Conservatory**. During his studies, he made a meager living by working as a clarinetist, copyist, teacher, and pianist, also composing **chansons** and **romances** and singing in local productions of Italian **operas** on the side. After working with touring Italian opera companies in 1843–1844 and working as *maestro de música* and director of primary and secondary schools in Salamanca (1844–1845), he returned to Madrid, joining a group of musicians who forcefully advocated for the formation of a Spanish national opera, a movement that gained significant momentum in the coming decade thanks largely to Barbieri's efforts.

Barbieri's reputation as a composer was established with the successful premiere of his one-act zarzuela *Gloria y peluca* (Glory and Wig) in 1850, and he almost single-handedly established the aesthetic competitiveness of the zarzuela as a genre in relation to Italian opera (the overriding preference of Spanish nobility) with his *Jugar con fuego* (Playing with Fire), the first three-act zarzuela. Continued successes led to the formation of a new company devoted to the genre and the construction of a new theater, the Teatro de Zarzuela, in 1856. Theatrical performances during Lent were forbidden, so in 1859 Barbieri initiated a special concert series featuring large chorus and **orchestra** in the new theater to be held on the six Lenten Fridays—another important new initiative in Spanish musical culture. He founded the Sociedad

Artístico-Musical de Socorros Mutuos (a fund for impoverished musicians and other artists) in 1860 and the Sociedad de Conciertos in 1866, and he was a founding member of the Sociedad de Bibliófilos Españoles in 1869.

Barbieri's renown as a composer was renewed with the premiere in December 1864 of *Pan y toros* (Bread and Bulls), and he organized his own series of orchestral concerts in 1866 (giving the first performance of a **Beethoven** symphony in Spain). He composed numerous subsequent successful works (e.g., *El barberillo de Lavapiés* [The Little Barber of Lavapiés, 1874] and *El Sr. Luis el tumbón* [Señor Luis the Idler, 1891]) but also worked assiduously to uncover Spain's great musical legacies of the past, including a general history of the zarzuela (1864). These efforts culminated in 1890 with the *Cancionero musical de los siglos XV y XVI* (Musical Songbook of the Fifteenth and Sixteenth Centuries). He authored a total of 11 books and numerous articles. In addition to his 42 zarzuelas, Barbieri also composed a number of works for chorus with accompaniment of orchestra or military band, several *concertante* works with orchestra and other independent orchestral compositions, and numerous dances for **piano** and orchestra. His style is a remarkable blending of elements of the Wagnerian **music drama** with rhythms, harmonies, and melodic formulas characteristic of Andalusian **folk song**. [JMC]

See also BRETÓN (Y HERNÁNDEZ), TOMÁS (1850–1923).

BARCAROLLE. (Fr.; via It. *barcarola* from Lat. *barca*, boat.) Originally, a Venetian gondola or boat **song** in duple or quadruple compound meter, suggesting a rowing rhythm; later an **operatic** or **chamber** composition (either vocal or instrumental) evocative of such a song and character. Many such works are designated as such by their titles, while others are only implicitly barcarolles (e.g., **Franz Schubert**'s *Auf dem Wasser zu singen*, D. 774, 1823). The *Venezianische Gondellieder* (Venetian Gondola-Songs) of **Felix Mendelssohn Bartholdy**'s *Lieder ohne Worte* (MWV U78, U110, and U151/Op. 19[b], no. 6, Op. 30, no. 6, and op. 62, no. 5, 1832, 1835, and 1844) occupy a middle ground between these two positions. Operatic barcarolles were composed by **D.-F.-E. Auber, Gaetano Donizetti, Giacomo Meyerbeer, Gioachino Rossini, Giuseppe Verdi**, and **Carl Maria von Weber**, among others. The best-known barcarolles of the **long 19th century** are **Fryderyk Chopin**'s Op. 60 (CT 6, 1845–1846), the Barcarolle from Act II of **Jacques Offenbach**'s *Les contes d'Hoffmann* (1881), and **Gabriel Fauré**'s 13 *Barcarolles* for piano solo (comp. and publ. separately, 1881–1921 passim). Others were written by composers such as **Adolphe Adam, Charles-Valentin Alkan, Mily Balakirev, Adrien Boieldieu, Cécile Chaminade, Félicien David, Alexander Glazunov, Fromental Halévy, Henri Herz, Anatoly Lyadov, Adolf Fredrik Lindblad, Edward Mac-**

Dowell, Sergei Rachmaninoff, Anton Rubinstein, Camille Saint-Saëns, Louis Spohr, Richard Strauss, Pyotr Il'yich Tchaikovsky, and Sigismond Thalberg, among a great many others. [JMC]

THE BARTERED BRIDE, JB 1: 100. (Cz., *Prodaná Nevěsta*, The Sold Fiancée; Ger., *Die verkaufte Braut*.) **Comic opera** in three acts by **Bedřich Smetana** to a **libretto** by Karel Sabina (1813–1877). It was premiered in the Provisional Theater, Prague, on 30 May 1866 in a version with two acts and spoken dialogue. This Smetana expanded and overhauled over the course of three subsequent revisions. The fourth, definitive version with recitative and three acts was presented in the same theater on 25 September 1870. The third version was published in piano/vocal score by Matice Hudební (Prague) in 1871 and reissued, with parallel German title and German text underlay, the following year. The final (fourth) version was first published in 1885, still in piano/vocal score but now with a German translation by Max Kalbeck (1850–1921). This version was first published in full score in 1892.

   Though initially less successful than Smetana's first opera, *Braniboři v Čechách* (The Brandenburgers in Bohemia, JB 1:87, 1862–1863, publ. posth. 1899), *The Bartered Bride* is now regarded as his most important stage work and his only **opera** to have won a standing place in the international repertoire; it ranks alongside *The Moldau* as his best-known composition. [JMC]

   See also MÁ VLAST; NATIONALISM, ROMANTIC NATIONALISM.

BATTLE OF VITORIA. See *WELLINGTON'S VICTORY, OR THE BATTLE OF VITORIA*, OP. 91.

BAYREUTH. Town in Bavaria, internationally famous as home to the Festspielhaus (Festival Theater) designed according to the wishes of **Richard Wagner**, and site of an annual music festival devoted exclusively to Wagner's works since 1876. Wagner initially developed the idea of a proprietary stage in order to realize his theories of the theater and establish a venue in which his **operas** could be ensured performance without alteration to suit the acoustic and architectural specifics as well as programming conventions of Europe's other opera houses. Wagner's plans had earlier centered on Munich and Nuremberg, but Munich's lively opera scene offered too much competition for a fledgling program devoted to a single comp oser, and Nuremberg (which at this point had no opera life) fell within the jurisdiction of Wagner's former creditors. He and Cosima thus settled on Bayreuth (home to an established opera culture and one of the best late Baroque theaters still in existence) and set about securing the necessary civic permissions and financial support from a network of patrons. **Ludwig van Beethoven**'s Ninth (**"Choral") Symphony** was performed at the laying of the cornerstone for the new theater on Wagner's birthday in 1872, and after several delays, the much-anticipated opening of the Festspielhaus occurred on 13 August 1876, with the first of three performance cycles of *The Ring of the Nibelung*. Since its inception, the Bayreuth Festival has been a site of musical and cultural pilgrimage, during the **long 19th century** attracting and inspiring composers including **Ernest Chausson**, J. W. Davison (1813–1885), **Claude Debussy, Paul Dukas, Henri Duparc, Edvard Grieg, Vincent d'Indy, Alberic Magnard, Jules Massenet, Hubert Parry, Max Reger**, and **Richard Strauss**, among a great many others.

Wagner had planned for his new theater to be free and open to the populace, but budgetary overruns during its construction made it necessary for tickets to be sold. Aside from that, the theater proved an ideal venue for Wagner's vision of the four operas of the *Ring* cycle and *Parsifal*—responding to acoustic, logistical, and **performance-practice**-related issues in ways that ingeniously alleviate issues encountered in modern performances of his works (especially in combination with the gut strings and smaller **orchestras** typical of his ensembles). To begin with, the issue of singers being able to project over the dense and often massive **orchestration** of Wagner's music was naturally addressed in Bayreuth by the fact that most of the orchestra's louder instruments (specifically the brass and percussion) were beneath and behind the lip of the stage rather than in a pit in front of it (what was reportedly described as the "mysterious space" or "mystic abyss" by the time of Albert Lavignac's important book *Le voyage artistique à Bayreuth*, 1897; see figure 1). The problem of clarity of texture (or lack thereof) in Wagner's complicated counterpoint is also addressed by the seating plan's retention, reversed, of the antiphonal distribution of most of the orchestra (e.g., first and second violins on opposite sides of the conductor; see figure 2). Finally, its use of a fan-shaped auditorium with only side entrances (no rear en-

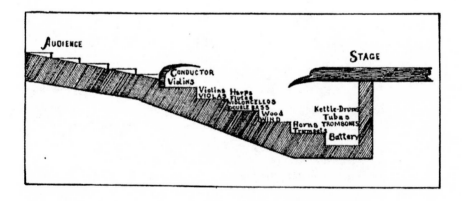

Figure 1. Cross section of orchestra pit in Bayreuth Festspielhaus.

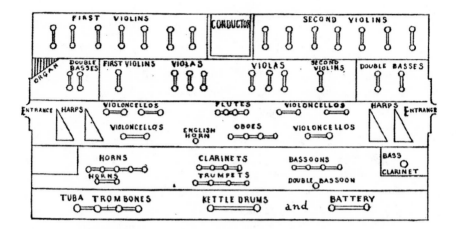

Figure 2. Arrangement of orchestra in Bayreuth Festspielhaus.

trances) and a single tier of seats combined with the use of steam curtains and a double proscenium to create an atmosphere that was at once egalitarian and mystical, facilitating audiences' sense of utter immersion in the world of the "acts of music made visible" (as Wagner put it in 1872) that were unfolding onstage. [JMC]

BEETHOVEN, LUDWIG VAN (1770–1827). German composer of seminal importance to virtually every aspect of music of the **long 19th century**. He published 135 numbered *opera* and another 43 works without opus number (*see* WOO); to these must be added three works published with posthumous opus numbers (opp. 136–38) and a great many more posthumous publications of music he withheld during his lifetime. His sizable output includes important contributions in virtually every major musical genre: one **opera** (the **rescue opera** *Fidelio*), **incidental music, ballet,** and **concert arias**; concerted works sacred and secular for chorus with and without **orchestra**; nine **symphonies**, five numbered piano **concerto**s, a violin concerto, and a "triple concerto" for violin, cello, **piano**, and orchestra; numerous **concert overtures** and other programmatic works; instrumental and vocal **chamber music** including 16 numbered **string quartet**s and 13 *opera* of **songs**; 32 numbered piano **sonatas**, four major sets of piano **variations** published with opus number during his lifetime and numerous others that were published without opus number or published posthumously; and more.

Beethoven's symphonies, string quartets, and piano sonatas are themselves canonical corpuses of work, each standing as a series of milestones in the history of its genre. Of the other works, the most important are certainly the concert aria *Ah, perfido!/Per pietà, non dirmi addio!* (Op. 65; comp. 1795–1796 and publ. 1805), the *"Eroica" Variations* for piano solo (Op. 35, 1802), the Violin Sonata No. 9 in A Major ("Kreutzer"), Op. 47 (1803), the Cello Sonata No. 3 in A Major (Op. 69, 1807–1809), the **cantata** *Meeresstille und glückliche Fahrt* (Calm Sea and Fair Sailing, Op. 112, 1815), the song cycle *An die ferne Geliebte* (Op. 98, 1816), and the *Missa solemnis* (Op. 123, 1823; *see* SOLEMN MASS) and *"Diabelli" Variations* for piano solo, Op. 120 (1823). Although his music generally enjoys a sacrosanct status today, some of his works that indulge in "trivial" styles (such as the "Battle Symphony" *Wellington's Victory*, the *Bundeslied* "In allen guten Stunden," Op. 122, or his many **folk song** arrangements) continue to pose aesthetic dilemmas, with the result that the modern Beethoven canon, extensive though it is, offers a perspective rather more selective and in some ways one sided than that enjoyed by his contemporaries.

Beethoven's career spans the societal and musical transition from the patronage system to the age of public patronage. Born and raised in Bonn, he was the son of a court tenor who, on recognizing his son's talent, set about promoting him as a prodigy. In the late 1770s and early 1780s, he received instruction in thoroughbass and organ, piano, and violin, finally studying more advanced composition with Christian Gottlob Neefe (1748–1798). By June of 1782 (at the age of 11½), he was acting as Neefe's assistant as court organist. In 1787, he made his first trip to Vienna, where he may have met **Wolfgang Amadeus Mozart** and taken a few lessons from him, and from 1789 he played viola in the court and theater orchestras of the Electoral chapel in Bonn alongside other musicians such as **Antoine Reicha, Andreas** and **Bernhard Romberg**, and **Nicolaus Simrock**, all the while socializing with the court's aristocratic and intellectual affiliates. Around 1790, he also seems to have begun composing regularly, producing his first compositions in a distinctive personal style and winning admirers for both his music and his abilities as a pianist.

In 1792, the Elector of Bonn sponsored a trip to Vienna for Beethoven to "receive Mozart's spirit from the hands of [**Joseph**] **Haydn**" (in the words of his future patron Count Ferdinand Waldstein). As the cultural capital of the Holy Roman Empire, Vienna was to prove a major source not only of inspiration but also of musical patronage; it was here that Beethoven devised a strategy of assembling an informal network of individual patrons who would commission music, subvent publication of his works, and ultimately (in the persons of Archduke Rudolf, Prince Ferdinand Kinsky, and Prince Karl Lichnowsky) provide an annuity that enabled him to live comfortably without having to enter into a contractual arrangement as performer or composer for a particular court or other institution. This arrangement proved prophetic as well as pragmatic, for the outbreak of the French Revolution, the Terror, and the Napoleonic Wars collectively conspired to end the Holy Roman Empire, whose electoral structure had comprised Beethoven's sole means of support to that date. While en route to Vienna, Beethoven had passed German troops heading west to meet Bonaparte's armies, which had invaded and occupied the Rhineland; the lesson that the old ways were in jeopardy would not have been lost on him. Later composers and biographers were to find in his skillfully crafted professional autonomy an inspiration for the notion of the artist as an independent spirit who created according to the biddings of the muses and personal inspiration rather than those of court and church—a view that runs aground in face of the facts of his creative life but that proved immensely influential nonetheless.

From the time of his arrival in Vienna, Beethoven was the very picture of a successful and socially outgoing musician. There he studied for a time with Haydn until the older composer's departure for London in 1794, also receiving his first strict and systematic instruction theory and counterpoint with Johann Georg Albrechtsberger (1736–1809) and perhaps dramatic composition in the Italian style with Antonio Salieri (1750–1825). Between 1792 and 1802, he concertized frequently, composing and publishing his first 33 numbered *opera*. The compositions of this Early Vienna Period are original from the outset—especially the op. 1 **piano trios**, the op. 2 piano sonatas, and the op. 5 cello sonatas—but a new and startling level of originality becomes evident with the works written in 1798 and afterward. Most important among these are the Piano Sonatas Nos. 8 ("Pathétique," Op. 13; comp. 1797–1798, publ. 1799) and 14 ("Quasi una fantasia"; comp. 1801, publ. 1802), the op. 18 string quartets (comp. 1798–1800, publ. 1801), and the First Symphony, Op. 21 (comp. 1799–1800, publ. 1801).

Concurrently with these successes, however, Beethoven realized that his hearing was worsening—a significant impediment for his performing, his composing, and his ability to interact with and win support from potential patrons. The realization that his deafness would eventually become complete provoked a personal and professional crisis that manifested itself partly in his contemplation of suicide (*see* HEILIGENSTADT TESTAMENT) but also renewed his resolve to forge a "new path" for composition (a statement of ca. 1802 to his close friend Wenzel Krumpholz, first reported by **Carl Czerny** in 1842). The new style of this Middle Vienna Period was characterized by a generally extroverted character, with exaggerated abundance of the engaging melodies, abrupt dynamic changes, innovative harmonies, colorful orchestration, and distended, end-weighted forms that by the mid-1790s had already become his trademarks. With it, his popularity rose to new heights, a situation that facilitated the performance and publication of major works for large ensemble, such as the first seven symphonies (Nos. 1 and 2 had been composed earlier but remained unpublished until 1803), the first two versions of *Fidelio*, the Mass in C (Op. 86), the last three piano concertos and the Violin Concerto, and the *Choral Fantasia*, Op. 80. Of the orchestral works, those generally considered most emblematic of this style are the **"Eroica" Symphony** (No. 3 in E-flat, Op. 55; comp. 1803–1804, publ. 1806); the Symphony No. 5 in C Minor, Op. 67; and the **"Pastoral" Symphony** (No. 6) in F Major, Op. 68 (the latter two both comp. 1807–1808 and publ. 1809).

The year 1812 was characterized by significant conflict in Beethoven's relationship with his brother Johann and an apparent affair with the "immortal beloved" (probably Antonie Brentano) as well the decisive turning point of the Napoleonic Wars. This year represented something of a watershed for the composer—one that led to the fourth and final period of his career and creative life (the Late Vienna Period). Although his creative spark was briefly renewed by his collaboration with **Maelzel** on *Wellington's Victory*, for much of 1813 he appears to have been depressed. Personal and familial concerns, chiefly surrounding the care of his nephew Carl and (after 1818) his complete deafness, continued to multiply for the remainder of the decade, impeding his productivity in quantitative terms. Indeed, the economic and political uncertainty that attended the end of the Napoleonic Wars, the redrawing of the map of Europe that occurred with the **Congress of Vienna**, and the establishment of the new governments (and new censorship) dramatically altered all the institutions of musical life, public and private—a circumstance that created new problems as well as new opportunities for every serious composer, not just Beethoven.

Nevertheless, during the early post-Napoleonic period, Beethoven produced a number of significant compositions, among them the cantata *Der glorreiche Augenblick* (The Glorious Moment, Op. posth. 136, 1814), the song cycle *An die ferne Geliebte*, the op. 102 cello sonatas (comp. 1815, publ. 1817), and the op. 106 (**"Hammerklavier"**) and op. 109 piano sonatas (comp. 1817–1818 and 1820 and publ. 1819 and 1821, respectively). These works may be characterized as possessing a new level of stylistic and aesthetic eclecticism: the works written for large ensembles and intended for public performance often celebrate accessibility, topicality, and triviality—*Wellington's Victory* and *Der glorreiche Augenblick* are prime examples of this tendency—while the vocal and instrumental chamber music increasingly cultivates intimate themes and a sense of introversion or introspectiveness.

Beginning around 1821, then, Beethoven's productivity increased dramatically, resulting in the last two piano sonatas (opp. 110 and 111; both comp. 1821–1822 and publ. 1823) and the last two *opera* of **bagatelles** (opp. 119 and 126; comp. 1820–1822 and 1824 and publ. 1823 and 1825, respectively), the *"Diabelli" Variations* (Op. 120; comp. and publ. 1823), the *Missa solemnis* (Op. 123; comp. 1819–1824, publ. 1827), the Ninth Symphony (op. 125; comp. 1822–1824, publ. 1826), and the last five string quartets and *Große Fuge* (opp. 127, 130, 131, 132, 133, and 135). Although most of the musical world would find these late Viennese compositions eccentric or simply baffling until the mid-1840s, Beethoven's fame was secure on the basis of the works of the previous decades. There were even plans (unrealized) for a complete edition of his music with the Mainz firm of Schott. He was able to live comfortably, but his nephew Karl's attempted suicide in July 1826 and his own declining health sullied the triumphs of the last year. His death on 26 March 1827 was followed by a large public funeral in Vienna, and the last three quartets, *Große Fuge*, and *Missa solemnis* were finally published in April and May of that year.

Just as Beethoven's career and music seem to chronicle the changes that swept through European life and culture between around 1770 and 1830, contemporary and posthumous responses to his life and works chronicle the significant changes that occurred in musical aesthetics and musical style over the course of the long 19th century, and various nations and localities within nations constructed their own versions of his identity, celebrating the aspects of his music and life that resonated with their own values while downplaying those that did not. There were also profound differences among the German, English, French, Italian, and other regional constructions of Beethoven's identity during the decades after his death and, within the German lands, among the Viennese, Prussian, and Bonn constructions of his life, works, and historical significance. These different posthumous **receptions** were shaped first and foremost by contemporary political and cultural pressures as artists, authors, and other cultural and political figures sought and found in Beethoven a cause célèbre that resonated with the values and cultural agendas of their own place and time. Additionally, few composers attempted to respond compositionally to the ideas, styles, and techniques represented in the works of the late Vienna years until the mid-1840s (**Hector Berlioz**, **Fanny Hensel**, **Felix Mendelssohn Bartholdy**, and **Robert Schumann** were important exceptions in this regard). As the more complicated late works became increasingly well known in the second half of the century, however, they found increasing champions not only in music criticism (especially the writings of **Franz Liszt**, **A. B. Marx**, and **Richard Wagner**) but also in new music. As a result, by the end of the 19th century, composers increasingly adopted Beethoven's more difficult works of the 1820s rather than the more accessible music of the Early and Middle Vienna Periods as models or starting points for their own new music. The symphonies of **Anton Bruckner** and **Gustav Mahler**, for example, almost all take Beethoven's Ninth Symphony as an obvious model, and it also significantly informed the symphonic output of **Johannes Brahms**.

The most far-reaching example of the complexity of Beethoven's reception history, however, is the conventional division of his creative life into three style periods rather than the four into which it naturally falls if one correlates the major caesurae of his life with the significant changes in musical style that occurred over the course of his compositions between the early 1780s and 1827. In the conventional tripartite view, the juvenilia and student

works of the 1780s are lumped together with the strikingly original compositions of the 1790s in a formative "period of imitation" that was followed by a
"heroic period" or "period of externalization" beginning around 1803 and
then by a cumulative synthesis in a late "period of internalization" during the
last decade or so of Beethoven's career. This view is not without its merits,
but it was formulated specifically in order to construe the life and works of
the celebrated composer as a self-fulfilling realization of a complete dialectical cycle—the Hegelian notion of historical development that emerged in the
1790s and that remained the predominant model until the mid-20th century—
see HEGEL, GEORG WILHELM FRIEDRICH (1770–1831). By viewing
the entire life and its works through this lens, based as it is on an ideological
preconception, subsequent commentators have inevitably subjected their
understanding of Beethoven's life and works to the prejudices and dogmatic
underpinnings of that ideology—most importantly, the tendency to diminish
or downplay the originality that made Beethoven's early and middle-period
works distinctive and influential in the eyes of his contemporaries, to recognize as representatives of the "late" style only those works that lend themselves easily to description as "forward-looking" fulfillments of specific antithetical ideas or techniques already recognized in earlier compositions, and
thus to rewrite the past in order to suit the ideologically predicated needs of a
present that was alien to Beethoven himself. [JMC]
   See also PROGRAM (PROGRAMMATIC) MUSIC.

BEL CANTO. (It., "beautiful singing," "beautiful song.") Term used since
the mid-19th century to identify as beautiful a style or styles of singing that
were under attack or considered to be either lost or endangered. The term *bel
canto* and a variety of semantically related expressions (e.g., *belleze dell'
canto* and *bell' arte del canto*) are typically applied to Italian styles of singing as they were cultivated in the early and mid-19th century, specifically in
the **operas** of **Vincenzo Bellini, Gaetano Donizetti, Gioachino Rossini,
Giuseppe Verdi** (especially works of his early and middle periods), and
others. By the mid- and later 19th century, it was used, often nostalgically, to
denote not only beauty of vocal tone (the literal meaning) but also more
specifically a light tone in the upper registers, variety of timbre across the
tessitura, and agility, flexibility, and taste in applying unwritten embellishments to the notated vocal line. This style of singing's privileging of inherently musical traits over others (such as the musical drama and clarity of text
declamation) earned it the scorn of **Richard Wagner**, who in 1849 dismissed
it as "the very gristle of vocal tone." [JMC]
   See also PERFORMANCE PRACTICE.

BELLINI, VINCENZO (SALVATORE CARMELO FRANCESCO) (1801–1835). Italian composer, with **Gaetano Donizeti** the dominant figure of the Romantic Generation in Italian **opera** between the de facto retirement of **Gioachino Rossini** and the emergence of **Giuseppe Verdi**'s mature style. Three of his mature operas are staples of the international operatic repertoire: *La sonnambula* (a **libretto** by Felice Romani, after **Eugène Scribe** and J. P. Aumer, 1831), *Norma* (a libretto by Romani, after Alexandre Soumet, 1831), and *I puritani* (a libretto by Carlo Pepoli, after J.-A.F.-P. Ancelot and Xavier, 1835). Most of his six other mature operas have maintained a presence in the active repertoire. Although his style is obviously influenced by that of Rossini, in most of his mature works he eschews repetition of phrases and aims instead for a direct style of text setting that achieves a stronger balance between the dramatic and melodic aspects of bel canto style than was typical of Rossini or Donizetti. This mature style usually (with some exceptions, such as the celebrated "Casta diva" from *Norma*) discourages excessive embellishment. Instead, it employs writing in a largely syllabic style and keeps passagi (at least as notated) closely related to the main melodic and motivic gestures of their contexts.

Bellini's collaborations with his librettists were difficult and intense. Despite his well-documented concern that the music reflect "*the verses, not the situations* [emphasis Bellini's]" of the drama (quoted from a letter to librarian and his eventual biographer Francesco Florimo), his sketchbooks and correspondence show that he sometimes presented his librettists with previously composed music, demanding that they write verses to fit his melodies. The result of this situation was that his librettists often delivered the final products to him only weeks before the work was to be staged, earning Bellini the reputation of being a notorious procrastinator and a "philosophical" composer who resisted writing music made to order. Although his operas written in Italy are number operas whose approach to the stage and to operatic form owes much to Rossini, his last opera, *I puritani*, written for the Paris Opéra, hints that a different style might well have emerged had he lived longer. In particular, its music relies more on continuity and less on contrast than does that of its predecessors, and its plot moves forward less by means of strong contrasts among characters and sharp breaks in action and more by fluidity and an approach to the operatic scene that creates greater parity between off- and onstage events.

Bellini wrote his first composition at the age of six and in 1819 entered the Real Collegio di Musica in Naples (now the Conservatorio di Musica San Pietro a Majella) on scholarship. He graduated in 1825 and later that year received his first professional commission (from the Teatro San Carlo). The resulting work, *Bianca e Gernando* (on a libretto by Domenico Gilardoni), was premiered in May 1826 after a delay of several months but was well received despite the delay. The work he was commissioned to compose as the principal opera of the fall season in 1827 by the Teatro La Scala (Milan), *Il pirata*, marked his first collaboration with the renowned librettist Felice Romani (1788–1865), author of 90 librettos for composers including Donizetti, **Giacomo Meyerbeer, Saverio Mercadante, Gioachino Rossini, Sigismond Thalberg**, and Verdi, among others, and established him internationally as a leading opera composer. Romani provided the librettos for each of Bellini's operas over the next six years (*La straniera* [The Female Stranger], 1829; *Zaira*, 1829; *I Capuleti e i Montecchi* [The Capulets and the Montagues], 1830; *La sonnambula* [The Female Sleepwalker], 1831, *Norma*, 1831; *Beatrice di Tenda*, 1833). Although the two had a falling-out over the blame for the hostile public reaction against the significant delay of their *Beatrice di Tenda*, they later repaired their friendship, and after working with Pepoli on *I Puritani*, Bellini vowed never again to work with any librettist other than Romani. He spent much of 1833 and 1834 in London and Paris and in September 1835 died in Paris of an outbreak of amoebic dysentery (an ailment that had plagued him chronically since 1831). He was 34. His output is small in comparison with most Italian opera composers of his day, a fact that may owe in part to his temperament (he worked best under a pressing deadline), partly to his extended negotiations with his librettists, and partly to his extended affair with the devoted wife of a wealthy nobleman—a situation that meant he could live without budgetary constraint and had generous support for the costs he incurred in day-to-day life. [JMC]

BENNETT, WILLIAM STERNDALE (1816–1875). English composer, conductor, pianist, and educator of the Romantic Generation, among the British Isles' most important composers of the **long 19th century**. He came from a family of church musicians; served as choirboy in King's College, Cambridge, from 1824 to 1826; and then studied composition and **piano** at the Royal Academy of Music (London) under William Crotch (1775–1847) and **Cipriani Potter** from 1827 to 1836. When his First Piano **Concerto** (Op. 1, 1832, publ. 1833) was performed at the Royal Academy on 26 June 1836, it was heard by **Felix Mendelssohn Bartholdy**, who requested to be introduced to the composer and invited him to visit Leipzig. This Bennett did, twice (1836 and 1837), being received enthusiastically by both Mendelssohn and **Robert Schumann** and winning praise in Leipzig for his performances at the piano as well as his compositions. He taught privately and was on the faculty of the Royal Academy from 1837 to 1858, also serving as director of the Philharmonic Society of London from 1856 to 1866 and professor of music at the University of Cambridge during those same years. He served as principal of the Royal Academy from 1866 to his death, also being knighted in 1871.

Bennett is best known today for works for piano and orchestra: four published solo concertos, a **Konzertstück** (1841–1843, rev. 1848), an unpublished concerto for two pianos (*see* PIANO DUET), and a **Caprice** in E major for piano and orchestra (Op. 22, 1836–1838, publ. 1840). He composed a total of six **symphonies** and nine **concert overtures** (including two on **William Shakespeare**'s *The Tempest* and *The Merry Wives of Windsor* and one after Thomas Moore's [1779–1852] *Lallah Rookh* [Op. 42, 1862, titled *Paradise and the Peri*]; cf. Robert Schumann's 1843 secular **oratorio** *Das Paradies und die Peri*). He also penned about three dozen works for piano solo or piano duet, a handful of chamber works, plentiful sacred works for chorus a cappella or with accompaniment of organ or **orchestra**, and four *opera* of **songs** as well as seven unpublished songs. [JMC]

BERLIN SCHOOL. *See* SECOND BERLIN SCHOOL, SECOND BERLIN LIEDER SCHOOL.

BERLIOZ, (LOUIS-) HECTOR (1803–1869). French composer, **conductor**, critic, memoirist, and writer on music of the Romantic Generation; iconic figure in French Romanticism and the first Frenchman to have achieved international renown in an age whose musical values were dominated by German and Italian music. He is best known today for a small portion of his sizable and varied output: the **program symphonies** *Episode in the Life of an Artist* and *Harold in Italy* (H. 68/Op. 16, 1848) and the "dramatic **symphony**" for soloists, chorus, and orchestra *Roméo et Juliette* (H. 79/Op. 17, 1839), the *Grande Messe des morts* (H. 75/Op. 5, 1837, rev. 1852, 1867; *see* REQUIEM), the **concert overture** *Le carnaval romain* (Roman Carnival, H. 95, 1843), the "dramatic legend" *La damnation de Faust* (H. 111/Op. 24, 1845–1846, publ. 1854), and the **song cycle** *Les nuits d'été* (Summer Nights, H. 81/Op. 7, 1840–41, publ. 1841, version with orchestra, 1856). His *Grand traité d'instrumentation et d'orchestration modernes* (Grand Treatise on Modern Instrumentation and Orchestration, Op. 10, 1843, 2nd ed., with new section on "Le chef d'orchestra" [The Conductor], 1855) remains one of the most influential writings on that subject and provided the basis for **Richard Strauss**'s treatise, and his quasi-autobiographical *Les soirées de l'orchestre* (Evenings with the Orchestra, 1852) and the late *Mémoirs* (1865) remain some of the most vivid and insightful published documents concerning mid-19th-century musical life. His personality—witty, outspoken, moody, prone to depression and violent mood changes, insistent that art and life must mirror each other, and resistant to compromise—has become, with those of **Pyotor Il'yich Tchaikovsky** in the Late Romantic Generation and **Gustav Mahler** in the Modern Romantic Generation, the archetypal Romantic temperament in music, much as the personality of **Lord Byron**, whom he admired, has become archetypal in literature. Despite his political conservatism and his efforts on behalf of German, Italian, and (to a lesser extent) French musical traditions, he is remembered chiefly for his progressive attitudes toward music and musical aesthetics and was one of few French musicians to be championed by the **New German School** and the **Allgemeiner Deutscher Musikverein**.

Berlioz was the son of a provincial doctor and was expected to pursue medicine as a vocation, but he displayed an early interest in music and learned the flageolet, flute, and guitar (but never **piano**). Sometime in his mid-teens, he procured copies of Jean-Philippe Rameau's (1683–1764) *Traité d'harmonie* (1722) and Charles Simon Catel's (1773–1830) *Traité d'harmonie* (1802). These texts, studied without recourse to the piano, provided the foundations of his views on music theory. He took music lessons with a local teacher and began composing around 1817. In 1819, his **romance** *Le dépit de la bergère* (H. 7) was published in Paris, but his family was determined that he would pursue medicine as a vocation. He thus continued his university studies in medicine at the Université René Descartes in Paris. His existing lack of interest in the profession was exacerbated by his experiences in the dissecting room, however. They coincided with his enthusiastic immersion in the French capital's vibrant musical life—both his experiences at the Opéra, where he saw works by **Adrien Boieldieu**, Christoph Willibald Ritter von Gluck (1714–1787), **Étienne Méhul**, Antonio Salieri (1750–1825), **Gaspare Spontini**, and **Carl Maria von Weber** (whose *Freischütz* was performed in Paris in **Eugène Scribe**'s adaptation as *Robin des bois* in 1824), and his acquaintance with **Jean-François Le Sueur**, who (on the basis works that are for the most part now lost and in any case speak little of the individuality that would later become Berlioz's trademark) prophetically pronounced him "no great apothecary but a great composer." In 1824, he officially gave up his studies in medicine, exacerbating existing family tensions and generating considerable hardship for himself, as the family's allowance was reduced and sometimes withheld. He formally enrolled in the Paris **Conservatory** in 1826.

Berlioz studied at the Conservatory from 1826 to 1830 and in 1830, on his fifth attempt, won first prize in the institution's **Prix de Rome** competition. He traveled to Rome in March 1831 under that prize and there became fast friends with **Felix Mendelssohn Bartholdy**. The two spent much time together and saw the sights of the Eternal City, but when Berlioz became aware that his fiancée, Camille Moke, had jilted him, he left Italy with plans to return to France and kill her and her lover. After his rage had abated, he returned to Italy, remaining there until May 1832. On returning to Paris, he finally met and soon married the Irish actress Harriet Smithson (1800–1854), with whom he had developed an intense obsession already in 1827 (*see* IDÉE FIXE). During the 1830s, he also organized several concerts per year of his own and others' music, earning money principally by contributing criticism to the Parisian music press, a chore he loathed but at which he excelled. His attempts to procure a regular position in Paris were unsuccessful, but he obtained two government commissions and several private commissions, among them one from **Niccolò Paganini** for the work that eventually became *Harold in Italy*. The compositions penned during the 1830s combined with his criticism to earn him a reputation in France and abroad as a musical voice that could be adored or abhorred but scarcely ignored. After his relationship with Harriet Smithson failed, he was able to launch a series of tours in Austria, Belgium, Switzerland, Russia, and the German lands, giving concerts of his own music in Europe's most important musical capitals.

Berlioz was in London when the **Revolutions of 1848** reached Paris and, politically conservative, was unsympathetic to the new direction taken in France with the Second Republic. He became increasingly less inclined to undertake new compositions, devoting himself instead to his prose (specifically the treatise on orchestration). He virtually ceased composing during the period 1850–1853, but the great and unexpected success of his "sacred trilogy" *L'enfance du Christ* (H. 130/Op. 25) at its premiere in 1854 renewed his creative energies for a time. The renewal was short lived, however, for the death earlier that year of Smithson, whom he had continued to support over the years, combined with the steady worsening of his Crohn's disease; the death of his second wife, Marie Recio (1814–1862), in 1862; the refusal of the Paris Opéra to stage his **opera** *Les Troyens* (H. 133a/Op. 5, comp. 1856–1858) in its entirety due to its overlarge scope and the failure of the truncated version that was finally given in 1863; and the death of his son from yellow fever in 1867 to leave him isolated and discouraged during his final years. He occasionally gave private readings of Shakespeare to a shrinking circle of intimates (among them **Jules Massenet** and **Camille Saint-Saëns**) but generally avoided music. In 1865, he completed his memoirs (adapted from compiled published and unpublished writings penned over the previous decades) and had 1,200 copies of them printed and stored in his office, intended for posthumous dissemination. His most important public ventures during these final years were two concerts he conducted in Vienna and Cologne (*La damnation de Faust* in Vienna in November 1866, followed by *Harold in Italy* and parts of *Béatrice et Benedict* [H. 138, comp. 1860–1862] in Cologne in February 1867) and a total of eight concerts in St. Petersburg and Moscow in the winter of 1867–1868 to a warmly receptive audience of Russian composers (including **Mily Balakirev, Aleksandr Borodin, César Cui, Modest Mussorgsky,** and **Nikolay Rimsky-Korsakov**). He died on 8 March 1869.

The task of inventorying Berlioz's output is complicated both by his predilection for generic innovation and by the fact that he destroyed some compositions, reused others in other works, and withdrew some works after their publication, assigning their opus numbers to new pieces (the last circumstance meaning that opus numbers are an even less reliable indicator of chronology for Berlioz than they are generally; *see* PRINTING AND PUBLISHING OF MUSIC). A rough inventory of his oeuvre as published by the end of his life includes three **operas**, four symphonies, five concert overtures, the instrumental romance for violin and orchestra titled *Reverie et caprice* (H. 88/Op. 8, 1841), three large-scale liturgical compositions, one **oratorio**, 15 numbered *opera* for chorus (some with soloists and/or orchestra), and 37 **songs** for solo voice with piano or orchestra. He stands as one of the **long 19th century**'s most extraordinary and imaginative figures in music and in Romantic culture generally. While his music was influenced by the ideas of **Antoine Reicha** (with whom he studied at Conservatory) concerning harmony, form, and orchestration, he also absorbed extracurricular influences into his creative persona with a brilliance and enthusiasm seldom rivaled elsewhere in the long 19th century.

Berlioz observed and sometimes adapted ideas and styles advanced in contemporary musics ranging from his friends **Ferdinand Hiller, Franz Liszt**, and **Felix Mendelssohn Bartholdy** (whose "elfin" **scherzi** he admired and apparently emulated) to **Richard Wagner** (for whose music he had little sympathy). But he also voraciously devoured the music of **Ludwig van Beethoven**, Christoph Willibald Ritter von Gluck, and Weber, becoming one of the latter two composers' most energetic and influential advocates in mid-19th-century France. He also absorbed and responded to literature with remarkable insight and imagination: his most important literary influences were certainly Byron, **Johann Wolfgang von Goethe**, Moore, Shakespeare, and Walter Scott (1771–1832), but he also read and drew inspiration from other historical and contemporary writers, including Honoré de Balzac, François-René de Chateaubriand, James Fenimore Cooper, Gustave Flaubert, Théophile Gautier, E. T. A. Hoffmann, **Victor Hugo**, Alfred de Musset, Gérard de Nerval, and Alfred de Vigny.

Berlioz's contemporaries often lampooned him, publicly and privately and in visual art as well as writing, for the enormous orchestral and choral ensembles he called for to realize his musical visions, but this perceived Romantic exorbitance on his part was the complement to an equally exceptional fluency at intimacy and spontaneity. This intimacy was often presented alongside those moments of grandeur in works such as the Requiem but also celebrated on its own in his many songs, including those for voice(s) and orchestra. Together with Mendelssohn and (later) Mahler and **Richard Strauss**, he created the modern conductor, being among the very first to use a baton (whose length was sometimes caricatured, sometimes in obviously phallic imagery) held at the tip rather than in the center. And as an observer, chronicler, and commentator on 19th-century musical life, he is without peer in his generation. [JMC]

BERUTTI (QUIROGA). Family of Argentine musicians, of which two brothers, *Arturo* (1862–1938) and *Pablo* (1866–1914), both of the Modern Romantic Generation, are the most distinguished. Both were important figures in Argentine musical **nationalism**. Their father was a composer and pianist, and both began their musical studies with him in their native San Juan, then relocated to Buenos Aires. Arturo was a prominent figure in Argentine musical life by 1882, when he began publishing not only his music but also a series of articles titled "Aires nacionales" in the *Revista Mefistófeles*. In 1884, he enrolled in the Leipzig **Conservatory**, where he studied with **Carl Reinecke** and Salomon Jadassohn (1831–1902), and in 1887 his **concert overture** *Obertura Andes* was performed by the Stuttgart Court Orchestra. He continued to represent South America to Europeans with further travels to Berlin, Paris, and Milan before returning to Argentina in 1896. There he focused mainly on **opera**. Although his musical style is an artful blend of Verdi's late style and ideas from Wagnerian **music drama**, the musical successfulness with which he gave voice to subjects that celebrated gaucho life and its issues rather than those typically cultivated in opera contributed to the growing cause of Argentine musical nationalism. The first of his operas completed in Argentina, *Pampa* (1897), is regarded as the first opera on a specifically Argentine subject; it was followed by *Yupanki* (1899), *Khrysé* (1902), *Nox horrida* (1908), and *Gli Eroi* (1919). He also translated Jadassohn's treatise on **orchestration** into Spanish.

Pablo Berutti's career ran a similar path. He was trained primarily as a pianist and toured widely as a performer before accepting a position as professor of **piano** at the Universidad Nacional de San Juan in 1887. He traveled to Leipzig and studied with Jadassohn in 1891 and, after the success of his *Gran sinfonia* and *Misa solemne* (both 1891), was offered a position on the faculty of the city's Conservatory. He declined the offer and returned instead to Buenos Aires, where he organized and founded a conservatory and worked as a teacher and inspector of military bands. His output includes much piano music and two operas. [JMC]

BERWALD. Swedish family of musicians of German descent. The first important musician in the family was Johann Friedrich Berwald (1711–1789). Its representatives during the **long 19th century** included the violinist (Christian Friedrich) Georg Berwald (1740–1825) and his brother (Georg Johann) Abraham Berwald (1758–1825, a bassoonist and violinist), plus Georg's sons Franz (Adolf) Berwald (1796–1868) and Abraham's son Johann Fredrik Berwald (1787–1861), a violin **prodigy**, composer, and conductor.

As a composer, the most significant member of this impressive musical family was Franz Berwald, who during his lifetime became the leading Scandinavian composer of the Early Romantic Generation. He is best known today for his four **symphonies** composed during the 1840s and published posthumously: No. 1 (*Sinfonie sérieuse*, 1842, rev. 1843–1844, publ. 1874), No. 2 (*Sinfonie capricieuse*, 1842, lost except for short score, publ., scored by E. Ellberg, 1945), No. 3 (*Sinfonie singulière*, 1845, publ. 1905), and No. 4 (1845, publ. 1911).

Berwald's influence on later composers derived largely from his original approach to harmony, his genius at large-scale formal structures, and his innovative **orchestration**. He trained as a violinist from age five and by the time he reached age 11 had performed in Uppsala and Västerås as well as his native Stockholm. For most of the period 1812–1828, he was a member of the Royal Court Orchestra, but he also developed a solid reputation as a composer during this period. He left Stockholm for Berlin in May 1829 in hopes of composing an **opera** that would be performed in the Prussian court, but when the two works he wrote for the city went unperformed, he turned to managing an orthopedic clinic and largely ceased composing. He married and moved to Vienna in 1841, a change of direction that coincided with the completion and successful performance of three new **tone poems** (*Erinnerung an die norwegischen Alpen* [Memory of the Norwegian Alps], *Humoristisches Capriccio* [Humoristic Capriccio], and *Elfenspiel* [Play of Elves]).

Despite the warm reception afforded Berwald's orchestral writing in Vienna, his four symphonies were failures when they were performed in Sweden in the 1840s; a second trip to Vienna in 1845 met with a significantly less enthusiastic reception. Although he made his living primarily as director of a glassworks in the 1850s, he continued composing, receiving public recognition as a composer only (but in increasing measure) in the 1860s: the performance of a revised version of his 1838 opera *Estrella de Soria* (comp. ca. 1838–1841, rev. 1862, publ. 1883), receipt of the Order of the North Star in 1866, and an important commission to revise Johann Christian Friedrich Hæffner's (1759–1833) collection of four-part **chorale** harmonizations (1820). He died of pneumonia before this effort could be completed.

In addition to the four symphonies, Berwald completed two surviving operas and two surviving **operettas**; a sizable body of sacred and secular choral music (both a cappella and accompanied); one **piano concerto**, one violin concerto, one concerto for two violins, and several other *concertante* works as well as several other large orchestral works; and much instrumental **chamber music** with and without piano, music for piano solo, and numerous **songs**. His **reception** in the 20th and 21st centuries has generally been more consistently enthusiastic than it was during his lifetime. His original harmonies and individualistic approach to orchestration exerted a significant influence on 20th-century Swedish nationalists such as Wilhelm Stenhammar (1871–1927) and Hugo Alfvén (1872–1960). [JMC]

See also NATIONALISM, ROMANTIC NATIONALISM.

BIEDERMEIER. *See* RESTORATION.

BIOGRAPHICAL FALLACY. Term used to denote the unqualified or excessive tendency, especially in biographical criticism, to explicate the meaning of a work by referring to the author's or composer's biography, thus reading the life in the work and vice versa; in literary criticism, the concept is also known as *inverted autobiography*. Those who find this method fallacious do not deny that artists' and composers' lives inform their works; rather, their objections reside primarily on two other concerns. First, although artists also employ their imagination in creating artworks and are thus able to make art of ideas and themes that are contrary to their life or even impossible, biographical criticism offers no means or method for differentiating between artifacts thus constructed and those that are confessional or autobiographical in nature. Second, biographical criticism's tendency to project the life onto the work tends to conflate biography with autobiography and confessional with professional utterance—serious logical errors that obscure any intended nonbiographical meanings with which the composer may have attempted to imbue the work. To these concerns may be added the fact that because few 19th-century listeners and performers knew any details of composers' biographies, composers are unlikely to have invested their works with any key to understanding that was biographical in nature, for such a key would have eluded most performers and listeners and left the music incomprehensible.

Like the **intentional fallacy**, the biographical fallacy came to light in the wake of the abuses of late 19th- and early 20th-century commentators: the ubiquity of interpretations of, for example, **Ludwig van Beethoven**'s **"Eroica" Symphony** as a confessional outpouring specifically centered on Napoléon Bonaparte; of *Die schöne Müllerin* as an allegory for **Franz Schubert**'s love life; of virtually everything **Robert Schumann** wrote in 1840 as a reflection of his relationship with **Clara Schumann**; of most of **Giuseppe Verdi**'s post-1840 **operas** as reflections of his devastation at the death of his wife and two daughters; and so on. This led some commentators to object that such interpretations, while not necessarily devoid of some element of truth, were restrictive and self-indulgent and ultimately substituted the composer's life for any other meaning he or she may have invested in the music, also obliterating any nonprivate themes that may have accounted for the works' public **receptions**.

At the same time, it must be remembered that many composers, performers, and listeners of the **long 19th century** prized music specifically for its (perceived) ability to give voice to deeply personal feelings and ideas. This situation lends credence, at least in principle, to some of the confessional or quasi-autobiographical criticism that at first blush appears to qualify as inverted autobiography: if Romantic composers believed that one task of their music was to give voice to their innermost selves, then it is not illogical to suppose that the "meaning" with which they strove to imbue it included confessional elements dealing with love, politics, sexuality, and so on. At the same time, to fix the perceived meaning of an artwork in such a fashion is to flirt dangerously not just with the biographical fallacy but also with the intentional fallacy and the affective fallacy while also blinding ourselves to the aspects of the work that more materially affected its contemporary and posthumous reception. [JMC]

See also ABSOLUTE MUSIC; HANSLICK, EDUARD (1825–1904); PROGRAM (PROGRAMMATIC) MUSIC.

BISHOP, (SIR) HENRY R(OWLEY) (1786–1855). English composer, conductor, educator, and impresario of the Early Romantic Generation; first English composer knighted, best remembered today for his **song** *Home, Sweet Home* (1829). He tried to become a jockey but, being found physically unsuitable, studied music instead with Francesco Bianchi (1752–1810). His first publications occurred in 1800–1803, and in 1804 he began to write for the stage. His first mature **opera**, *The Circassian Bride*, was produced at Covent Garden in 1809, followed by several other notable successes, leading to his appointment as composer and music director there in 1810. He became a founding member of the Philharmonic Society of London in 1813 and began adapting foreign operas for the English stage in 1814. He resigned from Covent Garden to become music director of Drury Lane in 1824, then assuming the same post at Vauxhall Gardens in 1830. He was principal conductor of the Concerts of Ancient Music (*see* HISTORICISM) from 1840 to 1848, served as Reid Professor of Music at Edinburgh from 1841 to 1843, and was knighted in 1842. He became professor at Oxford University in 1848, remaining there until his death.

Bishop composed some 135 works for the English stage, including adaptations of foreign composers' works (among them **Vincenzo Bellini, Wolfgang Amadeus Mozart**, and **Carl Maria von Weber**) as well as original compositions after **Johann Wolfgang von Goethe, William Shakespeare**, and other literary notables. He also composed an **oratorio** (*The Fallen Angel*, 1839), four large-scale **cantatas**, and several odes, as well as 327 glees, a great many **songs** and duets, one symphony, one *symphonie concertante*, two **overtures**, and some instrumental **chamber music**. [JMC]

BIZET, GEORGES (ALEXANDRE-CÉSAR-LÉOPOLD) (1838–1875). French composer, primarily of **operas** and orchestral works; also a highly skilled pianist and organist; member of the Late Romantic Generation. His final opera, *Carmen*, ranks as one of the most important works in the entire history of its genre.

Bizet came from a musical family and trained as a pianist, entering the Paris **Conservatory** at the age of 10 in 1848. There he formed close relationships with renowned **piano** pedagogue Pierre-Joseph-Guillaume Zimmermann (1785–1853), **Charles Gounod**, and especially **Fromenthal Halévy**, whose experience as an opera composer apparently influenced his pupil's aspirations in that direction. He also established an exemplary track record at the institution, winning its second prize for piano in 1851 and first prize for that instrument in 1852, its second prize for both fugue and organ in 1854 and its first prize for both in 1855. He finally won its highest honor, the coveted **Prix de Rome**, in 1857. Also, in April 1857, his second opera, *Le docteur Miracle* (posth. publ. 1962), won a competition organized by **Jacques Offenbach**; the work was performed publicly and well received at the Théâtre des Bouffes-Parisiens, establishing Bizet as a public figure several months before he left for Rome in December 1857. He remained in Italy for nearly three years, there encountering (but not liking) the music of **Giuseppe Verdi**, among others. He was back in Paris to witness the failed premiere of the Parisian version of **Richard Wagner**'s *Tannhäuser* in March 1861 and there also met **Hans von Bülow** and **Franz Liszt** (the latter is said to have declared Bizet's powers as a pianist to be equal to those of von Bülow and himself).

Bizet's first composition that is still well known today was *Les pêcheurs de perles* (The Pearl Fishers) and premiered to little acclaim at the Théâtre Lyrique in September 1863. His next major venture was the four-act *La jolie fille de Perth* (The Fair Maid of Perth, 1866), which, although better received than *Les pêcheurs*, still closed after only 18 performances. He produced a successful **suite** for **piano duet**, *Jeux d'enfants* (Childrens' Games), and orchestrated five of its movements as an orchestral suite in 1871, also producing incidental music for Alphonse Daudet's play *L'arlésienne* (The Maid of Arles) in 1872. His output also includes three **symphonies**, several programmatic **concert overtures**, sacred music, a number of *mélodies*, and works for solo piano, much of the last quite difficult. His best-known work in this category is the set of six *Chants du rhin* (1865, publ. 1866) modeled on the tradition of the **Lieder ohne Worte**. By far the most important work in his output is *Carmen*, which premiered as an **opéra comique** in 1875, just three months before his death. [JMC]

See also EXOTICISM; NATIONALISM, ROMANTIC NATIONALISM.

BLOCH, ERNEST (1880–1959). Jewish composer and teacher of the Modern Romantic Generation, born and raised in Switzerland; from 1916 primarily a resident of the United States, where he acquired citizenship in 1924. He studied violin and composition first in Geneva, then continued composition studies in Brussels, Frankfurt am Main, Munich, and Paris. From 1910 to 1911, he conducted concerts in Lausanne, and from 1911 to 1915, he lectured on aesthetics at the Geneva **Conservatory**. He emigrated to the United States in 1916, teaching at the recently founded **David Mannes** Music School from 1917 to 1919. He was director of the Cleveland Institute of Music from 1920 to 1925 and of the San Francisco Conservatory from 1925 to 1930. During the 1930s, he lived and worked mainly in Switzerland under a grant from the Stern family, composing and conducting free of the obligations of teaching. In 1940, he returned to the United States, holding a professorship and teaching summer classes at the University of California, Berkeley. He retired to Agate Beach, Oregon, in 1952, continuing to compose until shortly before his death from cancer in 1959.

Bloch's **reception** was well established during his lifetime. In addition to the two Ernest Bloch Societies founded during his lifetime, important festivals of his music were held in London in 1934 and 1937, Chicago in 1950, and Rome in 1953. He received some 17 prestigious prizes and other honors over the course of his career. Among these were honorary membership in Italy's Accademia di Santa Cecilia (1929); three honorary doctoral degrees, from Linfield College (1948), Brandeis University (1955), and Reed College (1955); the Elizabeth Sprague Coolidge Prize (1919); the Carolyn Beebe Prize of the New York Chamber Music Society (1926); the RCA Victor Award (1929); the Gold Medal in Music from the American Academy of Arts and Letters (1942); the American Jewish Congress's Stephen Wise Award (1952); the National Jewish Welfare Board's Frank L. Weil Award (1956); and the Henry Hadley Medal of the American Association of Composers and Conductors (1957).

Bloch's musical style on the whole is decidedly post-Romantic, but within this idiom his range of styles is eclectic, with rich, colorful orchestration and frequent recourse to Jewish folk and religious music. After a successful premiere of his only published dramatic work (the "lyric drama" *Macbeth*) in Paris in 1910, he created his first "Jewish cycle" in 1911–1916: a set of compositions that use distinctively Jewish subjects and musical techniques in a moving exploration of identity in the increasingly anti-Semitic climate of the early 20th century. These works—settings of Ps. 134 and 114 for soprano and **orchestra** (1912–1914), the **symphony** *Israel* for five solo voices and orchestra (1916), and the rhapsody *Schelomo* for cello and orchestra (1916)—feature the deeply personal, profoundly emotional tone that would remain Bloch's trademark for the remainder of his career. This style would also figure in his monumental Jewish sacred service (*Avodath hakodesh*) for baritone, chorus, and orchestra (1933) as well as various **chamber** works. Also important are his *America: An Epic Rhapsody* (for chorus and orchestra), which uses Native American themes, Negro spirituals, sea chanteys, patriotic tunes, and other elements associated with the United States. Though not known for his cultivation of more ardently progressive post-tonal styles, he did employ quarter tones in some works and compose in dodecaphonic and neo-Classical styles. [JMC]

See also FOLK SONG.

BOEHM, THEOBALD (1794–1881). German flute maker, goldsmith, and flautist whose inventions, calculations, and fingering system were indispensable in the development of the modern flute. As the son of a goldsmith, Boehm received training in the trade early on in his life. In addition to constructing his own instruments, Boehm received flute lessons from Johann Nepomuk Kapeller (1776–1843). In 1812, he became a flautist at the Isartor Theater and in 1818 joined the Royal Court Orchestra in Munich. Near the end of his tours across Europe as a flautist, Boehm established his first flute-making shop in 1828 in Munich. After many experiments, he developed the *Boehm flute*, which altered the position of the finger holes and employed a series of rings and levers that allowed for correct intonation regardless of the size of the player's hand. Boehm would make further developments on this system by combining it with a previous invention, the cylindrical flute and parabolic head. [MMM]

BOIELDIEU, (FRANÇOIS-) ADRIEN (1775–1834). French composer of the Early Romantic Generation, the early 19th century's leading French composer of **opera** and an important figure in the history of **opéra comique**. He trained as an organist and pianist in Rouen and had his first professional success in 1793 with *La fille coupable* (The Guilty Girl). By 1795, he was publishing large-ensemble instrumental works and vocal **chamber music** in Paris, and he established himself as one of his generation's leading dramatic composers when his *La famille Suisse* (The Swiss Family), *L'heureuse nouvelle* (The Happy News), *Le pari* (The Wager), and the **exoticist** *Zoraïme et Zulnar* were staged in 1797–1798. In 1798, he joined the faculty of the recently opened Paris **Conservatory**, and in 1800, his *Le calife de Bagdad* (The Caliph of Baghdad) won a resounding success. After his marriage failed, he left France in 1804 to take a post in the Russian imperial court, where he was made director of the French Opera.

Boieldieu returned to Paris in 1811 and renewed his standing with the Parisian operagoing public with *Jean de Paris* (John of Paris) in 1812. His successes accumulated once again: in 1815, he was appointed court composer and accompanist; in 1816, he joined the advisory board to the nominating committee of the Académie Royale de Musique; and in 1817, he succeeded **Étienne-Nicolas Méhul** as professor of composition at the Académie des Beaux-Arts. His *Le petit chaperon rouge* (Little Red Riding Hood, after Charles Perrault's fairy tale) was premiered in 1818 and earned him new accolades. As Paris became increasingly enthralled with the operas of **Gioa-chino Rossini** in the 1820s—Boieldieu referred to the craze as "notre convulsion musicale" (our musical convulsion)—Boieldieu's own fame was eclipsed. He retired to his home in the French capital's southern suburbs, revising earlier works and penning a number of minor new ones. His final major opera was *La dame blanche* (The White Lady), which won excellent reviews, although its two completed successors were less successful.

By the end of his life, Boieldieu had established himself as a proud standard-bearer of French opera in the tradition of Jean-Philippe Rameau (1683–1764) and André Grétry (1741–1813), one of the last holdouts against the tide of *rossinisme* (Rossini-ism) that swept France beginning in the mid-1820s. All totaled, he completed 40 staged musical dramas (including opéras comiques, serious operas, **ballets**, and **incidental music**); one **concerto** for **piano** (1792, publ. 1795) and one for harp (1801; this work is still popular today) and a few other orchestral compositions; one **piano trio**, six **violin sonatas**, and other instrumental chamber works; one lost harp sonata; numerous works for **piano**; and 124 vocal **romances**. He is known as an adept and sensitive melodist, and his operas reveal the sort of colorful and sensitive orchestration that would become characteristic of French opera for the remainder of the **long 19th century**. [JMC]

BOITO, ARRIGO (ENRICO GIUSEPPE GIOVANNI) (1842–1918). Italian **librettist**, poet, novelist, musicologist, journalist, and composer of the Late Romantic Generation; best known today as librettist of **Giuseppe Verdi**'s last two **Shakespeare** operas, although his own opera *Mefistofele* (1868, rev. and publ. 1876) is one of the most successful attempts to adapt **Johann Wolfgang von Goethe**'s recounting of the *Faust* legend as a staged musical drama. He was born in Padua and received his early musical training in Venice, moving to Milan to study at that city's **Conservatory** from 1853 to 1861. He was an important figure in the city's thriving **salon** culture in the early 1860s, also acquiring a reputation during these years as a prominent **nationalist** poet and a member of the *Scapigliatura* ("unkeptness" or "dishevelment"), a radical circle of musicians, painters, poets, sculptors, and writers critical of the orderliness and refinement of Italian art. His two published volumes of poetry—*Re Orso* (King Bear, 1865) and *Il libro dei versi e Re Orso* (The Book of Verses and King Bear, 1877)—exemplify the movement's aesthetics as well as Boito's striving to integrate musical values into his poetry. As a critic and journalist, he penned articles on German instrumental music in Italy, **Joachim Raff**'s Third **Symphony** (1872), the public **reception** of **Carl Maria von Weber**'s *Der Freischütz* at La Scala (1872), and **Felix Mendelssohn Bartholdy** in Italy (1864), among other things.

Boito's first collaboration with Verdi was on the *Inno delle nazioni* (Hymn of the Nations, 1862), arguably Verdi's most overt celebration of the victory of the **Risorgimento**. Although Boito's characteristically radical toast to the composer offended Verdi, their friendship was later repaired, and in 1881 Boito revised Francesco Piave's (1810–1876) initially unsuccessful **libretto** for Verdi's *Simon Boccanegra* and wrote the libretti for his *Otello* (1887) and *Falstaff* (1893). He also penned numerous other libretti (most famously that for **Amilcare Ponchielli**'s *La Gioconda*, 1876, rev. 1880), occasionally under the anagrammatic pseudonym Tobia Gorrio. His own musical compositions, in addition to *Mefistofele*, include the unfinished opera *Nerone* (posthumously premiered in truncated form in 1924) and another opera, *Ero e Leandro* (Hero and Leander, 1879), that he destroyed (its libretto was also set by **Giovanni Bottesini** in 1879 and by Luigi Mancinelli [1848–1921] in 1896). He also composed a small quantity of vocal **chamber music** and instrumental music. [JMC]

LA BONNE CHANSON, **OP. 61.** (Fr., "Good Song.") Iconic **song cycle** on poems by Paul Verlaine (1844–1896) composed by **Gabriel Fauré** in 1892–1894 and published in 1894; arranged for voice with string **quintet** 1898 and published in that format in 1900 (Paris: Hamelle). The original version was premiered privately in the **salon** of the Countess Henri de Saussine on 25 April 1894 and publicly in the **Société Nationale de Musique** on 20 April 1895; the arrangement for voice with strings was premiered in London on 1 April 1898 in the salon of the British arts patron Leo Frank Schuster (to whom **Edward Elgar**'s **concert overture** *In the South [Alsassio]* was dedicated). Although Marcel Proust, who was present at the private premiere, wrote that he adored the cycle, others expressed skepticism (e.g., Fauré's friend and mentor **Camille Saint-Saëns** reportedly said it should be burned). The cycle is stylistically indebted to **Jules Massenet** and **Hector Berlioz** (specifically Berlioz's 1841 cycle *Les nuits d'été*), but the subtle intensity of its **cyclic** construction set a new standard for such techniques in the song cycles of Fauré's contemporaries and successors (notably those of **Claude Debussy**).

Verlaine's original eponymous cycle consisted of 21 poems (1869–1870) addressed to his fiancée, celebrating amorous love against the backdrop of nature and using overtly sensual and unusually direct language to celebrate the beauties of both. Fauré extracted nine of these poems and reordered them, constructing a cycle whose constituent songs share various themes and motives. A tonal structure is unusual and roughly symmetrical, designed to heighten the emotional progress of the cycle while also reinforcing the thematic cross-references. The keys of the first four songs progress downward by step, turning to the minor mode with No. 4 and remaining there, a whole step lower, in No. 5. The latter two, the textual and emotional heart of the cycle, also introduce new thematic material that will be shared among the remaining four songs. The remainder of the cycle centers around the key of B flat, encircling it by minor thirds and bringing all five of the cycle's recurrent themes together in the final song. [JMC]

BORIS GODUNOV. Opera in prologue and four acts by **Modest Mussorgsky**, on his own **libretto** after **Aleksandr Pushkin**'s *The Comedy of the Distress of the Muscovite State, of Tsar Boris, and of Grishka Otrepyev* (1826), supplemented in the revised version by material based on several historical writings, most prominently Nikolay Mikhaylovich Karamzin's (1766–1826) *History of the Russian Empire* (1826). The original version, consisting of seven scenes, was composed in 1868–1869 but rejected by the St. Petersburg Opera in 1870. Mussorgsky thoroughly overhauled this material and added more to complete a second version comprising nine scenes organized into a prologue and four acts in 1871–1872. Three scenes from this version were performed by the St. Petersburg Opera in 1873, and after further revision the entire work was given on 8 February 1874 but withdrawn after 25 performances. That same year, it was published in piano-vocal score, as was usual for operas in the **long 19th century** (*see* PRINTING AND PUBLISHING OF MUSIC).

After Mussorgsky's death, his friend **Nikolay Rimsky-Korsakov** tried to revive *Boris Godunov*, introducing cuts, adding new material, and reorchestrating much of Mussorgsky's music. He conducted this version in a concert performance on 10 December 1896, and it was staged in Moscow on 19 December 1898. In 1906, Rimsky-Korsakov revised his version, restoring some of the previously cut original music, and conducted this version in Paris in 1908; it was produced in New York and London in 1913. The work entered the repertoire in this revised version by Rimsky-Korsakov. Mussorgsky's versions of 1869 and 1872 were published in an edition by Pavel Lamm in 1928, and a new performing edition, with some changes to the plot, was made in 1940 by Shostakovich, drawing on the 1874 piano-vocal edition. The first critical edition was published in piano-vocal score in 1968 and full score in 1975 by David Lloyd-Jones (Oxford: Oxford University Press). This two-volume edition, which draws on manuscript sources that had been unavailable to Lamm, presents Mussorgsky's 1872 version in volume 1 and the original 1869 version, plus other material from the work's complicated genesis, in volume 2.

Set in Russia in the period 1598–1605, *Boris Godunov* is generally considered the most important Russian opera of the 19th century, rivaled only by **Mikhail Glinka**'s *Zhizn' za tsarya* (A Life for the Tsar, 1834–1836, publ. ca. 1856) and *Ruslan and Ludmila* (after Pushkin, 1837–1842, publ. 1856). Its political subject matter has been from the outset a part of its appeal and one source of its problems. The opera is notable for bringing to the musical stage the epic historical grandeur of Fyodor Dostoyevsky (1821–1881), combined with scenes of great pageantry, a vivid style of declamation that is impeccably true to the Russian language, and a profound sense of psychology, especially in its characterization of Boris. [JMC]

See also NATIONALISM, ROMANTIC NATIONALISM.

BORODIN, ALEKSANDR PORFIR'YEVICH (1833–1887). Russian composer of the Late Romantic Generation; member of the **Mighty Handful.** He is best known for his contributions to Russian **nationalism** in the second half of the 19th century, especially his two **string quartets**, three **symphonies** (the last of which was completed by **Aleksandr Glazunov**), the opera *Knyaz' Igor'* (Prince Igor, 1869–1870, rev. 1874–1887), and the **symphonic poem** ("musical picture") *V sredney Azii* (In Central Asia, 1880, publ. 1882). Like most members of the Mighty Handful, he was not a musician by trade. Rather, he was a medical doctor and professor of chemistry in the Medical-Surgery Academy of St. Petersburg.

Borodin was the illegitimate son of a Russian prince and was registered as the son of a serf, but his mother (who later married an army doctor) afforded him an education in Western European languages and the arts, and he grew up playing the symphonies of **Ludwig van Beethoven** in **piano-duet** arrangements. He entered the Academy of Medicine in St. Petersburg in 1850, developed an interest in chemistry, worked as an assistant in general pathology and therapy, and graduated with his doctorate in 1858. He traveled to the German and Italian lands (all seething with nationalist fervor) in 1859–1862. Shortly after returning to St. Petersburg, he began lecturing in chemistry at the Institute of Forestry and assumed the position of assistant professor of chemistry at the Medical-Surgical Academy. In 1864, he was promoted to chair of the chemistry department with the rank of full professor. During the remainder of his career in this field, he achieved some notoriety through his investigation of the condensation products of valeraldehyde, enanthaldehyde, and acetaldehyde. In the meantime, however, in the **salon** of a faculty colleague, he had met **Mily Balakirev,** who by that point was emerging as the most magnetic personality among the composers of Russia's anti-**Conservatory** group.

The meeting was to prove life changing—for Borodin's experience with Western European culture and sympathies for the nationalist movement as he encountered it there and knew it in his native Russia combined with the brilliant and charismatic Balakirev's enthusiastic support to inspire a slow but steady stream of works that established him as one of his generation's leading composers. His first opera (the farce *Bogatïri* [The Heroic Warriors, 1867], little of which was original and most of which was parodied from works of Ferdinand Hérold, **Giacomo Meyerbeer, Jacques Offenbach, Gioachino Rossini,** and **Giuseppe Verdi**) was a failure, but he completed one symphony under Balakirev's guidance in 1867 and began two of the works that would contribute to his lasting fame—the Second Symphony and *Prince Igor*—in 1869. Meanwhile, after the Russian government in 1872 approved the teaching of advanced chemistry courses to women, Borodin eagerly contributed to the instruction of the Medical-Surgical Academy's new women students in both classroom and laboratory. From 1874 to his death, he served as director of the institution's laboratory, devoting less time to his own chemical research and more to instruction of his students. He also resumed intensive work on *Prince Igor*, and the Second Symphony was premiered by the Russian Musical Society in 1877.

In the summer of 1876, Borodin, having taken two of his female students to Jena to enroll in the university there, traveled to Weimar to meet Franz Liszt, who played through the Russian composer's two symphonies with him as piano duets and received them enthusiastically; the following month, Borodin learned that a Parisian salonnière was "wildly enthusiastic" about the Second and would be introducing it in her influential salon. His growing stature won for him the respect of the members of a St. Petersburg amateur choral and orchestral society (the St. Petersburg Circle of Music Lovers) whose members included the influential music patron Mitrofan Belyayev (1836–1904), patron to **Aleksandr Glazunov** and **Aleksandr Scriabin**, and after this point to Borodin himself. He also won the patronage of the wealthy Belgian countess Louise de Mercy-Argenteau (1837–1890) through Belyayev's mentorship and the efforts of Liszt. Together, these patrons effectively promoted Borodin's music in Western Europe as well as Russia. He joined France's Société des Auteurs, Compositeurs et Editeurs de Musique (Society of Authors, Composers, and Publishers of Music), in order to protect his copyrights, a move that also contributed to performances of his works throughout francophone Europe. He returned to Russia an international celebrity and continued work on both *Prince Igor* and his Third Symphony. Both were unfinished when he died of a sudden heart attack in the middle of a grand candlelit ball hosted by the faculty of the Medical-Surgery Academy in February 1887.

Borodin's chemical research and his heavy teaching and administrative duties made it difficult for him to make progress on large compositional projects; as a result, at his death many of his larger works lay incomplete but in progress or had been abandoned altogether. Some of these (such as *Prince Igor*, the opera-**ballet** *Mlada*, the Third Symphony, and a D-minor string **quintet** titled *Serenata alla spagnola*) were completed after his death by friends such as **César Cui**, Glazunov, **Anatoly Lyadov**, **Modest Mussorgsky**, and **Nikolay Rimsky-Korsakov**. Still, when one considers his extensive other obligations, his output is impressive quantitatively as well as qualitatively. All four of his orchestral projects (i.e., *In Central Asia* and the three symphonies) have a firm claim to a place in the repertoire; his cello **sonata,** two completed **string quartets**, two **string trios**, string **quintets, piano trio,** piano quintet, three works for string quintet, and **chamber** works for winds and strings, though written mostly before he met Balakirev and left in various stages of completion at his death, are original and colorful; and his handful of works for piano solo and piano duet evince many of the same qualities. Finally, his 20 solo **songs**, duets, and **part-songs**, mostly in the idioms of contemporary salon culture, represent important contributions to the literature of the Russian art song and are notable for their choice of texts (some are based on his own poems; others on works of literary notables, including **Heinrich Heine, Aleksandr Pushkin,** and **Leo Tolstoy**). His music bespeaks a thorough knowledge of the forms and styles of Western European cultivated music, but his melodic and rhythmic language is also informed by the idioms of Russian **folk song**. [JMC]

BÖSENDORFER. Austrian firm of **piano** makers, the first to be granted the title of königlich-kaiserlicher Kammer-Pianoforte-Verfertiger (official piano maker to the royal imperial chamber); still extant since 1966 as part of Kimball. It was founded in Vienna by Ignaz Bösendorfer (1794–1859), the son of a carpenter and apprentice to renowned piano maker Joseph Brodmann (1763–1848). Aware of increasing demands being placed on the fortepiano by **virtuosos** performing in large public spaces in the flourishing musical culture of the **Restoration**, Bösendorfer designed an instrument with Viennese action but increased stability and volume, winning the gold medal at an instrument makers' exhibition in 1839 and again in 1845.

In 1846, Bösendorfer's instruments won the enthusiasm of **Franz Liszt** (whose playing frequently placed so much strain on his instruments that they were unusable by the end of a single evening) after one withstood an entire evening's performance in good condition. They remained Liszt's favorites to the end of the virtuoso's life—a useful point of information for those interested in Liszt's style and pianistic tastes since Bösendorfer instruments resisted the trend toward bulk and homogenization (resulting from overstringing and solid metal frames) pursued by the U.S. firm of **Steinway** and (to a lesser extent) its German counterpart (Steinweg-Grobian). On Ignaz Bösendorfer's death, direction of the firm passed to his son Ludwig (1835–1919), who continued this tradition, declaring the increasingly popular Steinway duplex a "fraud" in the 1870s; during the early 20th century, the firm still offered a choice between Viennese or Érard-style instruments. The Bösendorfer sound, with its greater warmth and transparency, was apparently the preference of **Johannes Brahms**, who chose Bösendorfer instruments for most of his public performances after 1870 (*see* STREICHER). Despite these and other similar high-profile endorsements, the Bösendorfer firm remained primarily and characteristically Viennese until well into the 20th century, beginning to adopt the industrialized manufacturing techniques of Steinway and Chickering (and the consequent heavier action and fuller, more homogeneous tone) only in the 1890s and adopting them in earnest only in the 1920s. [JMC]

BOTTESINI, GIOVANNI (1821–1889). Italian double-bass virtuoso, composer, and **conductor** of the Late Romantic Generation. In his youth, he was actively involved in choral singing and performing as a timpanist and a violinist, but in 1835 he took up the double bass in order to study that instrument on scholarship at the Milan **Conservatory**. There, he studied composition, counterpoint, and harmony as well as his own instrument. In 1839, having won a prestigious prize in the amount of 300 francs, he purchased a new instrument, and with this he launched his first tour in 1840. In the **virtuoso** tradition, he achieved renown not only as a virtuoso bassist—a London critic dubbed him "the **Paganini** of the double bass"—but also as a composer. He was also an active conductor, especially of operas. His many appointments and engagements as bassist and/or conductor included Barcelona, Cairo, Havana, London, Madrid, Palermo, Paris, and San Miguel de Allende (Mexico); his friend **Giuseppe Verdi** also personally chose him to conduct the first performance of *Aida* in its sensational premiere in Cairo (1871).

As a composer, Bottesini is most remembered today for his virtuosic compositions for double bass (some with **piano**, some with **string quartet**, some with **orchestra**), but he was also widely respected for his other compositions. Among these were his 11 string quartets, his **oratorio** *The Garden of Olivet* (1887), and his 12 operas. Among the last, *Cristoforo Colombo* (1848, for the Teatro Tacón in Havana); *Marion Delorme* (after **Victor Hugo**, 1862); *Vinciguerra* (1870), which ran for 40 performances in Paris; and the exoticist comic opera *Ali Baba* (1871) were particularly noteworthy.

Just six months before his death, Bottesini accepted an appointment as director of the Parma Conservatory. His *Metodo completo per contrabbasso* (Milan, ca. 1869) was widely translated and reprinted; it still serves as the basis of modern technique for the instrument. His works featuring the double bass are rarely encountered today not because of any intrinsically musical deficiencies but because they are still considered extraordinarily difficult. [JMC]

BOURBON RESTORATION. In France, the period between Napoléon Bonaparte's abdication and the establishment of the short-lived **Second Republic**. The period was initiated when the Bourbon dynasty again became possessors of the Kingdom of France in April 1814 and validated by the **Congress of Vienna**. Although the period was generally peaceful—certainly less tumultuous than any other period since the 1780s in France—the tenu-

ousness of the peace was reflected in Napoléon Bonaparte's brief return to power from March to June 1815 and the July Revolution of 1830. Aside from Bonaparte's "Hundred Days," the Bourbon monarch of the first part of this period was Louis XVIII (fl. 1814–1824); he was succeeded by Charles X (fl. 1824–1830) and then, after the July Revolution, by the "citizen king" Louis Philippe (fl. 1830–1848). In French music and the arts generally, the most important aspects of the Bourbon Restoration were a renewed flourishing of salon culture and a gradual renewal of France's public educational and cultural institutions of music, especially the Conservatory and Opéra. [JMC]
See also RESTORATION.

BOYS' CHOIR. See CHILDREN'S CHORUS.

"BRAHMS THE PROGRESSIVE". Originally a radio lecture given by Arnold Schoenberg (1874–1951) in 1933 in honor of Johannes Brahms's centennial, published in substantially revised form in 1947. Schoenberg sought to rehabilitate Brahms and his music from the criticism of many of his late 19th-century and early 20th-century detractors, and in doing so he effectively changed later musicians' views of "Classical music" as well as of Brahms and his influence on later composers.

In "Brahms the Progressive," Schoenberg finds that the most influential musical trend of the past two centuries is "developing variation," or the complete integration of musical material based on the first theme. Any formal aspect that does not clarify, intensify, or complement that germinal material and its associated ideas is superfluous. Therefore, a passage that serves only to support the form of the work is unnecessary, and even repeated passages that lack variation are seen as "beneath" integrated compositional techniques. Though Schoenberg does not give any specific examples, Johann Sebastian Bach is seen as the progenitor of this development. Franz Joseph Haydn, Wolfgang Amadeus Mozart, and Ludwig van Beethoven each take up this trend in different ways, but Mozart and his music, which often eschewed balance and form to achieve greater expression and drama, is held up above the other two. [MMM/JMC]

BRAHMS, JOHANNES (1833–1897). German composer and pianist of the Late Romantic Generation. Brahms numbers among the handful of most significant compositional giants of the 19th century; he is often remembered today as one of Hans von Bülow's "three Bs." Despite efforts by contemporary proponents of the New German School to label him stylistically backward, Brahms synthesized late Romantic harmonic vocabulary and expanding notions of form with a love of structural succinctness and thematic development as practiced by Felix Mendelssohn Bartholdy, Robert Schumann, and like-minded Romantic Generation composers. Heralded by Robert Schumann in 1853 as a nascent great composer, Brahms was scrutinized heavily by many who measured him against acknowledged greats, such as **Ludwig van Beethoven**, and contemporary rivals, such as **Franz Liszt** and **Richard Wagner**. Among the highlights of Brahms's fairly well-rounded compositional output are four **symphonies**, two piano **concertos**, a violin concerto, a concerto for violin and cello, three **string quartets**, three **piano quartets**, three **piano trios**, a horn trio and clarinet trio, numerous **piano** works, **songs**, and large- and small-scale works for chorus.

Brahms was born in Hamburg to modestly bourgeois parents; his father Johann Jakob was a freelance musician on several instruments, including double bass and horn. Brahms studied **piano** with Otto Cossel (1813–1865) from age seven and Eduard Marxsen (1806–1887) a few years later; he was already contributing to the family income at 13 through freelance work. In 1853, Brahms became friends with **Joseph Joachim** and met numerous significant musicians of the time, including **Hector Berlioz**, **Ferdinand Hiller**, Franz Liszt, and Robert and **Clara Schumann**. Brahms's relationship with the Schumanns during these years was seminal. Robert's essay "Neue Bahnen" (New Paths) drew considerable attention to the promising young composer from publishers and patrons. Brahms put himself in the service of Clara and the children when Robert attempted suicide in February 1854 and forged a friendship with her that endured for the remaining decades of their lives.

After Robert's death in 1856, Brahms returned to Hamburg, where, after a brief pause in composing, he began to cultivate a career as **conductor**, composer, and concert pianist. The next several years of his life brought a number of failures. In 1859, Brahms's Piano Concerto No. 1 in D minor, Op. 15, was badly received on its Hanover premiere. When the Hamburg Philharmonische Konzertgesellschaft needed a new conductor in 1862, it was Julius Stockhausen—and not Brahms—who filled the position that fall. The death of his mother in 1865 was profoundly difficult for Brahms, but it was partly the inspiration for his *Ein Deutsches Requiem* (A German Requiem, Op. 45, 1868) for soloists, chorus, and orchestra. The popular success and critical acclaim for this work are largely why the late 1860s were a turning point for Brahms, in terms of his financial stability and reputation.

In 1871, Brahms moved to Vienna and made it his home; there, he conducted the **Gesellschaft der Musikfreunde** orchestra and chorus for the next four years. The remaining time line of Brahms's career is studded by the premieres of his most monumental works: his four symphonies in 1876, 1877, 1883, and 1885, respectively; his Violin Concerto in D major (Op. 77, 1879) for Joachim; his well-received Piano Concerto No. 2 in B-flat major (Op. 83, 1883); the *Academic Festival Overture* and *Tragic Overture* (respectively, Opp. 80 and 81, 1881); the Concerto for Violin and Cello in A minor (Op. 102, 1887) for Joachim and Robert Hausmann (1852–1909); the choral-orchestral *Nänie* (Op. 82, 1881) and *Gesang der Parzen* (Op. 89, 1883); and his final **chamber** works, especially the two String **Quintets** (Op. 88, 1882; Op. 111, 1891); the last two Piano Trios (Op. 87, 1882; Op. 101, 1887); the Trio in A minor for Clarinet, Cello, and Piano (Op. 114, 1892); and the Clarinet Quintet in B minor (Op. 115, 1891).

As an enthusiast of early music, Brahms was a significant agent of 19th-century **historicism**. In the late 1850s, when he was studying counterpoint with Joachim, he prepared editions of music by C. P. E. Bach and W. F. Bach. Decades later, he helped edit the works of Couperin. As conductor of the Gesellschaft der Musikfreunde, Brahms programmed works by **J. S. Bach** and other Baroque composers alongside mainstream fare (Brahms had compiled his own library of compositions from past eras). As an editor, Brahms was increasingly called on during his later years to assist in the complete works editions of 19th-century composers, too, such as those of **Franz Schubert** and Robert Schumann.

Brahms's place in **long 19th century** music is inseparably bound up with the rift between himself and some composers associated with the New German School, particularly Liszt and Wagner. Brahms's stylistic and aesthetic congruences with Robert Schumann—carved into stone by the latter's 1853 "Neue Bahnen"—made the young composer all the more susceptible to accusations that the "**absolute music**" he composed amounted to **Restoration**-era anachronism. Brahms himself helped draft an 1860 manifesto against the pro-NGS program of **Franz Brendel**'s *Neue Zeitschrift für Musik*, published prematurely with only four signatures including Brahms's, cementing his position at the other end of the divide. Consistently an advocate of Brahms's music—particularly during Brahms's years in Vienna—was **Eduard Hanslick**, who was also famously a tireless critic of Wagner. Many Modern Romantic Generation composers, affected far less by the musical politics of Brahms's time, held Brahms's music in high esteem while also drawing from elements of Wagner's style; these include **Edward Elgar**, **Gustav Mahler**, Arnold Schoenberg, Alexander von Zemlinsky, and numerous others. [RK]

See also ABSOLUTE MUSIC; "BRAHMS THE PROGRESSIVE"; EDITING AND EDITIONS; HANSLICK, EDUARD (1825–1904).

BREITKOPF & HÄRTEL. German publishing firm (still in existence), with C. F. Peters and **Simrock** one of the German lands' most prestigious publishers of music during the **long 19th century**. The first was founded in 1719 in Leipzig by Bernhard Christoph Breitkopf (1695–1777), whose son Johann Gottlob Immanuel Breitkopf (1719–1794) took over the printing works in 1745 and in the early 1750s introduced a number of music-printing innovations that facilitated the production and marketing of much larger editions of music; virtually every notable composer of the mid- and late 18th century published with the firm. It and its printworks passed to Gottlob Breitkopf's sons at his death, and in 1795 Gottfried Christoph Härtel (1763–1827) joined the firm. In 1796, Härtel, trained in law and classics, bought the firm and took over the publishing house, soon introducing the new technique of lithography to music printing and publishing sets of *oeuvres complettes* of Muzio Clementi (1752–1832), J. B. Cramer (1771–1858), J. L. Dussek (1760–1812), **Franz Joseph Haydn**, and **Wolfgang Amadeus Mozart**, also becoming one of **Ludwig van Beethoven**'s primary publishers.

The Breitkopf firm had remained active in printing letters as well as music, and it soon established two important journals: the Leipzig-based *Allgemeine musikalische Zeitung* (1798–1848) and the *Leipziger Literaturzeitung* (1812–1834). In 1807, it also began manufacturing fortepianos in the Viennese style (*see* PIANO), instruments that were used by **Franz Liszt**, **Felix Mendelssohn Bartholdy**, **Clara Schumann**, and **Richard Wagner**, among others. The firm was run by Härtel's nephew until his sons Raymund (1810–1888) and Hermann (1803–1875) entered the business beginning in 1832. Over the course of the 19th century, it continued to introduce printing innovations and became widely known as one of Europe's most reputable publishers of music.

Breitkopf & Härtel's contributions to 19th-century music's cultures of print have been rivaled by few and surpassed by none. The *Allgemeine musikalische Zeitung* remained one of the most important venues for music criticism, rivaled in the German lands only by the *Neue Zeitschrift für Musik*, for the entire period prior to the **Revolutions of 1848** (and beyond, albeit under different publishers). It also quickly became a major publisher for musical scholarship ranging from biographies and thematic catalogs to aesthetic and theoretical writings. It was among the first German music publishers to print **operas** and **operettas** in quantity, releasing works by **Adolphe Adam, D.-F.-E. Auber, Vincenzo Bellini, Luigi Cherubini, Gaetano Donizetti, Fromenthal Halévy, Albert Lortzing, Heinrich Marschner, Étienne Méhul, Giacomo Meyerbeer, Robert Schumann, Johann Strauss (II), Ambroise Thomas, Giuseppe Verdi, Richard Wagner,** and **Carl Maria von Weber**, among many others. In addition to those composers' operas and the collected-works series mentioned above, it was an important publisher for **Hector Berlioz, Fryderyk Chopin, Stephen Heller, Adolf Henselt, Friedrich Kalkbrenner, J.-F. Le Sueur,** Liszt, Mendelssohn, Clara and Robert Schumann, **Richard Strauss,** and **Sigismond Thalberg**, also becoming an important force in the mid-19th century's **Schubert** revival and serving as the publisher for the *Gesamtausgaben and Sämtliche Werke* of **Johann Sebastian Bach,** C. W. von Gluck, Haydn, Mozart, Lully, Palestrina, and Rameau. [JMC]

See also COPYRIGHT AND PERFORMANCE RIGHT; PRINTING AND PUBLISHING OF MUSIC.

BRENDEL, KARL FRANZ (1811–1868). Aesthetician, historian, pedagogue, and writer on music of the Romantic Generation; with **Robert Schumann** one of the German lands' most influential music critics in the middle third of the 19th century. He had little formal training in music, instead viewing the musical art and its history from perspectives derived from the philosophy of **Georg Wilhelm Friedrich Hegel**, which he studied at the universities in Leipzig, Berlin, and Freiburg. He devoted himself to the full-time study of music history and musical aesthetics in 1841, lecturing at universities in Freiburg and Dresden between then and 1844. His knowledge of history and aesthetics, his eloquent prose, and most of all his convictions concerning the necessity for a celebration of progress and rejection of philistinism in the worlds of music led to his appointment as Schumann's successor as editor-in-chief of the *Neue Zeitschrift für Musik* in 1845. This post he held until his death, contributing numerous articles of his own and taking the journal in a direction that would be profoundly reflective of the aesthetic and political crosscurrents of musical life in Europe in the century's second half. To this influential position was added a professorship in music history at the University of Leipzig beginning in 1846, and in 1848 he augmented his influence by publishing selected lectures from the earlier 1840s on the history of music in his widely read and reprinted *Grundzüge der Geschichte der Musik* (Essentials of Music History, 1845).

Brendel's combination of aesthetic, historical, and philosophical knowledge resonated strongly with the sense of urgency that characterized musical life after the **Revolutions of 1848**, and his influence consequently expanded still further in post-Revolutionary Europe. In 1850, as editor of the *Neue Zeitschrift für Musik*, he encouraged and printed pseudonymously the first version of **Richard Wagner**'s notoriously anti-Semitic essay "Über das Judentum in der Musik" (On Jewry in Music) in the journal, and he developed his staunchly progressive, neo-Hegelian, German **nationalist** perspectives further in his influential *Geschichte der Musik in Italien, Deutschland und Frankreich von den ersten christlichen Zeiten bis auf die Gegenwart* (History of Music in Italy, Germany, and France, from the Earliest Christian Times to the Present), first published in 1852 and published in at least seven new and expanded editions numerous times between then and 1907. He advocated for the progressive German nationalist agenda of Wagner in his *Die Musik der Gegenwart und die Gesammtkunstwerk der Zukunft* (The Music of the Present and the **Gesamtkunstwerk** of the Future, 1854), and with **Richard Pohl** he also edited the periodical *Anregungen für Kunst, Leben und Wissenschaft* (Incitements for Art, Life, and Knowledge) from 1856 to 1861. His importance to the progressive side of the German lands' musical polemics was further enhanced in his keynote address for the first annual Versammlung deutscher Tonkünstler (Conference of German Musicians) in 1859, in which he for the first time described the aesthetics and musical styles cultivated by **Franz Liszt**, Wagner, and certain works of **Hector Berlioz** as representing a **"New German School."** He was a founding member and first president of the **Allgemeiner Deutscher Musikverein**, another post that he held until his death. He published three other full-length books: *Franz Liszt als Symphoniker* (Liszt as Symphonist, 1859), *Die Organisation des Musikwesens durch den Staat* (On State Sponsorship of Musical Life, 1865), and *Geist und Technik im Clavier-Unterricht* (Spirit and Technique in Piano Pedagogy, 1867).

Although many modern readers take issue with Brendel's proclivities for abstract philosophizing and lack of technical detail, his ability to explain the complex crosscurrents of mid-19th-century music in terms of the issues of day-to-day life and contemporary politics was largely unrivaled in his day. It is not least through his efforts that large segments of the amateur musical public were able to view complex concepts such as the *Gesamtkunstwerk*, **music drama**, and **symphonic poem** as exciting innovations in an age of crucial change for the musical art. His role in shaping the late 19th-century reception of Berlioz, Liszt, **Felix Mendelssohn Bartholdy**, Robert Schumann, and Wagner cannot be overestimated; indeed, his historiography of music continues to provide the essential outlines represented in many mainstream music-history textbooks even today. [JMC]

BRETÓN (Y HERNÁNDEZ), TOMÁS (1850–1923). Spanish composer, **conductor**, and violinist of the Modern Romantic Generation; an important figure in Spanish musical **nationalism**. He grew up in extreme poverty, playing **piano** in local and circus orchestras, and studied first at the **Conservatory** of Madrid, followed by other studies after 1881 in Milan, Paris, Rome, and Vienna. In 1878, he founded the Unión Artístico-Musical, where he conducted many Spanish and foreign compositions; this was followed by what became Madrid's most important **orchestra**, the Sociedad de Conciertos de Madrid, which he conducted from 1885 to 1901. Also in 1885, he began lecturing and publishing articles and pamphlets outlining a program for developing a Spanish national **opera**. From 1901 until his retirement in 1921, he worked at the Madrid Conservatory, first as a teacher and then as director.

Bretón's program for a Spanish national opera consisted of three points: the operas must be in Castillan and should use national subjects and **folk songs**, Spanish opera should not be "purist" but should be willing and able to avail itself of idioms and techniques characteristic of other national traditions (e.g., the grandeur of French **grand opera** or the **Leitmotivic** techniques of Wagnerian **music drama**), and developing a national opera would serve Spain's economic as well as cultural interests because it would provide a means for Spain's citizenry to support native composers and performers rather than foreign ones (who typically visited Spain for performances but invested most of their livelihood into other nations' economies). He is best known for his more than 40 **zarzuelas**—most importantly *La verbena de la paloma* (The Paloma Fair, 1893)—but he also penned serious operas, such as *Los amantes de Teruel* (The Lovers of Teruel, 1889) and *La Dolores* (1895). He also composed one oratorio (*El apocalipsis* [The Apocalypse], 1882), six **program symphonies**, three **string quartets**, one string **trio**, one piano **quintet**, and one **sextet** for piano and winds as well as **songs** and choral pieces. [JMC]

BROADWOOD. London manufacturer of **pianos** that began with the partnership of Swiss harpsichord manufacturer Burkat Shudi (1702–1773) and Scottish cabinetmaker John Broadwood (1732–1812). **Franz Joseph Haydn,** Muzio Clementi (1752–1832), J. L. Dussek (1760–1812), and **Ludwig van Beethoven** admired Broadwood's instruments; Beethoven owned a Broadwood grand piano.

Broadwood had begun working for Shudi in London in 1761; he married Shudi's daughter in 1769, and partnered with Shudi in 1770. In 1782, after working with his brother-in-law, Broadwood ran the company by himself. The firm became "John Broadwood & Son" in 1795 and "Sons" in 1808, when John's children James and Thomas became partners. Broadwood's heyday lasted from the early 19th century through the 1840s, when its instruments were eclipsed by those of **Érard** and others.

The company's initial emphasis on harpsichords gave way to one on square pianos (based initially on those of Johannes Zumpe [1735–1783]) and grand pianos. Broadwood also assisted Americus Backers in inventing the English grand-piano action by about 1771; this experience was evident in Broadwood grands, which adopted Backers's action and harpsichord cabinetry. In some 20 years, Broadwood had widened his grand piano's range to six octaves, and adjustments in striking point and in the tension of the brass and steel strings effected notable increases in the grand piano's resonance. In the early 19th century, Broadwood's grand pianos grew capable of increasingly powerful dynamics; he achieved this with tenser, harder, heavier-gauge strings and—in the following decades—larger, heavier hammers. The leather hammer coverings, often noisier in these conditions, gave way to felt. To facilitate the increased string tension, Broadwood began bracing the frame with iron in the 1820s; a full iron frame, made of separate components bolted together, was introduced in the 1840s. [RK]

BRUCH, MAX (CHRISTIAN FRIEDRICH) (1838–1920). German composer, conductor, and teacher of the Late Romantic Generation. He was something of a **prodigy** in composition, completing a **septet** by the age of nine and having a **symphony** performed in Cologne by the age of 14. In the same year, he also won a prize from the Frankfurt am Main **Mozart**-Stiftung that allowed him to study composition with Ferdinand Breunung (1830–1883), **Ferdinand Hiller**, and **Carl Reinecke**. After living and composing in Mannheim from 1862 to 1864, he worked as court music director and conductor in several cities (Koblenz, Berlin, Liverpool, and Breslau), finally accepting a position as composer and conductor at the Hochschule für Musik in Berlin in 1890 and remaining there until his death. To the end of his life, he rejected the self-styled progressivism of **Franz Liszt**, **Richard Wagner**, and the **New German School**, continuing to espouse the styles of **Felix Mendelssohn Bartholdy**, **Robert Schumann**, and **Johannes Brahms** instead. Those preferences were out of step with the stauncher ideologies of German **nationalism**, but that did not prevent Bruch from becoming one of the most widely revered and performed German composers of the 1870s and early 1880s.

Today, Bruch is best known for his G-minor Violin **Concerto** (Op. 26, 1868), his "Scottish **Fantasy**" for Violin and **Orchestra** (Op. 46, 1880), and his *Kol Nidrei* (Op. 47, 1881), for cello and orchestra. The last are two of several works that reflect his absorption of **folk song** into cultivated music as a source of melody. During his day, he was also known for his sacred and secular choral works with and without orchestra (among them two **oratorios**, *Arminius* [Op. 43, 1877] and *Moses* [Op. 67, 1895], and a setting of **Friedrich Schiller**'s *Das Lied von der Glocke* [Op. 45, 1879] and a set of three *Hebräische Gesänge* on texts by **Lord Byron** [1888]). He also penned three **operas**: the first (Op. 1, 1858) on **J. W. von Goethe**'s *Scherz, List und Rache*; the second, *Die Lorelei* (Op. 16, 1862) on the libretto by Emanuel Geibel (1815–1884) that had been partially set by Mendelssohn; and the third, *Hermione* (Op. 40, 1870), after **William Shakespeare**'s *The Winter's Tale*. He composed three **symphonies**, a sizable corpus of instrumental **chamber music**, a number of pieces for **piano** solo and **piano duet**, and 14 published *opera* of vocal **chamber music** (most of it for solo voice with piano). [JMC]

BRUCKNER, (JOSEPH) ANTON (1824–1896). Austrian composer and organist, one of the most innovative members of the Late Romantic Generation, especially in the genres of the **motet** and **symphony**. He grew up near Linz in rural upper Austria, the son of a schoolmaster and church organist and music director. Despite his own gifts in music, he elected in 1840 to pursue the career of a schoolteacher, training in that field in nearby Windhaag beginning in 1841 but also assisting with church music and working in the fields, supplementing his income by playing violin in community occasions. From 1845 to 1855, he was first assistant teacher at the basilica and priory at St. Florian, also serving as singing instructor for the choirboys there from 1849. Meanwhile, he also served as organist for a small local church and independently continued his education in counterpoint and music theory. In December 1855–January 1856, he earned a permanent position as organist at the cathedral in Linz. During his Linz tenure, he also completed a rigorous six-year study of harmony and counterpoint with the legendary pedagogue **Simon Sechter**, followed by study of form and orchestration with theater conductor Otto Kitzler (1834–1915). Kitzler introduced him to **Richard Wagner**'s *Tannhäuser* (WWV 70, 1845), thus setting Bruckner on the path to a profound revolution in his own musical style, one predicated in no small degree on the music of the composer he later referred to as the "Meister aller Meister" (master of all masters). He met Wagner and **Hans von Bülow** in Munich in 1865, also attending the premiere of *Tristan und Isolde* that year. (He attended all subsequent Wagner premieres.)

After Sechter's death (1867), Bruckner applied for and was awarded his position as professor of harmony and counterpoint at the Vienna **Conservatory**; in the Austrian capital, he also secured two other teaching positions (one at a teacher's college for women, the other, beginning in 1875, as lecturer in harmony and counterpoint at the University of Vienna—despite the resistance of **Eduard Hanslick**). He also served as one of the organists (usually in charge of the afternoon service) in the Vienna Hofkapelle until 1892. He retired from the Vienna Conservatory in 1891 and from the university in 1894. Already in 1869, his skills as organist were well received in international competitions in Nancy and Paris (where he performed in the Cathedral of Notre-Dame), and a new level of acclaim in this capacity was achieved in 1871, when he performed in Royal Albert Hall and the Crystal Palace (London).

An important early acknowledgment of Bruckner's skill as symphonist came in 1874, when Wagner granted permission for him to dedicate the new Third Symphony (WAB 103, publ. 1875) to him. During the 1880s and early 1890s, his reputation increased steadily: in addition to increasingly frequent performances of his music (Vienna, Karlsruhe, Leipzig, and Linz) and a growing throng of admirers that included **Gustav Mahler** and **Hugo Wolf**, in 1885 he was named an honorary member of the Vienna Akademischer Wagner-Verein (Academic Wagner Association), in 1886 he was awarded the Order of Franz Joseph, in 1889 he became an honorary member of the Vienna Akademischer Gesangverein, and in 1891 he received an honorary doctorate from the University of Vienna. In 1895, by imperial decree, he was granted apartments in the caretaker's wing of Belvedere Palace, and a bust of him was posthumously installed in Vienna's Stadtpark in 1899.

Bruckner's music throughout his career was strongly influenced by that of fellow Austrians **Ludwig van Beethoven** and **Franz Schubert**, and the works of the 1850s also betray the influence of **Felix Mendelssohn Bartholdy** and **Robert Schumann**. The defining influence on his mature style, however, was Wagner, especially in his powerful **orchestration**, his avoidance of periodicity, and his employment of perpetual sequence and evaded cadence in order to generate expansive forms. Bruckner's most important compositions are his eight completed and numbered **symphonies** (which were prefaced by two earlier symphonies, one in F minor and one in D minor, and followed by an incomplete Ninth Symphony, WAB 109); his three Masses; his many Latin motets and a Te Deum in C Major (WAB 45, 1886); the **cantata** *Helgoland* for TTBB chorus, organ, and **orchestra** (WAB 71, 1893); a handful of **songs** and a considerable number of choral **part-songs** for mixed voices and *Männerchor*; half a dozen preludes and fugues for organ and a small number of **piano** compositions; and some impressive instrumental **chamber** works (in particular a String **Quintet** in F Major, WAB 112).

Bruckner's symphonies in particular present serious problems for modern performers. Most of these were revised at least once, partly of Bruckner's own volition and partly in response to suggestions from friends and conductors; since it is often unclear which changes are authentic and which are not, it is difficult to determine which version is most authoritative. The situation worsened in the 1930s and 1940s, when the symphonies were published in the series of Bruckner's *Sämtliche Werke* (Collected Works) under the general editorship of musicologist Robert Haas: most of these editions—still today the versions in which the symphonies are best known—were highly corrupt conflations of multiple chronologically discrete versions intermingled with tacit editorial patchwork. The result is that modern musicians must search diligently among the various source-critical editions that have emerged in the last few decades in order to find a version of Bruckner's symphonies that corresponds to his wishes. [JMC]

See also EDITING AND EDITIONS; RECEPTION.

BULL, OLE (BORNEMANN) (1810–1880). Norwegian violinist of the Romantic Generation. Bull was significant as a violin **virtuoso**, as an ambassador of European music to the United States, and as an outspoken representative of Norwegian national identity around the world. Contemporaries, including **Robert Schumann** and Mark Twain, noted his high level of musical skill as well as his gregarious, larger-than-life personality.

As a child violinist in Bergen, Bull played chamber music at home and orchestral and solo work with the Bergen Harmonic Society **Orchestra**. Bull left his home in 1828 to study theology at the University of Christiania (Oslo, Norway, was called Christiania before 1925) but failed the entrance exam. Bull also joined Christiania's music society, the Musical Lyceum, and quickly replaced its conductor Waldemar Thrane (1790–1828) after the latter's death. Bull's first foray from Scandinavia was an 1829 trip through Copenhagen to Kassel; he left Christiania again in 1831 for a remarkably eventful seven-year journey to Paris and subsequent performing tour through Switzerland, Italy, Paris again, Great Britain, Germany, and Russia. Despite initial struggles with poverty and illness, Bull gained considerably from the trip and encountered significant contemporaries such as **Maria Malibran** and **Nicolò Paganini.**

By the time Bull returned to Norway in 1838, he had cemented his reputation as internationally famous Norwegian virtuoso violinist. Before the decade ended, Bull embarked on another international tour that reached several new places, including the United States (where Bull remained from 1843 to 1845). Bull developed a special interest in the United States and visited it many times subsequently, engaging there in business ventures and philanthropy; he even met his second wife there. In Norway, Bull founded a Norwegian national theater in Bergen in 1850, paid Henrik Ibsen (1828–1906) to write for it, and brought in Bjørnstjerne Bjørnson (1832–1910) to do the same in 1857. Bull also encouraged a number of young Norwegian musicians who later distinguished themselves, including **Edvard Grieg.** [RK]

BÜLOW, (FREIHERR) HANS (GUIDO) VON (1830–1894). German **conductor,** composer, pianist, and writer on music of the Late Romantic Generation, his generation's most celebrated conductor of orchestral works of composers as diverse as **Johannes Brahms, Franz Liszt, Richard Strauss, Pyotor Il'yich Tchaikovsky,** and **Richard Wagner.** He received his early training in **piano** under Friedrich Wieck (1785–1873; father of **Clara Schumann**) and later studied at the Leipzig **Conservatory.** He originally set out to study law, at his mother's wishes, but after hearing Wagner conduct in Dresden in 1849 and seeing the premiere of *Lohengrin* under Liszt's direction in 1850, he abandoned that pursuit in favor of music. In 1850–1851, he held **opera**-conducting posts in Zurich and St. Gallen, drawing attention in part for his successful interpretations and in part because he (unusually for the time) conducted from memory. In 1851, he went to study with Liszt in Weimar, fundamentally rethinking his piano technique, touring widely, and writing provocative music criticism. In 1855, he was appointed to the Stern'sche Conservatory in Berlin, a post that was followed by his assumption of the position of Hofkapellmeister in Munich (1864).

The Munich position was to be a milestone in Bülow's life in several ways. On the one hand, his conducting of the premieres of Wagner's *Tristan und Isolde* (1865) and *Die Meistersinger* (1868) won him lasting and enthusiastic acclaim as one of the most brilliant musical advocates for the cause of the **New German School.** On the other hand, during this same period, his wife, Cosima, whom he had married in 1857, began an affair with Wagner, ultimately leaving her husband for the composer whose music he championed. The public cuckolding humiliated Bülow deeply (he never set foot in **Bayreuth**), but he continued to champion the music of Wagner as well as Liszt to the end of his career. He withdrew from public life for a time, but in

1872 he began touring as a pianist again, also giving 139 concerts in the United States in 1875–1876 and 1889–1890 and there premiering Tchaikovsky's First Piano **Concerto** in 1875 (Boston). He conducted the court theater in Hannover in 1878–1880 and the Meiningen **Orchestra** in 1880–1885, making the latter group (48 members) into one of Europe's finest and most disciplined orchestras and becoming very close to both Brahms and Richard Strauss. He also conducted the Berlin Philharmonic Orchestra from 1887 to 1893 and toured widely during his last years, with performances in London and Glasgow. He was institutionalized when his mental health began to deteriorate in 1893 and in 1894 went to Cairo in hopes that the dry air and warm temperatures would facilitate a recovery—but he died in a hotel room there in 1894.

Although some contemporaries viewed Bülow's conducting and pianism with dislike, others (among them **Amy Fay**, Liszt, Clara Schumann, and Richard Strauss) considered him phenomenal. Certainly his effectiveness in championing the music of both Brahms and the New German School bespeaks an exceptional musical diversity and intellectual stamina. In addition to the important premieres of *Tristan* and *Die Meistersinger*, he once conducted **Ludwig van Beethoven**'s Ninth **("Choral") Symphony** twice in a single evening and later gave the premiere of Brahms's Fourth **Symphony** (Op. 98, 1885), as well as giving the first public performance of Liszt's B-minor **Sonata** (LW A179) in Berlin in 1857 and conducting Brahms's First Piano Concerto (Op. 15) from the keyboard. He also published editions of keyboard works by C. P. E. Bach (1714–1788), **Johann Sebastian Bach**, Beethoven, **Hector Berlioz, Fryderyk Chopin, Antonín Dvořák**, Christoph Willibald Ritter von Gluck (1714–1787), **George Frideric Handel**, Liszt, **Felix Mendelssohn Bartholdy, Wolfgang Amadeus Mozart, Joachim Raff, Franz Schubert**, Tchaikovsky, and **Carl Maria von Weber**, among others, and prepared the first published piano/vocal score of *Tristan* (Leipzig: Breitkopf & Härtel, 1859). His own compositions were deemed successful but overly dependent on his models. They include works for orchestra, solo piano, and solo piano with orchestra, including **incidental music** to **William Shakespeare**'s *Julius Caesar*, the **symphonic poem** *Nirwana*, and others. His critical writings and notes on interpreting the music of other composers are also insightful documents concerning 19th-century **performance practice**. [JMC]

BURLESQUE. (Fr.; Ger., Burleske; It., Burlesca; Sp., Burlesco.) An entertainment distinct from comedy or farce in that it achieves its effects through caricature, distortion, and ridicule and from satire in that it lacks any ethical element. In music in the **long 19th century**, the term has three broad applications: (1) an instrumental composition (either **chamber music** or a work for **orchestra**) that adopts a playful or jocular attitude toward a genre or style

normally treated seriously; (2) a European (usually English) theatrical presentation, typically one that parodies other stage works; or (3) in the United States since about 1860, a comedic variety show that parodies serious or other comedic works and typically includes a striptease. Instrumental burlesques date from the 17th century but proliferated in the early 19th century and flourished after about 1850; notable examples include **Étienne Nicolas Méhul**'s *Ouverture burlesque* (1808; for piano, violin, percussion, and three mirlitons); François Prume's (1816–1849) *La danse des sorcières: Scherzo burlesque et caractèristique* (Op. 13, 1847; a burlesque on the scherzo); Maurice Strakosch's (1825–1887) popular *Flirtation Polka: A Burlesque Musicale* (1849; a burlesque on the polka); **Henri Herz**'s *Impromptu burlesque . . . sur des melodies populaires des Christy's Menestrels* (Op. 162, 1849, which parodies tunes by **Stephen Foster** and others); Jean-Madeleine Schneitzhoeffer's (1785–1852) *Quatour burlesque* (for string quartet; 1833), which parodies the **string quartet** as a genre; and, most importantly, **Richard Strauss**'s *Burleske* for **Piano** Solo and Orchestra (AV 145, 1885–1886), which parodies the *Konzertstück*. The leading librettists of theatrical burlesques without striptease during the long 19th century include James Robinson Planché (1796–1880) and W. S. Gilbert (1836–1911); important works of this sort included John Barnett's *Olympic Revels; or, Prometheus and Pandora* (1831, libretto by Planché) and *Dulcamara; or, The Little Duck and the Great Quack* (1866), the latter a spoof on **Gaetano Donizetti**'s *L'Elisir d'amor* with a libretto by Gilbert and music arranged by a Mr. Van Hamme (unidentified). The third variety of burlesque, represented in varieties put on by Laura Keene (1826–1873), emerged from this tradition but featured elaborate spectacles that included women whose costumes exposed their legs. [JMC]
See also EXTRAVAGANZA.

BUSONI, FERRUCCIO (1866–1924). Italian composer, **virtuoso** pianist, and writer on aesthetics as well as world affairs; member of the Modern Romantic Generation. Though he regarded himself most highly as a composer, he was widely known as a concertizing pianist during his own time. Like others of the Late Romantic Generation and Modern Romantic Generation, Busoni established himself as a musician and composer during his own lifetime in relation to the "Greats" of the past, whom he considered to be **Johann Sebastian Bach, Ludwig van Beethoven**, and **Franz Liszt**.

Busoni began **piano** studies with his father and in 1873 made his debut as a virtuoso. Most of his compositions date from this early period. Two years later, he enrolled at the Vienna **Conservatory**, where he encountered **Johannes Brahms, Eduard Hanslick**, and **A. W. Ambros**. He left Vienna after two years but continued his studies in composition first in Graz with Wilhelm Mayer, then in Leipzig from 1885 to 1888. In 1890, he won the

Rubinstein Prize for piano and composition and a year later began teaching at the Helsinki College of Music, where he became acquainted with **Jean Sibelius**.

After three years in the United States, Busoni settled in Berlin in 1894. Though he spent most of the 1890s concentrating on piano performance, his focus increasingly shifted to composition in the later part of the decade and onward. During this time period, he began to support, through financial and promotional means, young composers such as Bartók, Varèse, and Schoenberg. From 1902 to 1909, he also supported concerts featuring new orchestral music by composers such as **Edward Elgar** and **Vincent d'Indy** as well as Bartók. In his writings as well as in his performances, Busoni recognized the importance of the past in the way forward for the future of music. Influenced by the late works of Liszt, Busoni experimented with atonality but preferred a system that would not totally discard the past. In *Entwurf einer neuen Ästhetik der Tonkunst* (1911), he set forth these views and called for the use of microtones and mechanical or electronic instruments as a way to build upon past developments in music. His works include the **opera** *Doktor Faust*, two scenes of which were unfinished at this death, as well as arrangements and transcriptions of works by Bach, **Wolfgang Amadeus Mozart**, Schoenberg, and **Felix Mendelssohn Bartholdy**, only some of which are published. [MMM]
See also HISTORICISM.

BYRON, LORD (GEORGE NOEL GORDON) (1788–1824). English poet; iconic biographical figure and literary source of inspiration for musical Romanticism. The emotional turbulence of his life, his passionate engagement with political causes (he died at the age of 36 from a fever contracted while in Greece fighting for that country's liberation from the Ottoman Empire), and his hyperemotional art, which always seemed tinged with either melancholy or exuberance and willing to defy convention and rules in the interest of expressivity, made him a dramatically and artistically appealing symbol of Romantic values. Percy Bysshe Shelley described him as "the Pilgrim of Eternity," and **Johann Wolfgang von Goethe** compared him favorably to **William Shakespeare**. His writing (both prose and poetry) and lifestyle were widely imitated by Romantics ranging from **Heinrich Heine**, Alphonse de Lamartine (1790–1869), Alfred de Musset (1810–1857), and **Aleksandr Pushkin** to **Hector Berlioz** and **Pyotor Il'yich Tchaikovsky**, among others. He won international fame beginning in 1812 with the first two cantos of *Child Harold's Pilgrimage*, and much of his work was almost immediately translated into all the major European languages, enhancing his influence and offering the archetype of a Romantic biography and quintessential lifestyle to many who otherwise had little direct exposure to British Romanticism. Of particular and as-yet-underexplored influence was the collection of poems titled *Hebrew Melodies*; these originally appeared coupled with Jewish tunes by Isaac Nathan (1790–1864), but the texts' evocative beauty coupled with their topicality in an increasingly anti-Semitic Europe to lead numerous other composers to set them to their own music.

Byron's writings provided the basis for more than 40 operas as well as countless instrumental compositions and songs. Among these are **operas** and **incidental music** by **Gaetano Donizetti** and **Giuseppe Verdi**; programmatic instrumental works by **William Sterndale Bennett**, Berlioz, **Franz Liszt, Carl Loewe, Robert Schumann**, and Tchaikovsky; and vocal **chamber music** by **Mily Balakirev, Ludwig van Beethoven, Ferruccio Busoni, Charles Gounod, Fanny Hensel, Ferdinand Hiller**, Loewe, **Alexander Mackenzie, Felix Mendelssohn Bartholdy, Ignaz Moscheles, Modest Mussorgsky, Elias Parish-Alvars, Nikolay Rimsky-Korsakov**, Robert Schumann, and **Hugo Wolf**, among a great many others. **Rossini**'s *Il pianto delle muse in morte di Lord Byron* (The Muses' Lament on the Death of Lord Byron, 1824) was occasioned by Byron's death. [JMC]

C

CALDERÓN DE LA BARCA (Y BARREDA GONZÁLEZ DE HENAO RUIZ DE BLASCO Y RIAÑO), PEDRO (1600–1681). Spanish playwright, poet, and writer of the *siglo del oro*; with Miguel de Cervantes (1547–1616), he was the most influential figure in 17th-century Spanish literature. In his own day, Calderón (as he is more commonly known) was significant as the inventor of the genre of the **zarzuela** as well as an author of *mohigangas* (short comic works, sometimes with music, performed between the acts of a play by characters wearing animal masks) and of the one-act allegorical religious plays known as *autos sacramentales*. His influence extended into the **long 19th century** initially through the efforts of August Wilhelm Schlegel (1772–1829) and his brother Friedrich (1767–1845). He remained a prominent figure in German and French Romanticism through the end of the century, with his relevance to music and musical drama focused by **Richard Wagner**, among others. Both **Johannes Brahms** and **Robert Schumann** considered a text by Calderón as the source for an **opera** (never composed). Other long-19th-century composers who penned music after Calderón include **Felix Draeseke, Franz Liszt, Felix Mendelssohn Bartholdy, Joachim Raff**, and **Bernhard Romberg**. [JMC]

CANON. (from Gr. *kanon*, "rule, standard, model"; the reed or rod used for measurement.) In cultural studies generally, the body of works that are considered to be the most important for a given tradition, thus providing models for emulation and establishing implicit or explicit standards and expectations. Although in other areas of cultural enterprise the concept of a generally acknowledged corpus of authoritative or sacred texts (i.e., of *canonicity*) is at least as old as literate society, composers in the Western European musical tradition before the 19th century generally expected that their works would remain known for perhaps a generation, until their style was supplanted by another one. They thus published little of their work and addressed themselves to specific localized audiences rather than to posterity.

The Western musical canon is thus largely a creation of the **long 19th century**. Its emergence may be traced to a variety of factors. Most generally, it reflects the late Enlightenment and Romantic cult of individual genius and the long 19th century's view of history as an organized, unilinear continuum in which "forward-looking" historical figures leave manifestations of their individual genius for all posterity (a view that was fueled by developments in evolutionary theory over the course of the century). These interests and perspectives were abetted by the burgeoning of the music-publishing industry and the public concert during the **Restoration**, by the writing of new histories of music that attempted to embrace all Western European notated music (especially that of France and the German and Italian lands) into a single coherent narrative, and, especially during the second half of the 19th century and beyond, by the publication of scholarly series of editions of music that strove to make accessible to the musical public authoritative texts both of the complete works canonical composers and of selected *Kleinmeister* (literally, "small masters") representing various national traditions and genres. The former were intended to flesh out and reaffirm the genius of already-recognized musical geniuses, while the latter were intended to collectively provide a framework that would both contextualize and validate the established canon of "masterworks."

The importance of the spread of canonicity over Western music—in the words of Lydia Goehr, of an "imaginary museum of musical works" (*The Imaginary Museum of Musical Works: An Essay in the Philosophy of Music* [Oxford: Clarendon, 1991])—is reflected in the fact that latter-day musical culture (both vernacular and cultivated) is suffused with the products and by-products of canonicity, from the "three *B*s of Classical music"—**Bach** (J.S., not C.P.E.), **Ludwig van Beethoven**, and **Johannes Brahms**—to the broader manifestations of the concept that embrace **Claude Debussy, Edward Elgar, Franz Joseph Haydn, Franz Liszt, Felix Mendelssohn Bartholdy, Gustav Mahler, Wolfgang Amadeus Mozart, Arnold Schoenberg, (Robert) Schumann**, Igor Stravinsky, **Pyotor Il'yich Tchaikovsky, Richard Wagner**, and so on or The Beatles, Chuck Berry, Jackson Brown, Ray Charles, Patsy Cline, Billie Holiday, Madonna, Elvis Presley, The Rolling Stones, and so on. Those canons' existence is also reflected in the oft-encountered proposition that we know the music that we know "for a reason"—the suggestion being that canonical music is "the best" music, the embodiment of enduring standards of quality that transcend social context and history, while noncanonical music implicitly is somehow inferior, unable to pass "the test of time."

In recent decades, musicians and others have increasingly challenged both the Western musical canon itself and the validity of the very concept of canonicity—not least of all because the canon is an inherently exclusionary rather than representative or inclusive construct that reflects the normative biases of an exclusive and often politically motivated group more than any inherently musical or artistic traits or worth on the part of the compositions granted canonical status.

To put it more simply, if those works that become canonical achieve that status because they meet some abstract set of criteria for greatness, then we must ask who chose those criteria and how do they rather than others become the standards and standard-setters? The paucity of, for example, British, Canadian, Latin American, Native American, and Spanish names in the accepted list of canonical composers of Romantic music reflects neither some vague and generalized defect in those musical cultures nor any pervasive artistic or musical inferiority in the works of those cultures' composers, nor does the at-best marginal presence of women composers' names in such listings reflect any inability of women to compose good music. Instead, the accepted canons of Romantic music reflect the fact that the criteria were set by white (mostly German) Western European males in order to propagate, through published and private writings, concert programming, and print culture, the cultural and political values reflective of white (mostly German) European males who believed that white European (mostly German) male culture was the perfect embodiment and telos of musical culture and music history. Canonicity is thus first and foremost a function of cultural and political hegemony and only secondarily a function of artistic content and merit. What is more, while the concept of the canon implicitly and theoretically requires detailed understanding of music and its contexts in order to facilitate emulation, canonicity in practice has tended to encourage increasingly solipsist celebration of an increasingly unrepresentative corpus of works—effectively discouraging the very values it aspires to support.

Increased recognition of the "covert and casual values" (a phrase used in an important article published by Janet Levy in the *Journal of Musicology* 5 [1987]: 3–27) embodied in the accepted canon of Romantic music has also yielded a more nuanced understanding of the powers and limitations of traditional canonicity. For example, canonical status is also a function of "extra-musical" considerations, such as historiographic and generic labeling: a work penned in the late 19th century or early 20th century and labeled "classicizing" or "classicist" (refer to the beginning of this book's introduction) was implicitly designated as recidivist or reactionary and thus denied a place in the growing canon of compositions that collectively traced the great narrative of music's evolutionary progress, and when a work was labeled as "**salon** music," it was automatically consigned to the vast trash heap of music rich in style but lacking in substance, thus perpetuating post-Rousseauian prejudices against salon culture while permitting commentators to dismiss it without necessarily ever having played or even heard it. Similar damnation by feigned objectivity and faint praise was afforded by the label "occasional"; compositions dubbed "occasional pieces" were (and still often are) assumed to be lacking in inspiration, necessary evils produced of composers' need to earn a living rather than of artistic vision and individual genius. The same goes for other slippery but authoritative semantic ubiquities—e.g., "lyrical" (as opposed to dramatic), "**miniature**," and so on.

Finally, there is the nature of the musical work itself: since the early 19th century, the cult of genius (an attribute rarely recognized in women and other groups on the periphery of the canon), the practical necessity of being able to perform only a single version of a given work at a given time, and the equation of genius with authorship has combined with the self-affirming prejudices of hegemonic cultures to grant canonical or near-canonical stature to compositions that surely would warrant no such standing if assigned to a different, noncanonical author. (Mozart's **Requiem** would surely be less ubiquitous if its primary authorship were rightly accorded to Süßmaier in the popular imagination.)

Attempts to de- (or re-)center the canon and make it less myopically reflective of a small group of individuals in a relatively small geographic space (Western Europe) from a relatively short time span have made great progress in recent decades, especially in the domains of music historiography and musical scholarship generally. As a practical matter, however, every noncanonical work introduced into the limited time and space afforded by concert programs or courses in music history and music theory inevitably diminishes the time and space remaining for canonical works: to represent even a canonical concept such as large-scale cyclical form in the **piano** literature by programming or studying, for example, **Charles-Valentin Alkan**'s *Les mois*, **Ernesto Elorduy**'s *Anastasia*, or **Fanny Hensel**'s *Das Jahr* rather than Robert Schumann's *Carnaval* would be perceived in many quarters as heretical. Such a venture might (as hoped) revivify a Classical-music canon that is increasingly perceived as moribund and hopelessly bound up with socioeconomic elitism, especially in the United States—or it might equally well release a storm of protest that would further jeopardize the survival of Classical music in the Western world. The fact that the prestige of Romantic cultivated music began to diminish coterminously with the reification of the canon suggests that the former scenario is more likely, as does the success of many constructive critiques of the canon to date. Nevertheless, the balance is precarious. [JMC]

CANTATA. (Fr., cantate; Ger., Kantate.) In the **long 19th century**, a multimovement, nonliturgical composition, either sacred or secular, for chorus and/or soloists with **orchestra** or other accompaniment; different from the **motet** primarily in that it is always in the vernacular, never a cappella, and often (but not always) **narrative** or dramatic in nature. In the Italian lands, most cantatas were explicitly narrative in character by the turn of the 19th century (**Gioachino Rossini**'s works being a case in point). By contrast, in

France and the German lands during the first few decades of the 19th century, most cantatas were lyrical rather than dramatic in character—for example, **Ludwig van Beethoven**'s *Der glorreiche Augenblick* (Op. 136, 1814, publ. posth. 1837), **Carl Maria von Weber**'s *Jubel-Kantate* (Op. 58/J. 244, on a text by Friedrich Kind)—or only implicitly dramatic (Beethoven's *Meeresstille und glückliche Fahrt*, Op. 112, on a pair of poems by **Johann Wolfgang von Goethe**).

During the 1830s, composers of the Romantic Generation began to produce a number of hybrid variants that were more obviously dramatic in nature: **Felix Mendelssohn Bartholdy**'s first setting of Goethe's *Die erste Walpurgisnacht* (The First Walpurgis Night, MWV D3; 1830–1833), which he described as "a new kind of cantata"; his "symphony-cantata" *Lobgesang* (Hymn of Praise, MWV A18/Op. 52, 1840–1841) and the revised version of the *Walpurgisnacht* in 1843–1844; and **Robert Schumann**'s "completely new genre for the concert hall" *Das Paradies und die Peri* (Op. 50, after Thomas Moore's *Lallah Rookh*) and his 1852 *Vom Pagen und der Königstöchter* (Op. 140, on texts by Emanuel Geibel). In the Late Romantic Generation, the most important cantatas were penned by **Johannes Brahms** (especially *Rinaldo*, Op. 50, 1869, on a text by Goethe) and **Anton Bruckner** (*Helgoland*, WAB 71, 1893, a text by August Silberstein). Arguably the most prominent cantatas in a distinctly Romantic style from the Modern Romantic Generation are **Gustav Mahler**'s *Das klagende Lied* (The Plaintive Song, 1878–1880, rev. 1898–1899, on a text by Ludwig Bechstein) and **Claude Debussy**'s **Prix de Rome** cantata *L'enfant prodigue* (1884, rev. 1907–1908, on a text by Edouard Guinod). [JMC]

CAPRICCIO. (It., "fancy," "whim"; Eng., Fr., caprice.) A humorous, witty, or whimsical composition, distinguished as such sometimes by means of its character or style and sometimes by its downplaying or eschewing of current formal categories or stylistic norms. By the middle of the 18th century, the term had come to be applied to ad libitum passages in **concertos** (cadenzas), and by the century's end it had become synonymous with **fantasies** or potpourris based on others' music (as in Muzio Clementi's [1752–1832] Capriccio op. 17, 1787, rev. 1807; or **Camille Pleyel**'s *Capriccio for the Piano Forte, in Which Is Introduced a Favorite Air from Rossini's Opera of "Othello"* [1821]) as well as études that focus on figural or technical repetition rather than falling into a standard form such as binary, rondo, and so on and thus are "capricious" in their organization (e.g., **Pierre Baillot**'s *XII caprices ou études: Pour le violon, avec accompagnement de basse ou de forté piano*, Op. 2 [1803]). The most famous and influential application in the latter sense is found in **Nicolò Paganini**'s *24 Caprices*, Op. 1 (ca. 1805). The term retained the connotation of an étude, often for stringed instruments, well into the 19th century but after the 1820s increasingly became associated with more substantial solo compositions for the piano, particularly lively, energetic pieces that possessed a **scherzo**-like character. **Felix Mendelssohn Bartholdy**'s op. 5 Capriccio (MWV U50, 1825) belongs to this category, as do **Franz Liszt**'s *Trois caprice-valses* (LW A57, 1839, publ. 1850; *see* WALTZ) and the seven capriccios contained in **Johannes Brahms**'s opp. 76 (1879) and 116 (1892).

The noun also has two adjectival applications. The first of these, *a capriccio* ("after the manner of a capriccio"), occurs in works such as **Ludwig van Beethoven**'s *Rondo a capriccio* (Op. 129, 1798, publ. posth. 1828), the third-movement "Scherzo a capriccio" of Mendelssohn's Piano **Concerto** No. 2 in D Minor (Op. 40/MWV O11, 1837), or the second-movement "Presto a capriccio" from **Robert Schumann**'s *Six Intermezzos* (Op. 4, 1833). In these and other such works, the term seems to refer to the music's structure and seriousness. They are less rigorously organized than are scherzos, **sonatas**, and the like but more so than, for example, **fantasies**. Other compositions (such as **Carl Maria von Weber**'s *Momento capriccioso*, J. 56/Op. 12, 1808 [publ. 1811] or **Ferruccio Busoni**'s *Menuetto capriccioso*, Op. 61, 1880) bear the adjective *capriccioso* ("capricious") and seem to use the term to denote character or tone more than form.

The **long 19th century** also produced a number of **chamber**, concerted, and **orchestral** works titled *capriccio*. Most important among these are Mendelssohn's Capriccio in E Minor for String Quartet (MWV R32/Op. posth. 81, no. 3, 1843); **Camille Saint-Saëns**'s *Introduction and Rondo Capriccioso* for solo violin and orchestra, Op. 28 (1863, publ. 1870); and three great Russian **exoticist** works: **Mikhail Glinka**'s *Capriccio brillante: En forme d'ouverture pour grand orchestre sur le thème de la Jota Aragonesa* (1845, publ. 1858, also known as his "First Spanish **Overture**"), **Nikolay Rimsky-Korsakov**'s *Kaprichchio na ispanskiye temï* (Capriccio on Spanish Themes, Op. 34, 1888), and **Pyotor Il'yich Tchaikovsky**'s *Capriccio Italien*, Op. 45 (1880).

Capriccio is also the name of **Richard Strauss**'s final opera (1942), presumably because of the capricious nature of its **libretto**. [JMC]

CARMEN. **Opera** (opéra comique) in four acts by **Georges Bizet** after Prosper Mérimée's (1803–1870) eponymous novella (1845); libretto by Henri Meilhac (1831–1897) and Ludovic Halévy (1834–1908); premiered in Paris at the Opéra-Comique on 3 March 1875. It remains one of the most frequently performed works in the entire operatic repertoire. The premiere was not a failure, as is frequently suggested. In its authorized version as an opéra comique with spoken dialogue, it ran for 45 performances in Paris in 1875 and another three there in 1876; meanwhile, it had been adapted by Bizet's friend **Ernest Guiraud** for performance at the Vienna Court Opera, with the whole translated into German, the original dialog replaced by recitatives, and a **ballet** (itself reorchestrated from Bizet's *L'Arlesienne* **Suite**) inserted into Act II. It was in this Viennese adaptation as a German-language **grand opera** and French retrotranslations of that adaptation that *Carmen* became an international sensation. It remained best known in that version for much of the 20th century. Although this trend has been reversed and the work is now usually done without the Viennese adaptations, the edition still used in most productions (ed. Fritz Oeser, Kassel: Alkor-Verlag, 1964) remains corrupt, including a significant amount of music that Bizet explicitly cut in preparing the first edition of the work (Paris: Choudens fils, 1875).

Carmen is an iconic operatic essay in a number of defining trends of 19th-century music and society generally. First, its frank portrayal of middle- and lower-class individuals and groups (rank-and-file soldiers, cigarette girls, orange sellers, urchins) engaging in mundane and lewd activities and swept up in the forces of a love that was avowedly sexual but devoid of the noble or magical attributes typical of previous opera resonated powerfully with the trend toward realism that had emerged in French and German literature and art since the mid-1840s (including not only Mérimée's novella but also major works by Honoré de Balzac, Gustave Flaubert, Fyodor Dostoyevsky, Gustav Freytag, Adalbert Stifter, Theodor Storm, and Edith Wharton, as well as visual artworks by artists such as Gustave Courbet and Wilhelm Leibl, among others). Similarly, Bizet and his librettists tapped into the politics of national identity (*see* NATIONALISM, ROMANTIC NATIONALISM) and **exoticism**. The entire opera is set in Seville (southern Spain), and its colorful orchestration and much of its thematic material differ conspicuously from the sounds and styles typical of mainstream European cultivated music in the late 19th century.

Moreover, Carmen and many of the other characters are Roma Gypsies and thus represent one of European cultivated music's most potent exotic **topics**. At the same time, because Don José himself comes from northern Spain, is assigned music that is generally not exoticist in character, and is arguably the most sympathetic character in the opera, his role is one with which the opera's presumed primary audiences could readily identify: the northern Self is thus entrapped and ultimately threatened with negation by the beautiful and alluring but promiscuous and deceptive Other represented by the exotic Carmen and the remainder of the cast. Only by negating the Other (Don José's murder of Carmen in the final scene) can the Self retain its own identity. The fact that Don José, Self to the opera's primary presumed audiences, is male while the Gypsy title character whose seductive promiscuousness leads to his own humiliation and downfall is female further reinforced the strongly male-biased and often misogynist tendencies of 19th-century gender hierarchies. This affirmation of existing societal biases almost certainly amplified the appeal generated by the opera's (for the time) scandalously overt sexuality and violence and contributed to its extraordinary success—as did the fact that Bizet died on the night of the opera's 33rd performance in Paris (3 June 1875).

Bizet's score stands as one of the most remarkable in the entire literature of 19th-century opera—not only for its colorful and enticing (albeit mostly quite inauthentic) pseudo-Spanish and pseudo-Gypsy elements but also for its calculated and highly effective use of reminiscence themes and its vivid musical character portrayals. Composers as diverse as **Johannes Brahms** (who reportedly saw it 20 times), **Camille Saint-Saëns**, **Pyotor Il'yich Tchaikovsky**, and **Richard Wagner** hailed it, and it provided the dramaturgical as well as musical starting-point for the entire *verismo* school associated with **Ruggero Leoncavallo, Pietro Mascagni**, and (in an extended sense) **Giacomo Puccini**. The opera as a whole has been the basis of many adaptations to film, the theater, and other venues (including Cecil B. DeMille's 1915 film, Otto Preminger's 1954 *Carmen Jones*, Robert Townsend's 2001 television movie *Carmen: A Hip Hopera*, and Vicente Ardana's 2003 film *Carmen*). **Ferruccio Busoni**'s Piano Sonatina No. 6 (1920) is based on themes from *Carmen*. [JMC]

See also FEMINISM.

CARNAVAL: SCÈNES MIGNONNES SUR QUATRE NOTES, OP. 9.

(Fr., "Carnival: Little Scenes on Four Notes.") **Cycle** of 16 **character pieces** for **piano** by **Robert Schumann**. Initially titled *Fasching: Schwänke auf vier Noten für Pianoforte von Florestan* (Carnival: Pranks on Four Notes for Piano by Florestan) and published in 1837 as Schumann's Op. 12 (later changed to Op. 9), this deeply significant early work in Schumann's oeuvre incorporates his interest in literature, artistic autobiography, **virtuosity**, and **fantasy** into a multimovement work made cyclical through both recurring motives and a collection of poetic images. *Carnaval* emerged several years into a period when the composer was immersed in Romantic literature, particularly the works of **Jean Paul Richter** and **E. T. A. Hoffmann**, and after he already had composed several collections of short, evocative piano works. One particularly notable precursor to *Carnaval* is Schumann's *Papillons* for piano (Op. 2, 1832); both sets of character pieces are unified by the image of a masked ball, and the fact that *Carnaval* quotes themes from *Papillons* (including the **Kehraus**) draws further attention to the connection. In *Carnaval*, the titles and styles of the pieces evoke not only dance but also *commedia dell'arte* characters, names and nicknames of people important to Schumann (such as Estrella, Chiarina, [**Fryderyk**] **Chopin**, and [**Nicolò**] **Paganini**) and names tied to Schumann's fictional **Davidsbund** (i.e., Eusebius and Florestan).

Especially compelling is the manner in which Schumann inflects these pieces' nominal meanings (individual and collective) with a provocatively expressive, sometimes challenging (and even riddle-like) musical style. *Carnaval* has been regarded as difficult not only technically but also stylistically; **Stephen Heller** famously recalled Chopin having refused to consider *Carnaval* to be music. Scattered throughout *Carnaval* are peculiar displacements of rhythms and accents, rhythmically emphasized dissonances, and sparkling chromaticism. A handful of symbolic recurring motives—cipher-like adaptations of the Renaissance practice of *soggetto cavato*—calls the musician to strive even more to understand the work: E-flat–C–B–A (SCHA), A-flat–C–B (AsCH), and A–E-flat–C–B (ASCH). Two of these motives are mentioned in the title of the movement "A.S.C.H.—S.C.H.A: Lettres Dansantes," and all are featured in the mysterious "Sphinxes," which seems to exist solely to spell them out plainly as a sort of code key.

A layer of autobiography in *Carnaval*, already present in the pieces' titles, is reinforced by these motives; Asch, for example, was the hometown of Schumann's girlfriend Ernestine von Fricken ("Estrella"), and the S-C-H-A motive takes its letters from the name "Schumann." Schumann created additional stylistically odd moments in the work that suggest interpretation: the tempestuous "Florestan," for example, ends abruptly in dissonance and without tonal closure, but the beginning of the following movement "Coquette" seems to answer with a cadential gesture in a playful, lighthearted style. An air of mystery and intrigue emerges from these elements, which work well with the overarching *Fasching* image, with its masks and concealed identities. [RK]

CASTIL BLAZE [BLAZE, FRANÇOIS-HENRI-JOSEPH] (1784–1857). French composer, arranger, critic, translator, and writer on music; one of the most influential French music critics of the mid-19th century who was also trained in music. He began studying music at an early age and continued his musical pursuits when he went to Paris to study law in 1799, taking lessons at the **Conservatory**. After working as a government administrator in the provinces for a time, he returned to Paris in 1820 to pursue music full-time. The provocative ideas, technical proficiency, and witty, readable style reflected in his *De l'opéra en France* (On Opera in France [vol. 1], 1820) won him a wide readership, and beginning in 1822 he wrote reviews for influential mainstream papers such as the *Journal des débats*, *Le constitutionnel*, *La France musicale*, and the *Revue de Paris*. *De l'opéra en France* (a second volume of which was published in 1826) and Castil Blaze's other major surveys of French **opera** and its history (*Mémorial du grand-opéra, épilogue de l'Académie royale de musique: Histoire littéraire, musicale, choréographique, pittoresque, morale, critique, facétieuse, politique et galante de ce théâtre, de 1645 à 1847* [Memoir for the Opéra (and) Epilogue of the Académie royale de musique: A Literary, Musical, Choreographic, Scenic, Moral, Critical, Irreverent, Political, and Galant History of That Institution from 1645 to 1847] and *Théâtres lyriques de Paris* [3 vols., 1855–1857]) are unusual and in some ways prophetic in their blunt criticisms of the dramaturgical conventions and musical styles of French opera. His other book-length publications include analyses of **Carl Maria von Weber**'s *Der Freischütz* (1841) and **Gaetano Donizetti**'s *Anna Bolena* (1845), a history of the **piano** (1840), and a history of dance and **ballet** (1845).

Castil Blaze was also one of the mid-19th century's most energetic figures in devising a way to introduce non-French (especially German) music to a French musical public that generally had little direct exposure to such music. Among his most important efforts in this regard were his numerous arrangements, transcriptions, and translations into French of works by German composers including **Wolfgang Amadeus Mozart, Gioachino Rossini,** and Weber (*Der Freischütz* [with **Hector Berlioz**], *Euryanthe,* and *Oberon*). His own compositions included a number of **romances,** four operas, several Mass settings, and other sacred music. [JMC]

CASTILLON (DE SAINT-VICTOR), (MARIE-)ALEXIS, VICOMTE DE (1838–1873). French composer of the Late Romantic Generation, significant primarily for his **chamber music** and his role in cofounding (with Romain Bussine [1830–1899], **Camille Saint-Saëns,** and other younger composers) the **Société Nationale de Musique** in 1871. He was sent to the military academy at St. Cyr in 1856 but in 1861 left in order to pursue a career in music. He earned some success with his chamber and **piano** works of the mid-1860s but reached a turning point in 1869, when he met and came under the spell of **César Franck.** He fought in the **Franco-Prussian War** but was demobilized by his always-frail health. He cultivated a consciously Gallic style, characterized by refinement, elegance, and delicate but intense expression, within the forms and genres typically associated with German Romanticism. He arranged works by **Franz Schubert** and **Robert Schumann** for **orchestra** and composed two **symphonies,** a piano **concerto,** one **concert overture,** and several other orchestral works, plus a Wedding Mass (*Missa nuptialis,* Op. 14, 1872) and a *Paraphrase du psaume lxxxiv* for 3 S, T, B, double chorus and orchestra (Op. 17, 1872, publ. 1874); two **piano trios,** one **piano quartet,** one piano **quintet,** one violin **sonata,** and two **string quartets;** 12 *mélodies;* and several works for **piano** solo. His piano quartet, piano quintet, and *Pensées fugitives* (publ. posth. 1899–1900) for piano are still performed today. [JMC]

CASTRO (HERRERA), RICARDO (1864–1907). Mexican composer, pianist, and teacher of the Modern Romantic Generation. In 1877, at the age of 13, he entered the Conservatorio Nacional de Música (*see* CONSERVATORY), which had just become a state-sponsored institution, studying composition and **piano** there and graduating in 1883. He was invited to perform his *Aires nacionales mexicanos* (Mexican National Melodies) at the Bolivar Centenary celebration in Venezuela in that same year and in 1885 undertook a successful tour to Chicago, New Orleans, New York, Philadelphia, and Washington, D.C. With his reputation growing, he became actively involved with **chamber music** and **opera** on his return to Mexico in 1885, forming the Sociedad Filarmónica Mexicana (for the promotion of chamber music) and the Sociedad Anónima de Conciertos (for *concertante* works). In 1902, he completed his **opera** *Atzimba* (on the subject of the conquest of Michoacán), which was triumphantly premiered later that year, and gave a concert tour consisting of 30 performances in 17 cities in Mexico. In 1903, the government awarded him a scholarship that enabled him to travel to Europe. He remained there until 1906, performing and lecturing at Europe's leading conservatories (Berlin, Brussels, Leipzig, London, Milan, Paris, and Rome). He was named director of Mexico's own National Conservatory upon his return and began modernizing that institution on 1 January 1907 but died of pneumonia at the age of 43 on 28 November of that year.

Castro is best known today for his *Vals Capricho* for piano solo (Op. 1, 1892) and his *Thème Varié*, Op. posth. 47 (n.d.). He also composed numerous **character pieces** and stylized dances for piano solo that, while indebted to **Fryderyk Chopin** and **Robert Schumann**, also incorporate elements of Mexican popular music. His 1902 opera *Atzimba* remains his most important staged musical drama, but he also orchestrated **Ernesto Elorduy**'s **zarzuela** *Zulema* (1902). His other works include two **symphonies**, one **symphonic poem**, one cello **concerto**, and one piano concerto. [JMC]

See also NATIONALISM, ROMANTIC NATIONALISM.

CAVAILLÉ-COLL, ARISTIDE (1811–1899). Organ builder; the most influential figure in perfecting the French Romantic organ of the 19th and 20th centuries. Cavaillé-Coll was descended from organ builders centered around Barcelona and Toulouse, where he constructed a reed organ that so impressed **Gioachino Rossini** that the composer urged him to study in Paris. There he rose to prominence when he won the competition for a major instrument to be built and installed in the abbey in St. Denis. Over the course of his career, he built nearly 500 organs throughout Western Europe (excluding Germany) and South America. His instruments have from two to five manuals and, depending on the size and shape of the room in which they were installed, as many as 50 stops; his largest instrument (for Saint-Sulpice in Paris) includes five manuals and 100 stops. He maintained regular contact with contemporary scientists and in accordance with 19th-century developments in the science of acoustics quickly adopted the technique of geometric scaling proportions for the pipes. His instruments are notable for their timbral richness and variety (they were often likened to an **orchestra**), their ability to produce a seamless crescendo from *pianissimo* to *fortissimo*, and their ability to bring out treble lines even in the context of dense and potentially overpowering activity in the middle and lower registers. [JMC]

CAVALLERIA RUSTICANA. (It., "*Rustic Chivalry.*") One-act **opera** composed by **Pietro Mascagni**. The **libretto**, written by Giovanni Targioni-Tozzetti (1863–1934) and Guido Menasci (1867–1925), was based on an 1884 play of the same name by realist playwright Giovanni Verga (1840–1922). The premiere took place on 17 May 1890 at the Teatro Constanzi in Rome. Together with **Ruggero Leoncavallo**'s *I Pagliacci, Cavalleria Rusticana* serves perennially as a textbook example of late 19th-century operatic *verismo*.

The action is set on Easter Sunday morning in an unnamed Sicilian village in 1880. In the first few scenes, the audience learns that Santuzza's fiancé, Turiddu, has spent the night with his old flame Lola, who happens to be married to the wagon driver Alfio. Much of the drama unfolds at the home of Turiddu's mother Lucia as various characters stop by on the way to and from Easter Mass. Santuzza then confronts Turiddu—who abandons the conversation to go to church—and finally Alfio, who then accepts Turiddu's challenge to a duel when the men meet in the after-church revelry. Turiddu asks his mother to look after Santuzza and then walks offstage to his doom, which onlooking women announce dramatically.

Mascagni was only 26 years old when *Cavalleria Rusticana*, his first opera, won the Sonzogno competition and thereby earned its premiere in the spring of 1890. While Mascagni went on to enjoy a long operatic career that would be considered successful by any reasonable measure, this opera brought him a brilliant flash of worldwide fame. The dramatic content of the opera—for example, the class of the characters, the rapidly rising intensity of the plot, the bloody conclusion, and the startling juxtaposition of all of these elements against the offstage sounds of an Easter Mass—has much in common with other *verismo* operas. In contrast, the musical style (though rich in chromatic harmonies and declamatory singing) is relatively traditional in its patterned, clearly articulated musical numbers. [RK]

CECILIAN MOVEMENT. A variety of cultural trends supporting return to past traditions, including use of Gregorian chant, a cappella performance, *stile antico* polyphony, and priority of liturgical function and textual clarity over what was perceived as excessive musical expression, theatricality, and profanity; named after St. Cecilia of Rome (d. ca. 230), the patron saint of music and musicians in the Roman Catholic tradition. Although the Cecilian movement is sometimes defined more narrowly as the active, concerted effort to rally for the Catholic Church to change its official policy on music, it may be applied to the broad spectrum of individuals, associations, events, and musical compositions that reflect any number of these ideas not only in Catholicism but in Protestantism as well. While many of the movement's sentiments were held centuries earlier, they gained new significance in the 19th century, with its Romantic **historicism** and industrial-age, postrevolutionary nostalgia for a simpler, more pious golden age in Europe's collective imagination.

Part of the groundwork for the Catholic music reform movement was a resurgent interest in **Giovanni Pierluigi da Palestrina**, other high Renaissance composers, a cappella choral polyphony, and Gregorian chant in the early 19th century. The Roman composer and scholar Giuseppe Baini (1775–1844) published a substantial volume on the life and works of Palestrina in 1828, and he and Pietro Alfieri (1801–1863) edited the *Raccolta di musica sacra*, a set of early-music editions that made much of Palestrina's output accessible in print for the first time ever. In Regensburg, Carl Proske (1794–1861) began in 1830 to make that city the second most important city in the Cecilian movement after Rome. Proske, who became canon and Kapellmeister that year, was also a Renaissance choral music enthusiast and a tireless collector and editor; his labors helped establish a lasting Cecilian stronghold in Regensburg, out of which would come new editions of approved new church music, editions of old choral polyphony and Gregorian chant, and numerous movement leaders such as Francis Xaver Haberl (1840–1910, editor of **Breitkopf & Härtel**'s complete Palestrina edition) and Francis Xaver Witt (1834–1888). In 1870, Witt founded the *Allgemeiner Deutscher Cäcilienverein* (General German Society for St. Cecilia), a powerful vehicle for the promotion of Cecilian ideals, the distribution of acceptable church music repertoire, and the composition, editing, and publishing of that repertoire.

Ideas concordant with the Cecilian movement had circulated in Protestant Europe for many years as well, as revealed in the writings of such figures as Johann Gottfried von Herder (1744–1803), Johann Friedrich Reichardt (1752–1814), **E. T. A. Hoffmann**, and **A. F. J. Thibaut**. Herder lamented the state of church music in *Cäcilia* (1793), arguing that a cappella choral music best suited religious experience and that the style of stage music was an unsuitable accompaniment to encountering God. Reichardt advocated for the music of Palestrina in his capacity as music critic and concert programmer. Hoffmann, too, reserved his highest praise for a cappella choral church music in the style of Palestrina ("Alte und neue Kirchenmusik," 1815) and argued that familiarity with this repertoire would be edifying. Thibaut, the director of an amateur early music chorus in Heidelberg starting in 1811, argued along the same lines in his *Über Reinheit der Tonkunst* (On the Purity of the Musical Art, 1825, 2nd ed., 1826).

Also shaping the Cecilian movement's development in Protestant Europe was the enduring popularity of **George Frideric Handel** and—especially in Berlin—the **Bach revival**. To composers such as Carl Friedrich Zelter (1758–1832), **Felix Mendelssohn Bartholdy**, and **Johannes Brahms**, these figures from the past were significant not only as great paragons but also for how they themselves (as well as **Franz Joseph Haydn, Wolfgang Amadeus Mozart**, and **Ludwig van Beethoven**) used polyphonic choral writing, fugal textures, and *stile antico* polyphony as **topics** in their own sacred music. As a result, the northern manifestations of the Cecilian movement were much more often blended with elements of contemporary music than those of their Catholic counterparts, which were more inclined to embrace older styles of music at the expense of the new. The Cecilian movement's ideas found brilliant advocacy in the latter half of the 19th century, especially in the motets of **Anton Bruckner**. [RK]

CERVANTES (KAWANAG), IGNACIO (1847–1905). Cuban composer, pianist, and teacher, one of the first Cuban composers to assimilate cadential formulas and melodic and rhythmic devices typical of Cuban popular music into the genres and harmonic language of European cultivated music and an important early figure in Cuban musical **nationalism**. He studied with **Louis Moreau Gottschalk** from 1859 to 1861 and then with one of Gottschalk's teachers, the Cuban pianist Nicolás Ruiz Espadero (1832–1890), then in 1866–1870 continued his studies at the Paris **Conservatory** with **Charles-Valentin Alkan** and Antoine François Marmontel (1816–1898). He won the Conservatory's first prizes in composition (1866) and harmony (1867). He returned to Cuba in 1870 but, because of his concertizing on behalf of the rebel side in that country's Ten Years' War, was forced to leave in 1875. He continued to give benefit concerts for that cause in the United States until the conflict ended in 1878. Returning to Cuba in 1879, he began actively teaching and became orchestral **conductor** of the Payret and Tacón Theaters in Havana. He left Cuba again when the Cuban War of Independence erupted in 1895, living in Mexico from 1898 to 1900.

Cervantes composed numerous **orchestral** works and pieces of instrumental **chamber music**, one **opera** (*Maledetto* [Cursed, 1895]), and several **zarzuelas**. He also composed a number of other compositions that fall into the tradition of the European **character piece** (including two *Lieder ohne Worte*), but he is best known today for his 41 *Danzas cubanas*. [JMC]

CHABRIER, (ALEXIS-)EMMANUEL (1841–1894). French composer and pianist of the Late Romantic Generation, known for his wit and his pianistic abilities (**Vincent d'Indy** would compare him to **Franz Liszt** and **Anton Rubinstein**). He began studying **piano** and composing for the instrument at the age of six and by age 14 was able to publish a work titled *Aïka*, ironically assigned the genre of a "polka-**mazurka**." Family tradition impelled him to study law, receiving his degree in 1861 and working as a clerk in the Ministry of the Interior from then until late in 1880. A member of the French cult of **Richard Wagner**, he had continued composing and performing as a **salon** pianist during the intervening years—but his Wagnerian loyalties were attested to by spontaneous sobbing on hearing the opening cello line of *Tristan und Isolde* in Munich in March of that year. After his resignation, he performed widely in Parisian salon culture and supplemented his income by working as choirmaster, rehearsal pianist, and secretary for a new concert series founded by the Wagnerian **conductor** Charles Lamoureux (1834–1899). His Wagnerian enthusiasm soon was graphically famous through Henri Fantin-Latour's massive canvas of French Wagnerians titled *Autour du piano* (Around the Piano, 1885), and his pianism was brilliantly caricatured by Édouard Detaille (1848–1912) in a color lithograph published as the cover of *La revue illustrée* in 1887—a depiction of a short, heavyset, pug-nosed Chabrier with stubby, widespread arms, wearing a top hat and overcoat and sitting at the **piano** with three empty bottles and a half-empty glass at one foot and an unruly mass of music manuscripts at the other.

Meanwhile, in 1881, Chabrier had published his *10 pièces pittoresques* (Ten Picturesque Pieces), an important contribution to the repertoire of the French **character piece**. In 1882–1883 he had visited Spain and in response to that colorful experience composed the rhapsody *España*, which tapped into the late 19th-century French **exoticist** movement and became his best-known work. The late 1880s witnessed new and important operatic projects, but around 1890 his syphilitic condition began to advance. When his **opera** *Gwendoline* premiered at the Paris Opéra in December 1893, he did not recognize the music as his own. He was eventually paralyzed completely and died on 13 September 1894. His last opera, *Briséïs*, after **Johann Wolfgang von Goethe**'s *Die Braut von Korinth*, was begun in 1888 and left unfinished at his death. It premiered in a concert version at the Concerts Lamoureux in 1897 and first staged in Berlin in 1899 with **Richard Strauss** conducting.

Chabrier is best known today for his *España* (1883), originally written for **piano duet** (two pianos, four hands) and later tremendously popular as an **orchestral** showpiece, a colorful rhapsody whose musical language is indebted to the **exoticist** rhetoric of **Georges Bizet**'s *Carmen* and may have influenced **Nikolay Rimsky-Korsakov**'s *Kaprichchio na ispanskiye temï* (Spanish **capriccio**, Op. 34, 1887). He devoted most of his serious creative efforts, however, to serious and comic operas (six works) and **operettas** (three works). By all accounts, his most important work in these genres is *Gwendoline* (1885–1886). He also produced an appreciable body of **songs** and other vocal **chamber music**, music for piano solo and piano duet, and a handful of works for orchestra. Despite the small size of his output, his music was an important influence on French composers of the early 20th century, including **Claude Debussy**, Maurice Ravel, and Eric Satie. [JMC]

CHACONNE. (Fr., also Chacony; It., ciaccona, ciacona; Sp., chacona.) Originally a brisk dance type based on continuous **variations**, imported into Spain and the Italian lands from Latin America. The genre was appropriated in France in the mid-17th century, now assuming a stately character and abandoning the character of spontaneous improvisation typical of Spanish and Italian specimens in favor of a more regular, clearly structured harmonic plan alternating half and full cadences. The French tradition was in turn adapted into a distinctly German species that maintained the essential features of a majestic or severe set of triple-meter continuous variations but also called for increasing technical virtuosity over the course of the variations within the form's various sections. During the **long 19th century**, it typically employed either a ground bass or a melodic-harmonic ostinato and was usually in triple meter. The term was often used interchangeably with **passacaglia**, although composers and theorists differentiated between the two in varying fashions from region to region.

 George Frideric Handel's G-major Chaconne (or passacaglia) with 62 variations (HWV 442, publ. 1732 as part of his Op. 1) was familiar during the 19th century, but the work that became the archetypal Baroque specimen of the genre was the concluding "ciaconna" from **Johann Sebastian Bach**'s Partita No. 2 for Violin Solo, BWV 1004 (1720). Bach's "Chaconne" (as it is commonly known) was first published in 1802 in the context of a facsimile of the **holograph** for the complete Sonatas and Partitas and widely discussed in writings concerning Johann Sebastian Bach during the following decades, but it was not given publicly until 8 February 1840, when **Ferdinand David** performed the work with an improvised **piano** accompaniment by **Felix Mendelssohn Bartholdy** in a chamber-music *Abendunterhaltung* (soirée) in the Leipzig Gewandhaus. David included the work along with the rest of the Sonatas and Partitas in his teaching at the Leipzig **Conservatory** and published an edition of the complete set, including detailed information on his bowings, fingerings, and articulations, with **Breitkopf & Härtel** in 1843. During the last months of his life, Mendelssohn made preparations to publish his piano accompaniment with the London firm of J. J. Ewer & Co. (also published by Hamburg: Crantz), and this accompaniment appeared at the turn of 1847–1848. Mendelssohn's arrangement inspired **Robert Schumann** to write piano accompaniments to all the **Sonatas** and Partitas in 1852–1853 (WoO 2, publ. 1853), and David's realization of the work's three arpeggiated passages provided the model not only for **Johannes Brahms**'s virtuosic transcription of the work for **piano** solo, left hand only (McCorkle Anh. 1a/5, ca. 1877, publ. 1881), but also for the even more virtuosic transcription by **Ferruccio Busoni** (?1897) and the fanciful and virtuosic post-Romantic transcription for full orchestra by Leopold Stokowski (ca. 1934).

Bach's "Chaconne" was also transcribed by R. E. Bockmülhl (1822–1881; for cello solo, 1880), Friedrich Hermann (1828–1907; for two violins, ca. 1888), **Joachim Raff** (1874), **Carl Reinecke** (for **piano duet**, 1874), August Wilhelmj (1845–1908; for violin with **orchestra** or piano, 1884), and Géza Zichy (1849–1924; for piano, left hand, 1895), among many others. It thus became a **topic** of its own right over the course of the long 19th century. As such, it inspired a number of new chaconnes by Romantic composers, most of them modeled primarily on the atypical concept of the genre as represented in BWV 1004. Among the most significant such original tropes are **Ludwig van Beethoven**'s 32 Variations in C Minor (WoO 80, 1806, publ. 1807) and **Franz Liszt**'s *Praeludium on "Weinen, Klagen, Sorgen, Zagen"* (LW A198, 1859) as well as his *Variations on the Motive [F—E—E flat—D—D flat—C—C—F] from Bach's "Weinen, Klagen, Sorgen, Zagen" and the B-Minor Mass* (LW A214, 1862, publ. 1864). Other original chaconnes were submitted by **Cécile Chaminade** (1879), Cotsford Dick (1846–1911; 1875), Auguste Durand (1830–1909; 1872), Sigfrid Karg-Elert (1877–1933; 1910), **Franz Lachner** (Op. 170, 1875), Georges Lamothe (1837–1894; 1876), Henri Marteau (1874–1934; 1905), **Carl Nielsen** (Op. 32, 1917), Joachim Raff (Op. 150, 1870), **Carl Reinecke** (1875), **Max Reger** (Op. 117, 1909–1912), and Berthold Tours (1838–1897; 1875). [JMC]

See also HISTORICISM

CHADWICK, GEORGE WHITEFIELD (1854–1931). U.S. composer, **conductor**, organist, pianist, and teacher; leading U.S. composer of the Modern Romantic Generation. He is generally recognized as the first composer to achieve a distinctly "American" style, although he did not consider himself a nationalist composer and was skeptical of **nationalism**. He authored the first book-length biography of **Horatio Parker** as well as a widely circulated harmony textbook (*Harmony: A Course of Study*, 1897; 73 subsequent editions) and composed in virtually every genre available at the time: stage music (**operetta, opera,** and **incidental music**); large **orchestral** works ranging from four-movement **symphonies** to **concert overtures, fantasies, marches,** and **symphonic poems**; music for wind ensemble; instrumental **chamber** compositions with and without **piano**; works for piano and for organ; works for chorus and children's chorus with piano, organ, and orchestral accompaniment; and many solo **songs**, some with piano and some with orchestral accompaniment. He scoffed in 1923 at "the poly-tonal fad" and the use of "unresolved dissonances for a raison d'être" but despite frequent use of traditional forms and idioms (especially **sonata form**) developed a compositional style that was obviously modern. As a member of the faculty—teaching harmony and orchestration and directing the chorus and orchestra—of the New England **Conservatory** of Music from 1881 and its director from 1897 to 1930, he transformed that institution from a relatively parochial finishing school to a prestigious conservatory after the model of the great institutions in Leipzig and Paris. As a conductor, he was also active as director of the Springfield Music Festival (1889–1899) and the Worcester Festival (1897–1901). His pedagogical and other musical achievements in the Conservatory combined with his prodigious compositional activity to make him one of the most influential figures of his generation in U.S. music.

Chadwick was born and raised in New England and spent most of his career there. Although his family was musically inclined, his father, an insurance salesman, was opposed to his pursuing a career in music; consequently, Chadwick had to pay for his own musical instruction from an early age. Nevertheless, he had learned piano and organ by the age of 15 and seems to have decided to pursue that vocation after participating in the chorus of Patrick Gilmore's 1869 Peace Jubilee (celebrating the fifth anniversary of the end of the U.S. Civil War), followed by greater involvement in Gilmore's 1872 World's Peace Jubilee and International Music Festival. During the summer of 1872, he entered the New England Conservatory as a special student, continuing his study there until 1876. He accepted a temporary post as professor of music at Olivet College (Michigan) in 1876–1877, then traveled to Leipzig in 1877 to formalize his musical education first by private study with Salomon Jadassohn (1831–1902) and then by formal enrollment at that city's renowned conservatory; he spent his last year abroad studying with **Josef Rheinberger** at the Königliche Hochschule für Musik in Munich.

Upon returning to Boston in 1880, Chadwick immediately began working as conductor and church organist, also setting himself up as private teacher of piano and composition. After the premiere of *The Viking's Last Voyage* (for baritone, men's chorus, and orchestra on a text by Sylvester Baxter) in April 1881, he was offered a position teaching composition at the New England Conservatory, an offer he eventually accepted and one that eventually led to his being named director of that institution in 1897. His repute continued to grow along the way: in 1892, he was commissioned to compose an ode for the World's Columbian Exposition in Chicago, and in 1894 his Third **Symphony** was awarded a prize by the National Conservatory of Music (under **Antonín Dvořák**'s direction at the time).

Chadwick was awarded an honorary AM degree by Yale University in 1897 and an honorary LID by Tufts University in 1905. He was also elected to the National Institute of Arts and Letters in 1898 and the American Academy of Arts and Letters in 1909. A sabbatical in 1905–1906 took him back to Europe, where, in addition to securing performances of his music in Leipzig, he visited more than a dozen conservatories. Upon his return, he resumed his heavy teaching and administrative loads at the New England Conservatory but continued to compose, primarily during the summer months. His most important works from the period following his return were the *Suite Symphonique* in E-flat Major (1905–1909, publ. 1911), the **oratorio** *Noël* (1907–1908), the *verismo* opera *El padrone* (1912–1913), the "symphonic ballad" *Tam O'Shanter* after Robert Burns (1914–1915, publ. 1917), and the symphonic poem *Angel of Death* (1917–1918). Between the end of World War I and his death, his compositional energies declined, though he continued to produce choral works until the late 1920s and in 1930 finally published a revised version of his 1879 concert overture *Rip Van Winkle*—the composition that had established a solid foothold for him in Europe and the United States half a century earlier.

Chadwick's sizable output is distinctly eclectic and his **reception** history problematic. He was a master of conventional forms and a virtuosic orchestrator but was also adept at using rhythmic and melodic idioms from U.S. and Caribbean vernacular musics. On the whole, he must be regarded as one of the most important symphonists in U.S. musical history, having penned three full-length symphonies and a wide array of other symphonic works. His choral compositions are many and varied, and his operas, though little known today, represented important contributions to U.S. music for the stage (*Judith* and *El Padrone* are most important in this regard). At the turn of the 20th century, he was widely regarded in the United States and abroad as a leading composer, but his disdain for modernism, the importance of the academy in his professional persona, and music historiography's tendency to dismiss as inconsequential all but the most aggressive exponents of modernism came to overshadow his music and his influence in the years following his death. The list of his pupils and protégés includes Frederick Shepherd Converse, Arthur Farwell, Edward Burlingame Hill, **Daniel Gregory Mason**, **Horatio Parker**, and William Grant Still, among others. [JMC]

CHAIKOVSKY, PYOTR ILYICH. *See* TCHAIKOVSKY [CHAIKOVSKY, CHAYKOVSKY, TSCHAIKOWSKI], PYOTR [PETER] IL'YICH (1840–1893).

CHAMBER MUSIC. (Fr., musique de chambre; Ger., Kammermusik; It., musica da camera.) Until about 1830, music that was written for use in a private or domestic setting rather than for the concert hall, theater, or church. Music written in this original sense of the term was scored for a small ensemble, typically with one performer per part. Over the course of the **long 19th century**, it became increasingly common for chamber music to be performed publicly. This change did not affect the scoring or musical "content" of the works being performed, but it transformed the dynamic of performance by placing the characteristically intimate interactions among the players onstage in front of an audience. Consequently, the music-making more closely resembled a public round table than a private "conversation" (to borrow **Johann Wolfgang von Goethe**'s characterization of **Franz Joseph Haydn**'s and **Wolfgang Amadeus Mozart**'s **string quartets**). As this integration of passive consumers who were not integrally involved in the praxis of chamber music became increasingly accepted, many composers incorporated compositional techniques borrowed from larger public genres into their chamber works. By the time of the string quartets of composers in the Modern Romantic Generation, the musical styles of chamber music differed less from those of public genres, such as the **symphony**, than they had in the Early Romantic Generation or the Romantic Generation. Larger chamber compositions are sometimes performed today with a **conductor**, but the presence of such an authoritarian figure fundamentally contradicts the egalitarian spirit of chamber music as it was cultivated throughout the long 19th century.

In principle at least, the term *chamber music* embraces solo music (e.g., **sonatas** for one performer), although some prefer to discuss such works as a separate category ("solo music"). Chamber music may be either vocal, instrumental, or vocal with instrumental accompaniment. Most vocal chamber music of the long 19th century falls into one of three types: **songs** (classified and categorized by language), duets (usually for two voices with keyboard accompaniment), or **part-songs**. Much of the long 19th century's instrumental chamber music is cast in the **sonata plan** and is typically classified according to the number of parts, ranging from "solo music" to works for two performers (classified as "duets" when the two parts are both vocal or written for the same instrument, e.g., two violins), through **trios**, quartets, **quintets**, **sextets**, **septets**, **octets**, and even **nonets**. Such works are then classified according to types of scoring, the most common varieties being chamber music for strings, chamber music for strings and keyboard, chamber music for wind and strings, or chamber music for winds. Chamber music for winds is often further divided into two subcategories, depending on whether the instrumentation is for woodwinds (often including the horn) or for brass. [JMC]

See also QUARTET, PIANO; QUINTET; TRIO, PIANO; TRIO, STRING.

CHAMINADE, CÉCILE (LOUISE STÉPHANIE) (1857–1944). Composer and **pianist** of the Modern Romantic Generation; with **Ethyl Smyth**, her generation's most important female composer and with **Clara Schumann** one of the **long 19th century**'s most important **virtuosa** pianist-composers. She received her earliest instruction in music from her mother and was writing music by the mid-1860s, displaying exceptional potential as a composer, but was unable to enroll in the Paris **Conservatory** because of her father's opposition. Instead, she studied composition privately with Antoine-François Marmontel (1816–1898) and Benjamin Godard (1849–1895), among others. **Georges Bizet** in particular was impressed by her abilities. Her reputation as a composer and pianist grew rapidly beginning in the 1880s, and she gave her London debut in 1892, followed by other tours there and followed in 1908 by a successful tour of 12 U.S. cities from Boston to St. Louis. In 1913, she became the first woman to be named to the Légion d'Honneur. She composed less after World War I but did make several piano-roll recordings that remain valuable evidence of her style.

Chaminade is unusual among women composers in that she was able to publish almost all of her approximately 400 compositions during her lifetime. She was typical, however, in that her output was viewed (especially in the 20th century) according to gender stereotypes that held that women were able composers of **miniatures** and "sentimental" genres but not of large-scale, "masculine" forms, such as the **concerto, sonata**, and **symphony**. Accordingly, over the course of the 20th century her large-scale works were increasingly marginalized (and dismissed or treated condescendingly when they were performed), while her smaller works were performed but treated as examples of "feminine" music that was suitable to her sex but not to be viewed as a peer of similar works by male composers. Her output includes one **opéra comique** (*La Sévillane*/The Woman from Seville, 1882), one orchestral **suite**, one "symphonie dramatique" for voices and **orchestra** (*Les amazones*, Op. 26, 1888), one "**ballet** symphonique" (*Callirhoë*, Op. 37, 1888, publ. 1890), a **Konzertstück** for piano and orchestra (Op. 40, 1897) and a concertino for flute and orchestra (Op. 107, 1902), instrumental **chamber music** including two **piano trios** (1881 and 1887), about 200 works for piano solo, and approximately 125 **songs**. Of the compositions for piano solo, her concert **étude** *Automne* (Autumn, Op. 35, no. 2, 1886) was especially popular, selling over 6,000 copies in one year. [JMC]

See also CANON; FEMINISM; RECEPTION.

CHARACTER (CHARACTERISTIC) PIECE. (Fr., pièce caractéristique; Ger., Characterstück.) In the **long 19th century**, any one of a wide variety of subgenres of **program music** whose primary emphasis was on the representation of the essence (or character) of an extramusical idea, mood, person, or thing rather than on creating a musical narration of events. Some such works are expressly labeled simply "character pieces," such as Carl Friedrich Zelter's (1758–1832) *La malade, pièce caractéristique* (1787), his student **Felix Mendelssohn Bartholdy**'s *Sieben Characterstücke* (MW SD1/Op. 7, 1827), **Robert Schumann**'s *Davidsbündlertänze* (Op. 6, 1837, subtitled "18 Characterstücke"), or **Bedřich Smetana**'s *Six morceaux caractéristiques* (JB 1:35/Op. 1, 1847–1848, publ. 1851). Others employ more specific designations intended to invoke a specific type of character—such as arabesque, **bagatelle, ballade, capriccio, impromptu, intermezzo,** *Lied ohne Worte,* or **nocturne.** Whether or not specifically designated as belonging to a particular subtype, character pieces often appeared in collections or **cycles.** Most often, they are scored for **piano** solo, but scorings for other individual instruments or small ensembles are plentiful, and some character pieces are scored for **orchestra.** In principle, the last group also embraces *battaglie* (such as **Ludwig van Beethoven**'s *Wellington's Victory* or **Pyotor Il'yich Tchaikovsky**'s *1812*). [JMC]

See also *CARNAVAL: SCÈNES MIGNONNES SUR QUATRE NOTES,* OP. 9; *DAS JAHR,* H-U 385

CHARACTERISTIC MUSIC. *See* PROGRAM (PROGRAMMATIC) MUSIC.

CHAUSSON, (AMÉDÉE-)1ERNEST (1855–1899). French composer of the Modern Romantic Generation. He had difficulty choosing a career and came late to music, initially through contact with musicians in Paris's **salon** culture; his training was in law. After receiving his doctorate in jurisprudence and being sworn in as an appellate lawyer (1877), he enrolled in the Paris **Conservatory,** where he studied composition with **Jules Massenet** and sat in on **César Franck**'s classes. The latter's enthusiasm for *wagnerisme* instilled in Chausson a deep reverence for **Richard Wagner,** and he made four pilgrimages to **Bayreuth** between 1879 and 1882, even spending his honeymoon there in 1883 in order to hear the premiere of *Parsifal.* With a generous private income, he lived comfortably with his family, devoting his life to composition and a lively salon of his own until he was killed in a cycling accident in 1899. He is best known for the **orchestral song cycle** *Poème de l'amour et de la mer* (Poem of Love and the Sea, Op. 19, 1890, rev. 1893), his song cycle for voice and piano *Serres chaudes* (Greenhouses, comp. 1893–1896, publ. posth. 1911), his **Symphony** in B-flat Major (Op. 20, 1889–1890), and two **programmatic** orchestral works: the *Poème* for violin and **orchestra** (Op. 25, comp. 1896, publ. 1898) and the **symphonic poem** *Soir de fête* (Op. 32, 1897–1898). He also composed three **operas,** three sets of **incidental music,** 10 *opera* of *mélodies,* 11 **motets,** and instrumental **chamber music.** [JMC]

CHERUBINI, LUIGI (CARLO ZANOBI SALVADORE MARIA) (1760–1842). French composer, **conductor,** teacher, administrator, and music publisher; one of the most widely respected figures in French musical life during the Revolutionary and Napoleonic eras and the **Bourbon Restoration,** also widely performed in the German lands. He was raised in Florence and began studying and composing there, earning a solid reputation in the Italian lands for his sacred and dramatic works before moving to London as composer to the King's Theatre in 1784. Because the two works he composed there were only moderately successful, he relocated in 1786 to Paris, where he roomed with Giovanni Battista Viotti (1755–1824) and through him became a part of the circle of Marie Antoinette. After the Revolution, he became well known for his Republican hymns and odes, also serving as director of an Italian **opera** company (the Théâtre de Monsieur) from 1789 to 1792 and scoring major operatic successes with his **opéras comiques** *Lodoïska* (1791), *Eliza* (1794), and *Médée* (1797) and especially the *comédie lyrique Les deux journées* (The Two Days, 1800). Meanwhile, in 1793, he had also been appointed instructor at the new Institut national de musique, which in 1795 became the Conservatoire National Superieur de Musique (*see* CONSERVATORY). He would retain his affiliation with that premier institution of French musical life for the remainder of his career, becoming its director in 1822 and holding that post until retirement (1842).

Because Cherubini's rigid personality and tendency toward seriousness did not sit well with the tastes of Napoléon Bonaparte, during the **First French Empire** he gradually turned away from composing for the stage and devoted his energies primarily to teaching and sacred music. With **Jean-François Le Sueur**, he worked as director of the Chapelle Royale from 1816 until the disbanding of that institution after the **July Revolution** in 1830. His most important work as a teacher and administrator of the Conservatory was a widely used and translated treatise on counterpoint and fugue that he coauthored with **Fromenthal Halévy** (1835; Ger. trans. 1836, Eng. trans. 1837). His secular output includes a total of 34 French and Italian serious and **comic operas**, pasticcios, and opéras-**ballets**; one set of **incidental music**; and one ballet-pantomime; among these works, *Medée*, *Les deux journées*, and the late masterpiece *Ali-Baba* are particularly notable (*see* GRAND OPERA). The other secular works include six **cantatas** and numerous odes and Revolutionary hymns, **concert arias** and much French and Italian vocal **chamber music**, one **symphony**, several **overtures**, six **string quartets**, one **string quintet**, and numerous other **orchestral** and instrumental chamber compositions.

Among the sacred works that predominated during the latter part of his career, his two **Requiems** (1816 and 1836) are particularly significant, followed by his 14 other Mass settings and numerous other sacred choral works. In particular, the 1836 Requiem ranks as one of the **long 19th century**'s most dramatic and moving, along with those of **Hector Berlioz, Giuseppe Verdi**, and **Gabriel Fauré**. Although his **reception** has been at best ambivalent—**Ludwig van Beethoven** considered him the best of contemporary composers, while Berlioz and others mercilessly mocked his rigid nature and supposedly pedantic style—he remains one of the early 19th century's most important composers, important not least of all for his strong sense of musical drama. **D.-F.-E. Auber, Adrien Boieldieu,** and Halévy were among his pupils. [JMC]

CHICKERING AND SONS. Piano-making firm of the United States founded by Jonas Chickering (1797–1853). At mid-century it was the largest, most significant piano manufacturer in the United States; it was also the first to produce metal-frame grand pianos.

Jonas Chickering, a native of New Hampshire, was an apprentice cabinet-maker prior to 1819, when John Osborne took him on as an apprentice piano builder in Boston. At some point in the next few years, Osborne went into business with English piano and organ maker James Stewart, who in 1823 left Osborne with the apprentice to start a new firm, Stewart and Chickering. These partners worked together for three years and produced fine instruments, one of which is housed at the Smithsonian. Stewart left the firm in 1826 to move to London. Chickering's partnership with John Mackay in 1830 improved the firm's distribution and facilitated increased production. In 1837, Alpheus Babcock (1785–1842) began working with Chickering; in 1825, Babcock had patented a one-piece cast-iron square piano frame, an improvement on wooden ones not only in strength (good for higher string tension) but also in its ability to better handle the full variety of North American climates with fewer intonation problems. Chickering developed such a frame for grand pianos and patented it in 1843.

Chickering died soon after a fire destroyed the original Boston factory but not before beginning work on a massive new facility that his oldest son, Thomas, oversaw. The sons of Jonas Chickering—Thomas, Frank, and George—ran the company as Chickering & Sons through the 1890s, when the company began to decline. Chickering & Sons merged with several other piano makers in 1908 to become the American Piano Company, which was bought out by the Aeolian Company in 1932. The latest company to manufacture Chickering pianos was Baldwin Piano Company, which was purchased in 2001 by Gibson Guitar Corporation (Gibson sells only Baldwin-brand pianos).

In the 1850s and 1860s, Chickering & Sons was at the zenith of its international significance, with **Steinway** as its nascent rival. It received awards at the London Great Exposition of 1851 and the Paris International Exposition of 1867. Piano virtuosos such as **Louis Moreau Gottschalk, Franz Liszt,** and **Hans von Bülow** were well-known Chickering advocates; the latter premiered **Pyotor Il'yich Tchaikovsky**'s Piano **Concerto** No. 1 on a Chickering in Boston in 1875. [RK]

CHILDREN'S CHORUS. (Fr., choeur d'enfants, Ger., Kinderchor.) A chorus comprised only of pubescent and prepubescent boys and/or girls. Such ensembles had existed as adjuncts for seminary schools for centuries, and composers and other musicians encountered them in these contexts. The ensembles were prized for their pure and transparent timbre. The ensemble was seldom specifically called for in scores until late in the **long 19th century**, although in practice such ensembles were used in the performance of religious works when performed in churches that did not permit women's singing.

The *boys' choir*, or *boychoir* (Ger., *Knabenchor*), is an autonomous subset of the children's chorus, rarely specified in scores but often used as a stand-in for a children's chorus comprised of both boys and girls. Notable works that specify the use of children's chorus are **Mily Balakirev's** *Kolïbel'naya pesnya* (Cradle Song, 1898), **Hector Berlioz's** *Te Deum* (H. 118/Op. 22, 1849, publ. 1855) and *La damnation de Faust* (H. 111/Op. 24, 1846, publ. 1854), **Théodore Dubois's** *Vingt mélodies* (1878), **Gabriel Fauré's** arrangement of *Il est né le divin enfant* (1888), **Horatio Parker's** *Ecclesia* (1889), **Engelbert Humperdinck's** *The Miracle* (EHWV 151, 1911), **Franz Liszt's** *Crux!* (LW J17, 1865), **Gustav Mahler's** Third **Symphony** (1896, rev. 1906) and Eighth Symphony (1907, publ. 1910), **Carl Nielsen's** *Hymnus amoris* (FS 21/Op. 12, 1897), and the "Chorus of Flowers and Insects" from **Pytor Tchaikovsky's opera** *Mandragora* (1870). [JMC]

CHOPIN, FRYDERYK (FRANCISZEK) |FRÉDÉRIC FRANÇOIS| (1810–1849). Polish composer, **virtuoso** pianist, and teacher of the Romantic Generation. He was born and educated near Warsaw but spent the bulk of his career after 1830 in France (mostly Paris), where he contributed as a composer and performer to the city's vibrant **salon** culture and community of Poles who had fled their homeland in the wake of the violence of the Polish-Russian War of 1830–1831 and Russia's brutal and repressive campaign against the rebellious Poles. Along with **Ludwig van Beethoven** and **Franz Liszt**, he ranks as the **long 19th century**'s most important composer of music for the **piano**. He stands (with **Franz Schubert**) as one of its most imaginative harmonists and, as a visionary and committed pedagogue, one of the century's most original and innovative creative voices generally.

Chopin's father, a Frenchman, was a tutor for several wealthy families and a French teacher in schools, and his mother began teaching him piano when he was young. He demonstrated obvious talent and developed a distinctive style and technique of playing at an early age. His first publication occurred in 1817 (the **Polonaise** in G Minor, CT 161). In 1822, he began taking composition lessons with Józef Elsner (1769–1854), rector of the recently founded Warsaw Music School (later the Warsaw **Conservatory**; now the Fryderyk Chopin University of Music), where he formally enrolled in 1826.

Shortly after graduating in 1829, he gave two successful concerts in Vienna, performances whose success was amplified with several further concerts in Warsaw in 1830. On 1 November, he left Poland again for Vienna, intending the Austrian capital to be the first stop on a European tour. He had no way of knowing that the November Uprising that would launch the Polish-Russian War was in the offing, still less that he was leaving his homeland forever.

Chopin's reception in Vienna was cooler this time, perhaps in part because the Polish revolt against tsarist Russia was not well received in the Hapsburg imperial capital. His **nationalist** sentiments and exile brought a new immediacy to the nationalist aspect of his music, however, for while in Vienna he produced the two sets of **mazurkas** that would largely define the Romantic understanding of the genre thereafter, and his subsequent polonaises and **songs** are more authentically Polish, imbued with elements of the country's folk music that are only subtly present in their predecessors (*see* FOLK SONG). From Vienna, he traveled to Paris by way of Munich and Stuttgart. Upon arriving in Paris (whose own July Revolution had been motivated in part by issues similar to those that had sparked the November Uprising in his homeland and where sympathy for the Polish cause was widespread), he immediately felt at home. Although the French capital was teeming with aspiring virtuoso pianists (**Ferdinand Hiller, Friedrich Kalkbrenner,** Liszt, and **Sigismond Thalberg,** among others), Chopin quickly earned a reputation for a unique style. He gave his first public concert on 26 February 1832 in the Salle **Pleyel** and was well received, also earning the praise of **François-Joseph Fétis.** By the year's end, he was a fixture of the city's salon culture and an active member of its community of notable composers (especially **Charles-Valentin Alkan, Hector Berlioz,** Hiller, and Liszt). He earned his living partly from sales of his music and from his father's estate but mostly from teaching.

Chopin's reputation for excellence as a teacher endured for the remainder of his life. Because he disdained the logistics of organizing public concerts, he gave few of them, preferring instead the intimacy and conversation of the salon. Most of his daylight hours were spent teaching and most of his evenings in the salons. Like many Parisian artists, he traveled little, though he and Hiller attended the Lower Rhine Music Festival (conducted by **Felix Mendelssohn Bartholdy**) in Aachen in 1834. In August 1835, he went to Leipzig for a reunion with his parents, also meeting his enthusiastic admirer **Robert Schumann** and renewing his acquaintance with a young Polish woman, Maria Wodzińska, whom he had known as a child and to whom he would propose marriage the following year. Wodzińska accepted his proposal, but the family pledged him to secrecy; during a short personal trip to London in 1837, he learned by letter that they had severed the engagement. He returned to Paris depressed but launched a 10-year relationship with the French cigar-smoking, pants-wearing novelist and memoirist George Sand (1804–1876), whom he had met the previous year. The two traveled with Sand's two children to the Mediterranean island of Majorca in November 1838, but when the Majorcan doctors diagnosed Chopin's illness as tuberculosis, they were evicted from their rented villa. When they reached Barcelona in February 1839, he was hemorrhaging badly, but his condition improved during the couple's stay at Sand's country estate at Nohant that summer. He was able to resume teaching by the time they returned to Paris in October.

The trip to Majorca set the pattern for most of the remainder of Chopin's life. He and Sand remained together into 1847, but his health continued to decline, and this seems to have brought an early end to their sexual relationship, leading Sand to adopt a more maternal attitude and eventually to enter into relationships with other men; family circumstances also complicated their relationship. They spent summers and the early autumn in Nohant, where he did most of his composing, then returned for the winter to Paris, where he maintained a busy schedule teaching and participating in salons, with a few rare public performances. His reputation as a composer had continued to grow steadily, but he was devastated after the relationship with Sand ended in 1847. The increasing political tensions in Paris and around Europe during the latter part of that year, including the legal suppression of the so-called banquet campaign in January–February 1848 and the ensuing riots—see REVOLUTIONS OF 1848 (SPRING OF NATIONS, YEAR OF REVOLUTIONS)—depressed him further and no doubt reminded him of the political situation in his homeland.

On 16 February 1848, encouraged by friends, Chopin gave what would be his last public performance in Paris, and at the urging of his Scottish pupil Jane Stirling (1804–1859), he traveled to Great Britain in April 1848. There he performed privately for Queen **Victoria** and the Prince Consort, gave lessons, and gave public concerts in Manchester (for an audience of 1,200), Edinburgh, and Glasgow, also partaking in a benefit concert for Poland held on 16 November in London. He made it back to Paris, but together these travels and strenuous performances were too much for his already declining health; by 1849, he was too weak to teach. He died on 17 October. His funeral (which included a performance of Süßmaier's completion of **Wolfgang Amadeus Mozart**'s **Requiem**) was attended by thousands. He was buried in Paris's Père Lachaise cemetery—except for his heart, which at his request was returned to Poland.

Although Chopin's standing as a central figure of Romanticism is secure, his output poses several particular problems, and his reputation continues to be bedeviled by issues founded on long-outdated information and assumptions. Because he preferred the intimacy of private performing to the grandeur and relative anonymity of public concerts, most of his output falls into the genres of shorter, smaller, and more intimate works associated with parlor and the salon rather than large-scale public genres, such as **symphony** or

opera. This circumstance has led many commentators to describe him as a "miniaturist," in the process turning a blind eye not just to the two early **concertos** (which very few regard as his finest works) but also to such large-scale works as the early **piano trio** (Op. 8, 1828–1829, publ. 1833–1834), the three piano **sonatas** (the early G-minor Sonata [CT 201/Op. 4, 1827–1828] and the mature sonatas in B-flat minor [CT 202/Op. 35, comp. 1837, publ. 1840] and B minor [CT 203/Op. 58, comp. 1844, publ. 1845]), the four **ballades** (CT2–5/opp. 23, 38, 47, and 52; comp. ca. 1835, 1839, 1841, and 1842–1843; publ. 1836, 1840, 1841, and 1843), the four **scherzi** (CT 197–200/opp. 20, 31, 39, and 54; comp. ca. 1835, 1837, 1839, and 1842; publ. 1835, 1837, 1840, and 1843), the F-minor **Fantasy** (CT 42/Op. 49, 1841), and the **Barcarolle** (CT 6/Op. 60, 1845–1846, publ. 1846) or the Cello Sonata (Op. 65, 1846–1847, publ. 1847). Like most composers of his age, he also wrote **variations** based on previously existing themes (for piano solo, instrumental **chamber** ensemble, and solo instrument with **orchestra**) and a variety of **character pieces**.

Moreover, posterity's disproportionate emphasis on Chopin's **miniatures** is not only misleading but also, given the obsession with Romantic grandeur characteristic of much of the later 19th century and the 20th century, dismissive, pitting masters of "small forms" against other composers, such as Beethoven and **Richard Wagner**. Such attributes have led commentators and performers alike to interpret Chopin's music (and, by extension, his life; *see* BIOGRAPHICAL FALLACY) as "effeminate" in a condescending or (for some) vaguely discomfiting sense. Such a view perpetuates not only late **Victorian** and post-Victorian notions concerning the artistic merits of national musics outside the French, German, or Italian repertoires that made up the core of the musical **canon** as it developed in the mid- and later 19th century but also outmoded gender and musical expression generally. It further fails to consider the individuality, depth, and expressive richness Chopin achieved in writing dance forms (mazurkas, polonaises, and **waltzes**) as well as his intensity and mastery of the rhetoric of gesture in writing his Polish **songs** (all published posthumously) or his series (some would say **cycles**) of short, traditionally nonautonomous pieces, such as the 24 **preludes** (CT 168–89/Op. 28, 1838–1839; to these may also be added the Prelude in C-sharp Minor, CT 190/Op. 45, 1841) or the two **opera** of **études** published during his lifetime (CT 14–25 and 26–37/opp. 10 and 25, comp. 1830–1832 and 1835–1837, publ. 1833 and 1837).

Finally, Chopin's preference for intimacy and its concomitant flexibilities of form and expression made him averse to the notion of a single definitive version that would remain fixed for all performers and all contexts. Consequently, the English, French, and German versions of most of his works, although mostly equally authorized, differ substantively in significant aspects of their voicing, pedaling, and sometimes form because of the significant differences among English, French, and German fortepianos and the different **performance practices** employed by players on those instruments. The result is that modern interpreters (historians, theorists, and performers alike) face considerable difficulties in determining a particular text to use as a starting point for their own approach to Chopin's music. This particular issue was evaded entirely in the edition of his collected works issued by the Fryderyk Chopin Institute (Warsaw) under the general editorship of **Ignacy Paderewski** beginning in 1949 and in the so-called Polish national edition of his collected works that began in 1967 under the editorship of Jan Ekier (*Wydarie Narodowe Dziel Frederyka Chopin* [Cracow: Polskie Wydawn, Muzyczne]). Performers and scholars willing to explore the complexities and nuances opened up by Chopin's characteristically rich approach to expressive variants can now avail themselves of Web resources that offer a complete set of his first editions (http://www.cfeo.org.uk), most of the early editions held in the University of Chicago library (http://chopin.lib.uchicago.edu), or, in an ongoing interactive project, the comprehensive *Online Chopin Variorum Edition* (http://www.ocve.org.uk). [JMC]

See also COPYRIGHT AND PERFORMANCE RIGHT; EDITING AND EDITIONS; RECEPTION.

"CHORAL" SYMPHONY. Popular epithet for the **Symphony** No. 9 in D Minor, Op. 125, by **Ludwig van Beethoven**, employing a text adapted from the poem *An die Freude* (To Joy, 1785, rev. 1803) by **Friedrich Schiller** in the finale. Beethoven reportedly expressed interest in setting Schiller's poem to music already in 1798—before the poet excised some of the more expressly political elements—but he ultimately employed the revised version of the poem, with his own adaptations, as the text for the finale of the Ninth. The earliest sketches for the symphony pertain to the second movement and date from 1811, six years before the Philharmonic Society of London commissioned a new symphony from Beethoven in 1817. Active composition occurred between the autumn of 1822 and February 1824 (*see* COMPOSITIONAL PROCESS, CREATIVE PROCESS). The work was premiered in Vienna's Kärntnertor Theater on 7 May 1824, with orchestra director Michael Umlauf (1781–1842) conducting and Beethoven present on stage.

The Ninth Symphony is scored for an expanded **orchestra** comprising doubled woodwinds, four horns, two trumpets, three trombones, timpani, and strings, plus (in the Finale) SATB soloists and chorus and a **Janissary** ensemble comprising piccolo, contrabassoon, bass drum, cymbals, and triangle. It is cast in four movements with the **scherzo** occurring in second position and the slow movement occurring in third, the first such ordering in Beethoven's symphonies but one with ample precedent in his other works as well as those of **Franz Joseph Haydn**. The first three movements are entirely instrumental, and the last begins with an extended instrumental introduction that functions in part to introduce the thematic and motivic material that will be taken up by the voices. The finale itself is a concatenation of genres and idioms, employing instrumental as well as vocal recitative, Janissary music, and extensive recourse to fugue and double fugue as well as techniques typically associated with the *ars combinatoria*. The finale also invokes a variety of established forms and genres in its tonal and thematic processes— among them **sonata form**, ritornello form, and a four-movement symphony within a symphony. Its text (paradoxically written during the period of Beethoven's life in which he was most personally isolated) is a Deist call for a unified brotherhood of humankind beneath the starry heavens presided over by a "loving father," but it was later invoked in the service of causes that were avowedly German nationalist or Christian in nature. It was also set to music by Carl Gottlob Hausius (1754–1825) in 1791, Friedrich Wilhelm Rust (1739–1796) in 1796, **Franz Schubert** (D. 189, 1815), Christian Jakob Zahn (1765–1830) in 1792, and Johann Zumsteeg (1760–1802) in 1802.

The Ninth Symphony has been a provocative work from the outset. Among its most remarkable features are its length (about 55–60 minutes), its technical difficulty, its inclusion of a chorus (a feature that was anticipated in Johann Friedrich Reichardt's [1752–1814] *Schlachtssymphonie* and Peter von Winter's [1754–1825] *Schlacht-Sinfonie* [both 1814], which Beethoven may well have known), and its celebration of both "trivial" and "elevated" styles (e.g., the conspicuous banality of the "Joy" theme and the suspended dissonance of the "über Sternen muß er wohnen" or the ensuing double fugue). Its critical **reception** was initially mixed, but over the course of the 19th century, as the critical and historiographic reception of Beethoven increasingly came to terms with Beethoven's Late Vienna Period, it became iconic of the greatness of the composer's last years; **Hector Berlioz** (*Harold in Italy* and *Romeo and Juliet*), **Anton Bruckner** (all eight completed and numbered symphonies), **Gustav Mahler** (Symphonies Nos. 2, 3, and 8 and *Das Lied von der Erde*), **Felix Mendelssohn Bartholdy** (the "symphony-cantata" *Lobgesang*, MWV A18/Op. 52), as well as numerous 20th-century composers wrote choral/orchestral symphonies clearly indebted to the Ninth.

More recently, the extraordinary forcefulness of the first movement's recapitulation, which begins *fortissimo* in D major and then returns to D minor, has become emblematic of the gendering of sonata form: the mode of the initial moment of recapitulation (mm. 301–12) is that of the second subject and closing areas of the exposition, which contemporary and later 19th-century writers characterized as "feminine," but the collapse of the main theme back into its "masculine" mode and the presentation of the originally "feminine" material in both the key and the mode of the main theme seem to allegorize the 19th-century gender hegemony requiring that femininity ultimately submit to masculinity. The perceived "violence" of this struggle between masculine and feminine, minor and major, and the subjugation of the feminine led Adrienne Rich to liken the movement to rape ("The Ninth Symphony of Beethoven Understood at Last as a Sexual Message," 1971), and musicologist Susan McClary expounded on the elements of this poetic reading to propose a new, critical interpretation of the gendering of musical form and discourse concerning musical form generally (Susan McClary, "Getting Down Off the Beanstalk: The Presence of a Woman's Voice in Janika Vandervelde's *Genesis II*," in her *Feminine Endings: Music, Gender, and Sexuality* [Minneapolis: University of Minnesota Press, 1991], 112–31). Although Rich's and McClary's critiques significantly postdate Beethoven and his contemporaries, many 19th-century composers, listeners, and performers firmly believed that composers' works gave voice to their inmost experiences, ideals, and values, and Beethoven himself was certainly no champion of **feminism**. Therefore, to assert that the structural process of the Ninth and of other works that draw on them allegorize societal gender values is perfectly reasonable. [JMC]

See also ABSOLUTE MUSIC; BIOGRAPHICAL FALLACY.

CHORALE. (Ger., Choral.) The congregational or communal hymn text of the German Protestant (Evangelical) Church and any accompanying melodies intended for such use. Because of its presumed communal function, the chorale (per tradition dating back to Martin Luther) was strophic and metrical in form, even in its rhythmic language, and predominantly syllabic in its text setting. Many chorales are in **bar form**. These essential characteristics facilitated the production (by poets and theologians) of a sizable corpus of texts that shared a same basic set of forms and could be mixed and matched with a correspondingly large set of tunes, each of which could be used with any text whose stanzas contained the same number of lines as the musical phrases in that strophe and the same number of syllables in each line within the strophes. For example, the text "O Haupt voll Blut und Wunden" (familiar to many from **Johann Sebastian Bach**'s *St. Matthew Passion*) contains eight lines per strophe, with a syllabic distribution of 7–6–7–6–7–6–7–6–5; the tune that is paired with this text as No. 54 of that work is also used in the same work—but with different texts—as movements 15, 17, 44, and 62 as well as in numerous other works by Bach and other composers. Each of those texts, in turn, is also known in association with numerous other tunes that have the same form. This mix-and-match procedure (shared also with hymnody in Catholicism and other Protestant denominations as well as with some **folk song**) facilitated not only the use of any given tune in a variety of liturgical contexts but also a sense of congregational enfranchisement in communal worship.

For the purposes of the values of Romantic music, the chorale thus came to occupy something of an ambivalent stature. On the one hand, because chorale tunes were strophic and any given tune could be (and usually was) associated with multiple texts, the chorale as a genre was poorly suited to the **long 19th century**'s increasing emphasis on close, often graphic text–music relationships. On the other hand, the well-established formal, textural, and other stylistic traits of the body of familiar chorale texts and tunes made the chorale as a musical genre into a potent **topic**—one that could be employed to invoke, for example, German identity (*see* NATIONALISM, ROMANTIC NATIONALISM), Protestantism, communal worship, and many more themes.

This topical potency applied even if the chorale tune was newly rather than previously composed. Thus, although composers as diverse as **Johannes Brahms, Gaetano Donizetti, César Franck, Fanny Hensel, Franz Liszt, Felix Mendelssohn Bartholdy, Giacomo Meyerbeer, Max Reger, Robert Schumann, Arthur Sullivan, Giuseppe Verdi**, and **Richard Wagner** employed actual chorale tunes to suit the specific musical and/or dramatic needs of certain individual compositions, those same and other composers also used newly composed tunes (often called *pseudochorales*) whose formal, melodic, rhythmic, or textural characteristics evoked the topical associations of chorale even though their metrical organization often is inconsistent with that of actual chorales and their melodies were original. At the same time, a similar musical vocabulary without the predominantly even durational values characteristic of congregational singing could be employed to suggest religious inspiration of a Catholic or universal rather than Protestant variety. The latter capacity is illustrated by a comparison of the bona fide chorales in Meyerbeer's *Les Huguenots* and Mendelssohn's *St. Paul* with the pseudo-chorale in Mendelssohn's C-minor **Piano Trio** (MWV Q33/Op. 66) or Wagner's *Die Meistersinger* (WWV 96) or the hymn-like tunes that could never pass for actual chorales in Brahms's First **Symphony** or the symphonies of **Anton Bruckner** and **Gustav Mahler**. [JMC]

CHRYSANDER, (KARL FRANZ) FRIEDRICH (1826–1901). German music critic and musicologist of the Late Romantic Generation; a pioneer in the comparatively new disciplines of musical biography and musical philology in the 19th century and discoverer of the **autograph** score for **Johann Sebastian Bach**'s so-called B-Minor Mass (BWV 232). He originally earned his living as a private tutor, then began publishing reviews and writings on music in local journals in and around Rostock. He was awarded a PhD from the University of Rostock in 1855. By then, he had begun work on what was to be his *Lebensarbeit* (life's work), a full-length scholarly biography of **George Frideric Handel**, three volumes of which appeared between 1858 and 1867. Realizing the deplorably corrupt state of the Handel editions currently available, however, he also began a systematic effort to sort out the complicated compositional histories and sources of that sizable oeuvre and disseminate Handel's music in authoritative **editions**. Together with the literary historian Gottfried Gervinus (1805–1871), he received a grant from the Hanoverian crown to found the German lands' first *Händel-Gesellschaft* (Handel Society), which undertook the creation and publication of a new series of source-critical editions of Handel's music. This series began publication in 1858, but the state funding for the project ceased when Hanover was annexed to Prussia in 1866. Chrysander then assumed personal responsibility for seeing it through to completion, setting up a small printing press in his garden. In 1868, he assumed the general editorship of the resuscitated *Allgemeine Musikalische Zeitung* and in 1876 sold part of his musical estate to the state of Hamburg. The Handel edition finally ceased publication after its 48th volume in 1894. Although it has since been superseded and must be regarded in part as a component of German scholars' **nationalist** program to reclaim Handel from England as a German composer, it still stands as a monument of source-critical editing in the **long 19th century**.

In addition to helping the newly revived Leipzig-based *LAmZ* regain its position of centrality in German musical life, Chrysander cofounded the influential *Vierteljahrsschrift für Musikwissenschaft* (Quarterly Journal of Musicology) with **Guido Adler** and Philipp Spitta (1891–1894) in 1885 and was a founding editor of the *Denkmäler deutscher Tonkunst* (Monuments of German Musical Art), a seminal series of critical editions. He also produced critical editions of works by a wide range of composers, including C. P. E. Bach, Johann Sebastian Bach, **Ludwig van Beethoven**, Buxtehude, Carissimi, Clari, Clementi, Corelli, Couperin, J. L. Dussek, Keiser, **Felix Mendelssohn Bartholdy**, **Wolfgang Amadeus Mozart**, G. B. da Palestrina, Pergolesi, Alessandro Scarlatti, **Louis Spohr**, and Stradella. His first major published writings were a study of the minor mode in **folk song** (*Über die Molltonart in den Volksgesängen*, 1853) and a survey of the history of the **oratorio**. [JMC]

See also BACH REVIVAL, BACH AWAKENING, BACH RENAISSANCE; EDITING AND EDITIONS; HISTORICISM.

CIACCONA. *See* CHACONNE.

COLOR AND MUSIC. *See* SYNAESTHESIA.

COLOR KEYBOARD. *See* SYNAESTHESIA.

COMIC OPERA. (Fr., opéra comique; Ger., komische oper; It., opera buffa.) Umbrella term for any variety of staged musical drama with a humorous or lighthearted subject matter. The term is also used in more specific sense to refer to **operas** that share certain musical characteristics—most commonly, the use of spoken dialogue (instead of or in addition to recitative). In this sense, English ballad operas, French *opéras bouffes* and *opéras comiques*, German **Singspiele** and **Spieloper**, Italian *opere buffe*, Spanish *tonadillas*, and any of the international types of **operetta** are all varieties of comic opera. **Richard Wagner**'s *Die Meistersinger* qualifies as a comic opera in the first sense but not the second, while works such as **Ludwig van Beethoven**'s *Fidelio* and **Georges Bizet**'s *Carmen* qualify in the second sense but not the first. [JMC]

COMMUNE OF PARIS. The brief insurrectionary government formed in Paris after the **Franco-Prussian War**; it was formally declared on 28 March 1871 and ended on 28 May 1871, following the **Second Empire** and preceding the **Third Republic**. The Commune's roots lie in the various utopian and socialist movements that proliferated in France during the **Bourbon Restoration** and Second Empire, but it was the immediate result of the French (Parisian) citizenry's dissatisfaction with the Republic's government as too conservative, too royalist, and too willing to concede defeat to Prussia. Most of France was subject to neutrality after the country's defeat in the war, but the *communards* arose within Versailles and created a nationalist insurgency that became increasingly bloody over the coming weeks, culminating in "bloody week" (21–28 May), the insurgency's defeat, and fierce Prussian reprisals that resulted in more than 18,000 Parisians dead and 7,000 more deported.

The Commune was brief, but it represents an important stage in French cultural as well as political history. In addition to providing a potent national memory and source of inspiration for French **nationalist** (and anti-German) movements during the **long 19th century**'s last few decades, it inspired significant amounts of popular music. A series of four spectacular concerts given at the Tuileries in particular represented the movement's attempt to put high culture to use in the sacred cause of the French resistance. Mikhail Ippolitov-Ivanov's (1859–1935) socialist **opera** *Poslednyaya barrikada* (The Last Barricade, 1933) is set in the Commune. [JMC]

COMPOSITIONAL PROCESS, CREATIVE PROCESS. (Fr., processus de composition, processus compositionell; Ger., Entstehungsgeschichte, Kompositionsprozeß, kompositorische Prozeß; It., processo compositivo.) Term for the process by which musical compositions are created, revised, and disseminated in manuscripts, performance, and print. The term embraces a variety of facets including music's conception or inspiration (Ger. *Einfall*), sources (Ger. *Quellen*), performance history (Ger. *Aufführungsgeschichte*), and publication history (*Editionsgeschichte*). Serious interest in the compositional process in music of the **long 19th century** first emerged in connection with the **Wolfgang Amadeus Mozart**/Süßmaier **Requiem** (KV 626), the authenticity of which could be tested only by means of close study of the work's compositional history and musical sources. The study of the creative process intensified over the course of the 19th century in connection with the cults of genius and individualism. The most important scholar to synthesize those essentially biographical interests with methodologies employed in textual scholarship in order to win interpretive insights was **Gustav Nottebohm**, whose pioneering researches with regard to **Ludwig van Beethoven**, though now dated in their particulars and some aspects of their methodology, remain valuable both as models and for the musical and interpretive insights they offer.

During the 20th century, as scholars and other musicians became increasingly aware of the ubiquitous corruptions and other deficiencies that characterized editorial practice in the 19th century, investigations of the compositional process flourished. These inquiries led to new sophistication in techniques for distilling interpretive insight from archival documents and to explorations of the compositional process of virtually every major composer and a host of minor ones (*see* EDITING AND EDITIONS). Such studies typically draw extensively on contemporary concert programs, correspondence, diaries, printed librettos, and other such sources in order to construct a detailed time line for the genesis of the work at hand, in all its different versions. Such time lines typically include all such epistolary documents and musical documents, both those that still survive and those that are known to have existed but have since been destroyed or can no longer be traced or accessed.

The creative process in music is popularly construed as a unilinear, unidirectional process—one that begins with sketches and drafts and then leaves these preparatory stages behind as compositions proceed either to publication and then performance or through first performance to publication and thence to further performance. In fact, in the vast majority of cases, the process is highly recursive, even for small compositions: during the long 19th century, composers typically returned to sketching or drafting stages after the work had been completed and performed and, not infrequently, after publication as well. A fundamental step in understanding the compositional process as it was practiced in the long 19th century, then, is to recognize that preparatory documents (sketches and drafts) and final versions do not somehow stand apart from the finished product but rather offer complementary insights into the nature of the musical work, performance issues attendant to it, and its composer's goals, priorities, and values in creating and revising it.

Beyond this, it is essential to recognize that the compositional process varies widely. Although individual composers tended to devise their own methods for notating their musical ideas and developing their compositions from embryonic states to full-fledged musical texts, those methods typically varied significantly by genre and on a case-by-case basis with individual works. Moreover, different composers viewed the creative act differently— some as a process of refining and evolving an initially rough concept over the course of the process of composition, others as a process of refining the notation in order to realize better a "pure" initial conception, and others in still other ways. Finally, it is essential to recognize that for most of the long 19th century, few composers strove to achieve a single definitive version of their music, preferring instead for the musical text to be flexible and adaptable in terms of the needs of its varying constituent contemporary audiences. Since musical instruments, listening habits, and **performance practices** varied from location to location and changed over the course of the long 19th century, a reified version of any given musical text might be convincing or satisfying in any given location but less so in other places. **Operas** and their **librettos,** in particular, were continually rewritten to suit the needs of different locales and address (or duck) the many different issues that existed from place to place and time to time in the long 19th century's volatile politics. *See* especially AUBER, (DANIEL-FRANÇOIS-) ESPRIT (1782–1871); BELLI-NI, VINCENZO (SALVATORE CARMELO FRANCESCO) (1801–1835); DONIZETTI, (DOMENICO) GAETANO (MARIA) (1797–1848); MEY-ERBEER [BEER], GIACOMO [JAKOB LIEBMANN MEYER] (1791–1864); ROSSINI, GIOACHINO (ANTONIO) (1792–1868); VERDI, GIUSEPPE (FORTUNINO FRANCESCO) (1813–1901); WAGNER, (WIL-HELM) RICHARD (1813–1883); and WEBER, CARL [KARL] MARIA (FRIEDRICH ERNST) VON (1786–1826).

With these considerations in mind, it is possible to offer a few general observations on the various types of sources that forensically document music's creative processes as they existed during the long 19th century. **Auto-graph** sources are usually classified in three broad groups: *sketches* (Fr., *ésquisses*; Ger., *Skizzen*; It., *schizzi*), *drafts* (Fr., *ébouches* or *avant-projets*; Ger., *Entwürfe*; It., *scheme*), and *fair copies* (Fr., *copie au propre* or *partition au propre*; Ger., *Reinschriften*; It., *belle copie*). *Sketches* typically were hastily notated, fragmentary jottings that served to capture musical ideas (and, where applicable, the texts they would convey) for further working out; typically sketches were written on a single stave or on two staves with only sporadic interjections in one or the other of the staves. *Drafts,* too, might be written on only one or two staves, or they may be in short score or (less commonly) full score. Their primary function was to flesh out, connect, or develop material on a larger scale and in more complete form than is typically the case with sketches. Drafts that seem to be concerned primarily with working out connections among the various sections or parts of works are known as *continuity drafts. Fair copies* (sometimes *fair-copy scores*) typically were intended, at least initially, for use by others—either (in instances of chamber music for one or two performers) for performance or (in larger works) for use as the source of a copyist's score, which may in turn be engraved or typeset and used to generate parts for the singers and instrumentalists who will perform the work (*see* HOLOGRAPH).

Finally, composers often continued to revise their compositions extensively after they had been submitted to publishers and/or used in performance, either in order to produce another version for use under different circumstances or to revise the project as it had previously been completed. In these instances, they often returned to the sketching and drafting process, made changes to printed materials, and initiated new threads of communication in the form of letters and other documents. Studies of the compositional process in music often assemble all this information into a time line and glean insights into it in much the same fashion as criminal investigations work backward from the scene of a crime through its history in order to discover what happened and assess its significance.

The creative process itself typically varied significantly, depending on the presence or absence of a text in the work at hand—that is, between vocal and instrumental music. In vocal music, the process was naturally shaped by the fact that the music was a setting of a preexisting text that had its own form and posed its own expressive and linguistic issues and opportunities. Although some composers (notably **Hector Berlioz**, **Aleksandr Dargomïzhsky**, Gaetano Donizetti, **Felix Mendelssohn Bartholdy**, **Ethel Smythe**, **Arthur Sullivan**, and **Richard Wagner**) penned their own librettos for large-scale vocal music such as operas, **operettas**, and **oratorios** and this process became more common in the last third of the century, for most of the long 19th century most composers set to music texts that had been written by others. Decisions as to the form, instrumentations, text paintings, voicedness (*see* VOICE, VOICEDNESS, VOCALITY), and of course harmonies, melodies, and rhythms of text settings were therefore founded on composers' readings of the texts they set and their understandings of those texts' expressive import and linguistic style. Studies of the compositional process of vocal works often locate and study any printed books, periodicals, or other sources that composers had at hand in composing their settings of those texts and study any annotations or sketches contained in those documents.

The process of composing instrumental music in the long 19th century, conversely, was strongly informed by the need to achieve musical coherence and a sense of musical direction without the presence of words to help generate the form and musical language. In **absolute music**, the process often relied on performers' and listeners' as well as composers' assumptions about the needs, expressive potentials, and formal expectations of a given work's envisioned genre (what musicologist Jeffrey Kallberg has termed a "generic contract"). In the case of **program music**, these issues were further complicated by composers' aims of responding to or conveying an extramusical idea, situation, or story via tones alone, without the help of a sung or

spoken text. Sometimes composers' manuscripts for programmatic compositions contain verbal cues or annotations that reflect the role of this function in
the genesis of the music. (**Richard Strauss**, for example, often provided the
musical sketches for his **tone poems** with programmatic annotations.) [JMC]
   See also FASSUNG LETZTER HAND; PERFORMANCE PRACTICE;
PRINTING AND PUBLISHING OF MUSIC.

CONCERT ARIA, SCENA AND ARIA. (Fr., air de concert; Ger., Konzer-
tarie; It., aria di concerto, scena ed aria.) A composition, usually for one or
two voices with accompaniment of **orchestra** or **piano**, in the style of an
operatic recitative and aria. Although usually dramatic in nature, it is intended for use in the concert hall rather than in a larger dramatic or quasi-
dramatic setting (such as **opera** or **oratorio**) and for delivery in concert dress
rather than using costumes, scenery, and the like. Apparently in compensation for the lack of costumes and other visual aids, such works frequently
entail significant amounts of text painting. They typically begin with an
introduction that establishes a general dramatic context, then move through a
section in recitative to a lyrical, contemplative section before closing with a
rapid, episodic, often virtuosic section that may or may not include an orchestral ritornello. This pattern is frequently encountered in opera as well. It
is sometimes referred to as a "two-tempo aria" (with reference to the lyrical
and virtuosic sections); the lyrical section of the aria proper is sometimes
designated a "cavatina" (little carved-out section; i.e., set apart from the
surrounding material in quicker tempo), while its concluding virtuosic section is sometimes called a "cabaletta" (little intrigue). Because the dramatic
scenes implicit in such works and hence the texts of their recitatives tend to
be formulaic, it is customary to identify two-tempo arias by the textual incipits of both the recitative and the aria sections—thus, **Wolfgang Amadeus
Mozart**'s K. 431/425b (1783) is properly identified as *Misero! o sogno/Aura
che intorni spiri*.
   Virtually every major composer of the **long 19th century** composed concert arias. By consensus, the most important ones are those by **Ludwig van
Beethoven** (a total of nine works, most important among them *Ah, perfido!/
Per pietà*, Op. 65, 1796), **Felix Mendelssohn Bartholdy** (*Infelice!/Ah, ritorna, età dell' oro*, MWV H4, 1834, and *Infelice!/Ah, ritorna, età felice*, MWV
H5/Op. posth. 94, 1843), and Mozart (a total of 54: 35 for soprano, one for
alto, 11 for tenor, and seven for bass). Other notable contributors to the genre
include Luigi Boccherini (1743–1805), **Franz Joseph Haydn, Louis Spohr**,
and **Carl Maria von Weber**. [JMC]

CONCERT OVERTURE. (Fr., ouverture de concert; Ger., Konzertouvertüre.) Term for a one-movement **orchestral** composition not originally composed to precede a larger work (cf. **Overture, Prelude**). The distinction between concert overtures and **overtures** to dramatic works was murky until the early years of the 19th century because the introductory orchestral movements of **operas** and **ballets** were often also performed in concert settings. By the early 19th century, especially in the German lands, it had become common to open concerts with one-movement orchestral compositions titled simply *overture*. **Mikhail Glinka** (1820s), **E. T. A. Hoffmann** (1801), **Étienne Nicholas Méhul** (1793, 1808), **Antoine Reicha** (12 works between 1795 and 1824), **Andreas Romberg** (1815), **Franz Schubert** (1811, 1812, 1817, 1819), **Louis Spohr** (1806, 1819, 1842), and **Carl Maria von Weber** (1806 and 1807) penned such works, as did **Johannes Brahms** (1880–1881), **Anton Bruckner** (1863), **Antonín Dvořák** (1871, 1891–1892), **Niels W. Gade** (1846), **Fanny Hensel** (1830), **Nikolay Rimsky-Korsakov** (most prominently the *Russian Easter* Overture, Op. 36; 1888), and **Richard Wagner** (1831, numerous lost works from 1830). The work now known as the overture to **Franz Schubert's** **incidental music** to *Die Zauberharfe* (D. 644, 1820) was originally a concert overture of this sort, and **Ludwig van Beethoven's** *Coriolanus* Overture (Op. 62, 1807, publ. 1808) was first performed in concert. Although this ostensibly **absolute** variety of overture was less prominent than its programmatic counterpart after the mid-19th century, presumably because of the ascendance of the ideologies of the **New German School**, later contributions were penned by major composers including **Jules Massenet** (1863), **Giacomo Meyerbeer** (1862), **Camille Saint-Saëns** (1910), and **Arthur Sullivan** (1858, 1866, 1870). The term also embraced medleys based on national melodies; **Antonín Dvořák**, **Edward Elgar**, **Mikhail Glinka**, **Edvard Grieg**, **Aleksandr Glazunov**, **Nikolay Rimsky-Korsakov**, and **Bedřich Smetana** contributed to this group.

More important for the century as a whole was the **programmatic** or characteristic concert overture. Arguably launched by Weber's overture *Der Beherrscher der Geister* (J. 122/Op. 27, 1811–1813; actually a revision of an opera overture), these works attempted to suggest, portray, or respond to an extramusical idea or subject in a one-movement composition for large ensemble. **William Shakespeare** provided the inspiration for two of the earliest works of this sort, **Felix Mendelssohn Bartholdy's** *Midsummer Night's Dream Overture* (MWV P3/Op. 21; 1825–1826, publ. 1832) and **Hector Berlioz's** **fantasy** (titled "overture") based on *The Tempest* (H. 52, 1830). Berlioz later incorporated the *Tempest* fantasy unchanged into *Lélio, ou la retour à la vie* (H. 55/Op. 14b) in 1831–1832, while Mendelssohn published the *Midsummer Night's Dream Overture*, *The Hebrides* (MWV P7/Op. 26, comp. 1829–1830, publ. 1833), and *Calm Sea and Prosperous Voyage*

(MWV P5/Op. 27, 1828, rev. 1833, publ. 1835) serially as a set of three concert overtures in 1830–1835. (Mendelssohn requested that these overtures be released under a single opus number, thus implying that they made up a collective whole, but this wish was not realized.) Important contributions followed from **Robert Schumann** (*Die Braut von Messina* [Op. 100, 1850, publ. 1851] and *Julius Caesar* [Op. 128, 1851, publ. 1854]) and **Pyotor Il'yich Tchaikovsky** (*1812, Hamlet* [Op. 67, 1888, publ. 1890], *Francesa da Rimini* [Op. 32, 1876, publ. 1878], and *Romeo and Juliet*, among others).

The programmatic concert overture occupied a middle ground between the full-fledged **program symphony** and implicitly abstract one-movement works for orchestra. Functionally, it required less time and fewer resources than the former and thus took up less space on concert programs; it was also less expensive than symphonies and other large works to publish. At the same time, it solicited performers and audiences to listen and interpret more imaginatively than did the latter, thus engaging them in the increasingly heated polemics surrounding the "progressive" aesthetic agenda of the **New German School** without posing the logistical problems of larger works espoused by those composers.

Most works classified as concert overtures used a conventional musical form—usually **sonata form**. Programmatic concert overtures, beginning with Mendelssohn's *Midsummer Night's Dream*, typically also employed techniques of **thematic transformation**, generating most or all of the themes from a single melodic or motivic idea and altering its character over the course of the work in response to narrative or conceptual developments in the extramusical subject. Often the influence of the extramusical content is discernible via some sort of **deformation**—as, for example, in Mendelssohn's *Midsummer Night's Dream Overture*, in which the coda is longer than the development because of an extended musical denouement reflecting the structure of Shakespeare's play (specifically, Puck's epilog in Act 5). Such meldings of tonal and thematic musical processes with **narrative** literary strategies and philosophical propositions made the concert overture a genre whose engagement with the issues of the day was exceptional. They continued to play a significant role in the late 19th century in the **symphonic poems** of Liszt and the **tone poems** of Richard Strauss. [JMC]

CONCERT OVERTURE "1812". *See 1812: SOLEMN OVERTURE FOR LARGE ORCHESTRA, OP. 49.*

CONCERTO. (Fr., concert; Ger., Konzert; from It. *concertare*, to join together; related to Lat. *concertare*, to fight or contend.) In the **long 19th century**, an instrumental composition for one or more solo instruments with orchestral accompaniment; among public instrumental genres, the preeminent vehicle for the display of technical **virtuosity** in instrumental music. Most concertos follow the **sonata plan**. During the early 19th century, the individual movements typically follow the Type 5 **sonata form** or a modified version thereof. After the 1830s, **Felix Mendelssohn Bartholdy** and other composers increasingly employed a variant of this that merged the opening ritornello and the first solo section in a single unrepeated exposition. Beginning with Mendelssohn's Violin Concerto (MWV O14/Op. 65, comp. 1844, publ. 1845), it also became increasingly common to have two or more of the movements played without pause and to move the cadenza from its traditional position just before or within the coda to the end of the development section, so that it served the function of both development and retransition. The latter approach also encouraged some composers (such as **Franz Liszt** and **Robert Schumann**) to treat the concerto not as a series of movements but as a **cycle**, sharing thematic and motivic material among movements and sometimes distributing the various elements of sonata form across the series of interlinked movements (e.g., in Liszt's Piano Concerto No. 1, LW H4, comp. 1853–1856, publ. 1857).

The most common varieties of concerto during the 19th century were the *piano concerto, violin concerto,* and *cello concerto.* The most important piano concertos of the long 19th century were contributed by **Ludwig van Beethoven, Johannes Brahms, Fryderyk Chopin, Edvard Grieg,** Liszt, Mendelssohn, **Serge Rachmaninoff, Clara Schumann,** Robert Schumann, and **Pyotr Il'yich Tchaikovsky,** with other notable works by **Mily Balakirev, William Sterndale Bennett, Adrien Boieldieu, Max Bruch, Ferruccio Busoni, Carl Czerny, Gaetano Donizetti, Antonín Dvořák, John Field, Aleksandr Glazunov, Adolf Henselt, Ferdinand Hiller, Johann Nepomuk Hummel, Friedrich Kalkbrenner, Georges Kastner, Carl Loewe, Ignaz Mosceheles, Ignacy Paderewski, Hubert Parry, Max Reger, Carl Reinecke, Nikolay Rimsky-Korsakov, Anton Rubinstein, Camille Saint-Saëns, Aleksandr Scriabin,** and **Carl Maria von Weber.**

Violin concertos were penned by composers including **D.-F.-E. Auber,** Beethoven, Charles de Bériot (1802–1870), Brahms, Bruch, **Ferdinand David,** Dvořák, **Edward Elgar,** Glazunov, **Édouard Lalo,** Mendelssohn, **Carl Nielsen, Nicolò Paganini,** Saint-Saëns, Robert Schumann, **Jean Sibelius, Louis Spohr,** and Tchaikovsky. Particularly important among the cello concertos are those by Dvořák, Elgar, and Saint-Saëns, with others having been written by composers including Auber, Glazunov, **Bernhard Molique, Ignaz Pleyel, Joachim Raff,** and Robert Schumann. Other important solo concertos were written to feature the oboe (**Richard Strauss**), clarinet (Weber), horn (Richard Strauss), and trumpet (Hummel), among other instruments. The long 19th century also produced a number of *double concertos* (for two soloists plus orchestra; the most important such works are Brahms's Concerto for Violin, Cello, and Orchestra, Op. 102, 1887, publ. 1888, and Liszt's

Concerto Pathétique for Two Pianos and Orchestra, LW C18, 1856, publ. 1866, rev. 1877). The most important *triple concerto* is Beethoven's Concerto for Violin, Cello, Piano, and Orchestra, Op. 56, 1804–1807, publ. 1808). [JMC]

See also KONZERTSTÜCK.

CONCERT SPIRITUEL. Originally, a concert series founded in Paris in 1725 and lasting until 1790, producing up to 24 events annually. In the first *concerts spirituels*, royal chapel *sous-maître* Anne Danican Philidor (1681–1728) held concerts at the Tuileries Palace on Catholic holidays and during Lent, when the theaters closed. Performers were brought in from the Opéra, the royal chapel, and elsewhere in Paris; musicians visiting from far away were an increasingly common feature during the series's 65 years. Philidor and later directors of the concert series were granted a privilege by the Académie Royale de Musique to perform instrumental and sacred vocal music; the concerts nevertheless sometimes featured secular vocal music as well. In general, the series represented a rich variety of genres; musically, the concerts emphasized fresh new styles and high-quality performance. The later decades of the series saw a growing emphasis on orchestral repertoire, due in part to the influence of the Mannheim court orchestra (Johann Stamitz visited during the 1750s) and the vogue for the *symphonie concertante*. During the period 1773–1790 and under the direction of Pierre Gaviniès (1728–1800), Simon Leduc (1742–1777), François-Joseph Gossec (1734–1829), and Joseph Legros (1777–1790), works by **Wolfgang Amadeus Mozart** and **Franz Joseph Haydn** were programmed frequently.

Although the original concert series ended in 1790, the concert spirituel survived the French Revolution in name and in spirit. Even before the series ended, the term "concert spirituel" was sometimes used to describe other kinds of public concert. Johann Friedrich Reichardt (1752–1814) founded a concert series by that name in Berlin in 1783, for example, although in contrast to the current offerings of the Paris series, Reichardt was interested in promoting older works. At the beginning of the 19th century, the early Napoleonic era saw the resurgent use of the term to describe French Lenten and feast-day concerts, although in most of these cases the quality of the music was far below that in the original Paris concerts. An example along these lines in Vienna was the concert spirituel series with an entirely amateur orchestra, founded in 1819 by Francis Xaver Gebauer (1784–1822) and Eduard von Lannoy (1787–1853). Although this Viennese concert series set out to satisfy the demand for excellent contemporary and older orchestral music, the connotation of high performing quality was not retained from the original Paris series. [RK]

CONDUCTOR. (Fr., chef d'orchestre; Ger., Dirigent; It., direttore d'orchestra.) Since the turn of the 20th century, the term *conductor* has generally denoted an individual who neither sings nor plays any instrument in the performance of a given work but rather supervises and coordinates virtually all aspects of its preparation, interpretation, and execution and directs the performance from the front of an ensemble, back to the audience, often using either the hands or a baton and expressive facial and corporal gestures to guide the other performers in their interpretation of the notated musical text. In this view, the conductor's charges include rehearsal preparation and scheduling, detection and resolution of errors within the ensemble, seating, decisions concerning tempo and tempo changes, dynamics and dynamic changes, balance, phrasing, ensemble arrangement, and other performance parameters. When a concert is recorded or video-recorded, the conductor is usually centrally involved in the editing process as well. On the whole, the 21st-century conductor is responsible for the coherent interpretation of ensemble compositions and for giving expressive shape to the music by means of gestures directed at the performers.

The term had significantly different denotations for most of the **long 19th century**. These denotations and their historical development varied according to genre and location. The practice of conducting (Fr., *direction d'orchestre*; Ger., *Dirigieren*; It., *direzione d'orchestra*) entailed certain responsibilities in concerted music, others in **opera** and stage music, and others in church music. In general, it is fair to say that between about 1790 and 1830, most ensembles were directed from within the ensemble, either by the principal violinist or by a keyboardist (the latter being an extension of continuo practice); that during the years between around 1830 and 1880, more ensembles began employing a central and more-or-less authoritarian time beater who supervised and coordinated the ensemble without also playing; and that by about 1880, most ensembles were led by a time-beating maestro who did not otherwise perform in the music and who assumed overall interpretive control of the expressive issues named above. Historically speaking, the emergence of such a figure may well have been a practical necessity as much as an aesthetic desideratum—a function of larger ensembles used to fill larger halls and of the fact that the larger scale of large-ensemble music of the mid- and later 19th century increasingly included changes in tempo and meter, factors that are more easily coordinated by a central conductor rather than a participant of the ensemble itself.

Historical changes in the art of conducting are intricately bound up with broader issues of interpretation and **performance practice**. If one accepts that the presence or absence of a conductor affects the interactions among performers and the manner in which scores are executed and that composers generally consider such interactions and interpretive issues in creating their scores, then it stands to reason that the practical aspects of large-ensemble music during the Early Romantic Generation (e.g., in the **symphonies** of **Ludwig van Beethoven**, the **operas** of **Carl Maria von Weber** and **Gioachino Rossini**, and the sacred choral works of **Franz Schubert**) differed significantly from those same aspects of the Romantic Generation (the symphonies of **Robert Schumann**, the operas of **Giuseppe Verdi** and **Giacomo Meyerbeer**, and the sacred music of **Felix Mendelssohn Bartholdy**)—and the latter in turn differed from their counterparts in the Late Romantic Generation (**Johannes Brahms** and **Anton Bruckner**) and the Modern Romantic Generation (**Gustav Mahler, Richard Strauss,** and **Gabriel Fauré**). Performers who are concerned with any degree of fidelity to historical composers' wishes must consider the assumptions on which those various composers' works are based; differentiate between accrued subsequent practices and those germane to the genre, location, and composer at hand; and choose which (if any) of the former to employ despite their inauthenticity. For example, in music of the 1790s, interpretive gestures (such as a change in tempo, whether sudden or gradual) that require a modern conductor may be aesthetically attractive today, but the fact that those works were executed without a conductor in their own day strongly suggests that those changes in tempo are alien to the composers' expectations of how the works would be performed.

The transition from within-ensemble to fore-of-ensemble direction occurred earlier in choral music and opera than in concerted works. Already in the 16th and 17th centuries, it had been common for the leader of choral ensembles (i.e., one of the performers themselves, not an autonomous maestro) to beat time in such works using a roll of paper or a short stick gripped at the center. Similarly, by the late 17th century, at least some performances of operas in France used a *batteur de mesure* (time beater) to help the onstage musicians keep time and coordinate their music with that of the orchestra; indeed, in the French tradition, the conductor beat time audibly, tapping a violin bow or other object on a music stand. Both these traditions persisted into the long 19th century, but by the 1790s, outside the north German lands and England (where keyboard conducting prevailed), the most widespread practice in ensemble music was for the concertmaster to lead from his position at the head of the orchestra, using head motions and dramatic arm gestures to direct the music. (Sometimes the concertmaster stood.) By the 1820s, the choral/operatic tradition of using a wooden stick or a roll of paper was introduced into concerted-music ensembles as well; alternatively, the concertmaster might stand and use his bow to lead such ensembles, holding the bow at the frog or in the center and reading either from an annotated Violin 1 part that also included cues for other instruments or from a short score that included the main melody lines and bass written on two staves, similar to the *partimenti* used in pedagogy of counterpoint in the late 18th and early 19th centuries.

The practice of rudimentary rather than authoritarian baton, rolled-paper, or violin-bow conducting endured well into the long 19th century, but during the first few decades of the century, the prevalent practice was one of shared leadership, with one individual at the **piano** at the front of the ensemble, with the full score before him, observing the performance and correcting any mistake while the concertmaster (or *leader* in British parlance) both executed his own part "with exemplary accuracy and firmness" being observed by the other ensemble members for the tempo and being followed by them for his beat (as critic George Hogarth [1783–1870] would describe the practice in 1862). The increasing complexities of **orchestral** scores during the early 19th century made this coadjuvancy increasingly restrictive, however. Consequently, during the early years of the century, it became common for the direction to be entrusted to a single individual using a baton (Fr., *baguette*; Ger., *Taktstock*; It., *bacchetta*) at the fore of the ensemble. The batons in question were not, however, the modern slender tapered sticks grasped at one end but sturdy wooden staves with rounded knobs at each end—grasped at the center inside the conductor's fist.

According to legend, the initiator of this practice was **Louis Spohr**, although the evidence seems to indicate that Spohr used the baton only in rehearsal; Mendelssohn's use of the baton when he conducted the Philharmonic Society of London in 1829 raised eyebrows and met with objection from the concertmaster, and the practice was still objectionable from the perspective of critics such as **Robert Schumann** when Mendelssohn used the baton to conduct the Gewandhaus Orchestra in Leipzig in 1835. (Schumann reported in the *Neue Zeitschrift für Musik* that he was "disturbed" by Mendelssohn's use of the baton and felt that "in a symphony the orchestra must be like a republic, subordinate to no higher authority.") On the Continent, in England, and in the New World alike, conductors typically conducted from short scores or annotated violin parts until the final years of the 19th century.

Moreover, until late in the 19th century, protocol required all performers—including the conductor—to face the audience. Here, too, Mendelssohn appears to have initiated a move in the direction of the modern practice, turning sidewise at the fore of the orchestra, facing the first violins (with his back to the second violins) and his left shoulder to the audience. This practice, apparently adopted also by conductors such as Berlioz, **Gaspare Spontini**, Weber, and later **Richard Wagner**, was not without its problems, but it provided for much more rigorous direction and discipline. The interpretive control afforded by this new, centralized authority in the person of the conductor was further enhanced by **Franz Liszt**, who disparaged time beating as a "senseless, brutal habit" and attempted, in his own conducting, to shape the enfolding succession of notes by marking accents and developing an expressive vocabulary of gestures. Contemporary orchestras were often mystified by

Liszt's conducting and audiences distracted and amused by his exaggerated gestures, and his musical results were reportedly mixed. Nevertheless, his ideas became foundational to Wagner's theories of conducting as expressed in his later treatise *Über das Dirigieren* (On Conducting, 1861; rev. 1869), to the practices of **Hans von Bülow**, Hermann Levi (1839–1900), Hans Richter (1843–1916), and other conductors of the Late Romantic Generation, and to virtuoso conductors of the next generation, such as **Gustav Mahler, Richard Strauss**, and Felix Weingartner (1863–1942).

Although French and Italian practices were slow to adopt these principles—notwithstanding the reforms introduced by **Françoise-Antoine Habeneck** and Angelo Mariani (1821–1873)—by the end of World War I they were generally embraced there as well, as witnessed by the accomplishments of conductors such as Franco Faccio (1840–1891), Giuseppe Martucci (1856–1909), Pierre Monteux (1875–1964), and Arturo Toscanini (1867–1957).

The late 19th century's centralization of musical authority in a single powerful individual who commanded large ensembles with a baton and detailed expressive gesture marked the emergence of the conductor in the modern sense—but if one accepts that the changes in the art of conducting and the responsibilities of the conductor affected the way that ensemble members realized the musical notation before them, then it follows that certain practices that are facilitated by the presence of a baton-wielding maestro are anachronistic and in some ways contrary to the performance practices that composers of the long 19th century before, for example, 1880 envisioned as governing the realization of their large-ensemble music. Most obvious in this regard are fluctuations in tempo, of course, but there are also others. To name but one example, Wagner in 1861 criticized contemporary orchestras' rendering of the first movement of **Ludwig van Beethoven**'s Fifth **Symphony** for allowing the sustained note in mm. 4–5 to decay and for supposedly paying insufficient attention to the continuously flowing *melos* created by the rapid exchanges of the movement's central motive across the voices of the orchestra. Many, perhaps most, subsequent conductors have followed his admonitions—yet whatever the intrinsic musical merits of his ideas, the fact remains that the practices Wagner criticized half a century after that symphony's composition and premiere were those that had been in place during Beethoven's lifetime and that he had certainly envisioned when imagining how contemporary performers would realize his score. Wagner's ideas on conducting certainly tell us how to interpret his own scores and those of later composers and conductors who were influenced by him—but Beethoven was not a part of that group, and by following Wagner's recommendation for interpreting Beethoven, modern performers depart from rather than follow more closely the composer's own expectations and intentions (*see* INTENTIONAL FALLACY).

Finally, the rapid globalization of culture since World War II, abetted by the emergence of a new culture of recorded and broadcast musical sound, has created a new sort of conductor, one who travels widely (often internationally) and whose style is mingled with or grafted onto the widely varying performance styles employed by singers and instrumentalists in different locations around the globe. The result has been, in part, a homogenization of global choral and orchestral sounds and other interpretive practices and a significant reduction in the regional variants that were central to the compositional and performance practices of the long 19th century. Consequently, understanding the sounds of Romantic music as it was created and cultivated before this homogenization occurred—in a word, being faithful to the expectations of various historical composers from different times and places within the long 19th century—amounts in part to exploring and rediscovering practices that have been submerged beneath and obscured by other ones geographically as well as historically alien to those that surrounded the creation of the historical repertoires. Resources for this venture are abundant: in addition to a few historically aware secondary sources (e.g., José Antonio Bowen, ed., *The Cambridge Companion to Conducting* [Cambridge: Cambridge University Press, 2003], and Clive Brown, *Classical and Romantic Performance Practice, 1750–1900* [Oxford: Clarendon, 2002]), the mid- and later 19th century witnessed the publication of dozens of widely circulated books and articles on conducting as it was developing in different ways in different locales. [JMC]

See also EDITING AND EDITIONS.

CONGRESS OF VIENNA. Diplomatic gathering of the major European powers convened in order to restore peace, redraw the map of Europe after the demise of the Napoleonic Empire (*see* FIRST FRENCH EMPIRE), and establish international order after the defeat of Napoléon Bonaparte and the end of the Napoleonic Wars. Its representatives were the four victorious powers (Austria, Great Britain, Prussia, and Russia) plus (thanks to the diplomatic efforts of French foreign minister Charles Maurice de Talleyrand-Périgord) the vanquished France. The Congress was convened on 15 September 1814 and adjourned on 9 June 1815. The ensuing period of relative peace and stability, lasting until the **Revolutions of 1848**, is generally known as the **Restoration** (or, in France, the **Bourbon Restoration**).

From the perspective of musical romanticism, the Congress of Vienna marks an important caesura in the institutions and practices of musical life. Musical production and consumption in Europe had historically relied on the institution of the patronage system. But when the authority of the aristocracy was thrown into question by the Revolution and largely destroyed by the Reign of Terror and its aftermath, music making in the public sphere proliferated—even as the crowned heads of Europe, especially on the Continent, increased censorship in order to prevent the disintegration of the social order that they were witnessing in France from spreading to their own lands. The Napoleonic Wars then threw the Continent into a state of war, with men, material, and financial resources that previously could have been (and were) committed to peaceful civic activities, such as concerts, being committed to defense needs instead.

Moreover, when French troops occupied any given territory that had resisted the tide of the French emperor's armies, its government and governance structure were essentially replaced by personnel and new laws that supported the French Empire and French culture (including music and the other arts) while suppressing opposition, driving resistance underground, and bringing **nationalist** sentiment into focus for the subjects of the Napoleonic regimes. Public compositions more often than ever sported French titles, emulations of French genres and styles proliferated, and the ever-present threat of invasion, eruptions of resistance, and transferrals of governmental authority made the publication and performance of any text or artwork, even if not explicitly political in nature, a risky and sporadic business. In the domains of music, **Ludwig van Beethoven**'s Third **("Eroica") Symphony** and *Fidelio* are but two of innumerable case studies in these causes and effects; in literature, one celebrated instance is **Johann Wolfgang von Goethe**'s *Faust*.

With the Congress of Vienna, much of that changed. Because the male citizenry was no longer away on active duty or awaiting conscription, the Congress of Vienna facilitated a new domestic peace that encouraged both private music making (*see* HAUSMUSIK; SALON) and large-scale public music making (in the form of performances of **opera**, public orchestral concerts, and large public music festivals). The stability of domestic life in turn produced a sizable new market for published instrumental and vocal **chamber music**—a market that led to a burgeoning of the industry of music publishing, developments in **copyright** and intellectual property, and significant advances in the technologies of printing music (*see* PRINTING AND PUBLISHING OF MUSIC).

Perhaps in part because the citizenry had tired of the politically charged rhetoric of recent decades and in part because of the watchful eye of government censors intent on discouraging a proliferation of dissidence sympathetic to the goals that had launched the Revolution to begin with, vocal music more often than before dealt with themes that were domestic and philosophical: love, death, life cycles, childhood, parenting, and so on. Finally, with the Congress of Vienna, the generally pro-French and specifically Napoleonic propaganda and historiography that had been institutionalized in the Revolutionary and Napoleonic regimes ceased, resulting in a need for the various cultures of the Restoration to recenter their narratives of European history and to recover, write, or construct new narratives that were more consistent with the needs of the day. Music, of course, was a potent tool in these cultural/political projects, and it was accorded an important place in the process of education and self-betterment that in the German lands came to be known as *Bildung* (self-realization). These developments resulted in the cultivation, for the first time in musical history, of a stable musical **canon**, the emergence of a newly intense interest in establishing a coherent narrative for the history of music, and a proliferation of journals and other implicitly didactic publications, written by professional musicians with an eye to making contemporary music and its place in larger historical narratives comprehensible to amateurs. [JMC]

CONSERVATORY. (Fr., conservatoire; Ger., Konservatorium, Hochschule für Musik or Musikhochschule; It., conservatorio.) Term for a school specializing in the cultivation of music and, often, one or more of the other fine and performing arts. The first music schools were designated "conservatories" because they were established as orphanages—establishments (usually sponsored by the church and/or the monarchy) that employed music as an important component in the general custodianship of children and young adults. Such schools appeared in Naples and Venice in the early 16th century and continued to proliferate in Europe and the Americas throughout the **long 19th century** with the founding of conservatories in Würzburg (1804), Milan (1807), Florence (1811), Prague (1811), Breslau (1815), Vienna (1816), Warsaw (1821), Vienna (1821), Berlin (1822), London (1822), Königsberg (1824), Rio de Janeiro (1847), Boston (1853), Baltimore (1868), Chicago (1868), Havana (1885), and Buenos Aires (1893).

Conservatories in the modern sense (i.e., secular or only loosely ecclesiastical institutions designed to train professional as well as amateur musicians) began to emerge during the years immediately following the French Revolution, as private, municipal, and state sponsorship increasingly supplanted the authority and responsibility formerly assumed by the church and crown. Despite their differences, these institutions had in common one feature that was otherwise absent or only inconsistently present elsewhere in formal education: they included "applied" or "practical" as well as "academic" education (i.e., instruction in vocal and instrumental technique, often coupled with institutionally sponsored ensembles) as well as "academic" (historical and theoretical) instruction. By far the most influential institution of this new sort was the Conservatoire National Superieur de Musique, established by the French National Convention in 1795 and formally opened for instruction in 1796. Even a partial list of faculty, administrators, and students of the Paris Conservatory (as it is more commonly known) gives an idea of its influence as a shaping institution in musical life during the long 19th century. Among its faculty and directors during this period were **Adolphe Adam, Pierre Baillot, Adrien Boieldieu, Luigi Cherubini, Théodore Dubois, Gabriel**

Fauré, Charles Gounod, Françoise-Antoine Habenek, Fromenthal Halé-vy, Vincent d'Indy, Georges Kastner, Rudolfe Kreutzer, Jean-François Le Sueur, Jules Massenet, Ferdinando Paer, Antoine Reicha, Ambroise Thomas, and Charles-Marie Widor, and among its students were Charles-Valentin Alkan, Hector Berlioz, Georges Bizet, Claude Debussy, Paul Dukas, César Franck, and Camille Saint-Saëns.

In 1828, under Habenek's leadership, the institution sponsored the *Société des concerts du Conservatoire*, a series that ran uninterrupted through 1967 and introduced the Parisian public to some of the most important works of the long 19th century and much of the 20th century. In addition to being the first ensemble to establish **Ludwig van Beethoven**'s presence in French musical life, it gave the premieres of Berlioz's *Episode in the Life of an Artist* and *Grande Messe des morts* (*see* REQUIEM), Saint-Saëns's First Cello **Concerto**, and César Franck's **Symphony** in D Minor, among other works. Finally, the curriculum at the Conservatoire was centered around a series of instruction methods in all courses written by the appropriate faculty members; these texts were periodically updated and replaced as tastes and techniques changed. Because all students at the Conservatoire learned from these texts and based their own teaching on them, the influence of the institution's curriculum and faculty extended far beyond its walls.

The Paris Conservatory as it existed until the mid-19th century still differed from the modern model in that it was primarily regional or national rather than international in makeup, students were admitted from a very early age, and many completed only part of the curriculum. Still, the idea of a specialized formal education designed to rear capable professional musicians under the tutelage of a faculty community of well-known experts was widely emulated (often with the conservatory closely affiliated with a **university**) around the world during the remaining decades of the long 19th century. Important institutions along this line opened in Graz (1817), Innsbruck (1819), Klagenfurt (1828), Pest (1840), and Brno (1862).

The next and final major step in the emergence of the modern conservatory model was taken in the German lands, where King Friedrich Augustus II of Saxony, at the instigation of **Felix Mendelssohn Bartholdy** and several other cultural leaders, chartered a new *Konservatorium* based in Leipzig (today the Hochschule für Musik und Theater Felix Mendelssohn Bartholdy) with an initial roster of six faculty members and 22 students. While based on the Parisian model, the Leipzig Conservatory self-consciously strove for a greater degree of integrated study than its predecessors, chartered as it was to achieve a "higher education [i.e., education for adults and young adults, not children] in . . . all branches of music, seen as a science as well as an art" (i.e., to devote equal or very nearly equal importance to intensive study of applied, historical, and theoretical disciplines). It was closely connected to the Gewandhaus Orchestra, the Leipzig Singakademie, the Leipzig Opera, and the city's lively concert and publishing life. Because of these ties, a new and truly international series of students flocked to the institution; nearly half of the 6,000 students who studied there during its first 50 years were from countries outside the German lands. The roster of faculty includes Mendelssohn, **Ferdinand David, Niels W. Gade, Ignaz Moscheles, Max Reger, Carl Reinecke**, and **Robert** and **Clara Schumann**, and the list of distinguished alumni includes **Isaac Albéniz, Ferruccio Busoni, Frederick Delius, Edvard Grieg, Leoš Janáček, Ethel Smyth**, and **Arthur Sullivan**.

The Leipzig Conservatory's university-like integration of comprehensive knowledge, to which applied and academic areas of study alike were subject, set a new model that was quickly emulated by similar institutions that opened in Cologne (1845), Munich (1846), Berlin (1850, 1855, 1869), Strasbourg (1855), Dresden (1856), Stuttgart (1857), Bern (1858), Lausanne (1861), St. Petersburg (1862), Basel (1866), Moscow (1866), Weimar (1872), Hamburg (1873), Budapest (1875), Zürich (1876), Frankfurt am Main (1878, 1883), Brno (1882), and Karlsruhe (1884), among other places. These institutions, like those more closely modeled on the Paris Conservatory, actively promoted the performance and study of new and challenging contemporary compositions as well as historical repertoires by composers such as **Johann Sebastian Bach, George Frideric Handel**, Beethoven, and **Franz Schubert**.

Although most modern conservatories and schools and colleges of music within universities would acknowledge the Leipzig and/or Paris models as their progenitor, the fact that those institutional cultures emerged and flourished coevally with the establishment of academic, concert, and recital **canons** also had a more problematical consequence: by the end of the 19th century, the meaning of *conservatory* had come to connote musical conservatism rather than custodial education of orphans. That such aspersions did not apply to conservatories as they existed before the highly polemicized musical culture that resulted from the **Revolutions of 1848** and the controversies surrounding the **New German School** did not prevent them from being retroactively applied to conservatory culture as a whole. [JMC]

See also FÉTIS, FRANÇOIS-JOSEPH (1784–1871); RUBINSTEIN [RUBINSHTEYN].

CONTREDANSE, CONTRADANCE, CONTRA DANCE. (Ger., Kontertanz, Contratanz; It., contraddanza; Sp., contradanza.) A family of dances for paired couples, typically in duple meter (either simple or compound) and constructed as a series of eight-measure repeated strains that often are unrelated (though composers sometimes repeated individual strains episodically, thus creating rondo or rondo-like structures). Its prototype was the English country dance, which enjoyed a great vogue in the court of Louis XIV (fl. 1661–1705); the term *contredanse* may be a false cognate of "country dance." The dances were most commonly titled in this Gallicized form during the **long 19th century**. Composers of *contredanses* (designated as such rather than as one of their subtypes) during the long 19th century included **Charles-Valentin Alkan** (1862), **Ludwig van Beethoven** (1802), **Johann Nepomuk Hummel** (1850), **Anatoly Lyadov** (1835), **Wolfgang Amadeus Mozart**, and **Anton Rubinstein** (1854). [JMC]

See also HABANERA; QUADRILLE.

COPYRIGHT AND PERFORMANCE RIGHT. (Fr., droit d'auteur; Ger., Urheberrecht; It., diritti d'autore). The legal right to disseminate a text, musical composition, or other artwork in print, performance, broadcast, and recording. It is both domestic and international, the latter being governed, in whole or in part, on a country-by-country basis by one of seven international copyright conventions: the Bern Convention for the Protection of Literary and Artistic Works (1886) or similar conventions held in Paris (1896), Berlin (1908), Rome (1928), Brussels (1948), Stockholm (1967), and Paris (1971). Although the general intention of international copyright conventions has been to ensure certain basic rights internationally and the basic purpose of domestic copyright law in most countries is to offer the same protections to all who publish or otherwise disseminate a copyrighted work within those countries, these provisions and protections vary from place to place, and not all countries have accepted the copyright provisions of these international conventions. Since the Bern Convention, most countries concur that copyright protection is not contingent on, for example, a claim of copyright being filed or a copy of the work being deposited in the national library, and since the Bern Convention, it has been generally accepted that copyright resides with the original author and his or her heirs for a designated period after his or her death. Beyond these general provisions, however, copyright law and the methods of its implementation vary widely from one country to another.

Until 1886, copyright law and its protections differed significantly from this modern scenario. To begin with, copyright resided with the composer only until he or she arranged for a work's publication; the act of publishing was itself a broad transferral of legal ownership provided that it occurred with the original author's permission. This situation meant that composers had little or no control over the fate or state of their music once they released it for publication: publishers were not obligated to obtain permission from or the collaboration of composers in order to edit, rerelease, resell, or commission and sell arrangements or editions of composers' music. What control the composers did retain was a matter of commercial leverage and a gentlemen's agreement: if a publisher's handling of a given work's dissemination was disagreeable to a composer, he or she was under no obligation to work further with that publisher, a situation that would represent a loss of business for the offending publisher. As a result, composers whose music sold reliably enjoyed greater protection from publishers' abuses, while young and little-known composers were less able to stand up to publishing abuses, copyright infringement, or generally objectionable publishing practices.

Moreover, because there was no international copyright convention until 1886, up to then copyright existed solely within individual countries. This situation meant that the rights and protections afforded individual composi-tions varied according to the various countries in which they were published and that a work published in, for example, France was protected by copyright there but not in, for example, England unless it was also published in Eng-land. As a practical matter, copyright holders before the Bern Convention found no measure of secure protection of their intellectual property unless the work was published simultaneously in at least two different countries; more-over, the works in question were free for publication by other publishers or even other composers until publication under the true original author's name had occurred—a situation that effectively required that publication occur in all countries on a date agreed on by all publishers. Composers who were less well known and works that were nationally specific and therefore less likely to be sold elsewhere were sometimes published in only a single country, but this practice afforded no protection against publishers or individuals in other countries profiting off of the original composer's work.

Most commonly, the necessity of publishing in at least two countries si-multaneously meant that either the original composer or a publisher who had agreed to disseminate the work would arrange for another publisher in an-other country to disseminate it there. Because of the practical and logistical issues of 19th-century printing technologies and publication processes, this led to two production scenarios, neither of which was necessarily advanta-geous for the integrity of the editions produced. In the first scenario, extra copies of the score (*see* HOLOGRAPH) would have to be made (one for each publisher) and delivered to the foreign publishers, who would then produce their own set of proofs and publish the work essentially indepen-dently, either working with in-house proofreaders and engravers or typeset-ters or corresponding with the work's primary publisher. Composers were rarely involved in proofing these editions. Alternatively, once one or more foreign publishers had been designated, a work's primary publisher would have a set of plates delivered to the foreign publisher(s) (ideally after the composer had proofread them), who would then print and distribute the work from those plates. Then as now, larger publishing houses opened branches or partnerships in multiple countries and arranged for the delivery of proofs and other materials among these houses in order to improve accuracy and effi-ciency, control costs, and maximize profit.

These processes, complicated enough for purely instrumental music, be-came all the more complicated in the case of vocal music, regardless of whether the printed scores were to include texts in more than one language or only the foreign translation of the text, since in this situation the best-qualified translators were usually connected to the foreign (secondary) publishers rather than the primary ones. Equally troubling from a modern perspective was that poets had no right to control or profit from composers' settings of their texts once they were printed (a significant difference from today's practice, which requires composers to obtain permission to disseminate music that makes use of others' words). As long as a poem or a **libretto** remained in manuscript and in the possession of the poet, he or she could sell it to a composer or an opera company—but once that transaction had occurred, the text could be freely used, altered, or even appropriated as the basis of a new poem or libretto. This situation was at least partly responsible for **Victor Hugo**'s involvement with the movement that ultimately led to the Bern Convention. [JMC]

See also EDITING AND EDITIONS; PERFORMANCE PRACTICE.

CORNELIUS, (CARL AUGUST) PETER (1824–1874). German composer, actor, poet, translator, and writer on music of the Late Romantic Generation; nephew of the celebrated Nazarene draftsman and painter Peter von Cornelius (1783–1867). He is best remembered today for his German **comic opera** *Der Barbier von Baghdad* (1858; to Cornelius's own **libretto** after the *Thousand and One Nights*; see SHEHERAZADE, OP. 35) and his Christmas **song** *Die Könige* (The Three Kings, Op. 8, no. 3, 1856, rev. 1859), an artful combination of elegant solo vocal melody with the well-known chorale *Wie schön leuchtet der Morgenstern*.

Cornelius was born into a theatrical family and was trained for a dual career as musician and actor, studying violin and music theory from an early age and having a number of songs, choral works, and **string quartets** to his credit by the time he reached age 16. From 1844 to 1852, he lived in Berlin, there studying for two years with Siegfried Dehn (1799–1858), penning his own poems and writings on music, and becoming a well-known figure in the Prussian capital's literary and musical circles. He then moved to Weimar, where he worked as secretary and translator for **Franz Liszt** and published articles arguing for the emergent agenda of the **New German School**. His ardent support for that agenda led to the failure of *Der Barbier von Baghdad* when Liszt conducted its premiere in 1858 and marked the beginning of a souring of Liszt's relationship with the court that led to his resignation in 1861. From 1859 to 1865, Cornelius lived in Vienna, there meeting and becoming a member of the inner circle of **Richard Wagner**. He moved to Munich in 1865 and became professor of harmony and rhetoric at the Munich **Conservatory** in 1867. His second **opera**, the **grand opera** *Der Cid* (The Cid, 1865; libretto by Cornelius), was a success when it was premiered at Weimar and, though rarely heard today, stands as one of the most remarkable German grand operas of the late 19th century. His third opera, *Gunlöd* (to Cornelius's own libretto after the *Edda*), remained unfinished at his death and was posthumously completed by Carl Hoffbauer and Eduard Lassen (first performed Weimar, 1891).

Cornelius designated himself as a *Dichter-Musiker* (poet-musician), an apt characterization of his contributions to the turbulent musical cultures of the mid-19th century in the German lands. As a composer, he was prolific, original, and highly respected, penning five Mass settings; some 16 sacred and secular *Männerchöre*; numerous works for a cappella mixed chorus and vocal duets; 96 **songs** on sacred and secular texts by authors ranging from Cornelius himself through Joseph von Eichendorff (1788–1857), **Johann Wolfgang von Goethe**, **Heinrich Heine**, and Friedrich Hölderlin (1770–1843); four string quartets; and a small quantity of other **orchestral** and instrumental **chamber** works. He also prepared the German translations of numerous works by **Hector Berlioz** and Liszt (including the latter's song cycle based on texts of **Victor Hugo**, 1859). Despite his intense advocacy for the ideas of the New German School, he was never a central figure in that movement, shying away from its polemics and drawing on the styles developed by Liszt and Wagner only occasionally, intermingled with that of other composers as diverse as **Albert Lortzing**, **Felix Mendelssohn Bartholdy**, and **Robert Schumann**. His prose writings and poetry run to four volumes and include, in addition to his original poetry, essays on the artistic relationship between **Fryderyk Chopin** and Liszt, Berlioz, Liszt's **oratorio** *Die Legende der Heiligen Elisabeth*, Wagner, and Wagner's *Lohengrin*, *Die Meistersinger*, and *Tannhäuser*. [JMC]

COUSSEMAKER, (CHARLES-)EDMOND(-HENRI) DE (1805–1876). French musicologist and composer; along with **François-Joseph Fétis**, one of the most influential scholarly voices in the Romantic rediscovery of music of the Middle Ages and Renaissance both as a historical phenomenon and as a source of inspiration for modern musical creation. Although his career was in the field of law (which he studied in Paris from 1825 to 1830) and he held numerous positions in the legal professions from 1830 on, he also studied composition with **Ferdinando Paer** and **Antoine Reicha** in Paris and was a well-respected composer of **overtures**, choral works, **part-songs**, and numerous smaller instrumental and vocal compositions. He was an avid collector and scholar of medieval music manuscripts and treatises on music, eventually amassing a library totaling some 1,600 early manuscripts and instruments.

Coussemaker was also an influential scholar of the development of musical notation, early theories of polyphony, medieval liturgical dramas, and **folk song**—especially Flemish folk song and its relationships to developments in cultivated music in France. He published individual books on Hucbald, medieval instruments, and the development of polyphony between the ninth and 14th centuries, but his most important works were probably his four-volume collection of medieval treatises on music (*Scriptorum de musica medii ævi novam seriem a Gerbertina alteram collegit nuncque primum*, 1860–1876) and his edition of the complete works of Adam de la Halle (*Oeuvres complètes du trouvère Adam de la Halle [poésies et musique]*, 1872), which provided essential documentary evidence to support the emerging contemporary construction of Adam as the quintessential folk hero who created great literature and music.

Coussemaker was a recipient of the Légion d'honneur and titleholder of the Ordre de Saint-Grégoire le Grand as well as being a member of the Académie royale de belgique correspondent of the Institut de France and a member of some 25 academic societies. His meticulous attention to detail and comparatively objective scholarly method made his work less readily appealing and immediately influential than the more populist and generalized contemporaneous work of, for example, Fétis, but these same attributes increased his appeal to scholars and composers of later generations. [JMC]

CSÁRDÁS (CZÁRDÁS). *See* STYLE HONGROIS.

CUI, CÉSAR |KYUI, TSEZAR ANTONOVICH| (1835–1918). Russian **nationalist** composer and critic of the Late Romantic Generation; member of the **Mighty Handful** and one of the **long 19th century**'s most important contributors to the genre of the **romance**. The son of a Lithuanian peasant and a French army officer who stayed behind after Napoléon Bonaparte's retreat in 1812, he trained primarily as a structural engineer in Vilnius. He graduated from the Academy of Military Engineering in 1857 and worked as a lecturer at that institution until 1879, when he became a professor there; he was regarded as an expert in the field of structural fortifications. He also published numerous reviews and articles on music in Russian and French papers, including the *Revue et gazette musicale de Paris* (*see REVUE MUSICALE*). Among his most important books in music were a study of **Richard Wagner**'s *Ring of the Nibelung* (1889, 2nd ed. 1909) and *Russkiy romans: Ocherk yego razvitiya* (The Russian Art **Song**: A Study of Its Development, 1896).

That Cui made his living outside the domains of music was typical of the Mighty Handful, and so was his ardency in asserting the necessity of a distinctively Russian musical style based on language and informed by **folk song**. He was unusual among the composers of that group, however, in his cultivation of **miniatures** and **opera** and his relatively small output of large **orchestral** works. He composed a modest quantity of **part-songs** and small choral works, three **string quartets** and 11 other *opera* of short instrumental **chamber** works, two **mazurkas**, and 27 other *opera* of miniatures for **piano** solo. The most important portion of his orchestral oeuvre is his four **suites** (1882, 1887, 1887, and 1890), and in 1916 he composed *Slava* for military band. He composed a total of 16 **comic** and serious **operas** and collaborated with **Nikolai Rimsky-Korsakov** to complete the **overture** to **Aleksandr Dargomïzhsky**'s *The Stone Guest*. Of his operas, the most important are considered to be *Vil'yam Ratklif* (William Ratcliff, 1869; the first opera by a member of the Mighty Handful to be staged), *Saratsin* (The Saracen, 1896–1898), *Pir vo vremya chumï* (A Feast in Time of Plague) and *Kapitanskaya dochka* (1900 and 1909; both after **Aleksandr Pushkin**), and the children's opera/fairy tale *Kot v sapogakh* (Puss in Boots, 1913). He was made a member of the Institut de France in 1894. [JMC]

CUNHA, BRASÍLIO ITIBERÊ DA (1846–1913). Brazilian composer, pianist, diplomat, and lawyer of the Late Romantic Generation, author of the **piano fantasy** *A sertaneja* (The Hinterland, 1869), one of the earliest contributions to Brazilian musical **nationalism**. Da Cunha was trained as a pianist from an early age in his native São Paulo but received his degree in law, continuing to perform and study music while engaged in that venture. Upon graduation, he entered the diplomatic corps, serving in Italy, Belgium, Germany, Paraguay, and Peru and winning the respect of European musical luminaries, including **Franz Liszt** and **Anton Rubinstein**. Although the forms of his music and his style in general reflect his fluency in the idioms of Western European musical Romanticism, he is important as one of the first composers to integrate specifically Brazilian elements of urban popular music into his works. In addition to many compositions for piano solo, his output includes many choral compositions and some instrumental **chamber music**. [JMC]

CYCLIC FORM. Term coined by **Vincent d'Indy** in describing the music of **César Franck**. It denotes any music in which thematic material from one section or movement is reintroduced later in the same work; it was one of the most widely cultivated conceits of music in the **long 19th century**. Strictly speaking, only works that bring back material from the opening at the conclusion are truly cyclic, but Romantic views of the concept also embraced more general applications: important to 19th-century composers was not only the sense of ordered form and unity provided by returning to a given theme but also the rhetorical gesture of closure, of arriving at a goal that affirmed the figurative journey undertaken over the course of the work. Coupled with more specific thematic procedures, such as developing variation, **idée fixe**, *Leitfaden* and **Leitmotiv**, and **thematic transformation**, this general rhetorical model imparted to Romantic music a means of enriching the **narrative**

processes of music and creating a sense of direction and fulfillment that were, in the eyes of the Romantics at least, greater than those provided by "simple" linear form or series of unrelated movements.

Well-known literal examples of cyclic form include **Ludwig van Beethoven**'s **concert aria** *Ah, perfido!*/*Per pietà* (Op. 65, 1796) and A-major Piano **Sonata** (Op. 101, 1816, publ. 1817); Brahms's Third **Symphony** (Op. 90, comp. 1883, publ. 1884); **Felix Mendelssohn Bartholdy**'s String Quartet in A Minor (MWV R22/Op. 13, 1827, publ. 1830), *Hebrides Overture* (MWV P7/Op. 26, 1829, publ. 1832), and A-minor ("Scottish") Symphony (MWV N18/Op. 56, comp. 1829, 1841–1842, publ. 1842); the first movement of **Franz Schubert**'s "Great" C-major Symphony (D. 944, ca. 1825–1828); and **Pyotor Il'yich Tchaikovsky**'s **Serenade** for Strings (Op. 48, comp. 1880, publ. 1881) and Fourth and Fifth Symphonies (opp. 36 and 64, comp. 1877–1878 and 1888, publ. 1880 and 1888, respectively). Freer applications of the idea occur most famously in Beethoven's Fifth Symphony (Op. 67, comp. 1807–1808, publ. 1809) and **Hector Berlioz**'s *Episode in the Life of an Artist* (H. 48/Op. 14[A], 1830, publ. 1845) and *Harold in Italy* (H. 68/Op. 16, comp. 1834, publ. 1848) but also in **Anton Bruckner**'s Seventh Symphony (Op. 107, comp. 1881–1883, publ. 1884), **Antonín Dvořák**'s Eighth and Ninth Symphonies (S. 109/Op. 88 and S. 117/Op. 95, comp. 1889 and 1893, publ. 1892 and 1894), Franck's Symphony in D Minor (Op. 48, comp. 1886–1888, publ. 1890), **Fanny Hensel**'s String Quartet in E-flat Major (H-U 277, 1834), **Franz Liszt**'s B-Minor Piano Sonata (LW A179, comp. 1852–1853, publ. 1854), most of **Gustav Mahler**'s symphonies, and **Robert Schumann**'s Second and Fourth Symphonies (opp. 61 and 120, comp. 1845–1846 and 1841/1851, publ. 1847 and 1853), to name but a few examples.

Two of the most important examples of the **long 19th century**'s fascination with cyclic form occur in the **piano** cycle (such as Robert Schumann's *Papillons* [Op. 2, comp. 1830–1831, publ. 1831] and *Carnaval* [Op. 9, comp. 1834–1835, publ. 1837]) and the **song cycle**. Although many song cycles (e.g., Schubert's *Die schöne Müllerin* and *Winterreise*) do not restate previously given material, some do (among them Mendelssohn's 1830 song cycle [MWV K57–60] and Schumann's *Dichterliebe* [Op. 48, comp. 1840, publ. 1843–1844]). [JMC]

See also ORGANICISM; VARIATION.

CZERNY, CARL [KARL] (1791–1857). Austrian **piano** teacher, pianist, composer, arranger, theorist, and historian. He was instrumental in establishing **Ludwig van Beethoven**'s **piano** works in the emergent concert and recital **canon**, and his editions of Beethoven's piano music combined with his other writings to help shape the late 19th-century construction of Beethoven (*see* RECEPTION). He was also active in disseminating other composers' works to the musical public, authoring and publishing several hundred highly regarded arrangements for piano solo or **piano duet** (*see* PRINTING AND PUBLISHING OF MUSIC). His many theoretical and didactic writings are a rich source of information concerning piano technique during a profound period of change for both the instrument and its technique. His 861 numbered *opera* include six **symphonies**, one piano **concerto**, and one concerto for piano duet; six **sonatas** and eight sonatinas for piano duet; five **piano trios**; one violin sonata and two violin sonatinas; and a sizable body of Catholic choral music. In addition to these published works there are several unpublished concertos and a number of unpublished instrumental pieces as well as 11 unpublished Mass settings and many other sacred choral works.

Czerny's influence as a pedagogue was achieved in part through his many widely disseminated, translated, and reprinted didactic works for piano solo or **piano duet**. His most important original compositions include the *48 Études en forme de préludes et cadences* (48 Études in the Form of Preludes and Cadenzas, Op. 161, 1829), *Fantasie-Schule* (School of Improvisation, 2 vols., opp. 200 and 300, 1829 and 1833), *Schule der Geläufigkeit* (School of Velocity, Op. 229b, 1835), *Die Schule des Legato und Staccato* (School of Legato and Staccato, Op. 335, 1834), *Die Schule des Virtuosen* (School of Virtuosity, Op. 365, ca. 1837), *Die Schule des Fugenspiels und des Vortrags mehrstimmiger Sätze und deren besonderer Schwierigkeiten auf dem Piano-Forte* (School of Playing Fugue and of Performing Polyphonic Music, and of Its Particular Difficulties on the Piano, Op. 400, 1836), *Vollständige theoretisch-praktische Pianoforte-Schule* (Complete Theoretical and Practical School of Piano, Op. 500, 3 vols., 1839), and *Schule der praktischen Tonsetzkunst* (School of Practical Composition, Op. 600, ca. 1849). He also published an *Umriß der ganzen Musik-Geschichte* (Outline of the Whole of Music History, Op. 815, 1851) and made the ideas of the irreverent French composer and theorist **Antoine Reicha** accessible to German speakers by translating five of his most important treatises into German. The four-volume *Vollständiges Lehrbuch der musikalischen Composition* (Complete Textbook for Musical Composition, 1834) is a translation of Reicha's *Cours de composition musicale* (1816–1818), *Traité de mélodie* (Treatise on Melody, 1814), and two-volume *Traité de haute composition musicale* (1824–1826), and *Die Kunst der dramatischen Composition* (The Art of Composition for the Stage, 1835) is a translation of Reicha's *Art du compositeur dramatique* (Art of the Dramatic Composer, 1833).

Czerny was born in Vienna and studied piano with his father from the age of three; by the age of 10 he was able to play most of the standard repertoire at a professional level. He was introduced to Beethoven in the winter of 1799–1800 and studied with him for a time; Beethoven eventually entrusted him with the proofreading of many of his scores and with preparing the piano/vocal arrangement of *Fidelio* in 1805. He was one of Vienna's most respected piano teachers by the time he reached the age of 15 and reported (credibly) that he gave 12 lessons per day (from 8:00 a.m. to 8:00 p.m.) from then until he retired from teaching in 1836. **Robert Schumann** described him and his music in decidedly unflattering terms, but the volume of Czerny's publications and their translations (usually an indication that a composer's reputation was sufficient to make his or her music commercially viable) and the roster of his pupils and admirers paint a different picture: he taught the young **Franz Liszt** for two years beginning in 1821 and was a friend and correspondent of **Fryderyk Chopin**, and the roster of his many other distinguished students includes **Stephen Heller** and **Sigismond Thalberg**. [JMC]

D

DANCE OF DEATH. *See TOTENTANZ.*

DARGOMÏZHSKY, ALEKSANDR (SERGEYEVICH) (1813–1869).
Russian amateur composer, pianist, and vocal pedagogue, after **Mikhail
Glinka** one of the most important figures in Russian **opera** and **song** before
the rise of **Pyotor Il'yich Tchaikovsky** and the **Mighty Handful**. His third
opera, *Rusalka* (1848–1855), on his own **libretto** after **Aleksandr Pushkin**,
is a landmark in Russian opera. He carried its approach further in his subsequent works, most importantly his sixth and final opera, *Kamennïy gost'*
(The Stone Guest), begun in 1866 and posthumously completed by **César
Cui**, a literal setting to music of Pushkin's poetic drama of the same name
(1830) after the Spanish legend of **Don Juan** (with elements from Lorenzo
Da Ponte's and **Wolfgang Amadeus Mozart**'s *Don Giovanni*). Pushkin's
text was ideally suited to Dargomïzhsky's goals by this point in his career—
he wrote in 1857, "I want the note to express the word directly. I want
truth"—since aside from a duel, it consists entirely of dialogue, which
Dargomïzhsky set in a new style of accompanied recitative. On the whole,
the style of *The Stone Guest* vividly anticipates the approach to music, drama, declamation, and a distinctively Russian character that was later realized
more famously in **Modest Mussorgsky**'s *Boris Godunov*.

Dargomïzhsky was the son of a wealthy landowner and moved easily in
the aristocratic circles of imperial Russia, performing as a pianist in St.
Petersburg's **salons** and writing **songs** for performance in those venues. He
was a friend and artistic colleague of Glinka from 1833 until the end of the
older composer's life and also enjoyed the respect of the Mighty Handful. In
addition to his six operas, he authored four **programmatic** or characteristic
orchestral works, nearly 100 vocal **chamber** works (songs, vocal duets, and
part-songs), and a number of **character pieces** for **piano** solo and **piano
duet**. [JMC]

DAVID, FÉLICIEN (-CÉSAR) (1810–1876). French composer of the Romantic Generation. David began to encounter Middle Eastern music cultures in his early 20s; ultimately, this would mark his compositional output and legacy indelibly. His *Le désert* (1844, publ. 1845) gained him immediate and fairly lasting recognition as a significant composer, and it initiated a long line of French orientalist compositions (*see* EXOTICISM).

Orphaned at age five when his father died, David sang as a choirboy and received formal musical training in the Maîtrise Saint-Sauveur at Aix-en-Provence. He attended Lycée at the Jesuit college in that city at age 15. When he finished three years later, he found work briefly as an assistant theater conductor and then—for one year—as chapel master at Saint-Sauveur Cathedral. In 1830, David left for Paris and studied briefly at the Paris **Conservatory**, where he encountered monumental figures such as **François-Joseph Fétis** and **Luigi Cherubini**. In 1831, David joined the Saint-Simonians, among whom he thrived and for whom he provided many new ceremonial compositions, particularly choral music. He traveled with some of his cohorts eastward across the Mediterranean in 1833 after the Saint-Simonians were disbanded. David lived in Cairo until 1835. While there, he developed a profound enthusiasm for a collection of musical styles and **topics** that, when translated into the idiom of Western art music, eventually was to find welcoming audiences in a France soon to be smitten by orientalism.

For nearly a decade after returning to Paris, David struggled for success as a composer and produced works in a variety of genres, including **songs**, instrumental **chamber music**, and **symphonies**. David's 1844 composition *Le désert*, an *ode-symphonie* for narrator, solo tenor, men's chorus, and **orchestra** in three movements, finally established his reputation as a formidable composer when it premiered that December. This work transports the listener with a vivid blend of imagery-laden titles, depictive settings, and sounds from David's time in Cairo, the boldest among them certainly being the surprisingly realistic Muslim call to prayer in the third movement ("Chant du Muezzin"). In the wake of *Le désert*, numerous other French composers capitalized on the thrill that the notion of the East brought to listeners, particularly in opera; notable examples include **Giacomo Meyerbeer**'s *L'Africaine* (1865), **Georges Bizet**'s *Les pêcheurs de perles* (1863) and *Djamileh* (1872), and **Camille Saint-Saëns**'s *Samson et Dalila* (1877). [RK]

DAVID, FERDINAND (1810–1873). German violinist, composer, and pedagogue of the Romantic Generation; the most important German violinist before **Joseph Joachim**. He studied violin with **Louis Spohr** and theory with Moritz Hauptmann (1792–1868) before undertaking a tour with his pianist sister in 1823–1825 and playing in the Königstadt Theater (Berlin) from 1826 to 1829. From 1829 to 1835, he played in a private quartet in Tartu (Estonia), then returned to Leipzig in 1836, serving as concertmaster of the

Gewandhaus Orchestra under the direction of **Felix Mendelssohn Bartholdy** (whom he had befriended in Berlin in the 1820s) until 1873. He became director of the violin department at the newly opened Leipzig **Conservatory** in 1843 and over the coming decades was also increasingly active as a **conductor.** In 1840, he gave the first public performance of two movements from **Johann Sebastian Bach**'s Sonatas and Partitas for Unaccompanied Violin (the Preludio from the E-major Partita, BWV 1004, and the "**Chaconne**" from the D-minor Partita, BWV 1006, both with improvised **piano** accompaniment by Mendelssohn), and in 1845 he gave the first performance of Mendelssohn's Violin **Concerto** in E Minor (MWV O14/Op. 64).

David's many compositions include 50 numbered *opera* of original compositions comprising instrumental and vocal **chamber** music, one psalm setting, five violin concertos, one trombone concertino (Op. 4, 1837) and one bassoon concerto (Op. 12, 1850) as well as other works for **orchestra** with and without solo instruments. His *Die Hohe Schule des Violinspiels: Werke berühmter Meister des 17ten und 18ten Jahrhunderts* (The Fine Art of Playing the Violin: Works of Celebrated Masters of the 17th and 18th Centuries, 1863) was widely used and reprinted. Although he was widely respected as a composer in the 19th century, his most long-lasting contributions were as a teacher and editor. His edition of Bach's Sonatas and Partitas presents the Urtext of those previously obscure works along with David's detailed realization, the latter demonstrating how they were performed and taught in his classes at the Leipzig Conservatory. [JMC]

DAVIDSBUND. (Ger., "league of David.") Imaginary society of progressive musicians leagued together to combat the forces of philistinism in music. The society was invented by **Robert Schumann**, probably after the model of the *Doppelgänger* in **Jean Paul Richter**'s *Flegeljahre* (1804–1805), in his music criticism in the *Neue Zeitschrift für Musik*. The league comprised a set of narrative personae, each possessing a distinct personality and espousing different aesthetic values, who interacted with one another in novelistic fashion and thus made music criticism into a work of creative imagination rather than third-person reportage. Some of the names of the *Davidsbündler* (the league's members) were taken from Jean Paul's writings. others from the *commedia dell'arte.* Many represented individuals from Schumann's own immediate circle of friends and colleagues: "Florestan" (brash, impulsive, and passionate) and "Eusebius" (contemplative and melancholy) represented Schumann's own impetuous and reflective sides, respectively. "Chiara" or "Chiarina" represented his eventual wife **Clara Schumann**; "Felix Meritis," **Felix Mendelssohn Bartholdy**; "Jeanquirit," **Stephen Heller**; and "Master Raro," Friedrich Wieck (1785–1873), the respected piano pedagogue (and Schumann's eventual father-in-law) whose persona tends to be old-fashioned or pedantic.

The *Davidsbund* also made appearances in Schumann's music. The set of **character pieces** published in 1837 as his op. 6 was titled *Davidsbündlertänze* (Dances of the *Davidsbund*) in its first edition and then revised and retitled simply *Davidsbündler* (Members of the League of David) in the second edition (issued in 1850–1851). Similarly, his *Carnaval* (Op. 9, 1834–1834, publ., 1837) includes movements specifically titled "Eusebius" (no. 5), "Florestan" (no. 6), and "Chiarina" (no. 11) as well as a concluding *Marche des Davidsbündler contres les Philistins* (March of the *Davidsbündler* against the Philistines) that vividly contraposes music readily associable with the League of David with the traditional Grandfather's Dance (*see* KEHRAUS). Although the presence of the *Davidsbündler* in Schumann's music and prose is sometimes held to be an early manifestation of a sort of split personality and a prefiguring of his mental collapse in February 1854, that collapse is now known to have been a comparatively sudden phenomenon, and the notion that he suffered from gradual mental deterioration is widely considered fiction. Rather, his creation and use of the *Davidsbund* represents a sophisticated and innovative application to music and music criticism of an important conceit of literary Romanticism. [JMC]

DE CASTILLON, ALEXIS. *See* CASTILLON (DE SAINT-VICTOR), (MARIE-)ALEXIS, VICOMTE DE (1838–1873).

DEATH AND THE MAIDEN. A **topic** in European art, dating back at least as far as the 16th century, in which a beautiful young woman is abducted by Death, often inflected erotically with kissing, groping, and nudity. An offshoot of the *Totentanz* (in which numerous stations of humanity are encountered by Death), the "Death and the maiden" topic can be found in such early examples as Hans Baldung Grien's *Der Tod und das Mädchen* (1517) and *Tod und Frau* (Death and Woman, 1518–1520), Niklaus Manuel Deutsch's Bern *Totentantz* fresco (Dance of the Dead, 1517), Hans Schwarz's *Der Tod und das Mädchen* (ca. 1520), and Hans Sebald's *Der Tod und das stehende nackte Weib* (Death and Nude Standing Woman, 1547).

As with the *Totentanz* itself, this topic saw a revival in the 19th century, most famously in **Franz Schubert**'s **Lied** "Der Tod und das Mädchen" (D. 531, 1817) and his String Quartet No. 14 in D minor (D. 810, 1824). Schubert sets a 1775 poem of the same name by Matthius Claudius (1740–1815). In Claudius's eight-line poem, the first four lines are written in the **voice** of the maiden, who recognizes Death and begs him to leave her alone. Death responds by complimenting the maiden's beauty, promising not to hurt her, and assuring her that she will sleep well in his arms. Schubert wrote most of the Lied—including the **piano** prelude, Death's four lines, and a postlude—in a hauntingly simple style consisting almost entirely of dactylic rhythms, with the maiden's four lines the one passionate episode that pulls away from the otherwise solemn, processional song. In the string quartet, which Schubert composed in the spring of 1824 while seriously ill, Schubert transformed the simple melody from his Lied into a slow movement, a theme and **variations** in G minor (the other movements are in D minor). [RK]

DEBUSSY, (ACHILLE-)CLAUDE (1862–1918). French composer, **conductor,** pianist, and writer on music of the Modern Romantic Generation; one of his generation's most influential sources of inspiration for musical innovation in the 20th century. His imaginative harmonies and cultivation of an aesthetic that celebrated sensual beauty and pleasure rather than traditional values centering on tonal coherence, large-scale developmental forms, and a sense of telos made him the personification of musical **impressionism** as well as a leading figure in fin-de-siècle France's attempts to develop and cultivate a distinctively and unequivocally Gallic style of music that could rival and surpass the tides of *Wagnerisme* that swept that country and the worlds of European-influenced music during the late 19th and early 20th centuries. His originality in embracing influences as diverse as Javanese gamelan, symbolist poetry, and (paradoxically) **Wagnerism** was matched by his imagination in using whole-tone, pentatonic, and octatonic scales; streaming series of functionally unrelated chords; and his seventh, ninth, and eleventh chords as dissonances that neither required nor solicited resolution, enabling him to profoundly rethink the melodic, harmonic, and structural idioms post-Romantic music's celebration of intense, lushly beautiful sound.

Debussy had little formal education in music or anything else but in 1872 was admitted to classes in piano and theory at the Paris **Conservatory,** where he also later studied **conducting.** In 1879, he began to compose *mélodies,* and in 1880, Nadezhda von Meck (patron of **Pyotor Il'yich Tchaikovsky**) engaged him to teach her children and travel with her and her children to Vienna, Switzerland, and Moscow. Despite his general absence and his lackluster performance in most of his classes, in 1884 he won the Conservatory's prestigious **Prix de Rome,** under which he spent two years (1884–1885) in Rome; it was to one of the works he sent home from that sojourn that the term *impressionism* now so indelibly associated with his name was first applied, with derisive reference to the contemporary vogue in French graphic arts. In 1888 and 1889, he visited the **Bayreuth** Festival, and in 1889 he also was enthralled by the sounds of a Javanese gamelan at the Paris Exposition universelle. After the public success of the premiere of the *Prélude à "L'après-midi d'un faune"* (a **tone poem** after Mallarmé's eponymous poem) in 1893, his fame began to increase, and by 1901 he had begun his work as a critic, employing in much of his witty and incisive writing the fictitious persona of "M. Cloche" (a critical strategy similar to that of Robert Schumann's **Davidsbund**). He traveled widely in England, Russia, and the

Continent and was named to the Légion d'Honneur in 1903. In 1909, at **Gabriel Fauré**'s invitation, he became a member of the directorial board of the Conservatory. His renown continued to grow—by 1913, he had been the subject of some six book-length life-and-works studies—but in 1910 he began exhibiting symptoms of cancer, and it was this illness that took his life in 1918.

Although Debussy's name is indelibly associated with the post-Romantic idiom of impressionism, the outbreak of World War I seems to have prompted a stylistic change; many of his works after 1914 adopt a more detached and austere aesthetic that lends itself less readily to description as "Romantic." His creative output as whole, both literary and musical, consists of nearly as many incomplete as completed projects. The musical oeuvre for the stage comprises one completed **opera** and three incomplete ones, two completed **ballets** and a children's ballet, one set of **incidental music** and the flute piece *Syrinx* (written for use in Gabriel Mourey's *Psyché [Flûte de Pan]*), and the *12 Chansons de Bilitis* for recitation and performance with **tableaux vivants** and pantomime, performed in a **salon** in 1901. He also composed one **symphony** (for **piano duet**, 1880–1881), four concertante works, one tone poem, and six **suites** for **orchestra**; 10 **cantatas** and other works for vocal soloists, chorus, and orchestra; one **piano trio**, one **string quartet**, three **sonatas**, and several other instrumental chamber works; three **part-songs** and 88 **mélodies** and vocal duets; and much music for solo **piano**, piano duet, and two pianos. His best-known works are the opera *Pelléas et Mellisande* (1902, rev. and publ. 1907), the *Prélude à "L'après-midi d'un faune"* (1894, publ. 1895), and the ***Nocturnes*** for orchestra (1897–1899, publ. 1901); the symphonic suite *La mer* (1903–1905, publ. 1905, rev. and publ. 1910); the piano collections *Estampes* (1903), *Images* (two sets, 1905 and 1907), and ***Préludes*** (two books, 1910 and 1913); the string quartet (1893, publ. 1894) and cello sonata (1915); and numerous **songs**, including the *Ariettes oubliées* (texts by Verlaine, 1885–1888, publ. together 1903), *Cinq poèmes de Baudelaire* (1887–1889), and *Trois poèmes de Mallarmé* (1913). [JMC]

DEFORMATION. Term coined by musicologist James A. Hepokoski (1946–) in collaboration with music theorist Warren Darcy to describe a given work's deviation, usually near the end, from expectations established by its genre, **paratextual** elements, and intrinsic processes. Indebted to theories of musical cognition, genre, hermeneutics, intertextuality, narratology, and semeiotics, the concept of deformation views deviations from established norms not as deficiencies—a common and arbitrarily invoked tendency of much earlier scholarship—but as compositional choices taken in response either to some intrinsic aspect of a given work (especially a programmatic subject or theme) or to a particular message or interpretation that the composer wished to suggest to listeners. Hepokoski first developed the concept in essays on **Richard Strauss**'s *Macbeth* and *Don Juan* (refer to the bibliography). Despite criticisms that this concept, developed in part to explain nonnormative processes, can itself become normative, the theory continues to figure centrally in scholarly explanations of complex instrumental forms and processes, especially **sonata forms** of the late 19th and early 20th centuries. It has been usefully applied to works by **Anton Bruckner, Franz Liszt, Gustav Mahler, Jean Sibelius,** and Richard Strauss. [JMC]

See also NARRATIVE; PROGRAM (PROGRAMMATIC) MUSIC.

DELIBES, (CLÉMENT-PHILIBERT-)LÉO (1836–1891). French composer of the Late Romantic Generation. After studying at the Paris **Conservatory**, the young Delibes began to compose **operetta** prolifically while working as a church organist, accompanist, and theater chorus master until his mid-30s. Among his earliest successes were his operetta *Deux vieilles gardes* (Two Old Guards, 1856) and the **ballet** *La Source* (The Spring, 1866).

The early 1870s was a turning point for Delibes, whose ballet *Coppélia, ou La fille aux yeux d'émail* (Coppelia, or The Girl with Enamel Eyes) premiered in 1870 at the Opéra. The success of *Coppélia*, which is based on **E. T. A. Hoffmann**'s *Die Puppe* (The Doll) and *Der Sandmann* (The Sandman), prompted Delibes to limit his professional activities to composition. He married in 1871. Another ballet, *Sylvia, ou La nymphe de Diane* (Sylvia, or The Nymph of Diana, 1876), was not particularly well received; its current fame (with its iconic "Pizzicati") owes largely to the 1952 revival by the British Royal Ballet. Delibes was appointed to the Paris Conservatory in 1881. His opera *Lakmé* (1883, Opéra-Comique), on a love affair between a Hindu priestess and a British military officer, is best known today for its famous Flower Duet. *Lakmé* is among the most salient examples of mid- to late 19th-century European **exoticism**. [RK]

DELIUS, FREDERICK [FRITZ] (THEODOR ALBERT) (1862–1934). British composer of German parentage; member of the Modern Romantic Generation. Born into a family of merchants, he studied **piano** and violin as a child but was expected to go into the family's wool business. After his father became convinced that he would not succeed in that field, he arranged for him to assume managerial duties on an orange plantation in Solana Grove (on the Atlantic coast of Florida) in 1884—a venture that failed but that initiated a friendship and intensive music lessons with Thomas F. Ward (ca. 1856–1912) and exposed Delius, much to his delight, to African American slave music. In 1886, he enrolled at the Leipzig **Conservatory**, where he studied with Salomon Jadassohn (1831–1902) and **Carl Reinecke** and befriended **Edvard Grieg**. The Scandinavian composer both convinced Delius's father that his son's musical aspirations were appropriate and necessary and recommended Delius to his own publisher, Augener & Co.—an act of musical mentorship comparable to **Robert Schumann**'s on behalf of **Johannes Brahms** or Brahms's on behalf of **Antonín Dvořák**.

Delius moved to Paris in 1888 and became part of the circle that included French painter Paul Gauguin (1848–1903), modernist composer Maurice Ravel, Norwegian painter and printmaker Edvard Munch (1863–1944), and Swedish playwright August Strindberg (1849–1912)—but in 1895 he also contracted syphilis. His reputation began to grow especially in Germany during the 1890s, and by the early 1900s he was also known in his native England. His health declined steadily after 1918. Over the course of the 1920s, he continued composing even as he became paralyzed, blind, and increasingly dependent on an amanuensis; his last public appearance was at a six-day London festival of his music organized by Sir Thomas Beecham in 1929.

Delius's life as a composer is unusual in the **long 19th century** because he got a late start and matured rather slowly; only at age 37 was he able to complete a composition generally deemed a masterpiece (*Paris: A Nocturne [Song of a Great City]*, for **orchestra**, 1901). Other important works include the First Piano **Concerto** (1896, rev. 1906), *Appalachia* (orig. written for orchestra, 1896, rev. for chorus and orchestra, 1903); the nonliturgical *Mass of Life* (1904–1905; on texts from **Friedrich Nietzsche**'s *Also sprach Zarathustra*), and the **tone poems** *Brigg Fair* (1907), *On Hearing the First Cuckoo in Spring* (1912), and *North Country Sketches* (1914). His 1901 **opera** *A Village Romeo and Juliet* (troped from **William Shakespeare**) is generally considered the best of his six works in that genre. He also composed numerous **songs** and **part-songs** on Danish, English, French, German, and Norwegian texts and a small quantity of music for **piano** solo and instrumental **chamber** ensemble. [JMC]

EIN DEUTSCHES REQUIEM, **OP. 45**. (Ger., "A German Requiem.") Title of a work by **Johannes Brahms** for soprano and baritone soloists, chorus, and **orchestra**, with ad libitum organ. Its full title is *Ein deutsches Requiem: Nach Worten der Heiligen Schrift* (A German Requiem, after Words from the Holy Scripture). The work's texts were compiled by Brahms himself from Martin Luther's translation of the Bible (including the Apocrypha). It consists of seven movements: (1) *Selig sind, die da Leid tragen* (texts from Matthew 5:4 and Psalm 126:5–6), (2) *Denn alles Fleisch, es ist wie Gras* (1 Peter 1:24; James 5:7; 1 Peter 1:25; Isaiah 35:10), (3) *Herr, lehre doch mich* (Psalm 39:5–8 [Engl. vv. 4–7] and The Wisdom of Solomon 3:1), (4) *Wie lieblich sind diene Wohnungen* (Psalm 84:2,3,5 [Engl. vv. 1,2,4]), (5) *Ihr habt nun Traurigkeit* (John 16:22; Ecclesiastes 51:35 [Engl. v. 27]; Isaiah

66:13), (6) *Denn wir haben hier kleine bleibende Statt* (Hebrews 13:14; 1 Corinthians 15:51–52,54–55; Revelation 4:11), and (7) *Selig sind die Toten* (Revelation 14:13).

Brahms began composing the *Deutsches Requiem* in 1865 and conducted the first three movements in Vienna on 1 December 1867. He conducted a version including all but the fifth movement in Bremen on 10 April 1868. A month later he inserted the fifth movement in memory of his mother, and **Carl Reinecke** conducted a revised version of the complete work in Leipzig on 18 February 1869. It was published in full score and piano-vocal score by J. Rieter-Biedermann (Leipzig) in 1869, with English and French translations appearing in 1873 and 1875, respectively.

The title of the work reflects the fact that while all its texts are ruminations on death, making it conceptually appropriate as a funeral composition (like a **Requiem**), it is specifically German, drawing on Martin Luther's translations of biblical rather than liturgical texts. The use of the Apocrypha as well as authorized canonical texts further removes the work from any possible liturgical use. The movements adopt the clearly sectional, phrase-by-phrase form of text setting familiar from both the Latin Mass and the **motet**. [JMC]

DIABELLI, ANTON (1781–1858). Austrian music publisher and composer; the most important early publisher of the music of **Franz Schubert** and of early reissues of several works by **Ludwig van Beethoven**, among others. He studied music as a child and learned from Michael Haydn (1737–1806) in Salzburg before entering a monastery in Raitenhaslach at age nine, but in 1803 the Bavarian government dissolved the country's monasteries and convents in the wake of the expansion of France (*see* FIRST FRENCH EMPIRE). Diabelli relocated to Vienna, where he composed and made a living teaching **piano** and guitar, also working as a proofreader for the music publisher S. A. Steiner & Co. In 1818, he and Pietro Cappi (a former joint proprietor of **Artaria** who owned an art dealership in Vienna) set up the new firm of Cappi & Diabelli, renamed Diabelli & Cie when Cappi retired in 1824. Cappi was succeeded as Diabelli's partner by Anton Spina (1790–1857).

The firm developed an enormous list in the prosperous musical culture of the **Restoration** and was able to take over several other, smaller firms. On Diabelli's retirement in 1851, it passed to Spina's son Carl Anton, who in turn was succeeded by his son, who renamed it *C. A. Spina, vormals Diabelli* (formerly Diabelli) and in 1856 was able to purchase the competing firm of Mechetti. The firm continued to prosper, publishing the music of **Johann Strauss (II)**, among others, but in 1879 it merged with the Hamburg firm of August Cranz. The numbers of the plates (one number per edition, including the editions of the firms subsumed into Diabelli) had reached 24,670 by the time of the merger with Cranz.

From the outset, Diabelli's firm and its successors demonstrated a shrewd business approach that amounted to publishing sizable quantities of entertainment music in order to effectively subsidize the higher costs and smaller profits of lengthier, more serious works that would sell in smaller quantities. This approach made it possible for Diabelli to publish the *opera* 1 and 2 of the then relatively obscure Franz Schubert in 1821 (*Erlkönig* [D. 328, 1815] and *Gretchen am Spinnrade* [D. 118, 1814]), establishing a lifelong relationship with Schubert that would also make him the most important posthumous publisher of the composer's music. Diabelli's abilities as a composer—he penned numerous **cantatas**, Mass settings, and other Catholic sacred works as well as **operettas** and *Singspiele*, **songs** and **part-songs**, and instrumental **chamber music** for piano solo, **piano duet**, and **chamber** ensembles including flute, guitar, and violin—led him to compose the **waltz** theme that would become the subject of Beethoven's *33 Variations on a Waltz by Diabelli* (Op. 120, 1824). [JMC]

See also PRINTING AND PUBLISHING OF MUSIC.

DICHTERLIEBE, **OP 48.** (Ger., "Poet's Love.") Iconic **song cycle** by **Robert Schumann** on texts from the 55 poems in the "Lyrisches Intermezzo" of **Heinrich Heine's** *Buch der Lieder* (Book of Songs, 1827). Schumann's cycle was composed in 1840 and published in two volumes in 1843 (Volume 1) and 1844 (Volume 2). As Schumann composed it and first submitted it to publishers, the cycle comprised 20 songs, but in this form it was rejected three times (by Bote & Bock, Berlin, in 1840; Jan Hofmann, Prague, in 1843; and **Breitkopf & Härtel**, Leipzig, in 1843). It was accepted quickly by C. F. Peters (Leipzig), but Schumann revised it further and released it in two volumes comprising a total of 16 songs (eight songs in each volume) in 1843–1844. Both volumes were reissued (still in separate volumes) in 1850. Two of the four deleted songs ("Dein Angesicht" and "Es leuchtet meine Liebe") were eventually published in Schumann's *Fünf Lieder und Gesänge*, Op. 127, and the other two were published in his *Vier Gesänge*, Op. 142 (both assembled late in 1853; publ. 1854 and 1858, respectively).

Dichterliebe is widely considered Schumann's greatest contribution to the literature of the song cycle. Like the cycles *Die schöne Müllerin* and *Winterreise* by **Franz Schubert**, whom Schumann revered, it traces a **narrative** of unrequited love with a lyric persona (*see* VOICE, VOICEDNESS, VOCALITY) who projects his thoughts and feelings onto abundant nature imagery. Although the cycle's effectiveness derives in part from the fact that its texts constitute a series of fragments, snapshots of various points along the way in the narrative, Schumann also provided for **cyclical** coherence and narrative continuity by means of thematic references and smooth tonal connections among the songs. The first volume traces the lyric persona's recounting of his desperate hopes of love, events of the past, to his recognition, in the present, that those hopes were in vain. It parallels this progression by moving mostly through sharp keys from F-sharp minor and A major to C major and A minor at the end of "Und wüßten's die Blumen." The second volume (songs 9–16) moves from rage through grief and resolution to recognition of the irony of love and then to acceptance in the extended piano postlude, tracing this progression by moving from D minor to D-flat major, the latter being the enharmonic equivalent of the final sonority of song 1. Throughout, Schumann ingeniously captures the irony of Heine's poems through intricate piano accompaniments and interactions between the piano and the vocal line, together with beautiful melodies in the vocal line.

From structuralist and poststructuralist perspectives, *Dichterliebe* may be considered a *misreading* of the plot archetype of **Ludwig van Beethoven**'s *An die ferne Geliebte*, which Schumann knew and overtly quoted in several other works (most notably Opp. 17 and 61): whereas the lyric persona in Beethoven's cycle, the precursor, creates a cycle affirming love through song despite the distance that separates him from his lover, the lyric persona of *Dichterliebe*, the ephebe, first clings desperately to the notion that there was a love and then bitterly encases those misguided hopes in a giant casket that is plunged into the Rhine River and washed away. [JMC]

DIES IRAE. (Lat., "Day of Wrath.") A rhymed liturgical sequence attributed to Thomas of Celano (d. ca. 1250) and intended for use in the Proper of Roman Catholic Mass for the Dead (*see* REQUIEM). It was one of only four sequences retained after the Council of Trent (1545–1563). Although its text was consistently used in the Requiem Mass and on All Souls' Day until it was removed from the Roman Rite in 1969–1970, the associated melody was used almost exclusively in monophonic settings until around 1700.

The text of the 18 rhymed strophes of Celano's sequence, a trope on the Vulgate version of Jephaniah 1:15 and Joel 2:31, describes the Day of Judgment in vivid detail. Apparently, the first attempt to respond graphically to its depiction of the Day's terrors is that found in the *Dies irae* of the Requiem fragment by **Wolfgang Amadeus Mozart** (completed by Franz Xaver Süßmaier [1766–1803]). Other composers who responded compositionally to the stark drama and sometimes horrific imagery of the text in their Requiem settings include **Hector Berlioz** (1837–1839), **Anton Bruckner** (1849 and 1895), Alfred Bruneau (1857–1934; 1896), **Luigi Cherubini** (1816–1817 and 1836–1838), **Gaetano Donizetti** (1835), **Antonín Dvořák** (1890–1891), **François-Joseph Fétis** (1850), José Maurício Garcia (1767–1830; 1816), **Robert Schumann** (1852), and **Giuseppe Verdi** (1874–1877), among others.

The melody of Celano's chant acquired a new pedigree in Romantic music through its use in the final movement of Berlioz's *Episode in the Life of an Artist*. There, in accordance with the grotesquerie and horror of the Witches'

Sabbath depicted in the program, it is forcefully intoned in alternation and combination with the work's **idée fixe** by two bassoons, two ophicleides, celli, and basses in alternation with low brass and horns and interruptions by two large offstage church bells—a scoring that must have seemed obscene to the overwhelmingly Catholic contemporary audiences who were accustomed to hearing the melody only in a cappella settings (or with light organ accompaniment) in the context of one of the Church's most revered and solemn rites. So effective was Berlioz's horrific transformation of the venerable tune that other composers began to set it polyphonically, usually with grim, grotesque, or threatening characteristics, for the first time in its history soon after the first publication of the full score of Berlioz's Symphony in 1845.

Although Berlioz did not use the traditional *Dies irae* chant melody in his own setting of the Requiem (H. 75, 1837–1839), it was used prominently by **Charles Gounod** (*Faust*, 1859–1869), **Franz Liszt** (*Totentanz*, 1849–1859), **Gustav Mahler** (Symphony No. 2, 1888–1894, rev. 1903), **Modest Mussorgsky** (*Night on Bare Mountain*, 1866–1867; *Songs and Dances of Death*, 1875–1877), **Serge Rachmaninoff** (Symphony No. 1, 1895; Symphony No. 2, 1906–1907; Symphony No. 3, 1909; *The Isle of the Dead*, 1909; *The Bells*, 1913; *Rhapsody on a Theme of Paganini*, 1934; *Symphonic Dances*, 1940), **Camille Saint-Saëns** (*Danse macabre*, 1874–1875; Symphony No. 3, 1886), and **Pyotor Il'yich Tchaikovsky** (Orchestral Suite No. 3, 1884–1885; *"Manfred" Symphony*, 1885–1886), among others. In the 20th and 21st centuries, the tune ranks as one of the most frequently encountered **topics** in film scores as well as other art music. It figures prominently in films as diverse as Ingmar Bergman's *The Seventh Seal* (1957), Frank Capra's *It's a Wonderful Life* (1946), Walt Disney's *The Lion King* (1994), Stanley Kubrick's *The Shining* (1980), Harold Ramis's *Groundhog Day* (1993), Rintaro's *Metropolis* (2002), Joseph Ruben's *Sleeping with the Enemy* (1991), Henry Selick's *Nightmare before Christmas* (1993), Bryan Singer's *X-Men* (2000), and Orson Welles's *Citizen Kane* (1941), among dozens of others. [JMC]

***DON GIOVANNI*, K. 527.** (It., "Don Juan.") **Opera** (*opera buffa*) by **Wolfgang Amadeus Mozart** on a **libretto** by Lorenzo Da Ponte (1749–1838), after the folk legend of **Don Juan** and literary treatments by de Tirso de Molina (ca. 1630), Molière (1665), Carlo Goldoni (1736), and Giovanni Bertati (1782). More than any other work of Mozart (with the arguable exception of the **Requiem**, K. 626), it came to personify Romantic mythologized views of his life and works—and indeed, via its interpretations at the hands of later composers, to epitomize the myriad variety of Romantic ideologies. In **Fryderyk Chopin**'s hands, it provided the musical springboard for **Robert Schumann**'s first published review of music (1831); in Karl Immermann's (1796–1840) translation/adaptation, it created an embarrassing scandal at the beginning of **Felix Mendelssohn Bartholdy**'s career (1833); and it likewise provided the inspiration for **Franz Liszt**'s *Réminiscence de Don Juan: Grande fantaisie pour le piano* (LW A80, 1843). It inspired a famous short story (1813) by **E. T. A. Hoffmann** as well as a novella (1855) by Eduard Möricke (1804–1875) that treats the opera as a metaphor for Mozart's too-brief life and tragic death. Virtually every individual of artistic or aesthetic eminence in the 19th century grappled with it in a major work; the list also includes **Lord Byron, Johann Wolfgang von Goethe, Aleksandr Pushkin**, and **Richard Wagner**.

The most important factor in the work's extraordinary **reception** was the fact that the *Don Giovanni* most of the Romantics knew bore little resemblance to what Da Ponte and Mozart had written. Even during Mozart's lifetime, it existed in two substantially different versions, the first written for the premiere in Prague in 1787 and the second for the first Viennese performance in 1789. Almost immediately, German authors such as the composer and actor Christian Gottlob Neefe (1788), Friedrich Ludwig Schröder (1789), and the composer and poet Friedrich Rochlitz (1801) began translating Da Ponte's Italian libretto into their native tongue, in the process altering it to conform to contemporary German tastes and make it worthy of Mozart's music. These alterations included the substitution of spoken dialogue for Mozart's recitatives (a change that single-handedly made the work into a *Singspiel* rather than *opera buffa*), the division of the original two-act structure into four acts, and, most important, the deletion of the original's light-hearted epilog. The latter change, evidently first introduced by Franz Xaver Süßmayr when he conducted it in Vienna in 1798, meant that instead of Mozart's and Da Ponte's concluding affirmation of the late Enlightenment values of reason, order, and justice, the opera's closing moments portrayed a defiant *Don Giovanni* whose repeated exclamations of "Nein!" were followed by *fortissimo* orchestra punctuations in D minor. The *Don Giovanni* that served as the creative springboard for Liszt's "reminiscence" is one that clearly reflects the Romantics' perception of Mozart's opera as a decidedly **Faustian** German tragedy. [JMC]

DON JUAN. Legendary Spanish profligate and iconic figure in literature, music, and the visual arts; along with **Faust** and **Ossian**, one of the most important cultural themes of the **long 19th century**. The first major literary treatment of the legend is found in Tirso de Molina's (1579–1648) *El Burlador de Sevilla y convidado de piedra* (The Trickster of Seville and the Stone Guest, 1630), which, in addition to establishing the legendary character's seat as being Seville (a feature that has remained constant in the many subsequent treatments of the story), also introduced the theme of the unrepentant libertine's inviting a statue to dinner and meeting his own demise in retribution. Molina's version of the story was adapted by Molière (*Dom Juan, ou le* *festin de pierre*, 1660) and later by any number of other writers—the most authoritative tally to date suggests a staggering 3,300—among them Honoré de Balzac (1831), **Lord Byron** (1821), Alexandre Dumas *père* (1831), Gustave Flaubert (1851), **E. T. A. Hoffmann** (1813), Nikolaus Lenau (1844), Prosper Merimée (1834), José Zoririlla y Moral (1844), **Aleksandr Pushkin** (1830), **Friedrich Schiller** (1797), **George Bernard Shaw** (1903), and Leo Tolstoy (1860).

The reasons for the Don Juan story's immense—and continuing—appeal are obvious. On the surface, it has its fair share of sex, violence, deception, and revenge. It also provided the basis of **Wolfgand Amadeus Mozart**'s last serious **operas** and thus held great appeal for the long 19th century's Mozart cult (*see* RECEPTION). Perhaps most important, however, from Hoffmann's recounting onward, the Don was cast not primarily as a villain but as a tragic hero: a rebel against the mores of society and its institutions and one whose life bespoke impetuousness, daring, and defiance, revealing both some of the noblest aspects of human existence (in the eyes of some Romantics) and its propensity for self-destruction.

Among the long 19th century's many musical treatments of the Don Juan theme, three are particularly well known today: Mozart's opera *Don Giovanni* (K. 527, 1787) on a libretto by Lorenzo da Ponte; Liszt's virtuosic piano **fantasy** *Réminiscences de Don Juan*, based on themes from that opera (LW A80, 1840, publ. 1843); and **Richard Strauss**'s tone poem *Don Juan* (TrV 156/Op. 20, 1889). [JMC]

DON QUIXOTE. Title character in the iconic novel (*romanza*) *Don Quixote de la Mancha, El ingenioso hidalgo* (Mr. Quixote of La Mancha, The Ingenious Gentleman) by the *siglo de oro* Spanish writer Miguel de Cervantes (1547–1616). The novel is in two parts. The first part was published in 1605, the second in 1615. Its tale of an idle nobleman so carried away by the adventures of heroic knights in literature that he comes to believe himself such a knight and sets out to redress the world's wrongs is, at face value, a mockery of the exaggerated chivalric romances of Cervantes's day. During the **long 19th century**, it was often seen as a parable concerning a frustrated idealist in a materialistic world, a commentary on the stratification of social classes and a satire of the aristocracy, or a veiled attack on the Roman Catholic Church. The Don's inability to distinguish reality from imagination—a theme also prominent in the works of **Calderón de la Barca** and **Johann Wolfgang von Goethe**, among others—also played on important themes in Romantic literature and psychology.

Don Quixote has been an iconic work since its first publication. During the **long 19th century** it inspired music by composers including **Gaetano Donizetti, Felix Mendelssohn Bartholdy, Saverio Mercadante**, Giovanni Paisiello (1740–1816), Niccolò Piccinni (1728–1800), and Antonio Salieri

(1750–1825). The most famous such work is **Richard Strauss**'s eponymous **tone poem** (TrV 184/Op. 35, 1897), subtitled "Fantastische Variationen über ein Thema ritterlichen Charakters" (Fantastic Variations on a Theme of Knightly Character). Strauss's work—his first tone poem to dispense entirely with **sonata form**—combines some aspects of double-**variation** procedure (one main theme is associated with Quixote, the other with his sidekick Sancho Panza) with others appropriated from the double **concerto** (the Don is represented by the solo cello, Sancho Panza by the viola), synthesizing these within an overall structure that draws on the technique of **thematic transformation** best known from the **symphonic poems** of **Franz Liszt**. It also represents a vivid incorporation of the idea of **voicedness** into the instrumental composition in that the solo instruments seem to represent the protagonists' voices themselves, not simply their actions. As a work centering on the theme of a heroically motivated nonhero, the work is (in Strauss's terms) a "pendant" to his tone poem *Ein Heldenleben* (A Heroic Life, TrV 190/Op. 40, 1898), composed at the same time and in the same sketchbooks (*see* COMPOSITIONAL PROCESS), which quotes it extensively and appropriates the rhetoric of **Ludwig van Beethoven**'s **"Eroica" Symphony** to reflect its own theme of true heroism and domestic respite in the face of a philistine world. [JMC]

See also PROGRAM (PROGRAMMATIC) MUSIC; PROGRAM SYMPHONY *OR* CHARACTERISTIC SYMPHONY.

DONIZETTI, (DOMENICO) GAETANO (MARIA) (1797–1848). Iconic **opera** composer and composition teacher; with **Vincenzo Bellini**, the Romantic Generation's leading composer of Italian opera between the de facto retirement of **Gioachino Rossini** and the emergence of **Giuseppe Verdi**'s mature style. He composed more than 66 operas, both **comic** and serious, for Italian, French, and Viennese stages, plus revisions and adaptations of several of these. He also wrote 28 secular **cantatas**; sacred choral music; many solo **songs**, duets, and **part-songs**; 18 **string quartets** and other instrumental **chamber music** with strings; **symphonies, concertos**, and other **orchestral** compositions; and works for **piano** solo and **piano duet**. His influence as a composer of Italian opera was augmented by his work as teacher of counterpoint and composition at the Naples **Conservatory** (1833–1838). By the late 1820s, he had begun to exhibit symptoms of syphilis; these worsened over the course of the 1840s, until he was unable to compose at all by December 1845 and in January 1846 had to be confined to an asylum. In 1847, authorities granted permission for him to be relocated to his native Bergamo, where he was cared for privately in the home of Baroness Rosa Rota-Basoni until his death on 8 April 1848.

Donizetti was arguably the most influential figure in the **long 19th century**'s translation and adaptation of the traditions of *bel canto* singing into a style that was distinctively Romantic. Even more than Bellini (whose style was usually syllabic, with rare exceptions), Donizetti appropriated the tradition of the number opera that foregrounded the display of vocal **virtuosity** into a new style of opera whose subjects were modern (or at least post-Antiquity) and whose dramatic content was based on strong contrasts in situations and among characters, using vocal display and virtuosity as expressive vehicles for exploring the tensions generated by the plot: vocal ornament thus becomes an integral function of drama rather than a superficial ornament. At its simplest, this approach is reflected in Donizetti's application in his arias of a lyric prototype consisting of a four-line text set to music with the form $a\ a^1\ b\ a^2$ or c, in which the opportunity for embellishment is reserved for the culminating final section, informed as it is by the contrast between a and b. Moreover, Donizetti generally reserves this prototype for characters who are somehow "other" to the cast and/or plot of the opera. In the process of revising (*see* COMPOSITIONAL PROCESS, CREATIVE PROCESS), he typically strove for an economy in his motivic material that would make his melodies as a whole more malleable and susceptible to development in response to the characters' changing emotional states and events in the plot. Although the particulars of Donizetti's application of this style vary widely between serious and **comic opera**, from opera to opera, and between the works written for French and Italian stages, it resonated deeply with his contemporaries and provided a stylistic model that was also appropriated in the piano literature (especially in the works of **Fryderyk Chopin** and other Parisian virtuosos) as well as in the operas of Verdi.

Donizetti's prolificness and the breadth and diversity of his work even within the genres of Romantic opera make it difficult to single out a few works that illustrate his contribution. By consensus, his most important operas include *Anna Bolena* (1830; libretto by Romani after Pindemonte and Pepoli), *L'elisir d'amore* (The Elixir of Love, 1832; libretto by Romani after Eugène Scribe's text for **Daniel-François Esprit** Auber's Le philtre), *Lucrezia Borgia* (1833; libretto by Romani after **Victor Hugo**), *Lucia di Lammermoor* (1835; libretto by Salvatore Cammarano after Sir Walter Scott), *Maria Stuarda* (Mary Stuart, 1835; libretto by Bardari after Schiller, Milan, La Scala), *Roberto Devereux, ossia Il conte di Essex* (Robert Devereux; or, The Earl of Essex, 1837; libretto by Cammarano after François Ancelot), *La fille du régiment* (The Daughter of the Regiment, **opéra comique**, 1840; libretto by Saint-Georges and Bayard), *La Favorite* (The Favored One, 1840; libretto by Royer and Vaëz), and *Don Pasquale* (1843; libretto by Ruffini and Donizetti). On the whole, Donizetti's more adventurous writing is concentrated in the operas on serious subjects, while his comic operas tend to adhere to accepted tradition. [JMC]

DRAESEKE, FELIX (AUGUST BERNHARD) (1835–1913). German composer and composition teacher. Though rarely heard today, his music won high accolades from the likes of **Hans von Bülow, Peter Cornelius,** and **Franz Liszt** and was performed in highly competitive venues, such as the annual festivals of the **Allgemeiner Deutscher Musikverein** and the Berlin Philharmonic Orchestra. He was admitted to the Leipzig **Conservatory** at the age of 17 but found it too conservative and left in 1855, continuing private study with Julius Rietz (1812–1877) and then coming under the informal mentorship of **Franz Brendel** and especially Liszt (from 1857); he met and won the respect of **Richard Wagner** in Lucerne in 1859.

A professional crisis of sorts emerged when Draeseke's *Germania-Ode* (text by Heinrich von Kleist) was performed at the festival of the ADMv in 1861: the work as a whole bespoke the progressive musical language championed by the **New German School,** but its third movement was a march that—in keeping with the conventions of military music—was thoroughly diatonic and conservative; when it was repeated at the close of the concert, it met with hissing and catcalls. Discouraged, Draeseke relocated to Switzerland, where he taught privately while renewing his grounding in counterpoint and struggling to regain a sense of direction. This was followed by one year of study in Spain and another year in Switzerland. By 1876, he was ready to return to Germany, in that year publishing his first theoretical work (*Anweisung zum kunstgerechten Moduliren* [Instructions for Artistically Correct Modulation]) and beginning work at a private music school in Dresden. He was appointed to the Dresden Conservatory in 1884 and promoted to professor there in 1892.

Draeseke's music is stylistically diverse, although in general he became more invested in counterpoint and less avowedly supportive of the avant-garde of music during his last few decades. He completed seven **operas,** all to his own librettos (*König Sigurd,* 1853–1857; *Herrat,* 1877–1885; *Gudrun,* 1875–1884; *Bertran de Born,* 1892–1894; *Fischer und Kalif,* 1894–1895; *Merlin,* 1903–1905; and *Gotha,* 1913). Among his many sacred works are a Grand Mass in A Minor (Op. 85, 1909), a **Requiem** in E Minor (1909–1910), and the *Osterszene aus Goethes "Faust,"* Op. 39 (1889). His op. 38 Clarinet **Sonata** and op. 36 Piano **Concerto** are still performed, as are some of his instrumental **chamber** compositions and **songs.** He also composed five **symphonies** and five **symphonic poems,** among other works. His magnum opus is the **oratorio** tetralogy titled *Christus* (1895–1903), intended as a sacred counterpart to Wagner's *Ring of the Nibelung.* He also published several widely read writings about music. In addition to the *Anweisung* mentioned above, these include *Die Lehre von der Harmonia in lustige Reimlein gebracht* (The Study of Harmony Presented in Merry Rhymes, 1883) and *Der gebundene Styl: Lehrbuch für Kontrapunkt und Fuge* (The Strict Style: Handbook for Counterpoint and Fugue, 1902). The most famous was an essay titled "Die Konfusion in der Musik" (published in the *Neue Stuttgarter Musikzeitung*, 1906), a vehement condemnation of **Richard Strauss**'s *Salome* that (like most things associated with that opera) provoked bitter controversy. [JMC]

DRAFT. *See* COMPOSITIONAL PROCESS, CREATIVE PROCESS.

DRAME LYRIQUE, DRAMMA LYRICA. *See* LYRIC DRAMA.

DUBOIS, (FRANÇOIS-CLÉMENT-)THÉODORE (1837–1924). French composer, organist, and teacher of the Late Romantic Generation, one of the most influential composition and theory pedagogues of the late 19th century in France. He studied first in Rheims and then at the Paris **Conservatory** (1854–1861), winning prizes in harmony, fugue, and organ in 1856–1859 and then the prestigious **Prix de Rome** in composition in 1861. He served as organist at St. Clothilde under **César Franck** from 1858 to 1863 and choirmaster there from 1863 to 1869. In 1871, he joined the faculty of the Conservatory, where he became a highly respected teacher of harmony, counterpoint, and fugue. In 1877, he succeeded **Camille Saint-Saëns** as organist of the Madeline in Paris, a post he retained until 1906, also serving as director of the Conservatory beginning in 1896. Protests following his notorious systemic exclusion of Maurice Ravel from the competition for the Prix de Rome forced him to resign from the institution later that year.

Dubois's widely disseminated pedagogical works include *L'accompagnement pratique du plainchant* (Practical Rules for Accompanying Plainchant, 1884), *Traité de contrepoint et de fugue* (Treatise on Counterpoint and Fugue, 1901), *Petit manuel théorique de l'harmonie* (Short Handbook on the Theory of Harmony, 1919), and *Traité d'harmonie théorique et pratique* (Treatise on Harmony, 1921). He was also a prolific and well-respected composer. He is best known today for his organ music (especially the *Fantaisie triomphale* for organ and orchestra, 1889) and his sacred choral music (including two **Requiems** and 10 other Mass settings, plus five **oratorios**, several **cantatas**, and 71 **motets**). He also composed two **opéras comiques** and three other **operas**, one **ballet**, three **symphonies**, three **concert overtures**, six orchestral **suites**, three **symphonic poems**, one piano **concerto**, one violin concerto, several other *concertante* works, two woodwind suites, one **piano quartet**, one piano **quintet**, about 40 other instrumental **chamber** compositions, and 94 works for **piano** solo or **piano duet**. [JMC]

DUKAS, PAUL (ABRAHAM) (1865–1935). French composer, critic, and teacher of the Modern Romantic Generation. He studied **piano** as a youth and entered the Paris **Conservatory** at age 16, there studying harmony with **Théodore Dubois** and composition with **Ernest Guiraud** as well as conducting, orchestration, and piano. He won second prize in the **Prix de Rome** for composition in 1888 but left the Conservatory in discouragement after he received only three votes out of nine the following year. He maintained his musical activities during his tour of military service and, in addition to composing, began his lifelong career as a music critic—a career that between 1892 and 1934 would ultimately produce some 410 review articles in the leading francophone publications of the day. His public Parisian premiere (the **concert overture** *Polyeucte*, 1891) was well received, but his international standing was achieved with his **tone poem** *L'aprenti sorcier* (The Sorcerer's Apprentice, 1897, based on **Johann Wolfgang von Goethe**'s 1797 **ballad** after Lucian's *Philopseudes*, ca. CE 150). He also was actively involved in editing and promoting historical repertoires, notably those of **Johann Sebastian Bach**, **Ludwig van Beethoven**, Jean-Philippe Rameau (1683–1764), and Domenico Scarlatti (1685–1757). His reputation as composer and critic led to his appointment in 1910 to the faculty of the Conservatory, where he taught orchestration from 1910 to 1913 and succeeded **Charles-Marie Widor** as professor of composition in 1928. He served as member of Conseil supérieur du Conservatoire and the Conseil des émissions radiophoniques, was president of the Union syndicale des compositeurs, and was an officer of the Légion d'Honneur. In December 1934, six months before his death, he was elected to the Académie des Beaux-Arts.

Dukas was highly self-critical and destroyed much of his work. He is best known today for *L'aprenti sorcier*, a piano **sonata** (1899–1900), and the three-act **opera** *Ariane et Barbe-bleue* (Arianna and Bluebeard, 1899–1907). His other surviving works include a **symphony** (1895–1896), a **ballet** (*La péri*, 1912), several smaller piano works, four **cantatas**, and several works for chorus with **orchestra**. [JMC]

DUPARC [FOUQUES DUPARC], (MARIE EUGÈNE) HENRI (1848–1933). French composer, important figure in the founding of the Société Nationale de Musique. He trained as a pianist, studying with **César Franck**, and formally studied law but while doing so began composing under Franck's supervision. In 1885, at the age of 37, he was forced to abandon composition due to a neurasthenic condition indicated by hyperaesthenia or allodynia (experiencing pain in response to stimuli, such as light, sound, or touch, that do not normally induce pain), eventually leading to blindness and paralysis. The last 48 years of his life he essentially spent in retirement in southwestern France and Switzerland with his family, reading, executing sepia drawings and watercolors, and following musical events but not composing. He destroyed many of his compositions and is best remembered today for the total of 16 **songs** that survive. He was an avid and highly sensitive reader of poetry, a trait that is readily evident in his settings of texts. His musical style, while thoroughly imbued with the refinement and sense of intimacy stereotypical of Gallic taste in the late 19th century, is also intensely chromatic and characterized by pervasive sequencing of short phrases. In addition to his songs, he is known to have begun an **opera** (*Roussalka*, after **Aleksandr Pushkin**; later destroyed), and he completed five **orchestral** works; a handful of instrumental **chamber** compositions (of which a cello **sonata** is best known today); a **motet** for soprano, tenor, and bass; and a duet for soprano and tenor with **piano** on a text by Théophile Gautier ("La fuite," 1871, publ. 1903).

In addition to his work as a composer, Duparc was an avid French **nationalist** and a major influence in the assimilation of elements of German musical culture into French musical language. Like all students of Franck, he was an admirer of the music of **Johann Sebastian Bach** (as it was understood in France in the late 19th century; see RECEPTION) and the works of **Ludwig van Beethoven**'s late Vienna period. He was also an admirer of **Richard Wagner**, having heard performances of his music, met him in 1869, and traveled to **Bayreuth** numerous times; he also corresponding with him but later destroyed those letters. His **symphonic poem** *Léonore* (comp. 1874, publ. ca. 1895) reflects the style developed by **Franz Liszt** and promulgated by the **New German School**. Duparc's dedication to the progressive cause of French nationalism led to his involvement in the creation of the Sociéte Nationale de Musique Française in 1872 and his founding of the Concerts de musique moderne in 1878. [JMC]

DVOŘÁK, ANTONÍN (LEOPOLD) (1841–1904). Bohemian (Czech) composer of the Late Romantic Generation; with **Bedřich Smetana** one of Central Europe's most important musical **nationalists** in the **long 19th century**. He trained as a violist and church organist. He attained a distinct musical style by around 1875 but stands as one of very few composers who were able to move fluidly between conflicting stylistic forces, such as the Viennese tradition (as represented by **Johannes Brahms** and **Franz Schubert**), Bohemian dance and **folk song**, and the experimental, aggressively modern idioms of **Franz Liszt**, **Richard Wagner**, and the **New German School**, in an output that embraces virtually every genre available to musicians of his generation. Any overview of his output is complicated by the fact that he destroyed or withdrew most of his early works, resulting in doubled numberings, reused opus numbers, and a tangled web of titles. In the interest of clarity, this entry uses the numbering from the Burghauser thematic catalog (refer to the bibliography) and the complete rather than the final/authorized serial and opus numbers.

Dvořák displayed musical talent at an early age but encountered obstacles to pursuing a career as a musician. A butcher's son, he worked as an apprentice butcher during his teens but also took lessons in organ and harmony. He studied at the Prague Organ School in 1857–1859 and composed his earliest works (a polka for **piano**, a Mass in B-flat Major, and several small works for **orchestra**; all now lost) during these years. After graduation, he supported himself by working as a violist in local restaurants and theaters. One of these theaters, the Provisional Theater, hired him as principal violist in 1861, when he also wrote his earliest surviving compositions (a **string quintet** and a **string quartet** [B. 7 and 8/opp. 1 and 2], two **symphonies** [B. 9 and 34/opp. 3 and 10], a Cello Concerto in A Major [B. 10], and the **song cycle** *Cypresses*, B. 11). He was playing in the viola section in 1863 when Wagner came to Prague to conduct his *Faust Overture* and excerpts from *Tannhäuser*, *Tristan und Isolde*, *Die Walküre*, and *Die Meistersinger* and when Smetana assumed the directorship of the Provisional Theater on returning to Prague in 1866. He remained with the Theater until 1871, becoming acquainted with **operettas**, French **grand opera**, and the operas of Christoph Willibald Ritter von Gluck (1714–1787), **Wolfgang Amadeus Mozart**, and **Giuseppe Verdi**, among others. He composed his own first opera, the three-act *Alfred* (B. 16), in 1870, but it was never performed or published during Dvořák's lifetime.

Dvořák left the Provisional Theater in 1871, becoming known in Prague's **salons** for his instrumental and vocal **chamber music** and supporting himself by teaching. He gradually began to distance himself from the influences of the New German School and instead integrate elements of Slavonic folk music into his music with works such as the three string quartets (B. 17–19, ca. 1768–1770) and a new Cello **Sonata** (B. 20/Op. 11, 1871). His first major successes came with the revision in 1874 of his second opera, *Král a uhlíř* (The King and the Charcoal Burner, B. 21, rev. version B. 42, 1874). Also in 1874, Smetana conducted the premiere of his Third Symphony (B. 34, 1873), and he composed two more symphonies (B. 41 and 54) in 1874 and 1875. He won an increased reliable income for his growing family with his appointment as organist at the St. Vojtěch Church in February 1874, but truly life-changing events were set in motion a few months later when he submitted 15 compositions to the competition for the Austrian State Stipendium for Artists—winning the admiration of **Eduard Hanslick** as well as an appreciable stipend. His second application (1875) to the same competition earned him an even more valuable mentorship, that of Johannes Brahms (who had himself been propelled and mentored into the public spotlight by **Robert Schumann**). Brahms was so impressed by the *Moravian Duets* that Dvořák submitted in 1877 for his fourth successful application to the competition (B. 50/Op. 20, 1875) that he recommended them highly to one of his own preferred publishers, **Fritz Simrock**, thus putting the young Bohemian in contact with one of the more influential German agents in the burgeoning market for published music. Simrock in turn commissioned from Dvořák what became the first set of *Slavonic Dances* (for **piano duet**, B. 78/Op. 46; orch. B. 83, 1878). In a world pervasively fascinated with nationalism and **exoticism**, these three *opera* earned Dvořák an international reputation as the up-and-coming leading voice of Bohemian nationalism.

Now an international public figure in music, during the 1880s Dvořák devoted himself less to opera (composing only three during the decade) and more to **song** and **orchestral** music. He received increasing numbers of international commissions and invitations to travel abroad for performances of his music. England (historically always quick to embrace the Continent's current musical celebrities) welcomed him to its shores in performances with the Philharmonic Society of London in 1884, the first of a total of nine visits he would make to that country. So great was his success there that in 1884 he was commissioned to write a symphony (No. 7, B. 141/Op. 70, publ. 1885) for the Society's 1885 season and a choral work for the 1885 Birmingham Festival (*Svatební košile* [The Spectre's Bride], B. 135/Op. 69, publ. 1885), followed by the **oratorio** *Svatá Ludmila* (St. Ludmilla, B. 144/Op. 71), written for the 1886 Leeds Music Festival and published in 1887. In 1886, he was made an honorary member of the Philharmonic Society of London. He was also in increasing demand as a **conductor**, leading performances of his own music in Budapest, Dresden, Frankfurt am Main, Moscow, and St. Petersburg as well as Prague and London.

In 1890, Dvořák received an honorary doctorate from the University of Prague and was invited to join the faculty there, a position that he accepted and to which he would later return. The year 1891 included the awarding of an honorary doctorate from Cambridge University and the composition of both the celebrated "Dumky" **Piano Trio** (B. 166/Op. 90, publ. 1894) and a trilogy of **concert overtures** that were to be collectively titled *Příroda, Život a Láska* (Nature, Life, and Love): *V přírodě* (In Nature's Realm, B. 168/Op. 91), *Karneval* (Carnaval, B. 169/Op. 92), and *Othello* (B. 174/Op. 93; after **William Shakespeare**). All three would be published in 1894.

Dvořák's success in discovering and earning international appreciation of the musical voice of his own native Bohemia led in 1891 to the invitation to teach composition and serve as director of the recently (1885) founded National **Conservatory** of Music in New York—an invitation that he accepted at least in part because of the position's generous financial terms. From September 1892 through May 1895, he lived in the United States except for trips to Europe during the summer intersessions. While there, with the expectation that he would (as he put it) lead the United States "to the Promised Land, the realm of a new, independent art, in short a national style of music!," he studied transcriptions of Native American melodies and asked an African American student of the Conservatory to sing spirituals and plantation songs for him. He also attempted to infuse his own music with elements of his American experience, most notably in the Symphony No. 9 ("Z Nového světa" [From the New World], B. 178/Op. 95, comp. 1893, publ. 1894), the F-Major String Quartet (B. 179/Op. 96, comp. 1893, publ. 1894), and the *Biblické písně* (Biblical Songs, B. 185/Op. 99, comp. 1894, publ. 1895). His music was frequently performed and widely applauded, and the Conservatory renewed his contract for 1894–1896, but despite a summer (1893) with the Czech community in Spillville, Iowa, he missed the culture of his homeland. In the summer of 1895, back in his native Bohemia, he decided that he could not return, canceling his New York contract and resuming his position at the Prague Conservatory.

The remainder of Dvořák's life was devoted primarily to opera. He revised the earlier *Dimitrij* (B. 127, rev. version 186/Op. 46) and *Jakobín* (The Jacobin, B. 159, rev. version B. 200/Op. 84) and composed three new works in the genre: the **comic opera** *Čert a Káča* (The Devil and Kate, B. 201/Op. posth. 112, comp. 1898–1899), the "lyric fairy tale" *Rusalka* (B. 203/Op. posth. 114, comp. 1900; after de la Motte Fouqué's *Undine*), and the four-act *Armida* (B. 206/Op. posth. 115; after Tasso's *Gerusalemme liberata*). He also completed the Cello **Concerto** in B Minor (B. 191/Op. 104, comp. 1894–1895, publ. 1896), two new string quartets (B. 192/Op. 106 and 193/Op. 105, both publ. 1896), and several notable successors to his earlier trilogy of concert overtures: the **symphonic poems** *Vodník* (The Water Goblin, B. 195/Op. 107, 1896), *Polednice* (The Noon Witch, B. 196/Op. 108, 1896), *Zlatý kolovrat* (The Golden Spinning Wheel, B. 197/Op. 109, 1896), *Holoubek* (The Wild Dove, B. 198/Op. 110, comp. 1896, publ. 1899), and *Píseň bohatýrská* (A Hero's Song, B. 199/Op. 111, comp. 1897, publ. 1899). *Rusalka* was a resounding success at its premiere in February 1901, and later that year Dvořák was appointed director of the Prague Conservatory, but his last opera, *Armida*, was considerably less successful.

The multifacetedness of Dvořák's oeuvre, while perhaps not surprising in view of his long life, is remarkable. Overall, his creative life is usually divided into six periods: an early period of assimilation during which, largely self-taught, he attempted to develop his proficiency in the Romantic idiom of earlier 19th-century composers such as **Ludwig van Beethoven, Felix Mendelssohn Bartholdy**, and **Robert Schumann**; a phase strongly influenced by the New German School (1864–1872); a new phase that assimilates elements of Slavonic folk music into a more conventional Romantic idiom sometimes characterized as "Brahmsian" (1873–1877); a more intensely dramatic period (1877–1886); a second Slavonic period that cultivates less elaborate and pretentious musical forms than the first Slavonic period (1886–1892); and a final phase that synthesizes **programmatic** elements, musical drama, and national styles (including, for a time, those of the United States), extending from 1892 to the end of his life. Interspersed almost equally throughout that long creative life are 11 operas (several of them revised at least once); nine symphonies; one piano concerto, one violin concerto, and one cello concerto; eight concert overtures and six symphonic poems and two series of *Slavonic Dances* and other orchestral works; 10 large-scale works for chorus and orchestra (including a Mass in D [B. 153/Op. 86, 1887, publ. 1893], a **Requiem** [B. 165/Op. 89, 1890, publ. 1891], and the **cantata** *The American Flag* [B. 177/Op. 102, 1892–1893, publ. 1895]); nine collections of smaller choral works and **part-songs** (comprising 27 individual pieces); 33 songs and vocal duets, both sacred and secular, with accompaniment of **piano** or organ; and 14 string quartets, three string **quintets**, four piano trios, two **piano quartets**, two piano quintets, one string **sextet**, one violin **sonata**, and other instrumental **chamber** works for piano or piano duet with or without strings. [JMC]

See *also* ALBUMBLATT; CYCLIC FORM; HAUSMUSIK; STABAT MATER (DOLOROSA); STYLE HONGROIS.

DWIGHT, JOHN SULLIVAN (1813–1893). U.S. music critic and author of the Romantic Generation. Dwight was one of the first important music critics in the Western Hemisphere. Like his contemporary **Margaret Fuller**, his aesthetics were indebted to Romanticism and Transcendentalism, and his writings encouraged more widespread and thorough American acquaintance with the European concert tradition.

Dwight was born and raised in Boston; he graduated from Harvard College in 1832 and Harvard Divinity School in 1836. He emerged an amateur music devotee and an avid reader interested in recent German thinkers and writers such as Immanuel Kant (1724–1804), **Johann Wolfgang von Goethe**, and **Friedrich Schiller**. That interest led Dwight to publish an English-language anthology of poetry by Goethe and Schiller in 1839. During those years he also befriended minister and Transcendentalist George Ripley (1802–1880), who in 1849 made Dwight director of his utopian commune Brook Farm; Dwight remained until its demise six years later. There, Dwight organized music activities and wrote music criticism for the Brook Farm organ *Harbinger*.

Issues of *Dwight's Journal of Music* came out every Saturday from 1852 to 1864; beginning in 1865, the journal was printed every two weeks until its end in 1881. It was a bona fide music journal, with discussions of various musical topics—such as composers, compositions, performers, aesthetics, and music history—and coverage of the Boston classical music scene and correspondence from elsewhere in the Americas and Europe. Like Fuller, Dwight aimed at encouraging greater U.S. involvement in great music, but his emphasis on quality and **canon**-forming agenda set him apart from contemporaries. Interest in **Ludwig van Beethoven** in the United States during the 19th century was due largely to the efforts of Dwight, whose tastes were typically Teutonic across all genres (**Richard Wagner** was one of few Austro-German composers who did not win his critical approbation). Dwight's magazine also provided a forum for later important figures in American history, including **John Knowles Paine** and Beethoven biographer Alexander Wheelock Thayer (1817–1897). [RK]

E

ÉCOSSAISE. (Fr., "Scottish"; Ger., *Schottische*.) A stylized country dance supposedly of Scottish origin. Its tempo was lively and its meter typically 2/4; most often, it consisted of a series of musically unrelated eight-measure strains, each repeated. It was a ballroom favorite during the first half of the 19th century. *Écossaises* and sets of *écossaises* were composed by **Ludwig van Beethoven** (WoO 22 and 23 [1810], 83 [1825], 86 [1806]), **Cécile Chaminade** (Op. 151, 1903), **Stephen Foster** (*Holiday Schottische*, 1853), **Louis Moreau Gottschalk** (*Fairy Land*, 1863), **Fryderyk Chopin** (CT 13/Op. 72, no. 3, ca. 1829, publ. 1855), **Johann Nepomuk Hummel** (Op. 52, no. 5, 1810, publ. 1815), **Franz Schubert** (D. 145 [1815–1821], 158 [1815], 299 [1815], 421 [1816], 511 and 529 [1817], 643 [1819], 697 [1820], 734/Op. 67 [1822, publ. 1826]), 735/Op. 49 [ca. 1822, publ. 1825], 781 and 782 [1823], 783/Op. 33 [1824, publ. 1825], and 977 [?1825]), **Robert Schumann** (Op. 109, no. 7, 1851, publ. 1853), and **Pyotor Il'yich Tchaikovsky** (Act III of *Eugene Onegin*, Op. 24 [1878, publ. 1879]), among others. The term is also used as a modifier for other genres and forms (*marche écossaise*, *rhapsodie écossaise*, and so on). [JMC]

EDITING AND EDITIONS. The process of preparing musical texts for dissemination in print (*editing*), and the printed products of that process (*editions*). Although scholars have begun to focus on these issues and their implications for performers in relation to the music of the **long 19th century** only comparatively recently (since the last third of the 20th century), the issues first made themselves felt already in the early years of the 19th century, for few matters are more consequential for interpreters of every stripe (analysts, biographers, historians, and of course performers) than the state of the musical scores that provide the starting points for their interpretations. The issues multiply with increasing historical distance because musical notation is a system of symbols that attempt to suggest certain pitches, durations, timbres, and other interpretive parameters to its own contemporary performers, while performance traditions themselves are in a constant state of change. Any given reading of a given notated passage of music at a given time thus differs substantively from the way that earlier performers would have interpreted that same notation or what later performers will do with it. In preparing a given musical text for use in performance and other interpretation, then, editors are re-creating and/or reinterpreting a dense set of historical musical symbols for modern interpreters to whom the original notation is unavailable, confusing, or incomprehensible.

The particular problems and potentials entailed in the process of editing music of the long 19th century vary according to historical position, geography, genre, scoring, language, and composer—indeed, they are often case by case since no two compositions are alike in content and most compositions differ significantly in varying contexts. Despite the significant variations that occur at these levels, however, it is possible to speak of modern editions of music of the long 19th century in terms of two broad and overlapping but self-consciously discrete families: critical editions and "practical" or "performing" editions.

Critical editions (also known as *source-critical editions* [Ger., *quellenkritische Ausgaben*] or, in some cases, **Urtext** *editions*) are those that seek to empower performers and other interpreters by presenting the musical text (both its lyrics, when present, and the remainder of the music) in a state that keeps editorial judgment calls to a minimum, clearly differentiates between authorial and editorial information, and offers documentation and explanatory material that will enable interpreters to view or reconstruct different information (*variants*) provided in different manuscript and printed sources for the music at hand. Such editions typically include two main elements in addition to the music itself: (1) an introduction that summarizes the work's compositional and performance histories during the composer's lifetime, its position in the composer's biography, its contemporary reception, and other issues, such as those pertaining to **performance practice** or the work's position in its genre and (2) a *critical report* or *critical apparatus* that explains the editor's methods of making decisions, classifies and identifies the musical sources (both manuscript and early printed sources when the latter exist), and lists *variants* that are transmitted in those various sources. Typically, the editor constructs a family tree, or *stemma*, of the work's musical sources by means of a technique known as *stemmatic filiation*. The critical report may also reproduce or describe excised or deleted passages or earlier readings of individual passages within the work. By using it in conjunction with the introduction and the music itself, performers should be able to make informed and responsible decisions, according to criteria that suit their own general values and immediate needs.

The goal of critical editions of music of the long 19th century is (usually) not to establish a single definitive text for that music but rather to empower interpreters by providing complete and thorough information of the interpretive issues the work raises. It is the responsibility of the editor to establish, on the basis of his or her knowledge and understanding of the work and the issues it presents, a coherent view of the work that will enable him or her to organize and explain its history and sources in a fashion that will enable interpreters to feel themselves in possession of the best knowledge available and to make their own decisions from there. For some works (e.g., the **Mozart/Süßmaier Requiem, Ludwig van Beethoven**'s op. 2 piano **sonatas, Felix Mendelssohn Bartholdy**'s A-major ["Italian"] **Symphony,** or **Johannes Brahms**'s **Piano Trio** No. 1), there is no readily performable, definitive, and pure version; for others (especially **operas** and works that remained unpublished during their composers' lifetimes but also in the music of **Fryderyk Chopin**), there are multiple, significantly different versions with competing claims to authority; and for others, the composer arrived at a single definitive form and saw the work through the publication process in this version. The decision as to which case best applies to any given work is that of the editor, and that decision will affect—sometimes significantly—the musical text of the edition itself.

At the other end of the methodological spectrum are the editions informally known as *performing editions* or *"practical" editions*. These editions' rationale is that because the goal of scores is to facilitate performance, the proper function of the editor is the same. They do not strive to facilitate performance by offering performers and other interpreters a detailed landscape of historical and textual information to use in formulating their own interpretation. Rather, they make those decisions themselves and present the music in an affordable and straightforward guise. Because the complexities that must be discussed in the introduction and critical apparatus of critical editions are time consuming and expensive and require additional paper and binding, performing editions typically minimize or dispense altogether with the introductory material and critical report, also tacitly interjecting the editors' decisions concerning the issues presented by the musical sources as well as other interpretive aspects (such as articulations, dynamics, and tempos), to say nothing of pitches and durations. The advantages of these editions are primarily matters of convenience and cost; the disadvantage is that in using such an edition, interpreters willingly suspend their own critical judgment regarding the music text entirely, trusting entirely in the judgment of often-anonymous editors whose credentials may be no greater than their affiliation with the press. These editors' knowledge of the work and the relevant sources and other issues may be minimal, and their needs and values may differ significantly from those that the interpreter brings to bear on the work.

These two broad classes of edition are in some ways antagonistic to one another or perhaps mutually exclusive since printed music is expensive and few musicians have the money or time to assemble among the many competing editions of the music they intend to perform or study before choosing the edition that best suits their needs. In the face of the financial realities of the Classical music industry, it is often tempting to bypass the frequently more expensive critical editions of a given work and instead use a "practical" edition that may itself be a reprint of an edition, good or bad, that is now in the public domain—largely on the assumption that the different information provided in a critical edition would not be discernible to audiences. Yet this assumption, too, requires qualification—for even if an audience member seated in row 19 (or even row 1) does not notice the difference between, for example, the long slurs introduced in many 20th-century "performing" editions where their 19th-century counterparts provided a series of short slurs (or no slurs at all), the performers working from those different slurrings will interpret that same music differently, and these interpretive differences almost inevitably will shape the larger interpretation of the work—not only subtle matters, such as bowings and fingerings, but also more readily evident ones, such as tempos. The general interpretive consequences of these differences will be noticeable to any reasonably attentive listener. The editor's work is thus consequential not only for **performance practice** but also for **reception** and for understandings of the edited work's position in musical aesthetics generally.

Three instances of the problems that can be created by uncritical (or insufficiently critical) use of ostensibly authoritative editions and the insights that can be offered by using critical editions will have to suffice for purposes of this short entry. First, Beethoven originally intended for the third-movement scherzo of his Fifth Symphony to include full repeats of both the scherzo and trio and in this version had included two superfluous bars just after the C-major trio. In a letter to the work's publisher, **Breitkopf & Härtel**, he deleted these bars during the publication process—yet through an engraver's error, the first editions of the work's score and parts retained the two superfluous measures, and they were retained intact until 1846, when the German and French musical world erupted in an imbroglio that had **Hector Berlioz, Françoise-Antoine Habeneck**, and Beethoven's personal secretary, Anton Schindler (1795–1864), arguing for the measures' inclusion and the rest of the world (and posterity) arguing for their excision. Vexingly, however, editions based on the flawed first edition still continue to circulate. As a result, this textual dilemma, once solved, has been brought back to life through the expediencies of "performing" editions. Similarly, the retransition from the central B section of Chopin's celebrated E-major **Étude** Op. 10, no. 3 (CT 16, 1832), though well known and compelling in the version in which it appeared in 1833 (Paris: Maurice Schlesinger; Leipzig: Kistner), was altered by the composer in the exemplar owned by his pupil Jane Stirling approximately a dozen years after the piece was first published—and this version, whether didactically or compositionally motivated, represents the *Fassung letzter Hand* of the work. Yet most published editions, both critical and "practical," remain blind to this authorized and musically attractive version of the étude's B section, thus also leaving performers and other interpreters blind to a version that might refresh or reinvigorate a work all too hackneyed while shedding light on its history and on the genre of the étude in general.

Finally, **Anton Bruckner** revised most of his symphonies extensively in response to his "own" evolving compositional desiderata, experiences in performance, and suggestions from contemporaries, with the result that most existed in at least two substantially different versions, all authorized, by the end of his life. These revised versions were published with Bruckner's involvement and thus represent fully authorized and seemingly authoritative versions of the works' musical texts. Yet some elements of the later versions may be clearly identified as artifacts of others' intervention (although Bruckner himself authorized them), while others are indisputably authentic and better reflections of Bruckner's goals in writing and revising the scores. The editor of these works has the unenviable job of sorting out which of these variants belong to which class and determining the most authoritative version of the work at hand. The versions of most that are most commonly performed today are those issued as part of the so-called Bruckner *Gesamtausgabe* under the general editorship of Robert Haas between 1930 and 1953 (refer to the bibliography)—yet some of Haas's versions are conflations of the versions of different passages that Haas found most satisfying. As such, they represent versions of the works as a whole that never existed during Bruckner's lifetime and were never authorized by him. Interpreters who use Haas's ostensibly critical "performing" editions (which are advertised as "authoritative" in the widely disseminated Dover Reprints editions that most libraries and students use to study and perform them) unwittingly fly blindly into a dense web of textual corruptions that starkly contradict any presumable intentions of fidelity to the composer's wishes. [JMC]

See also AUTOGRAPH; HOLOGRAPH; COMPOSITIONAL PROCESS, CREATIVE PROCESS; COPYRIGHT AND PERFORMANCE RIGHT.

1812: SOLEMN OVERTURE FOR LARGE ORCHESTRA, OP. 49. Programmatic **concert overture** by **Pyotor Il'yich Tchaikovsky**, composed in 1880 for the 1882 commemoration of Napoléon Bonaparte's retreat from Moscow after the Battle of Borodino (1812). It was premiered on 20 August 1882 in the Cathedral of Christ the Savior, Moscow, and published in arrangements for **piano** solo and **piano duet** as well as in full score later that year (all Moscow: Jurgenson). It is scored for a large orchestra, including a specification that "any extra brass instruments available" be used during the final section, plus carillon and cannon. Like **Ludwig van Beethoven**'s *Wellington's Victory*, on which it is apparently modeled, *1812* quotes well-known previously composed themes in order to personify the protagonists in the battle. The strength and courage of the Russian government and its subjects are represented by the Slavic Orthodox hymn *God Preserve Thy People*; the suffering of the Russian people is represented by the Russian folk dance *U Vorot, Vorot* (At the Gate, the Gate); Bonaparte's armies are represented by the *Marseillaise*; and at the conclusion, after the French retreat, the Russians celebrate with a bombastic presentation of the Russian national anthem *Bozhe, Tsarya khrani* (God Save the Czar).

Tchaikovsky's overture belongs to a long tradition of programmatic battle pieces (*battailles*, *battaglie*) written during the **long 19th century**. That tradition includes not only *Wellington's Victory*, the first movement of **Felix Mendelssohn Bartholdy**'s D-minor ("Reformation") **Symphony** (MWV N15; Op. posth. 107, 1830–1832), and **Franz Liszt's symphonic poem** *Hunnenschlacht* (The Battle of the Huns, LW G17; 1857–1861) but also Frantisek Kotzwara's (1730–1791) *The Battle of Prague*, **Charles Villiers Stanford**'s *The Battle of the Baltic* (Op. 41, 1891), Charles Grobe's (ca. 1817–1879) *The Battle of Buena Vista* (Op. 101, 1847) and *The Battle of Roanoke Island* (Op. 1395, 1862), Theodore Moelling's (ca. 1822–ca. 1894) *The Battle of Waterloo* (Op. 54, 1863), and dozens of others. Along with Mendelssohn's D-minor Symphony and Liszt's symphonic poem, *1812* is the only one of these works to have maintained a stable position in the symphonic **canon**. [JMC]

See also NATIONALISM, ROMANTIC NATIONALISM; PROGRAM (PROGRAMMATIC) MUSIC; THEMATIC TRANSFORMATION, THEMATIC METAMORPHOSIS; TOPIC.

ELGAR, SIR EDWARD WILLIAM (1857–1934). English composer of the Modern Romantic Generation. Elgar is widely known today for his *"Enigma" Variations* (Op. 36, 1898–1899) and *Pomp and Circumstance March No. 1* (Op. 39, 1901), and popular culture tends to associate him with English **nationalism** and imperial nostalgia despite the marginality he experienced as a rural working-class Catholic in a strongly class-conscious Protestant England.

Elgar was born near Worcester and raised in a Catholic home in Worcester. His father was a **piano** tuner, music-shop owner, and church organist. Elgar therefore grew up surrounded by instruments; he revealed himself very early in life to have tremendous musical talent. Largely self-taught, Elgar received only some violin lessons as a teenager. Elgar's failure to afford to study at the Leipzig **Conservatory** did not prevent him from embarking on a career as a freelance musician; in his 20s, Elgar took charge of the Worcester Philharmonic and Worcester Amateur Instrumental Society, led an **orchestra** at the Worcester County Pauper and Lunatic Asylum, played bassoon in a wind **quintet**, assisted his father in his church organ duties, and taught violin and piano lessons. Worcester hosted the Three Choirs Festival triennially, and Elgar played the violin in the orchestra until he left for London in the

1890s. Elgar's work with the asylum, his quintet, and the festival gave him opportunities to compose and to have his work performed. His *Sevillaña* [*sic*]*: Scène Espagnole* was the most important of these earliest works; Elgar's violin teacher Adolf Pollitzer shared it with Crystal Palace music director August Manns, who gave the work its London premiere in 1884. By now, Elgar knew the venue well as an audience member.

In 1889, Elgar married his piano student Caroline Alice Roberts, who was nearly 10 years his senior and from a higher class than his shop-keeping family; Roberts's family disapproved of the union. The two moved to London, where they remained for only a couple of years; Elgar enjoyed only limited success there, even despite his unprecedentedly strong **concert overture** *Froissart* (Op. 19, 1890, rev. 1901), which did not receive a London premiere. Now living in Malvern, Elgar continued to finish new compositions and garner attention while *Froissart*, published by **Novello**, spread his name. Particularly noteworthy is a series of works for chorus and orchestra: *The Light of Life* (Op. 29, 1896, rev. 1899), *Scenes from the Saga of King Olaf* (Op. 30, 1896), and the **cantata** *Caractacus* (Op. 35, 1898). *Caractacus*, composed for the Leeds Festival, was dedicated to Queen **Victoria**, who accepted (*see* PRINTING AND PUBLISHING OF MUSIC). Elgar also continued to expand his knowledge of the concert repertoire on several trips to Germany with his wife.

The turn of the century brought Elgar considerable fame. The *Variations on an Original Theme ("Enigma")*, an orchestral work that revisits Elgar's melody in the spirit of 13 friends and finally himself, combines his previously demonstrated melodic and orchestrational skill with an inventive approach to the concept of orchestral variations. Renowned **conductor** Hans Richter (1843–1916) directed the premiere on 19 June 1899 at St. James's Hall in London. Another crucial work at this time, the **oratorio** *The Dream of Gerontius* (Op. 38), was premiered in London under Richter's baton on 3 October 1900. Based on the poem by Cardinal John Henry Newman, who—like Elgar—was no stranger to the cultural alterity of English Catholicism, the oratorio attracted continental attention; its German premiere was in Düsseldorf on 19 October 1901, and the work was performed there again the following May at the Lower Rhine Music Festival (both times under Julius Buths [1851–1920]). The lion's share of Elgar's other most important works emerge from the 20 years after the *"Enigma" Variations*: the orchestral **song cycle** *Sea Pictures* (Op. 37, 1899), *Pomp and Circumstance March No. 1*, the two numbered **symphonies** (opp. 54 and 63, 1908 and 1911), the Violin Concerto in B minor (Op. 61, 1909), *The Music Makers* for chorus and orchestra (Op. 69, 1912, based on the eponymous O'Shaughnessy poem), and the Cello **Concerto** in E minor (Op. 85, 1918–1919). Elgar was knighted in 1904, inducted into the Order of Merit in 1911, and appointed Master of the King's Musick in 1924. He received honorary degrees from many universities, including Cambridge, Oxford, and Yale. Elgar composed far less after Alice's death in 1920, although he did continue to write into the early 1930s.

Elgar's sudden fame as a great English composer during the early 20th century came despite an apparent recurring depression that ran counter to the consistent underlying tenacity that fueled his ultimate success. Another feature of Elgar's personality brought out by the spotlight was a typical frankness, which occasionally got him into trouble—at rehearsals, for example, or with influential critics such as Ernest Newman (1868–1859). The notion that Elgar's style was overly sentimental, saccharine, or old-fashioned during the 1920s and 1930s has not overpowered the prevailingly positive reception of Elgar as a sensitive, original composer with new ideas about musical style in the wake of **Richard Wagner** and **Johannes Brahms**. [RK]

ELIJAH (ELIAS), **MWV A25/OP. 70. Oratorio** in two parts by **Felix Mendelssohn Bartholdy** on his own **libretto** compiled from Scripture in consultation with the pastor and philologist Julius Schubring (1806–1889) and the diplomat Carl Klingemann (1798–1862); the English version of the libretto was prepared by Mendelssohn's preferred English translator, William Bartholomew (1793–1867), in intensive collaboration with the composer. The work is scored for SATB and boy soprano soloists, chorus and boys' choir (*see* CHILDREN'S CHORUS), and **orchestra**.

Mendelssohn began planning a second oratorio shortly after completing his first—*see ST. PAUL (PAULUS)*, MWV A14/OP. 36—and references to the Old Testament prophet Elijah in this connection date from the late 1830s. Actual composition took place mainly in 1845, after Mendelssohn received a commission to write a new oratorio for the 1846 Birmingham Music Festival; this compositional stage included **orchestration** of the a cappella chorus "Denn er hat seinen Engeln befohlen" (MWV B53, text from Psalm 95), which he had composed and sent to the Prussian monarch Friedrich Wilhelm IV after an assassination attempt in 1844. The original version of the finished work (in English) was premiered to great acclaim at the Birmingham Festival, with an orchestra of 125 and a chorus of 271, on 26 August 1846, but Mendelssohn immediately set about overhauling it extensively, conducting the revised version (again in English) in London on 16 April 1847. Both these performances were in English; the composer never heard the work in German. The London firm of J. J. Ewer & Co. published the choral parts for the first version already in 1846, and in 1847 the Bonn-based firm of **Simrock** published the **piano**/vocal score (including the Prelude arranged for **piano duet**) prepared by the composer, along with choral, orchestral, and soloists' parts and a bilingual full score in English and German. The piano/vocal score was published in France with a translation by Maurice Bourges in 1851 (Paris: Brandus & Cie).

The system of thematic and motivic recollections in *Elijah* adumbrates the idea of the *Leitfaden* as it would be cultivated by **Richard Wagner** and others beginning after 1849 (*see* LEITMOTIV). It is generally considered dramatically tighter and more vivid than *St. Paul*. Its colorful orchestration, vivid musical illustrations of its text, and stirring choruses have made it a favorite of professional as well as amateur performers, although later critics, such as **George Bernard Shaw** and others, criticized both it and *St. Paul* as examples of Mendelssohn's "despicable oratorio mongering" and deplored the supposed "great gulf" between "true religious sentiment and our delight in Mendelssohn's exquisite prettiness" (Shaw). Such objections became common only in the late 19th century, however, when Mendelssohn's music had become widely regarded as emblematic of the inadequacy of Jewish culture and Jewish composers in relation to the demands of Romantic musical expression. Its celebration of an Old Testament prophet is often considered a gesture that reflects the Lutheran Mendelssohn's embracing of his Jewish heritage, but musicologist Jeffrey Sposato and others have shown that Mendelssohn never self-identified as Jewish and never received instruction in Judaism. Together with *St. Paul*, *Elijah* revived the genre of the oratorio as a fruitful venue for musical and dramatic expression in the mid- and later 19th century. [JMC]

See also RECEPTION.

ELORDUY (MEDINA), ERNESTO (1853–1913). Mexican composer and pianist of the Modern Romantic Generation, one of the first Latin American composers to perform his own works successfully in both Europe and Mexico. He is best known for his approximately 100 short **piano** compositions, most of which are tailored to **salon** performance and nominally refer to the various subgenres of European **character pieces** and dances but infuse their musical language with rhythms and other stylistic elements of Mexican popular music (*caprichosas, polonesas, valses*, and so on). His piano **cycle** *Anastasia, o de las evocaciones de Oriente* (Anastasia; or, Some Evocations of the Orient, ca. 1900) and his **zarzuela** *Zulema* (1903) are two of the most important manifestations of orientalism in the Western Hemisphere of the early 20th century (*see* EXOTICISM).

Born in Mexico City, Elorduy undertook a European tour as a pianist and composer in 1871 at the age of 18. As things turned out, the tour became a long-term residence. He remained for a time in Hamburg (where he studied with **Joachim Raff, Anton Rubinstein**, and **Clara Schumann**) and toured the Balkans and Turkey in 1880. Later that year, he settled in Paris, where he remained until 1884. From 1884 to 1891, he served in the Mexican consulate in Marseilles, Santander, and Barcelona, and in 1891, he returned to Mexico and gave three successful recitals. He taught at the Mexico Conservatory from 1901 to 1906. Although much of his music reflects the exoticist interests of his day, his zarzuelas and his integration of Mexican styles into genres characteristic of European Romanticism represent important steps toward Mexican musical **nationalism**. [JMC]

ENGLISH MUSICAL RENAISSANCE. Popular term for an informal British **nationalist** movement in music of the late 19th and early 20th centuries. The movement was a backlash against the centuries-long predominance of continental music in British musical life. It attempted to discover and realize a distinctively English musical culture largely free of continental (especially German and Italian) influences and based instead on English **folk song** and English poetry and other literature. The movement also attempted to recover and celebrate the extraordinary musical accomplishments of Tudor and Elizabethan composers as well as (to a lesser extent) English medieval music, repertoires that had largely escaped extensive discussion in mainstream histories of European music to that point. It was postulated primarily in writings of Francis Hueffer (1845–1889), music critic of *The Times*, and musicologist J. A. Fuller-Maitland (1856–1936), especially in the latter's *English Music in the XIXth Century* (1902). Its principal composers are generally considered to have been **Alexander Mackenzie, Hubert Parry,** and **Charles Villiers Stanford**. [JMC]

EPISODE IN THE LIFE OF AN ARTIST: FANTASTIC SYMPHONY IN FIVE PARTS, **H. 48|OP. 14|A|.** (Fr., *Episode de la vie d'un artiste: Symphonie fantastique en cinq parties.*) **Program symphony** in five movements by **Hector Berlioz**. Along with **Ludwig van Beethoven's** Sixth **("Pastoral") Symphony**, one of the iconic pieces of 19th-century **program music,** the *Symphonie fanstastique* (as it is most commonly known in the English-speaking world) was initially composed in 1830 and premiered in December of the same year by the **orchestra** of the Paris **Conservatory,** conducted by **François-Antoine Habeneck**. It was first published as Berlioz's Op. 4 in 1834 in an arrangement for **piano** solo by **Franz Liszt** and in this guise was the subject of an important review by **Robert Schumann** in the *Neue Zeitschrift für Musik*. Berlioz continued to revise both the music and program substantively for more than a decade thereafter; the orchestral version was first published in parts and full score in 1845, now bearing the opus number 14. Berlioz made further revisions in the program through 1855, most importantly rewriting the entire program as a representation of an opium-induced dream rather than an actual biographical episode. The latter change was introduced in tandem with the publication of Berlioz's completion of the "episode" in the sequel **melodrama** *Lélio, ou Le retour à la vie* (Lelio, or the Return to Life, Op. 14[b]/H. 58).

From the outset, Berlioz conceived the *Episode in the Life of an Artist* as comprising five movements that collectively traced an episodic **narrative**. This program underwent many changes, some of them minor, some of far-reaching significance, over the course of the work's protracted compositional and performance history, but the overall outline is consistent. The first movement is titled *Rêveries, passions* (Day-dreams, Passions); the second, *Un bal* (A Ball); the third, *Scène aux champs* (Scene in the Countryside); the fourth, *Marche au supplice* (March to the Execution); and the fifth, *Songe d'une Nuit du Sabbat* (Dream of a Witches' Sabbath). This narrative would be perilously loose if not for three structural devices: the detailed prose narrative that Berlioz provided in order to explain the extramusical events traced by each movement's music (although Berlioz in 1855 conceded that the prose narrative could be omitted when the Symphony was performed independently of *Lélio*), the persona of the "artist" created by the main title and identified in the third person in the prose program, and the persona of the artist's beloved, who is musically personified by what Berlioz termed an **idée fixe** (a term that possessed both psychoanalytical and musical meaning).

In the prose program, Berlioz explains that this melody symbolizes the beloved; it thus serves the threefold function of interjecting her into the narrative (via the artist/protagonist's thoughts or experiences) whenever it occurs, clarifying that the remainder of the narrative is *not* the beloved's but the artist/protagonist's own, and musically unifying the Symphony as a whole. In these senses, the idée fixe represents the first symphonic application of the technique of **thematic transformation** represented in the **Leitmotivs**, **Leitfaden**, and reminiscence themes of contemporaneous opera and the **concert overtures** of **Felix Mendelssohn Bartholdy**, the later **symphonic poems** of **Franz Liszt**, and eventually the **tone poems** of **Richard Strauss**. The work's programmatic content is further depicted by Berlioz's extensive use—in a work written primarily for an overwhelmingly Catholic French musical public—of the sequence **Dies irae** from the Latin rite for the dead in frankly grotesque scoring in the "Dream of a Witches' Sabbath." While the *Episode* as a whole is broadly indebted to ideas with which Berlioz was familiar from Beethoven's "Pastoral" Symphony, that work was little known in Paris until the mid-1840s. Berlioz's Symphony may thus be seen as his attempt to advocate to the Parisian musical public for the ideas represented in Beethoven's Sixth Symphony as he understood them.

The music of the *Episode* is also notable for its harmonic adventurousness, its structural novelty, its thrifty (and programmatically vivid) recycling of material from previously composed works, and its innovative **orchestration**. The first two of these (discussed perceptively already in Schumann's 1835 review) include features such as repeated oscillations between harmonies whose roots are a diminished fifth apart (fourth movement, mm. 154–59), distinctive tropes on **sonata form** in the first and fourth movements, and a summative *grande réunion des themes* (grand recombination of themes) standing in for the recapitulation of the last movement (mm. 413–35). Its orchestration, while indebted to that of contemporary French **opera** and to ideas advocated for by **Antoine Reicha**, is unprecedented in any known symphony by composers still familiar today. [JMC]

ÉRARD. French firm of harp and **piano** manufacturers and music publishers, known for its instruments' enhanced key and pedal action. The firm was founded by Sébastien Érard (1752–1831) in Paris, where he secured the patronage of the Duchesse de Villeroy. In 1777, he manufactured his first known piano (a five-octave bichord); in 1779, a mechanical harpsichord (*clavecin à expression*) that included a pedal that would allow *crescendo* effects; and in 1791, a square piano. Such was Érard's success in these ventures—which trace the comparatively new fortepiano's triumph over the harpsichord—that he had to enlist the help of an older brother and eventually his nephew in order to complete his orders. His instruments of the late 1780s usually were triple-strung with four pedals, a range of five and a half octaves, and a single-escapement action. He continued to improve the technology and cabinetry of his instruments throughout the first half of the 19th century, significantly influencing composers' writing for the piano. (Both **Franz Joseph Haydn** and **Ludwig van Beethoven** owned one of these instruments, and Beethoven rewrote the last two movements of his Third Piano **Concerto** [Op. 37] to take advantage of its capabilities.)

Érard's most important contribution to piano technology was his introduction of double-escapement action (patented in 1822) that revolutionized piano technique by greatly facilitating rapid repeated notes. It was on such an instrument (with a seven-octave range) that the young **Franz Liszt** made his sensational début at the Paris Exhibition of 1823 and for it that he wrote his *Huit variations* (LW A3/Op. 1) as they were published (also by Érard) in 1824. The firm's pianos remained instruments of choice for a number of the **long 19th century**'s great pianists, among them **Friedrich Kalkbrenner, Felix Mendelssohn Bartholdy, Ignaz Moscheles**, and **Sigismond Thalberg**.

Érard's comparably important engagement with the manufacture of the harp dates from the early 1790s, when he fled the violence of Revolutionary France (where the social turmoil left few resources for ordinary citizens to purchase new instruments and learn to play them). His first patent for that harp was issued in 1794, for an instrument that differed substantially from its predecessors in several regards—most importantly, the use of a new tuning mechanism that permitted the harp to play in eight major and eight minor keys. This new harp was an immense success; an astonishing 1,374 of his harps had been sold by 1810. In 1801 Érard first developed a double-action version of the tuning mechanism that enabled the harp to play in all the major and minor keys, and he perfected and patented this instrument in 1807 and again in 1810. This new 43-string instrument was the basis of many developments in harp writing that emerged over the course of the 19th century. This is the instrument that facilitated the extraordinary innovations introduced by **Elias Parish-Alvars** and probably the one that **Hector Berlioz** envisaged for the second movement of his *Episode in the Life of an Artist*. [JMC]

See also BÖSENDORFER; BROADWOOD; GRAF; STEIN; STEINWAY; WALTER.

"EROICA" SYMPHONY. Popular term (authentic) for **Ludwig van Beethoven**'s Symphony No. 3 in E-flat major, Op. 55. This composition is significant as an emblem of Beethoven's eponymously "heroic" Middle Vienna Period, a **symphony** of unusual length and an atypical approach to dramatic structure for its time.

Beethoven composed most of the "Eroica" in Oberdöbling, near Vienna, during the summer of 1803; the apartment still exists as a museum, the *Eroica-Haus*. Beethoven dedicated the symphony to patron Prince Lobkowitz (1772–1816), who reportedly heard the work in June 1804 in his castle in Raudnitz an der Elbe (now Roudnice nad Labem, Czech Republic) and that December in his Palais in Vienna. Beethoven conducted the public premiere in Vienna on 7 April 1805 at the Theater an der Wien. **Breitkopf & Härtel** published the work as *Sinfonia Eroica* (It., "Heroic Symphony"), subtitled "composta per festiggiare il sovvenire di un grand Uomo" (composed to celebrate the memory of a great man); originally, the subtitle referred to Napoleon Bonaparte.

With respect to orchestration, the "Eroica" is comparable to Beethoven's First and Second Symphonies (opp. 21 and 36, comp. 1799–1800 and 1801–1802, publ. 1801 and 1804). Its length, on the other hand, is likely unprecedented, at roughly twice that of the two predecessors, and seems to have precipitated new approaches to form and proportion. In the first movement's **sonata form**, the monumental exposition is matched by an equally weighty development featuring a new theme in distant E minor. After the recapitulation—famously anticipated by two quasi-errant horns—fails to recall and resolve the development's theme, Beethoven inserts a substantial coda that accomplishes the task and pulls the movement's center of gravity closer to the end. Concern for the entire symphony's dramatic structure is evident in the finale, which grafts a kind of rondo form onto variations on a theme from Beethoven's **ballet** *Die Geschöpfe des Prometheus* (The Creatures of Prometheus, Op. 43, 1800–1801; he had also used the same theme in two earlier works). In this otherwise fast movement, after the end of a tempestuous fugato episode midway though the movement, the theme is presented twice more in an extended, pathos-filled *andante* grand enough to act as dénouement for the entire work. In addition to the symphony's length and

Beethoven's structural adjustments toward end-weightedness, references to contemporary French orchestral **topics** (particularly in the second movement, a funeral march) and extensive, disorienting use of hemiola (most extremely in the **scherzo**) are expressions of the "new path" Beethoven sought from 1802 on. Fugato passages throughout the symphony manifest Beethoven's ever-growing interest in imitative counterpoint.

Although symphonies of such formidable scope were uncommon for the Early Romantic Generation, Beethoven composed several comparably grand symphonies. Given that responses to Beethoven's model by subsequent generations of Romanticism, especially the Romantic Generation, typically also incorporated the attributes discussed above, it is unsurprising that Beethoven's other lengthy symphonies—the Fifth, "**Pastoral**" Sixth, Seventh, and "**Choral**" Ninth—lent themselves the most readily to **canon** formation later in the century. Another similarly large-scale symphony of the Early Romantic Generation is **Franz Schubert**'s "Great" C-major Symphony, No. 7, D. 944 (1825).

The "great man" of the 1806 title page may have been one of several people, including respected military leader Prince Louis Ferdinand of Prussia, dedicatee of Beethoven's Piano Concerto No. 3 and a friend of Lobkowitz who died fighting Napoleonic forces near the end of that year. Nevertheless, we know that Beethoven intended to name the work for Napoléon Bonaparte at various points from sketch to publication, both before and after the famous moment in May 1804 when, according to Ferdinand Ries, Beethoven ripped in half the "Buonaparte"-inscribed title page upon learning that the French leader had made himself emperor. Beethoven's letter to Breitkopf & Härtel that August indicates that the composer intended for the time being to name the symphony after Napoleon. Ries's assertion that Beethoven destroyed the title page and renounced Bonaparte as the work's subject is false since the supposedly destroyed manuscript still exists and Beethoven, during the late stages of the publication process, informed Breitkopf & Härtel that the "actual subject" of the work was Bonaparte. [RK]

ÉTUDE. (Fr., "study"; Ger., Etüde, Studie; It., studio; Sp., studio.) Originally, a composition intended to develop a performer's technique by isolating and developing a specific technical problem and enabling the performer to master the problem by integrating it into a musical context. Études are thus defined first and foremost by their emphasis on technique. The term was originally used interchangeably with *exercise* (Fr., exercise; Ger., Übung; It., essercizio), but by the early 19th century, *exercise* typically connoted a short, repetitive work of little (or no) intrinsically musical merit, often to be repeated ad libitum in different keys. Études tend to be compact and very often simple in form (ternary structures and rondos are common, with internal sections of these often focusing on a different problem of technique than the opening section or the refrain of the rondo). Because of their characteristic brevity, études were often composed and/or published in collections. Études are usually instrumental, and among instrumental études, those for **piano** predominate—but works designated *étude* (and its variants) were also published for the voice as well as many other instruments.

During the early 19th century, especially from the **Restoration** on, the flourishing culture of domestic music making and the growing cult of **virtuosity** increased the demand for studies that would develop the technique of aspiring performers. This market trend led noted pedagogues and performers to publish sets of études for their instruments, often supplementing the method books and treatises on performance that had proliferated since the late 17th century. During the early years of the century, few of these sets of études were intended for concert or recital use, but études that cultivated musical worth and were well suited for domestic and public performance became increasingly common. Examples of the original didactic application of the term *étude* include J. B. Cramer's (1771–1858) *Studio per il pianoforte* (London, 1804–1810), early portions of Muzio Clementi's (1752–1832) *Gradus ad Parnassum, or The Art of Playing on the Piano Forte* (1817–1826), and **Ignaz Moscheles**'s *Studien*, Op. 70 (1825–1826). The Early Romantic Generation's most consequential set of études, however, was written by **Nicolò Paganini**: the set of virtuosic studies composed around 1805 and published as the *24 Caprices*, Op. 1, in 1820.

As the early Romantic virtuoso par excellence, Paganini captured the imagination of all Europe, and as his fame spread through his own performances and publications of his music—especially the *24 Caprices*—the Romantic Generation effectively redefined the term *étude* from a utilitarian genre into one of considerable musical merits. **Franz Liszt** published a set of these new concert études as his Op. 6 (LW A8) in 1827, but the new standard was set by **Fryderyk Chopin**'s *12 Grandes études*, Op. 10 (CT 14–25, comp. 1830–1832, publ. 1833) and their op. 25 counterparts (CT 26–37, publ. 1837). These were quickly followed by **Robert Schumann**'s *Symphonic Études* (Op. 13, comp. 1834–1837, publ. 1837), whose title made these works' increased scope explicit, as well as Moscheles's *Charakterische Studien*, Op. 95 (1836–1837; these appropriated the function of the **character piece**), Liszt's *Grandes études* (LW A39, 1839), **Charles-Valentin Alkan**'s *Douze études dans les tons majeurs* (12 Études in the Major Keys, Op. 35, 1848) and *Douze études dans les tons mineurs* (Op. 39, 1857), and Liszt's revised version of the *Grandes études* as the *Études d'exécution transcendante* (LW A172, publ. 1852). Other significant collections of concert études for piano were published by **Claude Debussy, Stephen Heller, Adolf von Henselt, Ferdinand Hiller, Friedrich Kalkbrenner, Felix Mendelssohn**

Bartholdy, Serge Rachmaninoff, Aleksandr Scriabin, and Sigismond Thalberg, among many others. There were also many collections of études published for instruments other than piano. [JMC]

EWER. London music-publishing and -importing firm. John Jeremiah Ewer went into business in 1823 as a music publisher and importer of music and musical instruments. Ewer worked with partner Julius Johanning from 1823 to 1829. From then until a 1867 merger with Novello, the firm was known as J. J. Ewer & Co. The firm took over fellow London importer Gustavus André in 1839; André's substantial catalog featured works such as Johann Sebastian Bach's so-called B-minor Mass (BWV 232). When Ewer retired in the same year, the business was acquired by wool broker and music lover Edward Buxton. After contacting Raymund Härtel (of Breitkopf & Härtel) about Felix Mendelssohn Bartholdy, Buxton became Mendelssohn's main publisher in England in 1840 just as the composer's negative experiences with Novello came to a breaking point. William Witt became manager of Ewer in 1852 and took over when Buxton retired in 1859. Witt introduced a considerably large universal circulating music library when he took over Ewer. After the 1867 merger, the two parent companies became Novello, Ewer & Co.; the name "Ewer" was taken out in 1898. [RK]

EXOTICISM. (Fr., exotisme; Ger., Exotismus; It., esotismo.) In music and the other arts, the evocation of a people, place, or social milieu whose attitudes, customs, morals, or location are considered substantively different from those of a work's composer and presumed body of performers, listeners, and other interpreters (hereinafter collectively termed "auditors"). The character and manifestations of exoticism in any given instance varies according to the time, geography, and cultural and social attitudes, customs, and morals of a work's creator and presumable auditors. On the whole, however, exoticist artworks deal with the issue of identity—the Selfhood of the creator and/or presumable auditors and the perceived Otherness of the people, place, or social milieu being exoticized. They evoke the "Other" (uppercase O) in order to assimilate, exorcize, or romanticize it while also implicitly affirming the collective identity of the creator and presumed auditors.

Exoticism in music of the long 19th century is thus sometimes a pendant of nationalism (although historical and cultural themes may be exoticized as well): nationalism seeks to affirm collective identity by *authentically* dealing with themes or drawing on material associated with a given national identity, while exoticism deals with themes of an alien Other and imitates or caricatures that Other *inauthentically*, thereby affirming the composer's and presumable auditors' national identity by underscoring the difference between that national Self and the alien Other. Exoticism thus differs also from the practice (increasingly common in the Modern Romantic Generation) of drawing on outside musical subjects and idioms in order to enrich one's own musical palette (e.g., as in the music of **Claude Debussy**) because that practice aspires to authenticity of original expression rather than to a romanticizing or exorcizing of something that remains alien to the musical idiom as a whole.

Musical exoticism dates back to (at least) the 15th century, but its importance increased in Europe during the long 19th century because the industrial revolution, with its improvements in transportation and communication, made it possible for individuals to experience other cultures and peoples not just through literature and secondhand accounts but also in person—an experience that was naturally Other to the individuals' own frames of reference. Sometimes such encounters took the form of traveling to and returning from a foreign culture (resulting in the travelers' attempts to import an exotic *couleur locale* into their music), but frequently individuals and groups from foreign cultures were brought into a new locale and observed there. Both modes of encounter emphasized difference.

In the early long 19th century, the most common form of musical exoticism was the *alla Turca* style, represented, for example, in **Wolfgang Amadeus Mozart**'s *Die Entführung aus dem Serail*(The Abduction from the Seraglio, K. 384, 1781), the second subject of the last movement of **Ludwig van Beethoven's** Ninth **("Choral") Symphony** (Op. 125, 1824), or—a bit incongruously—**Peter Cornelius's** *Der Barbier von Baghdad* (1858). Other prominent forms of exoticism include the *Style hongrois*, Indianism (exoticizing Amerindians), American blackface minstrelsy (**Louis Moreau Gottschalk**'s *Le banjo: Grotesque fantasie*, 1855), and Russian orientalism. Orientalism itself is an umbrella term that embraces anything regarded by a given Western culture as "Eastern"—including such diverse subjects as the Islamic Middle East (e.g., Arabia, North Africa, Persia, Turkey), the area known in the Western Hemisphere as the "Far East" (i.e., East and South Asia, including China, India, Indochina, and Japan), or the Greater Middle East (all of the above taken together).

The various sorts of **folk songs** (real or imaginary) and "national" dances and **songs** penned during the long 19th century by composers not of the nationality supposedly represented—such as **barcarolles**, boleros, **écossaises**, fandangos, "hindostannies" **mazurkas**, polkas, **polonaises**, saltarellos, or tarantellas—are also manifestations of musical exoticism. So are, for example, non-German composers' musical evocations of Germanness via chorales and fugues (**Giacomo Meyerbeer**'s *Les Huguenots*, 1836), non-Italian composers' evocations of Italianness by means of melodies whose phraseology falls into *quinario doppio* and whose melodies are in compound triple meter and proceed in parallel thirds and sixths, and so on. Exoticism also flourished in the New World as well as the Old—in works of North and South America, in idioms that exoticize Amerindian cultures, and in North American works that exoticize Latin American ones.

The central techniques of musical exoticism were both **paratextual** and textual; that is, poets and composers employed foreign-sounding names, titles, and other verbal identifiers extrinsic to the musical text per se in order to signify the alterity of the exoticized subject, usually in tandem with musical idioms that were somehow alien or foreign to those of the exoticizer. Some of the most potent tools in the rhetorical arsenal of musical exoticism during the long 19th century were styles and **topics**, conventionalized rhetorical aggregates of melodic, harmonic, rhythmic, timbral, and structural features that collectively signified the alterity of the exoticized subject by departing from the assumptions and norms of the cultural Self of composers and their presumed auditors. Pentatonic and other gapped scales, modal melodies and harmonies, drone and ostinato accompaniments (particularly those outlining open fifths and octaves rather than triads), unconventional phraseology, persistent and tinkling or jangling percussion (e.g., sustained rather than sporadic use of cymbals, tambourines, and triangles), and highly sectional and repetitive forms are thus common indicators of the musically exotic. That such features usually have little or nothing to do with the actual idioms of the exoticized cultures is immaterial, for their rarity (especially in aggregate) in many of the accepted idioms of cultivated music in the Western European sphere of influence is enough to signify the alterity of the exoticized subject even if the musical idioms ascribed to it are fictitious or interchangeable with other musical or cultural Others.

Finally, it is useful to distinguish between *exoticism of creation* and *exoticism of consumption* or **reception** and to recognize that exoticism during the long 19th century (and before and after) was implicitly gendered. For instance, **Antonín Dvořák** composed his two sets of *Slovanské tance* (**Slavonic Dances**, B. 83/Op. 46 and B. 47/Op. 72, 1878 and 1887) as nationalist works, but those works were commissioned and published by a German firm (**Simrock**) for a market of Germans, French, and others, the overwhelming majority of whom got to know Dvořák's nationalist music as something distinctly Other to their own musical idioms and therefore exotic in content if not in intent. Moreover, 19th-century gender ideologies typically associated strength (authority, intellect, power, and imperial/colonial rule) with masculinity and weakness (uncultivatedness, simplicity, and colonial subjugation) with femininity. During the long 19th century, therefore, the exoticizing creator, regardless of nationality or cultural identity, often exaggerated musical features stereotypically associated with femininity in the exoticized subject, and since the stereotypical Self was usually male and intellectual, the stereotypical exoticized Other frequently was female and intuitive, often erotically enticing. Alternatively, the exoticized Other was frequently an assembly of cutthroat savages who betrayed and/or murdered the civilized Self in rage, thus demonizing the Other while warning of the dangers of accepting or welcoming such unintellectual attributes.

Providing even a minimally representative inventory of notable examples of the musically exotic in music of the long 19th century would exceed the limits of this entry. It is fair to observe, however, that **Georges Bizet**'s *Carmen* (1875) is the archetypical exoticist masterpiece: composed on a French libretto by a French composer for predominantly French audiences, it is set in Spain and centers on the seductive treachery of the Roma Gypsy Carmen, leading to the downfall of Don José (whose affinity with the French selfhood of the opera's presumed auditors is betrayed by the fact that his music is consistent with the norms of contemporary French musical idioms). Other notable examples include **Isaac Albéniz**'s *Iberia* (1905–1909); **Hector Berlioz**'s *L'enfance du Christ* (1855) and *La révolution grecque* (1825–1826); Bizet's *Les pêcheurs de perles* (1863); **Aleksandr Borodin**'s *In the Steppes of Central Asia* (1882) and *Prince Igor* (1869–1870, rev. 1874–1887); **Johannes Brahms**'s *Hungarian Dances* (1869, 1880); **Emmanuel Chabrier**'s *España* (1883); **Fryderyk Chopin**'s *Boléro* (1834); **Léo Delibes**'s *Lakmé* (1881–1882); **Mikhail Glinka**'s two *Spanish Overtures* (1845 and 1848); **Gaetano Donizetti**'s *La zingara* (1822); **Ernesto Elorduy**'s *Zulema* (1902); **Félicien David**'s *Le desert* (1845), *Christophe Colombe* (1847), and *Le perle du Brésil* (1851); **Carlos Gomes**'s *Il Guarany* (1870); **Édouard Lalo**'s *Symphonie espagnole* (1875); **Franz Liszt**'s 19 *Hungarian Rhapsodies* (1846–1853, 1882–1885 passim); **Edward Macdowell**'s *"Indian" Suite* (1895); **Pietro Mascagni**'s *Iris* (1898); **Jules Massenet**'s *Hérodiade* (1881, rev. 1884); **Felix Mendelssohn Bartholdy**'s *On Lena's Gloomy Heath* (1846); **Giacomo Meyerbeer**'s *L'Africaine* (1865) and *Il crociato in Egitto* (1824); **Jaques Offenbach**'s *La Périchole* (1868, rev. 1874); **Giacomo Puccini**'s *Madama Butterfly* (1896) and *Turandot* (1926); **Nikolay Rimsky-Korsakov**'s *Capriccio espagnol* (1888) and *Sheherazade* (1889); **Gioachino Rossini**'s *L'italiana in Algeri* (1813); **Camille Saint-Saëns**'s *Suite algérienne* (1881); **Gaspare Spontini**'s *Fernand Cortez, ou La conquête du Mexique* (1809); the Dance of the Seven Veils from **Richard Strauss**'s *Salome* (1905); **Arthur Sullivan**'s *Utopia Limited* (1893); **Giuseppe Verdi**'s *Il Trovatore* (1853, Fr. version 1857) and *Aida* (1871); and **Carl Maria von Weber**'s *Abu Hassan* (1811), among many others. [JMC]

See also JANISSARY MUSIC.

EXTRAVAGANZA. In general, term for any lavish production (with or without music), more specifically, a musical work characterized by extravagant fancy, often of a humorous or satirical sort. Extravaganzas may be either instrumental or vocal; the latter are usually staged. **Wolfgang Amadeus**

Mozart's *Ein musikalischer Spaß* (A Musical Joke, K. 522, 1787) and **Charles Villiers Stanford**'s *Ode to Discord* (1909) are well-known instrumental extravaganzas, as is the less well known final movement of **Louis Spohr**'s "Historical" **Symphony** (No. 6, Op. 116, 1842).

The staged vocal extravaganza is a subgenre of the **burlesque**, effectively defined by dramatist James Robinson Planché (1796–1880) as "the whimsical treatment of a poetical subject." The "poetical subjects" were sometimes serious or even tragic in nature, often based on well-known myths or fairy tales, and the satirical or parodying character of the extravaganza was typically enhanced by lavish sets, costumes, and staging. The lampooning character was further emphasized by the use of rhyming verse replete with puns and by consciously simple music orchestrated and otherwise treated as if it were complicated and sophisticated. W. S. Gilbert and **Arthur Sullivan** designated several of their collaborations as extravaganzas (e.g., *Trial by Jury*, 1875), and **John Philip Sousa** composed the music for at least one (*Chris and the Wonderful Lamp*, 1899). [JMC]

See also COMIC OPERA; OPERETTA, OPERATTA.

F

FANTASIA, FANTASY, FANCY. (It., from Gr. *phantasia*; Fr., fantaisie; Ger., Fantasie, Phantasie; Sp., fantasia.) In the **long 19th century**, term for compositions (usually instrumental) whose salient characteristics seem to be dominated by flights of the imagination or fancy and a freedom from any other set pattern of forms and styles. These may include episodic, sectional, or irregular form and improvised or improvisatory styles, or they may be new, apparently "free" acts of musical creation based on preexisting works. Many of these works are full-length compositions (the length of a **sonata** movement) but freer in form and at least occasionally improvisatory in style (e.g., **Ludwig van Beethoven**'s Fantasia in G Minor, Op. 77 [1810], **Fryderyk Chopin**'s F-minor Fantasy, CT 42/Op. 49 [1841, publ. 1842], **Felix Mendelssohn Bartholdy**'s *Trois fantaisies ou caprices*, MWV SD4/Op. 16 [1829, publ. 1830/1831], or **Wolfgang Amadeus Mozart**'s C-minor Fantasy, K. 475 [1785]). The term could also be applied (often with semantic modifiers) to short, ternary-form **character pieces**, such as **Johannes Brahms**'s op. 116 *Fantasien* for piano (the individual works of which are titled either "**Capriccio**" or "**Intermezzo**"; 1892, publ. 1893) or **Robert Schumann**'s *Phantasiestücke*, Op. 12 (originally titled simply *Phantasien*, 1832–1838). **Johann Sebastian Bach**'s *Chromatic Fantasy and Fugue in D Minor* for organ (BWV 903, 1723 or earlier) became a major **topic** and source of inspiration in the context of the **Bach revival** and the Romantics' appropriation of the Baroque composer.

Most ubiquitous in the long 19th century, represented by hundreds if not thousands of individual works, especially for **piano** solo or violin solo, were compositions labeled "fantasy" that were **virtuoso** showpieces based on themes from well-known **operas**. Many of these works took the form of improvised or improvisatory theme-and-**variation** sets that showcased spectacular technique but placed less emphasis on musical integrity, sometimes leaving behind the work on which they were based for extended stretches in order to explore a particular figuration. The names most commonly associated with this sort of fantasy are Charles de Bériot (1802–1870), **Louis Moreau Gottschalk, Nicolò Paganini**, and **Sigismond Thalberg**. These fantasies (sometimes labeled *potpourris*, *reminiscences*, or *concert paraphrases*) are frequently regarded with suspicion because of those plentiful instances of musical abuse, but the genre also includes many remarkable compositions. **Franz Liszt** is generally considered its master. Among his most important contributions are the *Grande fantaisie di bravura sur "La clochette" de Paganini* (often known simply as "La campanella"; LW A15, 1832–1834, publ. 1834, rev. 1839), *Réminiscences de* [**Gaetano Donizetti**'s] *"Lucia di Lammermoor"* (LW A22, 1835–1836, publ. 1840), *Grande fantaisie sur des thèmes de l'opéra Les Huguenots* [of **Giacomo Meyerbeer**] (LW A35, 1836–1842, publ. 1842), and *Réminiscences de Don Juan* [on Mozart's *Don Giovanni*] (LW A80, 1841, publ. 1843).

Occasionally in the long 19th century, the term *fantasia* could be used as a stylistic and/or formal modifier in conjunction with other, more obviously structured forms. The most well-known examples of this usage are probably Beethoven's piano sonatas Op. 27, nos. 1 and 2 (1801, publ. 1802); Robert Schumann's Op. 17 (a three-movement de facto sonata that quotes from Beethoven's *An die ferne Geliebte* and prefaces each movement with a **paratextual** subtitle: "Ruinen" [Ruins], "Siegebogen" [Triumphal Arch], and "Sternbild" [Image of a Star]); and Liszt's *Après une lecture du Dante, fantasia quasi sonata* (ca. 1843) from the second volume of the *Années de pélèrinage*, LW A55. **Franz Schubert**'s celebrated *"Wanderer" Fantasy* (D. 760, 1822, publ. 1823) is actually a **sonata** in four movements (played without pause), all movements of which are based in part on the theme that is the subject of the second movement. His Fantasia in F Minor for **piano duet** (D. 940, 1828, publ. 1829) is also cast in four thematically interrelated movements but is not based on a specific preexisting theme.

Although most common in connection with works for a single player (usually keyboard), the term *fantasy* and its variants were also appropriated for instrumental **chamber music** and **orchestral** works in the long 19th century. Important examples of the chamber variety include Robert Schumann's *Fantasiestücke* for clarinet, violin, or cello and piano (Op. 73, 1849) and his *Phantasiestücke* for violin, cello, and piano (Op. 88, 1842, publ. 1850) and **Gabriel Fauré**'s Fantasy for Flute and Piano, Op. 79 (1898). Among the best-known examples of the orchestral fantasy are Beethoven's *Choral Fantasy*, Op. 80 (1808, R/1809, publ. 1810); **Hector Berlioz**'s *Fantaisie sur la Tempête de Shakespeare* (Fantasy on Shakespeare's *The Tempest*, No. 6 of *Lélio, ou Le retour à la vie*, Op. 14[b], 1830); **Max Bruch**'s *Fantasie unter freier Benutzung schottischer Volksmelodien (Schottischer Fantasie)*, Op. 46 (1880); **Nikolay Rimsky-Korsakov**'s *Fantasia on Two Russian Themes* (Op. 33, 1886–1887); the first version (1841) of Robert Schumann's D-minor Symphony (assigned the serial number "4" and the opus number 120 when it was published in overhauled form in 1851) or his Fantasy in C Major for Violin and Orchestra (Op. 13, 1853, publ. 1854);

Richard Strauss's "symphonic fantasy" *Aus Italien* (TrWV 147/Op. 16, 1886); and **Pyotor Il'yich Tchaikovsky**'s *Romeo and Juliet* (1869, rev. 1870, 1880), which is subtitled "fantasy overture after Shakespeare." [JMC] *See also* CAPRICCIO; VIRTUOSO (M.), VIRTUOSA (F.).

FANTASTIC SYMPHONY. See EPISODE IN THE LIFE OF AN ARTIST: FANTASTIC SYMPHONY IN FIVE PARTS, H. 48/OP. 14[A].

FASSUNG LETZTER HAND. (Ger., "latest authorized version.") An editorial ideology that dictates that when there are multiple versions of an artwork or text that stem from the original creator, the latest one represents the creator's final thoughts and therefore supersedes all earlier versions, which are in turn relegated to a compositional status somewhere between a draft and the final version (*see* COMPOSITIONAL PROCESS, CREATIVE PROCESS). For most of the 20th century, source-critical **editions** of 18th- and 19th-century music were prepared according to this ideology. Increasingly, however, scholars have become aware that for most of the **long 19th century** (as well as earlier musical history), most composers held a more nuanced view of the relative authority of different versions. Although within a given composer's oeuvre there may be some instances in which the composer wished the final version to supersede earlier ones, within that same composer's output there are usually others in which the composer deliberately authorized multiple versions, sometimes differing significantly among one another, and considered many, most, or all of these "simultaneous variants" equally valid. When the composer did not consider any single version superior to any other ones, it is awkward to argue for the exclusion of all versions but the last on the basis of the authority of an editorial ideology whose foundation is the composer's presumable intentions (*see* INTENTIONAL FALLACY).

Therein lies the crux of the authority, and problematicality, of the *Fassung letzter Hand* as an editorial ideology. In philology generally, the notion began to gain strength as a by-product of the cult of genius: texts were to be interpreted as utterances of a single mind more than as products of their contexts. In music, the philological imperative for a single definitive version of any given "text" (i.e., composition) was abetted by the drive to create a **canon** of authoritative musical works and by the fact that only one version of a piece could be performed at any given time (one cannot perform two or more different versions of a work simultaneously). Together with the growth of the music-publishing industry over the course of the 19th century and, at century's end, the move to redefine principles of musical **copyright** so that authorship resided with the composer rather than the initial publisher, this

202 • FASSUNG LETZTER HAND

imperative discouraged any egalitarian perspective on "simultaneous variants" in favor of a single, authoritative musical text (*see* EDITING AND EDITIONS).

Few would suggest that such an ideology is problematical when composers themselves held such views. The problems arise when one considers that this editorial ideology was also applied to works that were created prior to and during the emergence of the drive to establish a musical canon—that is, before the ideology came into being. Since authorial intentionality justifies the selection of the *Fassung letzter Hand* as the definitive musical text, other ideologies logically should be employed when there is no evidence or other reason to believe that the composer wanted the final version to supersede all earlier ones. At the same time, any ideology arguing for the ultimate authority of the final, most heavily revised version of a composition also runs afoul of the notion, likewise increasingly prominent in writings about music over the course of the 19th century, that the composer's authority is greatest and purest in the version of a work that was (supposedly) created with the least consideration of specific, limiting contextual or circumstantial factors—that is, with the *first* complete notated version (*Fassung erster Hand*). One might well argue that the struggle between these two mutually exclusive editorial ideologies accounts for many or most of the misguided or philologically corrupt editions by which many compositions have been known since the late 19th century.

Whether the editor and performer should employ the *Fassung letzter Hand* or some other editorial ideology in any given editorial task is often a composer-by-composer or sometimes case-by-case decision. Although it is generally safe to assume that most compositions written in the last decade or so of the 19th century probably were intended to exist in a single authoritative version and that the latest version was conceived and executed as an improvement, there are known exceptions to this rule, and many more exceptions certainly have yet to be recognized. Similarly, it is probably safe to assume that until the century's end, few composers would have sympathized with an ideology that strove for a single authorized text to the exclusion of all others and with no regard to circumstance—but here, too, there are certainly exceptions. Editors, performers, and other scholars will continue to grapple with these issues and their consequences; indeed, a single overriding approach that is viable across repertoires spanning the long 19th century is probably not desirable. The complexities of the situation ultimately emphasize the importance of relying on source-critical editions and of their using the scholarly apparatus as well as the main musical texts of those editions.

Significant musicological contributions concerning the methodology of the *Fassung letzter Hand* have been made by Dadelson (1961), Finscher (1980), Feder (1989), Kallberg (1990), and Boorman (1997). [JMC]

See also BEETHOVEN, LUDWIG VAN (1770–1827); BRAHMS, JO-HANNES (1833–1897); BRUCKNER, (JOSEPH) ANTON (1824–1896); CHOPIN, FRYDERYK (FRANCISZEK) [FRÉDÉRIC FRANÇOIS] (1810–1849); MENDELSSOHN BARTHOLDY, (JACOB LUDWIG) FE-LIX (1809–1847); SCHUMANN, ROBERT (ALEXANDER) (1810–1856).

FAURÉ, GABRIEL (URBAIN) (1845–1924). French composer of the Late Romantic Generation. Fauré, who lived nearly 80 years, is often regarded as a transitional figure between mid-19th- and early 20th-century stylistic currents. While Fauré's compositional style did transform throughout his career from restrained elegance in the 1860s to a subtle, dissonance-friendly flavor of French Modernism, his style was original at every stage. Of his large compositional output, Fauré's more than 100 **songs** and 66 **piano** works provide the fullest testimony of his stylistic breadth. At various points in his life, Fauré worked in many other genres, producing several sets of **incidental music,** the **operas** *Prométhée* (1900) and *Pénélope* (1913), choral music (most of it sacred), orchestral **suites** based mainly on his stage music, a violin **concerto** and other orchestrally accompanied solo works, two **piano quartets** and **quintets,** a **string quartet,** and various other works of instrumental **chamber music.**

In 1855, Fauré's father sent him to Louis Niedermeyer's École de Musique Classique et Religeuse in Paris (later called the École Niedermeyer). Initially, the repertoire he studied there focused on church music, particularly plainchant, Renaissance polyphony, and organ works. After Niedermeyer's death in 1861, **Camille Saint-Saëns**—then 25—joined the faculty as an instructor in **piano** and composition; he added the works of recent and living composers to the conservative curriculum. After finishing at the École in 1865 with many prizes, Fauré served St. Sauveur at Rennes as an organist and composer; he built a reputation there as an excellent private teacher. Fauré enlisted in the infantry when the **Franco-Prussian War** began in 1870; he served for seven months. In the fall of 1871, he reconnected with Saint-Saëns, frequented his **salon,** and through him became acquainted with **Emmanuel Chabrier, Vincent d'Indy, Édouard Lalo,** and other significant Parisian musical figures. He also joined the **Société Nationale de Musique,** which Saint-Saëns and others had formed earlier that year. Fauré began filling in for Saint-Saëns at La Madeleine from 1874; he became choirmaster three years later when Saint-Saëns left permanently. While abroad in the late 1870s, Fauré met **Franz Liszt** and **Richard Wagner,** whose *Ring of the Nibelung* he heard multiple times through 1882 in addition to *Lohengrin, Die Meistersinger, Tannhäuser,* and *Tristan und Isolde.* Despite Fauré's appreciation for Wagner, his own compositions do not suggest any influence.

Fauré married Marie Fremiet in 1883; his work at the Madeleine supported their family of two boys (b. 1883 and 1889). In the 1880s, he composed many songs and piano pieces, several chamber works including the Piano Quartet No. 2, and a few sacred choral works. The first version of Fauré's **Requiem** premiered at his church in 1888. Fauré's career began to pick up rapidly in the early 1890s with his appointment as inspector of national conservatories in 1892 and the publication of his *Cinq mélodies* (Five **Mélodies**, Op. 58) and the **song cycle** *La bonne chanson.*

Fauré began teaching composition at the Paris **Conservatory** in 1896; he became director nine years later. His students there included Nadia Boulanger, Maurice Ravel, and Florent Schmitt. Fauré's directorship was a breakthrough for his reputation as a composer; his works finally were being performed more often. His opera *Pénélope* (1913) was a tremendous hit, and it was revived at the conclusion of World War I. Other significant works from these years include the song cycles *Le jardin clos* (The Walled Garden, Op. 106, 1914) and *Mirages* (Op. 113, 1919), the orchestrally accompanied piano *Fantaisie* (**Fantasy**, Op. 111, 1918), accompanied **sonatas** for violin and cello, and numerous piano **barcarolles, impromptus, nocturnes,** and **preludes.** Fauré's health declined in the years after his retirement (1920), but he produced some of his most spectacular chamber works during this time, including his second piano quintet and his only **piano trio** and **string quartet.** [RK]

FAUST. Iconic tragedy based on history, folklore, and a variety of literary treatments stemming from as early as the 16th century; one of the most potent and frequently troped **topics** of music, literature, painting, and general culture in the **long 19th century.** The tragedy's historical origin is found in the life and reputed deeds of a learned magician who supposedly entered into a pact with the devil and died some sort of unnatural death in 1540. The rumors and legends surrounding this historical Faust were compiled in a manuscript assembled by Christoph Rosshirt in 1575, published in a moralizing chapbook in 1587, and adapted into English in 1589 or 1593 in Christopher Marlowe's (1564–1593) moralistic drama *The Tragicall History of the Life and Death of Doctor Faustus* (publ. posth. 1604). Over the course of the 17th and 18th centuries, new, more elaborate adaptations of the story proliferated, and in the 18th century these stories began to portray Faust as a womanizer who took advantage of naive girls who stepped outside their social class and station in life as women. The saga was effectively redefined in the four treatments published by **Johann Wolfgang von Goethe** (see below), but other authors continued to pen new works based on the legend and lore outside Goethe's version as well as troping further on that version. Among these later treatments in the long 19th century are Christian Dietrich Grabbe's (1801–1836) *Don Juan und Faust* (1829), **Aleksandr Pushkin's** *A*

Scene from Faust (1830), Nikolaus Lenau's (1802–1850) Faust (1836), **Heinrich Heine**'s Der Doktor Faust: Ein Tanzpoem (1851), and **W. S. Gilbert**'s Gretchen (1879).

Goethe's version of the Faust saga centers around three principal characters: Faust, the demon Mephistopheles, and the humble, pure maid Margarete (Gretchen). In many ways, it represents the first "modern" Faust—partly because he recast the traditional moralizing tone of the tale as a tragedy set in motion by a wager between the Mephistopheles and Faust and partly because Goethe's profoundly conflicted Faust was, in an age obsessed with the acquisition and codification of knowledge and experience, both noble and empathetic. Equally important in the context of the changing societal structures of the long 19th century was that Goethe's Gretchen was not merely an object of male desire, as Faust's women had been in earlier recountings of the story, but a character who was fully worthy of Faust and in some ways the driving force behind the tragedy.

The Faust project occupied Goethe from the late 1760s to the end of his life. In 1775, he completed his first recounting of the first part of the tragedy in a document now known as the Urfaust (publ. posth. in 1887), and in 1790 he publicly staked his claim in the growing Faust discourse by releasing Faust: Ein Fragment. In 1797, he returned to the project of completing the first part, also beginning work on a Helena-Dichtung (Poem about Helen—i.e., ideas conceptualizing Faust's fabled conjuring of Helen of Troy) that would eventually figure in the tragedy's conclusion. Faust: Der Tragödie erster Teil (Faust: Part One of the Tragedy) was published with an extraordinary cliff-hanger ending in 1808, and the completed Helena-Dichtung was published as a "Classic-Romantic Phantasmagoria: Interlude to Faust" in April 1827. Finally, Goethe submitted the completion of the tragedy in Faust: Der Tragödie zweiter Teil for publication just weeks before his death; the work was published posthumously. The second part of the tragedy ranks as one of the most difficult works of German literature and is virtually incomprehensible without a thorough grounding in Greek mythology and medieval alchemy. This situation made adaptation into a faithful opera **libretto** or other musical setting extraordinarily difficult.

The complicated textual history of the Faust saga produced a correspondingly complex corpus of musical works based on Faust during the long 19th century: some settings derive completely or primarily from sources other than Goethe's recounting, others from Goethe's version as it existed until 1832, and others (written after 1832) from Goethe's completed tragedy; still others focus on one part while incorporating material from the other. To the first of these categories belong Johann Friedrich Reichardt's (1752–1814) **incidental music** (1790), **Louis Spohr**'s opera Faust (1816, rev.1852; on a libretto by Joseph Carl Bernard), which incorporates elements from Goethe's Faust I and Faust-Fragment but is based primarily on other versions; and

Franz Liszt's *Zwei Episoden aus Lenaus Faust* for **piano duet** (LW B15, 1856–1861), based on Lenau's version of the story (1836), among others. The many settings based on or extracted from *Faust I* include all of Carl Friedrich Zelter's (1758–1832) and **Franz Schubert**'s *Faust* settings (D. 118, 126, 367, and 440 and the incomplete scene D. 564) as well as **Ludwig van Beethoven**'s *Flohlied des Mephisto* (Op. 75, no. 3, 1810); **Giuseppe Verdi**'s *Perduta ho la pace* and *Deh, pietoso, oh Addolorata* (1838); Franz Liszt's *Studentenlied aus Goethe's "Faust," Der König in Thule*, and *Soldatenlied aus "Faust"* (1844); and **Hugo Wolf**'s *Gretchen vor dem Andachtsbild der Mater Dolorosa* (1878). Lesser-known works in this class include compositions by Spohr (1809), **Vaclav Tomášek** (1815), **Rudolfe Kreutzer** (1820), Ignaz Seyfried (1776–1841; 1820 and 1829), Bernhard Klein (1793–1832; 1830), Wilhelm von Lenz (1809–1883; 1830), Peter Josef von Lindpaintner (1791–1856; 1830 and 1854), **Carl Loewe** (1836), **Giacomo Meyerbeer** (1837), Julius Rietz (1812–1877; 1841), Moritz Hauptmann (1792–1868; 1850), **Franz Lachner** (1850), **Anton Rubinstein** (1864), Henry Litolff (1818–1891; 1875), Eduard Lassen (1830–1904; 1876), and Henrich Zöllner (1854–1941; 1887).

The corpus of works that straddle *Faust I* and *Faust II* includes some of the long 19th century's most provocative musical engagements with Goethe's recounting of the legend. **Hector Berlioz**'s original op. 1, the *Huit scenes de Faust* (H. 33, based on Gérard de Nerval's French translation), was composed in 1828–1829 and thus based entirely on *Faust I*, but Berlioz later withdrew this opus and subsumed much of its material into *La Damnation de Faust* (H. 111, 1846), a work that celebrates *Faust II* and its theme of redemption. **Richard Wagner**'s *Seven Compositions for Goethe's "Faust"* (WWV 15, 1831) ranks among his youthful ephemera, and his programmatic *Faust Overture* (WWV 59, 1839–1840) exerted little influence. While preparing to conduct Beethoven's Ninth Symphony in Dresden in 1846, he penned a program for that work based on excerpts from *Faust II*—a document that represented an important step in the development of his ideas on the **music drama** and a milestone in the critical reception of both Beethoven and Goethe. Liszt's ***"Faust" Symphony*** in three movements is constructed, according to its subtitle, as a series of "character studies after Goethe" (*Charakterbilder nach Johann Wolfgang von Goethe*); the movements' respective subjects—Faust, Gretchen, and Mephistopheles—are included in both *Faust I* and *Faust II*, but when Liszt added an optional concluding "Chorus mysticus" (T solo, TB chorus) in 1857, he explicitly embraced *Faust II* in the work as well.

The most enduringly popular musical setting of *Faust I* is **Charles Gounod**'s opera *Faust* (1859), on a libretto by Jules Barbier (1825–1901) and Michel Carré (1821–1872) after Nerval's 1828 translation of *Faust I*. Although Gounod's opera is based on the first part of the tragedy, he and his librettists dispensed with the conspicuously unresolved ending of Goethe's text and concluded their text with the chorus "Christ est ressuscité!" (adapted from Nerval's translation of ll. 737–41 of Goethe's text for Part I), thus adopting the rhetorical gesture of redemption that is utterly lacking in *Faust I* but concludes *Faust II*. The same gesture occurs at the close of Mahler's Eighth Symphony, which (like the revised version of Liszt's *"Faust" Symphony* and Schumann's *Szenen aus Goethe's "Faust"*; see below) quotes the concluding "Chorus mysticus" from Goethe's drama and thus implicitly aligns itself with that literary source.

Among the earliest composers to set texts from *Faust II* to music was **Fanny Hensel**, who in 1843 composed the opening of Act I in a setting for soprano solo, women's chorus (*see* FRAUENCHOR), and **piano**. **Robert Schumann** began contemplating using *Faust II* as well as *Faust I* as subjects for musical treatment in February of the following year, a venture that ultimately produced his *Szenen aus Goethe's "Faust"* for chorus and orchestra (WoO 3, 1849, rev. 1853, publ. posth. 1858)—by far the most extensive musical setting of texts from Part II of the drama to that point, with two of its three numbered sections taken from *Faust II*. The two most important compositional engagements with the complete tragedy in the late 19th and early 20th centuries were penned by Italians: **Arrigo Boito**'s *Mefistofele* (1868, rev. 1875, 1876) and **Ferruccio Busoni**'s incomplete *Doktor Faust* (1916–1924), which also draws on the early puppet plays and Marlowe's recounting of the tale. Other, less well known settings were composed by Loewe (1833), **Albert Lortzing** (1849), Meyerbeer (1862), Pietro Raymondi (1786–1853; 1837), and Carl Reissiger (1798–1859; 1849), among others. [JMC]

See also "CHORAL" SYMPHONY; FEMINISM; PROGRAM (PROGRAMMATIC) MUSIC.

A "FAUST" SYMPHONY, **LW G12.** (Ger., *Eine Faust-Symphonie.*) **Symphony** in three movements by **Franz Liszt**; with **Ludwig van Beethoven**'s **"Pastoral" Symphony** and **Hector Berlioz**'s *Episode in the Life of an Artist*, one of the most important **program symphonies** of the **long 19th century**. The full title is *Eine Faust-Symphonie: In drei Charakterbildern nach Goethe* (A *Faust* Symphony: In Three Character Pictures after [**Johann Wolfgang von**] **Goethe**). Liszt had been introduced to Part I of Goethe's recounting of the Faust legend (initially in Gérard de Nerval's very free French translation) by Berlioz already in 1830; at that point, Goethe was still working to complete Part II of the tragedy. When Liszt read the tragedy's conclusion is uncertain, but he sketched portions of his Symphony in 1839. As the mid-century cult of Goethe gained strength and after Liszt himself assumed the musical direction of the Weimar court (where Goethe had lived and worked for most of his career), Liszt encountered several other responses to the great poet's treatment of the old legend—most notably **Robert Schumann**'s *Szenen aus Goethes "Faust"* (WoO 3, 1848, rev. 1853, publ. posth. 1858), whose complete premiere Liszt conducted on 29 August 1849, and Berlioz's *La damnation de Faust* (H. 111/Op. 24, 1846).

Liszt composed the *"Faust" Symphony* in its essentials between August and October 1854, but in this state it contained little if anything to reflect the conclusion or completion of the tragedy as Goethe had finally published it in 1832. Perhaps in order to address this issue, in 1857 Liszt appended an optional section for solo tenor and *Männerchor* (with organ and **orchestra**), intoning the "Chorus mysticus" from the end of *Faust II*. The premiere took place in Weimar under Liszt's baton on 5 September 1857, and he continued to revise the work between then and its publication in parts and full score (1861) and his own arrangement of the first two movements for **piano duet** (two pianos, LW C19, 1862, rev. 1870) (all Leipzig: Schuberth).

The second, often-omitted portion of the Symphony's title is telling in several respects. To begin with, "nach Goethe" (*after* Goethe; emphasis added) makes clear that the work does not respond literally to Goethe's version of the tragedy but rather is simply based on it; that is, it does not attempt to re-create the **narrative** of the story, even though it does evoke certain specific moments in the drama. Moreover, *drei Charakterbilder* makes clear that each of the three movements portrays the character of the three main personages in Goethe's version: the first movement (titled "Faust") is a portrayal of the title protagonist as a whole, not (necessarily) his experiences; the second movement (titled "Gretchen") is a portrayal of her character taken as a whole; and the third movement (titled "Mephistopheles") portrays Mephistopheles. The first movement introduces thematic material that Liszt's friend and intrepid public apologist **Richard Pohl** (1826–1896) described as representing Faust, but its second, sharply contrasting subject represents Gretchen, while other material seems to represent Mephistopheles. In the second ("Gretchen") movement, material based on the Gretchen theme from the first movement predominates, but the material associated with Faust and Mephistopheles is also present, and in the third ("Mephistopheles") movement, the Mephistopheles theme is foregrounded, while Faust and Gretchen's material, further transformed, is also included. The three movements thus represent an unusual version of **cyclic** form in that they not only share thematic material but also offer different perspectives on the same drama, seemingly through the eyes of each of the protagonists, creating a centripetal rather than linear cycle. Only with the optional conclusion with tenor solo and *Männerchor* does the work abandon this approach, apparently in order to reflect the conclusion of Goethe's narrative.

A "Faust" Symphony also represents Liszt's most extended and virtuosic deployment to that point of the synthesis of conventional form and **thematic transformation** that he had initiated with his series of **symphonic poems** begun in 1846 (most of which had been composed but not completed when Liszt returned to the idea of his *Faust* symphony in 1854). Each of the three movements includes an extended **sonata form** at its core, but these conventional structures are framed by highly unstable and lengthy introductions and conclusions, and the musical language in general is so unstable that the form's large-scale tonal anchors contribute far less to the sense of musical structure than they did even in the most adventurous previous sonata forms. Instead, musical coherence is achieved by the recurrence of continually changing versions of the themes associated with each of the main characters, with the alterations reflecting the change in perspective noted above.

Finally, the tonal language of *A "Faust" Symphony* is extraordinary—its hyperchromatic language rivaled perhaps only by **Richard Wagner**'s *Tristan und Isolde* as a milestone in the late 19th century's unraveling of tonality as a governing force in musical form. The slow introduction to the first movement, a continuous sequence that outlines a downward spiral of ascending augmented triads and that uses all 12 notes of the chromatic scale without cadential articulation, is itself keyless—sometimes described as the first atonal passage in Western music. That description is an exaggeration, but it is fair to note that the tonal structure of the introduction replaces the conventional triad with an augmented triad, beginning on a unison *A flat*, emphasizing *C* and then *E* at its midsection (using *E* as what would later be termed a *substitute dominant* or *altered dominant*), and then closing on the original *A flat*. That tonal organization adumbrates the structure of the movement as a whole, for the principal theme itself, while highly unstable, is centered on *C*, and the closing section of the exposition is centered on *E* (major). Gretchen's movement, too, is centered on *A flat* (with prominent material in C and E), and both versions of the Mephistopheles movement foreground *C* and conclude in C major. This elevation of the augmented triad to an **organic** generator of the overall structure of the individual movements and the tonal cycle as a whole is unprecedented even in Liszt's own earlier works. [JMC]

FAY, AMY (1844–1928). U.S. pianist and author of the Late Romantic Generation. Fay's memoir *Music-Study in Germany* (1880) offers an illuminating glimpse of musical life in *Gründerzeit* Germany. Her significance as a prominent female concert pianist and teacher cannot be underestimated; among her students was composer John Alden Carpenter.

Fay was born in Bayou Goula, Louisiana, on the Mississippi River; her mother taught her and her siblings **piano** as children. When her mother died in 1856, Fay moved in with her sister Melusine ("Zina") Fay in Cambridge, Massachusetts. There, she studied with Otto Dresel (1826–1890) at the New England Conservatory and **John Knowles Paine** (who returned from Germany in 1861); she also did some work with Jan Pychowski (1818–1900), who was based in New York City. In 1869, Fay traveled to Berlin, where she participated in the studio of Polish pianist Carl Tausig (1841–1871) until his death. Fay studied with Theodor Kullak (1818–1882), **Franz Liszt**, and Ludwig Deppe (1828–1890)—her favorite—before returning to Boston in 1875. After establishing herself quickly as a concert pianist (she gave her American debut at New York's **Chickering** Hall), Fay relocated in 1878 to Chicago, where she formed a piano studio based on Deppe's pedagogy, published books and articles on music, and embarked on lecture-recital tours across the Midwest. There, her brother, businessman Charles Norman Fay, would go on to found the Chicago Symphony Orchestra in 1891 with conductor **Theodore Thomas** (by then husband to the Fays' sister Rose Emily). Amy Fay moved to New York City in 1890 and there continued most of the activities for which she was known in Chicago; her leadership of the New York Women's Philharmonic Society was the pinnacle of her lifelong effort to encourage and raise awareness of female involvement in concert life and music scholarship.

Fay's greatest accomplishment was her 1880 book *Music-Study in Germany*, which she drew from her correspondence during her years abroad and prepared with the help of her sister and her friend Henry Wadsworth Longfellow (1807–1882). In just a few years, it appeared in French and German translations, and the fact that over two dozen editions have been published since the first edition attests to the enduring relevance of Fay's memoir. With remarkable freshness, it reports Fay's impressions of such figures as **Joseph Joachim**, **Clara Schumann**, and especially Liszt, her most famous piano teacher. [RK]

FEMINISM. The broad struggle for the legal, economic, social, and political equality of women with men. In the history of music during the **long 19th century**, feminism was significant to public and private performance (including **conducting**, composition and publication, and teaching and learning). These activities were open to women only to the extent and in the manner afforded by notions of appropriate or prudent female behavior. Although it is easy to assume that the status of women musicians improved gradually throughout the long 19th century, feminism in 19th-century music history is not altogether a success story. Women's gains were frequently accompanied by antifeminist reactions and expressions of misogyny that otherwise might have gone unarticulated.

During the late 18th and early 19th centuries, Western women were predominantly at a significant disadvantage compared to men in terms of legal, political, economic, and social liberty, and the Enlightenment was of surprisingly little help in correcting widespread assumptions that women were mentally inferior to men, more prone to emotion and sensibility, and better relegated to the roles traditionally assigned to them. The French Revolution, which made palpable the possibility of a new social order, also fell short; the *Declaration of the Rights of Man and of the Citizen* (1789) left women disenfranchised. The response, significant even though it was ignored, included the Women's Petition to the National Assembly the following fall, an appeal in 1790 by Nicolas de Condorcet, and Olympe de Gouges's parody document, *Declaration of the Rights of Women and of the Female Citizen* (1791).

A shift from church instruction to secular **conservatory** training helped make musical instruction more available to women, but that instruction (when available) was typically tailored to gender, with programs for women less substantial and excluding such topics as harmony and counterpoint. Opportunities beyond training, however, were limited. The exclusion of women from **orchestras** altogether, for example, was common not only throughout the long 19th century but in many cases well into the 20th century; the Vienna Philharmonic and the Czech Philharmonic were male only until the late 1990s. One response to this problem, the all-female orchestra, was established increasingly in European cities toward the end of the 19th century. The dearth of female conductors in the 19th century was an extension of the orchestra problem, and the growing idea of conductors as baton-wielding authority figures became an additional barrier for women in that field.

Composition, as an act of creation rather than reproduction, was widely considered the province of the male sex and to challenge this order as a woman sometimes amounted to imperiling one's marriageability or reputation as wife and mother. **Fanny Hensel** (1805–1847), for example, despite her gifts, was warned by her father not to pursue composition professionally; she confined her compositions largely to her **salon** and published few of her compositions until she was 42 years old. That she and others introduced their works into the public sphere in the face of societal pressures deserves admiration and interest. Some other notable long-19th-century women composers include Amy Beach (1867–1944), **Cécile Chaminade** (1857–1944), **Chiquinha Gonzaga** (1847–1935), Johanna Kinkel (1810–1858), Louise Adolpha Le Beau (1850–1927), Alma **Mahler**-Werfel (1879–1964), Clara Rogers (1844–1931), **Clara Schumann** (1819–1896), **Ethel Smyth** (1858–1944), and **Maria Szymanowska** (1789–1831). At issue in these women's efforts to become professional public figures in the fields of music was not only their sex but also their class: those from upper socioeconomic classes (most notably Hensel) faced more powerful obstacles, while those from middle-class backgrounds (e.g., Clara Schumann) were viewed somewhat less skeptically for their subversion of traditional gender hierarchies.

Women were more widely permitted to flourish in the field of performance, albeit (as elsewhere) through the lens of gender. As an ornamental art, female music making was encouraged domestically, and ideas on how to perform, what music to choose, and even what to wear while performing were discussed in such women's literature such as *Godey's Lady's Book*. As with composition, however, women performers also brought their practice into salons as well as in front of public audiences. On **piano**, Clara Schumann is well known for this; other major women pianists include Marie Bigot (1786–1820), Chaminade, **Amy Fay** (1844–1928), Gonzaga, Marie **Pleyel** (1811–1875), and Szymanowska. Even better known were opera singers, the most famous of whom were **Jenny Lind** (1820–1887), **Maria Malibran** (1808–1836), **Giuditta Pasta** (1797–1865), and Pauline Viardot (1821–1910). Women violinists who gained public distinction in the 19th century include Wilma Neruda (1838–1911), Camilla Urso (1842–1902), and Maud Powell (1867–1920). Teaching was common for performers regardless of gender, but women were far less likely to be hired as **conservatory** instructors; notable female hires include Marie Pleyel at the Brussels Conservatory in 1848 and Clara Schumann at the Hoch Conservatory (Berlin) in 1878. [RK]

FERNÁNDEZ CABALLERO, MANUEL (1835–1906). Spanish **conductor** and composer of the Late Romantic Generation. Caballero was born in Murcia and raised in close contact with a musically inclined extended family. In 1845, he moved to Madrid to study with a brother-in-law; five years later, he became a student at the Madrid **Conservatory**. A superb musician, Caballero won several awards in Madrid, including a conducting post in Cuba in 1853 (which he, then 18, was too young to accept) and the conservatory's first prize in composition in 1856. During his student years, Caballero began playing violin in the Royal Theater and then embarked on a career as conductor at the Teatro Variedades. Caballero's time in Madrid so far had coincided with a strengthening revival there of the **zarzuela**, and therefore it comes as no surprise that he added the genre to his budding compositional oeuvre with *Tres madres para una hija* (Three Mothers for One Daughter, 1854); this would be the first of many zarzuelas from Caballero. In 1864, after working at several theaters in Madrid, Caballero moved to Cuba, where he continued to conduct and compose zarzuelas for seven years. Back in Madrid, Caballero became much more widely known with the success of *La Marsellesa* (The Girl from Marseilles, 1874). His best-received works came toward the end of his career: *El dúo de La africana* (The Duet from [**Giacomo Meyerbeer**'s] *L'Africaine*, 1893), *La viejecita* (The Little Old Lady, 1897), and *Gigantes y cabezudos* (Giants and Big-Heads, 1898)—all three on **libretti** by Miguel Echegaray (1848–1927). It should be noted that although these three compositions conform largely to the one-act, dance-inflected *género chico* zarzuela type that was popular on his return from Cuba, Caballero continued to compose many of the longer, more elaborate zarzuelas during his last few decades. [RK]

FESCA, FRIEDRICH ERNST (1789–1826). German composer and violin-ist of the Early Romantic Generation, possibly of Italian descent. He left his native Magdeburg in 1805 to study composition in Leipzig with the Thomas-kantor August Eberhard Müller (1767–1817) and serve as solo violinist in the Gewandhaus Orchestra. He worked in the musical courts of Oldenburg and Kassel, where he acquired a reputation for his **string quartets** and **symphonies**, but when the Kassel court was dissolved in 1813, he relocated to Karlsruhe, where he worked as concertmaster of the Grand Duke of Baden until his death. Although he is little known today, his music was esteemed by **Louis Spohr** and **Carl Maria von Weber**, among others. His reputation rests primarily on his 20 string quartets and four string **quintets**, but he also composed three symphonies, two **overtures**, an Andante and Rondo for horn and **orchestra** (Op. 39, 1825/1826), two **operas**, three psalm settings and a *Vater unser*, 10 **part-songs**, and 35 **songs**. His son Alexander Ernst Fesca (1820–1849) was also a composer, known for his three operas, several songs, and **chamber music** (six **piano trios**, two string quartets, a piano quintet, one piano **sextet**, and two piano **septets**). [JMC]

FÉTIS, FRANÇOIS-JOSEPH (1784–1871). Belgian musicologist, critic, composer, and teacher of the Early Romantic Generation; one of the most influential figures in Franco-Belgian musical life during the **long 19th centu-ry** and a scholar whose contributions remain immensely useful for research into many aspects of 19th-century music. He came from a family of musi-cians and instrument makers; played **piano**, organ, and continuo in sacred music in his youth; and began composing while still in his teens. At age 16, he entered the Paris **Conservatory**, where he studied with **Adrien Boieldieu** and won the attention of **Luigi Cherubini**. The latter sparked his interest in the music of **Giovanni Pierluigi da Palestrina**—an interest that in turn led him to pioneering research into the notation and **performance practice** of Renaissance and late medieval music. In 1821, he was appointed professor of counterpoint and fugue at the Conservatory and five years later became li-brarian of that same institution, a post he held until he was removed in 1832 because of excessive absenteeism occasioned by his research. He created a series of *concerts historiques* in 1832. In 1833, he relocated to Brussels, where he became first director of the newly founded Conservatory, a post he held to the end of his life.

Fétis was a respected composer, author of numerous serious and **comic operas**, a great deal of sacred choral music, three **symphonies**, two piano **concertos**, a flute concerto, three **string quartets**, a number of other instru-mental **chamber** works, much organ music (including 60 now-lost preludes and fugues), and several works for piano solo. His historical significance, however, lies primarily in his assiduous research concerning historical music and musical instruments and his integration of knowledge of those historical matters into contemporary musical life. He founded the *Revue musicale* and edited that important journal until 1833, also publishing many historical, theoretical, and didactic articles in various journals over the course of his career. The eight-volume *Biographie universelle des musiciens et bibliographie générale de musique* (Brussels, 1835–1844; 2nd ed., 1860–1865) was the single most important scholarly encyclopedia of contemporary and historical music until the appearance of **George Grove**'s *Dictionary of Music and Musicians* in 1878–1889. [JMC]

See also COUSSEMAKER, (CHARLES-)EDMOND(-HENRI) DE (1805–1876); GEVAERT, FRANÇOIS-AUGUSTE (1828–1908); HISTORICISM; PRIX DE ROME (PARIS); WIDOR, CHARLES-MARIE (-JEAN-ALBERT) (1844–1937).

FIBICH, ZDENĚK [ZDENKO] (ANTONÍN VÁCLAV) (1850–1900). Czech composer of the Late Romantic Generation. Fibich cultivated a less consciously Czech compositional style than did **Bedřich Smetana** or even **Antonín Dvořák**, but his ample works for **piano**, his **symphonic poems**, and above all his stage works testify to a boldly unique voice. Unfortunately, Fibich's blend of German **conservatory** elements with **Wagnerian** harmonic language and melodic structures worked against his success in Prague in the 1880s and 1890s. Fibich composed the first **tone poem** on a Czech national topic, *Záboj, Slavoj a Luděk* (Záboj, Slavoj, and Luděk, 1873) and the first trilogy of stage **melodramas** on a grand, Wagnerian scale, *Hippodamia* (1888–1891).

Born to a Czech father and German mother in tiny Všebořice (in today's Czech Republic, halfway between Prague and Jihlava), Fibich composed as a child and as a Gymnasium student in Vienna and Prague. He studied at the Leipzig Conservatory with theorist Ernst Richter and pianist **Ignaz Moscheles** in 1865–1867, then traveled to Paris and Mannheim. Beginning in these years, Fibich produced a steady stream of **songs** that would shift in the early 1870s from predominantly German texts to Czech ones; along with these was a more modest output of instrumental **chamber** works and piano music. After a brief return to Bohemia and the composition of his **opera** *Bukovín*, Fibich moved with his wife to Vilnius for a choirmaster post. They returned in late 1874 to Prague, where his wife and two infant sons died; Fibich then married his sister-in-law according to his wife's wishes.

The late 1870s and early 1880s saw Fibich's most extensive activity in Prague's public sphere. Fibich contributed to the Czech music magazine *Dalibor* as a critic. He also joined the Provisional Theater as deputy conductor and choirmaster in 1875, and he became choirmaster at the Russian Orthodox Church three years later. In 1881, after failing to get a teaching job at the Prague Conservatory, Fibich shifted to a life of composing and private teaching, which he maintained for most of the rest of his life. This final period saw the premieres of some of Fibich's most important works, including *Hippodamia* and the still-popular opera *Šarka* (1897). Among his best-known students are **Franz Lehár**, Otakar Ostrčil, and Anežka Schulzová; Schulzová also became his lover and wrote the **libretti** for his later operas, including *Šarka*. [RK]

***FIDELIO, ODER DIE EHELICHE LIEBE*, OP. 72.** (Ger., "Fidelio; or, Conjugal Love.") **Rescue opera** in two acts by **Ludwig van Beethoven** on a **libretto** by Joseph von Sonnleithner (1766–1835), based on the play *Léonore, ou L'amour conjugal* by Jean-Nicolas Bouilly (1763–1842). *Fidelio*, Beethoven's only **opera**, was originally titled *Leonore*. It entered the repertory nine years after its premiere (in 1814), and its position in the **canon** is closely tied to that of Beethoven himself. Composed at approximately the same time as the **"Eroica" Symphony**, *Fidelio*—with its rescue-opera plot of the "tyrant" variety, end-weighted structure, and intense C-major resolution—seems tailor-made to the conventional notion of Beethoven's "heroic" Middle Vienna Period.

Beethoven agreed to write an opera for the Theater an der Wien in 1803. For most of the year, he intended to set Emanuel Shickaneder's (1751–1812) *Vestas Feuer*, but instead he turned his attention largely to the Third Symphony. Ultimately, he composed very little for *Vestas Feuer*. By the end of the year, he had shifted his attention to a different text, Bouilly's play *Léonore* (1798), which was thematically similar to Bouilly's libretto for **Luigi Cherubini**'s *Les deux journées, ou Le porteur d'eau* (The Two Days; or, The Water Carrier, 1800). Beethoven composed the first version of *Fidelio*, in three acts, in 1804 and 1805.

Fidelio's initial production (Vienna, Theater an der Wien, 1805) ended after only three performances. While the failure was likely due in large part to the theater's unusual patrons (French military officers; Vienna was occupied by Bonaparte's troops at the time—hardly an auspicious turn of events for performance of an opera about tyranny), the slow dramatic pacing was also blamed. When *Fidelio* was staged again at the Theater an der Wien the next year, Beethoven slightly abbreviated the opera, organized it into two acts (like the original play), rearranged some of the numbers, removed Rocco's aria, and made many additional, minor revisions. Beethoven also revised the overture; the older version later became known as the Leonore Overture No. 2, the 1806 version No. 3.

Fidelio remained unsuccessful until 1814, when, in the wake of his popular "Battle Symphony" *Wellington's Victory*, Beethoven was invited to have *Fidelio* performed at Vienna's Kärntnertor Theater. For this performance, Beethoven prepared a third and final version that featured yet another overture (the one in E major typically performed today), the reintroduction of Rocco's aria from the first version, and even more extensive reordering of various arias and ensembles. He gave the first act a new finale and largely rewrote the finale of the second act. Poet Georg Friedrich Trieschke (1776–1842) reworked the libretto along with Beethoven. The young pianist **Ignaz Moscheles** prepared the vocal score, working closely with the composer. The premiere of this third, final version was a resounding success. The cast included soprano Anna Milder (1785–1838), veteran of the 1805 and 1806 versions, returning as *Leonora* and baritone Johann Michael Vogl (1768–1840) as Pizarro. Both singers later went on to become proponents of the **songs** of **Franz Schubert**, who was present at the 1814 performance. [RK]

FIELD, JOHN (1782–1837). Irish composer and **virtuoso** pianist of the Early Romantic Generation, widely considered the first to cultivate the elegant, expressive style of **piano** playing more famously associated with **Fryderyk Chopin.** He was born of Protestant stock to a family of musicians in Dublin and aroused considerable attention in three public concerts there when he was 10, moving in 1793 with his family to London, where he was apprenticed to Muzio Clementi (1752–1832). By the turn of the 19th century, his reputation had begun to widen, and in 1802, Clementi took him to Paris and Vienna, then to St. Petersburg, where their relationship soured. Field remained in Russia (Moscow and St. Petersburg) for the next 27 years. His reputation continued to grow, but an early fondness for drink advanced to alcoholism, and by 1822, his health failing, he had largely ceased to compose. He returned to London in 1831 and there experienced a brief recovery in concertizing and composing, also undertaking a tour on the continent (France, Switzerland, and the Italian lands) in 1833. He collapsed while in Naples and was hospitalized for nine months there, returning to Russia with his son Adrien in 1835. He gave his last concert there in March 1836 and died in January 1837. Because of his extended stay in Russia on the eve of that vast country's significant musical growth (these were also the early years of **Aleksandr Dargomïzhsky** and **Mikhail Glinka**) and his influence on many piano pupils there, he is sometimes considered a founder of the Russian school of pianism.

In 1812, Field became the first to publish dreamy, sectional, treble-dominated **character pieces** for **piano** solo with the genre designation "**nocturne.**" The contemporary press noted nothing special about those works, but other composers did—among them J. B. Cramer (1771–1858), Henri Herz (1803–1888), Glinka, **Maria Szymanovska**, and, most significantly, Chopin, who apparently modeled his own nocturnes after Field's pieces in the genre. Field published another 13 works in that genre between 1812 and 1836 as well as seven piano **concertos** and several other works for piano with or-

chestra, six independent **chamber** works for strings with and without piano, one vocal duet and two Italian **songs**, and numerous **fantasies**, rondos, *pastorales*, and other works for piano solo and **piano duet**. [JMC]
See also VIRTUOSO (M.), VIRTUOSA (F.).

FIRST FRENCH EMPIRE. (Fr. Empire Française.) The Napoleonic Empire, the period of imperial rule in France under Napoléon Bonaparte, beginning with Napoléon's coronation as emperor of the French on 2 December 1804, interrupted with his abdication on 11 April 1814, and briefly restored when he returned to the throne during the so-called *hundred days* (actually 111 days) between 11 March and 8 July 1815. The First Empire is part of the larger period generally known as the *Napoleonic era* (or *period*), which spans from Napoléon's coup d'état establishing himself as first consul of the French Republic (10 November 1799) to the end of the empire. It includes the Napoleonic Wars (1803–15), which witnessed the French Empire's aggressive invasion of countries and territories from North Africa to Moscow (eastern Russia) and installation of puppet regimes in its conquered territories, as well as the formation of alliances of armies to repulse their subsumption into the empire. The empire was ended with the Congress of Vienna and followed by the **Bourbon Restoration** in France and the **Restoration** in the remainder of Europe.

Like most imperial expansion, the empire and the Napoleonic Wars exerted a profound influence on music and culture generally—partly through the (admittedly unsolicited) intercourse of French music and other ideas with those of the peoples subsumed into the empire and partly through the travels of musicians both as conscripted soldiers and as parts of court retinues. Moreover, the French Revolution had demonstrated anew the potency of music as an instrument of propaganda and a means for winning hearts and souls to a given societal cause through stirring music—often music that valorized protagonists, disparaged the resistance, and sacralized the cause itself: *see* CHERUBINI, LUIGI (CARLO ZANOBI SALVADORE MARIA) (1760–1842); LE SUEUR [LESUEUR], JEAN-FRANÇOIS (1760–1837); and MÉHUL, ÉTIENNE-NICOLAS (1763–1817). Because of this persuasive power, composers of imperial France as well as its various opponents wrote a great deal of public and private music that implicitly or explicitly took up the issues attendant to the great societal turmoil that largely ruled the day-to-day lives of Europe's citizenry. This new industry of music in the service of social activism is most famously reflected in works such as **Beethoven**'s Third **("Eroica") Symphony**, his **ballet** *The Creatures of Prometheus*, or his much-maligned *Wellington's Victory* and the **cantata** *Der glorreiche Augenblick*. It is also reflected in more general trends, such as the flourishing of genres such as the march and **rescue opera**. [JMC]

THE FIVE. *See* MIGHTY HANDFUL.

FOLK SONG. (Fr., chanson folklorique; Ger., Volkslied; It., canto popolare; Sp., canción popular.) Broad term used to distinguish music of vernacular tradition and oral transmission from "cultivated" or "art" music. In accepted usages of the **long 19th century**, the term was used to denote both vocal and instrumental music, but *folk song* is best understood as a subset of *folk music.* Thus, *folk music* denotes any instrumental or vocal music that originates in vernacular tradition, is transmitted by oral practice rather than notation, and is used and understood by a linguistic, ethnic, or geographically defined group of people as its own. *Folk song* denotes the specifically vocal repertoires of these groups. The melodic characteristics of *folk song* are defined largely by the stresses, durations, and poetic patterns of the vernacular at hand. The long 19th century's interest in folk song also led many poets and composers to attempt to capture the character of folk song in poetry and music written for the cultivated tradition (*see* VOLKSTÜMLICHKEIT).

The long 19th century's interest in folk song was manifested partly in extensive scholarly enterprises and partly through institutional innovations created in response to those enterprises. The methods employed in amassing this data and 19th-century analytical techniques for interpreting and understanding it have since been largely rejected by folklorists. Those rethinkings, however, by and large postdated the period central to this dictionary and at any rate did not hinder composers from reading their works and appropriating what they found useful in their own compositions for their own purposes, whether aesthetic or political (*see* NATIONALISM, ROMANTIC NATIONALISM).

Published collections of folk poetry and folklore began to emerge already in the 17th century (most notably in Charles Perrault's [1628–1703] *Histoires ou Contes du Temps passé: Les Contes de ma Mère l'Oye* [Stories and Tales from the Past: Tales of Mother Goose, 1695]), but during the late 18th century, scholarly ventures that attempted to systematically collect, classify, and transfer to the cultures of print (sometimes in translation) the originally oral and vernacular repertoires of folk song, folk poetry, and folklore proliferated. These projects were born of two main impulses: (1) the late Enlightenment quest for a universal and orderly codification of human knowledge and experience, rooted in nature and codified by reason, and (2) the politically ambivalent and culturally marginal statuses of much of Central and Eastern Europe, specifically the German lands and Russia. The power of those impulses grew significantly in the wake of the general societal disruptions of the French Revolution and the political turmoil of the 1790s and the Napoleonic era. Two of the first important products of this impulse were the Russian anthologies *Sobraniye russkikh prostïkh pesen s notami* (Collection of Simple Russian Songs with Music, 4 vols., 1776–1795) by Vasily Trutovsky (ca.

1740–1810) and *Sobraniye narodnïkh russkikh pesen s ikh golosami* (Collection of Russian Folk Songs with Their Vocal Parts, 1790) by Ivan Prach (d. 1818). These Russian contributions, together with their counterparts in the German lands, prepared the way for subsequent investigations of Russian and other Central and Eastern European folk song published in the 19th century by the otherwise obscure Kirsha Danilov (a collection of 50 Siberian folk songs published as *Drevnie Russkie Stihotvoreniya* [Ancient Russian Poetry, 1804]) and Jan Rittersberk (1780–1841) (*České národní písně* [Czech National Songs], 1825), Oskar Kolberg (1814–1890) (the 36-volume serial anthology *Lud*, 1857–1890), and Karel Jaromír Erben (1811–1870) (*Písně národní v Čechách* [Folk Songs of Bohemia, 1842–1845] and *Prostonárodní české písně a říkadla* [Czech Folk Songs and Nursery Rhymes, 1864]), to name just a few.

Contemporaneous with these important investigations in the German lands was Johann Gottfried Herder's (1744–1803) enormous anthology of folk song from various peoples, *Stimmen der Völker in Liedern* (Voices of the Peoples in Songs, 1778–1779), which coined the term **Volktümlichkeit** to denote the (perceived) essential character of folk song. Herder's comparative collection laid the groundwork for Jacob (1785–1863) and Wilhelm Grimm's (1786–1859) collections of *Märchen* (fairy tales), first published in 1812 and revised and reprinted many times, and (more importantly for Romantic music) Arnim and Brentano's seminal three-volume collection of more than 700 folk song texts published under the title **Des Knaben Wunderhorn** (The Boy's Miraculous Posthorn, 1805–1808). None of these German investigations included actual folk melodies, but the predominantly syllabic style of folk music enabled musicians to get a strong sense of the rhythmic and phrasal organization of folk music from the texts and then to devise their own tunes whose melodic and tonal organization departed from the norms of cultivated music.

Francophone studies of folk song emerged on a comparatively informal level early in the 19th century—most importantly in Théodore Hersart de la Villemarqué's (1815–1895) *Barzaz Breiz* (Bardic Ballads of Brittany, 1839), but the year 1852 saw the official launching of a general compilation of French popular poetry on the suggestion of Hippolyte Fortoul (1811–1856), a venture that resulted in the collection of 3,250 songs and texts classified as "folk." These and related studies were rapidly disseminated in the second half of the century by scholars such as **Edmond de Coussemaker** (1856 and 1862–1864), Max Buchon (1863), Prosper Tarbé (1863), Achille Durieux and Adolphe Bruyelle (1864), Théodore de Puymaigre (1865), Théophile Marion Dumersan (1866), François-Marie Luzel (1868–1890), and Jérôme Bujeaud (1895), among others. In the Italian lands, important researches were conducted and published by Costantino Nigra (1888), Alessandro D'Ancona (1878), Antonio Casetti (1866, 1870, 1871), Giuseppe Ferraro

(1870, 1877, 1887, and 1888), and Giuseppe Pitrè (1875). The most important milestone in the scholarly study of Scandinavian folklore was the publication of the Finnish national epic *Kalevala* (parts of which inspired music by **Jean Sibelius**) by Elias Lönnrot (1802–1884) in 1835–1826 (first edition) and 1849 (second, expanded edition). Other scholarly compilations of folklore, folk poetry, and folk song of Scandinavia were submitted by scholars such as Svend Hersleb Grundtvig (1853), Axel Olrik (1877, 1886), and Carl Wilhelm von Sydow (1907).

Important Iberian studies were contributed by Sixto de Córdova (1822) and José Inzenga (1888). In the British Isles, the **Ossian** saga was for a time during the 18th century considered a legitimate source of folk materials, a sort of national epic comparable to the *Illiad* and *Odyssey*, the *Aeneid*, *Kalevala*, or the German *Nibelungenlied* (*see* THE RING OF THE NIBELUNG). Ossian proved to be a literary hoax, but legitimate scholarly documentary explorations of the Isles' folklore and folk song were submitted by Davies Gilbert (1822 and 1823), William B. Sandys (1833), John Broadwood (1843), Sabine Baring-Gould (1889–1891, 1895), Cecil Sharp (numerous collections, 1904–1923), and especially Francis J. Child (1882–1898), whose *The English and Scottish Popular Ballads* (10 vols., 1892–1898) interrelate English and Scottish folk songs (texts and melodies) with their North American counterparts by means of techniques typically associated with hymnody (*see* CHORALE).

Attempts to collect and catalog folklore and folk song in the Western Hemisphere emerged later and were complicated by the fact that the 19th-century scholars who engaged in the effort were of European descent and were therefore confronted with two bodies of lore and song—those of the hemisphere's indigenous peoples and those of its European settlers outside the cultivated tradition. Important long-19th-century studies of the Americas' folk repertoires were compiled by J. Murphy (1902), F. O'Neill (1903, 1907, 1910), H. Russell (1895), Ventura R. Lynch (1883), F. J. de Santa-Anna Nery (1889), and others. These scholarly efforts also led to the founding of a number of state and institutionally sponsored organizations devoted to the collection, analysis, and dissemination of folk music. These organizations, seated in all the cultural capitals of the Western world, sponsored publications of folk song texts and related scholarship, supported research, and in many cases constituted archives that would make folk song, folklore, and relevant research readily available to musicians and other scholars. The methodologies they employed for most of the long 19th century were unequivocally comparative and Eurocentric, but they provided a foundation for ethnographically and ethnomusicologically mature studies of folk materials in the 20th century after World War I. [JMC]

FORKEL, JOHANN NICOLAUS (1749–1818). German bibliographer, music historian, organist, and theorist, often regarded as a founder of modern musicology because of his bibliographic and biographical contributions. Largely self-taught until he enrolled as a chorister at a choir school in Lüneberg, he matriculated at the University of Göttingen in 1769 and served in various academic and musical posts there for the remainder of his career. In 1787, he was awarded an honorary doctorate and given professorial rank. In these posts, he organized an annual series of about 20 concerts per year as well as attendant lectures; the concerts' repertoire and lectures strove to make often-unfamiliar musical repertoires comprehensible to performers and music lovers through the works' underlying compositional principles and their position in history. These concerts continued until 1815 and the lectures until Forkel's death.

In 1787, Forkel published the first volume of his *Allgemeine Geschichte der Musik* (General History of Music), followed in 1788 by the groundbreaking *Allgemeine Litteratur der Musik* (General Music Bibliography) and in 1801 by the second volume of the *Allgemeine Geschichteder Musik*. Meanwhile, his tireless efforts to discover a coherent narrative for the history of European music and to make that heritage accessible to amateurs led Franz Anton Hoffmeister (1754–1812) and Ambrosius Kühnel (1770–1813), who had published the first serious attempt at a complete edition of **Johann Sebastian Bach**'s harpsichord works in 1800, to invite him to become the head of a new series titled *Oeuvres complettes de Jean Sebastien Bach* (Complete Works of J. S. Bach); *see* BACH REVIVAL, BACH AWAKENING, BACH RENAISSANCE.

Forkel's most consequential legacy for Romantic music lies in his advocacy of Bach, both as a composer and as a personification of German nationhood during the years of ascendant German **nationalism**. At a time when the elder Bach's music was familiar chiefly in extremely limited circles, Forkel acquired biographical information from family and professional sources and familiarized himself with the music—both the few works that were known at the time and many others that existed only in archival manuscripts. He assimilated this information into his impressive knowledge of other ideas, styles, and compositional trends in the history of music and drew on that knowledge to produce the first book-length biography of the Baroque composer—portraying him as an icon of German cultural greatness who could serve as a rallying call for Germans everywhere (*Ueber Johann Sebastian Bachs Leben, Kunst und Kunstwerke* [On Johann Sebastian Bach's Life, Art, and Artworks, 1802]). This portrayal further fueled public political and cultural interest in Bach's life and music, facilitated a number of editions and performances of some little-known works, and ultimately prepared the ground for the public **Bach revival** inaugurated by **Felix Mendelssohn Bartholdy**'s performances of the *St. Matthew Passion* in the spring of 1829. This movement was arguably the most important in the various early 19th-century "rediscoveries" that also included Albrecht Dürer and **Wolfgang Amadeus Mozart**, significantly fueling the drive for German national unity that erupted full force with the **Revolutions of 1848**. [JMC]

FORTEPIANO. *See* PIANO.

FOSTER, STEPHEN COLLINS (1826–1864). U.S. composer of the Late Romantic Generation, generally considered the greatest U.S. composer of **ballads** and **songs** in the mid-19th century. He grew up in a large family on the outskirts of Pittsburgh and learned **piano** and flute as a child, publishing his first **songs** in 1844. He worked as a clerk in Cincinnati beginning in 1846 and was placed on the track to a career as a songwriter in 1848 with his *Oh, Susannah* and *Uncle Ned*—both published without attribution or monetary gain to him. In 1850, he gave Cristy's Minstrels the rights to introduce and perform his songs, and in 1851 his *Old Folks at Home* was published with Christy as named author. He moved to New York in 1855 and there signed a contract with a publisher who promoted his music (with attribution to him) successfully. He continued composing popular songs but by the 1860s had become a chronic alcoholic; his late songs (including some written for the U.S. Civil War) were not successful, and he died obscure and impoverished.

Foster's songs are notable not only for their memorable melodies and their ability to evoke a sense of plantation culture (despite his lack of firsthand knowledge of the U.S. South) but also for their lyrics, which were mostly his own poems. These texts are often overly sentimental and racially insensitive by latter-day standards but also clever and witty and far less racially insensitive than most other contemporary lyric poetry in the United States. His output comprises 287 authenticated complete works—not only songs with piano accompaniment but also arrangements of these with guitar accompaniment, piano pieces, and numerous other smaller works. Among his best-known songs are *Nelly Bly* (1850), *Massa's in de Cold, Cold Ground* (1852), *My Old Kentucky Home* (1853), *Camptown Races* (1854), *Jeanie with the Light Brown Hair* (1854), *Come Where My Love Lies Dreaming* (1855), *Old Black Joe* (1860), and *Beautiful Dreamer* (1864, his final completed song). [JMC]

FRANCK, CÉSAR (-AUGUSTE-JEAN-GUILLAUME-HUBERT) (1822–1890). French composer of Belgian birth, member of the Late Romantic Generation; late in life and in posthumous **reception**, one of the most influential figures in French musical **nationalism**. He displayed talent at the **piano** at an early age and studied at the Liège **Conservatory** from 1830 to the spring of 1835, when his father, hoping to put his son's talent to lucrative ends, took him on a performance tour throughout Belgium. That summer, the family moved to Paris, the capital of piano **virtuosi**, and there Franck began private study in piano with renowned pedagogue Pierre-Joseph-Guillaume Zimmermann (1785–1853) and composition with **Antoine Reicha**. In 1837, he formally enrolled in the Paris Conservatory, there continuing studies with Zimmermann and studying counterpoint and composition, organ, and violin (the last with **Françoise-Antoine Habeneck**). In April 1842, his father formally withdrew him from study at the institution in order to resume promoting him as a touring virtuoso.

Franck was increasingly frustrated by his father's single-minded determination to force him into a career as a virtuoso at the expense of his formal advancement in education and composition of a more serious sort. He found some solace, however, in the warm reception afforded his **piano trios** (M 1–3/Op. 1) when they were published on a subscription basis in 1843—for among the subscribers were many of the current Parisian celebrities of the day (including **Daniel-François Esprit Auber, Fryderyk Chopin, Gaetano Donizetti, Fromenthal Halévy, Franz Liszt, Giachomo Meyerbeer**, and **Ambroise Thomas**). In 1845, he formally left his parents' home for a career of his own, and by 1848, now free of his father's control, he had married and settled into a life as a teacher of organ, improvisation, and composition and as organist in the small church of Notre Dame de Lorette. A major positive development was his appointment as organist in the church of St. Jean–St. François, which had an early organ by master builder **Aristide Cavaillé-Coll**. In 1858, he was appointed organist and precentor of the new Basilica of Ste. Clotilde, where another Cavaillé-Coll instrument, the most advanced yet, was at his around-the-clock disposal—no doubt a major source of inspiration for the powers of improvisation for which he would soon become known.

Franck retained the position at Ste. Clotilde until his death, and by the late 1860s, aspiring young composers were flocking to hear his compositions and improvisations—among them **Alexis de Castillon, Ernst Chausson, Paul Dukas**, and **Vincent d'Indy**. By the time of the surge in interest in discovering and celebrating a great contemporary French composer in the wake of France's humiliating defeat in the **Franco-Prussian War** set in, this circle of devotees had grown considerably; eventually, they would become known as the *Franckistes*.

In 1872, Franck was appointed professor of organ at the Paris Conservatory, where his teaching (in keeping with the traditional responsibilities of organists as improvisers, composers, and organizers of all aspects of music in their churches) centered as much on improvisation and composition as on other aspects of organ technique. The appreciation shown him by his circle—which mounted concerts and other performances of his music and touted his significance widely in the contentious but resolutely optimistic outlook of **Third Republic** politics and culture—was beneficial to his own compositional energies, resulting in a number of works that won appreciation in the 1880s: the **oratorio** *Les béatitudes* (M. 53, 1869–1879, publ. 1880), the Piano **Quintet** in F Minor (M. 7, 1879, publ. 1881), the ***Prélude, choral et fugue*** for piano (M. 21, 1884, publ. 1885; *see* CHORALE), the Violin **Sonata** in A Major (M. 8, 1886), the **String Quartet** in D Major (M. 9, 1889), the *Trois chorals* for organ (M. 38–40, 1890, publ. 1892), and the four **symphonic poems** *Les Éolides* (The Breezes), *Le chasseur maudit* (The Accursed Huntsman), *Les Djinns* (The Genies), and *Psyché* (M. 43–45 and 47, 1875–1888 passim). The **Symphony** in D Minor (M. 48, 1886–1888, publ. 1896), now considered one of his greatest works, met with incomprehension when it was premiered in the Concerts du Conservatoire in 1889.

Franck was unassuming by nature and (unlike some of his contemporaries) little interested in self-promotion or self-aggrandizement. Nevertheless, by the 1880s he had become a central figure in French musical life, specifically in the cause of promoting music as *utilité publique* and discovering a specifically French national style that would assimilate the progressive ideas from other countries (specifically Germany) into that style without compromising its quintessentially Gallic character. In 1885, he was named Chevalier de la Légion d'Honneur, and in 1886, he became president of the **Société Nationale de Musique**. Today, much of his output is well known and widely performed despite its complex chromaticism, dense counterpoint, and technical difficulty. Of the works that he considered his most important, only the **opera** *Hulda* (M. 49, 1879–1885, publ. 1894), the **lyric drama** *Ghiselle* (M. 50, 1888–1890, publ. 1896), and the two earlier **oratorios** *Ruth* (M. 51, 1844–1846, rev. 1871, publ. 1872) and *La rédemption* (M. 52 first version comp. 1871–1872, publ. 1872; second version 1874–1875, publ. 1875) have remained obscure. He also composed a sizable body of difficult music for piano solo (publishing nine numbered *opera* between 1834 and 1838) and a number of ***Lieder ohne Worte*** (published posthumously) and other smaller pieces for that instrument as well as 20 *mélodies* and 16 secular vocal works for forces ranging from solo voice with piano accompaniment to various combinations of voices and **orchestra**. [JMC]

See also CHORALE.

FRANCO-PRUSSIAN WAR, FRANCO-GERMAN WAR. Conflict between the **Second French Empire** and the Kingdom of Prussia, aided by the North German Confederation and three other German states, declared by France on 19 July 1870 and concluded by the Treaty of Frankfurt on 10 May 1871. The war was a humiliating defeat for France and the final step in the political unification of the German lands (other than Austria) into the German Empire under Otto von Bismarck (fl. 1862–1890). In France, it led to the unseating of Napoléon III (Louis-Napoléon Bonaparte; fl. 1848–1852 as president of the **Second Republic** and 1852–1870 as emperor of the French) and the establishment of the **Third Republic**. In Germany, it articulated Bismarck's victory over liberal opposition and consolidated a near-feudal socioeconomic structure and made the German Empire second to none in Europe in terms of economic strength and military power.

The Franco-Prussian War was enormously consequential for music, especially in terms of **nationalism**. The tensions that led to the conflict fueled nationalist sentiment on both sides of the Franco-German divide, while the growing European cult of **Richard Wagner** also created an ardent and brilliant minority cult of *Wagnerisme* in French musical life. Like most wars, the conflict itself produced much patriotic music on both sides (both in popular song and in cultivated music), and in France it spurred the formation of many institutions and concert societies dedicated to French music both contemporary and historical (*see* HISTORICISM). These societies continued to proliferate in the war's wake—most obviously in the founding of the **Société Nationale de Musique** for the express purpose of fostering the creation and performance of nonoperatic works by French composers but also in the active governmental cultivation of the doctrine of music as *utilité publique* in the Third Republic, revisions to the music curricula taught in schools, a new approach to programming at the Opéra and other French institutions, and so on. **Charles Gounod**'s moving motet *Gallia* (on a text Gounod assembled from the Lamentations of Jeremiah), for soprano solo, chorus, and organ, is a response to France's defeat in the war (Gounod later indicated that it was but not merely composed but "exploded in [his] head like an artillery shell"). [JMC]

See also COMMUNE OF PARIS; REVOLUTIONS OF 1848 (SPRING OF NATIONS, YEAR OF REVOLUTIONS).

FRANZ [KNAUTH], ROBERT (1815–1892). German composer of the Romantic Generation, best known for his *Gesänge* and **Lieder**. His formal education in music began in the Gymnasium in Halle and theory lessons with Friedrich Schneider (1786–1853) in Dessau as well as through self-education. Throughout his studies, he was immersed in works by **Johann Sebastian Bach, George Frideric Handel, Franz Joseph Haydn**, and **Wolfgang Amadeus Mozart** as well as 19th-century composers including **Franz Schubert, Felix Mendelssohn Bartholdy**, and **Robert Schumann**. He took his first position as organist at the Ulrichkirche (Halle) in 1841 and in the next year became conductor of that city's Singakademie. In 1851, he assumed responsibility for the music program at the University of Halle. His work there combined with the success of the city's reinvigorated Singakademie and his publications to spread his reputation (he earned the respect of **Franz Liszt**, whose 1872 short monograph *Robert Franz* extolled his talents). The university awarded him an honorary doctorate in 1861, but his deteriorating hearing forced him to resign from his official positions in 1867. In retirement, he was increasingly plagued by a nervous disorder but continued to compose until 1886. He remained a highly respected musical figure. His supporters (most importantly Liszt) succeeded in winning for him a handsome stipend. In 1883, King Ludwig II of Bavaria named him a Knight of the Order of Maximilian; he was made an honorary citizen of Halle and received the Order of the Crown from Kaiser Wilhelm I.

Franz published three numbered *opera* of sacred choral music, six numbered *opera* of **part-songs** for SATB or *Männerchor*, and four other part-songs without opus number. He also published a number of arrangements and editions of works by other composers, including Bach, Handel, Mendelssohn, Mozart, Schubert, and Giuseppe Tartini (1692–1770), but his realizations of the continuo parts in the music of the last two of these elicited criticism from **Eduard Hanslick**, and Franz was compelled to defend his practice in a public response (*Offener Brief an Eduard Hanslick über Bearbeitungen älterer Tonwerke* [Open Letter to Eduard Hanslick concerning Arrangements of Early Music, 1871]; *see* PERFORMANCE PRACTICE).

Franz is best known today for his more than 300 **songs** published in 43 numbered *opera* between 1843 and 1884 (opp. 1–14, 16–23, 26–28, 30–31, 33–44, 48, 50–52). In them, Franz's approach is distinctive, imaginative, and sensitive; they were admired by Robert Schumann, who reportedly arranged for their publication without Franz's prior knowledge or permission (perhaps because Franz's family was opposed to his working as a publishing musician). He aspired to "compose feelings, not words" in his songs, and he drew on an array of influences in doing so (German **folk song**, imitative counterpoint, Protestant **chorales**, and a harmonic richness sometimes reminiscent of Schubert). [MMM/JMC]

FRAUENCHOR. (Ger., "Women's Chorus.") A chorus comprising women and/or girls, or a composition written for it. Such works are usually scored as SSAA, but other combinations are possible. During the **long 19th century**, works scored for *Frauenchor* (pl. *Frauenchöre*) tended to deal with textual themes of domesticity, innocence or purity, benevolent spirituality, or spiritual comfort in nature. Notable examples include numerous *Ave Maria* compositions, the conversion scene in **Felix Mendelssohn Bartholdy**'s **oratorio** *St. Paul*, and **Franz Schubert**'s setting of Psalm 23. [JMC]
    See also CHILDREN'S CHORUS; MÄNNERCHOR.

DER FREISCHÜTZ, **J. 277/OP. 77.** (Ger., "The Free-Shooter" or "The Magic Shot.") **Opera** in three acts by **Carl Maria von Weber** on a libretto by Friedrich Kind (1768–1843), after the first German folktale published in the first volume of August Apel's (1771–1816) and Friedrich August Schultze's (1770–1849) *Das Gespensterbuch* (The Book of Spooks; 5 vols.,

1811–1817). The tale as published by Apel and Laun immediately attracted attention for staged musical drama: composer Carl B. Neuner (1778–1830) and librettist Franz Xaver von Caspar produced a **ballet** version that was staged in Munich already in 1812 and again in a revised version in 1813, and two further versions were produced in Vienna in 1816. In 1817, Weber approached the well-known poet and playwright Kind, a fellow member of the Dresden literary *Liederkreis* (*see* LIEDERTAFEL) whose **synaesthetic** "painterly play" *Van Dycks Landleben* (The Country Life of Van Dyk, 1816) was enjoying considerable success. Kind quickly produced a libretto. The ensuing opera progressed slowly due to Weber's busy schedule and poor health but was finally produced in the Berlin Schauspielhaus on 18 June 1821, to great acclaim.

Der Freischütz has two counterparts in the early 19th century's quest for a distinctively German form of opera, which gained momentum and was renewed with the changes in society facilitated by the **Congress of Vienna** and **Restoration** culture generally: **Louis Spohr**'s *Faust* (1816; rev. 1852) and **E. T. A. Hoffmann**'s *Undine* (1816). All three works draw on distinctively German lore and literature for their subject, feature rich and innovative **orchestration** within an eclectic and cosmopolitan mixture of national styles, and employ strategic recollections of previously stated thematic and motivic material in order to enhance musicodramatic coherence. *Der Freischütz* also employs **melodrama** and spoken dialogue. Despite these shared general features, however, *Der Freischütz* is generally recognized as the most effective of the three, and its influence eclipses theirs utterly: virtually the entire Romantic Generation of composers was captivated by it, and so great was its importance as an inspiration in **Richard Wagner**'s own quest to develop an authentically German genre of opera that many textbooks and other narratives of music history that otherwise proceed in chronological order first discuss it *after* their treatments of **Hector Berlioz, Franz Liszt, Felix Mendelssohn Bartholdy, Robert Schumann**, and **Giuseppe Verdi** in order to emphasize its conceptual significance for Wagner's mature operas. All of these composers were materially influenced by the work (Berlioz was one of its most influential early advocates). Such narratives obliterate readers' opportunity to observe the influence of *Der Frieschütz* those earlier composers. [JMC]

See also LEITMOTIV; NATIONALISM, ROMANTIC NATIONALISM.

FRY, WILLIAM HENRY (1813–1864). U.S. composer of the Romantic Generation; author of *Leonora*, usually considered the first staged **grand opera** by a U.S. composer. He studied music privately in his native Philadelphia and at age 18 composed an **overture** that was awarded a medal and public performance; subsequently, he studied with a former bandsman in Bonaparte's army who introduced him to the music of **Daniel-François-**

Esprit Auber, Vincenzo Bellini, Adrien Boieldieu, Fromenthal Halévy, Ferdinand Hérold, Saverio Mercadante, and Gioachino Rossini, powerful influences on the young composer's style and artistic outlook. He continued to compose, penning three more publicly performed **concert overtures** and numerous smaller works while earning a living as music critic for several newspapers and correspondent for several more. Although his first **opera**, *The Bridal of Dunure*, on a **libretto** by his older brother, is now lost, by 1838 he was at work on a new opera, *Aurelia the Vestal*, which was completed in 1841 but apparently not performed. The year 1845 witnessed the premiere of *Leonora* (after Edward Bulwer-Lytton's [1803–1873] **melodrama** *The Lady of Lyons*, 1838), a much-discussed event widely hailed (correctly) as the first American grand opera. A second performance was given in 1846 in New York City.

The notoriety generated by these events combined with Fry's reputation as a strong writer and speaker, leading the New York *Tribune* to send him to Europe as a correspondent. This position he held until 1852, meeting **Hector Berlioz** and other European notables during his time on the Continent. Upon returning to the United States in 1852, he became an important advocate for the development of a distinctively "American" style of composition in cultivated music (*see* NATIONALISM, ROMANTIC NATIONALISM), working as editorial writer and chief music critic for the *Tribune*. His contributions to the progressive cause in U.S. music were reflected in two **program symphonies**: the *Santa Claus (Christmas) Symphony*, premiered by **Adolphe Jullien**'s **orchestra** on Christmas Eve 1853, and the *Niagara Symphony* (1854). He revised *Leonora* as a four-act Italian opera for performance in 1858 as *Giulio e Leonora*, and his last opera, *Notre Dame of Paris* (after **Victor Hugo**), was unsuccessful when given as a benefit performance for the wounded in the U.S. Civil War. He was also a prominent lecturer on music, current political events, and the imperative for U.S. composers to rid themselves of their European inheritance and speak with a distinctively American voice.

Fry's health began to fail in the early 1860s, forcing him to spend days bedridden in New York, using a lover's telephone to listen to some of the music being performed in the nearby New York Academy of Music. He finally relocated to Santa Cruz (Saint-Croix) in the Virgin Islands, where he died of tuberculosis. His output includes four surviving symphonies (plus three lost ones), three **programmatic** concert overtures, the *Metropolitan Band March*, 11 **string quartets**, one **sextet**, one **piano trio**, one **oratorio**, and one Mass setting. [JMC]

FULLER (OSSOLI), (SARAH) MARGARET (1810–1850). U.S. author, critic, and journalist of the Romantic Generation. Fuller's writings on music offer vital clues toward understanding the state of Western art music in the first half of the 19th century; they also help us piece together how Transcendentalist thought—an American strain of **Romanticism**—engaged with music.

Fuller was born in Cambridgeport, Massachusetts, to a privileged family. Her father, Timothy Fuller, an attorney and Democratic Republican, was active in state and federal politics; he served from 1817 to 1824 as a U.S. representative. Throughout her childhood, Fuller demonstrated a high aptitude and interest in reading, writing, learning, and engaging with the ideas of others—and relatively little enthusiasm for more mainstream women's interests at the time, such as mastering etiquette and optimizing one's suitability for marriage. **Piano** lessons were part of Fuller's childhood education. Already in her early 20s, she was submitting essays, stories, and reviews to literary journals. Her highest aspiration at the time was to write an English-language biography of **Johann Wolfgang von Goethe**, a project that would require her to travel to Europe. When her father passed away in 1835, Fuller chose to remain near her family temporarily; her youngest brother at the time was nine years old.

Fuller was invited to Concord to meet Ralph Waldo Emerson (1803–1882) and his circle in 1836, beginning a lifelong relationship with the Transcendental Club. For the next three years, she taught at Transcendentalist-run schools, including Bronson Alcott's Temple School (Boston) and Hiram Fuller's Green Street School (Providence, Rhode Island). In 1839, with the money saved from her teaching income, Fuller moved her family close to Boston, where she began to hold her famous Conversations, a five-year series of women's lecture-discussions on humanities topics with increasing emphasis on abolitionism and **feminism**. In 1840, Emerson invited Fuller to become editor of *The Dial*, a journal intended to disseminate Transcendentalist ideas and counteract misinformation spread by the movement's opponents; she held the position for two years. While in Boston, Fuller attended many concerts and wrote about them in *The Dial*; among the offerings she heard there were **Ludwig van Beethoven's Symphonies** No. 5 and 7, **George Frideric Handel's** *Messiah*, and **Franz Joseph Haydn's** *The Creation*.

Horace Greeley hired Fuller in 1844 to write for the New York *Tribune* as a literary critic. There, she became a more prolific music critic, covering a broad variety of musical phenomena, such as the **virtuoso** violinist **Ole Bull**, **operas** by **Gioachino Rossini**, and Beethoven's Ninth ("**Choral**") **Symphony**. In 1846, she moved to Europe to serve the paper as foreign correspondent. In Italy, Fuller met Marquis Giovanni Angelo Ossoli (1821–1850), a supporter of *Risorgimento* leader Giuseppe Mazzini (1805–1872), and the two fell in love and married secretly, having a son on 5 September 1848. The entire family died when their ship sank near the coast of Fire Island, New York, as they were returning to the United States in 1850.

Fuller's writings on European music were as inviting as they were educational. Fuller was not a polemic; her discussions of various composers and performers rarely nitpicked and tended to emphasize the intrinsic value of hearing and enjoying music. On the occasions that Fuller critiqued or asked more of New York's musical life—whether declaring that a work should be performed in its entirety rather than separated piecemeal into movements, that concert tickets should not be prohibitively expensive, or that concert-goers should remain quiet during a performance for one another's sake—the apparent goal was to optimize the listening experience. Along with **John Sullivan Dwight**, Fuller left a wealth of information about how Americans understood and consumed European music in the 19th century. [RK]

G

GADE, NIELS WILHELM (1817–1890). Danish composer and **conductor** of the Romantic Generation. Recognized internationally for his compositional skill, he was also known as the foremost Danish musician of his time.

Gade was born in Copenhagen. His father made cabinets and musical instruments, giving him access to music early in life. Gade studied violin as a youth, and he was already playing with the Royal Danish **Orchestra** at age 17. Gade composed numerous works as a young adult. His *Efterklange af Ossian* ("Echoes of **Ossian**"), a **concert overture**, won a Danish composition contest sponsored by the Copenhagen Musikforeningen in 1840. In 1843, he submitted his **Symphony** No. 1 in C minor ("Paa Sjølunds fagre sletter" [On Zealand's Fair Plains], Op. 5) to **Felix Mendelssohn Bartholdy** and quickly won his favor. The Gewandhaus Orchestra in Leipzig premiered the symphony to considerable acclaim. Gade moved to Leipzig for a few years, where he worked and studied with Mendelssohn, **Ferdinand David**, **Robert Schumann**, and numerous other important figures. Schumann's estimation of Gade was high enough that he included the young composer in his list of "new and significant talent" near the beginning of his famous "New Paths" essay (1853).

Although Gade succeeded Mendelssohn as chief **conductor** of the Gewandhaus Orchestra in 1847, the First Schleswig War—which broke out in 1848—occasioned his return to Denmark. Now, Gade served Denmark as a musical leader, taking charge of the Musikforeningen. He also developed a new permanent orchestra in Copenhagen (today the Copenhagen Philharmonic Orchestra), with which he delivered the Denmark premieres of **Ludwig van Beethoven**'s Ninth **("Choral") Symphony** and—carrying Mendelssohn's baton in the **Bach revival**—the *St. Matthew Passion*. He became a joint director of the new Copenhagen **Conservatory** (now the Royal Danish Academy of Music) in 1866.

Gade's compositional style combines his interest in Danish subjects and literary works with his personal and aesthetic proximity to composers such as Mendelssohn and Schumann. Although this was problematic in the increasingly **nationalistic** decades after the **Revolutions of 1848**, Gade continues to be remembered as an important figure in the history of Danish music. [RK]

GARCÍA, MANUEL (DEL PÓPULO VICENTE RODRÍGUEZ) (1775–1832). Spanish tenor, composer, and director; one of the most influential vocal pedagogues of the **long 19th century** and father of two of the mid-19th century's most celebrated sopranos (**Maria Malibran** and Pauline Viardot-García [1821–1910]). He was known as a composer by 1792 and in 1807 left Spain and settled in Paris. In 1816, he created the role of Almaviva in **Gioachino Rossini**'s *Il Barbiere di Siviglia*, and he later became especially known for his Rossini roles. He left for New York in 1825 to establish an Italian **opera** company there and gave the U.S. premiere of **Wolfgang Amadeus Mozart**'s *Don Giovanni* but returned to Paris in 1829 after being robbed of all his belongings while in Mexico in 1828. He published a widely translated vocal method (*Esercizj per la voce con accompto. del pianoforte: Con un discorso preliminaire sull'arte del canto* [Exercises for the Voice with Piano Accompaniment, plus a Preliminary Essay on the Art of Singing, 1830]). His son, Manuel (Patricio Rodríguez) García (1805–1906), was also a renowned vocal teacher (with **Jenny Lind** among his pupils), inventing the laryngoscope and penning two of the long 19th century's most important writings on vocal technique: *Mémoire sur la voix humaine* (Notes on the Human Voice, 1840) and *Traité complet de l'art du chant* (Complete Treatise on Singing, 1840). [JMC]

GARDNER, ISABELLA STEWART (1840–1924). U.S. patron of the arts. A New Yorker by birth and daughter of a wealthy investor, a teenage Isabella befriended classmate Julia Gardner at a Paris boarding school. In 1860, she married Julia's brother John Lowell Gardner, and the new couple settled in Jack's hometown, Boston. The Gardners were avid world tourists, and they were enthusiastic about experiencing great art and music wherever they went, above all Venice. Gardner and her husband cultivated friendships with an ever-widening circle of American artists, authors, musicians, and scholars whom they entertained regularly at the parties they hosted; these figures include Arther Foote, Wilhelm Gericke, Henry Lee Higginson, Henry James, **Edward MacDowell**, Susan Metcalfe, Karl Muck, George Santayana, and John Singer Sargent.

Gardner was an important patron of the Boston Symphony Orchestra, which Higginson founded in 1881, as well as many individual composers and performers. Gardner also amassed an impressive collection of paintings, sculptures, rare books, and other valuable items from around the world, which she made available to the Boston public in 1903 with a newly constructed Isabella Stewart Gardner Museum. Intending more than a mere museum, Gardner built gardens in and around the building and used it as a venue for musical performances. [RK]

GERBER, ERNST LUDWIG (1746–1819). German lawyer, music lexicographer, composer, and organist. From Gerber's time to the present, the lexicons, dictionaries, and catalogs he published in the early 19th century have provided readers and scholars with an abundance of information about 18th-century European musical culture.

Gerber's father, Heinrich Nikolaus Gerber, court organist to the prince of Schwarzburg-Sondershausen and a student of **Johann Sebastian Bach**, trained Ernst on the organ; Ernst learned cello as well. At Leipzig University, Gerber studied law. After working as a solicitor's assistant, Gerber became the prince's court secretary and estate management accountant. When Heinrich Gerber died in 1775, Ernst took over his position as court organist.

It was predominantly later in his life that Gerber became the lexicographer remembered today. His work developed from a growing private collection of music manuscripts, prints, images of organs, and portraits and other likenesses of musicians. These materials were the impetus for Gerber's two-volume *Historisch-biographisches Lexikon der Tonkünstler* (Historical and Biographical Lexicon of Musicians, 1790 and 1792) and a four-volume updated edition in 1812–1814, publications widely read in German and imitated by authors of similar reference works in other languages. [RK]

A GERMAN REQUIEM. See EIN DEUTSCHES REQUIEM, OP. 45.

GESAMTKUNSTWERK. (Ger., "complete artwork" or "cumulative artwork.") Term submitted by **Richard Wagner** in the essay *Die Kunst und die Revolution* (Art and Revolution, 1849) to describe the synthesis of all the arts (most notably poetry, music, and dance but also the visual arts) achieved in ancient Greek tragedy and to articulate this multivalent synthesis as the goal of the **artwork of the future**, particularly where staged musical drama was concerned. In Wagner's view, "the great Greek *Gesamtkunstwerk*" had reached its greatest perfection in the works of Aeschylus (ca. 525–456 BCE), especially his *Prometheus*; the subsequent history of the arts was a narrative of specialization and creative fragmentation. The imperative of the artwork of the future was to undo this dissolution in order to achieve a new Romantic perfection of artistic expression forged in the heat of the universal social revolution manifested in the **Revolutions of 1848**. The new form, Wagner asserted, would dispense with both the "chaos of unconnected sensual elements" that he perceived in contemporary French and Italian **opera** and the unbecomingly derivative revivals of classical Greek drama characteristic of contemporary philhellenism and neoclassicism.

The term *Gesamtkunstwerk* is Wagner's invention, but in many ways the concept was hardly new. Whereas the 18th and 19th centuries' earlier calls for cumulative syntheses of the arts appealed to the greatness of Classical antiquity and argued that the arts were natural and scientific phenomena whose division into separate spheres of activity was a matter convention and artifice, Wagner's concept was unique in its forceful assertion that the truly cumulative artwork was the only way to realize, in the arts, the democratic impulse driven by "the people" (*das Volk*) that had led to the revolutionary tide of 1848. The concept was rooted in Wagner's (largely unacknowledged) appropriation of a well-established Enlightenment and Romantic project aimed at a cumulative synthesis of the arts in the context of staged drama with music. In a general sense, the *Gesamtkunstwerk* was theorized and advocated for in various ekphrastic and synaesthetic writings of the 17th and 18th centuries.

Most directly relevant for Wagner's purposes was Gottfried Ephraim Lessing's (1729–1781) unfinished theoretical essay *Laocoon*, which argued for a synergistic fusion of "natural" (visual or synoptically comprehensible) and "arbitrary" (literary or musical, i.e., temporally dependent) arts into a new expressive mode whose content would be greater than the sum of its parts. The works of **Carl Maria von Weber, Hector Berlioz**, and others which employ attitudes, **melodrama**, and *tableaux vivants* at particularly important moments in larger dramatic contexts reflect this thinking. Friedrich Kind (1768–1843), author of the libretto of *Der Freischütz* and explicator of the aesthetic premises that underlay that opera revered by Wagner, argued in the prefatory note to the second edition of his immensely successful play *Van Dyck's Landleben* (1817) that "just as there is *one* light that is, however, seen in many different refractions, so too there is only *one* art, which manifests itself in different media and forms." Similar arguments for a synergistic reunion of the arts echo also in the words of **Friedrich Schiller, Johann Wolfgang von Goethe**, and **Robert Schumann**. Although this well-established field of precursory concepts certainly aided Wagner in the formulation of his own ideas regarding the *Gesamtkunstwerk*, they are more directly relevant because their acceptance, to one degree or another, in various sectors of the musical world of the mid-19th century increased the public's readiness to embrace Wagner's arguments and, in turn, his **music dramas** based on those arguments.

In the event, Wagner himself was never able to synthesize the arts as equally as he hoped, and he eventually ceased using the term *Gesamtkunstwerk*. Nevertheless, the term represents a milestone in 19th-century aesthetics because it distilled a number of diverse efforts at synaesthetic thought into a new, compactly expressed, and socially committed idea, at the same time offering a firm aesthetic foundation for a number of other, more practicable ideas that revolutionized Wagner's approach to opera after 1849. His own return, by the time of his essay "Über die Benennung 'Musikdrama'" (On the Designation "Music Drama," 1872), to a view of musical drama not as a *Gesamtkunstwerk* but as "acts of music made visible" ("ersichtlich gewordene Thaten der Musik"—that is, an art form that privileged music and expressed musical ideas in visual terms)—did not prevent later creators of opera, **ballet**, and especially film music from setting the *Gesamtkunstwerk* as their own creative goal. [JMC]

See also BAYREUTH.

GESANG (PL. GESÄNGE). German term denoting either (1) voice; (2) the vocal line(s) in a work for voice(s) and/or accompaniment or the performance of same; (3) the text and/or music of a German art-song that, unlike the **Lied**, does not cultivate an air of simplicity or *Volkstümlichkeit*; or (4) vocal music generally. The last potentially includes sacred and or secular music and simple as well as complex vocal music, on a case-by-case basis.

The first usage is encountered in ubiquitous title phrases and descriptions, such as "für Gesang und Pianoforte" (for voice and piano, as in the title given for **Robert** and **Clara Schumann**'s collaborative **song cycle** *Liebesfrühling*, Op. 37). The second usage occurs frequently in prose descriptions and reviews (e.g., when a reviewer might observe that the vocal line—*Gesang*—is insufficiently melodious). The third usage—which generates the greatest confusion for nonnative speakers of German—is reflected in the ubiquity of titles such as *Gesang der Geister über den Wassern* (poem by **Johann Wolfgang von Goethe**), set by **Franz Schubert** as a solo **song** (D. 484, 1816) as the **part-song** for a cappella *Männerchor* (D. 538, 1817), as a song for male voices with piano (D. 705, 1820; sketch only), and as a song for male voices with orchestra (D. 714, 1820–1821), but also in frequently encountered titular distinctions, such as *Lieder und Gesänge* (e.g., **Gustav Mahler**'s Op. 27 or various collections by Robert Schumann). The fourth usage occurs in the many *Gesang-Bücher* (*Gesangbücher*; sing. *Gesangbuch*) published during the **long 19th century**, many (but not all) of which are sacred. It is important to note that the term *Gesang*, like the term *Lied*, does not necessarily refer to a musical setting per se; equally often (as in the case of Goethe's *Gesang der Geister über den Wassern*), it refers to a poetic text that the poet considered suitable for musical composition. [JMC]

GESELLSCHAFT DER MUSIKFREUNDE. (Ger., "society of friends of music.") Viennese musical association, still in existence, organized in 1812 by Joseph Sonnleithner (1766–1835) as the Gesellschaft Adeliger Frauen

(Society of Noblewomen) and officially chartered as the Gesellschaft der Musikfreunde in 1814. Its founding coincides with the end of the Napoleonic Wars and the beginning of the **Restoration**. In that period of momentous social and political change, the aim of the Gesellschaft was to promote music in all its facets and ensure that stewardship of music and musicians not be left to chance, accomplishing this by allying the city's moneyed aristocracy, elite Jewish bankers, and burgeoning music-loving middle class. It organized the founding of the Vienna **Conservatory** in 1817 and of the Vienna Singverein (Vocal Union) under the direction of Antonio Salieri (1750–1825) in 1819. The *Singverein* was involved in the premieres of **Ludwig van Beethoven**'s *Missa solemnis* (Op. 123, 1819–1823, publ. 1827; *see* SOLEMN MASS) and Ninth **("Choral") Symphony, Johannes Brahms**'s *Ein Deutsches Requiem*, and **Anton Bruckner**'s Te Deum, among many others. The Gesellschaft's archives rank highly among the Austrian capital's many musical collections. [JMC]

GEVAERT, FRANÇOIS-AUGUSTE (1828–1908). Belgian musicologist, composer, and music educator. Originally trained as a pianist and organist, he studied at the Ghent **Conservatory** beginning in 1841 and was subsequently employed as organist at the Jesuit College there. After completing his first two **operas** (*Hugues de Zomerghem*, 1848, and *La comédie à la ville* [The Village Comedy, 1849]) and having them produced, he traveled to France, the German and Italian lands, and Spain in 1849–1852. To the end of his life, he remained highly respected as a composer, penning a total of 12 operas and a substantial number of sacred and secular **cantatas** as well as **orchestral** and **chamber** music. Over the course of his career, he was named Composer to the King of Belgium; became a member of the Belgian Royal Academy, the Institut de France, and the Royal Academy in Berlin; and held the Leopoldsorde and the Order of the Queen of Spain.

For all his success as a composer, Gevaert's chief accomplishments are in the fields of education and scholarship. In 1867, he succeeded **Fromenthal Halévy** as Chef de chant at the Académie de Musique in Paris and was named music director at the Opéra. He held the latter post until 1872, when he succeeded **François-Joseph Fétis** as director of the Brussels **Conservatory**, there instituting a number of reforms that were widely emulated. Like **Edmond de Coussemaker**, he researched medieval and Renaissance music (especially liturgical music) extensively and laid the foundation for the intensive explorations and mythologizing of those repertoires that occurred in the final years of the **long 19th century**. In particular, his edition of 15th-century French secular **songs** (1875) was widely disseminated.

Gevaert's *Vade-mecum de l'organiste* (Organist's Handbook, 1871) and *Traité d'harmonie théorique et pratique* (Theoretical and Practical Treatise on Harmony, 1907) were likewise well known and much praised. His most

influential pedagogical works, however, were centered on musical instruments and the rapidly changing art of **orchestration**. The *Traité général d'instrumentation: Exposé méthodique* (General Treatise on Instrumentation, 1863) was followed by a significantly expanded *Nouveau traité d'instrumentation* (New Treatise on Instrumentation) in 1875 and then by a *Cours méthodique d'orchestration* (Methodical Course of Instruction in Orchestration) in 1890. The second of these was translated and published in English (1906), German (by Hugo Riemann [1849–1919]), and Russian (by **Pyotor Il'yich Tchaikovsky** in 1866 and Vladimir Rebikov in 1900). [JMC]
  See also ORCHESTRA; PRIX DE ROME (PARIS).

GILBERT, HENRY (FRANKLIN BELKNAP) (1868–1928). U.S. composer and writer on music; member of the Modern Romantic Generation. He was proficient on **piano** and violin and studied composition informally with **Edward MacDowell** and George E. Whiting (1840–1923) but until the early 20th century earned his living primarily by playing in small orchestras in his native Massachusetts and working in his uncle's print shop. At the World's Columbian Exposition in Chicago, he became acquainted with ragtime and thereafter increasingly championed the cause of musical **nationalism**, undertaking to make his living as a composer after hearing Gustave Charpentier's (1860–1956) **opera** *Louise* in Paris in 1901. His works draw on a wide variety of folk and ethnic elements—among them jazz, ragtime, African American spirituals, and Irish poetry and song—but by far the most important influence is that of Native American music as Gilbert understood it; this influence also made him an important collaborator with Arthur Farwell (1872–1952) in the creation and flourishing of the Wa-Wan Press.
  Among Gilbert's most important works are the opera *Fantasy in Delft* (1915–1920) and its incomplete predecessor, *Uncle Remus* (ca. 1906); the **symphonic poem** *The Dance in Place Congo* (1908), which was premiered as a **ballet** in New York's Metropolitan Opera in 1916; **incidental music**, such as *The Intimate Story of Indian Tribal Life (The Story of a Vanishing Race)* (1911); other orchestral works (most importantly the *Negro Rhapsody [Shout]*, 1912, the *Comedy Overture on Negro Themes*, 1912, and the *Nocturne after Whitman*, 1925–1926); and many **songs**. As a writer on music, he made important contributions (most of them centering on nationalism) to journals such as *Etude*, *The Musical Quarterly*, and *The New Music Review*. [JMC]
  See also EXOTICISM.

GILMAN, LAWRENCE (1878–1939). Influential U.S. music critic and author of books about music; member of the Modern Romantic Generation. Trained in studio art, he was largely self-taught in music theory and on organ and **piano**. Between 1901 and 1913, he served in a variety of increasingly important capacities for *Harper's Weekly*, joining the staff of *Harper's Magazine* in 1913 and becoming music, drama, and literary critic for the *North American Review*, the oldest literary magazine in the United States, in 1915. He served as program annotator for the New York Symphony Orchestra (later the New York Philharmonic) and the Philadelphia Orchestra from 1919 to 1939. He also authored several monographs and collections of essays, the latter comprising substantively revised versions of his previously published critical essays. He was also a composer; in particular, his recitation for voice and piano titled *A Dream of Death* (1903; text by W. B. Yeats) was widely performed and disseminated during the years leading up to World War I.

Throughout his career, Gilman was an ardent and influential champion of U.S. composers and of progressive currents in Western music. The former interest is reflected in his insightful reviews of music by Charles Ives and Charles Griffes and especially in his important biography of **Edward MacDowell** (1906, 2nd ed. 1909) and his survey titled *Phases of Modern Music: Strauss, MacDowell, Elgar, Loeffler, Mascagni, Grieg, Cornelius, Verdi, Wagner, "Parsifal" and Its Significance* (1904). His advocacy of progressive Romantic composers includes important essays on the composers of the **New German School** (especially **Franz Liszt** and Richard Wagner) as well as influential "thematic guides" to **Claude Debussy**'s *Pelléas et Mellisade* (1907) and **Richard Strauss**'s *Salome* (1907). His *Stories of Symphonic Music* (1907), addressed specifically to "the intelligent concert-goer who desires to listen understandingly" to "all modern delineative music" from **Ludwig van Beethoven** through Strauss and Debussy, with the strong suggestion that the essays be read *before* the concert rather than during it, is representative of Gilman's commitment to making sophisticated issues comprehensible to the educated layperson. [JMC]

See also PROGRAM (PROGRAMMATIC) MUSIC.

GLAZUNOV, ALEKSANDR (KONSTANTINOVICH) (1865–1936). Russian composer, **conductor**, writer on music, and pedagogue; member of the Modern Romantic Generation. He was director of the St. Petersburg **Conservatory** and an active contributor to Russian public musical life from 1905 to 1928 (although he retained his post at the Conservatory in absentia until 1830). He began composition studies at the age of 11 and at the age of 14 was recommended by **Mily Balakirev** to study with **Nikolay Rimsky-Korsakov**, a course of studies that he completed in 18 months. His First **String Quartet** (Op. 1) and First **Symphony** (Op. 5) were performed in 1882, and he soon was accepted into the informal society of Russian nationalist composers who were sponsored by the timber merchant and publisher Mitrofan Belyayev (1836–1904). Belyayev became Glazunov's patron, in 1884 taking him on a tour of Western Europe, including Weimar, where his

First Symphony was performed and he met **Franz Liszt**. Through Belyayev's support, he had his Second Symphony (Op. 16, 1886) performed at the World Exhibition in Paris in 1889, and during the 1890s he was extraordinarily productive, composing four symphonies, two string quartets, and three **ballets**, including the renowned *Raymonda*, Op. 57, among other works.

In 1899, Glazunov was hired as professor of orchestration and music theory at the St. Petersburg Conservatory, and during the revolutionary year 1905 he was made director of that institution. His productivity subsequently dropped off, no doubt due to his energetic efforts to reform the curriculum (including the creation of an **opera** studio and a student reading **orchestra**), improve standards, and raise the institution's profile while also offering special assistance and support to meritorious but needy students, such as Dmitri Shostakovich (who studied there from 1919 to 1930). Still, it was during this tenure that he produced some of his best-known works, including the Violin **Concerto** (Op. 82, 1905), the Eighth Symphony (Op. 83, 1907), and the Saxophone Concerto (Op. 109, 1934). In 1907, while in England, he received honorary doctoral degrees from Oxford University and Cambridge University.

Despite the hardships of World War I and the serious crisis in arts funding during the postwar years, Glazunov organized and conducted concerts in factories, clubs, and Red Army posts and participated in organizational work for the All-Russian Union of Professional Musicians and the Leningrad Philharmonic Orchestra. In June 1928, he left Russia for Vienna, where he served as chair of the committee tasked with evaluating original scores commissioned in celebration of the centennial of **Franz Schubert**'s death. Between then and 1932, he conducted concerts in Czechoslovakia, England, the French provinces, the Netherlands, Paris, Poland, Portugal, Spain, and the United States, returning in 1932 to Paris and dying there. [JMC]

GLINKA, MIKHAIL (IVANOVICH) (1804–1857). Russian composer of the Romantic Generation; the most important musical figure for Russian **nationalism** before the rise of **Pyotor Il'yich Tchaikovsky** and the **Mighty Handful**. He composed **songs** in Russian, French, and Italian; **piano** music and much instrumental **chamber music**; **incidental music**; and a number of **orchestral** works. He is best known for two of his five **operas**: *Zhizn' za tsarya* (A Life for the Tsar, 1834–1836, publ. ca. 1856) and *Ruslan and Ludmila* (after **Aleksandr Pushkin**, 1837–1842, publ. 1856). His musical education was unsystematic, and his tastes and stylistic influences were eclectic; he traveled widely within Russia and in Western Europe (France, the German and Italian lands, and Spain), meeting and learning from diverse notables including **Vincenzo Bellini, Hector Berlioz, Gaetano Donizetti, John Field, Felix Mendelssohn Bartholdy**, and **Giacomo Meyerbeer**. He also found important inspiration in the teachings of the Prussian theorist, archivist, and writer on music Siegfried Dehn (1799–1858), whose pupils included **Peter Cornelius** and **Anton Rubinstein** and with whom Glinka studied counterpoint in 1833–1834 and Renaissance polyphony in 1855–1857.

Glinka was the first Russian composer of the **long 19th century** (or earlier) to assimilate the various crosscurrents of Western European Romantic music into a personal style that was both distinctive and, in some ways, distinctively Russian. He was based in St. Petersburg for most of his professional life in Russia and won much appreciation in that city's cosmopolitan culture because of his ability to compose fluently in the idioms of **Ludwig van Beethoven**, Bellini, Field, **Franz Joseph Haydn**, **Wolfgang Amadeus Mozart**, and especially **Franz Schubert**, with which the aristocracy was acquainted through its own travels to the West and which it considered hallmarks of artistic accomplishment. His late works stemming from his study of Spanish music (most notably the First and Second Spanish **Overtures**, 1845 and 1848) were both cosmopolitan and **exoticist** in nature, reflecting his experiences in Spain in 1845–1857 and employing exoticist styles but doing so more authentically than, for example, **Georges Bizet** would in *Carmen* (1875) or **Nikolay Rimsky-Korsakov** would in the *Spanish Capriccio* (1887). At the same time, Glinka's use of specifically Russian subjects and his use of Russian folk tunes—even within a musical language in which French, German, and Italian influences are readily evident—won for him the admiration of the growing nationalist movement within Russia and a level of respect among Western European composers that few (if any) other Russian composers enjoyed at the time. It is significant that despite all their other many and important differences, both the Balakirev and the Tchaikovsky camps of Russian nationalism in the late 19th century viewed Glinka as their progenitor and a major source of inspiration. [JMC]

See also DARGOMÏZHSKY, ALEKSANDR (SERGEYEVICH) (1813–1869).

GODOWSKY, LEOPOLD (1870–1938). U.S. pianist and composer of Polish-Jewish birth; along with **Ferruccio Busoni** and **Serge Rachmaninoff**, one of the most influential **virtuoso** pianist/composers of the Modern Romantic Generation. He had acquired a considerable reputation in the United States (especially Boston and New York) by the 1890s and was a protégé of **Camille Saint-Saëns** in Paris, where he was well known as a **salon** performer from 1897–1899. His fame broadened further after a triumphant performance on 6 December 1900 (with the Berlin Philharmonic) at the Berlin **Beethoven** Hall, featuring **Johannes Brahms**'s First Piano **Concerto** (Op. 15) and **Pyotor Il'yich Tchaikovsky**'s First Piano Concerto (Op. 23) along with his own *Contrapuntal Paraphrase on [Carl Maria von] Weber's Invitation to the Dance* (J. 260/Op. 65) and seven of his highly original *Studies on* *the [Fryderyk] Chopin Etudes* (1894—1914). Over the course of the remainder of his career, he toured extensively and held teaching positions in Berlin, Chicago, New York, Philadelphia, and Vienna. His *Java Suite* (*Phonoramas*), published in 1925, was a substantive attempt to respond compositionally, without **exoticizing**, to the sounds, textures, and rhythmic language of Javanese Gamelan, which he had encountered during a tour of East Asia in 1922.

As a pianist, Godowsky is best remembered for his extraordinary virtuosity (Vladimir Horowitz declared that one would need six hands, not two, to play his 1927 *Passacaglia*) and his theories of weight release and economy of motion. As a composer, he extended the highly chromatic tonal language of the mid- and later 19th century but was also famous for his intricately polyphonic textures; the latter applied also to his transcriptions, arrangements, and **fantasies** based on other composers' works—among them vocal works by **Charles Gounod, Franz Schubert, Robert Schumann, Giuseppe Verdi**, and **Richard Wagner** as well as instrumental compositions by **Isaac Albéniz, Johann Sebastian Bach**, Beethoven, **Franz Liszt**, Schumann, Saint-Saëns, **Johann Strauss (II)**, and **Richard Strauss**, among others. [JMC]

GOETHE, JOHANN WOLFGANG (VON) (1749–1832). German poet, playwright, novelist, scientist, statesman, theater director and actor, critic, artist and art critic, privy councillor, and administrator; collector and transcriber of **folk song**. Although controversial during his lifetime and for several decades beyond, he is today reckoned as the towering German literary figure of the modern era. He is rivaled only by **Shakespeare** as a literary influence on music's Romanticisms.

The prevalent image of Goethe's relationship to music is that he was a marginally literate amateur prone to conservative tastes that were reinforced by a supposed reliance on Carl Friedrich Zelter (1758–1832), who is in turn viewed as largely reactionary because of his interest in cultivating the music of the past, especially that of **Johann Sebastian Bach**, alongside that of the present (*see* HISTORICISM). Like most myth, this image contains a kernel of truth but is hardly factual. The distortion resulted from a shift in the teleology of the historiography of music and the polemics surrounding the direction of Romanticism at mid-century (*see* NEW GERMAN SCHOOL and the introduction to this dictionary). Two of the myth's fundamental components—Goethe's relationships with **Franz Schubert** and **Hector Berlioz**—are deeply misleading. On the one hand, the conventional notion that Goethe disdained the Viennese composer and returned unopened a package of his settings (including *Erlkönig* and *Gretchen am Spinnrade*, among others) is at best half true (the package never reached the poet, being returned by his secretary), and in 1825, Goethe accepted Schubert's petition to dedicate his op. 19 songs to him (D. 161, 369, and 544). The latter interaction was required by law, and by 19th-century convention such permissions were granted only selectively and considered implicit but very real endorsements of the work being published (*see* PRINTING AND PUBLISHING OF MUSIC). Goethe thus respected Schubert enough to allow a public dedication—an acknowledgment of esteem, not disdain.

Similarly, Goethe's rejection, after receiving feedback from Zelter, of **Hector Berlioz**'s *Huit scèenes de Faust* must have reflected Zelter's opinion of the work, but that assessment was also shared by most of musical Germany; even **Adolf Bernhard Marx** and Berlioz's other early advocates accepted the work only with reservations. In point of fact, despite his amateur status, Goethe was passionate and well informed about many facets of music. A baritone, he could sight-sing and he performed in the private choir directed by Carl Eberwein (1786–1868). He also studied **piano** and cello, and he actively researched and developed well-formed ideas on music's history, theory, performance, and aesthetics generally.

Goethe's significance for music's Romanticisms is further attested to by his **reception** history in music. Composers' decisions to read certain authors' works and to set one or another of those works to music naturally reflect their own views of what those authors represented in historical and political terms and of how those works distilled some aspect(s) of the original authors' identity into a single text. Conversely, the various engagements with any author's works at any given time and place reflect contemporary views of that author and those texts. When Schubert began setting Goethe's texts in 1815, he was implicitly lending artistic endorsement to a poet who was regarded as radical and arch-Romantic (indeed, whose works had until recently been banned by the censors in Vienna); when **Felix Mendelssohn Bartholdy** and **Robert Schumann** set Goethe's texts, they were responding to a figure whose controversiality was of an entirely different sort than that with which Schubert engaged, and when the Frenchman Berlioz engaged compositionally with that same figure, he invited a different sort of controversy. But Goethe was anything but controversial by the time of **Hugo Wolf**'s 51 Goethe settings (1888–1889). Those settings therefore invited controversy only because of the ways in which they dealt with the words of a figure who had by then become the reigning deity of German letters, not because of what Goethe and his works had represented a half-century earlier. This constantly shifting reception history makes it useful to recognize that the modern image of Goethe as German patron saint of great literature is one that did not gain predominance until the last few decades of the 19th century, and that earlier compositional engagements with Goethe and his works accordingly represent significantly different perceptions of him and his works. Understanding those earlier engagements requires an awareness of this shifting context.

Goethe today enjoys the sort of canonical status and near-universal veneration typically afforded **Johann Sebastian Bach, Ludwig van Beethoven,** and **Wolfgang Amadeus Mozart.** For much of the 19th century, that was not the case. *Die Leiden des jungen Werther* (The Sorrows of Young Werther, 1774, rev. 1787) established him as an international literary figure who could not be ignored, but this renown entailed considerable controversy and widespread suspicion that he represented eccentricity or brazen immorality more than greatness. This skepticism persisted to the end of his life. It resulted from a variety of factors beyond his works themselves: his religious views (a pantheist, he described himself as "neither anti-Christian nor un-Christian, but decidedly non-Christian") and his politics (although firmly opposed to absolutist monarchy, he was deeply suspicious of the lower classes and popular sovereignty, found the counterweight to this in the aristocracy rather than the lower or middle classes, and favored reform of the monarchical and aristocratic status quo to revolution), and his increasing neoclassicism during precisely the period in which the aesthetic mandate for values celebrating emotion over intellect and the sublime over the beautiful began to gain wider currency.

Goethe's literary works themselves only fueled these suspicions: *Werther* made him known—much to his distress—as an "apologist of suicide"; the *Roman Elegies* and *Venetian Epigrams* equate artistic beauty with sensual, erotic, and homoerotic pleasure; *Faust* celebrates evil at least as much as goodness; and *Die Wahlverwandtschaften* (The Elective Affinities, 1816) justifies marital infidelity as a human manifestation of the same natural laws that cause chemical elements to realign and regroup. By the end of his life, the political and artistic views of this former radical were conspicuously out of touch with those of social and artistic progressives: representative are the views of Friedrich Schlegel (1772–1829), who in 1797 proclaimed Goethe the poet who had "ushered in an entirely new period in the history of art," and **Heinrich Heine,** who in 1828 (i.e., four years before Goethe's death) declared that the "old prophecy that the period of art that began at the cradle of Goethe [would] end beside his coffin seems close to its fulfillment. Today's art must be disposed of entirely because its principles are based on the old, now-rejected regime and have their roots in the Holy Roman Imperial past."

Goethe in turn regarded the effects of his influence with skepticism or outright contempt, and by the turn of the 19th century, he was disappointed with many of the currents in Romantic thought that had taken *Werther* and his other works from the 1770s and 1780s as their starting points. Most important among these movements was that of German **nationalism.** That movement sought in its formative years to discover a historical "German spirit" (*deutscher Geist*) in the art and culture of the remote past, to portray that past as one whose legacy had been neglected or betrayed by subsequent culture, and to articulate that spirit anew in modern artwork that, newly infused with a sense of national identity born of that heritage, addressed itself to its own world. Goethe sympathized with this national spirit. As mainstream German nationalism became increasingly xenophobic and determined to weed out "corrupting" or "compromising" elements, however, Goethe became increasingly committed to a pan-cultural, cosmopolitan variety of nationalism that would be represented in a supranational, if also German-chauvinist, *Welt-Literatur* (world-literature), a philosophy that alienated him from the ardent nationalism of most German Romantics and European Romanticism generally.

The view of Goethe as an erstwhile arch-Romantic grown outmoded still predominated the mid-19th century when terms such as "Goethe-Philistines" and "Goethe-pedants" were common in the popular press. By the 1860s, however, the cause of German nationalism and sympathies for the cult of the individual began to rally increasingly around Goethe as an icon of German cultural greatness and accordingly to downplay those of his views that were out of touch with current ideologies while emphasizing those that were in touch with it (or could be construed as being so). The last third of the century thus saw the emergence of a heterogeneous but near-universal Goethe cult; any number of deeply contradictory or mutually exclusive ideologies found in him an early champion, emphasizing elements of his vast and diverse output that seemed to foreshadow their own contemporary ideas. [JMC]

GOMES, (ANTÔNIO) CARLOS (1836–1896). Brazilian composer of the Late Romantic Generation, of Portuguese descent; although not a committed **nationalist**, his international success as a Brazilian composer who attempted to incorporate Luso-Brazilian and *modinha* folk styles (*see* FOLK SONG) into the idioms of cultivated music made him an important role model for later Brazilian nationalist composers such as **Alexandre Levy**. Gomes was born into a musical family, learning to play several instruments and beginning composition at an early age; when he was 18, he had his first Mass setting performed in a church in his native Campinhas. An 1859 concert tour led to his enrollment (against his father's wishes) in the Imperial **Conservatory** of Music in Rio de Janeiro. There, through performances of works **Vincenzo Bellini**, **Gaetano Donizetti**, **Gioachino Rossini**, and **Giuseppe Verdi**, he discovered the fascination with **opera** and flair for musical drama that would characterize his mature style. In 1864, he went to Milan to study at the Conservatory there. He settled quickly into the musical life of the Lombard capital and spent most of the rest of his life there, becoming successful as a composer and earning the praise of (among others) Verdi, who spoke of him as "a truly musical genius."

Gomes was widely feted in his native Brazil on a tour in 1873 and in consequence of this native fame was offered the directorship of the Conservatory in Rio de Janeiro upon his return by Brazilian Emperor Dom Pedro II (fl. 1831–1889). Shortly after he returned in 1889, however, the emperor was overthrown, and the Republic of the United States of Brazil established. Gomes's own monarchist sympathies finding little support in the new context, he returned again to Milan. There his new opera, *Condor*, was performed to great acclaim in 1891, leading to a new composition from him for the celebrations of the quadricentennial of Christopher Columbus's discovery of America. The resulting work, the four-part **oratorio** *Colombo*, led the Brazilian government to name him first representative to the Chicago quadricentennial celebrations in 1893. A successful trip to the United States included a performance (under his own baton) of excerpts from his own works at the Chicago Exposition. Further commissions and successes led to his being offered the directorship of the Liceo Civico Musicale "Benedetto Marcello" and that of the Music Conservatory of Belém (in the state of Pará in his native Brazil) almost simultaneously in 1896. He accepted the latter but died just months after his return.

Gomes composed successfully in a variety of genres, including (in addition to the oratorio *Colombo*) **cantatas, marches** and occasional pieces for **orchestra,** *modinhas*, other **songs** on Italian texts, and pieces for **piano** solo. He is best known, however, for his 12 **operas** (both serious and **comic**). Of these, *Fosca* (1873, rev. and publ. 1878), *Maria Tudor* (1879, after **Victor Hugo**), *Lo schiavo* (The Slave, 1889), and *Condor* (1891) were the best known during his lifetime. The work generally considered his masterpiece is the 1870 four-act "opera-ballo" *Il Guarany*, based on the well-known eponymous novel (1857) by the Brazilian Indianist novelist and playwright José de Alencar (1829–1877). With its noble Indian heroes and stylized dances, the opera succeeded in Europe not least of all as an **exoticist** drama. The *verismo*-influenced *Lo schiavo* likewise centers on Gomes's native land (in this case, the struggle for the liberation of Brazil's black slaves, although for the work's Italian premiere, the slaves were recast as local Indians, and the setting changed from the 19th century to the 16th). [JMC]

GONZAGA, CHIQUINHA (1847–1935). Brazilian composer, pianist, and **conductor** of the Late Romantic Generation; one of the most important progressive leaders in the movements to end slavery in Brazil and establish Brazilian independence. She was a prolific and widely respected composer of *modinhas*, dances, and **operettas.** Daughter of a wealthy officer in the Brazilian military and a mulatto mother, she received a thorough liberal arts education that also included instruction in music. Her marriage was an arranged one, to a commander in the Brazilian Merchant Navy, who forced her to accompany him as he transported weaponry and slaves in the War of the

Triple Alliance (1864–1867). The marriage was never a happy one, and when her husband forbade her to pursue a career in music, she divorced him, teaching **piano** lessons to earn money for herself and her children.

In 1877, the renowned flautist Joaquim Antônio da Silva Callado (1848–1880) invited Gonzaga to become the rehearsal accompanist of the Choro Carioca, and this social outlet provided increasing opportunities for her to display her musicianship. In 1885, she became the first woman to conduct an **orchestra** in Brazil, and in 1902 and 1904, she also traveled to Europe, settling in Lisbon from 1906 to 1909. During the early 20th century, she was also a leader in the movement to establish **copyright** protection for composers and playwrights.

Gonzaga's musical output is notable not only for its consistently tuneful melodies and colorful harmonies but also for the fact that so much of it was published: during her lifetime, more than 300 of her *modinhas*, other **songs**, dances, and **character pieces** for piano solo were published. She also composed 77 operettas and other works for the musical stage. By far the most important of these was the operetta *Forrobodó* (1912), which received 1,500 performances. Her first successful work was the polka *Atraente* (Attractive, 1877). Her march *Ô abre-alas* (1899) and tango *Corta-Jaca* (1912) remain immensely popular today. [JMC]

DIE GÖTTERDÄMMERUNG. See THE RING OF THE NIBELUNG.

GOTTSCHALK, LOUIS MOREAU (1829–1869). U.S. composer and **virtuoso** pianist of the Late Romantic Generation. Gottschalk was born in New Orleans to a German Jewish father from London and a Haitian mother. After childhood organ lessons revealed his musical aptitude, his father sent him to Paris, where he studied with English pianist **Charles Hallé** and composer Pierre Maleden (1801–1871). Gottschalk was famous across Europe by his 21st birthday, due in large part to four **piano** dances on melodies from the United States and the West Indies: *Bamboula, La savane* (The Savanna), *Le bananier* (The Banana Tree), and *Le mancenillier* (The Manchineel). The lively syncopations of these pieces, the faraway origins of their source material, and Gottschalk's own seemingly exotic heritage were a powerful mix in Europe, where **exoticism** was increasingly prevalent. Gottschalk was a prolific composer through the early 1850s, focusing primarily on the piano. After touring Switzerland briefly in 1850, Gottschalk composed and performed under the patronage of Spanish Queen Isabella II until his return to the United States in 1853.

Gottschalk's first several years in the United States were crucial in their productivity and adversity. On the one hand, they were foundational years for Gottschalk's stateside popularity as touring performer and composer; two of his most important works—*Le banjo* (1853) and *The Last Hope* (1854)—stem from this period. On the other, the death of his father (1853) and an unmanageably strenuous touring schedule contributed to a nervous breakdown in 1857, followed by five years in the Caribbean. The beginning of the U.S. Civil War saw Gottschalk's return to the United States, where he began touring again, this time as an agent for **Chickering & Sons**. A false accusation of sexual assault in 1865 prompted him to flee to South America, where he toured Argentina, Brazil, Chile, Peru, and Uruguay. Plagued by malaria, Gottschalk died in 1870 from a quinine overdose intended as treatment. [RK]

GOUNOD, CHARLES(-FRANÇOIS) (1818–1893). French composer, **conductor**, and organist of the Late Romantic Generation, best known today for his **opera** based on **Johann Wolfgang von Goethe**'s recounting of the **Faust** legend, his free discant on Prelude I from Volume I of **Johann Sebastian Bach**'s *Well-Tempered Clavier* (BWV 846), his *Messe solennelle de Ste. Cécile* (1855; *see* SOLEMN MASS), and his moving **motet** *Gallia* (1871). His output includes a total of 12 **comic** and serious operas, four sets of **incidental music**, two **symphonies** and several other works for **orchestra**, four **string quartets** and 11 other works for instrumental **chamber** ensemble, and many works for **piano** solo, **piano duet**, and organ as well as two **Requiems** and 19 other Mass settings, 52 motets and individual Latin sacred works for chorus, a sizable body of other sacred music on English or French texts, 30 **part-songs**, 10 multimovement secular **cantatas** and "petits **oratorios**," one **song cycle** (*Biondina*, 1872), and 162 other **songs** sacred and secular on English, French, and Italian texts and many songs and part-songs for children's voices (*see* CHILDREN'S CHORUS).

Gounod studied counterpoint and composition with **Fromental Halévy** and **Jean-François Le Sueur** at the Paris **Conservatory** from 1836 to 1839. He won the second **Prix de Rome** in 1837 and the Grand Prix de Rome in 1839, traveling to Italy in accordance with the prize's terms and there not only immersing himself in the music of **Giovanni Battista da Palestrina** but also meeting **Fanny Hensel**, who was instrumental in developing his familiarity with the music of Bach, **Ludwig van Beethoven**, and her younger brother **Felix Mendelssohn Bartholdy**. On returning to France, he continued to concentrate primarily on sacred music and from 1846 to 1848 trained for the priesthood—an avocation that was at odds with his reputation as an insatiable womanizer.

Gounod's introduction to the French capital's thriving culture of **grand opera** came through his acquaintance with famed soprano Pauline Viardot-García (1821–1910), who sang the title role in his first opera, *Sapho* (1851). The work was a failure, but he continued to compose, and his reputation grew. In 1852, he was appointed director of the Paris **Orphéon**, for which he wrote a great many choral works over the coming eight years, and director of vocal music in the capital's public schools. In 1856, he began collaborating with librettists Michel Carré (1821–1872) and Jules Barbier (1825–1901) on what was to be his greatest operatic success, *Faust* (completed and produced at the Théâtre Lyrique in 1859). He produced two more important operas over the course of the 1860s (*Mireille*, 1864, and **Roméo et Juliette**, after **William Shakespeare**, 1867). He seemed destined for enduring success in Paris but fled to England in September 1870 in the wake of the **Franco-Prussian War**. His French patriotism was strong and found expression in a number of moving works written over the course of his career (most notably the lamentation motet *Gallia*, based on texts selected from the Lamentations of Jeremiah by Gounod himself and composed for the London International Exhibition of 1871 after France's humiliating defeat). But his commitment to his family was also strong; he moved them first to Dieppe and then to London when it became clear that France would fall to Prussia and French lives would be endangered.

Gounod's stay in London was initially intended to be one of convenience, born of the warm reception his music had begun to enjoy in the British capital as well as of the need to flee the war—but it turned out to be much more than that. By the time he returned to Paris in 1874, he had established strong working relationships with several English publishers and written a respectable quantity of vocal music on English texts, becoming one of Great Britain's most beloved continental composers. Equally important (and detrimental) were complications that arose from his womanizing when he took up residence with an amateur singer, Georgina Weldon, and her estranged husband; this relationship was reportedly the reason for his wife's and children's abrupt return to France in May 1871. But while these events exerted significant adverse influence on his family life and mental health, in England they were publicly fodder for the rumor mill, insufficient to prevent his receiving a commission for an oratorio for the prestigious Birmingham Festival (*La rédemption*, 1882).

The same cannot be said of their effects on his reputation in France. There, the Parisian tabloids plumbed the prurient details surrounding his breakup with Georgina Weldon and his marital and extramarital affairs generally, sometimes implying that these amorous indiscretions were part of a general lack of character that had led Gounod to flee his country in its hour of need in 1870. He continued to draw solace in his religious faith and compose deeply felt Catholic church music as well as opera, also taking new interest in the **pedal piano** and writing the *Petite symphonie* for winds (*see* NONET). In 1893, he composed *Les drames sacrés* (The Sacred Dramas), incidental music for a series of 12 **tableaux vivants** based on Renaissance painted depictions of scenes from the Bible. [JMC]

See also LA BONNE CHANSON, OP. 61; ROMANCE.

GRAF. Viennese firm of **piano** makers, among the most respected and valued instruments in the style of **Stein** and **Walter**. The firm was founded in 1804 by Conrad Graf (1782–1851) and flourished until it was sold to Johann Andreas Stein (grandson of the founder of the **Stein** firm) in 1840. Among the significant composers and performers who regularly used Graf instruments were **Ludwig van Beethoven** (who received an unusual quadruple-strung instrument from the maker as a gift in 1823), **Johannes Brahms, Ignaz Moscheles,** and **Robert** and **Clara Schumann**. Other composers, including **Fryderyk Chopin, Friedrich Kalkbrenner,** and **Franz Liszt,** performed on them publicly. Beethoven's instrument was severely damaged in 1824 but has since been fully restored, and the Graf piano that Robert Schumann gave to Clara as a wedding present, bequeathed to Brahms after Robert's death, likewise still exists (albeit with numerous "modernizations" that reflect later trends in piano manufacture). The Graf firm produced over 3,000 instruments and provided each with a unique opus number; of these, 61 have survived.

Like most Viennese pianos until the final decades of the 19th century, Graf's instruments were triple-strung in straight fashion (all strings parallel rather than crossing the bass strings over the treble, as in the modern **Steinway**), were made entirely of wood except for a metal gap spacers, and had a thin soundboard and light, leather-covered hammers. They featured a light touch, a quick decay, and a clear, delicate tone with considerable variance in timbre across the registers (in contrast to the comparatively monochromatic timbre of the modern piano). Graf's instruments typically had a span of six and a half octaves and between three and five pedals (*una corda*, bassoon, *piano*, *pianissimo*, and **janissary**). Their all-wood casing was heavier than most fortepiano casing of the day, employing five-ply laminated spruce or (more commonly) oak with exceptionally careful joinery. [JMC]

GRANADOS (Y CAMPIÑA), ENRIQUE [ENRÍC] (1867–1916). Catalan composer and pianist of the Modern Romantic Generation; one of the most important figures in Spanish musical **nationalism** of the early 20th century. He is best known today for his two piano **suites** based on paintings of Francisco Goya (1726–1848) and collectively titled *Goyescas, o Los majos enamorados* (Goyescas; or, The Gallants in Love, Bk. 1, 1909–1911, publ. 1912; Bk. 2, 1911–1912, publ. 1913) as well as the *12 danzas españolas* composed around 1888–1890 and posthumously published in 1966. He also composed two **operas**, one children's opera, two sets of **incidental music**, and several smaller staged musical dramas; three choral compositions; three **symphonic poems**, two piano **concertos**, and two orchestral suites; much instrumental and vocal **chamber music**; and a sizable body of music for **piano** solo. Although he was Catalan by birth and upbringing and considered himself a Catalan nationalist, he rejected the contemporary movement for Catalan independence. His music reflects a thorough grounding not only in the *tonadilla* and **zarzuela** traditions of his homeland but also in the traditions of French **salon** culture and **opéra comique**.

Granados was born and raised in Barcelona, studying composition with Felipe Pedrell (1841–1922) from 1883 to 1887 and with Charles de Bériot (1802–1870) in Paris from 1887 to 1889. He made his living as a pianist/composer in his native Barcelona, achieving his first major success with the three-act opera *María del Carmen* (Madrid, 1898). In 1900, he founded a concert society and in 1901 the Acadámia Granados, where he collaborated with notables including Pablo Casals, Ivan Manén, and **Camille Saint-Saëns** over the coming decade. He began work on the *Goyescas* in 1909, premiering Book I to great acclaim in Barcelona in 1911. The work's success prompted a friend from the United States, pianist Ernest Schelling (1876–1939), to propose adapting the concept into an opera. Granados undertook that project enthusiastically, producing a work whose concept (a staged narrative pieced together from scenes depicted in well-known paintings) fused the concept of the *tableau vivant* with the dramaturgy of *verismo* opera. Granados traveled to New York for the work's premiere at the Metropolitan Opera. Although the performance was underrehearsed and received mixed reviews, Granados met with U.S. President Woodrow Wilson while in the country. He drowned in the English Channel while trying to save his wife after the ship on which they were traveling back to Spain was hit by a German torpedo. [JMC]

GRAND OPERA. In common parlance, any **opera** in which not a single syllable is spoken (i.e., no dialogue); typically long and lavish, dealing with a serious or historical subject and placing great emphasis on effect. That general definition is abstracted from the basic criteria that rendered a work acceptable for performance at the Paris Opéra from the 1820s through the 1880s. Those criteria were in turn distillations of earlier, less formal practices that had emerged during the **First French Empire** in the works of, especially, **Luigi Cherubini** (*Ali-Baba, ou Les quarante voleurs* [Ali Baba; or, The 40 Thieves, 1833]), **Étienne-Nicolas Méhul** (*Adrien*, 1799), and **Gaspare Spontini** (*La vestale* [The Vestal Virgin, 1807] and *Fernand Cortez, ou La conquête du Mexique* [Fernando Cortez; or, The Conquest of Mexico, 1809–1824]). There were also other, more specific criteria: grand operas had to comprise four or (more commonly) five acts, actively involve the chorus and include a ballet (the latter typically in the second act), and typically deal with conflicts between private emotion and public or civic duty and responsibility.

Like other forms of opera, grand opera began with its **libretto**—a work typically crafted by a professional poet or *littérateur* to bring high literary standards to the musical stage, then sold either to the Opéra (or another house that performed this repertoire) or, less commonly, to a composer directly. The most important figure in developing the dramaturgy of grand opera—and one of its most prolific librettists—was **Eugène Scribe**, who worked with virtually every major composer who wrote for the French musical stage (both serious and comic) during the first half of the **long 19th century**. Scribe's principal successors as librettists for grand opera were Michel Carré (1822–1872) and Jules Barbier (1825–1901).

The works of the Romantic Generation that came to epitomize grand opera as a genre are **Daniel-François-Esprit Auber**'s *La muette de Portici* (The Mute Girl of Portici, S. 16, 1828); **Giacomo Meyerbeer**'s *Robert le diable* (Robert the Devil, 1831), *Les Huguenots* (The Huguenots, 1836), and *Le prophète* (The Prophet, 1849); and **Gioachino Rossini**'s *Guillaume Tell* (1829). Later grand operas include **Hector Berlioz**'s *Les troyens* (The Trojans, H. 133, 1858–1863); **Charles Gounod**'s *Sapho* (1851, rev. 1858, 1883, 1884), *Faust* (1859), and *Roméo et Juliette* (1867); **Félicien David**'s *Herculanum* (1859); **Jules Massenet**'s *Le roi de Lahore* (The King of Lahore, 1877), *Hérodiade* (1881), and *Le Cid* (1885); **Camille Saint-Saëns**'s *Ascanio* (1890); **Ambroise Thomas**'s *Hamlet* (1869) and *Françoise de Rimini* (1882); and **Giuseppe Verdi**'s *Les vêpres siciliennes* (1855).

The genre of grand opera (strictly construed) also accounts for the French versions—many of them considered revisions or reworkings of their original versions—of the operas of **Vincenzo Bellini, Gaetano Donizetti**, Rossini, and Verdi as well as the third version (1861) of **Richard Wagner**'s *Tannhäuser* (WWV 70, 1845–1867). Berlioz also reworked **Carl Maria von Weber**'s *Der Freischütz* (J. 277, 1821)—unacceptable in its original form partly because of its language and partly because it included spoken dialogue—for performance at the Opéra as *Le Freyschütz* (H. 89, 1841). Although **Georges Bizet**'s *Carmen* is sometimes given today as a grand opera with recitatives and an inserted ballet, Bizet composed it as an **opéra comique** and had nothing to do with the recitatives (which were composed by his friend **Ernest Guiraud**). [JMC]

GRANDFATHER DANCE. *See* KEHRAUS.

GRIEG, EDVARD (HAGERUP) (1843–1907). Norwegian composer, **conductor**, occasional critic, and pianist of the Late Romantic Generation; his generation's most important exponent of Norwegian **nationalism** in music and the **long 19th century**'s most influential advocate for improving musical life and musical standards in Norway. On **Ole Bull**'s recommendation, he went to Leipzig in 1858 to train at the **Conservatory** there, studying **piano** with Louis Plaidy (1810–1874) and **Ignaz Moscheles**, theory with Moritz Hauptmann (1792–1869), and composition with Ernst Friedrich Richter

(1808–1879) and **Carl Reinecke**. He returned to Norway after graduation in 1862 but in 1863 moved to Copenhagen, where he befriended and was influenced by the ardent young nationalist Rikard Nordraak (1842–1866, composer of the music of the de facto Norwegian national anthem), planning a tour of the German and Italian lands with him. After a sojourn in Rome late in 1865, he moved to Christiania (now Oslo) in 1866 and there became conductor of an amateur **orchestra**, also helping to found the Norwegian Academy of Music in 1867 and founding a Christiania Music Society for the promotion of orchestral music in 1871.

Meanwhile, in 1868, Grieg had won the admiration of **Franz Liszt** and an invitation to visit him in Weimar. Although Grieg was unable to make good on this invitation, he did visit the older master in Rome in the autumn of 1869. He attended the first complete production of **Richard Wagner**'s *The Ring of the Nibelung* in **Bayreuth** in 1876. He served as conductor of the Bergen Philharmonic Society from 1880 to 1882. In 1883, after traveling again to Bayreuth to hear *Parsifal*, he began a long concert tour that included Amsterdam, Arnhem, Breslau, Cologne, Dresden, Frankfurt am Main, The Hague, Karlsruhe, Leipzig, Meiningen, Rotterdam, and Weimar. He would retain this tradition, performing only his own music (with his wife performing his **songs**) in musical capitals including Paris, Prague, and Warsaw, until the last year of life despite increasing difficulties from a pulmonary disorder that had first emerged in 1860.

Grieg had established himself as a Scandinavian celebrity by the mid-1860s, and by the end of his career his renown was international. He is best known today for the concert **suites** (opp. 46 and 55) drawn from the 26 numbers in his **incidental music** to the play *Peer Gynt* (Op. 23, 1874–1875, publ. 1876, rev. 1885–1902) by Henrik Ibsen (1828–1906), whom he had met in 1865. He is also known for his Piano **Concerto** in A Minor (Op. 16, 1868, publ. 1872), the **song cycle** *Haugtussa* (The Mountain Maid, Op. 67, 1895, publ. 1898), the suite *Fra Holberg tid* (From Holberg's Time) for piano solo (Op. 40, 1884, publ. 1885; also orchestrated), and selected numbers from the 10 volumes of *Lyric Pieces* (*Småstykker*, literally "tiny fragments" or "miniatures") for piano solo published between 1867 and 1901. Throughout his life, he professed difficulty with "large forms," but he nevertheless completed a **Symphony** in C Minor (1863–1864; this he withheld), three impressive violin **sonatas** (opp. 8 [1865], 13 [1867, publ. 1871], and 45 [1886, publ. 1887]), a cello sonata (Op. 36, 1882–1883), and a **string quartet** (Op. 27, 1877–1878, publ. 1879). His nationalist output is vividly original, including the *Album for mandssang, fritt efter norske folkeviser* (Album of *Männerchöre*, Freely Arranged from Norwegian Folk Songs, Op. 30, 1877–1878), numerous **part-songs** published without opus number or posthumously, and a collection of *Slåtter* (Norwegian peasant dances, Op. 72, 1902–1903) composed after the model of the tunes performed by Knut Dale on the traditional Hardanger Fiddle. During his lifetime, he was well known for his 22 numbered *opera* of songs, although only the op. 67 song cycle and two songs (nos. 2 and 3) from the op. 33 set are widely performed today. He also composed sacred music and a handful of works for **piano duet** (both two pianos and one piano with two players). [JMC]

GROßE FUGE, OP. 133. (Ger., "grand fugue.") Fugal movement in B-flat major for **string quartet** by **Ludwig van Beethoven**. Beethoven composed the piece in 1825–1826 as a finale for his String Quartet, Op. 130. He later replaced it with another, shorter movement to end that quartet, publishing the *Große Fuge* in 1827 with **Artaria**, with a dedication to Archduke Rudolph.

In 1822, Beethoven received a commission for several string quartets from Prince Nikolay Golitsïn (Galitzin; 1794–1866) of St. Petersburg. Beethoven went to work on three quartets: No. 12 (Op. 127, in E minor), No. 15 (Op. 132, in A minor), and No. 13 (Op. 130, in B-flat major). Beethoven completed Opp. 127 and 132 in 1825, and both were premiered that year in that order. Beethoven began composing Op. 130 at least as early as July 1825, a few months after the therapeutic trip to Baden that he memorialized in the "Heiliger Dankgesang eines Genesenen an die Gottheit, in der lydischen Tonart" (A Convalenscent's Holy Song of Thanks to the Deity, in the Lydian Mode) of the Op. 132 quartet. When the Schuppanzigh Quartet premiered Op. 130 on 21 March 1826, its sixth and final movement was an expansive fugato fantasia lasting approximately 15 minutes. Beethoven had visited this concept in previous works, such as the **"Hammerklavier" Piano Sonata** (No. 29 in B-flat major, Op. 106) and the finale of his Ninth **("Choral") Symphony** in D minor (Op. 125). Following the premiere, Beethoven was asked by Maurice Schlesinger—who was to publish Op. 130—to replace the fugal finale with a new, less challenging one.

Much about this movement has challenged listeners since its genesis. The *Große Fuge*'s pungent dissonances tend to overwhelm descriptions, but additional difficulties dwell in its disorienting rhythmic displacements and sometimes indiscernible beat. The fugal subjects themselves, presented in the oddly named *Overtura* introduction (*see* OVERTURE), are harmonically ambiguous enough in isolation that Beethoven is able to apply them contrapuntally with considerable flexibility throughout the work. In the final section, the subjects fit surprisingly well into the comparatively conventional, harmonically closed coda. [RK]

GROßVATER-TANZ. *See* KEHRAUS.

GROVE, GEORGE (1820–1900). English musicologist, biblical scholar, and civil engineer of the Late Romantic Generation. He was born in London and originally achieved distinction as a civil engineer, erecting the first two cast-iron bridges in the West Indies during his time there and working as assistant to Edwin Clark in the construction of the Brittania Bridge across the Menai Strait in 1847–1848. As a biblical scholar, he made many contributions totaling nearly 1,000 pages to Sir William Smith's *Dictionary of the Bible* (3 vols., 1860–1863; many reprints, continuations, and subsequent editions). In this capacity, he also visited the Holy Land in 1858 and 1861, helping to found the Palestine Exploration Fund by 1865 and working tirelessly on its behalf thereafter, an important contribution to the disciplines of archaeology and geography.

Grove's early musical activities included serving as secretary to the recently formed Society of Arts (now the Royal Society of Arts) (1848–1852) and secretary and director of the Crystal Palace from 1852 to 1873. He served as editor of *Macmillan's Magazine* from 1868 to 1883. Together with **Arthur Sullivan**, he traveled to Vienna in 1867 to examine manuscripts of **Franz Schubert**, whose popularity was growing in the German lands but who remained little known in England. There they discovered the previously unknown music to Schubert's *Rosamunde* **incidental music** (D. 797, 1823).

Diligent exploration of primary sources ranging from letters to musical autographs became one of the signature aspects of Grove's scholarship. This he combined with his lucid, consistently jargon-free prose in many periodical contributions and letters to the editor as well as his monograph *Beethoven's Nine Symphonies* (first publ. 1884, rev. and expanded under the title *Beethoven and His Nine Symphonies* in 1896 and reprinted many times thereafter). He received an honorary doctor of civil law degree from the University of Durham in 1875 and was knighted in 1883, also becoming first director of London's second **conservatory** of music, the Royal College of Music, in that year and continuing in that capacity until his retirement in 1894. In addition to his lifelong advocacy of **Ludwig van Beethoven, Felix Mendelssohn Bartholdy**, and **Robert Schumann**, he was a longtime friend of **Hubert Parry, Clara Schumann**, and **Charles Villiers Stanford**. He also met and respected **Richard Wagner**, though he retained reservations about his music.

Grove's most important contribution to musical scholarship was his *Dictionary of Music and Musicians (A.D. 1450–1878)*. This dictionary began as an outgrowth of the many program notes he wrote while secretary of the regular orchestral concerts of the Crystal Palace Company. He began informing friends in 1873 that he had resigned from his long term in that position in order to begin the project. It was first published in four volumes containing 25 parts issued serially in 1878–1889. By 1980, the dictionary was in its sixth edition (ed. Stanley Sadie) in 20 volumes; these produced many offspring dictionaries (devoted to American music, jazz, and opera) and books. It entered its seventh edition with *Grove Music Online* (now part of *Oxford Music Online*) in 2000 and remains the most authoritative standard music reference resource in English. [JMC]

GRUNDTHEMA. *See* LEITMOTIV.

GUILLAUME TELL. (Engl., *William Tell*; Ger., *Wilhelm Tell*; It., *Guglielmo Tell*.) **Grand opera** (*opéra*) in four acts by **Gioachino Rossini** on a libretto by Étienne de Jouy (1764–1846), Hippolyte Bis (1789–1855), and Rossini himself, with input from others, after **Friedrich Schiller**'s *Wilhelm Tell* (1804). The work stems from a contract with the French government into which Rossini entered when he moved to Paris in 1824. The contract specified only that he write a new grand opera (subject unspecified). He considered two librettos by **Eugène Scribe** for the project but ultimately decided on Schiller's 1804 play. The new work was premiered at the Paris Opéra on 3 August 1829. Engraving of the French first edition had begun already before the premiere (with the result that the first edition lacks corrections and changes made during rehearsal and immediately after the performance, many of them significant; *see* COMPOSITIONAL PROCESS, CREATIVE PROCESS), and the opera was published in its entirety and in excerpts in piano/vocal score (with the overture arranged for **piano duet**) by Eugène Troupenas (Paris), **Schott** (Mainz), **Artaria** (Vienna), **Novello, Ewer, & Co.** (London), **Ricordi** (Milan), and others that same year. The full score was published already in 1830, an unusually quick venture for operas at that point in the **long 19th century** (*see* PRINTING AND PUBLISHING OF MUSIC).

Rossini's decision to set Schiller's play was shrewd in the context of French politics during the **Bourbon Restoration** as well as artistically fruitful. The play is based on the legend of the 14th-century Swiss national hero and was first translated into French in 1818 by the historian and statesman Amable Guillaume Prosper Brugière, baron of Barante (1782–1866). It deals principally with two themes: the revolt of the Swiss cantons against Austrian tyranny and the relationship between Tell and the villainous governor who oppressed the citizenry and had personally humiliated Tell by forcing him to shoot an arrow off his son's head. The first of these themes resonated with a French public whose growing discontent with the monarchy of the Bourbon monarch Charles X (installed at the **Congress of Vienna**) would erupt in the July Revolution less than a year after the opera's premiere. The second Restoration culture's general interest in the ethical and moral interstices of domestic/private life and public/civic responsibility. Rossini dealt with these themes and their ramifications with extraordinary subtlety and insight, creating a title protagonist who is capable of heroism when circumstances so dictate but who is an ordinary citizen with whom the middle-class public can identify rather than a hero in the usual sense.

Guillaume Tell is extraordinarily long (it is rarely performed uncut despite significant damage done to the plot by the usual alterations) and is also unusual for its **overture**. The latter is a specimen of **program music** that was celebrated (with reservations) by **Hector Berlioz**, among others, partly for its unusual form (four sharply contrasting sections, each anticipating an aspect of the drama and none recurring within the overture itself) and partly for the vividness of its programmatic effects. The third of these sections—a quotation in the English horn of the *ranz des vaches* ("process of cattle" in Swiss French) stereotypically played by cowherds as they drive their cattle to or from pasture—also recurs in various forms throughout the opera, thus functioning as a sort of reminiscence theme (*see* THEMATIC TRANSFORMATION, THEMATIC METAMORPHOSIS). Whether by coincidence or by design, *Guillaume Tell* was Rossini's final opera, just as *Wilhelm Tell* was Schiller's final play. [JMC]

GUIRAUD, ERNEST (1837–1892). French composer born in the United States; member of the Late Romantic Generation. He was born in New Orleans and received his early training there, moving to Paris and entering the **Conservatory** in 1849. He is best remembered today for having adapted **Georges Bizet**'s *Carmen* as a German-language **grand opera** for performance in Vienna (adding recitatives and reorchestrating part of *L'arlesienne* for insertion as a **ballet** in Act II). A close friend of Bizet, he also arranged both *Carmen* **suites** (1875), the second suite from *L'arlesienne* (1880), and four of **Camille Saint-Saëns**'s **symphonic poems**, including the *Danse macabre* (for two pianos, eight hands, 1883; *see* TOTENTANZ). He also orchestrated **Jacques Offenbach**'s *Les contes d'Hoffmann* (1881).

Guiraud was professor of harmony at the Paris Conservatory from 1876 and professor of composition there from 1880; **Claude Debussy** and **Paul Dukas** were among his pupils. His own original output includes one Italian **opera**, five French serious operas (the last of which was completed by Saint-Saëns), five **opéras comiques**, one **ballet**, one Mass setting, one **cantata**, two suites for orchestra, two **concert overtures** and one **symphonic poem**, an *Allegro de concert* for **piano** and **orchestra**, and a **Caprice** for violin and orchestra. His *Traité pratique d'instrumentation* (Practical Treatise on Instrumentation) was published in 1892 and went through several editions. [JMC]

GYPSY STYLE. *See* STYLE HONGROIS.

HABANERA. (Sp.; Fr., havanaise.) The name used outside Cuba for the Afro-Cuban *contradanza* (*see* CONTREDANSE, CONTRADANCE, CONTRA DANCE). It is duple meter and slow to moderate in tempo and was popular in Europe, the United States, and elsewhere in the Western Hemisphere in the late 19th and 20th centuries. Evolved from the French **contredanse**, which had arrived in Cuba via Haiti, it typically employs the rhythm shown in figure 3, itself evolved from the three-against-two vertical hemiola characteristic of much sub-Saharan African music and known in Spanish as *tresillo*. The habanera departed from the earlier forms of this contradanza in that it was typically sung as well as danced; it became immensely popular elsewhere in Latin America and was an important influence on the Mexican danza.

The first known notated example of the habanera was "San pascual bailón" (1803). The dance witnessed a surge in popularity in Europe in the 1850s and 1860s, as numerous Spanish composers began publishing their own works in the genre from Barcelona- and Madrid-based publishing houses. It is most popular today via the celebrated Habanera from Act I of **Georges Bizet**'s *Carmen* (1875), but countless other composers composed and published habaneras in the wake of Bizet's immensely popular contribution. Among these were Georges Bachmann (1848–1894; 1893), **Emmanuel Chabrier** (1886), Justin Clérice (1863–1908; 1888), Felix Dreyschock (1860–1906; 1885), Augusta Mary Anne Holmès (1847–1903; 1898), Ethelbert Nevin (1862–1901; 1893), Maurice Ravel (1909), **Camille Saint-Saëns** (1888), and Michael Watson (1840–1889; 1886). [JMC]

Figure 3.

HABENECK, FRANÇOISE-ANTOINE (1781–1849). French **conductor**, educator, violinist, and composer of the Early Romantic Generation, one of the most influential figures in French musical life during the first half of the 19th century. As a violinist, he trained in the studio of **Pierre Baillot** at the Paris **Conservatory**, where in 1804 he won the *premier prix* for violin. Between 1804 and 1821, he occupied a series of important posts as violinist, beginning at the Opéra-Comique and moving almost immediately to the more prestigious Opéra. He became director of the Opéra in 1821 and retained that position until 1846. In 1828, he founded the Orchestre de la Société des Concerts du Conservatoire, which he conducted through its 1848 season, a total of some 188 concerts; this ensemble later was conducted by important conductors such as Charles Münch and André Cluytens and remained in existence until 1967, when it was disbanded and succeeded by the Orchestre de Paris. He also taught violin at the Conservatory (1808–1816, 1825–1848) and authored a *Méthode théorique et pratique de violon* (Method for the Theory and Practice of the Violin, 1835) that, like most of the Conservatoire's instruction methods, remained influential into the 20th century.

As a conductor and music director, Habeneck was important for his advocacy of new, little-known, and controversial music. In addition to his work as one of France's most energetic promoters of the music of **Ludwig van Beethoven** (he conducted the French premieres of the First, Third, Fifth, and Ninth **Symphonies** along with numerous smaller works), he directed the premieres of **Hector Berlioz**'s *Episode in the Life of an Artist* (1830), **Requiem** (1837), and *Benvenuto Cellini* (H76A; 1838) as well as **Fromenthal Halévy**'s *La Juive* (1835), **Giacomo Meyerbeer**'s *Robert le diable* (1831) and *Les Huguenots* (1836), and **Gioachino Rossini**'s *Guillaume Tell* (1829). [JMC]

HALÉVY, (JACQUES FRANÇOIS) FROMENTAL (ELIE) (1799–1862). French composer, teacher, and writer on music, member of the Early Romantic Generation. He was of Jewish descent, son of a noted Hebraic scholar. In keeping with 19th-century proscriptions regarding Jews, the family changed its name from Levy to Halévy in 1807. Between 1819 and 1858, he completed some 38 serious and **comic operas**, winning the praise of composer/critics such as **Hector Berlioz** and **Richard Wagner**. He is best known today for these works.

Although Halévy's fame rests on his vocal music, those works are well known by name but have all but disappeared from the performed **canon**. His **orchestration** was also admired by contemporaries: he was among the first composers to exploit the possibilities of chromatic brass instruments, and his scoring for woodwinds is frequently imaginative. His most important serious opera was *La juive* (The Jewess, 1835), the second of many collaborations with **Eugène Scribe**, followed by *La reine de Chypre* (1841) and *Charles VI*

(1843). He also composed an Italian **opera**, *La tempesta* (The Tempest), at the invitation of Her Majesty's Theatre (London) in 1850, but the work's literary foundations—its text is Scribe's adaptation of Pietro Giannone's translation of **William Shakespeare**'s play—compromise its success. His most important comic operas are *L'éclair* (The Lightning Flash, 1835), *Le shérif* (The Sheriff, 1839), *Le guitarrero* (The Guitarist, 1841), *Les mousquetaires de la reine* (The Queen's Musketeers, 1846), *Le val d'Andorre* (The Valley of Andorra, 1848), and *Jaguarita l'Indienne* (Jaguarita the Indian [set in Dutch Guyana], 1855). He also penned a sizable quantity of music for chorus with and without **orchestra** or **piano** and vocal **chamber music**, to which may be added one **concert overture** (1822), a few smaller instrumental works, and one opera left incomplete at his death. The three-act *Noé* (Noah) was completed by **Georges Bizet** and given the new title of *Le déluge* (The Flood, 1868–1869); it remained unperformed until 1885 and was published under its original title in 1886.

Halévy was chief vocal coach at the Théatre-Italien from 1826 to 1829 and at the Opéra from 1829 to 1845. He joined the faculty of the Paris **Conservatory** in 1827, beginning as professor of harmony and accompaniment and advancing to professor of counterpoint and fugue in 1833 and then to composition in 1840. He was also an accomplished and insightful prose stylist, drafting an unfinished biography of **Luigi Cherubini** (1845) and publishing critical and historical writings from 1844 on. Some of these writings were collected in his *Souvenirs et portraits: Études sur les beaux-arts* (Recollections and Portraits: Studies in the Fine Arts, 1861), and more appeared in the posthumously published *Derniers souvenirs et portraits* (Last Recollections and Portraits, 1863). He also published a primer on reading music for use in the Paris city schools (*Leçons de lecture musicale . . . pour les écoles de la ville de Paris* [Lessons for Reading Music . . . for the Schools of the City of Paris, 1857]). Although he acquired a reputation as a lax and inattentive teacher, the list of his pupils includes some of the leading names of the Romantic Generation (e.g., Bizet, **Charles Gounod**, and **Camille Saint-Saëns**). [JMC]

HALLÉ, CHARLES [HALLE, CARL] (1819–1895). English composer, **conductor**, pianist, and educator of the Late Romantic Generation, of German birth; an early and influential advocate of **Ludwig van Beethoven**'s **piano sonatas** in performance in Paris and England. The son of a musician, he exhibited musical talent early on; by age 11, he was able to take over the direction of **Carl Maria von Weber**'s *Der Freischütz* and *Preziosa* and **Wolfgang Amadeus Mozart**'s *Die Zauberflöte* when his father fell ill. He was an outstanding pianist and was proficient on the organ and violin. In his youth, he was mentored by **Louis Spohr** and gave his first piano recital at age nine. He moved to Darmstadt in 1835 to study with Johann Rink and

Gottfried Weber and then to Paris in 1836, there befriending **Hector Berlioz**, **Fryderyk Chopin**, **Stephen Heller**, **Franz Liszt**, **Ignaz Moscheles**, and **Richard Wagner**, performing Beethoven's sonatas in the city's flourishing **salons** and becoming the first pianist to offer Beethoven's complete piano sonatas in a series.

Civic disturbances and a decline in attendance at public concerts during the **Revolutions of 1848** prompted Hallé to flee to London, where he quickly rose to prominence as the first pianist to perform any of Beethoven's piano sonatas on a public program (at his first performance at the flourishing Musical Union). He accepted an invitation from Manchester to resettle there and revive the city's "dormant" (his own term) musical life. There, he had a large studio of aspiring students at the outset and launched a series of **chamber** concerts in 1849 as well as a series of private performances in his own home in 1850; he also maintained a residence in London during the summer months and performed there regularly. In 1849, he was also entrusted with the directorship and conducting of the well-established Gentlemen's Concerts.

Such was Hallé's progress in developing Manchester's orchestral culture that in 1857–1858 he founded a new orchestra whose playing was considered among the finest in England. He conducted this ensemble—today the Hallé Orchestra—in almost every one of its concerts offered over the next 30 years, including performances in Bradford, Edinburgh, Liverpool, and London. Its programming was innovative and up to date: under his direction, the orchestra offered the first British performances of Berlioz's *Episode in the Life of an Artist* (January 1879) and **Pyotor Il'yich Tchaikovsky**'s Fifth **Symphony** as well as performances of Berlioz's *La damnation de Faust* and *L'enfance de Christ*, **Johannes Brahms**'s Second Piano **Concerto**, and **Grieg**'s Piano Concerto (the latter two with Hallé as soloist); new works by **Antonín Dvořák** were also quickly incorporated into its repertoire. Hallé also accompanied his second wife on chamber-recital tours to Australia and South Africa in 1888.

Hallé was also active as a piano pedagogue, composer, and editor of music. His *Practical Pianoforte School*, first published in 1873, was issued in a new and enlarged edition in 1884. He prepared significant English editions of collections of music by **Johann Sebastian Bach** (both volumes of *The Well-Tempered Clavier*), Beethoven (the complete piano sonatas), and **Felix Mendelssohn Bartholdy** (all the *Lieder ohne Worte* known at the time) as well as editions of individual works by Berlioz, Chopin, **John Field**, **Niels W. Gade**, Christoph Willibald Ritter von Gluck (1714–1787), **Stephen Heller**, **Adolf von Henselt**, **Johann Nepomuk Hummel**, **Franz Liszt**, **Wolfgang Amadeus Mozart**, Jean-Philippe Rameau (1683–1764), **Carl Reinecke**, Domenico Scarlatti (1685–1757), **Franz Schubert**, **Robert Schumann**, and Weber.

Hallé's name was originally Carl Halle, but he later added the acute accent and changed his first name to ensure correct pronunciation in France and Great Britain. He was knighted in 1888. [JMC]

"HAMMERKLAVIER". (Ger., "Hammer Keyboard.") Title (authentic) of the Piano **Sonata** No. 29 in B-flat Major (Op. 106) by **Ludwig van Beethoven**, composed in 1818 and dedicated to Archduke Rudolf of Austria. The term "Hammerklavier" appears on the title pages of the Opp. 101 and 109 piano sonatas as well, but over the years it has come to identify Op. 106 specifically.

The genesis of the "Hammerklavier" Sonata followed a period marked by professional success and personal sorrows. On the one hand, Beethoven received a great deal of attention for his *Wellington's Victory* and works related to the **Congress of Vienna**; the Kärntnertor Theater invited him to stage *Fidelio* there in what would be its final version. On the other, Beethoven's hearing loss reached a point in 1818 where conversation books became necessary. He also suffered considerable grief over his brother Carl Caspar's death and the subsequent battle with his sister-in-law Johanna over his nephew Karl. This struggle, not settled until 1820, was particularly bitter while Beethoven was composing Op. 106. The years before "Hammerklavier" were relatively fallow; notable works from that time amount mainly to the two Cello Sonatas op. 102 (1815), the **song cycle** *An die ferne Geliebte* (To the Distant Beloved, Op. 98, 1816), and the Piano Sonata No. 28 in A major (Op. 101, 1816).

Perhaps spurred on by the London Philharmonic Society's commission of two **symphonies** (which he accepted and then retracted), Beethoven began composing the "Hammerklavier" Sonata in 1817 "in difficult circumstances," as he wrote two years later. When he completed it in the fall of 1818, it had grown into an enormous and technically challenging sonata in four movements. Typically Beethovenian by this point was the recurring structural significance of the submediant and the descending third. The lengthy fugato last movement, on the other hand, was far more in the spirit of later compositions, such as the famous finale of the Ninth (**"Choral"**) **Symphony** and the *Große Fuge* intended originally to conclude the **String Quartet** Op. 130. The "Hammerklavier" Sonata was published in 1819 in Vienna (**Artaria**) and London (Regent's Harmonic Institution). [RK]

HANDEL [HÄNDEL, HENDEL], GEORGE FRIDERIC [GEORG FRIEDERICH] (1685–1759). English Baroque composer and organist of German birth; important figure in **historicism** and **nationalism** in the **long 19th century**. With Jean-Philippe Rameau, Georg Philipp Telemann, and Antonio Vivaldi, he was arguably the most celebrated composer of his generation.

Unlike **Johann Sebastian Bach**, with whom he is frequently paired and compared in modern performances and writings about music, Handel did not lapse into near oblivion in the decades after his death. Rather, his **oratorios** and other choral works were heard regularly in Great Britain and occasionally in France, the German lands (especially in the Berlin Singakademie under the direction of C. F. C. Fasch [1736–1800] and Carl Friedrich Zelter [1758–1832]), Vienna (through the mediation of Baron Gottfried van Swieten [1733–1803]), and the Italian lands (notably Florence). This enduring popularity despite the significant changes in musical style, the institutions of music, and society generally that occurred during the late 18th century earned Handel a reputation as a composer whose genius was historically and socially transcendent, a quality that appealed to the universalizing, idealist aspirations of the Early Romantic Generation and Romantic Generation. (**Ludwig van Beethoven**, for example, called Handel "the greatest composer who ever lived," and **Fryderyk Chopin** remarked, after hearing a performance of Handel's *Ode for St. Cecilia's Day* [HWV 76, 1739] at the Berlin *Singakademie* in 1828, that his music "came nearest to the ideal which I had formed of great music.")

These ambitions of grandeur are most readily evident in the long 19th century's massive performances of Handel's oratorios at music festivals and choral festivals. The most famous such instance was the centennial celebration of Handel's death with 2,765 singers and 460 instrumentalists under the direction of Michael Costa (1808–1884) at the rebuilt Crystal Palace at Sydenham in 1859, but there were a great many others: the Westminster Abbey celebration of his (supposed) birth in 1784, with 525 performers. Comparably sized performances were given under the direction of **Franz Liszt, Ferdinand Hiller**, and **Felix Mendelssohn Bartholdy** at the Lower Rhine Music Festival in the 1830s, 1840s, and 1850s (Liszt conducted an ensemble of 417 singers and an orchestra of 137 in the festival held at Aachen in 1857). In general cultural terms, these performances are significant because they almost always presented oratorios—that is, works on sacred subjects in Handel's case—in public venues that included upper as well as middle and lower socioeconomic classes, thus integrating religion into a seemingly classless public life independently of ecclesiastical authority.

In France, too, massive performances of Handel's music were accompanied by writings in the popular press celebrating him as a "popular" composer who, because of his understanding of the musical public, was not only

Republican but also (paradoxically) non-Christian (i.e., free of unseemly indebtedness to the Roman Catholic Church). This late 19th-century French construction of Handel became especially popular in the three years after the **Franco-Prussian War**, providing inspiration for a number of conspicuously Handelian new compositions by **Théodore Dubois, César Franck, Charles Gounod, Jules Massenet**, and **Camille Saint-Saëns**. In particular, it found in Handel's music a consummately "masculine" style free of the weakening influences of excessive chromaticism, a voice that was "virile and national" and that mirrored the character of the "valiant, austere, and liberal [English] nation" (in the words of his French biographer, the great abolitionist Victor Schoelcher [1804–1893], whose biography of the composer was first published in 1857).

The established cult of Handel also offered fertile soil for Germans who sought to reclaim their celebrated native son/émigré and for German musicologists as well as the German lands' burgeoning industry of music publishers: he maintained a solid presence in German concert life already in the early decades of the 19th century, and this foothold grew even firmer as knowledge of his music and the century's interest in rediscovering the musical past increased. A collected edition of Handel's works had been attempted by the London-based publisher Samuel Arnold beginning in 1787, but these editions were corrupt even by the lax philological standards of the time. This situation provided occasion for "rediscoveries" of Handel's original editions in the 1830s and 1840s: in 1833, Mendelssohn conducted a restored version of *Israel in Egypt* (translated into German and lacking trombones since these parts had become separated from the rest of the score in the late 18th century) at the Lower Rhine Music Festival. In light of this contribution, Mendelssohn was also prevailed upon to edit *Israel in Egypt* for a new complete edition of the Baroque composer's works published by the English Handel Society, in so doing producing one of the 19th century's first credible attempts at an **Urtext** edition that distinguished systematically between authorial and editorial information.

Finally, in 1856, German musicologist **Friedrich Chrysander** organized the founding of a German *Händel-Gesellschaft* (Handel Society) whose goals included the production of source-critical editions of Handel's complete works. These editions have now been superseded by those of the Hallische Händel-Ausgabe (Halle Handel Edition), but they remained standard well into the 20th century. [JMC]

See also EDITING AND EDITIONS; PRINTING AND PUBLISHING OF MUSIC.

HANSLICK, EDUARD (1825–1904). Austrian music critic of the Late Romantic Generation; one of the most influential figures in advancing the notion of musical communication as a phenomenon that legitimately embraced inherently musical expression as well as the expression of emotion or extra-musical content. He was also crucially important in advancing the concept of an **absolute music** during the ascendance of an aesthetics of music that correlated musical value and music-historical progress with "poetic" content. Perhaps more importantly, he was the first to distinguish between music's inherent properties and performers' or listeners' subjective responses to them.

Son of a music bibliographer, Hanslick trained as a pianist, studying music with **Václav Tomášek** in Prague and then successfully pursuing a degree in law at the University of Vienna. Meanwhile, he also composed a small body of music and wrote music reviews for papers including Prague's *Ost und West* and then the *Wiener Allgemeine Musik-Zeitung* (1846–1848), the *Wiener Zeitung* (1849–1855), *Die Presse* (1855–1864), and the *Neue Freie Presse* (1864–1895). He retired from regular work as a critic in 1895 but continued to write occasional pieces, covering important premieres such as **Gustav Mahler**'s *Lieder eines fahrenden Gesellen* (Songs of a Wayfarer, 1897) and *Des Knaben Wunderhorn*, **Richard Strauss**'s first two **cycles of tone poems**, and **Giuseppe Verdi**'s *Falstaff*.

Hanslick's widely reprinted and translated early treatise *Vom Musikalisch-Schönen* (On the Musically Beautiful, 1854) stands as a milestone in musical aesthetics, and his two-volume autobiography is an important document of musical life and musical polemics during the second half of the 19th century. His 1875 book *Die moderne Oper: Kritiken und Studien* (Modern Opera: Criticisms and Studies) became a series of widely read, translated, and re-printed books containing critical and historical writings about music and musicians (many of them revisions of articles published previously in the press): volume 2 (1880), *Musikalische Stationen* (Musical Waystations); volume 3 (1884), *Aus dem Opernleben der Gegenwart* (From Today's Opera World); volume 4 (1888), *Musikalisches Skizzenbuch* (Musical Sketchbook); volume 5 (1889), *Musikalisches und litterarisches: Kritiken und Schilderungen* (Musical and Literary Matters: Criticisms and Accounts); volume 6 (1892), *Aus dem Tagebuche eines Musikers* (From a Musician's Diary); volume 7 (1895), *Fünf Jahre Musik, 1891–1895* (Five Years of Music, 1891–1895); volume 8 (1899), *Am Ende des Jahrhunderts* (At Century's End); and volume 9 (1900), *Aus neuer und neuester Zeit* (From Recent and Most Recent Times). Other notable writings include "Richard Wagners 'Judenthum in der Musik'" (**Richard Wagner**'s "On Jewry in Musik," first published in the Vienna *Neue Freie Presse* on 9 March 1869 in response to Wagner's recent release under his own name of an expanded version of the 1850 polemic, re-released together with an article by Wilhelm Lübke on Wagner's *Die Meistersinger von Nürnberg*, which viciously caricatured Hanslick); a memoir of the Paris World Exhibition of 1878 (*Musik und Musiker in Paris. [Erinnerungen aus dem Weltausstellungs-Sommer 1878]*);

an article on **Ludwig van Beethoven** in Vienna, published as part of a commemorative book on the unveiling of Vienna's Beethoven Monument in 1880; *Suite: Aufsätze über Musik und Musiker* (Suite: Articles on Music and Musicians, 1884); and the two-volume *Geschichte des Konzertwesens in Wien* (History of Concert Life in Vienna, vol. 1, 1864, vol. 2, 1870).

Hanslick is frequently portrayed as a single-minded champion of **Johannes Brahms** and **absolute music** and an opponent of both **program music** and the musicodramatic agenda of **Franz Liszt**, Wagner, and the **New German School**. The truth is more nuanced—for while he did defend the music of Brahms, **Felix Mendelssohn Bartholdy**, and **Robert Schumann** against the polemics of the New German School and sharply criticize the music promoted by the **Allgemeiner Deutscher Musikverein**, what he rejected about that party's agenda was neither the notion of program music per se nor the idea of a greater integration of drama into staged music. Rather, he rejected the assertion that extramusical or poetic content and the Wagnerian aesthetic of the **Gesamtkunstwerk** were *essential* or *imperative* to musical value and music-historical significance. His other writings on other composers' attempts to imbue music with the aesthetic essence of literature reveal him to be a significantly more thoughtful, broad based, and less biased skeptic of the New German School's agenda than commonly held viewpoints allow. His writings on Wagner, for example, are both more informed and more favorable than is often suggested. More generally, his writings collectively represent an important station in the advent of modern music criticism and crucial documentations of fin-de-siècle Viennese liberalism's project of civic integration of society's various conflicting economic and ethnic groups into a pro-German intellectual whole dominated neither by the Catholic church nor by the fragmenting, anti-intellectual factions that, from around 1880 on, increasingly claimed predominance in Austria and elsewhere in Germany. [JMC]

HARTMANN, JOHAN PETER EMILIUS (1805–1900). Danish composer of the Romantic Generation. For textual and topical sources, Hartmann often looked to Danish and Scandinavian literature and mythology, especially those of Danish poet/playwright Adam Oehlenschläger (1779–1850) and Danish author Hans Christian Andersen (1805–1875). To later generations of Romanticism, much of Hartmann's oeuvre—particularly his **concert overtures, cantatas,** and **operas**—suited **nationalist** projects as effectively as those of many composers of the **long 19th century,** such as later Danish composer **Carl Nielsen.**

Because Hartmann's parents were both Danish court employees, Hartmann's Copenhagen childhood was graced with many privileges of the aristocracy, including wanting for nothing, education, and connections to people in high places, including childhood friend Prince Christian VIII. Much of his early musical training came from his father, August Wilhelm Hartmann, court violinist and Garnisonskirke organist and choirmaster. Young Hartmann took his father's organ post in 1824. After studying law at the University of Copenhagen, Hartmann worked from 1828 to 1870 as a civil servant. During these years, Hartmann became increasingly prominent as composer and teacher. Hartmann helped found and lead the Copenhagen Musikforening, which from 1836 on was a fundamental element in the city's concert life. In 1867, when son-in-law **Niels W. Gade** founded the Copenhagen **Conservatory** (today the Royal Danish Academy of Music), Hartmann signed on as a codirector.

Hartmann began touring Europe in the late 1830s, bringing greater international attention to his work. After his first trip in 1836, accompanied by **Heinrich Marschner**, he met Kassel court chapel master **Louis Spohr**, who then premiered Hartmann's **Symphony** No. 1 in G minor, Op. 17, in 1837. Other new allies from this period include **Robert Schumann**, who wrote favorably and regularly about the composer, and **Franz Liszt**, who gave the Weimar premiere of Hartmann's one-act **opera** *Lidon Kirsten* (Little Christine, 1844, on a text by Hans Christian Anderson) in 1856. [RK]

HAUSMUSIK. (Ger., "home music.") Vocal or instrumental **chamber music** intended for informal use in domestic settings. *Hausmusik* is similar to other varieties of parlor music (such as **salon** music) except that it connotes music that not only aspires to be of a high quality but also is intended to be accessible to musically informed amateurs and used by them. Also unlike salon music, *Hausmusik* does not assume the presence of an audience. It is written for its performers, with the hopes of providing intimate and salutary, sometimes didactic, musical communication among them rather than between them and an audience.

The term *Hausmusik* apparently came into use in the 17th century in connection with the proliferation of published collections of sacred **songs** in households in the Protestant German lands, but it became more common and assumed a new sociological significance with the heightened domesticity of musical culture during the **Restoration**. It was regarded as a means of making cultivated music accessible to musical amateurs young and old, of educating youth in the values of the day, and sometimes (but not always) as an expression of the "German spirit"—always primarily by means of active music making (*Musizieren*) rather than passive consumption. Accordingly, *Hausmusik* does not abstain from the inclusion of passages that are showy if not actually difficult or free of all technical challenges, but it deliberately eschews virtuosity of the sort associated with **Franz Liszt** or **Sigismond Thalberg** and even the more intimate variety associated with **Fryderyk Chopin**. Also in keeping with the aims of facilitating music making in domestic contexts, ensemble *Hausmusik* often provides for flexible or alternate scorings. The **piano** is central to most (although the proliferation of a cappella **part-songs** in the mid- and late 19th century may be regarded as an outdoor species of *Hausmusik*), but works such as **Robert Schumann**'s *Drei Romanzen*, Op. 94 (1849–1851; scored for piano with either oboe, violin, or clarinet) or **Johannes Brahms**'s **Trio**, Op. 40 (1865–1866; scored for piano with violin and either natural horn or cello) are typical.

Among the most important and influential varieties of *Hausmusik* during the **long 19th century** were the many compositions written or arranged for **piano duet** (two pianists, one keyboard). Original compositions for this medium such as **Franz Schubert**'s **Fantasy** in F Minor (D. 940, 1828); Robert Schumann's *Bilder aus Osten* (Op. 66, 1848–1849); **Antonín Dvořák**'s *Legends* (Op. 59) and two volumes of *Slavonic Dances* (B. 78/Op. 46 and B. 145/Op. 72, 1879 and 1886); or Brahms's *Variations on a Theme of Robert Schumann* (Op. 23, 1861–1863) offered musically educated but nonexpert amateurs a chance to explore the musical and timbral possibilities of the piano in close company and are the qualitative compeers of their composers' compositions composed for large ensembles and performance in pubic venues.

Equally important—and even more overshadowed in today's world driven largely by passive and essentially public consumption of music—are the many arrangements for **piano duet** of larger public works, such as **concertos, symphonies, string quartets** and **quintets, oratorios**, and (less frequently) **operas**. Normally, large-ensemble works were published first in arrangements for piano duet (sometimes with ad libitum obbligato instruments; *see* PRINTING AND PUBLISHING OF MUSIC) simultaneously with **orchestral** and/or vocal parts. Only after the arrangements and performance materials had established that the work could reasonably be expected to turn a profit did publishers normally undertake the complicated and expensive process of engraving and publishing the works in full score. For this reason, composers as well as the musical public typically did not regard piano-duet and other arrangements as inferior by-products, as is often the case today; rather, they had every reason to view them as influential primary tools for either making or breaking the reputation of large compositions before they were performed publicly. [JMC]

HAYDN, (FRANZ) JOSEPH (1732–1809). Austrian composer, icon of Classicism and viewed by the Romantics as the "father of the **symphony**." His compositional output is immense and varied. The works best known in the 19th century include the late **oratorios** *The Creation* (*Die Schöpfung*, Hob. XXI: 2, 1798) and *Die Jahreszeiten* (The Seasons, Hob. XXI: 3, 1801), **symphonies** (a total of 108, about a dozen of which were regularly performed during the 19th century), **string quartets** (a total of 70, 10 of them well known during the 19th century), and 47 keyboard **sonatas** (six of which were familiar to the Romantics). In these works, Haydn employed numerous stylistic features that would become central features of Romantic musical language via their absorption into the idioms of **Wolfgang Amadeus Mozart** and **Ludwig van Beethoven** and later composers' emulations of those idioms. In particular, the styles of the *Sturm und Drang* elements of the works from around 1765–1772 were thoroughly absorbed as topics in Haydn's own later works, emulated in the more turbulent and tempestuous works of Mozart and Beethoven in the late 1780s and 1790s and, via other composers' absorption and emulation of those works, subsumed into the mainstream of musical Romanticism as represented especially in the works of German/Austrian composers such as Beethoven, **Johannes Brahms, Fanny Hensel, Johann Nepomuk Hummel, Felix Mendelssohn Bartholdy, Franz Schubert, Clara** and **Robert Schuman, Louis Spohr,** and **Carl Maria von Weber**, among others. Schubert, Mendelssohn, and the Schumanns absorbed Haydn's flair for achieving dramatic orchestral effects with conventional means, and Mendelssohn and Brahms in particular appropriated his assimilation of intricate counterpoint into functional tonal structures.

Haydn's **reception** in the 19th century is complicated. On the one hand, in performance his music retained a strong presence in England, essentially his adopted musical home of the 1790s, for most of the century. In France, he was a peripheral figure in public concerts, but the string quartets and oratorios were performed in excerpts in private venues, such as **salons**, especially during the early and middle parts of the century. And in the German lands, he was known primarily for the late symphonies and oratorios (the latter figuring prominently in music festivals for much of the century). On the other hand, this reasonably steady position in the performance **canon** was accompanied by a critical and historiographic shift that increasingly favored the image of "Papa Haydn" as the genial and good-natured antecedent of Mozart and Beethoven, overlooking the technical and emotional "depth" of his music and creating an increasingly one-dimensional view of his development as a composer and his compositional personality as a whole. The Romantics' Haydn as he was known around 1860 bore little resemblance to the Haydn who so strongly influenced the Early Romantic Generation and Romantic Generation. [JMC]

HEGEL, GEORG WILHELM FRIEDRICH (1770–1831). German philosopher of the Early Romantic Generation. Along with fellow philosopher Friedrich Schelling (1775–1854) and (to a lesser extent) epic poet Friedrich Hölderlin (1770–1843), Hegel submitted the 19th century's most influential critique of the idealist philosophies of Immanuel Kant (1724–1804) and his follower Johann Gottlieb Fichte (1762–1814). He became a professor at the University of Jena in 1805 but during the Napoleonic occupation (1807–1808) fled to Bamberg, where he edited a local newspaper. He left this position in 1808 to become rector of a *Gymnasium* (secondary school) in Nuremberg, subsequently returning to a professorship at Heidelberg (1816–1818). From 1818 until his death, he was professor at the University of Berlin (now the Humboldt-Universität, Berlin).

Hegel's most important publications include *Phänomenologie des Geistes* (Phenomenology of the Spirit, 1807), *Wissenschaft der Logik* (Science of Logic, 1812–1816), *Encyklopädie der philosophischen Wissenschaften im Grundrisse* (Encyclopedia of the Basics of the Philosophical Sciences, 1817), *Grundlinien der Philosophie des Rechts* (Basics of the Philosophy of Right, 1821), and the posthumously published *Vorlesungen über die Aesthetik* (Lectures on Aesthetics, 1835). The last of these presumably documents Hegel's aesthetic and philosophical thought as it was encountered by **Adolf Bernhard Marx, Felix Mendelssohn Bartholdy**, and other Prussian artists and intellectuals during the 1820s and early 1830s. Other Romantic musicians who were strongly influenced by Hegel's thought include the composers **Franz Liszt, Giacomo Meyerbeer**, and **Richard Wagner** as well as the scientist, playwright, and poet **Johann Wolfgang von Goethe**, the critic and historian **Franz Brendel**, the critic and aesthetician **Eduard Hanslick**, and the philosopher Arthur Schopenhauer (1788–1860).

Hegel's philosophy aspired to be comprehensive and universal, embracing the disciplines of aesthetics, history, law, psychology, science, and theology within a philosophical system that privileged logic over feeling. In particular, he strove to update Kant's transcendental idealism, which argued that reality is an individually constructed and therefore infinitely subjective phenomenon, by infusing it with more rigorous logic, arguing that there is in fact an objective reality—a *Weltgeist* (world-spirit)—whose nature and movements can be discerned as truth and understood when subjected to logical examination. His principal mechanism for identifying this reality was to subject it to principles derived from Aristotelian philosophy—most importantly, the notion that the real or phenomenal world is a concrete manifestation of an abstract ideal or nuomenal universe, and the notion that all reality is part and product of an eternal dialectical process: for any given phenomenon ("thesis"), there is also a negation ("antithesis"), and for any given thesis–antithesis pair, there is also a "synthesis" that possesses attributes of both the phenomenon and its negation. While this essential dialectic was found already in the writings of Aristotle and other philosophers of Classical Antiquity, Hegel lent it new power and appeal by applying it not only to nature and art but also to history and to the passage of time within the experience of individual phenomena. That application offered an elegant philosophical explanation for rhetorical and theoretical practices such as **sonata form**, a system for developing ideas on the sociology of music, and a philosophical foundation for the processes of the emergent **canon** as well as the historiography of Romantic music. [JMC]

HEILIGENSTADT TESTAMENT. Popular name for a letter drafted by **Ludwig van Beethoven** to his brothers Carl and Johann. It was written in Heiligenstadt, a suburb of Vienna. The main body of the unsent letter spans three pages and was concluded on 6 October 1802; perhaps on this date Beethoven addressed the letter (leaving an empty space where Johann's name should be). On 10 October, he appended a note to the intended recipients beginning "So nehme ich den Abschied von dir" (Thus I bid you farewell). The document as a whole details Beethoven's anguish at the knowledge that his rapidly advancing deafness will be incurable and at the virtually complete retreat from society that the malady had forced upon him; it reads as a suicide note. Although Beethoven decided not to take his life and never sent the letter, it serves as a valuable source of information concerning his values and state of mind in the early 19th century and the thinking that led to the "new way" reflected in the works of his Middle Vienna Period. The document was recovered by Anton Schindler (1795–1864) and Stephan von Breuning (1774–1827) as part of Beethoven's estate after his death and published by Schindler in October 1827. [JMC]

HEINE, HEINRICH (1797–1856). German-Jewish poet, journalist, travel diarist, and memoirist; generally regarded as the master of Romantic irony. He was one of the **long 19th century**'s most perceptive and influential cultural and social critics and, with **Johann Wolfgang von Goethe**, one of the Western world's most important composers of texts to be set to music. (At present, at least 8,000 settings of his words are known.)

Composers of Heine's own generation who set his texts or translations thereof or based their works on his texts include Moritz Hauptmann (1792–1868), **Carl Loewe, Heinrich Marschner, Giacomo Meyerbeer,** and **Franz Schubert.** In the Romantic Generation, his works found even more fertile soil, inspiring music by **William Sterndale Bennett, Robert Franz, Niels W. Gade, Fanny Hensel, Adolf von Henselt, Ferdinand Hiller, Franz Lachner, Franz Liszt, Felix Mendelssohn Bartholdy, Otto Nicolai, Jacques Offenbach, Clara Schumann, Robert Schumann, Sigismond Thalberg,** and **Richard Wagner,** and his influence increased further in the Late Romantic Generation through settings by composers such as **Aleksandr Borodin, Johannes Brahms, Peter Cornelius, César Cui, Felix Draeseke, Edvard Grieg, Engelbert Humperdinck, Joachim Raff, Carl Reinecke, Nikolay Rimsky-Korsakov, Anton Rubinstein, Camille Saint-Saëns, Franz von Suppé,** and **Pyotor Il'yich Tchaikovsky.** Composers of the Modern Romantic Generation who based works on his texts include **Alexander Glazunov, Anatoly Lyadov, Edward MacDowell, Gustav Mahler, Pietro Mascagni, Horatio Parker, Richard Strauss,** and **Hugo Wolf.**

From within this impressive roster, several works merit special mention: the six settings published posthumously in Schubert's *Schwanengesang* (D. 957, comp. 1828, publ. 1829), Hensel's *Schwanenlied* (Op. 1, no. 1, comp. 1831, publ. 1846), Mendelssohn's *Auf Flügeln des Gesanges* (MWV K86/ Op. 34, no. 2, comp. 1834 or 1835, publ. 1837), and especially Robert Schumann's **song cycles** *Liederkreis* (Op. 24, 1840) and *Dichterliebe*, Op. 48 (comp. 1840, publ. 1843/1844). The text of Wagner's early **opera** *Der fliegende Holländer* (The Flying Dutchman, WWV 63, comp. 1840–1841, publ. 1844) was based in part on Heine's *Aus den Memoiren des Herrn Schnabelewopski* (From the Memoirs of Herr Schnabelewopski, 1833). Heine's *William Ratcliffe* (1822, publ. 1823) provided the source material for **librettos** set by Cui and Mascagni, among others.

Most of these composers and their contemporaries knew Heine not only as a master of irony and lyric poetry but also as a critic and commentator whose incisive and occasionally vicious satires of society and its mores had resulted in an 1835 ban on publications of his works in the German lands. Having relocated to Paris in 1831, he served as French correspondent for the Augsburg *Allgemeine Zeitung* and various other papers. His Parisian writings (most notably *Zur Geschichte der neueren schönen Literatur in Deutschland* [On Recent Developments in German Literature, 1833] and *Die romantische Schule* [The Romantic School, 1835]) included searing critiques of the mystical and essentially traditionalist tendencies he discerned in German literature, observations he applied brilliantly in lampooning German **nationalist** myth and self-satisfied bluster in *Deutschland: Ein Wintermärchen* (Germany: A Winter's Tale, 1844) and *Atta Troll: Ein Sommernachtstraum* (Atta Troll: A Midsummer Night's Dream, 1841–1843, rev. 1847). These works, together with his earlier collections *Die Harzreise* (The Harz Journey, 1826) and *Buch der Lieder* (Book of Songs, 1827), made the exiled Heine one of **Restoration** and post-Revolutionary culture's leading poetic voices—one whose appeal to musicians was further enhanced by the fact that his writings on music dealt expressly with its social and political dimensions.

Heine grew up in the Rhineland province of Düsseldorf, worked in his uncle's Hamburg banking firm from 1816 to 1819, and in 1819 began studying law at the University in Bonn. He continued his legal studies at the universities in Berlin and Göttingen, receiving his doctorate in jurisprudence from the latter in 1825, in the same year converting from Judaism to Christianity in order to obtain full civil and professional rights in the contemporary legal system. Although his subsequent attempts at gainful employ in law were unsuccessful, during his years in Berlin he had won a substantial following through his contributions to the flourishing **salons** of Elise von Hohenhausen (1789–1857), Friederike Robert (1795–1832), and Rahel Varnhagen von Ense (1771–1833). These generated widespread receptiveness to his (for the day) radical social views as they were reflected in his first volume of *Reisebilder* (Travel Scenes, 1826). The *Buch der Lieder* was an astonishing success, going through some 13 editions during his lifetime.

After his move to Paris in 1831, Heine became something of a celebrity. He remained in the French capital for the rest of his career, except for two short visits to Berlin (1843–1844). In 1848, he was diagnosed with spinal tuberculosis of syphilitic origin, a condition that confined him to what he termed his "mattress-tomb" for the remaining eight years of his life. He continued to create, however, publishing a new three-volume collection of poems (*Romanzero*) and the **ballet libretto** *Der Doktor **Faust*** in 1851, plus another three-volume set of *Vermischte Schriften* ("Assorted Writings") in 1854. [JMC]

HEINRICH, ANTHONY PHILIP (1781–1861). American composer of German-Bohemian descent, during his lifetime dubbed "the **Beethoven** of America" as well as the first "professional" composer in the United States; member of the Early Romantic Generation. In 1817, at the age of nearly 40, after the death of his wife and several failed business ventures, he decided to become a full-time composer. He set out on a wilderness trek southward from Pittsburgh, eventually spending a winter, alone, living in a log cabin in Kentucky. Due to these travels and encounters with Native Americans, he gained a new appreciation of what it meant to be an American and sought to express this "Americanism" and his patriotism through the use of popular tunes and vivid descriptive passages in his works. While most of his works fall within this category, he continued to compose works about his Bohemian homeland throughout his career.

Heinrich's highly individualized style garnered him fame and respect in the United States and across Europe, where he became acquainted with many prominent people of his day, including John James Audubon, John Howard Payne, and President John Tyler. Concerts were given in his honor in Boston (1846), Graz (1836), and New York (1846), and a series of concerts organized in Prague (1857) was the first time in his career that his technically challenging works were not only well received by critics and the public but also properly rehearsed and performed. Some of his notable works include *The Dawning of Music in Kentucky or The Pleasures of Harmony in the Solitude of Nature* (1820), *The Western Minstrel* (1820), *A Chromatic Ramble* (1820), *Pushmataha, a Venerable Chief of a Western Tribe of Indians* (1831), *The Jubilee* (1841), and *The Ornithological Combat of Kings* (1847). [MMM]

See also NATIONALISM, ROMANTIC NATIONALISM; PROGRAM (PROGRAMMATIC) MUSIC.

HELLER, STEPHEN [ISTVÁN] (1813–1888). French composer, pianist, and critic of Hungarian birth and Jewish descent; member of the Romantic Generation. His output consists entirely of vocal and instrumental **chamber music**: song settings of texts by **Johann Wolfgang von Goethe** and **Heinrich Heine**, two compositions for violin and **piano** written in collaboration with the prominent violinist Heinrich Wilhelm Ernst (1814–1865), and a great many works for **piano** solo, many of them widely disseminated, reprinted, and praised by the likes of **Robert Schumann** (who regarded Heller as a kindred spirit, corresponded with him, and invited him to be the Augsburg correspondent of the *Neue Zeitschrift für Musik*). Among the piano works are four **sonatas** (opp. 9 [1829], 65 [1844], 88 [1856], and 143 [1878]), three sonatinas (opp. 146, 147, and 149, 1878–1879; *see* SONATA), 42 published *opera* of **character pieces** (including **Albumblätter, ballades,** *Lieder ohne Worte,* and others), nine sets of **variations** on themes by **Ludwig van Beethoven, Fromenthal Halévy, Nicolò Paganini,** Robert Schumann, and **Carl Maria von Weber**), and 13 *opera* of **etudes** (some of them concert etudes and others for didactic purposes, such as *L'art de phraser* [The Art of Phrasing, Op. 16, 1840] and the *21 technische Studien als Vorbereitung zu den Werken Chopins* [21 Technical Studies as Preparation for the Works of **Fryderyk Chopin,** Op. 154, 1879]). Less well known today but equally prominent in the 19th century were 28 published *opera* of transcriptions, **capriccios,** and **fantasies** based on works by **Daniel-François-Esprit Auber, Vincenzo Bellini, Gaetano Donizetti, Fromenthal Halévy, Giacomo Meyerbeer,** and **Johann Strauss (II),** among others. His brilliant transcriptions and arrangements of songs and other works by German composers made that music and those composers' names familiar to Parisian musical public that otherwise had little direct access to German music (*see* BOURBON RESTORATION).

Raised in a rural area, by the age of nine Heller was able to perform Jan Ladislav Dussek's (1760–1812) Double **Concerto** at the theater in Pest. He moved to Vienna to study with **Carl Czerny** but soon learned that the celebrated pedagogue's lessons were beyond his budget; instead, he took lessons with Anton Halm (1789–1872), who also introduced him to Beethoven and Schubert. He undertook a two-year concert tour beginning in 1828 but collapsed of nervous exhaustion while in Augsburg in 1830. He intended to remain there for only two weeks to recover but remained there for nearly eight years, teaching and composing. He moved to Paris in 1838 to study with **Friedrich Kalkbrenner,** soon parting ways with him and becoming a part of the circle of friends that included **Hector Berlioz,** Chopin, **Charles Hallé, Ferdinand Hiller,** Victor Hugo, and **Franz Liszt,** among others. In Paris, he earned a living by teaching as well as from his compositions, also writing criticism for the *Gazette musicale* (*see REVUE MUSICALE*). His sight failed him increasingly over the last five years of his life. [JMC]

HELMHOLTZ, HERMANN VON (1821–1894). German philosopher and leading scientist of the 19th century. His research and writings on a wide range of topics, including the law of conservation of energy, electrodynamics, and epistemology, changed the way people in the 19th century perceived themselves and the surrounding physical and metaphysical worlds. Specifically within the field of music, his groundbreaking research in physical acoustics made possible the just-temperment tuning system, which created a standard for tuning and scales. His work also aided in the production of a more resonant piano that could consistently maintain its tuning and produce the increased volume needed to fill the large concert halls that proliferated during the late 19th and early 20th centuries (*see* BÖSENDORFER; CHICKERING AND SONS; STEINWAY). His comments on consonance and dissonance, the scientific foundation for Western cultivated music, and the evolution of musical systems led many later 19th- and 20th-century aestheticians to use his work to justify the triumph of **absolute music** over the supposedly less evolved music of the **New German School**, which relied on image and word to convey meaning and achieve unity.

Helmholtz's findings and theories were first published in *Die Lehre von den Tonempfindungen als physiologische Grundlage für die Theorie der Musik* (On the Sensations of Tone as a Physiological Basis for the Theory of Music, 1862) and were later expanded into several more editions; the final, fourth edition appeared in 1877. Through the experiments outlined in that volume, Helmholtz made important discoveries about the physiological perception of musical tones and the scientific properties of sound and harmonics. He defined sound as a sensation, one that is a reaction of the ear to external stimuli. As the only organ able to perceive and understand these external stimuli, the ear and the faculty of hearing achieved greater importance than ever before. Helmholtz also discovered that musical tones were not solely made up of a fundamental or primary tone, as was widely assumed before, but of upper harmonic partials, which are perceptible only to the trained ear. He used these upper harmonics to develop the just-tuning system, which utilized these harmonics to retemper the octave and create a more resonant, full-bodied sound. Helmholtz's work also led to the Steinway innovation of the duplex scale.

Though not the first to do so, Helmholtz described the history of tonality in evolutionary terms, presenting the modern system as more "perfect" than "lesser" systems that came before it. But he does not attempt to further extend his empirical data to theories of aesthetics. As mentioned in the introduction to this dictionary, logical induction of natural sciences is aided by aesthetic induction of human sciences, but ultimately the methods and conceptual foundations of both fields should remain separate, not combined in a **Hegelian** framework. [MMM]

HENSEL (NÉE MENDELSSOHN), FANNY (CÄCILIE) (1805–1847).

German composer and pianist of the Romantic Generation. She was a prolific composer whose works—most of them unpublished during her lifetime and intended for private audiences—are engaging expressions of her own creativity and of her rich musical environment.

The firstborn of four children in her family, Fanny was just over three years older than the elder of her two brothers, **Felix Mendelssohn Bartholdy**. Among her childhood **piano** teachers were her mother Lea, pianist/composer Ludwig Berger (1777–1839), and Parisian pianist Marie Bigot (1786–1820). Hensel began studying music theory with Carl Friedrich Zelter (1758–1832) in 1819. That same year, she composed her first compositions, a set of 12 gavottes (now lost); her earliest surviving work is a birthday **Lied** (H-U 2) for her father Abraham. In 1820, she began to study composition with Zelter and joined the Berlin Singakademie; in the same year, Abraham famously articulated that professional composition was out of the question for Fanny, who was destined for marriage and domestic life. Nevertheless, she composed numerous **songs** and **piano** pieces over the next several years as well as a piano **quintet** and an accompanied violin piece. She also published Lieder under her brother Felix's name; among these were *Das Heimweh* (Homesickness, H-U 129), *Italien* (Italy, H-U 157), and the duet *Suleika und Hatem* in his *Zwölf Gesänge*, Op. 8 (1827, H-U 149), and *Sehnsucht* (Longing, H-U 219), *Verlust* (Loss, H-U 213), and *Die Nonne* (The Nun, H-U 46) in his *Zwölf Lieder*, Op. 9 (1830).

In 1829, Fanny married painter Wilhelm Hensel, and in her ensuing years as wife and mother, she also cultivated the **salon**-like *Sonntagsmusiken*, to which she contributed a steady stream of new works. During this period, she composed her only works in genres that fell outside the instrumental and vocal **chamber** realm normally accepted for women composers: the choral-orchestral **cantatas** *Lobgesang* and *Hiob* (H-U 257 and 258, both 1831), her *Cholera Cantata* (H-U 260, 1831), and a partially incomplete C-major **Overture** for **orchestra** (H-U 265, ca. 1830). Her 1820 setting of the *Ave Maria* trope from Sir Walter Scott's *Lady of the Lake* was published in the London musical periodical *The Harmonicon* in 1832—the first appearance of her music in print under her own name. She continued producing many works for piano and accompanied voice; a **string quartet** in E-flat major (H-U 277), a structurally innovative exploration of four-movement cyclic form, also comes from these years. In the mid-1830s, she seriously considered publishing a set of difficult piano compositions under her own name, even though her father had disallowed such activity. Although these works were originally composed separately, Hensel eventually ordered them into a large tonally coherent series (H-U 294, 301, 299, 304, 303, 321, 300, 313, 322, and 308), creating a large-scale **cycle** whose technical and musical demands fell well outside the usual contemporary perception of "feminine" composition.

The series of piano works from 1836 to 1837 represented a personal and professional crossroads for Hensel. On the one hand, it can hardly be coincidental that she first contemplated a major contravention of her father's proscription on publishing under her own name during the year after his death in 1835—an event that moved her deeply and represented a profound shift in the authority structures of the family. The personal distress to Abraham Mendelssohn's death also provided an opportunity of sorts in this episode, for in the summer of 1837, Lea Mendelssohn herself actually encouraged Hensel to publish her works—an encouragement that hardly would have been possible if Abraham were still alive. That summer, Lea also wrote to Felix (now the eldest male in the profoundly patriarchal family) suggesting that he convince her to publish some of her music. Lea used the verb *zureden*—a verb that means "encourage" in a specific sense, namely, to talk someone into doing something (to which he or she is opposed). Felix himself loathed the convoluted processes of publishing, however, and he demurred, responding that as soon as Fanny decided to publish, he would spare no effort to support her; "but *to talk her into publishing* is something I cannot do, because it is contrary to my views and convictions." Had Felix offered the encouragement his mother proposed, it seems likely that Fanny would have published the new cycle (clearly she made some steps in that direction since the manuscripts bear engraver's markings). As it turned out, however, she published only one of the works in question (H-U 301/Op. 2, no. 2), and that only a decade later (1846). The remainder of the cycle remained unpublished until 1994.

Although the 1840s were Hensel's last years, they also represent a significant turning point for the composer. Her Italian journeys in 1839–1840 and in 1845 seem to have made strong impressions on her; the first trip was part of the inspiration for her set of 12 **character pieces**, *Das Jahr* (The Year, H-U 385, 1841). After her second trip, she set out to publish her works and succeeded in doing so. In her final year, she saw through to publication her *Sechs Lieder* for voice, Op. 1; *Vier Lieder* for piano, Op. 2; the *Sechs Gesänge* for SATB, Op. 3 (*see* PART-SONG); her *Mélodies* for piano, Opp. 4 and 5; *Vier Lieder* for piano, Op. 6; and *Sechs Lieder* for voice, Op. 7. More of her piano and vocal works were published posthumously in 1850, as was her only **piano trio** (H-U 465/Op. 11). If Hensel's untimely death had not brought to such an abrupt end this public stage of her career, her public **reception** likely would have been far stronger. Much of her output remains unpublished and, by and large, obscure to classical audiences today. [RK/JMC]

See also FEMINISM.

HENSELT, (GEORG MARTIN) ADOLF VON (1814–1889). German piano **virtuoso** and composer of the Romantic Generation. Henselt was raised in Bavaria; his father worked in the textile industry. He took lessons first on violin and then on **piano**, which he took on as his primary instrument. At age 12, he began studying with Josepha von Fladt, herself a student of Abbé Vogler (1749–1814). Henselt spent much of 1832 in Weimar, where he studied with **Johann Nepomuk Hummel** with financial aid from King Ludwig I. After his first public recital that fall, Henselt moved to Vienna, became a pupil of **Simon Sechter**, and continued improving his technique. In 1838, he moved to St. Petersburg, which remained his home for the rest of his life. It was also at this point that Henselt, who had already written a few piano pieces, began producing a steady stream of compositions; his **Etudes** opp. 2 and 5 were critically well received. During the 1840s, Henselt taught at the School of Jurisprudence. **Franz Liszt** and **Clara** and **Robert Schumann**, by now Henselt's old friends, met with him in those years while visiting St. Petersburg. In the early 1850s, Henselt toured widely, performing in Kharkov, Kiev, and Odessa as well as cities in England, France, and the German lands. He performed far less in public and composed less in the decades that followed; in this later stage of his life, Henselt became a piano pedagogue of considerable renown, teaching at various institutions in St. Petersburg and Moscow. Henselt was editor of the music journal *La Nouvelliste* in the early 1870s. In 1887, Henselt joined the faculty of the St. Petersburg **Conservatory**, an institution he had opposed at its founding in 1862. Among his most widely reputed compositions is his Piano **Concerto** in F minor, Op. 16 (1847). [RK]

HILLER, FERDINAND (VON) (1811–1885). German composer, **conductor**, and pianist of Jewish descent, member of the the Romantic Generation; one of the mid-19th century's most multifaceted and respected musical voices on the conservative side of the polemics sparked by the emergence of the **New German School**. He demonstrated exceptional talent at an early age and for a while studied with the respected pedagogue Alois Schmitt (1788–1866) in his native Frankfurt am Main, giving a public performance of a **concerto** by **Wolfgang Amadeus Mozart** at age 10 and arousing the attention of **Felix Mendelssohn Bartholdy, Ignaz Moscheles,** and **Louis Spohr** before moving to Weimar to study with **Johann Nepomuk Hummel**. He lived in Paris from 1828 to 1835, becoming a member of the circle that included **Charles-Valentin Alkan, Hector Berlioz, Fryderyk Chopin, Stephen Heller,** and **Franz Liszt** and actively promoting their music to considerable acclaim. He also promoted the works of **Ludwig van Beethoven** (he gave the first public performance in Paris of Beethoven's Fifth Piano **Concerto**).

For most of the period 1836–1842, Hiller was in the Italian lands, where he studied Italian music and culture and devoted particular energy to studying Italian Renaissance polyphony (see CECILIAN MOVEMENT; HISTORICISM). In 1843, he went to Leipzig, where he served as director of the Gewandhaus Orchestra in the 1843–1844 season. On relocating to Dresden, he founded a series of subscription concerts and became a close friend of **Clara** and **Robert Schumann** as well as **Richard Wagner**, but in 1847 he was called to succeed Julius Rietz (1812–1877) as municipal music director in Düsseldorf. His successes there were such that in 1849 he was invited to serve as municipal Kapellmeister in Cologne. There he remained until illness compelled him to retire in 1884, except for a brief stint as director of the Théâtre-Italien in Paris in 1852–1853; in the meantime, he succeeded Heinrich Dorn (1804–1892) in 1850 as director of Cologne's Hochschule für Musik (music school) and reorganized it into a successful **Conservatory** modeled on that of Leipzig, directed an important concert series, and was active internationally as adjudicator, teacher, and conductor (he directed the Lower Rhine Music Festival a total of 11 times). His position at the Cologne Conservatory went to Franz Wüllner (1832–1902) on his retirement, but it is indicative of Hiller's vision and insight that his own recommendation for his successor had been for his friend **Johannes Brahms** or his pupil **Max Bruch**.

Hiller's reputation today rests largely on his accomplishments as a teacher, conductor, and writer on music: he published some 12 books and numerous articles between 1864 and 1884, and his voluminous correspondence with contemporary cultural and musical luminaries offers vivid insights into the musical crosscurrents of mid-19th-century music (especially in France and the German lands). He was a polished and well-respected composer, but most of his sizable output remains little known today. He penned one Italian **opera** and five German operas, two **oratorios** and numerous other compositions for chorus or solo voices with **orchestra**, about 150 *Gesänge* and **Lieder**, one **program symphony**, four **concert overtures**, two **piano** concertos, one *Konzertstück* for violin and orchestra, and a violin concerto and much instrumental **chamber music**, including three **string quartets**, six **piano trios**, one piano **quintet**, and about 200 works for piano solo. Much of this music remains unpublished. [JMC]

HISTORICISM. (Fr., historisme, Ger., Historismus.) In general, the tendency "to view all social and cultural phenomena, all categories, truths, and values, as relative and historically determined" (*OED Online*). As first used by Friedrich Schlegel, Novalis, and other German philosophers at the turn of the 19th century, the term was derived from arguments by Giambattista Vico (1668–1744) and Johann Gottfried Herder (1744–1803) which submitted that truth and aesthetic value transcend history and that human understandings of truth are conditioned by their respective historical settings. This original mode of historicism was a plea to appreciate historical artifacts on their own terms and as artworks or bodies of knowledge in their own right, not simply as ancestors or primitive versions of the present. By the late 19th century, the term had come to connote an attitudinal or stylistic contrast to modernism, one that celebrated the past to the implicit or perceived detriment of modernity and originality. By this point, the original ahistorical approach had largely given way to one that treated historical moments and systems of history as themselves historical, governed by natural laws of change that usually traced progressive developments toward the realization of transcendent truth and knowledge. This view of historicism is succinctly explained in **Friedrich Nietzsche**'s *Vom Nutzen und Nachteil der Historie für das Leben* (On the Advantages and Disadvantages of History for Life, 1874).

During the **long 19th century**, the starting point for historicism was the notion that the romantic present stood on one side of a historical caesura, on the other side of which was a vast repertoire of music that represented an even vaster range of ideas, styles, genres, and compositional techniques that were accessible to the present as artifacts, as sources of new ideas and new inspiration, or both. The world of the Early Romantic Generation (and before) was one in which few if any composers expected their music to be known and performed for more than a generation after their death or even throughout their career; accordingly, by the early 19th century, even the music of **Johann Sebastian Bach** and **George Frideric Handel** was not only chronologically remote but also (in the case of Bach's more learned works of the 1730s and 1740s) stylistically almost incomprehensible. Next to nothing was known about any composers who worked before the early 18th century, and no music written before the 1780s was performed with any regularity.

As historicism spread to the world of music, however, interest in the music of the past, the formation of a concert **canon** comprising both contemporary and early music, and the development of music historiography as a discipline resulted in a rapid and steady increase in interest of the music of the past. By the 1880s, there was a widespread use of the term "early music" to define music extending back to the early Renaissance (though earlier music was also becoming known in limited circles, thanks to the efforts of **Edmond de Coussemaker** and his pupils). Little music written before 1600 was performed with any frequency before the late 1940s, but by the time of World War I, scholarly knowledge of medieval music was sufficiently developed to permit composers of the post-Romantic generation to draw on those historically remote repertoires in their own works.

Historicism as movement comprises two opposing but interacting attitudes toward the relationship of the musical past to the present: in the terms of Walter Wiora, "relativistic" and "retrospective" historicism (see Walter Wiora, ed., *Die Ausbreitung des Historismus über die Musik: Aufsätze und Diskussionen* [Regensburg: Gustav Bosse, 1969]). Relativistic historicism offers a self-consciously objective historiographic stance, submitting that all phenomena are immanently historical and as such possessed of inviolable historical integrity: the task of history is to understand and appreciate the past "as it was." Retrospective historicism, by contrast, signified an appropriative or subjective attitude whereby the past's historical realization lay in the present, that is, in its use, adapted as deemed necessary, to suit the needs and tastes of modern composers, performers, and audiences. Both stances advocated for the active reintroduction of music from the distant past into the musical present, but whereas the retrospective mode was centered largely on issues surrounding concert programming, editing, and performance practice, the relativistic mode also extended to contemporary composition as composers responded in their own works to rapidly expanding knowledge of historical ideas, styles, techniques, and topics. The most obvious manifestations of these appropriative gestures are the Romantics' many arrangements and transcriptions of earlier music; their incorporation of chorales, fugues, *stile antico* polyphony, and imitations of these elements into original compositions; and their use of historical subjects and motives (most prominently, the B-A-C-H motive) in compositions that are otherwise thoroughly of a contemporary pedigree. The conflicts between these two modes are well exemplified in the quarrel that emerged between **Eduard Hanslick** and **Robert Franz** in the second half of the century.

Both of these modes of historicism are generally associated with two major trends: the **Bach revival** and the **Cecilian movement**. The controversies over the nature of historical progress that erupted after the **Revolutions of 1848** also intertwined historicism inextricably with several of the century's other movements, most importantly **nationalism** and the revival of interest in **folk song**. [JMC]

HOFFMANN, E(RNST) T(HEODOR) A(MADEUS) (1776–1822). German critic, novelist, prose stylist, and composer; one of the most important literary and stylistic influences on **Robert Schumann**, important figure in the Romantic **reception** of **Wolfgang Amadeus Mozart** and **Ludwig van Beethoven**, and author of works that inspired compositions by **Adolphe Adam, Ferruccio Busoni, Léo Delibes, Jacques Offenbach, Carl Reinecke**, Schumann, **Pyotor Il'yich Tchaikovsky**, and others. His career is characterized by achievement in the positions of law, literature, and music alike.

Hoffmann studied composition and piano from an early age, then studied law at the University of Königsberg from 1792 to 1795, working in the legal professions and civil service in Glogau, Berlin, Poznán, Płock, and Warsaw (where he conducted works of Beethoven, **Luigi Cherubini**, Christoph Willibald Ritter von Gluck [1714–1787], **Franz Joseph Haydn**, and Mozart in an amateur concert society) until he lost his position during Napoléon Bonaparte's occupation of Prussia in 1806. During those years, he studied composition with Johann Friedrich Reichardt (1752–1814) and continued composing, penning a **Singspiel** titled *Die Maske* (The Mask, 1799–1800) and another titled *Die lustigen Musikanten* (The Merry Musicians, 1805). The latter was staged in Warsaw in 1805. He was appointed conductor of the Bamberg Opera in 1808, and with the publication in the Leipzig-based *Allgemeine musikalische Zeitung* in 1809 of his short story "Ritter Gluck" (a fantastical exploration of Gluck meeting a modern composer 20 years after his death), Hoffmann established himself as an important literary voice in musical romanticism. Between 1808 and 1815, he published some 32 reviews of music and essays on music in that same periodical, also returning to the legal profession with a new appointment as judge in Berlin in 1814. His first novel, *Die Elixiere des Teufels* (The Devil's Elixirs), was published in 1815, and in 1816, his 21st opera, *Undine* (Op. 70), was premiered in Berlin to great acclaim. Between then and his death, he completed one more opera and the better part of a new novel (*Kater Murr*, 1820).

As a composer, Hoffmann created two Mass settings and other sacred music, a **concert overture**, a **symphony**, and three instrumental **chamber** works as well as about a dozen works for **piano** solo and numerous **songs**, **part-songs**, and other vocal chamber music. He is best known for *Undine* and his 21 other operas, which anticipate many of the dramatic and musical effects that would typify **Carl Maria von Weber**'s approach to operatic composition in the 1820s. He was more influential as a critic and prose stylist. His stories provided the basis for Delibes's *Coppelia*, Offenbach's *Les contes de Hoffmann*, and Tchaikovsky's *The Nutcracker*, and his predilection for combining obsessive detail with exaggerated fantasy provided important literary impetus to Romantic culture throughout the remainder of the **long 19th century**. In particular, Hoffmann's cultivation of *Zerrissenheit* (the state of profound conflict between personal or emotional forces and the practical needs of the real world) in his characters, probably born of the discussions of insomnia, mental illness, and psychopathology that he enjoyed with a number of medical doctors during his Bamberg days, added new levels of psychological depth and complexity to Romantic understandings of identity and emotional expression. [JMC]

HOFMEISTER, FRIEDRICH (1782–1864). German music publisher and bibliographer. He opened a music shop in Leipzig in 1807 and in 1808 extended this to become a music publisher. His sons assumed the leadership of the business in 1852, followed by one of their partners (Albert Röthing) in 1877 and then by Hofmeister's great-grandson Carl Wilhelm Günther (1878–1956) in 1905.

Although Hofmeister's business never rivaled that of **Breitkopf & Härtel**, it was decidedly reputable and influential. In addition to being the main German publisher of **Heinrich Marschner**'s works, it published music by **Ludwig van Beethoven, Hector Berlioz, Luigi Cherubini, Fryderyk Chopin, Carl Czerny, Gaetano Donizetti, Antonín Dvořák, Adolf von Henselt, Franz Liszt, Carl Loewe, Gustav Mahler, Felix Mendelssohn Bartholdy, Ferdinando Paer, Clara** and **Robert Schumann, Louis Spohr, Gaspare Spontini, Richard Strauss**, and **Carl Maria von Weber**, among others. It was also an important publisher of reference works and pedagogical literature. In the former category are manuals on harmony, **piano** technique, and vocal and instrumental technique by Johann Gottlob Werner (1777–1822), Bernardo Mengozzi (1758–1800; the official treatise on singing adopted by the Paris **Conservatory**, posthumously published in French and in German, 1804–1825), Iwan Müller (1756–1824; on the modern clarinet, 1826), and more. In particular, Hofmeister was influential in publishing didactic collections for individual instruments (cello, clarinet, horn, and so on). In the latter category—and still of great use to researchers of 19th-century music—are Hofmeister's periodical (often monthly) supplements to Carl Friedrich Whistling's (1788–1849 or later) *Handbuch der musikalischen Literatur* (1819ff). These supplements were published under the title *Musikalisch-literarischer Monatsbericht neuer Musikalien, musikalischer Schriften und Abbildungen* (Musical-Literary Monthly Report of New Publications of Music, Writings on Music, and Illustrations [on Music]) from 1829 on, with annual summaries published from 1852 on. Also in 1829, Hofmeister founded the Verein der deutschen Musikalienhändler (Union of German Music-Sellers), an organization that played a vital role in the revision of **copyright and performance right** over the course of the **long 19th century** and is still in existence today. [JMC]

HOLOGRAPH. A manuscript or portion of a manuscript in the hand of an author or composer but not signed; also, copies of earlier manuscripts by persons other than the named author or composer. Holographs differ from **autographs** in that the latter are identifiably written, without aid of external documentation, by the named author or composer him- or herself, whereas holographs are attributable only through the aid of secondary sources or not at all.

During the **long 19th century**, many composers were reluctant to hand over the autograph scores for their works to publishers for fear that those scores, the products of intensive labor, might be damaged or lost. Yet publishers had to have the music in order to have it engraved or (later) typeset. To resolve this situation, a copy of the autograph was generally made by a professional copyist and then proofed by the composer. These copyists' manuscripts themselves are holographs; when they contain corrections or changes in the handwriting of the composer, those corrections and changes are considered autograph emendations to the holograph manuscript.

One well-known such instance is the sole surviving manuscript score for **Ludwig van Beethoven**'s Third (**"Eroica"**) **Symphony**: the composer's autograph score is lost, but the copyist's score based on it survives and contains plentiful changes to the musical text and title in Beethoven's own handwriting (those to the title page belying the famous anecdote about Beethoven having destroyed the score and retitled the piece when he learned of Napoléon Bonaparte's having been crowned emperor). Composers' copies of other composers' works occupy a dual status: **Gustav Mahler**'s copies of the symphonies of Beethoven are his own autographs but are holographs of Beethoven's works. [JMC]

See also COMPOSITIONAL PROCESS, CREATIVE PROCESS; EDITING AND EDITIONS; PRINTING AND PUBLISHING OF MUSIC; URTEXT.

HUGO, VICTOR (1802–1885). French writer of plays, novels, and poetry; member of the Romantic Generation. Perhaps best known today for his novels *Notre-Dame de Paris* (The Hunchback of Notre Dame, 1831) and *Les Misérables* (1862), Hugo compelled contemporaries with the breadth of his oeuvre.

Born in Besançon to a republican army officer father and monarchist Catholic mother, Hugo seems to have been destined for a politically charged life. Hugo married Adèle Foucher in 1822, and the two had several children in the years that followed. His writing career flourished as well: Hugo's *Odes et poésies diverses* (Various Odes and Poems, 1822), the first of many poetry collections, earned him a royal pension. Hugo completed several novels and plays in his first few decades of adulthood, but none matched the extraordinary success of *Notre-Dame de Paris*, which helped precipitate Eugène Viollet-le-Duc's (1814–1879) cathedral restoration projects beginning in 1845. The 1840s saw an increasingly republican Hugo, whose participation in the **Second Republic** government necessitated his 15-year exile in 1851. Hugo was politically active and vocal for the remainder of his life.

Hugo's plays, novels, and poems inspired many dozens of musical settings and instrumental responses. Several composers reworked *Hernani* (1830) into **operas**, including **Vincenzo Bellini** (1830) and **Giuseppe Verdi** (1844). Hugo's novel *Notre-Dame de Paris* was reborn many times as **ballets** and operas; notable examples include operas by **Aleksandr Dargomïzhsky** (1847), **William Henry Fry** (1864), and Franz Schmidt (1874–1939; 1914). **Gaetano Donizetti** made an opera on Hugo's *Lucrèce Borgia* (1833) the year it was published. *Angelo, tyran de Padoue* (1835) was reworked by **Arrigo Boito** into the libretto for **Amilcare Ponchielli**'s *La gioconda*

(1876). *Ruy Blas* (1838), perhaps best known as the source for **Felix Mendelssohn Bartholdy**'s **concert overture** (MWV P15/Op. posth. 95, 1839), exists in numerous other musical incarnations, including **serenades** by **Emmanuel Chabrier** (1863), **Camille Saint-Saëns** (1870), and **Léo Delibes** (1879). Hugo's many poems, above all those published in *Odes et ballades* (1828), *Les orientales* (1829), and *Les rayons et les ombres* (Beams and Shadows, 1840), were composed into **songs** by dozens of composers, most notably **Hector Berlioz, Franz Liszt,** and **Camille Saint-Saëns.** [RK]

LES HUGUENOTS. (Fr., "The Huguenots.") **Grand opera** (*opéra*) in five acts by **Giacomo Meyerbeer** on a libretto by **Eugène Scribe**, with contributions by **Émile Deschamps** (1791–1871). The idea for the opera arose in Scribe's discussions with the Opéra director Louis Véron in September 1832, and Meyerbeer, whose *Robert le diable* (1831) had been an enormous success, was contractually brought into the project the following month. *Les Huguenots* was premiered in Paris at the Opéra on 29 February 1836 to great acclaim. Along with **Daniel-François-Esprit Auber**'s *La muette de Portici* and **Fromenthal Halévy**'s *La juive*, it became the iconic example of grand opera—so much so that **Robert Schumann**, no fan of Meyerbeer's music, the grandeur of French opera, or French music generally and wary of the opera's mixture of serious and comic, sacred and profane, and popular and vernacular styles, in 1837 contrasted it with **Felix Mendelssohn Bartholdy**'s contemporaneous **oratorio** *St. Paul*, proclaiming Meyerbeer's opera to be "a comprehensive list of all the defects and some few advantages of his age" and concluding that Mendelssohn's music led "to good"; Meyerbeer's, "to evil."

Schumann's review is largely a reaction to the immense acclaim that *Les Huguenots* had achieved even in the German lands. This acclaim derived in no small part on the **opera**'s resonance with contemporary European politics. Its plot is based on the plight of the French Calvinists (Huguenots) in the 16th century, situating the love of the Protestant nobleman Raoul and the Catholic Valentine, lady-in-waiting to the Queen of Navarre, amid the French Wars of Religion and culminating in the St. Bartholomew's Day Massacre (1572), in which the French government slaughtered thousands of Protestants in order to rid France of Protestant influence. In the political climate that gave rise to the bloody July Revolution (1830) and the June Rebellion (1832), two of the most important European political upheavals between the **Congress of Vienna** and the **Revolutions of 1848**, the antiestablishment rhetoric implicit in *Les Huguenots'* condemnation of the French state was quite stylish; the work's subject matter resonated all the more because of the rise of debates concerning religious tolerance in 19th-century England, France, Germany, and Italy, and these issues may have held further appeal because Meyerbeer was himself Jewish. The political topicality of the opera, while hardly new in the genre, newly legitimized the aesthetic agenda and commercial viability of such approaches to the genre and thus set the tone for French opera for the remainder of the **long 19th century**. [JMC]

HUMMEL, JOHANN NEPOMUK (1778–1837). Austrian composer, **conductor**, pianist, and teacher of the Early Romantic Generation; after **Ludwig van Beethoven** the most highly regarded Austrian composer of his generation in his day. He was the son of a violinist and conductor and a true child **prodigy**, able to read music at four, play violin at five, and play the **piano** at six. In 1786, he moved with his family to Vienna, where he became a close friend of **Wolfgang Amadeus Mozart** and took lessons with him until 1788, when Mozart reportedly recommended that Hummel make himself known to the world. Accordingly, he and his father toured the German lands, Denmark, Scotland, and England (London).

Over the next decade, Hummel studied with Johann Georg Albrechtsberger (1736–1809), **Franz Joseph Haydn**, and Antonio Salieri (1750–1825) in Vienna and became friends with Beethoven, whose presence he found both intimidating and inspiring. During these years, he was widely sought after as a teacher (he later wrote that most days he taught for nine or 10 hours in succession and had to arise at 4:00 a.m. in order to find time for composing). He served as Haydn's de facto successor as music director at Esterházy from 1804 to 1808 and again from 1809 to 1811 but ultimately resigned out of dissatisfaction with conditions there, returning to a life giving private instruction in Vienna.

Hummel returned to public life as a performing pianist in 1814, creating a sensation at the **Congress of Vienna** and undertaking a new tour of the German lands (Berlin, Breslau, Dresden, and Leipzig) and Prague in 1815. He served briefly as Kapellmeister of the court in Stuttgart in 1818 but left this in 1819 to take up a more favorable position at the court in Weimar. The latter not only facilitated a long friendship with **Johann Wolfgang von Goethe** but also provided him with three months' vacation in the springtime, the height of the touring season for participants in the growing cult of the **virtuoso**. He toured widely from England and France to Poland (where he met **Fryderyk Chopin**) and Russia (where he met **John Field**), also teaching privately (pupils including **Adolf von Henselt** and **Ferdinand Hiller**) and conducting works by **D.-F.-E. Auber, Vincenzo Bellini, Fromenthal Halévy, Giacomo Meyerbeer, Gioachino Rossini**, and **Louis Spohr**, among others. Traveling to Vienna with his pupil Hiller to visit the ailing Beethoven in 1827, he also made the acquaintance of **Franz Schubert**, who requested and received permission to dedicate his last three piano **sonatas** (D. 958, 959, 960) to him (*see* PRINTING AND PUBLISHING OF MUSIC). As it turned out, the works were not published until 1839, after both composers' deaths; the publisher thus changed the dedication to **Robert Schumann**.

Hummel continued to compose, conduct, and tour into the 1830s. His health began to fail and his productivity to decline in 1834. His death was widely lamented and honored with a performance of the Mozart/Süßmaier **Requiem** in Vienna. In addition to his musical compositions, he wrote *Ausführliche theoretisch-practische Anweisung zum Pianofortespiel: Vom ersten Elementar-Unterrichte am bis zur vollkommensten Ausbildung* (Detailed Theoretical and Practical Method for Playing Piano, from the Most Basic Instruction to the Most Advanced Education, 1828), which was widely translated and reprinted throughout the 19th century.

Hummel's music plays a peripheral role in the latter-day **canon** of the **long 19th century**, but before the 1840s, he ranked as a leading composer and virtuoso pianist; his influence is obvious in various early works of Chopin, **Felix Mendelssohn Bartholdy**, and Robert Schumann, among many others. His most important compositions are the **Septet** in D Minor, Op. 74 (ca. 1816); the widely emulated **polonaise** *La bella capricciosa* (Op. 55, 1815); a Trumpet **Concerto** in E Major (WoO 1, 1803) (today frequently transposed down to E-flat major); and four piano concertos (Opp. 85, 89, 110, and 113). He also penned a sizable body of sacred music, secular **cantatas**, and other choral works; some 16 **operas**, several **ballets**, pantomimes, and sets of **incidental music**; numerous **songs**, **part-songs**, and **folk song** arrangements; 26 numbered *opera* of instrumental **chamber music** and further chamber works that were published without opus number during his lifetime (*see* WOO); many works for piano solo, **piano duet**, and organ; and some orchestral music. [JMC]

HUMPERDINCK, ENGELBERT (1854–1921). German composer of the Modern Romantic Generation. Humperdinck is remembered for his folk-like **operas** in the tradition of **Richard Wagner**, above all the wildly successful **Märchenoper** *Hänsel und Gretel* (EHWV 93.3, 1893). In it, as in much of his stage music, Humperdinck combined Wagner's harmonic wanderings, use of themes, and knack for gravitas with his own orchestrational genius and ability to channel folk idioms.

As a child Humperdinck sang, played **piano**, and composed. After a year studying architecture, Humperdinck attended the Cologne **Conservatory** in 1872, where he studied with **Ferdinand Hiller** and Gustav Jensen (1843–1895). In 1877–1879, Humperdinck studied in Munich at the Königliche Musikhochschule under **Josef Rheinberger** and **Franz Lachner** and composed two significant **cantatas**: *Die Wallfahrt nach Kevlaar* (The Pilgrimage to Kevlaar, EHWV 55, 1878) and *Das Glück von Edenhall* (The Luck of Eden Hall, EHWV 60, 1879). Humperdinck's ongoing interest in Richard Wagner peaked when he attended the Munich premiere of Wagner's *Ring of the Nibelung* in 1878. In 1880, while in Italy on the Berlin **Mendelssohn** Prize, Humperdinck met Wagner in Naples, and in 1881 he moved to

Bayreuth on Wagner's invitation to assist in preparing *Parsifal*. Another trip to Bayreuth in 1882 to help prepare Wagner's **Symphony** in C for a Christmas Eve performance was Humperdinck's last time with Wagner, who died a few months later.

The next several years included a brief Iberian tour (inspiring his 1887 *Maurische Suite* [Moorish Suite], EHWV 87), first meetings with **Johannes Brahms** and **Richard Strauss**, and a short gig as pianist for the Krupps. Humperdinck taught at the Barcelona Conservatory in 1885–1886 (authoring a Spanish-language harmony text while there), the Cologne Conservatory in 1887–1888, and at the Hoch Conservatory (Frankfurt am Main) in 1890–1897. Besides composing, Humperdinck's other work during these years included writing music criticism, assisting at the Bayreuth Festival, and reading and editing for publisher Schott.

In 1890, Humperdinck set to music four of his sister's poems on the Grimm "Hansel and Gretel" tale; this became the basis for a **Singspiel** and, in 1893, an opera *Hänsel und Gretel* that premiered in Weimar under Strauss's baton. *Königskinder* (Children of the King) began as **incidental music** for an eponymous play by Ernst Rosmer (pseud. Elsa Bernstein-Porges, 1866–1949) but rapidly transformed, to the playwright's chagrin, into a kind of **melodrama** (EHWV 106.1, 1897) and then into a *Märchenoper* (fairy-tale opera, EHWV 160.2). Humperdinck devised for it a *Sprechgesang* notation ("Sprechnoten") designating approximate pitches for the singer, but certain critics complained that according to Wagner's own words, the melodrama was an un-Wagnerian genre. The work performed well nevertheless, as did its 1910 full operatic revision (Metropolitan Opera, New York). The Humperdincks moved to Berlin in 1900, where Engelbert taught composition through the Königliche Akademie der Künste through 1920. [RK]

HUNGARIAN RHAPSODIES, **LW A132.** Nineteen solo **piano** compositions by **Franz Liszt**, based largely on Hungarian and Romanian melodies and drawing on a combination of Hungarian and Roma stylistic elements. Significant both as masterworks of the concert piano repertoire and (in large part) as showcases of the *style hongrois*, these works represent the fusion of Liszt the **virtuoso** pianist and Liszt the unabashed, costumed Hungarian ambassador to the world.

The *Rhapsodies* did not all emerge at the same time; Liszt published the first 15 between 1846 and 1853 and Nos. 16–19 in 1882–1886. Moreover, Liszt based most of them on earlier, nominally Hungarian piano compositions, especially his *Magyar dallok* (Hungarian Melodies, LW A60a, 1840–1843) and *Magyar Rhapsodiak* (Hungarian Rhapsodies, LW A60b, 1847). The form of most of these works is based on a Hungarian *verbunkos* pattern, which typically features a slow, dotted-rhythm *lassú* section and a quicker, virtuosic *friss* section. Liszt's notions about Gypsy origins of the

Hungarian folk idioms displayed in his *Hungarian Rhapsodies* was partly to the fact that he himself became acquainted with them—and many with many Hungarian folk melodies (*see* FOLK SONG)—through Gypsy band performances. Of the six that Liszt and Franz Doppler (1821–1883) arranged for **orchestra** in the late 1850s and published in 1874–1875, the *Hungarian Rhapsody No. 2* is the most well known today (in both versions). [RK]

See also NATIONALISM, ROMANTIC NATIONALISM.

I

IDÉE FIXE. (Fr., "fixed idea" or "obsession.") Term developed in early 19th-century German and French phrenology and psychology to describe monomania or other fixation-related psychological disorders; it first appears in Franz Joseph Gall (1758–1828) and Johann Spurzheim (1776–1832), *Anatomie et physiologie du système nerveux en général et du cerveau en particulier*, Vol. 2 (1812). In this usage, it denotes a compelling idea or emotional obsession; its victims might not be aware that their frame of mind is not real.

Drawing on this application and on the contemporary French understanding of the term *idée* to mean "melody" or "theme," the term *idée fixe* was appropriated by **Hector Berlioz**—who studied medicine in Paris from 1821–1824 and thus may well have come into curricular contact with its medical usage. Beginning around 1830, Berlioz employed the term in connection with numerous works to denote a musical theme that was relatively stable, recurring numerous times over the course of a composition to signify a particular idea, image, or element in the program (most notable among these works are the *Episode in the Life of an Artist*, its sequel *Lélio, ou le retour à la vie* [Lélio; or, The Return to Life, H. 55/Op. 14b, 1831, rev. 1855], and *Harold in Italy*, H. 68/Op. 16, 1834). The character of the idée would be altered in accordance with its programmatic context by changes in harmonic underpinnings, scoring, tempo, and so on, and it might be presented in only fragmentary form. But unlike *Leitmotivs* and *Leitfaden*, the idée fixe was a full-fledged melody (idée), not merely a motive, and unlike them and reminiscence themes, it usually retained its exact intervallic structure, not just its general melodic contour. [JMC]

See also THEMATIC TRANSFORMATION, THEMATIC METAMORPHOSIS.

IMPRESSIONISM. (Fr., impressionisme; Ger., Impressionismus.) Term for an aesthetic approach that downplays clarity of line, form, and detail in order to emphasize light, color, texture, and an ultimately subjective "impression" of the moods, emotions, or ideas elicited by a subject rather than its objective nature or form. The term was occasionally applied to music in connection with composers of the Late Romantic Generation (most notably **Emmanuel Chabrier, Antonín Dvořák,** and **Edvard Grieg**) or certain later works of Romantic Generation composers, including **Franz Liszt** (*Nuages gris* [Grey Clouds], 1881) and **Richard Wagner** (Forest Murmurs from *Siegfried* and portions of *Tristan* and *Parsifal*). It is most strongly associated, however, with the music of **Claude Debussy** in works such as *Prélude à "L'après-midi d'un faune"* (**Prelude** to *The Afternoon of a Faun*, 1894), *Nocturnes* (1897–1899), *La mer* (1905, rev. 1910), *Reflets dans l'eau* (Reflections in the Water, 1905), *Les Sons et les parfums tournent dans l'air du soir* (Sounds and Fragrances Swirl in the Evening Air, 1910), and *Brouillards* (Mists, 1913). Its widespread use is associated with the graphic arts primarily via the Parisian engraver, painter, and art critic Louis Leroy (1812–1885), who in 1874 labeled Claude Monet's (1840–1926) painting *Impression: soleil levant* (Impression: Sunrise) as "impressionist" and associated the aesthetic with other contemporary painters such as Paul Cézanne, Edgar Degas, Eduard Manet, Camille Pissarro, Henri Regnault, and Pierre-Auguste Renoir. The term has also been applied to other composers, including **Ernest Chausson, Gabriel Fauré,** Maurice Ravel, and **Aleksandr Scriabin,** by extension of its characteristics in Debussy's music: foregrounding of timbre; static, nonclimactic melodies; coloristic harmonies; continually evolving but nondevelopmental forms; and so on.

Musical impressionism is typically associated with 20th-century developments because of its avoidance of functional tonality and rejection of the theoretical and compositional conventions of Romantic and post-Romantic form. Nevertheless, impressionist music's cultivation of rich, often luxuriant and sensually beautiful sonorities reflects its foundations in the musical idioms of post-Romanticism, as do its emphasis on subjectivity and its celebration of the fragmentary moment rather than telos and the architectonic whole. While it is true that many avant-garde 20th-century composers drew on aspects of impressionism, those works almost without exception depart from two salient features of the style: its cultivation of sensual beauty and lush sonorities and its celebration as dissonance not as an end itself but in the service of beauty. Few works generally considered impressionist date from after 1914 (the end of the **long 19th century** that generally corresponds to the heyday of Romantic music; see the introduction to this dictionary). [JMC]

IMPROMPTU. (Fr., "unpremeditated.") Term for a short composition, usually for **piano** or instrumental **chamber** ensemble, written in a style that suggests spontaneity or improvisation rather than careful planning and elaborate musical structure. Impromptus are typically miniatures and may be considered **character pieces.** Although music reference sources commonly report that the term was first applied to music as the title of a short piano piece by **Jan Václav Voříšek** published in the *Allgemeine Musikalische Zeitung* (Leipzig) in 1817 and then published independently in 1821, as well as to **Heinrich Marschner**'s 12 impromptus opp. 22 and 23 (also early 1820s), in fact the term emerged earlier and in different works. In 1813, the London firm of Chappell & Co. published J. B. Cramer's (1771–1858) *Kutusoff's Victory: An Impromptu for the Piano Forte. Founded on **Handel**'s Celebrated Air Disdainful of Danger* (from *Judas Maccabeus*) and two *Impromptu[s] for the Piano-Forte, with an Accompaniment for Flute* by Irish composer Francis Tatton Latour (1766–1845). The first of these two compositions drew on the term's connotations of spontaneous or improvisatory character and falls readily into the category of the **fantasy** on existing themes, but the second is a short, comparatively informal composition in the sense of the term better known today. In 1815, François-Joseph Gossec (1734–1829) published a **motet** titled *O salutaris hostia* whose subtitle, somewhat cryptically, designated it as an "impromptu à 3 voix sans accompagnement" (impromptu for three unaccompanied voices), and in 1818, guitarist Fernando Sor (1778–1839) published an *Impromptu dans le genre du Bolero fait au sujet du grand bruit que l'on fait avec les Cloches l'après midi de la Toussaints en Espagne* (Impromptu in the Genre of a Bolero on the Subject of the Great Noise Made with Bells in Spain on the Afternoon of All Saint's Day). Also sometime during the century's second decade, the German composer Daniel Steibelt (1765–1823) published *Le depart: Impromptu pour le pianoforte*. As of the 1820s, then, the term *impromptu* embraced two discrete meanings: a seemingly offhand or improvisatory composition based on preexisting material or a likewise unstudied miniature of modest length that was *not* based on preexisting material.

During the remainder of the **long 19th century**, the second of these applications assumed predominance, although the genre's continued connotations of building on previously composed music persevered in a fashion that was more substantive than vestigial. Thus, in the 1820s, the inventory of pieces designated impromptu (in both of these senses) grew rapidly. In 1824, **Franz** composed an *Impromptu brillant sur des thèmes de **Rossini** et **Spontini*** (LW A5, publ. 1825), but Liszt's later impromptus (LW A84c and 256, comp. 1850–1852 and 1872, respectively) are autonomous works that also adopt features of other genres (the **waltz** and the **nocturne**, respectively). In the summer or fall of 1827, **Franz Schubert** composed four lyrical piano pieces (D. 899), two of which were published with the designation *impromptu* as his Op. 90 later that year (nos. 3 and 4 of that set were published posthumously, in 1857). Although the designation *impromptu* was apparently the publisher's decision in connection with D. 899, it was evidently authentic as applied to Schubert's next set of impromptus (D. 935, December 1827, publ. 1828). Other important composers who worked in the genre in the long 19th century include **Fryderyk** (four impromptus, Op. 66 [1834], 29 [ca. 1837], 36 [1839], and 51 [1842]), **Clara Schumann** (opp. 5 and 9, 1836 and 1838), and **Robert Schumann** (Opp. 5 [1833], 66 [1848], and 124, nos. 1 and 9 [comp. 1832 and 1838 and publ. 1854]).

During the mid- and late 19th century, thousands of impromptus were produced; virtually every composer who wrote any quantity of piano or instrumental chamber music penned impromptus. A selective list of those composers includes **Isaac Albéniz, Charles-Valentin Alkan, Anatoly Arensky, William Sterndale Bennett, Georges Bizet, Franz Brendel, Hans von Bülow, Cécile Chaminade, César Cui, Carl Czerny, Antonín Dvořák, Ferdinand David, Gabriel Fauré, Aleksandr Glazunov, Mikhail Glinka, Louis Moreau Gottschalk, Charles Gounod, Enrique Granados, Edvard Grieg, Anthony Philip Heinrich, Stephen Heller, Adolf von Henselt, Johann Nepomuk Hummel, Friedrich Kalkbrenner, Ruggero Leoncavallo, Albert Lortzing, Anatoly Lyadov, William Mason, Edward MacDowell, Jules Massenet, Bernhard Molique, Ignaz Moscheles, Ignacy Paderewski, John Knowles Paine, Joachim Raff, Max Reger, Carl Reinecke, Josef Rheinberger, Nikolay Rimsky-Korsakov, Anton Rubinstein, Aleksandr Scriabin, Jean Sibelius, Pyotor Il'yich Tchaikovsky,** and **Sigismond Thalberg.** [JMC]

INCIDENTAL MUSIC. (Fr., *musique de scène*; Ger., *Bühnenmusik* or *Schauspielmusik*; It., *musica di scena.*) Instrumental and/or vocal music to be used in connection with a staged dramatic work that was predominantly spoken (as opposed to **melodrama**, which was concerted rather than staged and to predominantly sung genres such as **opera** and *Singspiel*). At its simplest, this might comprise theatrical **overtures**, *entr'actes*, and interludes, but by convention it also embraces music that sounds simultaneously with danced, pantomimed, or spoken events on stage. Strictly speaking, such music dates to the earliest uses of music in dramatic contexts. Its more systematic use seems to date from the 17th century, especially in the stage music of Henry Purcell and Jean-Baptiste Lully, however.

During the **long 19th century**, the concept of incidental music, especially the instrumental variety, broadened considerably as composers and audiences became more invested in notions of music's capacity for expressing the inexpressible: when music intrudes into a predominantly nonmusical drama, it necessarily attracts attention; moreover, audiences naturally relate the music to the drama that has preceded it and incorporate the music that intruded into their understanding of the subsequent dramatic events. The result is that while incidental music at its most elementary might simply fill otherwise dead stage time, for Romantic composers it was also able to comment on the drama, foreshadow later events and recall earlier ones, suggest different temporal or **narrative** frames, and occasionally suggest a hidden narrative different from what is discernible if one experiences either the text or the music alone. The aesthetic status of incidental music has been problematical since the mid-19th century. On the one hand, because theories of music tend to revolve around recognized genres and incidental music lacks the consistency of defining characteristics necessary to articulate a genre, it escaped theoretical and aesthetic evaluation until comparatively recently, with the first systematic attempts to explore it emerging only in the 1980s. Moreover, as the theory of music and polemics of musical aesthetics increasingly centered on either the autonomy of instrumental music or the necessity for a complete integration of musical and extramusical content into **program music** or something approaching the **Gesamtkunstwerk**, music that by definition achieved its function and aesthetic essence by means of the supplementarity of separate music and drama—that is, incidental music—had little chance of competing. Nevertheless, virtually every composer of any repute during the long 19th century was called on to compose incidental music and did so with considerable imagination. The best-known examples are those by **Ludwig van Beethoven** (for **Friedrich Schiller**'s *Egmont*, 1809–1810), **Felix Mendelssohn Bartholdy** (for Sophocles' *Antigone* and **William Shakespeare**'s *A Midsummer Night's Dream*; 1841 and 1843, respectively), **Robert Schumann** (for **Lord Byron**'s *Manfred*, 1848–1849), **Georges Bizet** (for Alphonse Daudet's *L'Arlesienne*, 1872), **Edvard Grieg** (for Henrik Ibsen's *Peer Gynt*, 1874–1875), **Gabriel Fauré** and **Jean Sibelius** (for Maurice Maeterlinck's *Pelléas et Mélisande*; 1898 and 1904–1905, respectively), and **Richard Strauss** (for Hugo von Hoffmannsthal's adaptation of Molière's *Le bourgeois gentilhomme* as *Der Bürger als Edelmann*, 1912). Except for Bizet, all of those composers also wrote other incidental music that is less well known. Other composers of incidental music include **Claude Debussy, Antonín Dvořák, Charles Gounod, E. T. A. Hoffmann, Engelbert Humperdinck, Friedrich Kuhlau, Franz Liszt, Albert Lortzing, Heinrich Marschner, Hubert Parry, Gioachino Rossini, Camille Saint-Saëns, Franz Schubert, Arthur Sullivan, Carl Maria von Weber,** and **Hugo Wolf.** [JMC]

See also MELODRAMA; SINGSPIEL; *TABLEAU VIVANT* (PL. *TABLEAUX VIVANTS*).

INDY, VINCENT D' (1851–1931). French composer, music editor, polemical writer, teacher, and director of the Schola Cantorum (from 1904) whose **nationalist** activities and opinions were aligned with right-wing sentiments in fin-de-siècle France. Born into an aristocratic Catholic family, d'Indy began studying harmony at an early age. After serving in the National Guard during the **Franco-Prussian War**, d'Indy was admitted into the organ class at the Paris **Conservatory** in 1872. His composition teacher there, **César**

Franck, fostered an appreciation of **sonata form** as well as the music of **Ludwig van Beethoven** and **Richard Wagner**. In 1876, d'Indy traveled to **Bayreuth** to see the premiere of Wagner's *Ring of the Nibelung*; Wagner's as well as Franck's negative views of French **grand opera** and the supposedly frivolous nature of French 19th-century music in general affected not only d'Indy's own music but also his attempts to reform French musical institutions such as the Conservatory.

In 1885, d'Indy won the **Prix de Rome** in composition for the **cantata** *Le chant de la cloche* (Song of the Bell, **after Friedrich Schiller**). The same year, he became the secretary for the **Société Nationale de Musique**. That position eventually allowed him some political leverage on a national commission formed to reform the Conservatory. Unfortunately, most of his suggestions to develop the music-history curriculum and institute a more varied instructional approach than solely the preparation of musicians and composers for the **opera** were disregarded. Therefore, in 1894, he founded, with Charles Bordes (1863–1909) and Alexandre Guilmant (1837–1911), the Schola Cantorum, assuming the position of full director in 1904.

The Cantorum was initially established as an alternative to the Conservatory by promoting not only religious music, such as Gregorian chant and the study of counterpoint, but also pre-19th-century French music in general (d'Indy himself edited the music of Jean-Philippe Rameau). Many of these changes were informed by d'Indy's increasingly anti-Semitic and anti-republican political activities following the Dreyfus Affair within the nationalistic *Ligue de la Patrie Française*. Eventually, the Cantorum began to be associated with such views. Though not all of his musical works are as overtly polemical as his political activities, some of his works engage the same issues, such as Catholicism and republicanism, as in the musical drama *La légende de Saint-Christophe* (1908–1915). [MMM]

INTENTIONAL FALLACY. Term first coined in literary studies by the literary theorist and critic W. K. Wimsatt (1907–1975) and the philosopher Monroe Beardsley (1915–1985) and subsequently appropriated by musicology as well as other disciplines of art criticism (see W. K. Wimsatt and Monroe Beardsley, "The Intentional Fallacy," *Sewanee Review* 54 [1946]: 468–88; reprint in Wimsatt, *The Verbal Icon: Studies in the Meaning of Poetry* [Lexington: University of Kentucky Press, 1954], 3–18). Although the term is sometimes used to suggest that authorial/compositional intentions cannot be known and are therefore immaterial to the interpretation of artworks, that application is both inconsistent with Wimsatt's and Beardsley's meaning and untenable (as the well-established disciplines of philology and textual criticism demonstrate). Rather, the *intentional fallacy* asserts (1) that authorial and textual intentions often change or fluctuate and therefore cannot be "fixed"; and (2) that those intentions, in all their forms, are immaterial to the *critical worth* of the artwork.

The first of these assertions means that because a given artwork often possesses or reflects no single, stable intention, any attempt to assign such a fixed intent is fallacious. The second means that because authorial intention falls in the province of biography, not aesthetics, the task of the critic is to judge the text or artwork (and, by extension, its variants) as an artwork *without recourse to biography.* After all, since artworks—especially those that are published or presented publicly—address themselves to audiences who have little or no knowledge of the creator's biography, knowledge of that biography cannot be a precondition for understanding or judging the artwork and its meaning. For example, **Ludwig van Beethoven** may well have intended for his *Wellington's Victory* to deploy the expressive intensity of **program music** in order to heighten the experience of communal celebration after the Duke of Wellington's defeat of Josef Bonaparte at the Battle of Vitoria on 21 June 1813, but to invoke that compositional intention in judging the work is to commit the intentional fallacy—for Beethoven's intentions, however lofty or not, do not necessarily guarantee an aesthetically successful or unsuccessful artwork.

In musical discourse, the widespread misuse of the term "intentional fallacy" was a backlash against a number of interrelated issues: the cult of individualism and the concomitant proliferation of examples of the **biographical fallacy**, the coming of age of the discipline of philology with regard to musical source studies pertaining to 19th-century music in the decades following World War II (*see* COMPOSITIONAL PROCESS, CREATIVE PROCESS; EDITING AND EDITIONS; PRINTING AND PUBLISHING OF MUSIC), and the application of sophisticated philological techniques to issues of **performance practice**, resulting in a widespread upsurge in "historically informed" performance practices that rejected anachronistic modern instruments, styles, and techniques in favor of those that were demonstrably consistent with those of historically remote composers.

In the specific realm of Romantic music, the composer who became the flashpoint for these debates was Beethoven, whose compositional processes and biography had been vigorously studied since the late 19th century (especially through the efforts of **Gustav Nottebohm** and Alexander Wheelock Thayer [1817–1891]). The post–World War II proliferation of studies of compositional process, particularly concerning Beethoven's sketches and drafts, reached a critical mass in the years following the bicentennial of Beethoven's birth and eventually led one of the most important scholars of Beethoven's compositional process, Douglas Johnson, to renounce sketch studies, focusing instead on the final products on the grounds that prefinal documents cannot enhance the analyst's understanding of the finished product ("Beethoven Scholars and Beethoven's Sketches," *19th-Century Music* 2 [1978]: 3–17). Johnson has since moderated his position, and numerous other scholars have continued to demonstrate the essential applications of compositional-process research not only for Beethoven's music but also for that of most composers.

The debate continues, however, and it is beyond the charge of this dictionary to try to resolve it. For purposes of this entry, it may be useful to advocate for a compromise based on clarification of terms, distinguishing between *authorial/compositional intention* and *textual intention*. The former certainly is a legitimate candidate for the concerns voiced by Wimsatt and Beardsley. The latter falls under the aegis of philology and textual criticism and clearly refutes what is denoted in the popular misapplication of the term "intentional fallacy"—for in the vast majority of cases, it most certainly *is* possible to determine which version or versions of a musical artwork (or passage therein) a composer did or did not intend to serve as the basis or bases of interpretation. [JMC]

See also FASSUNG LETZTER HAND.

INTERMEZZO (PL. INTERMEZZI). (Fr., entr'acte; Ger., Zwischenspiel.) A short, comparatively lighthearted musical or dramatic performance presented between the acts, scenes, or movements of a larger, more serious instrumental or vocal work, or a musical composition exhibiting these traits; less commonly, a title or subtitle applied to an independent composition. In the music of the Early Romantic Generation, the term is encountered primarily in the context of **incidental music** (e.g., as in the two intermezzi from **Franz Schubert**'s incidental music to *Rosamunde* [D. 797, 1823]) or other staged musical dramas. This application continued later in the 19th century (e.g., in the well-known intermezzo from **Felix Mendelssohn Bartholdy**'s incidental music to **William Shakespeare**'s *A Midsummer Night's Dream* or the "intermezzo sinfonico" from **Pietro Mascagni**'s iconic *verismo* opera *Cavalleria rusticana*).

During the Romantic Generation and afterward, it was increasingly common to substitute movements designated *intermezzo* for the customary **scherzo** in works that employ the **sonata plan** or other collections of instrumental movements: **Johannes Brahms**'s **Piano Quartet** in G Minor (Op. 24, 1861, publ. 1863) and the third movements of his Second and Third symphonies (1877–1878 and 1883–1884, respectively), **Edward Elgar**'s *"Enigma" Variations* (Op. 36, 1898–1899), and **Nikolay Rimsky-Korsakov**'s *Valse, intermezzo, scherzo, nocturne, prelude et fugue (six variations) sur le thème B-A-C-H* (Op. 10, 1878) all contain intermezzi of this sort. The term could also be appropriated for vocal **chamber music** that fulfilled the structural function of the intermezzo, as, for example, in the second song (*Dein Bildnis wunderselig*) of Schumann's *Eichendorff-Liederkreis*, Op. 39 (1840, publ. 1842).

In a further development of the concept, the intermezzo was eventually emancipated from its dependency on context, emerging instead as a kind of **character piece**—a development similar to the Romantic conceit of the autonomous **prelude** or (in the realm of large-ensemble music) **concert overture**. The most important specimens of this autonomous type are Robert Schumann's *Six Intermezzos* (Op. 4, 1832–1833) and Brahms's *Three Intermezzos* (Op. 117, 1892). Others were penned by **Anatoly Arensky** (*Intermezzo* for string **orchestra**, Op. 13, 1882), **Aleksandr Glazunov** (*Intermezzo romantico*, Op. 69, 1900), **Stephen Heller** (*Two Concert Intermezzi*, Op. 135, 1873), **Modest Mussorgsky** (*Intermezzo in modo classico* for orchestra, 1867), and **Max Reger** (*Six Intermezzi* for piano, Op. 45, 1900), among others.

Intermezzo is also the term of **Richard Strauss**'s ninth **opera** (a quasi-autobiographical *bürgerliche Komödie* [bourgeois comedy] on his own **libretto**, TrV 246/Op. 72; comp. 1918–1923, perf. and publ. 1924). Strauss's use of the term alludes to the early-18th century Italian practice of presenting a two-act domestic comedy between the acts of an *opera seria* (the most famous example being Pergolesi's *La serva padrona*). [JMC]

J

DAS JAHR, H-U **385.** (Ger., "The Year.") **Cycle** of 12 thematically inter-connected **virtuosic character pieces**, plus postlude, for **piano** solo by **Fanny Hensel**. Composed in 1841–1842 and lasting nearly an hour, the cycle was conceived as a synesthetic evocation of the cycles of change, transience, liminality, and loss in human existence: Hensel's music was paired with epigrams by **Friedrich Schiller**, Ludwig Uhland (1787–1862), Joseph Freiherr von Eichendorff (1788–1857), Ludwig Tieck (1773–1853), and **Johann Wolfgang von Goethe**, and each of these epigrams was illustrated through a vignette prepared by Hensel's husband, Wilhelm (1794–1861), a painter in the court of the Prussian monarch Friedrich Wilhelm III.

The cycle as a whole exists in two different versions. Both begin with January, announcing the core motive that will connect the various movements, and move progressively through the months of the year to December; both "March" and "December" incorporate seasonally appropriate Lutheran **chorales** (the Easter chorale "Christ ist erstanden" in "March"; "Das alte Jahr vergangen ist" in "December"), as does the concluding Postlude ("Vom Himmel hoch, da komm' ich her"). The cycle is also tightly unified tonally: several movements end in keys that serve as a transition to the following movement, and the cycle of keys for the movements as a whole favors sharp-centered keys, then progresses increasingly to flat-centered keys in the second half, closing in a pure C major.

Despite its length, virtuosity, and aesthetic ambitions, *Das Jahr* was familiar only in private circles during Hensel's lifetime and forgotten thereafter. The autograph for the first version was rediscovered the 1980s and that for the final version in 1993. Since its reemergence, it has generated a significant amount of scholarly commentary. By consensus it now ranks not only as one of Hensel's most important works but also as a worthy compeer to **Robert Schumann**'s *Carnaval* and **Franz Liszt**'s *Anées de pélèrinage*. [JMC]

JANÁČEK, LEOŠ (1854–1928). Czech (Moravian) composer, **conductor**, music educator, organist, teacher, theorist, and writer on music; member of the Modern Romantic Generation. He is best known today for his work in studying the rhythms and inflections of **folk song** and folk music, for devising ways to build on these in cultivated music (arguably the most important such investigations of his generation, succeeded by Bartók in the next generation), and for his development of the concept of *speech melodies*. The last proposes that the rhythms, phrasings, and contours of vocal lines must follow as closely as possible those of speech rather than conforming to intrinsically musical patterns of phrase, period, cadence, and so on.

Janáček originally trained as an organist and music educator and first undertook systematic study of musical composition in 1879–1880. In 1881, he founded the Brno Organ School (later the Brno **Conservatory**) and in 1888 began collecting and studying Moravian folk song with the pioneering ethnomusicologist and folklorist František Bartoš (1837–1906). After his first major **opera**, *Její pastorkyňa: Jenůfa* (Her Stepdaughter Jenůfa), was successfully produced in Brno in 1904, he gave up teaching at the Conservatory, although he remained its director until 1919. Over the next 20 years, he devoted himself almost entirely to writing numerous articles on music and to composition, his style becoming more dissonant and less observant of tonality after about 1918. In 1920, he began giving composition master classes in Brno for the Prague Conservatory, and his already considerable reputation broadened to the anglophone world over the course of the decade: each of his new operas was published by Universal Edition as it was completed, and his 70th birthday (1924) occasioned numerous honors, not least among them his receipt in January 1925 of an honorary PhD from the Masaryk University (Brno). His increasing fame in Germany was reflected in his election, together with Paul Hindemith and Arnold Schoenberg, to the Preußische Akademie der Künste in 1927.

Janáček is best known today for a small portion of his considerable output: the **operas** *Její pastorkyňa: Jenůfa* (Her Stepdaughter Jenůfa, 1904) and *Příhody Lišky Bystroušky* (The Adventures of Vixen Bystroušky, 1924; better known in English as *The Cunning Little Vixen*); his final work, *Z mrtvého domu* (From the House of the Dead, 1928; after Fyodor Dostoyevsky); two **string quartets**; the choral *Glagolitic Mass* (1926); and the *Sinfonietta* (also 1926). In addition to his dozens of short and long writings on contemporary music, folk song, and music theory and his five major editions of Central European folk songs, his surviving output includes 11 operas (counting those named above), 16 liturgical choral works, nine choral/**orchestral** compositions, approximately 45 settings of traditional Moravian texts for ***Männerchor***, one **melodrama**, numerous **songs** and folk song arrangements, 18 orchestral works, and numerous instrumental **chamber** works for **piano** solo, **piano duet**, or small instrumental ensemble. [JMC]

JANISSARY MUSIC. Music composed in emulation of the sounds created either by the band associated with Turkish sovereign's elite personal bodyguard corps or by the musical ensembles (*mehter*) modeled after that band that accompanied Turkish troops into battle during the Ottoman era from the 14th century until 1826 (when the bodyguard was disbanded after rebelling against the sultan's decision to raise a regular force). Often labeled *alla turca*, such music became a major **topic** in Western European music over the course of the period from around 1650 to around 1830. When scoring is used to evoke the style, composers frequently used generally noisy percussion instruments (cymbals and bass drum in unison, with triangle playing more rapid notes), often accompanied by field instruments that are unusual in concerted ensembles—especially piccolo and contrabassoon. Early and mid-19th-century **pianos** often featured a Janissary pedal that would mimic these timbres. The style could also be suggested without those instruments, however. In such instances, composers could draw on simple, repetitive harmonies and melodies that feature repeated notes with downbeats accented by prominent grace notes, square phrases, extensive doubling at the unison or octave, and more. While none of these features by itself necessarily indicated Turkishness, as an aggregate of stylistic traits they were quite effective at doing so for contemporary listeners and performers.

The first important appearances of Janissary music in Western art music are in the **operas** *Le bourgeois gentilhomme* (The Would-Be Gentleman, 1670, by Jean Baptiste Lully and Molière) and *Cara Mustapha* (1686) by the Hamburg composer J. W. Franck (1644–1710). The former was expressly requested by the French monarch Louis XIV after unsuccessful attempts at a diplomatic resolution in the growing conflicts with the Ottomans, and the latter was composed just three years after the Battle of Vienna, which marked the start of the Western European powers' systematic effort to remove the Turkish presence. By the mid-18th century, the musical vocabulary of the "Turkish style" had become sufficiently established to function effectively in **Ludwig van Beethoven**'s *Die Ruinen von Athen* (The Ruins of Athens, 1811) and the last movement of his Ninth **("Choral") Symphony**. Other well-known instances occur in Christoph Willibald Ritter von Gluck's (1714–1787) French **comic opera** *La rencontre imprévue* (The Unexpected Meeting, 1764) and **Franz Joseph Haydn**'s 1775 *L'incontro improvviso* (on the same story) and **Symphony** No. 100 (1793–1794), **Wolfgang Amadeus Mozart**'s **Singspiel** *Die Entführung aus dem Serail* (The Abduction from the Harem, 1782) and Piano **Sonata** in A Major (K. 331, 1778), **Franz Schubert**'s *Suleika II* (1821), and **Carl Maria von Weber**'s *Abu Hassan* (J. 106, 1811). [JMC]

See also EXOTICISM; ORCHESTRATION.

JEAN PAUL. *See* RICHTER, JEAN PAUL (JOHANN PAUL [FRIE-DRICH]) (1763–1825).

JOACHIM, JOSEPH (1831–1907). Austro-Hungarian violinist, composer, **conductor**, and teacher, of Jewish descent; member of the Late Romantic Generation and after **Nicolò Paganini** the most important violin **virtuoso** of the **long 19th century**. After studying at the Vienna **Conservatory** from 1839 to 1843, he relocated to Leipzig to study with **Ferdinand David** and **Felix Mendelssohn Bartholdy**, also taking composition lessons with Moritz Hauptmann (1792–1868). Word of his abilities spread widely, and in 1844 he gave his debut in London, performing **Ludwig van Beethoven**'s Violin **Concerto** there to great acclaim. **Franz Liszt** called him to serve as concertmaster in the Weimar Court **Orchestra** in 1850, but the two artists' temperaments were poorly matched, and in 1853 he accepted the position of concertmaster in the Hanover Court Orchestra, also befriending **Johannes Brahms**. While in Hanover, he converted to Lutheranism, founded his first **string quartet**, and composed prolifically. When the polemics of the **New German School** erupted, he rejected the agendas of Liszt, **Franz Brendel**, and **Richard Wagner** and aligned himself instead with **Robert Schumann** and **Johannes Brahms**.

In 1868, Joachim and his new wife relocated to Berlin, where, with sponsorship of the Königliche Akademie der Künste, he founded a school of instrumental music that from 1872 would be known as the Königliche Hochschule für Musik, the German lands' first Hochschule (academy) dedicated to music. His relationship with Brahms cooled after Brahms decided that Joachim's suspicions of his wife's affair were baseless, but he remained an influential advocate of his friend's music to the end of his life, and their rift was somewhat mended after Brahms wrote his Double **Concerto** for him (Op. 102, 1887). He was the dedicatee of violin concertos by **Max Bruch** and **Antonin Dvořák** as well as Schumann. He served as conductor of the Berlin Philharmonic Orchestra from 1882 to 1887.

Joachim composed a total of 56 works, publishing 14 of these as numbered *opera* during his lifetime and either publishing the others without opus number or leaving them unpublished (*see* WOO). Among these are three violin concertos, of which No. 2 in D minor (Op. 11, 1861, "in ungarischer Weise" [in the Hungarian style]; *see* STYLE HONGROIS) is best known today. He also composed two programmatic **concert overtures** based on works by **William Shakespeare** and two other **overtures**, several other works for violin with orchestra and a **march** for orchestra, a set of *Hebrew Melodies* for viola and piano that are still widely performed (Op. 9, 1855) and several other **chamber** works, one **concert aria** and three **songs**, and arrangements of works by other composers, including **Johann Sebastian Bach**, Beethoven, Brahms, Bruch, Arcangelo Corelli (1653–1713), Mendelssohn, **Wolf-**

gang **Amadeus Mozart**, and **Franz Schubert**. He was more important, however, as a performer. He was known for his sensitive and subtle rubato, his tasteful use of vibrato as an ornament, and his ability to blend superb technical mastery and musicianship with the music in such a fashion that he seemed to subordinate his own personality to that of the composer—a marked difference from many of the long 19th century's great virtuosi. [JMC]

See also AUER, LEOPOLD (1845–1930); BALLADE; FAY, AMY (1844–1928); PARRY, (CHARLES) HUBERT (HASTINGS) (1848–1918); ROMANCE; SMYTH, ETHEL (MARY) (1858–1944).

JOURNAL DES DÉBATS. (Fr., "Journal of Debates.") French newspaper running from 1789 to 1944; by the mid-19th century, one of the most influential venues for music criticism. It was founded shortly after the first meeting of the Estates-General in 1789 and after the outbreak of the Revolution served as a public record of the debates and decrees of the National Assembly. Although conceived as a political organ and published as such throughout its run, it also included reports on cultural life (which was integrally bound up with politics). The journal's most important and prolific music critic was certainly **Hector Berlioz**, who contributed some 936 items to it between 1834 and 1863. (Many of these were subsumed into Berlioz's *Memoirs*, completed in 1865.) Other notable contributors include Charles Baudelaire (1821–1867), **Castil-Blaze**, Alexandre Dumas, *père* (1802–1870), Jules Janin (1804–1874), Adolphe Jullien (1845–1932), **Victor Hugo**, **Franz Liszt**, Joseph d'Ortigue (1802–1866), Ernest Reyer (1823–1909), **Eugène Scribe** (1791–1861), and Stendahl (1783–1842). [JMC]

JULLIEN, LOUIS (ANTOINE) (1812–1860). French **conductor**, composer, and impresario of the Romantic Generation. Among the first of the 19th-century celebrity conductors, Jullien is remembered principally for his showmanship and specialization in light genres. His broad, sometimes lowbrow appeal extended from his lavish style of dress and flamboyant onstage manners—having his baton handed to him on a platter, for example—to his concert programs, which were heavily populated with **virtuoso** instrumental showpieces and popular dances (above all his own **quadrilles**). Jullien's ensembles were typically just as showy and larger than life. Sometimes billed as "monster concerts," Jullien's orchestral performances featured increasingly distinguished rosters of musicians, some of them on new, unusual instruments (e.g., the saxophone) or even non-traditional instruments such as cannon fire. Among the more substantial fare Jullien offered were **opera overtures** and movements from **symphonies**, including those of **Ludwig van Beethoven**.

Born to a bandmaster in the Provençal town Sisteron, Jullien studied at the Paris **Conservatory** in the early to mid-1830s. From 1836 to 1838, he conducted the band at the popular *Jardin Turc* (Turkish Garden) and founded his reputation as a thrilling and mercurial maestro. Fleeing from debt collectors, Jullien traveled to London in 1838, where he spent roughly 20 years as a concert conductor, composer, and producer of **grand opera**. During those years, Jullien toured England regularly and made significant trips abroad, most famously in 1853 to the United States, where he collaborated with P. T. Barnum (1810–1891). This period was also marked by further problems with debt, failed investments, and unprofitable productions of his own **operas**. In 1859, one year before he died, Jullien returned to France profoundly in debt. **Hector Berlioz**, who conducted some of Jullien's Drury Lane opera productions of the late 1840s, wrote about his struggles and failures humorously in his *Les soirées de l'orchestre* (Evenings with the Orchestra, 1852) and more seriously in his *Mémoires* (1865). [RK]

K

KALKBRENNER, FRIEDRICH (WILHELM MICHAEL) (1785–1849).
French composer, pianist, and teacher of German extraction; with **John Field**
and **Johann Nepomuk Hummel**, the leading **virtuoso** pianist of the Early
Romantic Generation. His compositions for **piano** solo include 13 **sonatas**
and a variety of **character pieces**, but he is best known for his many **fantasies**, potpourris, reminiscences, and other virtuosic works based on themes
and motives from others' compositions. He also composed several works for
piano duet (one *Grand Duo* for two pianos Op. 128, 1835, and numerous
four-hand compositions) as well as one **concerto** for two pianos and **orchestra** (Op. 125, 1835) and four piano concertos, plus nine other works for solo
piano and orchestra and numerous instrumental **chamber** works with piano.
He was renowned for the refinement and elegance of his technique and the
clarity of his tone; central to his technique was the idea that all arm movement should be lateral, with maximum independence of the fingers, and he
actually patented a hand guide that ran parallel to the keyboard and assisted
in this pedagogical goal. His eight large-scale didactic *opera* offer vivid
insights into the pianism of one of his generation's most influential virtuoso
pianists. The esteem with which his contemporaries regarded him is attested
to in part by **Fryderyk Chopin**'s dedication of his E-minor piano concerto to
him (*see* PRINTING AND PUBLISHING OF MUSIC).

Kalkbrenner entered the Paris **Conservatory** in 1799 and studied there
until 1801, when he took first prize in the institution's competition in both
harmony and piano. He met Muzio Clementi (1752–1832) and **Franz Joseph
Haydn** and studied with Johann Georg Albrechtsberger (1736–1809) during
a trip to Vienna after graduation, then gave a series of performances in the
German lands (Frankfurt am Main, Munich, and Stuttgart). He returned to
Paris briefly but relocated to London in 1814 and remained there for 10
years, establishing himself as one of Europe's leading pianists and becoming
a partial owner of the **Pleyel** firm, whose pianos he promoted. He returned to
Paris in 1824 and began touring widely (Berlin, Dublin, and Vienna). Until
the emergence of **Franz Liszt** and **Sigismond Thalberg**, his reign as the

supreme piano virtuoso was unchallenged. His health began to decline after about 1835 due to gout and nervous disorders, and he ceased performing publicly after 1839. [JMC]

KASTNER, JEAN-GEORGES (JOHANN GEORG) (1810–1867). Alsatian composer, theorist, and musical commentator. His sizable compositional output includes four **operas**, numerous choral works and vocal **chamber** pieces, a piano **concerto**, three **symphonies**, seven **overtures**, about a dozen **suites** and other compositions for wind band, works for **piano** solo and **piano duet**, instrumental chamber music with strings, and several compositions including the recently invented saxophone. These compositions are obscure today, but they were well regarded in their day. Since he studied on scholarship under **Antoine Reicha** at the Paris **Conservatory**, they naturally reflect the progressive French styles represented also in the works of **Hector Berlioz**, **Charles Gounod**, **Franz Liszt**, and **Georges Onslow**, all of whom also worked closely with Reicha during Kastner's years at the Conservatory.

Kastner's most important contributions are probably his various writings, which in their breadth and encyclopedic ambitions rival those of Michael Praetorius (1571–1621). They include pedagogical methods for cello, cornet, flageolet, flute, horn, oboe, ophicleide, piano, saxophone, trombone, timpani, violin, and voice as well as the most important manual on instrumentation before that of **Hector Berlioz** (Kastner's being written in 1837 and revised in 1844; Berlioz's first being published in 1844). He also penned a number of treatises that offer insights into contemporary views on important but generally neglected elements and themes from contemporary musical life. Most important among these were *Manuel général de musique militaire à l'usage des armées françaises, comprenant l'esquisse d'une histoire de la musique militaire* (General Handbook on Military Music as Used by the Armies of France, Including an Essay on the History of Military Music; 1848), *Les danses des morts: Dissertations et recherches historiques, philosophiques, littéraires et musicales sur les divers monuments de ce genre qui existent ou qui ont existé tant en France qu'à l'étranger, accompagnées de la Danse macabre, grande ronde vocale et instrumentale . . .* (Dances of Death: Historical, Philosophical, Literary, and Musical Essays and Inquiries on Sundry Monuments in This Genre That Exist or Have Existed in France as Well as Abroad, plus a Vocal and Instrumental Rondo Titled *Danse macabre*, 1852), *La Harpe d'Éole et la musique cosmique, études sur les rapports des phénomènes sonores de la nature avec la science et l'art, suivies de Stephen ou la Harpe d'Éole, grand monologue lyrique* (The Aeolian Harp and the Music of the Spheres: Essays on the Relationships between Natural Sonorous Phenomena, Science, and Art; Followed by a Grand Lyric Monologue Titled *Stephen, or the Aeolian Harp*, 1854 [*see TOTENTANZ*]), and others. These historical, philosophical, and theoretical contributions typically included one or more compositions by Kastner, after the model of Reicha's *Traité de haute composition musicale*. [JMC]

KEHRAUS. (Ger., "get out.") In the German lands, term for the last dance at a wedding, party, or feast. During the **long 19th century**, the tune used for this function was the first of the three strains in the so-called *Großvater-Tanz* (Grandfather's Dance) reportedly composed by Karl Gottlieb Hering (1765–1853), a melody known in France as "Grand-père, ou Le cotillion" (Grandfather; or, The Ball). The tune and its connotations—a shooing out from some fairly large event by an older and/or old-fashioned personage in authority—were sufficiently well known for it to serve as an important **topic** for quotation or allusion in Romantic music. The best-known instances of this usage occur in **Robert Schumann**'s *Papillons* (Op. 2, 1830–1831) and *Carnaval* (Op. 9, 1834–1835, publ. 1837) and in **Pyotor Il'yich Tchaikovsky**'s **ballet** *The Nutcracker* (Op. 71, 1891–1892); it also occurs in **Louis Spohr**'s *Festmarsch* (WoO 3, 1825). Literary references include Tolstoy's *War and Peace* (1892). [JMC]

KINDERTOTENLIEDER. (Ger., "Songs on the Death of Children.") Iconic **song cycle** for voice with accompaniment of **piano** or **orchestra**, composed in 1901–1904 by **Gustav Mahler** on texts of Friedrich Rückert (1788–1866), an orientalist and scholar of Classical, African, and Asiatic languages. The collection of texts by Rückert from which Mahler selected the ones he set in his song cycle was neither composed as poetry nor intended for publication. Rather, it was a private poetic grief diary comprising a total of 425 poems, compiled over the course of some 34 years, from 1833 to 1866. Some of the texts were written following the deaths of two of Rückert's youngest children in 1833, and more were added to those over the remaining years of his life. Rückert never reviewed, revised, or ordered them, and they were first published posthumously under the title *Kindertodtenlieder* in 1872. A second edition was published in 1881 with the new title *Leid und Lied: Ist die neue Ausgabe der 1872 zum ersten Mal veröffentlichten "Kindertodtenlieder"* (Sorrow and Song; i.e., The New Edition of the *Kindertotenlieder* First Published in 1872). In both editions, the poems were arbitrarily ordered by the editor.

Mahler set three of Rückert's texts (Nos. 374, 57, and 304 of the first edition) to music with orchestral accompaniment in the summer of 1901 and two more (Nos. 70 and 342) in the summer of 1904, then arranged these settings in the order 374–70–57–306–342 to create his own poetic and musical cycle. He conducted the premiere on 29 January 1905, and the works were published in full score, parts, and piano/vocal arrangement that same year (*see* PRINTING AND PUBLISHING OF MUSIC). Mahler emphasized the indivisibility of the cycle in a note on the first page of the full score: "Diese 5 Gesänge sind als ein einheitliches, untrennbares Ganzes gedacht und es muß daher die Continuität derselben (auch durch Hintanhaltung von Störungen wie z.B. Beifallsbezeugung am Ende einer 'Nummer') festgehalten werden" ("These five *Gesänge* are conceived as a unified, indivisible whole, and the continuity of the whole must therefore be preserved [also by delaying any disruptions such as applause between the 'numbers']").

In creating his music-poetic cycle of songs on the death of children Mahler did more than generate a new, indivisible, and—perhaps most importantly— public artistic whole out of a set of private diary ruminations. He also replaced the originally Christian philosophical orientation of Rückert's texts with eschatological perspectives that are more ambivalent, applicable to other religions as well as Christianity, and created a **narrative** cycle with a coherent philosophical message and a definite end that went beyond anything the poet envisioned. In so doing, he himself, arguably more than Rückert, became the de facto author of the poems. His aggressiveness of this assertion of authorial identity is evident partly in the numerous repetitions of significant words in the text, partly through changes in the words, partly through musical recasting of the form of some of the poems, and partly through a distinctive and clearly symbolic approach to the **orchestration** of the version for voice and orchestra.

In the popular and scholarly literature on Mahler, the *Kindertotenlieder* (begun in 1901 and completed in 1904) are often interpreted autobiographically as reflections on the death of either Mahler's brother Ernst or that of his daughter Maria. However poetically attractive such tales may be, they are also untenable: Mahler's brother had died 27 years earlier and his daughter had just been born when Mahler began work on his cycle, was in good health when he completed it, and died only in 1907, fully three years after the cycle's completion. More plausible would be to assert that Mahler, who (like many other Romantics) was fascinated to the point of obsession with the irrevocable and universal phenomenon of death, chose to set these texts partly out of personal experience but also as means of societal communication through song. Since mortality rates for children five and under in early 20th-century Western Europe apparently hovered between 23 and 27 percent, Mahler's contemporary audiences would have found in the *Kindertotenlieder* a poignant and all-too-rare opportunity to commune in sorrow and song (as the title of the second edition of Rückert's texts indicates) on a subject that had directly or indirectly touched a great many lives from among their midst. [JMC]

See also BIOGRAPHICAL FALLACY; INTENTIONAL FALLACY.

DES KNABEN WUNDERHORN. (Ger., "The Boy's Miraculous Posthorn.") A collection of the texts of more than 700 German **songs**, collected and published by archaeologist Achim von Arnim (1781–1831) and poet Clemens Brentano (1778–1842) (Heidelberg: Mohr und Zimmer, 1805–1808). Like other 18th- and 19th-century "transcriptions" of folk materials (most importantly, those of Jacob and Wilhelm Grimm, Joseph Görres, and Thomas Percy), the *Wunderhorn* texts were freely reworked; subsequent research has revealed that some were lyric poetry by minor poets rather than actual **folk songs**. Despite their shaky philological foundations, however, as a vast corpus of previously obscure high-quality texts written in German, the *Wunderhorn* poems quickly came to represent a historically based literary source of patriotic fervor and artistic inspiration for millions of German speakers who were troubled by the German lands' deep political fragmentation. They provided a cultural rallying point for German **nationalism** as it gained strength over the course of the mid-19th century.

These strong cultural and political associations attracted some of Romanticism's most important composers and hosts of minor ones. Apparently, the first published settings were Friedrich Heinrich Himmel's (1765–1814) *Zwölf alte deutsche Lieder des Knaben Wunderhorn mit Begleitung des Pianoforte (oder der Guitarre)* (12 Old German Songs from *Des Knaben* Wunderhorn, with Accompaniment of Piano [or Guitar], Op. 27, 1808) and Luise Reichardt's (1779–1836) *Frühlingsblume* ("Herzlich tut mich erfreuen," 1809). Individual texts were later set by **Johannes Brahms** (1852–1853, 1868, 1887), Ignaz Brüll (1846–1907; 1898), August Bungert (1845–1915; 1884), August Conradi (1821–1873; 1871), **Friedrich Fesca** (ca. 1824), Heinrich von Herzogenberg (1843–1900; 1889), Salomon Jadassohn (1831–1902; 1887), **Adolf Jensen** (1864, 1875), **Felix Mendelssohn Bartholdy** (1828, 1834), **Joachim Raff** (1864), **Carl Reinecke** (1884), **Robert Schumann** (1840, 1848, 1849, 1851, 1852), Christian Sinding (1856–1941; 1890), **Richard Strauss** (1896), Wilhelm Taubert (1811–1891; 1840, 1843, 1845, 1870), Otto Tiehsen (1817–1849; 1845), and **Carl Maria von Weber** (1818). By far the most influential settings are those of **Gustav Mahler**, who set a total of 24 of the *Wunderhorn* texts for solo voice with piano and solo voice with **orchestra** between 1887 and 1898. Mahler also quoted from those settings in other contemporaneous works (most importantly his Second, Third, and Fourth **Symphonies**). [JMC]

See also NATIONALISM, ROMANTIC NATIONALISM; OSSIAN.

KNABENCHOR. *See* BOYS' CHOIR.

KÖHLER, CHRISTIAN (LOUIS HEINRICH) (1820–1886). German piano pedagogue, composer, and critic of the Late Romantic Generation, affiliated with the **New German School.** A young pianist from Braunschweig, he
traveled to Vienna to study with pianist Carl Maria von Bocklet
(1801–1881); while there, he also studied with conductor Ignaz von Seyfried
(1776–1841) and music theorist **Simon Sechter.** In 1845, Köhler moved to
the East Prussian city of Königsberg (now Kaliningrad, Lithuania), where he
began in earnest his career in music journalism; he had begun submitting
correspondence to the Leipzig *Signale für die musikalische Welt* in 1844 and
later to the *Neue Zeitschrift für Musik*, and in 1849 he began his lifelong
role as music critic for Königsberg's *Hartungsche Zeitung* (a job he kept for
the rest of his life).

While Köhler spent much of his time in Königsberg teaching piano and
writing exercises, techniques, and graded **etudes**, his music criticism helped
bring him into contact with figures later associated with the New German
School, starting with his submissions to the *Neue Zeitschrift für Musik*
(edited by **Franz Brendel).** The publication of his book *Die Melodie der
Sprache in ihrer Anwendung besonders auf das Lied und die Oper* (The
Melody of Speech as Applied Specifically to Song and Opera, 1853) put him
in touch with **Franz Liszt** and **Richard Wagner,** both of whom corresponded with him about his ideas on poetically sensitive, expressive text
setting. Köhler was among those who attended the 1859 *Tonkünstler-Versammlung* (Conference of German Musicians) and helped establish the *Allgemeiner Deutscher Musikverein.* His creative interest in musical theater is
also evinced by the **ballet, incidental music,** and three **operas** he composed.
[RK]

KONZERTSTÜCK. German term for a composition featuring one or more
soloists and accompaniment (usually **orchestra** but also **piano**); usually in
one movement or three continuous movements. The term is usually translated as *pièce de concert* in French and "concert piece" in English, but "concertino" or the less elegant "**concerto** piece" would be more accurate since these
denote the *Konzertstück*'s essential feature of creating a concerto-like dialogue between soloist(s) and accompaniment within a composition whose
length and structural complexity are usually less imposing than those of the
concerto proper. Such works grew out of the 18th-century tradition of *concertante* **symphonies** that featured two or more soloists within the framework of an orchestral work that lacked the comparatively strict thematic and
tonal structures of concertos.

The term *Konzertstück* apparently originated around the turn of the 19th
century, as indicated by works bearing that title published by J. E. Brandl
(1760–1837) and others. The same period witnessed a proliferation of *con-
certinos* (such as **Carl Maria von Weber**'s E-minor Concertino for Horn

and Orchestra, J. 188/Op. 45, 1806, rev. 1815, publ. 1816). **Franz Schubert** composed a D-minor "Concertstück" for Violin and Orchestra in 1816 (D. 345), but this remained unpublished until 1897 and was therefore external to the mainstream series of *Konzertstücke* that emerged earlier in the century. The first major published composition designated using the German term is Weber's *Konzertstück* in F Minor for Piano and Orchestra (J. 282/Op. 79, comp. 1821, publ. 1823). Important later works so designated were written by **Franz Berwald** (Op. 2, 1827), **Felix Mendelssohn Bartholdy** (MWV Q23 and Q24/opp. posth.113 and 114, 1832–1833), **Franz Liszt** (LW C31, 1834), **Robert Schumann** (Op. 86, 1849/1851; Op. 92, 1849/1852), **Ferruccio Busoni** (K 240/Op. 31a, 1890), **Cécile Chaminade** (Op. 40, ca. 1893), and **Max Bruch** (Op. 84, 1911). [JMC]

KREUTZER, CONRADIN (1780–1849). German composer and **conductor** of the Early Romantic Generation. He served as Kapellmeister in Stuttgart (1812–1816), Donaueschingen (1818–1822), and Cologne (1840–1842) and was conductor of Vienna's Kärtnertor Theater from 1822 to 1833 and 1835 to 1840 as well as of the Josephsstadt Theater from 1833 to 1840. He also directed the Lower Rhine Music Festival in 1841, a highly visible appointment. As a composer, he was best known for his 41 serious and **comic operas** (most of them German) and *Singspiele*, but he also composed two sets of **incidental music** and two **ballets**, and his 1820 setting of scenes from **Johann Wolfgang von Goethe**'s *Faust* is an important early compositional engagement with that seminal work of German culture. He also composed three piano **concertos** and other works for **orchestra** with or without soloist as well as a great deal of instrumental **chamber music**, two **oratorios**, much music for chorus a cappella and with accompaniment, more than 150 solo *Gesänge* and **Lieder**, and **part-songs**. His best-known work is the **opera** *Das Nachtlager in Granada* (The Boot Camp in Granada, 1834). Conradin Kreutzer is no relation to the violinist **Rudolfe Kreutzer**, to whom Beethoven dedicated his A-major Violin Sonata (Op. 47). [JMC]

KREUTZER, RUDOLFE (1766–1831). French **virtuoso** violinist, composer, **conductor**, and pedagogue of the Early Romantic Generation; with **Pierre Baillot** and **Pierre Rode**, the most influential exponent of the Franco-Belgian school of violin playing in the early 19th century. After studying with Anton Stamitz (from 1750 to between 1796 and 1809) in Mannheim, he made his debut at the **concerts spirituels** in 1780 and was received there as a **prodigy** (a generous use of the term). He was taken under the patronage of Marie Antoinette, joining the Royal Court **Orchestra** in 1785 and relocating permanently to Paris in 1789. During the 1790s, he wrote **operas** for the Opéra-Comique and in 1795 was appointed to the faculty of the newly founded **Conservatory**. There, he continued to teach until 1826.

Meanwhile, word of Kreutzer's talents as a supremely capable violinist possessed of a fine tone and elegant touch continued to spread, thanks in part to a tour of the Italian lands. He succeeded Rode as solo violinist of the Paris Opéra in 1801, also joining the imperial chapel orchestra in 1802 and Napoléon Bonaparte's private orchestra in 1803. In 1804, he met **Beethoven**, whose A-major Violin **Sonata** (Op. 47, "Kreutzer," 1802–1803) was composed before their introduction but whose dedication to Kreutzer with its publication in 1805 reflected the Viennese composer's esteem for his French acquaintance's standing and style (*see* PRINTING AND PUBLISHING OF MUSIC). Kreutzer's career as a soloist was cut short when he broke his arm in a carriage accident in 1810, but he continued to play in ensembles until 1815, when he was named conductor of the Royal Chapel. Thereafter, he worked primarily as a composer and conductor, serving as general music director of the Opéra from 1824 to 1826, when he retired from most of his public positions due to declining health.

Kreutzer was a prolific and talented composer, penning a total of 43 serious and **comic operas** and opéras-**ballets**, one set of **incidental music**, six ballets and ballets-pantomimes, 19 violin **concertos**, four *sinfonies concertantes*, one clarinet (or oboe) **quintet**, 17 **string quartets**, five string **trios**, 16 duos, 13 violin **sonatas**, and a total of 60 *études ou caprices* (*see* CAPRICCIO) for solo violin. The first 42 of the last named (1796, first publ. 1807) were pedagogical in nature, and he was well known for his *Méthode de violon* (Violin Method, 1803), co-authored with Baillot and Rode and published in 1803. His brother Jean Nicholas Auguste (1778–1832) and his nephew Léon Charles François (1817–1868) were also able composers, although they did not achieve Rudolfe's distinction. The three were no relation to **Conradin Kreutzer**. [JMC]

See also PERFORMANCE PRACTICE.

KUHLAU, (DANIEL) FRIEDRICH (RUDOLPH) (1786–1832). German-born Danish composer and pianist of the Early Romantic Generation, best known today for his piano compositions and his chamber music with flute. The son of a military bandsman, he studied **piano**, organ, and composition as a youth and by 1804 had earned a reputation in Hamburg as a pianist, but in 1810 he was forced to flee to Copenhagen in order to avoid conscription into Napoléon Bonaparte's army. There, too, he rapidly gained fame, being named a court Kammermusikus (chamber musician) by 1813, rising to the rank of court composer by 1818. In 1828, after the considerable success of his **incidental music** to nationalist playwright Johan Ludvig Heiberg's (1791–1860) play *Elverhøj* (Elves' Hill), he was named professor to the

Faculty of Royal Danish Court Composers. He also toured successfully as a pianist and composer in Austria, the German lands, and Scandinavia throughout the 1820s.

Much of Kuhlau's output was destroyed when his home burned to the ground in 1830. His most important vocal works are his five **operas** and *Singspiele* (one a fictional biography of **William Shakespeare**) and three sets of incidental music, but he also composed a number of **songs** with Italian and German texts, several **part-songs**, and a few secular choral compositions. His output for piano solo includes some 20 **sonatas**, plus sonatinas, **variation** sets, rondos, and **fantasies** as well as many works for **piano duet**. His other instrumental works include a piano **concerto** and a concerto for two horns and **orchestra**, one **string quartet** (Op. 122, publ. posth. 1841), two **piano quartets**, and two violin sonatas, plus three **quintets** for flute with strings (Op. 51, 1823) and a great deal of other **chamber music** for solo flute with or without accompaniment. [JMC]

L

LACHNER. German family of musicians, all sons of Anton Lachner (1756–1820), an organist and watchmaker in the village of Rain am Lech in Upper Bavaria. Of the four sons, the composer, **conductor**, organist, and pianist Franz (Paul) (1803–1890) was the most prominent and is best remembered today, followed by the composer and conductor Ignaz (1807–1895) and then by their older stepbrother, the organist and composer Theodor (1788–1877), and the youngest brother, the conductor and teacher Vinzenz (1811–1893).

All three Lachner sons received early training in **piano**, organ, and composition from their father. Franz left in 1822 for Munich, where he earned a meager living as a music teacher, organist, and instrumentalist (horn, violin, cello, and bass) in a municipal **orchestra**. He relocated in 1823 to Vienna, where he soon befriended **Franz Schubert** and studied composition and music theory with Abbé Maximilian Stadler (1748–1833) and **Simon Sechter.** All the brothers were Catholic, but Franz was able to procure a position as organist at a Lutheran church, also serving as a violinist in the orchestra of the Kärntnertor Theater. He brought Ignaz to Vienna to join him in 1824, continuing his younger brother's instruction in organ and music theory and arranging for him to join the orchestra. Franz quickly rose to prominence in Viennese musical life, becoming vice-Kapellmeister of the orchestra in 1827 and being promoted to Kapellmeister in 1829, whereupon Ignaz succeeded Franz as vice-Kapellmeister.

Meanwhile, in 1828, Franz had also arranged for their stepbrother, Theodor, to succeed him as organist as the Lutheran church where he had been employed since 1823; this post Theodor retained until his death, also earning a reputation as a composer of *Gesänge*, **Lieder**, and **part-songs**. Franz and Ignaz, too, enjoyed growing reputations, and in 1831 Ignaz left the Austrian capital to assume the position of court music director in Stuttgart. He was succeeded as vice-Kapellmeister by the youngest brother, Vinzenz, who had recently moved to Vienna after working as a private music teacher in Poland for several years.

By the early 1830s, the brothers' lives had converged closely, and all were rising stars in the musical world of the **Restoration**—but they now began to pursue separate paths. Theodor remained in Vienna, but Franz left the city in 1834 to become Kapellmeister of the renowned Court Orchestra in Mannheim and then moved again in 1836 to Munich, where he served for nearly 30 years as director of the Court **Opera**, leader of a concert series, and choirmaster in the Royal Chapel until **Richard Wagner**'s arrival in 1864 forced his de facto demotion, an event that spawned much bitterness. Vinzenz, however, succeeded Franz as Kapellmeister in Mannheim, remaining there for the next 37 years, with occasional travels for performances of his music in cities as far afield as London. Ignaz joined Franz in Munich in 1842 and served as vice-Kapellmeister in Franz's orchestra until 1853, but that same year the two brothers again parted ways when Ignaz became Kapellmeister of the Municipal Theater in Hamburg. The geographic distance between them increased when Ignaz was called to Stockholm to serve as Kapellmeister there. Ignaz returned to Germany in 1861 to become the conductor of the Municipal Theater in Frankfurt am Main, a post he held until his retirement in 1875. Vinzenz relocated to Karlsruhe in 1872 and taught music at the **Conservatory** there until his retirement in 1884.

All the Lachner brothers composed **songs**, and all except Ignaz composed for the solo organ. Ignaz's output includes four **operas** (the most important of which is the one-act **Singspiel** *Alpenszenen* [Scenes from the Alps, 1850], which draws extensively on Bavarian **folk song**). He also composed a set of Vespers for chorus and organ, several songs and works for piano solo, one violin **sonata**, three sonatinas for string **trio**, six **piano trios**, and seven **string quartets**, these last reflecting his intimate knowledge of stringed instruments. Franz, for his part, composed a total of four operas and two sets of **incidental music**, plus a **Requiem** and eight other Mass settings, a **Stabat mater**, one **cantata**, one **oratorio**, and numerous smaller sacred works. His secular oeuvre includes many songs and part-songs, eight **symphonies**, seven **suites**, two harp **concertos**, much instrumental **chamber music** for ensembles ranging from two to nine players, and numerous works for piano solo, **piano duet**, organ, and harp (three *Lieder ohne Worte*, 1856). Franz also received the prestigious Bayerischer Maximilians-Orden für Wissenschaft und Kunst (Bavarian Maximilian Order in Science and Art) in 1853 and an honorary doctorate from the University of Munich (1862). In 1883 he became an honorary citizen of Munich. [JMC]

LALO, ÉDOUARD (VICTOIRE ANTOINE) (1823–1892). French composer of the Late Romantic Generation. His musical education in cello and violin began at the Lille **Conservatory**. He later studied violin with **Françoise-Antoine Habeneck** at the Paris Conservatory and pursued private composition studies with Julius Schulhoff (1822–1898).

As a performer and a composer, Lalo directly participated in the revival of **chamber music** in France during the mid-19th century. As **Hector Berlioz** had aimed to introduce the works of **Ludwig van Beethoven** to the Parisian public in the first half of the century, Lalo, as a founding member of the Armingaud Quartet (1855), attempted to do the same for Austro-German chamber music. The Armingaud Quartet performed the works not only of Beethoven but also of other composers, such as **Franz Joseph Haydn, Felix Mendelssohn Bartholdy, Wolfgang Amadeus Mozart,** and **Robert Schumann**. Additionally, Lalo composed two string **trios** (both 1853) and a **string quartet** (Op. 19, 1859, rev. 1880).

Lalo continued to compose instrumental works as well as **songs** and stage works, but he did not always receive performance opportunities for his stage works. For example, Lalo's **grand opera**, *Fiesque*, based on **Friedrich Schiller**'s play *Fiesco*, was never performed. Another stage work, *Le roi d'Y*, remained unperformed until 1888. Lalo's instrumental works, however, received performances more often, especially with the formation of the **Société Nationale de Musique** in 1870. Some such works include the *Symphonie espagnole* (1875), the D-minor Cello **Concerto** (1877), and the *Concerto russe* for violin (1879). [MMM]

LÄNDLER. (Ger.) Austrian country dance, usually slow and in 3/4 or 3/8 time, in which couples or groups spin or hop and clap; also the music to this dance. The dance itself predates the term, and there are significant regional variations, but during the years before the popularizing of the **waltz, mazurka,** and polka, the Ländler was the best known and most easily recognizable vernacular dances that were appropriated, in stylized form, in cultivated music. **Ludwig van Beethoven, Wolfgang Amadeus Mozart,** and **Franz Schubert** were among the early composers to write *Ländler*. **Franz Joseph Haydn** used one in the Minuet of his **Symphony** No. 97 (1792), and his **oratorio** *Die Jahreszeiten* (The Seasons, Hob. XXI: 3, 1799–1801), and **Anton Bruckner** and **Gustav Mahler** drew on the style evocatively in individual movements of their symphonies. As a whole, the style is a potent **topic** for suggesting *Volkstümlichkeit*. [JMC]

LE SUEUR [LESUEUR], JEAN-FRANÇOIS (1760–1837). French composer and writer on music of the Early Romantic Generation. His training was in church music, and most of his musical successes lay in that domain and that of **opera**. He was appointed choirmaster of the Cathedral of Notre Dame in 1786, but the large **orchestras** and operatic singing he introduced there led to his dismissal in 1788 on charges of inappropriate theatricality. (It was also a time of budgetary crisis for France generally, and under such circumstances, the financial burdens generated by such large performing forces were difficult to justify.)

Le Sueur composed 10 hymns, odes, and other large-scale choral/orchestral works for the Festivals of the Revolution and established himself as an operatic composer during the Revolutionary and Napoleonic Wars with works such as *La Caverne, ou Le Repentir* (The Cavern; or, Repentance, 1793) and the **rescue opera** *Paul et Virginie* (1794). Among his Revolutionary works, the *Chant du Ier vendémiaire an IX* (Song of the Year 9, Vendemiaire 1), scored for four spatially dispersed orchestras and choruses, is particularly notable. He was also first inspector of the newly formed Paris **Conservatory** and taught solfège there until 1802, when his publication of a pamphlet sharply criticizing the institution and its methods led to his dismissal. Deprived of his income, he fell into poverty but was rescued in 1804 when Napoléon Bonaparte named him as choirmaster at the Tuilleries, succeeding Giovanni Paisiello (1740–1816). His fame was renewed with the immensely successful opera *Ossian, ou les bardes* (1804), and he remained one of the most popular and esteemed composers in France through the remainder of the Napoleonic era and into the **Bourbon Restoration**. He succeeded André Grétry (1741–1813) at the Académie des Beaux-Arts in 1813 and served as professor of composition at the Paris Conservatory from 1818 until his death.

In addition to his seven operas, Le Sueur penned a large number of extravagant sacred works (Masses, **motets**, and **oratorios**) plus numerous smaller ones and with **Luigi Cherubini** was considered France's leading composer of sacred music during the first half of the 19th century. He also was a prolific writer on music, taking particular interest (as his Revolutionary works suggest) in music's ability to enhance the spiritual effectiveness of civic and other celebrations (this was the focus of some of his research on music in ancient Greece). His enormous *Histoire de la musique* (History of Music), announced for publication in 1810 but never released, is now lost, but his four-volume *Exposé d'une musique imitative et particulière à chaque solemnité* (Exposé concerning Music Fitted and Particular to Every Solemnity, 1787) provides much information about his aesthetic outlook and understanding of music's place in society. His many distinguished pupils include **Charles Gounod** and **Ambroise Thomas**, but the one most obviously influenced by Le Sueur's lofty ideals and expansive views on musical expression was **Hector Berlioz**. [JMC]

LEHÁR, FRANZ CHRISTIAN (1870–1948). Austro-Hungarian composer and bandmaster of the Modern Romantic Generation, best known for his **operetta** *Die lustige Witwe* (The Merry Widow, 1905) and associated broadly with the genre. This early 20th-century hit, along with Leo Fall's *Die Dollarprinzessin* (The Dollar Princess, 1907), Emmerich Kálmán's

Tatárjárás (The Gay Hussars, 1908) and Oscar Straus's *Der tapfere Soldat* (The Chocolate Soldier, 1908), ushered in a new golden age of operettas stretching into the 1930s, in effect one of the few bastions of the Modern Romantic Generation.

Lehár was born in Komárom, Hungary (now Komárno, Slovakia), to a German Moravian military bandmaster-composer and Hungarian mother. At age 10, Lehár moved to Sternberg (now Šternberk, Czech Republic) to study music with his uncle in a German-speaking environment. Two years later, Lehár started at the Prague **Conservatory**; while in Prague, he also met and studied with **Zdeněk Fibich**. Lehár's military service began in 1888 when he joined his father's band of the 50th Austrian infantry regiment. Lehár became a bandmaster himself in 1890 and continued into 1902; in those years, he led military bands in Budapest, Losoncz, Pola, Trieste, and Vienna.

As a composer, Lehár finally achieved his first major successes in Vienna; these include his famous **waltz** *Gold und Silber* (Gold and Silver, 1902) and *Die lustige Witwe* in 1905. Lehár composed some 20 additional operettas in the ensuing quarter of a century, most successful among them being *Der Graf von Luxemburg* (The Count of Luxemburg, 1909), *Zigeunerliebe* (Gypsy Love, 1910), and *Das Land des Lächelns* (The Land of Smiles, 1929). As the film industry boomed in the wake of World War I, Lehár reworked his operettas as films. *Die lustige Witwe*, for example, was reborn twice as a silent film: first in 1918 under the direction of Manó Kaminer Kertész (who later directed such hits as *Casablanca* as Michael Curtiz) and then in 1925 by MGM's Erich von Stroheim; MGM produced a talkie version in 1935. Lehár also composed five original film soundtracks during those years. In 1935, Lehár established the publishing house Glocken-Verlag, with which he regained the rights to most of his earlier compositions. Under the Nazi regime, Lehár's music was celebrated by Hitler and other party leaders despite the contributions to his operettas by Jewish librettists (such as *Die lustige Witwe* collaborators Viktor Léon and Leo Stein). Also Jewish was Lehár's wife Sophie, whom the Nazis designated an "honorary Aryan" (*Ehrenarierin*) in 1938. Lehár's wife died in 1947; he followed a year later. [RK]

LEITFADEN. *See* LEITMOTIV.

LEITMOTIV. (Ger., "leading motive.") Term generally used to describe the network of dramatically or textually allusive musical **motives** characteristic of the **music dramas** of **Richard Wagner**. Wagner appears to have regarded the term itself skeptically, at least as it was employed by Hans von Wolzogen (1848–1938) in his thematic guide to the *Ring of the Nibelung* (publ. 1876). He did, however, use it himself in his 1879 essay *Über die Andwendung der Musik auf das Drama* (On the Application of Music to Drama), there giving the impression that his concern with Wolzogen's "thematic guide" resulted not from the term *Leitmotiv* itself but from the guide's simplistic treatment of a self-consciously sophisticated and multivalent concept. Wagner's own lexicon of apparently synonymous terms includes *melodisches Moment* (melodic turning point), *thematisches Motiv* (thematic motive), *Ahnungsmotiv* (conceptual motive), *Grundthema* (fundamental theme), *Hauptmotiv* (principal motive), *Leitfaden* (leading thread), or simply *Motiv* (motive).

Common to all these terms is the notion of a melodic and/or harmonic gesture that can be used in noncontiguous situations in order to serve two main functions: to increase the work's musical and dramatic unity and to enable performers and listeners to comprehend more readily the **narrative** or otherwise extramusical aspects or implications of any given moment in the work. This structural and perceptual duality of function is most obvious in Wagner's characterization of the *melodische Momente* of the projected *Ring* cycle as "to some extent . . . emotional guideposts through the complete labyrinthine structure of the drama." In 19th-century German parlance, *Gefühlswegweiser*—the term that here is best understood as "emotional guideposts"—was commonly used to denote "expressive indications," such as *agitato, con fuoco*, and so on.

The term *Leitmotiv* was not Wagner's invention. It was apparently first used in print in 1860 in an essay by **August Wilhelm Ambros** on the contemporary polemic surrounding the music of the future (*see ARTWORK OF THE FUTURE*). Although Ambros applied it equally to the **symphonic poems** of **Franz Liszt** and to Wagner's **operas** up to that point—stating that the former are "Wagnerian Operas without Words" and the latter are "symphonic poems with sung text"—it became more specifically applied to stage music in **Eduard Hanslick**'s 1868 review of *Die Meistersinger*. F. W. Jähns (1809–1888), in an 1871 discussion of **Carl Maria von Weber**'s *Abu Hassan* (J. 106, 1811), *Der Freischütz*, J. 277 (1821), *Oberon*, J. 306 (1826), and the unfinished *Die drei Pintos* (1820–1821), also used the term, and it appears in Gottlieb Federlein's (1835–1922) analyses of *Das Rheingold* and *Die Walküre* (1871–1872). As these applications suggest, the term has a long conceptual history tracing back not only to Weber's operas (which Wagner knew well) but also to the reminiscence motives of early Romantic Italian opera, the **thematic transformation** of the orchestral music of **Felix Mendelssohn Bartholdy** and **Robert Schumann**, and the **idée fixe** of **Hector Berlioz**. Contemporary remarks on the Wagnerian version frequently refer to it as *Leitfaden* (leading thread), thus associating the technique with classical mythology via the thread that Ariadne provided Theseus so that he could escape from the labyrinth containing the minotaur of Crete. As a compositional technique, however, Leitmotiv is more successful than these other concepts in facilitating large-scale musical forms that rely on traditional structural schemas little or not at all since Leitmotivs can overlap or sound simultaneously; cross-refer to other points in the music, text, or dramatic elements; and develop symphonically.

The most vexing aspect of Leitmotiv in its Wagnerian incarnation is perhaps precisely what rendered it appealing and flexible to Wagner's contemporaries and later composers: its multivalence. In addition to addressing the ever more pressing need to discover alternatives to traditional forms and tonal paradigms in the late 19th century, it satisfied contemporary composers' interest in creating expansive, organically unified **narrative** forms—yet as semiotic devices, individual Leitmotivs operate at several levels simultaneously. Thus, the motive associated with the ring and with the wealth of the world at the end of Act I, scene 1, in *Das Rheingold* becomes the Valhalla motive at the beginning of scene 2, establishing a connection between the two located in the power they both possess. The labels employed by "thematic guides" such as Wolzogen's were incapable of conveying this semantic and semiotic malleability.

As a key element in the **Gesamtkunstwerk** and a concept that is applicable to instrumental as well as vocal music, Leitmotiv proved to be one of the most influential aspects of Wagner's rethinking of dramaturgy, staged musical drama, and musical narrativity in general. It strongly influenced the music of the **songs** of **Hugo Wolf**, the songs and **symphonies** of **Mahler**, and the **tone poems** and music dramas of **Richard Strauss** as well as the music of other composers ranging from **Modest Mussorgsky, Giacomo Puccini**, and **Giuseppe Verdi** to Alban Berg, **Claude Debussy**, and Arnold Schoenberg. Leitmotiv has been a standard feature of film music ever since George Steiner employed it in his celebrated score to *King Kong* (1933). [JMC]

LEONCAVALLO, RUGGERO (1857–1919). Italian composer and **librettist** of the Modern Romantic Generation; with **Pietro Mascagni** and (arguably) **Giacomo Puccini**, one of the most important representatives of the *verismo* movement in music. He became enamored with Wagnerian **music drama** while studying at the Naples **Conservatory** and set out to compose an operatic trilogy centered on the Italian Renaissance, but when the influential music publisher **Ricordi** rejected the first work in that **cycle** (*I Medici*[The Medicis, 1892]), he turned instead to *verismo*, producing the work for which he is best known today, *I Pagliacci* (The Clowns, 1893). The opera was an immediate success and established Leoncavallo's position in his generation; his opera based on Henry Murger's *Scènes de la vie de bohème* was able to compete with Puccini's *La bohème* for a time. His works were successful in Germany, but the Italian public wearied of his *verismo* style, and around 1912 he began to turn from *verismo* to **operetta**. He also composed one **ballet**, one **symphonic poem**, one **Requiem** and several other works for chorus and **orchestra**, 20 works for **piano** solo, and a number of **songs** on English, French, and Italian texts. [JMC]

See also OPERA.

LEVY, ALEXANDRE (1864–1892). Brazilian composer of French descent; important early figure in Brazilian musical **nationalism** because of his successful integration of contemporary Brazilian popular idioms (chiefly dance styles) into the genres and instrumentations of cultivated music. He was born into a family of musicians, trained by European immigrants, and was a founder of the **Franz Joseph Haydn** Club of São Paolo (1883). After spending the summer of 1887 in Milan and Paris, he returned to Brazil energized, attempting (unsuccessfully) to start an **orchestra** and writing music criticism. He took over his parents' music store and, along with his brother, ran it for the remainder of his short life, also composing works for **piano** and for **orchestra**. A number of his compositions self-consciously cultivate the traditions of the European **canon** (e.g., the **suite** *Schumanniana*, Op. 16, 1891), while others draw on its ideas but are less overt in their obeisance to its ideologies (most notably the four-movement *poème musical* for **piano duet** titled *En mer* [At the Sea, n.d.]). He is best known today for his piano works (especially the **tone poem** *Comala* and the *Tango Brasileiro*, both for piano, 1890) and the *Suite brésilienne* for orchestra (also 1890). He composed a number of *maxixes*, *modinhas*, sambas, and tangos for piano. [JMC]

LIBRETTO. (It., "small book"; Fr., livret; Ger., Buch *or* Textbuch.) The literary content of a staged musical drama (e.g., **ballet, opera,** or **Singspiel**) or the printed book by which such text is disseminated. The term is also often applied to the literary content of unstaged dramatic works set to music such as **cantatas** and **oratorios**. Construed as literary content, the libretto is taken to include, at a minimum, the work's sung and spoken text, its constituent verse forms (e.g., strophic **song** or da capo aria), and musical styles (e.g., recitative or chorus). It may also denote any written or printed stage directions or other **paratextual** materials. During the **long 19th century**, printed libretti sometimes included an "argument" or other summarizing text that was not performed as well as information on the performance venue, names of performers, and so on.

Attitudes toward libretti varied greatly from place to place and changed considerably over the course of the long 19th century. In contrast to the latter-day perspective, which tends to consider the libretto as a more or less fixed and authorized text and the musical realization of that text, for most of the long 19th century staged and unstaged musical dramas alike were usually created with an eye to performance that would vary according to location and circumstance. Usually the question of eventual publication—and thus a more-or-less fixed and stable text for the work as a whole—became relevant only if the work enjoyed a sufficiently successful performance history to suggest reasonable prospects for profit in performance elsewhere, altered as necessary to suit local resources and conventions of taste in different locales. Until late in the century, then, the literary content and music of operas were inherently unstable, conceived and written at least partially with an eye to mutability. Accordingly, the criteria for aesthetic success were largely determined by their topicality in different locales or by other factors that resist definition because they were circumstantially determined. Major works by composers such as **Hector Berlioz, Giacomo Meyerbeer, Wolfgang Amadeus Mozart, Giacomo Puccini, Gioachino Rossini, Giuseppe Verdi**, and **Carl Maria von Weber**, among others, thus exist with significantly different authorized libretti. (By contrast, in the 1870s, **Richard Wagner** attempted— not entirely successfully—to establish a single definitive version of the texts of his **music dramas**, and in the early 20th century **Richard Strauss** acknowledged no authorized variant versions of any of his mature operas.)

A second important development in the art of the libretto during the long 19th century was an increase in librettos based on contemporary novels rather than plays or classical dramas. It is axiomatic that because it takes longer to sing any given text than it does to speak it, vocal settings of originally spoken or otherwise unsung texts must truncate those texts significantly if the musical works based on them are not to become overly long. This historically established difficulty in setting words from spoken drama to music became all the more pressing over the course of the long 19th century, however, partly because of increasing interest in the aesthetic value and expressive potential of instrumental music and partly because of increasing interest in musical repetition as a means of providing intrinsically musical coherence and continuity. But the unprecedented expansion of the reading public in the late 18th and early 19th centuries resulted in a vast new body of literary works—novels, plays, and poems—whose popular appeal made them naturally appealing as potential subjects for staged musical drama. The librettist's task in adapting novels and plays was complicated by the fact that crucial information in those literary texts was often provided not in words that would be spoken or sung but in the surrounding **narrative** or poetic discourse. The process of adapting such literature into a libretto that could be set to music and staged thus compelled librettists and composers to alter previously created literary sources more extensively than ever before, omitting significant characters, cutting or combining important scenes, and making other invasive significant changes. The extensiveness of these necessary alterations raised the risk of not only alienating audiences who were familiar with the literary source but also potentially damaging the literary integrity of the work without somehow creating a satisfactory new aesthetic balance.

Because of these difficulties, the long 19th century saw renewed and intensified levels of collaboration between librettists and composers. By consensus, some of the most successful fruits of these collaborations in the long 19th century were composed by Mozart (with Lorenzo Da Ponte [1749–1838]), Verdi (with Francesco Maria Piave [1810–1876]), and Richard Strauss (with Hugo von Hofmannsthal [1874–1929]). Among Verdi's more literarily successful adaptations are *Rigoletto* (with Piave, after **Victor Hugo**'s play *Le roi s'amuse*), *La traviata* (with Piave, after the short story and play *La dame aux Camélias* by Alexandre Dumas, *fils*), *Otello* (with **Arrigo Boito**, after **William Shakespeare**'s *Othello*), and *Falstaff* (also with Boito, after Shakespeare's *The Merry Wives of Windsor* and *King Henry IV*). Strauss's two most notable such instances are *Elektra* and **Der Rosenkavalier** (both with Hugo von Hofmannsthal). Additional notable collaborations of this sort were penned by Rossini (**Guillaume Tell**, 1829, after **Friedrich Schiller**), Georges Bizet (**Carmen**, 1874–1875, after Prosper Merimée [1803–1870]), Puccini (*Madama Butterfly*, 1904, after a short story by Luther Long [1861–1927]), and **Nikolay Rimsky-Korsakov** (*Skazka o Tsare Saltane* [*The Tale of Tsar Saltan*], 1900, after **Aleksandr Pushkin**).

One further major development in the art of creating librettos was the notion that the composer should author the libretto him- or herself. Traditionally, the primary literary and dramaturgical responsibility entailed in creating an opera had been entrusted to a professional poet or librettist whose words were then used by a professional composer to create music. This method obviously was capable of great success, but its inherently collaborative nature by definition entailed an extraordinary amount of time and frequently necessitated artistically problematic compromises between librettist and composer (e.g., extensive dramaturgically pointless repetitions of text to fill the time until the completion of the musical period). It also ran contrary to the century's widely cultivated emphasis on the artwork as an organic unity because text and music were assembled through collaboration rather than born organically of a single, unified artistic vision.

The first major composer to create his own libretti on the basis of previously composed drama or literature was **Gaetano Donizetti**, first in his *Le convenienze teatrali* (The Usages of the Stage, 1827) and later in *Il campanello di notte* (The Night Bell, 1836), and *Betly, ossia La capanna svizzera* (Betly; or The Swiss Chalet, 1836). The notion that libretto and music would be aesthetically superior if produced by the composer won more influential support, however, in the post-1848 music dramas of Wagner and the late operas of Berlioz (specifically *Les troyens* [The Trojans, H. 133, 1856–1858, publ. 1863] and *Béatrice et Benedict* [H. 138, 1860–1862]).

Wagner had written his own libretti from the start, beginning with his "große germanische Oper" *Die Feen* (WWV 32, 1833–1834), but only at mid-century did he implement and theorize his own brilliantly original solution to the age-old problems of combining words and music to enact a drama. The first work to employ these techniques was *Lohengrin* (WWV 75, 1845–1848), although he later viewed that libretto as still overly indebted to the old poetic practice of structuring verse around the number of syllables per line of verse and basing its coherence on assonance. As he explained in the seminal tract *Oper und Drama* (Opera and Drama, 1850–1851), the appeal of medieval **Stabreim** and 16th-century **Knittelvers**, both central to the new variety of libretto that would characterize the **Gesamtkunstwerk** as he intended to implement it, especially the music dramas of the **Ring of the Nibelung**, was partly historical and **nationalistic** in character. Equally important, however, was that by employing those prosodic techniques syllabically within a dense vocal/orchestral texture of organically developing *Leitfaden*, the composer-cum-librettist could produce a continuous rather than sectional musical/dramatic synthesis whose organic nature would eradicate the problematic conflicts between music and poetry that had troubled composer/librettist collaborations for centuries. Wagner later implicitly acknowledged that this complete synthesis of the composer's, librettist's, and dramaturg's art was not fully practicable—advocating for terms such as *Wort-Ton-Drama* and *musikalisches Drama* rather than the more strident **Gesamtkunstwerk**, **Musik-Drama**, and *Handlung*—but he continued to employ this new style of libretto to the end of his life.

The aesthetic aspirations of the libretto articulated in *Opera and Drama* and implemented in Wagner's late operas deeply influenced later composers who collaborated with librettists (most notably Richard Strauss). Composers ranging from **Arrigo Boito** and **Aleksandr Borodin** to Alban Berg, **Claude Debussy**, Sergei Prokofiev, and Arnold Schoenberg followed Wagner's lead in combining the historically discrete roles of composer and librettist into the single creative persona of the composer alone. [JMC]

See also FASSUNG LETZTER HAND; LEITMOTIV.

LIED (PL. LIEDER). A German poem, usually lyrical and strophic, intended to be sung, or any musical setting of such a poem; during the **long 19th century**, the term was typically used in contradistinction to *Gesang*, **ballad**, **romance**, and other varieties of vocal **chamber music**. In German, the term embraces both **folk song** and "art **song**" (i.e., *Volkslied* and *Kunstlied*). The latter—the subject of the present entry—is typically characterized first and foremost by the fact that its texts are usually composed by a poet or other individual other than the composer, written out, and then set to (notated) music by a composer: art song is thus a cultivated tradition that involves discrete literary and musical creative acts, relies on notation rather than orality for its transmission, and, like most notated art of the long 19th century, aspires to a certain implicit fixity in its texts and/or music. During the long 19th century, the term *Lied* embraced solo songs (both secular and sacred) with accompaniment of **piano** or other instrument(s), other nondramatic vocal chamber music, and **part-songs**. For much of the century, especially in the flourishing domestic music making of **Restoration** culture, the Lied was primarily a commodity for use in domestic or other intimate contexts. Only beginning around 1870 did the modern tradition of offering public recitals of Lieder and *Gesänge* become common.

The creative autonomy of both text and music in the Lied significantly affected its aesthetics and sociology. On the one hand, the fact that the texts were first and foremost poetry created as poetry meant that, in principle, the words that composers eventually chose to set to music were words that aspired to full aesthetic legitimacy as literature. In particular, late 18th-century German poetry, responding in part to Johann Gottfried Herder's (1744–1803) assertion that language was neither a God-given faculty nor a human imitation of animal sounds, as was generally believed at the time, but rather a manifestation of the distinctively human capacity for reflection increasingly treated poetry as the voice of the spontaneous and unmediated self. This Romantic approach opened poetry itself to levels of drama previously unanticipated and made every poem an implicit drama staged within the human imagination—crucial developments for Romantic poetry in general and the Romantic Lied in particular.

Moreover, the unprecedented increase in the reading public in the German lands over the course of the long 19th century—only perhaps 5 percent of the public was literate in the mid-18th century, but by the end of the 19th century, Germany was one of the world's most assiduously well-read countries— meant that members of the musical public who (so composers hoped) would perform musical settings of those texts were already familiar with them through reading. The process of realizing a musical setting in sung performance was thus not primarily a musical one but rather more akin to heightened reading—an enriched synthesis of text and music whose richness derived from the fact that the singer presumably brought some measure of interpretive understanding of the text itself to the process of singing and playing. The process also naturally brought any given setting of a particular text into a kind of implicit dialogue or, perhaps, competition with other settings of the same text, a process that raised the stakes for composers to create settings that were (in their view) faithful to the sense of the words and in many ways alluded or responded to other settings of the same text.

For example, more than 100 composers set **Johann Wolfgang von Goethe**'s *Wandrers Nachtlied II* ("Über allen Gipfeln ist Ruh," 1780). By the end of the 19th century, the iconic status of not only the poet but also the other composers who had set the poem (among them **Franz Liszt, Carl Loewe, Franz Schubert**, and **Robert Schumann**) combined with ideas and approaches represented in those composers' music as well as that of still more, less well known today, to make the task of creating a setting that was both original and appropriately cognizant of the accomplishments already occasioned by that text particularly daunting for, for example, **Max Reger**, who set it as an SA duet with piano accompaniment (Op. 14, no. 2, 1894–1895). The almost obsessive cultivation of the **canon** over the course of the long 19th century raised the stakes even further; for in the 1790s composers were not competing to win what James Parsons has aptly called "the plaudits of posterity" or "the permanence of a musical **canon** not then invented" (*GMO*, s.v. "Lied"), but a century later they were.

The long 19th century established the Lied as a genre with a rich and, more importantly, imposing tradition comparable to that of the **string quartet** or the **symphony**. Until the end of the Napoleonic Wars, that tradition was dominated by the aesthetic premises typically associated with the **Second Berlin School**, treating the accompaniment as a vehicle—usually unobtrusive—for the voice's musical conveyance of the text: a song's artfulness resided not in the sophistication of its music, the beauty of its melody, or the complexity of its harmonies but in its perceived success in achieving parity and harmony between the text and the music that conveyed it as well as its accessibility to the musically literate members of the reading public. Within this tradition, however, composers of the Early Romantic Generation began to experiment with more active accompaniments, more sophisticated harmonic techniques, and more imaginative musical treatments of those aspects of their texts that call out for interpretation.

The most important composer in this comparatively traditional school of Lied composition in the early 19th century was **Ludwig van Beethoven**, whose 13 *opera* of published songs (plus a number of other songs published without opus number or published posthumously; *see* WOO) reflect the new century's growing emphasis on nuanced interpretive readings of carefully chosen poetic texts. Despite **Johann Wolfgang von Goethe**'s controversial status at the time, particularly in Vienna, Beethoven was an avid reader and composer of Goethe's texts, including Op. 52 (nos. 4 and 7), four settings of Goethe's *Sehnsucht* ("Nur wer die Sehnsucht kennt") from *Wilhelm Meisters Lehrjahre*, and "Es war ein König von Thule" from *Faust I*. Additionally, *Adelaide* (Op. 46, 1794–1795, publ. 1797) and the *Six Lieder on Texts by C. F. Gellert* (1715–1769), Op. 48 (1801–1802, publ. 1803), are notable for their detailed interactions between voice and accompaniment and their harmonic richness. Other composers of the Early Romantic Generation active in this style of Lied composition include Ludwig Berger (1774–1839), Leonard von Call (1768–1815), August Harder (1775–1813), Carl Gottlieb Hering (1766–1853), Friedrich Heinrich Himmel (1765–1814), **Ignaz Moscheles**, Sigismund Neukomm (1778–1858), Ferdinand Ries (1784–1838), **Andreas Romberg**, **Louis Spohr**, and **Carl Maria von Weber**.

The Early Romantic Generation opened new paths for the Romantic Lied on 19 October 1814, when Franz Schubert composed *Gretchen am Spinnrade*, D. 118. With this setting of words from Part I of Goethe's rendering of the *Faust* tragedy, Schubert imported into the genre of the Lied a sort of complex accompaniments, graphic musical illustrations of textual imagery, and complex form that belied the apparent simplicity of the Lied as a genre of poetry and invested it instead with the sort of profound sophistication that in vocal chamber music had previously been reserved for the **ballad** and the *Gesang*—a sense of drama, penetrating psychology, and compositional intensity that Goethe and others questioned because in such settings the music tended to detract attention from the words it conveyed. Nevertheless, the new approach emancipated composers of Romantic Lieder from the self-consciously understated aesthetic appearance of the texts they set. The same is true of *Gretchen*'s close successor, *Erlkönig* (The Erl-King, D. 328, October 1815; likewise on a text by Goethe). These two works remained obscure until they were published as Schubert's Opp. 1 and 2 in 1821. That event, however, not only established Schubert's reputation as a composer but also created a groundswell of interest in this new Schubertian aesthetic of the Lied. His contributions to the genre were further enhanced, especially in the eyes of posterity, by his two late **song cycles** on texts by Wilhelm Müller (1794–1827): *Die schöne Müllerin* (D. 795/Op. 25, comp. 1823, publ. 1824) and *Winterreise* (D. 911, comp. 1827, publ. 1828).

In the Romantic Generation and Late Romantic Generation, the early Romantic approach to the Lied represented by Beethoven, Spohr, and Weber continued, most importantly in the works of composers such as **Fanny Hensel**, **Felix Mendelssohn Bartholdy**, and (to a lesser extent) **Clara Schumann** and eventually **Johannes Brahms**. The tide turned increasingly in favor of the Schubertian aesthetic, however. By far the most important contributor influence by that approach was **Robert Schumann**. In 1827 and 1828, Schumann had composed a total of 13 songs thoroughly in the early Romantic style (they were first published posthumously, in 1927 and 1928), but during the 1830s, he composed no songs and left most reviews of contemporary song publications in the *Neue Zeitschrift für Musik* to his second in command at the journal, Oswald Lorenz (1806–1889). Indeed, in 1839, Schumann confided privately that he had "always considered music for the human voice inferior to instrumental music." That same year, however, he and his fiancée Clara began jointly keeping a notebook titled *Abschriften von Gedichten zur Composition* (Copies of Poems to Be Set to Music)—an undertaking that is of course consistent with the heightened aesthetic expectations of poetry and song in contemporary Romantic Europe. In early 1840, then, Robert Schumann embarked on one of the most staggeringly productive periods of song composition in the history of the musical art, between February 1840 and January 1841 composing a total of 125 songs in a style that took the Schubertian aesthetic as its starting point, with sophisticated piano accompaniments and complex musical forms that sometimes obscured the predominantly strophic forms of the poems themselves in order to elaborate on or (in some instances) contradict the literal sense of the words. This feature proved particularly effective in realizing musically the intense irony associated particularly with the poetry of **Heinrich Heine**.

In all, Schumann's so-called year of song produced nine numbered *opera* of songs (designated variously as Lieder, *Gedichte* [poems], *Balladen* [**ballads**], and *Romanzen* [**romances**]), including the song cycles *Myrthen* (Op. 25), *Dichterliebe* (Op. 40, publ. 1843–1844), and *Frauenliebe und -leben* (Op. 42, publ. 1843). Also in the early 1840s, **Franz Liszt** turned to song composition, composing some 60 songs on German texts over the next decades and revising many of them at least once over the course of the 1840s, 1850s, and 1860s. Schumann returned to the Lied in the late 1840s and 1850s, now adopting a more austere, less lyrical, and sometimes more declamatory style that would remain absent from the mainstream song repertoire until it was taken up again by **Gustav Mahler** two generations later. Schumann's late Lieder remained unfashionable until comparatively recently. Since the late 1990s, however, late settings such as *Herzeleid* (Heartache, Op. 107, no. 1, comp. 1849, publ. 1853); "Warnung," Op. 119, no. 2 (Warning, 1851, publ. 1853); and the late song cycles opp. 96, 98a, 117, and 135 have become increasingly popular, part of the current reappraisal of Schumann's late styles.

Of the other major German composers of the Romantic Generation, only **Richard Wagner** produced an output of Lieder that is still deemed important today—this being the so-called *Wesendonck-Lieder* (WWV 91, formally titled *5 Gedichte von Mathilde Wesendonck*), on poems by Wagner's mistress, first written for voice and piano in 1857–1858 and later orchestrated by Felix Mottl (1856–1911) under Wagner's supervision. But the repertoire was much richer at mid-century than it is today, for many composers highly regarded then but now forgotten figured prominently in the publishers' rosters and on the music stands of private music rooms (e.g., Franz Abt [1819–1885], **Peter Cornelius**, **Robert Franz**, and **Joachim Raff**).

The mature Romantic emphasis on the aesthetic claims of poetry led composers of the Early Romantic Generation and Romantic Generation to focus on texts written by poets generally regarded as leaders in their day (even if posterity has a different assessment of their contributions): Hans Christian Andersen (1805–1875), Robert Burns (1759–1796), **Lord Byron**, Adalbert von Chamisso (1781–1838), Joseph Freiherr von Eichendorff (1788–1857), Goethe, Heine, Ludwig Heinrich Christoph Hölty (1748–1776), Justinus Kerner (1786–1862), Friedrich Rückert (1788–1866), and Theodor Storm (1817–1888). This emphasis appears to weaken in the most important composer of Lieder in the Late Romantic Generation, Johannes Brahms. Although Brahms's approximately 240 songs include two important song cycles focused on a single textual source—the *Romanzen aus Tiecks Magelone* (Op. 33, nos. 1–6, publ. 1865, and nos. 7–15, publ. 1868–1869) and the extraordinary valedictory cycle *Vier ernste Gesänge* (Four Serious Songs, Op. 121, 1896, on texts from the Bible)—his song output as a whole reveals no clearly focused gravitation toward particular poets. His songs written before the early 1860s (Opp. 3, 6, 7, 14, and 19) engage primarily with the early Romantic song aesthetic represented by Beethoven and Weber, but beginning with the *Lieder und Gesänge* op. 32 (1864, publ. 1865), his settings become more ambitious. Even in those more complex later settings, however, the form of the poem remains visible in the form of Brahms's music; his approach eschews a level of musical complexity that would detract from the artfulness of the poem itself or place it in competition with music. Other composers of Lieder in this generation include **Bruckner**, Adolf Jensen (1837–79), Eduard Lassen (1830–1904), **Josef Rheinberger**, and Carl Riedel (1827–1888). The many composers who traveled to the German lands for study during this generation also produced works in the genre of the Lied. Among these composers were **Edvard Grieg** and **Anton Rubinstein**.

The final major chapter in the Lied of the long 19th century owes to the distinctive approach of the composers of the Modern Romantic Generation—foremost among them **Gustav Mahler, Richard Strauss,** and **Hugo Wolf**. In these composers' works, the Lied as a lyrical, strophic poem, often of a folk-like nature, written to be sung in middle-class domestic system, recedes to a vestigial presence. Their Lieder are post-Wagnerian essays in the appropriation of the deepest sophistications of the human psyche for purposes of Romantic expression.

Of these three composers, Wolf was the one whose career was most defined by the Lied. He composed some 343 songs for solo voice between around 1875 and the onset of his syphilitic insanity in 1897—240 of those songs after 1888. He is also noted for having focused intensively on individual poets or textual sources for entire groups of songs composed in a close chronological period: Eichendorff (20 songs published in 1889), Goethe (51 songs published in 1890), and Mörike (53 songs published in 1889); the *Spanisches Liederbuch* (Spanish Songbook, 1890–1891, texts by Paul Heyse in translation by Geibel); the *Italienisches Liederbuch* (Italian Songbook, 1891–1892, on anonymous Italian poems translated by Heyse); and other collections focused on **Lord Byron**, Heine, Robert Reinick (1805–1852), and **William Shakespeare**. Although his songs were conceived for voice and piano, their dramatic (not to say symphonic) intensity is reflected in the fact that he arranged 31 of them for **orchestra** (two of those with chorus). Wolf's commitment to expressing what he viewed as the inner truth of his poems, as expressed in their individual words, their imagery, and their allusions to other works, led him to realize his texts in ways that often all but completely denature those texts' meanings as their poets and contemporary readers would have understood them.

This profoundly subjective treatment of text also applies to the songs of Mahler—but in a radically different way, for whereas Wolf believed that his approach ultimately served to express the meaning conveyed by the poets whose words he set, Mahler deliberately altered original poetic purpose to suit his own expressive needs, changing words, reordering songs and stanzas, and musically suggesting meanings that stand in ironic contradiction to the texts they convey. Most of the six groups of songs he published in his maturity were originally conceived for voice with orchestra—most importantly, the *Lieder eines fahrenden Gesellen* (Songs of a Wayfarer, comp. 1883–1885 and publ. 1896, then rev. 1891–1896 and publ. 1897), the *Lieder aus Des Knaben Wunderhorn* (Songs from *Des Knaben Wunderhorn*, 1892–1899), the *Kindertotenlieder* (Songs on the Death of Children, 1901–1904, publ. 1905), the *7 Lieder aus letzter Zeit* (Seven Recent Songs, 1905, publ. 1907), and *Das Lied von der Erde* (The Song of the Earth, 1908–1909, publ. 1911). Of these, the *Lieder eines fahrenden Gesellen*, *Kindertotenlieder*, and *Lied von der Erde* are explicitly conceived as song cycles, although they are perhaps more at home in the symphonic tradition than they are worlds away in the genre of the Lied as their poets had understood it.

Richard Strauss, too, was a master of the orchestral song, although he, like Mahler, imbued his more than 200 songs with an appreciation of beautiful melody rivaled by few compeers even in the lush world of post-Romantic music. Strauss's Lieder span the complete range of years from 1870 (the *Weihnachtslied* [Christmas Song], TrV 2) to 1948 (*Malven*, TrV 297), although most were composed between 1877 and 1906. As with Wolf, Strauss's choice of poets reflects a preference for those well established in the **canons** not only of poetry but also of Romantic song—specifically as reflected in the oeuvres of Schubert and Robert Schumann. He, too, occasionally eschewed the designation "Lied," with its implications of strophic form and simple or folk-like style, designating some collections as *Gesänge* (e.g., *Drei Gesänge älterer deutscher Dichter* [Three *Gesänge* on Texts by Old German Poets], TrV 196, Op. 43, 1899–1900) or *Gedichte* (e.g., *5 Gedichte von Rückert*, TrV 199/Op. 46, 1899–1900) or by original titles (the brilliantly burlesque parody of music publishing composed and published in 1918 as *Krämerspiegel* [Shopkeepers' Mirrors], TrV 236/Op. 66). Some of Strauss's individual songs remain among the most popular in the modern concert repertoire (*Zueignung* [Devotion, TrV141/Op. 10, no. 1, 1885; text by Gilm] and *Morgen!* [TrV 170/Op. 27, no. 4, 1894; text by McKay]), but his most important collection is probably the posthumously assembled cycle for voice with orchestra, *Vier letzte Lieder* (Four Last Songs, TrV 296, 1948; texts by Joseph Freiherr von Eichendorff [1788–1857] and Hermann Hesse

[1877–1962]). Also important as a composer of Lieder in the Modern Romantic Generation are **Max Reger** (six numbered *opera* of solo songs) and Arnold Schoenberg, who penned 12 numbered *opera* of German songs before his seminal *Pierrot lunaire* (1912). [JMC]

See also FOLK SONG; *LIEDER OHNE WORTE*; ROMANCE; SONG; SONG CYCLE; *TONADA*; VOICE, VOICEDNESS, VOCALITY.

DAS LIED VON DER ERDE. (Ger., "The Song of the Earth.") **Symphony** or **song cycle** for tenor, alto, or baritone and orchestra or piano by **Gustav Mahler** based on secondary translations by the German poet and sinologist Hans Bethge (1876–1946) of eighth- and ninth-century Chinese poems. Bethge's anthology, titled *Die chinesische Flöte* (The Chinese Flute, 1907), was described in its subtitle as "Nachdichtungen chinesischer Lyrik" (poetic paraphrases of Chinese lyric poetry) and was in fact a free imitation of poetry contained in Hans Heilmann's *Chinesische Lyrik* (Chinese Lyric Poetry, 1905), which was in turn freely translated from two French collections: the reputable sinologist Marquis L'Hervey-Saint-Denys's (1822–1892) *Poesies de l'Époque des Thang* (Poems from the Tang Dynasty, 1862) and, more extensively, the dilettante Judith Gautier's (1845–1917) *Livre de Jade* (Book of Jade, 1867).

The texts that Mahler set thus have little about them that is authentically Chinese. He combined seven of Bethge's texts to form the six movements of his song cycle. As with the ***Kindertotenlieder***, he also made his own significant alterations to the text—so significant, in fact, that after the work's first publication, Bethge apparently requested that the second printing also include side-by-side presentation of his texts and Mahler's so that users would clearly recognize the readings that were not his own. That second printing also subtly but substantively changed the textual attribution from the original "Dichtung aus Hans Bethge's 'Chinesischer Flöte'" (Poetry from Hans Bethge's *Chinese Flute*) to "nach Hans Bethges 'Die chinesische Flöte'" (after Hans Bethge's *The Chinese Flute*).

Das Lied von der Erde was premiered posthumously on 20 November 1911 and that same month published in a piano/vocal version prepared by Josef Venantius von Wöss (1863–1943), who had also prepared the piano/vocal score of *Das klagende Lied* and the **piano-duet** arrangements of the Third, Fourth, and Eighth Symphonies. The full score was published in 1912, as was the above-mentioned second issue of the **piano**/vocal version. Wöss's piano/vocal version, based on Mahler's own autograph piano/vocal score, differs substantively from the orchestral version, so that it cannot be treated as a rehearsal score but must be regarded as an independent version of the work (*see* EDITING AND EDITIONS; FASSUNG LETZTER HAND).

Mahler privately designated *Das Lied von der Erde* "a symphony for contralto (or baritone), tenor, and orchestra" but refused to designate it as his ninth symphony publicly. This refusal was reportedly due to superstitious reasoning, since **Ludwig van Beethoven** and most other 19th-century composers known to Mahler died before writing a tenth symphony. (There is an oft-repeated assertion that this superstition and his plan to skip from his Eighth to his de facto Tenth Symphony—the latter actually being the nominal Ninth—had to do with the heart condition with which he had been diagnosed in 1907. This notion is weakly supported and improbable, however, since Mahler's heart condition usually was not life threatening.)

Das Lied von der Erde comprises six movements: (1) *Das Trinklied vom Jammer der Erde* (The Drinking-Song of the Ruefulness of Earth), (2) *Der Einsame im Herbst* (The Solitary Man in the Autumn), (3) *Von der Jugend* (On Youth), (4) *Von der Schönheit* (On Beauty), (5) *Der Trunkene im Frühling* (The Drunken Man in Springtime), and (6) *Der Abschied* (The Farewell). Although the anthology by Gautier that comprised the main textual foundation of the cycle/symphony reduced the original Chinese texts to dilettantish *chinoiserie*, in Mahler's setting based on Bethge's poetry, the songs are widely held to represent some of the most deeply personal and profound meditations on liminality and mortality of the entire pre–World War I period. Within Mahler's output, *Das Lied* is also distinguished by its prominent use of heterophony, which seems to represent an attempt to evoke the prevalent texture of Chinese music rather than simply appropriating pseudo-Chinese texts as the basis for creation in a Western European symphonic idiom. [JMC]

LIEDER OHNE WORTE. (Ger., "Songs without Words"; Fr., romances sans paroles.) Genre of **character piece** typically scored for solo **piano**, although there are also such compositions for other instrumental **chamber** ensembles (e.g., **Felix Mendelssohn Bartholdy**'s posthumously published *Lied ohne Worte* in D Major for cello and piano, MWV Q34/Op. posth. 109, 1845 or 1847). The genre designation *Lieder ohne Worte* is usually translated "songs without words," but because the German term is *Worte*, not *Wörter*, "songs without texts" would be more accurate. The term derives from the fact that such works are typically simple in character and style, after the model of the **Lied** rather than the **ballad** or *Gesang*, and that they typically emulate the texture of one of three types of vocal chamber composition: the solo Lied, the Lied as vocal duet (usually for two high voices or soprano and tenor), or the **part-song**.

The genre was apparently developed by either **Fanny Hensel** or **Felix Mendelssohn Bartholdy** sometime in the 1820s for private use in domestic contexts and widely emulated by other composers thereafter. The earliest such piece is a *Lied ohne Worte* in E-flat major composed by Felix Mendelssohn and notated in an album by Fanny Hensel on 14 November 1828 (MWV U68; first published Kassel: Bärenreiter, 1997). The first published collection by Felix (MWV SD6/Op. 19[a]), containing works dating back to 1829, appeared in 1832 in an English edition published by **Alfred Novello**, without opus number and titled *Original Melodies for the Piano Forte*; the same collection was published in 1833 with the opus number 19 as *Sechs Lieder ohne Worte* by **Nicholas Simrock** (Bonn) and without opus number by Maurice Schlesinger (Paris) as *6 Romances sans paroles*. The opus number 19 was also used for Mendelssohn's collection of vocal songs published in 1833 (*Sechs Gesänge für eine Singstimme und Klavier* [Six Vocal Pieces for Voice and Piano MWV SD6], published by Breitkopf & Härtel [Leipzig] in 1833). By convention, the vocal collection is now usually labeled Op. 19[a] and the collection of *Lieder ohne Worte* Op. 19[b].) The genre quickly became popular. Mendelssohn published another five collections during his lifetime (MWV SD9, 16, 23, 29, and 32/opp. 30, 38, 53, 62, and 67) and left many more unpublished. Meanwhile, beginning in 1829, Fanny Hensel also composed in the genre, in the last two years of her life publishing 14 of her own, distinctive works as her opp. 2, 4, 5, and 6 (1846 and 1847). The many other composers who wrote and/or published works in the genre include **Carl Czerny** (1872), **Charles Gounod** (1861), **Charles Hallé** (1845), **Stephen Heller** (1863, 1868), **Friedrich Kalkbrenner** (1849), **William Mason** (1845), **Louis Spohr** (1840), **Pyotor Il'yich Tchaikovsky** (1869, 1879), **Sigismond Thalberg** (1840), and **Richard Wagner** (WWV 64, 1840).

As a genre, the *Lieder ohne Worte* , along with the **ballade**, belong to a category of instrumental chamber music whose genre designation and musical style suggest that they are **programmatic** or characteristic but whose music (in most cases) in fact is conceived and presented without any text or specific extramusical reference. The apparent paradox of the genre designation—if there are no words, why is it called a song?—led many 19th-century musicians and editors to suggest that these works had in fact been conceived as texted vocal songs but then disseminated with the text removed. This notion may account for **Franz Liszt**'s and his publishers' decisions to publish his transcriptions of songs by **Franz Schubert** as "Lieder ohne Worte" and for **Georges Bizet**'s six *Chants du Rhin* (1865, publ. 1866), which are stylistically germane to the genre but are based not just on vocal prototypes but also on specific poems by Joseph Méry (1797–1866).

A widespread fancy thus ensued of retroactively inventing titles and/or texts that were supposed to have inspired the music of the *Lieder ohne Worte* and in some cases performing or publishing the works with those texts fitted to their music. Such ventures were alien to the idea of the works as it had been promulgated by the Mendelssohn siblings, whose private correspondence shows that the generic designation was at most an invitation to other musicians to invent or discover texts that expressed the idea and feeling of the music as those other musicians understood it, with the assumption that no single set of words would, could, or should "correctly" express the music. (Mendelssohn occasionally provided general character designations, such as "Jägerlied" [Hunters' Song, Op. 19(b), no. 2], "Venezianisches Gondellied" [Venetian Gondola Song, Op.19(b), no. 6], or "Abendlied" [Evening Song, Op. 30, no. 4], and Hensel typically eschewed such designations altogether, except for her "O Traum der Jugend, o goldener Stern," Op. 6, no. 3—but these labels are very general.) Nevertheless, the spread of such ventures and the dubious aesthetic worth of the products combined with the fact that the *Lieder ohne Worte* were patently conceived as **Hausmusik** or **salon** music and the later 19th century's suspicion of small-scale compositions to create a widespread perception that the songs without words were by nature sentimental, trivial concessions to dilettantism and were appropriate only for women since women supposedly were generally incapable of the "masculine seriousness" that mid- and late 19th-century commentators found in other music by male composers (*see* FEMINISM). [JMC]

LIEDERKRANZ. *See* LIEDERTAFEL.

LIEDERSPIEL. (Ger., "Song-play.") A type of musical play featuring simple, usually strophic **songs** (**Lieder**) that predominantly set familiar poems to new melodies. The genre was fostered among certain composers of the Early Romantic Generation, many of them in Berlin, and is not to be confused with ballad **opera** or **vaudeville**, in which the songs primarily underlay familiar melodies with new texts.

The inventor of the Liederspiel was Johann Friedrich Reichardt (1752–1814), who did not envision an elite operatic subgenre but rather something easily singable and musically simple and straightforward; aesthetically, it was very much in line with the **Second Berlin School** with which Reichardt and others are associated. In 1800, Reichardt premiered his *Lieb' und Treue* (Love and Faithfulness) at the Berlin Royal Opera House; the work featured Reichardt's own settings to known texts, such as **Johann Wolfgang von Goethe**'s "Heidenröslein" and the folk song "Wenn ich ein Vöglein wär." Other significant *Liederspiele* (pl.) include *Frohsinn und Schwärmerey* (Cheerfulness and Sentimentality, Berlin, 1801) by Friedrich Heinrich Himmel (1765–1814), *Der Teppichhändler* (The Carpet Dealer, Weimar, 1830) by Carl Eberwein (1786–1868), and *Der Pole und sein Kind, oder Der Feldwebel vom IV. Regiment* (The Pole and His Child; or, The Sergeant of the Fourth Regiment, 1832) by **Albert Lortzing**. At least as early as the 1820s, the term was sometimes used more broadly to describe works that resemble the original concept of Liederspiel on some level, such as **Felix Mendelssohn Bartholdy**'s *Aus der Fremde* (From Abroad, MWV L6/Op. posth. 89, 1829) or **Robert Schumann**'s *Spanisches Liederspiel* (Op. 74, 1849). [RK]

LIEDERTAFEL. (Ger., "Song-Table.") Strictly speaking, an organization that brings together a small number of men for the purpose of conviviality and the singing of **part-songs** or smaller, secular choral works. *Liedertafeln* (pl.) were originally composed of poets, composers, and amateur music lovers and specifically encouraged the composition of new part-songs on new German texts—thereby fostering a sense of creativity and national identity centered on language and shared cultural ties (*see* NATIONALISM, RO-MANTIC NATIONALISM). The first such organization—and the term itself—was created by Carl Friedrich Zelter (1758–1832) after the model of King Arthur's legendary round table and convened in Berlin on 21 December 1808. Similar groups rapidly sprang up elsewhere in the domestically centered, music-loving culture of the **Restoration**: Frankfurt an der Oder (1815), Leipzig (1815), Turingia (1818), Magdeburg (1819), Münster (1822), Hamburg (1823), Minden (1824), Potsdam (1826), Bremen (1827), Bielefeld and Mainz (1831), Mannheim (1840), Linz (1845), and Salzburg (1847). Central to this original species of Liedertafel was the nation of private, exclusive, male-centered, and implicitly nationalist conviviality that commingled song, food, and conversation—in some sense a male-centered and explicitly musical counterpart to the traditionally female-led and conversationally centered institution of the **salon**. Occasionally, women were invited to hear performances by *Liedertafeln*.

The success of the original *Liedertafeln* and the congruence between their edifying functions and larger societal themes also led to the formation of larger, less exclusive (i.e., public or semipublic) organizations that centered on secular choral **song** (not necessarily newly composed, as had been the focus in the original *Liedertafeln*) and less on conviviality and conversation. These organizations typically were named or described as *Liederkränze* (sing. *Liederkranz*, "wreath of songs") to emphasize their more inclusive (but still male) memberships. During the later 19th century, they were frequently known as *Männergesangvereine* (sing. *Männergesangverein*, "union for men's song"), and public competitions among the groups were an important part of the century's larger music festivals. [JMC]

See also MÄNNERCHOR; ORPHÉON.

LIND (LIND-GOLDSCHMIDT), JENNY |JOHANNA MARIA| (1820–1887). Legendary Swedish soprano, nicknamed "the Swedish nightingale" for the agility, breath control, purity, and range of her singing in **opera** and **oratorio**. She trained at the Kungliga Teaterns Operascen (Royal Opera

School) in Stockholm beginning in 1830 and made a sensational public debut in the role of Agathe in **Carl Maria von Weber**'s *Der Freischütz* in 1838. In the next few years, she won acclaim for her performances in **Vincenzo Bellini**'s *Norma*, **Gaetano Donizetti**'s *Lucia di Lammermoor*, **Giacomo Meyerbeer**'s *Robert le diable*, **Wolfgang Amadeus Mozart**'s *Don Giovanni*, and **Gaspare Spontini**'s *La vestale*. In 1841, her voice showing signs of strain and overuse, she went to Paris to study with the renowned pedagogue **Manuel García** the younger (1805–1906), who prescribed an extended vocal rest and then worked as a private pedagogue to restore and retrain her voice.

Lind returned to the stage in Stockholm in the role of Norma in November 1842 to great acclaim, her fame mounting with her successive performances in a variety of roles over the next several years: in Donizetti's *Anna Bolena*, Christoph Willibald Ritter von Gluck's (1714–1787) *Armide*, Meyerbeer's *Les Huguenots*, Mozart's *Le Nozze di Figaro*, and **Gioachino Rossini**'s *La gazza ladra* and *Il turco in Italia*. She conquered the German and Austrian stages beginning in 1845 with her role as Norma at the Theater an der Wien and in other operas including Donizetti's *La fille du regiment* and Meyerbeer's *Ein Feldlager in Schlesien*. In December 1845, she made her debut at the Leipzig Gewandhaus under the direction of **Felix Mendelssohn Bartholdy**, followed by acclaimed performances at the Lower Rhine Music Festival in Aachen (including a performance in a recital given by **Clara** and **Robert Schumann**) in 1846. She visited London for the first time in 1847, taking Great Britain by storm both in London and in numerous performances in the provinces (e.g., in the Norwich Festival). Beginning in 1848, she donated most of her substantial fees to charitable causes.

By 1850, Lind had acquired the status of a living legend. She was engaged by the American showman P. T. Barnum (1810–1891) to tour the United States extensively, and while the two parted ways over business issues in 1851, she did extend her tour, alongside the pianist Otto Goldschmidt (1829–1907; her eventual husband), into mid-1852—for a total of 93 performances and more than $350,000 in profits (for the time, a truly extraordinary sum that she donated to U.S., English, and Swedish charities). After returning to Europe, she made only concert performances (no operatic roles) and gradually withdrew from public life as a *sola* performer, living in England from 1855 to her death and becoming a British subject in 1859. In 1882, she joined the faculty of the newly founded Royal College of Music in London; there she was known for insisting on her students' general education as well as their vocal work. She was widely mourned and eulogized after her death in 1887 and has been memorialized on postcards, banknotes, and the names of countless cities, institutions (chapels, children's hospitals, hotels, parks, and pubs), street names, and even machines (the last including a locomotive, a clipper ship, and a schooner). She was the first woman to be memorialized in the Poets' Corner of Westminster Abbey.

Lind's claims to historical fame reside partly in her vocal legacy and partly in her commercial success. As a singer, she was notable partly for her range (from *b* to *g³*), partly for her reportedly impeccable taste in improvising and writing her own cadenzas in opera as well as her renditions of Swedish and Polish **folk song** (many of the latter are transmitted in the appendix to H. S. Holland and W. S. Rockstro, *Memoir of Madame Jenny Lind-Goldschmidt: Her Early Art-Life and Dramatic Career, 1820–1851* [London, 1891]), and partly for her extraordinary *pianissimo*. She performed in more than 40 operatic roles during her career. [JMC]

See also PERFORMANCE PRACTICE.

LINDBLAD, ADOLF FREDRIK (1801–1878). Swedish composer and teacher of the Romantic Generation, the most important of his generation. As a child, he demonstrated talent on flute and **piano** and began composing, and in 1823 he began studying music at the University of Uppsala. He traveled in the German lands and went to Paris between 1825 and 1827, also befriending the young **Felix Mendelssohn Bartholdy** during his brief studies with Carl Friedrich Zelter (1758–1832). From 1827 to 1861, he directed a music and piano school in Sweden, with the "Swedish nightingale" **Jenny Lind** among his most famous pupils. Although he composed one **opera** (*Frondörerna* [The Rebels, 1835]) and much instrumental music (two **symphonies**, two string **quintets**, seven **string quartets**, one string **trio**, and three violin **sonatas**), his importance resides chiefly in his vocal music—especially his 215 **songs** (among them two **song cycles**), some on German texts but most on Swedish texts composed by Lindblad himself. His songs began a new tradition in Swedish art song and are considered a milestone in Swedish musical **nationalism**. [JMC]

LISZT, FRANZ [FERENC, FRANCISCUS] (1811–1886). Hungarian composer, pianist, teacher, and writer on music of the Romantic Generation; one of music history's greatest **virtuosos** and (with **Richard Wagner**) one of the most ardent and influential champions of progressive music in the second half of the 19th century. Born in a German-speaking portion of western Hungary, he demonstrated exceptional talent early on and in 1822 was taken by his father to Vienna, where the prohibitive fee **Johann Nepomuk Hummel** charged for lessons led to his study instead with **Carl Czerny** and Antonio Salieri (1750–1825), both of whom waived their fees for the boy. By the end of 1822, he had given several public performances in Vienna whose success prompted plans for a trip to Paris later that year. He gave a farewell Viennese performance in April and, after a conspicuously patriotic farewell recital in Pest, undertook a tour deliberately modeled on the young **Wolfgang Amadeus Mozart**'s tour of 1763–1764, arriving in Paris in December.

As a foreign pianist, he was refused admission to the **Conservatory**, but he was able to take private lessons with **Ferdinando Paer** and **Antoine Reicha**, also establishing warm relations with the piano manufacturer **Érard** (whose double-escapement action would be foundational to his mature technique). He toured to growing acclaim in England (1824, 1825, and 1827), the French provinces, and Switzerland (1826). After a personal and professional crisis triggered by the death of his father and an abortive relationship with a pupil, he became involved with the St.-Simonians—an affiliation that he later downplayed but whose ideas remained central to his views on the social project of music for the remainder of his life.

In Paris, Liszt became a part of the circle of young artistic, literary, and musical geniuses that included **Charles-Valentin Alkan**, Honoré de Balzac (1799–1850), **Hector Berlioz**, **Fryderyk Chopin**, Eugène Delacroix (1798–1863), **Stephen Heller**, **Ferdinand Hiller**, and **Victor Hugo**, but the defining professional influence was that of **Nicolò Paganini**, whom he first heard in April 1832 and who became a model for a comparable level of pianistic virtuosity and showmanship. By 1833, he was producing new works of staggering technical difficulty and unprecedented fertility of composition-al imagination: the *Malédiction* for piano and orchestra (LW H1, 1833–1840), the *Album d'un voyageur* (LW A40a,b,c, 1835–1838), and the *Études d'exécution transcendante d'après Paganini* (Transcendental Etudes after Paganini, LW A52, 1838–1840). In 1834, he also began publishing his writings on music, a lifelong vocation that would only augment the influence won for him by his extraordinary musicianship and personal charisma. On tour almost constantly from 1839 to 1847 (Bonn, Great Britain, Dresden, Ireland, Leipzig, Pest, Portugal, Prague, Russia, Spain, and Weimar), Liszt was captivated with the music of the Hungarian Roma during a concert in Pest in 1840—a force that would be a dominant factor in his professional persona for years to come (*see* STYLE HONGROIS). Europe was swept by what has since been termed *Lisztomania*, though his brilliant showmanship and public displays of staggering virtuosity left him susceptible to charges of "empty virtuosity" from many, among them Chopin, **Fanny Hensel**, **Felix Mendelssohn Bartholdy**, and **Clara** and **Robert Schumann**.

Liszt reached a turning point in 1848. Already in 1842, the grand duke of Saxe-Weimar had invited him to become Kapellmeister Extraordinary at the Weimar court, and now (February 1848) Liszt settled down with his new mistress, the Polish princess Carolyne zu Sayne-Wittgenstein (1819–1887), to help turn the already distinguished city that had been home to **Johann Sebastian Bach**, **Johann Wolfgang von Goethe**, and **Friedrich Schiller** into an "Athens of the North." Although his skills as a **conductor** were at best unconvincing, he increased the size of the court's core **orchestra** to 45 players (supplemented as needed) and in 1850 hired the young **Joseph Joachim** to serve as concertmaster. His efforts to revive the Weimar court's musical culture succeeded brilliantly, with him teaching lessons and hosting musical and cultural luminaries from around Europe. He began committing to print new works and revised versions of many of the compositions he had written and performed from memory or manuscript while on tour during the previous decade and continued penning his lengthy and often eloquent prose publications, including important essays on his friend Wagner's *Lohengrin* and *Tannhäuser* (1851), Robert Schumann (1854), **Hector Berlioz**'s *Harold in Italy* (1855), and a book-length biography of Chopin (1852). The 1850s also saw the composition of major new works including most of his **symphonic poems**, the *"Faust"* and *"Dante" Symphonies* (LW G12 and G14, 1854–1857, rev. and publ. 1860, and 1855–1856, publ. 1859), the final (printed) version of the two piano **concertos** (LW H4 and H6, publ. 1857 and 1863), and the B-minor Piano **Sonata** (LW A179, 1852–1853, publ. 1854) as well as the *Fantasy and Fugue for Organ on the Chorale "Ad nos, ad salutarem undam"* from **Giacomo Meyerbeer**'s *Le prophète* (LW B8, 1850, publ. 1852).

With his reputation as a virtuoso showman receding into the historical distance, Liszt's influence as a key figure in musical culture after the **Revolutions of 1848** increased further in 1859, when he published the first edition of his widely read book on the music of the Hungarian Gypsies (*Des bohémiens et de leur musique en Hongrie* [Paris: Librairie nouvelle, 1859]). Also in 1959 he joined with historian and journalist **Franz Brendel** to organize the first annual Conference of German Musicians (*Versammlung deutscher Tonkünstler*; later known as the **New German School**), championing the self-styled progressive works of Wagner, Liszt himself, and other German composers as the rightful heirs to the musical legacies of Gluck, Mozart, **Carl Maria von Weber**, and **Ludwig van Beethoven**. He was instrumental in the founding of the more formal **Allgemeiner deutscher Musikverein** in 1861 and in that same year went with Sayn-Wittgenstein to Rome to petition the pope for an annulment of her marriage and then to wed her. The annulment fell through and with it the couple's plans for marriage—but they remained in Rome, and Liszt, inclined toward mysticism since his youth, became increasingly entranced with Catholic Renaissance polyphony, the history of church music, and Catholicism generally. He was tonsured a reader in the Roman Catholic Church on 25 April 1865.

Liszt would hereafter be known as "Abbé Liszt," wearing a cassock and concentrating primarily on sacred music, most importantly the **oratorios** *Die Legende von der heiligen Elisabeth* (The Legend of St. Elizabeth, LW 14, publ. 1867) and *Christus* (LW 17, 1866–1872). After 1869, he began to spend more time abroad, teaching in Weimar and helping to found the National Academy of Music in Pest in 1867. He reconciled with Cosima and Richard Wagner in 1872 and was invited by his old friend to settle in **Bayreuth** but continued to travel widely, rarely performing publicly as pianist but frequently conducting his own and others' works. It was to him, the Abbé, that Wagner dedicated his own profoundly spiritual final opera, *Parsifal*, in 1882. A final trip to London (his first in more than 40 years) in 1886 won another audience with Queen **Victoria**, and even after his health began to fail in the summer of that year, he traveled to Bayreuth to see that theater's premiere of *Tristan und Isolde* (25 July), sitting slumped in a chair in the back of the theater with a handkerchief over his mouth to suppress his coughing. He was diagnosed with pneumonia and died of a heart attack on 31 July.

The task of even a rudimentary inventory of Liszt's musical output is formidable in part because of his longevity and his prolificness: he began composing in 1822 and continued almost without interruption until 1885. Moreover, like his generational compeers Chopin and Mendelssohn, he continually reworked and revised his compositions in arrangements and alternate forms that sometimes were intended to supersede earlier versions but more often were intended as simultaneous variant versions—with the result that many of his works exist in multiple chronologically discrete and substantially different authorized versions (*see* EDITING AND EDITIONS; FASSUNG LETZTER HAND). The so-called *Gesamtausgabe* issued under the joint editorship of **Ferruccio Busoni**, Peter Raabe, and others between 1907 and 1936 ranks as one of the most corrupt and incomplete available for any major 19th-century composer (rivaled only by those of Chopin and Mendelssohn), and the *New Edition of the Complete Works* begun in 1970 is still many years from completion. Liszt's compositional output also includes many free transcriptions and arrangements of other composers' works that proved influential in those composers' **reception** histories—most famously Beethoven's **string quartets** and symphonies, Berlioz's *Episode in the Life of an Artist* and *Harold in Italy* (the latter prepared in 1836, rev., publ. 1879), many **songs** and **chamber** works of **Schubert**, and songs of Robert Schumann and **Robert Franz**. His genius and originality in rendering these compositions in a fashion commensurate with his profound understanding of the expressive capabilities of the fortepiano makes the terms *transcription* and *arrangement* awkward half-truths for these works. The inventory of the works published by British composer Humphrey Searle in the first edition of the *New Grove Dictionary of Music and Musicians* (1980) reflected the state of research at the time but is now seriously outdated. A full thematic catalog of all the works, prepared by Rena Charmin-Mueller and Mária Eckhardt, is in progress.

The same problems obtain (on a somewhat smaller scale) with regard to Liszt's published writings, but there they are further complicated by questions of attribution because he allowed some writings by others to be published under his own name and allowed others (most notably Marie d'Agoult and Sayn-Wittgenstein) to interpolate their own material—sometimes in substantial quantities—into texts of his own making. Only comparatively recently have scholars begun to make progress in the complex and often-frustrating task of constructing an accurate, philologically robust inventory of the surviving, missing, and lost manuscript and printed sources that document his creative life—the essential foundation for any reasonably reliable edition of his music and his writings. Source-critical editions of the collected prose works in the original French and German is in progress under the editorship of Detlef Altenburg (*Franz Liszt: Sämtliche Schriften* [Wiesbaden: Breitkopf & Härtel, 1989–]), and a reliable English translation of that same corpus is an even more recent venture (see Janita R. Hall-Swadley, *The Collected Writings of Franz Liszt*, 7 vols. [Lanham, MD: Scarecrow Press, 2011–]).

With those qualifications in mind, it is possible to single out a few compositions from within Liszt's oeuvre as being particularly important and/or representative accomplishments in the various genres in which he worked. Among the works for piano solo, the most important of the fantasies and potpourris based on other composers' works are the *Fantaisie sur des motifs favoris de l'opéra La sonnambula [of **Bellini**]* (LW A56, 1839–1842), the *Réminiscences de Don Juan* (LW A80, 1841, publ. 1842; after Mozart's ***Don Giovanni***), the transcriptions of the **overtures** to **Gioachino Rossini**'s ***Guillaume Tell*** (LW A54, 1838–1841, publ. 1842) and Weber's ***Der Freischütz*** (LW A129, 1846, publ. 1847), and the overture to Wagner's *Tannhäuser* (LW A146, 1847, publ. 1849) and the so-called "Liebestod" from *Tristan und Isolde* (LW A239, 1867, publ. 1868). The most imposing of the many original works for piano solo include the three volumes of *Années de pèlerinage* (Years of Pilgrimage, LW A159, 1848–1855, publ. 1858; A197, 1859, publ. 1861; A283, 1877–1882, publ. 1883), the B-minor Sonata (see above), the 22 ***Hungarian Rhapsodies***, the *Études d'exécution transcendante pour le piano* (LW A172, 1840 and 1851, publ. 1851), and the *Harmonies poétiques et religieuses* (LW A18, 1833–1834) and several late works whose presaging of quartal harmony, atonality, and serial technique is extraordinary (most famously *Trübe Wolken/Nuages gris* [Gray Clouds], LW A301, 1881, *R.W.—Venezia* [LW A320, 1883], and the *Bagatelle ohne Tonart/Bagatelle sans tonalité* [LW A338, 1885]). He also arranged and composed much music for **piano duet** (both for two pianos and for one piano, four hands). The orchestral compositions include his 13 **symphonic poems** (LW G1–4, 6–7, 9–10, 13, 15, 17, and 38; most famously *Les Préludes*), the "Faust" Symphony (see above), the *Totentanz* (LW H8, 1847–1862, publ. 1865), and transcriptions of most of the *Hungarian Rhapsodies*. The sacred choral music includes, in addition to the oratorios *St. Elisabeth* and *Christus* (see above), settings of Psalms 13, 18, and 96 (LW I3, I5, and I6; 1855–1866, 1860–1871, 1875, publ. 1871). Least well known today but remarkable in many ways are his instrumental and vocal **chamber** works—especially his

songs on French, German, and Italian texts (among them a recently recognized **song cycle** on texts of **Victor Hugo**; LW N11–12, N24–25, 1842, rev. 1859). [JMC]

See also BÖSENDORFER; PROGRAM (PROGRAMMATIC) MUSIC.

LJUBAV I ZLOBA. (Cro., "Love and Malice.") **Opera** composed by Croatian composer Vatroslav Lisinski (1819–1854) on a libretto by Janko Car (1822–1876) and Dimitrija Demeter (1811–1872). Performed in 1846, it was the first Croatian opera.

Ljubav i zloba came on the heels of the so-called Illyrian movement, a Croatian (and in some respects generally southern Slavic) **nationalist** literary movement that flourished in the 1830s and 1840s through the work of linguist Ljudevit Gaj (1809–1872), poet and lexicographer Ivan Mažuranić (1814–1890), and poet Petar Preradović (1818–1872). Especially in the wake of Gaj's *Kratka osnova horvatsko-slavenskoga pravopisaňa* (Brief Basics of the Croatian-Slavonic Orthography, 1830) and Mažuranić's *Njemačko-ilirski slovar* (German-Illyrian Dictionary, 1842), there was a proliferation of native-language literature in Slavic-speaking parts of the Austrian Empire. In that context, the appearance of a first Croatian opera was profoundly significant.

Vatroslav Lisinski, the composer, was a German-Jewish native of Zagreb originally named Ignacije Fuchs. Lisinski associated himself with the Illyrian movement fairly early in his life; in 1841, he composed the melody to the Croatian patriotic song *Pjesma Hrvata* (Song of the Croats), penned by Demeter. Another Illyrian activist, winemaker and amateur tenor Alberto Ognjen Štriga (1821–1897), suggested to Lisinski that he compose an Illyrian opera. In 1845, Lisinski completed a two-act opera set in 16th-century Split, in which a princess and her young lover struggle against forces threatening to keep them apart; in an intense finale that recalls elements of **Ludwig van Beethoven**'s *Fidelio*, the male protagonist's gun-wielding friend steps in to save the day, with a mob of justice-thirsty townspeople behind him. Although the premiere of *Ljubav i zloba* in Zagreb on 28 March 1846 was an internationally noted success, the years after the Hungarian Revolution of 1848–1849 were less hospitable to Croatian artistic nationalism and to such manifestations of Illyrianism as this opera. The post–World War I era saw a resurgence of interest in Lisinski and *Ljubav i zloba*. [RK]

LOEWE, (JOHANN) CARL (GOTTFRIED) (1796–1869). German composer and singer of the Early Romantic Generation. He is best known today for his hundreds of **Lieder** and dramatic **ballads**, but during his lifetime those works' reputation was enhanced by the reported intensity of his own performances of them; he was a favorite of the Prussian court of Friedrich

Wilhelm III (fl. 1797–1840) and toured extensively, winning praise for his songs and his singing in Vienna (1844), London (1847), Sweden and Norway (1851), and Paris (1857). He also composed four **operas**, two *Singspiele*, one set of **incidental music**, and three **concert arias** as well as 16 completed **oratorios**, 10 other sacred works, and a number of secular duets and **part-songs**. He also penned a sizable corpus of instrumental music: two **symphonies**, two piano **concertos**, five **string quartets**, five published *opera* of instrumental **chamber music** with **piano** and an unpublished *Duo espagnol* for violin and piano, and about a dozen works for piano solo. Many of the instrumental works reflect his gift for melodic gifts, but some—especially the oratorios—also reflect his dramatic abilities.

Loewe also published a *Gesang-Lehre* (Vocal Method) that ran to five editions between 1826 and 1854, a *Practisch-theoretische Klavier- und Generalbass-Schule für Lehrer und Lernende* (Practical and Theoretical Piano and Thoroughbass Method for Teachers and Students, 1834, 2nd ed. 1851), and a *Musikalischer Gottesdienst: Methodische Anweisung zum Kirchengesange und Orgelspiel* (Musical Worship Service: Methodic Instruction in Sacred Song and Organ Performance, 1851).

Loewe trained as a choirboy beginning in 1807, moving to Halle and studying there with Daniel Gottlob Türk (1750–1813) from 1809 to 1812, when his studies were interrupted by the outbreak of war with Napoléon Bonaparte's army. He had received a stipend from King Jerome of Westphalia in 1809 to support his studies, but when the king was forced to flee, this support ended abruptly. Loewe became the organist of a local church in 1814 and in 1817 entered the University of Halle to study philosophy and theology. In 1819–1820, he made the acquaintance of **Johann Wolfgang von Goethe**, **Johann Nepomuk Hummel**, and **Carl Maria von Weber** and in February 1820 was appointed organist of the Jacobikirche in Szczecin (Poland), a major port city and Prussian outpost. Having won the approval of Carl Friedrich Zelter (1758–1832), he was appointed Szczecin's municipal music director in February of that year, a post he retained until his failing health forced him to resign in 1866. He spent his last years in Kiel, but after his death his heart was found buried near the organ in the Jacobikirche.

From his original op. 1 ballad (*Klothar*, on a text by Friedrich Kind, 1812, publ. 1813) through the late songs and ballads published around 1860, Loewe demonstrated his sensitivity to prosody; a strong affinity for the supernatural, grotesque, or generally sublime aspects of Romantic poetry; and an ability to use the piano for sonorous and evocative effects. After 1817, when the influence of Rudolf Zumsteeg (1760–1802) increased significantly, his vocal chamber music parallels that of **Franz Schubert** in the complexity and musical sophistication of his accompaniments (albeit in a completely different manner). His oratorios *Die Zerstörung Jerusalems* (The Destruction of Jerusalem, Op. 30, 1829, publ. 1832) and *Johann Hus* (Op. 82, 1842), though obscure today, rank with the oratorios of **Louis Spohr** as the **Restoration**'s most important works in that genre after **Felix Mendelssohn Bartholdy**'s *St. Paul* and *Elijah* and **Robert Schumann**'s *Das Paradies und die Peri* and *Der Rose Pilgerfahrt*. [JMC]

LONG 19TH CENTURY. Term first coined by British historian Eric Hobsbawm (1917–2012) to denote the period between the outbreak of the French Revolution (1789) and World War I (1914). In traditional music historiography, this period is often considered to include two contrasting styles, Classicism and Romanticism, but that dichotomy is made problematic by the difficulty of applying and discerning the values perceived in each style with any consistency or objectivity, by the fact that most if not all composers who lived and worked during the long 19th century cultivated both "classical" and "Romantic" idioms, and by the fact that both styles are governed by a single approach to harmony (tonality, with varying degrees of chromaticism) and a single, relatively stable set of genres. This set of problems was described as "the confluence of classicism and romanticism" by musicologist Paul Henry Lang (1901–1991) in his seminal *Music in Western Civilization* (New York: Norton, 1941). Refer also to the introduction to this dictionary, pp. 2–4. [JMC]

LORTZING, (GUSTAV) ALBERT (1801–1851). German composer, actor, and singer best known for German-language adaptations of the French genre of **opéra comique** (i.e., German operas with spoken dialogue that were not based on folklore or legends, as **Singspiele** were, but were in contemporary settings). He was born into a family of actor-singers and spent his youth traveling and performing in theatrical roles. Although he began composing in the early 1820s, his first important work was the **oratorio** *Die Himmelfahrt Jesu Christi* (The Ascension of Jesus Christ, LoWV 15), premiered in 1828 and performed again in 1829. In November 1833, he began working as an actor in the Leipzig Stadttheater, a post that he retained until 1845. His first full-length **comic opera**, *Die beiden Schützen* (Misunderstandings by Resemblance, LoWV 35), was composed in 1835 but not premiered until 1837. It was a success, and Lortzing immediately began composing what would become his most popular **opera**: *Zar und Zimmermann, oder die beiden Peter* (Tsar and Carpenter; or, The Two Peters, 1837), which was premiered in Leipzig and quickly entered the repertoire in other major theaters as well. Recognition of his growing reputation led to his appointment as Kapellmeister of the Leipzig Stadttheater, but his success in this capacity was mixed, and he was dismissed in 1845.

In 1846, Lortzing and **Franz von Suppé** were jointly hired as Kapellmeister at the Theater an der Wien in Vienna, but the Viennese preference for Italian over German opera and the city's well-known operatic rivalries were not to his liking. He sympathized with the events of the **Revolutions of 1848** and like most Europeans saw in them a hope for a new beginning; when the Revolution collapsed in Vienna, however, his hopes were dashed—and when the opera company of the Theater an der Wien was dissolved in November of that year, he was once again jobless. Plans were made for him to resume his post in the Leipzig Stadttheater, and he moved his entire family (a wife and 11 children) there in 1849, spending almost the entire previous year's salary on the move—only to have the post fall through. He was hired by the Friedrich-Wilhelmstädtisches Theater in Berlin in May 1850, but this, too, proved a disappointing post. A new opera, *Die vornehmen Dilettanten, oder die Opernprobe* (The Distinguished Dilettantes; or, the Opera Rehearsal, 1850–1851), had a successful premiere in Frankfurt am Main on 20 January 1851, but Lortzing did not live to enjoy its success: he died unexpectedly of a stroke the following morning.

Zar und Zimmermann remains Lortzing's most popular work and is still widely performed in Germany. His other most important operas are likewise still done in Germany: *Der Wildschutz, oder die Stimme der Natur* (The Poacher; or, The Voice of Nature, 1842), the Romantic *Zauberoper Undine* (LoWV 64, 1843–1844, premiered 1845), and *Der Waffenschmied* (The Armorer, LoWV 66, 1846). In addition to his 20 completed operas and **operettas**, he penned 18 sets of **incidental music** (including an incomplete score for Part II of **Johann Wolfgang von Goethe**'s *Faust*), many **part-songs** for **Männerchor** and mixed chorus, the above-mentioned oratorio, and a number of occasional works. [JMC]

LYADOV, ANATOLY (KONSTANTINOVICH) (1855–1914). Russian composer, teacher, and **conductor** of the Modern Romantic Generation, associated with the **Mighty Handful**. Born to a musical family in St. Petersburg (father Konstantin conducted the Mariinsky Theater), Lyadov went in 1870 to the St. Petersburg **Conservatory**, where he excelled in counterpoint and worked particularly closely with August Vasilyevich Johanson (1826–1904) and **Nikolay Rimsky-Korsakov**. Lyadov undermined his own academic success with a poor attendance record and thereby delayed his graduation until 1878. He began teaching theory that year at the Conservatory, which was to be his lifelong employer; in later years, he taught advanced counterpoint and composition as well. Among his students there were Sergei Prokofiev (1891–1853) and Nikolay Myaskovsky (1881–1950). In the 1880s, Lyadov became friends with timber merchant and arts patron Mitrofan Belyayev (1836–1904), who held weekly musical gatherings and founded his own music publishing company in 1884 to promote the music of Russian composers. Lyadov was named a trustee of the firm after Belyayev's death. Among Lyadov's best-known compositions today are the orchestral *Eight Russian Folksongs* (1906) and the **tone poems** *Baba Yaga* (1904), *The Enchanted Lake* (1909), and *Kikimora* (1910); among his other notable works are four *opera* of **songs** and over 100 pieces for **piano**. [RK]

LYRIC DRAMA. (Fr., drame lyrique; Ger., lyrisches Drama; It., dramma lirico.) Term for a staged musical drama that does not fit into the traditional categories of **comic opera** and serious **opera** (in their various national/linguistic classifications). In general, works designated as "lyric dramas" shared with comic opera settings that were contemporary and European rather than historical or allegorical and based in Classical antiquity or mythology, but unlike **opéras comiques** and *Singspiele*, they typically do not employ spoken dialogue. Like serious operas, however, they were typically serious rather than satirical or humorous in tone; their subject matter was often intimate or centered on the private sphere rather than on broad issues of public history. For purposes of characterizing the nature of the work being performed and promoting it, more lighthearted lyric dramas (e.g., **Jules Massenet**'s *Thaïs*, 1894, and **Giuseppe Verdi**'s *Falstaff*, 1893) were termed "lyric comedies" (*comédies lyriques, commedias liricas*). As with other designations for staged musical drama during the **long 19th century**, such terms were intended to be broadly suggestive rather than strict and definitive—that is, they were inherently subjective and used inconsistently.

The number of works billed as lyric dramas increased significantly in the wake of the French Revolution, presumably in order to emphasize those works' contemporary political and societal topicality. Important French works of the sort were composed by **Jean-François Le Sueur** and **Étienne-Nicolas Méhul**. Later French exponents were penned by composers including **Adolphe Adam, Daniel-François Esprit Auber, Ernest Chausson, Félicien David, César Franck, Charles Gounod, Jules Massenet, Giacomo Meyerbeer, Georges Onslow, Camille Saint-Saëns, Charles-Marie Widor**, and most famously **Claude Debussy** (*Pelléas et Melisande*, 1902, rev. 1907). Important Italian *dramme lirici* were submitted by **Gaetano Donizetti, Fromenthal Halévy, Saverio Mercadante, Amilcare Ponchielli, Giacomo Puccini**, and **Giuseppe Verdi**, among others. Although the term was most commonly applied to French and Italian operas, it also occurred in connection with English and German ones—most notably **George Whitefield Chadwick**'s *Judith* (1901) and **Frederick Delius**'s *A Village Romeo and Juliet* (1899–1901, publ. 1910) or **Ernest Bloch**'s *Macbeth* (1910) and **Peter Cornelius**'s *Der Cid* (1865). The French version of **Ludwig van Beethoven**'s **rescue opera** *Fidelio* (Paris: A. Farrenc, 1826) was billed as a *drame lyrique*. [JMC]

M

MÁ VLAST. (Cz., "My Country.") **Cycle** of six **symphonic poems** composed by **Bedřich Smetana** between around 1872 and 1879 on subjects from his native Bohemia. Collectively, they represent important milestones in Bohemian **nationalism** as well as Bohemian applications of the ideas of **program music** and the genre of the symphonic poem as cultivated in the **New German School** by **Franz Liszt** and others. Smetana also strengthened the cyclicity of the group by quoting the main theme of the first work within the second.

The cycle's six constituent works are as follows: (1) *Vyšehrad*, 1872–1874 (the 10th-century castle overlooking the River Moldau, according to legend the location of the city's first settlement); (2) *Vltava*, 1874 (*The Moldau*); (3) *Šárka*, 1875 (in Czech legend, a mythical woman warrior and leader of the Bohemian amazons in the tale of the Maidens' War first recounted in the 14th century by Cosmas of Prague); (4) *Z českých luhů a hájů*, 1875 (From Bohemian Woods and Fields); (5) *Tábor*, 1878 (a Bohemian city that according to legend was the site of the Transfiguration of Christ); and (6) *Blaník*, 1879 (a mountain near Prague where, according to legend, St. Wenceslas and an army of his knights slumber, ready to spring to their country's defense in the event of an attack by four or more armies). Of these six works, *The Moldau* is by far the best known outside the Czech Republic. Smetana published Nos. 1 and 2 in **piano-duet** arrangements and **orchestral** parts in 1879 and Nos. 3–6 in 1880; Nos. 1 and 2 were also published in full score in 1880, while No. 4 was published in full score in 1881, No. 3 in 1890, No. 5 in 1892, and No. 6 in 1894. [JMC]

See also DVOŘÁK, ANTONÍN (LEOPOLD) (1841–1904).

MACDOWELL, EDWARD (ALEXANDER) (1860–1908). U.S. composer and pianist of the Modern Romantic Generation. His compositional output, featuring several **orchestral** works and numerous **songs** and **piano** compositions, was partially influenced by **New German School** ideas and tastes through teacher **Joachim Raff**. In 1876, a 15-year-old MacDowell traveled with his mother to Paris, where he studied **piano** at the **Conservatory**. Two years later, he moved to Germany, where he studied at the Hoch Conservatory (Frankfurt) with Raff and was heard on multiple occasions by **Franz Liszt**. Fort the next several years, he taught piano and began publishing his own compositions. Early successes included his *Erste moderne Suite* for piano (Op. 10, 1880–1881, publ. 1903, rev. 1904–1905, rev. version publ. 1906) and Piano **Concerto** No. 1 (Op. 15, 1882, publ. 1884). MacDowell settled in Boston in 1888 with his wife, also from the United States. MacDowell established stateside renown through such compositions as the Piano Concerto No. 2 (Op. 23, 1884–1886, publ. 1890), *Woodland Sketches* for piano (1896, featuring the famous **character piece** "To a Wild Rose"), and the **programmatic** "Indian" **Suite** No. 2 for orchestra (Op. 48, 1891–1895, publ. 1897). In 1896, he was made the first music professor at Columbia University (New York), where he spent the rest of his life. MacDowell's last few years were impaired by mental illness. In 1907, his wife transformed their summer home in Peterboro, New Hampshire, into the MacDowell Colony for artists. [RK]

MACKENZIE, ALEXANDER (CAMPBELL) (1847–1935). Scottish composer, **conductor**, and educator of the Late Romantic Generation; with **Hubert Parry** and **Charles Villiers Stanford** one of the leading figures of the **English Musical Renaissance**. Like many British musicians of his generation, he studied on the Continent before returning to his homeland, where he strove to reinvigorate British musical education and culture. Eventually he became committed to discovering or realizing a distinctively English musical language. His initial occasion for returning (1885) was the directorship of the **Novello** Choir, but in 1888 he was elected principal of the Royal Academy of Music, an institution that he reorganized and revivified over the course of the next 36 years (*see* CONSERVATORY). He also conducted the Royal Choral Society and Philharmonic Society Orchestra and from 1892 to 1899 toured widely, championing music by English composers alongside their compeers in the Classical continental canon. He served as president of the Royal College of Organists from 1893 to 1897 and 1914 to 1916 and president of the International Musicological Society from 1908 to 1912. He was knighted in 1895, elected Fellow of the Royal College of Music in 1918, and created Knight Commander of the Royal Victorian Order in 1922.

Born into a musical family, at the age of 10 Mackenzie was sent to Sondershausen (Turingia), where he joined the court **orchestra** and participated in premieres of numerous works by **Hector Berlioz, Franz Liszt,** and **Richard Wagner**, along with other composers of the **New German School**. He returned to London in 1862, continuing his orchestral experience in the orchestra of the Royal Academy of Music. He rose steadily through the channels of the United Kingdom's musical culture while working in his native Edinburgh between 1872 and 1879, but by 1879 the strain of his activities forced him to relocate to Florence, where he began composing full-time. His first major success came with the performance of his **cantata** *The Bride* at the Three Choirs Festival in Worcester in 1881. It was on the foundation of this and a string of similar successes that his later fame was built: until his retirement from public life in the mid-1920s, he remained one of the most prominent British composers of his generation.

In addition to book-length life-and-works studies of Liszt and **Giuseppe Verdi** and numerous shorter published writings, Mackenzie's output includes five serious and **comic operas** (among them *The Cricket on the Hearth*, 1901), five *opera* of **incidental music**, two **oratorios** (most famously *The Rose of Sharon*, 1884, rev. 1910), eight secular **cantatas** and several other works for chorus with **orchestra**, a handful of sacred a cappella works, 23 orchestral compositions (most famously the ***Overture to Shakespeare's "Twelfth Night,"*** Op. 40, 1888; the **nationalist** *Britannia Overture*, 1894; and the *Scottish Concerto* for piano and orchestra, 1897), 13 *opera* of instrumental **chamber music**, 11 *opera* of **character pieces** for **piano** solo, and many **part-songs** and solo **songs**. [JMC]

See also NATIONALISM, ROMANTIC NATIONALISM.

MAGIC OPERA. *See* ZAUBEROPER.

MAGNARD, ALBÉRIC (1865–1914). French composer of the Modern Romantic Generation. Born to the well-off family of a successful author and journalist, Magnard's turn toward a career in composition began in 1886, when his friend Augustin Savard (1861–1942) won the **Prix de Rome** and when he himself witnessed Felix Mottl's (1856–1911) **Bayreuth** performance of *Tristan und Isolde*. Magnard then entered the Paris **Conservatory**, where he distinguished himself under the tutelage of **Jules Massenet**. Within a few years Magnard had met **César Franck** and, through him, **Vincent d'Indy**, whose significance as teacher and mentor to Magnard is difficult to exaggerate. By the end of Magnard's studies with d'Indy in 1892, the young composer had finished a first **opera**, *Yolande* (1891), and a **symphony** (1890); his Second Symphony followed in 1893. Magnard taught counterpoint at d'Indy's Schola Cantorum beginning in 1896. Significant later works include the operas *Guercoeur* (1901) and *Bérénice* (1909), Symphonies No. 3 and 4 (1896 and 1913, respectively), the **orchestral** pieces *Chant funèbre* (1902) and *Hymne à la justice* (1904), and a small collection of **songs**, **piano** works, and instrumental **chamber music**. Magnard's symphonies, grand and fascinating four-movement works, are equally distinctive and overlooked contributions to the genre. The *Chant funèbre* poignantly mourns the death of the composer's father, and *Hymne à la justice* is Magnard's statement on the

Dreyfus Affair, an orchestral *j'accuse*. Magnard's death in 1914 is among the most impressive in music history: after firing upon invading German soldiers from his house, the soldiers set the house on fire with him inside. [RK]

MAHLER, GUSTAV (1860–1911). German-Jewish Austrian **conductor** and composer of the Modern Romantic Generation. Today Mahler is best known for his nine richly orchestrated, large-scale **symphonies**, many of which contain references to his **songs**. Mahler was famous during his own lifetime as an **opera** conductor whose exacting rehearsal manner and perfectionism made enemies among singers, **orchestra** members, and administrators. Mahler's compositions reveal brilliantly colored, finely detailed orchestration, an eclectic vocabulary of musical **topics**, and a highly original approach to traditional structural concepts, such as **sonata form** and the **sonata plan**. A modern Romantic in the truest sense, Mahler drew from numerous German Romantic sources from earlier in the **long 19th century**, including **Johann Wolfgang von Goethe**'s *Faust*, Friedrich Rückert's (1788–1866) *Kindertotenlieder*, Arnim and Brentano's *Des knaben Wunderhorn*, and **Jean Paul Richter**'s *Titan*. His oeuvre includes nine completed symphonies, four of which incorporate singers; 46 *Gesänge* and **Lieder**, most of which he accompanied with orchestra either originally or later; the vocal-orchestral *Das Lied von der Erde* (Song of the Earth, comp. 1908–1909, premiered 1911); and a folkloric **cantata,** *Das klagende Lied* (The Plaintive Song, comp. and rev. 1878–1899, premiered and publ. 1901).

A native of Kalischt, Bohemia (now Kaliště near Humpolec, Czech Republic), Mahler moved with his family to larger Iglau, Moravia (now Jihlava), at an early age; he grew up there and learned **piano**. He went to the Vienna **Conservatory** in 1875–1878, studied piano there with Julius Epstein (1832–1926), and began composing. He began his conducting career at a theater in Bad Hall (1880); his next posts were in Ljubljana (1881), Olomouc (1883), Kassel (1883–1885), Prague (1885–1886), and Leipzig (1886–1888). After distinguishing himself in 1888 by completing **Carl Maria von Weber**'s substantially unfinished **comic opera** *Die drei Pintos* (The Three Pintos, J. Anh. 5), he conducted the Budapest Royal Opera through 1891; **Johannes Brahms** was among those impressed with his conducting there. Mahler premiered his Symphony No. 1 in 1889 as a five-movement **symphonic poem**; its critical failure hurt him. Also that year were the deaths of Mahler's father, mother, and sister Leopoldine. Mahler was left in charge of four younger siblings, two of whom no longer lived at home; Mahler moved the other two to Vienna.

Mahler moved to Hamburg in 1891 to conduct at the Stadttheater for the next six years. There he worked with highly capable singers and expanded his repertoire to include such works as **Richard Wagner**'s *Tristan und Isolde*; he also befriended an aging **Hans von Bülow**, whose subscription concerts he took over after his death in 1894. In 1892, Mahler published his *Lieder und Gesänge* (on texts by Leander, Braunfels, and Mahler himself and from Arnim and Brentano's *Des knaben Wunderhorn*). In 1894, **Richard Strauss**, an ally since Mahler's Leipzig years, premiered Mahler's First Symphony (featuring **programmatic** movement subtitles) at the **Allgemeiner Deutscher Musikverein** festival. Mahler's greatest compositional success of his Hamburg years was the Berlin premiere of his Symphony No. 2 in 1895. The **song cycle** *Lieder eines fahrenden Gesellen* (Songs of a Wayfarer) premiered in Berlin in 1896 (publ. 1897). Conductor Bruno Walter (1876–1962), who worked with Mahler in Hamburg, would serve as a fierce advocate for a full half-century beyond the composer's death.

In 1897, after converting to Catholicism, Mahler began his decade with the Vienna Court Opera; he was promoted to director within months. He also conducted the Vienna Philharmonic in 1898–1901. In 1902, Mahler married Alma Schindler (1879–1964), daughter of landscape painter Emil Jakob Schindler (1842–1892) and stepdaughter of Secessionist painter Carl Moll (1861–1945). Schindler was a composer who had trained with Josef Labor (1842–1924) and Alexander von Zemlinsky (1871–1942), but Mahler married her on the condition that she stop composing. At the Opera, Mahler raised standards tremendously and drew enthusiastic audiences for its productions. Through Moll, Mahler met Alfred Roller, whom he employed to design numerous sets. During his Vienna years, Mahler also premiered his Symphony No. 4 (Munich, 1901), Symphony No. 3 (Krefeld, 1902), Symphony No. 5 (Cologne, 1904), *Kindertotenlieder* (Songs on the Deaths of Children, Vienna, 1905), and Symphony No. 6 (Essen, 1906). He also attracted a growing crowd of supporters who continued to popularize his works in the decades after his death, including composers Alexander Zemlinsky (1871–1942) and Arnold Schoenberg (1874–1951), musicologist Guido Adler (1855–1941), conductors Willem Mengelberg (1871–1951) and Oskar Fried (1871–1941), critic Richard Specht (1870–1932), and singer Marie Gutheil-Schoder (1874–1935).

In 1907, Mahler lost his four-year-old daughter (the oldest of two) to scarlet fever. That same year, he was diagnosed with a heart condition (a valvular defect) and advised to reduce strenuous activity. Despite his achievements in Vienna, he faced rising hostility at the Austrian court and among disgruntled factions at the Opera. He moved his family to New York City near the end of 1907; there, he conducted the Metropolitan Opera and the New York Philharmonic for the rest of his life. Mahler spent the summers in Europe, where he did the bulk of his composing and conducted various ensembles. These trips also occasioned the premieres of Mahler's Symphony No. 7 (Prague, 1908) and Symphony No. 8 (Munich, 1910). Mahler traveled to Vienna in the spring of 1911; he died there of bacterial endocarditis. *Das Lied von der Erde* and Symphony No. 9 were premiered within about a year of his death; a Symphony No. 10 was left incomplete. [RK]

MALIBRAN (NÉE GARCÍA), MARIA(-FELICIA) (1808–1836). Spanish *bel canto* mezzo-soprano of the Romantic Generation. A celebrity from a celebrity family, Malibran was known for her voice's power and range (from *g* to *e³*). She and her sister Pauline Viardot (1821–1910) were trained by their father, **Manuel García**, internationally famous in his own right as a composer, tenor, impresario, and vocal pedagogue. In 1825, she emerged as an **opera** singer in London, where she performed the role of Rosina in **Gioachino Rossini**'s *Barber of Seville*, among others. When Manuel García moved to New York City that fall to establish an opera company there, Maria repeated her role as Rosina there. She married banker François Eugène Malibran in 1826; he went bankrupt within months, and the marriage failed within a year. Maria returned to Europe, where she earned her legendary reputation.

A few years later, Malibran became romantically involved with **virtuoso** violinist Charles de Bériot (1802–1870), who fathered her son in 1833 and married her in 1836. She made her Paris debut in the title role of Rossini's *Semiramide* (Théâtre-Italien, 1828). Malibran's London performance as Amina in an English adaptation of **Vincenzo Bellini**'s *La Sonnambula* (1833, Drury Lane) did wonders for that production, which was able to transfer to Covent Garden; two years later, her Amina helped the financially struggling Teatro Emornitio (Venice), which renamed itself Teatro Malibran one year after she died. Malibran created the title role in **Gaetano Donizetti**'s *Maria Stuarda* (based on the play by **Friedrich Schiller**) at Milan's Teatro alla Scala in 1835. The plot, which resonated powerfully with the **Risorgimento**, had already caused the composer trouble in an earlier attempt to stage the opera, but after Malibran refused to observe the censor's changes at the premiere, the opera was promptly banned. Malibran also created the title role in Nicola Vaccai's (1790–1848) *Giovanna Grey* at the same theater in 1836.

Among Malibran's numerous acclaimed roles were Rosina in Rossini's *Barber*, Desdemona in Rossini's *Otello*, Arsace in Rossini's *Semiramide*, Tancredi in Rossini's *Tancredi*, and Romeo in both Vaccai's *Giulietta e Romeo* and Bellini's *I Capuleti e I Montecchi* (the very end of which Malibran replaced with that of the Vaccai at an 1832 performance in Bologna). The last role created for her was that of Isoline in Michael Balfe's (1808–1870) *The Maid of Artois* (London, Drury Lane, 1836). She had been in a riding accident a month before the May premiere, and she performed the role in crutches. In September 1836, she died of complications from her injuries. [RK]

MÄNNERCHOR. (Ger., "male Chorus" *or* "men's chorus.") A chorus comprised exclusively of men (usually TTBB) or a work scored for this ensemble, with or without accompaniment. During the 19th century, such works were usually performed with one or, at most, two singers per part. The texts were rarely sentimental or philosophical, occasionally nature-centered or religious, and most commonly based on folk, **nationalist**, or patriotic themes. The genre is most commonly associated with predominantly homorhythmic textures. Important *Männerchöre* in the **long 19th century** were composed by **Hector Berlioz, Johannes Brahms, George Chadwick, Peter Cornelius, César Cui, Niels W. Gade, Charles Gounod, Edvard Grieg, Franz Liszt, Felix Mendelssohn Bartholdy, Camille Saint-Saëns, Franz Schubert, Robert Schumann, Jean Sibelius, Richard Strauss,** and **Pyotor Il'yich Tchaikovsky.** The genre was also emulated in the harmony, registration, and texture of the coda of the last movement of Mendelssohn's Third ("Scottish") **Symphony** (in A Minor, MWV N18/Op. 56, 1843), a gesture that to contemporary performers and listeners would have imparted a patriotic or **nationalist** import to the work as a whole. [JMC]
See also CHILDREN'S CHORUS; FRAUENCHOR.

MÄNNERGESANGVEREIN. *See* LIEDERTAFEL.

MANNES, DAVID (1866–1959). Violinist, **conductor**, and pioneering music educator in the United States, member of the Modern Romantic Generation. After studying violin with some of the late 19th century's leading pedagogues, in 1891 he was invited by Walter Damrosch (1862–1950) to join the New York Symphony Society. He served as its concertmaster until his retirement in 1912. Meanwhile, using his means and his authority to help introduce cultivated music to the young, the underprivileged, and amateurs in the United States, he joined the faculty of the Music School Settlement (later the Third Street Music School Settlement, still in operation) in 1901 and eventually became its director; in 1912, he founded a separate Music School Settlement for Colored Children, directed until 1914 by David I. Martin (eventual cofounder of the Martin-Smith Music School). In 1916, he founded the David Mannes Music School (now the Mannes College of Music), whose early faculty members include **Ernest Bloch** and Hans Weisse (1892–1940), a student of Heinrich Schenker. In Weiss's courses, the Mannes School became the first U.S. institution to include Schenkerian analysis in its curriculum.

Mannes's contributions were not without their detractors. Some viewed his efforts to bring cultivated music to the economically disenfranchised as catering to amateurism, while others felt that his cultivation of European "classical" music on U.S. soil detracted from a mission of indigenous composers' attempts to escape the hegemony of European music (*see* NATION-ALISM, ROMANTIC NATIONALISM). Despite these criticisms, he is generally acknowledged as one of the early 20th century's most energetic and influential advocates for the cause of U.S. music education. [JMC]

MÄRCHENOPER. (Ger., "fairy-tale opera.") A term for German-language **opera** based or drawing on fantastical, supernatural folklore or newly crafted stories in that style. Although composers outside of German-speaking Central Europe produced operas on fairy-tale subject matter, the tradition was especially strong in the German lands and endured throughout the **long 19th century**. More a post hoc category than an actual genre, *Märchenoper* runs the gamut from full opera to *Singspiel*. It is not to be confused with *Zauberoper*, a category that overlaps with *Märchenoper* but that usually refers to *Singspiel* and implies extensive special effects. Notable examples are **E. T. A. Hoffmann**'s *Undine* (1816), **Engelbert Humperdinck**'s *Hänsel und Gretel* (1893), **Heinrich Marschner**'s *Der Vampyr* (The Vampire, 1828), **Louis Spohr**'s *Alruna, die Eulenkönigen* (Alruna the Owl Queen, comp. 1808, publ. 1812, unperformed), **Richard Wagner**'s *Der fliegende Holländer* (The Flying Dutchman, 1843), and **Carl Maria von Weber**'s *Rübezahl* (Woodwose, comp. 1805, unperformed), *Der Freischütz* (1821), and *Oberon* (1826). [RK]

MARQUÉS (Y GARCÍA), (PEDRO) MIGUEL (1843–1918). Spanish composer of the Late Romantic Generation. Notable for various other reasons as well, Marqués composed five **symphonies**. He was born in the Majorcan city of Palma de Mallorca and was a considerably talented child violinist. At age 16, he left for Paris, where he studied with violinist Jean-Delphin Alard (1815–1888), entered the **Conservatory**, and befriended **Hector Berlioz**. After a brief return to Majorca, Marqués moved to Madrid for further conservatory study. While in Madrid, Marqués became involved with **zarzuela** production, first as a theater violinist and then as a composer, beginning in 1872 with *Justos por pecadores* (The Just [Pay] for the Guilty). The breakthrough zarzuela of Marqués's career was *El anillo de hierro* (The Iron Ring, 1878); other successes include *El reloj de Lucerna* (The Lucerne Clock, 1884) and *El montaguillo* (The Altar Boy, 1891). Marqués composed all five of his **symphonies** between 1867 and 1880; their use of thematic recurrence among movements and **programmaticism** suggests Berlioz's influence. As a Spanish symphonist, Marqués belonged to a small cohort including **Tomás Bretón** and Ruperto Chapí (1851–1909); the Sociedad de Conciertos de Madrid was crucial in bringing his **orchestral** repertoire to an audience. [RK]

MARSCHNER, HEINRICH (AUGUST) (1795–1861). German composer, **conductor**, and pianist of the Early Romantic Generation; the most important exponent of German Romantic **opera** between **Carl Maria von Weber**'s *Der Freischütz* and **Richard Wagner**'s post-1848 **music dramas**. He was a choirboy and had begun to compose by 1811 but in order to avoid conscription into the Prussian army in 1813 went to Prague, where he studied composition with **Václav Tomášek**. At his father's wishes, he went to Leipzig to study law at the university there but was increasingly drawn to music. He began appearing as a pianist and composing **songs** and guitar pieces by 1815, and in 1820 Weber accepted his opera *Heinrich IV und d'Aubigné* (Henry IV and d'Aubigné, 1817–1818) for production at the Deutsche Oper in Dresden. He was appointed as Weber's assistant in 1823. As Weber's health declined between then and 1826, Marschner increasingly filled in for both him and the director of the Italian Opera (Francesco Morlacchi, 1784–1841).

Despite his services to the Dresden Opera, Marschner was passed over as Weber's successor in 1826. He resigned and toured for a time with his wife, a well-known singer, and while on these travels hit upon the idea of collaborating with his brother-in-law, an actor, of creating an opera about vampires (in connection with the literary movement known as *Schauerromantik* or *schwarze Romantik*, "horror Romanticism" or "black Romanticism"). The collaboration produced Marschner's first major success, *Der Vampyr* (The Vampire, 1827; **libretto** by Wilhelm August Wohlbrück), which opened at the Leipzig Stadttheater on 29 March 1828. That triumph combined with the success of *Der Templer und die Jüdin* (The Templar and the Jewess, 1829; after Walter Scott's *Ivanhoe*) the following year to make Marschner one of the most important figures in German opera. In 1831, in acknowledgment of this renown, he was appointed director of the Court Opera in Hanover. In 1833, he completed another major success, *Hans Heiling*, but his remaining eight operas all failed; apparently, his claims to preeminence in the world of German opera were diminished by Wagner's emergence as a major figure after 1849. He traveled frequently to conduct his earlier operas and was appointed Court Kapellmeister in 1852 but was forced to resign from this post in 1859.

Marschner's reputation today rests almost entirely on *Der Vampyr*, *Templer und Jüdin*, and *Hans Heiling*, works whose expansive **orchestration** and use of recurrent themes and motives relate closely to Weber's **Leitmotivs** and Wagner's *Leitfaden*. He also composed 193 published *opera* of solo **songs** with **piano** or guitar accompaniment as well as a great many accomplished **part-songs** for mixed chorus and *Männerchor*, a *Grande ouverture solennelle* on "God Save the King" (Op. 78, 1834; *see* OVERTURE), two piano **quintets**, seven **piano trios**, and other instrumental **chamber music**, including 47 *opera* of music for **piano** solo. [JMC]

LA MARSEILLAISE. **Song** written and composed in 1792 by Claude-Joseph Rouget de Lisle (1760–1836), best known today as the French national anthem. The melody quickly came to evoke France in various ways, at times in a spirit of **nationalism** but often to represent France's invading and occupying forces. It was originally titled *Chant de guerre pour l'armée du Rhin* (War Song for the Rhine Army).

Among the numerous appearances of the anthem in musical literature, a few examples stand out. In 1840, **Richard Wagner** set **Heinrich Heine**'s poem *Die Grenadiere*, in a French translation by François Adolphe Loeve-Veimar, as a **song**, *Les deux grenadieres*, for voice and piano (WWV 60); Wagner sets the last verses—a French soldier's monologue—to a rendition of *La Marseillaise* in the accompaniment. **Robert Schumann**, too, set Heine's poem that year and used it to begin his *Romanzen und Balladen*, Vol. 2 (Op. 49, comp. 1840, publ. 1844); Schumann's *Die beiden Grenadiere* ends similarly, only here the last two verses are sung to the French tune. In his **concert overture** *Hermann und Dorothea* (Op. 136, comp. 1851), based on **Johann Wolfgang von Goethe**'s epic poem set near French-occupied Mainz, Schumann uses *La Marseillaise*'s opening phrases as a theme and draws motives from it. Best known is **Pyotor Il'yich Tchaikovsky**'s **concert overture** *1812*, which thematizes the song's opening bars to represent Napoléon Bonaparte's forces; initially, the theme is pervasive and overwhelming, but in its final instances, it is slowed down fatally before the grand Slavonic chant-inflected conclusion.

With its strong duple meter, martial dotted rhythms, and numerous verses alternating with the refrain, *La Marseillaise* is a marching song in style and function. As such, it has served as a model for many subsequent march-style national anthems. Rouget de Lisle, a French army captain, penned the song in Strasbourg on the evening of 27 April 1792; it was then printed under its original title and became popular remarkably quickly. By the end of the year it was increasingly known by its current title, derived from the soldiers from Marseilles who sang the song while marching in Paris. It was made France's official national anthem in 1795. [RK]

MARX, (FRIEDRICH HEINRICH) ADOLF BERNHARD [SAMUEL MOSES] (1795–1866). Composer, critic, music theorist, and music educator of the Early Romantic Generation; one of the most influential theorists and critics of the mid-19th century. He studied law and composition (the latter with Daniel Gottlob Türk [1750–1813]) at the University of Halle until Türk's death, practicing law in nearby Naumberg from 1815 to 1821 and converting from Judaism to Lutheranism in 1819. After moving to Berlin in 1821, he became increasingly involved in music, most notably studying with Carl Friedrich Zelter (1758–1832), being named editor of the *Berliner allgemeine musikalische Zeitung* (*BamZ*) in 1824, and becoming an intimate friend of Zelter's pupil **Felix Mendelssohn Bartholdy**. In 1828, he applied for a PhD from the University of Marburg, a degree that was "conferred in philosophy and particularly music" in 1831. Meanwhile, he had received a supernumerary appointment as professor of musicology (*Musikwissenschaft*) at the University of Berlin, where he also became director of music in 1832 after the deaths of Zelter and Bernhard Klein (1793–1832).

Marx's influence as a music educator was further expanded in 1850, when he collaborated with Julius Stern (1820–1883) and Theodor Kullak (1818–1882) to form a private *Berliner Musikschule* (Berlin School of Music)—a venture from which Marx withdrew in 1856 but which remained in existence until it was merged with the Berlin Universität der Künste in 1966. He was also an active editor of music by **Johann Sebastian Bach, Ludwig van Beethoven**, and **George Frideric Handel**, preparing the first published editions of Bach's *St. Matthew Passion* and B-Minor Mass, the **piano-duet** editions of Beethoven's op. 132 and 135 **string quartets**, several Bach **cantatas**, and individual smaller pieces by Handel. In addition to his numerous important writings in the *BamZ*, he published numerous highly influential books: *Die Kunst des Gesangs, theoretisch-praktisch* (A Theoretical and Practical Introduction to the Art of Singing, 1826), *Über Malerei in der Tonkunst: Ein Maigruß an Kunstphilosophen* (On Musical Tone-Painting: A May Greeting to Philosophers of Art, 1828), *Die Lehre von der musikalischen Komposition, praktisch-theoretisch* (Theory and Practice of Musical Composition; 4 vols., 1837–1847, with numerous subsequent editions), *Die Musik des neunzehnten Jahrhunderts und ihre Pflege: Methode der Musik* (The Music of the 19th Century and Its Culture, 1854–1855), *Ludwig van Beethoven: Leben und Schaffen* (Beethoven: His Life and Works, 1859); *Vollständige Chorschule* (Complete School of Choral Singing, 1860), *Gluck und die Oper* (Gluck and Opera, 1863), *Erinnerungen: Aus meinem Leben* (Memoirs, 1865), and the posthumously published *Das Ideal und die Gegenwart* (The Ideal and the Present, 1867). *Die Lehre von der musikalischen Komposition*, although deeply indebted to **Carl Czerny** and **Antoine Reicha**, is the principal source for the latter-day understanding of **sonata form**. Marx contributed early ideas for Mendelssohn's **oratorio** *St. Paul*. His most important musical composition was the oratorio *Mose* (Moses, Op. 10, 1841, publ. 1844), premiered in Breslau in 1841 and later performed by **Franz Liszt** in Weimar in 1853.

Marx was one of the first to argue that thorough knowledge of the history and theory of music was not only an essential component of the training of composers but also an opportunity for the organic development of any human being within an overall educational system. This view, asserted in his *Die alte Musiklehre im Streit mit unserer Zeit* (Traditional Methods of

Teaching Composition in Conflict with Our Time, 1841), led to a well-publicized controversy with the theologian and influential music critic G. W. Fink (1783–1846).

Marx was also one of the 19th century's most influential exponents for the application to music of the ideas of **Georg Wilhelm Friedrich Hegel**, whose lectures at the University of Berlin he may well have heard in the 1820s. He viewed the history of music as a dialectical process of evolution based on the conflict and synthesis of opposing forces that continually strive to realize the *Weltgeist* (world-spirit). This process applied not only to the musical art as a whole but also to musical genres, composers, and individual compositions and their inner workings. All were concrete manifestations and agents of abstract ideas that were subject to these great historical forces: musical **motives** combine to form themes, whose combination and arrangement in larger form was a unique expression of the emotions, external events and actions, and overall personality of the composer, who personified a particular idea in the historical advancement of the musical art, of the arts generally, of society, and of the world as a whole. For Marx, this process required recognition of a profoundly antithetical relationship between, for example, **Ludwig van Beethoven** and **Gioachino Rossini**, between **opera** and **symphony**, and between Italian and German music: historical process required a synthesis of these dialectically oppositional forces. This Hegelian outlook and its pronounced telos made Marx a champion of progressive currents. His writings submitted eloquent support for Beethoven's late works at a time when these were little appreciated as well as for **Hector Berlioz, Franz Liszt**, and (before their friendship ended in 1836) Mendelssohn. They also provided important historical and philosophical scaffolding for the arguments of the **New German School.** [JMC]

See also BIOGRAPHICAL FALLACY; CONSERVATORY; ORGANICISM.

MASCAGNI, PIETRO (1863–1945). Italian composer, **conductor**, and educator of the Modern Romantic Generation, known today primarily for his *verismo* opera *Cavalleria rusticana*. He studied music theory and composition from an early age, in 1882 enrolling in the Milan **Conservatory**, where he studied with **Amilcare Ponchielli** and roomed for some time with **Giacomo Puccini**. He failed to keep up with his studies, however, and was expelled in 1884. Thereafter, he began conducting **operettas** with various touring companies until his wife became pregnant. The family settled in Puglia, and Mascagni taught private lessons and conducted a local theater **orchestra** to earn money. When the Milan-based music publisher Edoardo Sonzogno (1836–1920) announced a competition for a one-act **opera**, open to all Italian composers who had not yet had an opera produced, with the three winning operas performed in Rome at the publisher's expense, Mascagni asked his friend Giovanni Targioni-Tozzetti (1863–1934) to write a libretto after Giovanni Verga's (1840–1922) well-known *verismo* play *Cavalleria rusticana* (1884) for him to use in the competition. The hastily composed opera was adjudicated one of the winners and created a sensation when it was premiered in Rome on 17 May 1890, rapidly spreading throughout Europe and amassing a considerable fortune for publisher and composer alike.

Mascagni composed several other successful operas—notably *L'amico Fritz* (Friend Fritz, 1891), the **exoticist** *Iris* (1898), and *Il piccolo Marat* (The Lesser Marat, 1921)—and several failures, but he never managed to replicate the success of *Cavalleria rusticana*. In 1895 he was appointed director of the Conservatory in Pesaro but lost this position in 1903. He became an active conductor of his own and others' music and was appointed director at La Scala in 1929 when the anti-Fascist Toscanini resigned. He made a 50th-anniversary recording of *Cavalleria rusticana* in 1940. In addition to his 17 operas and **operettas**, he composed a **Requiem** and a sizable body of sacred choral music (almost all of it still unpublished), plus 35 **songs** (mostly still unpublished, although some were reused in Mascagni's operas). He also composed a **symphony** (1881, unpublished), an *Elegia* on **Richard Wagner**'s death (1883, unpublished), **incidental music** for the play version of Sir Hall Caine's (1853–1931) 1901 novel *The Eternal City* (1902), a **symphonic poem** titled *Rapsodia satanica* for the 1915 film *Alfa*, several pieces of instrumental **chamber music** (all still unpublished), and five early pieces for **piano** solo and **piano duet**. [JMC]

MASON. U.S. family of musicians; with the **Steinways**, one of the most influential musical families of the 19th century in the United States. The initiator of the family's historical distinction was Lowell Mason (I) (1792–1872), a composer and music educator whose sons Daniel Gregory (1820–1869), Lowell (II) (1823–1885), William (1829–1908), and Henry (1831–1890) contributed actively to U.S. musical culture as composers, educators, performers, and publishers. Grandson Daniel Gregory (II) (1873–1953) carried the family's legacy of musical distinction well into the 20th century as a composer, educator, and writer on music.

Lowell Mason (I), often cited as the father of U.S. music education, was born in Medfield, Massachusetts, to musically inclined parents and by age 16 had studied singing, learned to play several instruments, and served as church choir director. He moved to Savannah, Georgia, in 1812 at the age of 20. There, he became a successful banker and community personage, leading concerts and singing schools from 1813 to 1824 and, as superintendent of a Presbyterian church's Sunday School, opening the first Sunday School for black children in the United States in 1826. He published his first collection of hymns, *The Boston* **Handel** *and* **Haydn** *Society Collection of Church Music*, all contrafacta of tunes by European composers, anonymously in

1822, and the collection's success led to his acceptance in 1827 of an offer to supervise music in Boston's three Congregational churches. His work as a choirmaster earned him a national reputation, and in 1834 he and George James Webb (1803–1887) founded the Boston Academy of Music in order to promote church music and raise musical standards. That institution, too, was a resounding success. In addition to facilitating the acceptance of music as an element of the curriculum in Boston grammar schools, its annual 7- to 10-day conventions became a national phenomenon involving thousands of choral singers around the united States. He traveled to Europe (England, France, the German lands, and Switzerland in 1837 and 1851–1853), collecting music, observing European music education, and lecturing.

Over the course of his career, Mason composed more than 1,600 hymn tunes and many more parodies of existing melodies. His publications include 49 hymnals, psalters, and other collections of music for church; 15 collections of mixed sacred and secular melodies; and 18 collections for Sunday Schools and grammar schools. His success at integrating sophisticated harmonies and styles of singing into the structures of the U.S. educational system was unfortunate in that it diminished the standing of indigenous folk-like traditions of hymn singing as well as the distinctive sounds of 18th-century hymn and psalm singing, but it was a remarkable accomplishment that remains foundational to musical life in the United States today.

Of Mason's sons, Daniel Gregory and Lowell (II) Mason were most important as publishers of music and other educational materials, mostly through the firm of Mason Brothers; together (for a time in partnership with their brother Henry), they published English and French dictionaries, histories, school textbooks, and music periodicals, including *The New York Musical Gazette*, as well as much music. Henry Mason is important for his work as cofounder of Mason & Hamlin, a leading U.S. manufacturer of melodeons, **pianos**, and flat-topped cabinet organs, while William Mason, an accomplished pianist, became a respected composer. William studied at the Leipzig Conservatory with **Ignaz Moscheles** and in Weimar with **Franz Liszt** and traveled widely on the Continent and in England before returning to the United States, where he performed for a time before settling down to compose **virtuoso** piano music and glees, publish pedagogical manuals, and teach.

Daniel Gregory Mason (II), son of Henry, followed in his grandfather's footsteps as an exponent of European-based sophistication in U.S. music, studying with **John Knowles Paine**, **George Whitefield Chadwick**, and renowned music theorist Percy Goetschius (1853–1943). He began publishing in 1894 and working as a writer on music in 1902. He was appointed as lecturer in music at Columbia University in 1905—an affiliation he retained, with promotions up to the rank of **MacDowell** Professor, until his retirement in 1942. He received publication prizes from the Juilliard Foundation and the

Society for the Publication of American Music, was elected to the National Institute of Arts and Letters in 1938, and was awarded honorary doctorates from Tufts College (1929), Oberlin College (1931), and the Eastman School of Music (1932). He authored and coauthored 18 books on subjects ranging from major European composers of the 19th century (**Ludwig van Beethoven, Johannes Brahms,** and **Edvard Grieg**) to the **string quartet** and contemporary composers. His compositional output includes three **symphonies**; two orchestral preludes and fugues; many **songs, part-songs,** and choral works; 13 *opera* of instrumental **chamber music**; and several works for piano or organ. [JMC]

MASSENET, JULES (ÉMILE FRÉDÉRIC) (1842–1912). French composer of the Late Romantic Generation; the most prolific French composer of **opera** in the late 19th century and early 20th century. He grew up in poverty but was able to enroll in the Paris **Conservatory** in 1851, running away and returning to Paris in order to continue his studies when his family moved to Savoy in 1854. In order to support himself while studying harmony, counterpoint, and composition (the last with **Ambroise Thomas**), he played in cafés and worked as timpanist at the Théâtre Lyrique, thereby gaining valuable experience with the operas of **Ludwig van Beethoven** (*see FIDELIO, ODER DIE EHELICHE LIEBE,* OP. 72), Christoph Willibald Ritter von Gluck (1714–1787), **Wolfgang Amadeus Mozart,** and **Carl Maria von Weber.** He was also impressed by **Hector Berlioz**'s, **Jules Étienne Pasdeloup**'s, and **Richard Wagner**'s performances in the French capital, and his progress as a composer was such that by 1862 he was able to win the *Prix de Rome,* an honor that brought him a two-year stay in Italy, much travel, a meeting with **Franz Liszt,** and the acquaintance of his future wife. After returning to Paris, he began publishing his work and received a commission for a one-act work to be performed at the Opéra-Comique (*La grand' tante* [The Great Aunt, 1867]). He also became a member of the circle of aspiring composers that included **Georges Bizet, Alexis de Castillon, Léo Delibes, Henri Duparc, Édouard Lalo, Gabriel Fauré,** and **Camille Saint-Saëns.** His concentrated work as a composer for the stage was interrupted by the **Franco-Prussian War,** in which Massenet served in the infantry.

Massenet's rise to fame began in earnest after the war, not least of all through the **oratorios** *Marie-Magdeleine* (1871–1872, publ. 1873; this work occasioned Pauline Viardot-García's return to the public stage) and *Eve* (1874, publ. 1875) but also through his colorful themed **orchestral suites** (especially Nos. 3 and 4, both 1874) and especially the **exoticist grand opera** *Le roi de Lahore* (The King of Lahore, 1877). In 1878 he succeeded Thomas in a professorship at the Paris Conservatory, holding the post until he was offered the directorship in 1896. (He declined the latter because it was not a permanent appointment and resigned his professorship at the same time.) There, he became known as an industrious and inspiring pedagogue. Despite several stinging failures and halfhearted successes, wealth and honors were abundant during the remainder of his career: he traveled widely to conduct his works, chose his own **librettists** and subjects, and became known as the urbane epitome of his generation's aspirations toward an international career centered on French music. Although the Opéra declined *Hérodiade* (1881, rev. 1884), it was a resounding success when it was premiered in Brussels, and *Manon* (1884) and *Werther* (1892) immediately won long-standing positions in the international repertoire.

Massenet's output includes some 39 serious and **comic operas** on subjects adapted from **Lord Byron**, Gustave Flaubert (1821–1880), **Johann Wolfgang von Goethe**, and **Victor Hugo**, among others. His vocal output also includes 14 sets of **incidental music**; four oratorios; one **motet** and six other surviving sacred choral works; two surviving **cantatas**; seven smaller choral works for mixed chorus a cappella and with accompaniment of **piano, orchestra**, or organ; 11 works for male chorus (*see* ORPHÉON); some 250 *mélodies* and three **song cycles**; and 17 **part-songs** for various combinations of voices. His instrumental oeuvre includes four **ballets**, one piano **concerto**, five numbered and three other orchestral **suites** based on stage works, one **symphonic poem**, two **concert overtures**, a **fantasy** for cello and orchestra, and several smaller works. There are also several works for instrumental **chamber** ensemble, piano solo, and **piano duet** and arrangements of music by Luigi Boccherini (1743–1805), **Léo Delibes**, **Édouard Lalo**, and **Franz Schubert**. Of these, the operas are the best-known genre—especially *Manon*, *Werther*, *Thaïs* (1894), and *Cendrillon* (1899)—but other works, such as the *10 pièces de genre* for piano solo (Op. 10, 1866; *see* CHARACTER (CHARACTERISTIC) PIECE), the third and fourth orchestral suites, the oratorio *Marie-Magdeleine*, and the song cycle *Poème d'avril* (Op. 14, ?1866, publ. 1868), have also retained their place in the repertoire. The Meditation from *Thaïs*, an accompanied violin solo that exemplifies Massenet's elegant melodic style and delicate imagination, has acquired a life as an instrumental composition independent of the opera from which it is taken. His operas are notable for their celebration of important and strong female central roles. [JMC]

MATTHÄUS-PASSION. See ST. MATTHEW PASSION.

MAZURKA. Umbrella term for a family of traditional Polish dances that originated in eastern Poland in the 16th century. Such dances could be either fiery and war-like (*mazurs* or *mazureks*), lively and merry (*obertas* or *obereks*), or slower and melancholy (*kujawiaks*); all were typically danced by groups of 4 to 12 dancers. Musically, they were in triple meter, with accents on the second and third beats (accompanied by heel tapping), organized into two or four repeated sections of six to eight measures each; they often employed bagpipe-like drone harmonies in the accompaniment and cultivated the raised fourth scale degree typical of Slavic **folk song**.

Works designated *mazurka* began to be cultivated west of Poland (specifically in the German lands) during the late 17th and 18th centuries and were well known in the flourishing **salon** culture of Paris by the early 19th century. Their archetypal composer during the **long 19th century** was **Fryderyk Chopin**, who between 1830 and 1846 published some 45 works so designated in 11 numbered *opera* (opp. 6, 7, 17, 24, 30, 33, 41, 50, 56, 59, and 63) and another four without opus number, with another nine published posthumously (*see* WOO). Chopin's highly stylized masterpieces were preceded by published mazurkas by **Adrien Boieldieu** and **Maria Szymanowska**, among others. Further notable examples were penned by **Mily Balakirev, Francisco Barbieri, Hans von Bülow, Cécile Chaminade, César Cui, Claude Debussy, Léo Delibes, Antonín Dvořák, Edward Elgar, Gabriel Fauré, Alexander Glazunov, Mikhail Glinka, Louis Moreau Gottschalk, Adolf von Henselt, Henri Herz, Friedrich Kalkbrenner, Franz Liszt, Albert Lortzing, Anatoly Lyadov, William Mason, Modest Mussorgsky, Joachim Raff, Nikolai Rimsky-Korsakov, Bernhard Romberg, Anton Rubinstein, Camille Saint-Saëns, Alexander Scriabin, Louis Spohr, Johann Strauss (II), Pyotor Il'yich Tchaikovsky,** and **Charles-Marie Widor.** [JMC]

See also EXOTICISM; NATIONALISM, ROMANTIC NATIONALISM.

MÉHUL, ÉTIENNE-NICOLAS (1763–1817). French composer of the Early Romantic Generation; with **Luigi Cherubini** and François-Joseph Gossec (1734–1829) one of the most influential of the Revolutionary and Napoleonic eras, admired by **Ludwig van Beethoven, Hector Berlioz, Felix Mendelssohn Bartholdy, Richard Wagner,** and **Carl Maria von Weber** for his music's novel instrumentation and his keen sense of musical drama. Trained as a church organist, he was encouraged to write for the stage by Christoph Willibald Ritter von Gluck (1714–1787) while in Paris in 1778. He first gained attention for his arrangements of other composers' works and his keyboard compositions, but his reputation as a composer for the stage was secured with the **operas** *Euphrosine, ou Le tyran corrigé* (Euphrosine, or The Tyrant Reformed, 1790), *Stratonice* (1792), and *Le jeune sage et le vieux fou* (The Wise Young Man and the Old Fool, 1793), all performed at the Théâtre-Italien (later the Opéra-Comique).

Méhul's strong sense of drama, orchestration, and graceful melody resonated powerfully with the operagoing public, and in recognition of that reputation he became an inspector of the newly formed Paris **Conservatory** when it was formed in 1795. He was also a successful composer of Revolutionary hymns for the Republic's music festivals (e.g., the *Hymne à la raison*, 1793, publ. 1794; later titled *Hymne patriotique*). The climax of his career as a composer of **comic operas** came with *Joseph* in 1807. During the Napoleonic era, he also composed five **symphonies** and a number of **cantatas** on Napoleonic themes as well as a Mass in A-flat major (ca. 1804; written for Napoléon Bonaparte's coronation but not performed there). His output includes a total of 34 **comic** and serious operas, four **ballets**-pantomimes and three sets of **incidental music**, many choral works with orchestral or wind and brass accompaniment, much instrumental **chamber music**, two works for wind ensemble, and seven piano **sonatas** as well as the five symphonies mentioned above. [JMC]

DIE MEISTERSINGER VON NÜRNBERG, **WWV 96**. (Ger., "The Mastersingers of Nuremberg.") **Comic opera** in three acts by **Richard Wagner**. Wagner wrote the prose draft of the **libretto** while reading Georg Gottfried Gervinus's *Geschichte der poetischen National-Literatur der Deutschen* (History of the Poetic National Literature of the Germans, 1835–1842), also considering it a satyr pendant to the tragic *Tannhäuser* (WWV 72, 1842–1845), just as Greek tragedies were often followed by satyr plays. He returned to the libretto in 1861, completed the poem in January 1862, and began composing the music in April of that year. The score was completed in October 1867, and the immensely successful premiere took place at the Royal Court and National Theater, Munich, under the direction of **Hans von Bülow** on 21 June 1868.

Die Meistersinger is the only comic opera from Wagner's mature period and his only mature **opera** situated in an actual historical setting rather than a mythic or legendary one. It is also significant because in it, Wagner, strongly influenced by Arthur Schopenhauer's (1788–1860) argument that music's ability to express ideas without recourse to words rendered it aesthetically superior to the other arts, effectively renounced a number of ideas that had been central to his writings during the Revolutionary period 1848–1851. Most importantly, the aesthetic of the *Gesamtkunstwerk* is here scarcely in evidence, if at all, as is Wagner's rejection of the clearly delineated arias, duets, ensembles, and other "numbers" characteristic of conventional opera at mid-century.

Finally, despite its comic spirit, the opera is also strongly informed by Wagner's overriding artistic and political agenda of the 1860s: to rid "the German spirit" of impure or corrupting influences, chief among them (in Wagner's view) the Jews. Whereas the protagonist Hans Sachs is based on the actual historical cobbler and guild master by that name (1494–1576) and the young knight Walther von Stolzberg possesses all the character traits appropriate to a *Heldentenor*, the mastersinger Beckmesser, who also serves as town clerk, is a genuine philistine; Wagner's linguistic and musical portrayal, as well as his actions, are a veritable catalog of the anti-Semitic clichés cultivated by him and other anti-Semites of his day. Beckmesser's eventual onstage humiliation as he is unable to sing Walther's Prize Song is a de facto enactment of Wagner's ideas of why Jews are incapable of great artistic expression, first expressed pseudonymously in "Über das Judenthum in der Musik" (On Jewry in Music, 1850) in the *Neue Zeitschrift für Musik*, explicated in expressly musical terms in "Über das Dirigieren" (On Conducting, 1869), and then amplified, with attribution to Wagner, in a separate publication of "Das Judenthum" (Leipzig: J. J. Weber). The latter two were published in 1869, just one year after the premiere of *Die Meistersinger*. [JMC]

MELODRAMA. (Gr., "action with music"; Fr., *mélodrame*; Ger., *Melodram*; It., *melologo*.) Not to be confused with Italian *melodramma*, which denotes musical drama or simply "**opera**." In popular parlance, the term *melodrama* generally denotes any musical drama that relies heavily or disproportionately on disaster, hyperemotionalism, and sensational action; in this application, the term *melodramatic* is pejorative. In professional usage, it denotes a work or section of a work in which speech sounds simultaneously with music or, more specifically, a staged musical drama in which spoken dialogue occurs during brief pauses in the musical accompaniment. The latter application differs from the various forms of light opera in that the musical portion is instrumental or choral, never cast as an aria or ballad. Sometimes, such works include only a single protagonist or two protagonists and are designated as *monodramas* or *duodramas*. In the **long 19th century**, the performance of melodrama also typically involved a fairly stable rhetoric of gestures (sometimes known as *attitudes*) as well as pantomime and dance. Although melodrama is no longer in vogue in staged musical drama, the concept is central to film and television music, specifically in film's ubiquitous use of a musical sound track that unfolds simultaneously with speech in order to underscore the emotional or dramatic significance of the moment. The subjects of melodramas could be either comic or serious, and the musical accompaniment could be provided by **piano** solo or **piano duet**, by chamber ensemble, or by **orchestra**, with or without chorus.

Although the use of melodrama in the third sense outlined above predates the concept's theorization in Classical Greece (where the term was coined to explain an already-existing practice), its applications in the long 19th century date from J. E. Eberlin's (1702–1762) little-known Latin drama *Sigismund* (1753) and J.-J. Rousseau's (1712–1778) "scène lyrique" *Pygmalion* (1762, first set to music 1770 by Horace Coignet [1735–1821]). The latter, no doubt partly because of Rousseau's notoriety, was quickly translated into English, German, Spanish, and other languages, with music composed by Franz Asplmayr (1728–1786; Vienna, 1772), Anton Schweitzer (1735–1787; Weimar,

1772), and Georg Benda (1722–1795; Gotha, 1779), creating a vogue for melodrama in the late 18th century. Well-known examples from the long 19th century include the Prison Scene from **Ludwig van Beethoven**'s *Fidelio*, passages in **Hector Berlioz**'s *Lélio, ou le retour à la vie* (H. 55/Op. 14b, 1831–1832, publ. 1855), **Heinrich Marschner**'s *Hans Heiling* (1833), **Felix Mendelssohn Bartholdy**'s incidental music to Racine's *Athalia* (MWV M16/Op. posth. 74, 1842–1845), **Gioachino Rossini**'s *La gazza ladra* (1816, publ. 1854), **Bedřich Smetana**'s *The Two Widows* (1873–1874, rev. 1877), **Giuseppe Verdi**'s *Macbeth* (1847, rev. 1865) and *La traviata* (1853), **Richard Wagner**'s *7 Kompositionen zu Goethes "Faust"* (WWV 15/Op. 5, 1831), and the Wolf's Glen scene from **Carl Maria von Weber**'s *Der Freischütz* (J. 277, 1817–1821, publ. 1822).

Complete works in the genre of the melodrama include **Adrien Boieldieu**'s *La dame blanche* (1825), **Franz Liszt**'s *Der traurige Mönch* (LW P3, 1860, publ. 1872), **Franz Schubert**'s "Abschied von der Erde" (D. 824, 1826), **Robert Schumann**'s *Schön Hedwig* (Op. 106, 1849, publ. 1853), **Richard Strauss**'s *Enoch Arden* (TrV 181/Op. 38, 1897), and **Pyotr Il'yich Tchaikovsky**'s *The Voyevoda* (Op. 3, 1867–1868, publ. 1869). [JMC]

See also CHAMBER MUSIC; GESAMTKUNSTWERK; OPERA; SYNAESTHESIA; *TABLEAU VIVANT* (PL. *TABLEAUX VIVANTS*).

MENDELSSOHN BARTHOLDY, (JACOB LUDWIG) FELIX (1809–1847). German composer, **conductor**, pianist, organist, and music educator; member of the Romantic Generation. He is best known today as the composer of perennial favorites such as his Violin **Concerto** in E Minor (MWV O14/Op. 64, comp. 1844, publ. 1845), the A-minor ("Scottish"), D-minor ("Reformation"), A-major ("Italian"), and **Symphonies** (MWV N18, N15, and N16/Op. 56 and opp. posth. 90 and 107, comp. 1829–1843, 1832, and 1833–1834), the *Midsummer Night's Dream* and Hebrides **Overtures** (MWV P3 and P7/opp. 21 and 26, comp. 1826 and 1830–1832, publ. 1832), and the **oratorios** *St. Paul* and *Elijah* (MWV A14 and A25/opp. 36 and 70, comp. 1833–1836 and 1845–1856, publ. 1836 and 1847) as well as several Psalm settings for soloists, chorus, and **orchestra** an **Octet** in E-flat Major for Strings (MWV R20/Op. 20, comp. 1825, publ. 1833), two **piano trios** (MWV Q29 and Q33/opp. 49 and 66, comp. 1839 and 1845, publ. 1840 and 1846), numerous works for **piano** solo. The inventor of two of the 19th century's most important genres of **program music**, the programmatic **concert overture** and the **Lied ohne Worte** (song without words), he was also a **virtuoso** pianist and organist and one of the mid-19th century's most innovative and sought-after conductors. He was the organizer and director of the German lands' first **conservatory** of music, brother and musical confidant of **Fanny Hensel**, and a friend or close acquaintance of luminaries as diverse as

Hector Berlioz, Fryderyk Chopin, Johann Wolfgang von Goethe, Franz Liszt, Adolph Bernhard Marx, and Clara and Robert Schumann. He was one of the most successful cultural leaders of the Restoration in England as well as his native Germany, and he was highly regarded in France and the Italian lands as well. He is also widely regarded as one of the 19th century's most notable prodigies and influential promoters of the music of Johann Sebastian Bach (*see* BACH REVIVAL, BACH AWAKENING, BACH RENAISSANCE).

Mendelssohn was a grandson of the Jewish Enlightenment philosopher Moses Mendelssohn (1729–1786), whose arguments for religious tolerance had proven decisive for the assimilation of Jews into European society in the early 19th century. He apparently regarded this illustrious ancestry with understandable pride, but he never received any formal instruction in Judaism; he was baptized and raised Lutheran and remained a devout Lutheran to the end of his life. He was born in Hamburg, where father's banking firm supported the resistance to Napoléon Bonaparte in the composer's native Hamburg, but when the firm ran into trouble with the French emperor's puppet government in 1811 the family fled to Berlin. Felix, then two, soon began to demonstrate extraordinary ability in a variety of endeavors. His pianistic abilities were widely recognized during his first decade and his first original compositions were written when he was age 10. He began study in composition with Carl Friedrich Zelter (1758–1832) in 1819, and in 1821 Zelter introduced him to Goethe, who took a strong paternal and intellectual interest in him and became an important mentor and source of artistic inspiration.

Mendelssohn's growth in the mid-and later 1820s was extraordinary by any measure. He published his Opus 1 (the Piano Quartet in C Minor, MWV Q11) in 1823, at the age of 14, and by 1825–1826 (age 16–17) he was able to pen the works whose final versions stand as his first mature masterpieces: the Octet for Strings and the *Midsummer Night's Dream Overture*. By age 20 he had authored accomplished works in an astonishing array of genres—including, in addition to the Octet and the *Midsummer Night's Dream Overture*, the first version of the *Hebrides Overture*; an early string quartet and his first two mature quartets; Catholic as well as Protestant sacred choral works; secular choral music with piano and orchestral accompaniments; six staged musical dramas (comic opera, Liederspiel, operetta, and Singspiel); numerous works for organ and for piano solo (the latter category including several *Lieder ohne Worte* and other character pieces, plus seven sonatas, several études, and several fantasies and capriccios); and much vocal chamber music.

Meanwhile, in the mid-1820s Mendelssohn had also set out on his career path as promoter of early music and conductor. Early in 1824 his maternal grandmother gave him a manuscript copy of Johann Sebastian Bach's *St.*

Matthew Passion; this he conducted publicly (with assistance, counsel, and support from Zelter) with the Berlin *Singakademie* in two much-anticipated performances on 11 and 21 March 1829. Immediately after the second of these concerts he embarked on a tour of England, Scotland, and Wales, meeting cultural luminaries and performing his own and others' music as conductor and pianist. He was offered a chair in music at the University of Berlin in 1830, but refused; and from March to June 1832 he traveled extensively in Switzerland, the Italian lands, France, and London and arranging for public and private performances of his music in order to prepare the way for a secure post as a professional musician. After an unsuccessful bid for the position as Zelter's successor at the *Singakademie* (January 1833), he accepted an invitation to serve as Municipal Music Director in Düsseldorf. He held this position until August 1835, when he assumed the directorship of the renowned Gewandhaus Orchestra in Leipzig. Such was his success in the Saxon capital that the well-known Cäcilienverein (**Cecilian** Society) in Frankfurt am Main planned to recruit him to assume the direction of that ensemble, but in March 1836 the University of Leipzig awarded him an honorary doctorate, citing him as a "most illustrious man" for his "contributions to the art of music."

Mendelssohn would remain associated with Leipzig to the end of his life, even as his international fame grew. His reputation reached new heights with the sensational premiere of *St. Paul* at the Lower Rhine Music Festival in May 1836. In the early 1840s he built steadily on this growing prestige: he worked energetically to garner financial and public backing for the first monument to Bach (still extant today, outside the St. Thomas Church in Leipzig); supported the new Prussian monarch Friedrich Wilhelm IV's (fl. 1840-61) efforts at reform by serving as *General-Musik-Direktor für kirchliche und geistliche Musik* (General Music Director for Ecclesiastical and Sacred Music) in 1841-42; and in August 1842 met with King August II of Saxon to persuade him to found the German lands' first conservatory of music, in Leipzig. The institution's doors opened in April 1843, and Mendelssohn both directed and taught there for the remainder of his career. The pinnacle of fame was reached with the premiere of Elijah at the Birmingham Festival in August 1846, but his triumph was not to last—for the death of Fanny Hensel in May 1847 threw him into a deep depression, followed by his own death on 4 November, the result of a series of subarachnoid hemorrhages. He was 38.

Mendelssohn maintained a high public profile as a performer (pianist, organist, and conductor) throughout his career. As a pianist he appeared as soloist in his own and others' music in public and private concerts in England and around the continent and was renowned for his impeccable technique and his powers of improvisation. As an organist, too, he was known for his improvisations, but his intimate knowledge of that instrument enabled him to enhance its repertoire through two major published *opera* (the Three Preludes and Fugues, MWV SD 15/Op. 37 and the Six Sonatas, MWV SD 31/ Op. 65). His 1840 benefit concert for the German lands' first monument to J. S. Bach was another milestone in the Baroque master's posthumous reception. As a conductor, in addition to regular work in Düsseldorf, Leipzig, and Berlin he directed the Lower Rhine Music Festival in 1833, 1835, 1836, 1838, 1839, 1842, and 1846, also conducting his **oratorios** *St. Paul* and *Elijah* at the Triennial Birmingham Music Festival in 1837 and 1846, and conducting the concerts of the Philharmonic Society of London during a total of 10 visits to that city. Important performances of his own works (among them the premieres of his A-major ["Italian"] Symphony [MWV N16/Op. posth. 90] and *Hebrides Overture* [MWV P7/Op. 26) were given there under his baton, and he also performed as pianist with that orchestra (including performances of his two **piano concertos**).

Mendelssohn's efforts to promote new and recent works in his work as a conductor, music director, and pianist were unsurpassed in their day: in addition to the premières of works by **Niels W. Gade** (the First and Second Symphonies), Robert Schumann (the First and Fourth symphonies), and **Louis Spohr** (the Seventh Symphony), he programmed and conducted the first performance of **Franz Schubert**'s "Great" C-Major Symphony (D. 944). The ranks of the dozens of contemporary composers whose music he programmed and/or played or conducted in Leipzig alone include: **William Sterndale Bennett**, Charles de Bériot (1802–1870), **Hector Berlioz**, Norbert Burgmüller (1810–1836), Heinrich Wilhelm Ernst (1812–1865), Auguste Franchomme (1808–1884), Moritz Hauptmann (1792–1868), Fanny Hensel, **Adolf von Henselt**, Jan Kalivoda (1801–1866), Carl Koßmaly (1812–1893), **Franz Lachner**, Peter Josef von Lindpaintner (1791–1856), **Franz Liszt, Heinrich Marschner, Saverio Mercadante, Giacomo Meyerbeer, Bernhard Molique, Ignaz Moscheles, Otto Nicolai, Jacques Offenbach, Elias Paris-Alvars**, Ferdinand Ries (1784–1838), Julius Rietz (1812–1877), Friedrich Schneider (1786–1853), Clara Schumann, and **Sigismond Thalberg**. To these engagements on behalf of contemporary music must be added his promotions of composers of the recent and more distant past (especially Bach, **Ludwig van Beethoven**, Christoph Willibald Ritter von Gluck [1714–1787], **George Frideric Handel, Franz Joseph Haydn**, and **Wolfgang Amadeus Mozart**, among others). Beginning with his works of the late 1820s—especially the Viola Sonata (MWV Q14, 1823), the string quartets (MWV R25 and R22, 1827–1829) and the little-known "Dürer Cantata" (MWV D1, 1828)—he was one of the first composers to deal compositionally with the legacy of Beethoven's Late Vienna Period. Contemporary reviewers consistently commented on his "modernity" (Robert Schumann's usual term) and many viewed him as a standard-bearer for integrity in an age threatened by charlatanism. The result was a new approach to concert programming and performance: the developing concert **canon** provided a historical and musical context into which new music was systematically embedded.

Mendelssohn's own music famously reflects this integrative approach to historical and contemporary styles and techniques. He composed in virtually every genre available in the **long 19th century**: Lutheran and Catholic sacred music for large and small ensembles, accompanied and a cappella; sacred and secular **cantata**; oratorio; **concert aria**, **incidental music**, opera, and Singspiel; German secular partsong, song, and **song cycle**; concert overture, concerto, symphony; piano trio, piano quartet, string quartet, and other ensemble chamber music; and much music for piano solo, **piano duet**, and organ.

On the other hand, Mendelssohn's embrace of historical idioms and techniques—most prominently **chorale**, fugue, and *stile antico* polyphony—as equals or peers to contemporary idioms have combined with his conservative instrumentation (his ensembles are usually smaller than those requested by, say, Berlioz) and the smoothness of his forays into remote or chromatic harmony to provoke considerable criticism; 20th-century commentators often treated him as a composer who never quite managed to outgrow the proverbial "period of imitation." His self-critical faculty was relentless: he composed a total of about 750 works but published only seventy-two of these with opus number and another 24 without opus, leaving the remainder unpublished. His immense popularity at the time of his death led the musical public to clamor for the release of these published works. In response to this pressure, his family and others arranged for the posthumous publication of a number of works that he had withheld—a total of 50 posthumous *opera* (numbered 73–121) that increasingly drew on what he termed *Jugend-* or *Knabenarbeiten* (works of youth, works of a boy). These works include some whose previous suppression is puzzling (most notably the D-minor and A-major symphonies), but ultimately they also distorted public perception of his growth as a composer by presenting to the public compositions that he certainly would have continued to withhold.

Mendelssohn's conflicted **reception**—to his contemporaries he was a personification of modernity and originality, while to much of posterity he was an unbecomingly derivative archaism—was further exacerbated by the artistic and social polemics of the second half of the 19th century and the first half of the 20th. His obviously Jewish surname (which he refused to drop when he added "Bartholdy," despite his father's urgings that he do so) and his extraordinary celebrity in the Restoration culture that would be vehemently rejected with the **Revolutions of 1848** (which he did not live to see) branded him as Jewish to the increasingly anti-Semitic and anti-Judaic world of the late 19th and early 20th centuries; **Richard Wagner**'s tract *Das Judentum in der Musik* (Jewry in Music, 1850) and the chapter on "Les Israé-

lites" in Liszt's widely read and translated *Des Bohémiens et de leur musique en Hongrie* (On Gypsies and Their Music in Hungary, 1859) were but two of countless such overtly anti-Semitic attacks. Collectively, these developments discouraged serious scholarly investigation of Mendelssohn's music and life during the years when musicology as a discipline was finally beginning to mature (as witnessed by the substantial advances made in scholarship concerning Bach, Mozart, Beethoven, Schubert, and Robert Schumann at the turn of the 20th century). The nadir of this posthumous reception history was certainly the Nazi period, during which Mendelssohn's music—along with that of other composers of Jewish descent such as Meyerbeer—was banned in Adolf Hitler's empire. A widespread reappraisal began after World War II and has gained increasing momentum since then, with the result that public and scholarly understanding of Mendelssohn and his significance is now greater than ever before. [JMC]
    See also CONSERVATORY.

MENDELSSOHN HENSEL, FANNY. *See* HENSEL (NÉE MENDELS-SOHN), FANNY (CÄCILIE) (1805–1847).

MERCADANTE, (GIUSEPPE) SAVERIO (RAFFAELE) (1795–1870). Italian composer, **conductor**, and teacher of the Early Romantic Generation. During his lifetime, his fame was great, and his influence on music of the **long 19th century** was accomplished partly through his music and partly through his work as a teacher and head of the Naples **Conservatory**. As a youth, he lied about his age and birthplace in order to gain free tuition to the Collegio di San Sebastiano (Naples), where he studied with Niccolò Antonio Zingarelli (1752–1837) from 1808 to 1820 and became leader of the **orchestra**. He won public attention with his **ballets** *Il califfo generoso* (The Generous Caliph, 1818), *Il flauto incantato o Le convulsioni musicali* (The Magic Flute; or, The Musical Seizures, 1818), and *I portoghesi nelle Indie o La conquista di Malacca* (The Portuguese in the Indies; or, The Conquest of Malacca, 1819). His success with these works led in turn to commissions from theaters in Milan, Rome, and Venice, followed by an invitation to Vienna for that city's premiere of his 1821 **opera** *Elisa e Claudio*. He worked in Spain and Portugal between 1827 and 1831, then returned to the Italian lands with his phenomenally successful *I normanni a Parigi* (The Normans in Paris, 1832).
    Mercadante worked as *maestro di cappella* of the Novara Cathedral from 1832 to 1840 and composed much sacred music while there, but in 1835, at **Gioachino Rossini**'s invitation, he went to Paris, where he composed *I briganti* (The Pirates) for that city's Théâtre-Italien. In 1838 he lost the sight in one eye due to an inflammation. In 1840 he was offered and accepted the

directorship of the Naples Conservatory (also sought by **Gaetano Donizetti**), and in 1844 he became director of the opera theater at Teatro San Carlo (the oldest continuously active public opera house in Europe), posts whose heavy teaching and administrative responsibilities slowed his production of new operas considerably. He continued to receive regular invitations to write for theaters in Paris but in 1862 suffered a stroke that left him completely blind. Thereafter, he taught and composed primarily by dictating new compositions to students, among these works the autobiographical **symphonic poem** *Il lamento del bardo* (The Bard's Lament, 1862–1863). The last major event of his career as a composer was the premiere in 1866 of *Virginia*, a work allegorically set in ancient Rome in which the titular protagonist's actions result in a revolt of the plebeians and the institution of tribunes of the people—clearly intended as a commentary on the royal suppression of the constitution of 1849 and accordingly banned before it could be performed (*see* RISORGIMENTO).

Mercadante is best known today for his 62 operas, including *Violenza e costanza* (Violence and Faith, 1820), *Elisa e Claudio* (1821), *Caritea, regina di Spagna* (Caritea, Queen of Spain, 1826), *Gabriella di Vergy* (1828), *I Normanni a Parigi* (1832), *I briganti, Il giuramento* (The Oath, 1837), *I due illustri rivali* (The Distinguished Rivals, 1838), *Elena da Felta* (1839), *Il bravo* (The Good Man, 1839), *La Vestale* (The Virgin, 1840), *Leonora* (1844), *Gli Orazi ed i Curiazi* (The Horatii and the Curiatii, 1846), *La schiava saracena* (The Saracen Slave Girl, 1848), and *Virginia*. He also composed a great deal of sacred and secular choral music and much **orchestral** music, including **program symphonies, symphonic poems, concert overtures,** 20 **concertos,** and much instrumental and vocal **chamber music.** [JMC]

MESSE SOLENNELLE. *See* SOLEMN MASS.

METRONOME. Device for measuring musical time and/or setting tempo. The first such devices developed in the 19th century were invented separately by Dietrich Nikolaus Winkler (ca. 1780–1826) of Amsterdam in 1812–1814 and the Viennese court mechanician Johann Nepomuk Maelzel (1772–1838) in 1815, but references to the need for a reliable means of measuring time and setting tempo date from the 16th century, as do various inventions devised with these goals (most involved some variation of the term applied to the *chronomètre* invented by the French musician, pedagogue, and music theorist Etienne Loulié ca. 1694). Numerous other devices were also developed after Maelzel's device had been patented. Common to all these was the principle of a pendulum that oscillated regularly from one side to the other. The main contributions of the Winkler/Maelzel device were its use of a double-ended pendulum (an innovation that basically quartered the necessary length of the stem, greatly reducing the size of the instrument) and, in Maelzel's case, the labeling of musical time in terms of beats per minute on the device itself.

Winkel's and Maelzel's metronome—the term is Maelzel's—was not an original conception but rather the most successful product of a surge in chronometric mechanical devices that had begun in the 1780s. The harpist Dominique Renaudin invented a *plexi-chronomètre* in 1785 (this was later improved by Thomas Jefferson and marketed at a lower price) and the watchmaker Duclos (possibly Dubos) a *rhythmomètre* in 1787. By 1793, an English clock maker named William Pridgin had developed a "chronometer" or "musical time beater." In 1800, G. E. Stöckel advertised subscriptions for his *Taktmesser* (time measurer), a device that won the approval of respected musicians including J. F. Reichardt, D. G. Türk, and (most notably) **Ludwig van Beethoven**, among others. The latter device was the immediate starting point for the metronomes developed by Winkel and Maelzel.

It would be difficult to overestimate the significance of Winkel's and Maelzel's devices for editorial practices (*see* EDITING AND EDITIONS), **performance practice**, and understandings of musical time in general. On the one hand, the long history of attempts to develop such a contraption illustrates not only the general interest in mechanization characteristic of the modern era as a whole but also a specific need for such a device; clearly, there was widespread concern that tempos should be more reliable and fluctuate less than was the case in actual performance. The metronome addressed this perceived need directly.

On the other hand, before the advent of chronometric tempo specifications, the essentials of musical literacy dictated that musicians determine the proper tempo for a piece on the basis of three considerations—meter, predominant note values, and verbal specifications—so that, for example, the designation "Andante" would designate a quicker beat for music with a time signature of 3/2 or 2/2 and prevalent note values of half notes and quarter notes with occasional eighth notes than it would with a time signature of 4/4, 3/4, or 2/4 and smaller note values. The spread of the metronome supplanted these intuitive, subjective, and flexible approaches to musical time with one that was objective and theoretically inflexible. The result is that whereas most musicians from, for example, the 1810s might have regarded scores that provided specific metronome markings as overly prescriptive and implicitly inflexible, musicians from, for example, after 1880 tend to regard scores that provide only verbal tempo specifications as ambiguous. Additionally, until recently, the notion was widespread that early metronome numbers (specifically those of Beethoven, **Felix Mendelssohn Bartholdy**, and **Robert Schumann**) were skewed by imperfect mechanical functioning of early metronomes, but research has shown this assumption to be incorrect: although

Romantic composers tended to eschew metronome markings in solo and chamber works until the last few decades of the 19th century, by the 1840s most had accepted their usefulness in large-ensemble music. [JMC]

MEYERBEER [BEER], GIACOMO [JAKOB LIEBMANN MEYER] (1791–1864). German composer of Jewish descent; member of the Early Romantic Generation; the most frequently performed **opera** composer of the early and mid-19th century, a virtuoso orchestrator, and an important influence on French music well into the 20th century. He spent most of his career in Paris, where he consolidated the genre of French **grand opera** through such masterpieces as *Robert le diable* (Robert the Devil, 1831), *Les Huguenots* (The Huguenots, 1836), *Le prophète* (The Prophet, 1849), and *L'Africaine* (The African Maid, 1864). He also composed four German **comic operas** (most notably the **Singspiel** *Ein Feldlager in Schlesien* [A Silesian Boot Camp, 1844]) and six Italian operas (most notably *Il crociato in Egitto* [The Crusader in Egypt, 1824]). The remainder of his output, though little known today, is also impressive. It includes two sets of **incidental music** and other smaller works for the stage; 27 secular choral works (for mixed chorus, *Männerchor*, or other combinations of voices with **piano** or **orchestral** accompaniment); 15 individual or collected sacred choral works; many **songs** (*mélodies*, **folk song** arrangements, *Gesänge*, and **Lieder**); one **symphony**, one piano **concerto**, and several other *concertante* works; and several other smaller compositions for orchestra or *Harmoniemusik*.

Meyerbeer was born into a wealthy Jewish banking family and was the son of Amalie Beer, one of Berlin's leading *salonnières* (*see* SALON). He received private lessons and showed promise as a pianist at an early age, making his public debut with a performance of **Wolfgang Amadeus Mozart**'s Concerto in D Minor (K. 466, 1785) at the age of 11. He went to Darmstadt to study counterpoint with Abbé Vogler (1749–1814) and penned two operas and an **oratorio** while there, also traveling to Paris and London in 1814 and 1815. In 1816 he traveled to Italy, where he fell under the spell of **Gioacchimo Rossini** and composed his own Italian operas that give the first real evidence of the abilities as dramaturg and orchestrator that would later make him famous. The success of the last of these works, *Il crociato in Egitto*, at its Venetian premiere yielded an invitation to revise the work for performance in Paris, produced in the Théatre-Italien by Rossini, with **Giuditta Pasta** in the leading role—a brilliant success that sealed Meyerbeer's decision to remain in the French capital. He signed a contract to produce a grand opera for the Opéra, on a **libretto** by **Eugène Scribe**, in 1826, but family circumstances delayed completion of the work until 1831.

The long-delayed and much-anticipated opening of *Robert le diable* created a sensation—one of the most spectacular successes in opera history. Meyerbeer and Scribe were immediately signed for another contract with a starkly unrealistic due date of December 1833, and Meyerbeer paid the Opéra's contractual indemnity of 30,000 francs when they were unable to meet that deadline—but the money was returned and the institution's director forced to resign when it became clear that the unhappy composer and librettist were going to grant first-performance rights for the new work to another company. The Opéra's reversal was wise, for *Les Huguenots* was an even greater success than *Robert*. Meyerbeer thus stood at the forefront of European opera, and in 1842, despite his Jewish faith, he was hired to succeed **Gaspare Spontini** as *General-Musikdirektor* to the Prussian court in Berlin. He officially remained there until 1848, although ongoing difficulties with the intendant and the German public's skepticism about a Jewish composer who had become the personification of French opera made the appointment an unhappy one. In December 1846 he took a permanent leave of absence and returned to Paris, where he completed *Le prophète*, a work that resonated profoundly with the **Revolutions of 1848** and renewed the luster of his reputation.

Meyerbeer remained based in Paris for the remainder of his career and was enormously popular with the public even after the post-Revolutionary impulse for avant-garde music began to eclipse his fame with the critics. An overhauled French version of *Ein Feldlager in Schlesien*, given in the Opéra-Comique in 1854 as *L'étoile du nord* (The North Star), was a major success. The work that was to be his final opera, *L'Africaine*, had been begun in 1837, and Meyerbeer was still finishing it when he died suddenly in May 1864.

To overestimate the extent of Meyerbeer's influence on European-sphere-of-influence cultivated music of the mid- and later 19th century would be difficult. He was a profoundly original dramatist in an age increasingly concerned with musical drama, a brilliant orchestrator in a critical age of emancipation of the orchestra in the context of musical drama, a psychologically insightful delineator of characters in a world increasingly committed to music's ability to explore and celebrate the human psyche, and a cultural figure unrivaled in his ability to tap into themes and topics that resonated with contemporary politics and societal conflicts. Nevertheless, he was never fully accepted in the German lands: **Robert Schumann** harshly contrasted *Les Huguenots* with **Felix Mendelssohn Bartholdy**'s *St. Paul*, and he was the explicit subject of vituperative anti-Semitic attacks from **Richard Wagner**, especially in his notorious "Das Judenthum in der Musik" (On Jewry in Musik, 1850), and Liszt (in *Des Bohémiens et de leur musique en Hongrie* [On the Gypsies and Their Music in Hungary, 1859]). By the turn of the 20th century, such anti-Semitic assertions of Meyerbeer's supposed facile superficiality had become common in the musical literature, and today few outside France know any of his music. [JMC]

See also RECEPTION.

A MIDSUMMER NIGHT'S DREAM. (Ger., *Ein Sommernachtstraum.*) Programmatic **concert overture** (MWV P3/Op. 21) and **incidental music** (MWV M13/Op. 61) by **Felix Mendelssohn Bartholdy**, based on **William Shakespeare**'s eponymous play and the German translation thereof by August Wilhelm Schlegel (1767–1845; 1795) and its 1843 revision by Ludwig Tieck (1773–1853). The Overture was written during the summer of 1826 as a **programmatic** distillation of the main elements of the play into a one-movement **orchestral** composition; it was not intended to introduce the play. It was premiered in Stettin (Szczecin, Poland) on 20 February 1827 alongside **Ludwig van Beethoven**'s Ninth **("Choral") Symphony** and published in the composer's own arrangement for **piano duet** as his Op. 21 in 1831; the orchestral parts were published in 1832 (London: Cramer, Addison & Beale; Leipzig: **Breitkopf & Härtel**), and the full score was first published around May 1835. Mendelssohn intended this Overture, the *Hebrides Overture* (MWV P7/Op. 26), and the *Calm Sea and Prosperous Voyage Overture* (MWV P5/Op. 27) to be a triptych published under a single opus number—that is, comprising a single, three-part work—but this wish was not realized. The *Midsummer Night's Dream Overture* thus bears the opus number 21. As in its counterpart overtures in the triptych, all the thematic material is based on a single melodic cell whose character changes according to its position in the **sonata form** and its role in the Overture's implied extramusical content (*see* THEMATIC TRANSFORMATION, THEMATIC METAMORPHOSIS).

The incidental music to Shakespeare's play was written in 1842–1843 to accompany a performance of Ludwig Tieck's revision of Schlegel's translation, which had been criticized for its many liberties with Shakespeare's text. Mendelssohn learned of this project in November 1842 and began writing the 13 movements of the incidental music almost immediately. The complete incidental music, including the overture originally published as Op. 21, was premiered in the context of the Shakespeare/Tieck play in Potsdam on 14 October 1843 to great acclaim. This incidental music was published as Mendelssohn's Op. 61 in piano-duet arrangement (again by the composer) and orchestral parts by Breitkopf & Härtel (Leipzig) and **Novello & Co.** (London) in 1844; the full score was not published until 1848. Some of the incidental music's numbers were omitted from the score as published in the series of *Mendelssohns Werke* published by Breitkopf & Härtel under the editorship of Julius Rietz in 1874–1877. Because that edition was the source for most of the late 19th- and 20th-century publications, this music remained obscure until it was published in Christian Martin Schmidt's edition in Series V, Vol. 8, of the *Leipziger Ausgabe der Werke von Felix Mendelssohn Bartholdy* in 2000. [JMC]

See also EDITING AND EDITIONS.

MIGHTY FIVE. *See* MIGHTY HANDFUL.

MIGHTY HANDFUL. (Rus., moguchaya kuchka.) Term coined by Russian critic Vladimir Stasov (1824–1906) in an 1867 newspaper article to denote the small coterie of composers who, in his view, were working successfully to promote Russianness over European traditions in their music. The most important composers in the group to which Stasov referred were **Mily Balakirev** (the central figure in the group), **Alexander Borodin, César Cui, Modest Mussorgsky,** and **Nikolai Rimsky-Korsakov**; Stasov's grouping also included Apollon Selivyorstovitch Gussakovsky (1841–1875) and Nikolai Nikolayevich Lodïzhensky (1842–1916), although the last two are no longer considered part of the coterie (perhaps because of their posthumous obscurity). In addition to their devotion to Russian musical **nationalism** and their interest in **folk song** and folk subjects, the group also had in common the fact that they were mostly self-taught, as well as their determination to resist the refined (westernized) traditions represented in the Russian **Conservatory** movement most firmly associated with **Anton** and **Nikolay Rubinstein**. The group is also frequently referred to as *The Five* or *The Mighty Five*. [JMC]

MISSA SOLEMNIS. *See* SOLEMN MASS.

MODINHA. During the 18th century and **long 19th century**, term for a Brazilian or Portuguese art song; with the *lundu*, the most important **salon** genre in those two countries. The lyrics were typically amorous in character and the musical style simple, similar to that of the **romance** and its cognates elsewhere. Some 19th-century *modinhas* also exhibit influences of florid melodies derived from Italian **opera**, which was the predominant variety of staged musical drama in Iberia and South America for most of the 19th century. Important composers who worked in the genre include **Carlos Gomes, Chiquinha Gonzaga, Alexandre Levy,** and Heitor Villa-Lobos. [JMC]
See also SONG.

THE MOLDAU. (Cz., *Vltava.*) **Symphonic poem** by **Bedřich Smetana** composed in 1874 and published in versions for **piano duet** (1879) and **orchestra** (1880). *The Moldau* is the second installment of the programmatic **cycle** *Má vlast* (My Country) and by far the best-known work from that cycle.

Like the other works in *Má vlast, The Moldau* is based on subject important to Smetana's native Bohemia (the western portion of what is today the Czech Republic)—in this case, the country's longest and most important river. Smetana's music depicts a number of scenes along the course of this river in the context of a musical structure that employs the technique of **thematic transformation** within a rondo form. The slow introduction uses increasingly complicated interlocking lines presented by two flutes and clarinets to depict graphically the two streams that merge to form the beginning of the river, then introduces the theme in E minor (modal) that will symbolize the river in the remainder of the work. The score provides labels for five individual scenes along the course of the river, functioning as episodes within the rondo form: hunt in the forest, a peasant wedding, round-dance of mermaids by moonlight, and finally the St. John's Rapids, before the river widens and flows past the majestic 10th-century Vyšehrad Castle and vanishes into the distance. It symbolizes the castle by quoting the main theme from the eponymous first symphonic poem in the cycle. Not surprisingly, given the work's **nationalist** agenda, Smetana does not depict the end of the Moldau (where it merges with the Labe [Ger. Elbe] river, which is as important to Germany as it is to Bohemia). [JMC]

See also PROGRAM (PROGRAMMATIC) MUSIC.

MOLIQUE, (WILHELM) BERNHARD (1802–1869). German violinist, composer, and pedagogue of the Romantic Generation. He began his musical studies with his father, a municipal bandmaster in Nuremberg, but completed much of his musical training and early professional work in Munich and Vienna. From 1826 to 1849, he was concertmaster and royal music director of the Stuttgart Court **Orchestra**, an ensemble that won the praise of **Hector Berlioz**, among others. Beginning in 1840, he toured extensively, including Russia, but resettled in London in the wake of **Revolutions of 1848**. (In the meantime, he had also refused prestigious academic appointments in Hanover and at the **conservatory** in Prague.) After a successful debut in the Musical Union, he worked there as a chamber musician, pedagogue, and composer, becoming professor of composition at the Royal Academy of Music in 1861 and teaching there until his retirement (1866).

Molique's reputation rested equally on his technical prowess as a violinist (he was not a **virtuoso** but did possess unusually strong left-hand technique and infallible intonation) and on his compositions, of which the Violin **Concerto** No. 5 in A Minor (Op. 21), a piano **quintet** (Op. 35) commissioned by **Broadwood**, a Cello Concerto (Op. 45; conducted by Berlioz), the **oratorio** *Abraham*, several **string quartets**, and concertos for flute (written for **Theobald Boehm**) and oboe won him the praise of the musical public around Europe. He also penned a number of **songs** (in French and German) that were highly regarded as well as at least two Masses, one of which (for solo voices with orchestra and organ, with or without chorus) was praised in **John Sullivan Dwight**'s *Journal of Music* as "a work of elevated and touching beauty."

Molique authored a composition manual (*Studies in Harmony*, London, 1862) and was an honorary member of numerous prestigious musical associations, including the National Musical Association of Germany (1836), the Musical Association of Austria (1839), the Frankfurt am Main *Liederkrantz* (1840; *see* MÄNNERCHOR), the North German Musical Association, Hamburg (1842), the Academy of St. Cecilia, Rome (1843), and the Salzburg Mozarteum (1847), among others. [JMC]

MOMIGNY, JÉRÔME-JOSEPH DE (1762–1842). French composer and music theorist of Belgian birth, a member of the Early Romantic Generation. He set out to reformulate the principles of music theory entirely and argued a number of sophisticated concepts about the temporal organization of music and its bearing on human perceptions of melody, harmony, and form that would be taken up anew (and with greater impact) in the very late 19th and early 20th centuries. His most provocative concept was that the fundamental temporal organization of music is not from downbeat to downbeat but from upbeat to downbeat—an approach which meant that (in his words) "the real rhythmic unit . . . is not imprisoned . . . within two bar-lines, . . . [but] rather . . . straddles the bar-line, with its first beat to the left and its second to the right." Moreover, while harmony was based on resonance, the essential concord was based on seven contiguous thirds (not just three, as in Rameauian harmony), and any given tonality embraced 17 notes rather than seven—plus those 17 notes' enharmonic equivalents (which, he argued, diverged from a given key only by means of voice-leading and rhythmic arrangement, not by means of actual pitch). His overarching emphasis on music as a perceptual rather than notational phenomenon anticipated 20th-century theories on cognitive psychology of music, and his concepts for expanding tonality are strikingly similar to the approaches of both **Claude Debussy** and some dodecophonic composers.

Momigny began his career as organist in the church of the Belgian town of St. Omer, about 40 miles from Calais. He worked as organist in Lyon, but his involvement with the Revolution forced him to flee to Switzerland for a time. By 1800 he was in Paris, working as a teacher of **piano** and music theory. There he founded a music-publishing house and secured the patronage of the eminent French naturalist Bernard Germain de Lacépède (1756–1825), which provided him the security and stability necessary to continue his research, writing, and composing. In 1803–1805, he published in serial form his *Cours complet d'harmonie et de composition* (released as a book in 1806). The authority of these ideas was reinforced when Momigny was charged with supervising the musical portions of the 84-volume *Encyclopédie méthodique par ordre des matières* (Methodical Encyclopedia by Order of Subjects), a much-expanded version of Didérot's *Encyclopedie* originally published between 1751 and 1772.

Momigny's publishing house went bankrupt in 1828, but **Luigi Cherubini** assisted in his obtaining an annual pension. His last major theoretical and pedagogical publication was a *Cours générale de musique, du piano, d'harmonie et de composition, depuis A jusqu'à Z* (General Method for Music, Piano, Harmony, and Composition, from A to Z, 1831). His mental health worsened over his last years and he died in an asylum. Although his music is largely forgotten today, he was a prolific and well-respected composer, penning a number of **songs**, instrumental **chamber music** including **string quartets**, a **piano trio**, various smaller and larger works for solo piano, several **cantatas**, some sacred music, and three **operas**. [JMC]

MONTERO, JOSÉ ÁNGEL (1839–1881). Venezuelan composer, flautist, singer, and teacher of the Late Romantic Generation; composer of *Virginia* (1873), which was considered to be the first Venezuelan **opera** until José María Osorio's (1803–1852) *El maestro Rufo Zapatero* (1847) was discovered in 1977. He was the son of the *maestro de capella* at the Caracas Cathedral and in 1873 succeeded his father in that post; his two brothers were also respected musicians. He was also director of the Banda Marcial de Caracas from 1869 on. Aside from his contributions to the musical life of the Caracas Cathedral, he is important for having persuaded the country's government to found a musical institute that would serve as a national **conservatory**, print music by Venezuelan composers, and reprint foreign music. He also founded the journal *Arte musical* in 1878. His compositional output is dominated by his 16 **zarzuelas** and sacred music (including two **Requiems**, eight Mass settings, and numerous **motets**), but he also composed many dance pieces (polkas, **waltzes**, and so on), **symphonies**, and **concert overtures**. [JMC]
See also NATIONALISM, ROMANTIC NATIONALISM.

MOSCHELES, IGNAZ [ISAAC] (1794–1870). German composer, **conductor**, **virtuoso** pianist, and pedagogue of Bohemian birth and Jewish descent; member of the Early Romantic Generation. His pianistic abilities emerged early, and by 1804, he was studying with Bedřich Diviš Weber (1766–1842), director of the Prague **Conservatory**. Despite his teacher's conservative tastes, he was eager to learn everything new for **piano** by **Ludwig van Beethoven** and in 1808 relocated to Vienna, where he studied with J. G. Albrechtsberger (1736–1809) and Antonio Salieri (1750–1825). By 1814, his reputation was such that **Artaria** commissioned him to prepare the piano/vocal score of Beethoven's *Fidelio*, a task that he accomplished in collaboration with Beethoven himself.

Moscheles was also well known as a virtuoso, touring widely and giving a few finishing lessons on **piano** to the young **Felix Mendelssohn Bartholdy**, with whom he would remain fast friends to the end of the younger composer's life. His first appearance at a concert of the Philharmonic Society of London (1821) brought him great acclaim in the thriving musical culture of the English capital. In 1825 he settled there, teaching piano at the Royal Academy of Music and becoming a frequent conductor of the Philharmonic Society. Among his successes as an advocate for Beethoven—including the late works, which at the time were rarely heard—were the London premiere of the *Missa solemnis* (1832; *see* SOLEMN MASS) and performances of the Ninth **("Choral") Symphony** in 1837 and 1838. He also translated into English the Beethoven biography of that composer's longtime assistant and secretary, Anton Schindler (1795–1864), as *The Life of Beethoven* (1841). When Mendelssohn invited him to join the piano faculty at German lands' first conservatory of music (in Leipzig) in 1846, he accepted, retaining this position until his death and devoting himself increasingly to teaching. The roster of his pupils who went on to distinction as composers and/or pianists includes **Edvard Grieg**, **Arthur Sullivan**, and **Sigismond Thalberg**.

As a pianist, Moscheles was known for his crisp touch and sensitive phrasing. He admired the new pianistic techniques advanced by **Fryderyk Chopin**, **Franz Liszt**, and **Clara** and **Robert Schumann** and commissioned Chopin's *Trois nouvelles études* (CT 38–40, 1840) but made no effort to emulate the styles of that younger generation. He was also among the first major pianists to perform music of the 18th century on harpsichord rather than piano (*see* PERFORMANCE PRACTICE). His output includes six **sonatas** for piano solo and **piano duet**, eight piano **concertos** and nine other works for one or two pianos with **orchestra**, one **symphony** (1829) and one **concert overture** (1835), eight *opera* of solo **songs** and vocal duets, and numerous *opera* of instrumental **chamber music**. He also produced a number of widely used pedagogical methods and didactic works. [JMC]

MOTET. During the **long 19th century**, broad term for nonliturgical sacred or generally religious composition for chorus, with or without soloists and/or accompaniment. Nineteenth-century motets were usually in Latin except in the German Protestant lands, where they were usually in German. Aside from these general criteria, they vary enormously in style, form, and scoring; due to differences in liturgical practice from country to country, compositions that are "motets" in one country might be liturgical in another. One consistent feature of the Romantic motet, handed down from its Renaissance and Baroque counterparts, is that the form is highly sectional and strictly determined by the form of the text: each successive line of text is typically assigned a distinctive musical idea whose character and style respond to and interpret the textual import of that line; musical ideas are typically repeated only when the form of the text requires a repetition. In Protestant Germany, the Romantic motet often included a **chorale**, which served as a cantus firmus (as in the earlier motets of Heinrich Schütz and **Johann Sebastian Bach**).

Although the motet was often overshadowed by other, usually larger genres of sacred music (such as the **cantata**, the Mass Ordinary, or the **Requiem**) during the long 19th century, most major composers did contribute to the genre. These included notable composers from each of the major generations of Romanticism—most notably, from the Early Romantic Generation, **Gioachino Rossini** and **Franz Schubert**; from the Romantic Generation, **Hector Berlioz**, **Franz Liszt**, **Felix Mendelssohn Bartholdy**, and **Giuseppe Verdi**; from the Late Romantic Generation, **Johannes Brahms**, **Anton Bruckner**, **Antonín Dvořák**, **Gabriel Fauré**, **Charles Gounod**, and **Pyotor Il'yich Tchaikovsky**; and from the Modern Romantic Generation, **Edward Elgar**, **Giacomo Puccini**, and **Serge Rachmaninoff**. [JMC]

MOTIVE (MOTIF). In music and the other arts, a compact and easily recognizable idea that lends structural coherence through recurrence and manipulation. Motives are often the building blocks of musical themes and of polyphonic textures generally; many are identified on the basis of their general melodic, harmonic, or rhythmic contours, any or all of which may be modified—sometimes extensively—as they are repeated over the course of a work. The **long 19th century**'s increasing fascination with large-scale **cyclicity** and **organicism** led composers to focus increasingly on extended motivic techniques, especially in the German lands. Such techniques applied the central premises of motivic unity to multiple movements within larger compositions. The locus classicus for such practices is **Ludwig van Beethoven**'s **Symphony** No. 5, Op. 67 (1807–1808), although the idea of long-range motivic unity (sometimes as an extension of the figural unity characteristic of Baroque music) is at least implicit in compositions of the 1790s (among them **Franz Joseph Haydn**'s Symphony No. 103 ["Drumroll"], which **Jérôme-Joseph de Momigny** described explicitly in these terms in 1803). Beginning in the 1820s the idea became increasingly important in genres not typically considered **absolute music**, most notably in the programmatic **concert overtures** and **program symphonies** of **Hector Berlioz**, **Franz Liszt**, **Felix Mendelssohn Bartholdy**, **Robert Schumann**, and **Louis Spohr**; the **operas** of **Carl Maria von Weber**; and the post-1848 operas and **music dramas** of **Richard Wagner**. [JMC]

See also IDÉE FIXE; LEITMOTIV; THEMATIC TRANSFORMATION, THEMATIC METAMORPHOSIS; VARIATION.

MOZART, (JOHANN CHRYSOSTOM) WOLFGANG AMADEUS (1756–1791). Iconic and prolific composer and pianist, in the **long 19th century** widely regarded, along with **Franz Joseph Haydn** and **Ludwig van Beethoven**, as a member of a triumvirate who had first imparted the "Romantic spirit" to music. Born in Salzburg, he began composing at the age of four. He traveled widely with his father and performed before the crowned heads of Europe, quickly gaining fame as a child **prodigy**. In 1772, he received his first paid appointment in the court of the archbishop of Salzburg. He worked there as *Konzertmeister* from 1772 to 1779 and as court organist from 1779 until his dismissal in June 1781—having left his post in March of that year to attempt a career as a freelance performer and composer in Vienna. There, his fame continued to grow—as did his debts—but he fell ill in November 1791 and died on 5 December of that year.

The reasons for Mozart's appeal to Romantic Europe and the nature of that appeal evolved continually over the course of the long 19th century. It rested partly on his biography—or, rather, on his life and mythologized versions thereof—and partly on his music. During his lifetime, Mozart never managed to escape his youthful fame as a child prodigy—a situation that posed problems even as it also bolstered interest in his mature accomplishments—and that repute was accordingly a source of fascination for his early posthumous biographers. At the same time, the late Enlightenment's general fascination with the nature of genius—more specifically, with talent and intelligence that are innate and inspiration whose greatness is purest when untrammeled by intellect and reason—made Mozart, a child prodigy who (so the myths held) composed spontaneously and almost effortlessly, a cause célèbre for the Romantic movement. By the early 19th century, his well-known conflicts with his conservative father and with the church contributed to perceptions of him as the personification of the rebellious side of Romanticism—the side that was inspired by the French Revolution and the sense of momentous change accomplished by overthrowing the established order in pursuit of new ideas. Thus, Mozart was seen in the early 19th century as a compeer of and complement to Beethoven, whose Romanticism may have been purer in his instrumental music but who "breathed the same Romantic spirit" as Mozart.

These views prevailed during the early decades of the 19th century, when Romanticism was considered a "movement" rather than a "period." As the notion of Romanticism as a music-historical period that had succeeded "classicism" (now defined to embrace 18th-century music) gained currency around the mid-19th century, however, music historiography, fueled by **Georg Wilhelm Friedrich Hegel**'s notion of a *Weltgeist* (world-spirit) that propelled history in an ever-ascending dialectic process of increasing complexity, began to treat Mozart increasingly not as a child of Romanticism per se but rather as a predecessor to Beethoven, who was himself viewed alternately as a founding father of the Romantic period or a Janus-faced transitional figure who mediated between Classicism and Romanticism. Such views are of course consistent with the essential chronology of the long 19th century and had been anticipated in early 19th-century writings such as E. T. A. Hoffmann's celebrated essay on Beethoven's instrumental music. What is new about the post-1848 reception of Mozart, however, is that it integrated Mozart into a systematized, unilinear, and distinctly teleological view of music history: Mozart was now a composer whose Romanticism was anticipatory of rather than coterminous with that of Beethoven, and his music represented a "silver" age in music history that had led inexorably to the "true" Romantic era ushered in by Beethoven.

One important result of this reconsidered view of Mozart was that most of his music, with the exception of the last three **symphonies**, *Don Giovanni*, and the **Requiem** (most of which is by Süßmaier, not Mozart), came to play a peripheral role in the concert and recital canons, and Mozart thus exerted a less active influence on composers of the Modern Romantic Generation. During the last decades of the 19th century and the pre–World War I period, especially in Germany and Austria, one adopted a "Mozartean" demeanor when one wished to present an Apollonian foil to the daemonic or Dionysian persona that characterized much of the late 19th century's intensely subjective music. While narrowing the range of his musical presence in the cultural discourse of the day, however, the Modern Romantic Generation renewed its celebration of his biography—now focusing not on his accomplishments as a child prodigy but on his impetuous and occasionally radical nature and the well-known tensions entailed in his relationship with his father and with the Austrian courtly establishments.

By the early 20th century, then, Mozart had come to personify not the birth of Romanticism but rather the closing chapter of Classicism, and many early 20th-century musicians had little compunction about assisting the Romantic spirit they observed in his life in its perceived struggle to escape the fetters of the Classicism of its day by reorchestrating his music, removing the *lieto fine* (happy ending) of *Don Giovanni*, and generally appropriating (selectively) those aspects of his life and work that suited the image of Mozart not as an awe-inspiring *Wunderkind* but as a Romantic genius whose life was tragically cut short. These changes in Mozart's image over the course of the long 19th century are reflected in the active concert repertoire of Mozart's works, composers' compositional reception of Mozart's style, and biographical, lexicographic, and critical writings about his life and music. [JMC]

See also RECEPTION.

MUSIC DRAMA. (Ger., Musikdrama.) Term popularly used to designate **Richard Wagner**'s approach to **opera** in his works from *Lohengrin* (WWV 75, premiered 1848, publ. 1851) through *Parsifal* (WWV 111, 1882). Semantically, the term is an obvious cognate to one of the usual Italian terms for opera ("dramma per musica"), and it accurately reflects Wagner's and his followers' post-1849 avoidance of "numbers" and their endeavors to create a more perfect synthesis of music, plot, and poetry in staged musical drama. The term is not authentic to Wagner, however. In the theoretical writings penned during his Swiss exile (1849–1851), he expressed his ideas concerning this synthesis in terms such as "drama of the future" ("das Drama der Zukunft" or "Zukunftsdrama"), "the fulfilled **artwork of the future**" ("das vollendete Kunstwerk der Zukunft"), "the *universal* drama" ("das *allgemein-same* Drama"), or **Gesamtkunstwerk**. For his own works, he approached it in terms such as *Handlung* (literally, "plot"; used for *Tristan und Isolde*), though he designated other works by more conventional terms or ones that do not articulate the idea of a musicodramatic synthesis.

In his 1872 essay *Über die Benennung "Musikdrama"* (On the Designation "Music Drama"), Wagner rejected the term "music drama" outright, identifying it as a corrupt concept that attempted to fuse disparate entities: "music is an 'art,' while drama is an 'artistic act.'" In that 1872 writing, Wagner tentatively proposed the phrase "acts of music made visible" ("ersichtlich gewordene Taten der Musik") to reflect his thinking at the time and concluded by inviting suggestions as to more suitable terms. [JMC]

MUSSORGSKY |MOUSSORGSKY, MUSORGSKY|, MODEST PETROVICH (1839–1881). Russian composer of the Late Romantic Generation; one of the most influential Russian **nationalist** composers of the **long 19th century** and arguably the most intellectually incisive and stylistically original member of the **Mighty Handful**. By his own account, he was first inspired to improvise at the **piano** not by formal study of music but by Russian folktales. He had his earliest instruction in music from his mother and by age seven was able to play short pieces by **Franz Liszt**, later continuing his study privately. He continued to sing in the choir in the Cadet School of the Guards in St. Petersburg and in 1856 joined a regiment. In 1857, he was introduced into a circle of friends that included **Mily Balakirev, César Cui, Aleksandr Dargomïzhsky**, and the influential critic Vladimir Stasov (1824–1906). During this period he began composing actively, also studying music of **Ludwig van Beethoven, Franz Schubert**, and **Robert Schumann** as well as **Mikhail Glinka**. He was forced to resign his commission after a nervous breakdown in 1858, and financial burdens brought about through his developing alcoholism and the responsibility of managing the family estate after the emancipation of the serfs in 1861 led to his taking work in a menial position in the Ministry of Communications in 1863. In that year he also joined a commune.

Mussorgsky returned to St. Petersburg in 1867 and by 1868 was able to complete the first version of his historical **opera *Boris Godunov*** (after **Aleksandr Pushkin**). Despite his determined efforts, this version was never staged, but his frustration at that failure and his uninspiring government post (now in the Ministry of State Property) were insufficient to prevent him from completing his first **song cycle**, *Detskaya* (The Nursery), begun in 1868, completed 1872. While working on a revised version of *Boris*, he also began work on another historical opera, *Khovanshchina*, on his own **libretto**, left unfinished and unperformed at his death (completed and orchestrated by **Nikolay Rimsky-Korsakov** in 1883). By this point his drinking had worsened to the point where he was incapable of sustained periods of work. The same period witnessed the composition of his **programmatic** piano **suite** *Kartinki s vïstavki* (Pictures at an Exhibition), a series of *tableaux* inspired by paintings of his late friend Viktor Hartmann (1834–1873) and constructed as a quasi-narrative **cycle** by means of a recurrent "promenade" whose changes in character brilliantly illustrate the **narrative** potentials of techniques of **thematic transformation** even in noncontinuous music.

Mussorgsky's ideas on the ideal oneness of musical and verbal language in **song** found new realization in work on a new opera, *Sorochinskaya yarmarka* (Sorochintsky Fair, after Nikolay Gogol [1809–1852]), and in what was to be his final song cycle, the *Pesni i plyaski smerti* (**Songs and Dances of Death**). He toured as accompanist with a well-known contralto, his longtime acquaintance Darya Leonova, in 1879, and in 1880 was forced to resign his government post. Leonova offered him a position as accompanist and vocal coach in a singing school she had established, and two groups of friends offered him monthly stipends to facilitate his completion of *Khovanshchina* and *Sorochintsky Fair*—but his condition was too far advanced. After appearing as accompanist in a benefit concert for needy students at Leonova's academy on 21 February, he experienced a series of alcohol-related seizures (23–24 February) that led his friends to commit him to a military hospital on 26 February. A brief improvement in early March proved short lived; he died on 28 March.

Mussorgsky is remembered today primarily for *Boris Godunov*, *Pictures at an Exhibition*, the **tone poem** with chorus *Ivanova noch' na Lïsoy gore* (St. John's Night on Bald Mountain, 1866–1867; now familiar primarily through Rimsky-Korsakov's arrangement without chorus), and the *Songs and Dances of Death*. His "completed" (see below) output includes three serious operas and two **comic operas**, a handful of choral works based on texts ranging from the Bible to **Lord Byron**, *St. John's Night on Bald Mountain*, an orchestral march, and several other small orchestral compositions; 19 pieces for piano solo, many of them programmatic or characteristic; 48 **songs** on texts by authors including Byron, **Johann Wolfgang von Goethe**, **Heinrich Heine**, and Mussorgsky himself; and three song cycles. Many of his works were left unfinished at his death and were completed posthumously by his friends, while others that he did complete were promoted by his friends in versions whose harmony and orchestration were "refined" to be more readily palatable to tastes conditioned by French and German Romantic music. This is particularly true of *Boris Godunov* and the *Pictures at an Exhibition*, the latter having acquired its current canonic stature primarily through the colorful orchestrations of Maurice Ravel (1922) and others (Elgar Howath, Leopold Stokowski, and Henry Wood). Recent decades have witnessed concerted (and largely successful) attempts to restore his compositions to their authorized state. Coterminous with these revisitings has come a new appreciation for Mussorgsky's central quest to develop a distinctly Russian musical language whose rhythms, inflections, and forms analogized Russian verbal language as well as celebrating a Russian national identity profoundly informed by Russian cultures and experiences. [JMC]

N

NARRATIVE. In music and the other arts, the representation of an event or action or series of events or actions; *narration* denotes the process of such representation and *narrativity* the sense that such a representation is occurring or present. *Narrative* is distinct from *drama* in that the action in narrative is related or represented rather than enacted directly.

The **long 19th century** witnessed a surge in musical attempts to create narrativity in instrumental as well as vocal music and a proliferation of aesthetic and philosophical ideas that, while rarely dealing explicitly with narrative per se, raise questions concerning the potentials and problems of issues material to musical narrative and narrativity. These issues range from the Romantics' cultivation of both large-scale **cyclical** form and the idea of the fragment that captures the essential properties of a whole but is itself inherently incomplete, through their exploration of new and complex modes of **voicedness**, to new ideas concerning drama, memory, time, and temporality and new theories of musical expression and representation that center on issues ranging from text/music relationships to characteristic or programmatic content—*see* PROGRAM (PROGRAMMATIC) MUSIC—and the idea of **absolute music**. Writers ranging from **Johann Wolfgang von Goethe**, **Georg Wilhelm Hegel**, Immanuel Kant (1724–1804), **Friedrich Nietzsche**, and Arthur Schopenhauer (1788–1860) to **Hector Berlioz, Eduard Hanslick, Franz Liszt**, and **Richard Wagner** grappled with these issues in their private and published criticism and other writings, in turn stimulating further popular and professional attempts to address the relationship between narrativity and Romantic modernity.

Narrative and its attendant concepts apply most obviously to vocal music (which can avail itself of the discursive meanings of words in order to convey narrative content), but the Romantics were keenly aware that music was exceptionally well suited to narrativity because it, like verbal communication, conveys meaning through sequentially presented elements rather than simultaneously presented data (e.g., as in the graphic and plastic arts)—a fact that distinguishes narrative from description or characterization. (For example, the statement "my cat has fleas" describes the speaker's cat but does not narrate because it represents no event or action, whereas "my cat was bitten by a flea" conveys action and suggests a rudimentary narrative by postulating a time before, during, and after the flea bite.) The ability to convey a sequence of events that make up a narrative, Romantics noted, came naturally to an art whose successive durations, melodic pitches, harmonies, and timbres naturally unfolded in their own coherent and quasi-narrative succession. Yet Romantic ideas on musical narration also faced an important obstacle: the fact that music, unlike verbal language, has no past tense. This situation complicated the task of musically narrating with a sophistication even remotely comparable to the narratives of Romantic poetry and other literature.

Studies of musical narrative have identified a variety of considerations that formed and framed the narrativity of music—both instrumental and vocal— for composers, performers, and auditors during the long 19th century. These considerations operated both within and among individual compositions. Among the most important of the intrinsic narrative devices are *voice* (and *voicedness*); *narrative agency*; *narrative frame*; *thematic, timbral,* and *tonal structure*; and *narrative archetype*.

The terms *voice* and *voicedness* denote the vocality by which the narrative is conveyed—the source of utterance (whether specific or general and anonymous) who represents the events or actions to performers and listeners. Popular criticism often presents Romantic music as if the narrative voice is that of the composer or (more rarely) poet, but this is true only in very few highly exceptional cases (*see* BIOGRAPHICAL FALLACY). Most often, the source of narrative utterance in music is a fictitious and omniscient third-person construct whose thoughts and perspectives the composer him- or herself may or may not share but whose presence is discernible to interpreters and listeners. For example, although **Franz Schubert**'s setting of **Johann Wolfgang von Goethe**'s **ballad** *Erlkönig* creates discrete lyric personae for the narrator, father, son, Erl-King, and even the horse (*see* VOICE, VOICEDNESS, VOCALITY), the third-person narrator who delivers the grim twist ending is the primary narrative "I" of the work. This narrating "I" is a nonspecific and anonymous construct who neither participates in the action nor is specifically identifiable with Goethe himself (much less Schubert), however much poet and composer may have sympathized with the ballad's tale of unexplained child mortality and the conflict between reason and superstition, nature and the supernatural, and so on. Similarly, in **Nikolay Rimsky-Korsakov**'s **exoticist** symphonic **suite** *Sheherazade*, the internal narrative (the tales themselves) is recounted by Sheherazade herself, while the music programmatically illustrates not only the events of her stories but also the sultan (Shahryar) who is her audience. In both works, the narrative voices are discrete from the narrative agents (the latter being the individual *lyric personae* in Goethe's ballad and Schubert's music and the characters within the narratives, Sheherazade, and the Sultan in Rimsky-Korsakov's suite).

Like many **melodramas** and most **oratorios**, *Erlkönig* also creates an explicit *narrative frame*, with the narrator addressing listeners from his and their own present but recounting a series of events that occurred previously; his words begin in the present tense, and the events of the narrative are related in the present ("Wer reitet so spät durch Nacht und Wind?"/Who rides so late through night and wind?), but when he reaches the tale's grim twist ending, he switches to the past tense ("In seinen Armen das Kind *war* tot"/In his arms the child *was* dead; emphasis added), signifying that the narrator's tale had already taken place *before* he began recounting it and thus creating (at least) two temporal layers for the ballad's narrative. Schubert exploits this bivalence by plunging the listener into the travelers' urgent flight as the narrator is setting the scene (strophe 1) and before the narrative dialogue and attendant action of the poem begin (strophe 2) and underscores the bitemporality by switching to recitative—in oratorios and the like, the style typically associated with the narrator relating past events—for the poem's final line. In *Sheherazade*, by contrast, the narrative frame is only implicit since (as noted above) instrumental music possesses no discursive means for creating a past tense—yet Rimsky-Korsakov does manage to suggest the temporal layers in the first, second, and fourth movements by assigning distinct musical **motives** and instruments to the sultan and Sheherazade and then moving on to those movements' main narratives after a brief musical caesura.

The treatment of the lyric personae of the narrative framework in *Scheherazade* also illustrates another important element of narrative technique in Romantic music: that of assigning motives or themes to individual characters and presenting these materials in altered or original guises later in the work in order to trace the progress of a narrative through its effects on them. This technique, frequently termed **thematic transformation** (or thematic metamorphosis), provides musical as well as narrative coherence and is central to **opera** and oratorio as well as **song** and instrumental music; it is capable of providing essential narrative information not necessarily obvious or even present in the words of the drama itself (as most famously in the case of the "Samiel" **Leitmotiv** in **Carl Maria von Weber**'s *Der Freischütz* and in **Richard Wagner**'s treatment of the *Leitfaden* in his post-1849 music dramas). In **Hector Berlioz**'s *Harold in Italy*, for example, the narrative persona (the titular Harold, probably an admixture of **Lord Byron**'s Child Harold and Berlioz himself) is entrusted to the solo viola, whose sense of isolation in the Italian lands is conveyed in part by his environs' obliviousness to his presence (despite his sporadic efforts to join in) and in part by the absence of transformation to his **idée fixe** itself; the treatment of the idée fixe creates a layered narrative of ostracization based on but not coterminous with the narrative recounted by the musical events conveyed by the **orchestra**. Similarly, in **Felix Mendelssohn Bartholdy**'s *St. Paul*, the recurrence in No. 19 of the throbbing woodwind chords first introduced in No. 14 makes musically explicit the dramatic and theological connection between the voice of the risen Christ addressing Paul on the road to Damascus and instructing Ananias to find and retrieve Paul.

Romantic stereotypes regarding gender also facilitated timbral specification of narrative voice: instruments in the tenor, baritone, or bass register typically were employed to represent male narrative voices (the solo viola in Berlioz's *Harold*, the low brass in *Sheherazade*, or the solo cello in **Richard Strauss**'s *Don Quixote*), while those in the soprano or alto registers represented women (the solo violin in *Sheherazade* or Strauss's *Ein Heldenleben* or the solo flute in **Claude Debussy**'s *Syrinx*). So effective were these narrative gender associations in program music that the same instruments were able to assume the roles of narrators, implying the presence of an unstated but very real narrative, in **absolute music** as well (e.g., the solo oboe in the second movement "Romanze" of **Robert Schumann**'s D-minor **Symphony** [*see* ROMANCE] or the solo oboe and violin in the second movement of **Johannes Brahms**'s C-minor Symphony).

Finally, narrativity in Romantic music availed itself of **paratextual** devices (titles, subtitles, epigraphs, and printed programs) and established rhetorical conventions in order to convey narrativity by drawing implicit or explicit connections to other narrative works (what is sometimes referred to as *intertextuality*). The most common such technique in instrumental music was that of the textless recitative—instrumental passages stylistically modeled on the declamatory patterns of vocal recitative (with repeated notes, irregular phrases, and typically *secco* textures) but lacking words, as in **Mozart**'s Piano **Concerto** K. 271, **Beethoven**'s op. 130 **string quartet** or the last movement of his Ninth **("Choral") Symphony**, or the countless recitative-like passages in the music of other 19th-century composers. More generally, much music of the long 19th century, both programmatic and "absolute" and instrumental and vocal, uses stylistic, **topical**, and rhetorical associations established by other compositions in order to invoke a narrative *plot archetype*—a general pattern of musical events that suggests the presence of a narrative—such as illness and recovery or the circular or spiral quest (in which a narrative represents a protagonist's "spiritual journey" "through evil and suffering which is justified as a necessary means to the achievement of a greater good" (M. H. Abrams, *Natural Supernaturalism: Tradition and Revolution in Romantic Literature* [New York: Norton, 1971], 193). Such narratives—familiar through, for example, the progressions from C-minor to C-major in Beethoven's and Brahms's C-minor Symphonies—could be created through aggregates of gesture, including thematic quotation and allusion, processes of thematic transformation or recollection, and so on, or they could be subverted or misread (e.g., in Berlioz's *Episode in the Life of an Artist* or Richard Strauss's *Don Juan*). Either way, they served to enfranchise performers and listeners in the imagined construction of narrative progress both in staged musical dramas and in instrumental music. [JMC]

NATIONALISM, ROMANTIC NATIONALISM. Umbrella term for a variety of beliefs and concomitant social and political movements that sought, in both centripetal and centrifugal ways, to assert the primacy of nationhood in determining cultural, individual, and political identity. Implementations of these ideas varied so widely especially during the **long 19th century** that it is more accurate to speak of the term in the plural than in the singular. Nevertheless, it is fair to observe that most European 19th-century nationalisms were centered on issues of geography, culture, and language and were unleashed in part as cultural and political backlashes against French imperial expansion, intensified as resistance to the pan-European governance structures (and accompanying censorship) of the **Restoration**, and erupted with renewed fervor with the **Revolutions of 1848**. During the last few decades of the long 19th century, in the wake of the new science of Mendelian genetics, the understanding of individual and national identity began to shift to favor ethnicity over language, culture, and geography as the primary determinant of nationality.

In the United States and elsewhere in the Western Hemisphere, where any sense of cultural and political identity and of civic belonging based on shared beliefs was comparatively young, nationalisms may be characterized as strivings for cultural and political autonomy that was neither determined nor unduly informed by the hemisphere's colonial history. Cultural and political nationalisms thus also emerged later in the Western Hemisphere. When they did emerge, they, too, were concerned first and foremost with national identity as determined by geography, culture, and language; nationalist movements centered on ethnicity came into force only after World War I and are thus beyond the scope of this book. Because of this Eastern Hemisphere–Western Hemisphere division in the development and thematic fabric of nationalisms, this entry will treat European nationalisms and Western Hemisphere nationalisms separately.

Music and the other arts were potent tools in the long 19th century's various nationalist movements—partly because composers (and artists generally) were part of the profound societal restructurings that were both causes and effects of the century's nationalist movements and partly because in writing and disseminating their music composers engaged in discourse with performers and audiences who were themselves participants in Romantic nationalist discourse. The matter of translating such general ideas into specific musical actions that could engage in nationalist sentiment, however, was a complex one—for if composers simply rejected the techniques, styles, and sounds taught in contemporary music theory and wrote what came naturally to them, their music would be rejected in cultivated circles as primitive and irrelevant and would fail to further the cause. The nationalist project in cultivated music was further complicated by the fact that it mattered little to society's vast underclasses (serfs and peasants) what music was performed in the concert halls, salons, and theaters frequented by Europe's moneyed and ruling classes.

Composers and performers engaging in nationalist musical discourse thus had the task of bridging this socioeconomic divide. The first task of nationalist composers of any stripe, then, was to establish that a "native" music was as good as the foreign imports that already predominated. Typically, this was accomplished in two phases. In the first of these phases, composers typically chose subjects, topics, and themes that celebrated national culture, folklore, geography, and history but by and large retained the melodies, harmonies, rhythms, and general rhetoric of the prevalent hegemonies. In the second phase, they endeavored either to infuse the general idioms of the prevailing musical hegemony with new melodies, harmonies, rhythms, and forms that were found in the **folk song** of the nation being celebrated or, more radically, to replace the the "refinements" of foreign influence in melody, harmony, and rhythm with sounds and durational patterns that emulated those of the nation's folk idioms. These issues and patterns persevered through the long 19th century.

By most accounts, the rise of Romantic nationalism was a direct consequence of the French Revolution and the Napoleonic Wars. Drawing on ideas advanced in the *Declaration of the Rights of Man and of the Citizen* (1789), Napoléon Bonaparte and his government consciously strove to generate a substantially greater sense of the importance of national belonging among French citizens within France. His military exploits and political innovations also had another, decidedly unintended effect, however, for they generated a strong sense of nationhood as a natural and political imperative in the countries whose residents and leaders resisted, fought against, or were subjugated by and then liberated from the puppet governments of his empire. Certainly, Europe's citizenry was not entirely happy with the supranational Enlightened despotism of the late 18th century, but during the early 19th century, their subjugation to the French Empire provided occasion for the governed to join together, led in whole or in part by their erstwhile governors, and create a new and powerful sense of national community and national identity.

During the Revolutionary and Napoleonic periods, then, nationalism manifested itself differently in France and elsewhere in Europe. Within France, it was primarily a matter of patriotic music: it was cultivated in newly created national institutions and other organized public events that served to distill, crystalize, and promulgate Frenchness in law, letters, and sound (the consolidation in 1795 of France's main cultural institutions into the Académie des Beaux-Arts, the founding of the Paris **Conservatory**, and massive public festivals of music and oration celebrating the glory of the Revolution and of France generally). These were events and institutions to which composers such as **Luigi Cherubini**, François-Joseph Gossec (1734–1829), and **Étienne-Nicolas Méhul**, among others, contributed and which they valorized through music in their settings of patriotic texts and their cultivation of new genres, such as **rescue opera**. Outside France, the unrelenting bloodshed and plunder of French imperial expansion made it easy for Bohemians, Germans, Italians, Russians, and even Poles (who were liberated from oppressive Russian rule by Napoleon's armies) to rebel against Frenchness. This rejection found philosophical justification as increasing numbers of the non-French populace came under the influence of thinkers such as the German Johann Gottfried Herder (1744–1803), who since the mid-1770s had asserted geography as the "natural economy" of nations and located national identity in the local or regional vernacular of naturally determined economies. The musical nationalisms founded on these views were more subtle than their French counterparts, operating within the institutional structures cultivated primarily by the Enlightenment's cosmopolitan despots (the *Singspiele* performed in middle-class theaters that were rarely frequented by the aristocracy) or under the guise of scholarly historical inquiry (the **Ossian** craze in England and elsewhere and Luise Reichardt's [1779–1826] 1809 settings of songs from the Arnim/Brentano *Des Knaben Wunderhorn*). Nevertheless, they were substantive and influential assertions of a cultural identity that offered real hope for a political identity after the yoke of French Empire had been shed.

The situation changed after 1815—much to the encouragement of European nationalists. Within France, musical nationalism diminished somewhat (the great public festivals ceased, but rescue operas and grand **operas** that either were based on themes from French national history or resonated powerfully with it flourished). Outside France, the middle and lower classes who had tasted the ideologies of liberalism of the imagined national communities unintentionally occasioned by Bonaparte's exploits found the reversion to the pre-Revolutionary status quo deeply dissatisfying (*see* BOURBON RESTORATION; CONGRESS OF VIENNA; RESTORATION). In Austria and the German lands, the quest for national self-realization produced not only a proliferation of *Wunderhorn* settings but also renewed celebration of the Lutheran **chorale** within secular as well as sacred genres and the cults of national heroes such as **Johann Sebastian Bach**, Albrecht Dürer, Johannes Gutenberg, and, later, **Ludwig van Beethoven**, **Johann Wolfgang von Goethe**, and **Friedrich Schiller**, plus new celebrations in **song**, opera, and **program music** of German folklore (**Carl Maria von Weber**'s *Der Freischütz* and many works based on the legend of **Faust**). Prussian and

Saxon rulers and cultural elites labored assiduously to develop a sense of national belonging that would be dominated by North German, Protestant cultural identity rather than Austrian Catholicism, organizing great public **music festivals** that provided occasion for German speakers to come together and celebrate German composers past and present and founding new, specifically German cultural institutions. In the Italian lands, which were no less politically fragmented than their German counterparts outside Austria and which mostly still languished under Austrian dominion, this was the first flourishing of the *Risorgimento*, with rousing operatic choruses and themes that centered on issues of resistance and revolt against tyranny.

Central European nationalists in Bohemia and Poland, whose political challenges as nations were complicated by the nearly complete absence of naturally defensible borders in their lands, pursued the cause in songs that used texts in the vernacular (e.g., František Sušil's [1804–1868] publications of Moravian songs after 1835 or Karel Erben's [1811–1870] publications of Czech songs after 1842), in operas based on Czech and Moravian plays and performed in middle-class theaters, and in the subjects of operas and instrumental music generally. Some of these Central European nationalists, such as **Fryderyk Chopin**, operated in exile in Paris or elsewhere. In Russia, any sort of nationalist project was complicated by the country's geographic vastness and multitude of dialects, languages, and ethnic groups as well as by the enormous gap between the ruling elites and the uneducated masses and the fact that Russian leaders' reversal of their country's reputation for backwardness was quite recent and had been accomplished precisely by demonstrating their fluency in Western European idioms. Nevertheless, Russian nationalism also flourished during the Restoration, primarily through the Russian **romance** and through nationalist projects based on Russian literature and history (most importantly, works by **Aleksandr Dargomïzhsky, Mikhail Glinka,** and **Aleksey Verstovsky**). And in the United Kingdom, the glory of the British Empire was celebrated through a growth of glee clubs and, more grandly, through enormous choral festivals held in celebration of **George Frideric Handel,** that German expatriate who had reached the pinnacle of success in the British Isles.

These diffuse nationalist efforts came to a head with the wave of revolutions that swept the European continent in 1848—see REVOLUTIONS OF 1848 (SPRING OF NATIONS, YEAR OF REVOLUTIONS)—and, accordingly, composers and other musicians of the post-1848 era became increasingly engaged in writing works that gave musical voice and primacy to their "own" nation. In France, there was increased interest in *mélodie,* **chanson,** and the national idioms of **ballet, salon** music, and **grand opera**—including French adaptations of Italian operas by **Gioachino Rossini** and **Giuseppe Verdi.** In the Italian lands, the *Risorgimento* gained new support because of Pope Pius IX's announcement in 1848 that he would refuse to support Piedmont-Sardinia in its war with Austria, thus underscoring that Italians who wished to escape Austrian dominion would have to do so independently of the Church. This was the period in which Verdi's name was appropriated by the *Risorgimento*. The German lands developed a cult of **absolute music** whose main purpose was to celebrate and perpetuate the heritages of **Ludwig van Beethoven, Franz Joseph Haydn, Wolfgang Amadeus Mozart**, and (as a new addition to the growing **canon** of German instrumental music) **Franz Schubert**. At the other extreme of German nationalism was the self-styled progressivism of the **New German School** and the **Allgemeiner Deutscher Musikverein**, centering on the aesthetic agendas developed in eloquent writings and music by historian **Franz Brendel** and composers such as **Franz Liszt, Joachim Raff**, and **Richard Wagner** (the last most prominently in *The Ring of the Nibelung, Die Meistersinger von Nürnberg*, and *Parsifal*).

The period 1848–1870 was also a fruitful one for Bohemian and Russian nationalisms, witnessing the completion of **Smetana**'s *The Bartered Bride* and his cycle of **symphonic poems** collectively titled *Má Vlast* as well as the rise to prominence of the young **Antonín Dvořák**. In Russia, mid-19th-century nationalism was dominated by the pan-Slavist movement—a movement that fueled the rise to prominence of the **Mighty Handful** and occasioned works such as **Aleksandr Borodin**'s *Prince Igor* (based on the Russian national epic) and **Pyotr Il'yich Tchaikovsky**'s *Slavonic March*. Tchaikovsky's **concert overture** *1812*, celebrating the Russian expulsion from Moscow of Napoléon's troops, is another important manifestation of Russian nationalism.

Although strong nationalist sentiment (and artworks bespeaking these sentiments) continued to flourish in the German and Italian lands during the last quarter of the 19th century, nationalism became a less pressing issue there because the creation of the Kingdom of Italy under Vittorio Emanuele II in 1861 and of the North German Federation under Bismarck in 1866 had largely accomplished the goal of creating German and Italian nation-states that had been the major motivations of those countries' nationalists during the century's middle years. By contrast, France's defeat in the **Franco-Prussian War** sparked renewed determination to celebrate French composers of the past as well as the present and to cultivate a distinctively French national style untainted by the bombast, counterpoint, and self-satisfaction of German music. The **Third Republic**'s cultivation of the idea of *utilité publique*—the notion that even apparently luxurious projects (such as the arts) have public benefits worthy of government sponsorship not necessarily utilitarian in nature if they inspire critical awareness and instill national pride—fostered a large-scale project of newly written histories of music that reconceived and reframed music's roles in France's monarchical and revolutionary pasts. It also spawned a proliferation of musical societies and organizations geared toward cultivating French national identity—most important among these the **Société Nationale de Musique**, whose members included composers such as **Ernest Chausson, Henri Duparc, César Franck, Vincent d'Indy, Jules Massenet**, and **Camille Saint-Saëns**. In tsarist Russia, the cult of nationalism originally associated with Glinka continued with the successes of Tchaikovsky and the Mighty Handful (especially **Nikolay Rimsky-Korsakov**) as well as the younger **Anton Arensky** and **Aleksandr Glazunov**.

The last decades of the 19th century also witnessed the first rise to international prominence of English composers who, though in many cases still trained at least in part on the Continent, aspired to create a distinctly English national style imbued with elements of English folk song, using English texts and celebrating subjects of English national interest. It saw the flourishing of the distinctly English variety of **operetta** cultivated by Gilbert and **Arthur Sullivan**, the emergence of **Edward Elgar** and **Ethel Smyth** as internationally renowned English composers, the founding of the Royal College of Music (1882), and the beginnings of the movement known as the **English Musical Renaissance** (represented in the works of **Alexander Mackenzie, Hubert Parry**, and **Charles Villiers Stanford**).

The last years of the 19th century and the first of the 20th century also saw the emergence of several new separatist nationalist movements on the Continent—most importantly, in Denmark (a new appreciation of **Niels W. Gade** and **Friedrich Kuhlau**, as well as the emergence of **Carl Nielsen**), Finland (most prominently **Jean Sibelius** but also Selim Palmgren [1878–1951], Toivo Kuula [1883–1918], and Leevi Madetoja [1887–1947]), Norway (**Ole Bull, Edvard Grieg**, and **Thomas Tellefsen**), Spain (**Isaac Albéniz, Francisco Barbieri**, and **Thomas Bretón**), and Sweden (**Franz Berwald, Adolf Fredrik Lindblad**, and **August Söderman**).

In the Western Hemisphere, the matter of nationalism in cultivated music was even more complicated, for the institutions, genres, and forms of cultivated music—indeed, even the instruments on which it was played—were themselves of European provenance; the New World's composers of cultivated music would have to declare their independence not just from French, German, or Italian music but also from the music of an entire Continent and its history. (The centrality to European cultivated music of the **piano**, which was rare in domestic life in South America until the 1880s, underscores the enormity of this problem.) Even the fundamental concepts of music theory—most importantly, harmony, counterpoint, and tonality—were European constructs separated from those of indigenous musics of the Americas by a vast conceptual chasm. Perhaps most importantly, if the New World's composers of cultivated music were to celebrate their autonomy musically by infusing elements of true geographically indigenous music into the genres and forms of European art music (as many European nationalist composers did), the fact remained that those composers were trained in the European tradition.

Including indigenous musics in a nationalist project would affirm not themselves and their primary audiences but rather the exotic Other over whom they continued to exert dominion. (For example, a U.S. opera that celebrated rather than exoticized Native American or African American music would have been subversive to the audiences and the institutions of art music of which it was born and for which it was composed—thus, Dvořák's encouragement that U.S. composers find their own national voice by integrating African American spirituals and Native American music into their styles raised more questions than it answered.) In brief, nationalist cultivated music in the New World had to devise a substantially new set of conceptual premises and methods in order to meet Romantic nationalism's fundamental criterion of national self-affirmation.

For these reasons, nationalist ideologies in the Americas played out primarily in the realms of vernacular music and smaller-scale genres for much of the long 19th century: until at least the 1860s (according to location), most of the music played in churches, concert halls, and opera theaters in the Americas was composed by Europeans or written in direct imitation of European models. Both Canada and the United States experienced important efforts to collect folk song texts and set these to music—for example, Hubert LaRue's "Les chansons populaires et historiques du Canada" (Folk and Historical Song of Canada, 1863–1865) and Ernest Gagnon's "Les chansons populaires du Canada" (Folk Songs of Canada, 1865–1867), both published serially, or the many broadsides of folk and popular song published in the United States. Few of these songs were incorporated into cultivated music until the post–World War I period, however. Only with the flourishing of the brass band and revivalist culture in the years leading up to and after the U.S. Civil War did elements that would figure in post–World War I U.S. nationalism begin to come into focus. Nevertheless, a few composers set about the task of trying to achieve a distinctly "American" (i.e., U.S.) sound within the genres and forms of European cultivated music early on—first the Bohemian-born **Anthony Philip Heinrich**, then other composers, such as **Stephen Foster, William Henry Fry, Louis Moreau Gottschalk, Edward MacDowell, John Knowles Paine, Horatio Parker,** and **John Philip Sousa.** The first U.S. composer to achieve enduring international standing was **George Whitefield Chadwick.**

In Latin America, nationalist trends in cultivated music gained prominence even later—not least of all because those countries, unlike the United States and Canada, were slow to embrace culturally based notions of the concept of *nation.* In fact, such an embrace occurred only after 1910 in Mexico and after World War I elsewhere in South America, as the governments and state-sponsored institutions of Latin American countries sought to forge links between the ruling classes and those countries' culturally and economically disenfranchised indigenous peoples. Still, the long 19th century witnessed discernible steps toward a nationalist movement in cultivated music in some South American countries: in Argentina, the orchestral and piano compositions of **Arturo Berutti** and **Alberto Williams**; in Brazil, **Brasílio Itiberê da Cunha**'s *A Sertaneja* for piano solo (1869) and **Alexandre Levy**'s *Suite brésilienne* (1890); in Cuba, the *danzas cubanas* of **Ignacio Cervantes** (*see* HABANERA); in Mexico, the *danzas mexicanas* of **Ernesto Elorduy** and **Felipe Villanueva** and the operas of **Ricardo Castro Herrera** (*see* CONTREDANSE, CONTRADANCE, CONTRA DANCE); in Peru, **José María Valle Riestra**'s opera *Ollanta* (1900) and Quechua-influenced works of composers such as **Julián Aguirre** and **Daniel Alomía Robles**; and in Venezuela, **José Ángel Montero**'s opera *Virginia* (1873) and the **zarzuelas** of **Federico Villena**.

Despite their many and illustrious contributions to Romantic music, musical nationalisms continue to raise as many questions as answers. Like Romanticism itself, the meanings of the term *nationalism* differed so much from country to country, between the hemispheres, and from beginning to end of the century that they can scarcely be described as a single movement. Moreover, Romantic nationalisms were determined by their own proponents' widely varying understandings of what constituted a *nation*, by the specific conditions of the nation-state(s) to whose performers and audiences they addressed themselves, and by their own and their audiences' understandings of what did *not* qualify as nationally self-validating in those contexts: the surge in anti-Semitic and anti-Gypsy sentiment on the European continent (France as well as the German and Italian lands) during the years coterminous with the rise and flourishing of European nationalisms meant that the national selfhood of, for example, a self-consciously German composition was to a significant extent a function of its lack of (authentic) Gypsy or Jewish influence. For this reason, Romantic nationalisms are thus best understood not as a set of independent movements but rather as pendants of **exoticism** and racism. [JMC]

NEUE ZEITSCHRIFT FÜR MUSIK. (Ger., "New Periodical for Music.") Title of one of the **long 19th century**'s most important German-language music journals. The contract establishing the new journal was prepared in March 1834 by Julius Knorr (1826–1881; editor in chief), **Robert Schumann**, Ludwig Schunke (1810–1834), and Friedrich Wieck (1785–1873). The first issue appeared on 3 April 1834 under the title *Neue Leipziger Zeitschrift für Musik*, and the editorship was given as "durch einen Verein von Künstlern und Kunstfreunden" (by a group of artists and friends of art). Dissension erupted among the journal's contributors, however, and Schumann managed to gain full editorial control. The first issue prepared under the new editorial structure appeared on 2 January 1835, now titled simply *Neue Zeitschrift für Musik*. Schumann retained the editorship until his responsibilities at the Leipzig **Conservatory** forced him to relinquish the helm. He was succeeded by **Franz Brendel**, who further extended the periodical's consciously progressive stance and made it an unofficial organ of the **New German School** and later the **Allgemeiner Deutscher Musikverein**. It was also under Brendel's editorship that the journal published **Richard Wagner**'s notorious anti-Semitic essay "Über das Judentum in der Musik" (On Jewry in Music) under the disingenuous pseudonym "K. Freigedank" (C. Free-thought) as the lead article in the issues of 3 and 6 September 1850.

The *Neue Zeitschrift für Musik* has changed publishers, titles, and publication schedules several times over the years and during World War II was consolidated with several other German music periodicals (all run by the Nazi regime) under the title *Musik im Kriege* (Music in Time of War). Those changes notwithstanding, today it remains a leading periodical for music—one of very few that can claim more than 175 years of uninterrupted publication. To the end of the long 19th century, it remained remarkably consistent in delivering the essential components laid out in the prospectus of the first issue: (1) lengthy, often serialized, theoretical and historical articles; (2) belletristic pieces; (3) reviews of new music and of new editions of older music; (4) miscellaneous short notices concerning music, anecdotes, literature, and so on; (5) reports from foreign correspondents concerning music and musical life abroad; and (6) a "Chronik" (chronology—i.e., retrospective calendar) reporting recent and upcoming events. The journal also carried many advertisements from publishing houses, instrument makers, and so on and in this capacity is a rich source of information for latter-day scholars seeking information about early editions, instruments, and so on. Its periodic musical supplements are also valuable resources. [JMC]

See also ALLGEMEINE MUSIKALISCHE ZEITUNG.

NEW GERMAN SCHOOL. (Ger., [Die] Neudeutsche Schule.) Informal name for a group of musicians in the German lands centered around the socially and musically progressive ideas of **Hector Berlioz, Franz Liszt**, and **Richard Wagner**, among others. Critical perception of such a progressive group (also including **Robert Schumann**) dates from 1854, when the conservative Viennese music critic L. A. Zellner (1823–1904) and **Louis Spohr** both referred disparagingly to "*Zukunftsmusiker*" (musicians of the future). The group of philosophically affiliated musicians was still strictly informal at that point, but its "members" were centered around Liszt: they included (in addition to Berlioz and Wagner) Hans and Ingeborg von Bronsart (1840–1913), **Hans von Bülow, Peter Cornelius, Felix Draeseke, Louis Köhler, Richard Pohl, Joachim Raff**, and Carl Tausig (1841–1871).

In 1859, Liszt and **Franz Brendel** (since 1844 editor of the *Neue Zeitschrift für Musik*) organized the first annual Conference of German Musicians (*Versammlung deutscher Tonkünstler*), and at that gathering Brendel used the term *Die neu-deutsche Schule* as an alternative to the increasingly pejorative *Zukunftsmusiker* to refer to this circle and all who supported its progressive social and musical agendas. Also at that gathering, Liszt, Brendel, and others developed the idea of establishing an official organization centered on these artists' agreed-upon principles. That idea was formally proposed in June 1861, and at the *Tonkünstler-Versammlung* of 7 August 1861, the **Allgemeiner Deutscher Musikverein** (General German Musical Union) was founded. The *Allgemeiner Deutscher Musikverein* is thus a formal organization embracing the informal progressive circles generally referred to as the "New German School." Organized and led as it was by Brendel, the group was able to avail itself of the *Neue Zeitschrift für Musik* as its unofficial organ until 1892.

The specific goals of the New German School and *Allgemeiner Deutscher Musikverein* may be summarized as threefold: (1) to aspire for a fundamental rapprochement between the world of music and broader society; (2) to achieve this goal by recognizing that the music of the future would not be bound by conventional forms, genres, and compositional techniques but would instead possess a "poetic" content; and (3) to move music further along the path of progress on which it had been set especially by **Ludwig van Beethoven**. The first of these goals was derived from the New German School's members' understanding of the polis of Classical antiquity and shaped by **Georg Wilhelm Friedrich Hegel**'s and his followers' views of the nature of historical progress. The second implicitly recognized only two broad categories of music as progressive: **program music** and staged musical drama. The third, in the context of post-Revolutionary culture—*see* REVOLUTIONS OF 1848 (SPRING OF NATIONS, YEAR OF REVOLUTIONS)—also effectively dismissed as irrelevant or historically inconsequential all supposedly **absolute music** and much other music produced during the **Restoration**, especially after the death of Beethoven, while also rendering earlier music relevant and worthy of study not on its own terms but strictly as a step in the great historical narrative that had led to the post-Revolutionary present.

Although these core values were intended affirmatively and did much to support the work of young composers whose music might well find little respect in the existing structures of musical life and education, they also possessed a pronouncedly exclusionary tone. That tone (officially articulated by Brendel in the *Neue Zeitschrift für Musik* in March 1860) prompted **Johannes Brahms** and **Joseph Joachim** to draft a bitter rebuttal decrying *Zukunftsmusik* as running "contrary to the inner spirit of music." More generally, the increasing urgency and popularity of the aesthetic program that eventually led to the formation of the New German School was one prompt for **Eduard Hanslick**'s seminal tract *Vom Musikalisch-Schönen* (On the Musically Beautiful, 1854). [JMC]

See also GESAMTKUNSTWERK.

NIBELUNGENRING. See THE RING OF THE NIBELUNG.

NICOLAI, (CARL) OTTO (EHRENFRIED) (1810–1849). German composer, organist, and **conductor** of the Romantic Generation; founder of the Vienna Philharmonic **Orchestra**. Although he penned **part-songs**, **Lieder**, sacred music, orchestral works, and numerous instrumental **chamber** compositions, he is best known today for his **operas**, especially *Die lustigen Weiber von Windsor* (The Merry Wives of Windsor, 1849; after **William Shakespeare**). Nicolai ran away from home at age 16 and in 1827 was sent to study with Carl Friedrich Zelter (1758–1832) in Berlin; there, he later worked with Bernhard Klein (1793–1832), professor of music at the (Prussian) Royal Institute for Church Music and music director at the University of Berlin. In 1833, he accepted the position of organist at the Prussian embassy in Rome, where he also immersed himself in Italian sacred music of the late Renaissance—*see* PALESTRINA, GIOVANNI PIERLUIGI DA (1525–1594)—and Baroque and became well known as a **salon** pianist and pedagogue. He was also appointed *maestro compositore onorario* to the Accademia Filarmonica in Bologna, a title that **Wolfgang Amadeus Mozart** had held.

In 1837–1838, Nicolai was appointed conductor at the Court Opera in Vienna. He composed his first two mature Italian **comic operas**, *Enrico II* and *Il templario* (The Templar), in the wake of this experience, and the success of those two operas in Italian led to a successful career in opera in the Italian lands. They were followed by *Il proscritto* (The Proscribed Man), which was premiered at La Scala in March 1841. All three were translated into German in the early 1840s, when Nicolai was working as conductor of the Court Opera and the Kärtnertor Theater (Vienna) and of the Vienna Philharmonic Concerts, which he founded and which presented only works of "classical" masters such as Mozart and **Ludwig van Beethoven**. His *Kirchliche Fest-Ouvertüre* on the **chorale** "Ein' feste Burg" so impressed the Prussian monarch Friedrich Wilhelm IV that Nicolai was invited to Berlin to serve as director of the Berlin Cathedral Choir. In 1847, he was installed in that position and as Kapellmeister at the Royal Opera House in Berlin. Meanwhile, he had been at work on *Die lustigen Weiber von Windsor* since 1846. This was completed and premiered on 9 March 1849. Nicolai was elected a member of the Prussian Academy of the Arts on 11 May, but he collapsed and died of a stroke that same day without having received the news. [JMC]

NIELSEN, CARL (AUGUST) (1865–1931). Danish composer, **conductor**, violinist, and writer on music of the Modern Romantic Generation. He is best known today for his six **symphonies**, which were exact contemporaries of the symphonies of his fellow Scandinavian **Jean Sibelius** but exhibit a completely different development. He also composed the massive late masterpiece **Commotio** for organ (FS 155/Op. 58, 1930–1931) as well as two **operas**; two **melodramas** (both unpublished); 18 sets of **incidental music**; **concertos** for clarinet, flute, and violin as well as other **orchestral** works; 11 **cantatas** and five other works for chorus and orchestra; 26 a cappella choral works; approximately 60 **songs** and psalm settings for one voice and **piano**; a wind **quintet** that remains a staple of the literature for that ensemble, six **string quartets**, one **piano trio**, and about 20 other instrumental **chamber** works; and 14 works for piano solo. His opera *Maskarade* (FS 39, 1906, after Ludvig Holberg [1684–1754]), is considered a milestone in Danish music, and his memoir *Min fynske barndom* (My Childhood on Funen, 1927) is a classic of Danish literature.

Nielsen studied violin and trumpet as a youth and began composing at the age of nine. He became a military trumpeter at 14, also forming a string quartet and composing a few smaller pieces for piano solo or piano and other instruments between then and his entry into the Royal **Conservatory** (now the Royal Danish Academy of Music) in 1884. At the Conservatory, he studied music history with **Niels W. Gade** and theory with J. P. E. Hartmann (1805–1900) and Orla Rosenhoff (1844–1905), also joining the institution's orchestra as a violinist in 1886. In 1889, he became a violinist in the Royal Chapel Orchestra, and in 1892, he completed his First Symphony (FS 16/Op. 7), which, while clearly modeled on the symphonies of **Johannes Brahms**, **Antonín Dvořák**, and Gade, is tonally progressive (an unusual trait at that point) and reveals a distinctive rhythmic language as well as Nielsen's skills at dense orchestral textures. In 1901, he was awarded an annual government pension to support his composition. His **programmatic** Second Symphony ("De fire temperamenter" [The Four Temperaments], FS 29/Op. 16, 1901–1902) further broadened his reputation as a composer, and his renown as a conductor had been growing steadily. From 1905, he was a regular stand-in conductor with the Royal Chapel Orchestra, and the successful premiere of *Maskarade* in 1906 elevated him to the status of a national hero. In 1908, he formally succeeded his mentor as second Kapellmeister at the Royal Theater Orchestra, a post he held until 1914. His Third Symphony ("Sinfonia espansiva," FS 60/Op. 27, 1910–1911) increased his international fame, and he became conductor of the Danish Musical Society in 1915. He began teaching theory and composition at the Conservatory in 1916.

Nielsen's musical language changed dramatically with the outbreak of World War I. Although his Fourth Symphony ("Det uudslukkelige" [The Inextinguishable], FS 76/Op. 29, 1914–1916) ends on affirmative note, it

NIETZSCHE, FRIEDRICH (WILHELM) (1844–1900) • 407

marks the beginning of a more austere, less optimistic and idealistic style. His horror at the outbreak of war combined with his increasing involvement in music education to strengthen his commitment to Danish **folk song** and to music's social use generally. As his fame continued to grow, he became more involved in collecting folk song and more committed to developing a linear, posttonal idiom that could viably supersede the mainstream styles of post-Romanticism. His works over the last decade of his life became more concerned with chamber idioms, folk song, and other works that musically and generically fell outside the post-Romantic **canon**. His 60th birthday in 1925 was occasion for national celebration, but his health was on the decline. He composed fewer original works in the following years. He became director of the Conservatory in 1931 but died of a heart attack later that year.

Nielsen is considered a significant figure in Danish **nationalism** and Scandinavian nationalism generally, partly because of the international renown he achieved for his country and his region during the twilight of European nationalist movements in music. He also successfully forged a path for Danish national music that broke from the tonally governed Romantic and post-Romantic musical idioms characteristic of much other nationalist music while also cultivating the lush sonorities typical of late Romantic and post-Romantic music and forging an original and distinctive posttonal musical language. [JMC]

NIETZSCHE, FRIEDRICH (WILHELM) (1844–1900). German philosopher, poet, and amateur composer of the Late Romantic Generation, significant primarily for his early influential writings on behalf of **Richard Wagner** and his distinction between Romanticism (which he viewed as a naive and idealistic expression and consequence of weakness) and the *Dionysian impulse* (which he viewed as born of the individual's strength and will to power). He enrolled in the University of Bonn to study philosophy and theology but then went to Leipzig to study philology instead. In 1868, he became professor of classical philology at the University of Basel. He met and fell under the spell of Wagner in 1868, coming to view Wagner's ideas on music and drama as the revitalization of Classical Greek drama and espousing these views in his provocative first book, *Die Geburt der Tragödie aus dem Geiste der Musik* (The Birth of Tragedy from the Spirit of Music, 1872). In 1876, he and Wagner had a falling-out of unknown origin, leading him to pen a series of three pamphlets ridiculing Wagner's ideas and denouncing his influence. The most important of these pamphlets, *Der Fall Wagner* (The Case of Wagner) and *Götzendämmerung* (Twilight of the False Gods; a pun on the final opera of Wagner's **Ring of the Nibelung** tetralogy), argue instead for the approach to drama represented by **Georges Bizet**.

Nietzsche's health began to fail in the late 1870s. In 1879, he resigned from his post at the university, surviving thereafter on a small pension. His masterpiece of these years, the epic prose poem *Also sprach Zarathustra* (1883–1885), would inspire music by **Frederick Delius, Gustav Mahler,** and **Richard Strauss.** He lived a nomadic and increasingly ascetic existence over the next decade until his mental deterioration in December 1888–January 1889 led to his institutionalization. He was an excellent pianist and composed music for **piano** solo and **piano duet** as well as 17 **songs.** [JMC]

NOCTURNE. (Ger., Nachtstück.) Semantically, a composition intended to be performed at night or somehow evocative of the night. Linguistically, the term is the cognate of the 18th-century *notturno*, a multimovement instrumental or (more rarely) vocal ensemble composition akin to a **serenade,** intended to be performed with one person per part rather than by a larger ensemble. Musically, however, such works are far removed from the nocturne as the term emerged early in the 19th century and is best known today. In that usage, the term "nocturne" denotes a languid or dreamy composition, usually in slow tempo and scored for **piano** solo. The textures of such compositions are treble dominated and supported by an arpeggiated accompaniment; their melodic lines typically offer implicit or explicit opportunities for embellishment after the style of improvisation in Italian **opera;** the phrases are typically quadratic, the forms simple and sectional.

This style of writing for piano solo emerged in France already by the end of the 1790s and was often referred to as a **romance** (another vocal prototype), but only by the 1830s had it come to denote a piano **character piece** in the style just described. By the end of the **long 19th century,** that particular complex of stylistic traits had evolved further so that the term "nocturne" was understood to apply to virtually any composition in virtually any style provided that it had some sort of functional and/or characteristic affinity with night generally construed. **Claude Debussy's** *Three Nocturnes for Orchestra* (1897–1899, publ. 1901); the third-movement (labeled "Nocturne") of Vaughan-Williams's **Symphony** No. 2 (1912–1913, rev. 1920); **Robert Schumann's** *Nachtstücke* op. 23 (1839–1840); and the "Nocturne" from **Felix Mendelssohn Bartholdy's incidental music** for **Williams Shakespeare's** *A Midsummer Night's Dream* (1843, publ. 1844) are important examples of this rethinking.

The association of the term "nocturne" with a dreamy, sectional, treble-dominated style with improvisation and sectional forms, usually for piano solo, owes primarily to two composers. The first composer to publish works in this style with the genre designation "nocturne" was the Irish **virtuoso John Field,** who in 1812 published three nocturnes (so designated) that were eventually familiar to the genre's preeminent composer, **Fryderyk Chopin.** Although the Leipzig *Allgemeine Musikalische Zeitung* failed to note anything special about Field's nocturnes when it reviewed them in 1814, other composers and pianists (primarily ones associated with Field in some way) evidently took note, for between then and 1830, a number of new compositions in this style and bearing the designation "nocturne" appeared (works by J. B. Cramer, Simon Mayer, Henri Herz, **Mikhail Glinka**, and **Maria Agata Szymanovska**, among others). Although Field published another 13 piano nocturnes between 1812 and 1836, he was largely eclipsed after 1830 by Chopin, whose 21 nocturnes (CT 108–28/opp. 9, 15, 27, 32, 37, 48, 55, 62, and 72) expanded the emotional range of the genre and imbued it with new levels of musical sophistication as well as a distinctive style of pianistic **virtuosity** uniquely well suited to the **salon** as well as the public recital.

The list of composers who engaged with the Chopin-esque nocturne after 1830 includes some of the long 19th century's most respected names, among them **Mily Balakirev, Carl Czerny, Gabriel Fauré, Edvard Grieg, Friedrich Kalkbrenner, Franz Liszt, Ignaz Moscheles, Nikolay Rimsky-Korsakov, Clara Schumann, Aleksandr Scriabin, Pyotor Il'yich Tchaikovsky**, and **Sigismond Thalberg**. The extent to which Chopin came to personify the genre is evident from No. 12 of Robert Schumann's *Carnaval*, Op. 9 (1834–1835, publ. 1837), which is not labeled nocturne but is a brilliant parody of the Polish composer's nocturne style and is titled simply "Chopin." [JMC]

See also LIEDER OHNE WORTE.

NONET. (Fr., nonette; Ger., Nonett; It., nonetto; Sp., noneto.) Generally, an ensemble of nine solo performers or a composition written for it; a category of instrumental **chamber music**. Although earlier composers had specified as nine the total number of performers to be employed (e.g., **Ignaz Pleyel**'s *Symphonie concertante* in E-flat Major, B. 111, 1786), those works did not employ nine independent parts, instead calling for more than one player on some parts.

The first true nonets were penned in the Early Romantic Generation. **Franz Schubert**'s Wind Nonet for two clarinets, two bassoons, contrabassoon, two horns, and two trombones (D. 79, 1813, known as "eine kleine Trauermusik" [A Little Mourning Music]) is a modified version of the traditional *Harmoniemusik*, with flutes omitted and contrabassoon and trombones added for an appropriately funereal timbre. Since this remained unpublished until 1895, it could not provide a model for other nonets. By contrast, **Ludwig Spohr**'s *Grand Nonet* for Violin, Viola, Cello, Bass, Flute, Oboe, Clarinet, Bassoon, and Horn (Op. 31, comp. 1813, publ. in parts in 1818 and score in 1878) set the model for later works in the genre, combining soloists from the usual wind and string complements of the standard 19th-century **orchestra** in a composition laid out in the four-movement version of **sonata plan**. This structure—a kind of chamber **symphony**—was adopted in other nonets of the **long 19th century**, including those by Frans Coenen (1826–1904; 1858), Louise Farrenc (1804–1875; Op. 38, 1849), **Georges Onslow** (Op. 77, 1851), **Franz Lachner** (1875), **Josef Rheinberger** (Op. 139, 1885), and **Charles Villiers Stanford** (Serenade, Op. 95, 1905). Samuel Coleridge-Taylor (1875–1912) and William Wallace Gilchrist (1846–1916) wrote nonets with the piano replacing flute and oboe, respectively (1894 and 1910). [JMC]

NOTTEBOHM, (MARTIN) GUSTAV (1817–1882). German composer, teacher, musicologist, and philologist of the Romantic Generation; pioneer in the application of principles of philology to musical source studies. Nottebohm trained first in **piano** and theory in Berlin with Ludwig Berger (1777–1839) and Siegfried Dehn (1799–1858), respectively, also spending time with **Adolf Bernhard Marx**, whose pervasive interest in the relationship between composers' lives and works (*see* BIOGRAPHICAL FALLACY) left a lasting impression on him. In 1840, he secured his father's permission to pursue a career in music. This he did first in Dessau with Friedrich Schneider (1786–1853), who, recognizing his potential, sent him to study at the Leipzig **Conservatory**, where he was mentored by both **Felix Mendelssohn Bartholdy** and **Robert Schumann**. He relocated in 1846 to Vienna, where he continued his study of counterpoint with the renowned pedagogue **Simon Sechter**. In Vienna, his circle of friends and colleagues included **Joseph Joachim** and **Johannes Brahms**, the latter of whom recognized the significance of his scholarly endeavors and supported his efforts to get his work published.

Nottebohm served on the board of directors and as archivist and librarian for the **Gesellschaft der Musikfreunde** and in 1861 was invited by **Breitkopf & Härtel** to serve on the editorial board of the new *Gesamtausgabe* of **Ludwig van Beethoven**'s works, publication of which began in 1862. His contributions there along with his other scholarly publications led to his involvements in the edition of Mendelssohn's collected works (Breitkopf & Härtel, 1871–1874) and then in the **Wolfgang Amadeus Mozart** *Gesamtausgabe* (Breitkopf & Härtel, 1877–1905); his declining health prevented him from accepting the invitation to succeed Wilhelm Rust (1822–1892) as editor of Breitkopf & Härtel's edition of the complete works of **Johann Sebastian Bach**. In the meantime, he had published thematic catalogs of the works of both Beethoven (1868) and **Franz Schubert** (1874), works that remained standard reference works until they were succeeded in the mid-20th century by Georg Kinsky's and Otto Erich Deutsch's thematic catalogs of those composers' works (refer to the bibliography). He also published numerous scholarly essays and articles in the popular press concerning Bach,

Mozart, Beethoven, and Schubert. He also wrote and published the fourth volume of **August Wilhelm Ambros**'s seminal *Geschichte der Musik* (History of Music, 1878, 2nd ed. 1881).

Nottebohm's greatest contribution, however, lies in the area of philology and the advancement of knowledge concerning the **compositional process** in music, especially where Beethoven is concerned. Prior to Nottebohm's studies, Beethoven's manuscripts had been treated essentially as collector's items and never systematically applied to understanding of the composer's biography and creative process. Nottebohm sought out those primary sources, developed an understanding of the relationships among different kinds of documents and techniques for dating them, and transcribed and annotated his findings in short articles and several longer monographs, most importantly *Ein Skizzenbuch von Beethoven* (A Beethoven Sketchbook, 1865), *Beethoveniana* (1872), *Ein Skizzenbuch von Beethoven aus dem Jahr 1803* (A Beethoven Sketchbook from the Year 1803, 1880), and the posthumously published *Zweite Beethoveniana* (Beethoveniana Vol. 2, a collection of essays previously published in the *Musikalisches Wochenblatt*). His findings and methodologies are now dated, as are many other 19th-century philological techniques. Nevertheless, his work represented a vital first step in bringing the relatively new disciplines of musical scholarship up to pace with other scholarship in the humanities, basing knowledge of composers' lives on primary sources rather than merely recollections and criticisms, integrating the process of musical creation into biography, and using knowledge of the process by which music was created to enrich understanding of the final products as they were published and known in performance. [JMC]

NOVELLO. London-based firm of music publishers, still in existence and one of the United Kingdom's most influential firms in its field. The firm was founded in 1811 by Vincent Novello (1781–1861), himself a talented organist, choirmaster, and composer, one of the first to make the Masses of **Franz Joseph Haydn** and **Wolfgang Amadeus Mozart** available to the English musical public first through his and his choir's performances in the chapel of the Portuguese embassy in London and later in publication through vocal scores with **piano** or organ accompaniment, with **orchestral** parts available on a rental basis. In 1828, he also launched a similar series for Henry Purcell.

Vincent Novello's eldest son, (Joseph) Alfred (1810–1896), apprenticed as a music publisher in York, then returned to London, where he first worked independently and then (1830) joined with his father to form the firm of Novello & Co. Together, father and son continued publishing music, including choral series devoted to William Boyce (1830ff), **George Frideric Handel** (1834ff), and **Johann Sebastian Bach** (1845ff). They also founded two important periodicals, *The Musical World* (1836–1841) and *The Musical Times and Singing Class Circular* (1844–present; "and Singing Class Circular" was dropped from the title in 1904).

In 1867, the Novello business merged with its erstwhile rival, **Ewer & Co.**, to become Novello, Ewer & Co., and the name "Ewer" was finally dropped in 1898. Alfred Novello's successful pursuit of the English rights to **Felix Mendelssohn Bartholdy**'s oratorio *St. Paul* in 1836 proved to be a major financial success for the firm, as did its continuing editions of works by other, earlier composers. Beginning in 1857, it published a series of modern anthems by contemporary composers, adding the collection of *Hymns Ancient and Modern* (the most widely used hymnal in England) in 1861. During the late 1860s and 1870s, the firm added the genre of **opera** to its interests and became an aggressive leader in the world of concert promotion, ventures that added **Antonín Dvořák** and **Giuseppe Verdi** to the roster of major names associated with it. It began publishing *The School Music Review* in 1892, the first of a number of periodicals in the burgeoning discipline of music education. The firm's impact on choral music and amateur music making in the United Kingdom and its spheres of influence is incalculable. [JMC]

NUTCRACKER, OP. 71. (Rus., *Shchelkunchik*, Fr., *Casse-Noisette*.) Iconic ballet (*ballet-féerie*) in two acts by **Pyotor Il'yich Tchaikovsky**, composed in 1891–1892 and choreographed by Lev Ivanov (1834–1901), second ballet master for the Imperial Ballet in St. Petersburg and reputedly an able musician himself. It was first produced in St. Petersburg on 18 December 1892 and published in full score, parts, and **piano** reduction that same year (*see* PRINTING AND PUBLISHING OF MUSIC). The story is based on **E. T. A. Hoffmann**'s short story *Der Nußkracker und der Mäusekönig* (The Nutcracker and the King of Mice, 1816) as adapted and translated into French by Alexandre Dumas, *père* (*Histoire d'un casse-noisette*, 1844), and further adapted for the **libretto** by the ballet dancer, choreographer, and pedagogue Marius Petipa (1818–1910).

The many alterations and restructurings entailed in translating a short story intended for early 19th-century Germans into one for mid-19th-century French and then into a libretto that would be suitable for presentation as dance to a Russian public habituated to ballet necessarily resulted in a final product that resembles Hoffmann's original only in general terms, but this has not occasioned the sort of criticism that typically attends such substantial changes to literature. Rather, Tchaikovsky's score and the orchestral **suite** extracted from it have remained among his most popular works and are considered emblematic of his powers of musical invention, melodic imagination, and masterful **orchestration**. Among the ballet's most effective and well known numbers are the extended battle scene between the Nutcracker

Prince and the Mouse King (a scene whose turbulent musical language is also found in the *1812 Overture* and **Ludwig van Beethoven**'s *Wellington's Victory*), the "**Waltz** of the Snowflakes" and "Grandfather Dance" at the end of Act I (*see* KEHRAUS), and the nine **exotic** dances performed for Clara and the Nutcracker Prince in Act II. [JMC]

O

OCTET. (Fr., octette, octuor; Ger., Oktett; It., otteto; Sp., octeto.) Generally, an ensemble of eight solo performers or a composition written for it; a category of instrumental **chamber music**. Octets typically were in **sonata plan.** Four main varieties of octet were cultivated during the **long 19th century**: (1) octets for winds, (2) octets for winds and strings, (3) octets for winds and strings with piano, and (4) octets for strings. Although by the early 20th century such works were sometimes performed with a **conductor** (a practice that is not uncommon today), conductors were not used for this repertoire during the 19th century.

Wind octets may be regarded as indoor counterparts to the outdoor genre known as *Harmoniemusik*. Wind octets are typically scored for paired oboes, clarinets, bassoons, and horns. The best-known example of this variety of octet is that by **Ludwig van Beethoven**, which was composed while he was still in Bonn, revised in Vienna in 1793, overhauled in 1795 as the String **Quintet** in E-flat Major (Op. 4, publ. 1796), and posthumously published in 1830 as Beethoven's Op. 103. Other octets of this variety were composed by Louis Théodore Gouvy (1819–1898, Op. 1, ca. 1882), **Franz Lachner** (Op. 156, 1850), and **Carl Reinecke** (Op. 216, ca. 1892). The best-known *octet for winds and strings* is that of **Franz Schubert** for clarinet, horn, bassoon, two violins, viola, cello, and bass (D. 803), composed in 1824 and first published posthumously (movements 1–3 and 6 publ. as Op. posth. 166 in 1853 and published in its entirety in 1866). Although D. 803 may have been inspired by Beethoven's **Septet** (Op. 20, 1800, publ. 1802), it was also preceded in a similar scoring by Peter von Winter (1754–1824; 1812, for flute, clarinet, bassoon, two horns, violin, viola, and cello) and **Louis Spohr** (Op. 32, 1814; for clarinet, two horns, violin, two violas, cello, and bass). *Octets for winds and strings with piano* were penned by Frédéric Dolmetsch (1813–1892; 1858, for oboe, clarinet, horn, violin, viola, cello, bass, and piano), Prince Louis Ferdinand of Prussia (1772–1806; Op. 12, publ. 1808, for clarinet, two violins, two violas, two cellos, and piano), Paul Juon (1872–1940; Op. 27, for oboe, clarinet, bassoon, horn, violin, viola, cello, and piano), Ferdinand Ries (1784–1838; Op. 128, for clarinet, bassoon, horn, violin, viola, cello, bass, and piano), and **Anton Rubinstein** (Op. 9, 1856; for flute, clarinet, horn, violin, viola, cello, bass, and piano).

The *string octet*, scored for four violins, two violas, and two cellos functioning either as a double quartet or an ensemble of eight equal stringed instruments, emerged as a distinct subgenre in the 1820s and 1830s. Spohr penned four compositions of the double-quartet type: Opp. 65 (1823, publ. 1825), 77 (1827, publ. 1828), 87 (1832–1833, publ. 1833), and 136 (1847, publ. 1849). The archetypal "pure" string octet is **Felix Mendelssohn Bartholdy**'s Octet in E-flat, (MWV R20/Op. 20, comp. 1825, rev. and publ. 1833). Other works of this variety were composed by Woldemar Bargiel (1828–1897; Op. 15a, 1849–1850), **Niels W. Gade** (Op. 17, 1848–1849), Hermann Grädener (1844–1929; Op. 12, 1881), Ludvig Norman (1831–1885; Op. 30, 1866–67), **Joachim Raff** (Op. 176, 1873), and **August Svendsen** (Op. 3, 1867). [JMC]

OFFENBACH, JACQUES (1818–1890). French composer and **virtuoso** cellist of German birth and Jewish background, of the Romantic Generation; arguably the most influential figure in establishing the genre of **operetta** as it would be cultivated by later composers, including **Franz Lehár, Johann Strauss (II)**, and **Arthur Sullivan**. The son of a cantor, he trained as a violinist, cellist, and **conductor**, publishing his Opus 1 (the *Divertimento über Schweizerlieder* [Divertimento on Swiss Songs] for cello with two violins, viola, and bass) in 1833. He enrolled at the Paris **Conservatory** that same year but was forced to drop out the following year for financial reasons. He took a position as cellist in the **orchestra** of the Opéra-Comique and quickly made a name for himself as a solo cellist and composer of **romances, waltzes**, and instrumental **chamber music** in the Parisian capital's thriving **salon** culture and studying composition with **Fromenthal Halévy**. His growing reputation as a cellist included performances alongside **Franz Liszt** and **Anton Rubinstein** and took him to England in 1844, but his skills as composer also won him the admiration of prominent Parisian musical figures including **Adolphe Adam** and **Gioachino Rossini**.

Offenbach's fortunes as a composer for the stage changed with the Exposition Universelle of 1855. He rented a small theater on the Champs-Elysées and renamed it the Bouffes-Parisiens, programming original short, one-act musical entertainments with a cast of no more than three onstage performers. The immensely successful programs, featuring Offenbach's eminently tuneful, witty, colorful, and engaging music, made it possible for him to quit his job at the Comédie-Française in order to commit himself to composing for and managing the new company. Between the summer of 1855 and the autumn of 1858, he had composed and performed some 28 operettas. A new level of notoriety arrived with *Orphée aux enfers* (Orpheus in the Underworld, 1858, rev. 1874), and although critics decried Offenbach's music as cheap and frivolous, his reputation as a leading voice of the lighter, more hedonistic and occasionally cynical side of **Second Empire** France was soon acclaimed by such diverse figures as Anton Chekhov, **Friedrich Nietzsche**, and August Strindberg. Later works, including *La belle Hélène* (Fair Helen, 1864), *Barbe-Bleu* (Bluebeard, 1866), *La vie parisienne* (Parisian Life, 1866), *La Grande Duchesse de Gérolstein* (1867), and *La Périchole* (1868), spread quickly to England, the German lands, and the United States.

Offenbach's popularity declined in the changed French cultural climate after the **Franco-Prussian War**, but he traveled to the United States in 1876 for the Philadelphia Centennial Exhibition and gave some 40 highly successful concerts there, also publishing his impressions of the New World in a book titled *Offenbach en Amérique, notes d'un musicien en voyage* (Offenbach in America: Notes of a Traveling Musician) after his return. The main project of his later years was his five-act *opéra fantastique* based on short stories of **E. T. A. Hoffman**, *Les contes d'Hoffmann* (Hoffmann's Tales). The music was drafted in entirety and published in piano/vocal score in 1880 (*see* PRINTING AND PUBLISHING OF MUSIC), but the **orchestration**, at the family's request, had to be completed by **Ernest Guiraud** (also known for having supplied the recitatives for the Viennese production of *Carmen* by the composers' mutual friend **Georges Bizet**).

Les contes d'Hoffmann was premiered at the Opéra-Comique on 10 February 1881, four months after Offenbach's death from heart failure secondary to gout. Today, he is remembered almost entirely for a handful of his 97 surviving **operas**, operettas, and **opéras comiques** and, to a lesser extent, his many works for solo cello with accompaniment of piano, orchestra, or instrumental **chamber** ensemble. He also composed 35 sacred and secular works for accompanied and a cappella chorus, four **ballets**, numerous sets of **incidental music** and **vaudevilles**, much dance music for **piano** or orchestra, and several more serious orchestral works. [JMC]

ONSLOW, (ANDRÉ) GEORGES (LOUIS) (1784–1853). French composer of English descent, member of the Early Romantic Generation. He was born into England's landed aristocracy and maintained friendly professional relations with England throughout his career but spent most of his professional life in France—yet his music found little interest in either England or France but was widely sought after in the German lands, with leading publishers such as **Breitkopf & Härtel** and **Kistner** vying for the rights to his works. He studied with Jan Ladislav Dussek (1760–1812) in Hamburg (1799–1800) but decided to pursue music as a vocation only after hearing the overture to **Étienne-Nicolas Méhul**'s *Stratonice* (1792) in 1801. He then studied composition with Johann Baptist Cramer (1771–1858) in England and moved to Paris in 1808 to study with **Antoine Reicha**.

France remained Onslow's base for the remainder of his career—not Paris but his native Clermont-Ferrand, in Auvergne. He lost the hearing in one ear when a bullet became lodged in it during a hunting expedition in 1829. While convalescing composed the last three movements of the String **Quintet** No. 8, Op. 38, which became known as the *Quintette de la balle* ("Bullet" Quintet). As his reputation grew, he accrued numerous honors: in 1834, he was elected president of Paris's concert series titled L'Athenée musical; in 1839, he founded a Société Philharmonique in Clermont; in 1842, he succeeded **Luigi Cherubini** at the Académie des Beaux-Arts; in 1846, he was invited to the 28th Lower Rhine **Music Festival**, conducted by **Felix Mendelssohn Bartholdy** and starring **Jenny Lind**; and in 1847, his Fourth **Symphony** was conducted at the 29th convening of that festival (in Cologne). He is remembered today mostly for his instrumental **chamber music**, especially his wind **nonet** (Op. 77, 1849), wind quintet (Op. 81, 1852), 37 **string quartets**, 34 string quintets, and numerous chamber works with **piano**. He also composed four **operas**, one of which (the "drame lyrique" *Guise, ou Les états de Blois*, 1837; *see* LYRIC DRAMA) was enthusiastically reviewed by **Hector Berlioz**. Included in his 83 numbered *opera* are four symphonies, the third of which is an arrangement of his op. 32 string quintet. [JMC]

OPERA. (It., from Lat. *opera*, pl. of *opus*: "Work"; Fr., opéra; Ger., Oper.) Umbrella term for a variety of more specific genres, all of which denote staged musical dramas that are sung; generally the preeminent form of public vocal music during the **long 19th century**. The hypernym *opera* was employed casually, but by the time that sung, staged musical dramas were performed and published, they were usually provided with more specific designations that gave essential information concerning their language, subject matter, length or scope, tone or character, and other considerations when relevant. In part because a defining characteristic of the genre of opera since its emergence in the late 16th century had been continuous music (i.e., the absence of spoken dialogue of any sort), the primary distinctions among various genres were (1) the language used and (2) the presence or absence of spoken dialogue.

Because bringing an opera to stage was a complicated and enormously expensive venture, individual theaters typically developed requirements for works to be produced there that were suited to their size, location, audience demographics, stage resources and personnel, and of course budget; audiences in turn often frequented particular theaters whose profiles suited their tastes. Whether a given opera would be performed and in what state it would be given were thus often determined by the work's language, the presence or absence of speech, and its character or tone (amorous, humorous, satirical, serious, and so on) and subject matter (historical or contemporary, **nationalist** or **exoticist**, and so on). For example, for most of the 19th century, works performed in the Paris Opéra could include no spoken dialogue and had to include a **ballet**, typically in the second act. Accordingly, composers and **librettists** frequently made significant alterations to their operas according to changing expectations and requirements in the various locations and theaters in which their works were to be performed, the specific singers to be employed, and so on—and only rarely did they consider these "adapted" versions as illegitimate offspring of the original version. That situation complicates the task of modern editors and interpreters who need, whether for practical or ideological reasons, to determine a single "authoritative" version that best reflects the composer's and librettist's intentions (*see* FASSUNG LETZTER HAND; INTENTIONAL FALLACY).

Musicians (the primary assumed readership of this dictionary) naturally tend to view an opera as a musical product—that is, the work and intellectual property of the composer—and in some ways this perspective is correct. As a matter of practice and legality, however, during the long 19th century, composers were usually the last—and sometimes least, in terms of creative authority and intellectual ownership—in the creation of opera. Three models of creative process predominated. The most traditional of these models, typical especially of the Italian operas of **Vincenzo Bellini** and **Gaetano Donizetti** and in French operas of, for example, **Daniel-François-Esprit Auber** and **Giacomo Meyerbeer**, was a "top-down" procedure in which the composer was involved in the creation of the work only late in the process. In this creative model, the general subjects of the operas for a given season were chosen by the administrative directors of the court or theater in question, and the librettists for those subjects were selected according to their affiliation with the court or institution, their reputation, and so on. In this model, the **libretto** was usually the intellectual property of the theater that commissioned it rather than of the librettist. Sometimes the theater would designate both composer and librettist when the libretto was commissioned; sometimes the librettist could choose or suggest the composer. Either way, once a composer had been commissioned to create the music, he or she would set the libretto to music as the librettist provided it to him or her—a process that often unfolded piecemeal, resulting in last-minute completion of the score and delayed production.

The terms of such arrangements naturally reserved the right of first performance for the commissioning theater, but after the first performance run (or in some cases the opening of the first run), both the composer and the librettist had the right to pursue further performances of the work, subject to adaptation for the needs of other theaters. Depending on the terms of the original contract, the librettist had the right to have the libretto published or to sell it to other theaters or composers for setting to new music, while the composer had the right to sell performance rights to his or her music (and the librettist's text) to other theaters and/or publishers (*see* COPYRIGHT AND PERFORMANCE RIGHT).

This traditional model of creation persevered to the end of the 19th century (and beyond), but over the course of the 19th century, a second model that granted more authority to both librettist and composer became increasingly common. In this model (represented by **Carl Maria von Weber**'s *Der Freischütz* and typical of most of **Giuseppe Verdi**'s operas), composers and librettists—often individuals who had already worked together but sometimes ones who knew each other's work but had yet to collaborate directly—initiated the creative process collaboratively, then shopped the growing combination of text and music to an appropriate theater (either personally or through an agent). This marketing of the opera for production could occur either as the project was developing (often after the libretto had been completed but before the music was ready to show) or after it had been completed.

In this second model of the creative process, the copyright for the text and music of the opera typically resided with the librettist and composer, who either employed an agent to promote their works or freelanced and arranged for performance and/or publication themselves. This model also had the advantage of relative creative autonomy for the librettist and composer, at least in principle, since it permitted them to choose the subject, develop an approach, and pursue their own (shared) ideas as to appropriate theater(s) for performance. However, since the business of producing an opera entailed not only hiring an **orchestra** and singers but also designing and fitting costumes, creating sets, working out scene changes, developing a lighting design, setting rehearsal schedules and soloists' calendars, and scheduling and advertising the performances—all factors that entailed significant costs and contractual work for personnel and materials—that increased creative autonomy was anything but absolute. Once the sets had been built and the scene changes designed, the text and music of the work had to accommodate the staging, not the other way around. The annals of 19th-century opera are filled with accounts of composers and/or librettists needing to create more music to fill the time for a scene change or to abbreviate material text and/or music to accommodate other practical theatrical concerns.

The third model for operatic creation emerged latest and is least common but from the composer's perspective is perhaps most appealing. In this model, best known today through **Richard Wagner**'s creative process in his operas written after 1848, the libretto was penned by the composer, thus often removing a professionally credentialed *littérateur* from the process but uniting text and music as the products of a single, inherently unified creative vision—that of the composer. Such a process had obvious benefits from a strictly musical perspective and in terms of the legalities of copyright and performance right. Yet even this more streamlined creative process did not change the enormous complexity and cost of bringing an opera to the stage, for the librettist-cum-composer had to be able to present at least an overview of the entire final product—more commonly the entire work in most of its essentials—to the theater in order for that stage to undertake to produce the work, and the theater could develop a budget, production design, rehearsal schedule, performance calendar, and promotion plan only after that reasonably specific and detailed information had been received. The surviving parts and performance materials for works created according to this model reveal composer/librettists making extensive last-minute changes, sometimes after the first performances had begun, in order to make their work theatrically as well as musically successful (*see* COMPOSITIONAL PROCESS, CREATIVE PROCESS).

Finally, because the specifics of any given opera's text and music almost inevitably changed significantly from one production to another, for much of the long 19th century operas were typically disseminated in manuscript copies rather than in printed scores because the former could be more easily and cheaply altered. In those comparatively few instances when operas were committed to print, they were usually published not in full score but in piano/vocal arrangements only (sometimes with parts available on a rental basis). Committing an opera to print, however, was both time consuming and costly due to the length of the works. Because copyright law until the end of the 19th century assigned intellectual ownership to the publisher rather than the author (librettist and/or composer), publication of an opera actually limited rather than reinforced the ability of librettist and composer to safeguard the aesthetic quality of their collaborative artwork. For this reason, most operas were published only in excerpted arrangements—either piano/vocal transcriptions of particularly important portions that could be performed in private spaces (such as **salons**) or in public, arrangements of portions of the work for **piano duet** with or without singers, or **fantasies** and "reminiscences" (some virtuosic, others more modest) that promoted the opera through a trope based upon it. [JMC]

See also BALLET; BURLESQUE; *CARMEN*; CONDUCTOR; *DON GIOVANNI*, K. 527; DRAME LYRIQUE, DRAMMA LYRICA; EXTRAVAGANZA; FAUST; *DER FREISCHÜTZ*, J. 277/OP. 77; GRAND OPERA; INCIDENTAL MUSIC; LEITMOTIV; LIBRETTO; LIEDERSPIEL; MÄRCHENOPER; OPÉRA COMIQUE; OPERA SEMISERIA; OPERETTA, OPERATTA; ORATORIO; PERFORMANCE PRACTICE; POSSE, POSSE MIT GESANG; RESCUE OPERA; *THE RING OF THE NIBELUNG*; *ROMEO AND JULIET*; *DER ROSENKAVALIER*; *SAINETE*; SINGSPIEL; SPIELOPER; *TRISTAN UND ISOLDE*, WWV 90; VAUDEVILLE; ZAUBEROPER.

OPÉRA COMIQUE. Term for a French stage work that uses spoken dialogue to connect vocal and instrumental music; such works may also include recitative. The term *comique* is not synonymous with the English *comic* or the Italian *buffa* but rather derives from the Greek *komoidia*, itself a combination of *kōmos* (revel *or* community festival) and *aeidein* (to sing). The subjects and plots of operás comiques may thus be lighthearted, satirical, serious, tragic, or some combination of those characteristics. The term *opéra comique* thus embraces not only **Jacques Offenbach**'s *Les contes d'Hoffmann* (1881) but also tragedies such as **Georges Bizet**'s *Carmen* (1875) as well as the French version of **Ludwig van Beethoven**'s *Fidelio* and **Eugène Scribe**'s French adaptation of **Carl Maria von Weber**'s *Der Freischütz* or **Gioachino Rossini**'s *Barber of Seville*. The Opéra-Comique (hyphenated, with uppercase *c*) is the second of Paris's main opera houses, the most prestigious venue in which operás comiques were given during the **long 19th century**. (Paris's Théâtre Lyrique and Opéra-National also performed works in the genre.)

Opéra comique was immensely popular throughout the long 19th century not only in performance but also in publication: works in the genre were among the very few compositions for the musical stage that were quickly committed to publication in score as well as parts and were widely disseminated in quantity (*see* PRINTING AND PUBLISHING OF MUSIC). That situation owed partly to the topicality of its plots and the wit of many of its **libretti** but also to the tuneful and colorful music composers wrote for it. During the Revolutionary period and **First French Empire**, important contributions were made by composers of the Early Romantic Generation, including **Adrien Boieldieu, Luigi Cherubini, Jean-François Le Sueur**, and **Étienne-Nicolas Méhul**, but a new level of creativity and success arrived with the generally peaceful culture of the **Bourbon Restoration**—most importantly in contributions of other Early Romantic Generation composers, such as **Gaetano Donizetti, Fromenthal Halévy, Giacomo Meyerbeer, Georges Onslow**, and **Ferdinando Paer**. At mid-century, it flourished in the hands of Romantic Generation composers such as **Adolphe Adam, Daniel-François Esprit Auber, Hector Berlioz, Félicien David**, and **Ambroise Thomas**, among others. During the second half of the century, many operás comiques began using more sophisticated music and plots and more elaborate staging, a development that had as an unforeseen consequence the emergence and flourishing of more frankly lighthearted entertainments such as **burlesques, extravaganzas, operettas**, and **vaudevilles**. Despite that breakaway movement, the second half of the century witnessed further contributions by Late Romantic Generation composers including **Léo Delibes, Théodore Dubois, François-August Gevaert, Charles Gounod, Édouard Lalo, Jules Massenet, Jacques Offenbach, Camille Saint-Saëns**, and

Franz von Suppé. The Modern Romantic Generation, too, made significant contributions, with works by composers such as **Vincent d'Indy** and **Franz Lehár**, among a great many other composers less well known today. [JMC] *See also* OPERA.

OPERA SEMISERIA. (It., "half-serious opera.") General term for a subgenre of French or Italian **opera** that intermingles elements of serious opera with those of *opera buffa* or **opéra comique**. The term was originally applied to **rescue operas** (**Ferdinando Paer**'s *Camilla,* 1799, or Simon Mayr's [1763–1845] *Le due giornate* [The Two Days], 1801)—that is, to staged works that told a serious story but centered on class conflict and included ensemble finales. After the vogue of rescue opera, *opera semiseria* usually denoted a **comic opera** with an unusually serious plot. **Gaetano Donizetti**'s *Linda di Chamounix* (1842), **Giacomo Meyerbeer**'s *Marcherita d'Anjou* (1826), and **Gioachino Rossini**'s *La gazza ladra* (1817) are examples of the genre. [JMC]

OPERETTA, OPERATTA. (It., diminutive of "opera"; Fr., opérette; Ger., Operette; Sp., operetta.) An essentially popular form of light **opera**, originally in one act, that included spoken dialogue, brief instrumental numbers (**intermezzi** or *entr' actes*), and often dancing and whose plot was typically lighthearted, satirical, or farcical. Although the term was coined already in the early 18th century (e.g., **George Frideric Handel**'s *The Favourite Songs in the Operetta Call'd Hymen,* 1714), it gained widespread currency only in the early 19th century. Initially, its use appears to have been more common in England, the United States, and the Italian lands. In the English-speaking world, it denoted pieces, often in a single act, descended from the ballad opera tradition—the repertoire best known today as *musicals* or *musical comedies* (e.g., Julius Benedict's [1804–1885] *Un anno ed un giorno* [A Year and a Day, 1836] or Alexander Lee's [1802–1851] *The Fairy of the Lakes* [1840]). In Italy, its meaning was similar, although such works still often included recitative. Perhaps the best-known example is **Gaetano Donizetti**'s *Betly, ossia La capanna svizzera* (Betly, or The Swiss Chalet, on a libretto by **Eugène Scribe** and Mélesville after **Johann Wolfgang von Goethe**'s *Jery und Bätely,* 1780), composed and published as a one-act operetta in 1836 and revised in two acts, now redesignated a "dramma giocoso" in 1837. Similar works also existed in France (e.g., **Adolphe Adam**'s *Trois jours et une heure* [Three Days and an Hour, 1830] or his *Le Chalet* [1834], the latter after the same **Singspiel** by Goethe as Donizetti's *Betly*).

Around the middle of the 19th century, however, the genres of opera buffa, opéra comique, and Singspiel began to increase their aesthetic aspirations by increasing their length and the sophistication of their plots and music. That context produced the genre of the modern operetta. The term now came to serve as a sort of affirmative disclaimer, denoting short staged musical dramas that continued to cultivate easy accessibility and lightheartedness rather than participating in those efforts at "reform." The genre was born at the *Théâtre des Bouffes-Parisiens* in Paris (the company created by **Jacques Offenbach**), where Offenbach and others began presenting evenings comprised of short one-act sketches or chains of interrelated sketches that could collectively be designated *opéras bouffes*. The first such work by Offenbach himself was *Le trésor à Mathurin* (The Treasure of Mathurin, 1853, rev. as *Le mariage aux lanterns* [The Lantern Marriage] in 1857), but his two-act *Orphée aux enfers* (Orpheus in the Underworld, 1858) established the genre's runaway success. This and other works of its sort (most notably *La belle Hélène* [Fair Helen, 1864], *La vie parisienne* [Parisian Life, 1866], and *La Grande-Duchesse de Gérolstein* [1867]) were more indebted to the genre of opera than were contemporary **vaudevilles**, consisting of several acts and calling for full chorus and **orchestra** as well as solo **song**, but their brevity and their pronounced character of social satire also distinguished them from the worlds of opéra comique and *opéra*. Offenbach's German heritage caused his own popularity to wane in France after the end of the **Second Empire**, but by then, the genre of French operetta was well established. In the **Third Republic**, operettas tended to avoid political and social satire, focusing instead on amorous plots. Other important French composers of operetta during the **long 19th century** included Edmond Audran (1840–1901), Hervé (pseud. Florimond Ronger, 1825–1892), Charles Lecocq (1832–1918), Robert Planquette (1848–1903), and Louis Varney (1844–1908).

The operetta style created by Offenbach and his peers became an international sensation, partly by means of troupes that toured the German and Italian lands and England and partly (for more successful works) because of the practical necessity of publishing music in at least two different countries for purposes of **copyright** protection (*see* PRINTING AND PUBLISHING OF MUSIC). Viennese theaters began staging French operettas already in the 1850s. The success of those productions inspired composers such as **Franz Lehár, Johann Strauss (II)**, and **Franz von Suppé** to pen their own works in the genre, adding a distinctive flavor by means of plentiful polkas and **waltzes**. Like the French post-1870 operettas, these compositions tended to privilege romantic plots over social satire; they also frequently were set in **exotic** locales. Important works in this Austro-German tradition include Lehár's *Die lustige Witwe* (The Merry Widow, 1905), Carl Millöcker's (1842–1899), *Der Bettelstudent* (The Beggar Student, 1882), Strauss's *Die Fledermaus* (The Bat, 1874), and Suppé's *Franz Schubert* (a pseudobiography in music, 1864) and *Boccaccio* (1879). French and Austro-German operettas found an enthusiastic public also in Italy; indeed, by 1875, French operettas rivaled the popularity of Domenico Cimarosa (1749–1801) and **Gioachino Rossini** in Rome. In Spain, too, they inspired a new genre of opera, specifically in the revival of the **zarzuela**.

The Anglo-American world witnessed the emergence of its own distinctive variety of operetta in the last few decades of the 19th century. England had been enamored of the French and Viennese operetta traditions since the 1860s, and those works' success (in English translation) in English theaters facilitated the emergence of a new English variety (which was in turn exported to the United States) that integrated stylistic **burlesque** and parlor song into lighthearted plots that often blended social satire and romance. The first work in this new genre was **Arthur Sullivan**'s *Cox and Box, or The Long Lost Brothers* (1866, on a libretto by C. F. Burn and after J. Maddison Morton), but it was effectively defined in Sullivan's 14 collaborations with librettist W. S. Gilbert (1836–1911) between 1871 and 1896. Most important among these were *Trial by Jury* (1875), *H.M.S. Pinafore* (1878), *The Pirates of Penzance* (1879), and *Mikado* (1885). Other composers of the English operetta included Alfred Cellier (1844–1891), Frederic Clay (1838–1889), Edward German (1862–1936), Edward Jakobowski (1856–1929), and Edward Solomon (1855–1895). The English operetta also led directly to the "musical comedies" and "musical plays" cultivated in the early 20th century in works of Lionel Monckton (1861–1924) and Paul Rubens (1875–1917). [JMC]

ORATORIO. (Ger., Oratorium.) During the **long 19th century**, a continuously sung and played, unstaged, dramatic, **narrative**, or quasi-narrative multimovement composition, either sacred or secular, usually scored for soloist(s), chorus, and **orchestra**, with one or more solo voices typically narrating the plot rather than participating in it. The presence of the third-person narrator(s) was the main feature that consistently differentiated oratorios from **cantatas**, and that characteristic, together with the absence of costumes, sets, and other elements of staged musical dramas, was the main factor that differentiated oratorios from **operas**. As unstaged dramatic or quasi-dramatic works, oratorios' large-scale structural divisions were typically labeled as *parts* rather than the *acts* typical of operas and the like, and their parts were typically divided into *movements* comprising recitatives, arias, choruses, and so on. These general features apply reasonably well to most of the works that composers, performers, and audiences understood as *oratorio* during the long 19th century, but constructions of the term's meaning also varied by language and geography and changed over the course of the century.

For much of the long 19th century, the primary performance venue for oratorios was not the concert hall but rather the music festival or (in France and the Italian lands) the church—a fact that naturally influenced many aspects of oratorios' composition. Their difficulty needed to be sufficient to be rewarding to the professional musicians involved in the chorus and orchestra but not beyond the technical reach of the amateurs involved in the ensemble. Their duration/length needed to be sufficient to warrant the efforts and time of the many musicians assembled to perform them (since assembling a large ensemble for a short work is frustrating for performers and administrators alike) but not so long or uniform in style that it would unduly tax the attention or understanding the many amateur music lovers in the large audiences typically assembled for their performance. Their scoring needed to take advantage of the considerable timbral and dynamic variety afforded by large ensembles of vocalists and instrumentalists—ranging from quiet movements or sections whose instrumentation would project in large open-air spaces but impress as comparatively intimate to large-scale ones that celebrated the impressive sounds afforded by massed ensembles of hundreds of singers (sometimes more than a thousand) and orchestral players. And composers, aware that rapid and difficult figurations were difficult to execute with so many singers and instrumentalists (especially involving amateurs), typically adjusted their expectations for interpretation and performance practice accordingly, employing less complicated rhythmic and harmonic language in the large-scale *tutti* movements and confining challenging passages to more intimate moments and sections within individual large-scale movements.

Finally, because of the importance of civic or communal enfranchisement in the subjects of oratorios and because the acoustics of large and open-air performance spaces often made it difficult to understand the words being sung, oratorios' subjects (especially during the first half of the 19th century) tended to center on already familiar narratives or dramas whose themes resonated with current events and ideas of civic or communal edification or engagement so that audience members could know what was transpiring in the drama even if they did not understand the words relaying the dramatic action. For the same reasons, oratorios were almost always performed in the local vernacular rather than the original language of the composer (if different).

The early years of the genre's **reception** in the long 19th century were dominated by **Franz Joseph Haydn**'s late masterpieces *The Creation/Die Schöpfung* (Hob. XXI: 2, 1795, comp. in English; Haydn had little to do with the German translation) and *Die Jahreszeiten* (The Seasons, Hob. XXI: 3, 1801), which were themselves in many ways tropes on the oratorio tradition established by **George Frideric Handel**. Less well known today but central to musical culture for the first few decades of the long 19th century was Carl Heinrich Graun's (1704–1759) passion oratorio *Der Tod Jesu* (The Death of Jesus, 1755). During the Napoleonic period in France, works designated oratorios were either written for use in the imperial chapels and actually included in the Fore-Mass or conceived and performed as *drames sacrés* (sacred dramas)—that is, either as liturgical **cantatas** or as sacred operas (actually staged). The most important composers in these traditions were **François-Joseph Gossec, Jean-François Le Sueur,** and **Étienne-Nicolas Méhul.** There were also occasional performances of the oratorios of Handel and Haydn in French translation. In Great Britain, the genre continued to be dominated by the works of Handel and Haydn until the mid-1830s.

Elsewhere on the Continent, the social turmoil of the **First French Empire** tended to discourage the massed community gatherings that encouraged the composition and creation of new oratorios. Virtually the only noteworthy composition in the genre from this period was **Ludwig van Beethoven**'s *Christus am Ölberge* (Christ on the Mount of Olives, Op. 85, 1803, publ. 1811)—a work hastily composed after Beethoven was invited to write an opera for the Theater an der Wien in order to give him his first exposure, in a concert venue, as a composer of dramatic vocal music (an oratorio was more practical than an opera for these purposes because oratorios did not require staging). The return of peace and domestic tranquillity to life on the Continent during the **Restoration** witnessed a rapid growth in the culture of public music festivals and concerts generally, however, and with this growth, the oratorio as a genre also resurged.

The early years of the Restoration witnessed not only renewed interest in the oratorios of Handel and Haydn in the German lands and Scandinavia but also the appearance of new oratorios by composers of the Early Romantic Generation. Most notable in this group were **Carl Loewe**'s *Die Zerstörung Jerusalems* (The Destruction of Jerusalem, 1832), Friedrich Schneider's (1786–1853) 14 oratorios written between 1819 and 1838 (especially *Das Weltgericht* [The Last Judgment, 1819] and *Das befreite Jerusalem* [Jerusalem Liberated, 1835]), and **Louis Spohr**'s four oratorios written between 1812 and 1840 (most importantly *Das jüngste Gericht* [The Last Judgment, 1812] and *Die letzten Dinge* [The End of Days, 1827]). Although these compositions contained much rewarding music, none was able to obtain a lasting presence, mostly because their music was tailored to the sense of expansive scope germane to the music festivals where they were performed, but their dramatic and dramaturgical construction was insufficient for works of such great length; they impressed as assemblages of movements rather than coherent and compelling large-scale dramas.

A new chapter in the Romantic oratorio opened at the Lower Rhine Music Festival in May 1836 with the premiere of **Felix Mendelssohn Bartholdy**'s *St. Paul* (MWV A14/Op. 36, publ. 1837). The work had been much anticipated in part because of Mendelssohn's rapidly growing fame, and its premiere set a new standard for stylistic diversity and sacred drama presented on an epic scale—integrating elements of the oratorios of **Johann Sebastian Bach** (which were still little known in the 1830s) and their more familiar

Handelian counterparts into a large-scale narrative structure that drew on 19th-century concepts and techniques such as **Leitmotiv**, thematic recollection, and carefully organized large-scale tonal structure.

The sense of dramatic immediacy mingled with epic edification achieved in Mendelssohn's *St. Paul* was increased further in his second oratorio, *Elijah* (MWV A25/Op. 70, comp. 1845–1846, rev. 1846–1847, publ. 1847), but in the meantime other composers (most notably **Ferdinand Hiller** in his *Die Zerstörung Jerusalems* [The Destruction of Jerusalem, 1841–1842] and Loewe in quasi-sacred works on nominally secular topics such as *Palestrina*, 1841, and *Johann Hus*, 1842) had begun to emulate the new model of the genre. A particularly imposing (if now little-known) example from the last years of the century is **Felix Draeseke**'s oratorio tetralogy *Christus* (1895–1899), conceived and executed as a sacred, Christological counterpart to **Richard Wagner**'s *Ring of the Nibelung* cycle of **music dramas**. Another new model was introduced at mid-century with **Robert Schumann**'s secular "entirely new genre for the concert hall" *Das Paradies und die Peri* (Paradise and the Peri, Op. 50, 1843) and *Der Rose Pilgerfahrt* (The Pilgrimage of the Rose, 1851). Both were works that adopted the general idioms and techniques of the Romantic oratorio but were written with the concert hall rather than the music festival in mind and thus were able to take advantage of the concert hall's relative intimacy and commensurately greater potential for comparatively intimate, nuanced, and allegorical themes.

Der Rose Pilgerfahrt is one of the earliest manifestations of a new, more intimate model of dramatic oratorio that flourished in the German lands and France in the second half of the 19th century. Other important works in this new vein from German composers include **Franz Liszt**'s *Die Legende der Heiligen Elisabeth* (The Legend of St. Elisabeth, LW 14, 1862, publ. 1867) and *Christus* (LW 17, 1872) as well as **Joachim Raff**'s *Welt-Ende, Gericht, Neue Welt* (World's End—Judgment—New World, Op. 212, 1881) and especially **Max Bruch**'s *Arminius* (Op. 43, 1877) and *Gustav Adolf* (Op. 73, 1898). In France, the late 19th century witnessed a rebirth of the genre, most famously in **Hector Berlioz**'s *L'enfance du Christ* (The Childhood of Christ, H. 130/Op. 25, 1854) but also in important compositions by **Félicien David** (*Moïse au Sinaï* [Moses on Mount Sinai, 1846] and *L'Eden*, 1848), **Théodore Dubois** (especially *Les sept paroles du Christ* [The Seven Last Words of Christ, 1877, publ. 1899], *Le paradis perdu* [Paradise Lost, 1879], and *Le baptême de Clovis* [The Baptism of Clovis, 1899]), **César Franck** (*Ruth*, 1846; *La tour de Babel* [The Tower of Babel, 1865]; *Rédemption*, 1874; *Les béatitudes*, 1879; and *Rébecca*, 1881), **Charles Gounod** (*Tobie*, 1865; *La rédemption*, 1882; and *Mors et vita* [Death and Life, 1885]), **Jules Massenet** (*Marie-Magdeleine*, 1873; *Eve*, 1874; *La Vierge* [The Virgin], 1880; and *La* *terre promise* [The Promised Land, 1899]), and **Camille Saint-Saëns** (*Oratorio de Noël* [Christmas Oratorio, 1858] and *Le déluge* [The Flood, 1875]), among others.

Important oratorios in the Anglo-American world during the second half of the 19th century were penned by **Arthur Sullivan** (*The Prodigal Son*, 1869) and composers of the **English Musical Renaissance**, including **Alexander Mackenzie** (*Rose of Sharon*, 1884, rev. 1910), **Hubert Parry** (*Judith, or The Regeneration of Manasseh*, 1888; *Job*, 1892; and *King Saul*, 1894), and **Charles Villiers Stanford** (*Three Holy Children*, 1885, and *Eden*, 1891). By consensus, however, the genre's important English work of the Modern Romantic Generation is **Edward Elgar**'s *The Dream of Gerontius* (1900), followed by his oratorio pair *The Apostles* (1903) and *The Kingdom* (1906).

Oratorios were also composed in the United States during the long 19th century. The first known oratorio by a U.S.-born composer is John Hill Hewitt's (1801–1890) *Jephtha* (1845). By far the most important works by U.S. composers are **John Knowles Paine**'s *St. Peter* (1872), **Horatio Parker**'s *Hora novissima* (1892), and **George Chadwick**'s *Noël* (1908).

In the Italian lands, Iberia, and Latin America, the long 19th century witnessed few significant contributions to the oratorio. **Gaetano Donizetti**'s three-part "azione tragico-sacra" *Il diluvio universale* (The Great Flood, 1830), although eventually staged and published as an opera, was designated an oratorio in the composer's **autograph**—a feature that aligns it with **Gioachino Rossini**'s immensely popular *Mosè in Egitto* (the earliest version of which is likewise designated an "azione tragico-sacra"). Among the works more readily consistent with the oratorio in the Italian lands, the most adventurous is Pietro Raimondi's (1786–1853) trilogy *Giuseppe* (1847–1848), the three constituent works of which (*Putifar, Giuseppe*, and *Giacobbe*) were premiered in succession over the span of six hours in a single day in 1852, with a total of 430 performers involved. Notable Spanish oratorios include Francisco Andreví y Castellar's (1786–1853) *La dulzura de la virtud* (The Sweetness of Virtue, 1819 or earlier) and *El juicio universal* (The Last Judgment, 1822), Ruperto Chapí's (1851–1909) *Los ángeles* (The Angels, 1873), and **Tomás Bretón**'s *El apocalipsis* (1882). Although original oratorios were composed and performed in Central and South America during the long 19th century, the most important of these is the Brazilian **Carlos Gomes**'s *Colombo* (1892), written for the country's quadricentenary celebrations of Columbus's arrival in the New World. [JMC]

ORCHESTRA. (Fr., orchestre; Ger., Orchester; Sp., orquesta.) A performing body of diverse instruments. In today's usage in connection with Western music of the **long 19th century**, the term typically refers to the groups known alternately as *symphony orchestras* or *philharmonic societies* (abbrev.

philharmonic). As in the late 18th century, the core personnel of 19th-century orchestras comprised a string section (typically divided first and second violins, violas, and cellos and basses playing mostly in octaves) plus a group of woodwinds (usually paired flutes, oboes, clarinets, and bassoons) and a smaller contingent of brass (usually four horns, two trumpets, and often three trombones), with timpani being the only percussion instruments used consistently. Until the 1820s, many orchestras retained the presence of a keyboard *continuo*, but the growth of concert culture and the increasing complexity of orchestral scores made it increasingly practical after the 1830s to use a more-or-less authoritarian **conductor** to coordinate the ensemble. There were two main types of orchestra in the 19th century: theater orchestras and concert orchestras. To these may be added occasional orchestras: ad hoc ensembles assembled for music festivals or other special occasions as well as (during the late 19th century and early 20th century) smaller orchestral groups devoted largely to popular or lighthearted music: café orchestras, dance orchestras, **salon** orchestras, spa orchestras, and so on.

The number of established orchestras increased significantly in Europe and many times over in the New World during the long 19th century. Similarly, the expansion of orchestral culture in the relatively peaceful and prosperous environs of the **Restoration** encouraged an increase in the number of players in the core instrumentarium and increasing use of an expanded instrumentarium of the mid-18th century (most notably in the form of three trombones) and the addition of new instruments to that core ensemble. Even so, Romantic orchestral ensembles remained significantly smaller than even their smallest latter-day counterparts. At mid-century, the overwhelming majority of concert orchestras comprised 50 or fewer players; by the 1880s, due to the growth of the music-loving public, the concordant increase in large halls, and the need for more instruments in order to produce a volume of sound that would fill those halls, that number had risen to 70 in some larger orchestras, although many orchestras remained the same size as they had at mid-century. For example, the court orchestra at Meiningen, conducted by **Hans von Bülow** and **Richard Strauss** and highly esteemed by **Johannes Brahms**, comprised nine each of first and second violins and four each of violas, cellos, and basses, woodwinds, brass, and timpani to total 49 members. The numbers of **Richard Wagner**'s **Bayreuth** *Festspielhaus* Orchestra were only marginally larger, due partly to the fact that the orchestra was mostly beneath the stage and partly to Wagner's addition of other instruments (sometimes—as in the case of the six harps—with multiple players on those additional instruments because their sound was muffled by the overhanging stage). There were exceptions to these numbers. Festival orchestras, for example, often numbered in the hundreds in order to produce enough volume for open-air performance, demonstrate the wealth and power of civil society, and encourage the amateur populace's enfranchisement in the edifying experience of music making—but on the whole, the symphony orchestra of a hundred or more players remained the exception, not the rule, until the early years of the 20th century.

The comparatively small size of most 19th-century orchestras and the lighter, more natural composition of those ensembles' constituent instruments not only affected how and what composers wrote for their envisioned or presumed orchestral ensembles during the long 19th century but also had important ramifications for orchestral **performance practice**. Conversely, many of these performance practices have changed significantly over the course of the 20th and 21st centuries. Consequently, the sounds and effects envisioned by a given composer's orchestration in a given work in, say, the late 1880s are radically altered, masked, or even obliterated by latter-day practices, even though the notated score is the same. For example, when one uses a 19th-century-sized string section of 30 to 40 players performing on instruments with shorter necks, lower string tension, and mostly gut strings, together with the same-sized woodwind complement of woodwinds, the wind-to-string balance is much more even than that of the modern orchestra (60–70 strings), even though 19th-century woodwind instruments employed far more wood and far less metal than their latter-day counterparts. Similarly, whereas modern aesthetics of Romantic orchestral sound emphasize homogeneity, blend, and (in at least some instances) bulk, 19th-century orchestras envisioned for the music of composers ranging from **Ludwig van Beethoven**, **Franz Schubert**, and **Carl Maria von Weber** through **Antonín Dvořák**, **Franz Liszt**, **Pyotor Il'yich Tchaikovsky**, **Giuseppe Verdi**, and Wagner overwhelmingly strove for variety of color and antiphonal effects, with, for example, first and second violins placed across from each other at the front of the stage rather than next to each other (as is often the case today). Such seating practices, together with the subtle timbral difference that result from the second violins' projection toward the rear of the hall, explain Romantic composers' frequent use of first and second violins in dialogue, exchange, or extension of a single line from one part of the section to the other across a large range. Composers scored as they did in order to take advantage of the spatial and timbral choreography afforded by such aspects of Romantic orchestral practices. Latter-day conventions of practice rarely are able to capture the effects envisioned and prized by Romantic composers. [JMC]

ORCHESTRATION. (Ger., Orchestrierung.) The art of employing instruments and/or voices in various combinations; it includes the art of *instrumentation* (the study of the properties of various instruments and their selection for use in ensemble compositions). The art of orchestration grew significantly during the **long 19th century** due to a number of contextual factors—chief among them the development of new instruments and new varieties of existing instruments through new technologies facilitated by the industrial revolution, developments in Romantic aesthetic ideas concerning the dramatic and other expressive properties and potentials of music, and the growth of theater, concert, and occasional **orchestras** themselves. During the Napoleonic period (*see* FIRST FRENCH EMPIRE), the systematic study of orchestration was largely of a utilitarian or ad hoc nature. With the bourgeoning of public musical culture during the **Restoration** and beyond, however, theorists and composers increasingly came to view orchestration as a poetic enterprise that was equally important to the more traditional issues of counterpart, harmony, and form, not less so. Accordingly, the long 19th century after 1815 witnessed the production of a number of treatises and other, smaller writings on orchestration, texts that were in many cases widely translated, commented on in journals, and used as the basis for other texts as well as many rising composers' practical study. Some of the more important such writings were penned by **Georges Kastner** (1837), **Hector Berlioz** (1843, rev. 1855), **François-Auguste Gevaert** (1863, 1885, 1890), and **Nikolay Rimsky-Korsakov** (posth. publ. 1913). **Richard Strauss** in 1905 translated and updated Berlioz's treatise, which included examples from works by Beethoven, Christoph Willibald Ritter von Gluck (1714–1787), **Fromenthal Halévy**, **Giacomo Meyerbeer**, **Étienne-Nicolas Méhul**, **Wolfgang Amadeus Mozart**, **Gioachino Rossini**, **Gaspare Spontini**, and Weber, to include examples from the works of **Richard Wagner**.

Beyond these historical notes, the space limitations of this dictionary permit only a few generalizations about the many and complex developments in the art of orchestration during the long 19th century. First, it should be noted that some of the most important of the technological developments mentioned above centered on enhancing and perfecting the chromatic vocabulary of instruments that previously had posed difficulties in this regard: the invention of **Érard**'s double-action chromatic harp in 1810, the introduction of piston- and rotary-valved brass instruments beginning in the 1820s. These developments facilitated works such as **Robert Schumann**'s *Konzertstück* for Four Horns and Orchestra (Op. 86), the long melodic trumpet solos in **Louis-Moreau Gottschalk**'s First **Symphony** (1859), and Richard Strauss's *Ein Heldenleben* (1897), as well as the development of chromatic systems for various woodwinds in the 1830s and 1840s—*see* BOEHM, THEOBALD (1794–1881)—and the use of more timpani and development of increasingly sophisticated tuning mechanisms to expand the practical pitch vocabulary of those instruments within a given work. The century also witnessed the invention of dozens of new instruments—most importantly saxophones and new brass instruments such as the euphonium and Wagner tuba. Beyond this, it should be noted that because the high profit margins associated with successful **operas** and other theatrical works combined with those works' dramatic justifications for dramatic orchestral effects supported orchestral as well as vocal budgets, many of the long 19th century's orchestrational innovations and expansions took root first in the opera orchestra and only later became accepted into the concert orchestra.

Finally, these developments were highlighted in three overlapping but discrete approaches to the art of orchestration. First, and most traditionally, there were works that treated the ensemble as a heterogeneous set of choirs, foregrounding the voices (when present) and strings and granting subordinate roles to woodwinds, brass, and percussion. Additionally, some works treated the ensemble as a single instrument with full and essentially equal choirs of voices, strings, woodwinds, and brass, after the manner of the manuals on an organ. Still other works employed a coloristic, soloistic, or (as it is sometimes termed) "pointillistic" approach, highlighting individual splashes of color from individual instruments or heterogeneous groups of solo instruments and using these in sectional juxtaposition with massed choirs of woodwinds, brass, strings, chorus, or resplendent combinations of those choirs. Each of these approaches had advantages and disadvantages, and most composers employed all of them on occasion, depending on the musical needs of the work or passage at hand. [JMC]

See also PERFORMANCE PRACTICE.

ORGANICISM. Late Enlightenment and Romantic notion likening all human production, including musical and other artworks, to organic life forms. It is neither a philosophy nor a system of aesthetics per se but rather a theoretical attempt to explain how human creativity coheres with the beliefs in empirical order and the unity of knowledge that were characteristic of late Enlightenment philosophers. Art, in this view, is both like the natural world and a metaphor for it; therefore, artworks are like organic life forms sui generis, expressions of a single, unified whole and extensions of its essence that, like other life forms, grow from a single germ or seed. Temporal artworks (music and literature) lent themselves particularly well to organicist approaches because they could be experienced only sequentially over time: the time that it took to perform or listen to a piece of music, to read a poem or novel, or to watch a play was analogous to the life span of a living organism.

Like much Romantic theory, organicism represented an application of recent and contemporary scientific thought to the arts and thus also an attempt to make scholarship and aesthetic thoughts concerning the arts more "scientific." Applications of organicism to the arts and other areas of human endeavor were submitted by leading intellectuals of the era such as **Johann Wolfgang von Goethe, Georg Wilhelm Friedrich Hegel,** and Johann Gottfried Herder (1784–1803), among many others. It is an important aspect of the poetry and dramas of Goethe and of the visual artworks of Caspar David Friedrich (1774–1840) and Philipp Otto Runge (1777–1810), among many others. By the 1830s, it qualified as a major Romantic ideology.

Organicist theory is now largely rejected in the physical sciences, but it was the prevalent scientific worldview for much of the **long 19th century**— and it became an important tenet of musical Romanticism, eventually gaining such acceptance that it came to represent a central ideology and aesthetic criterion. The theory's lack of scientific viability did not mean that composers who subscribed to it were unable to use it in conceiving and executing their art, nor did it prevent theorists and aestheticians (most notably the early 20th-century theorist Heinrich Schenker [1868–1935]) from discussing and evaluating musical artworks in terms of their (perceived) organic unity. The roster of composers whose creative lives were created in the context of the musical world's growing fascination with organicism (and who therefore are likely to have attempted to build on it in their art) is extensive—indeed, organicist ideology is evident in the works of virtually every composer of the Romantic Generation and Late Romantic Generation.

Organicist ideas are also the source and theoretical justification for some of the mid-19th century's most significant developments in terms of musical form and process, including **idée fixe**, *Leitfaden*, **Leitmotiv**, and **thematic transformation**. They are arguably the raison d'être of the continuing metamorphoses of the initial motive of **Ludwig van Beethoven**'s Fifth **Symphony** (Op. 67, 1807–1808, publ. 1809) and are prominent organizing forces in the instrumental music of **Hector Berlioz, Fanny Hensel, Franz Liszt, Felix Mendelssohn Bartholdy, Franz Schubert, Robert Schumann**, and **Richard Wagner**, among many others. [JMC]

ORPHÉON. Name given to French-language amateur choral societies (usually adult working-class males but also for children and sometimes involving women as well as men). They were originally developed in imitation of German **Liedertafeln** and (more closely) *Liederkränze* or *Männergesangvereine* and remained one of the defining institutions of francophone middle-class musical life throughout the community- and domestically centered cultures of the **Bourbon Restoration, Second Empire**, and **Third Republic**. The movement to include such societies into French musical life emerged in the early years of post-Napoleonic France thanks to the efforts of music educator Guillaume-Louis Bocquillon-Wilhem (1781–1842) to integrate music into French elementary education and civilian life. Music, Wilhem and his supporters felt, had a moralizing effect on the masses. Like their German counterparts, *orphéon* societies came to possess a distinctively **nationalist** function, not only promoting music as a shared interest within a politically riven and culturally diverse French-speaking populace but also encouraging a sense of French community engendered by the making of music around French-language texts on themes that appealed to French citizens.

In their original form, the groups eventually known as *orphéons* were created for and composed of schoolchildren. By 1819, the administrative body responsible for primary schools in Paris had decided to adopt Wilhem's concept of integrating music into the city's educational system, and by 1833, Wilhem had begun organizing large musical assemblies that brought together student choirs from several schools to practice and perform together, designating the combined group *L'Orphéon* (after Orpheus; its members were dubbed *orphéonistes*). Similar groups were formed to include young adult workers, and the concept became central to the plans of utopian societies. The 1833 concert of Wilhem's group included 300 singers, a number that had risen to 1,600 by 1843. As the leaders of the **Second Empire** and **Third Republic** encouraged the societies as a means for "moral amelioration" among the working-class masses, the term *orphéon* came to denote a male-dominated or exclusively male group.

By 1859, France as a whole had 1,700 *orphéons* involving 9,000 working-class singers, including nearly 300 in Paris alone (the latter had been under the direction of **Charles Gounod** since 1852 and would pass to **Jules Étienne Pasdeloup** in 1860). At the Universal Exhibition of 1878, an astounding 15,000 singers performed in the groups. *Orphéons* also made it possible for working-class singers to commingle with the aristocracy, for example, bridging normally impenetrable socioeconomic barriers when *orphéons* and the regular memberships of Louis-Albert Bourgault-Duchoudray's (1840–1910) ensembles collaborated in performances of **George Frideric Handel**'s **oratorios** in Paris in 1872–1873. By 1880, there were some 1,500 *orphéons* in Paris (comprising about 60,000 members), and the movement peaked in the years leading up to World War I, with some 2,000 *orphéons* in France at the turn of the 20th century. In **Jacques Offenbach**'s iconic **operetta** *Orphée aux enfers* (Orpheus in the Underworld, 1858, rev. 1874), Orpheus is director of the *Orphéon* of Thebes. [JMC]

OSSIAN. Legendary Celtic poet and warrior (inauthentic), son of Finn Mac Cumhail; a cultural phenomenon and major **topic** in Romantic music, literature, and other art. The craze was unleashed in 1760, when the young poet James Macpherson (1736–1796) showed the Scottish playwright John Home (1722–1808) what he described as English translations of traditional Gaelic poetry, evocative poems filled with repetitive rhythms and recounting the lives and deaths of ancient Caledonian heroes in language filled with stark natural imagery and Celtic names. Macpherson persuaded Hugh Blair (1718–1800) of the University of Edinburgh that the poems were fragments of an ancient epic that was (in Blair's words) "coeval with the very infancy of Christianity in Scotland" and had been transmitted by oral tradition and (in some cases) in writing by generations of poets, beginning with Ossian, son of the legendary warrior Fingal. Macpherson traveled in Scotland in 1761 and later that year published *Fingal, an Ancient Epic Poem, in Six Books Translated from the Galic* [*sic*] *Language* along with several other poems that he described as "composed by Ossian, the son of Fingal." The 1761 volume was followed by another Ossianic epic, *Temora*, in 1763. Providing Great Britain and Ireland (and northern Europe generally) with an ancient, pre-Christian literary tradition that was comparable in scale, scope, and content to the great Homeric epics but not indebted to the Classical tradition, the poems created an immediate sensation. They were quickly translated into French and German and became a major cultural phenomenon in those countries as well. Macpherson's fabrication was exposed when he was unable to present manuscripts or other means of verifying his "translations," but in the meantime, the poetry had taken on a life of its own. The Ossianic lore remained a major **topic** throughout the **long 19th century**.

Ossianic poetry and its associated lore inspired countless artworks. Among the most important responses to the Ossianic craze in the visual arts are François Gérard's (1770–1837) *Ossian évoque les fantômes au son de la harpe sur les bords du Lora* (Ossian on the Bank of the Lora, Invoking the Gods to the Strains of a Harp, 1801), Anne-Louis Girodet's (1767–1824) *Apothéose des héros français morts pour la patrie pendant la guerre de la liberté* (Ossian Receiving the Ghosts of French Heroes, 1802), and Dominique Ingres's (1780–1867) *Le songe d'Ossian* (Ossian's Dream, 1813). Additionally, scholars have identified some 300 individual musical compositions based on the poem. Most important among these direct musical offspring are **Johannes Brahms**'s *Gesang aus Fingal* (Op. 17, no. 4, 1859–1860) and *Darthulas Grabgesang* (Op. 42, no. 3, 1861), **Niels W. Gade**'s **concert overture** *Efterklänge af Ossian* (Echoes of Ossian, Op. 1, 1840), **Jean-François Le Sueur**'s opera *Ossian, ou Les bardes* (Ossian; or, The Bards, 1804), **Étienne-Nicolas Méhul**'s one-act opera *Uthal* (1803, publ. 1806), and the nine **songs** that **Franz Schubert** composed on Ossianic texts (in German translation) between 1817 and 1819: "Lodas Gespenst" (Loda's Ghost, D. 150), "Kolmas Klage" (Colma's Lament, D. 217), "Ossians **Lied**" (Ossian's Song, D. 278), "Das Mädchen von Inistore" (The Maiden from Inistore, D. 281), "Cronnan" (D. 282), "Shilric und Vinvela" (D. 293), "Der Tod Oskars" (The Death of Oscar, D. 375), "Lorma" (D. 376), and "Die Nacht" (Night, D. 534). **Felix Mendelssohn Bartholdy** composed a **concert aria** (in English) titled *On Lena's Gloomy Heath* in 1846 (MWV H6, still unpublished), and **Camille Saint-Saëns**'s elegant *mélodie Le lever de la lune (poésie imitée d'Ossian)* (Moonrise [Poetry in Imitation of Ossian], 1855–1856) is a vivid evocation of the bardic style associated with Ossian-inspired music. **Georges Bizet** composed a concert overture (now lost) titled *La chasse d'Ossian* (Ossian's Hunt, 1860–1861), and in 1903 Arnold Schoenberg began a work for 14 voices with **orchestra** titled *Darthulas Grablegung* (Darthula's Burial), completing only 66 measures of music.

Additionally, the evocative language and stark imagery of the Ossianic poetry and the attraction it held as a body of epic literature not indebted to the Classical tradition facilitated the emergence of new variety of musical rhetoric. First cultivated at length in Le Seuer's *Ossian, ou Les bardes*, this "Ossianic manner" tended to privilege the harp or harp-like effects but otherwise to eschew refinement and grace, instead celebrating rough, stormy, turbulent musical language (Le Sueur's *Ossian* employs 12 harps accompanying the bards' singing). Mendelssohn's *Hebrides Overture* and A-minor **Symphony** ("Scottish," MW N18, begun 1829, completed and publ. 1841–1842) are among the best-known instrumental works indebted to it, and **Robert Schumann** adopted it in his late choral/orchestral ballads *Der Königssohn* (The King's Son, Op. 116, 1851, publ. 1853), *Des Sängers Fluch* (The Singer's Curse, Op. 139, 1852; posth. publ. 1858), *Vom Pagen und der Königstochter* (The Page and the King's Daughter, Op. 140, 1852, posth. publ. 1857), and *Das Glück von Edenhall* (The Fortune of Edenhall, 1853, posth. publ. 1860). The emergent Ossianic manner, rather than any actual knowledge of Scottish music, informed **Ludwig van Beethoven**'s musical language in his *25 Scottish Folksongs* (Op. 108, 1815–1818), and Le Seuer's *Ossian* seems to have provided the inspiration for the "Scottish" atmosphere of the final chorus in **Giuseppe Verdi**'s opera based on **William Shakespeare**'s *Macbeth* (1847; Fr. version 1865). [JMC]

OVERTURE. (Fr., ouverture; Ger., Ouvertüre; It., sinfonia.) An instrumental composition intended to open an act or part of an **oratorio, opera,** or other larger musical work (usually a staged musical drama such as a **ballet** or **incidental music**) but set apart from it by means of a full cadence (cf. PRELUDE [2]). In the early years of the **long 19th century**, overtures typically were constructed either as Type 1 **sonata form** (sonata form without development, often with a slow introduction) or as *reprise overtures* (i.e., ternary structures with tonally closed outer sections, both in quick tempo and with similar but not the same thematic material in both other sections). After the late 1780s, it became increasingly common for the overture either to adumbrate the whole of the ensuing drama or to articulate key elements of it, usually in general terms but occasionally by means of thematic quotation. The overture to **Wolfgang Amadeus Mozart**'s *Don Giovanni* is an important milestone in this regard, as are **Ludwig van Beethoven**'s three *"Leonore" Overtures* (Nos. 1 and 2, comp. 1804–1805 and 1805–1806, and Op. 138, 1807–1808) and **Felix Mendelssohn Bartholdy**'s overture to the oratorio *St. Paul* (MWV A14/Op. 36, 1837). **Franz Joseph Haydn**'s overture to his oratorio *The Creation* (Hob. XXI: 2, 1796–1798) represents a milestone in the development of the genre in that the overture's "Representation of Chaos" is not extrinsic to the plot but rather the first term of dramatic action.

Mendelssohn adopted a similar strategy in the Overture to his secular cantata *Die erste Walpurgisnacht* (MWV D3/Op. 60, comp. 1830–1833, rev. 1840–1843).

During the Romantic Generation, composers increasingly attempted to increase the organic connections between overture and the ensuing drama by drawing most or all of the overture's thematic and motivic material from the drama. **Carl Maria von Weber**'s overtures to *Der Freischütz* and *Euryanthe* and **Giacomo Meyerbeer**'s overture to *Les Huguenots* are important contributions of this sort. **Operettas** typically featured longer overtures comprised entirely of thematic material from the ensuing drama, known as *"potpourri" overtures*. This was the approach usually employed by composers such as **D.-F.-E. Auber, Charles Gounod, Jacques Offenbach, Johann Strauss (II), Arthur Sullivan**, and **Ambroise Thomas**. [JMC]

See also CONCERT OVERTURE; SYMPHONIC POEM; TONE POEM.

P

PADEREWSKI, IGNACY (1860–1941). Pianist, philanthropist, statesman, and composer of the Modern Romantic Generation; influential advocate for Polish **nationalism** and Polish independence from 1916 to 1919 and 1940 to 1941. From 1872 to 1878, he studied intermittently at the Warsaw **Conservatory**, where he also taught piano from 1878 to 1883. After study with Teodor Leszetycki (1830–1915) in Vienna and a teaching position at the Strasbourg Conservatory, he made a major concert debut in Vienna, followed by tours that took him to Paris (1888), London (1890), and the United States and Canada (1891). Although further tours took him to South America, southern Africa, Australia, New Zealand, and Hawaii, his fame was especially broadened by his numerous subsequent performances in the United States (1892–1893, 1895–1896, 1900–1901, 1901–1902, 1907–1908, and 1913–1914), where his debonair appearance and mannerisms combined with his pianistic artistry to lend him genuine star power. Together with his charismatic oratory, they also abetted his tireless efforts to generate funds and public support for the cause of Poland. So influential was Paderewski in these regards that the cause of Polish independence was among the stated aims cited when the United States entered World War I in 1917.

Having mediated between the Allied powers and the Polish government-in-exile during the war, Paderewski was appointed prime minister by the head of the new Polish state in 1919, representing it at the Versailles Peace Conference. In 1920 he resigned from this post, serving as delegate of the Republic of Poland to international conferences and the first delegate to the League of Nations. He withdrew from this post in order to return to performing, but through the 1930s, he gave benefit concerts for political causes and made prominent public statements. His philanthropic efforts results in significant funds established at U.S., Western European, and Russian conservatories and universities; unemployment funds for musicians in the United States and Great Britain; benefit concerts for Gypsy, Hungarian, Jewish, and Polish victims of Nazi aggression; and cosponsorships of monuments to **Ludwig van Beethoven, Fryderyk Chopin, Claude Debussy,** and **Franz Liszt,** among others. [JMC]

PAER (PAËR), FERDINANDO (1771–1839). Italian composer of the Early Romantic Generation, important chiefly for his success in reinvigorating the conventions of 18th-century Italian **opera** by infusing them with increased realism and both serious and comic elements as well as for his skillful treatment of the orchestra within Italian idioms and his influence on **Gioachino Rossini.** He produced at least 55 operas between 1791 and 1816. He began his career in his native Parma, composing and producing numerous successful operas, and in 1797 went from there to Vienna, where he became director of the prestigious Kärtnertor Theater (which was frequented by all social classes but gave premieres only in the elite genres of Italian opera). During his tenure there, he met and earned the esteem of **Ludwig van Beethoven,** also composing several operas in semiserious style (*Griselda*, 1798; *Camilla*, 1799; and *Achille*, 1801).

During the following years, Paer made a rapid succession of moves to increasingly prestigious positions. First he moved to Dresden, where in 1804 he composed *Leonora*, the same story that Beethoven would compose (on a **libretto** by Sonnleithner) as the first version of *Fidelio* the following year. Also in Dresden, he won the appreciation of Napoléon Bonaparte, following the Frenchman first to Warsaw and then to Posen before ultimately becoming his *maître de chapelle* in Paris. In Paris, he became director of the Opéra-Comique and the Théâtre-Italien, retaining the latter (with interruptions) until his de facto retirement in 1826. Though his compositional output slowed after 1816 (he completed only five new operas thereafter), he had established an excellent reputation as a teacher of voice and composition (**Franz Liszt** and **Nicolò Paganini** were among his students) and was able to live quite comfortably with earnings from his teaching.

A number of impressive honors were bestowed on Paer during the last decade of his life: he received the Cross of the Légion d'Honneur in 1828, became a member of the Académie des Beaux-Arts in 1831, became director of **chamber music** and *maître de chapelle* to Louis-Philippe in 1832, and was named superintendent of the Paris **Conservatory** in 1834, teaching composition there until his death. [JMC]

PAGANINI, NICOLÒ (1782–1840). Italian **virtuoso** violinist, teacher, and composer of the Early Romantic Generation. With his staggeringly high degree of technical ability, lifestyle as touring performer, and captivating (and, to some, demonic) public persona, Paganini was in many ways the prototypical 19th-century virtuoso. His international success occurred when many in the Romantic Generation were coming of age, **Giovanni Bottesini, Fryderyk Chopin, Franz Liszt, Elias Parish-Alvars,** and **Clara** and **Robert Schumann** among them.

With his long limbs and relaxed position (with the neck down and the instrument close), Paganini achieved extraordinary speed and employed techniques such as double harmonics, left-hand pizzicato, and ricochet bowing. In his hometown of Genoa, Paganini excelled on the violin early on, and as he grew up, he studied with several music teachers in Genoa and Parma, including **Ferdinando Paer**. In his early 20s, Paganini took up the guitar as well. He spent the years 1805–1810 in Lucca, performing in and conducting the **orchestra** there. Paganini's touring years began in 1810. In 1813, a strong performance at Milan's *Teatro alla Scala* set the stage for Paganini's later successes throughout the Italian lands. Likewise, his successes in Vienna in 1828 helped build momentum for his successful tours of Germany, France, and the British Isles through the early 1830s. Illness impeded Paganini's musical activities after about 1834. Notable compositions include his famous *24 Caprices* (comp. ca. 1805, publ. 1820; *see* CAPRICCIO), six guitar quartets (comp. 1805–1816, publ. 1820), and at least six violin **concertos** beginning with the first in E-flat major (comp. 1816, publ. 1851). **Hector Berlioz**'s *Harold in Italy* (1848) was the eventual result of Paganini's 1833 commission for a viola concerto. **Serge Rachmaninoff**'s *Rhapsody on a Theme of Paganini* (Op. 43, 1934) is among the best-known post-Romantic testaments to his legacy. [RK]

PAINE, JOHN KNOWLES (1839–1906). U.S. composer, organist, and teacher of the Late Romantic Generation; the first professor of music in the United States. After studying music in his native Portland, Maine, with a German émigré who had fled Berlin in the wake of the **Revolutions of 1848**, he went to Berlin in 1858 and enrolled in the Hochschule für Musik there. He remained in Europe for three years, beginning to compose, becoming an outstanding organist, and traveling widely during the intersessions (he gave recitals on piano and organ in England and France and met and played for **Clara Schumann**).

After returning to the United States in 1861, Paine gave a number of public lectures and recitals, leading to his appointment as organist of Harvard University in 1862, a post he held for 20 years. In that capacity, he also organized Harvard's new music department, the first in the United States, and over much opposition was appointed professor there in 1876. He also lectured at Boston University, was an adviser to the Board of Visitors of the recently founded New England Conservatory, and was a charter member of the American Guild of Organists and the National Institute of Arts and Letters. Much celebrated by **John Sullivan Dwight** in *Dwight's Journal of Music*, he was also a friend of musical notables such as **Amy Fay** and **Theodor Thomas**. The roster of his distinguished pupils includes Richard Aldrich (1863–1937), John Alden Carpenter (1876–1951), Frederick S. Converse (1871–1940), Mabel Daniels (1878–1971), Archibald Davison

(1883–1961), Olin Downes (1886–1955), Henry T. Finck (1854–1926), Arthur Foote (1853–1937), Edward B. Hill (1872–1960), Hugo Leichtentritt (1874–1951), **Daniel Gregory Mason**, Carl Ruggles (1876–1971), and Henry Lee Higginson (1834–1919; founder of the Boston Symphony Orchestra). He penned numerous prose articles on music and music education and was a leading figure in bringing **Johann Sebastian Bach**'s works into the active performance repertoire of the United States (*see* BACH REVIVAL, BACH AWAKENING, BACH RENAISSANCE).

The international recognition afforded Paine's music and his influence in organizing and leading the first music department at a U.S. university along a model of liberal arts education with a vigorous emphasis on composition make him a seminal figure in U.S. music. He was not a **nationalist**, however. Instead, his compositional style draws heavily and unapologetically on German models. His earlier works and writings are decidedly conservative and skeptical of the approaches to form and harmony characteristic of the **New German School**, but after the mid-1870s, he experimented with more chromatic harmony and techniques, such as **thematic transformation**. He was never able to have his *magnum opus*, the **grand opera** *Azara* (1883–1898) staged, but it was published in Leipzig in 1901 and given a concert performance in Boston in 1903. His most important works were the **oratorio** *St. Peter* (Op. 20, 1870–1872) and the Mass in D (Op. 10, 1865), which was premiered in Berlin by that city's renowned Singakademie in 1867. He also composed **incidental music** to Sophocles' *Oedipus tyrannus* (Op. 35, 1880–1881, rev. 1895, publ. 1908) and Aristophanes' *The Birds* (1900, publ. 1902), several **cantatas** and other works for unaccompanied chorus (both mixed chorus and *Männerchor*), and 11 **songs** (all on English-language texts, some of them translated from French or German). His instrumental music includes two **symphonies** (opp. 23 and 34, comp. 1875 and 1879, publ. 1908 and 1880, respectively); a **concert overture** after **William Shakespeare**'s *As You Like It* (1876, publ. 1907 with the German title for that play, *Was ihr wollt*); one **symphonic poem** (*The Tempest*, Op. 31, ca. 1876, publ. 1907); one **tone poem** (*Poseidon and Amphitrite: An Ocean Fantasy*, Op. 44, ca. 1888, publ. 1908) and a *Duo Concertante* for violin, cello, and **orchestra** (Op. 33, ca. 1877); several works for organ and **piano** as well as one **string quartet** (Op. 5, ca. 1855); one **piano trio** (Op. 22, ca. 1874); and several smaller pieces of instrumental **chamber music**. [JMC]

PALESTRINA, GIOVANNI PIERLUIGI DA (1525–1594). Italian Renaissance composer. Palestrina's polyphonic choral works became standard models of 16th-century counterpoint in later centuries, and that contrapuntal style in turn became the basis for the *stile antico* **topic**. Already at the outset of the **long 19th century**, Palestrina belonged to a then-small **canon** of great composers from previous eras. His reputation was preserved, even augmented, by his significance as contrapuntalist and his alleged role in defending church music from severe Tridentine reforms with his *Missa Papae Marcelli* (a tall tale at least as old as Agostino Agazzari's *Del sonare sopra il basso* [On Playing Over a Bass, 1607]). Palestrina figured regularly into treatises on counterpoint in the 17th and 18th centuries, including J. J. Fux's (1660–1741) seminal *Gradus ad Parnassum* (A Step to Parnassus, 1725).

Palestrina's significance continued to grow during the long 19th century. Within the **Cecilian movement**, certain leaders in church music were fervent advocates for 16th-century-style a cappella choral music in churches, and Palestrina became a kind of movement figurehead for many, including composer Giuseppe Baini (1775–1844), author of *Memorie storico-critiche della vita e delle opere di Giovanni Pierluigi da Palestrina* (Historical-Critical Memoirs of Giovanni Pierluigi da Palestrina's Life and Works, 1828). In the final years of the long 19th century, Hans Pfitzner (1869–1949) evoked the mythologized Palestrina in his third **opera**, *Palestrina* (comp. 1911–1915, perf. 1917). [RK]

See also HISTORICISM; RECEPTION.

PANIAGUA (Y VASQUES), CENOBIO (1821–1882). Mexican composer of the Late Romantic Generation; composer of the first *opera seria* by a Mexican composer. He was a violinist and a pianist and performed in the **orchestra** of Morelia until he moved to Mexico City, where he also became known for his works written for the city's **salon** culture. He decided to pursue his education independently after the city's leading composer of the day, José Antonio Gómez (1805–1876), refused to take him into his studio. Paniagua learned composition primarily from **Antoine Reicha**'s *Cours de composition musicale, ou Traité complet et raisonné d'harmonie pratique* (Course of Musical Composition; or, Complete and Ordered Treatise on Practical Harmony, 1816–1818). In 1845, he used a libretto by Felice Romano (1788–1865; best known for his collaborations with **Vincenzo Bellini**) to produce his own *opera seria*, *Catalina de Guisa*, and succeeded in having it performed in Mexico City in 1859.

Although *Catalina de Guisa* is in Italian, it was the first opera composed by a Mexican composer ever performed. It established an operatic tradition that endured in Mexico for several decades. It prompted the formation of a new company devoted to producing Italian operas and the creation of an Academia de Armonía y Composición (Academy of Harmony and Composition) directed by Paniagua. He composed one other opera (*Pietro d'Abano*) in 1863, but that opera was a failure and the same year witnessed the spread of rumors (untrue) that parts of *Catalinia* were plagiarized from Errico Petrella's (1813–1877) opera *Marco Visconti* (1855). His reputation damaged, Paniagua moved in 1868 to the small town of Córdoba, where he composed one further opera (*El paria*/The Outcast, date unknown), six **zarzuelas**, an **oratorio** (*Tobías*, 1870), several psalm settings, one **Requiem** (1882), and more than 70 other Mass settings as well as one **string quartet**. [JMC]

DAS PARADIES UND DIE PERI, **OP. 50**. (Ger., "*Paradise and the Peri*.") Secular **oratorio** by **Robert Schumann** on a text by Thomas Moore (1779–1852) translated by Emil Flechsig (1808–1878) and Schumann himself. It was composed in 1843 and premiered in Leipzig on 4 December of that year, with Schumann conducting, to great acclaim. It was published in parts and full score in by **Breitkopf & Härtel** (Leipzig) in 1844 and in piano/vocal score in the original German as well as French translation by Victor Wilder as *Le paradis et le Péri* that same year (*see* PRINTING AND PUBLISHING OF MUSIC).

The text of *Das Paradies und die Peri* stems from Moore's orientalist romance *Lalla Rookh* (1817), the story of a peri—in Persian mythology, a beautiful and benevolent mythical being descended from fallen angels and banned from paradise until penance is served—who gains entry into paradise after presenting the guardians of the gates with the tears of a repentant sinner. Schumann's original notes on the text designated it as "material for an **opera**," but while composing the music, he wrote to his friend Carl Koßmaly that "it is no opera—I believe it is an entirely new genre for the concert hall." Today, it is sometimes designated a **cantata**, although its scope and subject matter are more consistent with those of the oratorio. Running to about 90 minutes, it was Schumann's most ambitious choral/orchestral work to date and still stands as one of his more important contributions to the choral/orchestral repertoire. The music makes plentiful use of thematic recollections and reminiscence themes to enhance dramatic connections and ensure musical continuity (*see* LEITMOTIV). [JMC]

PARATEXT. In connection with music of the **long 19th century**, term for those elements of a musical text that stand apart from the sounding musical text per se but inform its meaning and potentially influence interpretation. In this context, *musical text* denotes the notated pitches, durations, dynamics, and other interpretative directions that interpreters realize or imagine in sound as well as any words that are declaimed or sung. By contrast, *paratexts* (occasionally *paratextual elements*) are usually verbal. Titles (especially characteristic or **programmatic** titles), section names, epigrams, and prefaces or programs are all paratexts. Thus, in **Ludwig van Beethoven**'s Sixth **("Pastoral") Symphony**, the paratexts may be considered as the titular designation "Pastoral": the subtitle "Erinnerung an das Landleben (mehr Ausdruck der Empfindung als Malerey)" (Recollection of Country Life [More an Expression of Feeling Than Tone-Painting]), the movement titles, and the labeling of the cuckoo, nightingale, and quail in the coda of the second movement. In other programmatic works (e.g., **Hector Berlioz**'s *Episode in the Life of an Artist*, **Franz Liszt**'s **symphonic poems**, and the **tone poems** of **Richard Strauss**), the printed and prefatory programs may be considered paratexts. In vocal and **absolute music**, paratexts include genre designations such as **nocturne** and labels of dance type (**écossaise**, furiant, and so on). The term was developed in structuralist literary theory by Gérard Genette (b. 1930) as a concept in intertextuality, denoting elements of a (literary) text that stand at the threshold of the text and help to control and direct the reader's reception of that text and its meaning. [JMC]

PARISH-ALVARS, ELIAS [PARISH, ELI] (1808–1849). Irish **virtuoso** harpist and composer, sometimes called the "king of harpists" and variously referred to in his day as "the **Paganini** of the harp" and "the **Liszt** of the harp." He toured widely and was praised as a composer and performer by such reputable critics as **Hector Berlioz** (who called him "a magician . . . in [whose] hands the harp becomes a siren . . . [that] utter[s] the music of another world") and Liszt (who dubbed him "a bard" and praised "the glowing imagination which lives in his compositions"). In his performances, he reportedly addressed the dearth of high-quality literature for the harp up to that point by performing **Ludwig van Beethoven**'s and **Johann Nepomuk Hummel**'s piano **concertos** and **Fryderyk Chopin**'s **études**, and in his original compositions he attempted to address this deficit, producing works that were idiomatic for the harp but less formulaic and more imaginative than the established harp literature of the day. His technique on the instrument also reportedly influenced that of the **piano**, specifically by creating textures that featured a melody in the middle registers surrounded by rapid, flowing arpeggios: this texture became known as the "three-hand technique" most famously associated with **Sigismond Thalberg** (though it was also used by other composers for the piano, notably Liszt, **Felix Mendelssohn Bartholdy**, and **Clara** and **Robert Schumann**). His output includes an **opera**, a **symphony**, a programmatic **concert overture** inspired by **Lord Byron**'s *Manfred*, and two piano concertos in addition to many works for harp solo and three harp concertos.

Parish-Alvars studied with the Flemish harpist François Dizi (1780–1847) and the French harpist Théodore Labarre (1805–1870) and toured as a virtuoso harpist on the Continent beginning in 1828 (performances in Brandenburg, Bremen, Constantinople, Copenhagen, Florence, Hamburg Magdeburg, Moscow, St. Petersburg, and Stockholm). During these years, he also performed in France, Hungary, Italy, and Switzerland, some of these with **John Field**. He was appointed solo harpist at La Scala (Milan) in 1834 and principal harpist of the Court Opera in Vienna in 1836, also studying counterpoint with renowned pedagogue **Simon Sechter** and composition with Ignaz von

Seyfried (1776–1841) while in the Imperial City. After returning to London from around 1838 to 1841, he toured the eastern Mediterranean and then returned to the German lands, where he won further renown in Dresden and Leipzig. In 1842, he made his first performances with the Philharmonic Society of London and, with **Bernhard Molique** and others, gave a special performance for Queen **Victoria** in Buckingham Palace. Apart from another triumphant set of performances in London in the spring of 1846, the remainder of his life was spent mostly on the Continent (Berlin, Cologne, Leipzig, Naples, and Stuttgart). He finally settled in Vienna, where in 1847 he was appointed imperial chamber virtuoso and began teaching harp at the **Gesellschaft der Musikfreunde**.

Parish-Alvars was in Vienna when riots and revolts erupted with the **Revolutions of 1848**. This instability prompted the Gesellschaft der Musikfreunde to halt payments, and because many of his pupils belonged to noble families who had fled the city in search of safety, Parish-Alvars and his family (which by now included a wife and two children) found themselves in dire financial straits. Having borrowed money from his publisher, **Artaria**, late in 1848, he sickened in January 1849 and died on 25 January 1849, apparently of pneumonia. [JMC]

PARKER, HORATIO (WILLIAM) (1863–1919). U.S. church musician, composer, **conductor**, organist, and teacher of the Modern Romantic Generation, best remembered today for his choral music and his role as teacher of Charles Ives. He began taking **piano** and organ lessons from his mother at age 14, then studied composition with **George Whitefield Chadwick** before enrolling in 1882 at the Munich Conservatory, where he studied with **Josef Rheinberger**. Upon his return to the United States (1885), he was active as a teacher and organist in New York City, teaching counterpoint at the National Conservatory and winning a prize from that institution in 1893 for his **oratorio** *Hora novissima* (Op. 30).

Parker worked as organist and choirmaster at Trinity Church (Boston) in 1893 and in 1894 was appointed to the music theory faculty at Yale University, also serving as dean there from 1904 to 1918. He was also director of the New Haven Choral Society from 1902 to 1910 and conductor of the New Haven Symphony Orchestra from 1903 to 1914. He also conducted the Three Choirs Festival in 1899 and 1900. Each of his two **operas** won a $10,000 prize and productions: *Mona* (Op. 71, 1910) from the Metropolitan opera (1912) and *Fairyland* (Op. 77, 1914) from the National Association of Music Clubs (1915). He was awarded an honorary doctorate from Cambridge University in 1902.

Parker is considered a member of the Second New England School. His musical style, like that of the others in this group, is deeply indebted to European post-Romantic traditions. Aside from his two operas, his stage works include one surviving set of **incidental music** (1905), a masque (*Cupid and Psyche*, Op. 80, 1916), and *An Allegory of War and Peace* (for chorus and band, 1916). His 36 published *opera* of choral music include **cantatas**, **motets**, odes, oratorios, and **part-songs**, to which may be added another 31 anthems and services (mostly unpublished). He also published many solo **songs** and vocal duets, 12 published *opera* of music for organ or **piano**, and a small quantity of instrumental **chamber music**. His **orchestral** output includes one **symphony** (1885), five **concert overtures** (both **programmatic** and occasional), two **symphonic poems**, and a **suite** adapted from his opera *Fairyland*. [JMC]

PARRY, (CHARLES) HUBERT (HASTINGS) (1848–1918). English composer, music historian, and teacher of the Late Romantic Generation; with **Alexander Mackenzie** and **Charles Villiers Stanford**, one of the most important members of the **English Musical Renaissance**. He studied with George Macfarren (1813–1887) and **William Sterndale Bennett** at Oxford University, earning his BMus degree from that institution at the age of 18—making him the youngest person ever to have achieved that distinction at that institution. He began publishing **songs** and **part-songs** that same year (1866) and through **Joseph Joachim** applied to study with **Johannes Brahms** in Vienna. That venture did not succeed, but it led indirectly to his studies with the brilliant **Wagnerian** partisan Edward Dannreuther (1844–1905).

In 1876, Parry attended the premiere of *The Ring of the Nibelung* at **Bayreuth** and, like many others, was profoundly inspired. Now converted to the aesthetic of the **New German School**, in 1879 he produced the work that would establish his public reputation: a Piano **Concerto** in F-sharp Minor (rev. 1895), which Dannreuther premiered at Crystal Palace in 1880. Meanwhile, he had met and befriended **George Grove**, who employed him as assistant editor for the first edition of his *Dictionary of Music and Musicians* beginning in 1875, ultimately secured from him 123 of the articles in that seminal work of musical scholarship, and appointed him as professor of composition and music history at the Royal College of Music in 1883. He succeeded Grove as director of the college in 1894 and retained that post until his death, also serving as professor at Oxford from 1900 to 1908. He was knighted in 1898 and made a baronet after composing music for the coronation of King Edward VII in 1903.

Although to latter-day ears the often-majestic, predominantly diatonic harmonies and homophonic textures of Parry's music are emblazoned with all the trappings of late **Victorian** privilege and political conservatism, in fact much of his music was written in service of progressive, class-conscious ideas quite remote from those assumed values. One example is the anthem

Jerusalem, a unison setting of a text by William Blake (1757–1827), which was written for a 1916 meeting of the suffrage union known as Fight for the Right, a group that both Parry and his wife supported actively.

Parry is best known for his vocal music. *Jerusalem* in particular acquired iconic stature in the rich tradition English choral music, and other choral works, such as *Blest Pair of Sirens* (1887), three **oratorios** (1888, 1892, and 1894), *The Soul's Ransom* (1906), *The Vision of Life* (1907), and the valedictory *Songs of Farewell* (1916), rank among the best-known choral compositions of the late 19th and early 20th centuries—despite the scorn heaped on them by the influential critic **George Bernard Shaw**. He also composed a number of English **songs** (most notably the 12 sets of *English Lyrics*, 1885–1920), one **opera**, one **ballet**, and seven sets of **incidental music** as well as much instrumental music. The last includes four **symphonies**, an *Elegy for Brahms* (1897), two piano **concertos**, and one **symphonic poem** plus three **string quartets**, one string **quintet**, and several other instrumental **chamber** works and a number of small and large works for **piano** solo or **piano duet**. His musicological work reflects the profound influence exerted on music historiography by Darwinian models of evolution. Among his most important writings (in addition to the 123 entries he penned for Grove's *Dictionary*) are *Studies of Great Composers* (1886), *The Art of Music* (1893, rev. as *The Evolution of the Art of Music*, 1896) and the volume on 17th-century music in *The Oxford History of Music* (1902). [JMC]

See also NATIONALISM, ROMANTIC NATIONALISM.

***PARSIFAL*, WWV 111.** Opera (*Bühnenweihfestspiel*, "festival-play for the consecration of the stage") in three acts by **Richard Wagner** to his own **libretto**, after the Minnesinger Wolfram von Eschenbach's (ca. 1170–ca. 1220) epic play *Parzival* (early 13th century) and the trouvère Chrétien de Troyes's 12th-century romance *Perceval, ou Le Conte du graal* (ca. 1190). Wagner's opera is based on Arthurian knight Percival's quest for the Holy Grail. It was written for the dedication of the Festspielhaus (Festival Theater) of **Bayreuth** and premiered in 1882 at the second Bayreuth Festival. Wagner had read Eschenbach's version of the tale as early as 1845 and in 1857 penned a prose sketch (now lost) for the work as a whole, followed by a prose draft in 1865. Most of the work on the libretto was done in March and April 1877. He drafted the music between August 1877 and April 1879 (preparing an **orchestral** version of the Prelude to Act I with concert ending in the fall of 1878) and composed the full score between August 1879 and January 1882 (*see* COMPOSITIONAL PROCESS, CREATIVE PROCESS). The Bayreuth Festspielhaus officially had exclusive claims to performances for the first 30 years—but the work was published in full score and piano/vocal arrangements (German, French, and English) in 1883, and numerous performances were given before that embargo elapsed (*see* PRINTING AND

PUBLISHING OF MUSIC). After the proscription elapsed, there was a veritable deluge of performances—being taken up by more than 50 European opera houses between 1 January and 1 August 1914 alone.

Parsifal reflects the profound occupation with religion and history that had emerged in Wagner's thinking during the last decade or so of his life. Like *Tristan und Isolde*, it is a revisiting of Arthurian legend, but in *Parsifal*, the themes of renunciation and redemption central to the immediate literary sources and Wagner's own beliefs are commingled with the pessimistic philosophy of Arthur Schopenhauer (1788–1860) and elements of Buddhism as Wagner understood them on the basis of the writings of Eugène Bernouf (1801–1852) and Karl Friedrich Köppen (1808–1863). (Some of this understanding reflects an unclear distinction between Buddhism and Hinduism.) By the time Wagner set about composing the music of *Parsifal*, he had distanced himself from the concept of **music drama** and **Gesamtkunstwerk**, as from many of the theories that generated *Der Ring des Nibelungen* and *Tristan* (although **Leitmotiv** and *unendliche Melodie* remain central to the work's musical dramaturgy). Instead, much of *Parsifal* unfolds as a series of *tableaux* that focus on the importance of ritual and epic narration—*see TABLEAU VIVANT* (PL. *TABLEAUX VIVANTS*). As indicated by Wagner's genre designation (*Bühnenweihfestspiel*), it was written to take advantage of Wagner's theories of the stage and the illusionist experience of theater as represented in the Bayreuth Festspielhaus (which was built according to his specifications): the auditorium is to be fan shaped, with a double proscenium and steam curtains, and the **orchestra** pit is hidden (mostly beneath the stage rather than in front of it). The result of this reimagined musical stage was to be one that both dispensed with the fourth wall and attempted to transport the listener into the mythical world of the "acts of music made visible" (Wagner's phrase) that constituted his drama. [JMC]

PART-SONG. Most generally, any setting of a secular or nonliturgical sacred text for two or more voices, either for mixed ensemble (usually SATB) or for female or male voices only. For much of the **long 19th century**, such settings were typically performed with one or (at most) two singers per part and without accompaniment. When accompaniment was provided, it was usually for **piano** only and contained no autonomous musical interest, being intended instead for rehearsal.

Part-songs were typically short and for this reason were cheap and easy to print and publish. This commercial viability combined with the amateur-centered musical life of the **Restoration** to make the genre exceedingly popular after about 1815. During the second half of the 19th century, such works were also frequently performed by choral ensembles. Consequently, during the century's closing decades, composers often conceived of them as choral works ("choral songs") rather than as vocal **chamber music** and wrote accordingly more sophisticated and challenging music in the genre. Important composers of part-songs include **William Sterndale Bennett, Aleksandr Borodin, Johannes Brahms, Anton Bruckner, Peter Cornelius, Aleksandr Dargomïzhsky, Claude Debussy, Léo Delibes, Gaetano Donizetti, Antonín Dvořák, Edward Elgar, Friedrich Fesca, Robert Franz, Edvard Grieg, Johann Nepomuk Hummel, Carl Loewe, Edward Macdowell, Heinrich Marschner, William Mason, Jules Massenet, Felix Mendelssohn Bartholdy, Otto Nicolai, Horatio Parker, Hubert Parry, Nikolay Rimsky-Korsakov, Camille Saint-Saëns, Franz Schubert, Robert Schumann, Ethel Smyth, Charles Villiers Stanford, Richard Strauss, Arthur Sullivan, Pyotor Il'yich Tchaikovsky, Richard Wagner, Carl Maria von Weber**, and **Alberto Williams**, among many others. [JMC]

See also HAUSMUSIK; LIEDERTAFEL; MÄNNERCHOR; ORPHÉON.

PASDELOUP, JULES (ÉTIENNE) (1819–1887). French **conductor**, composer, pianist, and music educator of the Late Romantic Generation; a shaping force in Parisian musical life for much of the **Second Empire** and **Third Republic**. Son of a conductor at the Opéra-Comique, he studied at the Paris **Conservatory**, where he won first prize in solfège in 1832 and in **piano** in 1834. He began giving music lessons at the age of 14 in order to make a living and by 1841 was appointed lecturer in solfège at the Conservatory, where he also served as lecturer in piano from 1847 to 1850.

Pasdeloup became an important organizer of musical events in France after the **Revolutions of 1848**, and in 1851, he began organizing the Société des Jeunes Artistes du Conservatoire (Society of Young Artists of the Conservatory), a youth **orchestra** comprised of his former pupils, unofficially contingent to the Orchestre des Societé des Concerts du Conservatoire, whose concerts in the Salle du Conservatoire were not open to the general public—*see* HABENECK, FRANÇOISE-ANTOINE (1781–1849). Far from the usual practices of latter-day youth orchestras, Pasdeloup's concerts focused on premiering new music and introducing Paris's young artists and musical public to new and unfamiliar music (rather than **canonical** works). During the 10 years of its existence, the orchestra offered the Parisian musical public French premieres of works by **Charles Gounod, Felix Mendelssohn Bartholdy, Camille Saint-Saëns, Robert Schumann**, and **Richard Wagner**, among many others.

The Société des Jeunes Artistes was a great success with the public but suffered financially. In response to this situation, Pasdeloup rented the French capital's Cirque Napoléon for a series of concerts by a new series of concerts open to the general public, the Concerts Populaires de Musique Classique (Popular Concerts of Classical Music), which continued Pasdeloup's tradition of presenting German as well as contemporary French music to a Parisian musical public for which such music was otherwise largely available only in arrangements for **piano duet**. The new series, launched on 27 October 1861, was given by an extraordinarily large **orchestra** of up to 110 in a hall that seated nearly 5,000 and was an immense success. Despite increasing anti-German sentiment in France, the series continued (with brief interruptions during the **Franco-Prussian War** and the **Commune**) until 1884.

Meanwhile, Pasdeloup's abilities as an energetic and effective conductor, impresario, and community organizer had won him a position as professor of choral music at the Conservatory (1855) and led to his appointment, alongside François Bazin (1816–1878), as director of the Paris *Orphéon* in 1860, succeeding **Gounod** in that highly visible position in French musical life. In 1868, he founded another new organization, the *Société des Oratories*, which gave the first complete public performance in France of **Johann Sebastian Bach**'s *St. Matthew Passion* in its opening year (*see* BACH REVIVAL, BACH AWAKENING, BACH RENAISSANCE; HISTORICISM). The post-1870 period contained increasing challenges in the form of other populist concert series (most notably those of the **Société Nationale de Musique Française** and the Nouveaux Concerts organized by Charles Lamoureaux [1834–1899]), and in 1884, Pasdeloup abandoned his own series. His final contributions, given during the last year of his life, were further extensions of his commitment to new music: a series of another five concerts in the Cirque Napoléon and a festival devoted to the music of **César Franck** (1886). [JMC]

PASSACAGLIA. (It.; Fr., passacaille; Ger., Passacalia; It., *also* passacaglio, passagallo, passacagli, passacaglie; Sp., pasacalle, passacalle.) A 16th-century genre rediscovered in the **long 19th century** and in the process unwittingly redefined; the long 19th century's understanding of the term was based on late Baroque specimens that were atypical of the genre's history. In the early 17th century, the term denoted a short ritornello, improvised or improvisatory in nature, played between the strophes of a song. From 1627, when Girolamo Frescobaldi published his *Partite sopra passacaglia*, the term frequently denoted continuous linked variations, often in triple meter and often based on a descending tetrachord in one voice. In its French, Italian, and Spanish guises, the term occasionally was used for an instrumental interlude in a vocal work; it could be in either duple or triple meter and could be in either the major or the minor mode (as the long 19th century understood modal theory). Beginning in the late 17th century, German composers began using newly composed melodic formulas as the basis of the variations, although they also preserved traditional forms (e.g., in the chorus "Weinen, Klagen, Sorgen, Zagen" from **Johann Sebastian Bach**'s eponymous **cantata** BWV

12 [1714]; its later contrafactum as the Crucifixus from the B-Minor Mass, BWV 232; or the opening movement of *Jesu, der du meine Seele*, BWV 78 [1724]).

When the long 19th century rediscovered the passacaglia, it was unaware of many of these inherited musical traits and consequently construed the term according to the characteristics of the specimens best known at the time: J. S. Bach's Passacaglia in C Minor for organ (BWV 582, ca. 1710) and (possibly) the passacaglia from **George Frideric Handel**'s Harpsichord **Suite No. 7** (HWV 255, 1720). Both of these works descended from a specifically German tradition based on the Frescobaldi model: they were extended sets of linked or continuous ostinato variations on an original melodic formula (rather than a more-or-less established version of the gesture of the descending tetrachord). Moreover, since Handel's passacaglia was overshadowed by BWV 582, 19th-century applications of the term tended to be in the minor mode and triple meter and usually for organ, **piano**, or **pedal piano**. Examples (scored for organ unless otherwise indicated) include Otto Barblan (1860–1943), Op. 6 (1895); Adrien Barthe (1828–1898; for woodwind **quintet**, 1899); Luigi Boccherini (1743–1805; Op. 30 for string quintet, 1779); Jacques Bosch (1826–1895; for guitar, 1885); Frédéric Brisson (1821–1900; for piano, 1887); Johann Georg Herzog (1822–1909; 1871); **Daniel Gregory Mason** (Op. 10, 1912); **Felix Mendelssohn Bartholdy** (MWV W7, 1823); Joseph O'Kelly (1829–1885; for piano, 1872); **Max Reger** (Op. 96, for two pianos, 1906); **Josef Rheinberger** (Op. 156, No. 11 [1888], Op. 132, No. 10 [1883]); Oskar Wermann (1875–1906, Op. 95, 1881; subtitled *Konzertstück*); Martin Roeder (1851–1895; 1878, for piano); Julius Röntgen (1855–1932; for piano, 1878); **Anton Rubinstein** (fourth movement of Suite for Piano, Op. 38, 1859); and Francis Thomé (1850–1909; for piano, 1881). The convention of referring to the last movement of **Brahms**'s Fourth **Symphony** (1884–85, publ. 1886) as a passacaglia is appropriate in terms of the late 19th-century understanding of the term but inauthentic. [JMC]

See also CHACONNE.

PASTA (NÉE NEGRI), GIUDITTA (ANGIOLA MARIA COSTANZA) (1797–1865). Legendary Italian soprano, after **Maria Malibran** the most famous exponent of the **bel canto** style associated with **Vincenzo Bellini, Gaetano Donizetti**, and **Gioachino Rossini**. Widely traveled and acclaimed already by 1818, she scored her first major success in Paris in 1821, singing the role of Desdemona in Rossini's *Otello* (1816). Further successes included the roles of Amina in Bellini's *La sonnambula* (1831), the title role in *Norma* (1831), and *Beatrice di Tenda* (1833). She created the title role in Donizetti's *Anna Bolena* (1830) and the role of Bianca in his *Ugo, conte di Parigi* (1832). Though she retired from the public stage in 1835, on rare occasions she did perform in prestigious venues thereafter. In 1839, she was elected an honorary member of the Accademia di Santa Cecilia in Rome and was given a valuable ring by Tsar Nicholas I of Russia (fl. 1855) after a series of acclaimed performances in St. Petersburg in 1840. That same year, she was also widely hailed for a series of performances in German cities (including Berlin, Leipzig, and Vienna).

Pasta's style was characterized both by her exceptional dramatic gifts and by her judicious *fioritura*. Though she was sometimes criticized for poor intonation, her musicianship was extraordinary by all accounts: the critic Henry Chorley (1808–1872), for example, noted that "there was a breadth, an expressiveness in her *roulades*, an evenness and solidity in her shake, which imparted to every passage a significance beyond the reach of more spontaneous singers." Her wide range—she possessed a full-volume low *A* and could extend upward to a high *C sharp*—was also celebrated for its diversity of timbres, a complexity that she brought to bear in making her interpretations not only musically beautiful but also dramatically intelligent. [JMC]

"PASTORAL" SYMPHONY. Popular name (authorized) for the **Symphony** No. 6 in F Major, Op. 68, by **Ludwig van Beethoven**. It was composed in 1808, premiered on the same concert with Beethoven's Fifth Symphony in Vienna on 22 December 1808, and published in parts and arrangements for **piano duet** (by William Watts) and for **piano** and violin or flute the following year. It was also published in an arrangement for piano duet in 1814 and arrangement for string **sextet** by Michael Gotthard Fischer (1773–1829) in 1816. The full score was first published in 1826. The work is dedicated to Prince Lobkowitz (1772–1816) and Count Andrey Rasumovsky (1752–1836), two of Beethoven's most important patrons.

The "Pastoral" Symphony comprises five movements, the last three of which are to be played without pause. These movements bear the individual characteristic titles (*see* PARATEXT): *Erwachen heiterer Empfindungen bei der Ankunft auf dem Lande* (Awakening of Happy Feelings on Arrival in the Countryside), *Szene am Bach* (Scene by the Brook), *Lustiges Zusammensein der Landleute* (Merry Gathering of the Country Folk), *Gewitter, Sturm* (Bad Weather; Thunderstorm), and *Hirtengesang. Frohe und dankbare Gefühle nach dem Sturm* (Shepherds' Song: Happy and Thankful Feelings after the Storm). Additionally, the three birdcalls that are graphically imitated in the coda of the second movement are specially labeled "Nightingale," "Quail," and "Cuckoo" in the first editions (but not the **autograph** full score). The first edition of the orchestral parts also includes an elaboration of the main title: "Erinnerung an das Landleben (mehr Ausdruck der Empfindung als Malerey)" (Recollection of Country Life [More an Expression of Feeling Than Tone-Painting]).

The "Pastoral" Symphony received mixed reviews at its premiere because of the graphicness with which it portrays extramusical events and labels these events using verbal language. As indicated by the parenthetical disclaimer ("more an expression of feeling than tone-painting"), such explicit programmaticism lent itself readily to accusations that the work's aesthetic essence was visual or experiential, not musical, and that its aesthetic worth as music was correspondingly diminished. Over the course of the 19th century, however, the ever-increasing investment in "poetic" content for instrumental music made the Sixth Symphony a work to be championed and invoked not only in defense of specific later **program symphonies** (most prominently **Hector Berlioz**'s *Episode in the Life of an Artist*) but also in service of the aesthetic agenda of **Franz Brendel, A. B. Marx**, and (after 1850) **Franz Liszt, Richard Wagner**, and the **New German School** generally. [JMC]

See also ABSOLUTE MUSIC; PROGRAM (PROGRAMMATIC) MUSIC.

PAUL, JEAN. *See* RICHTER, JEAN PAUL (JOHANN PAUL [FRIEDRICH]) (1763–1825).

PAULUS. See ST. PAUL (PAULUS), MWV A14/OP. 36.

PEDAL PIANO. (Fr., piano à pédalier, clavier de pédales; Ger., Pedalflügel, Pianoforte mit Pedal, Pedalklavier; It., pianoforte organistico.) A **piano** with a specially constructed pedal keyboard after the manner of the organ. It may be a descendant of the pedal clavier and pedal harpsichord used in the 17th and early 18th centuries. The instrument was apparently conceived as a practice instrument for organists, but during the **long 19th century** its popularity surged. **Wolfgang Amadeus Mozart** owned a pedal piano, made for him by **Anton Walter**, and may have used it for a performance of his Piano **Concerto** in D Minor (K. 466) in 1785. It was also championed by **Robert Schumann**, who reportedly persuaded **Felix Mendelssohn Bartholdy** to include a special class on it in the curriculum of the Leipzig **Conservatory** and wrote several important works for it (the *Six Pieces in Canonic Form* [Op. 56, 1845], *Four Sketches for the Pedal Piano* [Op. 58, 1846], and *Six Fugues on B-A-C-H.* [Op. 60, 1846]). Other composer champions of the instrument included **Charles-Valentin Alkan** (six works, 1859, 1870–1872), **Charles Gounod** (three works, 1886, 1888, 1896), **Franz Liszt** (the *Fantasy and Fugue on "Ad nos, ad salutarem undam" from* **Meyerbeer**'s *"Le prophète"* [LW E1, 1850, publ. 1852]), and **Camille Saint-Saëns** (the original version of the Piano Concerto No. 2, 1868), among others. [JMC]

PERFORMANCE PRACTICE. (Ger., Aufführungspraxis.) The conventions and knowledge that enable performers to create a performance. In the realm of Western notated music of the **long 19th century**, the concept embraces a complex intersection between musical notation and accepted conventions for interpreting notated texts and music; the technologies of manufacturing musical instruments and the resulting mechanical, tactile, and timbral properties of those instruments; the acoustics of the spaces in which performers realize and audiences hear and see the performances; and interactions among performers and between them and audiences.

Until the mid-1980s, it was widely assumed that the instruments, tempos, and sounds of musical performance during the long 19th century, unlike those of, for example, the Renaissance, Baroque, or early Classical periods, were largely the same as those of the 20th century. This is not the case, however. In recognition of the considerable, often profound, differences between the sounds of music in the long 19th century and the way the same musical works sound when realized according to latter-day performance conventions, for much of the post–World War II period it was customary to speak of *authentic* performance practices as opposed to *modern* ones. In recent decades performers and scholars have come to prefer the phrase *historically informed performance* (often referred to by the acronym HIP) for one basic reason: that phrase acknowledges the significant difference between historical and latter-day performance practices and their more recent counterparts while also recognizing that performance practices (and the interpretive expectations that composers assumed their performers would use in translating the notated musical text into sound) varied widely from location to location and time to time over the course of the long 19th century. Briefly put, *authentic* implies uniformity and authorially sanctioned stability, but *HIP* celebrates the more nuanced truth that interpretations have always varied widely.

Most musicians consciously endeavor to realize "the composer's wishes" in realizing notated musical texts as sound (*see* INTENTIONAL FALLACY)—or at least are reluctant to advocate for contravening the will of the composer in their own interpretation—and most accept that sound and duration (including tempo, phrasing, rhythm, and so on) are integral rather than incidental aspects of music. It follows, therefore, that the charge of those realizing the composer's wishes as he or she symbolically notated them for contemporary performers includes respecting the sounds and durations that composers of the long 19th century expected their notated scores to generate. Those sounds and durations changed profoundly in the last decades of the 19th century and the early 20th century as the continued urbanization and industrialization of society in the Old and New Worlds combined with the need for larger halls that would accommodate the growing audiences of cultivated music (a trend in audience size that reversed dramatically over the course of the 20th century, even in Europe), producing a musical culture that favored volume and homogeneity, blend, or bulk over variety and transparency of sound. Still further changes occurred as instruments were modified and performers adapted their techniques in order to take advantage of the vast new opportunities for dissemination of musical performance via the 20th century's advances in technologies for recording and broadcasting sound—a phenomenon that was unheard of for most of the long 19th century and a rarity for some time even after it had appeared.

Whatever the merits of these changes, they also resulted in a profound caesura in performance practices during the period around 1890–1920. Much like the restorations in the visual arts that recover the vibrant colors and clearly delineated lines that were obscured by accumulated dirt and changes in fashion, historically informed performances endeavor to filter out the accrued conventions of interpretation that accumulated after the music at hand was written and replace them with ones that are germane to the musical texts as composers and their contemporaries knew it.

Instruments: In the long 19th century as today, the **piano** was the central instrument of everyday life for amateur as well as professional musicians. Because of its centrality and because of the enormous differences between the **piano** for which, for example, **Ludwig van Beethoven, Johannes Brahms, Fryderyk Chopin, Franz Liszt, Felix Mendelssohn Bartholdy,** and **Clara** and **Robert Schumann** wrote and the instruments that modern performers use to realize those composers' music, the pianos of the 19th century are discussed in general terms in the PIANO entry in this dictionary and in more specific terms in the entries for the various makers (surveyed there). There were likewise significant differences between the organs of the long 19th century and their 20th- and 21st-century counterparts. Significant to voices and other instruments alike was the fact that pitch was generally lower: the modern standard of $a' = 440$ Hz was first recommended in 1834, but because this recommendation would result in significant changes in the manufacture of many instruments and require, for example, modifications to existing organs, pianos, and orchestral instruments already in use—at enormous expense—it was not widely adopted for more than a century. Recorded standards of pitch during the 19th century varied from place to place and (like most other aspects of performance practice) changed over the course of the century, but most standards ranged from A432 to A435. The lower pitch of, for example, **Giacomo Meyerbeer**'s, **Giuseppe Verdi**'s, or **Carl Maria von Weber**'s orchestras in turn meant that the pitch used by singers was also lower. The high notes that frequently tax performers' skills today thus fit somewhat more comfortably into the vocal tessitura than they do today.

Second to the piano in order of prevalence during the long 19th century were *stringed instruments*—primarily bowed strings. Commonly encountered assumptions that today's stringed instruments are essentially the same as those of long 19th-century composers are false. In fact, today's stringed instruments are heavy-metal powerhouses compared to those that inspired the music of Beethoven, **Hector Berlioz**, **Richard Wagner**, and Verdi. The instruments for which those composers wrote had shorter necks and fingerboards, lower bridges, and less tension on the strings; the strings themselves were made of gut rather than metal (or metal-wound gut), producing less volume but having a more transparent timbre. The chin rest (first used extensively by **Louis Spohr**) was positioned over the tailpiece rather than beside it, with the result that the instrument rested at an angle (**Pierre Baillot** recommended 45 degrees; Spohr, 25–30 degrees) and was semisupported by the left hand, with the right arm positioned higher than is usual today. The fingers and wrist were the focal points for cantabile bowing, and the vocabulary of bow strokes differed significantly from its modern counterpart. The prevalent variety of vibrato was not finger vibrato (the norm today) but the more subtle wrist vibrato or (most commonly) bow vibrato. Soloists applied vibrato selectively—apparently more selectively than in the middle of the 18th century—using it as an ornament to embellish individual notes rather than a staple of the instrument's tone; the same was true, apparently to a lesser extent, for **chamber** musicians. Until the early years of the 20th century, orchestral players almost never employed vibrato—but *portamento* was employed for expressive purposes (as famously specified in the scores of **Gustav Mahler** around the turn of the 20th century). These differences also resulted in greater timbral variety for bowed stringed instruments across their registers: the lower registers sounded more mellow and the upper ones more ethereal and less bulky than on the modern instrument.

Woodwind instruments, too, employed far less metal and far less tension than their modern counterparts, with a more natural tone that projected less but was clearly audible through the more transparent and less bulky timbre of strings in the same ensemble. They also generally had a shriller, more piercing tone in the upper registers. The century witnessed the development of **Boehm** woodwinds (two main systems, 1832 and 1847), but these were not widely adopted until about 1930—in fact, Boehm flutes were banned in some German orchestras as late as 1914.

Brass instruments likewise tended to be gruffer in their lower registers and more brilliant and piercing in their upper registers, but the higher registers were significantly easier to reach because the instruments used lighter metal, smaller bores, smaller mouthpieces, and less flair in the bell. (Those familiar with the fourth movement of **Robert Schumann**'s Third **Symphony** [1851] can compare the sound of the trombones in any modern-instrument recording with that of any period-instrument recording to hear the effects of these differences clearly.) Fully chromatic horns and trumpets were invented during the early years of the **Restoration** but became the norm only in the last decade or so of the 19th century. While some composers (most notably

Anton Bruckner, Mahler, and **Richard Strauss**) clearly exploited these instruments' expressive possibilities, others (such as Brahms, a generational compeer of Bruckner) clearly wrote for the more varied timbres of traditional brass.

As in previous centuries, the most common *percussion instruments* were the timpani. These were usually played with mallets that had hard disc-shaped heads made of wood or covered with leather; in some (apparently rare) instances, the mallets' heads could be covered with sponge. The drums' kettles themselves were smaller and shallower than their modern counterparts, making it possible for timpanists to strike the drum just off center (rather than close to the edge, as in today's practice) to produce a strong, crisp fundamental rather than the more rounded, overtone-rich sound employed in latter-day practice.

Voices: The physiology of the human voice was of course the same in the long 19th century as it is today (except that most humans were shorter during the long 19th century), but the differences in general principles of performance practice largely paralleled those of other instruments: vibrato was applied sparingly, as an ornament to emphasize individual notes, and primarily by vocal soloists, especially in staged vocal music (**opera, operetta**, and so on). On the other hand, vocal soloists, especially in Italian and French opera, employed extensive melodic embellishments much more freely than is usually the case today, taking the notated melodies of the score as descriptive general guidelines for melodic contour rather than prescriptive specifications of detailed, fixed melodies. Moreover, because **songs** remained primarily the domain of **salons** and other private chambers for much of the century, while most larger concert halls were considerably smaller than their modern counterparts, singers (like instrumentalists) needed to produce less volume than is the case in live performance today. This was true even in the most extreme well-known example (the "Wagnerian" techniques needed for singers to be heard over the densely orchestrated symphonic textures of Wagner's **music dramas**) since the **Bayreuth** Theater, engineered specifically in order to realize Wagner's own conception of what his music would sound like, placed the louder instruments underneath rather than in front of the stage (a placement whose effects were all the more pronounced because of the differences in the winds and strings discussed above). In choral/orchestral works, the chorus was often (despite regional and case-by-case variations) placed in front of the orchestra rather than behind it, with the result that except in music festivals and other such exceptional performances fewer choristers were needed than is usually the case today. That practice in turn facilitated brisk tempos, good intonation, and appropriate clarity and flexibility in imitative contrapuntal passages. In choral/orchestral and other choral works alike, sopranos were usually placed across from altos and tenors across from basses, facilitating antiphonal exchanges between the two principal groups of women's and men's sections. Alternatively, sopranos and altos were placed across from tenors and basses, accomplishing the same effect distributed differently.

That antiphonal disposition—consistent with the long 19th century's general preference for heterogeneity and transparency rather than blend and bulk in musical sound—is also consistent with Romantic orchestral seating practices. First and second violins were almost always placed on opposite sides of the stage at the front of the orchestra, with violas usually next to the firsts and cellos usually next to the seconds. Double basses, in a practice that seems decidedly odd from a modern perspective, were typically placed in different locations around the middle and rear of the orchestra rather than grouped together, for example, with one on either side of the orchestra behind first violins and violas and second violins and cellos and two others at the rear corners of the ensemble. In many orchestras, the first violins stood throughout the performance. Woodwinds and brass were typically placed on risers behind the strings with woodwinds in one or two straight rows and the brass behind them, horns and trumpets separated by trombones and (when present) tubas. The timpani and other percussion were in the rear of the ensemble, either centered or distributed on opposite sides of the center point. Harps, when present, were typically placed at or near the front of the ensemble on the side of the first violins.

Finally, orchestral ensembles, like choruses, usually were significantly smaller than their latter-day counterparts. As late as the mid-1890s, most German orchestras numbered fewer than 50 regular players and most French orchestras fewer than 65—another reflection of the fact that smaller halls required less bulk of sound to fill them. The smaller ensemble sizes combined with other aspects of historical instruments' construction and general performance practices to facilitate tempos that were, on the whole, quicker than those that have since become customary with the more metallic, heavier sounds of modern instruments being used in greater numbers in order to fill larger spaces.

The *balance* of orchestral and choral/orchestral sound in 19th-century combinations afforded a much greater (but not forced) presence to woodwind and middle-brass color, a much less opaque string-section timbre, and a significantly more bracing range of dynamic contrasts because of the increased brilliance of most instruments in their upper registers.

Tempos were also understood more flexibly than is usual today: for most of the century, chronometric tempo indications (i.e., metronome markings) were treated with skepticism, not because metronomes themselves were wildly inaccurate, as is sometimes asserted (it is true that they were not consistent, but they were not so far afield that they would utterly distort a tempo), but because tempos themselves were inherently flexible: for any given verbal tempo indication (e.g., *andante*) the chronometric value was understood to vary according to four basic features of the notated music: meter, note values, frequency of rapid notes (small note values), and types of rhythmic figuration. Small note values passed more quickly in the context of meters with higher denominators than in ones with lower denominators: in a 4/4 allegro, eighth notes (and consequently the beats themselves) were faster than those in a 4/2 allegro but slower than those in a 4/8 allegro. Moreover, the pulse of a given tempo designation in triple meter was assumed to be faster than that of the same tempo designation in a duple meter. Finally, verbal tempo designations reflected the fastest generally encountered note value so that a piece in which eighth notes are prevalent will tend to receive a slower tempo designation than one in which sixteenth notes are prevalent, even though the beat in the former may be quicker.

This fluid understanding of the intersections between metrical organization and notated duration also affected *phrasing*. For much of the long 19th century, melodies were not treated as the series of long, arching melodic lines usual today (the *melos* advocated in Wagner's *Über das Dirigiren* [On Conducting, 1869]). Rather, they were treated as the practice whose prevalence in the late 1860s prompted Wagner's criticism in that treatise—that is, as comparatively short, interlocking rhetorical figures that emphasized silence and the spaces between rhetorical phrases at least as much as the continuity of melodic line created by interlocking those phrases.

There were exceptions to all of the above observations. Some of these were aberrations, while others were taken up by later performers. Readers are encouraged to consult not only the many and detailed primary sources of the long 19th century that provide insights into both common and unusual performance practices that attended Romantic musics but also the by-now sizable body of secondary literature produced since the 1990s on virtually all aspects of performance practice (refer to the bibliography for a few selective recommendations). [JMC]

See also BEL CANTO; BÜLOW, (FREIHERR) HANS (GUIDO) VON (1830–1894); COMPOSITIONAL PROCESS, CREATIVE PROCESS; CONDUCTOR; COPYRIGHT AND PERFORMANCE RIGHT; EDITING AND EDITIONS; JOACHIM, JOSEPH (1831–1907); KREUTZER, RUDOLFE (1766–1831); MALIBRAN (NÉE GARCÍA), MARIA(-FELICIA) (1808–1836); MOSCHELES, IGNAZ [ISAAC] (1794–1870); ORCHESTRATION; OPERA; PASTA (NÉE NEGRI), GIUDITTA (ANGIOLA MARIA COSTANZA) (1797–1865); RODE, (JACQUES) PIERRE (JOSEPH) (1774–1830); TOPIC; URTEXT.

PIANO. (Fr., piano, piano droit; Ger., Hammerklavier, Klavier, Flügel; It., piano[forte].) Umbrella term for a variety of keyboard instruments that produce sound by means of hammers that strike strings inside a casing when corresponding keys are depressed. During the **long 19th century**, these instruments eclipsed the harpsichord as the preferred stringed keyboard instrument, so much so that pianos became anchors of private life in the middle and upper classes and staples of large-ensemble music written for public consumption. This ascent was facilitated in part by the increasing urbanization of society—more people lived close together in cities and had more time for recreational community than ever before—and in part by the spread of the industrial revolution. The latter not only facilitated more sophisticated mass production of more mechanically sophisticated instruments in factories and workshops around the industrialized world but also reduced the cost and increased the speed with which music for the piano could be printed and published.

As a staple of domestic life, especially from the **Restoration** to World War I, the piano provided opportunities for families to make music together and for young men and women to socialize with a level of intimacy that was otherwise suspect in polite society—sitting side by side on a bench while performing **piano duet**s, the one occasionally crossing hands with the other. This social dimension, coupled with the increased ease with which good instruments could be procured and maintained and the increased availability of printed music at low cost (*see* PRINTING AND PUBLISHING OF MUSIC), encouraged composers to write more music in intimate idioms, producing a new industry of *Hausmusik* and **salon** music. At the same time, the Romantic fascination with **virtuosity** and the fact that any aspiring virtuosos were reared in domestic environments in which the piano figured centrally meant that the long 19th century was the golden age of the piano virtuoso (**Ferruccio Busoni, Fryderyk Chopin, Franz Liszt, Clara Schumann**, and **Sigismond Thalberg**, to name but a few). In view of these changes, it is no exaggeration to say that the rise of the piano ranks as the most profoundly influential technological development in music history between the development of printing from movable type in the early 16th century and the advent of techniques for recording and broadcasting sound in the early 20th century.

Today, the terms "piano" and "pianoforte" are used for the relatively homogeneous descendants of the many and significantly varied versions of the basic concept of a hammered-string keyboard instrument of the long 19th century. Even if one considers only the wing-shaped grand piano, however, there was no single instrument that would have been understood as "the piano" from country to country and over the duration of the long 19th century (e.g., as **Steinway, Bösendorfer**, and a handful of other makers are understood today): the differences among instruments—in construction, tone, touch, and even tuning—were simply too significant. Because of the significant differences between the modern instrument and the ones for which composers of the long 19th century wrote, it is customary to refer to the modern instrument as the *piano* or *pianoforte* and to its 18th- and 19th-century counterparts as *fortepianos*.

Because of the many and diverse forms of the descendants of the instrument introduced by Bartolomeo Cristofori (1655–1731) in the early 18th century, this dictionary allocates discussion of specific issues to individual articles concerning specific makers (*see* BÖSENDORFER; BROADWOOD; CHICKERING AND SONS; ERARD; GRAF; PLEYEL; STEIN; STEINWAY; STREICHER). The present entry is concerned with general issues and the ways in which many or most instruments of the long 19th century differed from their latter-day counterparts (as represented especially by Bösendorfer and Steinway). This is not to deny or diminish the many important differences that exist among modern pianos, both across time and from maker to maker, but to clarify that those differences are small and few compared to the differences among the instruments that inspired and shaped the piano writing of 19th-century composers and the techniques of 19th-century pianists.

The shape of the piano's casing affects its stringing, timbre, and action. Today, there are three predominant forms of piano: the grand (also known as "concert grand"), the smaller baby grand, and the upright (known in German as a *Flügel* and in French as a *piano droit*). The baby grand did not exist during the long 19th century. Instead, the most common smaller alternative to the grand was the square piano (actually rectangular), also known as the *box piano*. Although squares had fallen from favor by the end of the 19th century in Europe and the early 20th century in the Americas, their comparatively compact design, minimally ornate casework, and sturdy construction made them well suited to salons and drawing rooms; additionally, they were frequently equipped with hand stops and/or knee levers that facilitated significant changes in timbre (a feature that was particularly appealing in sectional forms such as **variation** sets).

There were two principal varieties of grand piano: the Continental, Viennese, or German variety, which typically used two strings for each note and consequently had a light action and a comparatively small, transparent sound, and the English variety (also widely used in France), which was typically triple-strung with a heavy action and bigger, bulkier sound. The Viennese instruments represent the aesthetic for which, for example, **Wolfgang Amadeus Mozart, Ludwig van Beethoven, Franz Schubert,** and **Carl Maria von Weber** conceived their music, whereas the English ones are closer to what **Franz Joseph Haydn** probably imagined in his late **sonatas.** A major development occurred in 1821, when the Parisian maker **Sébastien Érard** patented his *double-escapement* action, which allowed the keys to be depressed repeatedly without first being fully released, thus facilitating rapid repeated notes. Moreover, the rapid growth of the concertgoing public in Restoration and post-1848 Europe and the United States necessitated everlarger concert halls, which in turn increased demands for more volume from fortepianos used in public venues. These demands resulted in increasing numbers of triple-strung instruments (even those with the Viennese action) and heavier-gauge wire. But more and heavier strings placed greater strain on the frame, and the instruments often eventually warped. Additionally, the fact that wood expands and contracts with changes in humidity made it difficult for instruments such as Beethoven's and Mozart's to retain their tuning.

In the second half of the 19th century, this situation led to the widespread adoption of metal frames (first patented by U.S. makers: Alpheus Babcock [1785–1842] for squares in 1825 and **Jonas Chickering** for grands in 1843), but metal frames in turn increased the bulk, weight, and expense of the instruments and produced a heavier, bulkier sound. The effects of this practice were amplified by the increasing prevalence of overstringing or crossstringing in grands during the last few decades of very late 19th century— that is, the practice of running the longest bass strings over and across the tenor strings. This development further homogenized the instruments' tone. The small, leather-covered hammers that had produced the sounds so favored by, for example, Beethoven, Chopin, Mendelssohn, and Liszt were also replaced by ever-larger, felt-covered hammers. While all these developments had their advantages, they also profoundly affected the striking mechanism, the materials that produced the sound, and the overall scale of the instruments' design in ways that made the instruments less well suited to music written for earlier instruments, simply because, for example, **Clara** and **Robert Schumann**, as composers writing primarily for performers using Viennese instruments, conceived their music at those instruments and wrote as they did partly in order to produce their ideal envisioned sound on those instruments rather than the bulkier instruments, more homogeneous tone, and less transparent timbres of the 21st-century piano.

Finally, the modern, electronically assisted tuning and temperament, dividing the octave into 12 equidistant notes—*see* HELMHOLTZ, HERMANN VON (1821–1894)—was utterly alien to the systems of tuning and temperament for which 19th-century composers wrote: because these instruments were well tempered rather than equal tempered, on them any given key or octave species retained a distinct intervallic structure different from those of all other keys and octave species—and these temperings naturally affected composers' choice of key in their music (indeed, they may well account for at least some of the significant differences among contemporary German, French, and English editions of the same music). As in other aspects of the instruments' design and construction in the 19th century, there was no uniform standard: Chopin's preferred tuning on his preferred **Pleyel** fortepiano was not the same as **Felix Mendelssohn Bartholdy**'s assumed tunings on the Érards he loved dearly, and these in turn differed significantly from those of the Graf, Streicher, and Bechstein instruments that **Johannes Brahms** is known to have used.

On the whole, then, fortepianos cultivated timbral variety rather than the comparatively homogeneous timbres of the modern piano: in most models, the upper registers were bright, middle registers were comparatively mild, and lower registers were full bodied with a slightly buzzing sound. The rapid decay time (even in the lower registers but especially in the upper ones) facilitated clarity of texture and pitch, even in thickly voiced chords and densely contrapuntal passages. Many models enhanced the range of colors by providing four or more shift mechanisms (*Verschiebungen*) in the form of foot or knee pedals, including an *una corda* device that reduced the number of sounding strings from two or three to one, creating a fortepiano sound closely akin to that of a harp. And the tuning and temperament differed significantly from the equal temperament employed today: transposing a piece from, for example, C minor to A minor affected not just the range and overall timbre of the music but also the intervallic structure of the work's constituent octaves, the quality of its respective chords (the intervallic structure of C minor would be different than that of A minor), and of course the intervallic structures of its melodic lines, since, for example, the distance between *A flat* and *G* would be different than that between *F* and *E*. The instruments that have survived and the detailed surviving information concerning the manufacture of fortepianos in their day makes it possible for modern musicians to hear vividly the immensely varied sounds that inspired composers and performers in the long 19th century. [JMC]

See also EDITING AND EDITIONS; PERFORMANCE PRACTICE; PRINTING AND PUBLISHING OF MUSIC.

PIANO DUET. A composition for two pianists, either at one keyboard or on two instruments. The former is usually described as being "for **piano** four hands" (*vierhändiger Klavierauszug* or *Klaverauszug zu 4 Händen*; Fr. *à quatre mains*), the latter "for two pianos."

During the **long 19th century**, the piano duet for two players at one keyboard represented one of the most important means of integrating music making into middle-class households. The rapid expansion of the musically literate middle class during the relatively peaceful and prosperous culture of the **Restoration** made the piano a symbol of domestic health and an anchor of middle-class life, thus generating a market for music for that instrument that was (ideally) of high quality yet also performable by musically literate but not expert musicians. **Ludwig van Beethoven, Franz Joseph Haydn, Wolfgang Amadeus Mozart,** and **Carl Maria von Weber** all wrote for this medium on occasion, but the first major composer to capitalize on it in a significant number of original works was **Franz Schubert**, whose compositions for it range from marches short and lengthy and collections of national dances to divertissements, theme-and-**variation** sets, full-length **sonatas**, and elaborate **fantasies**. Others included **Charles-Valentin Alkan, Mily Balaki-**

rev, Georges Bizet, Johannes Brahms, Emmanuel Chabrier, Cécile Chaminade, Fryderyk Chopin, César Cui, Carl Czerny, Aleksandr Dargomïzhsky, Claude Debussy, Felix Draeseke, Antonín Dvořák, Niels W. Gade, Mikhail Glinka, Louis-Moreau Gottschalk, Charles Gounod, Edvard Grieg, Adolf Henselt, Fanny Hensel, Friedrich Kalkbrenner, Franz Liszt, Felix Mendelssohn Bartholdy, Ignaz Moscheles, Gustav Nottebohm, Georges Onslow, Serge Rachmaninoff, Max Reger, Carl Reinecke, Anton Rubinstein, Robert Schumann, Camille Saint-Saëns, Johann Strauss (I), and Pyotor Il'yich Tchaikovsky, among others.

The piano duet was also one of the most influential means of familiarizing the middle- and upper-class musical public with works for **chamber** ensemble, organ, or large ensembles of instruments and/or voices during the long 19th century. Since any household with any disposable income was likely to have a box, cottage, or upright piano, works published in arrangements for piano could be purchased by those families and played and discussed in the home, thus promoting the works and their composers much more effectively than if those works were presented strictly or primarily through the expensive and comparatively passive media of public performances in churches, concert halls, and theaters.

Most music published during the long 19th century, from instrumental chamber works such as **piano trios** and **string quartets** through **concert overtures, symphonic poems,** and **symphonies** to **cantatas, operas,** and **oratorios** appeared in arrangements for piano duet. From the perspective of the public, this convention appealed because the piano-duet team could learn the music actively (and tactilely) rather than passively and could repeat and discuss movements or passages freely. It also made sense from the perspective of publishers (who in most cases held the **copyright** on music that they published) and composers because it musically nourished the burgeoning musically literate middle class. For this reason, few composers seem to have regarded piano-duet arrangements as practical necessities inferior to the large-ensemble versions of the same works, as is typical today. Rather, most devoted considerable time and energy to producing (or arranging for the production of) high-quality arrangements that would represent their music in the best possible light, especially in the case of major compositions.

Arrangements for piano duet rather than piano solo also appealed in the case of large-ensemble works because the availability of four hands rather than two made it possible for composers to incorporate complex textures and wide ranges more effectively and idiomatically than if the same music were arranged for one performer. In such publications—whether original works for piano duet or arrangements—the music was typically laid out with the "*primo*" and "*secondo*" parts on facing pages so that the player who covered the material in the upper registers would sit to the right and the one who covered the material in the lower registers on the left. Each pair of facing pages would contain the same number of measures in both parts, and the *primo* player would have responsibility for turning the pages. In choral works that required both a **conductor** and an accompanist (cantatas, oratorios, operas, and the like), the conductor would typically perform either the *primo* or *secondo* part during the **overture** or **prelude** (as applicable) and then would conduct from the fore of the ensemble during the remainder of the work while the other pianist continued accompanying.

The repertoire of compositions for two pianos is smaller than that for two players at one keyboard because even the booming piano culture of the long 19th century provided for only one piano in most homes. In the age of the **virtuoso**, a medium that provided for two pianists at two pianos offered a different set of musical rewards, not least of all because the range of each pianist was not limited as it was in works for two players at one piano. Since these works were often as not intended for public performance, they typically are less intimate in style and more inclined to technical display. The list of composers who wrote for the medium includes **William Sterndale Bennett**, Brahms, **Max Bruch**, **Ferruccio Busoni**, Chabrier, Chaminade, Chopin, Cui, Czerny, Debussy, **Aleksandr Glazunov**, Grieg, Mendelssohn, Moscheles, Mozart, Rachmaninoff, Raff, Reger, Reinecke, Rubenstein, Saint-Saëns, Robert Schumann, and **Bedřich Smetana**, among others. [JMC]
See also PRINTING AND PUBLISHING OF MUSIC.

PLEYEL. Austro-French firm and family of composers, instrument makers, performers, publishers, and teachers. It was founded in 1795, when the respected **opera** composer and **conductor** Ignace (Ignaz) Joseph Pleyel (1757–1831), former Kapellmeister in the Strasbourg Cathedral, opened a music shop and publishing house in Paris named the *Maison Pleyel* (Pleyel House). The firm's 39-year existence produced some 4,000 scores, including works by **Ludwig van Beethoven**, **Franz Joseph Haydn**, **Friedrich Kalkbrenner**, **Étienne Nicolas Méhul**, and **Gioachino Rossini**, among many others. Its series titled *Bibliothèque musicale*, launched in 1802, presented a series of works by Haydn and Beethoven in a comparatively compact format (it is often said that these were the first miniature scores, but the scores were only slightly more narrow than most scores already printed and just as tall). These scores served as important tools for facilitating French musicians' study of those Austrian composers' music and enhancing their standing in the **First French Empire**.

In 1807, the Pleyel firm entered the rapidly growing business of **piano** building, adapting many of the essential features of the English school of fortepiano construction (*see* BROADWOOD) and introducing them to the French musical public. In 1815, Ignace Pleyel's son Camille (1788–1855), an accomplished pianist, became a partner in the firm and worked energetically to expand its piano manufacture and sales. His close friend Kalkbrenner joined the firm in 1824, thus adding the visibility of a high-profile **virtuoso** (as well as financial support) to the growing roster of the firm's supporters. Kalkbrenner also introduced Camille to **Fryderyk Chopin** after the latter moved to Paris in 1831, and to the end of his life the Polish composer retained a strong affinity for Pleyel's instruments.

Meanwhile, Camille Pleyel had in February 1831 married a promising French pianist and composer, Marie Moke (1811–1875), after she broke off her engagement with the young **Hector Berlioz** during his stay in Rome. Marie and Camille Pleyel separated in 1835, and she resumed her career as a **virtuosa**, giving highly successful performances in Bonn, Dresden, Leipzig, London, St. Petersburg, Paris, and Vienna, eventually assuming a professorship at the Brussels **Conservatory**. A student of Henri Herz (1803–1888), Kalkbrenner, and **Ignaz Moscheles**, she enjoyed the esteem of most of the great composers and pianists of her day, among them **Daniel-François-Esprit Auber**, Berlioz, **Ferdinand Hiller, Franz Liszt, Felix Mendelssohn Bartholdy**, and **Clara** and **Robert Schumann**. She was the dedicatee of Chopin's op. 9 **nocturnes** (1833) and Liszt's *Réminiscences de* [**Vincenzo Bellini**'s] *Norma* (1841) as well as the latter's *Tarantelle di bravura d'après la Tarantelle de "La muette de Portici" d'Auber* (1846). [JMC]

POET'S LOVE. See DICHTERLIEBE, OP 48.

POHL, RICHARD (1826–1896). German critic of the Late Romantic Generation and intrepid proponent of the **New German School**. A native Leipziger, Pohl studied music with Ernst Ferdinand Wenzel (1808–1880). He also befriended and collaborated with **Robert Schumann** in the 1840s; their projects included the choral-orchestral **ballad** *Des Sängers Fluch* (The Singer's Curse, Op. 139, 1852, publ. posth. 1858) and a planned but uncomposed **oratorio**, *Luther*. Pohl moved to Dresden in 1852 and wrote and published on music; later, he moved to Weimar and finally to Baden-Baden. Much of his work appeared in **Franz Brendel**'s *Neue Zeitschrift für Musik*, which he eventually helped edit. In his writings, Pohl was an especially ardent advocate of **Hector Berlioz, Franz Liszt**, and **Richard Wagner**. Among his most notable books is a German translation (1864) of Berlioz's collected prose and a posthumously published *Richard Wiegand*, a novelized, fictionalized treatment of Wagner. [RK]

POLONAISE. (Fr., "Polish"; Ger., Polonäise; It., polacca.) In the strict sense, a festive processional couples' dance of Polish origin with either instrumental or accompanied vocal music; more broadly during the **long 19th century**, an instrumental work that emulates the musical features of that dance: moderate tempo; triple meter; phrases starting on or in the downbeat; short, repetitive rhythmic motives; and harmonic movement on the third beat of each measure.

Many titular polonaises of the 18th and 19th centuries—such as those of **Johann Sebastian Bach, Ludwig van Beethoven, Johann Nepomuk Hummel, Wolfgang Amadeus Mozart, Franz Schubert**, and **Carl Maria von Weber**—match these criteria but employ melodic and harmonic language that is not idiomatically Polish. Prince Michał Kleofas Ogiński (1765–1833), a Polish composer who was by profession a diplomat and politician, enhanced the folk-like character of the genre in 20 polonaises for **piano** or **piano duet**, but a genuine reinfusion of national character into the polonaise as a genre occurred only with **Fryderyk Chopin**, whose 13 polonaises are iconic in the genre's history. Other 19th-century composers who wrote in the post-Chopin tradition include **Anatoly Arensky, Carl Czerny, Ferdinand David, Antonín Dvořák, Stephen Heller, Ferdinand Hiller, Franz Liszt, Anatoly Lyadov, Modest Mussorgsky, Ignacy Paderewski, Carl Reinecke, Nikolay Rimsky-Korsakov, Anton Rubinstein, Robert Schumann, Aleksandr Scriabin**, and **Aleksey Verstovsky**, among a great many others. [JMC]

See also FOLK SONG; NATIONALISM, ROMANTIC NATIONALISM.

PONCHIELLI, AMILCARE (1834–1886). Italian composer, organist, and teacher of the Late Romantic Generation, after **Giuseppe Verdi** the most important Italian composer of opera before the emergence of the *verismo* style and the so-called *giovane scuola* (young school) represented by **Ruggero Leoncavallo, Pietro Mascagni**, and **Giacomo Puccini**. Ponchielli was raised in a village near Cremona, entered the Milan **Conservatory** in 1843, and remained there to 1854. His exceptional talent and invention were recognized, but he had difficulty obtaining anything more than local success for many years. He was appointed director of the Piacenza National Guard Band in 1861. When his Piacenza contract expired, he returned in 1864 to Cremona, continuing to work as local bandmaster throughout the 1860s—a post whose civic importance was enhanced by the impending unification of the Italian lands at the end of the decade (*see* NATIONALISM; RISORGIMENTO). He applied for the position of professor of composition at the Milan Conservatory, his alma mater, in 1870 and was adjudicated the winner—but the post went instead to composer/**conductor** Franco Faccio (1840–1891).

Ponchielli's career finally reached a turning point in 1872, when the revised version of his earlier opera *I promessi sposi* (The Betrothed, orig. 1856) achieved an unexpected success (partly due to growing anti-**Wagnerian** sentiment) in its performance in Milan's Teatro Dal Verme, winning him the support of the influential music publisher **Ricordi**. His **ballet** *Le due gemelle* (The Twin Sisters, 1873) and his next opera (*I Lituani* [The Lithuanians, 1874]) were also successful, and his career reached a new peak when his new opera *La gioconda* (The Happy Woman, on a libretto by **Arrigo Boito** after **Victor Hugo**'s *Angelo, tyran de Padoue* [Angelo, Tyrant of Padua, 1835]) was performed at La Scala in 1876. His fame continued to grow on the basis primarily of that work (though his following operas were also moderate successes), and in 1880 he was hired as professor of composition at the Milan Conservatory, a position he had won but been denied a decade earlier. In 1881 he assumed the additional post of organist at the Basilica di Santa Maria Maggiore in Bergamo, holding this and the position at the Conservatory until his sudden death from pneumonia in January 1886.

La Giaconda established Ponchielli as an international figure, with performances as far away as London and New York in 1883 and St. Petersburg in 1884. It remains his only work that has retained a regular place in the repertoire, and excerpts such as the "Dance of the Hours," the tenor aria "Cielo e mar," and the soprano *scena* "Suicido!" are among the finer moments in Italian opera of the 1870s. He also composed nine other operas, three surviving **ballets**, five secular **cantatas**, much sacred music, and about 20 pieces of vocal **chamber music**. His instrumental compositions include over 200 works for wind band and the earliest known **concerto** for euphonium (1872), plus several works for **orchestra**, much music for **piano** and **piano duet**, and two smaller instrumental chamber works (a *capriccio* for violin and piano and an *Elegia* for oboe and piano, both undated). The roster of Ponchielli's students includes such notables as Mascagni and Puccini. [JMC]

POSSE, POSSE MIT GESANG. (Ger., "farce" or "farce with singing.") A German-language staged farce with **songs**. The term is used often (but not always) to refer specifically to comic musical theater productions with fewer songs than *Singspiel*, but there is overlap between the terms. Vienna was an important center for the *Posse*, which flourished in the Volkstheater, Theater an der Wien, Theater in der Josefstadt, Theater in der Leopoldstadt, and other venues. Two significant Viennese *Posse* composers of the Early Romantic Generation were Ferdinand Kauer (1751–1831) and Wenzel Müller (1759–1839). Among Kauer's contributions are his music for Ferdinand Kringsteiner's *Die Kreuzerkomödie* (The *Kreuzer* Comedy, 1805) and Josef Alois Gleich's *Die Musikanten am hohen Markt* (The Musicians at the [Viennese] *Hoher Markt*, 1815). Notable examples by Wenzel Müller include his music for Ferdinand Raimund's *Der Barometermacher auf der Zauberinsel* (The Barometer-Maker on the Magic Island, 1823) and Gleich's *Herr Josef und Frau Baberl* (1826). Adolf Müller Sr. (1801–1886, unrelated to Wenzel) wrote songs for an important *Posse* by Johann Nepomuk Nestroy, *Der böse Geist Lumpazivagabundus, oder Das liederliche Kleeblatt* (The Evil Spirit Lumpazivagabundus; or, The Licentious Shamrock, 1833). In the 1840s, **Franz von Suppé** contributed to a series of Viennese *Possen* (pl.), including Josef Schick's *Die Hammerschmiedin aus Steiermark, oder Folgen einer Landpartie* (The Steiermark Hammersmith; or, An Outing's Consequences, 1842) and Alois Berla's *Der Dumme hat's Glück, oder Tolle Streiche* (The Fool Is Lucky; or, Great Pranks, 1850). [RK]

POTTER, (PHILIP) CIPRIANI (HAMBLY) |HAMBLEY| (1792–1871). English pianist, **conductor**, and composer of the Early Romantic Generation, remembered especially for his **symphonies**. In his youth, he studied **piano** with Thomas Attwood (1783–1856), William Crotch (1775–1847), and Joseph Wölfl (1773–1812). Potter, under Wölfl's influence, was taken with the music of **Johann Sebastian Bach**, whose *Well-Tempered Clavier* he not only mastered but also answered with his own *Studies in All the Major and Minor Keys* for piano (Op. 19, 1826). His relationship with the Philharmonic Society of London began in 1816, both as a pianist and as a composer. In 1817, Potter traveled to Vienna and studied briefly with **Ludwig van Beethoven**—whom he impressed—and Aloys Förster (1748–1823); his published accounts of his experiences with Beethoven (printed in the *Musical World* in 1836) were important in tempering negative or overblown notions of the old composer's turbulent personality. When the Royal Academy of Music was founded in 1822, Potter was appointed as its first piano teacher; he was principal there from 1832 to 1859.

Most of Potter's compositions date from between 1816 and 1837; among them are numerous piano works, a few **songs**, a horn **sonata**, a **string quartet** and various other instrumental **chamber** works, several **overtures**, at least three piano **concertos** and other solo works with **orchestral** accompaniment, and nine extant symphonies (there seem to have been more). Potter's career features numerous highlights: he conducted the English posthumous revival (1848) of **Felix Mendelssohn Bartholdy**'s A-major Symphony ("Italian," MWV N16/Op. posth. 90), and in 1855 **Richard Wagner** conducted his Symphony No. 10 and complimented him. [RK]

PRELUDE (1). (from Lat. *praeludere*, "to play beforehand"; Fr., prélude; Ger., Präludium; It., Sp., preludio.) During the **long 19th century**, either an instrumental work that prefaces or introduces a consequent complementary work, often in a free style (i.e., either improvisatory style or only loosely/sporadically contrapuntal in texture), or one that is autonomous or freestanding. At the turn of the 19th century the former application predominated; this was passed down to the Romantics most famously through the preludes of the two volumes of **Johann Sebastian Bach**'s *Well-Tempered Klavier* (BWV 846–69, 870–83; *see* BACH REVIVAL) as well as through a continuing tradition that is less well known today, represented in collections by composers such as J. G. Albrechtsberger (1736–1809; 1781), Charles Burney

(1726–1814; 1787), Ludwig Berger (1777–1839; 1821), and Christian Friedrich Ruppe (1753–1826; 1819), among others. (**Wolfgang Amadeus Mozart**'s Prelude and Fugue in C Major, K. 394/383a, 1782, fits into this tradition, but because it was first published only in the second half of the 19th century, it did not shape the Romantics' view of the genre.)

During the long 19th century, numerous composers contributed to this tradition of "attached" preludes, most important among them **Johannes Brahms, George Chadwick, Carl Czerny, Aleksandr Glazunov, Johann Nepomuk Hummel, Franz Liszt, Felix Mendelssohn Bartholdy, Giacomo Puccini** (for **string quartet**), **Max Reger, Anton Rubinstein, Camille Saint-Saëns**, and **Clara Schumann**. Almost all such preludes are for piano or organ. From Mendelssohn's first collection of preludes and fugues (MWV SD14/Op. 35, 1837) onward, these collections increasingly exaggerated the contrast between "free" and "strict" styles, employing conspicuously contemporary, predominantly homophonic idioms in the preludes and angular, severe, often densely contrapuntal and chromatic ones in the fugues. Ferdinand Ries's (1784–1838) *40 Preludes* (Op. 60, 1815) were intended "to serve as introductions to all sorts of [consequent] movements," and **Ignaz Moscheles**'s *50 Preludes* (Op. 73, 1832) were designated as "preludes in the major and minor keys, intended as short introductions to any movement and as preparatory exercises to [Moscheles's own] studies for the piano forte [Op. 70, 1825–26]".

The second (autonomous) variety of prelude is essentially the province of the 19th century and beyond. This variety, which ranges from diminutive miniatures seemingly improvised on fragmentary ideas to complicated, dramatic, and lengthy works, may best be considered an outgrowth of earlier preludes (e.g., **chorale** preludes) that were prefatory not explicitly to other music but to a service or an event. The absence of a complement or consequent evidently raised issues of structural and stylistic self-sufficiency in these compositions. Many are highly structured, and some are explicitly characteristic or **programmatic** in nature. Some were apparently intended to be performed as **cycles**—with the collection as published achieving a paradoxical completion by either creating a cycle of preludes prefacing preludes or serving as a heterogeneous collection from which smaller, more homogeneous cycles could be extracted and presented as a coherent whole. Some were explicitly didactic in nature. The paradigmatic example of this species is the cycle of 24 preludes published in 1839 as **Fryderyk Chopin**'s opus 28 (CT 166–89), but it was by no means the first. Other freestanding preludes and prelude cycles were submitted by composers including **Charles-Valentin Alkan, César Cui, Carl Czerny, Claude Debussy, Anton Diabelli, Gabriel Fauré, César Franck, Stephen Heller, Fanny Hensel, Adolf von Henselt, Johann Nepomuk Hummel, Friedrich Kalkbrenner, Anatoly Lyadov, William Mason**, Mendelssohn, **Serge Rachmaninoff, Josef**

Rheinberger, Anton Rubinstein, Aleksandr Scriabin, Simon Sechter, and Charles Villiers Stanford, among a great many others. Ludwig van Beethoven composed a Prelude in D Minor for string quintet (Hess 40, 1817; first publ. 1955). [JMC]

PRELUDE (2). (from Lat. *praeludere*, "to play beforehand"; Fr., prélude; Ger., Einleitung, Preambel, Vorspiel; It., Sp., preludio.) An instrumental composition intended to open an act or part of an oratorio, opera, or other larger musical work (usually a staged musical drama such as a ballet or incidental music), functionally distinct from the dramatic overture in that it elides directly into the dramatic action rather than coming to a full close before the drama ensues. Like overtures of the early 19th century, preludes often adumbrate the ensuing drama by drawing on themes, motives, or symbolic ideas from it. Preludes are often shorter than full-fledged overtures, and they rarely employ sonata form or any other sort of autonomous absolute musical structure. In this sense, preludes were frequently used by Vincenzo Bellini, Gaetano Donizetti, Giuseppe Verdi, and other Italian composers of the Romantic Generation to open their Italian operas (and French versions thereof). The prelude (*Einleitung* [Introduction]) to Felix Mendelssohn Bartholdy's *Elijah* (MWV A25/Op. 70, 1845–1847) is unusual in that it opens with the "curse" motive (*see* LEITMOTIV) and introduces the dramatic action by means of Elijah's pronouncement of the curse, then unfolds as the first element of dramatic action, programmatically depicting the worsening plight of the Israelites, and leads directly into their plea for help (*see* PROGRAM MUSIC): it is the first term of the dramatic action. A similar strategy is employed by Richard Wagner in all his operas of *The Ring of the Nibelung* (WWV 86A–D, 1853–1874), *Tristan und Isolde* (WWV 90, 1857–1859), *Die Meistersinger* (WWV 96, 1861–1865), and *Parsifal* (WWV 111, 1878–1881), although Wagner and others also penned musically closed versions of the preludes (*Vorspiele*) to the latter three works for use as independent compositions. With the exception of ballets, operettas, and oratorios, most staged musical dramas of the second half of the 19th century used preludes rather than overtures. [JMC]

LES PRÉLUDES, LW G3. (Fr., "The Preludes.") Symphonic poem "after Lamartine" by Franz Liszt. It was conceived and originally composed as the orchestral overture to a four-movement composition for *Männerchor* and piano on a text by Joseph Antoine Autran (1813–1877) titled *Les quatre éléments* (The Four Elements, LW L2, 1844–1848; perf. 1845, still unpublished). It was first orchestrated in 1848 by August Conradi, a copyist and assistant to Liszt, then reorchestrated by Joachim Raff in 1849. Liszt himself revised and reorchestrated the work in 1852–1854, retitling it *Les Pré-*

ludes and prefacing it with Alphonse de Lamartine's (1790–1869) poem of the same name around 1853. Liszt conducted the premiere in Weimar on 23 February 1854, and the work was published by **Breitkopf & Härtel** in an arrangement for **piano duet** (two pianos, two players) in 1855, followed by the full score in 1856. Liszt also created a piano-duet arrangement for two players at one keyboard and published this in 1857. He reused some of the work's thematic material in the song *Le vieux vagabond* (The Old Vagabond, LW N44, 1848) and in the second version of the solo-piano **etude** titled "Ab irato" (LW A63b, 1852), both of which were published before he decided to publish the symphonic poem.

Les Préludes is by far the most popular of Liszt's symphonic poems, well known not only for its application of the technique of **thematic transformation** within the context of a **sonata form** but also for its illustration of perceived aesthetic problems of **program music**: since the music was composed and performed before it was connected to Lamartine's poem, it cannot have been inspired by that seemingly programmatic text. Critics assert that it therefore cannot legitimately be considered program music. This argument, however, is specious, at least in terms of Liszt's own views on the nature of program music and programmatic titles. [JMC]

PRINTING AND PUBLISHING OF MUSIC. The aggregate process of producing multiple sets of copies of music by mechanical or (since the 1960s) photographic means (*printing*) and of disseminating music in print (*publishing*). The industrialization of society in the **long 19th century** facilitated the emergence of new technologies for printing music in greater volume, at less expense, and with more reliability than previously, and the rapid expansion of a middle-class, music-loving public, especially after the end of the Napoleonic era, generated vast markets for both public and private music. Those vast markets offered incentive for music publishers to improve technologies of printing, encourage new music from living composers, and forge partnerships with other publishers in order to reduce their own costs, maximize profits, and ensure **copyright**. The financial aspect of this situation was (and is) critically important, for the complexity of musical notation requires more highly skilled and specially trained printers and proofreaders than are needed for verbal texts; the complex network of symbols employed in musical notation means that printed music takes much more ink and space (i.e., more paper made from more wood from more trees) than printed words, and the increased amount of paper tends to require stronger or heavier bindings. In order to supply the rapidly expanding market and maintain profits, music printers and publishers of the long 19th century were thus continually compelled to find faster, more reliable, and less costly means of disseminating musical print than those that already existed.

Printing. At the beginning of the long 19th century, there were two princi-pal techniques for printing music, to which a third technique was added early in the 19th century. In the oldest of these techniques, *typesetting*, the com-poser provided an **autograph, holograph,** or other manuscript to the pub-lisher, who organized, funded, and directed the publication process. A *type-setter* or *compositor* then planned the page layout of the music, marking the manuscript to show page breaks and so on; a good typesetter knew how to balance the space efficiency and legibility of music, requiring as little paper as possible for the edition as a whole without compromising the legibility by using fonts or staves that were too small or creating a cluttered appearance by including too much information on each page. The typesetter then assembled the entire set of symbols for each page of music (staff lines, musical notes, dynamics and articulations, and, when applicable, words) onto a *galley*, which was secured by cord and set aside. There was one galley for each page of the edition (title pages, prefatory material, and music). Once all the galleys had been created, they were mounted onto the *press*, which then inked them and transferred the images onto sheets of paper. Typically, these were re-viewed for errors first by in-house personnel of the printer, then, after any obvious corrections had been made, by the composer. Any corrections or changes made by the composer were then made (usually requiring new type-setting on the affected portions of the galleys), and the revised galleys were then mounted to a press and printed page by page. The printed pages were then ordered, assembled, stitched together (by hand early in the 19th century, mechanically by the end of the century), and either sewn or glued into the *binding.*

Because 19th-century **copyright** law provided protection only if a work was published simultaneously in at least two countries, the process of pro-ducing galleys and printing had to occur in at least two countries—some-times in different branches of a single printing firm, sometimes by means of carefully coordinated scheduling and sharing of preparatory materials (either manuscripts or galleys) among different publishers who had entered into an agreement to collaborate (a process that required transporting galleys or the manuscripts from which galleys were to be generated across many miles, e.g., from Vienna to Paris). Sometimes composers negotiated the selection of second and third publishers; sometimes the selection and negotiation was taken care of by the primary publisher. Once those finished products were complete, they would be *published* and deposited in any legally required national libraries or archives on a set date that had been agreed upon by the publishers and the composer.

The second technique for printing music common in the early 19th centu-ry, *engraving*, was appropriated from techniques already used by mapmakers and other graphic fields already in the 17th century. The early stages of the process of engraving were more streamlined than those of printing, and the product was more flexible and capable of nuance and visually attractive layouts than were the mechanized products of typesetting. The downsides of engraving were that it perpetuated the susceptibility to scribal error that had always plagued manuscript dissemination of music and that engraving was itself a highly skilled activity—one whose practitioners were highly trained and therefore costly. In this process, once the printer had received the manuscript that would be used as the basis for the edition, the engraver would mark it up as he planned the layout of the edition. This accomplished, he would use a fine *burin* to engrave the music onto copper plates—*working in mirror image*, from right to left, and using punches for recurrent images such as clefs. Once the copper plates had been engraved, they were etched with weak acid, blotted, and then inked and mounted to presses. Thereafter, the process proceeds as with typesetting, except that the incidence of errors in the proofs—and therefore the possibility of errors slipping into the final product undetected as well as the cost of entering corrections—tends to be higher with engraving because the engraver must work in mirror image.

The third technique used in the 19th century, *lithography*, was invented in 1796 by the German actor and playwright Alois Senefelder (1771–1834). Lithography is based on the simple principle that water and oil repel each other. In lithography, a copyist or the composer him- or herself wrote the music on waxy paper using a specially prepared chemical ink. Once the ink was dry, the *verso* of each page was sponged with a weak acid and blotted to remove any superfluous liquid. The sheet was then laid face down onto a polished stone, which was then run through a press. The resulting mirror-image relief of the music manuscript could then be inked and pressed as usual. This process of *transfer* or *offset lithography* originally entailed producing the plates for pressing from stone, but by the mid-1820s, it had become more common to use cheap, soft metals, such as tin. Because clean correction of errors (i.e., corrections that do not smudge or otherwise damage the physical appearance of the final product) is more difficult in lithography than in typesetting and engraving, lithography considerably increased pressure on the scribe to produce a perfect visual image of the final product at the outset and limited composers' ability to correct mistakes or change their music once the process had begun. Nevertheless, the streamlined production method proved cost effective. Offset printing derived from lithographic methods forms the foundation of most noncomputerized form of printing used by presses today. It is often claimed that **Carl Maria von Weber** prepared the lithographic plates for the first edition of his Six Variations on an Original Theme (J. 7/Op. 2, 1800). This claim is false (the lithography was done by Theobald Senefelder, brother of Alois), but the Weber family, recognizing the new technique's potential for cutting costs and simplifying the process of printing, developed its own (ultimately unrealized) plans for starting a new lithographic firm. More famously, **Richard Wagner** himself lithographed the full score of *Tannhäuser* (WWV 70) in 1845.

Publishing. As noted above, during the long 19th-century, music publishers coordinated the entire dissemination of music in print, first mediating between composers and printers and then mediating between printers and the public; along the way, publishers had to consider the perspectives of the composer (and the need to keep successful composers happy with their products and the financial results so that they would supply more music), the public (which would not purchase the products of publishers' work if they were too expensive), and—because of 19th-century copyright law—the needs of other publishers who were, in principle, their competition but with whom they had to collaborate in order to secure copyright. Then as now, therefore, publishers tended to be concentrated in specific cities where other publishers as well as skilled printers were located, and individual printers frequently worked with more than one publisher. The most important cities for music publishing in the long 19th century were Amsterdam, London, Paris, and (after about 1780) Vienna.

For these reasons, many 19th-century music publishers also partnered with music stores. These stores—counterparts to the "distributors" now common in music publication—typically carried the products of one or a few particular publishers, which were in turn affiliated with certain composers: for example, a Parisian pianist interested in procuring a new work by **Fryderyk Chopin** would typically shop for such a work in a store that was affiliated with one of his preferred French publishers (e.g., Maurice Schlesinger), while one looking for a score by **Felix Mendelssohn Bartholdy** would search in a music store affiliated with Simon Richault. A London pianist looking for publications of music by those composers might look in stores affiliated with Wessel & Co. and **Ewer & Co.**, while German musicians would look in stores affiliated with **Breitkopf & Härtel**.

One final consideration that played an important part in the 19th century but is not immediately obvious to modern musicians is the importance of the *dedications* in publications of music. In today's protocols, dedications are usually inside-the-book public acknowledgments of private relationships or respects; rarely do they say much about the content or significance of the work being published. In the 19th and early 20th centuries, however, the choice of the dedicatee was a public statement about the work being published and its composer, and dedications were prominently displayed on the title pages of published music. Professional protocols and, in many places, law dictated that the composer would request the intended dedicatee's permission to publicly dedicate the work to him or her and could publish that dedication only after receiving permission; the dedicatee was chosen because of some substantive and professional (rather than private and personal) consideration that made him or her an appropriate dedicatee. For example, Chopin dedicated his Op. 10 and Op. 25 Études (CT 14–25 and 26–37) to the countess Marie d'Agoult, Franz Liszt's mistress, whose prominence in the salon milieu in which those works flourished and affiliation with Liszt made the dedication germane; Robert Schumann dedicated his C-major Fantasy (Op. 17, 1839) to Liszt; and Liszt dedicated his Études d'exécution transcendante d'après Paganini (LW A52, 1840) to the virtuosa Clara Schumann, his Études d'exécution transcendante (LW 172, 1852) to the master technician Carl Czerny, and his B-minor Sonata (LW 179, 1854) to Robert Schumann. The dedication itself thus functioned as one individual's endorsement of the work and its composer, and it foregrounded that substantive, professional communication in a few words for potential purchasers of the published work. Dedications thus played integral roles in the publication process.

These developments coexisted and varied significantly from country to country and firm to firm, and most have been outmoded since the late 1960s. Still, they strongly affected the sociology and in some ways the aesthetics of music over the course of the long 19th century. In Europe, they coincided with a significant reduction in the authority of the aristocracy, making it easier for independent music-publishing firms to commission and/or disseminate both new compositions and music of earlier eras (see BACH REVIVAL; HISTORICISM) and for composers to broaden their reputations by writing for the market of the middle-class music-loving public rather than for church and state (although these continued to be important patrons of music). But while these effects are generally regarded as beneficial, they also had their downsides—for example, raising complex new issues of intellectual ownership, copyright, and performance right and reducing composers' authority to revise and rework their compositions on an ongoing basis in response to, for example, changing circumstances or to developments or variations in technologies of musical instruments. Finally, because musical performance was (and is) an act in which performers interpret complex and highly nuanced musical symbols into sound by means of established techniques with which composers are more or less familiar, manuscript musical notation was capable of providing a level of nuanced information to performers that exceeded the capacities of even the most flexible and sophisticated technologies of music printing in the long 19th century. Because of these changes in the efficiency of symbolic communication between composers and performers, the growth of music publishing indirectly but substantially affected systems of musical notation during the long 19th century. [JMC]

See also ARTARIA; BREITKOPF & HÄRTEL; COMPOSITIONAL PROCESS, CREATIVE PROCESS; COPYRIGHT AND PERFORMANCE RIGHT; EDITING AND EDITIONS; EWER; NOVELLO; RICORDI; SIMROCK.

PRIX DE ROME (PARIS). (Fr., "Rome Prize.") In music, the first contest for musical composition. It was established in 1803 and awarded by the Académie des Beaux Arts (Paris) until 1968, suspended only during the two world wars. In the history of music, it is significant because it afforded music an artistic status similar to that of architecture, painting, and sculpture (for which the Académie had offered prizes since its founding in 1795).

The *Prix de Rome* competition was organized into two stages. The first emphasized the science of musical composition, requiring contestants to demonstrate proficiency in counterpoint and harmony. Contestants who passed this first stage proceeded to a second phase that, in principle, placed greater emphasis on artistry and invention: the contestants were sequestered and required to set a given text to music in the form of a **cantata** or "scène lyrique." A preliminary verdict was rendered by the judges from the music professorate, and the final decision was made through a vote of all members of the Académie. In some years, no one won the prize, while other years saw joint winners. From the outset, laureates were required to spend two years at the residence of the Institut National de France in Rome (the Villa Medici) and were awarded a stipend and support for the performance of their works plus military deferments and subventions for travel and cultural activities. After 1849, the rules were modified so that winners also spent time in the German lands and elsewhere in France.

Because the Prix de Rome was awarded by Académie members who were appointed for life and elected by the current membership, its standard tended to favor conservative rather than modern or innovative compositions; indeed, some remarkable composers were unsuccessful in their bids to win it (e.g., **Camille Saint-Saëns** and Maurice Ravel), and others won it only after several attempts (most famously **Hector Berlioz** and **Claude Debussy**), having first been eclipsed by other composers who are today forgotten. Nevertheless, the roster of its first- and second-prize winners includes some of the most important names in French music of the 19th and 20th centuries, among them **Adolphe Adam** (1825), Berlioz (1830), **Georges Bizet** (1857), Lili Boulanger (1913), Nadia Boulanger (1909), Debussy (1884), Marcel Dupré (1914), **François-Joseph Fétis** (1807), **Charles Gounod** (1839), **Fromenthal Halévy** (1819), **Jules Massenet** (1863), **Étienne-Nicolas Méhul** (1809), and **Ambroise Thomas** (1832). [JMC]

PRODIGY. (from Lat. prodigium, "prophetic sign"; Fr., prodigé; Ger., Wunderkind; It., prodigio.) In psychology, a child who demonstrates adult professional proficiency in one or more areas of endeavor before the age of 10. In music the term is used rather more loosely, usually denoting any musician who demonstrates exceptional (but not necessarily adult professional) skill at an early age (but not necessarily before the age of 10). The loose application of the term in music is sometimes justified when applied to performers—**Charles-Valentin Alkan**, Samuel Barber, Victor Borge, Sara Chang, Jacqueline Du Pré, **Johann Nepomuk Hummel**, and **Josef Rheinberger** were true prodigies as performers—but only rarely to composers, probably because ability as a composer must be preceded by ability to read and write music, skills that even the greatest musical geniuses only rarely acquire before the age of four or five, leaving only five years to reach adult professional proficiency in composition before the age of 10 (at which point they may qualify as exceptional or gifted but not true prodigies). By these criteria, other musicians frequently described as prodigy composers (such as **Ludwig van Beethoven, Georges Bizet, Fanny Hensel, Felix Mendelssohn Bartholdy**, and **Wolfgang Amadeus Mozart**) may well have been gifted or exceptional, but since their works composed before they were 10 do not measure up to adult professional standards, they were not true prodigies.

A more realistic application of the psychological concept of the prodigy within the time constraints that govern development in creating rather than performing music would subject musical giftedness to the general criteria characteristic of prodigies in other fields. These criteria, which operate in aggregate rather than individually, may be summarized as follows. First, the prodigy's development is asynchronous, dyssynchronous, and uneven: compositional prodigies are ahead of other children of his or her same age as composers but may well lag behind them in other areas of development, and their development proceeds in spurts and plateaus rather than at a steady pace. Second, prodigies tend to set significant restraints and self-imposed boundaries for themselves, effectively creating obstacles to further success so that their success will be more significant and convincing when they achieve it. Finally, prodigies' exceptional development in youth consistently produces a midlife crisis born partly of the exceptional treatment they received during their youth, partly of the burden of becoming an adult genius no longer dependent on the familial structures that were central to their youthful identities, and partly of a certain trepidation at the challenge of living up to one's youthful promise. When viewed against these criteria, some composers often casually referred to as prodigies actually do warrant the term (Hensel, Mendelssohn, and Mozart), while others (Beethoven, Bizet, and, as a composer, Hummel) do not. [JMC]

PROGRAM (PROGRAMMATIC) MUSIC. (Fr., musique à programme; Ger., Programmusik.) Instrumental music that is inspired by and/or attempts to portray, without recourse to sung or spoken words, extramusical events, ideas, images, or subjects. In today's usage, the term is often used in contradistinction to **absolute music**. Since the latter concept was not developed until the mid-19th century, however, and even then was more nuanced than today's usage typically recognizes, the dichotomy between absolute and program music should be understood as anachronistic with regard to most of the

long 19th century and thus also immaterial to the ways in which composers, performers, and audiences of the long 19th century created, interpreted, and understood such music.

During the long 19th century, it was common to distinguish between two categories of program music. In the century's early years, programmatic works usually strove to capture, reflect, or invoke in tones the general character or essence of some extramusical subject; such compositions were typically referred to as *characteristic music*, a designation that continued to be used throughout the long 19th century but became less common during the period after around 1850. Increasingly common after the mid-1820s were works that strove to depict not only the character or essence of an extramusical subject but also a specific series of events or ideas; these works gave rise to the term *program music* because their musical content and form was determined by a plan or scheme (program) of a not intrinsically musical nature.

The long 19th century's fascination with such **narrative** representations of extramusical content was neither entirely new (such representations date back at least to the battle pieces of the late Renaissance) nor illogical as an extension of the concept of characteristic music: since music's inherently musical processes unfold sequentially over time, it is reasonable to assert that characteristic content can be organized to create a specific narrative sequence of events. Nevertheless, the Romantics' fascination with instrumental music's ability to portray the extramusical by means of tones and **paratextual** materials alone drew new attention during the long 19th century because the expansiveness of instrumental music possessed of "poetic" content exceeded anything submitted previously, because it was seen in many quarters as posing a conflict between musical and extramusical form, and because music's engagement with such poetic content was submitted not as a novelty or a compositional option but as a criterion for aesthetic legitimacy (*see* NEW GERMAN SCHOOL). Over the course of the long 19th century, increasing numbers of composers and other musicians asserted that traditional structural process such as **sonata form** and rondo form, as intrinsically musical and generally a priori constructs, were ill suited to developing narratives that did not themselves employ elements such as recapitulations and other essential gestures of conventional instrumental music. In this view, the musical form of a composition must not determine the form of the extramusical content but rather be determined by it.

The challenge of meeting such aesthetic challenges and developing such ideas further spawned a number of new genres that grappled either implicitly or explicitly with the concept of characteristic and program music during the long 19th century. The most expansive such genre was that of the **program symphony** or *characteristic symphony*, represented in the 18th century by Carl Ditters von Dittersdorf's (1739–1799) *Trois simphonies, exprimant trois* *métamorphoses d'Ovide* (Three Symphonies Which Express Three of Ovid's *Metamorphoses*, 1791) and in the long 19th century most famously by **Ludwig van Beethoven**'s Sixth **("Pastoral") Symphony** (Op. 68, 1808, publ. 1809), **Hector Berlioz**'s *Episode in the Life of an Artist* (H. 48/Op. 14a, comp. 1830, publ. 1834), and **Franz Liszt**'s *"Faust" Symphony* (LW G12, 1857, rev. 1861). Beethoven's Op. 68 was designated a *sinfonia caratteristica*, and the first edition of the orchestral parts was provided with the subtitle "Erinnerung an das Landleben" (Recollection of Country Life) with the parenthetical disclaimer "mehr Ausdruck der Empfindung als Malerey" (More an Expression of Feeling than [Tone-]Painting). Nevertheless, the fact that each of its five movements is assigned a specific characteristic association and these movements were played in succession (the last three without pause) implicitly generated a narrative progression of characteristic events for the symphony as a whole such that it served as an obvious conceptual starting point for Berlioz's *Episode* (likewise in five movements). Berlioz's work amplifies considerably the detail of the paratextual descriptors—indeed, Berlioz required that the verbal program be distributed at every performance and in it described the programmatic significance of virtually every major musical event.

Other important Romantic species of program music were less expansive in scope but not in aesthetic challenges. At the opposite end of the spectrum from the century's sprawling program symphonies were the diminutive *Lieder ohne Worte* (Songs without Words) first cultivated by **Fanny Hensel**, **Felix Mendelssohn Bartholdy**, and their circle in the 1820s—miniatures whose generic designation implied at least vestigial extramusical inspiration (what, after all, was a **song** in the long 19th century if not a composition born of words?) and whose stylistic emulation of vocal **chamber music** led many contemporaries to underlay hypothetical texts or supply fanciful titles that supposedly expressed the "true meaning" that had inspired the music to begin with. In between these two extremes are other genres, such as the programmatic **concert overture** (e.g., Mendelssohn's *Midsummer Night's Dream*, MWV P3/Op. 21, 1833, or **Tchaikovsky's *1812***), **symphonic poem** (Liszt's *Les Préludes* or *Hamlet*), and **tone poem** (**Richard Strauss**'s *Don Juan* and *Don Quixote*). [JMC]

See also DEFORMATION; HANSLICK, EDUARD (1825–1904); NARRATIVE.

PROGRAM SYMPHONY *OR* CHARACTERISTIC SYMPHONY. A multimovement instrumental or mostly instrumental work that provides a descriptive or illustrative title or other **paratextual** material reflective or suggestive of a narrative or other extramusical aspect of the work. In theory, a *program* (or programmatic) *symphony* emphasizes its **narrative** (dynamic) elements, while a *characteristic symphony* offers a series of comparatively static tableaux that attempt to capture the character or essence of some extra-musical element. Thus, **Ludwig van Beethoven**'s Sixth (**"Pastoral"**) **Symphony** was designated a *sinfonia caratteristica*, while **Berlioz**'s *Episode in the Life of an Artist*, the last two movements of which seem to narrate the moment-to-moment events of a guillotining and a witches' Sabbath, was designated a "program symphony." This distinction was not always followed in practice, however, no doubt in part because any musical performance unfolds as a series of sequential events and thus resists synoptic perception. Nevertheless, the contemporary fascination with **synaesthesia**, as manifested for example in *tableaux vivants* and *tableaux mouvants*, enabled the distinction to persist.

The emergence of characteristic and program symphonies was a natural consequence of the rise of the symphony as a genre: new symphonies were created as contributions to the long-established field of **program music**. Eighteenth-century works of this sort include **Franz Joseph Haydn**'s Symphonies No. 6–8 (1761–1762, titled *Le matin, Le midi*, and *Le soir*, respectively; the fourth movement of No. 8 is titled "La tempesta" and quotes from C. W. von Gluck's [1714–1787] **opéra comique** *Le diable à quatre*, 1759) and Carl Ditters von Dittersdorf's 12 symphonies after Ovid's *Metamorphoses* (1781, three published 1791). Numerous other works were published with programmatically suggestive epithets, among them various "patriotic" characteristic symphonies published in response to the political turmoil in France in the 1790s (such as Paul Wranitzky's [1756–1808] *Grande symphonie charactéristique pour la paix avec la République Française* [Grand Characteristic Symphony for Peace with the Republic of France, 1797]).

The first lasting 19th-century contributions to the genre of the characteristic symphony were penned by Beethoven, whose Third and Sixth Symphonies (1806, 1809) bore obviously suggestive titles and whose Fifth and Ninth Symphonies (1809, 1826) conspicuously invited extramusical associations. Although these works were received skeptically in some quarters, they seem to have emboldened other composers to issue increasingly detailed programmatic works in the genre. Most important among these during the romantic generation was Berlioz, whose *Episode in the Life of an Artist: Symphonie fantastique in Five Movements* (1830–1843) and *Harold en Italie* (1834–1848) became paradigmatic for programmatic instrumental works in self-styled progressive quarters in the second half of the century (*see* NEW GERMAN SCHOOL). **Robert Schumann**'s First Symphony (Op. 38, 1841) was originally titled the *Frühlingssymphonie* ("Springtime" Symphony) and his Third the "Rhenish" Symphony (Op. 97, 1850, publ. 1851). Other significant contributions—less well known today but highly regarded and frequently performed in their day—were submitted by **Louis Spohr**, whose Symphonies Nos. 4, 6, 7, and 9 (1834, 1842, 1842, and 1853) all bore descriptive main titles and movement titles. Nor was the genre exclusively French and

German: most of the Italian **Saverio Mercadante**'s 60 symphonies (1826–1869 passim) are explicitly characteristic or programmatic, and Muzio Clementi's (1752–1832) *Great National Symphony* (1824) was highly regarded.

After 1848, some of the turf previously held by the program symphony was assumed by the **symphonic poem** and **tone poem**, genres that required less space on concert programs and were cheaper to publish but engaged many of the same aesthetic issues. Nevertheless, the post-1848 period did witness some major new program symphonies. These included, along with works by **Joachim Raff**, Karl Goldmark (1830–1915), and **Anton Rubinstein**, the *"Faust" Symphony* (LW G12, 1854–1857, rev. 1861) and *Dante Symphony* (LW G14, 1855–1856, rev. 1859) of **Franz Liszt**, the *Sinfonia domestica* (TrV 209/Op. 53, 1902–1903) and *Alpine Symphony* (TrV 233/ Op. 64, 1911–1912) of **Richard Strauss**, and the *Manfred Symphony* (Op. 58, 1885) of **Pyotor Il'yich Tchaikovsky**. Attendant to this shift in generic suppositions was a blurring of the distinctions between the symphony and other genres. This process had begun already with the introduction of a chorus in the last movement of the *Schlacht-Symphonie* (Battle symphony, 1814) of Peter von Winter and the Ninth **("Choral") Symphony** of Beethoven. Berlioz's *Harold en Italie* drew on aspects of the **concerto**, and his *Roméo et Juliette* (H. 79, 1839–1840) was designated a "dramatic symphony," while **Felix Mendelssohn Bartholdy**'s *Lobgesang* (MWV A18/Op. 52, 1839–1840), representing an integrated symphonic whole and including three full-scale symphonic movements followed by a series of choral movements, was designated a "symphony-cantata after the holy scripture." The second half of the century witnessed further such generic admixtures within works that were primarily symphonic, most importantly **Gustav Mahler**'s "Resurrection" Symphony (No. 2, 1888–1894, rev. 1903) and *Das Lied von der Erde* (The Song of the Earth, 1908–1909; publ. 1911). Significant 20th-century contributions indebted to the Romantic tradition were submitted by Corigliano, Harbison, Honegger, Messiaen, Shostakovich, Vaughan Williams, and others.

The historiography of the program symphony is complex, owing partly to its intermingling with other genres and partly to the role it came to play in the highly polemical musical world of the late 19th century. More influential in creating this fraught historiography, however, was some composers' belief that all music, an inherently subjective experience, necessarily gave voice to ideas that individual performers and listeners would interpret in their own way, *even if that music did not bear an explicitly programmatic or characteristic title*. The most significant works whose programmatic content or lack thereof is related to the former concern are the D-minor ("Reformation"), A-major ("Italian"), and A-minor ("Scottish") Symphonies of Felix Mendelssohn: the composer never published either of the former two and only privately referred to the D-minor Symphony as a "Kirchensymphonie" (church symphony), while the music of the A-major work cannot be connected to any music the composer reported having written during his Italian sojourn; indeed, the "Italian" sobriquet emerged only several years after Mendelssohn's death and probably stems more from Berlioz than from Mendelssohn himself. The A-minor Symphony, for its part, is biographically connected to Scotland only in the slow introduction to the first movement, and Mendelssohn never publicly identified the work as "Scottish" (this work, too, became geographically identified only posthumously).

If composers were occasionally reticent to provide descriptive titles because they feared those titles would become overly prescriptive, these worries were compounded by aesthetic concerns that music whose "content" was determined by ideas that were not inherently musical was mere imitation whose substance lay beyond the proper sphere of music and was thus not only ill suited to the nature of music itself but also alien to Romantic aesthetics' emphasis on the infinitely subjective. These concerns, familiar already by the first decade of the 19th century, probably underlay the unwieldy but telling disclaimer regarding the extramusical content of Beethoven's Sixth Symphony as it was presented in the first edition of the parts (1809): "Pastoral-Sinfonie/oder/Erinnerung an das Landleben/(mehr Ausdruck der Empfindung als Malerey)" (Pastoral Symphony; or, Recollection of Country Life [More an Expression of Feeling than (Tone-)Painting]). They also account for extended essays defending the practice of musical "tone painting" by Berlioz, **Adolph Bernhard Marx**, and Liszt, among others. Beethoven's Third **("Eroica") Symphony** (Op. 55) was composed with the title *Sinfonia grande/intitulata Bonaparte* and eventually published as *Sinfonia Eroica . . . composta per festeggiare il sovvenire di un grand Uomo* (Heroic Symphony . . . Composed to Celebrate the Memory of a Great Man); its second movement is written in the style of a French funeral march and may allude to one such march by **Luigi Cherubini**, and its last movement is a reworking of the finale of Beethoven's successful 1801 **ballet** *Die Geschöpfe des Prometheus*, thematically linked to the Promethean story of Bonaparte's rise to power and the liberal tendencies set in motion by the French Revolution. [JMC]

See also TOPIC.

PUCCINI, GIACOMO (ANTONIO DOMENICO MICHELE SECONDO MARIA) (1858–1924).

Italian composer of the Modern Romantic Generation, generally considered the greatest Italian composer of **opera** after **Giuseppe Verdi**. He was born into a long line of church musicians in Lucca and demonstrated his own musical talent at an early age, first studying organ and voice with an uncle, then enrolling in the Istituto Musicale Pacini (1874–1880), where he drew attention with his **motet** *Plaudite, populi* (1877) and a Credo that would later be subsumed into his *Messa a quattro* (1880). Further study at the Milan **Conservatory** (1880–1883) not only brought him into contact with the group of young intellectuals known as the *scapigliati* (a group that also included **Arrigo Boito** and composer/**conductor** Franco Faccio [1840–1891]) but also introduced him to the aesthetics of **Richard Wagner** via study with the composer and musicologist Amintore Galli (1845–1919) and enabled him to study with **Amicare Ponchielli**, newly installed in a professorship there. In the vibrant Milanese culture, he also encountered major French operas by composers including **Georges Bizet, Charles Gounod**, and **Ambroise Thomas**. Although he had reportedly recognized opera as his true métier already at a performance of Verdi's *Aida* in 1876, these encounters during his time in Milan cemented his commitment to the musical stage and provided a rich and multifaceted background that he would soon synthesize into his own distinctive style.

That synthesis was not long in coming. Puccini's absorption of the fluid harmonic movement and expansive tonal structures of Wagner's musical language is reflected in two works that he penned while still a student in Milan: a *Preludio a orchestra* (which includes a clear allusion to the end of the so-called *Liebestod* from **Tristan und Isolde**) and a *Capriccio sinfonico* that was submitted and performed in partial fulfillment of the requirements for Puccini's diploma. Faccio would perform the latter piece twice more in the following year, winning the attention of the influential Milanese critic Filippo Filippi (1830–1887). Puccini's first opera, *Le villi* (The Villages, 1883, 2nd version 1884) was initially rejected by a competition sponsored by the publisher Sonzogno but earned a commission for another opera from Sonzogno's rival, **Ricordi**, after the composer's friends arranged for its performance by subscription on 31 May 1884. The work that resulted from that commission, *Edgar* (1889; 2nd version 1892; 3rd version 1905), was only a minor success, but Ricordi recognized in the young Puccini a composer who was able to combine the emotional immediacy of *verismo* with the soaring melodies and dramatic pacing of Verdi and the expansive, fluid tonal and dramatic structures of Wagner.

Those gifts were confirmed in *Manon Lescaut*, the **libretto** of which was the painstaking work of five different authors and whose success enabled Puccini to purchase a villa on the lake at Massaciuccoli, living there until 1921. Premiered at Turin in 1893, the work was given on the London stage to great acclaim already in 1894—firmly establishing Puccini as the heir apparent to the aging Verdi. The rate of his compositional output thereafter appears slow at first glance, but the infrequency of new works is a consequence both of Puccini's laborious work on librettos and music of new compositions and of his far-flung travels to conduct his own music and of major overhaulings of works already composed for their revivals in new performances (*see* FASSUNG LETZTER HAND).

486 • PUCCINI, GIACOMO (1858–1924)

The remainder of Puccini's career may be characterized as a series of successes ranging from moderate to absolute, sullied only by his unhappy marriage and, in 1908–1910, the suicide of a servant and a widely publicized lawsuit involving his jealous wife, Elvira, whom he had married in 1904 and lived with since 1886. *La bohème* (The Bohemian Girl, 1896) was only a moderate success, but the reception of *Tosca* (comp. and publ. 1899, first perf. 1900) was immediately and wholeheartedly enthusiastic—despite (or perhaps because of) critics' protests at its celebration of violence and brutality. Audience protests (reportedly arranged by Puccini's rivals) at the premiere of *Madama Butterfly* at La Scala in 1904 failed to impede the work's success (2nd version premiered in Brescia, 1904; 3rd version, 1905; 4th version, 1906), and *La fanciulla del West* (The Golden Girl of the West, 1910) and *La rondine* (1917), while less enthusiastically received than *Tosca* and *Butterfly*, were still successful with the public if not with the critics.

Puccini then turned his attentions to a triptych of one-act operas collectively titled *Il Trittico* and written for the Metropolitan Opera, New York, and premiered there in 1918: *Il tabarro* (The Cloak), *Suor Angelica* (Sister Angelica), and *Gianni Schicchi*. His final opera, the **exoticist** *Turandot*, left incomplete at the composer's death, returned to the expansive structures synthesizing the hyperemotionalism of *verismo* with the sure dramatic pacing of Verdi and the symphonic breadth of Wagner. At the suggestion of Arturo Toscanini, contemporary composer Franco Alfano (1875–1954) wrote an ending based on the composer's notes and sketches, producing the version usually given today.

Aside from his 13 operas, Puccini's output includes one unfinished **Requiem** (before 1905) and one other Mass setting, one motet, one hymn, and one **cantata**; a small body of **songs**, the 1893 *Preludio a orchestra* and *Capriccio sinfonico*, and a march for orchestra (1896); several works for **string quartet** (most notably *Crisathemi*, 1890); and a handful of pieces for **piano** solo. [JMC]

See also LEONCAVALLO, RUGGERO (1857–1919); LYRIC DRAMA; MASCAGNI, PIETRO (1863–1945).

PUSHKIN, ALEKSANDR SERGEYEVICH (1799–1837). Russian poet, playwright, novelist, and short-story writer of the Early Romantic Generation; among Russian authors, his standing is comparable to that of **William Shakespeare** in England or **Johann Wolfgang von Goethe** in Germany. He was born into the landed aristocracy, received a first-class education, and led a fast-paced social life, but his literary expression of sympathies with tsarist Russia's disenfranchised masses landed him in trouble with the government and led to his expulsion from the capital in 1820. He was given permission to return in 1826 and in 1836 founded a literary journal, *Sovremmenik* (The Contemporary), but was killed the following year in a duel over his wife's unbecomingly close attachment to a guardsman.

Pushkin's importance for Russian culture and Russian Romanticism rests primarily on two considerations. First, he is generally credited with having enriched the Russian literary language by means of highly nuanced prose and poetry and by synthesizing an artful literary style with folk themes in his writing. These aspects of his writing both imported into Russian Romanticism the celebration of fantasy, poetic subjectivity, and epic historical appropriation that were important to Romanticism generally and paved the way for Russian **nationalism** in the later 19th century. Second, Pushkin deployed these techniques in order to produce outstanding work in virtually every major genre of his time, in the process facilitating an integration of literature, folk themes, and social criticism into the other arts in Russian (including music).

Even a brief survey of the musical compositions of the **long 19th century** that were based on Pushkin's works and words reveals the extensiveness of his influence on music. He inspired music by **Anatoly Arensky, Mily Balakirev, Aleksandr Borodin, César Cui, Aleksandr Dargomïzhsky, Aleksandr Glazunov, Mikhail Glinka, Ruggero Leoncavallo, Modest Mussorgsky, Serge Rachmaninoff, Nikolay Rimsky-Korsakov, Anton Rubinstein**, Igor Stravinsky, **Franz von Suppé**, and **Pyotor Il'yich Tchaikovsky**, among many others. Particularly important among those settings are Glinka's *Ruslan and Ludmila* (1837–1842, publ. 1846; a milestone in Russian nationalist music, after Pushkin's 1830 poem); Dargomïzhsky's *Rusalka* (1848–1855, rev. 1856, after Pushkin's 1819 verse play) and *The Stone Guest* (1866–1869, completed by Cui and Rimsky-Korsakov; a setting of Pushkin's brilliantly **Byronic** retelling of the **Don Juan** legend, 1830); Mussorgsky's *Boris Godunov* (1868–1869, rev. 1871–1872, after Pushkin's 1825 historical drama); Rachmaninoff's *Aleko* (1893, after Pushkin's 1827 poem *The Gypsies*); Tchaikovsky's *Eugene Onegin* (1877–1878, publ. 1879, after Pushkin's 1831 novel-in-verse); and Leoncavallo's blend of **exoticism** and *verismo*, *Gli Zingari* (The Gypsies, 1912; after the same poem). Cui and Tchaikovsky were among the most enthusiastic composers of music based on his works, penning three and four **operas** based on Pushkin, respectively. Pushkin's *Eugene Onegin* continues to be regarded by musicians and non-Russians alike as an essential literary source of Russian Romanticism. [JMC]

QUADRILLE. A **contredanse** originally for four couples in square formation, alternatively for six or eight couples; progenitor of the American square dance. With the **waltz**, it was one of the **long 19th century**'s most popular ballroom dances. The original functional quadrilles (i.e., those that were danced rather than simply musically performed) were created by stringing together four short dances in succession, followed by a finale. In dance and performance, every quadrille was in principle unique, as the constituent dances (known as *figures*) were chosen and ordered by the participants of the occasion at hand. Over the course of the long 19th century, the figures themselves and the dancing that went with them became more complicated; often the figures were based on well-known tunes from **operas**. **Johann Strauss (I) and (II)** were prolific composers of quadrilles. Other quadrilles were published during the long 19th century by composers including **Daniel-François-Esprit Auber**, Robert Nicolas-Charles Bochsa (1789–1856), **Adrien Boieldieu, Anton Bruckner, Hans von Bülow** (on melodies from **Hector Berlioz**'s opera *Benvenuto Cellini*), **Emmanuel Chabrier, Stephen Foster, Johann Nepomuk Hummel, Louis Antoine Jullien, Anatoly Lyadov, Saverio Mercadante, Ignaz Moscheles, Jaques Offenbach, Rossini, Arthur Sullivan**, and **Carl Maria von Weber**. [JMC]

QUARTET, PIANO. (Fr., quatour pour piano, violon, alto et violoncelle [nomenclature varies acc. to scoring]; Ger., Klavierquartett.) Generally, an ensemble consisting of **piano** and three other instruments or a composition written for it; a category of instrumental **chamber music**. Typically, such works are in **sonata plan**, although the scoring was also used for arrangements of large-ensemble works such as **symphonies**. Until about 1800, works designated *piano quartet* were usually scored either for two violins, cello, and piano or for violin, viola, cello, and piano; thereafter, the latter scoring predominates. The genre moved from the periphery of the chamber repertoire toward its center (rivaling the **string quartet** and **piano trio**) during the 1780s and 1790s, especially in Vienna. **Wolfgang Amadeus Mozart**'s piano quartets K. 478 and 493 (1785 and 1786) and **Ludwig van**

Beethoven's three posthumously published piano quartets (WoO 36, comp. 1785) are but a few of the many original works and arrangements that proliferated toward the end of the 18th century. Beethoven's op. 16 wind quintet and **"Eroica" Symphony** were also published in arrangements for this scoring in 1802 and 1807, respectively.

During the late 18th century and the Early Romantic Generation, the textural predisposition of the piano quartet as a genre tended to treat the keyboard and nonkeyboard instruments in *concertante*-like opposition, with the musical substance entrusted primarily to the piano; this is the case in the above-mentioned works by Mozart and Beethoven, as in **Franz Schubert**'s posthumously published *Adagio and Rondo concertante* (D. 487, 1816) and other works by composers including J. B. Cramer (1771–1858; 1803), Jan Ladislav Dussek (1760–1812; 1804), and **Carl Maria von Weber** (1810/1811).

A new approach to the piano quartet, more centered on the equality of voices among the stringed instruments and treating the piano as a subordinate rather than leading member of the ensemble, began to emerge with the piano quartets of **Felix Mendelssohn Bartholdy** in the 1820s (MWV Q11, 13, and 17/opp. 1–3, 1822–1825). By far the most important work of this generation, however, is the piano quartet of **Robert Schumann** (Op. 47, comp. 1842, publ. 1845). The genre experienced a new flourishing in the Late Romantic Generation, notably in works by **Johannes Brahms** (opp. 25 and 26, both comp. 1861, publ. 1863), **Antonín Dvořák** (1875 and 1889), **Joachim Raff** (1876 and 1877), **Josef Rheinberger** (1870), and **Camille Saint-Saëns** (1877), and in the Modern Romantic Generation in works by **Ernest Chausson** (1898), **Gabriel Fauré** (1884 and 1887), **Vincent d'Indy** (1888), **Max Reger** (1910 and 1914), and **Richard Strauss** (1884). **Gustav Mahler** began but did not complete a Piano Quartet in A Minor (ca. 1876–1878). [JMC]

See also QUINTET.

QUARTET, STRING. (Fr., quatuor à cordes; Ger., Streichquartett; It., quartetto d'archi; Sp., quarteto de cuerdas.) Generally, an ensemble of four stringed instruments (usually two violins, a viola, and a cello) or a composition written for it; a genre of instrumental **chamber music**. During the **long 19th century**, it was the preeminent and most tradition-laden genre of instrumental chamber music. Such compositions assumed a variety of forms, from **variation** sets to independent compositions in this scoring and arrangements of other compositions for four stringed instruments. Many **concertos** of the 19th century were published with accompaniment of solo instrument(s) with string quartet (as opposed to full orchestra). Most commonly, however, the term *string quartet* is reserved for multimovement original compositions in **sonata plan**.

Two main varieties of string quartet were cultivated during the long 19th century. The earlier of these, the *quatuor brillant* or *solo quartet*, featured a **virtuosic** solo part (usually the first violin) and granted a clearly subordinate role to the other instruments, creating a kind of chamber concerto. This variety descended from the *quatuor concertant* of the mid-18th century and flourished primarily during the first half of the 19th century (most notably in some of the quartets of **Ludwig Spohr**, who was himself a virtuoso violinist). Other composers of this variety include **Friedrich Fesca**, Anton Bernhard Fürstenau (1792–1852), **Rudolfe Kreutzer**, Kaspar Kummer (1795–1870), Carl Gottlieb Reissiger (1798–1858), Ferdinand Ries (1784–1838), **Pierre Rode**, and **Andreas Romberg**.

The other variety of 19th-century string quartet, sometimes termed the "grand quartet" (Fr., *grand quatuor*; Ger., *große Streichquartett*), descended from the conversational ideal first cultivated in **Franz Joseph Haydn**'s Op. 33 quartets (Hob. III: 29–34, 1788) and the later quartets of **Wolfgang Amadeus Mozart**. Such quartets exploit the homogeneity of timbre and breadth of range of the four-stringed instruments, creating textures of an essentially egalitarian character in which all four instruments are entrusted with the musical substance. They often employ sharply chiseled themes and concentrated **motivic** development as well as dramatic, occasionally **orchestral** effects. Imitative counterpoint, which has little place in the solo quartet, appears in thematic as well as developmental and transitional spaces in grand quartets. The overall rhetoric of the grand quartet was serious, whereas that of the solo quartet was geared toward display and entertainment.

Like other genres of chamber music, the string quartet was patently cultivated as a genre for private or quasi-private performance—one intended primarily for shared experience and musical communication among the musicians rather than for performance before an audience of relatively anonymous listeners who were not themselves a part of the music making. Nevertheless, public quartet performances were not uncommon in London during the 1780s and 1790s, and the early years of the **Restoration** witnessed the occasional performance of string quartets on public concert programs and the founding of numerous professional chamber-music societies on the Continent (most notably by **Pierre Baillot** in Paris, Karl Möser [1774–1851] in Berlin, and Ignaz Schuppanzigh [1776–1830] in Vienna). Although these rethinkings of the performance venues of the quartet as a genre were intended to foster the solo quartet, they also expanded to embrace the grand quartet. By the second half of the 19th century, they had collectively accomplished the migration of the string quartet from an intimate genre of true chamber music into a public analogue thereof.

The history of the canonical string-quartet repertoire of the long 19th century divides neatly around the mid-century revolutions. Preeminent among **canonical** works from the century's first half are **Ludwig von Bee-**

thoven's 16 string quartets and *Große Fuge* (1798–1826), works that cast a shadow over Romantic chamber music no less imposing than that cast by Beethoven's **symphonies** in large-scale instrumental music. Second in prominence today among quartets by composers of the Early Romantic Generation are the last few of **Schubert**'s quartets (15 works, 1811–1826 passim). Schubert's quartets reflect his immersion in the Viennese grand-quartet tradition and a brilliant engagement with Beethoven, also anticipating (most notably in the D-minor **"Death and the Maiden"** Quartet, D. 810, 1824) **Gustav Mahler**'s integration of **song** into serious instrumental music. Since only one of them (in A minor, D. 804) was published during Schubert's lifetime, however, they exerted little influence on other contemporary string quartets or Romantic understandings of the genre until they were published (mostly after ca. 1870).

Among other Early Romantic Generation composers of string quartets, the most important in the first half of the 19th century was Spohr, who composed a total of 36 string quartets, in both grand and solo styles, distributed over 22 numbered *opera* between 1804 and 1857 (all but four of these before 1850, the last two still unpublished). The Early Romantic Generation's other notable contributors to the string quartet as a genre included **Franz Berward**, Peter Hänsel (1770–1831), **Georges Onslow**, and **Antoine Reicha**.

The Romantic Generation's quartet contributions, too, fall almost entirely in the period to around 1850. By consensus, the most important contributions in this corpus are the quartets opp. 12 and 13, and op. posth. 80 (MWV R25, R22, and R37, comp. 1829, 1827, and 1847) of **Felix Mendelssohn Bartholdy** and the three quartets of **Robert Schumann** (Op. 41, comp. 1842, publ. in score in 1848 with a dedication to the late Mendelssohn [*see* PRINTING AND PUBLISHING OF MUSIC]). Other contributions from this generation were submitted by **Niels W. Gade, Mikhail Glinka, Fanny Hensel, Ferdinand Hiller, Franz Lachner**, G. A. Macfarren (1813–1887), Wilhelm Taubert (1811–1891), and Johannes Verhulst (1816–1891). Mendelssohn's opp. 12 and 13 quartets are highly experimental and draw directly on the challenges of internal structure, thematic and motivic construction, and especially **cyclic** form raised by Beethoven's quartets of the 1820s. Otherwise, few of these works make any obvious effort to address the legacy of Beethoven's late works, instead following in the more readily comprehensible paths of Beethoven's quartets of his middle Vienna period or (as in Schumann's case) those of Mendelssohn's and Spohr's grand quartets.

During the second half of the century, increasing numbers of composers took up the Beethovenian challenge. The most important quartets of the Late Romantic Generation are the three quartets of **Johannes Brahms**. The first two of these works (Op. 51, 1873), separated from the quartets of Mendelssohn and Schumann by some 25 years, are milestones in the genre, engaging a Beethovenian logic of thematic and motivic material within a structural tautness unprecedented in the genre, while Op. 67 (1876) echoes—or, in structuralist terms, "misreads"—the deliberate eccentricity of Beethoven's late quartets in a decidedly capricious fashion. The Late Romantic Generation also appropriated the string quartet for its celebration of **nationalist** ideas—most notably in several of the quartets of **Antonín Dvořák** (14 works, 1861–1895 passim) and those of his senior countryman **Bedřich Smetana** (two works, 1876–1893) but also in consciously Russian quartets of **Aleksandr Borodin** and **Nikolay Rimsky-Korsakov**, a Norwegian one by **Edvard Grieg**, and Gallic ones by **Charles Gounod, Camille Saint-Saëns**, and (especially) **César Franck**. As in other nationalist compositions, many of the Central and Eastern European and Scandinavian works in the genre drew directly or indirectly on **folk song** and avoided the approaches to tonality and form characteristic of French and German traditions. Other important quartets in this generation were penned by composers including **Felix Draeseke, Édouard Lalo, Joachim Raff, Carl Reinecke, Josef Rheinberger**, and **Pyotor Il'yich Tchaikovsky**.

By the end of the long 19th century, the tradition of the solo quartet had become all but extinct, replaced by a bifurcation that cultivated the post-Beethovenian (implicitly though not always **absolute**) grand quartet on the one hand and the nationalist quartet on the other. Because the post-Beethovenian quartet was increasingly considered the hallmark of Germanness (*see* RECEPTION), during the Modern Romantic Generation the string quartet as a genre may be viewed in primarily nationalist terms. Composers such as **Ferruccio Busoni, Carl Nielsen, Richard Strauss**, and **Hugo Wolf** continued to cultivate the Austro-German tradition, while other composers, including **George Whitefield Chadwick, Claude Debussy, Edward Elgar, Zdeněk Fibich, Aleksandr Glazunov, Albéric Magnard, Serge Rachmaninoff**, and **Charles Villiers Stanford**, worked to develop a distinct and recognizable national tradition. Other countries, such as Italy and the Netherlands, produced their own body of string-quartet literature but few works of distinction and no sense of a national tradition in the genre.

Finally, the string quartet's transformation from an essentially private genre to a public one over the course of the long 19th century combined with composers' increasing awareness of the genre's tradition to produce a gradual but definitive trend of professionalization. This trend in turn encouraged composers to write string quartets that were more obviously demanding for all players—in some cases employing almost symphonic textures. The professional quartets of the early years of the Restoration found many successors in the remaining years of the century, most notably in ensembles such as the Quatuor Armingaud (1820–1900), the New York–based chamber-music societies of **William Mason** (1829–1908) and **Theodor Thomas** (1835–1905), the Gewandhaus Quartet (1836–1873), the Dresden String Quartet (1840–1860), the London Quartet Society (from 1846), the Hellmesberger

Quartet (1849–1891), the Müller Quartet (1855–1873), the Trieste String Quartet (1858–1901), the Florentine String Quartet (1866–1880), the **Joachim** Quartet (1869–1907), and the Rosé Quartet (1883–1938), among many others. The significance of these ensembles' proliferation is not merely social and institutional, for when the string quartet moved out of private spaces and into large public venues (concert halls and the like), the fine, pure tone and intimacy of gesture for which the idiom had been primarily celebrated in the period to around 1850 was no longer adequate; increasingly, performers adopted a stronger, less delicate sonority so that the ensemble's sound would not be swallowed by the hall itself. The modern performance traditions associated with the quartets of, for example, Beethoven are thus far removed from the sounds and approaches that he and his contemporaries so prized about the string quartet as a genre. [JMC]

See also ORCHESTRA; PERFORMANCE PRACTICE.

QUINTET. (Fr., quintette, quintuor; Ger., Quintett; It., quintetto; Sp., quinteto.) Generally, an ensemble of five solo performers or a composition written for it. During the **long 19th century**, quintets usually were categories of vocal as well as instrumental chamber music. Vocal quintets may be understood as chamber-music expansions of the four-part writing typical for mixed vocal ensembles in the long 19th century and were most often scored for either SSATB or SATTB, usually with accompaniment. **Anthony Philip Heinrich** composed an *Elegiac Quintetto Vocale* in 1846, but most of the long 19th century's best-known vocal quintets occurred in **operas**, such as **Georges Bizet**'s *Carmen* (Act II), **Gioachino Rossini**'s *Il Barbiere di Siviglia* (Act II), and **Richard Wagner**'s *Die Meistersinger* (Act III).

Instrumental quintets during the long 19th century typically were in **sonata plan** and usually occurred with one of four instrumentations: (1) one woodwind instrument and **string quartet**, (2) piano and **string quartet** (*piano quintets*), (3) five stringed instruments (*string quintets*), or (4) *woodwind quintets*. Although the first of these categories tended to place the wind instrument in an obbligato or *concertante* role, the latter three generally strove for a more or less egalitarian scoring. The best-known quintets for one wind instrument and string quartet are the clarinet quintets of **Wolfgang Amadeus Mozart** (K. 581, 1789) and **Johannes Brahms** (Op. 115, 1891; clarinet optionally replaced by viola, making this a *string quintet*), but other string quintets with clarinet were penned by Heinrich Bärmann (1784–1847; three works), **Max Reger** (Op. 146, 1915), **Antoine Reicha** (Op. 107, 1821, publ. 1826; clarinet optionally replaced by oboe), and **Carl Maria von Weber** (J. 182/Op. 34, 1811–1815, publ. 1816). Related works scored for a different woodwind instrument and strings were composed by Luigi Boccherini (1743–1805; two *opera* of flute quintets, opp. 17 and 19). Other notable combinations of one woodwind instrument plus strings were penned by Mozart: the horn quintet with two violas (K. 407/386c, 1782) and the Adagio and Rondo for flute, oboe, viola, cello, and glass harmonica (K. 617, 1791). More prominent than quintets for one woodwind instrument and strings were *piano quintets*. This subgenre includes three works that are generally acknowledged as masterpieces, composed by Brahms (Op. 34, 1862, publ. 1865), **Franz Schubert** (D. 667, "Trout," 1819, posth. publ. 1829 as Op. 114), and **Robert Schumann** (Op. 44, 1842, publ. 1843). The multitude of other piano quintets includes works by **Aleksandr Borodin** (1862), **Felix Draeseke** (Op. 48, 1888), **Antonín Dvořák** (B 28 and 155/opp. 5 and 81, ?1872 and 1887, publ. posth. and 1888), **Edward Elgar** (Op. 84, 1918–1919), **Gabriel Fauré** (opp. 89 and 115, comp. 1887–1905 and 1919–1921, publ. 1907 and 1921), **César Franck** (Op. 7, comp. 1879, publ. 1881), **Vincent d'Indy** (Op. 81, 1924), **Franz Lachner** (opp. 139 and 145, 1868 and 1869), **Joachim Raff** (Op. 107, 1862, publ. 1864), **Max Reger** (in C minor, 1897–1898, publ. posth., and Op. 64, 1901–1902), **Carl Reinecke** (Op. 83, ca. 1866), **Josef Rheinberger** (Op. 114, 1879), **Anton Rubinstein** (Op. 99, 1876), **Camille Saint-Saëns** (Op. 14, ?1855, publ. 1865), **Louis Spohr** (Op. 130, comp. 1845, publ. 1846), and **Charles Marie Widor** (opp. 7 and 68, 1868 and 1894).

Finally, the most egalitarian varieties of instrumental quintet were the *string quintet* and the *woodwind quintet*. Three scorings predominated among string quintets: (1) for two violins, two violas, and cello; (2) for two violins, viola, and two cellos; or (3) for two violins, viola, cello, and bass. The most prolific composers in this genre were Boccherini and **Georges Onslow**, with 157 and 33 contributions, respectively. The iconic works among string quintets with paired violins are Mozart's six works in the genre (K. 174 [1773], 515 [1787], 516 [1787], 406/516b [1788], 593 [1790], and 614 [1791]) as well as those by Brahms (opp. 88 and 111, comp. 1882 and 1890, publ. 1882 and 1891) and Mendelssohn (MWV R22 and R33/Op. 18 and Op. posth. 87, comp. 1826 and 1845, publ. 1833 and 1850). Other notable such works were composed by **Ludwig van Beethoven** (opp. 4 and 29, comp. 1795 and 1801, publ. 1796 and 1802), **Anton Bruckner** (WAB 112, 1878–1879, three movements publ. 1881), **Gaetano Donizetti** (two works, n.d.), **François-Joseph Fétis** (three works, 1860 and 1862), **Adolf Fredrik Lindblad** (two works, one publ. posth. 1885), Onslow (opp. 8, 25, 39, 78, and 80, publ. 1823–1842 passim), **Ignaz Pleyel** (10 works, 1785–1789 passim), **Rheinberger** (six works, opp. 89, 93, and 147), **Anton Rubinstein** (Op. 59, 1859, publ. 1861), Spohr (seven works, opp. 33, 69, 91, 106, 129, and 144, publ. 1815, 1819, 1826, 1834, 138, 1845, and 1850), and **Charles Villiers Stanford** (Op. 25, 1886). *String quintets for two violins, viola, and two cellos* were composed by **Luigi Cherubini** (1837, posth. publ. 1907), Draeseke (Op. 77, 1901, publ. 1903), **Niels W. Gade** (Op. 8, 1845, publ.

1846), **Aleksandr Glazunov** (Op. 39, 1891–1892), Lachner (Op. 121, 1834, publ. 1864), Onslow (13 works, 1823–1845 passim), Schubert (D. 956, 1828, posth. publ. as Op. posth. 163, 1853), and **Ethel Smyth** (Op. 1, 1883, publ. 1884), among others. *String quintets for two violins, viola, cello, and bass* were composed by Dvořák (B. 49/Op. 77, 1875, publ. 1888), Onslow (13 works, 1821–1836 passim), and **Ambroise Thomas** (Op. 7, 1836). There are also many other quintets with further variant scorings.

Woodwind quintets (also known as *wind quintets*) are typically scored for flute, oboe, clarinet, bassoon, and horn, although the genre's sizable repertoire reveals many variants of this scoring. Wind quintets shared with their stringed counterparts an egalitarian approach to scoring but differed in that their constituent instruments possessed significantly different timbres and techniques. The genre emerged in the last three decades of the 18th century in the works of Giuseppe Cambini (1746–1825), Antonio Rossetti (1750–1792), and Nikolaus Schmitt (1723–1802), but the most important works in the genre are the 24 wind quintets that **Antoine Reicha** composed between 1811 and 1820 (publishing these in his opp. 88, 91, 99, and 100, 1817–1820), plus his four posthumously published movements for wind quintet, and the nine quintets published by Franz Danzi (1763–1826) in his opp. 56, 67, and 68 between 1819 and 1824. Other works in the genre were composed by Giulio Briccibaldi (1818–1881; Op. 124, 1875), Elgar, Lachner, Peter Müller (1791–1877), Onslow, **Carl Nielsen**, and Johann Sobeck (1831–1914). Unusual contributions to this repertoire were also penned by Mozart (the Quintet for oboe, clarinet, bassoon, horn, and piano, K. 452, 1784) and Beethoven (Op. 16, 1796, publ. 1801; for the same scoring as K. 452). Beethoven also began but did not finish a Quintet in E-flat Major for oboe, three horns, and bassoon (Hess 19; ?1793, publ. 1954). [JMC]

R

RACHMANINOFF [RAKHMANINOV, RACHMANINOV], SERGE
[SERGEY] (VASIL'YEVICH) (1873–1943). Russian composer, **conductor**, and **virtuoso** pianist of the Modern Romantic Generation, widely regarded as one of the greatest pianists of his generation. He had his earliest **piano** lessons from his mother and entered the St. Petersburg **Conservatory** in 1882, but his performance there was lackluster, probably because of his parents' separation in the wake of his father's lavish spending. On the recommendation of Alexander Ziloti (1863–1945), a pupil of **Anton Rubinstein**, his mother enrolled him in the class of Nikolai Zverev (1832–1893) at the Moscow **Conservatory**, where he also studied with **Anatoly Arensky** and Sergei Taneyev (1856–1915). After graduating with honors in piano in 1891, he arranged to continue at the Conservatory for another year in order to earn a diploma in composition; this he received with a gold medal. His career received a major boost when an opera completed during his extra year at the Conservatory was performed to great acclaim at the Bolshoy Theater in 1893, but the unsuccessful premiere of his First **Symphony** (under **Aleksandr Glazunov**'s direction) in 1897 so destroyed his self-confidence that he was unable to compose for the next three years.

Despite these difficulties, Rachmaninoff was also establishing himself as a conductor, working first at the Moscow Private Russian **Opera** (conducting **Georges Bizet**'s *Carmen*, **Aleksandr Dargomïzhsky**'s *Rusalka*, **Mikhail Glinka**'s *A Life for the Tsar*, Christoph Willibald Ritter von Gluck's [1714–1787] *Orfeo ed Euridice*, **Nikolay Rimsky-Korsakov**'s *May Night*, **Camille Saint-Saëns**'s *Samson et Dalila*, and **Pyotor Il'yich Tchaikovsky**'s *Queen of Spades* in the 1897–1898 season) and then with a concert of his own music at the Queen's Hall in London (1899). As a composer, however, he was at an impasse: ideas for new works continued to come to him, but he could not complete them. Relief came through his friendship with Nikolai Dahl (1860–1939), a physician who was also an amateur cellist. Rachmaninoff traveled to Italy in the summer of 1899 and there composed the a cappella chorus *Panteley-tselitel'* (Panteley the Healer), the love duet for his emergent opera *Francesca da Rimini*, and the Second Piano **Concerto**, which was premiered on 9 November 1901.

Rachmaninoff's creative powers were now unleashed, and his activities as pianist, conductor, and composer surged. In September 1904, he began what was supposed to be a two-year term as director of the Bolshoy but in February 1906 resigned in the wake of the political unrest in Russia and fled first to Italy and then to Dresden. He soon returned to Russia, but when the Bolshevik Revolution of 1917 erupted, he fled again, first to Stockholm, then to Copenhagen, and then to the United States. He remained based in Copenhagen for the rest of his life, with frequent concert tours to the United States and other parts of Europe during the period 1918–1939. When World War II broke out in 1939, he moved permanently to the United States (New York and Los Angeles) but continued touring extensively, even after his doctor diagnosed him with pleurisy and recommended canceling his tour in January 1943. It soon became clear that he was suffering from cancer, and he died in his Los Angeles home on 28 March 1943, four days before his 70th birthday.

Rachmaninoff was one of very few musicians to have excelled in not just one or even two careers but three. As a pianist, his abilities remain legendary, remarkably well preserved thanks to technology in a set of recordings from the years 1919–1942 that in 1973 were released by RCA under the title *The Complete Rachmaninoff*. As a conductor, too, he was one of the most sought after figures of his generation, twice being offered (and declining) the permanent directorship of the Boston Symphony Orchestra. As a composer, he (like his friend Tchaikovsky, whom he eulogized in the *Trio élégiaque* for **piano trio**, 1893) is celebrated for his long, sinuous melodies and his ability to craft and pace tunes, phrases, and entire movements with a sense of drama and emotion rivaled in his generation only by **Richard Strauss**.

Rachmaninoff is best known today for a handful of works: the early **Prelude** in C-sharp Minor (Op. 3, no. 2, 1892; popularly known as "The Bells of Moscow"), the Second Piano Concerto (Op. 18, 1900–1901), the **symphonic poem** *Ostrov myortvïkh* (The Isle of the Dead, Op. 29, 1909), the *Rhapsody on a Theme of* **Paganini** (Op. 43, 1934; a work whose compositional strategy follows the finale of **Ludwig van Beethoven**'s "Eroica" **Symphony**), the symphony-**cantata** *Kolokola* (The Bells, Op. 43, 1913), his Second Symphony (Op. 27, 1906–1907), the a cappella choral works *Liturgiya svyatovo Ioanna Zlatousta* (Liturgy of St. John Chrysostom, Op. 31, 1910) and *Vespers* (Op. 37, 1915), and the *Symphonic Dances* (Op. 45, 1940). Besides his substantial corpus of music for piano solo, he completed four **operas**, four *opera* of instrumental **chamber music**, and arrangements for piano of works by **Johann Sebastian Bach**, Bizet, Glazunov, **Felix Mendelssohn Bartholdy**, **Modest Mussorgsky**, Rimsky-Korsakov, **Franz Schubert**, and Tchaikovsky, among others. [JMC]

RAFF, (JOSEPH) JOACHIM (1822–1882). German composer, critic, and teacher born in Switzerland. Trained as a violinist and pianist, he was largely self-taught as a composer, producing his earliest original works during his years teaching primary school in Rapperswil (Switzerland) (1840–1844). Some of these works—a **serenade** for Piano, a set of **character pieces**, a **scherzo**, a **fantasy** on themes by **Gaetano Donizetti**, a set of **caprices**, and a set of **variations**—he submitted in 1841 to **Felix Mendelssohn Bartholdy**, who recommended them to the prestigious publisher **Breitkopf & Härtel**. In 1845, he traveled to Basel and met **Franz Liszt**, who quickly took him under his wing and mentored him, employing him from 1850 on in Weimar as a personal assistant, copyist, and orchestrator. His reservations about certain aspects of the emergent **New German School**'s philosophy led him to publish a critical essay titled "Die Wagnerfrage" (The **Wagner** Question) in 1854, and by the early 1860s, tensions had emerged between him and his Weimar mentors. In 1865, he moved to Wiesbaden, where his wife was employed. There, he gave private instruction in voice, piano, and harmony until 1877, when he was appointed director of the newly founded Hoch **Conservatory** in Frankfurt am Main. He was also active in the musical press and is responsible for some of the writings published with attributions to Liszt and Wagner.

Raff's style of the 1850s reflects the influences of the New German School, but his earlier and subsequent works are equally indebted to **Johannes Brahms**, Mendelssohn, and **Robert Schumann**. He published some 216 numbered *opera* and an additional 56 works without opus number (*see* PRINTING AND PUBLISHING OF MUSIC). He is best known today for his compositions for **piano** solo and other **chamber music**, but during his lifetime he also achieved renown for his larger compositions, including six **operas**, 11 numbered **symphonies** (preceded by another symphony that is now lost), an orchestral **suite**, numerous **overtures**, and **incidental music**. The three *Klavier-Soli* (Piano Solos), Op. 74 (1852), the **song cycle** titled *Maria Stuart* (Op. 172), the Third Symphony (Op. 153, 1869), and the **oratorio** *Welt-Ende—Gericht—Neue Welt* (World's End—Judgment—New World, Op. 212, 1881) rank among his most recognized efforts. [JMC]

RECEPTION. Umbrella term denoting a number of interrelated concepts and methodologies (reception history, reception theory, and aesthetics of reception) concerning the ways in which meaning and artistic identity, biographical as well as inherently musical, change in response to shifts in historical and cultural context. First developed in French and Russian literary studies in the early 20th century, reception-centered methodologies were quickly appropriated by a number of other disciplines, including historiography and history as well as critical and historical studies of all the arts. Although reception-centered methodologies are related to cognitive psychology and reader-response theory, they differ fundamentally in one regard: reception studies deal with *collective* perceptions of and responses to artworks, whereas cognitive psychology and reader-response studies focus on *individual* perceptions and responses.

Reception-centered methodologies vary considerably, but in connection with music, their basic premises are straightforward. Composers' contemporaries construct their own collective image of those composers and works based on their public actions and artistic utterances within a frame of reference established by the issues of the day. As those issues inevitably change, later performers, audiences, and critics will inevitably view the music and its creator through the lens of their own experiences and issues, emphasizing aspects of the works and life that seem more relevant to those later perspectives. Consequently, works that may seem to be the composer's greatest at the time of their composition and premiere may fall from favor in the eyes of posterity, while posterity elevates the status of works that the composer and his or her contemporaries demonstrably considered insignificant or trivial.

The same shifts in constructed identity may apply to composers, genres, and virtually any other element of artistic identity that is "received." Thus, Romantics around Europe and in the New World came to consider **Johann Sebastian Bach**, whose life and works were known and celebrated only in limited circles concentrated in Prussia and (to a lesser extent) Vienna until the early 19th century, as the personification not only of specifically German greatness during the early modern era but also of Baroque music (*see* BACH REVIVAL, BACH AWAKENING, BACH RENAISSANCE; HISTORICISM). Similarly, for most of the 19th century there were vast differences among British, French, Italian, and German constructions of **Ludwig van Beethoven**'s identity and profound differences among the Prussian, Rhenish, Saxon, and Viennese constructions of that same life and corpus of works. The same is true of the **zarzuela**, *tableau vivant*, and **melodrama**: owing largely to their provenance in the musical culture of Iberia, which traditional music historiography has dismissed as insignificant or outright inferior, zarzuelas and their composers have never won any measure of recognition outside their native lands, and the fates of the abundant *tableaux vivants* and melodramas that populate the landscape of 19th-century music have waxed and waned as the aesthetic principles of the genres with which they were associated were called into question and eventually dismissed. So, too, has the public reception of the composers who contributed to those enterprises. By extension, one might plausibly argue that the **Requiem** generally attributed to **Wolfgang Amadeus Mozart** would likely disappear from the performance repertoire entirely if the work were to be more accurately labeled as "Süßmaier's Requiem, with fragments by Mozart."

Reception theory has had its fair share of detractors, most obviously because it tends to diminish four cherished notions of canonicity and traditional historiography (*see* CANON): (1) the idea that artistic worth and historical greatness are intrinsic and immanent; (2) the assumption that the processes by which certain works, composers, and genres are selected for historical survival, while others are left on the proverbial scrapheap of history, is a pure and reliable function of artistic worth, uncorrupted by the vagaries of politics, cultural polemics, or other "extrinsic" (i.e., not inherently artistic) factors; (3) the proposal that a given work or composer possesses an aesthetic essence that is ontologically fixed from the moment of its creation and stable for posterity; and (4) the assumption that the creators and moments of creation of artworks occupy a privileged position that fixes those artworks' identity thereafter, thereby anchoring their essence and providing a stable ontological basis for the judgments of posterity. Taken to their logical extremes, reception-centered perspectives tend to replace these notions either with radically relativistic ones that dismiss any historically or textually centered criticism or value judgment in favor of moment-to-moment critical response or with dogma that rejects out of hand any realistic view of the autonomy of both the creator and the created (composer and work). In the musicological literature, the most influential exponent of these critiques of reception theory is Carl Dahlhaus (1928–1989).

Despite these points of controversy, the fundamental premise of reception-centered methodologies—that because the varying cultural and historical situations of performers and auditors profoundly affect the "ears" with which they experience and interpret music, any inherent meaning that a given musical artwork may have originally possessed is profoundly unstable and susceptible to obliteration in the face of radically different interpretive contexts—is beyond dispute. Advocates for these methodologies thus view them as essential complements to others that presume a level of work immanence that is untenable in view of the significant influences exerted by changes in historical and social context. The importance of the various "revivals" and critical reappraisals that have occurred over the course of the 19th, 20th, and 21st centuries testifies to these methodologies' importance to the ongoing discourse of musical life, for to them we owe not only the Romantics' appropriations of, for example, **Giovanni Pierluigi da Palestrina** and J. S. Bach but also far-reaching discoveries and reappraisals considering figures ranging from **Wolfgang Amadeus Mozart** through Beethoven to **Fanny Hensel, Felix Mendelssohn Bartholdy, Robert Schumann, Johannes Brahms, Franz Liszt**, and **Gustav Mahler**, to name but a few. [JMC]

See also BIOGRAPHICAL FALLACY; INTENTIONAL FALLACY.

REGER, (JOHANN BAPTIST JOSEPH) MAX(IMILIAN) (1873–1916).
German composer, **virtuoso** organist, and writer of the Modern Romantic
Generation. He studied first with his father, a schoolteacher who published a
harmony textbook and played several instruments, then with an organist who
introduced him to the music of **Johann Sebastian Bach** and **Ludwig van
Beethoven** and would later publish a biography of him. A turning point came
when he went to Bayreuth to hear *Die Meistersinger* and *Parsifal* in 1888.
He had already penned several works, but the visit sparked his compositional
muse. In 1890 he went to study with Hugo Riemann (1849–1919), at first
privately and then in Riemann's new position at the Wiesbaden **Conservatory**. Eventually, he became Riemann's teaching assistant.

Now having received a thorough introduction to the organ works of J. S.
Bach as well as **Felix Mendelssohn Bartholdy**, Reger was increasingly
drawn away from the aesthetic agendas of the **New German School** and
toward one that celebrated what he termed "architectonic beauty" buttressed
by "intellectual content." His reputation as an organist and as a composer
grew, and he began to travel widely as a performer, also making his living as
an organist in Munich and teaching counterpoint at the university there in
1905–1906. He taught at the University of Leipzig in 1907–1908 and was
music director of the court orchestra at Meiningen from 1911 to 1915. The
stress of the job, however, combined with his heavy drinking and poor
health, proved to be too much for him. He thus resigned and retired to Jena,
where he intended to sustain his family through payments from his publications and performances as a virtuoso organist. He died of a heart attack while
returning home from a tour to the Netherlands.

Reger's mature compositional style is, for the most part, densely contrapuntal and highly chromatic, a challenging and complex synthesis of German
styles from J. S. Bach through Beethoven, Mendelssohn, and **Johannes
Brahms** to **Franz Liszt** and **Richard Wagner**. His output is large considering his brief career. His 147 numbered *opera* include 28 large and small
works for organ; two **concert overtures**, four **tone poems**, one violin **concerto**, one piano **concerto**, and 14 other works for **orchestra**; 16 sacred and
secular works for chorus a cappella and with orchestral or keyboard accompaniment; 34 *opera* of solo **songs** and vocal duets (some of which he also
orchestrated); 34 *opera* of instrumental **chamber music** (most notably a
clarinet **quintet** [Op. 146, 1915] and five **string quartets**); and 30 works for
piano (mostly **character pieces**). To these must be added other works that he
published without opus number or left unpublished in all categories. He also
was an active music critic and the recipient of honorary doctorates from
universities in Jena and Berlin, and his private reply to a critic ("I am sitting
in the smallest room of my house. Your review is in front of me. Soon it will
be behind me.") remains one of the most often quoted bons mots of music
history. His seven chorale **fantasias** penned between 1898 and 1900 (opp.

30, 40, and 52) rank among the most extraordinary tropes on the J. S. Bach's works in the genre, and his *Variations and Fugue on a Theme of [Wolfgang Amadeus] Mozart* and *Acht geistliche Gesänge* (Eight Sacred Songs for 4–8 vv, opp. 132 and 138, both 1914) are widely celebrated for their synthesis of disparate styles. [JMC]

REICHA [REJCHA], ANTOINE(-JOSEPH) [ANTONÍN, ANTON] (1770–1836). French composer, flutist, teacher, and theorist of the Early Romantic Generation, of Czech birth; one of the 19th century's most influential music theorists. His influence as a teacher is testified to by the fact that by the time he himself applied for a position on the faculty of the Paris **Conservatory**, eight of his students were already on the faculty at that prestigious institution; his many successful subsequent pupils include **Hector Berlioz**, **César Franck**, **Charles Gounod**, and **Franz Liszt**. His 16 published writings on music theory and pedagogy of musical composition—most prominently the *Traité de mélodie* (Treatise on Melody, 1814), *Cours de composition musicale, ou Traité complet et raisonné d'harmonie pratique* (Course of Musical Composition; or, Complete and Ordered Treatise on Practical Harmony, 1816–1818), *Traité de haute composition musicale* (Treatise on Advanced Musical Composition, 1824–1826), and *Art du compositeur dramatique, ou Cours complet de composition vocale* (The Art of the Dramatic Composer, 1833)—rank among the most widely disseminated, reprinted, and translated such publications of the entire 19th century (the four treatises just cited were all translated into German by **Carl Czerny**). In particular, his views on contrapuntal experiment, **orchestration**, and **sonata form** opened up new possibilities in these facets of musical creation and analysis for generations to come, as evidenced in the writings of **Adolf Bernhard Marx** and **Hector Berlioz** and the compositions of Berlioz and **Giacomo Meyerbeer**, among a great many others.

As a composer, Reicha is best known today for his wind **quintets**, which are frequently performed and rank among the most original contributions to that genre. His knowledge of woodwind instruments and their contributions to the sound palette of the developing Romantic **orchestra** made him one of the most innovative and influential voices in 19th-century **orchestration**. He also published a series of 36 keyboard fugues (Op. 36, 1803) of striking originality in tonal organization (he penned some of the earliest known fugues at the sixth), meter, and harmony. His sizable output includes 16 completed and surviving comic and serious **operas**; one **oratorio**, one **Requiem**, three **cantatas**, and several other works for chorus with orchestra; seven choral works with accompaniment of harp, organ, or **piano** and several more for chorus a cappella; one **melodrama**, two **concert arias**, and a few other works for solo voice with orchestra; 11 pieces of vocal **chamber music** (**part-songs** and solo **songs** in French and German); 13 complete and surviving **symphonies** (most of them still unpublished) and 12 **concert overtures;** **concertos** for flute, clarinet, violin, viola, and piano, and several other *concertante* works; two quintets for four flutes, one **sonata** for four flutes, 24 **trios** for three horns, 24 wind quintets, and various other chamber works for woodwinds; 14 published *opera* of chamber music for strings and eight published *opera* of chamber music for strings and winds; eight published *opera* of chamber music for piano and strings; and 18 *opera* of works for piano alone. There are also numerous smaller compositions, many of them still unpublished.

Reicha was a talented flautist and by the age of 15 was a member of the court orchestra in Bonn, where he befriended the young **Ludwig van Beethoven** (who remained a friend and respected Reicha highly to the end of his life). He entered the University of Bonn in 1789 and in the early 1790s met **Franz Joseph Haydn** but in 1794 was forced to flee to Hamburg when Bonaparte's armies invaded Bonn. There, he devoted himself to composing and to teaching composition, harmony, and piano and received some success with performances of his earliest operas. In 1800, he moved to Paris (opera capital of northern Europe and seat of the ever-expanding **First French Empire**) in hopes of operatic success but then relocated to Vienna, where he renewed his friendship with Haydn and took compositions with Johann Georg Albrechtsberger (1736–1809) and Antonio Salieri (1750–1825). Despite the turmoil caused by the Napoleonic occupations, he managed to complete some 50 new works while in the German lands, returning to Paris in 1808. There, his reputation continued to grow, and in 1818, he was appointed professor of harmony, counterpoint, and composition at the Conservatory. His originality and occasional irreverence often brought him into conflict with the institution's more conservative faculty, but most of his students revered him. He was naturalized as a French citizen in 1829 and become a member of the Légion d'Honneur in 1831, succeeding **Adrien Boieldieu** as professor of composition at the Académie des Beaux-Arts in 1835. [JMC]

REINECKE, CARL (HEINRICH CARSTEN) (1824–1910). German composer, **conductor**, pianist, violinist, and music educator of the Late Romantic Generation. He is best known today for his **programmatic** flute **sonata** titled *Undine* (Op. 167, 1882) but was also widely known in the 19th and early 20th centuries for his **piano** music, his three **symphonies**, his **piano concertos**, his concerto for flute and harp, and much music for children (the *Kinderlieder* [Childrens' Songs], opp. 37, 63, 75, 91, 135, 138, 154b, and 196, and the *Kinder-Symphonie* [Childrens' Symphony], Op. 239, 1897). His published output runs to 288 numbered *opera*, including (in addition to the works just named), five **operas**, one **operetta**, and one set of **incidental music** (for **Friedrich Schiller**'s *Wilhelm Tell*, Op. 102, 1871); one **oratorio** and several **cantatas**; seven **concert overtures**, several **con-**

certos, and other *concertante* works; a great deal of instrumental and vocal chamber music; and many works for piano solo and piano duet, including cadenzas for more than 40 piano concertos by other composers. He was also an important conductor and an influential contributor to the didactic literature of music, with eight books to his name. Although his pupils were many and varied in their aesthetic outlooks—the list includes **Edvard Grieg**, Hermann Kretzschmar (1848–1924), James Kwast (1852–1927), Karl Muck (1859–1940), Hugo Riemann (1849–1919), **Johan Severin Svendsen**, **Arthur Sullivan**, and Felix Weingartner (1863–1942)—he took it on himself to instill in others a profound respect for the **canon** of composers of the 18th and earlier 19th centuries.

Reinecke received a solid basic education in the fundamentals of music from his father, a respected music theorist. He made his debut as a violinist in 1835 (age 11) and served for a while as an orchestral violinist but then became increasingly interested in piano and developed an international reputation in that regard. After serving as court pianist in Copenhagen from 1846 to 1848, he took a series of increasingly important teaching posts (Cologne, Barmen, and Breslau) before moving to Leipzig, where he was conductor of the famed Gewandhaus **Orchestra** from 1860 to 1895 and professor of piano and composition at the **Conservatory** from 1860 to 1897. He served as director of the Conservatory from 1897 to 1902. He was named a member of the Königliche Akademie der Künste in 1875 and received an honorary doctorate from the University of Leipzig in 1884. He retired from his official duties in 1902 but continued composing and performing to the end of his life. [JMC]

RELLSTAB, (HEINRICH FRIEDRICH) LUDWIG (1799–1860). German **librettist**, music critic, novelist, and poet. The son of music publisher and composer Johann Carl Friedrich Rellstab (1759–1813), he spent most of his life in and around Berlin. He was trained in music by Ludwig Berger (1777–1839) and Bernhard Klein (1793–1832), but his initial claim to fame was his poetry. His first collection of poems, *Griechenlands Morgenröthe* (Dawns of Greece), was published in 1822 and was widely disseminated. In 1823, he penned the libretto for Klein's *Dido* and his first review (an insightful critique of Anton Radziwill's [1775–1833] incidental music to **Johann Wolfgang von Goethe**'s *Faust*), and these were followed in 1824 by his first published play, the five-act tragedy *Karl der Kühne* (Charles the Bold). He also provided the German translations for several important **operas**, most notably J.-H.V. de Saint-Georges's libretto for **Halévy**'s *Le val d'Andorre* (The Valley of Andorra, 1848) and **Eugène Scribe**'s libretto for **Giacomo Meyerbeer**'s *Ein Feldlager in Schlesien* (A Silesian Boot Camp, 1844; publ. 1847) and *Le Prophète* (The Prophet, 1849). Although the emphasis of his literary work eventually shifted from poetry to prose (criticism and novels), he remained a respected and influential contributor to the discourses of musical Romanticism, especially where composers of the Romantic Generation were concerned.

Rellstab was an ardent proponent of the need for a style of German opera distinct from the styles of France and the Italian lands. His strong criticisms of the perceived superficialities of Italian opera and of the naïveté of Prussian audiences who submitted to those indulgences earned him enemies and twice led to his arrest. He argued for values articulated by Christoph Willibald Ritter von Gluck (1714–1787) and for the music especially of **Felix Mendelssohn Bartholdy** and **Carl Maria von Weber**, but considered **Richard Wagner**'s *Der fliegende Holländer* (The Flying Dutchman, WWV 63, 1843) and *Tannhäuser* (WWV 70, 1859–1860) largely unsuccessful. **Ludwig van Beethoven** reportedly solicited him to write a libretto for him (a project that remained unfulfilled), and his poetry was set by many composers. The most important of these was **Franz Schubert**, who set 10 of his poems (most notably *Auf dem Strom*, D. 943); other composers include Berger, Klein, **Franz Lachner**, Liszt, **Heinrich Marschner**, Mendelssohn, and Julius Stern (1820–1883). Rellstab's active life as a reviewer includes (in addition to many published reviews) work as the editor of two journals: *Berlin und Athen* (1836) and *Iris im Gebiete der Tonkunst* (1830–1841, issued weekly). [JMC]

REQUIEM. A musical and/or spoken celebration or commemoration of the dead. It was originally strictly a part of the Roman Catholic rite but was later appropriated and adapted to different spiritual denominations.

Like all Roman Catholic Masses, the *Missa pro defunctis* consists of both spoken and sung prayers, some of whose texts were the same for every day of the liturgical year (the Mass Ordinary) and some of whose texts were specific to the public celebration of the rite for the dead (the Mass Proper). Additionally, in the Requiem Mass, the Gloria and Credo are omitted, and the 13th-century sequence *Dies irae* (Day of Wrath, attr. Thomas of Celano, ca. 1250) occupies the central section instead. There are also regional variants, though these are significantly fewer in number and import than they had been in previous centuries. The resulting form for the texts of the liturgical requiem is shown on the following page.

Within this overall structure, the rich variety of emotions and images entailed in the texts of the various prayers led many composers to set them as multiple movements in contrasting styles, tempos, and textures, each responding to its particular text with a discrete musical style, after the manner of the **motet**. This is particularly true of the Sequence (Dies irae), by far the longest text of the Mass. In such instances, the decision as to the movement-by-movement distributions of the various strophes of the texts was made by the composer. In the Requiem of **Wolfgang Amadeus Mozart** and

Mass Proper		Mass Ordinary
Spoken	*Set to music*	*Spoken*
	Introit (Requiem aeternam . . .)	
Epistle		
	Gradual (Requiem aeternam . . . In memoriam aeternam erit iustis . . .)	
	Tract (Absolve, Domine, animas omnium fidelium defunctorum)	
	Sequence (Dies irae, dies illa), typically divided into multiple movements during the long 19th century	
Gospel		
	Offertory (Domine Iesu Christe, Rex gloriae . . .)	
Prayers		
Psalm		
Secret		
Preface		
		Canon
		Pater noster
	Communion (Lux aeterna luceat eis, Domine . . .)	
Prayers		
	Responsory (Libera me, Domine . . .)	
	Antiphon (In paradisum deducant te Angeli . . .)	

Süßmaier, for example, the Sequence comprises six discrete movements, but in **Hector Berlioz**'s Requiem, the same text comprises five movements. In **Giuseppe Verdi**'s it comprises 10 movements, and in **Antonín Dvořák**'s only one (with contrasting sections).

Over the course of the **long 19th century**, it also became common for composers to create settings of the texts of the Requiem Mass that were intended for concert rather than liturgical use, thus separating the Requiem from its liturgical raison d'être. Such settings naturally dispensed with the spoken portions of the Proper and Ordinary alike, and their independence from liturgical function also made it possible for the composer to combine, omit, reorder, or (in rare instances) change the wording of the liturgically prescribed texts. **Gabriel Fauré**, for example, omitted the Sequence and combined the Agnus Dei and Communion into a single movement.

The long 19th century can boast a great many remarkable settings of the Requiem Mass. Among those that are best known today, several warrant special mention here: most of Mozart's Requiem (KV 626, 1791) is not by Mozart at all but by Süßmaier. The settings by Berlioz (H. 75/Op. 5, 1837, publ. 1838) and Verdi (1874) are liturgically impracticable because of their scope and their rearrangement of the texts, respectively; **Johannes Brahms's** *Deutsches Requiem* (1865–1868, publ. 1869) is not only in German and not liturgical but also based in part on texts taken from the Apocrypha rather than the authorized Bible; and **Frederick Delius's** Requiem (1913–1914, publ. 1922) is based on a variety of texts by Delius himself and his close Heinrich Simon and Peter Warlock and intermingles "Alleluia" statements with invocations to Allah (this last was provisionally designated a "pagan requiem" by the composer until shortly before the premiere).

Other Requiems of the long 19th century include those by Nicolas-Charles Bochsa (1789–1856; 1816), **Anton Bruckner** (1849), **Luigi Cherubini** (two settings: 1816, publ. 1817, and 1836, publ. 1838), **Gaetano Donizetti** (two settings: 1835, for **Vincenzo Bellini**, and 1837, for Niccolò Antonio Zingarelli [1752–1837]), **Felix Draeseke** (1880), Dvořák (1890, publ. 1891), **François-Joseph Fétis** (1850), José Maurício Nunes Garcia (1767–1830; four settings, 1799–1816), **Charles Gounod** (three settings: 1842, 1873, ca. 1893), **Franz Lachner** (1856), **Franz Liszt** (1867–1868, publ. 1869), **Pietro Mascagni** (1887), **Camille Saint-Saëns** (1878), **Robert Schumann** (1852), **Charles Villiers Stanford** (1897), **Ambroise Thomas** (1833, publ. 1835), and Johannes Verhulst (1816–1891; 1854), among many others. [JMC]

RESCUE OPERA. (Fr., pièce à sauvetage; Ger., Rettugsoper *or* Befreiungsoper.) Term invented in the early 20th century and retroactively applied to **opéras comiques**, often of an expressly political nature, whose plots feature an endangered or imprisoned hero or heroine who is rescued through the valor of another character (usually not cast as stereotypically heroic). Although rescue had been a common conceit in opera since the genre's inception, the events leading up to the French Revolution and the political turmoil in France and elsewhere during the Terror and the **First French Empire**

made a specifically political variety of rescue, often foregrounding establishment oppressiveness of valorous citizens, particularly appealing between about 1790 and 1830.

Most works now regarded as rescue operas tend to fall into three broad categories: (1) those whose moral and material dilemmas are the product of tyranny or of power arbitrarily wielded, (2) those that include no tyrant figure per se but whose dilemmas are institutional or societal in nature and solved by means of individual courage and sacrifice in righting a wrong, and (3) those whose crisis is occasioned by some sort of natural catastrophe (such as a violent storm) that requires human intervention. By inverting the conventional divine-intervention ending (such as the clichéd *deux ex machina*) to one in which salvation is imparted through human agency, usually a combination of mental and moral fortitude, such operas resonated powerfully with the late Enlightenment as well as Romanticism. Those whose crisis was created by tyranny or institutional corruption also naturally were perceived as analogues of contemporary political and societal struggles. Their potency in this regard is testified to partly by the sheer number of operas that censors canceled, cut, or compelled to be rewritten during the first half of the 19th century and partly by the fact that those of an overtly political nature were often situated in another country and/or time, thus granting them a safe geographic and historical distance and winning for librettist and composers a measure of what would become known as "plausible deniability" in the 20th century.

The musical language of the rescue operas of Revolutionary and Napoleonic France drew heavily on that of the many hymns, **cantatas**, dirges, and other works written for the government's festivals and public celebrations designed to inspire patriotic fervor—not least of all because many of those works' composers also composed rescue operas. Arguably the most important such work indigenous to Revolutionary France is the *comédie héroïque Lodoïska* (a stereotypical "tyrant" opera) by **Luigi Cherubini**, first staged at the Théâtre Feydeau (Paris) in July 1791. Notable examples of the second variety include Nicolas Dalayrac's (1753–1809) *Raoul sire de Créqui* (1789) and Cherubini's *Les deux journées* (1800), the latter of which was widely known in the German lands as *Der Wasserträger* (The Water-Bearer) during the decade leading up to the **Revolutions of 1848**. Of the third type, the most important French examples include operas based on Bernardin de Saint-Pierre's 1787 novella *Paul et Virginie* by **Rudolfe Kreutzer** (1791) and **François-Joseph Le Sueur** (1794) as well as **Étienne-Nicolas Méhul**'s *Mélidore et Phrosine* (1794) and Cherubini's *Eliza* (1794).

During the 19th century, the genre of the rescue opera continued to flourish in France, but it was also widely troped in the German and Italian lands, perhaps because of its implicit appeal to idealistic patriotic fervor. Arguably the best-known 19th-century specimens are the three versions of **Beetho-**

ven's *Fidelio* (1805, rev. 1806; final version 1814), whose 1805 performances (both fittingly and paradoxically) were postponed by the censors and whose initial success was undermined because Vienna was occupied by French troops at the time. The "tyrant" variety of the genre also appealed to the *Risorgimento* in 19th-century Italy. Of these appropriations, the best known (using recitative rather than spoken dialogue) is **Verdi**'s *Il trovatore* (The Troubador, 1853, after an 1836 play by the great Spanish dramatist and **zarzuela** librettist Antonio García Gutiérrez [1813–1884]). [JMC]

See also OPERA.

RESTORATION. Term for the period in European history from around 1815 to 1848, between the **Congress of Vienna** and the **Revolutions of 1848**. Politically, the period is characterized by predominantly conservative and antinationalist monarchical structures that operated within the *Congress System* or *Concert of Europe* (Great Britain, the Habsburg Empire, the Kingdom of Prussia, and Imperial Russia, and, after 1818, France). Because it marked the first return of international peace since the turbulence that had been unleashed by the French Revolution, amplified by the Terror, and exported in the name of "liberating" puppet governments set up by Bonaparte during the Napoleonic Wars (*see* FIRST FRENCH EMPIRE), it was characterized by a renewed emphasis on domestic life and family values, a tendency profoundly reflected in music and the other arts.

On the other hand, because the victorious powers were determined to prevent the rise of another Napoléon Bonaparte, the Restoration also witnessed extensive political and artistic censorship. Such deliberate repression of the notions of individual liberties and self-determining nation-states was profoundly irksome even to the war-weary public of the day. This resulted in major revolts in 1830 and a wave of revolutions that swept the continent in 1848–1849. Because the structures of government strongly affected the institutions of music and the other arts, the years 1815, 1830, and 1848 also represent major caesuras in music history and milestones in the successive generations of musical romanticism.

In cultural criticism, the Restoration is usually spoken in terms of two complementary concepts: *Biedermeier* and *Vormärz*. The former is used primarily in conjunction with the German lands and corresponds largely to the tendencies associated with early **Victorianism** in the United Kingdom and petite bourgeoisie of the **Bourbon Restoration** in France, emphasizing Restoration culture's self-conscious domesticity, political conservatism, and emphasis on community participation. The term is derived from Jacob Biedermeier, the pseudonymous author of a series of poems written in the 1850s by Ludwig Eichrodt (1798–1844) and Adolf Kußmaul (1822–1902) to satirize the tastes and social conventions of the period.

By contrast, the term *Vormärz* (literally "pre-March") views the years 1815–1848 through an at least partially favorable lens, considering their relative political and social stability as the fertile soil in which the seeds of the idea of Europe as an amalgamation of self-determining nation-states sewn by the French Revolution and the Napoleonic Wars took root, ultimately producing the wave of revolutions that swept Europe in 1848–1849. The term apparently emerged in the press in March 1849. The term *Vormärz* is primarily political rather than cultural and implicitly treats the repressive political structures of the Restoration as forces that compelled liberal Europe's citizenry to call for artistic and social change by means that were hardly overt but clear and compelling to their contemporaries. Thus, seemingly timeless and apolitical themes, such as alienation, loss, or passionate dedication to nature, would be above the censors' reproach but in contemporary context would have allegorized more deeply social and topical concerns, such as social or political divisions, defeat, or nationalist sentiment, respectively.

Political repressiveness and differing historiographic interpretations aside, during the Restoration Europeans cultivated a wide variety of public and private venues for creating, performing, publishing, and conversing about music and the other arts in ways that had been impossible for a full generation previously. In England and the German lands, it witnessed a surge in widespread public participation in glee clubs, **music festivals**, public concerts, and **chamber-music** production and consumption (*see* HAUSMU-SIK). In France and the German lands, it was characterized by a flourishing press, much of which dealt with music criticism; this was matched in France by an equally influential **salon** culture in the middle as well as upper classes and by a flourishing culture of **vaudeville** and **opera**, the latter accompanied by a thriving cult of **virtuosity**. In the Italian lands, too, it witnessed a burgeoning operatic culture that coupled spectacular vocal virtuosity with a new emphasis on opera based on contemporary literature.

The Restoration is a period less effectively defined by its own content than by the events that frame it. Musicians who wish to understand its cultural production and consumption in context should differentiate between the periods before and after the 1830 revolutions and, within that differentiation, geographically between the cultures of Central Europe, England, France, the German lands, Iberia, and the Italian states. European culture during these years saw not only the creation and dissemination of some of the most important works of the Early Romantic Generation (e.g., **Gioachino Rossini**'s *Guillaume Tell*, the late **string quartets** and **sonatas** of **Ludwig van Beethoven**, **Carl Maria von Weber**'s *Der Freischütz*, and **Franz Schubert**'s late sonatas, **symphonies**, and **song cycles**) but also the professional emergence of the entire Romantic Generation whose works, for many, epitomize the concept of Romanticism: most famously **Vincenzo Bellini**, **Hector**

Berlioz, Fryderyk Chopin, Gaetano Donizetti, Mikhail Glinka, Franz Liszt, Felix Mendelssohn Bartholdy, Clara and Robert Schumann, Giuseppe Verdi, and Richard Wagner. [JMC]

REVOLUTIONS OF 1848 (SPRING OF NATIONS, YEAR OF REVOLUTIONS). A series of popular uprisings in Western and Central European countries and Latin America; enormously consequential for music, the institutions that cultivated it, and the creation of new music. While all the revolts may be considered backlashes against the cultural, economic, and political trappings of the Restoration, exacerbated by poor harvests and prolonged economic recession, their specific motives varied widely. Some were fueled by economic and political grievance, others by liberal and socialist aspirations (Marx's and Engels's *Communist Manifesto* was completed in 1848), and others by nationalism. There were increasingly significant signs of discontent during the years leading up to 1848, but the wave of revolutions was officially triggered by the Sicilian Revolution of 1848 (12 January), the overthrow of the Bourbon monarch Louis-Philippe in France in February 1848 (*see* BOURBON RESTORATION), and the establishment of the French Second Republic with the election of Napoléon III on 2 December. Between then and July 1849, more than 50 countries in Europe and Latin America experienced significant revolutionary outbreaks. The shock waves were greater than any experienced since the French Revolution (1789) and any others until the eruption of World War I (1914).

Most of the 1848–1849 revolts brought about significant political change via the institution of representative governments or the introduction of representative systems into monarchical structures, the creation of new sovereign or quasi-autonomous nation-states within empires, or the overthrow of existing governments. They resulted in liberal constitutions in Austria and many German and Italian lands, the most important (if also abortive) Irish uprising against British rule since the Act of Union (1801), and the creation and implementation of numerous socialist organizations (most importantly the cooperative system of production known in France as the National Workshops). However, because the established governments of Central and Western Europe were a relatively united political concert while the revolutions themselves were born of diverse causes and not coordinated with each other, many of the concessions granted in response to the uprisings proved to be either symbolic, short lived, or both.

In the realm of music and the arts generally, the most important outcomes of the 1848 Revolutions were a sense of sweeping and profound societal change and widespread perception that the revolts had yielded an opportunity to reclaim the ideals of the French Revolution that had been betrayed by Bonaparte and largely abandoned at the Congress of Vienna. In all affected countries, they produced a proliferation of songs and part-songs (*see*

MÄNNERCHOR; ORPHÉON). They are also accountable for major reforms in the affected countries' educational systems and reflected in a proliferation of new musical organizations that hoped to seize and affirm the moment of societal regeneration as well as in the composition and performance of specific compositions written on revolutionary themes: the concert performance of Poland's first major national opera, *Halka* (1846) by Stanisław Moiuszko (1819–1872); the *Freiheits-Marsch, Marsch des einigen Deutschlands*, and *Radetsky-Marsch* (opp. 226–28, 1848) of **Johann Strauss (I)**, and the *Revolutions-Marsch* (Op. 54, 1848) and *Studenten-Marsch* (Op. 56, 1848) of **Johann Strauss (II)**, among a great many others.

Although the immediate political consequences of the revolutionary years were less transformative than expected, the revolutions themselves ensured that musical Romanticism as it existed in the second half of the 19th century was a significantly different phenomenon than its pre-1848 counterpart. [JMC]

See also ALLGEMEINER DEUTSCHER MUSIKVEREIN; NEW GERMAN SCHOOL; RISORGIMENTO.

REVUE MUSICALE. (Fr., "musical review.") Influential music periodical based in Paris. It was founded in 1827 by **François-Joseph Fétis** and published weekly until November 1835, when it combined with the *Gazette musicale de Paris* to form the *Revue et gazette musicale de Paris*, published by the Prussian expatriot music publisher Maurice Schlesinger, in 1848. It ran until 1880, except for a cessation from September 1870 to September 1871 (*see* FRANCO-PRUSSIAN WAR, FRANCO-GERMAN WAR).

Under Fétis, the *Revue musicale* was conservative in nature, but under Schlesinger's auspices, it adopted a more progressive stance akin to that of the Leipzig-based *Neue Zeitschrift für Musik*. This new spirit was reflected in the Romantic Generation's efforts to introduce German music and musicians to the Parisian reading public as well as in its receptiveness to progressive composers such as **Hector Berlioz** and **Franz Liszt**. The contents of the *Revue* regularly featured biographies and life-and-works studies as well as longer articles on arts policy in the complicated world of French politics, music history, music theory, musical instruments, and pedagogy (especially at the Paris **Conservatory**). It also included reports of private and public musical performances, music festivals, and **salons** in the provinces and around Europe (particularly Berlin and London) as well as Paris. Its plentiful advertisements are a valuable source of information for music publications and new musical instruments. Among its contributors are **Adolphe Adam**, Honoré de Balzac (1799–1850), Berlioz, **Castil Blaze**, Fétis, **Fromenthal Halévy, Georges Kastner, Jean-François Lesueur**, Liszt, **Adolf Bernard Marx**, Heinrich Panofka (1807–1887), and **Richard Wagner**. [JMC]

RHEINBERGER, JOSEF (JOSEPH) GABRIEL (1839–1901). German composer, **conductor**, organist, and teacher of the Late Romantic Generation; with **Anton Bruckner, Théodore Dubois**, and **Max Reger**, one of his generation's most important organists. A child **prodigy** as an organist, he also took private lessons in composition with **Franz Lachner** and studied at the Munich **Conservatory** from 1851 to 1854. He began publishing his music in 1859, also that year becoming professor of piano at the Munich **Conservatory**—a post that he succeeded as professor of organ (1860–1865) and then harmony and composition (1867 to his death). Among his distinguished pupils were **George Whitefield Chadwick, Engelbert Humperdinck**, and **Horatio Parker**. From 1864 to 1877, he directed the Munich Oratorienverein (**Oratorio** Club), earning a reputation as an outstanding choral conductor. He was also a prolific composer. Much of his output comprises **fantasies** and **sonatas** for organ, but he also composed much music for **orchestra** (including two **symphonic poems**, and several **concert overtures**, and two organ **concertos**) as well as instrumental **chamber music**, music for piano solo and **piano duet**, about 70 **songs**, numerous **part-songs**, seven comic and serious **operas**, three **Requiems**, eight other Mass settings, two *Stabat mater* settings, and much other sacred choral music. [JMC]

RHEINGOLD, DAS. See THE RING OF THE NIBELUNG.

RICHTER, JEAN PAUL (JOHANN PAUL [FRIEDRICH]) (1763–1825). German novelist, satirist, and aesthetician; a significant influence on a number of composers and writers on music, including **E. T. A. Hoffmann, Gustav Mahler**, and **Robert Schumann**. He was unable to achieve public success until he changed his name to simply "Jean Paul" and published under that name a comic novel titled *Die unsichtbare Loge* (The Invisible Lodge, 1793). This was followed by the immensely popular *Hesperus: Hundposttage* (Hesperus: Dog's Mail Days) in 1795 and then by *Blumen-, Frucht- und Dornenstücke* (Still Lives with Flowers, Fruits, and Thorns, 1796–1797), his most popular work (usually known by its main character, *Siebenkäs*). His other important fiction includes *Titan* (1803) and *Flegeljahre* (The Awkward Years, 1804–1805).

Jean Paul's *Vorschule der Aesthetik* (Preparatory School of Aesthetics) ranks as his most important nonfiction work, profoundly influencing not only other writers of and thinkers on music but also Thomas Carlyle (1795–1881), Samuel Taylor Coleridge (1772–1834), Novalis (1772–1801), August Wilhelm Schlegel (1767–1845), Friedrich Schlegel (1772–1829), Karl Solger (1780–1819), Ludwig Tieck (1773–1853), and Friedrich Theodor von Vischer (1807–1887), among others. A friend of Gottfried Herder (1744–1803) and reader of Immanuel Kant (1724–1804), he developed a system of aesthetics that linked the concept of humor (*Witz*) with Kant's category of the sublime and postulated an affinity between aesthetics and ethics; in particular, his views of aesthetic experience as a phenomenon that was infinitely subjective and individualized, a deeply personal experience of the infinite and the universal, appealed to composers and other aestheticians of the Romantic Generation, Late Romantic Generation, and Modern Romantic Generation. Also important, especially later in the **long 19th century**, was his view of poetic genius as a faculty possessed of two complementary parts: "reproductive imagination" (*Einbildungskraft*) and "Phantasie," which creates new worlds wholly of the artist's own making, independent of external reality or experience. A work of genius, Jean Paul (and his followers) held, would synthesize these two faculties by means of a differentiating "poetic reflectiveness" that permitted artists to view their work with critical detachment.

Jean Paul's mature style is characterized in part by frequent and detailed references to music and musical performance as allegories for more general personal experience, and by extravagant, often digressive prose and long, florid, prolix and occasionally abstruse sentences. **Robert Schumann** was among those who idolized this distinctive style, the influence of which is especially evident in Schumann's works of the late 1830s and early 1840s. Schumann's *Papillons* (Op. 2) was apparently inspired at least in part by *Flegeljahre*, and Jean Paul's frequent conceit of the *Doppelgänger* (double) as expressions of contrasting aspects of the artist's own psyche, manifested in the characters Wulf and Walt in *Flegeljahre*, finds an apt counterpart in Schumann's use of different personae in much of his music criticism. **Gustav Mahler** in 1891 dubbed his First **Symphony** "Titan" after Jean Paul's 1803 novel, also labeling the Symphony's first movement, "Aus den Tagen der Jugend; Blumenstück, Fruchtstück und Dornstück" (From the Days of Youth: Still Life with Flowers, Fruits, and Thorns), after *Siebenkäs*. Other composers who were significantly influenced by Jean Paul include **Franz Liszt** and **Richard Wagner**. [JMC]

RICORDI. Italian firm of publishers of musical editions, books on music, and musical journals, preeminent during the **long 19th century** and still thriving. The firm was founded in Milan in 1808 by Giovanni Ricordi (1785–1853) and passed from him to his son Tito (1811–1888) in 1853, then to his grandson Giulio (1840–1912).

Giovanni Ricordi had worked as a copyist and in 1807 had spent several months in Leipzig, studying the techniques of leading German publisher **Breitkopf & Härtel** before returning to Milan and launching his own publishing enterprise in partnership with Felice Festa, an engraver and music seller. That partnership dissolved quickly, and Ricordi opened his own shop and printing works. The firm grew rapidly with the burgeoning of the music-publishing industry during the **Restoration**, with an average annual production of 300 editions during its second decade (up from an average of 30 during its first) and exclusive rights to publish music performed at La Scala. By the end of 1837, Ricordi had published more than 10,000 editions, and the firm opened independent pan-European branches in London and Paris in 1875 and 1888 and several others as the unification of the Italian lands gained pace and was accomplished (Naples, 1860; Florence, 1865; Rome, 1871; and Palermo, 1888).

Although the Ricordi firm used lithography on a few occasions, most of its editions before 1860 were prepared from engraved plates (*see* PRINTING AND PUBLISHING OF MUSIC). It was the preferred Italian copublisher of major English, French, and German publishers of the long 19th century (*see* COPYRIGHT AND PERFORMANCE RIGHT), and its roster includes some of the century's most important composers for the Italian stage and concert hall as well as non-Italian composers. Among these were **D.-F.-E. Auber, Ludwig van Beethoven, Vincenzo Bellini, Arrigo Boito, Carl Czerny, Gaetano Donizetti, Franz Liszt, Jules Massenet, Felix Mendelssohn Bartholdy, Saverio Mercadante, Giacomo Meyerbeer, Amilcare Ponchielli, Giacomo Puccini, Gioachino Rossini, Richard Strauss, Sigismond Thalberg, Giuseppe Verdi**, and **Richard Wagner**, among many others. [JMC]

RIMSKY-KORSAKOV, NIKOLAY (ANDREYEVICH) (1844–1908).

Russian composer, **conductor**, and pedagogue; a member of the **Mighty Handful** and one of the Late Romantic Generation's most influential exponents of **exoticism** as well as **nationalism**. His programmatic and characteristic **orchestral** works are still widely performed, as are his **orchestrations** and reorchestrations of others composers' works. His *Uchebnik garmonii* (Textbook on Harmony, 1884–1885) and his posthumously published treatise *Osnovï orkestrovki* (Principles of Orchestration, begun in the 1880s) were widely translated and reprinted and used well into the 20th century. He also authored numerous articles on music, music history, and music theory that were published in the popular Russian press of his day. Among his many pupils were **Aleksandr Glazunov, Konstantin Lyadov**, Nicolai Myaskovsky (1881–1950), Prokofiev, Respighi, and Igor Stravinsky.

Rimsky-Korsakov began playing piano at age six but trained in the Russian navy, graduating from the College of Naval Cadets as a midshipman in 1862. Having met **Mily Balakirev, César Cui**, and **Modest Mussorgsky** during his training, he renewed contact with them and began a friendship with **Aleksandr Dargomïzhsky** after returning from his tour of duty in 1865. During the late 1860s, he devoted increasing energy to composition, and in response to the reputation developed through performance of his music he was invited in 1871 to become professor of composition and instrumentation at the St. Petersburg **Conservatory**. The move damaged his relationship with the staunchly anti-Conservatory members of the Mighty Handful but won him additional authority in Russian musical circles. He became inspector of naval bands (a position created specifically for him) in 1873, conductor of the Free School Concerts after Balakirev's death in 1875, and assistant music director to the imperial chapel in 1883.

Meanwhile, Rimsky-Korsakov was increasingly in demand as a composer and conductor. Between 1873 and 1904, he completed some 14 **operas**, three **symphonies**, other orchestral works, original works and arrangements for military band, and a great deal of choral music both sacred and secular as well as vocal and instrumental **chamber music** and works for **piano** solo. During this time, he also conducted his own and others' music in Brussels and Paris (the Paris Exposition of 1899). His overt sympathy with the First Russian Revolution that culminated in "Bloody Sunday" on 22 January 1905 led to his dismissal from his post at the Conservatory, but support for him from the faculty and students of the institution as well as from the general public led to his reinstatement later that year when Glazunov became the institution's director.

Despite his commitment to Russian nationalism and his brilliant forays in musical exoticism, Rimsky-Korsakov was also deeply impressed by **Richard Wagner**'s **music drama**s and was an avid consumer of other Western music (although he hissed unabashedly at **Richard Strauss**'s *Salome* and expressed only guilty pleasure on hearing the music of **Claude Debussy**). His best-known works today are the characteristic *Kaprichchio na ispanskiye temï* (**Capriccio** on Spanish Themes or Capriccio espagnol, 1887, publ. 1888), the **programmatic** symphonic **suite** *Sheherazade* (1888, publ. 1889), and *Svetlïy prazdnik* (Russian Easter Festival **Overture**, 1888, publ. 1889). [JMC]

See also PROGRAM (PROGRAMMATIC) MUSIC; PROGRAM SYMPHONY *OR* CHARACTERISTIC SYMPHONY; SYMPHONIC POEM.

THE RING OF THE NIBELUNG. (Ger., *Der Ring des Nibelungen.*) Stage festival play (*Bühnenfestspiel*), WWV 86, by **Richard Wagner** comprising a **cycle** of four **music drama**s to be performed in a preliminary evening (*Vorabend*) and three subsequent performances; **libretti** by Wagner himself, after German and Norse mythology, poetry, and other literature, with indirect but substantive influences from ancient Greek tragedy. The constituent **operas** are *Das Rheingold* (The Gold of the Rhine), *Die Walküre* (The Valkyries), *Siegfried*, and *Götterdämmerung* (Twilight of the Gods). The first two works were premiered separately in 1869 and 1870, respectively, and the latter two as the last two nights of the premiere of the complete tetralogy (14–17 August 1876).

The *Ring* cycle is scored for an immense **orchestra** including piccolo, three flutes, three oboes, English horn, three clarinets, bass clarinet, and three bassoons; eight horns (doubled as needed by four Wagner tubas), three trumpets, bass trumpet, three trombones and contrabass trombone, and contrabass tuba; two sets of timpani, triangle, cymbals, and Glockenspiel; six harps; and strings (16 first violins, 16 second violins, 12 violas, 12 cellos, and eight basses). Other instruments are called for at select moments in the individual operas: bass drum, tam-tam, onstage harp, 18 anvils, and snare drum, and onstage bullhorn. In modern traditions, this scoring produces problems in balance, with the result that singers must possess an exceptionally powerful and resonant tone in order to be heard over the dense **orchestration**; however, Wagner's design for the **Bayreuth** *Festspielhaus* (where the cycle was premiered) in these operas and *Parsifal* places all the brass and percussion beneath the stage rather than in front of it. It also provides for an acoustic cover that forms a shell between the orchestra and audience and a downward-sloping stage extension that would further mute the instruments in the rear of the orchestra.

Aside from its remarkable orchestration, the *Ring* cycle and its constituent operas are extraordinary in their contrapuntal and harmonic technique and the unprecedented richness and complexity of dramaturgy. They are also a de facto compendium of ideas and compositional techniques that Wagner had developed as part of his conceptualization of the music drama, the *Gesamtkunstwerk*, and the **Artwork of the Future**—most importantly, *Leitfaden*, *Stabreim*, and *unendliche Melodie*.

The core text of Wagner's cycle is the anonymous 13th-century *Nibelungenlied* (Song of the Nibelung). This epic saga had been discovered in 1755 and by the early 19th century had aroused great enthusiasm in the German lands (composers who set or adapted it or planned to do so included Heinrich Dorn [1804–1892], **Fanny Hensel**, **Felix Mendelssohn Bartholdy**, and **Robert Schumann**, among others). Wagner's idea for the cycle may have come indirectly from the aesthetician and philosopher Friedrich Theodor Vischer (1807–1887) via the prominent feminist, poet, and women's-rights activist Louise Otto (later Otto-Peters, 1819–1895). In 1844, Vischer, in his lengthy *Kritische Gänge* (Critical Paths), called for a German national opera. Otto responded to this challenge in a lengthy serial article, with draft libretto based on the *Nibelungenlied* published in the **Neue Zeitschrift für Musik** under the editorship of Wagner's close friend and advocate **Franz Brendel** between August and October 1845. Around the same time (between July and November), Wagner drew on Otto's text in Act II, scene 4, of *Lohengrin* (WWV 75). Brendel echoed Vischer's and Otto's challenge again in 1846. Wagner set to work on the project in 1848, first sketching a prose summary of the entire cycle, then drafting prose summaries for the individual operas, and finally penning the individual libretti working backward from

Götterdämmerung to *Das Rheingold* and completing these in 1852. Only after completing the poetic text did he set about composing the music, now working forward from the beginning of the cycle to the end (*see* COMPOSITIONAL PROCESS, CREATIVE PROCESS).

In its original Middle High German form as discovered in 1755, the *Nibelungenlied* represented for German speakers a national epic whose significance was similar to that of the **Ossian** saga in the British Isles, the *Kalevala* for Finns, or the *Edda* for Icelanders: it was a work of great literature, historical in nature and epic in scope, that offered a worthy peer to the great works of ancient Greece and Rome and thus established a great and valorous—and distinctively German—distant past that could inspire a sense of national pride. In adapting the subject, Wagner infused it with a variety of other influences as well. Because Wagner's first active work on the project occurred amidst the political and cultural turbulence of the mid-19th century, it seems likely that he originally envisioned its core narrative of the decadence of the gods and the courage and valor of the individuals (especially Siegfried) who rose up against them to seize power as an implicit allegory of the many anarchical, socialist, and utopian movements that proliferated at mid-century. Wagner's own direct personal involvement in the **Revolutions of 1848** makes such a scenario all the more likely, as does his view of the **Gesamtkunstwerk** as an expressly political construct. Such a view underlies George Bernard Shaw's interpretation in *The Perfect Wagnerite* (1898). But the literary and dramaturgical multifacetedness of Wagner's cycle also invites other interpretations—most notably, Jungian and eco-centric ones. [JMC]

See also ALLGEMEINER DEUTSCHER MUSIKVEREIN; NEW GERMAN SCHOOL.

RISORGIMENTO. (It., "Resurgence.") In 18th- and 19th-century history, a period of cultural **nationalism** and political activism that strove for (and ultimately achieved) the political unification of the Italian-speaking countries. The Italian peninsula had not been a single political entity since the fall of the Western Roman Empire in the fifth century, and since the 16th century, it had been dominated continuously by foreign powers. The temporary expulsion of Habsburg Austria and other repressive powers during the Revolutionary period and the Napoleonic Wars encouraged hopes for eventual unification, and these hopes attained new ardency when the map of Europe was redrawn and the old order restored, with the Italian lands subject to foreign authority, after the **Congress of Vienna**.

The drive for unification produced numerous secret societies (such as the *Carbonari* and the *Giovine Italia*) whose goal was to generate political unrest and eventually unseat the establishment. The *Risorgimento* uprising against Austrian rule in 1848 was one of the most important events in that year of revolution and eventually led the various factions to unite around Vittorio Emanuele Maria Alberto Eugenio Ferdinando Tommaso, king of Sardinia, as leader of a future unified Italy. War erupted in 1859, and despite threats to the project of unification caused by wars among various Italian lands, the project did succeed. The Two Sicilies and the Kingdom of Sardinia were united with most of the rest of the peninsula under the former king of Sardinia (now Vittorio Emanuele II) in March 1861. With the acquisition of Venetia in 1866 and the papal lands in 1870, the project was complete.

The *Risorgimento* resided primarily in the middle and lower classes (not the ruling one, for obvious reasons). In an age of rapidly expanding public patronage and the music publishing industry (*see* PRINTING AND PUBLISHING OF MUSIC), this meant that **librettists**, poets, and composers used music as a potent means of sending politically seditious messages through the textual content, characters, and memorable melodies of Romantic **opera** and **song**. Opera in particular was an effective tool in this project. In the domain of opera buffa (*see* COMIC OPERA), important works included Salvatore Viganò's (1769–1821) *Giovanna d'Arco* (1820–1821) and Luigi Ricci's (1805–1859) *Il nuovo Figaro* (1832). There were also Italian stage adaptations of French **grand operas** associated with themes of oppression (most prominently, **Giacomo Meyerbeer**'s *Les Huguenots*). The operas of **Vincenzo Bellini**, **Gaetano Donizetti**, and **Gioachino Rossini** figured prominently as well, establishing the rousing opera chorus as an expression of a "voice of the people."

By far the most important figure associated with the *Risorgimento* was **Giuseppe Verdi**, whose name served as an acronym for the king-designate of the future unified Italy (Vittorio Emanuele, Ré D'Italia = Victor Emmanuel, King of Italy) in the slogan "Viva VERDI" beginning in 1859. Verdi was sympathetic to the *Risorgimento*—he composed the *Inno populare* (Hymn of the People) at the behest of the *Risorgimento* leader Giuseppe Mazzini (1805–1872) in 1848 and composed a new *Inno delle nazione* (Hymn of the Nations), on a text by **Arrigo Boito**, to represent the newly unified Italy at London's International Exhibition in 1862—and after the unification many of his operas were reinterpreted as operatic expressions of sympathy for the movement. Within his operas themselves, however, there are few overt gestures of support for the *Risorgimento*. The elements sympathetic to the movement are mostly allegorical or general in nature—noble citizens ruthlessly oppressed (*see* RESCUE OPERA) or intense expressions of love for the *patria* in *Nabucco* (1842), *I Lombardi* (1843), *Attila* (1846), and *Macbeth* (1847). Most obvious among the latter works is *La battaglia di Legnano* (The Battle of Legnano, 1849), whose (fictionalized) depiction of the 12th-century Lombards' expulsion of the cruel German Holy Roman Emperor Friedrich I ("Barbarossa") was intended as an overt allegory for contemporary Italians' overthrow of the Austrian rule—a gesture that did not escape the attention of the censors. The legend that the moving Chorus of Hebrew Slaves ("Va, pensiero") from *Nabucco* was encored because it resonated so strongly with the sentiments of Austria's contemporary Italian subjugates is untrue (it was instead the chorus "Immenso Jehova," sung by the Hebrew slaves as thanks to God for saving His people, that was encored). [JMC]

See also NATIONALISM, ROMANTIC NATIONALISM.

RODE, (JACQUES) PIERRE (JOSEPH) (1774–1830). French **virtuoso** violinist and composer of the Early Romantic Generation; with **Pierre Baillot** and **Rudolfe Kreutzer** one of the most influential exponents of the French Classical school of violin. He began playing violin at age six and, after several years of studying with a local violinist, went to Paris in 1787 to study with Giovanni Battista Viotti (1755–1824). This he did for three years, becoming the aging Italian virtuoso's favorite pupil and making his public debut in 1790, with further performances of Viotti's last two **concertos** in 1792. He was appointed to the faculty of the newly formed Paris **Conservatory** in 1795 but began teaching there only in 1799. During the period 1795–1799, he had already toured in the German lands, the Low Countries, and England, and he continued his international performing in 1800 with appearances in the Italian lands and Spain, there befriending Luigi Boccherini (1743–1805). On his return, he was named solo violinist to Napoléon Bonaparte, and during the Napoleonic era, his fame spread still further as he traveled extensively in the German lands (where **Louis Spohr**, among many others, admired his playing) before settling in Russia as solo violinist to the tsar (1804–1808) and living for a time with **Adrien Boieldieu** in St. Petersburg. Upon his return to Western Europe, contemporaries found that his skills had deteriorated; the Parisian public responded coolly to his concerts there, and **Ludwig van Beethoven**, who had composed his op. 96 Violin Sonata to fit Rode's style, was disappointed when he premiered that work in Vienna in 1812.

Rode settled in Berlin from 1814 through 1819 and there taught Eduard Rietz (1802–1832), the boyhood friend and informal violin instructor of **Felix Mendelssohn Bartholdy**. After retiring to his native Bordeaux for several years, he made a disastrous attempt at a Parisian comeback in 1828. His health subsequently failed him; he became paralyzed and died soon afterward. He is best remembered today for the *Méthode de Violon* (Violin Method), which he coauthored with Baillot and Kreutzer and published in 1803. He also composed a total of 12 violin concertos, of which No. 7 (in A Minor, Op. 9, 1803) is still well known, as well as four **string quartets** and several *quatuors brillants* and a small quantity of other instrumental and vocal **chamber music**. [JMC]

See also PERFORMANCE PRACTICE.

ROMANCE. (Fr., romance; Ger., Romanze, It. and Sp., romanza *or* romanzero.) In the **long 19th century**, a vocal or instrumental composition lyrical in style and usually moderate or slow in tempo, often with a strophic or other simple form and an amorous, epic, or sentimental character. Like *Gesang*, **Lied**, and *mélodie*, the term is both literary and musical: poets composed texts that they titled "romance" because of those texts' character, content, and form, independently of any music, and composers alternately set texts already designated as "romances" to music or composed instrumental music that emulated the style of vocal romances. (The usual French term for **Lieder ohne Worte** is *romances sans paroles*, or "textless romances," and **Robert Schumann** designated as "Romanze" the slow movements of his *Konzertstück for Four Horns and Orchestra* [Op. 86, 1849, publ. 1851] and his D-minor **Symphony** [Op. 120, first composed in 1841 and revised in 1853]). Romances figured prominently in French and Italian **opera** of the long 19th century, although these, unlike their counterparts in vocal **chamber music** and instrumental music, typically assumed an ominous, gruesome, or dramatic character.

César Cui, himself a prolific contributor to the genre of the vocal-chamber romance, published two essays on the history and development of the Russian romance. Composers of the long 19th century who penned autonomous vocal romances include **Anatoly Arensky, Ludwig van Beethoven, William Sterndale Bennett, Hector Berlioz, Adrien Boieldieu, Johannes Brahms,** Cui, **Aleksandr Dargomïzhsky, Gaetano Donizetti, Aleksandr Glazunov, Mikhail Glinka, Charles Gounod, Edvard Grieg, Adolf von Henselt, Franz Liszt, Carl Loewe, Étienne-Nicolas Méhul, Serge Rachmaninoff, Nikolay Rimsky-Korsakov, Franz Schubert,** Robert Schumann, **Aleksandr Scriabin, Gaspare Spontini, Pyotor Il'yich Tchaikovsky, Sigismond Thalberg,** and **Richard Wagner.** Operatic romances were composed by **Adolphe Adam, Daniel-François-Esprit Auber, Vincenzo Bellini,** Berlioz, **Henry Bishop, Luigi Cherubini,** Donizetti, **François-Auguste Gevaert,** Gounod, **Fromenthal Halévy, Heinrich Marschner, Giacomo Meyerbeer, Otto Nicolai, Jacques Offenbach, Amilcare Ponchielli, Gioachino Rossini, Camille Saint-Saëns,** Schubert, **Louis Spohr,** Tchaikovsky, **Ambroise Thomas, Giuseppe Verdi,** Wagner, and Weber, among others. The many composers who penned instrumental romances include **Mily Balakirev,** Beethoven, Bennett, Berlioz, **Max Bruch, Cécile Chaminade, Carl Czerny, Felix Draeseke, Edward Elgar, Gabriel Fauré, John Field, Louis Moreau Gottschalk,** Gounod, **Charles Hallé, Stephen Heller, Vincent d'Indy, Joseph Joachim, Édouard Lalo, Franz Liszt, Edward Macdowell, Felix Mendelssohn Bartholdy, Elias Parish-Alvars,** Rachmaninoff, **Joachim Raff, Max Reger, Carl Reinecke, Anton Rubinstein,** Saint-Saëns, **Clara Schumann,** Robert Schumann, **Maria Szymanowska,** Tchaikovsky, and Thalberg. [JMC]

See also SONG.

ROMBERG, ANDREAS (JAKOB) (1767–1821). Violinist and composer of the Early Romantic Generation; nephew of Bernhard Anton Romberg (1742–1814). He began touring with his father, his uncle, and his cousin, **Bernhard Heinrich Romberg**, in 1782, earning praise in Frankfurt am Main and Paris before joining the electoral court **orchestra** in Bonn in 1790. The invasion of Napoléon Bonaparte's armies in 1793 prompted the Rombergs' escape to Hamburg and engagement in the court orchestra there, followed by a two-year concert tour of the Italian lands in 1795 and a stay in Vienna in 1796. After 1800, Andreas Romberg settled in Hamburg and devoted his energies increasingly to composition but he relocated to Gotha in 1815, succeeding **Louis Spohr** as concertmaster of the court orchestra there. His best-known work, an 1809 setting of **Friedrich Schiller**'s lengthy (430-line) poem *Das Lied von der Glocke* (Song of the Bell) for SATB chorus and orchestra, remained popular throughout the 19th century. He also composed numerous other sacred and secular choral works, plus nine **symphonies**, 20 violin **concertos**, five double concertos (two for violin and cello, two for two violins, and one for clarinet and violin), 25 **string quartets**, one **octet**, and various other instrumental **chamber** compositions as well as eight **operas**. [JMC]

ROMBERG, BERNHARD HEINRICH (1767–1841). Cellist and composer of the Early Romantic Generation; son of Bernhard Anton Romberg (1742–1814), and after **Ludwig van Beethoven** his generation's most important German composer of music for cello solo. Until 1797, he pursued a career identical to that of his cousin, **Andreas Romberg**, then he toured London, Portugal, and Spain, earning the praise of Luigi Boccherini (1743–1805). He went to Paris in 1799 and began working as a cellist there before receiving a teaching appointment at the **Conservatory** (1801), where he taught on the faculty with **Rudolfe Kreutzer**. He moved to Berlin in 1805 and was based there until 1836, also touring widely. His compositions include 10 cello **concertos** and numerous other concertos and *concertante* works for cello or other instrument with **orchestra**, five **symphonies**, a great deal of instrumental **chamber music**, and a small quantity of vocal chamber music. He also penned three **operas**, one **operetta**, one **ballet**, and one set of **incidental music**. He is most important for the changes he introduced to the 19th-century cello and cello technique, especially his popularization and expansion of the bowing techniques and musical applications of the Tourte bow. [JMC]

ROMEO AND JULIET. (Fr., *Roméo et Juliette*; Ger., *Romeo und Julia.*) Iconic tragedy by **William Shakespeare**, first published in a corrupt edition in 1597 and then in a better one in 1599. Its tale of star-crossed lovers caught up in a feud between rival families and a well-meaning but largely ineffectual mediation from the Church combined with its vivid portrayals of characters and emotions to win for it a cult status in the **long 19th century**. This status was especially pronounced on the European continent, where Shakespeare's own persona (first cultivated in writings of the *Sturm und Drang* in the 1770s) as an impassioned breaker of rules who was possessed of virtually infinite imagination only enhanced the antiestablishment elements of the story in the eyes of the Romantics.

The story of Romeo and Juliet was not original to Shakespeare; he based his play on Arthur Brooke's (d. ca. 1563) poem *The Tragicall Historye of Romeus and Juliet* (1562) and William Painter's (ca. 1540–1595) *The Palace of Pleasure* (1580 or earlier), which was in turn based on a French translation of Matteo Bandello's (ca. 1480–1562) novella *Giulietta e Romeo* (1554). **Vincenzo Bellini**'s opera *I Capuleti e i Montecchi* (1830) stems from this Italian source and other Italian literature based on it, not from Shakespeare's play. **Frederick Delius**'s opera *A Village Romeo and Juliet* (1907) is based on a novel by Gottfried Keller (1819–1890) and may be considered an indirect descendant of Shakespeare's play.

Shakespeare's version of the old Italian tale—or, rather, various translations and adaptations of it, some of them quite free—was the one that exerted the greatest influence on Romantic music. By consensus, the most important versions of it from the long 19th century are **Hector Berlioz**'s "dramatic symphony" (1839), **Charles Gounod**'s opera (1867), and **Pyotor Il'yich Tchaikovsky**'s **concert overture** (1869, rev. 1870 and 1880). **Robert Schuman** drafted a scenario for a **libretto** on Shakespeare's play in 1850. In the early 19th century, Niccolò Antonio Zingarelli's (1752–1837) opera *Giulietta e Romeo* (1796), based on Shakespeare and other sources, remained quite popular, as did Nicola Vaccai's (1790–1848) opera by the same name (1826, rev. 1835). Other composers who used Shakespeare's tragedy as a starting point for **ballet**, concert overture, **incidental music**, or opera include Pietro Carlo Guglielmi (1810), Claus Nielsen Schall (1811), William Seaman Stevens (1815), George A. Macfarren (1838), Niels Ravnkilde (1846), **Stephen Foster** (1864), Filippo Marchetti (1866), Richard d'Ivry (1867), Louis Schlottmann (1867), William H. Callcott (1869), Alfred Lebeau (1869), Henry Hugo Pierson (1873), **Joachim Raff** (1879), **Julius Benedict** (1882), and Karl Kliebert (1886). [JMC]

DER ROSENKAVALIER. (Ger., "The Knight of the Rose.") **Opera** ("Komödie für Musik") in three acts by **Richard Strauss** on a **libretto** by Hugo von Hoffmannsthal (1874–1929), premiered in Dresden in 1911. Like its immediate predecessors in Strauss's oeuvre, *Salome* (1905) and *Elektra* (1909), *Der Rosenavalier* is a **music drama** thoroughly indebted to the Wagnerian tradition, especially in its pervasive use of *Leitmotiv*. It is a romantic comedy involving, like the operas by **Wolfgang Amadeus Mozart** that Strauss greatly admired, mistaken identity and class conflict, with the young lower-class Octavian beating out the lecherous Baron von Ochs for the hand of aristocratic Marschallin Marie Thérèse, Princess Werdenberg. The setting is the Viennese court around 1745. The libretto is the product of extensive collaboration between Strauss and Hoffmannsthal. It was adapted from the novel *Les amours du chevalier de Faublas* (The Loves of the Knight of Faublas, 1787–1790) by Louvet de Couvray (1760–1797) and Molière's (1622–1673) comedy *Monsieur de Pourceaugnac* (1669).

The musical language of *Der Rosenkavalier* is unabashedly tonal and consonant. This fact shocked a musical public that, in view of Strauss's well-established persona as one of the most aggressive modernists of the Modern Romantic Generation and the unrelenting dissonance and hyperchromaticism of *Salome* and *Elektra*, expected from this composer anything but a romantic comedy set to luxuriously post-Romantic tonal music. Some critics (most notably Theodor Adorno and Arnold Schoenberg) viewed the opera as a retrenchment on Strauss's part—an indication that, having ventured into the turbulent waters of unresolved dissonance and posttonal harmony, he became frightened by those prospects and retreated instead into the safety of a more comfortable, less challenging musical language. Others see in *Der Rosenkavalier* an even greater sophistication of harmonic and motivic technique than had been submitted in his previous works and—more importantly—an implicit ideological assertion that emancipated dissonance is not the only key to modernism. For the remainder of his career, Strauss would remain true to the opera's musical idiom and to its extraordinarily subtle yet provocative exploration of often-delicate subjects. [JMC]

See also WAGNER, (WILHELM) RICHARD (1813–1883).

ROSSINI, GIOACHINO (ANTONIO) (1792–1868). Italian composer and director of the Early Romantic Generation, generally considered his generation's greatest composer of Italian **opera**. In his day, he was the only serious rival to the fame of **Ludwig van Beethoven** as well as the leading composer of opera in Paris during the **Bourbon Restoration** prior to the rise of **Giacomo Meyerbeer** and **grand opera** in the 1830s.

Rossini's mother and father were employed as a singer and horn player by a local theater in his native Pesaro, and his boyhood experiences were repeatedly disrupted by Napoléon Bonaparte's Italian campaigns, inextricably intertwining opera and politics and French and Italian culture in the young composer's eyes. He studied cello, **piano**, and voice in Bologna beginning in 1804 and soon began composing as well as working as a rehearsal pianist in local theaters. His second opera (the one-act *La cambiale di matrimonio* [The Marriage Contract]), completed and produced at the Teatro San Moisè (Venice) on 3 November 1810, when he was 18, was an immediate success, encouraging a steady stream of no fewer than five operas from his pen over the next 18 months. His career as a leading figure in Italian opera of the Napoleonic era was cemented with *La pietra del paragone* (The Touchstone), which ran for a total of 53 performances after it was premiered at La Scala on 26 September 1812.

Ideas now came readily to Rossini, and so did success. In 1813–1814, he penned another six operas, including two that have retained a firm place in the repertoire (*Tancredi*, 1813, and *L'italiana in Ageri* [The Italian Girl in Algiers], 1813), followed by another two in 1815. Up to this point, Naples had remained largely immune to the growing Rossini mania, but it, too, would be conquered in the course of the nearly unbroken stream of successes that flowed from his pen over the next seven years: *Elisabetta, regina d'Inghliterra* (Elizabeth, Queen of England, Naples, 1815; after Walter Scott's *Kenilworth*), *Otello, ossia Il moro di Venezia* (Othello; or, The Moor of Venice, Naples, 1816; after **William Shakespeare**), *La Cenerentola, ossia La bontà in trionfo* (Cinderella; or, Goodness Triumphant, Rome, 1817), *Mosè in Egitto* (Moses in Egypt, Naples, 1818; subject of a celebrated **fantasy** by **Sigismond Thalberg**), *La donna del lago* (The Lady of the Lake, Naples, 1819; after Walter Scott), and, most importantly, *Il barbiere di Siviglia* (The Barber of Seville, Rome, 1816; after Beaumarchais), one of the greatest **comic operas** of the **long 19th century**. His conquest of the Italian stage continued in the early 1820s with works such as *Maometto II* (Mohammed II, Naples, 1820), *Zelmira* (Naples, 1822), and *Semiramide* (Venice, 1823). Collectively, these works raised the dramatic and musical stakes for Italian serious and **comic opera** to new heights—not only celebrating the beauty and agility of the human voice and the colors offered by the Romantic **orchestra** but also creating new approaches to operatic dramaturgy and musical pacing as well as techniques for generating variety and unity in large-scale dramatic structures.

In October 1823, Rossini and his wife left Bologna for London via Paris, where many of his 34 operas were already known (albeit in heavily altered versions) at the Théatre-Italien. The Rossini season that had been organized by the King's Theatre was unsuccessful, but the couple's wealth increased significantly by the largesse of English aristocracy who paid generous sums for music lessons. In February 1824, he signed a contract with the French government to stay for one year in Paris, writing new works for the Opéra and the Opéra-Comique as well as supervising new productions of his older ones. His conquest of Paris began on 7 September with an immensely successful production of *Il donna del lago* at the Théâtre-Italien, and in November he signed a new contract as *directeur de la musique et de la scène* (director of music and scene) at the theater. He brought the Théâtre-Italien to new heights of success with French reworkings of the earlier operas *Maometto II* (as *La siège de Corinthe* [The Siege of Corinth], 1826), *Mosè in Egitto* (as *Moïse et Pharaon, ou Le passage de la Mer Rouge* [Moses and Pharaoh; or, The Crossing of the Red Sea], 1827) and the new opera *Il viaggio a Reims* (The Journey to Rheims, 1825), an allegorical celebration of the coronation of Charles X (*see* BOURBON RESTORATION), and his productions of other composers' works (most notably **Giacomo Meyerbeer**'s *Il crociato in Egitto*, 1825). Fully cognizant of the special importance of language and declamation in French opera, he was slow to produce a new opera in French for the Parisian stage. The first such work, *Le comte Ory* (1828; on a libretto by **Eugène Scribe** and Charles-Gaspard Delestre-Poirson [1790–1859]), reused much music from *Il viaggio a Reims*. The next, **Guillaume Tell** (1829; after **Friedrich Schiller**), would be his final operatic masterpiece as well as an early milestone in the genre that was to become known as grand opera.

Rossini had been considering retirement for some time, and the success of *Tell* combined with his receipt of a handsome unconditional lifetime annuity from the French state to make it possible. Although he continued to work occasionally with the Théatre-Italien until 1836, he and his wife returned to Bologna in 1829. His physical and mental health began to suffer in 1832, and he composed little. He also separated from his wife in 1836 and after her death in 1846 married the artist's model Olympe Pélissier (1799–1878), with whom he had begun an affair in the early 1830s. The principal compositional fruits of his Italian retirement are the *Soirées musicales* (ca. 1830–1835, publ. 1835) and the *Stabat mater* (1841). He and his new wife fled to Florence in the wake of the Revolutions of 1848 but in 1855 returned to Paris. There, his condition and creativity improved markedly, producing two final musical gems: the *Péchés de vieillesse* (Sins of Old Age, mostly published posthumously), a collection of 163 **songs** and **piano** pieces, composed and gathered over the period 1857–1858 and reflective of the French capital's still-vibrant **salon** culture, and the *Petite Messe solennelle* (1st version, for 12 solo vv, two pianos, and harmonium, 1863, rev. 1864; 2nd version, for SATB, chorus, and orchestra, 1867; both versions publ. posth., 1869; *see* SOLEMN MASS). He fell ill in the autumn of 1868 and died in his villa near Paris on 13 November. He was buried in the Père-Lachaise Cemetery after a funeral attended by thousands and mourning throughout France and the Italian lands.

Rossini has often been portrayed as a facile, insouciant composer who tossed off hurriedly composed operas in order to cater to the superficial tastes of his contemporary bourgeois public while making as much money as possible—but this image is largely a product of the rivalry between him and Beethoven and of 19th-century German historians' cultivation of stereotypes contrasting Italians' simple and lighthearted nature with the ostensibly more artistically serious and authentically passionate personalities of Rossini's German Austrian generational compeers Beethoven and **Carl Maria von Weber**. While it is true that Rossini recycled much of his music from one work to another, he viewed this as rehabilitation, not reuse—and the reappropriation (a more neutral term) was always from failed works to successful ones: he did not reuse already successful music. He was aghast when he learned in the 1850s that **Ricordi** would be publishing all his operas:

> the publication . . . will bring all my operas together before the eyes of the public. The same pieces will be found several times, for I thought I had the right to remove from my fiascos those pieces which seemed best, to rescue them from shipwreck by placing them in new works. A fiasco seemed to be good and dead, and now look they've resuscitated them all!

Moreover, Rossini's successfulness in the *buffo* tradition has obscured his accomplishments in casting aside the reified conventions of Italian *opera seria* as they had been cultivated by earlier and contemporary composers such as Giovanni Paisiello (1740–1816) and Nicolò Zingarelli (1752–1837), developing new approaches to drama, musical form, and **orchestration** that would provide the essential framework for the compositions of other composers such as **Vincenzo Bellini, Gaetano Donizetti**, and all but the latest works of **Giuseppe Verdi**. In addition to his 39 operas, he composed six Mass settings and many other Catholic liturgical works, 17 **cantatas**, many hymns, and other nonliturgical sacred works; many Italian songs (including the *Soirées musicales*); and 24 works for **orchestra** or military band. [JMC]

RUBINSTEIN [RUBINSHTEYN]. Family name of Anton (Grigor'yevich) (1829–1894) and Nikolay (Grigor'yevich) (1835–1881), both Russian pianists, composers, **conductors**, and educators of Jewish descent. Both were highly regarded as pianists and composers, although Anton, by far the more prolific composer, tends to overshadow Nikolay in both these regards today. Their significance is amplified by their leadership in Russian cultural life: together with the German-born Grand Duchess Elena Pavlovna (1807–1873), they founded the Russian Musical Society in 1859, Anton serving as its director from 1859 to 1867 and Nikolay as director of a Moscow branch beginning with its founding in 1859. Additionally, Anton founded the St. Petersburg **Conservatory** (Russia's first conservatory; today the N. A. **Rimsky-Korsakov** Saint Petersburg State Conservatory) in 1862, and Nicolay founded the Moscow Conservatory in 1866. Their upbringing, too, had many commonalities: both began to exhibit musical talent at an early age, both studied **piano** with Theodor Kullak (1818–1882) and harmony and counterpoint with Siegfried Dehn (1799–1858) while the family was in Berlin in 1844–1846, and in Russia both studied piano with Aleksandr Villoing (1804 or 1808–1878), who took them on tours and promoted them as child **virtuosi**. Beyond these obvious and important parallels, the two brothers' lives read as a study in contrasts. Anton composed in large-scale public genres, producing some 19 **operas**, five published piano **concertos**, a concerto for violin and one for cello, six **symphonies**, and a number of occasional and programmatic **overtures**. He began his professional concert career with a tour of Western Europe in 1854 and in the winter of 1856–1857, while staying in an apartment of the Grand Duchess Helen of Nice, began planning to improve music education in Russia. A Russian patriot, he was instrumental in erecting the first monument to **Mikhail Glinka**; however, he was also aware that most of the best instrumentalists in Russia were of either French or German training and began crusading against the amateurism prevalent in Russian musical life early on. His dismissal of most of Russia's native talent as amateurish also earned him the enmity of the Russian **nationalist** circles represented by the **Mighty Handful**, but the same pursuit underlay achievements such as the founding of the Russian Musical Society and the St. Petersburg Conservatory. He served as director of that institution from 1862 to 1867 and again from 1887 to 1891, meanwhile composing prodigiously and continuing his pursuits as a virtuoso pianist comparable only to **Franz Liszt** in his technical and musical accomplishments and range.

After leaving the Conservatory in 1867, Anton toured Europe, and in 1871, he served as director of the Philharmonic Concerts in Vienna. At the behest of **Steinway** & Sons, he toured the United States, giving an extraordinary 215 concerts between 10 September 1872 and 24 May 1873. During these tours, his repertoire continued to broaden; in 1885–1886, for example, his tour of Europe and Russia included a series of seven historical concerts, beginning with William Byrd (1540–1623), John Bull (ca. 1563–1628), François Couperin (1668–1733), and Jean-Philippe Rameau (1683–1764), moving through the German and French **canon**, and concluding with contemporary Russian composers. After leaving the Conservatory again in 1891, he resettled in Dresden, also giving benefit concerts elsewhere in Germany and Austria. His prestige as a composer is attested to by the fact that his music was published by some 21 individual publishers in Russia and Western Europe (*see* PRINTING AND PUBLISHING OF MUSIC) and his importance as a teacher of composition and of piano by the roster of his pupils, which includes **Pyotor Il'yich Tchaikovsky** as well as the legendary Josef Hofmann (1876–1957).

Nicolay, by all accounts a gregarious bon vivant who enjoyed socializing in intimate circles, wrote primarily in intimate genres intended for private consumption. He, too, mentored Tchaikovsky, hiring him as professor of music theory at the Moscow Conservatory in 1866 and actively encouraging the performance of his works. (The two had a well-known falling-out when Nikolay criticized Tchaikovsky's First Piano Concerto as unplayable, but they later reconciled.) Nikolay was also an active supporter of the Mighty Handful. He gave the premiere of the first version of **Mily Balakirev**'s enormously difficult **exoticist** showpiece *Islamey*, Op. 18, just two months after its completion in 1869, also programming and conducting performances of works by the other members of the Mighty Handful. His own roster of piano students included Emil von Sauer (1862–1942), Sergey Taneyev (1856–1915), and Alexander Ziloti (1863–1945). [JMC]

S

SAINETE. (Sp., "farce" or "tidbit," diminutive of *sain*, "spicy sauce"; Fr., saynète.) Term for a one-act comedy (prototypically in Spanish) featuring middle- and lower-class characters in urban settings. Sometimes the texts of these plays were set to music or included musical numbers, and *sainetes* typically were presented between acts or at the conclusion of a larger, longer, and more serious work (tragedies and the like). *Sainetes* gained currency in the last third of the 18th century and were popular for much of the 19th century, with entire companies and theaters devoted to the genre. Like other genres of **comic opera**, they typically employed spoken dialogue rather than recitative.

Sainetes were set apart from other related forms by their sketch-like character and their realistic celebration of urban life, complete with coarse language and protagonists whose attributes were anything but noble. In this sense, the *sainete* not only gave expression in cultivated musical theater to the uneducated masses who otherwise found little direct empathy with the musical stage but also anticipated the aesthetics of realism and the emergence of *verismo* by decades. The genre also spawned a number of regional and stylistic variants, including the shorter and more farcical *sainetillo* ("little sainete"), the Argentine *sainete criollo* (whose social content and musical styles were informed by the realities of life in the River Plate region), and the French *saynète* and *saynète bouffe*. **Jules Massenet** described his *Bérangère et Anatole* (1876; lost) as a *saynète*.

The genre remains popular today. Important composers who wrote music for *sainetes* during the long 19th century included **Francisco Barbieri**, **Tomás Bretón**, Rafael Calleja (1870–1938), Ruperto Chapí (1851–1909), **Manuel Fernández Caballero**, Manuel de Falla (1876–1946), Ángel Rubio (1846–1906), and José Serrano (1873–1941), among many others. [JMC]

See also TONADA; TONADILLA, TONADILLA ESCÉNICA; ZARZUELA.

SAINT-SAËNS, (CHARLES) CAMILLE (1835–1921). French composer, **pianist**, organist, and writer of the Late Romantic Generation; a leader in the French musical renaissance of the 1870s and 1880s and one of France's most prolific composers of his generation. He was born in Paris and entered the **Conservatory** there at the age of 14, studying organ with François Benoist (1794–1878) and composition with **Fromenthal Halévy**. He frequently participated in the **salons** of **Gioachino Rossini** and others beginning around 1849. His abilities as a pianist, organist, writer, and intellectual fluent in discourse on subjects ranging from astronomy and Classical Antiquity to the natural sciences combined with his extraordinary memory, perfect pitch, and wit to make him a leading figure in French cultural life of the 1860s and 1870s. They also broadened his international reputation and impressed even those not ideologically suited to his music (most notably **Richard Wagner**, who in 1859 was astonished by his memory and his ability to sight-read and memorize his complex scores).

During the **Franco-Prussian War**, Saint-Saëns helped defend Paris, but during the ensuing **Commune**, he fled to London, where he was feted in public and private musical life. Returning to Paris in 1871, he helped to found the new **Société Nationale de Musique**, the primary purpose of which was to foster new French music. He was elected to the Académie des Beaux-Arts in 1881 and made an officer in the Légion d'Honneur in 1884, both honors bestowed only on the most esteemed members of French intellectual and cultural life. Although the honors continued to accrue, he became increasingly out of touch with progressive elements in French music. After losing a power struggle with **Vincent d'Indy** and the **César Franck** faction of the Société over the issue of whether the organization should perform the works of foreign as well as French composers, he broke with that group in 1886.

From the early 1880s on, Saint-Saëns toured widely as a pianist and composer, traveling not only to Germany, Italy, and Spain but also to the Canary Islands, East Asia, Russia, Scandinavia, South America, and the United States (Chicago, New York, Philadelphia, San Francisco, Washington, D.C.). He received an honorary doctorate from Cambridge University in 1893, assumed the general editorship of the Rameau *Gesamtsausgabe* (*see* EDITING AND EDITIONS) in 1894, composed a march for the coronation of King Edward VII and was made a Commander of the Victorian Order in 1902, and received an honorary doctorate from Oxford University in 1907. In 1908, he became the first established composer to write a film score (*L'assassinat du duc de Guise*). On 6 August 1921, he gave his final performance at the Dieppe Casino marking 75 years of his public concertizing.

Saint-Saëns was also widely respected as a lecturer and as a witty and insightful writer, publishing dozens of periodical articles, reviews, and public letters on subjects ranging from theater in Classical Antiquity through alchemy and the mystical issues raised by the idea of *musica mundana* to a treatise on harmony and melody (1885) and several sets of recollections. Today, his reputation rests almost exclusively on only four of his many works that resonated deeply with the musical culture of the late 19th century: his Third ("Organ") **Symphony** (Op. 78, 1886), the hastily composed quasi-programmatic set of **character pieces** titled *Carnaval des animaux* (Carnival of the Animals, 1886, publ. 1922), his **opera** *Samson et Delilah* (1859, rev. 1867, rev. 1873–1877, publ. 1878), and his *Danse macabre* (1872, publ. 1873, *see TOTENTANZ*). He also composed 12 other operas; numerous sets of **incidental music** and **ballets**; a large volume of sacred and secular choral music (including many **motets** and three completed **oratorios**); a great deal of vocal **chamber music**; three mature symphonies and two still-unpublished early symphonies; numerous **concert overtures**; two cello **concertos**, five piano concertos, three violin concertos, and numerous shorter works with one or more solo instruments; five works for military band; 30 numbered *opera* of instrumental chamber music; 36 numbered *opera* of works for piano solo or **piano duet**; and many works for harmonium, organ, or other keyboard instrument. [JMC]

SALON. (It., *salone.*) An interdisciplinary and egalitarian private gathering, usually intimate in character, centered on the informal exchange of ideas through conversation, performance of music, and readings or discussion of other art; usually (but not always) organized and directed by a woman (*salonnière*). Its institutional history dates to the *mujālasāt* of the Ummayad dynasty of ninth-century Iraq. From there, it was adopted in the Iberian Moorish Empire and in Counter-Reformation Italy before spreading to virtually every sector of European civilization in the Enlightenment.

The most famous music-inclusive salons of the **long 19th century** were based in Berlin, Paris, and Vienna. In Berlin, the most influential were led by Amalie Beer (ca. 1772–1854; mother of **Giacomo Meyerbeer**), Henriette Herz (1764–1847), Sara Levy (1761–1854; great aunt of **Fanny Hensel** and **Felix Mendelssohn Bartholdy**), Princess Luise Radziwiłł (b. Princess of Prussia; 1770–1836), Clara Simrock (1839–1928), Elisabeth von Stägemann (1761–1835), and Rahel Varnhagen von Ense (1771–1833). Notable Parisian salons were led by Marie d'Agoult (1805–1876; paramour of **Franz Liszt**); Delphine de Girardin (1804–1855); Juliette Récamier (1770–1849); Marguerite de Saint-Marceaux (née Jourdain; 1850–1930); Winaretta Singer, Princesse de Polignac (1865–1943); and Germaine de Staël (1766–1817). Notable Viennese salons were led by Fanny von Arnstein (Vienna, 1758–1818) and Alma **Mahler** Werfel (1879–1974). Other influential salons were led by Elizabeth Fox, Baroness Holland (1771–1845) in London; Nadine Helbig (1847–1922) in Rome; Maria Kalergis (1822–1874) in Warsaw; Cosima Wagner (1837–1930; wife of **Richard Wagner**) in **Bayreuth**; and Jane Francesca ("Speranza"), Lady Wilde, in Dublin (1821–1896).

The long 19th century also enjoyed several other egalitarian interdisciplinary gatherings that featured music while centering less on conversation. Most notable among these were the *Schubertiaden*(sing. **Schubertiade**) hosted by Josef Witteczek (1787–1859) and others in and around Vienna and the ***Sonntagsmusiken*** (Sunday musicales) hosted by the Mendelssohn family in Berlin. The latter were begun by Abraham and Lea Mendelssohn in the 1820s as an offshoot of the salons hosted by Sara Levy; their initial intended purpose was to foster the musical growth of Hensel and Mendelssohn. Hensel reinitiated them in the mid-1830s and continued them until her death in 1847.

Few institutions of musical life have been so pervasively misrepresented and consequently misunderstood as the salon. Latter-day commentators typically construe these gatherings as elitist, self-congratulatory celebrations of triviality and ephemera—comings together of like-minded individuals from close-knit circles within the upper socioeconomic strata to reaffirm tastes and values concerning matters of little contemporary relevance or enduring import. Some certainly were. But most salons were self-consciously interdisciplinary in nature, focused on pressing cultural, intellectual, and political themes and assiduous in their efforts to assemble individuals from diverse vocations and often diverse social standings with emphatically diverse disciplinary and political perspectives. In the context of the strict and pervasive censorship of **Restoration** culture and post-1848 Europe, especially in public and semipublic gatherings, the salon was valued for its potency as a venue that operated largely beyond the purview of the censors, one in which new and controversial ideas could be exchanged among conversants who, for purposes of that gathering, were essentially equal in stature and voice. Music written for such gatherings was thus only rarely elitist or ephemeral in its aspirations. Rather, despite its generally intimate media, it strove—most famously in the works of **Adolphe Adam, Isaac Albéniz, Arrigo Boito, Emmanuel Chabrier, Ernest Chausson, Fryderyk Chopin, Aleksandr Dargomïzhsky, Claude Debussy, Antonín Dvořák, Gabriel Fauré, Enrique Granados,** Hensel, Mendelssohn, **Cenobio Paniagua, Gioachino Rossini, Camille Saint-Saëns, Franz Schubert, Clara Schumann,** and **Václav Tomášek**—for a combination of topicality and aesthetic legitimacy that would not yield to more obviously imposing large forms and genres intended for public consumption.

The decidedly negative connotations of the term "salon music" in latter-day discourse stem from the historiographic polemics surrounding salon culture and **feminism** generally. From the *saloni* of the Counter-Reformation on, such gatherings had traditionally been organized and run by learned women because of their cultivated social graces and because such gatherings operated within the private rather than public sphere and thus did not violate contemporary values concerning women's societal roles and privileges. Influential figures such as Jean-Jacques Rousseau (1712–1778), however, beginning with the *Lettre à d'Alembert sur les spectacles* (Letter to d'Alembert concerning Spectacles, 1758), argued that women were intellectually inferior to men and that they could not productively lead men or engage with them in conversation. Men, such voices asserted, altered their behavior when in the company of women, becoming womanly and cowardly themselves. Rousseau and countless followers submitted that salon discourse celebrated elegance and *politesse* and was consequently superficial rather than substantive. As the tradition of salons as private-sphere gatherings led by women continued through the long 19th century, conservative critics perpetuated Rousseau's critique by categorizing "salon music" as charming, elegant, and sometimes **virtuosic** but generally lacking in depth or substance: women undermine seriousness, and institutions led by women inevitably cultivate superficiality and frivolity.

The issues raised by this critique are many: aside from the obvious aesthetic dismissal of femininity and anything resembling **feminism**, it implicitly denigrates "small forms" such as **character pieces**, instrumental **chamber** works that do not belong to tradition-bound genres such as **sonata** or **string quartet**, and most vocal chamber music. It also tends to regard with suspicion virtually any private music that is virtuosic. While some music written for use in salon culture is not of the highest quality, the same may also be said of much music belonging to large "public" genres. Aesthetic and gender-based prejudice aside, salon culture both inspired and cultivated important composition from virtually every composer of note during the long 19th century. [JMC]

SCENA ED ARIA, SCENA E DUETTO. *See* CONCERT ARIA, SCENA AND ARIA.

SCHERZO (*PL.* SCHERZI *OR* SCHERZOS). (It., "joke" or "jest.") In the **long 19th century**, a quick, lighthearted movement or piece, usually instrumental and often in triple or compound meter with a rounded-binary or ternary form. When used as a movement in the context of a work cast in the **sonata plan**, the scherzo usually falls in the position previously allotted to the minuet. In keeping with the literal sense of the term, many compositions designated as scherzi during the long 19th century exhibit humor, wit, or irony, sometimes by means of unexpected gestures (dynamic outbursts, sudden rests, or intrusions of serious material into lighthearted contexts or vice versa) and often by means of syncopations, cross rhythms or cross accents, or metrical, melodic, or harmonic jokes. In the 1820s and 1830s, a new type of scherzo emerged that was typically in duple rather than triple or compound meter and typically employed thin, transparent, gossamer textures and rapid, repetitive, scampering melodies or motives. The prototype for this new variety was **Felix Mendelssohn Bartholdy**'s *Midsummer Night's Dream Overture*(MWV P3/Op. 21, comp. 1826, publ. 1832). Because the style's **programmatic** association in that well-known work was with the fairies in **William Shakespeare**'s comedy (which were known as "elves" in German translations of the play at the time), scherzi in this new variety are sometimes referred to as "elfin" or "fairy" scherzi.

The long 19th century's application of the term *scherzo* seems to have come into use in the early 1780s, specifically with **Haydn**'s set of six **string quartets** published in 1782 as his Opus 33 (Hob. III: 37–43). These works are thus sometimes his "Scherzo" Quartets, even though their movements labeled "scherzo" are serious or somber in style—that is, "jokes" only in the sense that they are surprising departures from the typically good-natured minuet, which would normally occur in that position in the sonata plan. The term occurs regularly in the works of **Ludwig van Beethoven** from the earliest works of his Early Vienna Period on, beginning with the posthumously published Wind **Octet** of 1792 (Op. posth. 130; comp. before November 1792 and revised as the **String Quartet** in E-flat, Op. 4, in 1793; wind version published 1830) and the third movement of his **Piano Trio** in E-flat Major, Op. 1, no. 1 (1794–1795); the third movement of his First **Symphony** (Op. 21, comp. 1799–1800, publ. 1801) is titled "minuet," but its tempo designation (*allegro molto e vivace*) clearly identifies it as a scherzo in all but name. In keeping with Beethoven's fascination with the applications of **sonata form**, most of these works employ a full-fledged sonata form for at least the outer sections of their typical ternary structure or sometimes all three sections. Although most of Beethoven's are based on the traditional A—B—A—coda process, he began treating this process more flexibly beginning with the **"Eroica" Symphony**, the third section of which is fully written out and marked *pianissimo*, leading to a *fortissimo* coda that also quotes from the trio section. Except for the Eighth Symphony (which uses a slightly archaic stylized minuet rather than a scherzo), the expansion of form and additional modified repetition of sections observed in the "Eroica" would remain characteristic of all Beethoven's remaining symphonic scherzi.

Other composers of the Early Romantic Generation who employed this style of scherzo include **Johann Nepomuk Hummel** (especially the **Bagatelle** op. 107, no. 2, which is titled *Scherzo and Russian Rondo*), **Franz Schubert** (the *Scherzo and Allegro* [D. 570, 1817, publ. posth. 1897] and the Two Scherzi [D. 593, 1817, publ. posth. 1871] as well as the inner movements of the **piano** sonatas and symphonies), and **Carl Maria Weber** (the inner movements of his symphonies, piano sonatas, and instrumental **cham-**

ber works). This variety of scherzo continued to be the norm for the quick internal movement of works in the sonata plan for the remainder of the long 19th century.

Composers of the Romantic Generation, Late Romantic Generation, and Modern Romantic Generation followed the lead established by those central composers of the Austro-German tradition in using a quick triple- or compound-meter ternary form as the internal movement of a sonata cycle, but they also expanded the range of stylistic criteria, topical associations, and structural functions. **Hector Berlioz**'s "Queen Mab" Scherzo for his dramatic symphony *Romeo and Juliet* (H. 79/Op. 17; comp. 1839, publ. 1847), the scherzi of **Robert Schumann**'s Second and Fourth Symphonies (opp. 61 and 120, comp. 1845–1856 and 1841–1842, respectively, and publ. 1847 and 1853), the scherzo of **Johannes Brahms**'s Fourth Symphony (Op. 96, comp. 1884–1885 and publ. 1886), and the scherzi of **Gustav Mahler**'s Fourth, Sixth, and Seventh **symphonies** (comp. 1892, rev. 1910; comp. 1903–1904, rev. 1906; comp. 1904–1905, publ. 1906) rank among the most imaginative specimens of this expanded variety of scherzo within works in the sonata plan. Robert Schumann's *Overture, Scherzo, and Finale* (Op. 52; comp. 1841, rev. 1845, publ. 1846) and **Hugo Wolf**'s *Scherzo and Finale* (1876–1877, posthumously published 1940) may be considered tropes on the scherzo's traditional position in a sonata **cycle**.

Additionally, the 19th century witnessed the creation of a great many instrumental scherzi outside such a formal cycle, both as autonomous works and as components of suites or collections. In the former category, the most important exemplars are Brahms's Scherzo in E-flat Minor for piano solo (Op. 4; comp. 1851, publ. 1854), **Fryderyk Chopin**'s four Scherzi for piano solo (opp. 20, 31, 39, and 54, publ. 1835, 1837, 1839, and 1842–1843, respectively), and **Clara Schumann**'s Scherzi in D minor and C minor (Opp. 10 and 14, publ. 1838 and 1845, respectively). Other such compositions (both freestanding and as parts of collections) for piano solo, **piano duet**, or instrumental chamber ensemble were penned by **William Sterndale Bennett, Aleksandr Borodin, Ferruccio Busoni, Aleksandr Dargomïzhsky, Ferdinand David, Felix Draeseke, Antonín Dvořák, John Field, Niels W. Gade, Louis Moreau Gottschalk, Charles Gounod, Charles Hallé,** Stephen Heller, Adolf von Henselt, Friedrich Kalkbrenner, Édouard Lalo, Franz Liszt,** Mendelssohn, **Serge Rachmaninoff, Joachim Raff, Nikolay Rimsky-Korsakov, Anton Rubinstein, Camille Saint-Saëns,** Robert Schumann, **Louis Spohr, Pyotor Il'yich Tchaikovsky,** and **Sigismond Thalberg,** among a great many others.

The long 19th century also saw the production of scherzi for piano solo based on material from well-known operas, as well as scherzi for voices with and without orchestral or piano accompaniment. The best-known scherzo for piano solo based on an operatic theme is **Carl Czerny**'s *Scherzo brillant sur* *un air favori de l'opéra "Les Huguenots" de Giacomo Meyerbeer*, Op. 407 (1836). The best-known scherzo for voices is Berlioz's *Le trebuchet* for two voices and piano (H. 113/Op. 13, no. 3; comp. before 1846, publ. 1850 in *Fleur de landes*, H. 124), subtitled "scherzo for two voices and piano." Other vocal scherzi were composed by Giacomo Gotifredo Ferrari (1763–1842) and Lauro Rossi (1810–1885), among others. [JMC]

SCHILLER, FRIEDRICH VON (1759–1805). German aesthetician, dramatist, poet, historian, and theorist; with **Johann Wolfgang von Goethe**, the leader of the movement known as Weimar Classicism and after him one of the greatest German literary and political influences on Romantic music and Romanticism generally. His fame rests primarily on his plays, but his poetry and other writings have also remained widely read and influential. He exerted a significant influence on German Romantic philosophy and aesthetics, especially through his *Briefe über die ästhetische Erziehung des Menschen* (Letters on the Aesthetic Education of Man, 1795) and his *Über naïve und sentimentalische Dichtung* (On Naive and Sentimental Poetry, 1796). As a historian, his most famous work is *Die Geschichte des Dreißigjährigen Krieges* (History of the Thirty Years' War, 1792). From 1791 to his death, he served as professor of history at the University of Jena (now named for him), and he was ennobled in 1802. He was deeply influenced by Immanuel Kant (1724–1804). He was not a musician but is known to have esteemed Christoph Willibald Ritter von Gluck (1714–1787) highly.

In the music of the **long 19th century**, Schiller is best known for **Ludwig van Beethoven**'s adaptation of his poem *An die Freude* (To Joy) in the Finale of the Ninth **("Choral") Symphony** and for numerous instrumental and choral works, songs, and stage works inspired by his writings. Composers who have set his texts to music or composed works based on them include **Johannes Brahms** (*Nänie*, Op. 82, 1881), **Max Bruch** (*Das Lied von der Glocke*, Op. 45, 1879), **Gaetano Donizetti** (*Maria Stuarda*, 1835), **Franz Liszt** (*Lieder aus Schillers "Wilhelm Tell,"* LW N32, 1845–1855; *An die Künstler*, LW L9, rev. 1854 and 1857; *Die Ideale*, LW G15, 1856–1857), **Carl Loewe** (most importantly *Die Hochzeit der Thetis*, Op. 120a, 1851, two ballads), **Felix Mendelssohn Bartholdy** (*Festgesang An die Künstler*, MWV D6, Op. 68, 1846), **Franz Schubert** (*Hymne an den Unendlichen*, D. 232, 1815; numerous part-songs and solo songs including *Strophe aus Den Götter Griechenlands*, D. 677, 1819, and *An die Freude*, D. 189, 1815), **Robert Schumann** (most importantly the *Overture to Schiller's "Die Braut von Messina,"* Op. 100, 1851), **Bedřich Smetana** (*Wallensteins Lager*, JB 1: 72, 1859), **Pyotor Il'yich Tchaikovsky** (*Orleanskaya deva* [The Maid of Orléans], 1879, R/1882), **Giuseppe Verdi** (*Giovanna d'Arco*, 1845; *I Masna-*

dieri, 1847, *Luisa Miller*, 1849; *Don Carlos* and *Don Carlo*, 1867 and 1884), and **Carl Maria von Weber** (*Overture and marches for "Turandot, Prinzessin von China*," 1809). [JMC]

See also *ANNÉES DE PÈLERINAGE*; INDY, VINCENT D' (1851–1931); DON JUAN; DWIGHT, JOHN SULLIVAN (1813–1893); GESAMT-KUNSTWERK; HENSEL (NÉE MENDELSSOHN), FANNY (CÄCILIE) (1805–1847); LALO, ÉDOUARD (VICTOIRE ANTOINE) (1823–1892); NATIONALISM, ROMANTIC NATIONALISM; PROGRAM (PROG-RAMMATIC) MUSIC; REINECKE, CARL (HEINRICH CARSTEN) (1824–1910); ROMBERG, ANDREAS (JAKOB) (1767–1821); SECHTER, SIMON (1788–1867).

DIE SCHÖNE MÜLLERIN. (Ger., "The Fair Miller Maid.") A **song cycle** of 20 *Lieder* by **Franz Schubert**, D. 795, on poems of Wilhelm Müller (1794–1827), published as Schubert's Op. 25 in 1824. When Müller wrote the 23 strophic *Schöne Müllerin* poems in 1816–1817, he intended them as a *Liederspiel* for his literary circle in Berlin; they did not appear in print until 1821 as part of his *Sieben und siebzig Gedichte aus den hinterlassenen Papieren eines reisenden Waldhornisten* (77 Poems from the Posthumous Papers of a Traveling Hornist). Ludwig Berger's (1777–1839) *Gesänge aus einem gesellschaftlichen Liederspiele "Die schöne Müllerin,"* Op. 11 (1818), are the first settings from the collection. Schubert composed his settings in the fall of 1823 as he recovered slowly from a serious bout of illness (probably syphilis) earlier that year.

The poems, mainly in the **voice** of a wandering miller, trace his journey to a mill, where he falls for a young woman. When she falls in love with the hunter, the protagonist ends his pain by drowning himself in the brook that runs the mill wheel. In the poem of Schubert's penultimate Lied, the first person alternates between the miller and the brook, which is only a passive audience to the miller's songs until this point; in the final Lied, the brook sings a final lullaby to the miller. While the song cycle generally maintains a simple, folk-like style (*see* VOLKSTÜMLICHKEIT), it often astonishes the listener with harmonically bold gestures (such as the switching between major and minor in No. 16, "Die liebe Farbe" [The Dear Color], which also juxtaposes sweet sentiments with macabre images) and powerfully expressive **piano** accompaniment (e.g., the undulating, flowing accompaniment to No. 2, "Wohin" [Where To?], which addresses the brook). [RK]

SCHUBERT, FRANZ (PETER) (1797–1828). Austrian composer of the Early Romantic Generation; seminal figure in the history of the **song** and **song cycle** and one of the most prolific major composers of the **long 19th century.** He is renowned for the complexity, richness, and subtlety of his harmonic and melodic language, his lyrical melodies, his ability to depict and otherwise interpret text with unprecedented sensitivity, and his capacity for creating extended forms and expansive compositions. His sizeable oeuvre— all the more remarkable because he died at age 31—includes more than 600 songs (among them two song cycles, *Die schöne Müllerin*, D. 795 [1824] and *Winterreise*, D. 911 [1828]) and many **part-songs** as well as eight **operas** and *Singspiele*, seven Masses, eight **symphonies**, 17 **string quartets**, an **octet** for winds (D. 72, 1813) and another for strings and winds (D. 803, 1824), two **piano trios**, a piano quintet, 15 piano **sonatas, part-songs, character pieces** for **piano**, and more.

Schubert's life and career rank among the most mythologized of the major composers of the long 19th century—less so than those of **Ludwig van Beethoven** and **Wolfgang Amadeus Mozart** but on a par with those of **Hector Berlioz, Felix Mendelssohn Bartholdy**, and **Robert Schumann**. Above all, the popular notion of him as a largely self-taught composer who published little and enjoyed little or no public success is simply untrue. After studying piano, violin, organ, counterpoint, and fugue at an early age, he was admitted in 1808 into the choir of the Imperial Chapel in Vienna, where he received the best musical training available in the imperial capital at the time—for free. In 1811, he progressed to studies in counterpoint and advanced composition with Antonio Salieri (1750–1825) and by 1814 was sufficiently well known for his Mass in F (D. 105) to be selected as part of music to be performed at the **Congress of Vienna**. Meanwhile, late in 1813, he had entered a teachers' training school, and in 1814, he began teaching at his father's school, holding this post for two years and initiating a truly extraordinary streak of productivity: between 1814 and 1820, he composed hundreds of songs (including *Gretchen am Spinnrade*, D. 118, 1814, and *Erlkönig*, D. 328, 1815, both on texts by **Johann Wolfgang von Goethe**), many sonatas and string quartets, six symphonies, several operas and *Singspiele*, three more Masses and much Latin sacred music, many piano compositions small and large, and an appreciable body of chamber music.

Real renown reached the 24-year-old composer in 1821, when *Erlkönig* was performed (and repeated) to great acclaim at an annual benefit concert held on Ash Wednesday; the song was issued as his Op. 1 later that year, initiating a series of 101 published *opera* that would be released in a steady stream over the next eight years. Already in 1823, plans were made for a public academy devoted solely to his own music (an event rare even for Beethoven), and while the only such event that did occur (on 26 March 1828) was overshadowed in the press by **Nicolò Paganini**'s first performances in Vienna three days later, it was financially successful. By the end of his life, his music had been published by major firms including **Artaria, Diabelli**, Haslinger, Kistner, Probst, and **Schott**. Publishers in London and Paris had begun to publish his songs, part-songs, and smaller instrumental works already in 1824, and the year 1827 alone witnessed the publication of 29 works by his German and Austrian publishers. At his death, he was widely commemorated in epitaphs, eulogies, memorial poems, and other tributes. There is no doubt that his renown was greater in Vienna than elsewhere—but Vienna was, after all, the undisputed cultural capital of Europe at the time, rivaled (but probably not surpassed, at least in the 1820s) only by London and Paris.

Despite his professional successes, Schubert's personal life was difficult. After 1815, he never maintained a residence of his own, living instead with family, friends, and families of friends; despite an evidently intense sexual appetite and reported wishes to settle down, he never entered into a sustained relationship or marriage; and in 1820, on the eve of nascent fame, his apparent sympathy with the circles of radical reformists known as the *Bildungskreis* got him and four friends arrested and severely reprimanded by the oppressive police in Metternich's Vienna (*see* RESTORATION). Finally, he suffered from both depression and a recurrent serious illness, most likely syphilis, from 1823 until his death on 19 November 1828 from *Neverfieber* ("nervous fever"; i.e., probably tertiary-stage syphilis, although some biographers consider it to have been either typhus or typhoid fever).

After Schubert's death, his brother Ferdinand took care of his estate, quickly arranging for the publication and performance of many previously unknown works—among them 50 posthumous collections of songs (including the so-called third song cycle, *Schwanengesang*, which was assembled, titled, and published posthumously by its publisher, Haslinger, in 1828), the Piano Quintet in A Major ("Trout," D. 667), the **"Death and the Maiden"** String Quartet (in D minor, D. 810, 1824), and the B-flat-major Piano Trio (D. 898, 1827). His influence was further broadened by **Franz Liszt**, who published his transcriptions of Schubert songs and song cycles for piano solo in 1833 (*Die Rose*, D. 745; LW A17), 1839–1840 (LW A42, A45, A46, A49, A50), 1840 (the *Mélodies hongroises [d'après Schubert]*, LW A48, based on D. 818, and *Franz Schuberts geistliche Lieder*, LW A73), 1844 (LW A109), 1846 (*Schuberts Märsche für das Pianoforte solo*, LW A123), and beyond. In 1838, **Robert Schumann** was introduced to Schubert's "Great" C-major Symphony (D. 944) and collaborated with Mendelssohn to have it premiered at the concerts of Leipzig's celebrated Gewandhaus as well as its publication in parts the following year—events that significantly influenced the development of the 19th-century symphony thereafter (*see* PRINTING AND PUBLISHING OF MUSIC). More such "discoveries" followed. With the production of the first thematic catalog of his works by **Gustav Nottebohm** (*Thematisches Verzeichnis der im Druck erschienenen Werke von Franz Schubert* [Vienna, 1874]) and the initiation of a source-critical *Gesamtausgabe* under the leadership of Eusebius Mandyczewski (1857–1929), **Johannes Brahms**, and others (Vienna, 1884–1897), the full extent of Schubert's prodigious output became known (*see* EDITING AND EDITIONS).

To describe an immense and varied output such as Schubert's in terms of a single compositional style is at best difficult and at worst misleading. As Robert Winter noted in the Schubert entry for *GMO*, we may observe the presence of four discrete styles in the mature works: a conspicuously popular, unlearned style (e.g., represented in the fourth movement of the "Trout" Quintet); an "ambitious" style that tends toward expansiveness and discursiveness; a learned style characterized by extensive and often erudite counterpoint; and an avant-garde style whose harmonic adventurousness is largely unparalleled until the turn of the 20th century. His songs reflect the intensity and insight with which he read, setting words by more than 150 poets and ranging in style from the simplest *Volkstümlichkeit* to elaborate conceptions that entail multiple lyric personae and couple a penetrating psychology with vivid musical depictions of images, ideas, and rhetorical gestures in the texts themselves. The instrumental chamber works and partsongs are obviously produced by and directed primarily toward domestic uses (*see* SCHUBERTIADE), combining intimacy with (often) a sense of conviviality that lends itself well to music making among executants whose shared experiences facilitate deep understanding. Much the same may be said of his many works for piano solo and piano duet, which range from (apparently) simple marches to expansive sonatas and fantasies and take full advantage of the particular nuances of the Viennese fortepiano of the day.

Finally, Schubert's works in the major public genres—the operas, symphonies, and sacred choral works—offer a range of styles and a richness of harmonic and melodic material that reflects the influence not only of **Beethoven** and (to a lesser extent) **Weber** and **Rossini** but also of **Haydn** and **Mozart**. As a whole, this output constituted one of the most potent forces in mid- and late 19th-century music, influencing countless other composers and earning Schubert a firm position alongside Beethoven in the emergent concert and musicological **canons**.

Three milestones in 20th-century Schubert scholarship warrant inclusion in this entry. First, through a variety of contributions, the Viennese musicologist Otto Erich Deutsch (1883–1967) made Schubert one of the best-documented composers of the long 19th century by publishing an extensive documentary biography; source-critical editions of his letters, diaries, and other writings; and a new thematic catalog that established a new standard for such scholarship (refer to the bibliography for specific citations). Second, the year 1964 witnessed the initial publication of the *Neue Schubert-Ausgabe* by Bärenreiter-Verlag (Kassel) under the general editorship of Walther Dürr and others, an ongoing enterprise that supersedes the 19th-century *Gesamtausgabe* and makes Schubert's works and their many variant versions available in reliable scholarly texts. Finally, considerable controversy was aroused in 1989 when musicologist Maynard Solomon presented a thorough and, in the eyes of many, valid argument that Schubert was homosexual or possibly bisexual—a perspective that is based on extensive (if also necessarily oblique) documentary evidence but that sharply contradicts conventional heterocentric views (likewise based on ambivalent evidence) of the composer's mysterious romantic life. If there is any truth to the widely held notion that music expresses the inmost selves of its composer, then the issue of Schubert's sexuality bears materially not only on his biography but also on his music and its analysis and interpretation. [JMC]

See also GESANG (PL. GESÄNGE); LIED (PL. LIEDER); RECEPTION.

SCHUBERTIADE. Generally, a gathering to celebrate (usually in performance but also sometimes with discussion) the music of **Franz Schubert** and his contemporaries, consisting primarily of **songs** and instrumental **chamber music** for **piano** solo, **piano duet**, or chamber ensemble. In today's practice, the term applies to any such musical event centering on Schubert's songs and may be considered a subset of the song-centered recitals frequently referred to as *Liederabende* (sing. *Liederabend*) or even to recordings of such programming. In the strict (original) usage of the word, however, a *Schubertiade* was an intimate gathering whose nature precluded the sort of anonymity that attends public performances in the modern application of the term: friends and acquaintances gathered in a private setting for an evening of conviviality including the music of Schubert; readings and conversation also played a prominent or central role. The original *Schubertiaden* took place in the home of Josef Witteczek (1787–1859) beginning in 1816, but others also hosted the gatherings. They are similar to **salons** except that their content centered on music more than on conversation. [JMC]

See also SONNTAGSMUSIK.

SCHUMANN (NÉE WIECK), CLARA JOSEPHINE (1819–1896). German **virtuosa pianist** and composer of the Romantic Generation. Among the most influential concert pianists of the long 19th century, Schumann adhered to the now-predominant model of performing from memory a program of compositions mainly by other composers. In her long life as a performer, she also advocated for the works of husband **Robert Schumann** and her friend **Johannes Brahms** during years when many audiences did not accept them. As a composer, Schumann's youthful piano works of the 1830s—including her only piano **concerto**—reflect her sharp mind and virtuosic capabilities; her compositions from the 1840s on reveal her to be among the most engaging voices of the Romantic Generation.

Clara was daughter of Friedrich Wieck (1785–1873), a Leipzig piano teacher and music dealer well known as a pedagogue, and Marianne Tromlitz Wieck, a pianist and soprano. Her parents divorced when she was five; Marianne married Adolph Bargiel, and composer Woldemar Bargiel was one of their children. Clara, a **prodigy**, debuted as a pianist at the Leipzig Gewandhaus in 1830 and toured with her father throughout her teens to international acclaim; during these years, she came into contact with such figures as **Fryderyk Chopin, Franz Liszt, Felix Mendelssohn Bartholdy**, and **Nicolò Paganini**. She also composed numerous piano works, including her challenging and original Piano Concerto in A minor, Op. 7 (1835).

In 1840, she married **Robert Schumann**, whom she had met 10 years earlier when he began piano studies with her father. Robert did not meet the approval of Friedrich, who had fought against and postponed the wedding through legal action since spring 1839. Between then and Robert's 1854 hospitalization, Schumann gave birth to eight children, all but one of whom survived infancy. During these years, she also maintained an active, successful performing career; took on students; and composed the bulk of her oeuvre. Two of her most significant tours were in northern Germany (1842) and Russia (1843–1844). Among her compositions from this time are her **Piano Trio** in G minor (Op. 17, 1847); *Three* **Romances** for accompanied violin (Op. 22, 1855); over a dozen piano works featuring **character pieces**, a set of **variations** on a theme by Robert, and a few historically minded **preludes** and fugues; and numerous **songs**, including her three for *Liebesfrühling* (Spring of Love, 1841, composed jointly with Robert on poems from an eponymous **Rückert** collection) and her Op. 13 (1844) and Op. 23 (1856) collections of six each.

The entrance of Brahms into the Schumanns' lives in 1853 was a high point for all three. Brahms proved his friendship in the years through 1856 by remaining with Clara and the children during Robert's asylum years; he remained Clara's friend through their final years. Schumann stopped composing all but entirely at this point, choosing instead performance and teaching as her means for supporting her family. She taught piano for the rest of her life; in 1878, **Joachim Raff** gave her a position at the Hoch **Conservatory**. Schumann kept up her performing career until the age of 82. [RK]

See also FEMINISM; HISTORICISM; PERFORMANCE PRACTICE.

SCHUMANN, ROBERT (ALEXANDER) (1810–1856). German composer and music critic; cofounder of the *Neue Zeitschrift für Musik* and one of the Romantic Generation's most important creative and critical voices. Though he is best known today for his many *Gesänge* and **Lieder, string quartets**, and **piano cycles** written before the mid-1840s, during his lifetime his first real success as a composer came between around 1845 and 1853, the period that saw the composition and revision of his last three **symphonies** as well as a number of other works, both small and large in scale, that are less well known today.

Schumann's skeptical stance regarding the **New German School** and his championing of **Johannes Brahms** and **Felix Mendelssohn Bartholdy** during the years of the New German School's ascendance combined with his apparently sudden mental breakdown early in 1854 to raise questions about his aesthetic judgments during the late 1840s and early 1850s and the quality of his music composed during those years. Early critics and biographers who were supportive of the New German School and unaware of the details of Schumann's biography found in his periodic bouts of depression evidence of an inexorable decline that intensified over the course of the late 1840s and early 1850s. This image, which documentary and other evidence has since shown to be specious, was propagated in the popular press, countless biographies, and film during the late 19th and 20th centuries, engendering widespread disregard for most of Schumann's music written after around 1846 and leading editors and performers to ignore or willfully rewrite his music in ways that would be considered egregiously inappropriate in connection with most other composers' works. Since the mid-1990s, drawing largely on the groundbreaking research of musicologist John Daverio (1954–2003), there has been a broad resurgence of interest in his contributions during the last decade of his creative life, with the result that a new image of Schumann, his works, and his cultural and historical significance is taking root as this entry is being written.

Schumann's father was a bookseller, a fact that may have nourished his lifelong habit as a voracious reader and his general literary proclivities. He trained as a pianist and by 1823 was making frequent performances as a pianist in his school. Per his mother's wishes, he enrolled to study law at the University of Leipzig in 1828, also beginning study of piano and composition in the fall of that year with the respected pedagogue Friedrich Wieck (1785–1873), whose nine-year-old daughter **Clara**, already a well-known **virtuosa**, would eventually become his wife. In the summer of 1829, he moved to Heidelberg, ostensibly to study law at the university there, but he skipped many classes in order to practice piano and devoted more time to champagne, cigars, and travel to Switzerland and Italy than to his studies. He returned to Leipzig in the fall of 1830, having arranged (much to the concern of his mother) to devote himself full-time to the pursuit of a career as a virtuoso pianist/composer under the tutelage of Wieck.

Schumann's pianistic aspirations were scuttled in the early 1830s by the emergence of a numbness in the middle finger of his right hand, probably caused by his use of a new device known as a *chiroplast* to strengthen that finger, but in the meantime, he was composing for the piano with a vengeance and immersing himself in the music of **Ludwig van Beethoven,**

Ignaz Moscheles, Franz Schubert, and others. In 1831, he began studying counterpoint and thoroughbass with Heinrich Dorn (1804–1892) and publishing music reviews in local journals, culminating with the publication of his pathbreaking review of Fryderyk Chopin's op. 2 *Variations on "Là ci darem la mano"* (from Wolfgang Amadeus Mozart's *Don Giovanni*) in the prestigious Leipzig-based *Allgemeine musikalische Zeitung* (7 December 1831).

Despite deep depression occasioned by the unsuccessful performance of the first movement of his G-minor Symphony, the death of his sister-in-law, and his own attempted suicide, the early 1830s were characterized by a series of extraordinarily affirmative creative ventures: the beginnings of work on the *Studien nach Capricen von Paganini* (1832; *see* CAPRICCIO), the *Abegg-Variations* (Op. 1, 1830), *Papillons* (Op. 2, 1832), the Toccata in C (Op. 7, 1833), and *Carnaval* (Op. 9, 1834–1835, publ. 1837). Beginning in March 1834, he, together with Friedrich Wieck and his close friends Julius Knorr and Ludwig Schunke, began planning the new biweekly music periodical that would emerge on 3 April 1834 and eventually be titled the *Neue Zeitschrift für Musik*. Conceived and circulated as a periodical that would combat philistinism in the arts and promote the best of the music of the past and the present alike, the publication not only resonated with the interests and values of the burgeoning middle-class musical culture of the **Restoration** but also provided an alternative voice to the *Allgemeine musikalische Zeitung* (which was easily viewed as an organ of its own publisher, **Breitkopf & Härtel**). Schumann would serve as the new journal's editor in chief for most of the crucial first decade of its existence, from 1835 to 1844.

Schumann's tireless efforts on behalf of the *Neue Zeitschrift für Musik* and his brilliant contributions established him as one of the German lands' most insightful music critics (he was awarded an honorary doctorate from the University of Jena in January 1840), but as a composer he remained little known and less appreciated: the piano compositions of the late 1830s were neither heard nor understood easily in their day. In January 1840, he turned his creative energies to a new genre that did service to his musical imagination and his superior abilities as a reader of literature: that of solo **song**. Over the course of 1840, he produced about 125 *Gesänge* and Lieder (more than half his total output in the genres) including the seminal **song cycle** *Dichterliebe*, the **Heine**-Liederkreis op. 24, the Eichendorff-Liederkreis op. 39, and the collaborative song cycle on texts by Friedrich Rückert published as *Liebesfrühling*, Op. 37 (nos. 2, 4, and 11 of this cycle were composed by Clara). This chronologically concentrated burst of activity was followed by analogous concentrated explorations of **orchestral** genres (1841), instrumental **chamber music** (1842–1843), and **oratorio** (1843). Also in 1843, he was nominated by his friend Mendelssohn to serve as professor of piano and composition at Leipzig's newly founded **conservatory**, a post that he held until the Schumanns and their two children moved to Dresden in December 1844. Despite growing interest in his music, Schumann was passed over as a potential candidate for the directorship of the Leipzig Gewandhaus **Orchestra** (the post went to **Niels W. Gade** instead), and this, together with the fact that Clara was still the most publicly and financially successful member of the growing family, threw Schumann into a deep depression characterized, according to his physician, by auditory disturbances, bodily tremors, exhaustion, insomnia, and numerous phobias.

The depression lifted in late 1845 or early 1846, when Schumann developed "a completely new manner of composing" characterized by an integration of counterpoint into the overall thematic process, greater attention to continuity, and a renewed emphasis on music as an art form for constructive, even didactic communication as well as for impetuous or spontaneous self-expression. The fruits of this new style quickly became apparent, for despite deep personal losses such as the death of his first son, Emil, in 1846 and the deaths of Mendelssohn and **Fanny Hensel** in May 1847, Schumann's professional accolades, compositional productivity, and commercial success as a composer increased significantly. In 1845, he completed two old compositional projects (the op. 53 *Romanzen und Balladen* begun in 1840 and the A-minor Piano **Concerto** begun in 1841); in 1846, he completed his Second Symphony (Op. 61), and in 1847, he succeeded **Ferdinand Hiller** as director of the Dresden *Liedertafel* and completed his First **Piano Trio**, Op. 63. Deeply supportive of the communal and democratic impulses that led to the wave of revolutions that swept the Continent in 1848—*see* REVOLUTIONS OF 1848 (SPRING OF NATIONS, YEAR OF REVOLUTIONS)—he founded a *Verein für Chorgesang* (Choral Union) in January 1848 and in the same year completed the didactic *Album für die Jugend* (a milestone of *Hausmusik*) as well as the **opera** *Genoveva* and the dramatic scenes from **Byron**'s *Manfred*, also revising and reissuing many of his previously published works. The revolutionary year of 1849 was one of staggering productivity, witnessing the composition of numerous solo vocal works (opp. 51, 71, 74, 91, 98a, and 98b), **part-songs** for mixed voices (Opp. 67, 75, 141, 145, and 146), *Männerchor* (opp. 93 and 137), and **women's chorus** (opp. 69 and 91); instrumental chamber pieces (opp. 70, 73, 94, and 102); and orchestral works (the brilliant *Konzertstück* for four horns and orchestra, Op. 86, as well as the *Introduction and Allegro appassionato* for piano and orchestra, Op. 92). Yet more recognition came in July 1849, when Ferdinand Hiller, who had just accepted the offer to become music director in Cologne, invited Schumann to succeed him as municipal music director in Düsseldorf. Schumann accepted, beginning his official duties in that capacity in September 1849.

Düsseldorf had a history of difficult relations with its music directors despite its lively public musical life: it proved a serious disappointment to Schumann just as it had to Mendelssohn 20 years earlier. On the one hand, his tenure there witnessed some of his most remarkable compositional achievements: the successful revision of the D-minor Symphony originally composed in 1841 (overhauled in 1851 and published as his Fourth Symphony in 1852); the composition and publication of the E-flat Major ("Rhenish") Symphony, Op. 97; numerous instrumental chamber works and late song cycles such as the Kulmann-Lieder (Op. 104); the *Gedichte der Königen Maria Stuart* (Op. 135); and works for chorus and orchestra such as the choral ballads *Der Königsohn* (The King's Son, Op. 139), *Des Sängers Fluch* (The Singer's Curse, Op. 139), and *Vom Pagen und der Königstochter* (The Page and the King's Daughter, Op. 140); the oratorio *Der Rose Pilgerfahrt* (Op. 112); and the **Requiem** in D-flat Major (Op. 148).

On the other hand, Schumann was increasingly depressed and isolated by Düsseldorf's troubled musical politics. New hope came on 30 September 1853, when he received a surprise visit from Johannes Brahms, an occasion that he reported and described in what was to be his final essay in music criticism: the article "Neue Bahnen" (New Paths), published in the *Neue Zeitschrift für Musik* on 13 October 1853. Still, the situation in Düsseldorf continued to deteriorate, and he resigned from his post as music director in November of that year. Despite a tour to the Netherlands with Clara and a visit to his old friend **Joseph Joachim** in Hanover, his health deteriorated, and his depression, aural disturbances, and phobias worsened. On 26 January 1854, he demanded to be placed in an asylum but agreed to his physician's urging that he spend the night at home. The following day, he attempted suicide by jumping from a bridge into the Rhine, and his repeated requests to be institutionalized were finally granted in the following weeks. On 4 March 1854, he left for an asylum in Endenich (near Bonn), where he spent the remainder of his life, his condition inexorably declining as was normally the case in 19th-century asylums. He would not see Clara again until just two days before his death on 29 July 1856.

Schumann's reputation today rests on his work as a critic and as a composer. His criticism represents a milestone in the history of the genre. Although his generation had more than its fair share of composer/critics—**Hector Berlioz, Franz Liszt**, and **Richard Wagner** rank among the most brilliant, perceptive, and influential music critics of the **long 19th century**—Schumann's decision early on to employ a novelistic style modeled in part on the writings of **E. T. A. Hoffmann** and **Jean Paul Richter** both in its ebullience and in its novelistic creation of *Doppelgänger* to represent different perspectives on a single issue revolutionized the genre. It was a stroke of genius unprecedented in music criticism. This approach enabled Schumann to develop an argument in the first person (by quoting his fictitious personae's ideas) without venturing into the dry, often-academic tone characteristic of most contemporary criticism, thereby attracting lay audiences and transforming the writing of music criticism itself into an act of literary creation. It is to his credit that his first published review announced the then-obscure Polish pianistic marvel Chopin with a prophetic flourish ("Hats off, gentlemen, a genius!") and that his last presented the little-known Brahms as "a newblood at whose cradle the graces and heroes stood guard" to the musical public just as Brahms's Op. 1 was being published. During Schumann's 10 years as editor of the *Neue Zeitschrift für Musik*, he published astute commentaries on the music not only of major composers of his own day such as Berlioz (an important detailed analysis of the *Episode in the Life of an Artist*), **Luigi Cherubini**, Chopin, **Carl Czerny**, Gade, Liszt, Mendelssohn, **Giacomo Meyerbeer**, **Gioachino Rossini**, and Wagner but also advocated eloquently for then-underappreciated works by **Johann Sebastian Bach**, Beethoven, and Schubert. Few critics before or since can compare with his extraordinary powers of observation and his seeming prescience.

The most important works in the conventional **canon** of Schumann's works include the piano cycle *Carnaval* and the **Fantasy** in C Major (Op. 17, 1836–1838, publ. 1839); the song cycles *Eichendorff-Liederkreis* (Op. 39, 1840, publ. 1842, rev. 1850), *Dichterliebe*, and *Frauenliebe und -leben* (Op. 42, 1840, publ. 1843); three string quartets (Op. 41, 1842, publ. 1848), a piano **quartet** (Op. 47, 1842, publ. 1845), and a piano **quintet** (Op. 44, 1842, publ. 1843); four symphonies (Opp. 38, 61, 97, and 120, 1840–1851 passim); and a piano **concerto** (Op. 54, 1841 and 1845, publ. 1846). The modern reappraisal of Schumann has led to a resurgence of interest in the large choral/orchestral works of the 1840s and 1850s as well as the more intimate works of those same years. Most important among the larger works of these later years are the opera *Genoveva*, the dramatic music for Byron's *Manfred*, the oratorios *Das Paradies und die Peri* and *Der Rose Pilgerfahrt* (Op. 112, 1851, publ. 1852), the *Requiem für Mignon* (Op. 98b, 1849, publ. 1851), and the *Scenen aus Goethes Faust* (WoO 3,1853, publ. 1858). Most prominent among the more intimate musical rediscoveries are the late song cycles (esp. opp. 98a, 117, 135, 1849–1852 passim), three **piano trios** (opp. 63, 80, and 110, 1847–1852 passim), and numerous **character pieces** for instrumental chamber ensemble (especially the *Fantasiestücke*, Op. 73; the *Drei Romanzen*, Op. 94; the *Fünf Stücke im Volkston* [Five Pieces in Folk-Like Style], Op. 102; and the *Märchenbilder* [Fairy-Tale Scenes], Op. 113). The extraordinary sophistication of these late works continues to complicate their reception. [JMC]

See also EDITING AND EDITIONS; ORCHESTRA; ORCHESTRATION; PERFORMANCE PRACTICE.

SCRIABIN, ALEKSANDR (NIKOLAYEVICH) (1872–1915). Russian composer and pianist of the Modern Romantic Generation; with **Claude Debussy** and Arnold Schoenberg, one of the most profoundly original composers of his generation. He composed 74 numbered *opera* of **virtuosic** works for **piano** solo, a Piano **Concerto** in F-sharp Minor (Op. 20, 1896), three **symphonies** and several other major works for **orchestra**, and a handful of **chamber** works, leaving unfinished at his death work on a massive **synaesthetic** *Mysterium* that was to be performed in India and employ manipulations not just of sounds but also of colors, textures, and aromas and be realized by actors and dancers as well as chorus, **orchestra**, and piano. His Third Symphony (*Le poème divin* [The Divine Poem], Op. 43, 1902–1904), Fifth Piano **Sonata** (Op. 53, 1907), and *Le poème de l'ecstase* (The Poem of Ecstasy, 1905, rev. 1908) rank among the most tonally adventurous works of the first decade of the 20th century, and his use of harsh dissonances and relentlessly unstable tonal language in late piano works such as the last five piano sonatas (1911–1913), *Vers la flamme* (Through the Flame, Op. 72, 1914), and *Prométhée, le poème du feu* (Prometheus, the Poem of Fire, Op. 60, 1908–1910) legitimately qualify as pantonal or atonal, some of the new century's first works to warrant that designation.

Scriabin trained as a professional pianist and composer in the Moscow **Conservatory** beginning in 1888 and acquired substantial mentoring from the St. Petersburg impresario and music publisher Mitrofan Belyayev (1836–1904) in the early 1890s, publishing his first works (without opus number or compensation) through his agency. After touring to great acclaim in Russia and abroad in 1894–1897, he was awarded a professorship at the Moscow Conservatory, frequently traveling the nearly 500 miles from there to St. Petersburg for performances in one capital or the other during his tenure in Moscow.

He resigned from that position in 1902. Freed from his teaching duties, he continued work on his ever-more-complex and ambitious projects and was increasingly drawn to mystical philosophical ideas (in particular Belyayev's theosophy), joining the Moscow Philosophical Society. In 1904, he relocated to Switzerland, where, despite the collapse of his marriage in the wake of his long affair with a student, he managed to complete his Third Symphony, which he considered "the first proclamation of [his] new doctrine." The work met with a mixed reception, with responses ranging from enthusiasm to bewilderment, when it was premiered in Paris, but the attention it generated won him the patronage of the Russian émigré Serge Koussevitsky (1874–1951), who began acting as Scriabin's publisher and promoter and arranged for him to return to Russia in 1909. A tour of England and further performances in Russia in 1914 and 1915 met with increasingly ecstatic reviews, but this wave of success met with a most pedestrian end in 1915, when he died of blood poisoning stemming from an abscess underneath his moustache.

Scriabin's output divides neatly into two broad periods: pre- and post-1905. The pre-1905 music clearly takes the rich sonorities and tonally adventurous idioms of **Fryderyk Chopin, Claude Debussy**, and **Richard Wagner** as its aesthetic starting point, reflecting Wagner's influence also in its use of pervasive sequence and infrequent cadential resolution. After 1905, he began to think and compose in more explicitly and ambitiously **synaesthetic** terms, becoming increasingly fascinated after around 1908 with chromatically modified quartal harmonies (the most famous of which is the so-called *mystic chord* or *chord of the pleroma*, e.g., *C—F sharp—B flat—E—A—D*). Though he cultivated a lush post-Romantic idiom to the end of his life, his increasingly adventurous harmonic language provided fertile theoretical and sonorous soil for later composers. During the early years of the Soviet era, the enormous fame he had achieved by the end of his life made him an important icon of Russian brilliance, optimism, and originality; his success at developing a coherent and convincing post-tonal musical language provided an important foundation for Russian composers who lived further into the 20th century (such as Serge Prokofiev and Dmitri Shostakovich), even though they apparently viewed his philosophical ideas skeptically. [JMC]

SCRIBE, (AUGUSTIN) EUGÈNE (1791–1861). French dramatist and **librettist**; one of the most prolific and influential literary figures in musical Romanticism. He studied at the Collège Sainte-Barbe in Paris and began his career in law but moonlighted by writing librettos for use in the **vaudevilles** of the Théâtre des Variétés on the Boulevard Montmartre (the oldest extant theater building in Paris). By 1820, he had signed an exclusive contract for that theater among the French capital's secondary theaters, although he was still free to write without restriction for the major theaters (the Opéra-Comique, Opéra, and Théâtre Français). By the early 1830s, he had earned a reputation as Europe's leading librettist: already in 1827 he had been named to the Légion d'Honneur, and in 1836, he was elected to the Académie Française. He devoted significant amounts of the large fortune he amassed to a fund for impoverished musicians and dramatists.

Scribe's success as a librettist owed most of all to his exceptional dramaturgical abilities and his ability to focus on highly topical situations through the perspective of the middle classes, mirroring those classes' morality and life through drama that invited empathy without the bluntness of social realism. Among latter-day musicians, he is best known for his triumphs in the genre of French **grand opera** (a total of 30 libretti set to music by composers including **Adolphe Adam, Daniel-François-Esprit Auber, Adrien Boieldieu, Luigi Cherubini, Charles Gounod, Fromenthal Halévy**, and **Giaco-**

mo **Meyerbeer**) and works written for Italian composers working in France (**Vincenzo Bellini**, **Gaetano Donizetti**, **Gioachino Rossini**, and **Giuseppe Verdi**), but over half of his output consists of vaudevilles (some 250 of them). He also wrote the libretti for 97 **opéras comiques** and three **melodramas** as well as the French adaptation of Friedrich Kind's (1768–1843) **libretto** for *Der Freischütz* (*Robin des bois, ou Les trois balles*, 1824). [JMC]

SECHTER, SIMON (1788–1867). Bohemian-Austrian theorist, music educator, organist, and composer of the Early Romantic Generation. He was a legendary teacher of harmony and counterpoint and one of the most influential Viennese music theorists of the entire **long 19th century**. Among his pupils were Selmar Bagge (1823–1896), **Anton Bruckner**, Theodor Döhler (1814–1856), Franz Grillparzer (1791–1872), **Johannes Brahms**'s teacher Eduard Marxsen (1806–1887), **Gustav Nottebohm**, **Franz Schubert** (one lesson only), **Sigismond Thalberg**, and Henri Vieuxtemps (1820–1881). His three-volume *Die Grundsätze der musikalischen Komposition* (Fundamentals of Musical Composition, 1853–1854) was widely circulated, translated, and reprinted, going through multiple editions in German and English. In particular, his idea that even highly chromatic chord progressions are based on principles of diatonic voice leading, although adapted from Jean-Philippe Rameau (1683–1764) and Friedrich Wilhelm Marpurg (1718–1795), influenced early 20th-century modes of analysis, including the *Stufentheorien* (theories of stepwise progression) developed by Arnold Schoenberg and Heinrich Schenker. He also published numerous other theoretical writings, including an article on music education for the blind ("Musikunterricht für Blinde," 1819), a treatise on **piano** fingering (ca. 1828), and an edition (1843) of Marpurg's *Abhandlung von der Fuge* (Treatise on Fugue, 1753).

Sechter was born in Frimburk, Bohemia, and moved to Vienna in 1804. By 1810, he was teaching piano and voice at the Educational Institute for the Blind, and in 1824, he was appointed court organist. He was highly sought out as a private teacher of harmony and counterpoint. In 1850, he was appointed professor of composition at the University of Vienna, a post he held until his death. Over stiff opposition from **Eduard Hanslick**, he was succeeded in his professorship by his former pupil Bruckner. He was also a respected composer of sacred music as well as secular choral compositions, instrumental **chamber music**, and works for piano and (especially) organ. In particular, his 13 Mass settings and his setting of **Friedrich Schiller**'s *Die Glocke* (written for and sung by the students at the Institute for the Blind in 1813) were well known in the mid- and later 19th century. He also penned a **comic opera** (*Ali Hitsch-Hatsch*, 1844) and two **oratorios**. [JMC]

SECOND BERLIN SCHOOL, SECOND BERLIN LIEDER SCHOOL. Informal term for a group of composers based in Prussia whose approach to the composition of German art songs emphasized clear, musically unobtrusive settings of the text in order to provide for clarity of diction and respond first and foremost to the underlying ideas of the text rather than specific detailed ideas and images contained in it. Such songs typically avoid complicated accompaniments, striving instead for a balance between unobtrusiveness and sensitivity that errs on the side of the former.

The most important composers of the Second Berlin School are typically held to be Johann Friedrich Reichardt (1752–1814), Johann Abraham Peter Schulz (1747–1800), and Carl Friedrich Zelter (1758–1832). They are designated the "second" Berlin school because their aesthetics are related to but distinct from those of an earlier generation of Prussian composers whose style emphasized a folk-like quality (*Volkstümlichkeit*). That earlier group included Johann Friedrich Agricola (1720–1774), C. P. E. Bach (1714–1788), Johann Philipp Kirnberger (1721–1783), Friedrich Wilhelm Marpurg (1718–1795), and Johann Joachim Quantz (1697–1773).

The Second Berlin School's approach to text/music relationships won the approval of many poets and philosophers of the late 18th and early 19th centuries, among them **Georg Wilhelm Friedrich Hegel, Johann Wolfgang von Goethe**, Immanuel Kant (1724–1804), and Arthur Schopenhauer (1788–1860). Among latter-day musicians, who generally prefer the style associated first with **Franz Schubert**'s songs after 1814, it is often considered insufficiently musical, directed primarily at poets and philosophers rather than singers and other musicians. The best-known extensions of its approach were **Ludwig van Beethoven** and **Carl Maria von Weber** in the Early Romantic Generation, **Fanny Hensel** and **Felix Mendelssohn Bartholdy** in the Romantic Generation, and (to some extent) **Johannes Brahms** in the Late Romantic Generation. [JMC]

See also GESANG (PL. GESÄNGE); LIED (PL. LIEDER); SONG CYCLE.

SECOND FRENCH EMPIRE, SECOND EMPIRE. Period in France under the rule of the Emperor Napoléon III, extending from 1852 to 1870; preceded by the **Second Republic** and followed by the **Third Republic** (Third French Republic) in 1870. The period to around 1859 enjoyed economic prosperity and successful foreign policy that enabled its authoritarian policies to go uncontested, and France, highly industrialized and generally prosperous, generally championed the **nationalisms** of others. Over the course of the 1860s, the imperial regime liberalized its policies. The result was a greater flourishing of French musical and general artistic culture than any since the reign of Louis XIV (fl. 1661–1715). The government's adoption of economically unfavorable measures such as a low-tariff agreement with Great Britain increased opposition within the government, however, and a new, more conservative constitution was adopted in 1870. France's ill-considered declaration of war with Prussia and its humiliating defeat in the resulting **Franco-Prussian War** resulted in a popular uprising on 4 September 1870, the overthrow of the government, the abdication of Napoléon III, and the end of the Second Empire. [JMC]

SECOND REPUBLIC, SECOND FRENCH REPUBLIC. Period in French political and cultural history between the end of the **Bourbon Restoration** and the creation of the **Second Empire** (1852). The Second Republic (so named after the "First Republic" created in the wake of the French Revolution of 1789) was born of liberal, secular, republican ideals and the hopes of establishing an enduring democratic system of governance, ideals that eventually led to the **Revolutions of 1848**. After Louis-Napoléon (nephew of Bonaparte) was elected president and a monarchist majority elected to the legislature, those prospects began to fade: suffrage was sharply curtailed and freedom of the press reduced, and the Roman Catholic Church was given increased control over education. On the night of 1–2 December 1851, Louis-Napoléon organized a coup d'état and had himself granted another 10-year term of office, also reconstituting the legislature, securing a more conservative constitution that reduced the authority of the legislative assembly, and reducing the rights of the public to assemble. The Second Republic ended and the Second Empire was born when he was proclaimed Napoléon III, emperor of the French, on 2 December 1852. [JMC]

SEPTET. (Fr., septour; Ger., Septett; It., septetto; Sp., septet.) Generally, an ensemble of seven solo performers or a composition written for it; a category of instrumental **chamber music**. Most septets are laid out in expanded **sonata plan**, using five, six, or more movements. Most fall into one of two types, either (1) those scored for a mixture of winds and strings or (2) those for winds, strings, and **piano**. Throughout the **long 19th century**, the genre was typified by **Ludwig van Beethoven**'s Op. 20 (1799, publ. 1802, scored for clarinet, horn, bassoon, violin, viola, cello, and bass), a work whose ubiquity and light tone had by mid-century come to epitomize the most accessible genres of chamber music. **Richard Wagner** used it to exemplify the supposed superficiality of English taste in his early essay *Eine Pilgerfahrt zu Beethoven* (A Pilgrimage to Beethoven, 1840). Other composers who scored their octets for this ensemble or a variant of it include **Franz Berwald** (ca. 1828), Adolphe Blanc (1828–1885; Op.40, 1864), **Max Bruch** (1849), and **Franz Lachner** (1824).

During the long 19th century, the most popular septets with piano were written by composers of the Early Romantic Generation: **Johann Nepomuk Hummel** (opp. 74 and 114, 1816 and 1829) and **Ignaz Moscheles** (Op. 88, 1832–1833). Other septets with piano were composed by Alexander Fesca (1820–1849; opp. 26 and 28, 1839–1840), **Mikhail Glinka** (1823), **Friedrich Kalkbrenner** (op. 15 and 132, 1814 and 1835), Jean Frédéric Kittl (1806–1868; Op. 25, 1846), **Georges Onslow** (Op. 79, 1852), Ferdinand Ries (1784–1838; Op. 25, 1812), **Camille Saint-Saëns** (Op. 65, 1881), and **Louis Spohr** (Op. 147, 1853). [JMC]

SERENADE. (Fr., sérénade; Ger., Nachtmusik, Serenade, Ständchen; It., serenada, serenata.) An instrumental or vocal composition implicitly intended for performance in the evening (sometimes outdoors) and usually submitted with the connotation of pleasing or seeking favor from a friend, lover, or person of rank. During the **long 19th century**, vocal serenades were sometimes designated as **romances** or, more rarely, **barcarolles** or lullabies). The *Ständchen* from Schubert's *Schwanengesang* ("Leise flehn meine Lieder," D. 957, no. 4, 1828), remains a standard in the **song** repertoire, and it and many other vocal serenades adopt simple, treble-dominated textures with accompaniments that imitate strummed or plucked instruments such as the guitar or lute; many are included in **operas** (serious or **comic**) in scenes that depict an amorous serenade. Vocal serenades (either staged or chamber) were composed by **Daniel-François-Esprit Auber, Hector Berlioz, Henry Bishop, Georges Bizet, Johannes Brahms, Gaetano Donizetti, Gabriel Fauré, Friedrich Fesca, Stephen Foster, Robert Franz, Charles Gounod, Fromenthal Halévy, Conradin Kreutzer, Friedrich Kuhlau, Adolf Fredrik Lindblad, William Mason, Jules Massenet, Giacomo Meyerbeer, Jacques Offenbach, Louis Spohr, Richard Strauss, Ambroise Thomas,** and **Carl Maria von Weber,** among a great many others.

The long 19th century also witnessed a rise in the popularity of the instrumental serenade. Such works fell into two broad categories: single-movement lyrical works written in emulation of vocal serenades and multimovement compositions loosely laid out in **sonata plan**. The best-known work in the former category, a bit ironically, is the *Ständchen* from Schubert's *Schwanengesang* (see above), a work that has been transcribed as a sort of **Lied ohne Worte** for solo instrument, instrumental **chamber** ensemble, or even **orchestra** by countless composers (most famously **Franz Liszt** [LW A49, 1838–1839]) and whose romantic, lyrical, quasi-Italianate character was adopted by countless other single-movement instrumental serenades during the later 19th century.

Equally important was the multimovement instrumental serenade. Such works were similar to **suites** except that they were almost always scored for instrumental **chamber** ensemble or orchestra (rather than solo instrument) and were less likely than suites to cultivate a serious, somber, or melancholy attitude, instead adapting the connotations of "entertainment music" associated with the 18th-century cassation, divertimento, or serenade. In many ways, the tone for the 19th-century multimovement serenade was set by **Wolfgang Amadeus Mozart**'s eight works in the genre (K. 185/167a, 203/189b, 204/213a, 250/248b, 320, 361/370a, 375, and 388/384a, 1773–1783 passim), the last four of which were widely published, reprinted, and performed throughout the long 19th century. Instrumental serenades of both varieties were submitted by composers including **Pierre Baillot, Ludwig van Beethoven, Aleksandr Borodin,** Brahms, **Franz Brendel, Cécile Chaminade, Carl Czerny, Ferdinand David, Anton Diabelli, Felix Draeseke, Antonín Dvořák, Edward Elgar, John Field, Aleksandr Glazunov, Louis Moreau Gottschalk, Stephen Heller, Ferdinand Hiller, Johann Nepomuk Hummel, Franz Lachner, Ignaz Lachner, Édouard Lalo, Felix Mendelssohn Bartholdy, Camille Pleyel, Serge Rachmaninoff, Joachim Raff, Reinecke, Nikolay Rimsky-Korsakov, Robert Schumann, Gioachino Rossini, Anton Rubinstein, Camille Saint-Saëns, Richard Strauss, Maria Szymanowska, Pyotor Il'yich Tchaikovsky,** and **Charles Marie Widor,** among a great many others. Of these, the contributions by Beethoven, Brahms, Dvořák, Elgar, Richard Strauss, and Tchaikovsky are best known today. (In German, *Nachtmusik* denotes the multimovement variety, while *Ständchen* denotes either the vocal variety or the instrumental emulation thereof.) [JMC]

SEXTET. (Fr., sextette, sextuor; Ger., Sextett; It., sestetto; Sp., sexteto.) Generally, an ensemble of six solo performers or a composition written for it; a category of instrumental **chamber music.** Sextets typically were in **sonata plan.** During the **long 19th century,** three main varieties predominated: (1) *piano sextets* scored for strings and piano, (2) *string sextets* (typically scored for paired violins, violas, and cellos), and (3) sextets with a mixture of winds, strings, and piano. The most important sextets for strings with piano were composed by **William Sterndale Bennett** (Op. 8, ca. 1835, publ. 1845; for two violins, viola, cello, bass, and piano), **Mikhail Glinka** (1832; two violins, viola, cello, bass, and piano), Paul Juon (1872–1940; Op. 22, 1902, for two violins, viola, two cellos, and piano), **Ignaz Moscheles** (Op. 35, 1815, for flute, two horns, violin, cello, and piano), and **Georges Onslow** (Op. 30, for flute, clarinet, bassoon, horn, bass, and piano).

String sextets for paired violins, violas, and cellos were composed by **Aleksandr Borodin** (1860–1861), **Johannes Brahms** (opp. 18 and 36, 1859–1860 and 1864–1865, publ. 1866), **Antonín Dvořák** (Op. 48, 1879), **Niels W. Gade** (Op. 44, 1865), **Vincent d'Indy** (Op. 92, 1922), **Joachim Raff** (Op. 178, 1872), **Nikolay Rimsky-Korsakov** (1876), **Anton Rubinstein** (Op. 97, 1876), **Louis Spohr** (Op. 140, 1848), and **Pyotor Il'yich**

Tchaikovsky (the *Souvenir de Florence*, Op. 70, 1890–1892). **Ferdinand David** composed a string sextet for three violins, viola, and two cellos (Op. 38, 1861), and **Carl Reinecke** composed a woodwind sextet for flute, oboe, clarinet, bassoon, and two horns (Op. 271, 1904). [JMC]

SHAKESPEARE, WILLIAM (1564–1616). English dramatist and poet; together with **Lord Byron, Johann Wolfgang von Goethe, Heinrich Heine, Victor Hugo,** and **Friedrich Schiller** the most important literary inspiration for musical Romanticism. For modern viewers one of the thorniest problems attendant to Romantic musical responses to Shakespeare is that of authenticity or lack thereof (i.e., fidelity or changes to what Shakespeare wrote). Between the early 17th and late 18th century, however, there was no sense of fidelity to historical authors' works, so the texts of Shakespeare's works came down to the Romantics in decidedly corrupt form—with the overall structure changed (especially as regards the number of acts and scenes); characters added, deleted, or changed; events reordered; and verse forms changed or blank verse compressed into accepted verse forms. The problems were further compounded when Shakespeare's texts were used in translation. The result is that modern musicians and readers of Shakespeare, working from modern source-critical texts of the playwright's works, might accuse Romantic composers and/or their **librettists** of having willfully altered the texts that they were setting, often to the detriment of Shakespeare's work—when in fact those composers may have endeavored to be faithful to the bard's work as they knew it. Therefore, the first question to ask in dealing with any given Romantic music based on Shakespeare is almost always what the composer's and/or librettist's own textual source of Shakespeare was.

But Shakespeare's influence extended beyond settings of his work. The difficulties that poets and composers of the **long 19th century** experienced in trying to adapt his works to more recent continental conventions of literature and theater led them to view him as a breaker of rules, an iconoclastic Romantic rebel ahead of his time. Accordingly, it is difficult or misleading to speak of a single historical Shakespeare during the long 19th century—for the conventions and rules that Shakespeare challenged varied significantly along linguistic, cultural, and national lines, and the national appropriations and constructions of his identity and his works differed according to the ways in which his works adhered to and departed from those national conventions and rules (*see* RECEPTION). In his native England, Shakespeare's works had a more-or-less continuous posthumous life but had been continually reshaped in accordance with 18th-century literary and theatrical conventions. Consequently, to 19th-century English Romantics, Shakespeare—as he was transmitted to them after the 18th century's alterations—represented a great and noble English past and a source of national pride, a starting point for **historicism** of the sort that characterized, for example, the **Bach revival** in the German lands. By contrast, for the first part of the long 19th century little of Shakespeare's work was actually known in any form on the Continent: *Hamlet, King Lear,* and *Othello* figured most prominently before the **Congress of Vienna**; *Richard III, Romeo and Juliet, Macbeth,* and the *Tempest* became more common during the **Restoration**; and after the 1840s, *A Midsummer Night's Dream* likewise became well known. The range of literary texts increased in number and diversity as Shakespeare became more accepted over the course of the long 19th century, but even by the early 20th century, few French or German composers had access to the bard's original works in the quantity and range that modern readers take for granted.

In the German lands themselves "Saspar," "unser Shakspear," or "unser Wilhelm" was widely regarded as a prefiguring of the German Romantic spirit—initially through the affinities between works such as *Romeo and Juliet* or *Hamlet* and the German *Sturm und Drang* movement, then as a champion of natural individualistic dramatic expression unfettered by artifice and a **virtuoso** of character delineation. By the 1860s, it had become common for German speakers to refer to Shakespeare's "conquest" (*Eroberung*) of German culture, and in the world of the Modern Romantic Generation, Shakespeare had become inseparably linked with the Weimar Classicism of **Johann Wolfgang von Goethe** and **Friedrich Schiller**. Early agents of this appropriation included Gotthold Ephraim Lessing (1729–1781) and August Wilhelm Schlegel (1767–1845) as well as the writings and translations of Shakespeare by Goethe and Ludwig Tieck (1773–1853). Russian and Bohemian constructions likewise appropriated the notion of Shakespeare as iconoclastic tragedian who used vivid character delineations to communicate direct human emotions. The most famous such versions include **Pyotor Il'yich Tchaikovsky's** *Romeo and Juliet, Tempest,* and *Hamlet* **concert overtures** but also **Mily Balakirev's** **incidental music** for *King Lear* (1858–1861, R/ 1902–1905), **Anton Rubinstein's** concert overture *Anthony and Cleopatra* (Op. 116, 1890), and **Anatoly Arensky's** incidental music for *The Tempest* (Op. 75, 1905).

In the major countries of European Romanticism associated with the romance languages (France, Italy, and Spain), Shakespeare's success came more slowly. In France, an early and influential, if also ambivalent, advocate was the late Enlightenment philosopher and dramatist Voltaire (1694–1778), who regarded the English playwright as a drunken savage, perhaps, but one capable of genius, passion, and sublimity. The French adaptations contemporaneous with Voltaire attempted to compensate for Shakespeare's indecorousness: their *Hamlet* had no ghost or gravediggers, their *King Lear* no fool, their *Macbeth* no witches. More progress was made in the long 19th century by Germaine de Staël (1766–1816) and Stendahl (1783–1842). De Staël advocated for Shakespeare in *Corinne* (1807) by means of a conspicuous parallel to the balcony scene of *Romeo and Juliet,* while Stendhal—perhaps prompted by an 1822 incident in which a French audience pummeled the performers of *Othello* with eggs and tomatoes—contrasted the free forms and potent emotionalism of Shakespeare with the rigid rules and stale conventions of Jean Racine (1639–1699) in his widely read essay *Racine et Shakespeare* (1823–1835).

Most important in the French rehabilitation of Shakespeare, however, was **Victor Hugo**, who extolled the bard as the very essence of drama (*Préface de "Cromwell,"* 1827) and appropriated Shakespeare's dramaturgy (as he understood it) in his own construction of Romantic drama in *Hernani* (1830; source for **Giuseppe Verdi**'s *Ernani*, 1844). Hugo's attitudes, combined with those of the English troupe led by Charles Kemble (1775–1854) in performances at the Odéon Theatre in Paris, decisively shaped those of **Hector Berlioz**, whose lifelong fascination with Shakespeare produced some of French Romanticism's most imaginative and successful engagements (see below). An important but little-known late manifestation of Shakespeare's posthumous intercourse with French Romanticism is the **Suite** No. 3 for **orchestra** (*Scènes dramatiques*) by **Jules Massenet** (1874), whose three movements are based on *The Tempest*, *Othello*, and *Macbeth*, respectively.

Slower still but no less powerful was Shakespeare's canonization in the Italian lands. The peninsula's comparatively slow embrace of Shakespeare may well have been a result of the fact that many of his politically and socially critical plays were set there—a fact that posed additional difficulties for Italian Romantics who had somehow to get any adaptations of his work past the censors during the tumultuous years of the Austrian and French occupation and the rise of the **Risorgimento**. Gioachino Rossini's *Otello* (1816) follows Shakespeare's *Othello* in a general sense only, presumably because the English Renaissance playwright was little known (and certainly not revered) in the Italian lands in the early 19th century, so radically changing his texts was not sacrilegious—and if changing them made it possible for his works to get past the censors, then so much the better. Indeed, faithful renditions of the bard in Italy would occur mostly in the second half of the century—primarily at the hands of **Arrigo Boito** and Verdi, whose *Otello* manages to rewrite Shakespeare significantly while remaining remarkably true to the work as a whole.

Even a cursory inventory of the long 19th century's music based on Shakespeare's works gives an idea of his extraordinary influence on musical Romanticism. His texts were set as songs and **part-songs** by composers including Berlioz, **Johannes Brahms**, **Claude Debussy**, **Stephen Foster**, **Franz Joseph Haydn**, Franz Schubert, **Robert Schumann**, **Arthur Sullivan**, and **Maria Szymanowska**, among many others. His plays were adapted into **operas** such as Berlioz's *Béatrice et Bénédict* (H 138, 1862; based on *Much Ado about Nothing*); **Ernest Bloch**'s *Macbeth* (1910); **Charles Gounod**'s *Roméo et Juliette* (1867); **Fromenthal Halévy**'s *Le tempestà* (1850);

Otto Nicolai's *Die lustigen Weiber von Windsor* (1849); Rossini's *Otello* (1816); **Ambroise Thomas**'s *Hamlet* (1868); Verdi's *Macbeth* (1847), *Falstaff* (1893; after *The Merry Wives of Windsor* and *Henry IV*, parts 1 and 2), and *Otello* (1887); and **Richard Wagner**'s youthful *Das Liebesverbot* (The Ban on Love, WWV 38, 1836; after *Measure for Measure*). Shakespeare's *Romeo and Juliet* inspired Berlioz's "dramatic **symphony**" of the same name (for soloists, chorus, and **orchestra**), and the incidental music for voices and orchestra inspired by his works includes **Felix Mendelssohn Bartholdy**'s *A Midsummer Night's Dream* (MWV M13/Op. 61, 1843); **Louis Spohr**'s *Macbeth* (WoO 55, 1825); **Richard Strauss**'s *Romeo und Julia* (TrV 150, 1887); Sullivan's *The Tempest* (1861), *The Merchant of Venice* (1871), *The Merry Wives of Windsor* (1874), *Henry VIII* (1877), and *Macbeth* (1888); and Tchaikovsky's *Romeo and Juliet* (Op. 67a, 1869, rev. 1870, publ. 1871, rev. 1880, publ. 1881).

Shakespeare's works also provided the inspiration for many **programmatic** instrumental works (*see* CONCERT OVERTURE; SYMPHONIC POEM; TONE POEM). Apparently first of these was Mendelssohn's programmatic concert overture *A Midsummer Night's Dream* (MWV P3; comp. 1826, publ. 1832). Others include Antonio Bazzini's (1818–1897) *Re Lear* (Op. 68, 1874); Berlioz's *Fantaisie sur La Tempête de Shakespeare* (in *Lélio, ou Le retour à la vie*, H. 55/Op. 14[b], 1831) and *Le roi Lear* (H. 53/Op. 4, 1831–1833); Julius Benedict's (1804–1885) *The Tempest* (Op. 77, 1875); **Hans von Bülow**'s *Ouvertüre héroïque de la tragédie "Jules César" de Shakespeare* (Op. 10, 1860); **Antonín Dvořák**'s *Othello* (S. 113/Op. 93, 1894); **Edward Elgar**'s "symphonic study" *Falstaff* (Op. 68, 1813); **Niels W. Gade**'s *Hamlet* (Op. 37, 1862); **Franz Liszt**'s *Hamlet* (LW G22, 1858, publ. 1861); **Josef Rheinberger**'s *Der Widerspenstigen Zähmung* (Op. 18, 1874); Anton Rubinstein's *Antony and Cleopatra* (Op. 116, 1890), Robert Schumann's *Julius Cäsar* (Op. 128, 1851, publ. 1854); Richard Strauss's *Macbeth* (TrV 163/Op. 23, 1881, rev. 1891); and Tchaikovsky's orchestral **fantasies** on *Romeo and Juliet* (see above), *The Tempest* (Op. 18, comp. 1873, publ. 1877), and *Hamlet* (Op. 67, comp. 1888, publ. 1890), to name but a few. [JMC]

See also EDITING AND EDITIONS; HISTORICISM; NATIONALISM, ROMANTIC NATIONALISM.

SHAW, (GEORGE) BERNARD (1856–1950). Irish novelist, playwright, and music critic; one of the most eloquent and influential British advocates for **Richard Wagner** at the turn of the 20th century and the first of many English-language critics to interpret Wagner's *Ring* **cycle** from a socialist perspective. He was born in Dublin to a musical family (his father played trombone and his mother sang) and in 1876 moved to London, where he ghostwrote and pseudonymously published music criticism first for the *Pall*

Mall Gazette, then for *The Hornet* and *The Star*, before taking a position at *The World* in 1890 (a post he held until 1904). During these years, he also worked as art critic (for *The World*, 1886–1889) and drama critic (for *The Saturday Review*, 1895–1898). The last of his novels, *The Irrational Knot*, was published in 1905; aside from this work, he concentrated exclusively on plays, social commentaries, and retrospective collections of earlier writings after he retired from *The World* in 1904.

Shaw's views on music were profoundly informed by **Wolfgang Amadeus Mozart** (especially *Don Giovanni*), and his criticism is justly known for both its penetrating insights and its trenchant, often biting wit. He loathed **Felix Mendelssohn Bartholdy**'s "despicable **oratorio**-mongering" and derided **Johannes Brahms** as "a sentimental voluptuary" whose *Deutsches Requiem* "could only have come from the establishment of a first-class undertaker" (although in the 1920s he recanted the criticisms of Brahms, calling them his "only mistake"). Always a champion of modernity, he befriended and supported **Edward Elgar** and was an important English advocate for other continental composers of the Modern Romantic Generation, including **Aleksandr Scriabin** and **Richard Strauss**. [JMC]

SHEHERAZADE, OP. 35. Symphonic **suite** in four movements composed by **Nikolay Rimsky-Korsakov** in 1888, first performed in St. Petersburg in 1889. Based on the Arabic *1,001 Nights* (also known in English as *Arabian Nights*), *Sheherazade* manifests 19th-century European orientalism (*see* EXOTICISM) and demonstrates Rimsky-Korsakov's excellent **orchestrational** skill. *Sheherazade* mimics its literary source's form. Just as the varyingly numerous tales of the *Nights* are framed by a story in which captive Queen Sheherazade tells Sultan Shahryār those tales to keep herself alive, the suite *Sheherazade* situates four orchestral **character pieces**, each of them recalling images from the tales (such as a sailing Sinbad), within the **narrative** frame of a multimovement **cyclic form**. While various ideas connect the four movements, two do so conspicuously and in such a way that invites recollection of the king and queen, respectively: a bold, menacing orchestral *tutti* theme and a sweet, lyrical theme for solo violin. The manner in which these themes occur within the four movements (especially the major-mode conclusion with the solo violin theme) suggests the same happy ending that Sheherazade enjoys after telling her 1,001 tales. [RK]

SIBELIUS, JEAN [JOHAN] (CHRISTIAN JULIUS) (1865–1957). Finnish composer of the Modern Romantic Generation; significant figure in Finnish **nationalism** and, with **Edward Elgar, Aleksandr Glazunov, Gustav Mahler, Carl Nielsen**, and **Richard Strauss**, one of the most important **orchestral** composers of his generation. His compositional response to the dissonant Modernism that began sweeping the musical world during the early years of the 20th century was arguably the first manifestation of the aesthetics of objectivity that would later become better known as Neo-Classicism.

Sibelius grew up in the south of Finland in a family that spoke Swedish, learning Finnish only from the age of about eight. As a child, he played violin and composed, particularly influenced by **Adolf Bernhard Marx**'s *Die Lehre von der musikalischen Komposition, praktisch-theoretisch* (Practical and Theoretical Course in Musical Composition, first publ. 1837–1847), which was among the first treatises to present musical form as an essentially thematic rather than tonal process. He studied at the University in Helsinki from 1885 to 1889, then traveled to Berlin, Leipzig, and Vienna; during these travels he studied with Albert Becker (1834–1899), **Ferruccio Busoni**, Albert Fuchs (1858–1910), and Karl Goldmark (1830–1915) (the aging **Johannes Brahms** declined him). After returning to Finland in 1891, he was quickly established as a prominent exponent of Finnish nationalism and Finnish independence from tsarist Russia with the successful premiere of his choral/orchestral **symphonic poem** *Kullervo*, Op. 7 (1891–1892, rev. 1917–1918), a reputation that would earn him international fame and make him the personification Finnish nationalism for the remainder of his career.

Sibelius traveled widely during the first few years of the 20th century but returned to Finland in 1904 and remained based there for the rest of his life. Around this time he developed a leaner, sparer style of composition that emphasized continuous development through rotation of contrasting episodes, musical logic, and systematic progression, working in traditional genres but eschewing both conventional musical forms and what he seems to have considered the willful and self-indulgent chaos of modernism (e.g., as represented in Strauss's *Salome* [TrV 215/Op. 54, 1905]). His departure from convention and refusal to embrace the avant-garde left him in an uncomfortable position, and his reputation declined. Although the compositional output of these years was modest, around 1912 he entered into a new phase in which he seems to have embraced his peripheral position in relation to musical Modernism and the markets of Western European music, creating a new series of masterpieces that carry the intense musical logic of the works of the previous decade to new levels while also attempting to engage, philosophically, the mysteries of isolation in nature.

Sibelius continued to compose through World War I and visited the United States in 1914. The postwar years witnessed a resurgence of his popularity there and in England, but his compositional productivity declined sharply during the 1920s: his last major works were his Seventh **Symphony** (1924), the **tone poem** *Tapiola* (1925), and **incidental music** to Edvard Lembcke's (1815–1897) Danish translation of **William Shakespeare**'s *The Tempest* (Op. 109, 1925). He began work on an Eighth Symphony around 1928 and appears to have considered it ready for copying (i.e., for performance) in the early 1930s, but sometime in the 1940s he burned its score; its music remains utterly unknown. During the last 30 years of his life, he lived in isolation and composed virtually nothing, his most important surviving works being two additions, in 1946 and 1948, to a set of Masonic ritual compositions for chorus and **piano** (begun in 1927, first published in 1936, and published in final form in 1950).

Sibelius composed in virtually every genre available to composers of his day. His stage works include a one-act **opera** (*Jungfrun i tornet* [The Maiden in the Tower], 1896, still unpublished) as well as incidental music and stage music for a variety of plays and other stage productions (most importantly, a translation of Maeterlinck's *Pelléas and Melisande* and the above-mentioned translation of Shakespeare's *Tempest*). He also composed 16 numbered *opera* of music for chorus with piano or organ accompaniment, eight numbered *opera* of music for chorus a cappella, and 18 numbered *opera* of works for solo voice with accompaniment of piano or orchestra, plus numerous unpublished works in all these categories. His piano music (several dozen works) is dominated by **character pieces**, and his other instrumental **chamber music** (13 numbered *opera*) reflects his intimate knowledge especially of stringed instruments.

Sibelius is most important, however, for his Violin **Concerto**, his orchestral **suites** (especially the *Karelia* **Overture** and Suite, Op. 10/11 [1893, publ. 1906 and 1909]), his eight **tone poems** (notably *Finlandia*, Op. 26, 1900; *Pohjolan tytär* [Pohjola's Daughter], Op. 49, 1905–1906; and *Tapiola*, Op. 112, 1926), and his seven completed symphonies. The first two symphonies (opp. 39 and 43, 1899 and 1901–1902), while firmly rooted in the lush sonorities of post-Romanticism, established Sibelius as Finland's leading composer, but he broke with their lushness in the Third and Fourth Symphonies (opp. 52 and 63, 1907 and 1910–1911), producing a new sound palette whose tautness and sparseness seems to renounce the luxuriousness of post-Romanticism in favor of a more rigorous approach to form and sound that is governed by its telos and a deep inner logic. That trend is carried further in the last three symphonies (Opp. 82, 104, and 105, 1915 rev. 1919, 1923, and 1924, respectively), reaching its extreme in the one-movement Seventh. Although Sibelius is remembered for his contributions to Finnish nationalism, he never researched Finnish folk music rigorously and never quoted it directly, instead absorbing its flavor into his idioms (*see* FOLK SONG). He also developed one of the long 19th century's most profoundly original applications of the quintessentially Romantic doctrine of **organicism** within the parameters of an objective approach to musical expression whose distinctive pedigree belongs squarely in the mid-20th century. [JMC]

SIEGFRIED. *See THE RING OF THE NIBELUNG.*

SIMROCK. German firm of music publishers, for most of the **long 19th century** the principal competitor of **Breitkopf & Härtel** and C. F. Peters. The firm was founded by hornist Nicolaus Simrock (1752–1834) in Bonn in 1793 and opened new branches in Paris and Cologne in 1802 and 1812 under the direction of Heinrich (Henri) Simrock (1754–1839) and Johann Peter Simrock (1792–1868), his brother and son, respectively. Heinrich was himself a respected composer. Johann Peter took over the firm's Bonn office from his father in 1832 and in turn passed it on to his own son, Friedrich August (Fritz) Simrock (1837–1901), in 1768. Fritz moved the firm to Berlin in 1870. It established agencies in Germany's publishing capital, Leipzig, in 1904 as well as further agencies in New York and Paris. It exists today within the Benjamin–Rahter–Simrock publishing organization, with branches in Hamburg and London.

Throughout the long 19th century, the Simrock firm was noteworthy for its early embrace of young composers, its fastidious attention to detail in producing and marketing music, and its influential advocacy of works by established composers. It was among the earliest German publishers to embrace **Franz Joseph Haydn** as a part of its program (publishing three of the "London" **symphonies** in 1801 and a collection of 37 of his symphonies in 1810) and was the publisher of **Ludwig van Beethoven**'s *Fidelio* (Op. 72, 1814) and much of his vocal and instrumental **chamber music** as well as new editions of his first four symphonies during the 1820s. It was also one of **Carl Maria von Weber**'s principal publishers, publishing his one-act **opera** *Abu Hassan* (J. 106, 1819) and much of his vocal and instrumental chamber music. It published important early editions of the works of **Johann Sebastian Bach** and **George Frideric Handel** during the first three decades of the 19th century (a critical period in those composers' **reception** histories) and contributed to the **historicist** and **Caecilian** movements with editions of music by Josquin des Prez (1450–1521), Orlande de Lassus (1530–1594), and **Giovanni Pierluigi da Palestrina** (in its series *Classische Kirchenwerke alter Meister für Männerchor* [Classical Church Music for Men's Chorus by Early Masters]).

Other important composers in whose oeuvres Simrock figures prominently include **Felix Mendelssohn Bartholdy** (all six volumes of **Lieder ohne Worte** published during his lifetime and the **oratorios** *St. Paul* and *Elijah*), **Johannes Brahms** (all four of the symphonies and the *Deutsches Requiem*), and **Antonín Dvořák** (the Sixth and Ninth Symphonies and *Stabat mater*) as well as **Max Bruch, Max Reger, Johann Strauss (II)**, and many others. [JMC]

See also COPYRIGHT AND PERFORMANCE RIGHT; EDITING AND EDITIONS; PRINTING AND PUBLISHING OF MUSIC.

SINGSPIEL. (Ger., "sing-play.") A staged musical drama in German with spoken dialogue, usually **comic** in nature or derived from folklore. The musical style of *Singspiele* (pl.) typically is apparently simple or at least less obviously elaborate and sophisticated than those of other varieties of **opera** and **operetta**, and the works' settings are usually **exotic**, fantastic, or rural, featuring members of the middle and lower classes rather than aristocracy. Most *Singpsiele* are cast in one or two acts. The best-known 18th-century representative of the genre—well known and celebrated to the Romantics— is **Wolfgang Amadeus Mozart**'s *Die Zauberflöte* (The Magic Flute, K. 620, 1791). The genre's heyday passed in the 1790s, but its resonances are clearly felt in other works, such as **Ludwig van Beethoven**'s **rescue opera** *Fidelio* (Op. 72, 1814) and **Carl Maria von Weber**'s *Abu Hassan* (J. 106, 1811, rev. 1812–1813, rev. 1823) and *Der Freischütz* (1821). As a genre, it is the progenitor of other genres such as the **Posse** and **Spieloper**. Other 19th-century *Singspiele* were written by composers including **E. T. A. Hoffmann, Conradin Kreutzer, Friedrich Kuhlau, Carl Loewe, Albert Lortzing, Felix Mendelssohn Bartholdy, Giacomo Meyerbeer, Otto Nicolai, Jacques Offenbach, Carl Reinecke, Franz Schubert**, and **Gaspare Spontini**, among others. German translations and adaptations of French **opéras comiques** by composers such as **Luigi Cherubini** (e.g., *Les deux journées* as *Der Wasserträger*), **Adrien Boieldieu** (e.g., *Le nouveau seigneur du village* as *Der neue Gutsherr*), or **Étienne-Nicolas Méhul** (e.g., *Le trésor supposé* as *Die Schatzgräber*) were usually designated *Singspiele*. [JMC]

SKETCH. *See* COMPOSITIONAL PROCESS, CREATIVE PROCESS.

SKRYABIN. *See* SCRIABIN, ALEKSANDR (NIKOLAYEVICH) (1872–1915).

SLAVONIC DANCES. (Cz., *Slovanské Tance.*) Title for two collections (B. 78 and 145/opp. 46 and 72, 1878 and 1886) of stylized sets of dances for **piano duet** by **Antonín Dvořák**; iconic works in Bohemian **nationalism**. "Slavonic" refers to any of the people who speak the Slavonic languages (Serbo-Croat, Bulgarian, Ukrainian, Russian, Polish, Slovene, Czech, Slovak, Macedonian, Belarusian, and so on). The first set of Dvořák's dances was commissioned by **Simrock**, and both sets were published by that firm in their original guise and arrangements for **orchestra** (B. 83 and 147, 1878 and 1887). The first set comprises one *dumka* (Czech, Polish, and Ukrainian), two *furiants* (Czech), one *polka* (Czech), one *skočná* (Czech), and two *sousedskás* (Czech). The second set (B. 145/Op. 72, 1886) comprises two *dumkas*, one *kolo* (Serbian), one *odzemek* (Czech), one *polonaise* (Polish), one *skočná*, one *sousedská*, and one *spasírka* (Czech). Dvořák employed rhythms, phrase structures, and melodic gestures characteristic of the nominal dance types but did not use any actual tunes from the folk repertoires (*see* FOLK SONG). [JMC]

SMETANA, BEDŘICH (1824–1884). Bohemian composer, **conductor**, music educator, and music critic of the Late Romantic Generation, leading figure in Bohemian **nationalism**. He is best known today for his nationalist **opera** *Prodaná nevěsta* (*The Bartered Bride*, 1863–1870) and his **cycle** of six **symphonic poems** collectively titled *Má vlast* (My Fatherland), of which the most familiar today is *Vltava* (*The Moldau*).

Smetana was the son of a moneyed master brewer who also played in a **string quartet**, and he trained on violin and **piano** with aspirations of becoming a piano **virtuoso** after the model of **Franz Liszt**. In 1844, he began teaching private lessons in music theory, using **Adolf Bernhard Marx**'s writings as his principal source. As a composer, he was largely self-taught, inspired chiefly by Marx's approach to composition and the music of **Hector Berlioz** and Liszt. Between 1848 and 1855, he operated a financially successful music school in Prague and through Liszt's mentorship began publishing his music in 1851, such as the *Six morceaux caractèristiques* for piano solo, Op. 1—*see* CHARACTER (CHARACTERISTIC) PIECE. Smetana also won acclaim for his piano playing in the city's **Ludwig van Beethoven** and **Wolfgang Amadeus Mozart** festivals (1854 and 1856, respectively) and created his first substantial **orchestral** compositions during this period: the *Jubel-Overture* (JB 1:39, 1848–1849, rev. 1883) and the *Triumf-Sinfonie* (JB 1:59/Op. 6, 1853–1854, rev. 1881; *see* SYMPHONY). His increasing professional success was marred, however, by the deaths of three of his four daughters in 1854–1855, and when the G-minor **Piano Trio** (JB 1:64/Op. 15, 1855, rev. 1857, publ. 1870) he composed in response to his grief was poorly received, he decided to leave the country and test his fortunes elsewhere.

Disheartened by his misfortunes in Prague, Smetana left Prague for Göteburg (Sweden) in October 1856, interrupting the voyage with a stopover in Weimar, where he heard the premieres of his mentor's *"Faust" Symphony* and symphonic poem *Die Ideale*. Between his arrival in Göteburg and May 1861, he ran a successful music school, conducted a choral society, and organized chamber concerts, but these successes, too, were tainted with tragedy: the death of his wife in 1859 (an event whose emotional complexities were amplified by Smetana's affair with a married student during his previous years in Sweden). In 1860, at age 36, he fell in love with and married the 19-year-old daughter of friends and in May 1861 returned to Prague permanently with her. In 1863, he was elected head of the music section of the city's new Society of Arts and reopened his music school, and in 1864 he began publishing music criticism. His 1863 nationalist opera *Braniboři v*

Čechách (Brandenburgers in Bohemia, JB 1:87/Op. 3) won the prestigious prize of Prague's Provisional Theater in 1866. Despite his strong nationalist sentiments and his affiliation with nationalist organizations, he was accused of Wagnerism—a reasonable if also misguided charge, given the profound influence that Liszt, **Wagner**, and the **New German School** exerted on his thinking in general terms—and found his public support weakening in a Bohemia increasingly determined to free itself from the tainting influences of Austro-German culture during the late 1860s and the 1870s.

Early in 1874, Smetana's hearing began to worsen, probably as the result of syphilis. In October of that year, he was forced to resign his conducting post and sacrifice the performing rights to his operas in exchange for a pension. Although his symptoms continued to worsen, he composed actively over the coming years, completing the six symphonic poems of the cycle *Ma vlast*, four more operas, two **string quartets** (JB 1:105, 1876, publ. 1880; and JB 1:124, 1882–1883, posthumously published 1889), and other works over the next decade. By late 1883, his behavior had become increasingly erratic and occasionally violent, and in the early months of 1884, he suffered from increasing hallucinations and paranoia. He was institutionalized three weeks before his death, leaving unfinished an orchestral cycle titled *Pražský karneval* (Prague Carnival) and an opera titled *Viola* (based on **Shakespeare**'s *Twelfth Night*).

Smetana was an iconic figure in the late 19th century's advancement of the belief in music as a vehicle for communicating collective national identity generally. Although his thinking was influenced by that of the New German School, his use of national themes and subjects and his frequent and successful appropriation of the language of **folk song** helped to establish the aesthetic viability of musical nationalism—not just Bohemian nationalism—during the critical first decades after the **Revolutions of 1848**. His only symphony was written in celebration of the marriage of the Habsburg emperor Franz Joseph I and Elisabeth of Bavaria, and when he abandoned Prague for Scandinavia in 1856, his interests turned to various national interests that were not Bohemian in nature: Shakespeare (a Lisztian symphonic poem after *Richard III*, JB 1:70, Op. 11, 1857–1858, and a *Sketch to the Scene for Macbeth and the Witches* for piano solo, JB 1:75, 1859), German national literature (a symphonic poem after **Friedrich Schiller**'s *Wallensteins Lager*, JB 1:72/Op. 14, 1858–1859, and an orchestral **prelude** to a puppet play on *Faust*, JB 1:85, 1862), and Norwegian legend and literature (the symphonic poem *Hakon Jarl*, JB 1:79/Op. 15, 1858–1859). Yet his native Bohemia had been a part of the Austro-Hungarian Empire and subject to the rule of the Habsburg monarchy for nearly 300 years at his birth, and Smetana's sympathy with the calls for Bohemian independence had become increasingly common during the 75 years leading up to the Revolutions of 1848. Those calls came to little, but they did inspire renewed fervency in Bohemian nationalism during the second half of the 19th century. After his return to Prague in 1861, he devoted himself increasingly to the cause of Bohemian nationalism, especially in his seven post-1861 operas and his choral and orchestral works. By the early 20th century, the doubts that assailed his reputation during the last decade of his life had abated, and he had become, along with **Antonín Dvořák**, a personification of Bohemian nationalism. [JMC]

SMYTH, ETHEL (MARY) (1858–1944). English composer, suffrage worker, and writer on music; member of the Modern Romantic Generation. She was one of the most important figures in British musical life during the late **Victorian era** and the first half of the 20th century, and one of the early 20th century's most insistent and influential voices demanding that women composers be treated as equals. Over her father's opposition to the notion of women studying music, she entered the Leipzig **Conservatory** in 1878, initially studying there under **Carl Reinecke**, Salomon Jadassohn (1831–1902), and Louis Maas (1852–1889). She was disappointed with the institution and its students but chose to remain in Leipzig in order to study harmony and counterpoint privately with Heinrich von Herzogenberg (1843–1900). She remained in Germany until 1878, moving in circles that included **Johannes Brahms, Antonín Dvořák, Edvard Grieg, Joseph Joachim, Clara Schumann**, and **Pyotor Il'yich Tchaikovsky** and hearing her works performed both privately and publicly—most importantly in the Leipzig Gewandhaus.

Upon her return to London, Smyth's *Serenade* (1890) and **concert overture** on **William Shakespeare**'s *Anthony and Cleopatra* (1890) were performed in the Crystal Palace concerts under the authorship of "E. M. Smyth," to considerable acclaim—though reviewers were apparently surprised when they learned that the works were by a woman. Her Mass in D (1891, publ. 1893, rev. 1925) was less well received when it was performed in 1893. Her first **opera**, the two-act *Fantasio* (1892–1894, publ. 1899), on Smyth's (1805–1887) own German **libretto** adapted from Henry Brewster (1805–1887), was premiered in Weimar in 1898, and her second, *Der Wald* (The Forest, likewise in German on her own libretto), was premiered in Berlin in 1902. The latter was performed in Covent Garden later that same year and at the Metropolitan Opera (New York) in 1903.

Over the course of the 20th century's first decade, Smyth became increasingly involved with the suffrage movement, meeting Emmeline Pankhurst (1858–1928) in 1910 and devoting herself wholeheartedly to the movement thereafter. She composed a set of three works for **women**'s **chorus** with optional **orchestra** under the title *Songs of Sunrise* in 1911, and the second of these, "The March of the Women" (later adopted as the anthem of the English suffrage movement), was premiered under Smyth's own direction that same year. The following year, she spent time in prison for her involvement with the movement (and famously conducted the "March of the Women" with a toothbrush from a window overlooking the prison's courtyard when the renowned conductor Thomas Beecham [1879–1961] came to visit). She also penned numerous witty and insightful periodical articles and a total of nine books, among them a two-volume autobiography; these, too, contributed to her reputation and to the **feminist** cause of the early 20th century. She received two honorary doctorates (one from Durham University, 1910, and one from Oxford University, 1926) and in 1922 was made a Dame of the British Empire. By 1939, she was completely deaf and composed no more but continued to advocate for her own and other women's music.

Smyth was arguably the late 19th and early 20th centuries' most influential personal proof that women were fully capable of writing high-quality music in the large public genres and styles typically considered the domain of men as well as in the stereotypically "feminine" genres of instrumental and vocal **chamber music**. Some critics hinted that the ostensibly "unfeminine" style of her music stemmed from her well-known attractions to other women, but the enthusiastic reception that greeted her large-scale works ultimately undermined such sniping. She composed a total of six operas, both serious and light, of which *The Wreckers*, originally written as *Les naufrageurs* in French but premiered in Germany as *Standrecht* (Martial Law) in 1906, is generally considered her finest (it was premiered in English in London, 1909). In her operas; her Double **Concerto** for Violin and Horn (1927); her two **piano trios** for flute or violin, oboe, and **piano** (both 1927); or the 1930 *Hot Potatoes* for four horns, four trumpets, and percussion, Smyth reveals abilities at colorful and nuanced **orchestration**. She also composed a sizable body of **part-songs** and other vocal chamber music. Her Mass in D remains one of the 19th century's most original concert settings of the Mass Ordinary. [JMC]
    See also FEMINISM.

SOCIÉTÉ NATIONALE DE MUSIQUE. (Fr., "National Society for Music.") Private concert society founded in Paris in the wake of France's disastrous defeat in the **Franco-Prussian War** with the express purpose of fostering new, nonoperatic music by French composers; extant until 1939. The Society's formation reflected the **Third Republic**'s overriding view of music as *utilité publique* and was an attempt to facilitate modernization and revivification of French musical culture. It did so partly by encouraging the cultivation of **orchestral** and other instrumental music and partly by committing itself specifically to French and (eventually) other francophone composers, thus securing a place for them in concert programs that during the 1860s had increasingly been dominated by their German counterparts—particularly under the influence of **Richard Wagner** (*wagnerisme*). The presidency was first shared by Romain Bussine (1830–1899) and **Camille Saint-Saëns**, with other early members including **Alexis de Castillon, Henri Duparc, Théo-dore Dubois, Gabriel Fauré, César Franck, Ernest Guiraud,** and **Jules Massenet**. The Society's first concert was given on 17 November 1871, and in the 1880s it expanded its eligibility to Belgian composers. [JMC]

SÖDERMAN, (JOHAN) AUGUST (1832–1876). Swedish composer of the Late Romantic Generation. Raised in the family of a theater music director, Söderman went on to join the same profession. As a composer, he distinguished himself with his **operettas, incidental music, Lieder,** and choral music; his personal style strikes a successful balance between late Romantic individualism and a kind of folk music–imbued **nationalism** (*see* FOLK SONG). After studying at the Swedish Royal Academy of Music in 1847–1850, Söderman became music director for the traveling theater company of Edvard Stjernström (1816–1877). The troupe settled in Stockholm in 1853. In 1856–1857, Söderman studied in Leipzig, where he became interested in the music of **Robert Schumann**. In 1858, he attained his final position at the Royal Opera in Stockholm as chorus master and deputy **conductor**. Söderman's last significant journey abroad before his untimely death was a European tour in 1869–1870. Highlights of Söderman's compositional output include his **concert overture** *Svenskt festspel* (Swedish Festival, 1858, extracted from his **incidental music** for *Några timmar på Kronoborgs slott* [A Few Hours in Kronoborg Castle]), his operettas *Urdur* (1852) and *Hin Ondes första lärospån* (The Devil's First Lesson, after **Eugène Scribe**, 1856), and his incidental music for **William Shakespeare**'s *Richard III* (1872). [RK]

SOLEMN MASS. (Lat., missa solemnis; Fr., messe solennelle.) In the Roman Catholic liturgy generally, a Mass in which none of the prayers are omitted and almost all are sung. In music of the **long 19th century**, the term also denotes an exceptionally lengthy or elaborate setting of the five sung prayers of the Mass Ordinary. Composers of such Masses during the long 19th century include **Adolphe Adam** (1837), **Ludwig van Beethoven** (Op. 123, 1819–1823, publ. 1827), **Hector Berlioz** (1824, withdrawn and posthumously rediscovered 1992), **Anton Bruckner** (WAB 29, 1854), **Luigi Cherubini** (five works, 1816–1821 passim), **Théodore Dubois** (1900), **Charles Gounod** (four works, 1855, 1876, 1883, 1888), **Johann Nepomuk Hummel** (WoO 12, 1806), **Jean François Le Seuer** (three works, 1828–1830), **Franz Liszt** (LW 12, 1855–1858, publ. 1859, rev. 1871), **Etienne-Nicolas Méhul** (1804), **Saverio Mercadante** (1863), **Gioachino Rossini** (1863, rev., publ. 1869), **August Söderman** (1875, publ. 1881), **Ambroise Thomas** (1852, publ. 1858), and **Carl Maria von Weber** (J. 224 and 251, 1817–1818 and 1818–1819), among many others. Of these, the Solemn Masses of Beethoven and Gounod occupy special stature—especially Beethoven's because of its scale, vivid text painting, and the confessional conflict between the Roman Catholic ideas expressed in the text and Beethoven's own staunchly Deist views. During the long 19th century, the *Messes solennelles* of Cherubini and Gounod were widely performed. [JMC]

EIN SOMMERNACHTSTRAUM. See A MIDSUMMER NIGHT'S DREAM.

SONATA. (from It. *suonare*, "to sound.") During the **long 19th century**, a composition for one or more solo instruments, usually laid out in several movements and following **sonata plan**; with the **string quartet**, one of the preeminent genres of instrumental **chamber music**. Unlike the **symphony**, whose prestige and popularity increased dramatically over the course of the 19th century, or the string quartet, whose prestige increased but whose tradition seems to have encumbered the production of new works, the sonata apparently retained its prestige but actually diminished in popularity during the period after around 1830. The decline was apparently a result of the proliferation of **character pieces** and other miniatures that were cheaper to publish and more accessible to nonprofessional players, and of increasing perceptions after mid-century that the creative potentials explored so brilliantly in the sonata tradition as codified by **Franz Joseph Haydn, Wolfgang Amadeus Mozart,** and **Ludwig van Beethoven** had lost their potential for self-renewal in the works of composers of the Romantic Generation. Nevertheless, virtually every composer of the long 19th century worked in the genre, producing a corpus of works that are worthy compeers of their 18th-century counterparts.

Sonatas of the long 19th century may be grouped into two broad families: *solo sonatas* (usually written for **piano** but occasionally for other solo instruments, most commonly violin or cello) and *duo sonatas* (for other instrument with piano accompaniment). In the first of these categories, the works that defined the genre internationally for much of the century were the 32 piano sonatas published by Beethoven between 1796 and 1823—works that from the earliest set (Op. 2, 1793–1795, publ. 1796) were startling in their admixtures of structural and stylistic convention and innovation and their breadth and variety of expression. As Beethoven's reputation grew in the German lands, Great Britain, France, and (to a lesser extent) the Italian lands, his sonatas were widely reprinted and republished in editions that often differed significantly from those that he actually oversaw and authorized himself (*see* COPYRIGHT AND PERFORMANCE RIGHT) but that nevertheless contributed to the spread of his cultural authority and shaped contemporary and later understandings of the solo piano sonata as a genre. Beethoven's piano sonatas also drew on ideas and techniques from other sonata composers. Such was the canonization of Beethoven's sonatas that by 1861 pianists had begun programming them in complete **cycles.**

Other composers of the Early Romantic Generation who produced solo piano sonatas that circulated widely include Muzio Clementi (1752–1832), J. B. Cramer (1771–1858), **Carl Czerny,** Jan Ladislav Dussek (1760–1812), Ferdinand Hérold (1791–1833), **Johann Nepomuk Hummel, Friedrich Kalkbrenner, Friedrich Kuhlau, Carl Loewe, Ignaz Moscheles, Ferdinando Paer, Ignaz Pleyel, Cipriani Potter,** Ferdinand Ries (1784–1838), **Franz Schubert, Jan Václav Voříšek,** and **Carl Maria von Weber.** Also worthy of mention in this generation's output are several sonatas for **piano duet** (one keyboard, two players) by composers including **Anton Diabelli,** Hummel, **Heinrich Marschner,** Moscheles, and Schubert. Schubert's "Grand Duo" Sonata in C Major (D. 812, comp. 1824, publ. posth. as Op. 140, 1838) occupies a particularly important position in this subclass.

Composers of the Romantic Generation were slow to try their hand at the daunting legacy of their Early Romantic Generation predecessors. The first composer in this group to address the innovations of form, style, emotional breadth, and scale represented by Beethoven's late sonatas was **Felix Mendelssohn Bartholdy,** whose E-major Sonata (MWV U54/Op. 6, 1826), along with its posthumously published counterparts in G minor and B-flat major (MWV U30 and U64/opp. posth. 105 and 106, comp. 1821 and 1827, publ. 1868), is an obvious and conscious, if not entirely convincing, attempt to come to grips with Beethoven's late sonatas. More enduring success has been accorded the sonatas of Mendelssohn's generational compeers **Fryderyk Chopin, Franz Liszt,** and **Robert Schumann:** two mature piano sonatas by Chopin (CT 202 and 203/opp. 35 and 58, comp. 1837 and 1844, publ. 1840 and 1845), the B-minor Sonata of Liszt (LW A179, 1852–1853, publ. 1854), and three sonatas by Schumann (Op. 11, 1832–1835, publ. 1836; Op. 14, 1835–1836, publ. 1836, rev. 1853; and Op. 22, 1833–1838, publ. 1839). Of these, the B-minor Sonata of Liszt is particularly noteworthy as a **cycle** of four movements played without pause that collectively outline a massive **sonata form** tightly unified by the technique of **thematic transformation** central to Liszt's mature styles. These works are followed (in terms of significance) by the solo sonatas of **Charles-Valentin Alkan, William Sterndale Bennett, Niels W. Gade, Stephen Heller, Henri Herz, Ferdinand Hiller, Franz Lachner, Otto Nicolai,** and **Richard Wagner,** among others.

Significant solo piano sonatas of the Late Romantic Generation were penned by **Johannes Brahms, Gabriel Fauré, César Franck, Edvard Grieg, Max Reger,** and **Camille Saint-Saëns,** with other contributions by composers including **Mily Balakirev, Felix Draeseke, Hubert Parry, Joachim Raff, Joseph Rheinberger, Anton Rubinstein,** and **Pyotor Il'yich Tchaikovsky,** among others. The genre's popularity faded in the century's last few decades, but noteworthy contributions were made by composers such as **Isaac Albéniz, Ferrucio Busoni, Cécile Chaminade, Vincent d'Indy, Paul Dukas, Alexander Glazunov, Edward MacDowell, Carl Nielsen, Sergei Rachmaninoff, Alexander Scriabin, Richard Strauss,** and **Hugo Wolf.**

A special class of solo sonata during the long 19th century was the *organ sonata*. Because of the instrument for which they were written, organ sonatas were explicitly incompatible with use in domestic venues and instead presumed the presence of a church or church-like institution for their use. The first milestone in this genre is Mendelssohn's Six Sonatas for the Organ (MWV SD31/Op. 65, comp. 1829–1845, publ. 1845); other major organ sonatas were composed by **Vincenzo Bellini** (ca. early 1830s?), **Edward Elgar** (1895), **Josef Rheinberger** (20 sonatas, 1884–1901 passim), Reger (1899 and 1901), and **Charles Villiers Stanford** (five sonatas, all 1917–1918), among others.

The same issues of form, style, and tradition that complicated the generic history of the solo sonata over the course of the long 19th century also applied to the *duo sonata*. Here, however, the genre's move from the amateur-dominated spaces of domestic performance into the professional and **virtuoso** spaces of the concert and recital hall gradually exerted another important influence: a shift in the musical balance of the works in question, from essentially egalitarian partnership in the works of the 1790s and earlier to a relationship dominated by the soloist, with the accompaniment (usually piano) either relegated to supporting or subservient position or figuring as a *concertante* partner. The duo-sonata repertoire of the century as a whole may thus be viewed as a renegotiation of these fundamental issues of balance and texture as well as the more general issues of form and content that informed the history of the solo sonata.

In modern practice, duo sonatas of the long 19th century are typically designated by the non-keyboard instrument primarily for convenience (e.g., sonatas for violin and piano are typically termed *violin sonatas* in popular parlance). Two varieties of duo sonata predominated during the long 19th century: violin sonatas and cello sonatas. The early 19th century's understanding of the violin sonata was informed to some extent by some of the violin sonatas of **Wolfgang Amadeus Mozart** (K. 296, 376, 377, 481, 526)—described on their title pages, in keeping with the 18th-century balance of roles, as *sonatas for the harpsichord or pianoforte, with violin accompaniment*. The same formulation (and musical balance) "piano and violin" was also employed in all 10 of Beethoven's violin sonatas. Nevertheless, the violin sonatas of Mozart and Beethoven feature complex contrapuntal and conversational interactions between keyboard and violin, and the independence and level of difficulty of the violin part are greater than was usual in many other contemporary and earlier violin sonatas. Other important violin sonatas of the Early Romantic Generation include those of Hummel, **Rudolfe Kreutzer**, Kuhlau, Ries, Schubert, Weber, and especially **Louis Spohr** (himself a renowned violinist); unusually, the violin sonatas of the great virtuoso **Nicolò Paganini** (59 sonatas, most 1804–1809) were written for accompaniment of guitar rather than piano. Only three major composers of the Romantic Generation penned violin sonatas—Mendelssohn, Niels W. Gade, and Robert Schumann—and of these, only the two sonatas of Schumann (opp. 105 and 121, both comp. 1851 and publ. 1852 and 1853, respectively) were widely known during the 19th century.

During the second half of the century, the violin sonata experienced something of a resurgence. Major contributions were made by composers including Brahms, **Antonín Dvořák**, Fauré, Franck, **Édouard Lalo**, Saint-Saëns, and **Charles-Marie Widor**, with lesser-known works also being submitted by **Théodore Dubois**, Grieg, Raff, Reinecke, and Rubinstein, among others. The list of Modern Romantic Generation violin sonatas is even more impressive, with contributions by **Ernest Bloch, Ferruccio Busoni, Claude Debussy, Frederick Delius**, Elgar, **Zdeněk Fibich**, Indy, **Albéric Magnard**, Nielsen, Reger, **Jean Sibelius, Ethel Smyth**, Stanford, and Richard Strauss, among many others.

The issues of balance and scoring that presented themselves in the Romantic violin sonata were even more pronounced in the *cello sonata* of the long 19th century, largely because the instrument's usual range fell into the middle and lower end of the usual range of the accompaniment. In the traditional (18th-century and earlier) approach to the accompanied sonata, this was not a major issue, but the 19th century's increasing understanding of the sonata as a venue for accompanied soloist rather than two equal performers made it more difficult. Here, too, Beethoven's five sonatas (opp. 5, 69, and 102) outline the emergence of the newer approach and develop solutions. Whereas the two op. 5 sonatas reflect the earlier tradition, the arduous revision history of Op. 69 reflects, in part, the composer's recasting of scoring, texture, and (in some places) form in order to win greater prominence for the cellist (*see* COMPOSITIONAL PROCESS, CREATIVE PROCESS); the two op. 102 sonatas reflect this accomplishment. Other Early Romantic Generation composers of cello sonatas include **Adrien Boieldieu**, Paer, and **Bernhard Romberg** (the last himself a well-known cellist). The Romantic Generation submitted relatively few cello sonatas, but the contributions of Chopin, Mendelssohn, and (to a lesser extent) Alkan and Lachner were important attempts to keep the genre alive in part by building on the ideas and techniques reflected in Beethoven's op. 69 sonata (as well as Op. 102, although this Opus was less well known until the second half of the century).

The 19th century's subsequent cello sonatas continue to grapple with these issues—the nature and importance of which was only complicated as heavier, more monochromatic pianos became common in the last few decades of the century (*see* BÖSENDORFER; CHICKERING AND SONS; STEIN-WAY). Major sonatas were submitted in the Late Romantic Generation by Brahms, Fauré, Franck, Grieg, Lalo, and Saint-Saëns and in the Modern Romantic Generation by Magnard, Rachmaninoff, Stanford, Richard Strauss, and Reger, among others.

Although violin sonatas and cello sonatas were by far the most common varieties of duo sonata during the long 19th century, the Romantics also contributed notable sonatas for various other scorings: flute (**Gaetano Doni-zetti**, Ferdinand Ries, and especially Reinecke), oboe (Donizetti and Saint-Saëns), clarinet (Brahms, Draeseke, Mendelssohn, Reger, and Saint-Saëns), horn (Potter), and viola (Brahms, Mikhail Glinka, Reinecke, and Anton Rubinstein). [JMC]

See also "HAMMERKLAVIER".

SONATA FORM, SONATA-ALLEGRO FORM, FIRST-MOVEMENT FORM. (Fr., forme-sonate; Ger., Sonatensatz; It., forma-sonata.) Term for the family of related structural processes that predominated in Western European art music from the late 18th century to the early 20th century. The term refers not to an entire work but to the structure of a given movement or section within a multimovement or extended composition, either instrumental or vocal, such as a **sonata**, **string quartet**, **symphony**, or **opera**. It is best viewed as a complex of coordinated tonal and thematic events that collectively provide a broad and highly flexible template for musical process in such works. The term was apparently coined by **Adolf Bernhard Marx** in his *Die Lehre von der musikalischen Komposition, praktisch-theoretisch* (Theory and Practice of Musical Composition; 4 vols., Leipzig, 1837–1847) because of the form's ubiquity in the first movement of sonatas. The term *sonata-allegro* form is doubly misleading because the form is found in all tempos. *First-movement form* is likewise problematic because the form occurs in any movement, not only the first.

The variety of historical and musical contexts in which sonata form occurs, together with the flexibility that composers celebrated in exploiting its broad conceptual outlines for their own purposes, make the task of pinning down a single set of clear and consistent characteristics impossible beyond the general facts that all such forms (1) are tonally based and thematically articulated and (2) establish a tonic, depart from it, and return to it. Musicologist James Hepokoski and music theorist Warren Darcy have developed an extensive taxonomy of its variants that embraces the common-practice repertoire; this taxonomy provides the basis of the discussion below (James Hepokoski and Warren Darcy, *Elements of Sonata Theory: Norms, Types, and Deformations in the Late 18th-Century Sonata* [Oxford: Oxford University Press, 2006]). Additionally, keys are given in Roman numerals (with upper-case numerals indicating major mode and lowercase ones indicating the minor mode). In referring to thematic elements the discussion, P refers to the theme(s) associated with the primary key, T to a modulating passage (transition), t to a passage that is based on T but does not modulate, S to theme(s) associated with the secondary key(s), and K to cadential material. The discussion below focuses on what by convention is the central or main portion of the form; this may be preceded by an introduction (related or unrelated) and/ or followed by a coda (ditto).

Sonata form is prototypically a two-part form subdivided into four sections (two sections per part); various works specify that either or both of the two parts is to be repeated. Frequently, the first two sections are collectively referred to as the *exposition* (its first section establishing the tonic and its second establishing at least one other, conflicting key); the third, tonally unstable one (if present) as the *development*; and the concluding section that typically reaffirms the tonic as the *recapitulation* or *reprise*. Frequently, the constituent sections or stages in the processes are differentiated by pronounced changes in dynamics, texture, or (where applicable) orchestration.

Type 1 ("sonatina form" or "sonata without development"). This variety includes a tonally progressive first part, typically with discrete themes that articulate the major tonal divisions, and typically resolves any thematic material initially stated in a key other than the tonic back to the tonic; it includes only a minimal developmental or unstable section, however, or none at all. This variety of sonata form is common in opera **overtures** and slow movements of **sonata-plan** works and frequently contains no internal repeats. Most of **Gioachino Rossini**'s overtures belong to this variety. It may be diagrammed as shown in figure 4.

I (Exposition)					II (Recapitulation)			
P	T	S	K	(brief bridge, optional)	P	t	S	K
I	→	V--------			I		I---------	

Figure 4. Type 1 ("sonatina form" or "sonata without development").

I (exposition)				IIa (development)	IIb (recapitulation)			
1		2		3	4			
P	T	S	K		S	t	P	K
I	→	V--------		(unstable)	I		I---------	

Figure 5. Type 2 (binary or binary variant).

Type 2 (binary or binary variant). This variety begins the recapitulation not with P but with S or some other nondevelopmental element. It may be diagrammed as shown in figure 5.

Type 3. This "textbook" variety includes full-fledged exposition, development, and reprise. The reprise typically is initiated by P. Early 19th-century composers and theorists considered it binary (**Antoine Reicha** called it the "grande coupe binaire" [large binary form] in 1828), but Marx and other later theorists regarded it as ternary. It differs from the usual understanding of ternary form in that its first section is tonally progressive, whereas the first section of ternary form proper is tonally closed. It may be diagrammed as shown in figure 6.

Type 4 (sonata-rondo). This hybrid of sonata process and the thematic principles of the rondo is characterized by bivalent function: the expository space typically closes with a restatement of P (serving as *A* in the rondo form) in the dominant, treats the *C* section of the rondo as a developmental section, and ultimately resolves S (originally serving as *B* in the rondo form) to the tonic. It may be diagrammed as shown in figure 7 (rondo functions here given in parentheses).

I (exposition)		IIa (development)	IIb (recapitulation)	
1	2	3	4	
P T	S K		P t	S K
I →	V--------	(unstable)	I	I--------

Figure 6. Type 3 ("textbook" variety).

Ia (exposition)		IIa (development)	IIb (recapitulation)		
1	2	3	4		
P (A) T	S(B) K (A)	(C)	P(A) t	S(B)	K(A)
I →	V-------------	(unstable)	I	I-------------	

Figure 7. Type 4 (sonata-rondo).

Type 5 (concerto-sonata form or ritornello form). This variety, too, is characterized by functional bivalence, now occasioned by a hybridization of the tonal and thematic processes of Type 3 sonata form with those of the ritornello form associated with concerto movements and the A sections of da capo arias in the 17th and earlier 18th centuries. The opening ritornello and the statement of P in the solo section affirm the tonic, S in the first solo section affirms the secondary key(s), K confirms the latest secondary key, the soloist-dominated portion of the recapitulatory space reestablishes the tonic and resolves thematic material original presented in other keys to the home key, and the concluding section resolves K to the tonic while serving as a closing ritornello. This variety may be diagrammed as shown in figure 8.

Ia (exposition)			IIa (development)	IIb (recapitulation)	
Ritornello	Solo	Rit.	Solo		Rit.
1	2		3	4	
P t S K	P T S	K		P t S (cadenza)	K
I	I → V----------		(unstable)	I---------------------------	

Figure 8. Type 5 (concerto-sonata or ritornello form).

Finally, this family of templates may be applied to vocal as well as instrumental works or stretched across multiple movements or sections of larger works. **Felix Mendelssohn Bartholdy**'s setting of **Lord Byron**'s "There Be None of Beauty's Daughters" (MWV K76, 1833, publ. 1836–1837) is a Type 1 sonata form; composers from **Wolfgang Amadeus Mozart** to **Richard Strauss** (and beyond) applied the form to individual sections, numbers, scenes, or entire acts of **operas**; and composers such as **Fanny Hensel**, **Franz Liszt**, and **Pyotor Il'yich Tchaikovsky** stretched the form's constituent elements out over multiple movements. During the **long 19th century**, the form was also discussed in distinctly gendered terms, with analysts characterizing P as "masculine" and S as "feminine" and positing the rhetorical processes of the form as a whole as the competition or interplay among the two sexes and their vying for primacy or struggle against subordination. [JMC]

See also "CHORAL" SYMPHONY; DEFORMATION; NARRATIVE; SONATA PLAN.

SONATA PLAN. Term for the fairly standardized series of movements that characterized much instrumental music in the **long 19th century**; so termed because the opening movement of the series was typically in **sonata form**. It is most commonly used in **concertos**, instrumental **chamber music** (such as the **piano trio**, piano **quartet**, piano **quintet**, and **string quartet**), solo and accompanied or duo **sonatas** and **symphonies**, and (more loosely applied) **serenades** and **suites**. Within any given work that follows the sonata plan, the individual movements are typically in contrasting tempos, usually beginning and ending with a movement whose predominant tempo was lively or quick and containing one or more middle movements that are slow or moderate in tempo. The work as a whole was typically unified by a central tonality, normally the main (ending) key of the first movement.

The most common applications of the sonata plan consist of either three or four movements. In three-movement works, the first movement establishes the key of the work and is usually cast in sonata form (with or without introduction). The second movement is typically in a plagal, mediant, or submediant key (use of the dominant is rare in this position) and may be a theme with **variations** or double theme with variations, a Type 1 sonata form (without development), a binary form (Type 2), or a **song** form. The closing movement reaffirms the tonic and is often in sonata, rondo, or sonata-rondo form. In the late 18th century, the three-movement application of the sonata plan was most common in solo sonatas and concertos, although three-movement symphonies remained common in Central Europe into the 1790s (**Wolfgang Amadeus Mozart**'s "Prague" Symphony, K. 504 [1786] being but one of many examples).

Four-movement applications of the sonata plan, prevalent in the duo sonata, string quartet, and symphony and in the late 18th century, typically insert into this plan a stylized dance movement in moderate or quick tempo, often in triple meter. In the late 18th and early 19th centuries, this movement typically intervened between the slow movement and the **finale**; during the first half of the 19th century, it became increasingly common for the dance movement to precede the slow movement. The dance movement was typically in the tonic. In the late 18th century, it was typically in the style of a minuet and trio, but beginning in the 1790s, it was usually cast as a **scherzo**; by the second half of the 19th century, it was often set as a *Ländler* (e.g., in the symphonies of **Anton Bruckner** and **Gustav Mahler**).

Instrumental music of the long 19th century is also characterized by a number of elaborations on or expansions and adaptations of the sonata plan. Such variants are most common in works designated as **serenade** or **suite** but were not uncommon in other works typically associated with sonata plan. For example, **Ludwig van Beethoven**'s five-movement String Quartet in G Minor, Op. 18, no. 6 (1800, publ. 1801), begins with a sonata-form first movement and follows this with an adagio, scherzo, and finale but interpolates an intensely expressive movement titled "La malincolia" (Melancholy) between the scherzo and finale; his **"Pastoral" Symphony** (No. 6, Op. 68, 1808, publ. 1809) interpolates a movement titled "storm" between the scherzo and finale; and his string quartets opp. 131 and 132 (1825–1826, both publ. 1827), comprising seven and five movements, respectively, distribute elements of the slow movement and dance movement across the inner movements. **Hector Berlioz**'s *Episode in the Life of an Artist* (H. 34/Op. 14[A], 1830–1834, publ. 1834) interpolates its celebrated "March to the Scaffold" between its slow third movement and its finale. **Robert Schumann**'s Third Symphony (Op. 97, 1850, publ. 1851) interpolates a quasi-programmatic stylized movement featuring orchestral *stile antico* polyphony between its slow (third) movement and its finale, and Mahler's Third Symphony (1896) is cast in two parts, the first comprising one movement and the second five; the latter group includes both a "tempo di menuetto" and a "scherzando" as well as an adagio and follows the brisk finale with another extended adagio. Finally, Berlioz's "dramatic symphony" *Roméo et Juliette* (H. 79/Op. 17, 1839, publ. 1847) is cast in three parts comprising seven movements (those standing in for an adagio and a scherzo contained in Part II), and **Felix Mendelsohn Bartholdy**'s "symphony-cantata" *Lobgesang* (MWV A18/Op. 52, 1840, publ. 1841) tropes the overall form of Beethoven's Ninth (**"Choral") Symphony** by combining a symphonic sonata-form movement, scherzetto, and adagio with an extended choral finale that itself includes many of the essential gestures of a symphony.

The term *sonata plan* is a historical artifice, apparently invented in the early 20th century as a means of describing and theorizing a set of musical conventions that had assumed the function of a lingua franca. It is usefully applied as a framework for understanding how individual compositions within the instrumental practice of the long 19th century relate to one another and to the various generic and rhetorical conventions of the century. [JMC]

SONG. A relatively brief, usually unstaged vocal composition, sacred or secular, for a solo singer or a small group of singers, typically one on a part, with or without accompaniment; probably the most instinctual and primal form of human expression in music. For purposes of the **long 19th century**, it is useful to classify song into two broad categories—**folk song** and art song—and to divide these according to language, linguistic group, or geographical range (this often being coterminous with the language or linguistic group per se), then to subdivide the latter into different genres.

The most important characteristics differentiating folk song from art song are that folk songs typically rely primarily on oral transmission and therefore usually exist in multiple versions that differ substantively, whereas art songs typically rely primarily on notation and thus implicitly entail a certain—but by no means absolute—amount of fixity in text, music, and the relationship between the two. Moreover, the text and music of folk song are typically anonymous and thus not bound up with any notions of authorial identity or fidelity to the poet's or composer's wishes, whereas art song was typically created in the long 19th century by the setting of a previously notated and/or published poetic text to music by a specific named composer who then arranged for or permitted the performance and/or publication of the song. The practice for creating and disseminating art song thus not only emphasizes textual and musical fixity but also places the composer and the poet in the position of creators whose wishes performers are to realize. In so doing, it creates at least two new aesthetic criteria: that of the effectiveness of music in conveying the sense of the text and that of the success or failure of the intersection of the two primary creative voices, poet and composer.

Finally, by convention during the long 19th century, folk song was typically performed in relatively informal settings (often outdoors or in public indoor venues that were not specifically created for musical performance), while art song typically was performed in a more formal venue. For most of the long 19th century, the venues for performing art song were domestic and private (although such songs were occasionally performed in the context of public concerts), but by century's end, it had become common for art songs to be performed in public recitals (known in Germany as *Liederabende*—"song evenings").

Since the primary emphasis of this dictionary is on cultivated rather than folk music, the many varieties of folk song will be briefly surveyed in that entry. The remainder of this entry will discuss general issues that pertain to art song in the long 19th century.

Within the broad category of 19th-century art song, the principal linguistic/geographic categories are those of song in *Central and Eastern Europe*, *England and the United States*, *France*, *Germany and Austria*, *Italy*, and *Spain and Latin America*. Although many genres appear to transcend these linguistic and geographic categories (e.g., **romance**), the fact that each linguistic group has its own literary and poetic conventions that in turn provide the foundation for the musical settings of the text in art song leads to significant differences within each genre from one language group to another, even when the terms themselves are linguistic cognates.

The principal varieties of art song of Central and Eastern Europe were the **ballade**, *lullaby*, and *romance*; those of the English-speaking world, the *ballad* and *romance* (both generically referred to as "song"); and those of France, the **chanson**, **mélodie**, and *romance*. The most important forms of art song in the German lands were the **Ballade, Gesang, Lied**, and *Romanze*; those in Italy, the *ballatta, canzone, canzonetta*, and *romanza*; and those in Spain and Latin America, the *canción* and *villancico*.

Despite the important differences among these various linguistic and geographic families, the overarching tendency of art song to comprise a more or less stable and formally presented poetic text that was set to notated music by a trained composer and presented in performance generated a number of important techniques for interpretation and aesthetic assessment during the long 19th century. Most of these reflect the process of creation itself, beginning with the text and assessing the music in terms of its response to that text, interpreting this as a compositional decision that reflects the composer's interpretation or reading of the original poetic text. Thus, it is useful to begin with the *external* or *overall form* of the text and music. If the poem is a free, non-stanzaic or irregularly stanzaic form, such as a ballad or an ode, then cultivated music's aesthetic criterion of coherence in the long 19th century typically led composers to find musical means of providing a unifying element that would generate a sense of beginning, middle, and end. Conversely, if the poetic text is organized into stanzas, with or without refrain, the composer may decide either to reuse the same music for each stanza and/or the successive statements of the refrain (*strophic setting*), to set out in a strophic pattern but substantively change the music to one or more stanzas in order to emphasize them or bring out some significant difference between them and the other strophes (a *modified-strophic setting*), to provide no regular or discernible pattern of textual/musical repetition (a *through-composed setting*), or to graft an appropriate established musical form onto the text in order to attain a sense of direction and coherence: **Franz Schubert**'s *Gretchen am Spinnrade* (Gretchen at the Spinning Wheel, D. 118, 1814) is set as a rondo (achieved in part through Schubert's insertion of the poem's first four lines several times where poet **Johann Wolfgang von Goethe** does not include it); his setting of "Der König in Thule" (The King of Thule, D. 367, 1816), responding to the archaic atmosphere of the poem, groups and musically sets the stanzas in such a fashion as to suggest the **bar form** characteristic of medieval and Renaissance German song; **Felix Mendelssohn Bartholdy**'s setting of **Lord Byron**'s "There Be None of Beauty's Daughters" (MWV K76, 1833, publ. 1836/1837) is a miniature **sonata form**; and so on. Because these compositional decisions affect the way performers and listeners experience the poem, they are often crucial to the effectiveness, or lack thereof, of any given setting. The analyst's and interpreter's position is thus to recognize this compositional/interpretive means—or its absence, in those rare instances when this is the case—and understand whether and how it combines with the composer's other interpretive decisions to shape the song as a whole.

Also significant in the creation of art song in the long 19th century was what might be called the *internal form*, aspects of the text's construction that do not affect its overall shape but do affect its style and processes: sequence of stanzas, rhyme scheme and number of lines within stanzas, and so on. Keenly aware that one of the most effective ways of emphasizing a word or line of text is to repeat it one or more times, Romantic composers frequently elected to alter the original text by repeating, often extensively, parts of the text that appear only once in the original poem ("Gretchen am Spinnrade" obsesses musically on the final stanza of Goethe's text, stating them three times in close succession and with ever-greater intensity, thus emphasizing both Gretchen's growing physical fixation on **Faust** and implicitly prophesying her demise in the wake of that nascent relationship). Similarly, composers sometimes elected to omit or reorder the words, lines, or strophes of the poem so that their music would bring out the meaning of the text as they interpreted it. They were also resourceful in discovering ways for making the musical structure parallel the rhyme scheme of the text by means of musical rhymes—parallel melodic, harmonic, or cadential gestures that coincide with textual rhymes.

Perhaps more obvious than these general techniques are the issues of *text or word painting* and **voicedness**. Prior to the long 19th century, most genres of vocal **chamber music** tended to be sparing with graphic musical illustrations of the images or actions in their texts; text painting tended to be quite subtle except in public vocal and choral genres such as **motet, oratorio**, and **opera**. During the long 19th century, however, composers (and with them performers, audiences, and aestheticians generally) became increasingly interested in having the vocal line(s) and/or accompaniment respond pictorially to textual images. Such musical responses to the text could be general (e.g., the use of **topics** such as the epic, hunting, or military styles; the generalized use of chromaticism and severe harmonies to convey the idea of a text that is somehow sad, sorrowful, or tragic; or a musical evocation of a bagpipe through drone fifths and short, crude melodies in the accompaniment, as in "Der Leiermann" from Schubert's **Winterreise**, D. 911), or they could be highly detailed (the rapidly oscillating right-hand figure in the accompaniment of *Gretchen am Spinnrade*, the quiet duet in parallel thirds and sixths between the spirit of the rose and the woman who wore it at the ball at the end of *Le spectre de la rose* in **Hector Berlioz**'s *Les nuits d'été* [H. 81A-B and 82/Op. 7, 1840–1841/1856], or the graphic depiction of the stormy night in the last song of **Gustav Mahler**'s **Kindertotenlieder**). Similarly, Romantic poets exulted in the suggestion or depiction of multiple personae (poetic voices) within their texts, and composers were infinitely resourceful in devising musical means for depicting this divided vocality (the most famous example perhaps being Schubert's **Erlkönig**, which musically not only differentiates between the voices of the narrator, father, son, and Erl-King but also makes of the horse on which father and son ride a wordless but important poetic source of utterance). Against the backdrop of the 19th century's debates over the potentials and limitations of musical expression, composers' decisions as to which (if any) of these poetic elements to depict in their music were potentially fraught with controversy, liable to charges of having exceeded the limitations of music and unduly privileged the text— and as calculated risks, such compositional decisions naturally stand out as composers' attempts to emphasize aspects of the text that they deemed important. Careful examination of composers' text painting and voicedness thus provide important interpretive information.

Finally, analysis and interpretation of art song of the long 19th century must consider what might be termed *aggregate meaning*. Over the course of the century, composers increasingly felt free (or perhaps compelled) to present in close proximity poetic texts that were written and presented as discrete or unrelated texts by the poets themselves. Sometimes this aggregate meaning was fairly loose and general—*Les nuits d'été*, usually considered a **song cycle**, may also be viewed reasonably as a set or collection and is one obvious such instance. Sometimes it was much stronger: by requiring continuous performance of the songs and structuring the music as he did tonally and thematically, **Ludwig van Beethoven** made all but certain that the six songs of *An die ferne Geliebte* would not be separated from one another or deprived of their aggregate meaning in performance. **Robert Schumann** used a variety of elaborate and sophisticated musical devices to create a clear and compelling cycle among the 16 songs he selected from the 55 poems of **Heinrich Heine**'s *Buch der Lieder* for the final version of *Dichterliebe*. **Franz Liszt** created a compelling cycle where none had previously existed, in either the poet's mind or (apparently) his own, in his 1859 revision and reordering of four poems by **Victor Hugo** that he had originally composed and published, along with two others, in 1844. This proclivity for enhancing the poetic texts' meaning by grouping and ordering them into new wholes, in part a reflection of the long 19th century's general fascination with **cyclic form** and **organicism**, represents one of the most important overarching developments in the international cultivation of the art song. [JMC]

See also PART-SONG.

SONG CYCLE. (Fr., cycle de mélodies *or* cycle de chansons; Ger., Liederkreis, Liederzyklus.) Term for a group of three or more **songs** or **part-songs** presented as a collective whole (*see* CYCLIC FORM). Most song cycles of the **long 19th century** are for one solo voice with **piano** accompaniment, but some are written for more than one voice with accompaniment, while others are cycles of part-songs (with or without accompaniment) and some are written for one or more voices with accompaniment of orchestra rather than piano. The genre as a whole ranks as one of the most important in music's Romanticisms, a secular vocal counterpart to, for example, the **string quartet** or the **symphony** among instrumental genres—and its iconic works represent some of the long 19th century's most venerated composers: **Ludwig van Beethoven**'s *An die ferne Geliebte* (1816); **Franz Schubert**'s *Die schöne Müllerin* (D. 795, 1823, publ. 1824) and *Winterreise* (D. 911, 1827, publ. 1828); **Robert Schumann**'s *Dichterliebe* (Op. 48, 1840, rev. and publ. 1844) and *Frauenliebe und -leben* (Op. 42, 1840, publ. 1843); **Hector Berlioz**'s *Les nuits d'été* (for voices and piano, H. 81A, 1840–1841, for voice and **orchestra**, H. 81B, 1856); **Johannes Brahms**'s *Magelone-Lieder* (Op. 33, 1865–1869); **Gustav Mahler**'s *Lieder eines fahrenden Gesellen* (1897), *Kindertotenlieder* (1905), and *Das Lied von der Erde* (1911); and **Gabriel Fauré**'s *La bonne chanson* (version for voice and piano, 1894; version for voice and string **quintet**, 1900). The poets, composers, and texts represented in that list are all French or German, and the fact that the usual terms *Liederkreis* and *Liederzyklus* are both German accurately reflects the fact that German composers, followed by French ones, were more fascinated with the challenge of creating cycles of songs than were their counterparts from other linguistic groups. Nevertheless, virtually every nationality and linguistic group represented in Romantic music contributed to the genre—and indeed, the characteristic parameters are even more diverse and nuanced than the features of the iconic works just listed would suggest. Given the 19th century's widespread fascination with **organic** unity and cyclicity in general, it is hardly surprising that song cycles were written by virtually every 19th century composer included in this dictionary, including (in addition to those named elsewhere in the present entry) **Isaac Albéniz, William Sterndale Bennett, George Whitefield Chadwick, César Cui, Claude Debussy, Frederick Delius, Henri Duparc, Antonín Dvořák, Edward Elgar, Charles Gounod, Enrique Granados, Edvard Grieg, Leoš Janáček, Conradin Kreutzer, Heinrich Marschner, Daniel Gregory Mason, Jules Massenet, Gioachino Rossini, Anton Rubinstein, Bedřich Smetana, Charles Villiers Stanford, Richard Strauss, Arthur Sullivan, Pyotor Il'yich Tchaikovsky, Sigismond Thalberg,** and **Carl Maria von Weber,** among many others.

Poets and texts: As with most other cultivated song during the long 19th century, the starting point of the song cycle was the text—typically a previously written poem or set of poems by one or more authors other than the composer, assembled, ordered or reordered into a new musico-poetic whole and set to music by the composer him- or herself. The texts of the cycle may stem from a single poet or collection of poetry, or they may represent different poetic voices and textual sources assembled by the composer. Cycles such as *An die ferne Geliebte, Die schöne Müllerin, Winterreise, Dichterliebe,* and *Les nuits d'été* are all based on a single poet's texts, drawn from a single collection, while others (most notably Robert Schumann's *Myrthen* [Op. 25, 1840]) create a new narrative or exploration of a topic by using texts of several different poets, while still others focus on a single poet but create the cycle from texts extracted from different works (**Hugo Wolf'**s Goethe- and Möricke-Lieder). The texts need not have been envisioned as a cycle by the poet(s), but composers can create a cycle where none previously existed (e.g., Mahler's *Kindertotenlieder*). Nor were all song cycles written for a single voice or voice type: Schubert's *Abendröte* cycle based on texts of Friedrich Schlegel (1820–1823), the piano/vocal version of Berlioz's *Les nuits d'été* (1841), and Mahler's *Das Lied von der Erde* are all scored for two or more voice types (plus accompaniment). Finally, some song cycles not initially conceived as cycles were drawn together over the course of their compositional history, while others were not formally designated as such in their titles: Mendelssohn's 1830 song cycle (MWV K57–60) and op. 71 songs (MWV SD35) are not officially designated as cycles, but their textual and musical construction reveals them to be cycles in every usual sense of the word.

Given the considerable flexibility with which composers of the long 19th century handled the concept of song cycle, the obvious question becomes, What distinguishes a song cycle from a set or collection? Here, too, the answer is anything but simple. Regarding the texts themselves, cyclicity may derive from the songs' presentation of a **narrative** in detailed or fragmentary form (*external* or *internal plot cycles*), from the texts' focusing on a central general theme (known as *topical cycles*), or from the presence of a uniform lyric persona (*see* VOICE, VOICEDNESS, VOCALITY). These textual devices for creating cyclicity were subject to amplification and commentary through music: Beethoven structured *An die ferne Geliebte* as a tonally closed cycle in which the songs are played without interruption and the outer two songs, both in E-flat, frame a tonally coherent internal "package" of songs sent by the lyric persona to his beloved to transcend the distance that separates them. Although clearly reasoned large-scale tonal interrelationships among songs do not appear to have been material to Schubert, Schumann's criticism of others' song cycles suggests that key is an important criterion for him, and both his *Frauenliebe und -leben* and his Eichendorff-Liederkreis (Op. 39) reflect that concern; the same concern is evident in other composers' cycles, ranging from **Carl Loewe**'s *Esther* to **Ernest Chausson**'s *Poème de l'amour et de la mer* (1893). Many cycles do not create tonal closure but do employ a clear and logical tonal structure to create coherence (e.g., the cycles of Mahler or Fauré's *La bonne chanson*). Many others employ recurrent thematic, motivic, or other musical links to generate unity.

Finally, in keeping with Romantic understandings of cyclicity, because the meaning of the individual constituent songs of such a cycle is substantively informed by the other constituent songs, reordering the songs or performing them outside the cycle necessarily divests them of meaning envisioned by the composer (*see* INTENTIONAL FALLACY). It is one of the ironies of latter-day music-history pedagogy that while every music-history and music-literature course that deals with the 19th century teaches about the development of the song cycle and the importance of cyclicity to the very nature of those cycles' songs, most such courses study song cycles only in excerpt. [JMC]

SONGS AND DANCES OF DEATH. (Rus., *Pesni i Plyaski Smerti.*) Iconic **song cycle** by **Modest Mussorgsky** on poems of Arseny Golenishchev-Kutuzov (1848–1913); Mussorgsky's third contribution to the genre of the song cycle. (The first two were *Detskaya* [The Nursery, 1872] and *Bez solntsa* [Sunless, 1874].) The poetic source was a literary trope on the **topic** of the **Totentanz**, dealing with death from the perspectives of many various constituents of Russian society, and although Mussorgsky intended to set many of the texts, he ultimately composed only four: *Kolïbel'naya* (Lullaby, 1875), *Serenada* (Serenade, 1875), *Trepak* (1875), and *Polkovodets* (The Field Marshal, 1877). Mussorgsky's changes to the texts of the poems themselves were comparatively few (especially compared to the extensive changes introduced by, e.g., **Gustav Mahler** in his *Kindertotenlieder*) but of crucial importance: he deleted outer frames that commented on the scenes in the manner of a Greek chorus, thus creating a **narrative** distance and reducing the immediacy of the scenes themselves, and he recast all the poems in the present tense, likewise enhancing the texts' immediacy. The cycle remained unpublished at Mussorgsky's death but was posthumously published, edited by his friend **Nikolay Rimsky-Korsakov**, in 1882. Generally considered the masterpiece of the Russian song cycle, it is notable for its unorthodox harmonic syntax and success in conveying the rhythmic and metrical structure of the poems in the melodies. Mussorgsky intended to **orchestrate** the songs but was unable to do so before his own death; that project was undertaken by **Aleksandr Glazunov** and Rimsky-Korsakov for a transcription published in 1882 and again by Shostakovich in 1962. [JMC]

SONGS ON THE DEATH OF CHILDREN. *See KINDERTOTENLIEDER.*

SONGS WITHOUT WORDS. *See LIEDER OHNE WORTE.*

SONNTAGSMUSIK. (Ger., "Sunday musicale.") Term for the private Sunday-afternoon musical gatherings hosted by the **Mendelssohn** family from 1821 until the death of **Fanny Hensel** in May 1847 (with interruptions during the period 1829–1831 and occasionally during the 1830s and 1840s). Although often described as **salons**, the *Sonntagsmusiken* were not understood as salons by their organizers or participants, primarily because they entailed no conversation except before and afterwards. Rather, they are better understood as by-invitation-only private concerts on a rather large scale (with room for upwards of 100 guests), held in the *Gartenhaus* (Garden House) of the Mendelssohn family's palatial home at Leipzigerstraße 3, Berlin. Like leading salons, they were frequented by an interdisciplinary range of intellectual and cultural luminaries (among them historian Gustav Droysen [1808–1884], philosophers **Georg Wilhelm Friedrich Hegel** and Alexander [1769–1859] and Wilhelm von Humboldt [1767–1835], composer and music theorist **Adolf Bernhard Marx**, author Rahel Varnhagen von Ense [1771–1833], diplomat August Varnhagen von Ense [1785–1858], and many others).

The centerpiece of the *Sonntagsmusiken* (pl.) was generally choral music (both historical and contemporary), with instrumental **chamber music** (both works for solo **piano** or **piano duet** and small-ensemble works) interspersed. The musicales' repertoire included not only new works by Hensel and her younger brother Felix but also others by contemporary composers and others ranging from **Johann Sebastian Bach** and **George Frideric Handel** through

Christoph Willibald Ritter von Gluck (1714–1787), **Franz Joseph Haydn**, and **Wolfgang Amadeus Mozart** to **Ludwig van Beethoven, Louis Spohr, Carl Maria von Weber**, and others. Choral/**orchestral** works were typically performed in piano/vocal reduction, and occasionally concert or semistaged performances of **operas** were given. Despite their apparent resemblance to the usual male-dominated, male-organized concerts of the day, however, the fact that the *Sonntagsmusiken* were organized, programmed, and directed by a woman, thus subverting the usual social order in a major cultural event, was not lost on the events' contemporaries. [JMC]

See also SCHUBERTIADE.

SOUSA, JOHN PHILIP (1854–1932). U.S. composer and **conductor** of the Modern Romantic Generation. The most important bandmaster in U.S. music history, Sousa is remembered for many still-famous marches such as *The Washington Post* (1889) and *Stars and Stripes Forever* (1897, now the U.S. national march); he was also a significant **operetta** composer. Trained on the violin and several other instruments in his youth in Washington, D.C., Sousa apprenticed with the U.S. Marine Band in his teenage years; his father was trombonist in the ensemble. Sousa distinguished himself in the 1870s as a violinist, conductor, and composer. In 1880–1892 Sousa led the U.S. Marine Band, for which he transcribed classical pieces and wrote many marches with patriotic titles. Among his most successful works during this time were the operetta *Désirée* (Washington, D.C., 1884) and the march *The Gladiator* (1886). Sousa formed his own ensemble in 1892, the Sousa Band, which he led for the rest of his life; the ensemble toured annually and performed abroad five times in the early 20th century. During World War I, Sousa conducted the Naval Reserve Band in Illinois. Sousa's operetta *El Capitan* (Boston, 1896) was his greatest stage success. Well-known marches additional to the aforementioned include *The Liberty Bell* (1893) and the U.S. Marines' official march, *Semper Fidelis* (1888).

Although Sousa's band music was widely available as sheet music, the numerous recordings of the Sousa Band testify to the conductor's practice of diverging from the published dynamics and **orchestration** in concert performances; for example, Sousa would often require certain instruments, such as upper-range brass instruments or parts with countermelodies, to be *tacet* during the first repetition of a given section. Among the notable musicians who performed under Sousa were trumpeter Herbert L. Clarke, trombonist Arthur Pryor, and (then) flautist Meredith Wilson. Sousa's name also endures in the sousaphone, a kind of helicon developed upon his request in the early 1890s. [RK]

See also NATIONALISM, ROMANTIC NATIONALISM; PERFORMANCE PRACTICE.

SPIELOPER. (Ger., "play-opera.") Normally, a type of 19th-century German-language **comic opera** that employs spoken dialogue between set musical numbers. There is little to differentiate clearly between *Spieloper* and *Singspiel*, except that most *Spieloper* have genuinely comical plots rather than ones that are simply not serious. These characteristics apply to most works designated *Spieloper* during the **long 19th century**. Unfortunately, those same works have occasionally also been labeled *Sprechoper* ("speech operas"), leading to the occasional use of the term *Spieloper* to denote operas that are sung throughout and do *not* employ spoken dialogue—the exact opposite of the usual meaning of the term.

Notable examples of the primary application of the term *Spieloper* include **Peter Cornelius's** *Der Barbier von Bagdad* (The Barber of Baghdad, 1858), **Engelbert Humperdinck's** *Die Marketenderin* (The Victualer, 1914), **Conradin Kreutzer's** *Das Nachtlager von Granada* (The Bivouac of Granada, 1834), **Albert Lortzing's** *Zar und Zimmermann* (1839) and *Der Wildschütz* (The Poacher, 1842), and **Otto Nicolai's** *Die lustigen Weiber von Windsor* (The Merry Maids of Windsor, 1849). It is also used in the German-speaking world to refer to German versions of non-German comic operas that use spoken dialogue (e.g., **Bedřich Smetana's** *The Bartered Bride*, 1866). [JMC]

SPOHR, LOUIS [LUDEWIG, LUDWIG] (1784–1859). Composer, conductor, and virtuoso violinist of the Early Romantic Generation; after **Ludwig van Beethoven** and **Carl Maria Weber**, one of the most respected composers of his generation for most of the **long 19th century**. After **Nicolò Paganini**, he the most important violinist of the early and mid-19th century, and he was one of the first **conductors** to use a baton. Spohr's mother was a singer and pianist and his father a flutist who also began his instruction on violin before entrusting his training to more professional teachers. In 1796, he entered the Collegium Carolinum for more professionalized study and in 1799 was appointed *Kammermusikus* (chamber musician) in the court of the duke of Braunschweig. His abilities grew steadily and were further enriched in 1804, when he heard **Pierre Rode** perform. That experience inspired two new violin **concertos** that were enthusiastically reviewed in the Leipzig *Allgemeine Musikalische Zeitung*, and that review in turn led to his appointment as concertmaster at the court in Gotha. He remained there, producing compositions that drew increasing attention from his contemporaries—several compositions for violin and harp (the latter being the instrument of his wife), two clarinet concertos, three **operas**, a **symphony**, and an **oratorio**—until 1812, when, during a concert tour, he accepted the position of Kapellmeister of the **orchestra** of the Theater an der Wien (Vienna).

In Vienna, Spohr befriended and earned the respect of Beethoven and continued to produce works whose modernity and diversity won great admirers, but his politically liberal tendencies were ill suited to the city's conservative politics, and in 1815, he undertook a new concert tour, this time accepting a position as director of the Opera in Frankfurt am Main. That position, too, ended badly due to political frictions. He and his wife traveled to London in 1820 and initiated a veritable Spohr craze that was inspired by his compositions and his playing of the violin and fueled by his use of the baton in conducting during rehearsal. From London, they traveled to Paris (publishing four reports on the state of music in the French capital in the *LAmZ*) and from there to Dresden, finally accepting a post as Kapellmeister in Kassel. This he retained until 1857, even though Kassel's repressively conservative court politics were even more at odds with his disposition than those in his earlier posts in Vienna and Frankfurt had been.

Over the course of his remaining years, Spohr devoted increasing energies to composition and toured widely as a conductor, also working assiduously to secure benefits and stability for other court musicians. In 1845, he shared the direction of the great Beethoven Festival in Bonn with **Franz Liszt**, and on **Felix Mendelssohn Bartholdy**'s death, he was appointed to the place in the Prussian order *pour le mérite* left vacant at his friend's passing. He received an honorary doctorate from the University in Marburg and was awarded memberships in 38 German musical societies. **Ferdinand David** and August Wilhelmjh (1845–1908) are among his many accomplished pupils on the violin.

Few who witnessed Spohr's rise to fame or knew any quantity of his music during his lifetime could have anticipated the marginal status that posterity has accorded his music—indeed, that status also generally puzzles those who know his works today. His receptiveness to innovation, both as a composer and as a conductor, had few rivals, and he was among the most influential advocates for a full integration of both the music of the past and a variety of "progressive" styles into the music of his own time (he conducted **Richard Wagner**'s *Der fliegende Holländer* [The Flying Dutchman] in Kassel in 1843 and *Tannhäuser* in 1853). In particular, his operas *Jessonda* (1823) and *Der Alchymist* (1830) stand as milestones in the development of German opera between Weber and Wagner, and his **program symphony** *Die Weihe der Töne: Charakteristisches Tongemälde in Form einer Sinfonie* (The Consecration of Tones: Characteristic Tone-Painting in the Form of a Symphony, comp. 1832, publ. 1834), though little known today, stood alongside **Hector Berlioz**'s *Episode in the Life of an Artist* as one of the first works to require audiences to read a program in order to grasp a composition's extramusical meaning.

Spohr's oratorios, too, are remarkable for their musical invention and ability to convey musical drama without staging and within the limitations imposed by usual performance of works in that genre not in the concert hall but in open-air public music festivals. *Die letzten Dinge* (The End of Days, 1823) is arguably the most important oratorio between **Franz Joseph Haydn**'s *The Creation* (1795) and Mendelssohn's *St. Paul* (1837). He was also renowned for his sensitive and occasionally virtuosic **orchestration**—not least of all his writing for his own instrument (the violin) but also for the clarinet and for woodwinds generally.

Spohr's compositional career spanned nearly 60 years, from the late 1790s to 1857. His output includes 11 operas and three sets of **incidental music**; 10 symphonies; two **concert overtures**; 15 published violin concertos; four clarinet concertos and several other *concertante* works; numerous potpourris and **fantasies** for solo instrument(s) with strings; 36 **string quartets**; four string **octets** (double quartets); seven string **quintets**; an Octet in E Major for clarinet, two horns, string quartet, and bass (Op. 32, 1814); a **septet** for piano and winds and a **nonet** for winds and string quartet; three **piano trios**; and many other **chamber** works with strings. [JMC]

SPONTINI, GASPARE (LUIGI PACIFICO) (1774–1851). Italian composer and **conductor** of the Early Romantic Generation; a dominant figure in **grand opera** during the first half of the 19th century. After training in Naples and becoming a successful composer of **opera** there, he went in 1803 to Paris, the capital of Napoleonic Europe, where he began his career giving singing lessons. In 1805, the successful premiere of the grand opera *La vestale* (The Vestal Virgin) won him a commission to provide music in support of Napoléon Bonaparte's Spanish campaign; the result was *Fernand Cortez* (1809, rev. 1817, 3rd version 1824), glorifying the conquistador's conquest of Mexico. He later became court composer to Louis XVIII, and in 1810, he directed the first performance of **Wolfgang Amadeus Mozart**'s *Don Giovanni* in its original form.

By 1819, Spontini had become one of the most powerful composers and conductors in the court of Prussian King Friedrich Wilhelm III (fl. 1797–1840), celebrated for the pageantry of his operas as well as his authoritarian conducting. His output includes 23 Italian and French **operas** (several of which exist in multiple versions; *see* EDITING AND EDITIONS; FASSUNG LETZTER HAND); eight **cantatas, concert arias**, and other works for one or more solo voices with **orchestra**; 10 cantatas, hymns, and other works for chorus and orchestra (in French, German, Italian, and Latin); several pieces for military band or orchestra; and a small body of instrumental and vocal **chamber music**. Aside from *La vestale* and *Fernand Cortez*, his most important operas are *Olympie* (1819, rev. 1821, 1826) and *Nurmahal* (1822). [JMC]

ST. MATTHEW PASSION. (Ger., *Matthäus-Passion*, Lat., *Passio secundum Matthaeum*.) **Oratorio** in two parts by **Johann Sebastian Bach**, BWV 244, based on the Passion of Jesus Christ as recounted in the Gospel of St. Matthew, with free poetic texts by Picander (pseud. Christian Friedrich Henrici, 1700–1764); iconic work in the **Bach Revival** and **historicism** generally. Bach's oratorio was first performed in Leipzig in 1727 and revised for a second performance in 1736 and a third in 1742; there is also evidence of further revision, but no performance, in 1743–1746. In its final version, the work is scored for solo voices, double choir, double **orchestra**, and two organs.

Like most of Bach's music, the *St. Matthew Passion* remained in manuscript and largely unknown during the late 18th and early 19th centuries. In Prussia, however, interest in Bach's music was kept alive through the efforts of C. P. E. Bach (1714–1788), C. F. C. Fasch (1736–1800), and Carl Friedrich Zelter (1758–1832). Zelter began privately reading through certain passages of the *Passion*—four solo numbers and two short choruses—with a select group of singers from the Berlin Singakademie in 1815. Zelter's source for these readings was apparently a copy of a score prepared by J. C. Altnikol (1720–1759), a son-in-law of Bach, that had passed into the library of Bach's student J. P. Kirnberger (1721–1783)—a score that, significantly, omits the chorus "O Mensch, bewein' deine Sünde groß" at the end of Part I of the oratorio.

The result of these developments was that there was active—and apparently growing—interest in the sprawling, complex Lutheran masterpiece in Berlin already in the second decade of the 19th century. In late 1823 or early 1824, the Berlin **salonnière** Bella Salomon (1729–1824) commissioned Johann Friedrich Rietz (1766–1828), father of the Mendelssohns' family friends Eduard (1802–1832) and Julius Rietz (1812–1877), to prepare a manuscript score for the *Passion* on the basis of Bach's autograph parts for the work, which were held in the Royal Library in Berlin (now the Staatsbibliothek zu Berlin—Preußischer Kulturbesitz). She then gave this **holograph** to Zelter's student **Felix Mendelssohn Bartholdy** in early 1824 (possibly on his birthday, 3 February), thus placing the *Passion* in the hands of a Romantic Generation whose interest in history (and in the musical past as locus of German national history and identity) was profound. Mendelssohn and his circle studied the *St. Matthew Passion* intensely and began a series of private readings of portions of the Passion in the Mendelssohn family home in Berlin late in 1827, reportedly with a group of about 16 singers and with no intention of performing the work publicly.

Among those privy to these readings was the theorist and composer **Adolf Bernhard Marx**, a friend of Mendelssohn at the time, who wrote enthusiastically about the work and its composer in the *Berlinische Allgemeine musikalische Zeitung* and reported to the group in 1828 that he had persuaded the journal's publisher, Adolph Martin Schlesinger, to publish it. In December of that year, Mendelssohn and his friend Eduard Devrient (1801–1877) petitioned the Singakademie to use its hall for a performance of the work, and choral rehearsals began on 2 February 1829, with Mendelssohn conducting the chorus (which reportedly grew from rehearsal to rehearsal as excitement about the work spread) from the **piano**. The orchestral musicians (assembled from an amateur orchestra formed by Eduard Rietz) joined the chorus on 6 March, and the dress rehearsal was held on 10 March.

The Bach Revival became a public affair with three performances of the *St. Matthew Passion* given by the Berlin Singakademie in the spring of 1829. The first performance, held on 11 March, was attended by King Friedrich Wilhelm III and his retinue, as well as **Georg Wilhelm Friedrich Hegel**, **Heinrich Heine**, the influential Protestant theologian Friedrich Schleiermacher (1768–1834), **Gaspare Spontini**, Rahel Varnhagen von Ense (1771–1833), and Zelter, but was oversubscribed; reportedly a thousand Berliners were turned away at the door. A second performance, likewise given before a packed house under Mendelssohn's direction, was given on 21 March (Bach's birthday). Finally, the Singakademie decided to replace its traditional Good Friday performance of Carl Heinrich Graun's (1704–1759) well-known *Der Tod Jesu* with the newly revived Passion by Bach on Good Friday of 1829 (17 April)—this time conducted by Zelter, since Mendelssohn had left for a series of performances in the British Isles. During the spring of 1829, some 3,000 individuals who previously had heard little of Bach's large-scale works had come to know the Baroque master through the Passion.

The *St. Matthew Passion* was published, edited by Marx, in full score and piano/vocal score in 1830 (Berlin: A. M. Schlesinger). This version, based as it was on Zelter's copy of the Altnikol score, was not complete—it lacked a total of 22 of the movements of the final version as they are numbered in the *Neue Bach-Ausgabe*—and was essentially a mixture of the versions of 1727 and 1736, further corrupted (in a philological sense) by plentiful added dynamics, articulations, and other textual changes of a practical nature. In this guise, the work was taken up for many other performances over the next 40 years.

The 1829 performances of the *St. Matthew Passion* created a sensation and are generally considered defining moments in the 19th century's rediscovery of J. S. Bach. Although interest in Bach's life and music had been growing steadily, especially in the German lands, since the 1790s, those performances established that Bach's music was viable in the Romantic musical world. Those present at the performances regarded them as quasi-religious experiences, moving celebrations of the German Lutheran spirit as voiced by a

Lutheran composer who was only beginning to escape oblivion and assume his rightful place in German speakers' ongoing quest for a distinctively German national identity. [JMC]

See also NATIONALISM, ROMANTIC NATIONALISM.

ST. PAUL (PAULUS), MWV A14/OP. 36. Oratorio in two parts by **Felix Mendelssohn Bartholdy** on his own **libretto** compiled from Scripture in consultation with the pastor and philologist Julius Schubring (1806–1889), the orientalist Julius Fürst (1805–1873), and the composer and theorist **Adolf Bernhard Marx.** Mendelssohn began contemplating the idea of an oratorio on the subject of the Apostle Paul late in 1831 and was invited to compose an oratorio by the Cäcilien-Verein in Frankfurt-am-Main early in 1832. He worked out the libretto and composed the music, with extensive reworkings and excisions, from late 1833 to early 1835, and the premiere took place at the Lower Rhine Music Festival in Düsseldorf on 22 May 1836. Mendelssohn prepared a piano-vocal arrangement (with the **overture** arranged for **piano duet**), and this was published by **N. Simrock** (Bonn) and **J. Alfred Novello** (London) in 1836, the English text of the latter prepared by William Ball; the choral parts, **orchestral** parts, and organ part were also published separately in 1836. Mendelssohn was not actively involved in the creation of the English translation prepared by William Ball, but he did incorporate it into the full score first published in 1837.

St. Paul represents a milestone in the history of the oratorio as a genre. The most recent contributions to have any lasting impact in the genre before it were **Franz Joseph Haydn**'s *The Creation* (published in German as *Die Schöpfung*, Hob. XXI:2, 1796–1798) and *Die Jahreszeiten* (The Seasons, Hob. XXI: 3, 1798–1801); **Ludwig van Beethoven** wrote one work in the genre (*Christus am Ölberge* [Christ on the Mount of Olives, Op. 85; comp. 1803, rev. 1804, publ. 1811]), but neither it nor the contributions by other members of the Romantic Generation to which Mendelssohn belonged were able to address the early and mid-19th century's increasing interest in dramatic expression. *St. Paul* accomplished this partly by means of a sophisticated and intensely dramatic plot, partly through its colorful **orchestration**, partly through its effective use of **Leitmotivs** and thematic cross-references, and partly through its incorporation of well-known **chorales** as opportunities for communal/congregational reflection at critical points in the drama. [JMC]

See also ELIJAH (ELIAS), MWV A25/OP. 70.

STABAT MATER (DOLOROSA). (Lat., "sorrowfully his mother stood.") Extended Latin poem of 13th-century Franciscan origin, traditionally attributed to Jacopone da Todi (d. ?1306), contemplating the suffering of Mary as she beheld the crucified Christ. Although apparently neither originally conceived nor used as a liturgical sequence, it shares the general form of the later varieties of that genre and by the late 15th century was used as a liturgical sequence in the Mass of the Compassion of the Blessed Virgin Mary, with a plainchant melody that appears to be of the same date. It was removed from the liturgy at the Council of Trent but revived by Pope Benedict XIII in 1727 for use on the two feasts of the Seven Sorrows (Friday in the fifth week of Lent and the third Sunday of September, later 15 September). Around the same time, it came into use as a hymn in the Office for Friday in the fifth week of Lent. The text begins with third-person descriptions of the scene as Mary witnesses Christ's crucifixion, in the past tense and addressed to the listener (stanzas 1–8), and then moves to the lyric persona's (*see* VOICE, VOICEDNESS, VOCALITY) pleas addressed to Mary in heaven (stanzas 9–18) and a prayer directly to Christ for the lyric persona to be in His presence after death (stanzas 19–20).

The emotional poignancy and intense sorrow of the *Stabat mater* appealed deeply to composers during the **long 19th century**. Moreover, its celebration of Mary made it particularly important as a text of the **Cecilian movement**, and its focus on maternal suffering for deceased male offspring seems to have produced increased interest around the times of violent political upheavals in a century where many male offspring predeceased their mothers. Many of the long 19th century's settings use the poem's words only, but some treat the tune and text as a *cantus firmus*. Presumably because of the poem's great length (60 lines in 20 strophes), many composers did not set the complete text. The settings best known today are those by **Antonín Dvořák** (S. 38/Op. 58, 1876–1877, publ. 1881), **Franz Liszt** (LW A142, 1847; often erroneously considered part of the unrelated **oratorio** *Christus*, LW A141), **Gioachino Rossini** (1832–1833, publ. 1841; rev. 1841, publ. 1842), **Franz Schubert** (D. 175, 1815), and **Giuseppe Verdi** (1896–1897, publ. 1898 as no. 3 of the *Quattro pezzi sacri*). Other settings were penned by Pietro Alfieri (1801–1863; 1844), Louis Albert Bourgault-Ducoudray (1840–1910; 1873), Cándido Candi (1844–1911; 1874), **William Henry Fry** (as an oratorio, 1855), Henry J. Gauntlett (1805–1876; 1849), Marie de Grandval (1828–1907; 1872), **Charles Gounod** (in French trans., 1867), Friedrich Kiel (1821–1885; 1866), **Franz Lachner** (Op. 154, 1872), Nicolás Ledesma (1791–1883; 1837), Eduardo López Juarranz (1844–1897; 1876), Alexey L'vov (1799–1870; 1850), Julius Miller (1782–1851; 1850), **Wolfgang Amadeus Mozart** (K⁶ 33c, before ca. 1768; lost), Sigismund Neukomm (1778–1858; 1825), Pietro Raimondi (1786–1853; 1825), **Josef Rheinberger** (Op. 16, 1868, and Op. 138, 1903), Carl Friedrich Rungenhagen (1778–1851; 1826), Gaston Salvayre (1847–1916; 1877), Johann Baptist Vanhal (1739–1813; 1775), Joaquín Velázquez de Aparici (1832–1917; 1860), Peter von Winter (1754–1825; 1815), and Franz Witt (1834–1888; 1882). During the long 19th century, settings by Luigi Boccherini

(1743–1805; 1781 and 1800) and **Franz Joseph Haydn** (Hob. XXbis, 1767) also circulated widely, as did the earlier settings by Josquin des Prez and **Giovanni Pierluigi da Palestrina**. [JMC]

STABREIM. (Ger., "staff rhyme" or "stem rhyme.") A form of alliterative verse characteristic of old German poetry and revived in the **long 19th century** by Friedrich de la Motte Fouqué (1777–1843) in his dramatic trilogy *Der Held des Nordens* (The Hero of the North, 1810; an important influence on J. R. R. Tolkein's *The Lord of the Rings*). De la Motte Fouqué's trilogy in turn influenced **Richard Wagner** to employ *Stabreim* in *Der Ring des Nibelungen* (*The Ring of the Nibelung*). Wagner explained this new/revived aesthetic of verse and **libretto** creation in his tract *Oper und Drama* (**Opera and Drama**, 1851), proposing that because surviving literature documents the natural and intuitive means by which early Germanic tribes communicated and shared their great epic tales, by reviving this style of versification, librettos and other literature would disabuse themselves of the artifice that characterized the corrupt traditions of opera as they had existed earlier in the 19th century. They would thus regain for staged musical drama an authentic, primal, or organic means of expression that was consistent with its aesthetic aspirations.

The basic literary principles of *Stabreim* are simple: each line of poetry contains two half lines, each of which contains two or three stressed syllables separated by an indeterminate number of unstressed syllables. In theory (which Wagner did not always follow strictly), the stressed syllable of each second half line is the main stress, with which one of the other stressed syllables must alliterate. Thus,

> Verfluchter Reif! Furchtbarer Ring!
> Dein Gold fass' ich, Und geb' es nun fort

> Cursed richness! Fearful ring
> I grasp your gold, and now give it up.

> (from the closing scene of *Götterdämmerung*)

In Wagner's adaptation of these principles to suit the ends of musical-dramatic expression, emotional and dramatic emphasis should reside in the stressed syllables. In a truly music-dramatic mode of composition, therefore, the composer would musically emphasize those pent-up points of emotional and dramatic expression by means of melodic turns and modulations directed toward goals that coincide with the stressed syllables. From a practical perspective, this application resulted in continual wide melodic disjunctions (stressed syllables typically on high notes, unstressed ones often a least a third lower), an overwhelmingly syllabic style of text setting, pervasive sequence with sparing use of cadences (only at the primary points of arrival), and largely continuous modulation. The emphasis on consonants rather than vowels also reduced the problems of intonation that frequently occur in vocal music (since intonation problems occur on vowels, not consonants). By clearly delineating syllables by articulating their separating consonants, such verses made it easier for the text to be discerned by the audience despite the large orchestral accompaniment and the dense web of **motivic** material typical of Wagner's post-1849 operas. [JMC]

See also BAYREUTH; LEITMOTIV; MUSIC DRAMA.

STANFORD, CHARLES VILLIERS (1852–1924). Irish composer, **conductor**, teacher, and writer on music of the Modern Romantic Generation; leading figure in the **English Musical Renaissance** and English **nationalism** generally at the turn of the 20th century. He studied organ, **piano**, violin, and music theory in his native Dublin before enrolling in Queen's College, Cambridge, as an organ scholar in 1870. He received a BA from that institution in 1874 and an MA in 1877. He also studied with **Carl Reinecke** in Leipzig in 1874 and 1875 and Friedrich Kiel (1821–1885) in Berlin in 1876.

In 1873, Stanford became conductor of the Cambridge Musical Society in 1873 and in 1874 he was appointed organist of Trinity College, a post he held until 1892. He garnered attention as a composer beginning with his Opus 1, a setting of eight texts from George Eliot's *The Spanish Gypsy* (1877–1878). His reputation increased with his First **Symphony**, his **incidental music** for Tennyson's *Queen Mary*, and his **operas** *The Veiled Prophet of Khorassan* (1881), *Savonarola* (1884), and *The Canterbury Pilgrims* (1884). He was appointed professor of music at the Royal College of Music (London) in 1883 (*see* CONSERVATORY) and succeeded George A. Macfarren (1813–1887) as professor of music at Cambridge in 1887, also retaining his position at the Royal College of Music until 1894, when he resigned (succeeded by **Hubert Parry**).

Although Stanford's health began to deteriorate in the late 1890s, he continued to teach, compose, and conduct actively, occasionally leading the Philharmonic Society of London as well as the London Bach Choir (1886–1902), the Leeds Philharmonic Society (1897–1909), and the Leeds Triennial Festival (1901–1910). He received honorary doctorates from Oxford University, Cambridge University, Durham University, and Leeds University and was knighted in 1902. In his published writings, he was eloquent and articulate, especially in advocating for a distinctively English national opera. His pupils include Arthur Bliss, Frank Bridge, Gustav Holst, and Ralph Vaughan Williams, among many others.

Stanford is best known for his large choral compositions and other sacred works, but he was a prolific and accomplished composer in virtually every genre current in his generation. He worked mostly in England but was among the most successful composers of his generation in giving authentic voice to Irish and Celtic themes. His vocal output includes 10 operas and seven sets of incidental music, 30 numbered *opera* of sacred and secular choral works with **orchestral** accompaniment, three Mass settings and a great many other smaller sacred choral works (a cappella and with organ accompaniment), 123 **part-songs**, and 162 solo **songs** and duets. His instrumental oeuvre includes seven symphonies, two violin **concertos**, three piano concertos, six *Irish Rhapsodies*, and numerous other works for orchestra with or without *concertante* instrument(s); much instrumental **chamber music** including one piano **quintet**, two string quintets, eight **string quartets**, three surviving **piano trios**, two violin **sonatas** and a sonata for clarinet or viola and piano, and numerous smaller works for instrumental chamber ensemble; and one piano sonata, five organ sonatas, and many **character pieces** and other smaller compositions for piano or organ. His best-known works today are the operas *Shamus O'Brien* (1896) and *The Travelling Companion* (1919), the **oratorios** *The Three Holy Children* (1885) and *Eden* (1891), the choral **ballad** *The Revenge* (1886), and the First and Fourth *Irish Rhapsodies* (1902 and 1914). His textbook *Musical Composition* (1911) continued to be used well into the 20th century, with a sixth edition appearing in 1950. [JMC]

STEIN. Austrian firm of keyboard-instrument manufacturers, founded by organist and harpsichordist Johann Andreas Stein (1728–1792). The fortepianos developed by the Stein firm proved decisive in the **piano**'s eclipse of the harpsichord in popularity in the German lands in the late 18th century.

To the end of Stein's life, the firm was based on Augsburg. Although most of its instruments are harpsichords, clavichords, or other keyboard instruments, Stein's development of the so-called German (Viennese) action and the fully functional damper pedal remained central to the concept of the piano from the 1790s on. His instruments found great popularity with **Wolfgang Amadeus Mozart** and **Ludwig van Beethoven**, among a great many others. Before Stein's death, the firm produced some 700 instruments, of which only 13 pianos survive.

The earliest surviving Stein fortepianos were double-strung and had no leather on the wooden hammers, resulting in a sharp attack and quick decay; the hammers of the early 1780s were round and hollow (lighter), and the instrument was triple-strung, producing a greater volume and more mellow attack but with a more transparent timbre. In the mid-1780s, the firm reverted to double-strung instruments and solid hammers but covered the hammers with leather. From 1782 on, the firm's instruments employed the so-called A-frame, wherein the inner bent side does not follow the curve of the outer frame but continues in a straight line to the belly rail—another feature typical of Viennese instruments throughout the 19th century.

When Stein's failing health necessitated his withdrawal from active work in the firm around 1790, it was taken over by his son Matthäus Andreas (1776–1842) and his daughter Nanette (1769–1833). In 1794, Nanette, together with her brother and her husband, Johann Andreas Streicher (1761–1833), moved the firm to Vienna, where they opened a piano shop known alternately as *Geschwister Stein* (Stein Siblings) or *Frère et Soeur Stein* (Brother and Sister Stein). Nanette and her husband broke away and founded the independent firm of **Streicher** in 1802. Matthäus Andreas renamed the earlier family firm *Andre Stein, d'Augsbourg, à Vienne* (Andreas Stein, from Augsburg, in Vienna) and continued producing instruments according to family tradition until his death, when it passed to his son Karl Andreas (1797–1863). [JMC]

STEINWAY. U.S.-based firm of **piano** makers, today one of the leading producers of the instrument. The firm was founded by Heinrich Engelhardt Steinweg (1797–1871), a native German who worked as an apprentice organ builder and cabinetmaker in Goslar during the period before around 1830. Together with his six daughters and five sons, he began a prosperous firm in Seesen. By the mid-1830s, the firm was making several square and grand pianos per year, all with Viennese action and a six-octave range, and by the late 1840s, it reportedly had made about 400. In 1849, son Karl (1829–1865), worried by the unrest of the **Revolutions of 1848** and wishing to avoid military conscription, moved to the United States (New York) to explore business possibilities there, changing his name to Charles after his arrival. The rest of the family followed in 1850—all except for the eldest son, (C. F.) Theodor, who remained in Seesen and continued the firm's European line of instruments, receiving numerous patents for improvements over the course of the next decade. This European line retained the German form of the family name (Steinweg) and continued to flourish. Another successful German piano maker of Viennese-style instruments, Friedrich Grotrian (1803–1860), joined the firm in August 1858. Grotrian died two years after joining the firm but left his portion to his son, Wilhelm, who became a partner when he came of age in 1865. The German firm was still named *C. F. Theodor Steinweg* at this point.

Meanwhile, the U.S. branch of the family changed the family name from *Steinweg* to *Steinway* and Americanized their given names, learning English and the business ways of the United States for several years but beginning their own piano manufacture in 1853 and establishing a new U.S.-based firm under the name of *Steinway & Sons*. The U.S. firm's instruments differed significantly from the Viennese-style instruments manufactured by its German counterpart, using a seven-octave range; a one-piece metal frame; a heavier, English action (actually now French, centered in the firms of **Erard** and **Pleyel**); and, most importantly, cross-stringing (overstringing), a development that produced a powerful, long-lasting tone homogenized across the instrument's registers. The heavier action and thicker, more monochromatic tone of the New York firm's instruments were disappointing to many, but the larger range and sturdy metal frame were immensely attractive. The young firm's square pianos began winning prizes already in 1855, and this acclaim combined with its shrewd business practices, further technical refinements, and willingness to take advantage of industrial technology to facilitate its rapid growth. It was producing grands by 1856 and uprights by 1860. In 1859, it patented a design for overstringing grands, thereby introducing their trademark expanded range, sturdy structure, and even, monochromatic tone into that instrument's history. In 1860, the firm opened a large new factory on Fourth Avenue (now Park Avenue), and in 1866, they used its wealth to build a 2,000-seat concert hall (Steinway Hall, closed when Carnegie Hall opened in 1890).

A new chapter in the history of the two firms began with the deaths of two of Heinrich Steinweg's (now Henry Steinway's) sons and his son-in-law in 1864–1865. In order to join his aging father and the remainder of the family in New York, Theodor Steinweg bequeathed the German firm to his former partner's son, Wilhelm Grotrian (1843–1917), and two other colleagues, who now renamed the firm *Grotrian, Helfferich, Schulz, Th[eodor] Steinweg Nachf[olger]* (Grotrian, Helfferich, & Schulz, successors to Theodor Steinweg; the unwieldy name is often abbreviated to simply "Th. Steinweg Nachf."). His knowledge of acoustics (thanks in part to his familiarity with **Hermann von Helmholz**'s new theories on the science of musical sound) enabled him to make further improvements on the New York instrument's design—most famously the tunable duplex-scaling patent (1872), which assigned a perfect harmonic to the nonspeaking portions of the strings in order to speak in sympathy with the speaking portion, thereby increasing the richness of overtones and the overall resonance of the instrument.

The firm's reputation continued to grow. Although some competitors (most notably **Érard**) vehemently objected to the heavier action and thicker, comparatively muddy tone of the Steinway & Sons design, those efforts proved futile. The firm won medals at numerous international trade fairs, established a London salesroom in 1875, and built a Hamburg factory (in direct geographic competition with its former sibling, now named Grotrian-Steinweg) in 1880. Other firms (e.g., Bechstein, **Bösendorfer**, and **Chickering**) began to copy the concept. As Steinway's Sons signed on pianistic luminaries including **Anton Rubinstein** and **Ignacy Paderewski** to endorse and promote its instruments, other composers began to write their piano music to take advantage of those instruments' sound rather than the lighter, more transparent, and more colorful timbres of the pianos that predominated for most of the 19th century.

Today, Steinway & Sons pianos are the most commonly used instruments on the concert and recital stage worldwide, but even the "Romantic" sound of the modern Steinway differs appreciably from that of, for example, the Steinway & Sons instrument that **Johannes Brahms** requested in 1881 or the 1892 Steinway grand used by Paderewski (the latter is now owned by the Smithsonian Museum). Since the typical modern Steinway & Sons was not fully developed until 1930, only a few of the most recent members of the Modern Romantic Generation could have developed their pianistic sound and technique around that instrument—most notably, **Serge Rachmaninoff** and **Aleksandr Scriabin**. For most of the great Romantic virtuosos of the 19th century (as well as other composers and pianists), the sounds and techniques of Romantic pianism differed significantly. [JMC]

See also BÖSENDORFER; BROADWOOD; CHICKERING AND SONS; ÉRARD; GRAF; STEIN; STEINWAY; WALTER.

STRAUSS. Austrian family of musicians of Hungarian origin. Its members active during the **long 19th century** are (1) Johann (Baptist) Strauss (I) (1804–1849); (2) Johann (Baptist) Strauss (II) (1825–1899), eldest son of (1); (3) Josef [Joseph] Strauss (1827–1870), second son of (1); (4) Eduard Strauss (1835–1916); third and youngest son of (1); and (5) Johann (Maria Eduard) Strauss (III), eldest son of (4). All were composers, **conductors**, and violinists. Although all were important contributors to Austrian (especially Viennese) musical life, the most important two were Johann Strauss (I) and (II). This entry focuses on those two.

Johann Strauss (I), also known as Johann Strauss Sr. or Johann Strauss the Elder, was apparently a self-taught musician who played violin in his father's tavern and viola in a local dance **orchestra** in his youth. The flourishing of dance and entertainment ensembles during the **Restoration**, even in Metternich's comparatively repressive Austria, provided ample opportunities for his talents, and by 1825, he headed his own dance orchestra. In 1826–1827, he began publishing galops and **waltzes**, and by 1832, he had become the leader of a local regiment for which he wrote marches. He toured widely in the late 1830s (Belgium, Budapest, the German lands, Holland, London, and Paris). Most of his compositional energies were devoted to the genres utilized by his orchestra: galops, *Ländler*, marches, polkas, **quadrilles**, and waltzes. His compositions number about 250, and his *Radetsky March* (Op. 228, 1848) is still performed at every New Year's Eve concert of the Vienna Philharmonic.

Johann Strauss (II), also known as Johann Strauss Junior or The Younger, was intended by his father to go into business but secretly managed (with the help of his mother) to obtain private violin lessons with the concertmaster of his father's orchestra. He began studying the instrument and music theory openly after his father left the family to live with another woman in 1842. In

1844, he formed his own dance orchestra, which was initially a rival of his father's and eventually combined with it after his father's death. His orchestra began touring widely in 1846, traveling to Hungary, Prague, Romania, Serbia, Styria, and Warsaw as well as elsewhere in the German lands and spending 15 summers in a resort near St. Petersburg beginning in 1855. He began directing the music for Viennese court balls in 1853 but was not given this post officially for another decade. He resigned his post in 1871 and, now an international celebrity, participated in Patrick Gilmore's World's Peace Jubilee in Boston in 1872, an event that may have occasioned the waltzes *Greeting to America* and *Farewell to America* (these works' attribution to Strauss is not confirmed).

The younger Strauss's compositions may be classed into three broad periods of creativity. He was sympathetic to the liberal causes that incited the **Revolutions of 1848**, and during the years leading up to that broad social upheaval he became increasingly interested not only in penning works that were suitable for use at court but also in giving voice to the revolutionaries' cause—most notably the *Patrioten-Marsch* (Patriots' March, Op. 8, 1845), *Revolutions-Marsch* (Revolutionary March, Op. 54, 1848), and *Studenten-March* (Students' March, Op. 56, 1848). After the Revolutions' failure in Austria, he quickly affirmed his allegiance to the crown with works such as *Kaiser Franz Joseph-Marsch* (Op. 67, 1849), *Triumph-Marsch* (Op. 69, 1850), and *Kaiser Franz Josef I. Rettungs-Jubel-Marsch* (March in Celebration of the Rescue of Kaiser Franz Josef I, Op. 126, 1853); during this second phase, he also penned most of his famous orchestral waltzes, such as *An der schönen blauen Donau* (The Beautiful Blue Danube, Op. 314, 1867), *Künstlerleben* (Artists' Life, Op. 316, 1867), *Wein, Weib und Gesang* (Wine, Women, and Song, Op. 333, 1869), and *Wiener Blut* (Viennese Blood, Op. 354, 1873).

Finally, after his retirement from his post at the head of the Austrian Court Orchestra, Strauss (II) devoted his energies primarily to the relatively new (in Austria) genre of **operetta**, lending a distinctively Viennese flavor to these works by including in them plentiful polkas, waltzes, and other elements characteristic of the imperial capital (many of them appropriations of his own earlier well-known works). By far the most important of his 17 works in this genre are *Die Fledermaus* (The Bat, 1874; after an earlier work by **Fromenthal Halévy**) and the faux-**exoticist** *Der Zigeunerbaron* (The Gypsy Baron, 1885). [JMC]

STRAUSS, RICHARD (1864–1949). German composer, **conductor**, and writer on music of the Modern Romantic Generation; with **Gustav Mahler**, one of the most important influences on 20th-century music and 20th-century views on musical life as well as post-Romantic music generally. The only thread that pervades his lengthy career is that of **song**: he composed some

187 completed surviving songs (among them several **song cycles**) for voice with **piano** and 46 for voice with **orchestra** (many of these arrangements of the songs for voice with piano). The remainder of his output includes 15 completed **operas**, music for several other staged works (**ballets, incidental music,** and music for *tableaux vivants*), and a film score; eight **tone poems,** two **symphonies,** two **program symphonies,** one violin **concerto,** two horn concertos, and numerous other works for orchestra with or without soloist(s); four works for wind **chamber** ensemble and five works for brass ensemble with timpani; 10 surviving works for chorus with orchestra; two published *opera* of a cappella *Männerchöre,* one collection of German **motets,** and various other works for unaccompanied chorus; two **melodramas** and several other works for voice with piano accompaniment; two **piano trios,** one **string quartet,** one **piano quartet,** one cello **sonata,** one violin sonata, and 17 other autonomous instrumental chamber works; one piano sonata and two other published *opera* for piano solo; and numerous other works for piano. That sizable musical output embraces enormous stylistic variety, from (mostly early) compositions clearly indebted to a post-**Brahms**ian aesthetic to some of the most radically dissonant and conceptually challenging idioms of the early 20th century. He also published a German translation of **Hector Berlioz**'s treatise on orchestration, updated to include examples from the music of **Richard Wagner,** as well as many analytical, critical, and descriptive writings of remarkable insight and wit.

Strauss was born into a moneyed family of Bavarian brewers (the Pschorr family) and was the son of one of Europe's greatest hornists (Franz Strauss [1822–1905]), a conservative anti-Wagnerian who from 1875 until his death also conducted Munich's celebrated amateur orchestra titled *Wilde Gung'l.* Richard Strauss was a true **prodigy,** studying piano from the age of four, composing from the age of six, and beginning violin lessons at eight, publishing his op. 1 (the Festival March in E-flat Major, TrV 43) at 11, later joining his father's orchestra as a violinist and writing some of his earliest orchestral music for it. During these years, his most important musical influences—his father and his friend Ludwig Thuille (1861–1907), later an accomplished theorist in his own right—were decidedly conservative, vehemently opposed to the self-styled "progressive" agenda of **Franz Liszt, Richard Wagner,** and the **New German School** and **Allgemeiner Deutscher Musikverein.** Strauss subscribed to the same views (he even wrote Thuille a letter in *Stabreim* about awaiting a letter, mocking Wagner's **music dramas**), celebrating **Wolfgang Amadeus Mozart** above all others and also regarding highly the music of **Johannes Brahms, Franz Joseph Haydn, Albert Lortzing, Felix Mendelssohn Bartholdy, Franz Schubert, Robert Schumann,** and **Carl Maria von Weber.** He soon developed a brilliant reputation for his fluency in a post-Brahmsian idiom. His First **Symphony** (TrV 94, 1880) was premiered in 1881 by Hermann Levi (1839–1900) in

Munich, and the year 1882 saw the premiere of both his **Serenade** in E-flat Major for Winds (TrV 106/Op. 7, 1881) in Dresden and a piano-violin reduction of his Violin **Concerto** (TrV 110/Op. 8, 1880–1882) in Vienna. His trip to the Austrian capital for the latter performance also exposed him to its vibrant musical life and won him what he later described as his "first and only positive review" from the city's leading music critic, **Eduard Hanslick**.

But Strauss's days as a musical conservative were numbered. Much to his father's chagrin, he had attended performances of Wagner's *Die Walküre* and *Siegfried* and by 1879 had heard *Tristan und Isolde* and the entire *Ring of the Nibelung*. He matriculated in 1882 at the University of Munich, where he was introduced to the ideas of Arthur Schopenhauer (1788–1860) and **Friedrich Nietzsche**, but soon decided to abandon his university studies in order to pursue an independent career in music. He embarked on a critical new formative chapter in the winter of 1883–1884 with a trip to Berlin, where he attended concerts, theater, and opera performances and met **Hans von Bülow**, conductor of the court orchestra at Meiningen. Strauss was captivated by Bülow's conducting, and Bülow, impressed by Strauss's Serenade, invited him to compose a piece for the Meiningen Orchestra. This Strauss did (the **Suite** in B-flat Major, TrV 132/Op. 4), making his own debut as a conductor with its premiere in Meiningen on 18 November 1884. While in Berlin, he also composed a Second Symphony (in F minor, TrV 126, 1884), which was premiered under the baton of **Theodore Thomas** by the New York Philharmonic Society in December 1894 and then in Germany (Cologne) on 13 January 1895; it also won the admiration of Brahms.

In the summer of 1895, Strauss accepted von Bülow's invitation to become his assistant conductor in Meiningen. The appointment was for only one year but was of seminal importance for Strauss—for it not only offered him occasion to learn the comparatively new art of conducting from one of its greatest practitioners but also was his first professional position and gave him new independence from the dominating influence of his family's musical conservatism. Most importantly, while in Meiningen, he befriended the ardent Wagnerian composer and conductor Alexander Ritter (1833–1896), under whose influence he was converted to the Wagnerian cause. (Strauss later used the term *Bekehrung* to describe the experience—the expression used for a specifically religious conversion and no doubt an indicator of the profoundly spiritual nature of the turn for him.)

After the end of his stint in Meiningen, Strauss traveled briefly to Italy (where he penned his first contribution to "characteristic music" with the "symphonic **fantasy**" *Aus Italien*, TrV 147/Op. 16) and then assumed a position as third conductor of the Munich Court Opera. His new, avowedly progressive musical voice came gradually to the fore in the works he penned over the next few years—first with the tone poem *Macbeth* (TrV 163/Op. 23, after **William Shakespeare**) and then with the work whose opening measures the 20th-century musicologist Carl Dahlhaus identified as epitomizing the "dawning of 'musical modernism'": *Don Juan* (TrV 156/Op. 20), based on Nikolaus Lenau's (1802–1850) rendering of the legend, conducted by the composer at the Weimar Opera on 11 November 1889.

Over the next decade and a half, Strauss would establish himself as the *enfant terrible* of European musical life, producing two **cycles** of tone poems that stretched existing concepts of musical genre and the art of programmatic musical depiction of extramusical subjects to new philosophical as well as literary and pictorial limits. The first cycle included, in addition to *Macbeth* and *Don Juan*, the philosophical *Tod und Verklärung* (Death and Transfiguration, TrV 158/Op. 24, 1888–1889). After these three works, he tried his hand at the Wagnerian **music drama** with an opera, *Guntram* (TrV 168/Op. 25, 1892–1893), which he later disavowed, but then returned to poetic instrumental music with a new cycle of tone poems, these even brasher than their predecessors: *Till Eulenspiegels lustige Streiche* (Till Eulenspiegel's Merry Pranks, TrV 171/Op. 28, 1894–1895), *Also sprach Zarathustra* (Thus Spake Zarathustra, after Nietzsche; TrV 176/Op. 30, 1894–1995), *Don Quixote* (after Cervantes; TrV 184/Op. 35, 1897) and *Ein Heldenleben* (A Heroic Life, TrV 190/Op. 40, 1897–1898). These qorks were followed by the frankly autobiographical *Symphonia domestica* (TrV 209/Op. 53, 1902–1903).

Strauss had now established himself as musical modernism's most aggressive and brilliant champion, but he renewed (or exacerbated) his reputation as a provocateur with three operas that individually and collectively embody, onstage, many of the central challenges of modernity that faced his own and later generations. The first of these (*Salome*, after Oscar Wilde; TrV 214/Op. 54, 1903–1905) was based on a scandalously modern retelling of a biblical story that celebrated lust, betrayal, incestuous attraction, and violence. The second (*Elektra*, on a libretto by Hugo von Hoffmannsthal after Sophocles; TrV 223/Op. 58, 1906–1908) was a modernist recounting of an ancient Greek tale of extramarital betrayal, filicide, fratricide, homicide, matricide, and sororicide, complete with crazed erotic dance and vivid psychological depravity. And the third (*Der Rosenkavalier* [The Chevalier of the Rose, TrV 227/Op. 59, 1909–1910]) was an outwardly superficial romance about mistaken identity and romantic class subversion in Enlightenment Vienna, a work whose seemingly nostalgic take on Europe's dwindling aristocracy was, at its core, a genteel satire of the social mores of modern life. *Salome* and *Elektra*, while thoroughly tonal in their construction and descended in their musico-dramatic technique from Wagner's **music dramas**, were hyperchromatic and unremittingly dissonant (except for the moment of perverse consonance as Salome addresses and then kisses the severed head of John the Baptist); with *Der Rosenkavalier*, however, Strauss returned to an unabashedly consonant, sumptuously post-Romantic tonal idiom, one that synthesized the substance of a Mozartean romantic comedy with the rhetorical techniques of **Leitmotiv** and *unendliche Melodie* within an eclectic idiom that exalted banal **waltz** tunes and romantic love with equal brilliance.

If by the early 20th century Strauss had made a reputation for reaching new peaks of brilliance only to undercut himself with banality, with the three operas of the 1905–1913 he took this exploration of the profound disunity of modern life and modernism generally to even greater extremes—in the process inviting one of the great reception-historical quandaries of 20th-century music (*see* RECEPTION). Over the next 30 years, the aging composer saw the great German Empire born in his youth humiliated in the devastating World War I, then give birth to new hope in the Weimar Republic, only to witness that resurgence's disintegration into the heinous bizarreness of the Nazi era and the utter vanquishing of World War II, ending in a divided Germany whose reputation for greatness lay in tatters. In this context, he continued to devote most of his energies to the musical stage, that venue whose primary raison d'être had since the early 17th century been the musical exploration and probing of the great historical moments of humanity and problematical issues of society. Among most important works of the pre-Nazi years are two versions of *Ariadne auf Naxos* (TrV 228 and 228a/Op. 60, 1911–1912 and 1916) and the domestic sex comedy *Intermezzo* (TrV 246/ Op. 72, 1918–1923). During the 1930s, he penned a work that landed him in trouble with Nazi authorities, *Die schweigsame Frau* (The Silent Woman, TrV 265/Op. 80, 1935), followed by a retelling of the ancient Greek myth of the atonement of human violence through transfiguration into nature, *Daphne* (TrV 272/Op. 82, 1938). His final opera, the "conversation piece for music" *Capriccio* (TrV 279/Op. 85, 1940–1941), is an enactment in 18th-century France of the age-old question of which is more important, music or poetry. All these operas, like *Der Rosenkavalier*, were bold and brilliant musical explorations of a worldview that acknowledged the simultaneously base and grandiose, cruel and lovely, historical and ahistorical contradictions of life in the modern world—but they were also unabashedly tonal contributions to a musical world whose conception of modernity was increasingly focused almost exclusively on dissonance and the outright rejection of tonality.

After completing *Capriccio*, the 77-year-old composer declared his compositional career to be over (he actually declared, with characteristically dry humor, that his next work would be "scored for harps"). The declaration turned out to be premature, however. Strauss composed (in addition to a few occasional works) four more songs for voice with piano, three new *concertante* works (the Second Horn Concerto [TrV 283, 1942], an Oboe Concerto [TrV 292, 1945, rev. 1948], and the Duet-Concertino [TrV 293, 1947]), two new "sonatinas" for 16 winds (TrV 288 and 291, 1943 and 1944–1945), and the *Metamorphosen* for 23 solo strings (TrV 290, 1945). Perhaps most importantly, in his last year he orchestrated his early song *Ruhe, meine Seele* (TrV 170/1/Op. 27, no. 1, orch. 1948) and composed the orchestral songs posthumously published as his *Vier letzte Lieder* (Four Last Songs, TrV 296, 1948).

In modern music historiography, Strauss continues to be one of Western music's most complex characters. Most obviously, his passive complicity (at an age that few of his generation expected to outlive) in the horrors of Nazi Germany presses upon any historian of the 20th century some of the most difficult questions of ethics and morality. In a strictly musical sense, his abandonment of a Schoenbergian paradigm of music-historical evolution that was defined by the emancipation of dissonance and dissolution of tonality challenges the mores by which mainstream histories of 20th-century music have been (and in many cases continue to be) written. Perhaps most vexingly, despite his celebration of the sumptuous sonorities of post-Romantic idioms, he cultivated a decidedly un-Romantic artistic persona, turning from Schopenhauer to Nietzsche and dispensing with historically transcendent nobility and saintliness in favor of the quotidian joys and pettinesses of existence. For a composer whose music sounds so consummately Romantic to adopt and celebrate musically such an overtly pedestrian worldview challenges the very foundations of Romantic greatness as they had been conceived since the early years of music's Romanticisms. [JMC]

STREICHER. Austrian firm of **piano** manufacturers, significant for developing the Romantic Viennese action (in competition with **Graf** and **Walter**) to provide a balance of sensitivity and nuance with agility that made the fortepiano suitable for the cult of the **virtuoso** that flourished during the **Restoration**. The firm was founded when Nannette (Maria Anna) Streicher, née **Stein** (1769–1833), daughter of Johann Andreas Stein and herself a **salonnière** and able pianist, began building pianos independently of her father's firm, which she had taken over at his death in 1792. Between 1792 and 1802, she and her brother had continued the Stein firm, but in 1802, she and her husband, composer/pianist Johann Andreas Streicher (1761–1833), broke away and founded their own. The Streichers' son Johann Baptist (1796–1871) became a partner in 1823, and after his parents' deaths, the already prosperous firm flourished under his leadership (the firm being known first as "Nannette Streicher geb. Stein und Sohn" and then as "J. B. Streicher"). Already preferred instruments of **Ludwig van Beethoven** during his active performing career (1790s), as well as of **Johann Nepomuk Hummel** and **Carl Maria von Weber**, Streicher fortepianos now became enormously popular with Romantic Generation composer/pianists, including **Fanny Hensel**, **Clara** and **Robert Schumann**, **Franz Liszt** (until 1846, when the more robust **Bösendorfer** instruments won his loyalty), and **Felix Mendelssohn Bartholdy**.

In the second half of the century, the Streicher firm continued to procure many patents and increase the size and volume of its instruments as larger concert halls proliferated. But because the Viennese action typically became more unwieldy as the size of the instrument increased, the Streicher instruments' popularity lost ground to other makers of Viennese instruments (notably Bösendorfer) and of course to the heavier, louder, more homogeneous pianos of **Chickering, Steinway**, and other such makers of solid-metal, cross-strung instruments during the second half of the century. (In 1867, Streicher did exhibit a metal-framed, cross-strung instrument, but by this point crucial ground in the marketplace battle for a louder piano had been lost.) Nevertheless, Streicher instruments continued to be prized by many—most importantly **Johannes Brahms**, who wrote glowingly of them in 1864, apparently played almost exclusively on them when in Vienna from 1865 to 1875, and retained one as his studio piano until his death. At the death of Johann Baptist Streicher in 1871, the firm passed to his son Emil (1836–1916), who continued to run it until he sold it to the firm of Stingl when he retired (1896).

The Streicher firm's instruments were initially similar to those of Stein, but after about 1810, they began to introduce further refinements that set their action, touch, and tone apart from other contemporary fortepianos. Like most European firms, Streicher instruments retained parallel stringing throughout the century, using interlocking wooden frames, leather-capped hammers, and Viennese action and rejecting the duplex frames and cross-stringing typical of the more industrialized instruments of the United States branch of Steinway. In 1823, Streicher patented a down-striking mechanism that would facilitate repeated notes without compromising the sensitivity of tone and touch characteristic of the Viennese action—a development that was first produced in a piano for Hummel in 1825 and (judging from reports in the contemporary press and the number of surviving instruments) remained quite popular. Additionally, in the mid-1830s, the firm began developing its own alternative to the English action, and this, too, remained popular into the 1870s. By 1803, Streicher instruments' typical range had expanded from five and a half to six octaves, and mid-19th-century instruments typically include a seven-octave range and four pedals: in addition to a damper pedal and a *pianissimo* pedal, an *una corda* pedal and a bassoon pedal (a silk-padded rail pressed against the strings to produce a slightly reedy sound).

Like most parallel-strung instruments, Streicher's fortepianos have a clear, highly nuanced, and richly variegated sound, with crisp, distinct articulation facilitated by the leather-covered hammers. They are as mellow as modern Steinways at lower dynamic levels (albeit more transparent in tone), but there is a distinct contrast in tone between lower and higher dynamic levels (a feature that may explain Brahms's fondness for the instruments since it facilitates clarity and differentiation between primary and secondary lines in his dense textures that combine wide-ranging melodic lines with complicated polyphonic accompaniments). [JMC]

STYLE HONGROIS. (Fr., "Hungarian style.") Term applied to the stylistic evocation in cultivated music of the music and styles of music making (*romungro*) of the Romani Gypsies during the **long 19th century**; a subset of **exoticism**. Although the term suggests that the style is Hungarian, that is, evocative of the Magyars, the music in question imitates or evokes the exotic-sounding style of the Roma, themselves outcast and despised by their Hungarian peers. Western Europeans encountered the Roma repertoire as the Gypsy tribes traveled westward and composers such as Carl Ditters von Dittersdorf (1739–1799), **Franz Joseph Haydn**, and Michael Haydn (1737–1806) assumed positions in Hungarian courts. Elements of the style had appeared within the small repertoire of Hungarian dance music that began to circulate in the West in the late 15th century, but during the late 18th century, it became more common, assuming the status of a full-fledged musical dialect and **topic** by the early decades of the 19th century.

The *style hongrois* thus represents a trajectory from vernacular music to concert music; only in the Modern Romantic Generation did its ubiquity and potency as a musical topic begin to diminish. Prominent early examples from the long 19th century, sometimes mingled with the Turkish style (*see* JANISSARY MUSIC), are found in the third-movement *rondo alla zingarese* of Haydn's **Piano Trio** in G Major (Hob. XV:25, 1795), the third movement of **Wolfgang Amadeus Mozart**'s Violin **Concerto** in A Major (K. 219, 1775), and the fourth movement of his **String Quartet** in F Major (K. 590, 1790). In the Early Romantic Generation, it is most prominently represented in **Carl Maria von Weber**'s *Andante and rondo ungarese* (J. 79, 1809, solo part arranged for bassoon in 1813 and published as J. 158/Op. 35), the fourth of his *Huit pièces* for **piano duet** (J. 243/Op. 60, no. 4, 1818–1819, publ. 1820), and especially his **incidental music** for *Preciosa* (P. M. Wolff, after Cervantes; J. 279/Op. 78, 1820–1821). It also occurs in works by **Ludwig van Beethoven**—most importantly, the **overture** to his **incidental music** for *König Stephan* (Op. 117, 1811–1812, publ. 1822–1823) but also in the finale of his String Quartet in C Minor (Op. 18, no. 4, 1799–1800, publ. 1801) and the third movement of his youthful Piano Concerto in E-flat Major (**WoO 4**, 1784). **Franz Schubert** famously evoked the style in the *Divertissement à l'Hongroise* (D. 818, ca. 1824, publ. 1826) as well as in the F-minor *Moment musical* (D. 780/Op. 94, no. 3, 1828), the final movement of the **Octet** (D. 803, 1824), the String Quartet in A Minor (D. 804/Op. 29, no. 1, 1824), the *Grand Duo* for piano duet (D. 812, 1824; posthumously published as Op. 140 in 1838), and *Der Leiermann* from *Winterreise*, D. 911). To Hungarian ears of the day, the Hungarian-Gypsy style as represented in these and other such works was a distant memory of authentic Roma music—but to Western Europeans, it was authentic and current, capable both of lending a distinctly exotic flavor to the idioms of Western European art music and of "domesticating" the exotic Other through its assimilation into those idioms.

In the Romantic Generation, the style figures in the music of **Robert Schumann** in works such as the vocal trio *Zigeunerleben* (Op. 29, no. 3, for SAT and piano with *ad lib.* triangle and tambourine), the song *Zigeunerliedchen* from the *Lieder-Album für die Jugend* (Op. 79, no. 7, 1849), the third movement ("Zigeunertanz") from the *Clavier-Sonate für die Jugend* (Op. 118, no. 3, 1853), "Ungarisch" from *Ball-Szenen* for piano duet (Op. 109, 1851, publ. 1853), and the **Fantasy** in C Major for Violin and **Orchestra** (Op. 131, 1853, publ. 1854). In this generation, however, it is most famously associated with the music of **Franz Liszt**. In addition to authoring a widely disseminated and translated book titled *Des Bohémiens et de leur musique en Hongrie* (On the Gypsies and Their Music in Hungary, 1859, 3rd ed., 1884), Liszt also penned 19 *Hungarian Rhapsodies* for piano solo (LW A132; nos. 1–15 comp. 1846–1853 and publ. 1853, nos. 16–19 comp. 1882–1885 and publ. 1882–1886) and a *Fantasie über ungarische Volksmelodien* (**Fantasy** on Hungarian Folk Melodies, LW H12, 1849–1852, publ. 1864) based on No. 14 of that series. Although Liszt seems to have backed away from his extensive cultivation of the *style hongrois* in the last three Rhapsodies and in a few other late works on Hungarian topics, his mid-century explorations of the sorrow and desperations as well as the musical brilliance of the Roma in the concert and recital repertoire remain some of the long 19th century's most brilliant and persuasive.

The last decades of the 19th century witnessed a decline in uses of the *style hongrois* in cultivated music, even though it remained ubiquitous in café music and other "light" genres. In the Late Romantic Generation, its most prominent advocate was **Johannes Brahms**, who employed the style not only in several finales (those of the **Piano Quartet** in G Minor [Op. 25, 1861, publ. 1863], the Piano **Quintet** in F Minor [Op. 34, 1862, publ. 1865], the First Piano Concerto [Op. 15, 1859, publ. 1861], the Violin Concerto [Op. 77, 1878, publ. 1879], and the Double Concerto [Op. 102, 1887, publ. 1888]) but also in lighthearted works descended from the *Hausmusik* tradition, such as the two sets of *Ungarische Tänze* for piano duet (WoO 1, 1869 and 1880), the 11 *Zigeunerlieder* **part-songs**, Op. 103 (eight of which Brahms also arranged as solo songs), and the last four part-songs from Op. 112 (1891). The style also figures, appropriately, in **Antonín Dvořák**'s *Zigeunermelodien* (Gypsy Melodies, Op. 55, 1880). It is also found, assimilated into a more generally Viennese idiom, in **Johann Strauss (II)**'s **operetta** *Der Zigeunerbaron* (The Gypsy Baron, 1885).

In works of the Modern Romantic Generation, the *style hongrois* continues to occur in this lighthearted fashion. The most obvious examples are **Franz Lehár**'s operetta *Zigeunerliebe* (Gypsy Love, 1910) and Maurice Ravel's *Tzigane* (1924) as well as other works by **Isaac Albéniz**, Manuel de Falla (1876–1946), **Enrique Granados**, Joaquín Rodrigo (1901–1999), and Pablo de Sarasate (1844–1908). Although the fascination with the Gypsy as a general social topic has remained strong, the musical rhetoric of the *style hongrois* as it was cultivated in the works of the mid-19th century has essentially disappeared.

Like all musical topics, the *style hongrois* achieved its effectiveness through **paratextual** elements as well as the use of a conventionalized set of figures in a variety of contexts. The paratextual elements are evident from the titles of the works above. Simply by using the word "Gypsy" or its many variants (*bohémien, ongarese, tsigane, gitan, Zigeuner, zingarese,* and so on) in the title or other paratextual material of a work, composers could signify the Otherness of their music and specify its intended connotations and effects—even if the musical techniques specific to the work at hand are more or less generic in nature.

The musical gestures associated with the *style hongrois* increased their evocative or suggestive power through aggregation, but even individually they sufficed to evoke the Roma. Its stereotypical dance types are the *verbunkos* (a presentation dance in duple meter, originally used for military recruitment, that begins very slowly and gradually accelerates into a wild *friska* with rapid running notes) and its descendant, the *czardas*. Instrumentation in the *style hongrois* tended to emphasize the solo violin (in imitation of the stereotypical Gypsy fiddler) or middle-range woodwinds (especially the clarinet), typically involving rapid florid runs spanning registral extremes and (for the solo violin) double- or triple-stops in combination with the above gestures. In quick tempos, the style tended to employ extremes of registers in the solo instrument and (for the violin) pizzicatos or prominent, frequent double- or triple-stops.

In slow movements, the style typically required considerable flexibility of tempo in order for slow-moving chords in the ensemble to accommodate virtuosic-sounding, free ornamentation searching in the outer extremes of the instrument's register (a technique known as *hallgató*). As in other styles, drone harmonies in open fifths or octaves in the middle or lower register were also used—signifiers that are generally alien to cultivated music of the common-practice period but that are ubiquitous in folk and national repertoires of all sorts; the same is true of parallel fifths in the lower registers, especially when used in combination with one of the other gestures evocative of the *style hongrois*. Rapid, rhythmically free oscillations between two widely spaced pitches or sets of pitches could imitate the frequently encountered Gypsy cimbalom. Instrumental evocations of Gypsy vocal music typically involved the use of grace notes more than a fifth away from the principal notes and parallel homorhythmic doublings of the melody at the third or sixth in such a fashion that neither line is "the melody" but both are equal parts of it (another gesture common in folk and national repertoires).

Finally, the *style hongrois* also had a distinct melodic and rhythmic vocabulary. The most common elements of the melodic vocabulary were prominent use of the augmented second at the mediant and submediant, producing a symmetrical semitonal inflection of the dominant (e.g., *D—E—F—G sharp—A—B flat—C sharp—D*), and the *kuruc* fourth (a repeated rebounding between the two notes a fourth apart, usually the dominant and the upper prime). Among its most common rhythmic components was the *alla zoppa* ("limping") rhythm featuring two or three long notes flanked by two or three short ones, the first and last of which articulate the downbeat. [JMC]

SUITE. (Fr., "series" or "sequence.") Instrumental genre in multiple movements, usually involving either dance music or pieces extracted from a stage work. In the 19th century, the term had several possible applications. With the rise of genres such as the **sonata, serenade,** divertimento, and **symphony,** suites decreased in importance toward the end of the end of the 18th century. In the 19th century, while the publication of like stylized dances in a single opus (such as **mazurkas, polonaises,** or **waltzes**) may have carried on part of the earlier concept of the dance suite, the term "suite" was not often used before mid-century. By the turn of the 20th century, "suite" commonly referred to one of three kinds of pieces. The first, sometimes called an extract suite, consisted of movements drawn from stage sources such as **ballet, opera,** or **incidental music;** examples are **Georges Bizet** (posthumously) and **Ernest Guiraud,** *Carmen* Suite No. 1 (1882); **Edvard Grieg,** *Peer Gynt* Suites Nos. 1 (Op. 23, 1888) and 2 (Op. 55, 1891); and **Pyotor Il'yich Tchaikovsky**'s *Nutcracker* Suite (Op. 71A, 1892).

The second type of suite uses the term chiefly to distinguish it from multiple-movement works that follow or reference the **sonata plan** (such as the **symphony** or **string quartet**). In many cases, these bore only Italian tempo markings (such as **William Sterndale Bennett**'s 1842 piano *Suite de pièces* and **Leoš Janáček**'s 1877 *Suita* [Suite] for strings, JW 6/2), but more often the movements amounted to **character pieces** or even elaborate **program music.** Examples of these are **Nikolay Rimsky-Korsakov**'s *Sheherazade* (1888), **Joachim Raff**'s *Thuringian Suite* (1877), and **Jean Sibelius**'s *Lemminkäis-sarja* (Lemminkäinen Suite, Op. 22, 1896, rev. 1897, rev. 1939).

Finally, the term was used for works composed in the spirit of **historicism** and meant to conjure the dance suite of the 18th century and earlier (and not necessarily to emulate them entirely); among these are Woldemar Bargiel's (1828–1897) accompanied Violin Suite (Op. 17, 1859) and Piano Suite (Op. 21, 1860), **Claude Debussy**'s *Petite suite* (1888) and *Suite bergamasque*

(1890, rev. 1905), **Franz Lachner**'s **orchestral** suites (No. 1 in D minor, 1861; No. 2 in E minor, 1862; No. 3 in F minor, 1864; No. 4 in E-flat major, 1865, No. 5 in C minor, 1868; No. 6 in C major, 1871; No. 7 in D minor, 1881), Grieg's *Holberg Suite* (1884), **Hubert Parry**'s *Lady Radnor's Suite* (1894), and most of Raff's orchestral suites (No. 1 in C major, 1863; No. 2 "In Hungarian Style," 1874; Italian Suite, 1871), In many cases, 19th-century suites drew from more than one of these three types. Bargiel's Piano Suite No. 2, Op. 33, precedes its generically and characteristically titled movements with a "Präludium." Debussy's *Suite bergamasque* offers a prelude, minuet, and passepied, but it is famous for its evocative, lyrical third movement "Clair de lune" (Moonlight). [RK]

SULLIVAN, ARTHUR (SEYMORE) (1842–1900). English composer and **conductor,** contributor to a wide array of genres but famous primarily for his **operettas** written in collaboration with librettist W. S. Gilbert (1836–1911). He was the son of the theater clarinetist and learned to play many instruments, studying first at the Royal Academy of Music (1856–1858) and then at the Leipzig **Conservatory** (1858–1861), where he completed a score for **incidental music** to **Shakespeare**'s *The Tempest.* From 1862 to 1872, he worked as a teacher, accompanist, and church organist in London, where the *Tempest* music was performed in the Crystal Palace in 1862, his first major success. Other works from his early maturity include the **ballet** *L'île enchantée* (The Enchanted Isle, 1864), a Cello **Concerto** (1866), a **Symphony** in E Major ("Irish," 1866, publ. 1915), a set of **character pieces** for **piano** (*Day Dreams,* Op. 14, 1867), a **concert overture** (*Marmion,* after Walter Scott, 1867), an *Overture di ballo* (1867), and two **oratorios** on his own **libretti** after the Bible (*The Prodigal Son,* 1869, and *The Light of the World,* 1873, rev. 1890). With **George Grove,** he also discovered the complete score and parts for **Franz Schubert**'s incidental music *Rosamunde* (D. 797) during a trip to Vienna in 1867.

Over the course of his career, Sullivan also composed vocal **chamber music** (solo **songs,** duets, trios, and **part-songs**), a handful of works for instrumental chamber ensemble, dozens of hymn tunes (including *Onward, Christian Soldiers,* 1871), and a sizable body of other sacred music. He also wrote incidental music to *The Merchant of Venice* (1871, publ. 1898), *The Merry Wives of Windsor* (1874), *Henry VIII* (1877, publ. 1878), and *Macbeth* (1888) as well as Alfred Tennyson's (1809–1892) *The Foresters* (1892). His three-act **opera** *The Beauty Stone* (1898) was among his least successful stage works, closing after just 50 performances. Sullivan was knighted in 1883 and buried in St. Paul's at the command of Queen Victoria.

Sullivan's main claim to fame lies in the genre of operetta. His first work in the genre, the three-character, one-act *Cox and Box, or the Long-Lost Brothers,* on a libretto by Francis Cowley Burnand (1836–1917) after John

Maddison Morton (1811–1891), was first performed privately with piano accompaniment in May 1866 and then **orchestrated** and performed publicly on 11 May 1867. During its initial public run (264 performances), he met W. S. Gilbert, with whom he produced the now-lost *Thespis* in 1871. Their second collaboration, the one-act *Trial by Jury* (1875), a romantic comedy satirizing the legal profession, won them the support of the successful impresario Richard D'Oyly Carte (1844–1901), and the further successes of the two-act *The Sorcerer* (1877, publ. 1878) and especially *H.M.S. Pinafore, or The Lass That Loved a Sailor* (1878) established them as the leading composers in the new genre of English operetta. D'Orly Carte formed the D'Orly Carte Opera Company specifically to afford their operettas the highest-quality performances and in 1880–1881 built for it the state-of-the-art Savoy Theatre, a major venue for operetta, especially of the **exoticist** variety, for the next few decades. Gilbert and Sullivan's most important operetta collaborations, include, in addition to *Pinafore*, *The Pirates of Penzance* (1879), which opened on Fifth Avenue in New York City and ran for 363 performances after it opened in London in 1880; *Princess Ida* (1884); *The Mikado* (1885); *Ruddigore* (1887); *The Yeomen of the Guard* (1888); and *The Gondoliers* (1889). [JMC]

SUPPÉ [SUPPÈ], FRANZ (VON) (1819–1895). (Adopted name of Francesco Ezechiele Ermenegildo Cavaliere Suppé Demelli.) Austrian composer and **conductor** of Belgian descent, of the Late Romantic Generation; best known today for his tuneful **overtures** and his farces and **operettas** in the style of **Jacques Offenbach**. He demonstrated talent in composition at an early age and by 1834 had written a Mass and one **comic opera**. After his father's death in 1835, he and his mother settled in Vienna, where he studied composition with Ignaz von Seyfried (1776–1841) and **Simon Sechter** while working as a conductor in various municipal and provincial theaters. His first complete score of this mature period was the "comic portrait" *Jung lustig, im Alter traurig, oder Die Folgen der Erziehung* (Merry in Youth, Sad in Old Age; or, The Consequences of Education, 1841), and around that time he also met **Gaetano Donizetti**, in whose *L'elisir d'amore* he sang the *basso profundo* role of Dulcamara in 1842. By 1845, he had composed some 20 comic operas, and his success as a conductor continued to grow with performances such as a German version of **Giacomo Meyerbeer**'s *Les Huguenots* (as *Die Gibellinen in Pisa*) with **Jenny Lind** in 1846 and *Ein Feldlager in Schlesien* in 1847.

Suppé's claim to lasting fame was achieved in part as a backlash against the popularity in Vienna of the new style of operetta created by Offenbach and the Bouffes-Parisiens in the early 1850s. The genre had been enormously popular in Vienna since the 1858 premiere there of Offenbach's *Le mariage aux lanterns* (The Lantern Marriage, 1857), but until Suppé's *Das Pensionat*

(The Boarding School, 1860), no original German-language counterpart had successfully competed with French imports. Suppé's colorful **orchestration**, superb wit, tuneful melodies, and adeptness at surprise harmonies offered a competitive native species of the genre—and it flourished.

Between 1860 and 1895, Suppé produced 27 other significant *Operetten* and *komische Operetten* as well as dozens of **overtures** and other works. Aside from *Das Pensionat*, he is best known today for his fictionalized stage musical biographies *Franz Schubert* (1864) and *Joseph Haydn* (1887) as well as the march *O du mein Österreich* (Oh, My Austria, from *S'Alraund*, 1849), the *Dichter und Bauer* (Poet and Peasant) and *Leichte Kavallerie* (Light Cavalry) Overtures (1846 and 1866), and the operettas *Flotte Bursche* (Jolly Students, 1863), *Fatinitza* (1876), and *Boccaccio* (1879). His prestige is reflected in the fact that he was among those invited to the first **Bayreuth** Festival in 1876 and was widely sought after in musical capitals including Brussels, London, and Paris. He also composed a number of **songs**, dances, and marches. [JMC]

SVENDSEN, JOHAN SEVERIN (1840–1911). Norwegian composer, **conductor**, and violinist of the Late Romantic Generation. The most important Scandinavian conductor of the **long 19th century**, Svendsen—like **Grieg**—forged a distinctive, compelling compositional style that lent itself well to **nationalist** projects of his time. The son of a military bandsman in Christiania (now Oslo), Svendsen grew up hearing marches and dance music; in his teenage years, he performed and composed this music. In 1863–1867, Svendsen studied with **Ferdinand David** and **Carl Reinecke** at the Leipzig **Conservatory**; while there, he completed his first two **string quartets**, the Symphony No. 1 in D major (Op. 4, 1865–1867, publ. 1868) and an **octet** (Op. 3, 1865–1866, publ. 1867), both published by the prestigious firm of **Breitkopf & Härtel**. After touring the British Isles in 1868, Svendsen lived and performed in Paris for a few years. In the early 1870s, Svendsen befriended **Richard Wagner** in **Bayreuth**, where he completed his orchestral *Karnival i Paris* (Carnival in Paris, Op. 9, 1872, publ. 1877).

In 1872–1877, Svendson conducted for Christiania's Musical Society, together with Grieg for the first two seasons. After a few years' travel in Rome, London, and Paris (in which cities he encountered Giovanni Sgambati [1841–1914], Pablo de Sarasate [1844–1908], and Pauline Viardot-García [1821–1910], respectively), Svendsen continued his activities in Christiania in 1880–1883. Svendsen then moved to Copenhagen, where he spent the rest of his life and conducted the Danish Royal Opera from 1883 to 1908. Some of Svendsen's other major works are his *Romance* for violin and **orchestra** (Op. 26, 1881), his Symphony No. 2 in B-flat major (Op. 15, 1874, publ. 1877), and his four *Norwegian Rhapsodies* for orchestra (opp. 17, 19, 21, and 22. nos. 1–3 comp. 1876, publ. 1877, No. 4 comp. 1877, publ. 1878). [RK]

SYMPHONIC POEM. (Fr., poème symphonique; Ger., symphonische Dichtung.) Term for a **programmatic** instrumental work, usually in one movement, bearing a descriptive title and performed or published with a prefatory poem or other printed program. Such works date from early in the **long 19th century**, but the term itself was coined by **Franz Liszt** to distinguish between his own compositions of the sort and the programmatic **concert overtures** of **Hector Berlioz, Felix Mendelssohn Bartholdy, Robert Schumann, Louis Spohr**, and others during the first half of the 19th century.

In principle, the term *symphonic poem* foregrounded the works' poetic or programmatic elements while downplaying their use of conventional **absolute** musical processes, such as **sonata form**, rondo, and the like. In practice, works designated as symphonic poems still employ those conventional forms but place greater emphasis on continuity achieved via **thematic transformation** rather than on tonal, thematic, and **motivic** contrast and development. The term usually denotes a composition for full **orchestra** but is considered to embrace smaller works as well, ranging from **Richard Wagner**'s *Siegfried Idyll* (1870) for **chamber** orchestra of 15 players and Arnold Schoenberg's *Verklärte Nacht* (Transfigured Night, 1899) for string **sextet** to **Aleksandr Scriabin**'s *Vers la flame* (Through the Flame, 1914) for **piano** solo. These works sometimes appeared in **suite**-like groups (e.g., **Nikolay Rimsky-Korsakov**, *Sheherazade*, 1888; **Debussy**, *La mer*, 1903–1905; and Gustav Holst, *The Planets*, 1914–1918).

The term *symphonic poem* was first employed in 1854 for a performance of Liszt's *Tasso: Lamento e trionfo* (LW G2, after **Byron** and **Goethe**, 1847–1854; also arranged as LW B20, 1858, and C10, 1857). Liszt also applied it to a total of 12 other works, including some that also bore other generic designations: No. 1, *Ce qu'on entend sur la montagne* (LW G1, 1847–1857, after **Victor Hugo**; known in German as *Bergsymphonie* [Mountain **Symphony**] and bearing the French subtitle *Médidation symphonique*); No. 3, **Les Préludes** (LW G3, after Lamartine, 1849–1856); No. 4 *Orpheus* (LW G9, 1853–1856); No. 5, *Prometheus* (LW G6, after Herder, 1850–1856); No. 6, *Mazeppa* (LW G7, 1851–1856, after Hugo); No. 7, *Festklänge* (Festival Sounds, LW G10, 1853–1856, rev. 1861); No. 8, *Héroïde funèbre* (LW G4, 1849–1857); No. 9, *Hungaria* (LW G13, 1854–1857); No. 10, *Hamlet* (LW G22, after **William Shakespeare**, 1858–1861); No. 11, *Die Ideale* (The Ideal, LW G15, 1856–1858, after **Friedrich Schiller**); No. 12, *Hunnenschlacht* (Battle of the Huns, after paintings by Wilhelm von Kaulbach [1805–1874], LW G17, 1857–1861); and No. 13, *Von der Wiege bis zum Grabe* (From the Cradle to the Grave, LW G38, 1881–1883). The last of these works, separated from its predecessors by two full decades, is cast in three short thematically interrelated movements; Nos. 1, 3, 4, 5, 6, 7, and 8 in this series were originally designated as concert overtures.

The term *symphonic poem* was eagerly taken up by numerous other composers, among them **Mily Balakirev** (*Tamara*, 1867–1884), **Aleksandr Borodin** (*In Central Asia*, 1880–1882), **Paul Dukas** (*L'apprenti sorcier*, 1897), **Henri Duparc** (*Léonore*, 1874), **Antonín Dvořák** (*The Water Goblin*, Op. 107, 1896; *The Noon Witch*, Op. 108, 1896; *The Golden Spinning-Wheel*, Op. 109, 1896; *The Wild Dove*, Op. 110, 1896–1899; and *A Hero's Song*, Op. 111, 1897–1899), **César Franck** (*Les Eolides*, M43, 1875–1876, publ. 1892–1893; *Le chasseur maudit*, M44, publ. 1894; *Les Djinns*, M45, 1884, publ. 1893; *Psyché*, M47, 1887–1888, publ. 1898), **Aleksandr Glazunov** (*Kreml'*, Op. 30, 1892), **John Knowles Paine** (*The Tempest*, Op. 31, 1876, publ. 1907), **Serge Rachmaninoff** (*The Rock*, Op. 7, 1893, and *The Isle of the Dead*, Op. 29, 1909), **Camille Saint-Saëns** (*Danse macabre*, Op. 40, 1875), Scriabin (Symphonic Poem in D Minor, 1896–1897), **Bedřich Smetana** (the six symphonic poems in the **cycle *Ma Vlast***), and **Pyotor Il'yich Tchaikovsky** (*Fatum*, Op. posth. 77, 1868).

Like the concert overture and its generic consequent, the **tone poem**, the symphonic poem engaged performers and audiences in an experience that was quintessentially imaginative, whether by soliciting them to understand how the musical composition gave voice to a philosophical or quasi-philosophical idea (Liszt's *Les Préludes*), portraying a character or personality (*Orpheus*), responding to a visual image (*Hunnenschlacht*), or musically narrating an explicit series of extramusical events (Dukas's *The Sorcerer's Apprentice*). Along with the **program symphony**, it became the archetypal genre of instrumental ensemble music for "progressive" composers in the second half of the 19th century. Later composers such as Griffes, Honegger, Milhaud, Villa-Lobos, Gershwin, Copland, Jacob Druckman, Hans Werner Henze, David Del Tredici, John Tavener, and Philip Glass, have continued to invoke the genre in one-movement programmatic orchestral works, even if they are not officially designated symphonic poems. [JMC]

See also PROGRAM (PROGRAMMATIC) MUSIC; PROGRAM SYMPHONY *OR* CHARACTERISTIC SYMPHONY.

SYMPHONIE FANTASTIQUE. *See EPISODE IN THE LIFE OF AN ARTIST: FANTASTIC SYMPHONY IN FIVE PARTS*, H. 48/OP. 14[A].

SYMPHONY. (Fr., symphonie; Ger., Symphonie; It., sinfonia.) In the **long 19th century**, a multimovement composition in the **sonata plan** for **orchestra**, with or without voices and without designated instrumental soloist(s); by the second half of the century, the preeminent public genre of instrumental music. The symphony is distinct from other orchestral works such as the **suite** in that it follows the sonata plan and consists of a fixed number of movements (typically between three and five, with four being the norm) whose content is usually serious, and from other orchestral works in the sonata plan such as the **concerto** in that it does not (explicitly) designate a particular solo instrument or instruments to "compete" with the orchestra and/or voices. Although its historical origins and defining musical characteristics qualify it as a genre of so-called **absolute music**, the long 19th century also became increasingly interested in the **program symphony** or "characteristic symphony"; many symphonies whose titles do not explicitly mark them as programmatic are nevertheless directly and sometimes overtly linked to poetic or extramusical subject matter, thus occupying a middle ground between absolute and program music. Like most orchestral music before the advent of recorded and broadcast sound, symphonies were disseminated during the long 19th century first and foremost in transcriptions for **piano duet** or (more rarely) **piano** solo, sometimes with obbligato instruments. Until the 1870s, few symphonies were published in full score until sales of such transcriptions and orchestral parts had established their commercial viability (*see* EDITING AND EDITIONS; PRINTING AND PUBLISHING OF MUSIC).

Because the symphony was the preeminent public genre of instrumental music, its history during the long 19th century is best considered in terms of the major caesurae in public life: during the Revolutionary and Napoleonic eras (to 1815), the Restoration symphony (1815–1848), the Late Romantic Generation symphony (1848–1870), and the post-Romantic or "modern" Romantic symphony (many symphonies after 1870; for purposes of this dictionary, primarily those written before 1914). Within these broad divisions, the following discussion will highlight a few relevant general trends in the genre's history, followed by a brief review of the most important composers and a few particularly significant works.

The Symphony in the Revolutionary and Napoleonic Eras, 1789–1815. During the mid-18th century, the symphony as a genre flourished in a number of centers—Mannheim, London, Paris, Vienna—and by the 1780s, Paris was more appreciative than Vienna of the symphonies of **Franz Joseph Haydn** and **Wolfgang Amadeus Mozart**. But the political and economic turmoil unleashed with the French Revolution, the Terror, and the Napoleonic Wars largely removed Paris from the market for large-scale public instrumental music. Meanwhile, the vibrant public musical life engendered by the reforms of the Habsburg emperor Joseph II (fl. 1780–1790) and even the more moderate establishments of his successors, Leopold II (fl. 1790–1792) and Francis II (fl. 1792–1806), made Vienna's musical public more receptive than most to the large and complex genre of the symphony. The Habsburg capital was followed closely in these regards by London, where a densely urbanized environment, comparatively liberal government, and flourishing middle class created a sizable appetite for all manner of music making, including public concerts that typically entailed at least one symphony.

Vienna and, to a lesser extent, London were thus the most influential centers in laying the foundation of the 19th-century symphony. The Napoleonic era witnessed a continued flourishing of public musical culture in Vienna and elsewhere in the German lands and Central Europe whenever those areas were not subject to invasion or occupation. Consequently, during the period around 1790–1815, symphonies were produced by **E. T. A. Hoffmann** (1806), **Étienne-Nicolas Méhul** (1809), **Gioachino Rossini** (ca. 1806), **Louis Spohr** (1809), and **Carl Maria von Weber** (two symphonies, both 1807). Those same years witnessed the composition and performance of **Ludwig van Beethoven**'s first eight symphonies and the publication (in parts, arrangements for piano solo and piano duet, and eventually score) of the first six of those (nos. 7 and 8 being published in 1816 and 1817, respectively). Although the last years of Beethoven's initial surge of symphonic creation and the gap between it and the composition of his final (ninth) symphony coincided with the composition of the first seven of **Franz Schubert**'s eight completed symphonies, none of the younger composer's symphonies was published or performed publicly during his lifetime.

The Early Romantic Generation's contributions to the discourse of the genre before the premiere of Schubert's "Great" C-major Symphony (No. 7, D. 944) in 1839 were thus dominated almost exclusively by Beethoven. Precious few other composers contributed to the genre during the first 15 years of the 19th century. In France, these included Méhul (five symphonies, 1808–1810) and **Luigi Cherubini** (one symphony, 1815, but commissioned by the Philharmonic Society of London and premiered there) and in Great Britain the works of the German-born Ferdinand Ries (1784–1838; two works, 1809 and 1813); in the German lands, Spohr (one work, 1811); in Sweden, Carl Braun (1788–1835; six symphonies, 1810–14); and in Denmark, Peter Krossing (1793–1838) and Georg Gerson (1790–1825) (one symphony each, 1811 and 1813).

The Restoration Symphony, 1815–1848. The chronology of the symphony during the **Restoration** must be divided into two phases: 1815–1839 and 1839–1848. The sparseness of symphonic production during the Napoleonic era had been not least of all a function of socioeconomic concerns in a Europe that was constantly at war: the constant threat of invasion or occupation and the need for Europe's leaders to organize and fund military defense rather than peaceful social activities such as concerts, together with the fact that a career as a public musician was acceptable only for men (who were needed for the defense) during this period, was an obstacle to public concert life. The relative peace and prosperity of the Restoration improved this situation—but it also had its drawbacks. On the one hand, Vienna no longer offered a fully congenial environment for symphonic production because Prince Clemens von Metternich's culture of censorship and oppressive regulation made the Habsburg capital significantly less hospitable to new ideas in public music—indeed, to public gatherings generally—than it had been during the period around 1780–1815 (*see* VORMÄRZ). The fact that the Viennese Beethoven produced only one symphony (the Ninth) after the end of the Napoleonic era (and that at instigation of the Philharmonic Society of London) is indicative of this change in climate—as is the fact that Beethoven's Ninth was rarely heard and little understood until after the 1840s. Yet new centers for symphonic production emerged elsewhere in the German lands—most notably in Leipzig (in the Kingdom of Saxony), followed by Berlin (Kingdom of Prussia) and Kassel (Grand Duchy of Hesse-Darmstadt).

Moreover, even the relatively hospitable symphonic climate of Restoration Europe could not lessen the burden posed by the enormous symphonic legacy left by Beethoven and the few symphonies by Haydn and Mozart that were known at the time. Some important symphonies were composed between 1815 and 1839 but published only later, including **Felix Mendelssohn Bartholdy**'s D-minor ("Reformation") and A-major ("Italian") symphonies (MWV N15 and N16/opp. posth. 107 and 90, composed in 1832 and 1833–1834, respectively, and published posth. 1871 and 1851) and **Hector Berlioz**'s *Harold in Italy* (H. 68/Op. 16, comp. 1834, publ. 1848). But even the work that towers above all others from these years in terms of significance—Berlioz's *Episode in the Life of an Artist* (H 48/Op. 14[A], comp. 1830–1834)—was available only in **Franz Liszt**'s arrangement for piano solo until 1845, when it was finally published in parts and full score.

The remainder of the symphonic production of these years is of considerably less historical significance, at least in retrospect. In France, the symphonic milieu was dominated by the English-born **Georges Onslow** (three works, 1830–1834) and **Félicien David** (two works, 1837 and 1838). In the German lands, it was dominated by Spohr's Symphonies Nos. 2–5 (1820–1837), with other contributions by Jan Kalivoda (1801–1866; four works, 1826–1835), **Franz Lachner** (seven works, 1828–1839), Sigismund von Neukomm (1778–1858; two works, both 1822), **Andreas Romberg** (two symphonies, 1818 and 1828), and **Richard Wagner** (whose Symphony in C Major [WWV 32] was completed during this period but failed to make an impact and was first published posthumously). In Great Britain, new symphonies of the period 1815–1839 were dominated by **Cipriani Potter** (15 works, 1819–1834), Ferdinand Ries (five more symphonies, 1816–1835) and the German-born Mendelssohn (1829 and 1833), with other contributions by **William Sterndale Bennett** (five works, 1832–1836) and G. A. Macfarren (1813–1887; six works, 1828–1836). Scandinavia's symphonic output of these years included the First Symphony (1820) of **Franz Berwald** and the first version of **Adolf Fredrik Lindblad**'s First Symphony (1831), plus one symphony each by the Norwegian composers Frederik Frøhlich (1806–1860) and **Emilius Hartmann** (1830 and 1835). Finally, this period saw the first tenuous attempts at a Russian symphony in the two works in the genre by **Mikhail Glinka** (ca. 1824 and 1834), both of which remained incomplete.

The trigger for the symphonic breakthrough of the 1840s appears to have been the first performance of Schubert's "Great" C-major Symphony (D. 944, ?1825–1828) through the efforts of **Robert Schumann** and Mendelssohn on 21 March 1839. The performance created a sensation in the popular musical press, as German critics and foreign correspondents marveled at this latest milestone in the emergent Schubert renaissance (*see* RECEPTION). Although the Philharmonic Society of London balked at Mendelssohn's strenuous efforts to have it performed there in 1840, its publication later that year made it possible for Schubert's voice to join Beethoven's in the symphonic discourse of the second half of the 19th century.

Perhaps tellingly, the symphonic breakthrough of the 1840s emerged first not in the German lands but in France. Berlioz's expansive "dramatic symphony" *Roméo et Juliette* (H. 79/Op. 17, commissioned in December 1838 by **Paganini**) was premiered at the Paris Conservatory on 24 November 1839; it was followed by the first version of the now-little-known royalist *Grande Symphonie funèbre et triomphale* (Grand Funereal and Triumphal Symphony, H. 80/Op. 15) in July 1840 and by Félicien David's extraordinary (and, unfortunately, now-obscure) **exoticist** ode-symphony *Le désert* (The Desert) in 1844. In the German lands, the first major signs of this breakthrough occurred with the composition, performance, and publication of Mendelssohn's symphony-**cantata** *Lobgesang* (MWV A18/Op. 52, 1840, publ. 1841) and A-minor Symphony ("Scottish," MWV N18/Op. 56, begun 1829, comp. 1841–1842, publ. 1843), as well as the composition and performance of Robert Schumann's first two symphonies (opp. 38 and 61, 1841 and 1846) and the first version of his D-minor symphony (1841, later revised and renumbered as "No. 4," Op. 120, 1851). Only after 1839 did symphonic production and publication increase.

The resurgence of the Restoration's symphonic production also occurred elsewhere, resulting in new works by Spohr (three works, 1839–1847) as well as important contributions from composers of the Romantic Generation: Berwald (four works, 1842–1845), **Niels W. Gade** (three works, 1841–1847), Lindblad (the revision of his 1831 First Symphony in November 1839, now including quotations from Schubert's C-major Symphony), and Macfarren (one work, 1839–1840), among many others. Other important milestones in the symphonic history of the *Vormärz* include the publication in score and parts of Berlioz's *Episode in the Life of an Artist* and *Harold in Italy* in 1845 and 1848, respectively, as well as the increasing presence of Beethoven's voice in France via **François-Antoine Habeneck**'s performances with the Orchestre de la Société des Concerts du Conservatoire.

The Romantic Symphony in the Late Romantic Generation, 1848–1870. The third quarter of the 19th century witnessed an even greater revival of the symphony—partly in response to the new ideas introduced in the major works of the 1840s, partly through growing familiarity with (and acceptance of) Beethoven's Ninth Symphony, but mostly through the sense of opportunity and crisis that emerged with the **Revolutions of 1848** and the aesthetic polemics put forward with the emergence of the **New German School**, Richard Wagner's revolutionary tracts, and **Eduard Hanslick**'s treatise *Vom Musikalisch-Schönen* (On the Musically Beautiful, 1854). Already before 1848, composers of symphonies had (and took advantage of) the option of writing works in the genre that were instrumental or vocal, "absolute" or programmatic, abstract or politically topical—but in the post-1848 climate, these and other compositional issues came to be viewed more as imperatives than as choices.

The stimulus was clearly productive. During the years after the mid-century revolutions, composers of the Romantic Generation submitted new works of newly ambitious aesthetic and topical purport—most notably, the Third Symphony ("Rhenish," Op. 97, 1851) of Robert Schumann, the overhauled version of his earlier D-minor Symphony (Op. 120), and the avant-garde *"Faust" Symphony* (LW 19th century, 1856, rev. 1862) and *"Dante" Symphony* (LW 20th century, 1856) of Liszt. This is also the period that witnessed the entry of rising composers of the Late Romantic Generation into the symphonic fray. In France, the changing dynamic produced the two symphonies of **Georges Bizet** (1855 and 1860–1868, rev. 1871) and **Charles Gounod** (1855 and ?1856) and the first two symphonies of **Camille Saint-Saëns** (1853 and 1859), while in the German lands, it yielded **Anton Bruckner**'s first three symphonic attempts (WAB 99 [1863], 100 [1869], and 101 [1866, rev. 1877, 1884, 1889], all published significantly later) and the first three symphonies of **Joachim Raff** (1859–1861, 1861, and 1869) as well as **Johannes Brahms**'s early efforts on his First Symphony (which would be alternately hailed and criticized as "Beethoven's Tenth" when it was finally completed in 1876). Listeners in Great Britain heard new symphonies by **William Sterndale Bennett** (1863–1864) and **Arthur Sullivan** (1866), while those in Central Europe heard the *"Festive" Symphony* of **Bedřich Smetana** (JB 1:59, 1853–1854), the first two symphonies of **Antonín Dvořák** (B. 9 and 12, both 1865), and the first two symphonies of **Zdeněk Fibich** (both 1865, both now at least partially lost). In Scandinavia, the period 1848–1870 yielded the C-minor Symphony of Grieg (EG 119, 1863–1864) as well as five more symphonies by Gade and the First Symphony of **J. S. Svendsen** (1865–1867). And in Russia, it witnessed the birth of the Russian Romantic symphony in the first three symphonies of **Anton Rubinstein** (1850, 1851, and 1855); other symphonies by **Mily Balakirev**

(1864–1866, rev. 1893–1897), **Aleksandr Borodin** (1862–1867), and **Nikolay Rimsky-Korsakov** (1861–1865, rev. 1884); and the First Symphony of **Pyotor Il'yich Tchaikovsky** (1866, rev. 1874).

The Post-Romantic Symphony, 1870–1914. As noted elsewhere in this dictionary, the unification of German and Italian lands during the years leading up to 1870 reduced the **nationalist** fervor of those countries, while France's defeat in the **Franco-Prussian War** engendered both nationalist fervor and a cult of Wagner and Beethoven there. The determination of the United States after the end of its own Civil War in 1865 to forge a new presence on the international cultural stage also led to a surge of nationalism in U.S. music. Russian nationalism continued to flourish primarily in genres other than the symphony, while the Scandinavian countries that had previously been subject to German and Russian musical hegemony strove to develop real musical autonomy. Finally, during the last years of the long 19th century, Great Britain, long celebrated for embracing the European musical luminaries, saw its own serious project determined to develop and celebrate a distinctively English national school of composition.

These events changed the landscape of the symphony during the period 1870–1914. More than ever before, some composers cultivated the symphony as either an "absolute" or programmatic genre whose Beethovenian heritage was to be celebrated, while others viewed it as a venue for large-scale public musical exploration of the deepest, most personal, and most individualized elements of the human psyche, and still others viewed it as a public mode of communication that perhaps voiced individual experience but did so within the rhetoric of collective national identity. The first (post-Beethovenian) of these categories was, naturally enough, evident in the German lands, especially in the symphonies of Johannes Brahms (four works, 1876–1877, 1877, 1883, 1884–1885); the last eight of Bruckner's nine symphonies (1871–1896), the "Manfred" Symphony of Tchaikovsky (1885, after **Lord Byron**); the two "absolute" symphonies of **Richard Strauss** (TrV 94 and 126, 1880 and 1884) and his later *Symphonia domestica* (1902–1903) and *Alpensinfonie* (1911–1915); the Third ("Organ") Symphony of Saint-Saëns (Op. 78, 1886) and the symphonies of **Ernest Chausson** (1889–1890), **César Franck** (1886–1888), and **Vincent d'Indy** (four works, 1870–1918 passim); the three symphonies of **Serge Rachmaninoff** (1895, 1906–1907, and 1935–1938); and the later symphonies of **Jean Sibelius** (nos. 3 through 7, 1907–1924). The landmarks in the second category are the last three symphonies of Tchaikovsky (1878, 1888, and 1893) and the nine completed symphonies and symphony/**song cycle** *Das Lied von der Erde* of **Gustav Mahler** (1888–1909), which consistently commingle the orchestral and choral expansiveness of Beethoven's works in the genre with chamber-like scoring and the intimacy of the **Lied.**

Finally, the symphony as a highly individualized utterance of a distinctive national style is evident in the first two symphonies of Sibelius (1899 and 1901–1902) and the first four symphonies of **Carl Nielsen** (1892–1916); the post-1870 symphonies by Russian composers including Borodin, Anton Rubinstein, Glazunov, and Rimsky-Korsakov; the self-consciously Gallic symphonies of **Théodore Dubois** (1908, 1912, and 1924), **Édouard Lalo** (1874, 1886), **Albéric Magnard** (four symphonies, 1889–1913), and **Charles-Marie Widor** (five works, 1873–1908); the symphonies of **Edward Elgar** (three works, 1907–1933), **Hubert Parry** (five symphonies, 1880–1912), and **Charles Villiers Stanford** (seven symphonies, 1876–1911); and the symphonies of U.S. composers including **George Whitefield Chadwick** (three works, 1881–1894), **John Knowles Paine** (two symphonies, 1875 and 1879), and **Horatio Parker** (1885), among others.

The sheer volume and stylistic diversity of the post-1870 symphonic repertoire reflects not only the polyphony of contemporary voices engaged in that compositional discourse at various points in the history of the symphony as a genre but also other factors, such as the changing individual and national constructions of Beethoven; increasing familiarity with the earlier symphonies of Haydn, Mozart, and Schubert; and significant changes in **performance practice** triggered by the expansion of the modern orchestra, during the early years of the 20th century, beyond the deliberately heterogeneous 50 or 60 players envisioned and used by Beethoven, Mendelssohn, Schumann (or even the 70 envisioned and used by Brahms) into a highly blended instrument comprising more than 100 instrumentalists. These and other factors—most notably the development of technologies for broadcasting and recording sound—led to further radical rethinkings of the genre among composers of the early 20th century, but the contributions of these many and diverse Romantic symphonists enabled the genre to continue to flourish throughout that century and into the current one in its fundamentally Romantic guise—most notably in the work of later symphonists including Leonard Bernstein, Henryk Górecki, Charles Ives, Per Nørgård, Serge Prokofiev, Dmitri Shostakovich, and Ralph Vaughan Williams, among many others. [JMC]

See also "CHORAL" SYMPHONY; CONCERT OVERTURE; CONDUCTOR; "EROICA" SYMPHONY; "PASTORAL" SYMPHONY; PROGRAM (PROGRAMMATIC) MUSIC; PROGRAM SYMPHONY *OR* CHARACTERISTIC SYMPHONY; SYMPHONIC POEM; TONE POEM; "UNFINISHED" SYMPHONY.

SYNAESTHESIA. The aesthetic and cognitive phenomenon whereby a stimulus applied to one sense is associated with a response in one or more other senses. In connection with music, it most commonly denotes associations between color and timbre or color and pitch, though it may also refer to music inspired by visual art (or vice versa) as well as associations between music and any other nonauditory sense or experience (gustatory, olfactory, or tactile). A well-known fictional example based on the phenomenon is found in Marcel Proust's (1871–1922) *À la recherche du temps perdu* (In Search of Lost Time, 1913–1927), which famously associates a "little phrase" from a **sonata** for violin and **piano** by the fictional composer Vinteuil not only with some unspecified element of the music and/or plot of **Richard Wagner**'s *Tristan und Isolde* but also with the taste of a madeleine dipped in tea and the memory of "the mass of the piano-part beginning to emerge in a sort of liquid rippling of sound, multiform but indivisible, smooth yet restless, like the deep blue tumult of the sea, silvered and charmed into a minor key by the moonlight." This so-called Proustian experience, articulating aesthetic and cognitive stimulatory correspondences between timbre and color, harmony and color, musical texture and physical mass, states of matter, and tactile texture, was likely inspired by the Belgian composer Guillaume Lekeu (1870–1894) and either his well-known G-minor Violin Sonata (1892, publ. 1894) or the A-major Violin Sonata (Op. 8, 1886) of **César Franck** and may be regarded as a post-Romantic manifestation of the aesthetic significance of synaesthesia.

Interest in synaesthetic creation, experience, and theory dates back to Classical Antiquity, but it gained new momentum with the Enlightenment's impulse toward universal knowledge verified through empirical experience, most notably in writings by John Locke, Gottfried Wilhelm Leibnitz, and Isaac Newton (1690, 1704, and 1704, respectively) and in the French Jesuit monk Louis Bertrand Castel's (1688–1757) invention and description of several versions of a *clavecin pour les yeux* (ocular keyboard) beginning in 1725. More obviously, Romantic descriptions associating the physical and cognitive association of color and sound with emotion were submitted by Charles Baudelaire (1857 and 1860), J. G. Herder (1772), **E. T. A. Hoffmann** (*Kreisleriana*, 1810), Friedrich Kind (1816), and Ludwig Tieck (1828). Around 1833, Schumann's critical persona Eusebius declared that "the educated musician will be able to derive as much usefulness from the study of a Madonna by Raphael as will a painter from a Mozart symphony," whereupon the more impulsive Florestan replied, "The aesthetics of the two arts are the same; only the material is different."

The repertoire of Romantic compositions demonstrably born of the synaesthetic impulse is vast and diverse. **Liszt**'s *Totentanz* and *Lo Sposalizio* (*Années de pélerinage* II, 1838–1839; publ. 1846), the latter based on Raphael Sanzio's (1483–1520) 1504 painting *The Marriage of the Virgin*, are commonly cited as the first major examples, but they were preceded by **Felix Mendelssohn Bartholdy**'s posthumously published 1830 chorale cantata *O Haupt voll Blut und Wunden* (MWV A8), which was inspired by Antonio del Castillo y Saavedra's (1616–1668) painting *Mary and John Returning Home from Calvary* as well as (arguably) by Robert Schumann's **Carnival**

(1834–1837) and *Kreisleriana* (1838). The concept of synaesthesia is foundational to the theory and practice of *tableaux vivants* (and thus, by extension, to 19th-century practices of staging **oratorios** and other concerted works), to **Richard Wagner**'s theory of the *Gesamtkunstwerk*, and to the practice of describing the music of, for example, **Claude Debussy** as musical **impressionism** as well as to the aesthetic underlying such music. **Aleksandr Scriabin**'s 1910 **tone poem** *Prometheus: The Poem of Fire* was composed for piano, **orchestra**, chorus, and a *clavier à lumières* (color organ). [JMC]

SZYMANOWSKA (NÉE WOŁOWSKA), MARIA AGATA (1789–1831). Polish composer and pianist of the Early Romantic Generation; one of the **long 19th century**'s first touring **virtuoso** pianists. She made her debut as a pianist in Warsaw in 1810 and then traveled to Paris, where she probably performed in the French capital's thriving **salon** culture. In 1810, she married, bearing three children in 1811–1812. She began touring in 1815, traveling first to the major Russian musical cities (Kiev, Moscow, Riga, and St. Petersburg) and then (beginning in 1818) around the Continent: England, France, the German and Italian lands, and Holland. These tours included public and private appearances (the latter both in salons and in private performances for the nobility); some of the greatest performers of the day shared the stage with her, including **Pierre Baillot, Johann Nepomuk Hummel,** and **Giuditta Pasta**. Everywhere she was acclaimed, in language typical of the gendered rhetoric of the day, for her faultless technique, her gentle tone, and her sense of lyricism.

Szymanowska divorced in 1820 but continued touring, together with her children. She returned to her native Warsaw in 1826 and then, in 1827, settled permanently in St. Petersburg, where she had received the title of First Pianist to the Czar in 1822. There she ran an influential salon, concertized, and gave private instruction. Among the notables who admired and publicly praised her were **Luigi Cherubini, John Field, Johann Wolfgang von Goethe,** and **Gioachino Rossini**.

Szymanowska's historical significance resides partly in her life as a touring virtuosa and partly in her contributions as a composer. She authored some 100 compositions and began publishing her works in 1819. Apart from a fanfare for two trumpets and two horns (n.d.), her music is instrumental and vocal **chamber music** of the sort deemed appropriate for women at the time: three instrumental chamber compositions, many works for **piano** solo, and many **songs**. The works for **piano** solo include virtuosic concert **etudes** as well as caprices (*see* CAPRICCIO), **mazurkas, nocturnes, polonaises,** and **preludes**. Her style is similar to that of Field and an apparent influence on that of **Fryderyk Chopin**, particularly noteworthy for its use of unexpected harmonic twists to effect a quick modulation from remote keys back to the tonic within the context of textures that are modeled on those of vocal music (especially **opera**). [JMC]

T

TABLEAU VIVANT (**PL.** *TABLEAUX VIVANTS*). (Fr., "living scene" or "living picture"; Ger., lebendes Bild, *pl.* lebende Bilder.) In the **long 19th century**, a mostly or entirely immobile stage representation of a scene (often based on well-known visual artworks such as paintings or sculptures) presented simultaneously with music, declamation, poetry, or a combination thereof.

The history of the *tableaux vivants* dates to medieval performances in the context of mystery plays or nativity scenes and to the traditions of "attitudes" or *poses plastiques* cultivated in acting and **melodrama** in 17th- and 18th-century theater. It witnessed a new flowering in late Enlightenment aesthetic theory, most notably Denis Diderot's (1713–1784) theories of the theater and Gotthold Ephraim Lessing's (1729–1781) unfinished aesthetic treatise *Laokoon* (1766) as well as Lessing's play *Emilia Galotti* (1772). As theorized and applied during this more recent flowering, *tableaux vivants* achieved expressive power and aesthetic depth through their synthesis of "arbitrary" art forms that convey meaning sequentially, through a temporal succession of events (such as declamation, music, and poetry), with "natural" art forms that convey meaning synoptically (costume, decoration, gesture, painting, and sculpture). "Arbitrary" arts, according to such thought, are able to convey analytical concepts, abstract thoughts, and moral notions but are unable to offer concrete data concerning the external world of the senses; "natural" arts, by contrast, were able to present such information collectively and simultaneously but were unable to clarify its reasoning and import. By synthesizing the two families of art forms in *tableaux vivants*, one relieved each of its handicaps and granted the whole a **synaesthetic** and synergistic expressive depth. The expressive potential of *tableaux vivants* was further amplified by the fact that they were not necessarily entirely stationary: they could employ mime or pantomime to highlight specific moments in the accompanying music or speech, or they could gradually coalesce into or out of their central form as a stationary scene. The latter, represented in works such as Friedrich Kind's (1768–1843) well-known play *Van Dyk's Landleben* (Country Life in Van Dyk's Paintings, 1816) and more recently in Sondheim's 1983 *Sunday in the Park with George* (which animates Georges Seurat's [1859–1891] pointillist masterpiece *Sunday on the Isle of La Grande Jatte*, 1884), are sometimes referred to as *tableaux mouvants* (moving or animated scenes).

During the long 19th century, *tableaux vivants* were sometimes presented as independent phenomena and sometimes incorporated into larger artworks. When presented as independent phenomena, they were sometimes used to allegorize or emphasize the historical or moral significance of a particular occasion and sometimes for entertainment. Allegorical or instructive presentations occurred (to name but three of many examples) in Paris in the 1780s in exhibitions of paintings by Jacques-Louis David (1748–1825) and Jean-Baptiste Isabey (1767–1855), in an 1817 Berlin celebration of the arts with poetry by **Johann Wolfgang von Goethe** and music by Carl Friedrich Rungenhagen (1778–1851), and on the occasion of the first visit to the Prussian capital of the future Russian tsar Nicolas I and his wife, Princess Charlotte of Prussia, using scenes from Thomas Moore's (1779–1852) *Lalla Rookh* with music by **Gaspare Spontini.** Some of the long 19th century's most important composers penned music expressly designed for such presentations: **Aleksandr Borodin** (*In Central Asia*, 1880), **Claude Debussy** (the posthumously published 1901 music for Pierre Louÿs's *Chansons de Bilitis*), **Jean Sibelius** (the music that would eventually become his *Karelia Suite*, 1893), and **Richard Strauss** (*Musik zu lebenden Bildern*, 1892). They could also function as entertainments with decidedly immoral or prurient overtones since such presentations often took painted or sculpted nudes as their visual basis and were often presented to audiences consisting only of men.

Within larger artworks, *tableaux vivants* functioned as staged moments of concentrated illustrative and expressive import. Aside from Lessing's *Emilia Galotti*, notable such instances include Goethe's 1778 play *Der Triumph der Empfindsamkeit* (The Triumph of Emotionalism; music by Carl Eberwein [1786–1868]), his 1809 morality novel *Die Wahlverwandschaften* (The Elective Affinities), and **Victor Hugo**'s 1818 elegy *La Canadienne suspendant au palmier le tombeau de son nouveauné* (The Canadian Woman Hanging Her Dead Newborn from a Palm Tree), the last being a trope on the *stabat mater. Tableaux vivants* and *mouvants* frequently occurred near the ends of acts in **melodramas** and **operas.** One example that is at once well known and obscure is **Carl Maria von Weber**'s *Der Freischütz*: in Kind's libretto, the opera was to be preceded by a *tableaux vivant* featuring the hermit and Agathe and symbolizing purity and goodness; the celebrated Wolf's Glen scene at the end of Act II was a *tableaux mouvant* that antithetically symbolized concentrated evil, and the final scene of Act III was the synthesis of these two moral extremes represented in another *tableau vivant*. Ultimately. Weber excised the work's opening *tableau*, but the aesthetic effectiveness of the remaining scenes set an important precedent for the structural importance of *tableaux vivants* and *mouvants* in Romantic **opera** and provided an important conceptual antecedent for **Richard Wagner**'s theory of the *Gesamtkunstwerk*. (As a child, Wagner had played the role of an angel in private presentations of *tableaux vivants* in Weber's home.) [JMC]

TCHAIKOVSKY [CHAIKOVSKY, CHAYKOVSKY, TSCHAIKOW-SKI], PYOTR [PETER] IL'YICH (1840–1893). Russian composer and **conductor** of the Late Romantic Generation; iconic figure in the "cosmopolitan" variety of Russian **nationalism** represented by, for example, **Anton Rubinstein**. He took **piano** lessons as a child but at age 10 entered the St. Petersburg School of Law, studying there until 1859 and then taking a position as a civil servant. He took classes in music theory in the newly formed Russian Musical Society in 1861 and after being denied a promotion in the civil service applied to the newly opened music school that would later become the St. Petersburg **Conservatory**. There, he studied composition, flute, organ, piano, and theory.

In 1866, Tchaikovsky joined the faculty of the newly opened Moscow Conservatory at the invitation of its founder, **Nikolay Rubinstein**. There, he met **Mily Balakirev** (1868) and the other composers of the **Mighty Handful** and became an ardent Russian nationalist, though their separatist nationalism did not appeal to him and they came to regard him as too tainted by Western influences. By 1875, he had composed four **operas**, two **symphonies**, and his First Piano **Concerto**, also working as music critic for the newspaper *Russkiye vedomosti* (Russian news) from 1872 to 1876 and attending the premiere of **Richard Wagner**'s *Ring of the Nibelung* at the **Bayreuth** Festival in 1876. In 1875–1876, he composed the **ballet** *Lebedinoe ozero* (*Swan Lake*, Op. 20, publ. 1877) produced by the Bolshoy Ballet in the Bolshoy Theater in 1877.

By this point, Tchaikovsky was a social celebrity in Moscow, but despite his generous income, he notoriously overspent and had to request advances from his publisher (Jürgenson). He was also distressed by the little time and energy left for composition by his teaching at the Conservatory. Nearing financial and psychological collapse and despite his homosexuality, in 1877 he married a pupil who was coming into an inheritance, having clarified to her that the union would have to remain platonic. The marriage was a disaster and ended after nine weeks.

Over Rubinstein's objections, Tchaikovsky made arrangements late in 1877 to leave the Conservatory (although his departure would become official only in 1878). In September 1877, he attempted suicide. His fortunes were reversed, however, when the wealthy widow Nadezhda von Meck (1831–1894) out of admiration offered him a generous annual stipend that would allow him to devote himself entirely to composition. The two never met, but the arrangement, which lasted until 1890 and produced one of the great epistolary relationships of Western culture, proved extremely beneficial. He traveled to Italy and Switzerland and there resumed work on two major projects he had begun before marriage—the Fourth Symphony (Op. 36, 1877–1878, publ. 1880) and the **opera** *Eugene Onegin* (after **Aleksandr Pushkin**)—as well as composing the Violin **Concerto** and gathering ideas that would later be used in his *Capriccio Italien* (Op. 45, 1880). His music was still received with skepticism in Paris and Vienna—in particular, the Violin Concerto and the second version of the **concert overture** *Romeo i Dzul'etta* (*Romeo and Juliet*, comp. 1869, rev. 1870, publ. 1871, rev. 1880, publ. 1881) were rejected by the Austrian capital's audiences and the leading critic **Eduard Hanslick**. Nevertheless, by the early 1880s he was widely regarded in Russia as the country's leading composer and was eagerly watched abroad.

Several years as a widely traveled public figure had made Tchaikovsky yearn for peace and quiet. This desire he fulfilled beginning in 1885, establishing himself as a resident of the rural town of Kiln (about 60 miles from Moscow) and living and working there in isolation. In 1887, he made his public debut as a conductor with a Moscow production of a revised version of his early opera *Kuznets Vakula* (Vakula the Smith, 1873, publ. 1876, rev. 1878, rev. and publ. 1885 as *Cherevichki* [The Slippers]). He was soon in demand as a conductor, performing in Berlin, Cologne, Frankfurt am Main, Geneva, Hamburg, London, Moscow, Paris, and Prague in 1888 and 1889. After the successful premiere in 1890 of *Spyashchaya krasavitsa* (The Sleeping Beauty, Op. 66, comp. 1889, publ. 1890), he went to Florence to complete a new opera, *Pikovaya dama* (The Queen of Spades, after Pushkin). He accomplished this, and the new opera was slated for performance in St. Petersburg beginning in December, but on 30 September, he received a letter from von Meck ending her patronage and the relationship. The letter is lost; her grounds for terminating the friendship are variously attributed to purported bankruptcy, illness, or pressure from her family. In any case, the event was deeply hurtful to Tchaikovsky, and the loss of income put him in a financial position from which he had been removed for 15 years.

Still, his reputation continued to grow. On 5 April 1891 he conducted a successful concert of his own works in Paris, and on 17 April he left for the United States, where he was enthusiastically received as a conductor and composer in concerts in New York City (where he conducted his *Festival Coronation March* [1883] in the opening concert of the city's New Music Hall, later renamed Carnegie Hall) as well as in Baltimore, Buffalo, Niagara Falls, Philadelphia, and Washington, D.C. The coming year witnessed further travels and conducting in Brussels, St. Petersburg, Prague, and elsewhere as well as the premieres of the opera *Iolantha* and the ballet *The Nutcracker* and the composition of his final (Sixth) symphony (Op. 74). On 1 June 1893, he conducted his Fourth Symphony with the Royal Philharmonic Society in London, and on 13 June, together with **Arrigo Boito, Max Bruch, Edvard Grieg** (in absentia), and **Camille Saint-Saëns**, he received an Honorary Doctorate of Music from Cambridge University.

Tchaikovsky's Sixth Symphony was premiered under his baton in St. Petersburg on 28 October 1893, but a few days later, he began complaining of stomach pains. He was diagnosed with cholera on 2 November and died of the disease on 6 November. Although the diagnosis itself and the means by which he contracted the disease (drinking unboiled water) are uncontested, the circumstances of his death are not. Tchaikovsky had made unwanted sexual advances on a young man of high birth, and this scandalous news was about to be published. Some scholars have argued that Tchaikovsky's fellow alumni of the School of Law compelled him to drink the water before a "Tribunal of Honor" rather than bring dishonor on himself, themselves, their alma mater, and their profession. Others argue that the deadly drink was consumed in an innocent but fatal moment of carelessness. The evidence for suicide does not withstand scrutiny and no doubt appeals in part because of its sensationalistic qualities, but the other side of the argument is also not entirely convincing.

Today, the Western world knows Tchaikovsky's music better than that of any other Russian composer. Although the pervasive and central genre of his career as a composer was opera—he was constantly in search of a suitable libretto and completed 11 surviving works in the genre between 1868 and 1891—only two of these (*Eugene Onegin* and *The Queen of Spades*, 1890) have retained a place in the repertoire. His completed large-scale public music also includes three ballets (*Swan Lake, The Sleeping Beauty*, and *The Nutcracker*), seven sets of **incidental music** for plays ranging from Pushkin to **William Shakespeare**, a **melodrama**, and music for a *tableau vivant* as well as six symphonies, four independent orchestral **suites** and a suite from *The Nutcracker*, three piano concertos, a violin concerto, and seven smaller works for solo instrument with orchestra. Seven of his 19 other works for orchestra (the concert overtures *1812, Francesca da Rimini, Hamlet*, and *Romeo and Juliet*, plus the *Slavonic March* and the *Italian Capriccio*) have remained staples of the concert repertoire. His instrumental **chamber music** includes three **string quartets** published during his lifetime (opp. 11, 22, and 30; 1871, 1873–1874, and 1876, respectively) and a posthumously published **string quartet** (1865), a **piano trio** (Op. 50, 1881–1882), the well-known string **sextet** titled *Souvenir de Florence* (Op. 70, 1890), and 18 published *opera* of works for **piano** solo and **piano duet**, plus numerous unpublished, lost, or posthumously published instrumental **chamber** works. His concerted vocal music includes four **cantatas** for soloists, chorus, and orchestra; 19 **part-songs** and a cappella choral works, and 14 published *opera* of **songs** and vocal duets as well as unpublished and lost works of this type. He also composed *Albumblätter* and musical jokes and wrote poetry as well as a

Guide to the Practical Study of Harmony (1871), a *Short Manual of Harmony* (1875), and a short autobiography (1889). The reasons for the popularity of his music are obvious: he was a superb melodist and **orchestrator**, and the deeply emotional, often confessional nature of his style makes his music both accessible and emblematic of the heights and depths of Romantic passion. [JMC]

TELLEFSEN, THOMAS DYKE ACLAND (1823–1874). Norwegian composer and pianist of the Romantic Generation. A native of Trondheim, Tellefsen distinguished himself in his youth; his public debut on **piano** was in 1841. Tellefsen studied in Paris first with Charlotte Thygeson (1811–1872) and **Friedrich Kalkbrenner**, and in the late 1840s he studied with and became close to **Fryderyk Chopin**. Tellefsen gave his first Parisian concert in 1851. Paris remained his home for rest of his life, but he also gave concerts in England, Sweden, Norway, and elsewhere through the early 1860s. Tellefsen was significant as a piano teacher in Paris. Chopin's influence shined not only in his repertoire but also in his compositional output, which is mainly for piano and features many **mazurkas**, several **nocturnes** and **waltzes**, and a *Grande Polonaise*. Other significant works include his two piano **concertos**, his **Piano Trio** Op. 31, two violin **sonatas**, and a cello sonata. [RK]

THALBERG, SIGISMOND (1812–1871). Pianist and composer of the Romantic Generation; one of the greatest and most widely revered **virtuosos** of the **long 19th century** and rival of **Franz Liszt**. Born in Switzerland, Thalberg went to Vienna in 1822 and studied music there with **Johann Nepomuk Hummel** and **Simon Sechter**. He began touring internationally at age 18, encountering and studying with **Friedrich Kalkbrenner** (Paris) and **Ignaz Moscheles** (London). In 1837, Thalberg's popularity had risen to such an extent that an argument erupted in the *Revue musicale* over his status, with **François-Joseph Fétis** coming out pro-Thalberg and Liszt and **Hector Berlioz** contra. Thalberg toured South and North America in the 1850s and briefly lived in the United States before retiring in Posillipo, Italy. Thalberg's expertise as a performer was his balance of technical fireworks with melodic gracefulness; he made frequent use of the so-called three-hand technique. Thalberg's reputation as a composer rests largely on his **piano** music (which constitutes the overwhelming majority of his output), especially his **fantasias** on themes from **operas**. Among those, the most successful was Thalberg's *Fantasy on Rossini's "Moïse,"* Op. 33. [RK]

THEMATIC TRANSFORMATION, THEMATIC METAMORPHO-SIS. (Ger., Themenverwandlung or Themenmetamorphose.) Term for the process of altering a theme over the course of a work so as to change its character without altering its identity. It differs from traditional thematic/ motivic development in that traditional processes typically return to the theme's original or primary form, whereas in thematic transformation, the altered form is autonomous; indeed, in some instances, the altered version of the theme is the goal or telos of the process launched at the outset, so that the original version is best regarded not as a source for elaboration but rather as an incomplete or unfulfilled embryo of a thematic concept that will be revealed later. During the **long 19th century**, thematic transformation was a favorite means of enhancing the unity and cohesion of an **opera** or instrumental work; in the case of opera and **program music**, it could also be used to delineate character and trace the **narrative** progress of the drama or plot archetype.

In general terms, thematic transformation is closely related to the notion of **variation** sets and has its roots in 17th-century dance **suites** as well as other works that base multiple movements or themes on shared material (such as so-called monothematic **sonata forms**). It also appears for dramatic purposes in Act II of **Wolfgang Amadeus Mozart**'s *Così fan tutte* (Thus Do All Women, K. 588, 1790) and perhaps for narrative ones in the first movement of **Franz Joseph Haydn**'s Symphony No. 103 ("Drumroll," 1795), when the slow introduction returns in transformed version at the end of the movement. As a means for **organic** unity—one of its primary functions in Romantic music—it appears in the first movement of **Beethoven**'s **Piano Sonata** No. 8 ("Pathétique," Op. 13, 1797–1798, publ. 1799), the first movement of his **"Eroica" Symphony** (1803–1805, publ. 1806), and certain works of **Franz Schubert** (the last two symphonies, D. 759 [1822] and 944 [?1825–1828], and the A-minor String Quartet, D. 804/Op. 29, no. 1, [1824]).

Thematic transformation was first widely cultivated as a unifying structural device by composers of the Romantic Generation. Among those the first composers to employ the technique consistently was **Felix Mendelssohn Bartholdy**, whose first three programmatic **concert overtures** (*A Midsummer Night's Dream*, MWV P3/Op. 21 [1826, publ. 1832], *Calm Sea and Prosperous Voyage*, MWV P5/Op. 27 [1828, publ. 1835], and *The Hebrides*, MWV P7/Op. 26 [1829, publ. 1833]) and Third Symphony ("Scottish," MWV N18 [begun 1829, comp. 1841–1842, publ. 1843]) are all based on the principle of thematic transformation, the last at least implicitly narrative in function. A more explicitly narrative application was famously pursued by **Hector Berlioz** in the **idée fixe** of his *Episode in the Life of an Artist* (H. 48/ Op. 14[a] [1830, publ. 1834]), and the technique is central to the dramatic and musical structure of his *La damnation de **Faust*** (H. 111/Op. 24 [1845–1846, publ. 1854]). Also in the Romantic Generation, it was employed by **Robert Schumann** in the first movement of the C-major **Fantasy** (Op. 17 [1836–1838, publ. 1839]) and across the whole of his Second Symphony (Op. 61 [1845–1846, publ. 1847]), both works basing the process of transformation on the last song of Beethoven's *An die ferne Geliebte* and implying a narrative process of gradual revelation rather than mere variation or elaboration.

Within the Romantic Generation, however, thematic transformation is most famously associated with the music of **Franz Liszt**, who employed the technique for philosophical as well as structural and narrative purposes in his 13 **symphonic poems** (LW G1–4, G6–7, G9–10, G13, G15, G17, G22, G38 [1847–1848, 1881–1883]) as well as his *"Faust" Symphony* (LW G12 [1854–1857, rev. and publ. 1861]) and other works. In the Late Romantic Generation, it was also employed by **Johannes Brahms** (most notably in the Horn **Trio** [Op. 40, 1865–1866], in which the four movements are unified by a theme based on a **folk song** of autobiographical significance). In the Modern Romantic Generation, influenced by **Richard Wagner**'s closely related concept of the *Leitfaden* (*see* LEITMOTIV), the technique of thematic transformation also became a foundational principle in **Richard Strauss**'s **tone poems** (opp. 20, 24, 25, 28, 30, and 40, 1886–1898) and **program symphonies** (opp. 53 and 64, 1902–1903 and 1911–1915). It also figures prominently in **John Knowles Paine**'s Second Symphony ("Spring," Op. 34, 1879–1880) and in **Edward Elgar**'s *The Dream of Gerontius* (Op. 38, 1900). Important late uses of the technique are founded in Paul Hindemith's *Symphonic Metamorphosis on Themes of Weber* (1943) and Richard Strauss's *Metamorphosen for 23 Solo Strings* (TrV 290, 1945). [JMC]

THIBAUT, ANTON FRIEDRICH JUSTUS (1772–1840). Legal scholar, professor, amateur musician, and early-music advocate of the Early Romantic Generation. In addition to having a distinguished academic career in jurisprudence, Thibaut was an amateur singer who made a hobby of collecting copies of music from the previous 300 years, above all **folk song** and sacred choral works. His collection began as early as 1802, when he moved to Jena. In 1811, six years after his appointment as law chair at Heidelberg University, Thibaut founded an amateur early music chorus, the repertoire of which drew from his library and featured such composers as **Giovanni Pierluigi da Palestrina** and **George Frideric Handel**. The chorus attracted increasing attention; in the 1820s, its rehearsals attracted such visiting participants as **Felix Mendelssohn Bartholdy, Robert Schumann,** and **Louis Spohr**. In 1825, Thibaut published *Über Reinheit der Tonkunst* (On the Purity of the Musical Art, 1825), which argued that church music of such 16th-century masters as Palestrina, Orlande de Lassus (1530–1594), and

Cristóbal de Morales (1500–1553) was composed in a style unsurpassed in its suitability for religious contexts. This publication was significant in the development of the **Cecilian movement**, particularly in Germany. [RK]
   See also BACH REVIVAL, BACH AWAKENING, BACH RENAIS-SANCE; HISTORICISM.

THIRD REPUBLIC, THIRD FRENCH REPUBLIC. French government that existed from the fall of the **Commune** of Paris to 1940, ending with the fall of France to German troops in 1940. The Republic was created by means of complex maneuvers by the Legitimists (who supported continuation of the Bourbon dynasty), Orléanists (who supported continuation of the rule of Louis Philippe), and a small number of Bonapartists; the Republic was firmly established via the Constitutional Laws of 1875, which established parliamentary supremacy. In music, it supported not only the rise of a strong new sense of French **nationalism** but also a flourishing of state- and other publicly sponsored cultural initiatives in virtually all aspects of musical enterprise and endeavor. [JMC]
   See also OPERETTA, OPERATTA; xref href="C16-O.xml#ORPHEON" base="C16-O.xml#ORPHEON"/>; PASDELOUP, JULES (ÉTIENNE) (1819–1887); SOCIÉTÉ NATIONALE DE MUSIQUE.

THOMAS, (CHARLES LOUIS) AMBROISE (1811–1886). French composer, best known today for his light **operas**. He studied piano and composition with Pierre-Joseph-Guillaume Zimmermann (1785–1853) and **Jean-François Lesueur** at the Paris **Conservatory** from 1828 to 1832, taking first prizes in **piano** and harmony in 1829 and 1830 and winning the coveted **Prix de Rome** in 1832. Beginning with *La double échelle* (The Step Ladder, 1837), which won the admiration of **Hector Berlioz** and ran to 187 performances at the Opéra-Comique, plus other performances in Belgium, Berlin, London, New Orleans, and Vienna, and the **ballet** *La gypsy* (after Miguel de Cervantes's [1547–1616] short story *La gitanilla*, 1613), he had numerous works performed at the Opéra-Comique between his return to Paris in 1835 and 1849, when his *Le Caïd* (The Ringleader, a spoof of Italian opera) renewed his reputation as one of France's leading composers of light opera. His 1850 *Le songe d'une nuit d'été* (The Midsummer Night's Dream) has little to do with the eponymous play but does invest in the Romantic cult of **William Shakespeare**, having Elizabeth I, Falstaff, and Shakespeare himself in the cast of characters.
   In recognition of this success, Thomas was elected to the Académie des Beaux-Arts in 1851 and named professor of composition at the Conservatory in 1852, a post he held until he was named director of the institution in 1871. His opera *Mignon* (1866), based very loosely on **Johann Wolfgang von**

Goethe's *Wilhelm Meisters Lehrjahre*, ran to more than 1,000 performances at the Opéra-Comique, and his **grand opera** *Hamlet* (1868; **libretto** after Alexandre Dumas *père*'s translation of Shakespeare) ranks as his masterpiece, notable not only for the integrity with which it adapts its literary source but also for its vivid character delineations, its integration of the overture into the plot, and its colorful orchestration.

Although his reputation today rests largely on his operas, Thomas also composed a sizable number of sacred and secular choral works (including a **Requiem**, 1833, publ. 1835), much vocal and instrumental **chamber music**, several **orchestral** works, and pieces for piano. His pupils included **Daniel-François-Esprit Auber**, **Théodore Dubois**, **César Franck**, **Gabriel Fauré**, and **Jules Massenet**. [JMC]

THOMAS, THEODORE (CHRISTIAN FRIEDRICH) (1835–1905). German American violinist and **conductor**, founder of the Chicago Symphony **Orchestra**, and advocate for high-quality concert fare in the United States. Born in the North Sea town of Esens to a musician father, young Thomas was a talented violinist of regional note. The Thomas family emigrated to New York City in 1845. Thomas spent his teenage years in various orchestras, sometimes as conductor, in New York and elsewhere in the United States. Highlights of this period include stints in **Louis Jullien**'s orchestra and with the New York Philharmonic. He led the New York Academy of Music beginning in the late 1850s when he was needed as a replacement, and in 1862 he began conducting an orchestra of his own, presenting such progressive fare as the U.S. premiere of the **overture** to **Richard Wagner**'s *Der fliegende Holländer* (The Flying Dutchman, WWV 63, 1843).

Between 1862 and 1875, Thomas was extremely active, leading an annual concert series in Central Park and also cultivating an appetite for orchestral music in the United States and Canada with regular tours. Beginning in 1876, Thomas initiated several annual music festivals built around large-scale choral-orchestral performances of such works as **George Frideric Handel**'s *Messiah* and **Johann Sebastian Bach**'s *St. Matthew Passion*; these included events in Philadelphia, Cincinnati, and New York City. Thomas conducted the New York Philharmonic from 1877 until 1891, when he moved to Chicago on an invitation to conduct a new permanent resident orchestra supported by a team of businessmen—one of whom was a brother of pianist **Amy Fay**. Further solidifying that family connection was his marriage to the Fays' sister Rose in 1890. Thomas's post in Chicago was his pinnacle, and it was the last position of his life; in 1904, just before he died, Thomas gave his first concerts in Chicago's newly completed Orchestra Hall. [RK]

TOMÁŠEK, VÁCLAV (JAN KŘTITEL) (1774–1850). Bohemian composer of the Early Romantic Generation, once called a "musical pope" of Prague by **Eduard Hanslick**. Trained on violin as a child in eastern Bohemia, Tomášek went to Prague for secondary school in 1790–1794 and studied at Charles University in 1794–1797. Tomášek taught himself **piano** during these years with little help from teachers; by the late 1790s, he was composing and performing in **salons**. The success of Tomášek's **ballade** *Leonore* (Op. 12, 1801, on the poem by Gottfried August Bürger [1747–1794]) helped build his reputation, and in 1806–1824 he was court composer and family music tutor to Count Georg von Buquoy.

After moving back to Prague in 1822, Tomášek taught music; among his students were Hanslick and **Václav Voříšek**. By then a leader in Prague's musical life, Tomášek also led an important weekly salon beginning in the 1830s that was visited by such luminaries as **Hector Berlioz**, Muzio Clementi (1752–1832), **Clara Schumann**, and **Richard Wagner**. Tomášek was strongly impressed by **Wolfgang Amadeus Mozart** and regarded his 1790 encounter with *Don Giovanni* as formative; he also became acquainted with **Johann Sebastian Bach**'s music through **Johann Nikolaus Forkel** in 1801. These influences can be detected in his compositions; highlights among these are an **opera**, a few Masses and a **Requiem**, three **symphonies**, three **string quartets**, and 52 simply composed *eclogues* for piano. [RK]

TONADA. A general Spanish term for a Spanish folk or folk-like text of four-, five-, or 10-line strophes, with or without refrain, set to music of a prevailingly lyrical character. Unlike the **villancico**, the *tonada* was usually set for one, two, or at most three solo voices. Its textual content could be either sacred or (more commonly) secular. When cast as four-line strophes with refrain, the strophes and refrain often employ contrasting tempos and/or meters. Like **chorales**, **hymns**, and other **folk songs**, the text of any given *tonada* could be used with any tune of the same form, so that the genre's texts and tunes intermingled freely by means of the practice of contrafactum. [JMC]

See also *TONADILLA, TONADILLA ESCÉNICA.*

TONADILLA, TONADILLA ESCÉNICA. (Sp., "little song," "little song on stage.") An **intermezzo** sung and/or danced between the acts of a serious play or (more rarely) **opera** in Spanish theater of the late 18th and early 19th centuries. Like the *tonada*, the *tonadilla* tended to be of a folk-like character and usually took the form of a strophic **song** (with or without refrain). During the late 18th century, *tonadillas* were often used at the conclusion of short theatrical plays dealing with everyday life (known as *sainetes*). They were exported from the Spanish theater to that of Latin America.

During the later 18th century, it became common to expand the number of dramatic voices in the *tonadilla* from a single voice to two, three, or four voices, each acting out a different character or role, and to perform a number of *tonadillas* in sequence to create new interactions among characters and a new, often satirical plot. The result was a lighthearted or satirical musical play performed between the acts of a serious one, much like the intermezzo of the 18th-century Italian theater. Such staged adaptations of the *tonadilla* became known as *tonadillas escénicas* and were performed over and over in various locations. More than 200 are known to have been written between 1790 and 1814, although only the texts survive for most of these. [JMC]

TONE POEM. (Ger., *Tondichtung*.) **Richard Strauss**'s preferred term for his one-movement programmatic **orchestral** compositions that followed in the tradition of the **symphonic poem** established by **Franz Liszt**. The implicit reason for the generic distinction was to further distance these works from conventions of symphonic form (as Liszt had decided on the term *symphonic poem* in order to distance his compositions semantically from the conventions of the programmatic **concert overture**, thereby downplaying the **sonata form** that underlay many of the works while emphasizing the technique of **thematic transformation** and the inherent oneness of his compositions' musical and extramusical content). Strauss's works also draw on a wider range of generic prototypes than do works designated "symphonic poem." Among these other prototypes are rondo (*Till Eulenspiegel*), **concerto** combined with double theme and **variations** (*Don Quixote*), and **symphony** (*Ein Heldenleben*).

The term *tone poem* is not Strauss's exclusively, but neither did it achieve the common currency of the Lisztian designation—a paradox since Strauss's works are today better known than their Lisztian antecedents. Strauss's own works in the genre include *Macbeth* (TrV 163/Op. 23, 1881, rev. 1891), *Don Juan* (TrV 156/Op. 20, 1888–1889), *Tod und Verklärung* (Death and Transfiguration, TrV 158/Op. 24, 1888–1889), *Till Eulenspiegels lustige Streiche* (Till Eulenspiegel's Merry Pranks, TrV 171/Op. 28, 1894–1895), *Also sprach Zarathustra* (Thus Spake Zarathustra, TrV 176/Op. 30, 1895–1896), *Don Quixote* (TrV 184/Op. 35, 1897–1898), and *Ein Heldenleben* (A Heroic Life, TrV 190/Op. 40, 1897–1898). Other composers' works that explicitly invoke the Straussian model include Arnold Bax (1883–1953) (*Moy Mell*, 1918), **Jean Sibelius** (*Finlandia*, 1905; *The Bard*, 1914; and *Tapiola*, 1926), Arnold Schoenberg (*Pelleas und Melisande*, 1920), and George Gershwin (*An American in Paris*, 1929). [JMC]

TOPIC. (from Gr. *topos*, pl. *topoi*; literally, "place, region.") Appropriated from classical rhetoric, a conventionalized expression or passage in a text which becomes a resource for allusion and/or intertextual meaning in other texts; an important species or category. In the music of the **long 19th century**, topics may be regarded as extensions of the Baroque and Classical emphasis on the discipline of rhetoric and its attendant use of musical figures—that is, the use of conventionalized musical gestures to convey a general but relatively stable sense of meaning in varying contexts. Musical topics are crucial aspects of the ways in which **program music** and characteristic music convey their extramusical or poetic content, and they lend programmatic or characteristic suggestive power to works not explicitly presented as program music.

Some of these Romantic topics may be regarded as *types* (specific categories of musical organization or form that carry certain generic, musical, or extramusical associations) and others as *styles*. Most obvious among topical *types* are the various dance forms that were cultivated in music of the long 19th century. For example, a **waltz** possessed one set of connotations; a *Ländler*, a different set; a minuet, still others; and a mazurka, still others. Although these dance types share important musical features (they are all triple-meter dances typically organized into paired, symmetrical periods), differences in their other musical characteristics lend each a different set of connotations: the waltz is a couples' dance often associated with ballroom dancing; the *Ländler* is a dance more rustic in character and stereotypically evocative of rural or country life; a minuet is a courtly dance that was increasingly used in the long 19th century to evoke courtly life, refinement, and/or archaicness; and a mazurka is a dance associated with Poland and Polish peasant life.

The topical *styles* of Romantic music are the various harmonic, melodic, orchestrational, or textural conventions that were widely cultivated during the long 19th century. Most often, these styles acquire meaning and differentiations of meaning through aggregations of features or traits. For example, crisp, dotted rhythms in unison, open fifths, or at the octave tend to evoke military or martial contexts when presented in quick tempos but courtly pomp or fanfare when presented in slower ones. Homorhythmic, treble-dominated textures with predominantly conjunct melodies tend to suggest the hymn or **chorale** when they are presented in slow tempo and their phrases are irregular in length, but similar music is evocative of **folk song** when its tempo is moderate or quick and its phrase structure more balanced or regular. Imitative contrapuntal textures with closely spaced entrances at irregular intervals and a cappella or *colla parte* scoring tend to evoke the *stile antico* polyphony associated with the Roman Catholic Church during the late Renaissance and, by extension, with the idealized or romanticized notion of purity of musical expression associated with the **Cecilian movement**, whereas contrapuntal structures with more widely spaced entries in tonal answers, often episodic in form, in the long 19th century tend to evoke the music of **J. S. Bach** and the suggestion of conflict, strife, or struggle. Florid, treble-dominated textures with opportunities for melodic filigree or written-out ornamentation in moderate or slow tempo over an arpeggiated accompaniment, especially when written for piano solo, can suggest a **nocturne** in the style of **John Field** or **Fryderyk Chopin**, and so on. Among the most important styles for Romantic music are *empfindsamer Stil*, epic style, brilliant style, military style, hunt style, Ossianic style (*see* OSSIAN), singing style, strict or learned style, *style hongrois*, and Turkish style or *alla turca* (*see* JANISSARY MUSIC).

Musical topics, whether they be types or styles, can also provide essential information concerning broader issues such as **performance practice** and interpretation, often serving as tools for communicating or suggesting issues such as politics, nationalism, or (more broadly) interstices between popular and learned culture. Topics are inherently interwoven with other compositional practices and disciplines, including hermeneutics, intertextuality, **narrative**, rhetoric, and semeiotics. [JMC]

TOTENTANZ. (*Todtentanz*; Eng., "dance of the dead," Fr., danse macabre.) Literary, musical, and pictorial **topic** that arose in the 14th century contemporaneous with the Black Death and the Hundred Years' War and became a frequent theme in Romantic artists' and composers' fascination with death. The *Totentanz* (often translated more freely as "dance of death") typically personified Death as a dancing skeleton or corpse leading a procession of groups of living figures, usually grouped according to order of social precedence. The earliest literary manuscript on this subject originated in Spain (*Dança general de la muerte*, ca. 1400), and the earliest recorded pictorial treatments emerged in the 14th century: a fresco from the school of Orcagna (pseud. Andrea di Cione [1308–1368]) titled *Il trionfo della morte* (The Triumph of Death, 1344–1345); a series of paintings (destroyed 1699) dating from 1424 in the Cimetière des Innocents, Paris; a painting in the old St. Paul's Cathedral (destroyed 1666) from around 1450; and a series of prints published in Paris in 1485.

For 19th-century composers, the most important pictorial sources of the *Totentanz* were the so-called *Lübeck Totentanz* (1463), Hans Holbein the Younger's [1397–1543] series of 50 woodprints titled *Bilder des Todes* (Scenes of Death, ca. 1523–1524; publ. Lyons, 1538), and perhaps the Speuerbrücke (Speuer Bridge) in Lucerne, Switzerland, which contains a series of 67 paintings on the subject prepared around 1625–1635 under the supervision of the painter Kaspar Meglinger (1595–ca. 1670). Though less frequently discussed in the secondary musicological literature on the *Totentanz*, Meglinger's **cycle** was the largest pictorial illustration of the subject and would have been familiar to most 19th-century composers who dealt with the subject in their works. **Johann Wolfgang von Goethe**'s **ballad** *Der Todtentanz* (1815) likewise may have exerted a greater influence than is generally known.

Romantic explicitly titled musical engagements with the dance of the dead include ballad settings of Goethe's poem by **Carl Loewe** (Op. 44, no. 3, 1835), Wilhelm Berger (1861–1911; Op. 86, 1903), and Felix Woyrsch (1860–1944; Op. 51, 1905); **songs** by **Camille Saint-Saëns** (with orchestra, 1872/1873); **symphonic poems** by **Georges Kastner** (1852), **Franz Liszt** (for **piano** and orchestra; 2 versions, 1847–1862), and Saint-Saëns (Op. 40; 1874/1875); and **character pieces** for piano by Máximo Marchal (Op. 48, 1861) and **Joachim Raff** (Op. 181, 1890). To this list may be appended tropes on the theme, such as **Franz Schubert**'s *Der Tod und das Mädchen* (D. 531) and D-minor **String Quartet** (D. 810), the fifth movement of **Hector Berlioz**'s *Episode in the Life of an Artist* (1830–1843), **Adolphe Adam**'s ballet *Giselle* (1841/1848), **Modest Mussorgsky**'s *Songs and Dances of Death* (1875–1877), and **Gustav Mahler**'s *Das klagende Lied* (1878–1880/1888–1889). The most important of the explicitly titled works is probably Liszt's composition, the final version of which is subtitled "paraphrase on the **Dies irae**" and the first version of which was based on the chant setting of Psalm 129/130. The scholarly literature has concentrated on the visual treatments of the *Totentanz* theme by Orcagna and Holbein as sources of inspiration for Liszt in this work; however, the chronology and circumstances of the work's genesis suggest that Goethe's poem and the Speuer Bridge (which Liszt saw in 1835) deserve more attention than is generally acknowledged in this regard. Saint-Saëns's symphonic poem and song both draw on a well-known poem by Henri Cazalis (1840–1909) that was similar to Goethe's ballad. [JMC]

See also REQUIEM.

TRIO, PIANO. (Fr., trio pour piano, violon et violoncelle [nomenclature varies according to scoring]; Ger., Klaviertrio.) Generally, an ensemble consisting of **piano** and two other instruments or a composition written for it; a category of instrumental **chamber music**. During the **long 19th century**, works designated as piano trios were typically original compositions in **sonata plan**, but composers also transcribed **symphonies** and other large-ensemble works for the medium and used it in other genres, most notably **variation** sets (e.g., **Ludwig van Beethoven**'s Op. 44 or **Carl Maria von Weber**'s *Variations on the Air "Woher mag diess wohlkommen?" from the Opera "Samori" by Abbé Vogler*, J. 43/Op. 6, 1804) or collections of **character pieces** (e.g., **Niels W. Gade**'s *Noveletten*, Op. 29, 1854, or **Robert Schumann**'s *Phantasiestücke*, Op. 88, 1850).

Most piano trios typically entrust the non-keyboard parts to one treble instrument and one instrument in the tenor or baritone range. Although the usual scoring for such works was for violin, cello, and piano, other combinations were also used: violin, viola, and piano; two violins and piano; flute, cello, and piano; clarinet, cello, and piano (usually known as a *clarinet trio*); or violin, horn, and piano (usually known as a *horn trio*). In keeping with the tradition of **Hausmusik** as it was cultivated during the **Restoration** and beyond, some piano trios also specify ad libitum substitutions for one or (rarely) both of the nonkeyboard instruments (e.g., Beethoven's op. 11 trio [1798] specifies that the treble part is for either clarinet or violin, and **Johannes Brahms's** op. 40 trio [1866] specifies that the tenor part is for either horn or cello).

As a genre, the piano trio is descended from the 18th-century duo **sonata**, in which the bulk of the musical interest is invested in the keyboard instrument, while the other parts were geared largely toward amateur players and frequently doubled material in the piano *colla parte*. The piano trios of **Franz Joseph Haydn** and **Wolfgang Amadeus Mozart** retain these essential traits; early editions of them and contemporaneous works similarly scored frequently designated them as "sonatas for the pianoforte with accompaniments of violin and cello." Greater autonomy for the non-keyboard parts emerges in the piano trios of Beethoven's Early Vienna Period (opp. 1 and 11, 1795 and 1798) and his arrangement for piano trio (Op. 38, 1805) of the celebrated **Septet** (Op. 20, 1802). His most important contributions to the genre, however, are the three trios published during the renewed flourishing of chamber music characteristic of the **Restoration** (opp. 96 and 97, both publ. 1816). Other important contributions by composers of the Early Romantic Generation were made by **Franz Berwald** (four works, 1851–1854), **Adrien Boieldieu** (1800), **Carl Czerny** (eight works, 1820–1850), **Johann Nepomuk Hummel** (10 works, 1792–1822), **Friedrich Kalkbrenner** (five works, 1810–1841), **Heinrich Marschner** (seven works, 1823–1855), **Ignaz Moscheles** (1830), **Franz Schubert** (D. 898 and 929, both comp. ?1828 and publ. posthumously), and **Louis Spohr** (five works, 1842–1852).

A decisive step moving the genre from its traditional orientation toward amateur musicians was made with the two piano trios of **Felix Mendelssohn Bartholdy** (MWV Q29 and Q33/opp. 49 and 66, 1840 and 1846), the first of which prompted **Robert Schumann** to dub Mendelssohn "the most brilliant musician [of the 19th century] to penetrate the contradictions of the age and the first to reconcile them." Other contributions from the Romantic Generation were penned by **Fryderyk Chopin** (1832), **Félicien David** (three works, 1857), **Fanny Hensel** (1846, publ. posth.), **Adolf von Henselt** (1851), **Ferdinand Hiller** (six works, 1835–1879), **Franz Lachner** (two works, 1828 and

1830), **Bernhard Molique** (two works, 1846 and 1858), **Joachim Raff** (four works, 1864–1871), **Clara Schumann** (1847), and **Robert Schumann** (three works, 1848–1852).

On the whole, the corpus of piano trios produced in the first half of the 19th century generated a wide range of new expressive capabilities, most obviously evident in the frequent subdivision of the trio ensemble into smaller duo ensembles and occasional solo/unaccompanied passages: Hensel, Mendelssohn, and Clara and Robert Schumann in particular exploited poignant and occasionally **virtuosic** passages for piano solo, duets between the stringed instruments with subordinate piano accompaniment, and passages that function as if they were excerpted from a violin sonata, cello sonata, or other form of duo sonata. The interplay of these various ensemble textures is central to the piano trio as it was cultivated around 1850 and later. In the Late Romantic Generation, the most important piano trios are those of Brahms (three trios for violin, cello, and piano, 1854–1887; one for violin, horn or cello, and piano, 1866; and one for clarinet or viola, cello, and piano, 1892), **Antonín Dvořák** (three surviving works, 1880–1883), and **Pyotor Il'yich Tchaikovsky** (1882). Others were composed by **Max Bruch** (1858), **Théodore Dubois** (two works, 1904 and 1911), **César Franck** (five works, 1834–1844), **Édouard Lalo** (three works, ca. 1850–1881), **Hubert Parry** (three works, 1879–1893), **Carl Reinecke** (two works, ca. 1854 and ca. 1895), **Josef Rheinberger** (four works, 1870–1899), **Nikolay Rimsky-Korsakov** (1897), **Anton Rubinstein** (five works, 1855–1883), **Camille Saint-Saëns** (two works, 1867 and 1892), and **Bedřich Smetana** (1857, publ. 1880). Composers of the Modern Romantic Generation who penned piano trios include **Anatoly Arensky** (1894 and 1905), **Cécile Chaminade** (two works, 1881 and 1887), **Ernest Chausson** (1881, publ. 1919), **Claude Debussy** (1880), **Zdeněk Fibich** (1872), **Vincent d'Indy** (two works, 1887 and 1929), **Max Reger** (two works, 1891 and 1908), **Charles Villiers Stanford** (1889, 1899, and 1918), and **Charles-Marie Widor** (1874). [JMC]

See also QUARTET, PIANO; TRIO, STRING.

TRIO, STRING. (Ger., Streicher-Trio.) Generally, an ensemble of three stringed instruments or a composition written for it; a category of instrumental **chamber music**. The heyday of the genre seems to have been during the second half of the 18th century, with important contributions penned by **Ludwig van Beethoven** (1797 and 1798), **Franz Joseph Haydn** (1784), and **Wolfgang Amadeus Mozart** (1777, 1782, and 1788). During the **long 19th century**, compositions designated as string trios were usually scored for either two violins and cello or violin, viola, and cello, although works for two violins and viola were penned by **Antonín Dvořák** (1887) and Sergei Taneyev (1856–1915; 1909). Contributions in the more usual scorings were submitted by Luigi Boccherini (1743–1805), **Aleksandr Borodin** (1855), **Ferdinand Hiller** (n.d.), **Franz Lachner** (1874), **Ignaz Pleyel** (1806), **Max Reger** (1904), **Carl Reinecke** (1901), and **Franz Schubert** (1813). [JMC]

"TRISTAN CHORD". (Ger., *Tristan*-Akkord.) Informal term for the sonority on the downbeat of measure 2 and elsewhere in **Richard Wagner**'s **opera *Tristan und Isolde*** and its transpositions and enharmonic equivalents. At the outset of Wagner's opera, it is spelled *F—B—D sharp—G sharp* and occurs via the intersection of the chromatic descent in the cellos' melodic line *A—F—E—D sharp—D natural* with the initiation of a chromatic ascent (*G sharp—A—A sharp—B*) in the oboe and the dyads *F/ B—E /G sharp* in the bassoons. (Pitches in bold denote the notes of the chord itself.) See figure 9.

Although the *"Tristan* chord" itself appears to be an altered half-diminished seventh chord or a "French" augmented-sixth chord, Wagner's **orchestration** and voice leading reveal that it is a pre-dominant sonority whose intensity is created by the sustained appoggiatura (*G sharp*) in the oboe, which resolves belatedly but regularly to *A* before passing chromatically through *A sharp* to the fifth of the dominant-seventh chord on *E* in the following bar. Its effect of intense yearning is enhanced by the fact that the harmony at the end of this phrase does not resolve; instead, after a long pause, the opening measures are repeated, transposed up a step, in the following bars and then again (after more pauses and still without resolution) in the following ones. The persistent evasion of cadence and near emancipation of dissonance in the sonority proved iconic in the evolution of chromatic harmony in the late 19th and early 20th centuries, and Wagner's construction of this and other gestures in the harmony made it a milestone in the history of the *Leitfaden* and **Leitmotiv**.

The *"Tristan* chord" was not new to Wagner: it had been used by composers ranging from **Wolfgang Amadeus Mozart** (the String Quartet in E-flat major, K. 428/421b, 1783) and **Louis Spohr** (the **Zauberoper** *Der Alchymist*, 1829–1830, publ. 1831) to **Louis Moreau Gottschalk** (*The Last Hope*, Op.

Figure 9.

16, 1854). Although the sonority itself had been previously employed, however, Wagner's use of it in the context of a work whose entire plot centered on delayed resolution of longing and whose sexually charged **libretto** alone had generated much attention before the premiere earned it a new measure of notoriety. [JMC]

TRISTAN UND ISOLDE, WWV 90. (Ger., Tristan and Isolde.) Epoch-making **opera** (*Handlung* [drama]) in three acts by **Richard Wagner** to his own **libretto**, after Gottfried von Strassburg's (d. ca. 1210) version of the 12th-century trouvère Chrétien de Troye's rendition of an ancient Celtic legend. Wagner conceived the idea of an opera on the subject by the autumn of 1854 and had completed initial drafts of the libretto by mid-December 1856. The Prelude was premiered with a concert ending composed by **Hans von Bülow** on 12 March 1859, and the work's libretto was published by **Breitkopf & Härtel** later that year. The Prelude was performed again, now with a new concert ending composed by Wagner, on 25 January 1860, and both this and the entire opera were published in score and piano/vocal arrangement by Breitkopf & Härtel in the same year. The libretto was published in French translation by Paul Challemel-Lacour in 1861 (Paris: A. Bourdillat), and the Prelude was performed in combination with the conclusion of Act III (the latter designated "Isoldes Liebestod" [Isolde's Love-Death]) in 1863. The complete opera's premiere was slated for performance in Munich on 15 May 1865 but had to be postponed because Isolde (Malvina Schnorr) lost her voice that afternoon. The performance finally took place in the Königliches Hof- und Nationaltheater (Royal Court and National Theater), Munich, on 10 June 1865, with three repeat performances. Along with new editions of the score, excerpts, and potpourris and **fantasies** on the opera's themes by various other composers, the libretto took on a life of its own, appearing in 1876 in an Italian translation by **Arrigo Boito**, in 1882 in English (translated by H. L. and F. Corder), and in 1886 in a new French translation by Viktor Wilder (1835–1892).

Tristan was provocative from the outset. As the above publication history suggests, the libretto generated its own fair share of literary interest—partly because it was a new, self-consciously Romantic adaptation of an iconic cycle of medieval romances; partly because it thematized and valorized a romantic relationship that flew in the face of societal mores; and partly because its glorification of that illicit relationship offered an enticing parallel to Wagner's own suspiciously close (though perhaps unconsummated) relationship with Mathilde von Wesendonck, his own benefactor's wife. The music represented a new stage in the development of Wagner's contrapuntal and harmonic technique. Its hyperchromatic language, pervasive sequence and evasion of cadence, and extreme delays in resolution of dissonance proved foundational to the idioms of composers ranging from **Anton Bruck-**

ner (who attended the premiere) and **Claude Debussy** to Arnold Schoenberg, **Richard Strauss**, and many others. While the celebrated *"Tristan chord"* itself was hardly new, Wagner's deployment of that sonority in the context of a series of sequential statements of unrealized harmonic progressions to symbolize, from the work's second bar onward, the intense and unfulfilled longing central to the work's plot represented a new level of conceptual unity between music and drama. It was a brilliant manifestation of Wagner's ongoing revision of his understanding of music drama not as a *Gesamtkunstwerk* but as "acts of music made visible" ("ersichtlich gewordene Thaten der Musik") (as he would put it in an 1872 essay). [JMC]

IL TROVATORE. (It., "The Troubador.") **Opera** in four acts by **Giuseppe Verdi** on a libretto by Salvadore Cammarano (1801–1852), completed by Leone Emanuele Bardare (1820–1874), after the 1836 play *El Trovador* by Antonio García Gutiérrez (1813–1884). Descended from the "tyrant" variety of **rescue opera**, it premiered in Rome at the Teatro Apollo on 19 January 1853. It was performed in Vienna in the spring of 1854, in the United States in New York's newly opened Academy of Music on 2 May 1855, and in London in the Covent Garden Theater on 10 May 1855. All these performances presented the opera in a heavily adapted English translation, with popular songs inserted, as *The Gypsy's Vengeance* (trans. Charles Jefferys). Verdi revised it, with inserted **ballets** and a new libretto in French, as *Le trouvère* by Emilien Pacini, and this version was premiered in Paris at the Théatre-Italien in 1854 and subsequently performed in Brussels in 1856 and in Paris at the Opéra on 12 January 1857.

Il trovatore was published in the original Italian by Ricordi (Milan and London) in 1853 (the London publication including a translation by Charles Jefferys), in German translation by Gustav Friedrich Kogel (Vienna: Cranz, 1856), and in Pacini's French translation (Paris: Benoit, 1856). It also quickly became the subject for any number of **fantasies** for a variety of instruments, and individual excerpts were published in their own arrangements (many featuring harp or guitar). A **piano**/vocal score in the original language of Gutiérrez's play (Spanish) was published in 1866 (Madrid: B. Eslava).

Together with its more overtly experimental counterparts *Rigoletto* (1851) and *La traviata* (1852), *Il trovatore* signaled Verdi's arrival at a new style of composition that tipped the balance in Italian opera from vocal display toward musical drama. All three works have much in common with the subgenre of *melodramma* as it had been cultivated in the previous decades and with the styles of operatic vocal writing cultivated by **Vincenzo Bellini** and **Gaetano Donizetti**, but their cultivation of dramatic contrasts is more pronounced, their use of recitative more restricted, their **orchestration** more colorful, and their musical construction less regular and predictable, particularly in the pronounced rhythmic propulsion of the accompaniments. *Il trovatore* in particular was a resounding international success, at least in part because it taps into the **long 19th century**'s interest in **exoticism**. [JMC]

U

"UNFINISHED" SYMPHONY. (Ger., *Unvollendete Symphonie*). Popular name for **Franz Schubert**'s **Symphony** in B Minor, D. 759, of which only two movements and sketches for a third survive (*see* COMPOSITIONAL PROCESS). It is one of a great many unfinished symphonies penned during the **long 19th century** (notable others survive by **Ludwig van Beethoven, Edward Elgar, Gustav Mahler, Felix Mendelssohn Bartholdy**, and **Robert Schumann**) and one of five unfinished symphonies by Schubert: the others are D. 2b (?1811), 16 (1818), 708a (1820 or later), 729 (1821), and the "lost" "Gmunden-Gastein Symphony," D. 849, which is almost certainly the "Great" C-major Symphony, D. 944.

The reasons for Schubert's having abandoned the B-minor Symphony remain unclear. He began writing the **autograph** full score on 30 October 1822 and sent the first two movements, fully orchestrated, to his friend Josef Hüttenbrenner in September 1823 as a token of gratitude to the Styrian Musical Society (Graz) for having elected him to its membership. The work remained archived in Graz until 1865, when Johann Herbeck (1831–1877) brought the autograph to Vienna and on 17 December premiered the Symphony with the **Gesellschaft der Musikfreunde**. Although the Austrian capital's leading music critic, **Eduard Hanslick**, had previously warned against the rapidly growing Schubert cult, he hailed the torso of the B-minor Symphony in glowing language. News of the work spread rapidly, and it received its British premiere at London's Crystal Palace on 6 April 1867, followed by further performances by the Philharmonic Society of London (20 May) and the Hallé Orchestra in Manchester (5 December). The work was published as Schubert's Eighth Symphony (the serial number "7" would be more accurate) in 1867. [JMC]

See also PRINTING AND PUBLISHING OF MUSIC; RECEPTION.

URTEXT. (Ger., "primal text.") An edition of a musical or other text that is, or purports to be, free of undifferentiated editorial input; an ostensibly pure or uncontaminated reproduction, in modern notation, of the textual source at hand. Because changes are inevitably introduced into a given text in the process of copying and most Classical, biblical, and medieval texts existed in manuscripts (or prints based on manuscripts) that were the products of such copying, Enlightenment philologists and textual scholars developed sophisticated techniques for identifying variants and textual corruptions introduced by scribes or caused by the histories of manuscripts themselves and for reducing received versions of texts to "pure" or "authoritative" forms that predated those changes. In the second half of the 19th century, musical scholars, increasingly concerned with fidelity to historical composers' intentions (*see* INTENTIONAL FALLACY), appropriated this concept and adapted its techniques in an effort to correct the century's earlier tradition (facilitated by the complexities of **copyright**) of extensive, willful, and undifferentiated editorial changes to musical texts as composers had notated them. By rooting out these textual changes, the argument goes, one can arrive at a stable and authoritative text that will enable interpreters to start with what the composer created, not with a third party's interpretation of that original compositional product (or an interpretation or previous interpretations of it).

Although most modern musicians are concerned at least in principle with realizing historical composers' wishes—at any rate, few argue that, for example, **Ludwig van Beethoven**'s or **Anton Bruckner**'s wishes are immaterial to performers' and other interpreters' concerns in approaching those composers' music—the concept of the Urtext is deeply problematic in principle as well as in practice. The term aspires to textual fixity and authority but cannot deliver on that promise because the meanings of the term itself vary profoundly. To begin with, a true "primal text" is the first complete version of a musical work—that is, an implicitly complete version that does not incorporate any revisions, corrections, or other changes the composer him- or herself may have introduced later in the work's history. Such an approach would contravene the goals of its methodology by rejecting the composers' later realizations of their music. At the opposite extreme, editors have employed the ideology of the *Fassung letzter Hand* in identifying the textual source for Urtext editions—yet because these editions often rely on the latest *autograph* source for the composition(s) at hand and disregard published editions prepared and disseminated with the full involvement of the composer, they, too, explicitly disregard the very compositional intentions they aspire to respect.

More recently, many ostensible "Urtext" editions have employed a more realistic application of the concept of the *Fassung letzter Hand* by presenting, in modernized notation and with careful differentiation between authorial and editorial information and a detailed textual apparatus explaining textual variants and editorial decisions, the latest published version of a work in which the composer is known to have been substantively involved. Yet these approaches, too, are problematic with regard to the music of most of the **long**

19th century because few composers consistently viewed any single version of their works as *the* authoritative, final version that superseded all previous ones. On the contrary, composers' views on such issues tended both to vary from composition to composition and to change over time: the notion of a single, stable, fully authorized and definitive version of music of the long 19th century is thus at odds with the views of the composers whose intentions that ideology aspires to serve.

Finally, there is the fact that whatever their editorial approach, "Urtext" editions are commercial products that must be sold and understood by their consumers—a situation that means that many self-designated "Urtext" editions are anything but pure. After all, there is no legal standard for Urtext, and there are no legal penalties for marketing as "Urtext" an edition that utterly disregards editorial responsibility. At the lower end of the market are ostensible "Urtext" editions that provide no critical apparatus or source description and introduce substantial editorial information without differentiation. Such products are Urtext editions in name only. Better than these are "Urtext" editions that tacitly introduce "incidental" information (such as fingerings or phrase markings) that affect interpretation while also presenting in uncorrupted form the pitches, durations, and tempo indications as given in the source at hand—or even editions that introduce no such undifferentiated editorial material but do fail to tell the user what source(s) and editorial methods were used in preparing the edition, thus leaving the user blind regarding the reasons for the edition's putative authority.

The problems of Urtext editions do not, of course, mean that modern performers and other interpreters should simply throw up their hands and use any edition available. On the contrary, they increase the responsibility of those interpreters who are concerned with historical authority to choose an edition carefully and make decisions that are historically informed and textually aware. [JMC]

See also CANON; COMPOSITIONAL PROCESS, CREATIVE PROCESS; EDITING AND EDITIONS; PERFORMANCE PRACTICE.

V

VALLE RIESTRA (Y CORBACHO), JOSÉ MARÍA (1858–1925). Peruvian composer of the Modern Romantic Generation, notable for his incorporation of Inca and Mestizo elements into his **nationalist** compositions. He began his studies in Lima and continued them in London. He returned to Peru shortly before the Chilean occupation (1881–1883), which fueled his desire to find a way to give voice to Peruvian culture in his music. After returning to Europe to study at the Paris **Conservatory** with André Gedalge (1856–1926; teacher of Maurice Ravel, among others), he returned to Peru and completed his opera *Ollanta* (1900), one of the first major works by a Peruvian composer to draw on a subject of national and folk significance and assimilate elements of indigenous music into an idiom predicated on European late Romanticism. On further reflection, he decided that the work was too heavily indebted to **Giuseppe Verdi**'s *Aida* (1871) and completely overhauled the first two acts. This revised version was produced in 1920. He also composed a **Requiem** setting, several **motets**, and other Catholic sacred works. [JMC]

VARIATION. In the **long 19th century**, a technique of restating a given theme or melodic idea, often repeatedly, changing some features of the original while retaining others. The technique is related to others such as **motivic** development and **thematic transformation**, but variation technique generally keeps the original form of the theme in view, whereas those related concepts subject it to processes of more-or-less **organic** growth that are directed away from a return or affirmation of the basic theme or idea itself. Themes used for variation in the long 19th century typically contained a clear, balanced, and cadentially articulated phrase structure that would provide a firm general framework for extensive modification in other musical parameters. The themes could be either original (e.g., the second movement of **Ludwig van Beethoven**'s Piano **Sonata** in C Minor, Op. 111) or borrowed from a preexisting composition, either by the same composer (e.g., **Franz Schubert**'s variations on his **Lied** *Die Forelle* [The Trout, D. 550, 1817–1821] in the fourth movement of his Piano **Quintet** in A Major [D. 667, 1819]) or by another one (e.g., **Johannes Brahms**'s *Variations on a Theme of Haydn*, Op. 56a and 56b, 1873, publ. 1874, or **Fryderyk Chopin**'s *Variations on* [**Mozart's**] *"Là ci darem la mano,"* B. 225/Op. 2, 1825, publ. 1830). The technique also was frequently used in **fantasies** for piano or other instrumental **chamber** medium based on one or more arias from popular **operas**.

Depending on the degree of integration and cyclicity (*see* CYCLIC FORM), compositions based on variation technique could be constructed and regarded as either *variation sets* or *variation cycles*. Both could be either autonomous compositions or movements of larger works in genres such as **sonata** or **symphony**. As part of the **historicist** movement and **Bach Revival**, composers in the middle and later part of the long 19th century also revived the Renaissance and Baroque technique of *ostinato variation*. The most celebrated examples of this are **Franz Liszt**'s *Präludium nach J. S. Bachs "Weinen, Klagen, Sorgen, Zagen"* (LW A198, 1859, publ. 1863) and *Variations on the Motive [F—E—E flat—D—D flat—C—C—F] from Bach's "Weinen, Klagen, Sorgen, Zagen"* (LW A214, 1862, publ. 1864) and the fourth movement of Brahms's Fourth **Symphony** (Op. 98, 1884–1885, publ. 1886).

Composers of the 19th century also continued to use the genre of *alternating variations* cultivated in the 18th century. Such works (the best known of which by a "Classical" composer is probably **Franz Joseph Haydn**'s Andante with Variations in F Minor ["Un piccolo divertimento," Hob. VII: 6, 1793]) typically began by stating two contrasting themes in succession and then developing them in alternation, an approach that integrated elements of variation technique, rondo, and (depending on the presence or absence of a central developmental section) **sonata form**. The best-known examples of this approach are the second movements of Beethoven's Third (**"Eroica"**) and Seventh Symphonies (opp. 55 and 92, 1803–1805 and 1811–1812, publ. 1806 and 1816) and the second movement of **Robert Schumann**'s Third Symphony (Op. 97, 1850, publ. 1851). An adaptation of this approach appears in the Finale of Beethoven's Third Symphony and other works, such as the second movement of Brahms's C-Major **Piano Trio** (Op. 87, 1880–1882, publ. 1882) and **Rachmaninoff**'s *Rhapsody on a Theme of Paganini* (Op. 43, 1934). There, the composer treats a theme and its accompaniment as separate elements for variation (i.e., offers variations on each) and may eventually combine the two.

Although variation technique in one or more of these guises occurs in the outputs of virtually every major and minor composer of the long 19th century, the technique was viewed with suspicion in many quarters (most notably, Robert Schumann). Still, the long 19th century produced its fair share of milestones of variation technique. It was central to the works of both Beethoven (most notably the piano variations opp. 34, 35, 76, and 120, plus 16 sets of piano variations published without opus number or posthumously) and

Brahms (opp. 9, 21, 23, 24, 26, 35, 40, 56, 60, 88, 100, 120, no. 2, and numerous movements of larger works). Brahms also integrated variation technique into forms that were normally characterized by thematic and motivic development (most notably sonata form), producing a distinctive approach to variation technique sometimes referred to as *developing variation* (*See* "BRAHMS THE PROGRESSIVE"). Composers of other notable variation sets from the long 19th century include **Antonín Dvořák** (Symphonic Variations, B. 70/Op. 78, 1877), **César Franck** (*Variations symphoniques*, Op. 46, 1885, publ. 1892), **Louis Moreau Gottschalk** (*Le Carnaval de Venise*, Op. 89, 1850, publ. 1877), **Felix Mendelssohn Bartholdy** (*Variations sérieuses*, MWV U156/Op. 54, 1841), Schubert (the variations on *Der Tod und das Mädchen* in the second movement of the D-minor **String Quartet**, D. 810, 1824), Robert Schumann (the *Abegg Variations*, Op. 1, 1830, publ. 1831; *Impromptus sur une romance de Clara Wieck*, Op. 5, 1833, and Symphonic Etudes, Op. 13, 1834–1837, publ. 1837), and **Pyotor Il'yich Tchaikovsky** (*Variations for Cello and Orchestra on a Rococo Theme*, Op. 33, 1876, publ. 1889). **Edward Elgar**'s *"Enigma" Variations* (Op. 36, 1898–1899) is probably the most celebrated variation cycle by a British composer. An unusual extension of variation technique, synthesized with *concertante* technique in the context of program music, is **Richard Strauss**'s tone poem *Don Quixote* (TrV 184/Op. 35, 1897). [JMC]

VAUDEVILLE. In the **long 19th century**, term for a light comedy in English, French, or German with spoken dialogue interspersed with popular **songs**; vaudevilles are sometimes termed *musical comedies*. The term dates from the 16th century and since that point had connoted lighthearted or satirical texts set to music. During the second half of the 19th century, as **opéras comiques** began using more sophisticated plots and scenery and more elaborate music, the term *vaudeville* came to denote such works that remained true to their unpretentious and consciously frothy roots. By the 1890s, it had become closely related to the **burlesque**, distinguished primarily by vaudeville's lack of systematic satire and spoofing on other works or genres. Particularly in the United States, vaudeville was the predominant popular musical entertainment from about 1890 on. Notable 19th-century vaudevilles were composed by **Adolphe Adam, Adrien Boieldieu, Franz Lachner, Albert Lortzing, Jacques Offenbach**, and **Franz von Suppé**, among many others. [JMC]

VERDI, GIUSEPPE (FORTUNINO FRANCESCO) (1813–1901). Italian composer of the Romantic Generation and important symbolic figure in Italian **nationalism**. He is generally considered the greatest Italian musical dramatist of his generation, and all but one of the 13 operas he wrote after the

Revolutions of 1848 have remained in the repertoire—a distinction attained neither by **Vincenzo Bellini, Gaetano Donizetti,** nor **Gioachino Rossini.** He wrote for the Italian and French stages with equal fluency and was equally celebrated in the anglophone world. Even in the German lands—home also to his artistic nemesis **Richard Wagner**—his notoriety was considerable.

Verdi was born into a family of modest means in a village in the duchy of Parma and began his instruction in music at the age of 15, with the *maestro di cappella* at a church in Bussetto. He became actively involved in the city's musical life and by 1832 had decided to pursue a career in music. He traveled to Milan in order to apply to the **Conservatory** there and was accepted but was not allowed to register partly because of his **piano** technique and partly for administrative reasons. He remained in Milan, however, studying privately with the retired *maestro concertatore* at La Scala, Vincenzo Lavigna (1776–1836) and occasionally assisting in the city's local musical productions, including the Teatro Filodrammatico and Società dei Filarmonici. In mid-1835, he completed his instruction with Lavigna and in March 1836 assumed the recently vacated post responsible for secular music in Busseto, also directing the city's Philharmonic Society and giving lessons. This post he held for two and a half years, but in the meantime, he composed his first opera (originally titled *Rocester*) and remained in contact with Massini, completing a **cantata** for his society in 1836. He resigned from his position in Busseto in 1838 but with Massini's help was able to have *Rocester,* now retitled *Oberto, conte di San Bonifacio* (Oberto, Count of San Bonifacio), premiered at La Scala.

Oberto was sufficiently successful for Milan's leading music publisher, **Ricordi,** to commission three more operas from Verdi—but he vowed to give up composing after the death of his two daughters in 1838 and 1839, followed by the death of his wife in 1840 and the failure of the premiere of his **comic opera** *Un giorno di regno* (A One-Day Reign, 1840; retitled *Il finto Stanislao* [The Pretend Stanislaus], 1845). His mind was changed in 1841, however, and over the course of the coming decade, he developed a reliable pattern for creating new operas that would enable him to develop an original approach within the idioms of Bellini and (especially) Donizetti while also cultivating a distinctive style that resonated with the public in an Italy that was still under Austrian occupation. This method gave him increasing choice of subject. He preferred subjects with strong characters and dramatic contrasts, usually based on foreign literature whose literary worth was proven as spoken drama. Only after the **libretto** was finished did he begin composing the music (*see* COMPOSITIONAL PROCESS, CREATIVE PROCESS).

The method served him well—and his works of the 1840s renewed the already obvious connections between Italian opera and current political issues. His first great success, *Nabucco* (1842), although nominally about the plight of biblical Hebrews as they are assaulted and exiled from their homeland by Nebuchadnezzar, was quickly interpreted by the public as an allegory for the plight of the Italian peoples under the cruelties and strict censorship of Austrian occupation; in its first full season in Milan and Parma, ticket sales exceeded the population of those sizable cities (*see* RISORGIMENTO). Similarly veiled but vivid political topicality contributed to the growing success of his following operas. Most notable among these were *I Lombardi alla prima crociata* (The Lombards in the First Crusade, 1843), *Ernani* (1844, after **Victor Hugo**'s controversial play *Hernani, ou L'honneur Castillan*, 1830), *I due Foscari* (1844; a **rescue opera** after **Lord Byron**), *Giovanna d'Arco* (1845, after **Friedrich Schiller**'s *Die Jungfrau von Orleans*), *Alzira* (1845, after Voltaire's 1736 tragedy *Alzire, ou Les américains*, an exploration of the complications that arise when a wicked occupying governor falls in love with an humble maiden of the occupied land, in this case Peru), *I masnadieri* (1847, after Schiller's political play *Die Räuber*, 1781), *Il corsaro* (after Byron's *The Corsair*, 1814), *Macbeth* (1849, after **William Shakespeare**), *La battaglia di Legnano* (The Battle of Legnano, 1849, a fictionalized depiction about Italians' overthrow of the cruel German emperor Barbarossa in the 12th century), *Luisa Miller* (1849, after Schiller's *Kabale und Liebe*, 1784), *Rigoletto* (1851, after Hugo's *Le roi s'amuse*, 1832, a merciless satire of hegemonic exploitation by an inept monarch), and *Il trovatore* (1853, a rescue opera after Antonio García Gutiérrez's 1836 play). Although Verdi was not himself involved in the Risorgimento, his exploitation of themes that resonated powerfully with that growing movement's agenda earned him a powerful reputation as an Italian nationalist and made his name a symbolic acronym for the slogan Vittorio Emmanuele, Ré D'Italia (Victor Emmanuel, King of Italy). Contemporary audiences did not know that he carefully chose his subjects and librettos—but they responded enthusiastically to the vivid characterizations, tense drama, and rousing choruses that he created to bring those politically charged topics to the musical stage. In 1848, back on the Italian peninsula after an extended stay in Paris, the prosperous composer purchased a farm in Sant' Agata, near Busseto, installing his parents there in 1849 and moving there in 1851 with his mistress, Giuseppina Strepponi (whom he would secretly marry in 1866).

By the early 1850s, Verdi had thus become the new reigning force in Italian opera abroad as well as at home. He had also developed a leaner, more starkly dramatic style that demonstrated increasing flexibility with the conventions of Italian opera. In this new idiom, he frequently diminished the prominence and significance of recitative, compressed the conventional *scena ed aria* and minimized divisions between numbers, increased the prominence of the chorus (often entrusted with simple, rousing tunes sung in unison or in octaves), and employed more colorful **orchestration**. The flair for musical characterization that had been steadily developing in his operas of the late 1840s reached a new height in the less overtly political *La traviata* (1853, after Alexandre Dumas *fils* [1824–1895]). His reputation enabled him to negotiate for increasingly elaborate productions in order to explore topics more grandiose and sweeping in scale—a tendency evident in several works written for stages outside the Italian lands in the coming years: *Les Vêspres siciliennes* (for Paris, 1855, on a libretto by **Eugène Scribe**, a bloody tale about 16th-century Sicilians' massacre of the French), *Don Carlos* (for Paris, 1867, after Schiller), a revision of *Macbeth* for the Paris stage, *La forza del destino* (1862, written for St. Petersburg), and the **exoticist** political drama *Aida* (1871, written for Cairo to celebrate the opening of the Suez Canal).

The exhausting work on these increasingly elaborate works combined with Verdi's international success to still his creative impulse for opera for nearly 16 years, and the quest for unification of the Italian lands that had been such a powerful force in his earlier creative life was realized when Venezia joined the new kingdom in 1866, followed by the papal lands in 1870. He penned a **string quartet** in 1873, and the death of the brilliant *Risorgimento* poet Alessandro Manzoni (1785–1873) in March of that year inspired him to create his first major liturgical composition (if also one inspired by the death of a political leader): the *Messa da* **Requiem**. The new composition, initially completed in April 1874, was too lengthy and theatrical for liturgical purposes, but it constituted a new popular triumph for the 61-year-old composer, and he spent the better part of the next five years revising, promoting, and performing it in London, Milan, Paris, and Vienna. He eventually published it in piano-vocal score (1875) and full score (1877).

In 1879, Verdi met with a former Wagner partisan, **Arrigo Boito**, who had proposed through Ricordi that he and Verdi collaborate on an opera based on Shakespeare's *Othello*. Boito drafted a libretto, and Verdi, impressed with his former antagonist's work, bought the rights to it, but the first product of the new partnership was a revision of the 1857 *Simon Boccanegra*, now with a new libretto by Boito, premiered to great acclaim at La Scala in 1881. The two then engaged into an extended and complicated process of libretto creation and revision to complete *Otello*, one of the most brilliant and successful adaptations of Shakespeare in all operatic history, late in 1886. The new opera became an international sensation after it was premiered at La Scala in February 1887, and Verdi was soon arranging it for French and English stages and enjoying its success in Europe's leading theaters. He readily accepted when Boito proposed a new opera based largely on Shakespeare's *The Merry Wives of Windsor* and *King Henry IV*, resulting in his final masterpiece, *Falstaff*, premiered at La Scala in February 1893. Designated a "commedia lirica," *Falstaff* retains the colorful orchestration, freedom of form, and sense of taught dramaturgy characteristic of Verdi's earlier operas, but its rhythmic language is more varied, its musical text paintings are more plentiful and vivid, and its technique is more obviously contrapuntal than anything seen in any of his earlier works.

Despite renewed successes on the Parisian stage, Verdi's final years were spent in de facto retirement, and he felt increasingly discouraged about the state of music and society in his native Italy. His vision and hearing began to decline, and the death of his second wife in 1897 was a heavy blow. The retrospective collection of sacred works published in 1898 as his *Quattro pezzi sacri* (Four Sacred Pieces) was to become his last work. He spent much energy and a sizable portion of his accumulated wealth on two philanthropic projects (founding a home for retired musicians in Milan and the construction of a hospital near Busseto). In December 1900, he made arrangements for the posthumous destruction of the works he had written during his youth in Busseto, and on 21 January 1901, he suffered a stroke. After his death on 27 January, he was mourned internationally.

Verdi's surviving output includes a total of 28 operas, several of which were revised at least once, and it is on these and the Requiem that his fame rests. Besides the destroyed youthful compositions, the *Quattro pezzi sacri*, and the E-minor String Quartet, he also composed several other sacred choral works and songs, two surviving **symphonies** (one undated, the other ca. 1832–1835), a **waltz** for piano solo, and a *romanza senza parole* (**Lied ohne Worte**) for piano solo (1844, publ. 1865). [JMC]

VERISMO. (It., "realism" or "verism.") A post-Romantic movement in literature, music, and the other arts that attempted to democratize the arts, creating novels, operas, and plays out of ordinary contemporary lives and incidents such as those found in the daily press and showing that human passion and suffering were the same regardless of social status. *Verismo* art eschews the historical situations and noble characters typically celebrated in earlier opera and other art forms but not the **long 19th century**'s penchant for drama—indeed, drama in *verismo* art is, if anything, exaggerated by the tawdriness of the characters and circumstances and the sordid violence that tends to characterize their ends.

The *verismo* movement began in Italian literature as an outgrowth of the literary naturalism of Émile Zola (1840–1902) and Guy de Maupassant (1850–1893); its first products were the novels and plays of Giovanni Verga (1840–1922). The movement was quickly taken up in music, especially **opera**. Its musical prototype was **Pietro Mascagni**'s *Cavalleria rusticana* (Rustic Chivalry, 1890; based on a short story of the same title by Verga), a work whose veristic qualities were soon emulated in **Ruggero Leoncavallo**'s *I Pagliacci* (The Clowns, 1892), Umberto Giordano's (1867–1948) *Mala vita* (Bad Life, 1892), and **Giacomo Puccini**'s *Il tabarro* (The Cloak, 1918). Other works that subscribe to the movement's ideals in general terms include

Francesco Cilea's (1866–1950) *Adriana Lecouvreur* (1902); Umberto Giordano's (1867–1948) *Andrea Chénier* (1896); Puccini's *La bohème* (1896), *Tosca* (1900), and *Madama Butterfly* (1904; see EXOTICISM); and Ermanno Wolf-Ferrari's (1876–1948) *I gioielli della Madonna* (The Jewels of the Madonna, 1911). Although these last depart from the brevity and contemporaneity of the *verismo* movement as originally promulgated, they may also be regarded as maturations of the movement's ideals and its typical emotionalism. Viewed this way, the movement may also be regarded as the source of **Tomás Bretón's** (1850–1923) *La Dolores* (1895), Eugen d'Albert's (1864–1932) *Tiefland* (1903), Frédéric d'Erlanger's (1832–1911) *Tess* (1906), **Leoš Janáček's** *Her Stepdaughter Jenůfa* (1904), **Jules Massenet's** *La Navarraise* (1894), and **Ethel Smyth's** *The Wreckers* (1906). The movement's musical characteristics include a pronounced cultivation of extreme contrast; intense chromaticism; conspicuously unlyrical, declamatory vocal writing with wide ranges and use of extreme tessitura; and heavy doubling of the vocal lines in the **orchestra**. [JMC]

VERSTOVSKY, ALEKSEY (NIKOLAYEVICH) (1799–1862). Russian composer of the Early Romantic Generation whose **operas** of the 1830s and 1840s, inspired by French and German **comic opera**, helped form the foundation for later operatic Russian **nationalism**. Verstovsky studied piano, violin, and counterpoint independently with several instructors while enrolled at the Institute of the Corps of Engineers in St. Petersburg; among his teachers was pianist and composer **John Field**. Verstovsky began composing and staging **vaudevilles** when he finished school in 1817; his greatest early success was *Karantin* (Quarantine, 1820).

In 1824, one year after moving to Moscow, Verstovsky saw a Russian performance of **Carl Maria von Weber's** *Der Freischütz*, which changed the trajectory of Verstovsky's compositional ambitions; his regard for the work as 19th-century masterpiece is recorded in his 1825 essay "Fragments from the History of Dramatic Music." Earlier in 1825, Verstovsky became an administrator for the Moscow Theatrical Repertory, and his hand in Moscow's operatic repertoire decisions became another means for him to elevate the quality of musical theater there. In 1848, he was to be appointed head of the Moscow Imperial Theaters' board of administration. Verstovsky's greatest success, the opera *Askol'dova mogila* (Askold's Tomb, after the novel by Mikhail Zagoskin [1789–1852]), premiered in Moscow in 1835 and St. Petersburg in 1841. From the late 1830s on, despite this major success, Verstovsky was overshadowed by **Mikhail Glinka**, whom Russian composers of later generations were far more inclined to claim as a significant predecessor. [RK]

VICTORIAN ERA. Popular term for the period from 1837 to around 1901 in British, anglophone, and British-sphere-of-influence history (including the United States), those dates denoting the reign of Queen Victoria of England, empress of India (1819–1901). The values and social trends of the era emerged in the United Kingdom's legal and social structure with the Reform Act of 1832 and were consolidated and widely promulgated during Victoria's long and prosperous rule, a period of unprecedented expansion of the British Empire. Today, the era is regarded as conservative, but it is less so than both the preceding Georgian era and the following Edwardian era, witnessing the flourishing of progressive movements including liberalism, socialism, and organized **feminism**.

As a whole, the Victorian era witnessed transformative changes in nearly every aspect of the public and private spheres. In the public sphere, these changes occurred not only in industry but also in law, medicine, philosophy, and technology. In the private sphere, they led to renewed emphasis on domestic and family life (*see* RESTORATION) as well as on gender relations and sexuality. (This was the era that coined the terms "homosexual" and "heterosexual," for the first time in human history dichotomizing modes of sexual behavior, framing them in terms of natural identity, and attempting to encode them in societally prescribed and proscribed gender codes.) The era is also best understood as comprising two subperiods: an early period of idealism and vibrant optimism, extending just into the years immediately following the demise in 1861 of Victoria's husband, Albert, prince-consort of Saxe-Coburg and Gotha (1819–1861), and a late Victorian period characterized by a more predominant emphasis on the status quo and the cumbersome stodginess that the term *Victorian* typically connotes today, especially in popular culture.

In music, the Victorian era was characterized by a renewed surge in middle-class music making and musical consumption, both public and private. In the public sphere, the period witnessed a flourishing of music festivals and of Italian and (to a lesser extent) French **opera** throughout Britain, with a surge in **comic opera** and **operetta** in the final decades of the **long 19th century**. It was also a major period of growth for **orchestras** and large choral societies. In the private sphere, the period was characterized by a proliferation of glee clubs both in their traditional upper-class contexts and in the middle and lower social and economic classes and of **salon** and parlor music, developments that also generated vast new markets for music publishers (*see* PRINTING AND PUBLISHING OF MUSIC) and makers of musical instruments.

Paradoxically, although the Victorian era is primarily a British and British-sphere-of-influence phenomenon, its musical repertoires were dominated by non-British composers. During the early Victorian era, the public and private repertoires alike were dominated by **Ludwig van Beethoven, George Frideric Handel, Franz Joseph Haydn, Felix Mendelssohn Bartholdy, Wolf-**

gang **Amadeus Mozart, Gioachino Rossini,** and **Carl Maria von Weber,** followed at some distance by composers such as **Charles Gounod, Bernhard Molique, Otto Nicolai,** and **Giuseppe Verdi;** the only London-based or British composers who figured prominently were **William Sterndale Bennett,** William Crotch (1775–1847), and **Cipriani Potter.** During the late Victorian era, the same group of non-British composers remained central but shared the stage with other composers, such as **Hector Berlioz, Johannes Brahms, Max Bruch, Franz Liszt, Joachim Raff, Camille Saint-Saëns,** and **Richard Wagner,** while the British composers of the early part of the century yielded their ground to more recent ones. The latter fall into two groups: those such as **Edward Elgar, Ethel Smythe,** and **Arthur Sullivan,** who were schooled in the continental tradition and whose styles were strongly informed by continental idioms and those who made a concerted effort to draw on English **folk song** and music of the English Renaissance (most important among them **Alexander Mackenzie, Hubert Parry,** and **Charles Villiers Stanford**). [JMC]

See also BROADWOOD; ENGLISH MUSICAL RENAISSANCE; EWER; NOVELLO; RESTORATION.

VIENNA CONGRESS. See CONGRESS OF VIENNA.

VILLANUEVA, FELIPE (1862–1893). Mexican composer, educator, and violinist of the Modern Romantic Generation; one of the best-known representatives of Mexican Romantic **nationalism.** He began playing violin at an early age and by the age of 10 had completed a nationalist **cantata** for soloists, chorus, and piano titled *El retrato del benemérito cura Hidalgo* (Portrait of Hidalgo the Meritorious). He entered Mexico's National **Conservatory** of Music in 1873 and became a violinist in the **orchestra** of the Hidalgo Theater in 1876.

Villanueva's reputation as a composer was significantly bolstered in 1879 with the publication of the **programmatic piano** compositions *La erupción del Peñol* (The Eruption at Peñol) and *La llegada del ciclón* (The Arrival of the Cyclone). He became professor of music at the Colegio del Sagrado Corazón in 1884. During Villanueva's youth, public musical life and music education in Mexico were dominated by Italian opera, while the country's **salon** culture centered on French repertoires. In 1887, he and a circle of friends founded the Instituto Musical with the specific idea of promoting French and French-influenced music, specifically via the works of **Fryderyk Chopin, Franz Liszt,** and **Anton Rubinstein.** He died in at the age of 31, and in 1945 his remains were relocated to the Rotonda de las Personas Ilustres in Mexico City in recognition of his contributions to Mexican musical life.

Villanueva is best remembered today for his *Vals poético* (1890; *see* WALTZ). He also penned two **comic operas**, *Un día de asueto* (A Day Off, 1885) and *Keofar* (1892). Although much of his music reflects the stylistic influence of French and Austro-German traditions (including various **mazurkas**, **nocturnes**, *écossaises*, and waltzes), he frequently drew on dance rhythms of his native Mexico and wrote numerous works on national and patriotic subjects. [JMC]

VIRTUOSO (M.), VIRTUOSA (F.). An Italian term for an individual of great technical ability and accomplishment; during the **long 19th century** in the fields of music, usually reserved for **conductors** and other performers (e.g., pianists and singers). Exceptional speed and ability had long been prized attributes for musicians, but during the 19th century they grew in importance, acquiring cult-like status.

The emergence of the cult of virtuosity may be attributed to three primary factors. First, the increased urbanization of society and increased access of the middle and lower socioeconomic classes to public cultural events during the **Restoration** and beyond facilitated the rise of public concerts, events whose economic viability relied on the sustained support of large groups of middle-class audiences who were not necessarily well trained in music but were able to behold extraordinary technical achievement with awe and wonder. Second, developments in technology during the Restoration facilitated both extensive touring and new developments in the technology of musical instruments that made the formerly impossible possible—in the hands of a performer who was sufficiently skilled, willing to endure the hardships of a life on the rail and steamship, and adept at stagecraft and showmanship. Finally, the rise of Romantic values that celebrated the idea of superhuman accomplishment and artistic transcendence made the phenomenon of the virtuoso one that resonated with the age itself: these were not just humans who commanded their instruments to conspicuously new heights of musical expression but also personifications of the urbanization and industrialization of modern life. Virtuosos proved that the seemingly impossible was possible.

That same transcendence was not without its problems, however. First and foremost among these was the fact that virtuosity in performance was at least as much about technique as about substance or content—arguably more so since many virtuoso compositions (such as the many **fantasies** and potpourris central to the programs of traveling virtuosos) were tropes on works that were not original to the performers themselves. In the eyes of some, the fact that the virtuoso was often relieved of the personal responsibility of the primal creative act of composition and was therefore able to build by technical means on musical foundations laid by others deprived the creative products of virtuosity of some of their potency as Romantic utterance. Others were leery of the fact that virtuoso performance foregrounded technique before content—indeed, made it possible for music that was aesthetically lackluster or deficient to be presented in dazzling forms to an amateur-dominated musical public whose taste and discernment in matters of aesthetics were—so skeptics maintained—too easily impressed by showmanship and insufficiently schooled to appreciate more complex substance. The latter concern is reflected in the frequently encountered phrase "empty virtuosity" (*leere Virtuosität*), often leveled by musicians who were themselves virtuosi at others whose works found a supposedly less optimal balance between musical content and technical execution.

On the whole, however, few denied that the virtuosos' technical achievements, fueled by the intense competition among virtuosos for the favors of the vast music-loving public of peacetime Europe during the early and mid-19th century and abetted by their often-lucrative teaching, raised standards of performance in virtually all areas of musical endeavor during the long 19th century. By breaking free of the constraints of established technique in music that sounded unabashedly Romantic—and acknowledging that the concept of "Romantic" sound itself varied considerably (see the introduction to this dictionary)—the virtuosos inspired other performers to extend the expressive capacities of their own instruments and display their achievements to ever-larger crowds of enthralled audiences.

The archetype of the Romantic virtuoso instrumentalist was the Italian violinist **Nicolò Paganini**, whose extraordinary technical achievements and showmanship provided the model for the century's great piano virtuosos, including, most famously, **Franz Liszt**. A selective roster of influential virtuosos includes musicians as diverse as **Charles-Valentin Alkan** (piano), **Giovanni Bottesini** (double bass), **Pierre Baillot** (violin), **Ferruccio Busoni** (piano), **Fryderyk Chopin** (piano), **Domenico Dragonetti** (double bass), **John Field** (piano), **Leopold Godowski** (piano), **Louis Moreau Gottschalk** (piano), **Fanny Hensel** (piano), **Adolf von Henselt** (piano), **Johann Nepomuk Hummel** (piano), **Friedrich Kalkbrenner** (piano), **Joseph Joachim** (violin), **Rudolfe Kreutzer** (violin), **Jenny Lind** (soprano), **Maria Malibran** (soprano), **Felix Mendelssohn Bartholdy** (piano and organ), **Jacques Offenbach** (cello), **Ignacy Paderewski** (piano), **Elias Parish-Alvars** (harp), **Serge Rachmaninoff (piano)**, **Max Reger** (organ), **Pierre Rode** (violin), **Bernhard Romberg** (cello), **Anton Rubinstein** (piano), **Clara Schumann** (piano), **Louis Spohr** (violin), **Maria Szymanowska** (piano), **Sigismond Thalberg** (piano), and **Carl Maria von Weber** (piano). **Hans von Bülow, Gustav Mahler, Gaspare Spontini, Richard Strauss,** and **Richard Wagner** are considered virtuoso **conductors**. [JMC]

VOICE, VOICEDNESS, VOCALITY. Theoretical concept for the source or sources of musical and/or poetic utterance in an instrumental or vocal composition. Used in this sense, "voice" is neither the physical source of vocal or instrumental sound nor necessarily the composer's own presence but rather a source of utterance created by the poet and/or composer within the musical text itself. In vocal music, whether for solo voice or vocal ensemble, the voices present in the text and/or the composer's setting of it are referred to as *lyric personae* (sing. *lyric persona*). Different compositions may attempt to re-create the voicedness of a poetic text or alter that vocal structure; for this reason, it is important to distinguish, at least at the outset, between the vocal structure of the text and that of the music. The concept of voicedness helps to explain how Romantic music manages to **narrate** emotional, physical, and psychological events; create a sense of a differentiated past and present tense; or suggest different times and places within a single text.

A few examples will suffice to illustrate these basic points. **Johann Wolfgang von Goethe**'s 1782 **ballad** "Erlkönig" (later set by **Carl Loewe** and **Franz Schubert**, among others) contains four discrete lyric personae (none of them representing the poet himself): the narrator (who speaks in the third person), the father (who speaks in the first person and addresses his son), the son (who speaks in the first person and addresses the father), and the Erl-King himself (who speaks in the first person and addresses the son). In Schubert's setting (D. 328, 1814), each of these voices is entrusted with a discrete musical character and range. Additionally, the urgent pounding of the horse's hooves (repeated triplet chords in the right hand of the accompaniment) as the pair races through the night is also pervasive in Schubert's setting and creates a separate "voice" for the horse. Yet the voice of the horse abates twice: first when the Erl-King tries to lure the child with promises of games, flowers, and his mother's golden robes (mm. 56–61) and then at the end, when the narrator's voice returns to provide the poem's devastating final line: "in seinen Armen das Kind war tot" (in his arms the child was dead). The change of texture in the accompaniment at the first of these instances supports the Erl-King's voice by musically transporting the singer and listener into the Erl-King's own world, a separate space where the horse's hooves do not pound, while the sudden move to recitative style at the second instance removes us from the narrative space of the previous portion of the song entirely in order to underscore the dramatic conclusion.

Similarly, the six poems of Alois Jeitteles (1794–1858) that **Ludwig van Beethoven** used for his **song cycle** *An die ferne Geliebte* (Op. 98, 1816) possess no discrete or fixed lyric persona, but Beethoven's music creates two layers of narrative and geographic space. In the first song (E-flat major), the lyric persona, speaking in the first person, promises to transcend his and his lovers' separation by means of song; in songs 2–5 (G major, A-flat major, and C major), he submits four contemplations on loneliness, separation, and love, using abundant nature imagery to create the distance between himself and his beloved and reflect; and in the final song (E-flat major), he reflects on those previous four songs, which he has delivered as a sort of package to his beloved in order to overcome the distance that separates them, quoting from the first song and returning to the initial key to affirm the closure effected by his gift of song: "Nimm sie hin denn, diese Lieder, Die ich dir, Geliebte, sang, singe sie dann abends wieder, Zu der Laute süßem Klang" (So take, then, these songs that I have sung to you, beloved, and sing them again [yourself] some evening to the sweet sounds of the lute).

Composers of the Romantic Generation further extended these applications of vocality, so that, for example, in the opening song of **Robert Schumann**'s *Dichterliebe*, the piano accompaniment, replete with wide-reaching, angular melodic lines and dissonances that are resolved belatedly and consistently in F-sharp minor, may be seen as reflecting the sad (from the lyric persona's perspective) fact that the his love is unrequited, while the vocal melody itself is consistently in A major, reflecting his wistful imagining of a love that the piano tells us is unrequited. The poignant irony of the song's text is thus reflected in neither the words of the lyric persona nor the voice of the piano accompaniment per se but rather in the relationship between the two. [JMC]

VOLKSTÜMLICHKEIT. (Ger., "folk-like quality" or "folksiness.") Term employed in discussions of cultivated music and other cultivated art to denote a stylistic evocation, imitation, or "recapturing" of the quality of **folk song** and (as applicable) folk poetry or folk art; distinct from actual folk music. During the **long 19th century**, the term was applied most often to lyric poetry and to settings of such poetry in **song**. Poems that were described as *volkstümlich* (folk-like) were usually strophic and dealt with themes of nature or life in the country and were rarely narrative in content.

The term *Volkstümlichkeit* was first coined by Johann Gottfried Herder (1744–1803) in his enormous comparative anthology *Stimmen der Völker in ihren Liedern* (Voices of the Peoples in Their Songs, 1773). Although the term itself is German, during the long 19th century, the notion that the earth's nations were naturally defined by geographical boundaries and that the essence of any given nation was captured in its folklore and folk song was international. *Volktümlichkeit* is thus a term that applies to any European-sphere-of-influence cultivated music that emulates folk song and to any other art that is cultivated in European spheres of influence but attempts to adopt a folk-like character.

Musical settings of such poetry tended to be overwhelmingly syllabic, so that their melodic structures and phrase lengths were defined in large part by the rhythms, stresses, and poetic forms of their texts. Music that aspired to *Volkstümlichkeit* typically had unobtrusive accompaniments and primarily conjunct and syllabic melodies and employed strophic or modified strophic forms. Instrumental music emulated these characteristics. Genres frequently described and treated as *volkstümlich* included the **Lied** and the **Romance**, while works designated as **Ballade** or **Gesang** tended toward self-conscious complexity. The aesthetics of *Volkstümlichkeit* were most common in the **Second Berlin School** and in certain Lieder of **Johannes Brahms, Fanny Hensel, Felix Mendelssohn Bartholdy, Wolfgang Amadeus Mozart, Franz Schubert** (most famously "Heidenröslein," D. 257; text by **Johann Wolfgang von Goethe**), and **Robert Schumann**. [JMC]

See also NATIONALISM, ROMANTIC NATIONALISM.

VOŘÍŠEK, JAN VÁCLAV |WORZISCHEK, JOHANN HUGO| (1791–1825). Bohemian composer, pianist, and organist of the Early Romantic Generation, principal Bohemian exponent of the early Romantic styles associated with **Ludwig van Beethoven, Johann Nepomuk Hummel, Ignaz Moscheles**, and **Franz Schubert**. He studied organ and violin and toured Bohemia on foot during the first few years of the 19th century and studied at a Jesuit school in Prague under the patronage of a local countess from 1802 to 1810, also studying briefly with **Václav Tomášek** in 1804. He studied philosophy and then law at the University of Prague between 1810 and 1813, when he moved to Vienna in hopes of studying with Beethoven. During his time in the Austrian capital, he became acquainted with Beethoven, Schubert, and **Louis Spohr**, also studying **piano** with Hummel. In 1818, he was named conductor of the **Gesellschaft der Musikfreunde** and in 1822 became assistant court organist, defeating **Simon Sechter** and several other notable musicians in his bid for the post. He was promoted to principal court organist in 1823 and retained this position until January 1825, when he was forced to resign because of his rapidly worsening tuberculosis.

Voříšek's reputation during his lifetime was impeccable: he was considered one of Vienna's premier pianists, preeminent especially in the *brillante* style of virtuosity, and "the first among living organists." He is important chiefly for his lyrical piano pieces, especially his rhapsodies, **impromptus**, and other piano miniatures. He also composed one **symphony** (premiered by the Gesellschaft der Musikfreunde in 1823, publ. 1825), four *concertante* works for piano and **orchestra**, a small body of vocal and instrumental **chamber music**, and secular and sacred works for chorus and orchestra, including a Mass in B-flat Major (1825) that ranks among the more important Catholic liturgical compositions between **Franz Joseph Haydn** and Schubert. [JMC]

VORMÄRZ. (Ger., "pre-march.") German term for the period between the **Congress of Vienna** and the large public demonstrations in Vienna that heralded the arrival of the **Revolutions of 1848** in the German lands. By extension, in Germany, the Revolutions of 1848 are sometimes referred to in the singular as the *Märzrevolution* (March Revolution). [JMC]

See also RESTORATION.

W

WAGNER, (WILHELM) RICHARD (1813–1883). German composer, **conductor, librettist,** and writer on music of the Romantic Generation; after **Ludwig van Beethoven,** one of the most consequential figures in musical Romanticism and post-Romanticism as well as much of the music of the 20th century. He composed a small quantity of music for **piano** solo; several surviving insertion arias for **operas** by **Vincenzo Bellini, Heinrich Marschner,** and others; a number of **songs** on French and German texts; and one surviving completed **symphony** and some other orchestral works (most importantly the **symphonic poem** *Siegfried Idyll* [WWV 103, comp. 1870, publ. 1878]). His most important works, however, are his 14 operas and **music dramas,** especially the cycle of music dramas collectively titled *Der Ring des Nibelungen* (**The Ring of the Nibelung,** WWV 86a–d) and the individual operas *Lohengrin* (WWV 75, 1850, publ. 1851), *Die Meistersinger von Nürnberg* (WWV 96, 1868), *Tristan und Isolde* (WWV 90, comp. 1857–1860, libretto publ. 1859, score publ. 1860, premiered 1865), and *Parsifal* (WWV 111, 1877–1882). He was also an eloquent and influential critic and writer on music, especially via his pamphlets and tracts *Die Kunst und die Revolution* (Art and Revolution, 1849), *Das Kunstwerk der Zukunft* (*The Artwork of the Future,* 1849), *Das Judentum in der Musik* (Jewry in Music, 1850, rev. 1869), *Oper und Drama* (Opera and Drama, 1850–1851), and *Über das Dirigieren* (On **Conducting,** 1869). He also penned an autobiography (*Mein Leben* [My Life, 1865–1880]) that was widely read and translated.

Born in Leipzig, Wagner was the ninth child of a police actuary and a former mistress of the prince of Saxe-Weimar-Eisenach. His father died when he was an infant, and after his mother remarried in 1814, he became a favorite son of his stepfather. While in Dresden during the early 1820s, he met **Heinrich Marschner, Louis Spohr,** and **Carl Maria von Weber,** three of the major figures in German opera of the day. In 1828, he began his first instruction in composition; so rapid was his progress that two of his **overtures** (both now lost) were performed at the Königliches Sächsisches Hoftheater in 1830 and 1831. His self-consciously Beethovenian Symphony in C Major, having won the attention of **Clara Schumann** at a performance by the Leipzig-based civic **orchestra** Euterpe, drew favorable notice as far away as London when it was performed by the Gewandhaus Orchestra (Leipzig) on 10 January 1833.

By January 1834, Wagner had completed the score for his first opera, *Die Feen* (The Fairies, WWV 32), and in June of that year, his first published essay (*Die deutsche Oper* [German Opera]) appeared in the *Zeitung für die elegante Welt*. His growing reputation led to his being offered the directorship of a failing opera company based in Magdeburg in July 1834, an engagement that offered him opportunities to conduct major French, German, and Italian works from the current repertoire (Bellini, **Gaetano Donizetti**, Marschner, Spohr, and Weber, as well as numerous **operas comiques**). He became a member of the informal group known as Junges Deutschland (Young Germany), a group that rejected the neoclassicism of **Johann Wolfgang von Goethe** and the perceived sentimentality of **E. T. A. Hoffmann**, turning instead to Italian sensuality and the idealism of French utopian movements such as the Saint-Simonians. Under these influences, he completed his second opera, *Das Liebesverbot* (The Ban on Love, WWV 38, 1838; after **William Shakespeare**'s *Measure for Measure*). He accepted the music directorship of a company based in Riga, but when he learned in March 1839 that his contract with the financially struggling company was not being renewed, he and his wife, Minna (1809–1866), fled first to London and then to Paris in order to escape his creditors.

Although Wagner's Parisian period (1839–1842) proved to be a bitter disappointment (not least of all because of his lack of connections and money in the culture of the **Bourbon Restoration**), it was formative in several largely unforeseen ways: it launched his career as a musical journalist, via numerous articles produced for the *Revue et gazette musicale* and as Parisian correspondent for the Dresden *Abend-Zeitung*; it provided him with new exposure to the large-scale dramaturgy of French **grand opera**, also instilling in him an abiding resentment toward the successes of **Giacomo Meyerbeer** and what he perceived as the general Jewish predominance in public musical culture; it solidified his mature tendency to set operas on historical subjects; and it gave him the opportunity to complete and produce *Rienzi* (WWV 49, 1842; the first opera that hinted at his mature gifts in the genre) and draft the **libretto** and some music for *Der fliegende Holländer* (The Flying Dutchman, WWV 63, 1843; after **Heinrich Heine**). *Rienzi* was accepted for performance at the Dresden Hoftheater, and Wagner, once again under pressure from creditors in Paris, returned to Dresden with hopes of securing a position at the court there. The success of its premiere on 20 October 1842 was considerable, followed by a warm reception of the *Der fliegende Holländer* in January 1843.

With these two public successes under his belt, Wagner was appointed to the recently vacated post of second Kapellmeister of the Dresden Hoftheater. His activities in that position included not only the composition of libretto and music for his next opera, *Tannhäuser und der Sängerkrieg auf Wartburg* (Tannhäuser and the Singers' Contest on the Wartburg, WWV 70, comp. 1845, rev. 1847, rev. 1860), but also significant conducting experience (including widely recognized readings of works by Christoph Willibald Ritter von Gluck [1714–1787], **Wolfgang Amadeus Mozart**, and Weber, as well as a near-legendary performance of Beethoven's **"Choral" Symphony**). The production of *Tannhäuser* in 1845 furthered his reputation and won the attention of **Robert Schumann**, but Wagner's support for the revolt against the court that employed him when the **Revolutions of 1848** reached Dresden in 1849 forced him to flee—first to **Franz Liszt** in Weimar and then, under threat of arrest, to Zurich by way of Paris.

The personal and professional crisis posed by Wagner's desperate flight to Switzerland brought his composing to a temporary halt; instead, he produced a series of lengthy aesthetic and philosophical tracts in which he worked out an artistic and social agenda that, in his view, would both make good on the promise of social and political renewal born of the Revolutions of 1848 and win anew for music and drama the power for which those arts had been celebrated in ancient Greece. The notoriously anti-Semitic essay *Judentum in der Musik*, first published serially under the pseudonym K. Freigedank (C. Freethought) in **Franz Brendel**'s *Neue Zeitschrift für Musik* in September 1850, served primarily to vent his bitterness at the personal, professional, and financial setbacks that had plagued him, but other essays, such as *Die Kunst und die Revolution*, *Das Kunstwerk der Zukunft*, and especially *Oper und Drama*, collectively outlined an eloquent and profoundly new aesthetic agenda that would be pursued by Wagner himself in his compositions over the next two decades and by countless other composers thereafter.

The most important long-term projects born of Wagner's Zurich exile were the completion of the libretto for the *Ring of the Nibelung* and initial drafting of the music for the first two music dramas in that cycle. He conducted the Philharmonic Society of London in 1855 and received financial support from the wealthy Zurich merchant Otto von Wesendonck, with whose wife (author of the poems of the so-called *Wesendonck-Lieder*, WWV 91, 1857–1858) he began an affair whose parallels to his next completed opera, *Tristan und Isolde* (WWV 90), generated much controversy when that work was premiered. Privately, the affair also generated tensions between Mathilde von Wesendonck and Minna—and between Wagner and Wesendonck—such that Wagner and Minna were forced to flee to Venice. By September 1859 he was again in Paris, hoping for "great success" in the Parisian capital. He rented the Théâtre-Italien for a series of three concerts of his own music given between 25 January and 8 February 1860, winning a great following. The much-anticipated opening of a revised version *Tannhäuser* (whose chances for success were considerable because of its indebtedness to **grand opera**) at the Paris Opéra was spoiled by riots concerning the position of the ballet in the French version of the work. Withdrawing the work, Wagner and Minna fled to Karlsruhe.

In Karlsruhe, Wagner renewed his acquaintance with actor and renowned theater historian Eduard Devrient (1801–1877); finished the libretto for his only **comic opera**, *Die Meistersinger von Nürnberg* (The *Meistersinger* of Nuremberg, WWV 96); and began composing the music for that work. Again desperate for money, at the turn of 1862/1863 he published the libretto for his version of the *Ring* cycle, wondering in the Foreword whether there was somewhere a German prince with the will and means to support his vision. That solicitation was answered the following year when King Ludwig II of Bavaria offered Wagner his patronage and installed him in a sumptuous villa near Munich. His marriage to Minna was in tatters, and the two would soon separate permanently, but in 1864 he was joined in his villa by Cosima von Bülow (daughter of his friend Liszt and wife of **Hans von Bülow**), whom he would marry after her marriage to the famous conductor was annulled in 1870.

The final chapter of Wagner's life amounts to one of triumph. With the support of the Bavarian monarch, he set about planning and raising funds for the erection of a new Festspielhaus in **Bayreuth** that would reflect his vision for an ideal opera theater, also completing the music for *The Ring of the Nibelung* (first conceived in 1848). The theater officially opened with the first of three successive performance cycles of that tetralogy on 13 August 1876, and although the performances were financially disastrous, the event was a cultural sensation—probably the greatest such event in German music since the Berlin Singakademie's 1829 performances of **Johann Sebastian Bach**'s *St. Matthew Passion* (*see* BACH REVIVAL, BACH AWAKENING, BACH RENAISSANCE). He turned next to what was to be his final opera, *Parsifal*, completing the libretto in April 1877 and beginning work on the music shortly afterwards. While working on this project, he also continued to write prolifically, including the essays *Über das Dichten und Komponieren* (On Composing Poetry and Music, 1879) and *Religion und Kunst* (Religion and Art, 1880).

By the early 1880s Wagner's health had begun to fail, and in March 1882 he suffered a serious heart attack. The opening of *Parsifal* in July 1882 was another major event, partly because of the much-anticipated work (which he had announced in a published essay in 1877) itself and partly because much of musical Europe knew that it might well be the final musical utterance of the aging and near-legendary genius who had created *Tristan* and the *Ring*. The 69-year-old Wagner's infatuation and possible affair with one of the flower girls in the opera, Carrie Pringle (then 24), led to a major confrontation with Cosima in Venice on 13 February 1883; hours later, he was found slumped over a drafted essay on Goethe's "eternal feminine" (*see* FAUST), dead of a heart attack.

Wagner's consequentiality for music of the late 19th century and beyond derives in part from his eloquence in formulating a new set of premises for musical drama and German music generally (premises whose unforeseen consequences and backlashes were themselves momentous; *see* SOCIÉTÉ NATIONALE DE MUSIQUE), partly from his success in implementing those premises in his own music, and partly from his ability to synthesize diverse and contradictory impulses, such as German Romantic **nationalism**, **Singspiel**, French **grand opera** and opéra comique, Beethovenian symphonic technique, and intricate counterpoint. His notion of a unified creative vision that generated plot, libretto, and music successfully legitimized the practice (previously employed only sporadically and with limited success) of composers penning their own libretti. His augmentation of the orchestra, while largely a function of a vision of theater design and acoustics that have long since been left behind, set the standard for numerous later composers of opera as well as concerted music. And the threat to traditional tonality posed by the hyperchromatic musical language of *Tristan* provided a starting point for composers of later generations (such as **Anton Bruckner**, **Claude Debussy**, **Gustav Mahler**, **Aleksandr Scriabin**, **Richard Strauss**, and **Hugo Wolf**) whose extensions of tonality would articulate a caesura in the 20th century's challenges to that foundational aspect of form in Western music.

Wagner's views on the nature of the interpretive task of conducting—specifically, the idea of discovering the *melos* that pervades an entire composition and interpreting every musical composition not as an aggregate of rhetorically potent phrases but as a single long melodic line—would set the trend for most conductors for generations to come and be of enormous consequence for music theory and analysis (especially as represented in the ideas of Heinrich Schenker [1868–1935]) as well as later composers. The forcefulness and embittered eloquence of his autobiography and *Das Judenthum in der Musik* resonated profoundly with anti-Semitic currents that sought the sort of cultural authority he had achieved by the time of the publication of the expanded second edition of the latter tract, laying a cultural and artistic blueprint that would be appropriated by later anti-Semites (including, most famously, Adolf Hitler and Joseph Goebbels). That same persuasive power lent new and enduring life to the Romantic cult of the genius-cum-suffering/ persecuted artist—establishing, via his own self-mythologized account of his life, a paradigm that would become a de facto litmus test not only for later composers but also for the historiographic reception of earlier ones. His legacy also includes a family dynasty of musical notables: composer/conductor Siegfried Wagner (1869–1930), his son; stage designer Wieland Wagner (1917–1966), a grandson; and administrator and director Wolfgang Wagner (1919–2010), another grandson. [JMC]

See also ALLGEMEINER DEUTSCHER MUSIKVEREIN; GESAMT-KUNSTWERK; MUSIC DRAMA; NEW GERMAN SCHOOL.

DIE WALKÜRE. See THE RING OF THE NIBELUNG.

WALLASCHEK, RICHARD (1860–1917). Austrian scholar and critic of the Modern Romantic Generation who addressed issues of music aesthetics, music perception, and comparative musicology. By approaching long-debated questions of how people perceive and understand music, Wallaschek was a pioneer in the psychology of music. Wallaschek's most important publications include *Ästhetik der Tonkunst* (Aesthetics of the Musical Art, 1896), *Primitive Music* (1893, rev. 1903 as *Anfänge der Tonkunst* [Beginnings of the Musical Art]), and *Psychologische Ästhetik* (Psychological Aesthetics, publ. posth., 1930). In them, he applied his broad interdisciplinary skills to old questions of music's relation to other human behaviors, such as dance, motion, sense of time, and speech. Wallascek's first two degrees were in philosophy (University of Tübingen, 1885) and law (University of Bern, 1886). After teaching briefly at the University of Freiburg, Wallaschek did interdisciplinary work at the British Museum in London from 1890 until 1895. He then moved to Vienna, where he spent the rest of his career on the faculty of the University of Vienna. Between 1896 and 1908, he was a music critic for Viennese *Die Zeit*, a weekly publication that went daily during his tenure. [RK]

WALTER. Viennese firm of fortepiano manufacturers; most influential in developing the "German action" invented by the firm of **Stein**. The firm was founded by Anton Walter (1752–1826), who trained as a musician and **piano** maker in Neuhausen (near Stuttgart) and relocated to the Habsburg capital by 1772. By 1778, Walter had made several wing-shaped **pianos**. In July of that year, he requested legal permission to manufacture and sell instruments in Vienna, a request that the court granted in March 1779 despite resistance from the imperial capital's guild of organ builders. By 1790, Walter had become so successful that he was named Königlich-Kaiserlicher Kammeror-gelbauer und Instrumentenmacher (Royal-Imperial Chamber Organ Builder and Instrument Maker). In 1796, the *Jahrbuch der Tonkunst in Wien und Prag* (Musical Annual for Vienna and Prague) dubbed him the "most famous piano maker of our time." By that point, the firm had 20 employees and occupied a sizable number of apartments in Vienna, evidence of a thriving business. By the first decade of the 19th century, it was selling thousands of instruments annually. Sometime after 1810 (not 1800, as is commonly reported), Walter was joined in the business by his stepson.

Walter's instruments, of which about 40 survive, were played and praised by **Ludwig van Beethoven, Franz Joseph Haydn, Wolfgang Amadeus Mozart**, and **Franz Schubert**, among many others. Mozart purchased one shortly after moving to Vienna in 1782, and **Carl Czerny** reported in his memoirs (1842) that Beethoven described them as "the best" during the winter of 1799–1800. Beethoven in particular commissioned a mahogany instrument with an *una corda* stop from Walter for 30 ducats in November 1802 (the commission fell through, but Beethoven's surviving letter requesting the instrument details the musical and structural features that made the instrument desirable to him). The instruments were distinguished in part by their superior construction (including brass pivot forks, forward-leaning hoppers, and a back check that prevented unwanted rebound) and in part for their robustness, their ability to deal with the growing demand for more volume that emerged with the cult of the **virtuoso** and larger concert halls of the **Restoration**. This construction was emulated by Walter's competitors, most notably **Graf**, whose business seems to have surpassed Walter's in the 1820s.

Like all fortepianos built before **Érard**'s development of the double-escapement action, Walter's instruments have a single escapement, but their shallow touch largely compensates for that mechanism's requirement that the key rebound fully before being struck again. Also typical for the day, the instrument is characterized by great timbral variety from the lower to the upper registers and great clarity of texture, facilitating clarity of voice leading and making dense voicings, especially in the middle and lower registers, more transparent than is common on the modern piano. [JMC]

WALTZ. (Ger., Walzer, from *walzen*, "to turn about"; Fr., valse; It., valzer; Sp., vals.) A couples' dance in 3/4 time, part of the general category of dances known as *Deutsche* (sing. *Deutscher*). Probably descended from the *Ländler*, it emerged in the 18th century and gained popularity for its erotic appeal (since the two dancers hold hands and remain in close bodily contact throughout). It rose to new levels of popularity during the **Congress of Vienna**, becoming the most popular ballroom dance of the 19th century. There are two principal types, differentiated primarily in tempo: the original variety is the *Viennese waltz*, which typically moves at a brisk tempo of approximately one quarter note =180, and the slower *English waltz*, which typically moves at about half that tempo.

Today, the waltz is most famously associated with **Johann Strauss (I)** and **(II)** as well as the unrelated **Richard Strauss** and, of course, **Fryderyk Chopin** and **Pyotor Il'yich Tchaikovsky**. Most of the **long 19th century**'s major (and minor) composers produced notable compositions in waltz style, however. Among these are **Ludwig van Beethoven, Hector Berlioz, Aleksandr Glazunov, Mikhail Glinka, Charles Gounod, Johann Nepomuk Hummel, Franz Lehár, Franz Liszt, Jacques Offenbach, Camille Saint-Saëns, Franz Schubert, Jean Sibelius, Franz von Suppé,** and **Carl Maria von Weber.** [JMC]

"WAR OF THE ROMANTICS". *See* ALLGEMEINER DEUTSCHER MUSIKVEREIN; NEW GERMAN SCHOOL.

WEBER, CARL [KARL] MARIA (FRIEDRICH ERNST) VON (1786–1826). German composer, **conductor**, critic, and pianist of the Early Romantic Generation; one of the leading piano **virtuosos** and most influential music critics of his day and a seminal figure in the establishment of German Romantic **opera**. The son of an actress and a town musician who organized a touring theater company, he grew up in a thoroughly theatrical and unusually itinerant family, immersed in the contemporary repertoire of *Singspiele* and popular plays. He began taking music lessons at the age of three, but his instruction was erratic for a time because of the family's travels. During a stay in Salzburg in 1797–1798, he studied with Michael Haydn (1737–1806) and composed and published his Opus 1 (a series of six fughettas, J. 1–6). A short concert tour as a pianist and further studies in composition and singing, first with Johann Evangelist Wallishauser (1735–1816) and Johann Nepomuk Kalcher (1764–1827) in Munich and then with Abbé Vogler (1749–1814) in Vienna, led to his appointment as Kapellmeister of the Breslau theater in 1804 at the age of 17.

Weber's attempts to reform the repertoire and the musical organization of the Breslau theater engendered the enmity of the institution's older musicians, whose intrigues during his brief absence due to illness (he had drunk engraver's acid from a wine bottle) led him to resign in the autumn of 1806. He relocated to the court of the duke of Württemberg-Öls at Karlsruhe, where he found support for his composing and began his quasi-autobiographical novel *Tonkünstlers Leben* (Musician's Life), on which he worked at intervals over the remainder of his career but left unfinished at his death. His good fortunes in Karlsruhe came to an end after his father joined him there and appropriated for his own purposes money that the duke had given Weber to pay for some horses, leading to a financial scandal that resulted in both Webers' brief imprisonment and eventual banishment from the kingdom.

His fortunes began to turn during his subsequent travels. He gave two successful concerts of his music in Mannheim and met his future wife while in Frankfurt am Main to conduct the successful production of his opera *Silvana* (J. 87, 1808–1810, rev. and publ. in excerpt 1812). He also renewed his relationship with Vogler, who was now in Darmstadt, and with him formed a *Harmonischer Verein* (Harmonious Union) for the purpose of publishing music criticism (some of it pseudonymously). After a year in Darmstadt, he undertook further travels to Aschaffenburg, Augsburg, Bamberg, Frankfurt am Main, Gießen, Nuremberg, and Würzburg, settling in March 1811 in Munich. There he met the renowned clarinet virtuoso Heinrich Bärmann (1784–1847) and had his one-act Singspiel *Abu Hassan* (J. 106, comp. 1810–1811, rev. 1812–1813, publ. 1819, rev. 1823) performed in the Court Theater. With Bärmann, he undertook a concert tour to Dresden, Gotha, Leipzig, Prague, Weimar, and Berlin, where two successful concerts were followed by an enthusiastically received performance of *Silvana*. After several months in Gotha, he relocated to Prague and there accepted a three-year contract as director of the Prague Opera.

During his tenure in Prague, Weber's already weak constitution began showing signs of what would eventually become his fatal tuberculosis. Nevertheless, the position served him well. His tenure there enabled him to implement a program of reforming **orchestral** discipline, revitalizing the repertoire, and implementing an agenda that largely removed from active performance the Italianate works that up to then had predominated, instead using French **opéras comiques**, which he felt provided better models for German composers and were politically expedient during the Napoleonic era: works by **Adrien Boieldieu**, **Luigi Cherubini**, André-Ernest-Modeste Grétry (1741–1813), **Étienne-Nicolas Méhul**, and **Gaspare Spontini**, together with others by **Wolfgang Amadeus Mozart**, predominated. He also introduced Prague's musical public to **Ludwig van Beethoven**'s *Fidelio*, **Giacomo Meyerbeer**'s *Wirth und Gast*, and **Louis Spohr**'s *Faust*. In Prague, he also increased his activity as a music critic, promoting an agenda that paved the way for the concept reformulated as the **Gesamtkunstwerk** in the writings of **Richard Wagner** (whose family Weber visited frequently in 1817) after 1848. As Weber put it in a review of **E. T. A. Hoffmann**'s *Undine*, "the German ideal" would be "a self-sufficient artwork whose every feature and every contribution by the related arts are molded together in such a way that they dissolve, forming a new art."

With his fame growing, Weber entered the final chapter of his professional life in December 1816. As the German lands renewed their efforts to develop a distinctly German cultural identity in the wake of the devastation of the Napoleonic era, he was appointed music director of the new Deutsche Opera in the Saxon capital of Dresden. This he readily accepted. The post was later made permanent, and his position ranked equal to that of the director of the court's Italian opera—a major victory in advancing the status of German opera. Meanwhile, he married his longtime mistress, Caroline Brandt, and befriended the prominent **synaesthete** poet and playwright Friedrich Kind (1768–1843), whose commitment to the "liberation" of German opera through essentially synaesthetic musical and dramaturgical precepts accorded with Weber's own. Weber asked Kind to write a libretto for an opera based on the first folktale from August Apel's and Friedrich Laun's widely read *Das Gespensterbuch* (The Book of Spooks; 5 vols., 1811–1817). During the nearly four years of their collaboration on the project, Weber penned a number of highly successful compositions (his Masses in E-flat Major and G Major, the *Jubel* cantata [J. 221, 1817], and the **incidental music** to the Spanish drama *Preziosa* by P. A. Wolff [J. 279/Op. 78, 1821]). But when *Der Freischütz* was premiered in Berlin on 18 June 1821, it propelled both Weber and Kind to new levels of international fame. On the morning of the premiere, Weber also completed one of the 19th century's most popular *concertante* works for piano, the programmatic ***Konzertstück*** in F Minor (J. 282/Op. 79, publ. 1823), which was successfully premiered in Berlin just four days after the *Freischütz* opening.

In November 1821, the Vienna Opera commissioned a new opera (*Euryanthe*, J. 291, publ. 1823), and although this was only a qualified success at its premiere (25 October 1823), the continuing success of *Der Freischütz* in London led in August 1824 to an invitation to compose a new opera on the subject of either *Oberon* or *Faust*, on a libretto by James Robinson Planché (1796–1880), for performance in Covent Garden. By this point, Weber's tuberculosis had worsened, and he knew the stress would be too much for him, but he accepted the offer in order to provide for his family. Having received the libretto piecemeal, he was able to complete the score only after his arrival in London and apparently intended to rework it later for the German stage. The premiere (26 April) was a resounding success, and Weber conducted another 11 performances—but his strength was gone. He died in his sleep in London on 5 July, one day before his planned return trip to Dresden. He was initially buried in London, but in 1844, his remains were repatriated to his native Germany.

Der Freischütz remains a milestone in the history of German music and of opera generally, and Weber is best known today for it and *Euryanthe*, distantly trailed by *Oberon*. In particular, his skillful approach to musical dramaturgy and his ability to achieve startling orchestral effects without resorting to elaborate **orchestration** earned him the praise of such renowned orchestrators as **Hector Berlioz, Mikhail Glinka, Franz Liszt, Felix Mendelssohn Bartholdy, Nikolay Rimsky-Korsakov, Giuseppe Verdi**, and **Richard Wagner**. During the 19th century, he was equally renowned as a virtuoso pianist, however, and his compositions for piano solo or piano and orchestra rank among the finest of his generation, works whose **reception** has been complicated precisely because of their freedom from the aesthetic and technical presumptions of the Viennese concert **canon** (such as contrapuntal intensity, organic unity, and sustained motivic development). The compositions for piano solo or **piano duet** include the celebrated *Aufforderung zum Tanze*

(Invitation to the Dance, J. 260/Op. 65, 1819, publ. 1821), which employs an episodic form based on four separate **waltzes**; four surviving **sonatas** that serve as archetypes for the *brillante* sonata of the mid-19th century; several sets of themes with **variations** and rondos; and numerous compositions for amateurs. In addition to the F-minor *Konzertstück*, his works for solo instrument and orchestra include two piano **concertos** (J. 98 and 155/opp. 11 and 32, comp. 1810–1812 and publ. 1813 and 1814), one horn concertino (J. 188/ Op. 45, 1806, rev. 1815, publ. 1818), two clarinet concertos (J. 114 and 118/ opp. 73 and 74, comp. 1811, publ. 1823 and 1824), one clarinet concertino (J. 109/Op. 26, 1811, publ. 1813), one bassoon concerto (J. 127/Op. 75, 1811, rev. 1822, publ. 1824), and several other surviving works featuring the flute, viola, cello, or harmonichord.

The remainder of Weber's oeuvre embraces a variety of genres: a total of seven operas and another (*Die drei Pintos*, J. Anh. 5) that would be completed posthumously by **Gustav Mahler**, 25 sets of **incidental music** and numerous insertion arias and duets, five **concert arias** and duets, two Mass settings and several other sacred and choral works with and without accompaniment, 20 **part-songs** and 84 solo **songs**, two **symphonies**, several works for wind ensemble and *Harmoniemusik*, and 14 compositions for instrumental **chamber** ensemble. The concepts of *Gesamtkunstwerk* and *Leitmotiv*, both major sources of interest in the Romantic Generation, Late Romantic Generation, and Modern Romantic Generation, may be credited to him. [JMC]

See also JANISSARY MUSIC; *TABLEAU VIVANT* (PL. *TABLEAUX VIVANTS*); THEMATIC TRANSFORMATION, THEMATIC METAMORPHOSIS.

WELLINGTON'S VICTORY, OR THE BATTLE OF VITORIA, **OP. 91.** (Ger., *Wellingtons Sieg, oder die Schlacht bei Vittoria.*) **Programmatic** depiction by **Ludwig van Beethoven** of the Duke of Wellington's (1769–1852) defeat of Joseph Bonaparte (1768–1844; older brother of Napoléon Bonaparte and king of Spain during the Napoleonic era) in the Battle of Vitoria (Spain) on 21 June 1813. The battle was of little long-term strategic import in the Napoleonic Wars, but it did serve to strengthen the resistance movements against Bonaparte and offer an important symbolic victory both for Europeans who were subjects of the puppet regimes installed under Bonaparte's reign and for those who faced the prospect of becoming such subjects. Citizens of the German lands and the Habsburg Empire were anxiously following the progress of the wars with (eventually well-founded) concern that they, too, would eventually fall under Napoleonic rule. When word of the victory reached Vienna, the Viennese court mechanician Johann Nepomuk Maelzel (1772–1838; inventor of one of the ear horns Beethoven had used), who had earlier eased Beethoven's financial difficulties and arranged for the two of them to visit London together, engaged him to compose a new work for his "panharmonicon," a mechanical instrument that simulated the sounds of an **orchestra**, in celebration of the battle.

Maelzel suggested the essential thematic material to be quoted in the work, provided the overall plan, and sketched the drum and trumpet fanfares. He also suggested that Beethoven orchestrate the work and have it performed in that guise in order to generate funds to support their trip to London. Beethoven complied, and the work was an immense success when it was premiered in Vienna on 8 December 1813, greatly overshadowing Beethoven's Seventh **Symphony** (Op. 92, comp. 1811–1812, publ. 1816). The concert was repeated by popular demand on 12 December, but the success of the work also led to a split between the collaborative composers: Maelzel claimed it as his property, Beethoven arranged for a third performance solely for his own benefit (2 January 1814), and Maelzel arranged the piece for his instrument and retaliated against Beethoven's third performance by taking a copy of the orchestral score along with him on a trip to Munich, where he had the orchestral version performed in a concert for his own benefit. Beethoven sued in the Vienna courts and sent a letter to the musicians of London entreating them not to support Maelzel. That notwithstanding, the work was performed in London in 1815. Beethoven sold the rights to the Viennese firm of S. A. Steiner and published it, with no reference to Maelzel, in 1816—not only in the orchestral version (parts and full score, for piccolo, two flutes, two oboes, two clarinets, two bassoons, contrabassoon, four horns, two trumpets in E flat and two in C, three trombones, timpani, and divided percussion sections) but also in arrangements for nine-part *Harmonie-Musik*, string **quintet, piano trio, piano duet**, and **piano** solo. The full score and piano arrangements include a lengthy prefatory note in German and French explaining the construction of the piece and providing detailed instructions for performance.

Although Beethoven privately referred to *Wellington's Victory* as a "Battle Symphony," it belongs to the genre of the *battaglia* represented earlier by Frantisek Kotzwara's (1730–1791) *The Battle of Prague* (1788), enormously popular in the early 19th century and certainly familiar to Beethoven. Like Kotzwara's warhorse, the work depicts the preparations for battle, the battle itself, and the retreat of the vanquished army (with a brief reference to the plight of the wounded) before concluding with a hymnic celebration of the victors and the ensuing peace that they had secured; this concluding section accounts for the extended "Victory Symphony" that comprises the entire second half of the work. Apparently new to Maelzel's and Beethoven's conception, however, was the idea of symbolizing the competing forces through discrete themes taken from their actual musical cultures: the British, Spanish, and Portuguese forces allied under the duke of Wellington's command are symbolized by *God Save the King* and *Rule Brittania*, while the forces of

Joseph Bonaparte and his general are symbolized by the tune *Marlborough s'en va-t-en guerre* (also familiar as *For He's a Jolly Good Fellow*). The work thus represents an important contribution to the 19th-century discourse of musical **topics** based on quotation or allusion. The scores include specific **paratextual** identifiers for the work's programmatic elements: "English drums," "Rule Brittania," "French drums," "Marlbourgh," "Signal for Attack of the French," "Signal for Attack of the British," "English cannons" and "French cannons," and so on.

Wellington's Victory is today considered among Beethoven's weakest works, a veritable case study in the aesthetic liabilities of **program music**. Beethoven was unashamed of it, however, and it certainly represented a musical plot archetype that was later echoed (arguably more successfully) in **Pyotor Il'yich Tchaikovsky**'s still-celebrated *1812* **concert overture** (1882). [JMC]

See also METRONOME; NARRATIVE; PROGRAM SYMPHONY *OR* CHARACTERISTIC SYMPHONY.

WIDOR, CHARLES-MARIE (-JEAN-ALBERT) (1844–1937). French composer, organist, and teacher of the Late Romantic Generation. He came from a family of organists and organ builders and on the recommendation of **Aristide Cavaillé-Coll** entered the Brussels **Conservatory** in 1863, studying organ there with Jacques-Nicolas Lemmens (1823–1881) and composition with **François-Joseph Fétis**. After graduation, with the help of Cavaillé-Colle and **Camille Saint-Saëns**, he assumed the prestigious post of organist at the Church of St.-Sulpice in Paris, home to Cavaillé-Colle's magnum opus. He retained this post, which was originally designated as temporary, until 1934, when he retired at the age of 90. In the meantime he also succeeded **César Franck** as professor of organ at the Paris Conservatory (1890–1896) and then **Théodore Dubois** as professor of composition there. He was elected to the Académie des Beaux-Arts in 1910 and became its permanent secretary in 1914. His many distinguished pupils in organ and composition include Marcel Dupré (who succeeded him at St.-Sulpice), Arthur Honegger, Darius Milhaud, Albert Schweitzer, Charles Tournemire, and Louis Vierne.

Widor's output includes three **operas**; two sets of **incidental music**; one **ballet** and one ballet-pantomime; five **symphonies** for **orchestra** (nos. 3–5 with organ, No. 4 with chorus); one **tone poem** and one **concert overture**; one piano **concerto**, one violin concerto, one cello concerto, and several other works for solo instrument with orchestra; a sizable body of instrumental **chamber music** (including two piano **quintets**, one **piano quartet**, one **piano trio**, two violin **sonatas** and one cello sonata, and many smaller pieces); 15 *opera* for **piano** solo; numerous sacred and secular choral works (a cappella and with accompaniment of piano or orchestra); and 10 *opera* of *mélodies* and other vocal **chamber music**. He is best known for his 10 organ symphonies (opp. 13, 42, 70, and 73, 1872–1900), which brilliantly deploy the enormous timbral vocabulary of the French Romantic organ (post–Cavaillé-Coll) as a substitute for the sounds of a full post-Romantic orchestra. [JMC]

WIECK SCHUMANN, CLARA. *See* SCHUMANN (NÉE WIECK), CLARA JOSEPHINE (1819–1896).

WILLIAM TELL. See GUILLAUME TELL.

WILLIAMS, ALBERTO (1862–1952). Argentine composer, **conductor**, pianist, and poet of the Modern Romantic Generation; of English and Basque descent. He was born into a musical family and studied **piano** from an early age. In 1881 he published his opus 1, a **mazurka** titled *Ensueño de juventud* (Reverie of Youth). In 1882 he went to Paris with a scholarship from the Paris **Conservatory**, where he studied composition with **César Franck**. After returning to Argentina in 1889, he made a concerted effort to absorb the melodies, rhythms, and forms of Argentine folk music into his own works (*see* FOLK SONG). In addition to his published works that adopted themes, subjects, and musical elements from Argentine music, he founded the Buenos Aires Conservatory in 1893 (directing it until 1941) and several series of concerts that were devoted to promoting music and music education in his native land. He also served as vice president and then president of the Argentine National Arts Commission, and president of the Argentine Concert Association, the Argentine Association of Composers, the Chamber Music Association, and the Folklore Association. The significance of his contributions is evident in his having conducted a concert of his own music with the Berlin Philharmonic Orchestra, already one of Europe's finest, in 1900 and in his election to France's Légion d'Honneur in 1939. Although his works written after about 1910 also include elements from the European mainstream tradition, he is generally considered the founding figure of Argentine musical **nationalism**.

Williams's 117 numbered *opera* include 75 **songs** and numerous **part-songs** and choral works (many of them deeply indebted to Argentine folk styles), more than 100 compositions for piano solo, three violin **sonatas** and one cello sonata, nine **symphonies**, three *Argentine Suites* for string **orchestra**, and other works for orchestra. He is best known today for his piano works (especially the *Argentine Sonata*, Op. 74, 1917). Among his songs, the four *Canciones incaicas* (Op. 45, 1907) are particularly noteworthy. [JMC]

WINTERREISE. (Ger., "winter journey.") Iconic **song cycle** (D. 911) for male voice in two books by Franz Schubert, on poems from the *Gedichte aus den hinterlassenen Papieren eines reisenden Waldhornisten* (Poems from the Posthumous Papers of a Traveling Hornist, 2 vols. 1821–1824) of Wilhelm Müller (1794–1827), whose poetry Schubert had also used in his previous song cycle, *Die schöne Müllerin* (The Fair Miller Maid, D. 795, 1823). Müller's collection comprised a total of 77 poems. Schubert extracted 24 of these for *Winterreise* and arranged them into two volumes, reordering them to present a series of fragments depicting moments in a physical and psychological journey born of unrequited love and leading to utter alienation. He began composing the first volume (**songs** 1–12) in February 1827 and completed it that spring; it was published on 14 January 1828. Meanwhile, Müller had died on 30 September 1827, and Schubert had begun composing the sequel (designated *Fortseztung*, "continuation") in October of that year. Schubert was correcting the proofs for Volume 2 during his final illness, and it was posthumously published by Haslinger as his Op. 89 on 30 December 1828. Book 1 (Songs 1–12) originally was tonally closed, beginning and ending in D minor, but when Schubert began Book 2 he transposed the last song of the first book down a third (to B minor), thus creating a series of songs whose tonal structure invites continuation and/or completion. The final song of Book 2 (No. 24) then returns B minor, implicitly completing the tonal journey provisionally realized at the end of Book 1.

Winterreise raised to new levels of sophistication the essential concepts of the song cycle as they had been cultivated earlier in **Ludwig van Beethoven**'s *An die ferne Geliebte* and other, earlier cycles by composers such as Ludwig Berger (1777–1839), Friedrich Heinrich Himmel (1765–1814), **Conradin Kreutzer**, Sigismund Neukomm (1778–1858), Ferdinand Ries (1784–1838), and **Carl Maria von Weber**. Part of this sophistication (anticipated in the *Müllerin* cycle) has to do with the subtlety and psychological depth of the accompaniment, which not only engages in vivid text painting (e.g., the graphic depiction of birds singing, ravens croaking, dogs baying, the rotating weather vane, or the drones and cramped circular melodies of the hurdy-gurdy) but also establishes the contextual action for various moments in the cycle's progression (the plodding rhythms of the accompaniment evoke images of the protagonist's footsteps in the dreary winter landscape) and at times belies the lyric persona's assertions, musically telling the truth when the words of the text reflect his deepening cycle of denial. Situated in the context of Metternich's Vienna, the cycle's progressive decline into bleak isolation also reads as an allegory for the city's increasingly oppressive political situation, thus transforming the well-established **topic** of the *Wanderlieder* **cycle** into a metaphor for the individual human condition and that of society as whole. Schubert also constructs a set of subtly recurring **motives** and characteristic melodic gestures that reinforce its unity of conception.

Winterreise is among the longest of Schubert's compositions, with its total duration of 72 minutes exceeding even that of the "Great" C-major **Symphony** (D. 944). Although its individual songs are sometimes performed individually or transposed, such alterations fundamentally violate the compositional intentions on whose behalf Schubert went to elaborate means in creating and revising the work. As a cycle, it became paradigmatic for numerous later compositions, not least among them **Robert Schumann**'s *Dichterliebe* (Poet's Love, Op. 42, 1840, publ. 1840–1841) and **Gustav Mahler**'s *Lieder eines fahrenden Gesellen* (Songs of a Wayfarer, 1883–1885, rev. ?1891–1896) and *Kindertotenlieder*. [JMC]

See also CYCLIC FORM; VOICE, VOICEDNESS, VOCALITY.

WINTER'S JOURNEY. See *WINTERREISE.*

WOLF, HUGO (FILIPP JAKOB) (1860–1903). Austrian composer and writer on music of the Modern Romantic Generation, usually regarded, with **Richard Strauss** and **Gustav Mahler**, as the fin-de-siècle consummation of the approach to the German art **song** begun (by most accounts) with **Franz Schubert**'s "Gretchen am Spinnrade" (D. 118) in 1814. He worked in most of the genres current in his day, including **opera** (one completed and two others begun), **incidental music** (one completed set), choral music (five settings with accompaniment of **piano** or **orchestra**, plus 13 a cappella settings), **orchestral** music (one surviving **symphony**, one **symphonic poem**, three **serenades**, and a few other works), instrumental **chamber music** (including one complete **string quartet**, an *Intermezzo* and a **serenade** for string quartet, and several lost or abandoned works), and a handful of surviving works for piano solo (most importantly, one paraphrase on **Richard Wagner**'s *Die Meistersinger* and another on *Die Walküre*; *see* FANTASIA, FANTASY, FANCY).

Wolf made his most important marks, however, in music criticism and in the genre of the German art song. In particular, his 250 *Gesänge* and *Lieder* stand as milestones in the history of those genres and of German poetry, notable not only for their extraordinary expressive intensity and success at achieving congruity of mood and idea between text and music but also for their harmonic richness and their ability to transfer to the patently intimate genres of song a musical idiom that was born in the **symphonic poems** of **Franz Liszt** and the **music dramas** and **operas** of **Richard Wagner**. Most of his songs were published in collections devoted to a single poet or group of poet: 53 songs on poems of Eduard Mörike (1804–1875; WW I, 1888–1890, publ. 1890), 20 on poems of Joseph Freiherr von Eichendorff (1788–1857; WW II, comp. 1880, 1886–1888, publ. 1889), 51 on texts by **Johann Wolfgang von Goethe** (WW III, comp. 1888–1890, publ. 1890), 41 on German translations of Spanish poems (the *Spanisches Liederbuch* [Spanish Songbook], WW IV, comp. 1888–1890, publ. 1891), and 46 songs published in two volumes on German texts translated from Italian (the *Italienisches Liederbuch* [Italian Songbook], WWV V, vol. 1 comp. 1890–1891, publ. 1892; vol. 2 comp. and publ. 1896). His remaining songs are on translated texts by poets ranging from **Lord Byron** and Henrik Ibsen (1828–1906) to Miguel de Cervantes (1547–1616) and **William Shakespeare**, among others.

Wolf was born near Graz and studied music while young, in 1875 entering the Vienna Conservatory, where he studied harmony, piano, and composition and began composing. Also during these years, he was introduced to the music and writings of Wagner and became one of the elder composer's most ardent devotees in conservative Vienna, finding support and comparable enthusiasm in the ideas and music of his fellow student Gustav Mahler. He was dismissed from the Conservatory in March 1877 and tried to make a living as a private teacher but was forced to rely on support from his father and friends. From 1884 to 1887, he worked as music critic for the *Wiener Salonblatt* (Viennese **Salon**-Page), earning a reputation not only for the wit and incisiveness of his writing but also his outspoken criticisms of **Johannes Brahms** and his passionate pronunciations of Wagnerian idealism. By this point, Wolf had experienced several intense bursts of compositional activity—most notably 1875, 1878, December 1882–May 1883, and the winter of 1886 to the spring of 1887—but in 1888–1889 he composed nearly half of his mature songs: the Goethe songs, the Mörike songs, most of the Eichendorff songs, and 26 songs of the *Spanisches Liederbuch*. He also gave his first public performances accompanying his songs during this period and in 1888, thanks to the support of **Engelbert Humperdinck**, finally succeeded in having his music published (*Sechs Lieder für eine Frauenstimme*, WW VI, comp. 1877–1882, and *Sechs Gedichte von Scheffel, Mörike, Goethe und Kerner*, WWVI, comp. 1883–1887).

This sudden burst of creativity and public recognition was beneficial to Wolf. In the spring of 1890 he completed the *Spanish Songbook*, and in 1890–1891 he began work on the *Italian Songbook*. More importantly, he also turned his attention to the genre of opera, completing the **comic opera** *Der Corregidor* (after Pedro Antonio de Alarcón's [1833–1891] *El sombrero de tres picos* [The Three-Cornered Hat]) in March–December 1895 and completing the *Italian Songbook* in March–April 1896. The opera was a success when it was premiered in Mannheim on 7 June 1896 but failed to gain a secure following. Meanwhile, his health had been deteriorating from syphilis probably contracted in 1878. He composed three settings of texts by Michelangelo Buonarotti (1475–1564) in March 1897 and began work on a new opera that July but suffered a complete mental breakdown and was institutionalized in September. By January 1898, he had improved enough to be released but soon relapsed. He was returned to the asylum in October and died there four and a half years later, having been unable to compose or play music since 1899.

It is generally accepted that Wolf was able, in at least some sense, to bring out inner truths and ideas of the words he set to music through music that, by genre and style, would have been incomprehensible or offensive to his textual sources: certainly, his settings of folk-like texts are anything but folk-like (*see* FOLK SONG; VOLKSTÜMLICHKEIT), and certainly his distended settings of texts by Goethe, with their almost symphonic accompaniments, would not have been to the liking of their poet, who preferred the **Second Berlin School**'s approach to text/music relationships. That ability to enhance the verity of art through paradox appealed to modernist sensibilities of Wolf's own generation and the next—something similar was articulated in Pablo Picasso's well-known dictum that "art is the lie that makes us realize truth"—and underlies the expressive intensity of his compositions and his prose alike. His music criticism is incisive and insightful, bluntly taking contemporaries to task for catering to outmoded traditions and developing new ones (such as what he called the "epidemic" of song recitals that were public potpourris of popular favorites rather than concentrated private explorations of the expressive potentials of poetry). Here, as in his music, the forcefulness of his personality and the brilliance with which he conveyed his ideas are extraordinary and occasionally off-putting, a small-scale but equally potent counterpart and counterpoint to the massive staged and choral/orchestral explorations of post-Romantic culture of Mahler and **Richard Strauss**. [JMC]

WOO. (Ger., Werke ohne Opuszahl.) Works without opus number. The term was developed by music bibliographers in order to assign a relative chronological position to compositions that composers either left unpublished at their death or published without an assigned opus number. The latter category typically applies to minor compositions. WoO numbers do not correlate directly with opus numbers or other catalogers' numbers but only with each other; that is, WoO 2 chronologically follows WoO 1 and precedes WoO 3, but all three may fall at any point within the chronology of the composer's works that were published with opus number. [JMC]

See also COMPOSITIONAL PROCESS, CREATIVE PROCESS; COPYRIGHT AND PERFORMANCE RIGHT; PRINTING AND PUBLISHING OF MUSIC.

Y

YEARS OF PILGRIMAGE. *See ANNÉES DE PÈLERINAGE.*

THE YOUTH'S MAGIC HORN. *See DES KNABEN WUNDERHORN.*

Z

ZARZUELA. (Sp., from *zarza*, "bramble bush," "jumble," or, more literally, "thing that is all linked together and intertwined in itself.") A type of Spanish-language **operetta** or **vaudeville**, characterized by spoken dialogue intermingled with **song** and instrumental music; usually considered the most important traditional Spanish-language branch of **comic opera**. The genre had flourished in the mid-17th century to distinguish relatively informal musical plays in one or two acts with spoken dialogue from the usual courtly fare of three-act Spanish-language *comedias*, and its name may derive from the royal hunting lodge Palace of the Zarzuela on the outskirts of Madrid.

During the early 19th century the zarzuela as a genre was moribund, Italian opera being the predominant variety of staged musical drama on the Iberian Peninsula, followed in more popular venues by the *sainete* and the *tonadilla escénica*. It was revived in the early 19th century, however, first in an academic context and then publicly. The academic work first dubbed a *zarzuela* was a one-act opera titled *Los enredos de un curioso* (Entanglements of a Curious Man) with music in Italian and spoken dialogue in Spanish, composed by Ramón Carnicer (1789–1855) and Pedro Albéniz y Basanta (1795–1855) on a **libretto** by musicologist Baltasar Saldoni (1807–1889) for performance in the Madrid **Conservatory**. (In some sources, the composer Albéniz is incorrectly identified as Mateo Pérez de Albéniz [1755–1831], who was an organist and choirmaster, not affiliated with the Madrid Conservatory, and had died before *Los enredos* was composed.)

The genre's public reemergence, with music as well as dialogue in Spanish, was fueled by the growing Spanish **nationalist** sentiment, manifesting itself first in a collaboration by Italian composer Basilio Basili (1803–1895) and the poet/librettist Bretón de los Herreros (1796–1873), an outspoken opponent of Italian **opera**. The most important work in this revival was the one-act *El novio y el concierto* (The Groom and the Concert, 1839), followed by the same creators' *El ventorillo de Crespo* (The Inn at Crespo, 1842). The success of those two works made possible a stream of new zarzuelas over the coming decade, culminating in the premiere of *Colegiales y soldados* (Colleagues and Soldiers) by Rafael Hernando (1822–1888) and librettists Mariano Pina Bohigas and Francisco Lumbreras, the work that is considered the first modern zarzuela. Together with several other Spanish nationalist composers of the Late Romantic Generation—the so-called *grupo de los cinco* (group of five) that also included **Francisco Asenjo Barbieri** (1823–1894), Joaquín Gaztambide (1822–1870), José Inzenga (1828–1891), and Cristóbal Oudrid y Segura (1825–1877)—Hernando reestablished the zarzuela as the preeminent genre of Spanish popular musical theater. By 1856 its popularity was sufficient to warrant the founding of a theater specifically devoted to the genre (the Teatro de la Zarzuela, Madrid), and by 1885 Barbieri was able to list 475 librettists and 240 composers of the genre.

For much of the 19th century, the musical style of the zarzuela exhibited few influences of Andalusian or other Iberian folk music and was deeply indebted to that of Italian opera, while the plots themselves followed models established by French traditional **opéra comique** (known in Spanish as *teatro comico*). A new strand characterized by contemporary plots and middle-class characters, after the model of **Jacques Offenbach**'s operettas for the Bouffes-Parisiens, emerged in 1866 with *El joven Telémaco* (The Young Tememaco; music by José Rogel [1829–1901] and libretto by Eusebio Blasco).

The decisive turn toward the modern zarzuela emerged in the aftermath of the Revolution of 1868. This new variety of zarzuela, known as the *género chico* (little genre), was cast in one act, based on middle-class situations, and employed music influenced by popular and **folk song**. The genre was a tremendous success, with more than 1,500 works being produced in 11 theaters specifically devoted to it by the 1890s. Its best-known composers include **Tomás Bretón**, Federico Chueca (1846–1908), Joaquín Valverde (1846–1910), and Manuel Nieto (1844–1915). [JMC]

ZAUBEROPER. (Ger., "magic opera.") Most generally, term for any German-language **opera** in which magic plays an integral role in the plot and directly affects interactions among characters; more specifically, a **Singspiel** that exhibits these characteristics, usually along with elaborate special effects and scenery. Using the general definition of the term, **Richard Wagner**'s *Handlung* (drama) *Tristan und Isolde* (WWV 90, 1865) and **Richard Strauss**'s *Die Frau ohne Schatten* (TrV 264/Op. 65, 1919) may be considered *Zauberoper*. Construed more specifically (i.e., with spoken dialogue), the genre flourished in the late Enlightenment and the early 19th century, especially in Vienna. The most famous example is **Wolfgang Amadeus Mozart**'s *Die Zauberflöte* (The Magic Flute, K. 620, 1791), and the most influential 19th-century example is **Carl Maria von Weber**'s *Der Freischütz* (J. 277, 1821). Other notable examples include **E. T. A. Hoffmann**'s *Undine* (AV 70, 1816) and **Franz Schubert**'s *Die Zauberharfe* (The Magic Harp, D. 644, 1820). Weber's *Oberon* would qualify for the genre but for the fact that it is not in German (it was commissioned by Covent Garden and written in English), and **Gaspare Spontini**'s *Alcidor* (1825) would qualify except for its use of recitative. [JMC]

See also MÄRCHENOPER.

ZUKUNFTSMUSIK. (Fr., la musique de l'avenir.) German for "music of the future" or "future music," associated with **Richard Wagner** via his 1850 pamphlet *Das Kunstwerk der Zukunft* (The Artwork of the Future) but later discouraged by him. [JMC]

See ARTWORK OF THE FUTURE; GESAMTKUNSTWERK; NEW GERMAN SCHOOL.

Bibliography

CONTENTS

INTRODUCTION

This bibliography is designed to introduce the reader to the breadth of literature on 19th-century music: reference works, critical editions, published collections of primary sources, surveys of the era, and studies that address specific regions, contexts, issues, and individual people. Preference is given to English-language publications from the past 30 years; items beyond those parameters are included either because of their significance (e.g. *Die Musik in Geschichte und Gegenwart*) or because they have no worthy substitute in English.

The first set of entries, "General Encyclopedias and Lexica," identifies general music-historical references that are ideal for quickly gathering the basic facts on a variety of subjects. All address topics throughout history; none is restricted to the long 19th century. A vital starting point for any student must be *Grove Music Online* (*GMO*), an online reference edited by L. Deane Root. Based on the second edition of the *New Grove Dictionary of Music and Musicians*, *GMO* is in a constant state of development, with new updates occurring all the time. Many university and college libraries subscribe to this resource.

Below this, a list of source-critical series of editions is provided. Critical editions present a printed piece of music in a way that communicates clearly to the reader the source of its content and clearly differentiates between authorial and editorial information. Whereas a more conventional score or part (a "practical edition") delivers a single, plain reading of a composition while concealing ambiguities regarding conflicting versions, apparent mistakes or omissions in manuscripts, contradictions among sources and versions, and similar issues, a critical edition presents a musical work in all of its naked complexity. Above all, it reveals the source for every note and style marking, as well as when and why the editor might change or diverge from that source in a given instance. Typically, the reader of a critical edition can also expect to learn about a composition's history (from initial inspiration to premiere and later performances), its contemporary significance, reception history, and performance-practice issues. Where two series are listed under a single composer, usually the second, older source is listed to compensate for the incomplete state of the newer one (e.g., see those listed under Beethoven). In certain other cases (e.g., Bennett), multiple smaller-scale edition projects are listed to compensate for the lack of a complete works edition.

Entries pertaining to primary sources take the reader beyond explanations and descriptions to the documents themselves. The collections and anthologies of primary sources showcase 19th-century ideas about music in excerpts of select essays, articles, books, and letters, many of which are typically mentioned in surveys of music history. Also listed are significant treatises commonly available in later editions (e.g., A. B. Marx, *Die Lehre von der musikalischen Komposition, praktisch-theoretisch* [Theory and Practice of Musical Composition, 1837–1847]) and significant music periodicals from the era (e.g., the *LAmZ* or *Dwight's Journal of Music*).

The remainder of the bibliography is devoted to secondary literature. "Surveys of 19th-Century Music" provides sweeping book-length treatments of the era; currently, Taruskin's *The Oxford History of Western Music, Volume 3: The Nineteenth Century* stands out among the others in its depth and newness. A series of subtopics is addressed under the heading *Narrower Studies*, accounting for the most significant literature addressing musical genres, music and politics, reception history, and the like. Students interested in aesthetics might begin with the two anthologies listed: Dalhaus/Katz's *Contemplating Music* and Lippman's *Musical Aesthetics*. Those investigating performance practice would do well to start with Brown's *Classical & Romantic Performing Practice, 1750–1900*. And on the various issues concerning reception, Dahlhaus's chapter "Problems in Reception History" remains seminal.

Finally, specific composers are listed with major English-language scholarly publications, works catalogs, and, in some instances, relevant websites. Most composers are listed with only a few vital sources, but certain major names are accompanied by many more. For these, readers unsure where to begin might seek out research guides and "bio-bibliographies" published by Garland, Greenwood, Routledge, and others; these typically feature helpful biographical essays as well as thorough overviews of relevant research materials. For many composers, Cambridge University Press has published brief, high-quality biographies with similar titles: Kennedy's *The Life of Elgar*, Jones's *The Life of Haydn*, and so on. These are also ideal introductions. Those in need of further direction might consider these recommendations for initial readings: for Beethoven, Kinderman's biography and Cooper's *Beethoven Compendium*; for Berlioz, Cairns's biography and the Langford/ Graves research guide; for Brahms, Platt's research guide; for Chopin, Samson's *Chopin* and Smialek's research guide; for Debussy, Nichols's short biography; for Elgar, Kennedy's biography and Kent's research guide; for Haydn, Jones's biography; for Janáček, Tyrrell's *Janáček: Years of a Life*;

for Liszt, Saffle's research guide and Walker's biographies; for Mahler, Filler's research guide and Franklin's short biography (La Grange is essential but not the best place for a novice to start); for Mendelssohn, the Cooper/ Mace research guide and Mercer-Taylor's short biography; for Mozart, Rosselli; for Puccini, Budden's musical-biographical study; for Schumann, Daverio's work; for Sibelius, the biography by Barnett; for Richard Strauss, Gilliam's *The Life of Richard Strauss*; for Verdi, Rosselli's biography and Harwood's research guide; and for Wagner, Saffle's research guide and Millington's *Wagner Compendium*.

GENERAL ENCYCLOPEDIAS AND LEXICA

Finscher, Ludwig, ed. *Die Musik in Geschichte und Gegenwart: Allgemeine Enzyklopädie der Musik* (Music in History and in the Present: General Music Encyclopedia). 2nd ed. 27 vols. Kassel: Bärenreiter, 1994–2007.

Randel, Don Michael. *The Harvard Biographical Dictionary of Music.* Cambridge, MA: Belknap Press of Harvard University Press, 1996.

————. *The Harvard Dictionary of Music.* 4th ed. Cambridge, MA: Belknap Press of Harvard University Press, 2003.

Root, Deane, ed. *Grove Music Online.* Oxford: Oxford University Press, 2001–. Part of *Oxford Music Online* at http://www.oxfordmusiconline. com.

Sadie, Stanley, and John Tyrrell, eds. *The New Grove Dictionary of Music and Musicians.* 2nd ed. 29 vols. New York: Grove, 2001.

SELECTED SOURCE-CRITICAL SERIES OF EDITIONS

General

Hallmark, Rufus, ed. *Recent Researches in the Music of the Nineteenth and Early Twentieth Centuries.* Middleton, WI: A-R Editions, 1979–.

Beethoven

Werke. Edited by Joseph Schmidt-Görg and Martin Staehelin. Bonn and Munich: Henle, 1961–.

Ludwig van Beethoven's Werke. Edited by Ferdinand Davis et al. Leipzig: Breitkopf & Härtel, 1862–1888.

Bellini

Edizione critica delle opere di Vincenzo Bellini (Critical Edition of the Works of Vincenzo Bellini). Edited by Fabrizio Della Seta, Alessandro Roccatagliati, and Luca Zoppelli. Milan: Ricordi, 1999–.

Bennett

William Sterndale Bennett: Works for Pianoforte Solo. Edited by Nicholas Temperley. The London Pianoforte School 1766–1860: Clementi, Dussek, Cramer, Field, Pinto, Sterndale Bennett, and Other Masters of the Pianoforte, vols. 17–19. New York: Garland, 1985.
English Songs, 1800–1860. Edited by Geoffrey Bush and Nicholas Temperley. Musica Britannica, vol. 43. London: Stainer and Bell, 1979.
Sterndale Bennett: Piano and Chamber Music. Edited by Geoffrey Bush. Musica Britannica, vol. 37. London: Stainer and Bell, 1972.

Berlioz

Hector Berlioz: New Edition of the Complete Works. Edited by Hugh Macdonald. Kassel: Bärenreiter, 1967–.

Brahms

Neue Ausgabesämtliche Werke (New Edition of Complete Works). Edited by Johannes Behr et al. Munich: Henle, 1996–.
Sämtliche Werke (Complete Works). Edited by Hans Gál et al. Leipzig: Breitkopf & Härtel, 1926–1927.

Bruckner

Neue Bruckner Edition. Edited by Paul Hawkshaw et al. Kassel: Bärenreiter, 2012–.
Sämtliche Werke (Complete Works). Edited by Robert Haas et al. Vienna: Musikwissenschaftlicher Verlag der Internationalen Bruckner-Gesellschaft, 1951.

Chopin

Wydarie Narodowe Dziel Frederyka Chopin [Polish National Edition]. Edited by J. Ekier. Warsaw, 1967–.

Complete Works: According to the Autographs and Original Editions with Critical Commentary. Edited by Ignace J. Paderewski et al. Warsaw: Fryderyk Chopin Institute and Kraków: Polish Music Publications, 1949–1962.

Cornelius

P. Cornelius: Musikalische Werke. Edited by Max Hasse. 5 vols. Leipzig: Breitkopf & Härtel, 1905–1906.

Debussy

Oeuvres complètes de Claude Debussy (Complete Works of Claude Debussy). Edited by François Lesure et al. Paris: Durand, 1985–.

Delius

Frederick Delius: Complete Works. Edited by Thomas Beecham and Robert Threlfall. London: Stainer & Bell, 1951–1993.

Dvořák

Antonín Dvořák: Soubornévydánídíla (Complete Works Edition). Edited by Otakar Šourek et al. Prague: Artia, 1955–.

Elgar

The Elgar Complete Edition. Edited by Robert Anderson. London: Novello, 1981–.

Fauré

Gabriel Fauré: The Complete Works. Edited by Jean-Michel Nectoux. Kassel: Bärenreiter, 2010–.

Fibich

Souborné vydánídĕl Zdeňka Fibicha (Collected Edition of Zdeňek Fibich's Works). Edited by Ludvik Boháček et al. Prague: Státní hudební vydavatelství, 1950–1967.

Foster

The Music of Stephen C. Foster: A Critical Edition. Edited by Steven Saunders and Deane L. Root. Washington, DC: Smithsonian Institution Press, 1990–.

Gade

Niels W. Gade: Works. Edited by the Foundation for the Publication of the Works of Niels W. Gade, Copenhagen. Kassel: Bärenreiter, 1995–.

Grieg

Samlede verker (Complete Works). Edited by Dag Schjelderup-Ebbe et al. Frankfurt: Peters, 1977–1995.

Haydn

Werke. Edited by Jens Peter Larson et al. Munich: Henle, 1950–.

Heinrich

Heinrich: Complete Works. Edited by Andrew Stiller et al. Philadelphia: Kallisti Music, 1991–.

Hensel

Ausgewählte Klavierwerke (Selected Piano Works). Edited by Fanny Kistner-Hensel. Munich: Henle, 1986.
Ausgewählte Lieder für Singstimme und Klavier (Selected Lieder for Voice and Piano). Edited by Annette Maurer. Wiesbaden: Breitkopf & Härtel, 1994.

Weltliche a-cappella-Chöre von 1846 (Secular A Cappella Choral Works from 1846). Edited by Elke Mascha Blankenburg. Kassel: Furore-Edition, 1988.

Hoffmann

E. T. A. Hoffmann: Ausgewählte musikalische Werke (Selected Musical Works). Edited by Georg von Dadelsen et al. Mainz: Schott, 1971–2006.

Janáček

Leoš Janáček: Souborné kritické vydání (Complete Critical Edition). Edited by Jiří Vysloužil et al. Prague: Supraphon, 1978–.

Liszt

Neue Ausgabe sämtlicher Werke (New Edition of Collected Works). Edited by Zoltan Gárdonyi et al. Budapest: Editio Musica, 1970–.
Franz Liszts musikalische Werke (Franz Liszt's Musical Works). Edited by Ferruccio Busoni et al. Leipzig: Breitkopf & Härtel, 1907–1936.

Loewe

Carl Loewes Werke: Gesamtausgabe der Balladen, Legenden, Lieder und Gesänge (Carl Loewe's Works: Complete Edition of Ballads, Legends, Lieder, and Songs). Edited by Max Runze. Leipzig: Breitkopf & Härtel, 1899–1904.

Mahler

Sämtliche Werke: Kritische Gesamtausgabe (Collected Works: Critical Complete Edition). Edited by Reinhold Kubik et al. Vienna: Universal Edition, 1960–.

Mendelssohn

Leipziger Ausgabe der Werke von Felix Mendelssohn Bartholdy (Leipzig Edition of the Works of Felix Mendelssohn Bartholdy). Edited by the Sächsische Akademie der Wissenschaften. Leipzig: Breitkopf & Härtel, 1997–.

Leipziger Ausgabe der Werke Felix Mendelssohn Bartholdys (Leipzig Edition of Felix Mendelssohn Bartholdy's Works). Edited by the Internationale Felix-Mendelssohn-Gesellschaft. Leipzig: Deutscher Verlag für Musik, 1960–1977.

Felix Mendelssohn Bartholdy's Werke. Edited by Julius Rietz et al. Leipzig: Breitkopf & Härtel, 1874–1877.

Meyerbeer

Meyerbeer Werkausgabe (Meyerbeer Works Edition). Edited by Jürgen Selk et al. Munich: Ricordi, 2010–.

Mozart

Wolfgang Amadeus Mozart: Neue Ausgabe sämtlicher Werke (New Edition of the Collected Works). Edited by Ernst Fritz Schmidt. Kassel: Bärenreiter, 1955–1991.

Mussorgsky

Polnoyev akademicheskoye sobraniye sochineniy M. P. Musorgskogo (Complete Academic Collection of the Works of M. P. Mussorgsky). Edited by Eugene M. Levashev et al. Moscow: Muzyka, 1996–.

Nielsen

Carl Nielsen Udgaven (Edition). Edited by Niels Krabbe et al. Copenhagen: Royal Library, 1998–.

Paganini

Edizione nazionale delle opere di Niccolò Paganini (National Edition of the Works of Niccolò Paganini). Edited by Raffaello Monterosso. Rome: Istituto Italiano per la Storia della Musica, 1976–.

Paine

Complete Piano Music. Edited by John C. Schmidt. New York: Da Capo, 1984.

John Knowles Paine: The Complete Organ Works. Edited by Wayne Leupold and Murray Somerville. Boston: Wayne Leupold Editions, 1996.

Reger

Sämtliche Werke (Collected Works). Edited by Hermann Unger et al. 38 vols. Wiesbaden: Bärenreiter, 1954–1970 and 1974–1986.

Rheinberger

Sämtliche Werke (Collected Works). Edited by Günter Graulich et al. Stuttgart: Carus, 1988–.

Rimsky-Korsakov

Polnoye sobraniye sochineniy (Complete Collected Works). Edited by Andrey Rimsky-Korsakov et al. 50 vols. Moscow: Muzyka, 1946–1970.

Rossini

Edizione critica delle opere di Gioachino Rossini (Critical Edition of the Works of Gioachino Rossini). Edited by Philip Gossett. Pesaro: Fondazione Rossini Pesaro, 1979–.

Schubert

Neue Ausgabe sämtlicher Werke. Edited by Walter Dürr et al. Kassel: Bärenreiter, 1964–.
Franz Schubert's Werke. Edited by Eusebius Mandyczewski et al. Leipzig: Breitkopf & Härtel, 1884–1897.

Schumann, Clara

Sämtliche Lieder für Singstimme und Klavier (Complete Songs for Voice and Piano). Edited by Joachim Draheim and Brigitte Höft. Wiesbaden: Breitkopf & Härtel, 1990.

Schumann, Robert

Sämtliche Werke (Complete Works). Edited by Ulrich Conrad. Mainz: Schott, 1991–.
Robert Schumann's Werke. Edited by Clara Schumann et al. Leipzig: Breitkopf & Härtel, 1881–1993.

Sibelius

Jean Sibelius: Works. Edited by Fabian Dahlström et al. Wiesbaden: Breitkopf & Härtel, 1999–.

Spohr

Neue Auswahl der Werke (New Selection of Works). Edited by Folker Göthel and Herfried Homburg. Kassel: Verlag der Louis-Spohr-Gesellschaft, 1963–.
Selected Works of Louis Spohr. Edited by Clive Brown. New York: Garland, 1987–1990.

Tchaikovsky

Novoye polnoye sobraniye sochineniy (New Edition of the Complete Works). Moscow: Muzyka, 1993–.
P. I. Chaykovsky: polnoye sobraniye sochineniy (Complete Works). Edited by B. V. Asaf'yev et al. Leningrad: Gosudarstvennoe Muzykal'noe Izdat, 1940–1990.

Verdi

The Works of Giuseppe Verdi. Edited by Philip Gossett et al. Milan: Ricordi; Chicago: University of Chicago Press, 1983–.

Wagner

Sämtliche Werke (Collected Works). Edited by Carl Dahlhaus, Egon Voss, et al. Mainz: Schott, 1970–.

Weber

Sämtliche Werke (Collected Works). Edited by Gerhard Allroggen. Mainz: Schott, 1998–.

Wolf

Sämtliche Werke (Collected Works). Edited by Hans Jancik. Vienna: Musik-wissenschaftlicher Verlag, 1960–2001.

PRIMARY SOURCES

Collections and Anthologies

Le Huray, Peter, and James Day, eds. *Music and Aesthetics in the Eighteenth and Early Nineteenth Centuries*. Cambridge: Cambridge University Press, 1981.
Treitler, Leo, ed. *Strunk's Source Readings in Music History*. Rev. ed. New York: Norton, 1998.
Weiss, Piero, ed. *Opera: A History in Documents*. Oxford: Oxford University Press, 2002.
Weiss, Piero, and Richard Taruskin, eds. *Music in the Western World: A History in Documents*. 2nd ed. New York: Schirmer, 2007.

Treatises

Chenevert, James. "Simon Sechter's *The Principles of Musical Composition*: A Translation of and Commentary on Selected Chapters." 3 vols. PhD diss., University of Wisconsin, 1989.
Czerny, Carl. *The School of Practical Composition*. London: R. Cocks, 1848. Reprint, New York: Da Capo, 1979.
Helmholtz, Hermann. *On the Sensations of Tone as a Physiological Basis for the Theory of Music*. Translated by Alexander Ellis. London: Longmans, 1877. Reprint, New York: Dover, 1954.
Macdonald, Hugh. *Berlioz's Orchestration Treatise: A Translation and Commentary*. Cambridge: Cambridge University Press, 2002.
Marx, Adolph Bernhard. *Theory and Practice of Musical Composition*. Translated by Herrman S. Saroni. New York: Mason, 1860.
Reicha, Antoine. *Treatise on Melody*. Translated by Peter M. Landey. New York: Pendragon, 2001.

Reymann, Rita Marie. "François-Joseph Fétis, 1784–1871, *Traité complet de la théorie et de la pratique de l'harmonie*: Annotated Translation of Book I and Book III." MM thesis, Indiana University, 1966.

Riemann, Hugo. *The Nature of Harmony*. Translated by John Comfort Fillmore. Philadelphia: Theodore Presser, 1886.

Sechter, Simon. *The Correct Order of Fundamental Harmonies: A Treatise on Fundamental Basses and Their Inversions and Substitutes*. Translated by Carl Christian Müller. New York: Pond, 1871.

Periodicals

Allgemeine musikalische Zeitung. Leipzig, 1798–1848, 1863–1882.
Dwight's Journal of Music. Boston, 1852–1881.
The Harmonicon. London, 1823–1833.
The Musical World. London, 1836–1891.
Neue Zeitschrift für Musik. Leipzig, 1834–.
La Revue et Gazette musicale de Paris. Paris, 1835–1880.

SURVEYS OF 19TH-CENTURY MUSIC

Dahlhaus, Carl. *Nineteenth-Century Music*. Translated by J. Bradford Robinson. Berkeley: University of California Press, 1989.

Plantinga, Leon. *Romantic Music: A History of Musical Style in Nineteenth-Century Europe*. New York: Norton, 1984.

Samson, Jim, ed. *The Cambridge History of Nineteenth-Century Music*. Cambridge: Cambridge University Press, 2002.

Taruskin, Richard. *The Oxford History of Western Music, Volume 3: The Nineteenth Century*. Oxford: Oxford University Press, 2005.

NARROWER STUDIES OF 19TH-CENTURY MUSIC

General

Rosen, Charles. *The Romantic Generation*. Cambridge, MA: Harvard University Press, 1995.

Aesthetics

Chantler, Abigail. *E. T. A. Hoffmann's Musical Aesthetics.* Aldershot: Ashgate, 2006.

Dahlhaus, Carl, and Ruth Katz, eds. *Contemplating Music: Source Readings from the Aesthetics of Music.* 4 vols. Stuyvesant, NY: Pendragon, 1986–1993.

———. *The Idea of Absolute Music.* Translated by Roger Lustig. Chicago: University of Chicago Press, 1989.

Daverio, John. *Nineteenth-Century Music and the German Romantic Ideology.* New York: Schirmer, 1993.

Lippman, Edward, ed. *Musical Aesthetics: A Historical Reader.* Vol. 2, *The Nineteenth Century.* Stuyvesant, NY: Pendragon, 1986.

Nietzsche, Friedrich. "The Birth of Tragedy" and "The Case of Wagner." Translated by Walter Kaufmann. New York: Vintage, 1967.

Rehding, Alexander. *Music and Monumentality: Commemoration and Wonderment in Nineteenth-Century Germany.* Oxford: Oxford University Press, 2009.

Composing and Publishing Music

Cooper, Barry. *Beethoven and the Creative Process.* Oxford: Oxford University Press, 1990.

Kallberg, Jeffrey. "Chopin in the Marketplace: Aspects of the International Music Publishing Industry in the First Half of the Nineteenth Century." *Notes* 39 (1983): 535–69 and 795–824.

Krummel, Donald W., and Stanley Sadie, eds. *Music Printing and Publishing.* New York: Norton, 1990.

Parkinson, John A. *Victorian Music Publishers: An Annotated List.* Warren, MI: Harmonie Park, 1990.

Tyson, Alan. *Mozart: Studies of the Autograph Scores.* Cambridge, MA: Harvard University Press, 1987.

Genre

Charlton, David, ed. *The Cambridge Companion to Grand Opera.* Cambridge: Cambridge University Press, 2003.

Hibberd, Sarah, ed. *Melodramatic Voices: Understanding Music Drama.* Farnham: Ashgate, 2011.

Hirsch, Marjorie W. *Romantic Lieder and the Search for Lost Paradise.* Cambridge: Cambridge University Press, 2008.

Holomon, D. Kern, ed. *The Nineteenth-Century Symphony*. New York: Schirmer, 1997.

Horton, Julian, ed. *The Cambridge Companion to the Symphony*. Cambridge: Cambridge University Press, 2013.

Kant, Marion, ed. *The Cambridge Companion to Ballet*. Cambridge: Cambridge University Press, 2007.

Keefe, Simon P., ed. *The Cambridge Companion to the Concerto*. Cambridge: Cambridge University Press, 2005.

Lindeman, Stephan D. *Structural Novelty and Tradition in the Early Romantic Piano Concerto*. Stuyvesant, NY: Pendragon, 1999.

Newman, William S. *The Sonata since Beethoven*. 3rd ed. New York: Norton, 1983.

Parsons, James, ed. *The Cambridge Companion to the Lied*. Cambridge: Cambridge University Press, 2004.

Rosselli, John. *The Opera Industry in Italy from Cimarosa to Verdi: The Role of the Impresario*. Cambridge: Cambridge University Press, 1984.

Rowland, David, ed. *The Cambridge Companion to the Piano*. Cambridge: Cambridge University Press, 1998.

Stowell, Robin, ed. *The Cambridge Companion to the String Quartet*. Cambridge: Cambridge University Press, 2003.

Till, Nicholas, ed. *The Cambridge Companion to Opera Studies*. Cambridge: Cambridge University Press, 2012.

Todd, R. Larry, ed. *19th-Century Piano Music*. 2nd ed. New York: Routledge, 2004.

Tunbridge, Laura. *The Song Cycle*. Cambridge: Cambridge University Press, 2010.

Webber, Christopher, and Ignacio Jassa Haro, eds. *Zarzuela.net*. 1997–. http://zarzuela.net. Accessed 15 December 2012.

Harmony, Counterpoint, and Music Theory

Hepokoski, James, and Warren Darcy. *Elements of Sonata Theory: Norms, Types, and Deformations in the Late Eighteenth-Century Sonata*. Oxford: Oxford University Press, 2006.

Kinderman, William, and Harald Krebs, eds. *The Second Practice of Nineteenth-Century Tonality*. Lincoln: University of Nebraska Press, 1996.

Kopp, David. *Chromatic Transformations in Nineteenth-Century Music*. Cambridge: Cambridge University Press, 2002.

Rosen, Charles. *The Classical Style: Haydn, Mozart, Beethoven*. Rev. ed. New York: W. W. Norton, 1997.

———. *Sonata Forms*. Rev. ed. New York: W. W. Norton, 1988.

Place, Politics, and Social Issues

Bloom, Peter, ed. *Music in Paris in the 1830s*. Stuyvesant, NY: Pendragon, 1987.

Boyd, Malcolm, ed. *Music and the French Revolution*. Cambridge: Cambridge University Press, 1992.

Citron, Marcia J. *Gender and the Musical Canon*. Cambridge: Cambridge University Press, 1993.

Donakowski, Conrad. *A Muse for the Masses: Ritual and Music in an Age of Democratic Revolution, 1770–1870*. Chicago: University of Chicago Press, 1977.

Fulcher, Jane. *French Cultural Politics and Music from the Dreyfus Affair to the First World War*. New York: Oxford University Press, 1999.

———. *The Nation's Image: French Grand Opera as Politics and Politicized Art*. Cambridge: Cambridge University Press, 1987.

Huebner, Steven. *French Opera at the "Fin de Siècle": Wagnerism, Nationalism, and Style*. Oxford: Oxford University Press, 1999.

Johnson, James H. *Listening in Paris: A Cultural History*. Berkeley: University of California Press, 1995.

Loesser, Arthur. *Men, Women, and Pianos: A Social History*. New York: Simon and Schuster, 1954.

Saffle, Michael. *Music and Culture in America, 1861–1918*. New York: Garland, 1998.

Taruskin, Richard. *Defining Russia Musically: Historical and Hermeneutical Essays*. Princeton, NJ: Princeton University Press, 1997.

Temperley, Nicholas, ed. *Music in Britain: The Romantic Age, 1800–1914*. London: Athlone, 1981.

Tyrrell, John. *Czech Opera*. Cambridge: Cambridge University Press, 1988.

Walsh, Thomas J. *Second-Empire Opera: The Théâtre Lyrique, Paris, 1851–1870*. London: John Calder, 1981.

Weber, William. *Music and the Middle Class: The Social Structure of Concert Life in London, Paris, and Vienna*. London: Croom Helm, 1975.

Performance Practice

Bowen, José Antonio, ed. *The Cambridge Companion to Conducting*. Cambridge: Cambridge University Press, 2003.

Brown, Clive. *Classical & Romantic Performing Practice, 1750–1900*. Oxford: Oxford University Press, 1999.

Brown, Howard Mayer, and Stanley Sadie, eds. *Performance Practice: Music after 1600*. New York: Norton, 1989.

Reichwald, Siegwald, ed. *Mendelssohn in Performance*. Bloomington: Indiana University Press, 2008.

Rink, John, ed. *The Practice of Performance: Studies in Musical Interpretation*. Cambridge: Cambridge University Press, 1995.

Stowell, Robin. *Performing Beethoven*. Cambridge: Cambridge University Press, 1994.

Reception

Applegate, Celia. *Bach in Berlin: Nation and Culture in Mendelssohn's Revival of the St. Matthew Passion*. Ithaca, NY: Cornell University Press, 2005.

Bonds, Mark Evan. *After Beethoven: Imperatives of Originality in the Symphony*. Cambridge, MA: Harvard University Press, 1996.

Burnham, Scott. *Beethoven Hero*. Princeton, NJ: Princeton University Press, 1995.

Dahlhaus, Carl. "Problems in Reception History." In his *Foundations of Music History*, translated by J. B. Robinson, 150–65. Cambridge: Cambridge University Press, 1983.

Dennis, David B. *Beethoven in German Politics, 1870–1989*. New Haven, CT: Yale University Press, 1996.

Horton, Julian. *Bruckner's Symphonies: Analysis, Reception, and Cultural Politics*. Cambridge: Cambridge University Press, 2004.

Kreuzer, Gundula. *Verdi and the Germans: From Unification to the Third Reich*. Cambridge: Cambridge University Press, 2010.

Lawson, Colin, ed. *The Cambridge Companion to the Orchestra*. Cambridge: Cambridge University Press, 2003.

Senner, Wayne M., Robin Wallace, and William Meredith, eds. *The Critical Reception of Beethoven's Compositions by His German Contemporaries*. 2 vols. Lincoln: University of Nebraska Press, 2001.

Sipe, Thomas. "Interpreting Beethoven: History, Aesthetics, and Critical Reception." PhD diss., University of Pennsylvania, 1992.

STUDIES OF INDIVIDUAL COMPOSERS

Alkan

Eddie, William Alexander. *Charles Valentin Alkan: His Life and Music*. Burlington, VT: Ashgate, 2007.

Balakirev

Garden, Edward. *Balakirev: A Critical Study of His Life and Music.* New York: St. Martin's Press, 1967.

Barbieri

Henken, John Edwin. "Francisco Asenjo Barbieri and the Nineteenth-Century Revival in Spanish National Music." PhD diss., University of California, Los Angeles, 1987.

Beethoven

The Beethoven Gateway. San Jose, CA: The Ira F. Brilliant Center for Beethoven Studies, San Jose State University, 1991–. http://www.sjsu.edu/beethoven/bbd/bgateway.html. Accessed 15 December 2012.

Burnham, Scott, and Michael P. Steinberg, eds. *Beethoven and His World.* Princeton, NJ: Princeton University Press, 2000.

Cook, Nicholas. *Beethoven: Symphony No. 9.* Cambridge: Cambridge University Press, 1993.

Cooper, Barry. *Beethoven.* Oxford: Oxford University Press, 2008.

———, ed. *Beethoven Compendium: A Guide to Beethoven's Life and Music.* London: Thames & Hudson, 2010.

Dennis, David B. *Beethoven in German Politics, 1870–1989.* New Haven, CT: Yale University Press, 1996.

Jones, David Wyn. *The Life of Beethoven.* Cambridge: Cambridge University Press, 1998.

Kinderman, William. *Beethoven.* 2nd ed. Oxford: Oxford University Press, 2009.

Kinsky, Georg, and Hans Halm. *Das Werk Beethovens: Thematisch-Bibliographisches Verzeichnis seiner sämtlichen vollendeten Kompositionen* (Beethoven's Oeuvre: Bibliographic-Thematic Catalog of All of His Completed Compositions). Munich: Henle, 1955.

Lockwood, Lewis. *Beethoven: The Music and the Life.* New York: W. W. Norton, 2003.

Nettl, Paul. *The Beethoven Encyclopedia.* New York: Citadel, 1956.

Stanley, Glenn, ed. *The Cambridge Companion to Beethoven.* Cambridge: Cambridge University Press, 2000.

Stowell, Robin. *Performing Beethoven.* Cambridge: Cambridge University Press, 1994.

Bellini

Maguire, Simon. *Vincenzo Bellini and the Aesthetics of Early Nineteenth-Century Italian Opera*. New York: Garland, 1989.
Rosselli, John. *The Life of Bellini*. Cambridge: Cambridge University Press, 1996.
Willier, Stephen Ace. *Vincenzo Bellini: A Research and Information Guide*. New York: Routledge, 2009.

Bennett

Temperley, Nicholas, ed. *Lectures on Musical Life: William Sterndale Bennett*. Woodbridge: Boydell, 2006.
———. "Schumann and Sterndale Bennett." *19th-Century Music* 12 (1988–1989): 207–20.
Williamson, Rosemary. *William Sterndale Bennett: A Descriptive Thematic Catalogue*. Oxford: Clarendon, 1996.

Berlioz

Bloom, Peter, ed. *The Cambridge Companion to Berlioz*. Cambridge: Cambridge University Press, 2000.
Cairns, David. *Berlioz*. 2 vols. Berkeley: University of California Press, 2000.
Holoman, D. Kern. *Berlioz*. Cambridge, MA: Harvard University Press, 1989.
———. *Catalogue of the Works of Hector Berlioz*. Kassel: Bärenreiter, 1987.
Kemp, Ian. *Hector Berlioz: Les Troyens*. Cambridge: Cambridge University Press, 1988.
Langford, Jeffrey Alan, and Jane Denker Graves. *Hector Berlioz: A Guide to Research*. New York: Garland, 1989.
Rushton, Julian. *The Music of Berlioz*. Oxford: Oxford University Press, 2001.
Tayeb, Monir, and Michael Austin. *The Hector Berlioz Website*. 1997–. http://www.hberlioz.com. Accessed 15 December 2012.

Bizet

Curtiss, Mina. *Bizet and His World*. Westport, CT: Greenwood, 1977.

McClary, Susan. *Georges Bizet: Carmen*. Cambridge: Cambridge University Press, 1992.

Bloch

International Ernst Bloch Society. http://www.ernestblochsociety.org. Accessed 15 December 2012.

Kushner, David Z. *Ernest Bloch: A Guide to Research*. New York: Garland, 1988.

Strassburg, Robert. *Ernest Bloch, Voice in the Wilderness*. Los Angeles: Trident Shop, 1977.

Borodin

Dianin, Sergej. *Borodin*. Translated by Robert Lord. London: Oxford University Press, 1963.

Brahms

Frisch, Walter. *Brahms: The Four Symphonies*. New York: Schirmer, 1996.

McCorkle, Margit L., and Donald McCorkle. *Johannes Brahms: Thematisch-Bibliographisches Werkverzeichnis* (Johannes Brahms: Thematic-Bibliographic Catalog of His Works). Munich: Henle, 1984.

Musgrave, Michael. *A Brahms Reader*. New Haven, CT: Yale University Press, 2000.

———, ed. *The Cambridge Companion to Brahms*. Cambridge: Cambridge University Press, 1999.

Notley, Margaret. *Lateness and Brahms: Music and Culture in the Twilight of Viennese Liberalism*. Oxford: Oxford University Press, 2007.

Platt, Heather. *Johannes Brahms: A Research and Information Guide*. New York: Routledge, 2011.

Swafford, Jan. *Johannes Brahms*. New York: Knopf, 1997.

Bruch

Fifield, Christopher. *Max Bruch: His Life and Works*. Gollancz: London, 1988.

Bruckner

Grasberger, Renate. *Werkverzeichnis Anton Bruckners* (Catalog of Bruckner's Works). Tutzing: Schneider, 1977.
Howie, Crawford, Paul Hawkshaw, and Timothy Jackson, eds. *Perspectives on Anton Bruckner.* Aldershot: Ashgate, 2001.
Jackson, Timothy L., and Paul Hawkshaw, eds. *Bruckner Studies.* Cambridge: Cambridge University Press, 1997.
Williamson, John, ed. *The Cambridge Companion to Bruckner.* Cambridge: Cambridge University Press, 2004.

Bull

Haugen, Einar, and Camilla Cai. *Ole Bull: Norway's Romantic Musician and Cosmopolitan Patriot.* Madison: University of Wisconsin Press, 1993.

Bülow

Birkin, Kenneth. *Hans von Bülow: A Life for Music.* Cambridge: Cambridge University Press, 2011.
Walker, Alan. *Hans von Bülow: A Life and Times.* New York: Oxford University Press, 2010.

Busoni

Beaumont, Antony. *Busoni the Composer.* Bloomington: Indiana University Press, 1985.
Couling, Della. *Ferruccio Busoni: "A Musical Ishmael."* Lanham, MD: Scarecrow Press, 2004.
Roberge, Marc-Andre. *Ferrucio Busoni: A Bio-Bibliography.* Westport, CT: Greenwood, 1991.

Cavaillé-Coll

Douglass, Fenner. *Cavaillé-Coll and the Musicians: A Documented Account of His First Thirty Years in Organ Building.* 2 vols. Raleigh, NC: Sunbury, 1980.

Chabrier

Myers, Rollo. *Emannuel Chabrier and His Circle.* London: Dent, 1969.

Chadwick

Faucett, Bill F. *George Whitefield Chadwick: A Bio-Bibliography.* Westport, CT: Greenwood, 1998.
———. *George Whitefield Chadwick: The Life and Music of the Pride of New England.* Boston: Northeastern University Press, 2012.

Chaminade

Citron, Marcia J. *Cécile Chaminade: A Bio-Bibliography.* Westport, CT: Greenwood, 1988.

Chausson

Grover, Ralph Scott. *Ernest Chausson, the Man and His Music.* London: Athlone, 1981.

Cherubini

Deane, Basil. *Cherubini.* London: Oxford University Press, 1965.
Willis, Stephen. "Luigi Cherubini: A Study of His Life and Dramatic Music, 1795–1815." PhD diss., Columbia University, 1975.

Chopin

Bellman, Jonathan D. *Chopin's Polish Ballade: Op. 38 as Narrative of National Martyrdom.* Oxford: Oxford University Press, 2010.
Chomiński, Józef, and Teresa Turło. *Katalog dzieł Fryderyka Chopina* (Catalogue of Fryderyk Chopin's Works). Kraków: Polskie Wydawnictwo Muzyczne, 1990.
Goldberg, Halina. *Music in Chopin's Warsaw.* Oxford: Oxford University Press, 2008.
Kallberg, Jeffrey. *Chopin at the Boundaries: Sex, History, and Musical Genre.* Cambridge, MA: Harvard University Press, 1996.
Samson, Jim. *Chopin.* Oxford: Oxford University Press, 1996.

————, ed. *The Cambridge Companion to Chopin*. Cambridge: Cambridge University Press, 1992.
————, ed. *Chopin Studies*. Cambridge: Cambridge University Press, 1988.
Samson, Jim, and John Rink, eds. *Chopin Studies 2*. Cambridge: Cambridge University Press, 1994.
Smialek, William. *Frédéric Chopin: A Guide to Research*. New York: Garland, 2000.

Czerny

Gramit, David, ed. *Beyond "The Art of Dexterity": Reassessing Carl Czerny*. Rochester, NY: University of Rochester Press, 2008.

David, Félicien

Hagan, Dorothy Veinus. *Félicien David, 1810–1876: A Composer and a Cause*. Syracuse, NY: Syracuse University Press, 1985.

Debussy

Briscoe, James R. *Claude Debussy: A Guide to Research*. New York: Garland, 1990.
Code, David J. *Claude Debussy*. London: Reaktion Books, 2010.
Fulcher, Jane, ed. *Debussy and His World*. Princeton, NJ: Princeton University Press, 2001.
Lesure, Francois. *Catalogue de l'oeuvre de Claude Debussy* (Catalogue of Claude Debussy's Works). Geneva: Minkoff, 1977.
Nichols, Roger. *The Life of Debussy*. Cambridge: Cambridge University Press, 1998.
Roberts, Paul. *Claude Debussy*. London: Phaidon, 2008.
Smith, Richard Langham. *Debussy Studies*. Cambridge: Cambridge University Press, 1997.
Trezise, Simon. *The Cambridge Companion to Debussy*. Cambridge: Cambridge University Press, 2003.

Delibes

Studwell, William Emmett. *Adolphe Adam and Léo Delibes: A Guide to Research*. New York: Garland, 1987.

Delius

Carley, Lionel, ed. *Frederick Delius: Music, Art and Literature*. Aldershot: Ashgate, 1998.

Huismann, Mary Christison. *Frederick Delius: A Research and Information Guide*. Rev. ed. New York: Routledge, 2009.

Donizetti

Ashbrook, William. *Donizetti and His Operas*. Cambridge: Cambridge University Press, 1982.

Cassaro, James P. *Donizetti: A Research and Information Guide*. London: Routledge, 2009.

Gossett, Philip. *"Anna Bolena" and the Artistic Maturity of Gaetano Donizetti*. Oxford: Oxford University Press, 1985.

Draeseke

Krueck, Alan Henry. *The Symphonies of Felix Draeseke*. Roscoe, PA: Roscoe Ledger, 1967.

Duparc

Meister, Barbara. *Nineteenth-Century French Song: Fauré, Chausson, Duparc, and Debussy*. Bloomington: Indiana University Press, 1980.

Dvořák

Beckerman, Michael. *New Worlds of Dvořák*. New York: Norton, 2003.

———, ed. *Dvořák and His World*. Princeton, NJ: Princeton University Press, 2003.

Beveridge, David. *Rethinking Dvořák: Views from Five Countries*. Oxford: Oxford University Press, 1996.

Burghauser, Jarmil, and John Clapham. *Antonín Dvořák: Thematic kýkatalog, bibliografie přehled života a díla* (Antonín Dvořák: Thematic Catalog, Bibliography, and Summary of His Life and Works). Rev. ed. Prague: Bärenreiter Editio Supraphon, 1996.

Dwight

Saloman, Ora Frischberg. *Beethoven's Symphonies and J. S. Dwight: The Birth of American Music Criticism.* Boston: Northeastern University Press, 1995.

Elgar

Anderson, Robert. *Elgar.* London: Schirmer, 1993.

Grimley, Daniel, and Julian Ruston, eds. *The Cambridge Companion to Elgar.* Cambridge: Cambridge University Press, 2005.

Harper-Scott, J. P. E. *Edward Elgar, Modernist.* Cambridge: Cambridge University Press, 2006.

Kennedy, Michael. *The Life of Elgar.* Cambridge: Cambridge University Press, 2004.

Kent, Cristopher. *Edward Elgar: A Thematic Catalogue and Research Guide.* Rev. ed. New York: Routledge, 2013.

Riley, Matthew. *Edward Elgar and the Nostalgic Imagination.* Cambridge: Cambridge University Press, 2007.

Fauré

Caballero, Carlo. *Fauré and French Musical Aesthetics.* Cambridge: Cambridge University Press, 2001.

Nectoux, Jean-Michel. *Gabriel Fauré: A Musical Life.* Translated by Roger Nichols. Cambridge: Cambridge University Press, 1991.

Phillips, Edward R. *Gabriel Fauré: A Research and Information Guide.* Rev. ed. New York: Routledge, 2011.

Tait, Robin. *The Musical Language of Gabriel Fauré.* New York: Garland, 1989.

Fibich

Hudec, Vladimir. *Zdeněk Fibich: Tematický katalog* (Zdeněk Fibich: Thematic Catalogue). Prague: Editio Bärenreiter, 2002

Zemanová-Šustíková, Věra. *Zdeněk Fibich: Master of Scenic Melodrama.* Prague, 1996.

Field

Branson, David. *John Field and Chopin*. New York: St. Martin's Press, 1972.
Piggott, Patrick. *The Life and Music of John Field*. Berkeley: University of California Press, 1973.

Foster

Emerson, Ken. *Doo Dah! Stephen Foster and the Rise of American Popular Culture*. New York: Simon and Schuster, 1997.

Franck

Davies, Laurence. *César Franck and His Circle*. Boston: Houghton Mifflin, 1970.
———. *Franck*. London: Dent, 1973.
Stove, Robert James. *César Franck: His Life and Times*. Lanham, MD: Scarecrow Press, 2012.

Gade

Celenza, Anna Harwell. *The Early Works of Niels W. Gade: In Search of the Poetic*. Aldershot: Ashgate, 2001.

García

Radomski, James. *Manuel García (1775–1832): Chronicle of the Life of a Bel Canto Tenor at the Dawn of Romanticism*. Oxford: Oxford University Press, 2000.

Gilbert, Henry

Martin, Sherrill V. *Henry F. Gilbert: A Bio-Bibliography*. Westport, CT: Greenwood, 2004.

Glinka

Brown, David. *Mikhail Glinka: A Biographical and Critical Study*. Oxford: Oxford University Press, 1973.

Godowsky

Nicholas, Jeremy. *Godowsky, the Pianists' Pianist: A Biography of Leopold Godowsky*. Hexam: Appian, 1989.

Gottschalk

Perone, James. *Louis Moreau Gottschalk: A Bio-Bibliography*. Westport, CT: Greenwood, 2002.
Starr, S. Frederick. *Bamboula! The Life and Times of Louis Moreau Gottschalk*. New York: Oxford University Press, 1994.

Gounod

Flynn, Timothy. *Charles François Gounod: A Research and Information Guide*. New York: Routledge, 2009.
Huebner, Steven. *The Operas of Charles Gounod*. Oxford: Oxford University Press, 1990.

Granados

Clark, Walter Aaron. *Enrique Granados: Poet of the Piano*. Oxford: Oxford University Press, 2006.
Hess, Carol. *Enrique Granados: A Bio-Bibliography*. Westport, CT: Greenwood, 1991.

Grieg

Benestad, Finn, and Dag Schjelderup-Ebbe. *Edvard Grieg: The Man and the Artist*. Translated by William H. Halverson and Leland B. Sateren. Lincoln: University of Nebraska Press, 1998.
Fog, Dan. *Grieg-Katalog: En Fortegnelse over Edvard Griegs Trykte Kompositioner* (Grieg Catalogue: A List of Edvard Grieg's Published Compositions). Copenhagen: Fog, 1980.
Grimley, Daniel. *Grieg: Music, Landscape, and Norwegian Identity*. Woodbridge: Boydell, 2006.
Jarrett, Sandra. *Edvard Grieg and His Songs*. Aldershot: Ashgate, 2003.

Halévy

Jordan, Ruth. *Fromental Halévy: His Life & Music*. New York: Limelight, 1996.

Haydn

Clark, Caryl. *The Cambridge Companion to Haydn*. Cambridge: Cambridge University Press, 2005.
Heartz, Daniel. *Mozart, Haydn, and Early Beethoven 1771–1802*. New York: Norton, 2009.
Jones, David Wyn. *The Life of Haydn*. Cambridge: Cambridge University Press, 2009.
Sisman, Elaine, ed. *Haydn and His World*. Princeton, NJ: Princeton University Press, 1997.
Sutcliffe, W. Dean, ed. *Haydn Studies*. Cambridge: Cambridge University Press, 1998.

Heinrich

Clark, J. Bunker. *The Dawning of American Keyboard Music*. Westport, CT: Greenwood, 1988.
Upton, William Treat. *Anthony Philip Heinrich: A Nineteenth-Century Composer in America*. New York: Columbia University Press, 1939.

Hensel

Citron, Marcia J., ed. *The Letters of Fanny Hensel to Felix Mendelssohn*. New York: Pendragon, 1987.
Mace, Angela R. "Fanny Hensel, Felix Mendelssohn, and the Formation of the Mendelssohnian Style." Ph.D. dissertation, Duke University, 2013.
Tillard, Francoise. *Fanny Mendelssohn*. Portland, OR: Amadeus Press, 1996.
Todd, R. Larry. *Fanny Hensel: The Other Mendelssohn*. Oxford: Oxford University Press, 2009.

Hoffmann

Allroggen, Gerhard. *E. T. A. Hoffmanns Kompositionen* (E. T. A. Hoffmann's Compositions). Regensburg: Bosse, 1970.
Chantler, Abigail. *E. T. A. Hoffmann's Musical Aesthetics*. Aldershot: Ashgate, 2006.

Schafer, R. Murray. *E. T. A. Hoffmann and Music*. Toronto: University of Toronto Press, 1975.

Hummel

Christians, Ian. *The Hummel Project*. 2009–. http://www.jnhummel.info. Accessed 15 December 2012.

Kroll, Mark. *Johann Nepomuk Hummel: A Musician's Life and World*. Lanham, MD: Scarecrow Press, 2007.

Zimmerschied, Dieter. *Thematisches Verzeichnis der Werke von Johann Nepomuk Hummel* (Thematic Catalog of the Works of Johann Nepomuk Hummel). Hofheim am Taunus: Hofmeister, 1971.

Humperdinck

Humperdinck, Eva. *Engelbert Humperdinck: Werkverzeichnis zum 140. Geburtstag* (Engelbert Humperdinck: Works Catalogue on His 140th Birthday). Koblenz: Görres, 1994.

d'Indy

Thomson, Andrew. *Vincent d'Indy and His World*. Oxford: Oxford University Press, 1996.

Janáček

Beckerman, Michael, ed. *Janáček and His World*. Princeton, NJ: Princeton University Press, 2003.

Katz, Derek. *Janáček beyond the Borders*. Rochester, NY: University of Rochester Press, 2009.

Simeone, Nigel, John Tyrrell, and Alena Němcová: *Janáček's Works: A Catalogue of the Music and Writings of Leoš Janáček*. Oxford: Oxford University Press, 1997.

Tyrrell, John. *Janáček: Years of a Life*. 2 vols. London: Faber & Faber, 2007.

Wingfield, Paul, ed. *Janáček Studies*. Cambridge: Cambridge University Press, 1999.

Lehár

Grun, Bernard. *Gold and Silver: The Life and Times of Franz Lehár.* London: W. H. Allen, 1970.

Leoncavallo

Dryden, Konrad Claude. *Leoncavallo: Life and Works.* Lanham, MD: Scarecrow Press, 2007.

Levy

Béhague, Gerard. *The Beginnings of Musical Nationalism in Brazil.* Detroit: Information Coordinators, 1971.

Liszt

Allsobrook, David Ian. *Liszt: My Travelling Circus Life.* Carbondale: Southern Illinois University Press, 1991.
Gibbs, Christopher H., and Dana Gooley, eds. *Franz Liszt and His World.* Princeton, NJ: Princeton University Press, 2006.
Hamilton, Kenneth, ed. *The Cambridge Companion to Liszt.* Cambridge: Cambridge University Press, 2005.
Saffle, Michael. *Franz Liszt: A Research and Information Guide.* New York: Routledge, 2009.
Walker, Alan. *Franz Liszt: The Final Years, 1861–1886.* Ithaca, NY: Cornell University Press, 1997.
———. *Franz Liszt: The Weimar Years, 1848–1861.* Ithaca, NY: Cornell University Press, 1993.

MacDowell

Levy, Alan H. *Edward MacDowell: An American Master.* Lanham, MD: Scarecrow Press, 1998.

Mackenzie

Barker, Duncan J. "The Music of Sir Alexander Campbell Mackenzie (1847–1835): A Critical Study." PhD diss., University of Durham, 1999.

Mahler

Barham, Jeremy, ed. *Perspectives on Gustav Mahler*. Aldershot: Ashgate, 2005.

Filler, Susan. *Gustav and Alma Mahler: A Research and Information Guide*. New York: Routledge, 2008.

Fischer, Jens Malte. *Gustav Mahler*. Translated by Stewart Spencer. New Haven, CT: Yale University Press, 2011.

Franklin, Peter. *The Life of Mahler*. Cambridge: Cambridge University Press, 1997.

Johnson, Julian. *Mahler's Voices: Expression and Irony in the Songs and Symphonies*. Oxford: Oxford University Press, 2009.

La Grange, Henri-Louis de. *Gustav Mahler: A New Life Cut Short (1907–1911)*. Oxford: Oxford University Press, 2008.

———. *Gustav Mahler: Vienna: Triumph and Disillusion (1904–1907)*. Oxford: Oxford University Press, 2000.

———. *Gustav Mahler: Vienna: The Years of Challenge (1897–1904)*. Oxford: Oxford University Press, 1995.

Painter, Karen, ed. *Mahler and His World*. Princeton, NJ: Princeton University Press, 2002.

Malibran

Bushnell, Howard. *Maria Malibran: A Biography of the Singer*. University Park: Pennsylvania State University Press, 1979.

Fitz Lyon, April. *Maria Malibran: Diva of the Romantic Age*. London: Souvenir Press, 1987.

Marschner

Palmer, A. Dean. *Heinrich August Marschner, 1795–1861: His Life and Stage Works*. Ann Arbor, MI: UMI Research Press, 1980.

Mascagni

Flury, Ronger, *Pietro Mascagni: A Bio-Bibliography*. Westport, CT: Greenwood Press, 2001.

Mallach, Alan. *Pietro Mascagni and His Operas*. Boston: Northeastern University Press, 2002.

Mason

Broyles, Michael, ed. *A Yankee Musician in Europe: The 1837 Journals of Lowell Mason.* Ann Arbor, MI: UMI Research Press, 1990.
Pemberton, Carol Ann. *Lowell Mason: A Bio-Bibliography.* New York: Greenwood, 1988.
———. *Lowell Mason: His Life and Work.* Ann Arbor, MI: UMI Research Press, 1985.

Massenet

Irvine, Demar. *Massenet: A Chronicle of His Life and Times.* Portland, OR: Amadeus, 1994.

Mendelssohn

Brown, Clive. *A Portrait of Mendelssohn.* New Haven, CT: Yale University Press, 2003.
Cooper, John Michael. *Felix Mendelssohn Bartholdy: A Guide to Research.* 2nd ed.. Revised by Angela R. Mace. New York: Routledge, 2012.
Cooper, John Michael, and Julie D. Prandi, eds. *The Mendelssohns: Their Music in History.* Oxford: Oxford University Press, 2002.
Mercer-Taylor, Peter, ed. The *Cambridge Companion to Mendelssohn.* Cambridge: Cambridge University Press, 2004.
———. *The Life of Mendelssohn.* Cambridge: Cambridge University Press, 2000.
Todd, R. Larry. *Mendelssohn: A Life in Music.* 2nd ed. Oxford: Oxford University Press, 2005.
———, ed. *Mendelssohn and His World.* Princeton, NJ: Princeton University Press, 1991.
———, ed. *Mendelssohn Studies.* Cambridge: Cambridge University Press, 1992.

Meyerbeer

Everist, Mark. *Giacomo Meyerbeer and Music Drama in Nineteenth-Century Paris.* Aldershot: Ashgate, 2005.
Letellier, Robert Ignatius. *An Introduction to the Dramatic Works of Giacomo Meyerbeer: Operas, Ballets, Cantatas, Plays.* Aldershot: Ashgate, 2008.

Moscheles

Gresham, Carolyn Danton. "Ignaz Moscheles: An Illustrious Musician in the Nineteenth Century." PhD diss., University of Rochester, 1980.

Silver, Phillip Alan. "Ignaz Moscheles: A Reappraisal of his Life and Musical Influence." DMA diss., University of Washington, 1992.

Smidak, Emil F. *Isaak-Ignaz Moscheles: The Life of the Composer and His Encounters with Beethoven, Liszt, Chopin, and Mendelssohn.* Brookfield, VT: Scolar, 1989.

Mozart

Daverio, John. "Mozart in the Nineteenth Century." In *The Cambridge Companion to Mozart*, edited by Simon P. Keefe, 171–84. Cambridge: Cambridge University Press, 2003.

Eisen, Cliff, and Simon P. Keefe, eds. *The Cambridge Mozart Encyclopedia.* Cambridge: Cambridge University Press, 2006.

Köchel, Ludwig Ritter von, et al. *Chronologisch-thematisches Verzeichnis sämtlicher Tonwerke Wolfgang Amade Mozarts* (Chronological Thematic Catalog of the Collected Musical Works of Wolfgang Amadeus Mozart). 6th ed. Wiesbaden: Breitkopf & Härtel, 1964.

Rosselli, John. *The Life of Mozart.* Cambridge: Cambridge University Press, 1998.

Rushton, Julian. *Mozart.* Oxford: Oxford University Press, 2006.

Mussorgsky

Brown, David. *Musorgsky: His Life and Works.* Oxford: Oxford University Press, 2006.

Brown, Malcolm H., ed. *Musorgsky: In Memoriam, 1881–1981.* Ann Arbor, MI: UMI Research Press, 1982.

Emerson, Caryl. *The Life of Musorgsky.* Cambridge: Cambridge University Press, 1999.

Taruskin, Richard. *Musorgsky: Eight Essays and an Epilogue.* Princeton, NJ: Princeton University Press, 1993.

Nielsen

Grimley, Daniel M. *Carl Nielsen and the Idea of Modernism.* Woodbridge: Boydell, 2010.

Lawson, Jack. *Carl Nielsen.* London: Phaidon, 1997.

Reynolds, Anne-Marie. *Carl Nielson's Voice: His Songs in Context*. Copenhagen: Museum Tusculanum, 2010.

Offenbach

Faris, Alexander. *Jacques Offenbach*. London: Faber and Faber, 1980.
Harding, James. *Jacques Offenbach: A Biography*. London: Calder, 1980.

Paganini

Kendal, Alan. *Paganini: A Biography*. London: Chappell, 1983.

Paine

Schmidt, John C. *The Life and Works of John Knowles Paine*. Ann Arbor, MI: UMI Research Press, 1980.

Parker

Kearns, William K. *Horatio Parker, 1863–1919: His Life, Music, and Ideas*. Metuchen, NJ: Scarecrow Press, 1990.

Parry

Allis, Michael John. "The Creative Process of C. Hubert H. Parry." PhD diss., University of London, 1994.
Dibble, Jeremy. *C. Hubert H. Parry: His Life and Music*. Oxford: Clarendon Press, 1992.

Puccini

Ashbrook, William. *The Complete Operas of Puccini*. Rev. ed. Oxford: Oxford University Press, 1985.
Budden, Julian. *Puccini: His Life and Works*. New York: Oxford University Press. 2002.
Carner, Mosco. *Puccini: A Critical Biography*. 3rd ed. London: Holmes & Meier, 1992.
Fairtile, Linda B. *Giacomo Puccini: A Guide to Research*. New York: Garland, 1999.

Phillips-Marz, Mary Jane. *Puccini: A Biography*. Boston: Northeastern University Press, 2002.

Puccini, Simonetta, and William Weaver, eds. *The Puccini Companion*. Rev. ed. New York: W. W. Norton, 2000.

Wilson, Conrad. *Puccini*. London: Phaidon, 1997.

Rachmaninoff

Cunningham, Robert E. *Sergei Rachmaninoff: A Bio-Bibliography*. Westport, CT: Greenwood, 2001.

Harrison, Max. *Rachmaninoff: Life, Works, Recordings*. London: Continuum, 2005.

Norris, Geoffrey. *Rachmaninoff*. New York: Schirmer, 1994.

Reger

Bittman, Antonius. *Max Reger and Historicist Modernisms*. Baden-Baden: Koerner, 2004.

Grim, William. *Max Reger: A Bio-Bibliography*. Westport, CT: Greenwood, 1988.

Mercier, Richard, and Donald Nold. *The Songs of Max Reger: A Guide and Study*. Lanham, MD: Scarecrow Press, 2008.

Rimsky-Korsakov

Griffiths, Steven. *A Critical Study of the Music of Rimsky-Korsakov, 1844–1890*. New York: Garland, 1990.

Seaman, Gerald R. *Nikolai Andreevich Rimsky-Korsakov: A Guide to Research*. New York: Garland, 1988.

Rossini

Gallo, Denise P. *Gioachino Rossini: A Research and Information Guide*. 2nd ed. New York: Routledge, 2010.

Osborne, Richard. *Rossini*. 2nd ed. Oxford: Oxford University Press, 2007.

Senici, Emanuele. *The Cambridge Companion to Rossini*. Cambridge: Cambridge University Press, 2004.

Walton, Benjamin. *Rossini in Restoration Paris: The Sound of Modern Life*. Cambridge: Cambridge University Press, 2007.

Saint-Saëns

Flynn, Timothy. *Camille Saint-Saëns: A Guide to Research.* New York: Routledge, 2003.
Pasler, Jann. *Camille Saint-Saëns and His World.* Princeton, NJ: Princeton University Press, 2012.
Ratner, Sabina Teller. *Camille Saint-Saëns (1835–1921): A Thematic Catalogue of His Complete Works.* 3 vols. projected. Oxford: Oxford University Press, 2002–.
Rees, Brian. *Camille Saint-Saëns: A Life.* London: Chatto and Windus, 1999.

Schubert

Gibbs, Christopher. *The Life of Schubert.* Cambridge: Cambridge University Press, 2000.
———, ed. *The Cambridge Companion to Schubert.* Cambridge: Cambridge University Press, 1997.
McKay, Elizabeth Norman. *Franz Schubert: A Biography.* Oxford: Oxford University Press, 1996.
Newbould, Brian. *Schubert: The Music and the Man.* Berkeley: University of California Press, 1997.

Schumann, Clara

Chissell, Joan. *Clara Schumann: A Dedicated Spirit.* New York: Taplinger, 1983.
Reich, Nancy. *Clara Schumann.* Rev. ed. Ithaca, NY: Cornell University Press, 2001.

Schumann, Robert

Daverio, John. *Robert Schumann: Herald of a "New Poetic Age."* Oxford: Oxford University Press, 1997.
Finson, Jon W. *Robert Schumann: The Book of Songs.* Cambridge, MA: Harvard University Press, 2007.
Kok, Roe-Min, and Laura Tunbridge, eds. *Rethinking Schumann.* Oxford: Oxford University Press, 2011.
McCorkle, Margit L. *Thematisch-Bibliographisches Werkverzeichnis* (Thematic-Bibliographic Catalog of Works). Mainz: Schott, 2003.
Perry, Beate, ed. *The Cambridge Companion to Schumann.* Cambridge: Cambridge University Press, 2007.

Todd, R. Larry, ed. *Schumann and His World*. Princeton, NJ: Princeton University Press, 1994.

Scriabin

Baker, James. *The Music of Alexander Scriabin*. New Haven, CT: Yale University Press, 1986.
Schloezer, Boris de. *Skryabin: Artist and Mystic*. Translated by Nicolas Slonimsky. Berkeley: University of California Press, 1987.

Sibelius

Barnett, Andrew. *Sibelius*. New Haven, CT: Yale University Press, 2007.
Dahlström, Fabian. *Jean Sibelius: Thematisch-Bibliographisches Verzeichnis seiner Werke* (Thematic-Bibliographic Catalogue of His Works). Wiesbaden: Breitkopf & Härtel, 2003.
Goss, Glenda Dawn. *Sibelius: A Composer's Life and the Awakening of Finland*. Chicago: University of Chicago Press, 2009.
Grimley, Daniel M., ed. *The Cambridge Companion to Sibelius*. Cambridge: Cambridge University Press, 2004.
———, ed. *Jean Sibelius and His World*. Princeton, NJ: Princeton University Press, 2011.
Jackson, Timothy L., and Veijo Murtomäki, eds. *Sibelius Studies*. Cambridge: Cambridge University Press, 2001.

Smetana

Clapham, John. *Smetana*. London: J. M. Dent, 1972.
Tyrrell, John. *Czech Opera*. Cambridge: Cambridge University Press, 1988.

Sousa

Bierley, Paul E. *John Philip Sousa: American Phenomenon*. Rev. ed. Miami, FL: Warner Bros. Publications, 2001.
———. *The Works of John Philip Sousa*. Westerville, OH: Integrity, 1984.

Spohr

Brown, Clive. *Louis Spohr: A Critical Biography*. Cambridge: Cambridge University Press, 1984.

Göthel, Folker. *Thematisch-bibliographisches Verzeichnis der Werke von Louis Spohr* (Thematic-Bibliographic Catalog of Ludwig Spohr's Works). Tutzing: Schneider, 1981.

Strauss, Richard

Gilliam, Bryan. *The Life of Richard Strauss.* Cambridge: Cambridge University Press, 1999.

————, ed. *Richard Strauss and His World.* Princeton, NJ: Princeton University Press, 1992.

Richard Strauss Online. Verlag Dr. Richard Strauss. http://www.richardstrauss.at. Accessed 15 December 2012.

Schmid, Marc-Daniel, ed. *The Richard Strauss Companion.* Westport, CT: Praeger, 2003.

Trenner, Franz. *Richard Strauss: Werkverzeichnis* (Works Catalog). 3rd ed. Mainz: Schott, 1999.

Youmans, Charles. *Richard Strauss's Orchestral Music and the German Intellectual Tradition.* Bloomington: Indiana University Press, 2005.

————, ed. *The Cambridge Companion to Richard Strauss.* Cambridge: Cambridge University Press, 2010.

Sullivan

Dillard, Philip H. *Sir Arthur Sullivan: A Resource Book.* Lanham, MD: Scarecrow Press, 1996.

Eden, David, and Saremba Meinhard. *The Cambridge Companion to Gilbert and Sullivan.* Cambridge: Cambridge University Press, 2009.

Jacobs, Arthur. *Arthur Sullivan: A Victorian Musician.* Oxford: Oxford University Press, 1984.

Svendsen

Benestad, Finn, and Dag Schjelderup-Ebbe. *Johan Svendsen: The Man, the Maestro, the Music.* Translated by William H. Halverson. Columbus, OH: Peer Gynt, 1995.

Szymanowska

Dobrzański, Sławomir. *Maria Szymanowska: Pianist and Composer.* Los Angeles: Polish Music Center at the University of Southern California, 2006.

Kijas, Anna E. *Maria Szymanowska (1789–1831): A Bio-Bibliography.* Lanham, MD: Scarecrow Press, 2010.

Tchaikovsky

Brown, David. *Tchaikovsky: The Man and His Music.* New York: Pegasus, 2007.
Poznansky, Alexander, and Brett Langston, eds. *The Tchaikovsky Handbook: A Guide to the Man and His Music.* 2 vols. Bloomington: Indiana University Press, 2002.
Wiley, Roland John. *Tchaikovsky.* Oxford: Oxford University Press, 2009.

Thomas, Theodore

Horowitz, Joseph. *Wagner Nights: An American History.* Berkeley: University of California Press, 1994.
Schabas, Ezra. *Theodore Thomas: America's Builder and Conductor of Orchestras, 1835–1905.* Urbana: University of Illinois Press, 1989.

Verdi

Balthazar, Scott L., ed. *The Cambridge Companion to Verdi.* Cambridge: Cambridge University Press, 2004.
Budden, Julian. *Verdi.* 3rd ed. Oxford: Oxford University Press, 2008.
Chusid, Martin. *A Catalog of Verdi's Operas.* Hackensack, NJ: Boonin, 1974.
Giuseppe Verdi Official Website. Province of Parma Department of Tourism. http://giuseppeverdi.it. Accessed 15 December 2012.
Harwood, Gregory. *Giuseppe Verdi: A Research and Information Guide.* New York: Routledge, 1998.
Osborne, Charles. *Verdi: A Life in the Theatre.* New York: Alfred A. Knopf, 1987.
Phillips-Matz, Mary Jane. *Verdi: A Biography.* Oxford: Oxford University Press, 1993.
Rosselli, John. *The Life of Verdi.* Cambridge: Cambridge University Press, 2000.

Wagner

Deathridge, John, Martin Geck, and Egon Voss. *Wagner Werk-Verzeichnis: Verzeichnis der musikalischen Werke Richard Wagners und ihrer Quellen* (Wagner Works Catalog: Catalog of Richard Wagner's Musical Works and Their Sources). Mainz: Schott, 1986.

Deathridge, John, Peter Wapnewski, and Ulrich Müller, eds. *The Wagner Handbook*. Cambridge, MA: Harvard University Press, 1991.

Gregor-Dellin, Martin. *Wagner-Chronik: Daten zu Leben und Werk* (Wagner Chronology: Dates of His Life and Works). Munich: Carl Hanser, 1972.

Grey, Thomas S. *Richard Wagner and His World*. Princeton, NJ: Princeton University Press, 2009.

———. *Wagner's Musical Prose: Texts and Contexts*. Cambridge: Cambridge University Press, 1991.

———, ed. *The Cambridge Companion to Wagner*. Cambridge: Cambridge University Press, 2008.

Millington, Barry. *Wagner*. Rev. ed. Princeton, NJ: Princeton University Press, 1992.

———. *The Wagner Compendium: A Guide to Wagner's Life and Music*. London: Thames and Hudson, 2001.

Sabor, Rudolph. *Richard Wagner, "Der Ring des Nibelungen": A Companion*. 5 vols. London: Phaidon, 1997.

Saffle, Michael. *Richard Wagner: A Guide to Research*. New York: Routledge, 2010.

Weber

Meyer, Stephen C. *Carl Maria von Weber and the Search for a German Opera*. Bloomington: Indiana University Press, 2003.

Warrack, John. *Carl Maria von Weber*. 2nd ed. Cambridge: Cambridge University Press, 1976.

Widor

Near, John R. *Widor: A Life beyond the Toccata*. Woodbridge: Boydell & Brewer, 2011.

Thomson, Andrew. *The Life and Times of Charles-Marie Widor, 1844–1937*. Oxford: Oxford University Press, 1987.

Wolf

Glauert, Amanda. *Hugo Wolf and the Wagnerian Inheritance*. Cambridge: Cambridge University Press, 1999.

Walker, Frank. *Hugo Wolf: A Biography.* Rev. ed. London: J. M. Dent, 1968.

About the Authors

John Michael Cooper is professor of music and holds the Margarett Root Brown Chair in Fine Arts at Southwestern University (Georgetown, Texas). He is the author of three previous books: *Mendelssohn, Goethe, and the Walpurgisnacht: The Heathen Muse in European Culture, 1700–1850* (2007), *Mendelssohn's "Italian" Symphony* (2003), and *Felix Mendelssohn Bartholdy: A Guide to Research* (2nd ed., 2012). He is also coeditor, with Julie D. Prandi, of *The Mendelssohns: Their Music in History* (2002). He has published articles, book chapters, reviews, and translations on subjects ranging from 18th- and 19th-century aesthetics to performance practice, source studies, and editorial method, discussing composers ranging from Johann Sebastian Bach and Christoph Graupner through Hector Berlioz, Anton Bruckner, Antonín Dvořák, Franz Schubert, Robert Schumann, Louis Spohr, and Richard Strauss. His shorter writings have appeared in journals including *Ad Parnassum*, the *Choral Journal*, *Early Music*, the *Journal of Musicological Research*, *Music & Letters*, *19th-Century Music*, *Notes*, *Philomusica Online*, and *Richard-Strauss-Blätter*, and in books published by Ashgate, Bärenreiter, Breitkopf & Härtel, Laaber, Peter Lang, Schirmer Books, and the University of Rochester Press. He is also an active presenter of papers and public lectures in Europe as well as the United States.

Cooper's numerous published editions include a two-volume facsimile edition of the complete surviving autograph sources for Mendelssohn's A-major ("Italian") Symphony and the first published edition of the revised version of that work (Wiesbaden: Dr.-Ludwig-Reichert-Verlag, 1997–1999), the first complete version of Mendelssohn's setting of Johann Wolfgang von Goethe's *Die erste Walpurgisnacht* (Madison, WI, 2008), and four major works with Bärenreiter-Verlag's *Bärenreiter Urtext* series: Mendelssohn's *Three Motets* Op. 69 (2006), the a cappella Psalm settings Op. posth. 78 (2007), *St. Paul* (2008), the final (1843) version of *Die erste Walpurgisnacht* (2010), and *Psalm 42 (Wie der Hirsch schreit)*. His editions of music by Fanny Hensel and Felix Mendelssohn Bartholdy have been used in numerous live performances and in recordings released by Claves, Deutsche Grammophon, and Harmonia Mundi. He is currently preparing an article on music in 19th-century utopian societies and the United States, and writing a book on *Music and Secular Religion in the Long 19th Century*. A Fulbright scholar, he holds both a bachelor's and master's in music from Florida State University and a PhD from Duke University.

Randy Kinnett received his bachelor's in music theory at Furman University and completed his master's and PhD in musicology at the University of North Texas. His dissertation, "'Now His Time Really Seems to Have Come': Ideas about Mahler's Music in Late Imperial and First Republic Vienna," was written under the supervision of Margaret Notley. Kinnett's research interests include 20th-century music in central Europe before World War II, reception history, and interwar Viennese culture. He has presented his work on the music of Gustav Mahler and Alban Berg in the United States and in Europe. He is a recipient of the AMS-SW Hewitt-Oberdoerffer Award (2006) and the University of North Texas Toulouse School of Graduate Studies Thesis and Dissertation Award (2008).

FOR REFERENCE

Not To Be Taken From This Room